AIR WARS AND AIRCRAFT

AIR WARS AND AIRCRAFT

A Detailed Record of Air Combat, 1945 to the Present

VICTOR FLINTHAM

Facts On File

New York • Oxford • Sydney

Facts On File, Inc., 460 Park Avenue South, New York NY 10016,
USA.

Library of Congress Cataloging in Publication Data
Flintham, Victor.
    Air wars and aircraft.
    Includes bibliographical references.
    1. Air warfare – History.   2. Military history, Modern – 20th
    century.   I. Title.
UG630.F55 1990   358.4'009   89-23382
ISBN 0-8160-2356-5

Facts on File books are available at special discounts when purchased
in bulk quantities for business associations, institutions or sales
promotions. Please contact the Special Sales Department of our New
York office at 212/683-2244 (dial 800/322-8755 except in NY, AK or
HI).

Text design by Roger Chesneau.
Jacket design by David Gibbons.
Composition by Typesetters (Birmingham) Ltd.
Manufactured by Courier International Ltd.
Printed in Great Britain.

10 9 8 7 6 5 4 3 2 1

Contents

Introduction

AIRCRAFT IN ACTION SINCE 1945

Since the end of the Second World War in 1945 there have been numerous wars involving the use of military, and occasionally civil, aircraft. The purpose of this book is to describe those wars and catalogue the use to which aircraft were put. In doing this, I have considered it important to set the military action in a political context – not just to explain what happened, but why it did and to some extent with what outcome.

I write at 'third hand'. Although I do not work in aviation I have witnessed aircraft going about their warlike business. In 1967 I saw a mixture of US military types at Bangkok and Honolulu at the height of the Vietnam War. On trips to Belfast I watched helicopters at work. At Yeovilton in 1982 I saw the Sea Harriers return from the Falklands. Most of us have the opportunity of seeing the evidence of aircraft at war even if we are not there. Many 'enthusiasts' I have met seem content to collect serial numbers apparently without giving any real thought as to why aircraft are where they are and to the problems of operating them in conflict. This book is for those who are interested in why and how military aircraft are used operationally.

The contents are necessarily confined to wars or the use of aircraft to avoid war. For that reason there are sections on strategic reconnaissance, the Berlin airlift, the Cuban missile crisis and Kuwait. I have not included, except where it is appropriate, reference to the use of aircraft to combat smuggling or in humanitarian relief; neither have I catalogued the large number of hijacks of civil aircraft.

The book is designed for a wide audience. It is intended as a primer for researchers and enthusiasts – a source book from which those with an interest might pursue more detailed study. It is also for journalists and other writers not necessarily familiar with the subject matter, and for this reason appendices have been added to make the book as comprehensive as possible. It has also been written with modelmakers in mind: for this readership some familiarity with the subject is assumed and only summarized notes of markings are given.

I have no particular political axe to grind. For reasons of space the writing is necessarily economic and care has been taken in the choice of language to remain non-partisan: one man's 'terrorist' is another man's 'freedom fighter'. Inevitably some observations are made in analysis, but I hope that these will be perceived as being objective. If I seem unduly harsh on the Americans it is for one reason. The United States has freedom of information laws which expose the country's operations, flaws included. If all nations were as generous with details of actions committed in the name of their people this book would have been very much easier to write – and much longer.

My material has been collected from a wide variety of sources over many years. Much of it has been taken directly from original records, but even in these there is occasionally conflicting information. Most of the sections involving British, French or American actions have been based on primary research. The second level of information has been derived from reputable published sources, which themselves used prime references, or from first-hand accounts. The third level of information, used only to fill gaps, comes from newspaper and magazine reports, and I have prefaced such material accordingly.

The nature of the contents means that a truly reliable account of every air war is impossible to produce. I have tried to scrape away any veneer of 'disinformation', but many of the conflicts described were sensitive and it may be some time before hard facts become available, if ever. To the best of my knowledge I have used only that material which is in the public domain: it has not been my intention to prejudice the genuine security concerns of any nation. The accessibility of information has resulted in sections dealing with the Warsaw Pact, many third world countries and Israel being incomplete. For Latin America, in particular, apparently authoritative sources differ considerably in their accounts. For the future I would be delighted to hear from readers with suggested corrections or amendments but, ideally, only if such material can be verified.

HOW TO USE THIS BOOK

Each significant war or action is contained in a section, the sections being placed in geographically determined chapters. The chapters take the reader around the world in a logical fashion, starting with Europe and working eastwards. Not all the sections are covered in the same degree of detail: the war in Vietnam, for example, could have extended into several volumes. What I have tried to do is use some sections to highlight particular aspects of war in the air. The section on the Nigerian civil war, for example, gives insights into how rebels secure arms, while the section on the abortive invasion of Cuba explains how covert operations may be set up.

Most sections include tables of the units involved. Combat units are usually listed first, in date order, followed by support units. Where appropriate, I have tried to enable the reader to track the succession of units, and where units are listed for a given date I have attempted to give some assessment of numbers. In using the tables some care is called for: the size of a squadron, for example, can vary from three to several dozen aircraft, while flights similarly vary in size. It is extremely unusual for the number of aircraft on charge all to be serviceable at any given time. Dates, where given, are believed to be those from which and to which a given unit was operational, not necessarily the dates between which a unit might have been based at a particular location.

Throughout the book I have used contemporary spellings of place names. It is not possible to be dogmatic about names when the pronunciation determines phonetically the English spelling. What is clear is that the commonly used spellings have changed over time. When using abbreviations or acronyms, I have given the term in full on the occasion of its first use in each section, although all such terms are also listed in a separate glossary. I have also included a comprehensive bibliography. It is necessarily biased towards British publications since I have listed works to which I have had access or with which I am familiar; similarly, the list of magazine and journal references has a distinctly British inclination.

In each section I have given examples of aircraft markings. In each case I believe them to be accurate, but they are normally based on photographic evidence, which can occasionally be misleading as to time or location. With regard to colours, I have given the commonly used descriptions wherever possible, but again these need treating with care. Modellers will be familiar with the contention surrounding descriptions of colours, which change with age, wear and cli-

mate. For the sake of completeness, I have added appendices dealing with serials, codes and designations of aircraft used by the major powers. Examples of systems used by other countries will be found in the notes on aircraft markings contained in each section.

ACKNOWLEDGEMENTS

Apart from my long-suffering wife, who has helped in many ways in the production of this book, there are four people without whom it could not have been written. They are Jim Davilla (US), Jean-Pierre Dubois (France), Mike Robson (UK) and Mike Schoeman (South Africa). These gentlemen have several things in common. They all responded spontaneously to a published letter asking for assistance; they have all given generously of their time, I suspect at the expense of pursuing their own interests; and none of us has ever met. There is no way that I can repay their generosity.

I would also like to record my grateful thanks to the following for their help in providing information or photographs: Colin Baker, Winton Brent, J. D. Brown, A. R. Bruinen, Joe Carreras, John Cooke, Paul Crellin, Maj. John Cross, Joseph Dabney, Bob Dorr, Jeff Ethell, Harry Foot, Harry Gann, Nico Geldhof, Don Goult, Sam Katz, Ed Michalski, David Oliver, John Pike, Leonardo Pinzauti, Air Commodore Henry Probert, Bruce Robertson, Colin Shepherdson, Christopher Shores, Ken Smy, Terry Sykes, Andrew Thomas, Chris Thomas, Dick Tipton, Kenens Valentyn and John Winton. The staffs of the Air Historical Branch, Fleet Air Arm Museum, Imperial War Museum, Netherlands Air Force Museum, Public Records Office and Royal Air Force Museum have also been invariably helpful. Particular thanks go to Christine Flintham and Pauline Hart, who drew the maps, and lastly to David Dorrell, until recently editor of *Air Pictorial*. Without his guidance and help over many years I would not have embarked on the project.

Vic Flintham

1: Europe

After six years of war, Europe in 1945 was in turmoil. Even before the war against Germany had ended on 8 May 1945, Greece was struck by civil war. The Allies had met at Yalta in February 1945 to consider the future shape of Europe and had determined the borders of Poland and Yugoslavia and agreed on the partition of Germany. The agreements were consolidated at Potsdam in July 1945. The Western European nations were to retain national independence; Greece was to remain in the British sphere of influence, while Albania, Rumania and Bulgaria were to come under Soviet domination. The boundaries of the middle European nations were the subject of dispute until 1947, by which time Poland, Czechoslovakia, Hungary and East Germany were also subject to Soviet influence. Austria and Yugoslavia were able to retain a degree of neutrality.

The issue of union with Greece resulted in insurgency in Cyprus from 1955, and British forces made novel use of aircraft in their successful attempt to control the situation. But peace was not to last for long, and by 1963 there was serious fighting between Greek and Turkish Cypriots, resulting in war in 1974. The island remains physically divided, and a large UN peacekeeping force is present.

There were civilian uprisings in Poland and Czechoslovakia between 1945 and 1947, in East Germany in 1953 and in the USSR in 1955. More serious uprisings in Hungary in 1956 and Czechoslovakia in 1968 resulted in armed Soviet intervention. Despite apparent Soviet reluctance to exploit the Greek civil war, the Allies could not resist interfering in Albania and Yugoslavia in the early postwar years.

Determined to prevent the possibility of a reunited Germany, the Soviet Union effectively blocked access to Berlin in 1948, and only a massive airlift allowed West Berlin to retain its integrity. The city was to become the focus of further deterioration in East–West relationships in 1962 when the building of the Berlin Wall resulted in a rapid reinforcement of US forces in Europe as a demonstration of the West's determination to anticipate Soviet intentions.

With the drawing of the 'Iron Curtain' across Europe from 1946, the need for intelligence was paramount. Initially this need was met by human resources, but over time aerial reconnaissance assumed an increasingly important role. With the first Soviet atomic test in August 1949, US and British intelligence gathering increased dramatically, and Europe remains the location for many covert operations.

A nation relatively untouched by the Second World War was Ireland. However, the divisions between Catholic and Protestant in the north of the island are as strong as any between East and West, and to this day the security forces attempt to preserve law and order in what must be the saddest of Europe's conflicts.

1.1. The Greek Civil War, 1944–1949

Occupied by German forces since 1941, Greece was first re-occupied by British troops on 17 September 1944, and by the 23rd of that month Araxos airfield had been captured, while Athens and the surrounding airfields were retaken by mid-October after a paradrop on Megara airfield. Initially the British were welcomed, and Dakotas of 216 Sqn. were soon ferrying in supplies as Spitfires of 32 and 94 Sqns., Beaufighters of 108 Sqn. and Wellingtons of 221 Sqn., all under the aegis of 337 Wing RAF, flew into Kalamaki airfield (re-named Hassani from 1 December 1944), outside Athens. In November they were joined by two more Wellington squadrons and the two Greek Spitfire VB squadrons, Nos. 335 and 336. With northern Greece liberated, 32 Sqn. moved north to Sedes.

The communist-based National Liberation Front (EAM) and National Popular Liberation Army (ELAS) had been offered a limited role in the postwar government, but dissatisfaction with this arrangement resulted in demonstrations in Athens, and at one banned meeting on 2 December British troops opened fire and ten or eleven demonstrators were killed. Two days later police stations were attacked and RAF units at Hassani began flying attack sorties against ELAS and EAM targets, mainly in the Athens area. Spitfires of 73 and 94 Sqns. strafed soft targets, while the Beaufighters of 108 Sqn. attacked buildings with 25lb bombs. Bombing was of limited value, however, and from 15 December a flight of six rocket-equipped Beaufighters of 39 Sqn. was attached to 108 Sqn. until 18 January 1945. These aircraft were highly successful, and in just two weeks 39 Sqn. flew sorties against 105 targets as follows: radio stations (2); guns (7); HQs (19); buildings (55); ammunition and fuel dumps (10); and transit (12). The host unit flew 244 day and 21 night operational sorties in December. The Wellingtons of 221 Sqn. were involved in supplying 32 Sqn. at Sedes, dropping flares in support of night attacks and leaflet raids. On two nights the Wellingtons bombed targets with 250lb and 500lb bombs, all with delayed fuses. Although it had been decided to prohibit the use of the Greek fighter squadrons, 13 Sqn. HAF (Hellenic Air Force) assisted with the leaflet dropping task. On 19 December AHQ Greece at Kifisia was attacked by ELAS troops, and after a spirited defence by 2933 Sqn. RAF Regt. was overrun the next day. Many British prisoners were taken and marched north, being supplied by air by 221 Sqn.

By 7 January Athens was again in British control, with ELAS irregulars fleeing north. A ceasefire was announced on 11 January and confirmed in the Varkiza agreement on 12 February. Unkept promises led to continuing fighting through 1945, but the RAF fighter units were withdrawn by early summer. Three light bomber squadrons, Nos. 13, 18 and 55 – all of 252 Wing RAF – were flown into Hassani from September.

In mid-1946 the 'Greek' RAF squadrons formally transferred to the Royal Hellenic Air Force (RHAF) and by the end of the year all RAF units had gone. With Greek Communist Party (KKE) support, the Greek Democratic Army (DSE) was formed, initially with 11,000 men; it soon controlled much of rural Greece. The first major military operation by the Greek National Army (GNA) in April 1947 was 'Terminus' in the Pindus mountains: a cordon operation, it was unsuccessful. In March 1948 the RHAF identified and attacked two guerrilla landing strips near Lake Prespa; presumably they had been prepared to receive supplies and men from neighbouring Albania and Yugoslavia. The next operation, 'Dawn', was launched in the Gulf of Corinth in April 1948 with US advice. This was the first operation fully supported by the RHAF, which flew 370 offensive sorties of a total of 641 sorties

Among the first RAF aircraft to be based in Greece in late 1944 were Wellingtons of 221 and 38 Sqns. They were operated in the general support role, often supplementing the Dakotas of 216 Sqn. in shifting supplies. These GR.XIVs are from 38 Sqn. and they show clearly the contemporary Coastal Command white finish with faded Extra Dark Sea Grey/Dark Slate Grey upper surfaces. The nearest aircraft is NB895/G. (Via A. S. Thomas)

The Beaufighter played an important part in suppressing ELAS. The first unit to arrive in Greece after the reoccupation was 108 Sqn.: Mk. VIF X8079, illustrated, is believed to have belonged to the squadron. The need for rocket-firing aircraft to attack small targets with precision led to aircraft of 39 Sqn. being detached to Hassani for a month from mid-December 1944. The empty bomb rack is clearly visible on this well-worn aircraft. (IWM)

in May. In the operation, in which ten Spitfires were damaged and one destroyed, Dakotas of 355 Sqn. were occupied with supply and leaflet drops. This time the DSE was defeated in the area and the irregulars consolidated their northern bases on the Grammos and Vitsi mountains. In their operations in the extreme north the GNA and RHAF were hampered by the need to avoid creating international incidents through bombing or shelling neighbouring countries, and a five-mile limit south of the border was placed on all strikes.

In Operation 'Coronis' from 15 July 1948 the GNA attacked the Grammos base; 335 and 336 Sqns. were moved up to Yannina and Kozani, together with several AT-6s, and a flight of Harvards and Austers was forward-based at Argos Orestikon for artillery spotting; in addition, a flight of Oxfords was based at Sedes for photo-reconnaissance. With heavy casualties on both sides the result was inconclusive as the DSE withdrew to sanctuary in Albania. Strike aircraft were particularly important because of the limitations placed on the use of artillery.

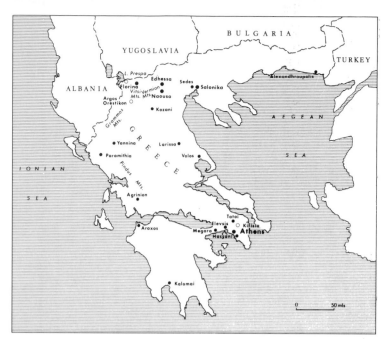

Typical of the targets designated for attack by RAF fighters was this ELAS headquarters outside Athens. The building has just received a direct hit by a rocket-firing Beaufighter of 39 Sqn. Targets included arms caches, fuel dumps, radio stations and vehicles and guerrillas on the move. (IWM).

These actions were well supported by the RHAF, which by now had a third Spitfire IX unit, 337 Sqn. Unfortunately the Spitfires lacked range and ammunition capacity and they proved vulnerable to ground fire. Not only Spitfires were used in attack sorties, but Harvards also dropped 20lb fragmentation bombs, while the Dakotas of 355 Sqn. were equipped to attack troop concentrations with 250lb and 500lb bombs fitted to underfuselage racks. Strikes were hampered by poor ground-to-air communications and were either pre-planned or carried out in response to a call-up from observation aircraft, normally the AT-6. It is believed that Mosquitoes of 13 Sqn. RAF assisted with photo-reconnaissance. During the operation 3,474 sorties were flown, peaking at 1,570 during August. Twenty-three Spitfires were hit by light anti-aircraft fire, and one crashed, killing the pilot.

In September the GNA launched an operation in the Vitsi area, supported by the RHAF, whose Spitfires were particularly effective against camouflaged targets marked by smoke by the GNA. Gradually ground–air communications, so important for fast response or close support, were improved. From May trials began with the use of napalm, carried by Spitfires and dropped in barrels from Dakotas, but the weapon remained unpopular with Greek air crews. The first operational use was in September. Between 22 and 24 December Spitfires harried a group of guerrillas who had attacked the village of Edhessa, killing

157 and forcing the remainder to split and make for the border. In the 1948 campaigns the RHAF flew 8,907 combat and 9,891 transport sorties, losing twelve air crew killed. On 12 February 1949 two guerrilla divisions attacked Florina and the RHAF was credited with having caused most of the casualties among the 900 who were killed or captured. Through the winter the Army continued on the offensive, although RHAF operations were hampered by bad weather.

The next rebel strike was on the village of Naousa, which was attacked early in June. Three hundred civilian hostages were taken, but RHAF Spitfires dive-bombed the retreating guerrillas in

TABLE OF UNITS: GREECE, 1944–1949

Unit	Aircraft (code)	Base	Role	Dates
RAF				
32 Sqn.	Spitfire VC (GZ)	Araxos, Hassani, Sedes	Fighter, ground attack	24/09/44 to 25/02/45
94 Sqn.	Spitfire VB/VC (GO)	Hassani, Sedes	Fighter, ground attack	00/10/44 to 30/04/45
6 Sqn.	Hurricane IV	Araxos	Ground attack	00/10/44 to 00/11/44
108 Sqn.	Beaufighter VIF/VIII	Araxos, Hassani	Ground attack	13/10/44 to 28/02/45
39 Sqn.	Beaufighter VIF	Hassani	Rocket-firing (support to 108 Sqn.)	15/12/44 to 18/01/45
252 Sqn.	Beaufighter X	Hassani, Araxos	Replaced 108 Sqn.	00/02/45 to 01/12/46
73 Sqn.	Spitfire LF.IX		Fighter, ground attack	08/12/44 to 28/01/45
221 Sqn.	Wellington XIII		Support, leaflet-dropping, bombing	24/10/44 to 00/04/45
38 Sqn.	Wellington XIII/XIV		General support	00/11/44 to 00/12/44
18 Sqn.	Boston V		Light bombing	00/09/45 to 00/03/46
55 Sqn.	Boston V, Mosquito XXVI	Hassani	Light bombing	00/09/45 to 01/11/46
13 Sqn.	Boston V		Light bombing	12/09/45 to 19/04/46
680 Sqn.	Spitfire XI		PR	00/01/45 to 00/02/45
216 Sqn.	Dakota IV (GH)		Transport	00/10/44 to 00/03/46
624 Sqn.	Walrus I		Mine spotting	00/02/45 to 00/04/45
SAAF				
40 Sqn.	Spitfire IX (ex 318 Sqn. RAF)	Hassani	Pilots only to 73 Sqn.	09/12/44 to 25/01/45
44 Sqn.	Dakota IV		Transport	00/12/44 to 00/03/45
RHAF				
13 Sqn.	Baltimore IV, Wellington XIII		General support, recce	00/11/44 to 31/10/46
336 Sqn.	Spitfire VB	Hassani	Training only	09/11/44 to 00/05/45
335 Sqn.	Spitfire VB		Training only	10/11/44 to 12/05/45
336 Sqn.	Spitfire VB/IX, SB2C-5	Sedes, Hassani	Replaced 94 Sqn.	00/05/45 to 30/06/46
335 Sqn.	Spitfire VB/IX/XIV	Sedes, Hassani	Supplemented 336 Sqn.	12/05/45 to 31/07/46
337 Sqn.	Spitfire IX/XIV	Hassani	Fighter, ground attack	00/07/47 to 31/10/49
355 Sqn.	C-47, Anson, Wellington XIII	Hassani, Elevsis	Bombing, transport, recce, liaison	31/10/46 to 31/10/49
345 Flt. 346 Flt. 347 Flt.	Auster 6, Harvard, Oxford	Various	Recce, liaison, light support	00/08/45 to 31/10/49

Note: Throughout the campaigns of 1948–1949, Spitfire and liaison units were based at Yannina, Kozani, Larissa and Elevsis as the need dictated.

This line-up of Spitfire Mk. Vs is of aircraft of 335 Sqn., Royal Hellenic Air Force. The squadron moved to Greece on 10 November 1944 but, in common with other Greek units, was not used operationally in the early stages of the civil war. From May 1945, 335 and 336 Sqns., both equipped with Spitfires, replaced 94 Sqn. RAF and began operations against guerrillas. The aircraft are in several colour schemes: nearest the camera, in patched camouflage, is JK612, while behind, in bare metal finish, is JK782. (Via A. S. Thomas) the Vermion mountains, forcing the release of the hostages. The final GNA push against the re-occupied Grammos and Vitsi mountains began in August 1949. By now 336 Sqn. had re-equipped with the potent SB2C-5 Helldiver, 40 of which were obtained from US Navy stocks. The oper-ation began on 5 August when the RHAF mounted its largest strikes to date, and by the 10th it was flying over 150 sorties a day. In the second stage, beginning on 24 August, the Hell-divers were used for the first time to great effect, dropping bombs and incendiaries in guerrilla hideouts. The operation ended on the 30th. Although many of the passes into Albania had been blocked, many DSE guerrillas escaped to Bulgaria and Albania, this time not to return. During August the RHAF flew 826 operational sorties, during which it dropped 288 tons of bombs, fired 1,935 rockets and made 114 napalm strikes. With guerrilla resistance finished, a ceasefire was declared from 16 October 1949.

The civil war cost the Government forces 12,777 dead and 37,732 wounded, the ELAS/DSE losing an estimated 38,000 dead and 40,000 wounded; 4,289 civilians were executed by anti-Government forces.

AIRCRAFT MARKINGS

RAF

Spitfire IX *Ocean Grey/Dark Green over, Medium Sea Grey under, with Sky fuselage bands, black serial and, where appropriate, grey code on rear fuselage: MA282 (94 Sqn.). Squadron marking in yellow and blue across the fuselage roundel: MJ238/X (73 Sqn.). Dark Earth/Middle Stone over, Azure Blue under: JK447 (32 Sqn.).*
Beaufighter VIF, X *Dark Earth/Middle Stone over, Azure Blue under, black serial, grey code on rear fuselage: KV962/L (108 Sqn.), NV597/P*

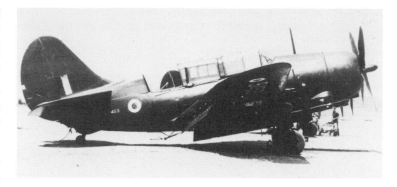

(39 Sqn.), NE472/D (252 Sqn.). Most had a very worn appearance.
Wellington XIII *Coastal Command white extending around the fuselage, with Extra Dark Sea Grey/Dark Slate Grey on upper wing and tail surfaces, black serial, grey code on rear fuselage: NB895/G (38 Sqn.), JA254/D (221 Sqn.).*
Dakota IV *Olive Drab over, Neutral Gray under, black serial, white code on rear fuselage: KN???/P-GH (216 Sqn.).*

RHAF

Spitfire V *Bare metal overall, black anti-glare panel on forward fuselage: JK782 (335 Sqn.).*
Spitfire IX *Ocean Grey/Dark Green over, Medium Sea Grey under, black serial on rear fuselage: MH322 (335 Sqn.), PV349 (336 Sqn.).*
Spitfire XIV *Ocean Grey/Dark Green over, Medium Sea Grey under, black serial on rear fuselage: TE382 (335 Sqn.).*
C-47 *Natural metal overall, black serial on fin: 492622 (355 Sqn.).*
Baltimore IV *Dark Earth/Middle Stone over, Azure Blue under, black serial, white code on rear fuselage: FW546/U (13 Sqn.).*
SB2C-5 *Semi-gloss Sea Blue overall, white serial on rear fuselage and under wing: 9453 (336 Sqn.).*

By 1949 the RHAF had replaced its Mk. V Spitfires with the Mk. IX and XIV, but as the war moved further north the British fighter lacked the necessary range and ground-attack capacity needed to support the Army. In the latter stages of the war, the RHAF took on charge some 40 SB2C-5 Helldivers from the United States. They equipped 336 Sqn., which used them from sping 1949 with great effect. E.9453 is shown, at an advance landing field. (Via A. S. Thomas)

1.2. Albania, 1949–1954

A Muslim principality, Albania was occupied by the Italians in 1939 and by the Germans from 1941 until late 1944. A strong partisan movement headed by Enver Hoxha assumed control of the cities, and a republican government was formed in November 1945, recognized by all the major powers. The government was Stalinist, and as the Iron Curtain fell across Europe Britain decided that Albania was ready for revolution and the establishment of a pro-western democracy. On 22 October 1946, 44 British seamen had been killed when two warships of a naval task force had been hit by mines in the Corfu channel. Early in 1948 Albania had been found guilty at the Hague, but no compensation was forth-coming. With internal support for the exiled King

Zog and with various exiled groups from which to draw indigenous forces, an invasion plan was prepared.

A training camp was established on Malta and two small-scale landings were made by boat in October 1949. These landings were unsuccessful and in due course the British lost interest. The US, who had funded the original British expedi-tions, decided to take up the reins and set up a training camp at Munich. On 19 November 1950 a larger group from 'Company 4000' was flown from Germany and parachuted into the marshy region in the south-east of the country. They were dropped via Greece by C-47 aircraft probably in spurious civilian markings. With radio con-firmation of success, further drops were made of

TABLE OF UNITS: UNITED STATES AIR FORCE OPERATIONS OVER ALBANIA, 1949–1954				
Unit	**Aircraft**	**Base**	**Role**	**Dates**
433 TCW	C-119C	Rhein-Main	Agent- and supply-dropping	29/07/50 to 14/07/52
582 ARG	C-119C, SA-16A, C-47, B-29A	Molesworth	Agent-dropping and recovery, supply	00/02/54 to 08/12/57

small groups until 31 December 1953 when Radio Tirana announced the capture of all agents. Their equipment had been used over several years to confuse the Americans, US intentions having been betrayed by the traitor Kim Philby. The survivors were tried in April 1954 and executed.

The Albanian episode is an interesting example of British and American attempts to 'roll back the Iron Curtain', as President Truman put it; the US also supported large numbers of agents in postwar Poland and the Ukraine. A specially formed air support unit, the 582nd Air Resupply Group, equipped with the SA-16A, C-47, C-119C and B-29A, moved from Wiesbaden to Molesworth in the UK in February 1954 to facilitate such projects.

1.3. Cyprus, 1955–1959

Subject to Turkish sovereignty until the First World War, Cyprus was annexed by Britain in 1914 and became a colony in 1925. With four-fifths of the population of Greek origin, pressure grew for *Enosis*, or amalgamation with Greece. Recognizing the difficulty of getting the British to concede such an important base, the National Organization of Cypriot Fighters (EOKA), under the leadership of the ex-Greek colonel George Grivas, resorted to arms. On 1 April 1955 a bombing campaign started with attacks on government buildings at Larnaca, Limassol and Nicosia. There was already a large British army presence following the departure in 1954 from Egypt, and in May a Sycamore helicopter flight was formed, initially for search and rescue duties, and based at Nicosia. After further attacks in the autumn, in which policemen and servicemen were killed, Field Marshal Sir John Harding arrived as Governor, declaring a state of emergency on 27 November 1955.

Immediately the number of troops was increased and the Sycamore flight split to provide an internal security unit. From late 1955 Operations 'Foxhunter', 'Pepperpot' and 'Lucky Alphonse' were mounted in vain endeavours to locate Grivas and his supporters. On 12 April 1956, the Fleet Air Arm (FAA) started operations from Nicosia with three Gannet AS.1 aircraft from 847 Naval Air Squadron (NAS), to prevent the smuggling of arms by sea. Perhaps by way of protest, EOKA blew up a Dakota aircraft on the airfield on the 27th; a Hermes on charter had already been destroyed on 3 March. September saw a further influx of troops prior to the Suez expedition, and during the month the first placement of soldiers by helicopter took place at Prodhomos. In October the Sycamore flights became consolidated as 284 Sqn. with fourteen aircraft.

All three services operated aircraft throughout the Cyprus emergency. In September 1955, 1910 Flt. with Auster AOP.6s had transferred to Nicosia for general reconnaissance and liaison work; such was the demand that it was joined by 1915 Flt. in April 1956. Eventually some fifteen airstrips were prepared for Army use and the robust Austers complemented the Sycamores admirably. From November 1956, when terrorist attacks increased to 416 in the month, several Whirwind HAR.2s were added to 284 Sqn.'s inventory and further attempts were made, with some success, to round up the EOKA cells. Although fighter aircraft were of little value in the cordon and search operations conducted by the Army, the RAF retained a flight of Meteor NF.13s of 39 Sqn. at Nicosia when the squadron transferred to Malta in March 1957. The only use of fighters is believed to have been in August 1958, when Sea Venom FAW.21s of 809 NAS, flying off HMS *Albion*, attacked hideouts in the Troodos Mountains.

The light aircraft resource was increased from November 1958, with 230 Sqn.'s Pioneer CC.1s based on Nicosia supplementing the Austers

Shortly after the start of the EOKA campaign against the British in Cyprus, the Fleet Air Arm re-formed 847 NAS with the Gannet AS.1. The role of the unit was primarily to monitor shipping around the island, to prevent arms smuggling. Aircraft of the squadron were supplemented from time to time by those of units embarked on carriers in the Mediterranean. Gannet AS.4 XG794/295R is from HMS *Ark Royal* and is seen taxiing at Akrotiri in March 1958. (C. Shepherdson).

Helicopters were of great use to the RAF in Cyprus, but those available had limited range and capacity. The Search and Rescue Flight became the Internal Security Flight in July 1955 and, equipped with the Sycamore HC.14, achieved squadron status as 284 Sqn. just over a year later. The handful of helicopters available were put to heavy use transporting troops to inaccessible areas. XG547/5 is seen here with what appear to be irregular troops disembarking in an olive grove; in the original photo, the tail of a second machine can be seen in the background.

which had re-formed as 653 Sqn. AAC in September 1957. With a greater payload, the short take-off and landing (STOL) Pioneers were able to use the Auster strips. During 1958, as the British military strength increased, there were diplomatic moves to end the conflict. The spiritual leader of the Greek community, Archbishop Makarios, suspected of supporting EOKA, had been deported in 1956, but he was released to Athens in April 1957. He announced his abandonment of support for *Enosis* in September 1958, and after a London conference in February 1959 he returned to the island.

From the previous autumn there had been outbreaks of violence, and in December five Chipmunk T.10s, making up 114 Sqn., operated unsuccessfully, flying anti-terrorist patrols for which they were not suited. The unit disbanded on 14 March 1959. Cyprus was a conflict in which the helicopter came into its own. Despite the fact that the Sycamores had a limited payload, they were able to place troops quickly in inaccessible parts of the mountainous countryside, thus keeping EOKA units constantly on the move. By the time the emergency ended in December 1959, 284 Sqn. had been renumbered 103 Sqn., having been operating continuously in support of the Army since 1955. In all, the

TABLE OF UNITS: THE CYPRUS EMERGENCY, 1955–1959

Unit	Aircraft	Base	Role	Dates
RAF				
SARF RAF	Sycamore HR.14		SAR	00/05/55 to 00/10/56
ISF RAF	Sycamore HR.14		Liaison, communications, recce	00/07/55 to 00/10/56
284 Sqn.	Sycamore HR.14, Whirlwind HAR.2		Ex SARF and ISF (to 103 Sqn.)	00/10/56 to 01/08/59
230 Sqn.	Pioneer CC.1	Nicosia	Light transport, liaison	00/11/58 to 00/04/59
114 Sqn.	Chipmunk T.10		Patrol, liaison, recce	00/12/58 to 14/03/59
JEHU	Whirlwind HAR.2		Transport	00/01/59 to 00/06/59
103 Sqn.	Sycamore HR.14, Whirlwind HAR.2		Transport, SAR (ex 284 Sqn.)	01/08/59 to 31/07/63
39 Sqn.	Meteor NF.13		All-weather fighter	00/01/56 to 30/06/58
FAA				
847 NAS	Gannet AS.1/AS.4	Nicosia	Anti-smuggling	08/04/56 to 30/11/59
809 NAS	Sea Venom FAW.21	*Albion*	Ground attack	00/08/58 to 00/08/58
British Army				
1910 Flt.	Auster AOP.6	Nicosia, Lakatamia, Kermia	Liaison, communications, recce	00/09/55 to 01/09/57
1915 Flt.	Auster AOP.6	Nicosia, Lakatamia, Kermia	Liaison, communications, recce	04/04/56 to 01/09/57
653 Sqn.	Auster AOP.6	Nicosia	(Ex 1910 and 1915 Flts.)	01/09/57 to 00/00/60

squadron flew 9,792hrs in 19,375 sorties, dropping 4,000 troops and 120 tons of supplies and lifting 268 casualties.

AIRCRAFT MARKINGS

RAF

Sycamore HR.14 *Dark Earth/Dark Green overall, black serial on boom, code on nose: XG547/5 (284 Sqn.).*
Whirlwind HAR.2 *Dark Earth/Dark Green overall, black serial on boom, code on rear fuselage: XK986/F (JEHU).*
Chipmunk T.10 *Silver overall, black serial on rear fuselage, yellow trainer bands on fuselage and wings: WK586 (114 Sqn.).*
Pioneer CC.1 *Silver overall, black serial on rear fuselage: XL517 (230 Sqn.).*

British Army
Auster AOP.6 *Dark Earth/Dark Green overall, black serial on rear fuselage: VF503 (1910 Flt.).*

FAA
Gannet AS.1 *Extra Dark Sea Grey over, Sky under, black serial on rear fuselage and black codes on fin and nose: WN417/087/HF (847 NAS).*
Gannet AS.4 *XA462/086 (847 NAS).*

1.4. Cyprus, 1963 to date

Cyprus was granted independence from Great Britain from 16 August 1960 but with little prospect of a lasting peace. A total of 990 Greek and 650 Turkish troops were based on the island, and there were two British sovereign base areas, at Dhekelia in the east and Akrotiri/Episkopi in the west. From 1962 both Greek and Turkish Cypriot factions began stockpiling weapons, and in early 1963 armed violence broke out, resulting in several hundred killed. On 27 March 1963 a UN peacekeeping force was established as United Nations Force In Cyprus (UNFICYP), comprising at its peak 7,000 troops with air support provided by 19 Liaison Flight and 21 Recce Flight of 651 Sqn. AAC operating Sioux helicopters and Auster AOP.9s. From 1972 the Whirlwind HAR.10s of B Flight, 84 Sqn. RAF were also committed.

George Grivas, not content with independence, still sought *Enosis* and in August 1964 took command of the Greek Cypriot National Guard. On the 8th of the month, Greeks attacked three villages north of Nicosia and the following day Turkish Air Force (THK) fighter-bombers struck targets in the immediate area. The aircraft comprised F-84Gs from 141 and 161 Filos and F-100C/Ds of 111 and 181 Filos. Napalm was reportedly used and two aircraft crashed in the attacks, killing the pilots. Fighting died down for some years, although THK F-100 fighters flew low over Nicosia on Christmas Day 1964.

With little warning, there was a coup on 15 July 1974 when President Makarios was deposed by the Greek National Guard. Two days later Nicos Sampson, a leading figure in EOKA-B, was declared president. The Turkish reaction was predictable, if leisurely.

On Saturday 20 July Turkish Army Bell UH-1 and AB.204 helicopters dropped troops behind Kyrenia while parachute troops were dropped around Nicosia by Transall C-160s and Dakotas of 221 and 231 Sqns. respectively; at the same time, a seaborne landing took place while THK F-100s of 111, 132 and 181 Filos and F-104Gs of 141 Filo attacked targets around Nicosia, including the National Guard barracks. During the air strikes the THK inadvertently sank the Turkish destroyer *Kocatepe* with one direct hit from a 1,000lb bomb. Greek naval vessels were reported in the area; both navies used similar warships, hence the mistake.

The attacks caused great concern for the safety of foreign nationals caught up in the fighting. The RAF contingent at Nicosia Airport was evacuated to Dhekelia, as were the families of troops living in the east of the island. They were subsequently flown out from King's Field airstrip by RAF Hercules, although 500 US citizens were evacuated by Sixth Fleet CH-46 and CH-53 helicopters to the USS *Inchon* on the 24th. Cover was provided by fighters from USS *Forrestal*. Holidaymakers in the Kyrenia/Nicosia area were transferred to HMS *Hermes* from the beach at Kyrenia on the 23rd by Wessex HU.5s of 845 NAS and Sea King HAS.1s of 814 NAS, aided by HMS *Devonshire*'s Wessex HAS.3. By the end of the day, 1,630 people had been evacuated.

There was no Greek intervention, although on the 23rd seven F-4Es of 117 Wing, Greek Air

On 20 July 1974 Turkish forces landed on Cyprus with cover from F-100 and F-104 units. The F-104G Starfighters were from 141 Filo, normally based at Murted but detached to Adana. They provided cover against air attack and bombed targets around Nicosia.

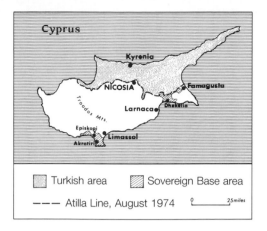

Cyprus

Kyrenia
NICOSIA
Famagusta
Troodos Mts.
Larnaca
Dhekelia
Episkopi
Akrotiri
Limassol

▨ Turkish area ▨ Sovereign Base area

——— Atilla Line, August 1974   0   25 miles

Force (EA) took off from Iraklion to attack Turkish positions. After US intervention they were recalled. Fighting had apparently drawn to a halt. At Akrotiri the RAF was busy evacuating families of servicemen to the UK, while bringing in supplies and troop reinforcements. Also brought in were four Puma HC.1s of 33 Sqn. to ease transport between bases. When the evacuation was complete on 8 August, 13,430 people had been returned in a well-organized operation, especially in respect of reception in England. The aircraft involved included Hercules, Belfasts, Comets, Britannias and VC.10s.

August 14 saw a renewed Turkish offensive, with air strikes on Famagusta by F-100s. The following day a ceasefire was agreed, with the 'Attila' ceasefire line cutting the island in two. Cyprus has remained partioned, with large Greek and Turkish Army contingents staying on the island. In March 1987 tension rose in the Aegean over disputed territory around Tasoz island, an area of oil exploration. Both Turkish and Greek forces were placed on full alert for some weeks. On Cyprus, Nicosia Airport has been renamed Ercan, and a new military airfield has been built at Gecitkale.

AIRCRAFT MARKINGS

THK

F-84F *Bare metal overall, black serial on fin, last three digits on nose: (5)28894/894 (14 Filo).*
F-100D *Shadow green/medium green/desert drab over, pale grey under: 0-(5)63399 (111 Filo).*
F-104G *Light grey overall, black serial on fin, buzz number on rear fuselage: (6)22344/FG-344 (141 Filo).*
Transall C-160D *Green/grey over, aluminium under, white serial on rear fuselage: 028 (221 Filo).*

EA

F-4E *Dark green/tan over, pale grey under, black serial on fin: (7)01512 (117 Pterigha).*

RAF

Strategic transports were polished metal with white upper fuselage decking and dark blue cheat line. Small black serial on fuselage, numbers repeated large on fin.
Belfast C.1 *XR364 (53 Sqn.).*
Comet C.4 *XR398 (216 Sqn.).*
Britannia C.2 *XL657 (99 Sqn.).*
VC.10 C.1 *XV107 (10 Sqn.).*
Hercules C.1 *Sand/dark brown over, gloss black under, white serial on rear fuselage, numbers repeated large on fin and forward fuselage: XV205 (Lyneham Wing).*

Puma HC.1 *Dark Green/Dark Sea Grey over, black under, black serial on boom: XW236 (33 Sqn.).*

FAA
Wessex HU.5 *Matt olive drab overall, white serial on rear fuselage, code on fin and mid-fuselage, squadron badge on upper fuselage:*

XT465/BH (845 NAS).
Sea King HAS.1 *Blue-grey overall, white serial on boom, codes on nose and mid-fuselage: XV672/271 (814 NAS).*

Note: *All British service helicopters had Union flags taped to the fuselage sides.*

1.5. Hungary, 1956

Hungary was declared a (communist) People's Republic on 20 August 1949. The Stalinist premier Mátyás Rákosi was dismissed in 1953 to make way for the liberal Imre Nagy. Further changes in 1955 and 1956 and the denunciation of Stalinism encouraged a sense of prospective independence, and on 23 October 1956 students rioted in Budapest, demanding the withdrawal of Russian troops. Soviet reaction was immediate, and at 2 a.m. on the 24th the 2nd Guards Mechanized Division entered Budapest with T-34 tanks. Later the 17th Mechanized Division from western Hungary and the 32nd and 34th Mechanized Divisions from Rumania moved on the capital. Fighting between Soviet forces and civilians occurred across the country, and by 30 October the Russians had lost an estimated 40 tanks. Nagy had been named Prime Minister on the 24th, and on 1 November, as Soviet forces appeared to be leaving, he announced Hungary's withdrawal from the Warsaw Pact, asking the UN to recognize the country's neutrality.

The Hungarian Air Force (ML) was one of the strongest in the Warsaw Pact. In 1956 there were three fighter regiments each with 70 MiG-15s and a fourth of 30 MiG-17s, two bomber regiments with 40 Il-28s and 40 Tu-2s and an attack regiment of 60 Il-10s. An airborne division with about 60 Li-2s and An-2s comprised two paratroop regiments at Taszár and one at Pápa, with an airborne artillery regiment at Baja. All units were supervised by Soviet 'advisers'. A truce had been negotiated on 28 October, by which time the ML had played no part in the fighting. On the 30th, however, the Air Force command announced that if all Soviet forces were not withdrawn from Budapest by the next day the ML would fight.

The Budapest airfields of Ferihegy, Budaörs and Tököl and three other main bases were under Soviet control but the ML had the use of some 200 combat aircraft on six airfields. On 31 October the Military Revolutionary Committee (HFB) was formed, and although it seemed that the Soviet withdrawal was under way, in fact supplies were being flown into Tököl and Ferihegy from Ukrainian bases. With the invasion of Sinai by the Israelis and the threat of an Anglo-French invasion of Egypt the Soviets had a change of mind, and by 3 November twelve armoured divisions, equipped mainly with the improved T-54 tank, surrounded all major towns and cities. At 4 a.m. on the 4th the Russians entered Budapest. Fierce fighting broke out and there were reports of Russian MiG-17s strafing buildings. The ML had begun flying reconnaissance sorties on the 28th and one aircraft was shot down by Soviet anti-aircraft fire at Debrecen on the 30th.

The Russians attempted to occupy all ML airfields, and three Mi-4s carrying assault troops were shot down by Hungarian airfield defence. As the airfields were cut off the ML still manged to fly some MiG-15 strafing sorties, while Il-28s from Kunmadaras attacked a pontoon bridge across the Tisza river. Il-10 sorties were also flown. On 4 November the ML was formally demobilized, however, and by 14 November all resistance had been crushed and a new government appointed. Estimates of Hungarian dead range from 3,000 to 20,000, and the Russians are believed to have lost 1,500 troops. In the aftermath there was an exodus of up to 200,000 mainly well-educated Hungarians to the USA, Canada and Western Europe.

Throughout November and December refugees flocked to temporary camps in Austria, flying out through Vienna to new lives. Included in the airlift were DC-3s of Air Kruise, Derby Aviation, Skyways, Cambrian and Starways; Vikings of Eagle Aviation; C-54/DC-4 Skymasters of Central Air Transport, Flying Tiger Line, General Airways, Icelandic Airways, Maritime Central Airways, Slick Airways, Trans American Airways and the Royal Canadian Air Force (RCAF); and L1049H Constellations of Flying Tiger.

ML

MiG-15 *Bare metal overall, nose code in red: '22' (? Fighter Regt.).*

MiG-17PF *Bare metal overall, nose code in red outlined in white: '838' (? Fighter Regt.).*

Il-10 *Drab green over, pale blue under: no codes applied (2 Assault Regt.).*

Il-28 *Bare metal overall.*

Mi-4 *Green over, light blue under, white code on rear fuselage: '28' (? unit.).*

An-2 *Green over, light blue under, white code on rear fuselage: '10' (? unit.).*

1.6. Czechoslovakia, 1968

Czechoslovakia occupies an important position in Europe as a 350-mile long corridor from Bavaria to the Ukraine. The country had been under communist rule since 1946, and resentment at perceived Soviet exploitation led to student demonstrations in October 1967. With the appointment of Alexander Dubcek as First Secretary on 5 January 1968, Czechoslovakia seemed set for liberalizing reform. At first the USSR seemed unconcerned, but at the end of July Dubcek was called to account at a conference at the frontier town of Cierna nad Tisou. Then at 2300hrs on 20 August 1968 the Russians struck to forestall a 'West German-inspired counter revolution'.

An An-22 transport aircraft of Aeroflot, purporting to have a malfunction, radioed Prague Ruzyne Airport, seeking permission to land. On landing, the aircraft remained at the end of the runway for a period. Early in the morning of the 21st the aircraft disgorged special forces troops, who took over the control tower. Meanwhile the aircraft, itself fitted out as a control centre, guided in the first of some 250 Military Air Transport (V-TA) An-12 sorties bringing troops and T-55 tanks of Soviet airborne divisions from bases in Poland. The transports, escorted by MiG-21s, were part of the 24th Tactical Air Army. Simultaneously four Soviet and one East German armoured divisions entered the country from Dresden, occupying Plzen and Ceské Budejovice in the west.

A total of five divisions, including the East German 7th Armoured Division, surrounded Prague from Polish and East German bases, while the central region was occupied by four Polish divisions. The occupation was completed by four Soviet divisions in the East and four Soviet, two Hungarian and one Bulgarian divisions around Bratislava. In all some 245,000 troops were in place, most within 24 hours of the initial invasion. All major airfields and airports were occupied, many by troops and equipment transported by Mi-6 and Mi-8 helicopters of Frontal Aviation (FA). Some FA MiG-21 and Su-7 units from East Germany subsequently took up temporary residence, but Czechoslovak forces made no attempt to resist, despite the provocation of having German troops on their soil, although there was some token resistance in Prague and about 70 civilians are believed to have died. In October a treaty was announced legalizing the presence of Soviet troops in Czechoslovakia.

AIRCRAFT MARKINGS

V-VS

An-12 *Natural metal overall, dark blue code on rear fuselage: '46' (24 Tactical Air Army).*

Mi-6, Mi-8 *Drab green over, blue under, dull red codes.*

1.7. The Berlin Airlift, 1948–1949

At the end of the Second World War, Germany was occupied by France, Great Britain, the Soviet Union and the United States; Berlin, the capital, was in the Soviet-controlled eastern zone but was also occupied by the four powers. With Russian influence extending throughout eastern Europe, Stalin felt that Berlin should be unified within the Soviet sphere of influence. Access to the city from the western zones was by three rail routes, one major and two lesser roads and by air, all carefully monitored by the Russians. On 31 March 1948, it was announced that all road traffic would be subject to inspection. The next day a US military train carrying 300 personnel was stopped and documentation sought and inspected. The Americans immediately started flying in all military supplies to Berlin and in eleven days moved 327 tons. In June, the Western occupying powers announced their intention to create a single West German state.

On 15 June all rail traffic into Berlin was stopped and on 19 June the British Air Forces of Occupation's (BAFO) Operation 'Knicker' was issued. This provided for the resupply of the British Berlin garrison by air. All rail and road passenger and freight traffic was formally cut from 0600hrs on 24 June, and the following day the Russians announced that they would not provide food for the 2.25 million people living in the western parts of Berlin. RAF Dakotas began flying into Germany from the UK, beginning with 30 Sqn. from Oakington, and the USAF made immediate arrangements to begin pulling in C-54 Skymasters to supplement the 105 C-47s of 60 and 61 Troop Carrier Groups (TCG). The decision to maintain the city, for an indefinite period and relying solely on air supply, had been taken.

The airlift began formally on 26 June 1948: the task was to transport a minimum of 4,500 tons of essential materials daily. Operation 'Knicker' was ordered on 28 June, and RAF Dakotas of 38 and 46 Groups flew in 44 tons in the first twenty-four hours of operations. Two days later, as Yorks of 47 Group joined the Dakotas in Germany, the exercise was updated to Operation 'Carter Paterson'; in July the British part in the airlift was renamed Operation 'Plainfare', while the US part was named Operation 'Vittles'. On 5 July Sunderland flying boats of 201 and 230 Sqns. from Calshot began flying in salt, and the first York sortie was flown to Gatow on the 10th.

The West German airfields in closest proximity to Berlin were in the British zone: Schleswigland in the north, Fühlsbuttel outside Hamburg, Lübeck on the border, Fassberg and Celle north of Hanover, and Wunstorf and Bückeburg to the west of Hanover. The Sunderlands used a stretch of the Elbe east of Hamburg at Finkenwerder. Much farther away, near Frankfurt in the US zone, were Rhein-Main and Wiesbaden. In Berlin there was Gatow (British sector) and Tempelhof (American sector), the Sunderlands alighting on Havel See which conveniently backed on to Gatow. In August construction of a third airfield began at Tegel, in the French sector, and it was operating from 7 December 1948. The aircraft flying into Berlin used one of two twenty-mile wide and 10,000ft high air corridors from Hamburg and Frankfurt and returned via a third towards Hanover or at low level using the Hamburg corridor. The northern and central routes were over flat country, but the longer southern route lay over mountains. Timing was critical, and aircraft were required to report at beacons at Wedding for Tempelhof and Frohnau for Gatow and Tegel within thirty seconds of scheduled time. Flights often arrived at the rate of one every four minutes.

Initially the RAF Dakotas had been based at Wünstorf, but the Yorks' arrival resulted in overcrowding. The Dakotas transferred to Fassberg on 19 July. By now some transports had been 'buzzed' by Soviet fighters, and with only one Fighter Group (FG) in Europe (the 86th, equipped with the F-51D) the US deployed the 56 FG with the F-80A to Fürstenfeldbruck. A second FG, the 36th, brought its F-80 Shooting Stars to Europe by sea and in August it replaced the 56th at Fürstenfeldbruck. The RAF maintained one Tempest Wing at Gutersloh, and 80 Sqn. joined it there on 14 July, having spent three weeks at Gatow. One B-29 Group was moved from the US to West Germany and a further three to East Anglia; these latter moves were intended to convince the Russians that the West regarded the situation seriously. The Bomb Groups (BG) were rotated every 90 days from the US. Later in the

During the Berlin Airlift, the Americans were quick to withdraw the C-47 in favour of the larger C-54, but it was late in 1948, when the Airlift was at its peak, that the RAF introduced the Hastings into service. The aircraft, which also had a much greater capacity than the Dakota, began operations with three squadrons in November. Shown here at Schleswigland is TG514/C of 297 Sqn. (Via A. S. Thomas)

month, on the 27th, the first British civil charter flight was made when a Lancastrian of Flight Refuelling Ltd. transported a load of M/T fuel. Liquid fuels were to provide much of the work for the charter companies flying mainly from Wunstorf and latterly Schleswigland.

The C-54 was now replacing the USAF C-47 in large numbers, being brought in from Panama, Hawaii, Alaska, the Aleutians, Guam and TAC. Overcrowding at the two US bases became a problem, and from 22 August some 50 C-54s moved into Fassberg, forcing the RAF Dakotas to move again, this time to Lübeck. By the end of September all USAF C-47s had been withdrawn and on the RAF side Australian, New Zealand and South African crews joined the effort. A joint Anglo-American organization was established as the Combined Air Lift Task Force (CALTF) on 15 October to ease the difficult scheduling and co-ordinating problems being encountered.

The commander of CALTF was the experienced Gen. William H. Tunner, who had earlier organized the massive airlift in South-East Asia from Assam over 'the Hump' to China. His resources were further enhanced from 11 November with the first RAF Hastings sortie from Schleswigland. Two days earlier two USN R5D units had also begun operations, attached to existing TCGs. By now the US had phased out the C-47 and operated the C-54 or R5D in five TCGs. From Rhein-Main, 60 TCG had moved to Wiesbaden to make room for 513 TCG; also at Wiesbaden was 317 TCG, which moved to Celle on 16 December, while 313 TCG was at Fassberg. The newer TCGs were formed from squadrons that had arrived from across the world in the summer. The extra resources more than compensated for the withdrawal of the Sunderlands from 14 December through concerns that the Havel See would ice over (the winter of 1947–48 was particularly vicious). The airlift continued through the winter with little sign of relief, but in March 1949 the Soviet delegate to the UN hinted that the blockade could be lifted. By 4 May the four powers had reached agreement, and free access was enabled from 0001hrs on 12 May. The airlift

TABLE OF UNITS: THE BERLIN AIRLIFT, 1948–1949

Unit	Aircraft (code)	Base	Home base	Dates
USAF/USN				
60 TCG (10, 12, 333 TCS)	C-47, C-54, C-82	Rhein-Main, Wiesbaden	Rhein-Main	00/06/48 to 00/10/49
61 TCG (14, 15, 53 TCS, VR-8 attached)	C-47, C-54	Rhein-Main	Rhein-Main	26/06/48 to 00/10/49
513 TCG (330, 331, 332 TCS, VR-6 attached)	C-54	Rhein-Main	Various	00/07/48 to 00/09/49
313 TCG (11, 29, 47, 48 TCS)	C-54	Fassberg	Various	21/08/48 to 00/08/49
317 TCG (39, 40, 41 TCS)	C-54	Wiesbaden, Celle	Various	00/08/48 to 04/08/49
VR-6 (513 TCG)	R5D	Rhein-Main	Guam	09/11/48 to 31/07/49
VR-8 (61 TCG)	R5D	Rhein-Main	Honolulu	09/11/48 to 31/07/49
18 WS	WB-29A	Rhein-Main	Rhein-Main	00/06/48 to 00/10/49
56 FG (13, 61, 62, 63 FS)	F-80A	Fürstenfeldbruck	Selfridge AFB	20/07/48 to 00/00/00
36 FG (22, 23, 53 FS)	F-80A/B	Fürstenfeldbruck	?	00/08/48 to 00/12/49
301 BG (32, 352, 353 BS)	B-29A	Fürstenfeldbruck, Scampton	Smoky Hill AFB	07/07/48 to 00/04/49
28 BG (77, 717, 718 BS)	B-29A	Scampton	Rapid City AFB	17/07/48 to 00/10/48
2 BG (20, 49, 96 BS)	B-29A	Lakenheath	Hunter AFB	18/07/48 to 00/10/48
307 BG (370, 371 BS)	B-29A	Marham, Waddington	MacDill AFB	08/08/48 to 00/11/48
86 CG (525, 526 FS)	F-51D	Neubiberg		
RAF				
30 Sqn.	Dakota IV (JN)	Wunstorf, Fassberg, Lübeck, Wunstorf	Oakington	25/06/48 to 29/08/49
46 Sqn.	Dakota IV (XK)	Wunstorf, Fassberg, Lübeck, Wunstorf	Oakington	28/06/48 to 00/07/49
18 Sqn.	Dakota IV	Wunstorf, Fassberg, Lübeck, Wunstorf	Waterbeach	28/06/48 to 29/08/49
53 Sqn.	Dakota IV (PU), Hastings C.1	Wunstorf, Fassberg, Lübeck, Schleswigland	Waterbeach	00/07/48 to 00/07/49
77 Sqn.	Dakota IV (YS)	Fassberg, Lübeck	Manston	00/07/48 to 01/06/49
238 Sqn.	Dakota IV	Wunstorf, Fassberg (to 10 Sqn. 11/48)	Abingdon	00/07/48 to 05/11/48
10 Sqn.	Dakota IV	Fassberg, Wunstorf	(Ex 238 Sqn.)	00/11/48 to 23/09/49
240 OCU	Dakota IV	Wunstorf, Fassberg, Lübeck, Wunstorf	Waterbeach	00/07/48 to 00/00/49
27 Sqn.	Dakota IV	Schleswigland, Wunstorf, Fassberg, Lübeck	Oakington	00/07/48 to 00/09/48
62 Sqn.	Dakota IV	Fassberg, Lübeck	Waterbeach	00/07/48 to 01/06/49
24 Sqn.	Dakota IV, York C.1	Lübeck, Buckeburg (passenger service)	Bassingbourn	00/08/48 to 00/07/49
40 Sqn.	York C.1	⎫	Abingdon	00/07/48 to 00/07/49
51 Sqn.	York C.1 (MH)		Bassingbourn	00/07/48 to 00/08/49
59 Sqn.	York C.1 (BY)		Abingdon	00/07/48 to 22/08/49
99 Sqn.	York C.1 (A)		Lyneham	00/07/48 to 00/08/49
242 Sqn.	York C.1 (KY)	⎬ Wunstorf	Abingdon	00/07/48 to 00/06/49
511 Sqn.	York C.1		Lyneham	00/07/48 to 26/08/49
241 OCU	York C.1 (YY)		Lyneham	00/09/48 to 00/07/49
206 Sqn.	York C.1	⎭	Lyneham	00/11/48 to 15/08/49
201 Sqn.	Sunderland V (NS)	Finkenwerder (as 235 OCU)	Calshot	05/07/48 to 14/12/48
230 Sqn.	Sunderland V (4X)	Finkenwerder (as 235 OCU)	Calshot	05/07/48 to 14/12/48
47 Sqn.	Hastings C.1	Schleswigland	Dishforth	01/11/48 to 15/08/49
297 Sqn.	Hastings C.1	Schleswigland	Dishforth	28/11/48 to 00/08/49
135 Wing (16, 26, 33 and 80 Sqns.)	Tempest II	Gutersloh (80 Sqn. to Gatow 22/06/48 to 14/07/48)		

Note: C-54s for 313 and 317 TCG came from 19 TCS (Hickam AFB), 20 TCS (Panama), 48 TCS (Bergstrom AFB) and 54 TCS (Anchorage).

BRITISH CIVIL OPERATORS

Operator	Type	Usual base	Sorties
Air Contractors	Dakota	Fühlsbuttel	386
Airflight	Tudor, Lincoln	Wunstorf	967
Airwork	Bristol Freighter	Fühlsbuttel	74
Air Transport (CI)	Dakota	Fühlsbuttel	205
Aquila Airways	Hythe	Finkenwerder	265
BAAS	Halton	Fühlsbuttel, Schleswigland	661
British Nederland AS	Dakota	Fühlsbuttel	76
BSAA	Tudor 2/V	Wunstorf	2,562
BOAC	Dakota	Fühlsbuttel	81
Bond Air Services	Halton	Fühlsbuttel	2,577
Ciros Aviation	Dakota	Fühlsbuttel	328
Eagle Aviation	Halton	Fühlsbuttel	1,504
Flight Refuelling	Lancastrian	Wunstorf, Schleswigland	4,438
Hornton Airways	Dakota	Fühlsbuttel	108
Kearsley Airways	Dakota	Fühlsbuttel	246
Lancashire Aircraft Corp.	Halton	Schleswigland	2,760
Scottish Airlines	Dakota, Liberator	Wunstorf	497
Silver City Airways	Bristol Freighter	Fühlsbuttel	213
Siewright Airways	Dakota	Fühlsbuttel	32
Skyflight	Halton	Fühlsbuttel	40
Skyways	York, Lancastrian	Wunstorf, Schleswigland	2,749
Transworld Charter	Viking	Wunstorf	118
Trent Valley Aviation	Dakota	Fühlsbuttel	186
World Air Freight	Halton	Fühlsbuttel	526
Westminster Airways	Dakota, Halton	Fühlsbuttel, Schleswigland	772

did not end, however, as stocks were built up. Apart from the C-47 and C-54, the USAF also used five C-82s from September 1948, and a sole C-74 and a C-97 towards the end of the operation.

From July, units began to return to other commitments, and on 1 September CALTF was disbanded. The airlift officially finished with a USAF flight on 30 September after 462 days; the last civilian flight was on 16 August, the last RAF flight on 23 September. After a precarious start the airlift ran smoothly, thanks to superb organization and commitment. Aircraft and air crews were to some extent pooled, and because of the demands on flying time completely new maintenance arrangements were made.

Despite the intensity of flying and the pressure on aircraft and their crews, accidents were relatively few. The US lost four C-47s, six C-54s and one R5D with a total of 27 killed. The RAF lost three Dakotas, one York and a Hastings with a loss of life of eighteen plus seven German passengers. Three civilian Haltons and a York were lost, together with ten air crew. During the airlift 2,325,800 short tons (=2,000lb) of supplies were delivered in 277,804 flights committing a total of 57,000 personnel. This averaged 5,560 tons a day, or one ton per Berliner over the period. The total included 1,586,539 tons of coal and 538,016 tons of food. Wet fuel made up most of the remainder and was generally handled by civilian contractors at a contract rate of £98 per hour. The RAF also handled backloading, which included the 'export' of 7,530 tons of mail, 6,800 tons of freight, 5,000 tons of manufactured goods and 35,600 people. The overall balance of activity of the three contributors is as follows:

	USAF/USN	RAF	Civilian
Tonnage	1,783,572	394,509	147,727
Sorties	189,963	65,857	21,984
No. of aircraft	441	147	104
Accidents (fatal)	11	7	6
Lives lost (total)	28	30	10

Berlin is, for the Western powers, a symbolic but tangible illustration of their determination to stand firm against the perceived threat of communist expansion in Europe. The organization of the airlift, bearing in mind the relatively small individual loads carried, was a major achievement, and it was clear that air supply could have kept the city sustained, if not thriving, indefinitely.

AIRCRAFT MARKINGS
Throughout the operation some aircraft of all services had large two- or three-digit codes applied to their vertical surfaces, normally the fin but sometimes the forward fuselage. Examples of these are given below in quotation marks; there was no single system for determining the codes applied.

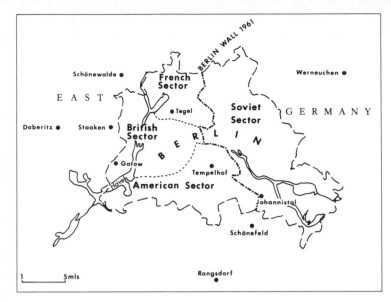

USAF
Transport aircraft were generally in a silver or bare metal finish, although some C-47s were Olive Drab over and light grey under. Some C-54s had complex cheat lines, especially those from the Pacific Division. The C-82s had red fins.
C-47 *BM: (4)316255 (60 TCG). OD, yellow serial on fin: (4)349029 (60 TCG).*
C-54 *(4)272581/'488' (61 TCG). 'The Air Transport Command' along fuselage: (4)50527/'440'.*
C-82 *4557743/'743' (60 TCG).*
C-74 *455414 (sole aircraft of type).*

RAF
Transport aircraft were generally in bare metal finish. Exceptions were some Dakotas which retained the wartime Olive Drab over and Neutral Gray under. The newly delivered Hastings had white upper decking divided from the bare metal by a blue cheat line.
Dakota *KN652 (10 Sqn.); KN499 (18 Sqn.); KN415 (27 Sqn.); KN419 JN-O (30 Sqn.); KN518 XK-Y (drab finish, 46 Sqn.); KN517 PU-Y (53 Sqn.); KN508 (62 Sqn.); KN660 YS-P '50' (77 Sqn.).*
York *MW206 (40 Sqn.); MW132 MH-C (51 Sqn.); MW309 BY-I (59 Sqn.); MW263 AG (99 Sqn.); MW286 (206 Sqn.); MW287 KY-N '16' (242 Sqn.); MW112 (511 Sqn.); MW172 YY-D (241 OCU.).*
Sunderland *White overall: RN273 NS-A (201 Sqn.); PP164 4X-X (230 Sqn.).*
Hastings *TG530 W (47 Sqn.); TG569 (53 Sqn.); TG572 '572' (297 Sqn.).*

Civilian aircraft
These were also generally in bare metal with a

range of added livery. Most were conversions of
bomber types, for example Halifax/Halton,
Lancaster/Lancastrian and Liberator.
Registrations were painted large on the fuselage
sides except in the case of the Tudors.
Avro Lancastrian G-AHVN (BOAC); G-AKDR
(Flight Refuelling).
Avro Tudor I G-AGRJ (BSAA).
Avro Tudor V G-AKBY (Airflight); G-AKBZ

(BSAA).
Avro York G-AHLV (Skyways).
Bristol Freighter G-AHJC (Silver City Airways).
Consolidated Liberator G-ANZP (Scottish
Airlines).
Handley Page Halton G-AIAP (Eagle Aviation);
GALEF, finished red overall (Eagle Aviation);
G-AIWP (London Aero Services); G-AIHY
(Lancashire Aircraft Corp.).

1.8. The Berlin Wall Crisis, 1961–1962

After the Berlin Airlift had demonstrated Western
determination to maintain the integrity of West
Berlin, the NATO allies pressed for the establishment of a tangible West German contribution
to European defence; Britain, France and the US
had many other commitments farther afield. On
5 May 1955 the German Federal Republic was
declared and just nine days later the formation of
the Warsaw Pact was announced. The Soviet
Union, mindful of the unthinkable prospect of a
re-united Germany, kept a tight control on
access to Berlin and in 1958 suggested the
handover of Berlin as a demilitarized city in
exchange for concessions. The Western powers
rejected the proposal. Resenting the embedded
example of capitalism, which had encouraged no
fewer than 2.25 million East Germans to cross to
the West between 1949 and 1959, the Russians
pressed for a resolution and early in 1961 threatened a bilateral solution with East Germany.

On 8 July the Soviet defence budget was
increased by 25 per cent and on 25 July President
Kennedy called for a build-up of conventional
forces and the mobilization of Reserve and
National Guard units. Then, on 13 August, 63 of
the 80 entry points from East Berlin were sealed
and the construction of a substantial physical
barrier was begun. The US, having committed
itself to a strong nuclear force, had no option but

to rely on reserve units, because, as Kennedy
said, '...we intend to have a wider choice than
humiliation or all-out nuclear action'. At the
end of August the Soviet Union resumed its
nuclear test programme. On 1 October 1961
18,500 ANG officers and men reported for duty,
while the six United States Air Force Europe
(USAFE) Tactical Fighter Wings, seven fighter
squadrons and two reconnaissance Wings were to
be supplemented by a number of ANG units in
Operation 'Stairstep'.

American reinforcements moved with the support of C-97 and C-124 transports of Military Air
Transport Service (MATS), including the 63
Troop Carrier Wing (TCW). In 1960 France had
demanded the withdrawal of US nuclear-capable
aircraft from French bases, but the reinforcements now flew into Chambley, Chaumont,
Dreux, Etain Toul-Rosières and Phalsbourg as
well as Ramstein in Germany and Moron AFB,
Spain. Most of the tactical units flew the F-84F,
still in service with a number of European air
arms, and a Wing of F-86H Sabres was also
involved; in November a Wing of F-104A Starfighters was flown over. The RAF also made
token gestures at the end of the year, but as
diplomatic progress was made the reserve units
gradually withdrew to the UK and US. The
Western allies had again demonstrated support

During the Berlin Wall
crisis, numerous Air
National Guard aircraft
were called to active
service and placed under
Federal control. While
some, such as this F-84F
of the 166th Tactical
Fighter Squadron, had
their ANG markings
removed, others also had
USAF markings applied.
The 'Ohio Air Guard' can
just be made out on the
nose of (5)26629,
photographed at
Wethersfield in the
summer of 1962.
(Author's collection)

USAFE units equipped with 'century-series' fighters were supported by veteran fighters from Air National Guard units through the winter of 1961–62. Illustrated is F-86H (5)22009, wearing the markings of the 131st Tactical Fighter Squadron, Massachusetts ANG, part of 102 TFW. Normally based at Barnes Field, Westfield, the unit was at this time temporarily based at Phalsbourg, France. (Author's collection)

for the position of West Berlin and the importance to them of a strong foothold in West Germany, together with their ability to back that support with tactical, conventional forces.

AIRCRAFT MARKINGS

USAFE fighters were bare metal overall, the exception being the F-102A, which was light grey overall; transports were also bare metal. The black serial was carried on the fin, the 'buzz number' on the rear or mid fuselage. The practice of carrying buzz numbers was in transition, but most fighter types displayed them. Fighter aircraft wore colourful unit markings, normally across the tail, although the ANG unit markings were generally less flamboyant.

USAFE

F-100D *(5)53690/FW-690 (20 TFW), (5)63321/FW-321 (48 TFW).*
F-101C *(5)41486 (81 TFW).*
F-102A *(5)61121/FC-120 (525 FIS, 86 FIW).*
F-104C *(5)60901/FG-901 (479 TFW).*
F-105D *(6)10150/FH-150 (36 TFW).*
RF-101C *(5)60216/FB-216 (66 TRW).*

ANG

F-84F *'Ohio Air Guard' on nose scrubbed out: (5)26629 (166 TFS). 'US Air Force' on nose: (5)26993/FS-993 (166 TFS). 'US Air Force' on nose: (5)26616/FS-616 (110 TFS). 'Ind-ANG' across fuselage national marking: (5)26426 (163 TFS). (5)31502 (141 TFS).*
F-86H *(5)22009/FU-009 (131 TFS); (5)25732, (5)31502 (101 TFS); (5)31495 (138 TFS).*
F-104A *(5)60851/FG-851 (151 FIS); (5)60844 (157 FIS).*
RF-84F *(5)37601/FS-601 (106 TRS).*
C-97A *(4)92589 (Oklahoma ANG); (4)92607 (Minnesota ANG).*
C-124C *(5)20950 (63 TCW).*

TABLE OF UNITS: THE BERLIN WALL CRISIS, 1961–1962

Unit	Aircraft	Base	Role	Dates
USAFE units, 1961				
20 TFW	F-100D	Wethersfield	} Fighter-bomber	
48 TFW	F-100D	Lakenheath		
81 TFW	F-101C	Bentwaters		
10 TRW	RB-66C	Alconbury	PR	
47 BW	B-66B	Sculthorpe	Medium bombing	
32 FIS	F-102A	Soesterberg	Fighter	
66 TRW	RF-101C	Laon	Fighter-recce	
479 TFW	F-104C	Moron AFB	Fighter	
36 TFW	F-105D	Bitburg AB		
49 TFW	F-100D	Spangdahlen AB } Fighter-bomber		
81 TFS	F-100D	Hahn AB		
496 FIS (86 FIW)	F-102A	Hahn AB	} Fighter	
525 FIS (86 FIW)	F-102A	Bitburg AB		
526 FIS (86 FIW)	F-102A	Ramstein AB		
RAF units in West Germany, 1961				
5 Sqn.	Javelin FAW.5	Laarbruch	} Fighter	
11 Sqn.	Javelin FAW.4	Geilenkirchen		
4 Sqn.	Hunter F.6	Jever		
118 Sqn.	Hunter F.6	Jever		
3 Sqn.	} Canberra B(I).8	Geilenkirchen	} Interdiction	
16 Sqn.		Celle		
88 Sqn.		Wildenrath		
213 Sqn.	Canberra B(I).6	Ahlhorn		
2 Sqn.	Hunter FR.10	Jever	Fighter-recce	
4 Sqn.	Hunter FR.10	Gutersloh	Fighter-recce	
17 Sqn.	} Canberra PR.7	Wildenrath	} PR	
31 Sqn.		Laarbruch		
80 Sqn.		Laarbruch		
US ANG detached units				
102 TFW (101, 131, 138 TFS)	F-86H	Phalsbourg	Fighter	01/10/61 to 20/08/62
141 TFS		Chaumont		01/10/61 to 17/08/62
166 TFS	} F-84F	Etain	} Fighter-bomber	01/10/61 to 15/08/62
163 TFS		Chambley		01/10/61 to 20/08/62
110 TFS		Toul-Rosières		01/10/61 to 20/08/62
106 TRS	RF-84F	Dreux, Chaumont	Fighter-recce	01/10/61 to 20/08/62
197 FIS		Ramstein AB		
151 FIS	} F-104A	Ramstein AB	} Fighter	01/11/61 to 15/08/62
157 FIS		Moron AFB		
USAF detached units				
55 TFS	F-100D	Chaumont	Fighter-bomber	00/12/61 to 00/00/62
? TRW	RB-57A	?	PR	00/11/61 to 00/00/62
US Army				
503 Army Div.	OV-1A	W. Germany	Observation	00/12/61 to 00/00/62
RAF detached units				
56 Sqn.	Lightning F.1A	Bruggen		00/10/61
111 Sqn.	Lightning F.1A	Gutersloh	} Fighter	00/12/61
228 OCU	Javelin FAW.5	Bruggen		00/10/61

Note: The following state ANG units were involved: 106 TRS (Ala.); 197 FIS (Ariz.); 163 TFS (Ind.); 101, 131 TFS (Mass.); 110 TFS (Miss.); 141 TFS (NJ); 138 TFS (NY); 166 TFS (Oh.); 157 FIS (SC); 151 FIS (Tenn.).

1.9. Northern Ireland, 1969 to date

The rift between Catholics and Protestants, Republicans and Loyalists in Ireland is impossible to untangle rationally. The 26 southern counties effectively achieved independence in 1922, leaving the six counties of Ulster an integral part of the United Kingdom. The Irish Republican Army (IRA) insists on a united, republican Ireland, using terrorism to achieve political ends. A series of incidents in the 1950s resulted in a detachment of AAC Auster 6s of 1913 Flt. to patrol the border with the Irish Republic. With the emergence of the Northern Ireland Civil Rights Association (NICRA) in the late 1960s, tension in the province rose. The 1969 Apprentice Boys' march resulted in riots and the Westminster Government was obliged to send troops to reinforce the Royal Ulster Constabulary (RUC). From an early date 666 Sqn. AAC was detached to Ballykelly outside Londonderry. The unit's two flights of four Sioux AH.1s and four Scout AH.1s provided liaison, reconnaissance and casualty evacuation with a limited troop-carrying capability.

The military presence increased and the situation worsened dramatically from 'Bloody Sunday', 30 January 1972, when thirteen civilians were killed in Londonderry by men of 1 Para. The security forces increased, to supplement the RUC and the locally raised Ulster Defence Force (UDF). In 1978 the Sioux of 3 Flt. AAC, operating from Omagh, were replaced by more capable Gazelles, although troop-moving capacity was still a problem. Wessex HC.2s of 72 Sqn. RAF were detached from their home base at Odiham and the unit moved into Aldergrove, with a detachment at Bessbrook, in 1981.

The Wessexes operate extensively in the dangerous countryside of South Armagh in support of regular Army units and the Special Air Service Regt. (SAS), and several have been damaged by ground fire. For more extensive exercises the Wessexes are supplemented by Puma HC.1s of 33 Sqn. and by naval Sea Kings. Since 1979 the Army has operated two mixed Squadrons of Gazelle AH.1s and Scout AH.1s on four-month rotations, nominally based at Aldergrove. The aircraft have been equipped with Nightsun search-

lights, and with image-intensifying and recording and infra-red detection systems. From 1982 the Lynx AH.1 began replacing the Scout. Since 1975 the Army has had a fixed-wing element of five Beaver AL.1s, for liaison work, based at Aldergrove. In addition the Irish Air Corps maintains regular border patrols using Alouette IIIs and Cessna-Reims FR.172Hs from Baldonnel and Gormanston respectively.

The Army and RAF helicopters, which are unarmed, perform a range of difficult tasks: they maintain a watch on demonstrations, assist security forces in emergencies and, in the case of the larger types, move heavy supplies such as concrete for new roadblocks. Many small Army posts are supplied by air, and troops are moved to and from ambush points by air. The flying is not without risk. At least nine helicopters have crashed in the province since 1970, including one Puma and several Lynx, one of which latter, from 665 Sqn., was brought down by heavy machine-gun fire at Silverbridge in June 1988. With the knowledge that the IRA has acquired some SA-7 missiles, the Army has fitted exhaust suppression kits to its helicopters, while the Lynx is currently being fitted with the ALQ-177 infra-red jamming

The Army's first helicopter unit in Northern Ireland was 666 Sqn. AAC, equipped with the Sioux and Scout. Earlier, in 1957, Auster AOP.6s of 1913 Flt. were based at Aldergrove for border patrols. The Sioux was replaced in due course by the Gazelle and the Scout by the Lynx, and all types have flown in the province with a wide range of surveillance equipment. Here three Sioux of 666 Sqn. are seen over typical Ulster terrain. (Museum of Army Flying)

TABLE OF UNITS: NORTHERN IRELAND, 1969 TO DATE

Unit	Aircraft	Base	Role	Dates
AAC				
1913 Flt.	Auster AOP.6	Aldergrove	Recce	13/02/57 to 00/08/57
666 Sqn.	Sioux AH.1, Scout AH.1	Ballykelly	Liaison, casevac, resupply, recce	00/10/69 to 00/00/73
4/7 RDG	Sioux AH.1	Omagh	Liaison, recce	00/00/71 to 00/00/73
Beaver Flt.	Beaver AL.1	Aldergrove	Liaison, resupply	00/00/75 to date
659 Sqn.	Sioux AH.1	?	Liaison, recce	Believed 1977
3 Flt.	Sioux AH.1, Gazelle AH.1	Omagh	Liaison, recce	00/08/77 to 00/00/80
653 Sqn.	Scout AH.1 Gazelle AH.1	Omagh Aldergrove	Resupply, casevac, placement Liaison, recce	00/10/77 to 00/00/80
655 Sqn.	Scout AH.1, Lynx AH.1, Gazelle AH.1	Omagh, Aldergrove, Ballykelly	Liaison, casevac, resupply, recce	00/00/82 to date
665 Sqn.	Gazelle AH.1, Lynx AH.1	Aldergrove	Liaison, casevac, resupply, recce	00/00/86 to date
RAF				
72 Sqn.	Wessex HC.2	Aldergrove, Bessbrook	Troop-carrying, supply, casevac	00/00/78 to date
33 Sqn.	Puma HC.1	Odiham (det. Aldergrove)	Transport	Detachments

device to counter the possibility of IRA acquisition of the Stinger SAM. At the time of writing, there is no end in sight to the eighteen years of unrelenting terrorism by both Republicans and Loyalists.

AIRCRAFT MARKINGS

AAC
Sioux and Scouts were originally brown/Dark Green all over, but by mid-1970s all aircraft were finished in Dark Green/black overall, with black serials and muted national markings.
Sioux AH.1 *XT502 (4/7 Royal Dragoon Guards); XT515 (3 Flt.).*
Scout AH.1 *XX373 (663 Sqn.).*
Gazelle AH.1 *XW899, XZ327, ZA774 (655 Sqn.).*
Lynx AH.1 *XZ188, XZ207 (655 Sqn.).*
Beaver AL.1 *Dark Green/black over, black under, black serial on rear fuselage and individually coloured spinners: XP771/blue, XV270/green (Beaver Flt.).*

NORTHERN IRELAND

RAF
RAF helicopters are finished Dark Green/Dark Sea Grey over, with matt black undersides. Aircraft have muted markings and black serials and codes on the rear fuselage.
Wessex HC.2 *XT671/AD, XV728/AA (72 Sqn.).*
Puma HC.1 *XW210/CG (33 Sqn.).*

1.10. Strategic intelligence-gathering, 1949 to date

Although a global activity, much postwar intelligence-gathering has focused on Europe; the international picture is thus described in one chapter for convenience. Where strategic reconnaissance has been applied to a particular confrontation, as in Vietnam and the Cuban missile crisis, the details are presented in the appropriate chapter. Satellite reconnaissance is not within the scope of the present work.

From the late 1940s there has been a need, particularly for Western powers, to use aircraft for intelligence-related work, since the closed borders of the Iron Curtain countries have meant that conventional espionage is extremely difficult. The range of aerial spying is extensive. Photographic reconnaissance (PR) was the first use to which military aircraft were put. Electronic Intelligence ('elint') is subdivided into Signals Intelligence ('sigint'), Communications Intelligence ('comint') and Telemetry Intelligence ('telint'). Aircrafts are also used for nuclear monitoring and in support of agents ('humint'). In broad terms, photo-reconnaissance is applied to determine *what* is in place *where* and elint is applied to ascertain *how* it works. Whereas PR aircraft usually operate alone, elint flights are more complex and often involve several aircraft: while one aircraft probes a border to stimulate defence systems, a second aircraft monitors and records reactions and especially signals and communications for subsequent analysis.

UNITED KINGDOM
The RAF maintained a small number of strategic

reconnaissance aircraft at RAF Benson after the war. Mosquito PR.34s of 540 Sqn. were replaced by the Canberra PR.3 from 1952, the PR version of the Canberra entering service before the bomber. No. 58 Sqn. converted from Lincolns to Canberras in January 1953, and by the mid-1950s there were five RAF strategic PR Canberra squadrons in the UK and Europe. The early unmarked aircraft were operated secretly from RAF Wyton and flew from German bases across the Soviet Union to Iran. In July 1953 one such sortie over the Kapustin Yar missile centre resulted in the aircraft being damaged by gunfire, although it landed safely. Also operating from Wyton from 1955 to 1974, first with Valiants then with Victor SR.2s, was 543 Sqn., engaged on radar reconnaissance. Currently the RAF's sole PR unit is 1 PRU based at Wyton with a handful of Canberra PR.9s.

From early 1949, the Western allies were concerned to monitor the extent of Soviet progress towards developing an atomic bomb, and USAF and RAF aircraft were hastily equipped to fulfil the task. In the event, the first Russian test took place on 29 August 1949. The RAF aircraft were probably Lincolns, but in due course the RAF operated 1323 Flt. at RAF Wyton with Canberras in 1952, and from 1954 No. 542 Sqn. (which in 1958 became 21 Sqn.) flew the Canberra B.6 and PR.7 out of RAF Upwood. In addition, Canberras of several basic marks were operated by 76 Sqn. from 1953 to 1957 in association with British nuclear tests in the Pacific. Some of the B.6 versions were fitted with the Double Scorpion rocket to extend the aircraft's operating ceiling.

The first RAF post-war elint work was conducted by the Radar Reconnaissance Flight, an offspring of 58 Sqn. equipped with Lincoln B.IIs at RAF Benson from 1951. In July 1951 No. 192 Sqn. formed with Lincolns at RAF Watton, which after adding the Canberra B.2 and B.6 and the Washington B.1 to its inventory became 51 Sqn. in 1958. The unit subsequently moved to RAF Wyton to re-equip first with the Comet 2R and then the Nimrod R.1 in 1971. Generally working around Scandinavia and the Baltic, the squadron's aircraft frequently operate farther afield; Falklands honours were accorded in 1982. Although the RAF does not appear to have suffered the operational loss of any elint aircraft, Lincoln B.II RF531/C of the CGS was shot down by four Soviet MiG-15s in March 1953. Flying along the Berlin corridor, it may have been assumed to have been on a probing flight.

The UK is believed to be preparing for its first comint satellite operation. The system, reportedly named Zircon, is thought to be due for launch within the next two years among the Skynet communications series as Skynet IVC.

UNITED STATES

The US government reacted swiftly to the news of a Soviet atomic weapon. Various types of aircraft were fitted with air sampling equipment, and after initial deliveries of the U-2 to the CIA from 1956 a number of the type were fitted for high-altitude air sampling and operated by the USAF. From 1959, 'weather' reconnaissance squadrons began equipping with the high-flying RB-57D, starting with the 4926 Test Sqn. (TS) at Kirtland Air Force Base (AFB). Located around the world, most of these units had disbanded by 1974, by which time they were being supplanted by the more capable WC-135B of the 55th Weather Reconnaissance Squadron (WRS), 41st Rescue and Weather Reconnaissance Wing (RWRW), at McClelland AFB.

Another variant of the C-135, the NC-135, is in service with the US Atomic Energy Commission, flying out of Forbes AFB. Keeping well away from national borders, the monitoring aircraft are able to collect fine atmospheric particles, and subsequent analysis enables scientists to determine a wide range of weapon characteristics. The sampling aircraft came into their own after the accident at the nuclear power station at Chernobyl, Ukraine, on 26 April 1986. Sweden first identified the explosion, and nuclear fallout samples were collected by J32D Lansens of F13M, based at Linköping. An RC-135U of 55 Strategic Reconnaissance Wing (SRW) flying out of RAF Mildenhall had also gathered evidence, and on the 28th an EC-135H of 10 Airborne Command and Control Squadron (ACCS) confirmed the accident through monitoring communications. From the 30th, samples were collected from the easterly airstream by two WC-135Bs of

55 WRS detached to Mildenhall. It is quite conceivable that without the evidence having been collected the Russians would have maintained secrecy, regardless of the risk to Western European nations.

The premier USAF strategic reconnaissance unit is the 55th SRW. From 1950, the Wing was equipped with the RB-29A and RB-50E, F and G models; in addition, the 91st Strategic Reconnaissance Squadron (SRS) flying out of Yokota Air Base (AB), Japan, was equipped with the RB-45C. The tasks of the Wing included a mixture of PR and elint, and with the higher risks involved in overflights the unit soon suffered casualties. A number of unarmed reconnaissance aircraft were shot down, typically by MiG-15 fighters, especially in the Far East. By 1954 they were often escorted and when, on 27 January of that year, an RB-45C was attacked over the Yellow Sea by eight MiG-15s, an escorting F-86 shot one of the latter down. In a similar attack on 5 February 1955 two MiGs were destroyed.

In Europe, one approach to the strategic reconnaissance task fell from 1956 to the 1st Air Division, headquartered at Offutt AFB but flying balloons out of Giebelstadt in West Germany, Norway and Turkey. Relying on the prevailing winds, 516 50ft-diameter 'Moby Dick' balloons with the WS-119L camera system were released from 10 January, to be retrieved in Alaska. So many landed in Russia that the programme was halted on 1 March, although a similar operation was mounted in the autumn of 1958. The programme was of limited value due to the vagaries of the weather and mechanical problems. Another novel development believed to have been used operationally was the FICON (Fighter Conveyor) project. A number of RB-36 bombers were converted as stand-off launchers to carry a fast reconnaissance model of the F-84 fighter, but the 91st SRS was equipped with the combination for only a year. More conventional platforms were the RB-45C of 19 RS, 91 RW, based at RAF Sculthorpe from 1954, an unusual unit in that some of the aircraft wore RAF markings (but not serials) and the RAF provided at least two crews.

With increasing concerns in the US about Soviet missile developments, it was essential that a safe reconnaissance platform be developed capable of extended, high-level flight. In 1954 a contract was let by the CIA to Lockheed for the production of an aircraft to fulfil the role. Built in great secrecy, the aircraft that first flew on 4 August 1955 from a new facility at Groom Lake was to be designated U-2. The U (Utility) designation was one attempt to disguise the type's function. Pilots for the U-2 were temporarily released from the USAF and contracted to Lockheed as civilians. The first CIA U-2 unit, 1 Weather Reconnaissance Squadron Provisional (WRSP 1) formed at Groom Lake in April 1956, moving to RAF Lakenheath in July.

The first overflight over Moscow took place on 4 July 1956. This sortie went undetected, but the remaining four of the first series, which ended on 10 July, were noted and a public complaint was made. At the time the Soviet Union had no fighters capable of coming anywhere near the U-2's altitude. Security was such that news of a new type in the UK soon leaked and the USAF was obliged to admit the existence of a 'weather reconnaissance' aircraft. The unit moved to Wiesbaden AB in West Germany from September. Shortly after, WRSP 2 (also known as Detachment 10/10) was formed at Incirlik in Turkey, while early in 1957 a third unit formed at Atsugi in Japan. The CIA continued the overflight programme until 1960 when the U-2 gained instant notoriety on 1 May. Piloted by Gary Powers, U-2C 566693 of WRSP 2 was shot down by one or more SA-2 missiles over Sverdlovsk. The Russians initially refrained from admitting that they had captured the pilot, but then humiliated President Eisenhower after he had made a denial which was then disproved.

The importance of the U-2 programme cannot be overstated. Without sound intelligence the Americans ran into the 'missile gap' controversy from 1957. Put simply, the USAF was alarmed at what it claimed was a fast rate of intercontinental ballistic missile (ICBM) development and deployment (although the CIA claimed a slower rate). The cost of making the wrong assumption was high, both in economic and political terms. During the four-year period of the programme, about 30 overflights were made, but many more were vetoed by the President, constantly worried about the implications of an accident. In the event the issue was not settled by the U-2 programme, but it did furnish invaluable data about bomber deployment, air defence systems and submarine development.

The U-2 overlights were halted, but the USAF suffered a further setback when an ERB-47H of

TABLE OF UNITS: STRATEGIC INTELLIGENCE, 1945 TO DATE

Unit	Aircraft	Base	Role	Dates
RAF				
540 Sqn.	Mosquito PR.34, Canberra PR.3/7	Benson, Wyton	PR	00/12/47 to 00/03/56
58 Sqn.	Mosquito, Canberra PR.3/7/9	Benson, Wyton	PR	00/00/50 to 30/09/70
541 Sqn.	Canberra PR.3	Buckeburg	PR	00/00/53 to 06/09/57
543 Sqn.	Valiant B(PR)K.1, Victor SR.2	Wyton	Radar recce	00/09/55 to 24/05/74
13 Sqn.	Canberra PR.7/9	Akrotiri, Luqa, Wyton	PR	00/05/56 to 00/01/82
39 Sqn.	Canberra PR.3/9	Luqa, Wyton	PR (to 1 PRU)	01/07/58 to 00/00/84
1 PRU	Canberra PR.9	Wyton	PR (ex 39 Sqn.)	00/00/84 to date
1323 Flt.	Canberra PR.3	Wyton	? Nuclear monitoring	00/00/52 to 00/00/54
76 Sqn.	Canberra B.6 Mod.	Wittering	Nuclear monitoring	09/12/53 to 00/00/57
542 Sqn.	Canberra PR.3/7, B.2/6	Wyton, Laverton (Aust.)	Nuclear monitoring	17/05/54 to 00/07/58
21 Sqn.	Canberra B.6, PR.7	Upwood	Nuclear monitoring	01/10/58 to 15/01/59
RRF	Lincoln B.II	Benson, Wyton	Elint	00/00/51 to 00/00/54
192 Sqn.	Lincoln B.II, Canberra B.2/6, Washington B.1	Watton	Elint (to 51 Sqn.)	15/07/51 to 00/08/58
51 Sqn.	Lincoln B.II, Canberra B.2/6, Comet 2R, Nimrod R.1	Watton, Wyton	Elint (ex 192 Sqn.)	21/08/58 to date
USAF SAC Wings				
91 SRW				
91 SRS	RB-29, RB-45C, RB-50	Barksdale AFB, Johnson AB	PR (to 71 SRFW)	00/00/50 to 00/12/54
322, 323, 324 SRS	RB-45C, YRB-47B, RB-47E	Barksdale AFB, Lockbourne AFB	PR	00/00/50 to 08/11/57
19 SRS	RB-45C, RB-66C	Sculthorpe	General int., inc. PR	00/05/54 to 00/08/59
71 SRFW				
91 SRS	GRB-36J, RF-84K	Larson AFB, Spokane AFB	PR (ex 91 SRW)	00/00/55 to 01/07/57
5 SRW				
31 SRS	RB-29, RB-45C, RB-50	Travis AFB, Kadena AB, Yokota AB, Johnson AB	PR	00/00/50 to 00/00/56
23, 31, 72 SRS	RB-36F	Travis AFB	PR	00/03/51 to 00/00/55
55 SRW				
338 SRS	RB-29A, RB-50E/F/G	Ramey AFB	General int., inc. PR	00/00/50 to 00/00/56
	RB-47E/H/K	Forbes AFB, Offutt AFB	General int., inc. PR	00/00/56 to 00/06/63
	RB-47K	Offutt AFB	General int., inc. PR (ex 343 SRS)	25/03/67 to 24/12/67
38 SRS	RB-29A	Barksdale AFB	General int., inc. PR	00/00/50 to 00/00/56
	RB-47E/H/K	Forbes AFB, Offutt AFB	General int., inc. PR	00/00/56 to 00/00/65
	RC-135	Offutt AFB	Elint	00/00/64 to date
343 SRS	RB-29A	Barksdale AFB	General int., inc. PR	00/00/50 to 00/00/56
	RB-47E/H/K	Forbes AFB, Offutt AFB	General int., inc. PR (to 338 SRS)	00/00/56 to 25/03/67
	RC-135	Offutt AFB		00/00/64 to date
Det. 4	EB-47E, ERB-47H	Incirlik AB	Elint	00/00/56 to 00/00/59
Det. 1	RC-135C/D/M/U/V	RAF Mildenhall		00/00/69 to date
922 SRS	RC-135U/V	Hellenikon AB		00/00/70 to date
1370 PMW	RC-135A	Turner AFB	PR	00/00/57 to 00/00/64
6 SW				
24 SRS	RC-135D/S/X	Eielson AFB, Shemya (Det. 1)	Elint	00/00/70 to date
376 SW				
82 SRS	RC-135T/W	Kadena AB	Elint	00/00/71 to 00/00/79
28 SRW				
77, 717, 718 SRS	RB-36F	Ellsworth AFB	PR	00/00/50 to 00/00/55

TABLE OF UNITS: STRATEGIC INTELLIGENCE, 1945 TO DATE (continued)

Unit	Aircraft	Base	Role	Dates
111 SRW (became 99 SRW 11/53)				
129, 130 SRS	RB-29A	Fairchild AFB	PR	00/08/51 to 00/00/54
72 SRW				
60, 73, 301 SRS	RB-36F	Little Rock AFB	PR	00/00/52 to 00/00/55
26 SRW				
3, 4, 10 SRS	YRB-47B, RB-47E	Lockbourne AFB	PR	00/09/53 to 01/07/58
90 SRW				
319, 320, 321 SRS	RB-29A, RB-47E	Forbes AFB	PR	00/00/54 to 14/05/58
70 SRW				
6, 26, 61 SRS	RB-47E	Little Rock AFB	PR	00/00/55 to 14/06/58
4080 SRW (to 100 SRW)				
4025 SRS	RB-57D	Turner AFB, Laughlin AFB (det. Yokota AB 1957)	General int., inc. PR	00/02/56 to 15/06/60
	DC-130A, CH-3E	Bien Hoa	Drone ops. (to 350 SRS)	20/08/64 to 00/02/66
4028 SRS	U-2A/C	Laughlin AFB, Davis-Monthan AFB (dets. Bien Hoa 1964–66)	General int., inc. PR (to 349 SRS)	11/06/57 to 11/02/66
100 SRW (ex-4080 SRW; to 9 SRW)				
349 SRS	U-2C/R	Davis-Monthan AFB (dets. U-Tapao, Bien Hoa)	General int., inc. PR (ex 4028 SRS)	15/06/66 to 00/04/76
350 SRS	DC-130A/E, CH-53A	Bien Hoa, U-Tapao	Drone ops. (ex 4025 SRS)	
4200 SW				
–	SR-71A	Beale AFB	General int., inc. PR (to 9 SRW)	07/01/66 to 06/06/66
9 SRW				
1 SRS	SR-71A	Beale AFB (dets. Kadena AB, Mildenhall)	General int., inc. PR (ex 4200 SW)	06/06/66 to date
99 SRS	U-2R, TR-1A	Beale AFB (dets. Akrotiri, Mildenhall, Osan AB)	General int., inc. PR (ex 349 SRS)	00/03/76 to date
17 RW				
95 SRS	TR-1A	Alconbury	General int., inc. PR	00/05/84 to date
USAF independent units				
1 AD	Balloons	Giebelstadt, Eielson AFB	PR	00/00/56 to 00/00/58
6091 RS	RB-57A/E, C-130A-II	Yokota AB, Don Muang AB	General int., inc. PR (to 556 RS)	00/01/58 to 00/06/67
556 RS	EB-57E, C-130B-II	Yokota AB, Don Muang AB	General int. (ex 6091 RS)	00/06/67 to 00/00/70
7406 CSS	C-130A-II/B-I	Rhein-Main AB	Elint	00/00/56 to 00/00/74
	RB-69A	Wiesbaden AB, Sculthorpe	Elint	00/03/57 to 00/00/59
	EC-97G	Wiesbaden AB	Elint	00/00/63 to 00/00/64
7407 CSS	RB-57D/F	Rhein-Main AB	General int., inc. PR (to 58 WRS)	00/06/59 to 00/01/64
USAF and AEC nuclear monitoring				
4926 TS	RB-57D		Nuclear monitoring (to 1211 TS)	00/09/59 to 00/06/61
1211 TS	RB-57D	Kirtland AFB	Nuclear monitoring (ex 4926 TS; to 58 WRS)	00/06/61 to 00/06/63
58 WR	RB-57D/F		Nuclear monitoring (ex 1211 TS; to 9 WRW)	00/06/63 to 00/05/72
55 WRS	RB-57D	McClelland AFB, Eielson AFB	Nuclear monitoring	00/11/60 to 00/10/63
54 WRS	RB-57D	Guam AFB	Nuclear monitoring	00/03/62 to 00/04/64
57 WRS	RB-57D	Avalon (Aust.)	Nuclear monitoring	00/06/62 to 00/05/65
56 WRS	RB-57F, WB-57F	Yokota AB	Nuclear monitoring (to 9 WRW)	00/00/67 to 00/05/72
9 WRW (to 41 RWRW)				
55 WRS	WB-47E, WC-135B	McClelland AFB	Nuclear monitoring	00/00/65 to date
56 WRS	RB-57F	Yokota AB	Nuclear monitoring	00/05/72 to 00/11/73
58 WRS	RB-57F	Kirtland AFB	Nuclear monitoring	00/05/72 to 00/08/74
AEC				
–	NC-135	Forbes AFB	Nuclear monitoring	00/00/72 to date
CIA				
WRSP-1	U-2A/C	Lakenheath, Wiesbaden	PR	00/04/56 to 00/11/57
WRSP-2	U-2C	Adana	General int., inc. PR	00/00/57 to 00/00/60
WRSP-3	U-2C	Atsugi	General int., inc. PR	00/00/57 to 00/00/60
	A-11, SR-71A	Groom Lake	General int., inc. PR	00/00/62 to 00/00/68
USN				
VP-26	PB4Y	Norfolk NAS	Elint	00/00/49 to 00/00/53
VQ-1	P4M-1Q, EC-121M, EA-3A/B, EP-3E	Guam AB	Sigint	00/00/52 to date
VQ-2	P4M-1Q, EC-121M, EA-3A/B, EP-3E	Port Lyautey, Rota AB	Sigint	00/00/54 to date
Other air forces				
IDF	C-97, Boeing 707 (var.)	?	Elint	00/00/70 to date
2St. 3MFG, WGN	Atlantique (Mod.)	Nordholz	Elint	00/00/77 to date
Esc. El 51, AA	DC-8 (Mod.)	Evreux	Elint	00/00/77 to date
F13M, RSwedAF	C-47, J32E, Caravelle	Malmslätt	Elint, nuclear monitoring	00/00/52 to date
60 Sqn., SAAF	Boeing 707 (var.)	Waterkloof	Elint	00/05/86 to date

Note: The Pakistan Air Force (PAF) and Chinese Nationalist Air Force (CNAF) have flown the RB-57F, and the U-2 and RB-57 respectively for the USAF or CIA.

55 SRW was shot down by two MiG-19s over the Barents Sea. The aircraft had flown from RAF Brize Norton, and only two of the crew of six survived. Various RB-36 and RB-47 units had been based in the UK since 1955, primarily on elint work, but this was the first reported casualty.

The CIA had recognized the potential vulnerability of the U-2 and had contracted with Lockheed in August 1959 for the manufacture of a far more revolutionary aircraft to fly not only very high but very fast. Initially known as the A-11 and flown on overflights from Groom Lake in total secrecy for some years from 1962, the aircraft evolved into the SR-71. As such, it entered USAF service in 1966 with 4200 SRW, which became 1 SRS, 9 SRW, later in the year. A potent reconnaissance vehicle, the SR-71 operates from detached units at RAF Mildenhall and Kadena AB and has flown from Osan AB in Korea; from August 1981 the type has regularly overflown North Korea with impunity. The few examples of SR-71 photographs released for publication demonstrate the high quality of the camera systems.

A type which supplemented the U-2 family was the RB-57. The original Canberra design was developed with a much longer wing span, and the RB-57D was operational from April 1956; although not capable of reaching the ceiling of the U-2, it could carry a heavier payload and had the benefit of a two-man crew. Four sub-types were introduced into service with 4025 SRS. The final RB-57 type was the RB-57F, a grotesque redesign with a wing span of 122ft against the original 64ft of the Canberra. It entered service in 1963. It could carry two tons of cameras and had an effective range of 60 miles. It was involved in border flights, although one was lost over the Soviet Union in 1965.

The CIA turned its attention to China from 1962 and in partnership with the Chinese Nationalist Air Force (CNAF) made many U-2 overflights of the Chinese mainland until at least 1970; RB-57s were also flown for the US by CNAF pilots. The cost of the programme was high. At least two pilots were killed in training and no fewer than nine U-2s, three RB-57s and two RF-101s were brought down over China in eight years. The successors to the original U-2 are the much improved U-2R and externally similar TR-1A currently operated by 99 SRS, 9 SRW, at Beale, with detachments at RAF Akrotiri and Osan AB, and 95 RS, 17 RW, at RAF Alconbury. These latest members of the U-2 family use a wide range of sensors and cameras and have the advantage over satellite systems that they can be used with discretion to suit need and weather conditions.

The US Air Force appears to have combined elint work with photo-reconnaissance within 55 SRW until the early 1970s. The first dedicated

elint unit in US service was probably the USN's VP-26 equipped with PB4Y Privateers at Norfolk NAS. The first casualty of the elint war was a PB4Y of VP-26 flying from Wiesbaden and shot down with the loss of ten crew members over Leyaya, Latvia on 8 April 1950. The USN suffered a series of losses over the next few years; these are also included in the table.

VQ-1 and VQ-2 were the two sigint units set up to interrogate Soviet and Chinese seaborne radars and communications. Covering the Pacific and Indian Oceans and the Atlantic/Mediterranean Sea respectively, they have operated continuously since 1952. Initially equipped with the P4M-1Q Mercator, VQ-1 suffered two early losses. The first was at Wenchow in eastern China on 22 August 1956 in which sixteen crew members died, but in the second incident over the Sea of Japan on 16 June 1959 the crew survived an emergency landing at Mihi, Japan. VQ-1 also lost an EC-121M, 135749, after it had overflown Chongjin, North Korea, on 15 April 1969. Modern elint work often demands large aircraft with extensive equipment, and numerous operators and the long time on station mean extra flight crew. The EC-121 loss cost no fewer than 31 lives.

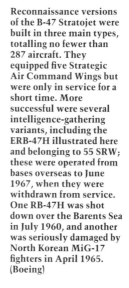

Reconnaissance versions of the B-47 Stratojet were built in three main types, totalling no fewer than 287 aircraft. They equipped five Strategic Air Command Wings but were only in service for a short time. More successful were several intelligence-gathering variants, including the ERB-47H illustrated here and belonging to 55 SRW; these were operated from bases overseas to June 1967, when they were withdrawn from service. One RB-47H was shot down over the Barents Sea in July 1960, and another was seriously damaged by North Korean MiG-17 fighters in April 1965. (Boeing)

The infamous U-2 operated covertly from European and Japanese bases for four years until one, piloted by Gary Powers, was brought down over Sverdlovsk on 1 May 1960. Hand-built in great secrecy by Lockheed, the early versions were extremely difficult to fly and suffered many accidents. When the type was first observed in 1956, it was stated to be used for F-104 fuel-flow testing and for weather research. This example, (56)6715, is shown while in service with 4080 SRW. (USAF)

On 13 June 1952 a DC-3 of the Royal Swedish Air Force (RSAF) was shot down north of Gotland in the Baltic Sea. Three days later a PBY5A of the RSAF was also shot down by a Soviet MiG-15 while searching for survivors from the DC-3. It has subsequently been suggested that the aircraft was using US electronic equipment, possibly with American personnel support.

Through the late 1950s the USAF operated, perhaps for the CIA, a number of units in West Germany equipped with a range of esoteric aircraft. From 1956, the 7406th Combat Support Squadron (CSS) at Rhein-Main AB operated the C-130A-II equipped for communications monitoring, often flying along the Berlin air corridors. One of the type, having flown out of Adana, Turkey, on 2 September 1958, crashed 30 miles north of Yerevan in Soviet Armenia. Six of the crew, which included nine civilians, died, and the fate of the eleven survivors is apparently known to the US government but kept secret.

The USN was not alone in flying the P2V Neptune; an undisclosed unit of the USAF operated the RB-69A model from Wiesbaden, possibly using the newly developed side-looking airborne radar (SLAR). This equipment would enable radar maps to be produced across boundaries but without the need for overflying. In 1963, 7406 CSS was also flying from Wiesbaden using the EC-97G, again on work along the Berlin corridors. Meanwhile 7407 CSS had formed at Rhein-Main with the RB-57 from 1959. RB-57F 6313287 was shot down by a surface-to-air missile (SAM) over the Black Sea on 14 December 1965 with the loss of the pilot and systems operator.

The 55th SRW moved from dual elint/PR capability to elint only from 1964 with the phasing out of the RB-47 and re-equipment with various marks of RC-135. Based at Offutt AFB, the Wing operates squadrons or detachments at RAF Mildenhall, Hellenikon, Eielson AFB and Kadena AB. The different sub-types of the durable Boeing 707 derivative carry a wide range of sensors, radars and communications fits and engage in every form of elint work. Several have been lost in operational accidents. In March 1987 it was reported that the Soviet Union had developed and was operating forms of lasers which were intended to blind, or had the effect of blinding, pilots of overflying reconnaissance aircraft. The equipment is claimed to have been used in the Middle East and Afghanistan.

Airliners of several nations have been known to be used for photo-reconnaissance work, although the diplomatic risks are high. Five or six – not necessarily involved in intelligence gathering – have been attacked and at least four brought down. On a smaller scale, the C-12A communications aircraft of the US ambassador to South Africa was fitted with cameras and used covertly from 1978 until its discovery in April 1979. KAL

WESTERN INTELLIGENCE-GATHERING AIRCRAFT: KNOWN OR ASSUMED LOSSES

Date	Type	Unit	Location
08/04/50	PB4Y	VP-26	Leyaya, Latvia
00/12/50	RB-45C	91 SRS	N. Korea
06/11/51	P2V-3	VP-6	Vladivostok
13/06/52	RB-29	91 SRS	Sea of Japan[1]
13/06/52	DC-3 (Tp-79)	Swed. AF	Gotland, Baltic
16/06/52	PBY-5A (47002)	Swed. AF	Baltic
03/07/52	RB-29	91 SRS	Far East
31/07/52	PBM-5S2	VP-731	Formosa[2]
07/10/52	RB-29A (4461815)	91 SRS	Kuriles
29/11/52	?	?	Manchuria
12/01/53	RB-29A (4294000)	91 SRS	Sea of Japan
18/01/53	P2V-5	VP-22	Formosa Straits
15/03/53	RB-50	55 SRW	Kamchatka[2]
00/07/53	Canberra PR.3	?541 Sqn.	Russia[2]
28/07/53	RB-50	55 SRW	Vladivostok
27/01/54	RB-45C	91 SRS	Yellow Sea[2]
04/09/54	P2V-5	VP-19	Sea of Japan
07/11/54	RB-29	91 SRS	Sea of Japan[2]
05/02/55	RB-45C	91 SRS	Yellow Sea[2]
22/06/55	P2V-5	VP-9	Bering Strait[2]
22/08/56	P4M-1Q	VQ-1	Wenchow, China
17/09/56	U-2A	WRSP-1	Kaiserlautern, WG[3]
31/10/56	Canberra PR.7 (WH799)	13 Sqn.	Syria
27/06/58	C-118A	?	Soviet Armenia
02/09/58	C-130A-II (560528)	7406 CSS	Yerevan
16/06/59	P4M-1Q	VQ-1	Sea of Japan[2]
24/09/59	U-2A (360)	WRSP-3	Fusigawa[3]
07/10/59	RB-57D	CNAF	Off China
01/05/60	U-2C (566693)	WRSP-2	Sverdlovsk
00/00/60	U-2	WRSP-2	Khartoum[3]
01/07/60	ERB-47H (534281)	55 SRW	Barents Sea
06/11/60	P2V-7	?	Off China
00/08/62	RF-101A	CNAF	Fukien, China
09/09/62	U-2C	CNAF	E. China
27/10/62	U-2C	4028 SRS	Cuba
20/11/62	U-2C	4028 SRS	Off Key West[3]
01/11/63	U-2C	CNAF	Shanghai
10/03/64	RB-66C	10 TRW	Gardelegen, WG
07/07/64	U-2G (3514)	CNAF	S. China
10/01/65	U-2C (3512)	CNAF	South of Beijing
21/01/65	Canberra PR.3 (WF926)	39 Sqn.	?[1]
00/03/65	RF-101A	CNAF	China
27/04/65	ERB-47H	55 SRW	N. Korea[2]
11/09/65	RB-57F	24 Sqn. PAF	India
14/12/65	RB-57F (6313287)	7407 CSS	Black Sea
01/01/66	KA-3B	?	S. China
28/07/66	U-2	4080 SRW	Bolivia
08/10/66	U-2A (566690)	4080 SRW	Bien Hoa
17/07/67	KC-135R (591465)	55 SRW	?[3]
09/09/67	U-2	CNAF	E. China
02/04/68	U-2	CNAF	China
05/06/68	A-12 (606932)	9 SRW	S. of Philippines[1]
00/01/69	U-2	CNAF	China
00/03/69	U-2	CNAF	Inner Mongolia
10/03/69	RC-135S (591491)	6 SW	Eilson[3]
15/04/69	EC-121M (135749)	VQ-1	SE Chongjin, N. Korea
05/06/69	RC-135E (624137)	6 SW	Bering Strait[3]
00/00/70	U-2	CNAF	China
13/10/74	WC-130	?	S. China Sea[4]
29/05/75	U-2C (566700)	349 SRS	Winterberg WG[3]
15/08/75	U-2R (6810334)	99 SRS	Gulf of Siam
07/12/77	U-2R (6810330)	99 SRS	Akrotiri[3]
23/04/78	Boeing 707	KAL	Murmansk
16/09/80	RC-135U	55 SRW	Libyan coast[2]
17/03/81	RC-135S (612664)	6 SW	Shemya[3]
01/09/83	Boeing 747 (HL7442)	KAL	Sakhalin
26/02/85	RC-135T (553121)	6 SW	Valdez, Alaska[3]

Notes:
1. Aircraft missing from potentially operational sortie.
2. Aircraft attacked by ground or air units but returned safely.
3. Aircraft crashed during potentially operational sortie.
4. Aircraft disappeared.
All other references are where an aircraft is known to have been shot or forced down, normally in hostile territory.

had a polar-routed Boeing 707 brought down by Soviet fighters well outside its flight plan at Murmansk on 23 April 1978, and the airline suffered a much greater loss when Boeing 747

HL7442 on Flight KE007 from Alaska to Seoul was shot down by an Su-15 off Sakhalin Island with the loss of all 269 aboard. A number of peculiarities of the flight support the idea that the aircraft might have been acting as a probe for several RC-135s of 24 SRS known to be flying in the area.

No account of US reconnaissance activity would be complete without reference to the new generation of 'stealth' aircraft, designed to emit low radar, infra-red (IR), acoustic and visual signatures. Lockheed, with its experience of producing the U-2 and SR-71 in conditions of extreme secrecy, was the contractor chosen for small fighter type, and the prototype aircraft, designated XST, flew from 1977. The production Covert Survivable In-weather Reconnaissance-Strike (CSIRS) aircraft, designated F-117, flew from 1982 and is believed to equip the 4450th Tactical Test Squadron. The F-117 is reported to have made overflights, some from overseas bases. The second 'stealth' type is the B-2 which should have flown by the time these words are read. A bomber, it may also generate reconnaissance or elint variants. In January 1988 it was reported that a new reconnaissance aircraft was under development in the US to replace the SR-71. With 'stealth' technology, it is intended to fly at Mach 5 and at an altitude in excess of 100,000ft.

OTHER AIR FORCES

Within NATO, the West German Navy (MFG) and French Air Force (AA) operate a limited number of Atlantiques and DC-8s respectively on elint work. The RSAF also operates two Caravelles with F13M. Farther afield both the Israeli Defence Force/Air Force (IDF/AF) and the South African Air Force (SAAF) operate elint versions of the Boeing 707, converted by Bedek Aviation, and Israel formerly flew the C-97 in the elint role.

The Soviet Air Forces have used a range of dedicated intelligence-gathering aircraft since about 1958. Long Range Aviation (DA) flew the huge Mya-4 'Bison-B' and 'C' until 1975, since when it has operated both the Tu-16 'Badger-K' and the Il-20 'Coot-A'. DA aircraft are normally based in the USSR, although the Il-20 has worked over the Indian Ocean from Aden. Shorter range types are used, generally for photo-reconnaissance, by Frontal Aviation (FA). The Yak-26 'Mandrake' has been in service since 1963 and the later MiG-25 'Foxbat-B' and 'E' have been operated in Europe and the Middle East since 1971. At least one, in Syrian Air Force markings, has been shot down by the IDF/AF.

The bulk of elint work for the Soviet Union has fallen to Naval Aviation (AV-MF), and its aircraft have long been a feature of western naval exercises. Since 1963 the elderly Tu-16 'Badger-E' and 'F' have plied the Mediterranean and Baltic Seas. The Tu-20 'Bear-C' (elint), 'D' (maritime

reconnaissance/elint) and 'E' (maritime reconnaissance/photo-reconnaissance) have been operated across the world, together with the elint Tu-142 'Bear-F'. The most recent type on the AV-MF inventory is the Il-20 'Coot-A'.

The V-VS also operates aircraft designed to monitor nuclear tests. On 11 May 1966 an An-8 was intercepted by Republic of Korea Air Force (ROKAF) F-5As while monitoring fallout from a Chinese test two days earlier.

Both DA and AV-MF aircraft are regularly intercepted almost daily as they approach national airspace across the world on elint missions, but losses have occurred only through accident.

AIRCRAFT MARKINGS

RAF

Lincoln B.II *Medium Sea Grey over, black under (extending up fuselage), grey spinners, white fuselage codes, red serial on rear fuselage: RE319/A (RRF); RA685/M (51 Sqn.); SX991/OT-C (58 Sqn.); SX980/M (192 Sqn.).*
Washington B.1 *Bare metal overall, black serial and large black codes on fin: WZ966/A (192 Sqn.).*
Canberra PR.3 *Medium Sea Grey over, PR Blue under (extending up fuselage sides), small white serial on rear fuselage: WE145 (540 Sqn.). Dark Green/Dark Sea Grey over, PR Blue under, small white serial: WF922 (39 Sqn.).*
Canberra PR.7 *Silver overall, small black serial: WH779 (542 Sqn.). Dark Green/Dark Sea Grey over, silver under: WT519 (13 Sqn.).*
Canberra PR.9 *Bare metal overall, small black*

The ultimate (and ugliest) development of the Canberra design was the RB-57F, with a wing span increased to 122ft and with two J60 jet engines in addition to the main powerplants, changes which enabled the aircraft to cruise at 63,000ft. One example, operated by the 7407th Composite Support Squadron, was shot down over the Black Sea in December 1965. RAF reconnaissance Canberras had their wing area increased by extending the chord inboard of the engine nacelles.

The probing of Soviet intelligence-gathering aircraft provides good interception practice for NATO fighters. In this instance, an An-12 'Cub-B' of the Naval Air Force has been picked up off the Norwegian coast by an F-104G Starfighter of 331 Sqn. from Bodo. Soviet strategic reconnaissance aircraft rarely carry markings apart from national insignia on fin and wings, making even the user service impossible to identify. (RNAF)

serial: *XH164 (58 Sqn.). Dark Green/Dark Sea Grey over, Light Aircraft Grey under: XH170 (39 Sqn.); XH134 (1 PRU).*

Canberra B.6 *White overall, large black serial, fin badge: WH962 (76 Sqn.). Silver overall, large black serial and 'Royal Air Force Signals Command' along fuselage, fin badge: WJ640 (51 Sqn.).*

Valiant B.1 *Bare metal overall, black serial on rear fuselage: WZ382 (543 Sqn.).*

Victor SR.2 *Dark Green/Medium Sea Grey over, white under, black serial, unit badge on fin: XM718 (543 Sqn.).*

Comet 2R *White over, bare metal under divided by blue cheat line: XK659/659 (51 Sqn.).*

Nimrod R.1 *Hemp overall, white serial, unit badge on fin: XW665/65 (51 Sqn.).*

USAF

Most strategic reconnaissance aircraft in USAF service have flown in bare metal finish with national markings appropriately placed.

RB-50E *47122 (55 SRW).*

RB-45C *480037 (91 SRW).*

RB-36H *5113722 (5 SRW).*

RB-47H *534280 (55 SRW).*

ERB-47H *536245 (55 SRW).*

RB-57D *533977 (55 WRS).*

RB-57F *6313291 (7407 CSS).*

C-130A-II *Light grey overall: 541637 (7406 CSS).*

U-2C *Black overall, white serial: 566722 (4028 SRS). Natural metal, bold national markings: 566708 (4028 SRS).*

U-2R *Black overall, no national markings, red serial: 6810339 (99 SRS).*

TR-1A *Black overall, no national markings, red serial: 801078 (95 SRS).*

SR-71A *Black overall, national markings, white serial: 6417955 (1 SRS). Black overall, no national markings, red serial: 6417974 (9 SRS, Det. 4).*

RC-135 *Originally light grey overall, latterly white upper decking: RC-135S 612663. RC-135U*

614849. RC-135V 614841. RC-135W 624135 (all 55 SRW).

USN

PB4Y *Dark Sea Blue overall, white codes: HA/5 (VP-26).*

P4M-1Q *Dark Sea Blue overall, white serial and code: 124373/PS3 (VQ-2).*

EC-121M *White over, light grey under, black radomes: 145940/PR (VQ-2).*

EA-3A *Gull Gray over, white under: 142672/JQ (VQ-2).*

EP-3E *White over, light grey under, small black serial on rear fuselage, black radome: 149668 (VQ-1).*

CIA

A-11 *Bare metal with black undersides and front fuselage: 606934/FX-934.*

U-2A *Black overall, no national markings or serial.*

V-VS

V-VS reconnaissance aircraft are almost invariably in bare metal finish and rarely carry distinguishing codes or serials. Where codes are carried, they appear as two digits on the forward fuselage, usually in pale blue. Some AV-MF Il-20s have appeared in a medium grey finish. National markings appear on the wings and fin.

POSTSCRIPT

Strategic reconnaissance overflights by the major powers have long been deemed to be high-risk operations. Most photo- and related reconnaissance is now undertaken by satellites with high-definition cameras. It is technically possible for these to be attacked and destroyed in space, and the American KH programme has suffered severe setbacks due to problems with the Shuttle programme. Cloud cover also poses problems, but at the time of writing a greater degree of openness between the superpowers may have reduced the need for covert intelligence gathering.

1.11. Miscellaneous conflicts and incidents

1. In August 1946 United States Army Air Force (USAAF) transport aircraft were brought down by Yugoslav fighters. On the 9th a C-47 was forced down and the ten on board later released; on the 19th an unspecified type was shot down and four of the crew of five killed.

2. There have been numerous uprisings in the Soviet Union since 1945, some of which may have been put down with the aid of aircraft. Major incidents are known to have occurred in 1946, 1947, 1953, 1962 and 1975.

3. The RAF and later the USAF dropped agents by parachute in the Ukraine from July 1949.

Later flights were allegedly flown from Cyprus. The first US drops were made on 18 August 1951. Drops continued, being recorded in 1953, 1957 and 1960.

4. There have been many defections to the West, particularly by pilots from the Polish, Czechoslovak and Hungarian Air Forces. The first MiG-15 to reach Western hands in Europe was an aircraft piloted by Lt. Jazwensky, who landed at Bornholm Island in the Baltic on 20 May 1953.

5. Many aircraft have been 'buzzed' by Soviet and East German fighters in the Berlin corridor and around Berlin itself. Some have been shot down, several allegedly for spying. In April 1965 West Berlin was overflown by Soviet fighters during a special session of the Bundestag, and in similar activities the following year a Yak-28P crashed in Lake Havel. In October 1968 American, British and French aircraft overflew the city to prevent incursions; British participation included two Hercules, three Pembrokes and two helicopters. The last reported 'political' overflights were on 26 April 1969, but on 18 September 1981 a MiG-23 overflew West Berlin after a LOT Polish Airlines An-24 was hijacked to Tempelhof airfield.

6. Soviet submarines have regularly penetrated Swedish waters since 1966. On 28 November that year a 'W' Class vessel was reported sunk. In October 1981 the 'Whiskey' Class submarine 137 ran aground near Karlskrona naval base only one month after Soviet spies were arrested in the area. The vessel was damaged, having been chased and depth-charged by Swedish Navy Hkp4 (Vertol KV-107) helicopters. After diplomatic activity the submarine was released. In February 1982 a Coast Guard Cessna was buzzed by a Russian Su-15. The most extensive operations were in 1982. In early June helicopters and Viggen fighters spent three days searching for a vessel off Umea. There was a further hunt in September, then on 3 October two submarines were identified off Musko naval base. In the hunt for the vessel some 3,000 troops were moved to the area to man coastal artillery and AAA, while forty ships were involved in blocking the Horsefjaerd. Although inconclusive, this was the largest search operation of sixty in the year.

In March and May 1983 more submarines were attacked off Musko and Sundsvall respectively, and there have been reports of Swedish attacks in February 1984 and June 1986. On 7 July 1985 Swedish Air Force Viggens which were shadowing a Soviet naval exercise were harried by a Soviet Su-15 which later crashed in the Baltic. On 26 July 1986 four Czechs flying a Piper Cherokee over restricted military areas were detained by police, having been forced to land. The Swedish anti-submarine effort is maintained by two units both equipped with the Hkp4 and Hkp6

(AB.206A). The 1st Helikopterdivisionen is based at Berga, the 3rd at Kallinge. The helicopters are supported by Viggen SF37 and SH37 reconnaissance and maritime surveillance fighters of F13 based at Norrköping/Brävalla and Coast Guard aircraft. Both torpedoes and depth charges are employed, although these are designed to disable rather than destroy. There were further reports of foreign submarines in June 1988.

7. On three occasions since 1945 – in 1958, 1972–73 and 1975–76 – Great Britain and Iceland have been at odds over fishing limits around the latter's shores. The most serious incidents occurred in the last two 'conflicts' when there were numerous collisions between Icelandic gunboats and British trawlers, fishery protection vessels or frigates. Wasp helicopters of 829 NAS embarked on frigates were used for reconnaissance and liaison tasks, while the Nimrod MR.1s of 120, 201 and 206 Sqn. from Kinloss flew maritime patrol sorties.

8. After a coup in Portugal in April 1974, which brought an extreme left-wing government to power, there were attempted counter-coups in 1975, which helped to modify the Government's stance. During one such action, on 11 March 1975, a pilot of the Portuguese Air Force (FAP), flying from Lisbon, attacked an army barracks in the capital in T-6G 1737, causing some damage.

9. On 27 June 1980 an Itavia DC-9 travelling at 27,000ft between Bologna and Palermo crashed in the Tyrrhenian Sea, killing 81 on board. The cause of the accident remains a mystery, and one that is heightened by the discovery of a crashed Libyan Air Force (LARAF) MiG-23 in Calabria on 18 July that year. On two occasions since, in August 1981 and on 16 May 1982, Aero Trasporti Italiana DC-9s have reported explosions in the area.

10. An Argentinian-registered CL-44 of Transportes Aéreos Rioplatenses (TAR) crashed near Yerevan on 18 July 1981. The aircraft was on a flight from Cyprus to Tehran with a cargo of 'food and medicine', and reports suggested that it had been shot down by Soviet fighters.

An unusual photograph of an Il-20 'Coot-A', taken by an RAF fighter in 1980. The type is operated by the Soviet Air Force to gather maritime elint and regularly shadows NATO vessels and exercises in the Baltic and Atlantic. The large fairing under the fuselage is believed to house side-looking airborne radar (SLAR), while the large blister on the forward fuselage contains optical/infra-red sensors. (RAF)

2: The Eastern Mediterranean

At the end of the Second World War British forces occupied Palestine, Jordan and Egypt, while the French occupied Lebanon and Syria which they were soon to leave. Palestinian Jews opposed to British policy fought the British in Palestine, forcing withdrawal in 1948. With the creation of the State of Israel, war with Arab neighbours was inevitable and the West made no effort to intervene. The Israeli Defence Force successfully held out until the ceasefire in 1949, after which began a process of re-equipment.

Britain withdrew from Egypt in the early 1950s, but with the nationalization of the Suez Canal in 1956 embarked on the ill-fated joint Anglo-French expedition. The only beneficiary was Israel, which simultaneously invaded the Sinai peninsula to the Suez Canal, capturing vast amounts of war *matériel* before retiring to her original frontier.

Two years later, unrest was to spill over into Lebanon and Jordan, with prospective external intervention, but in both cases the position was stabilized by Western intervention. Israel remained technically at war with her Arab neighbours and, anticipating an Egyptian invasion, in 1967 took pre-emptive action, again invading Sinai, West Jordan and the Syrian Golan Heights. This time the captured territory was not conceded.

Jordan was next to suffer war as Syrian forces invaded in 1970 in support of Palestinian irregulars. The Jordanian Government had put pressure on the Palestinians to stop using Jordan as a base for attacks on Israel, which offered to intervene in support of King Hussein against Syria.

As Egypt attempted to wear down Israel through a process of attrition, she was also planning an invasion across the Canal. The cost to the Israelis was high and, recognizing the difficulty of holding Sinai, a historic peace was negotiated, through the United States, with Egypt. The peace treaty was the signal for renewed Palestinian attacks on Israel, leading to the Israeli invasion of Lebanon. Although Israel has now withdrawn her forces, the civil war continues and the IDF/AF makes regular offensive sorties across the border to attack suspected Palestinian camps.

GENERAL NOTE

The Israeli Air Force in particular is exceedingly security-conscious. This means that all notes on markings applied to aircraft actually participating in wars should be treated with some caution. The overall colour schemes are believed to be accurate, but codes are changed regularly, making the identification of individual aircraft impossible. Unit numbers are not publicized, and any unit markings are invariably censored on photographs or obscured in public.

Israeli airfields are often misrepresented on maps, but the accompanying schedule is believed to be accurate. Egyptian and Syrian airfield names have enjoyed many spellings as the Arabic is phonetically translated to English; in addition, some airfields have been renamed. Spellings given in the text and on maps are those most commonly used at the time; the many alternatives are not scheduled. In general, units operated from their normal bases, so dates are given exceptionally.

ISRAELI AIRFIELDS

Name	Alternative name(s)	Nearest town	Notes
Aqir	Tel Nof, Ekron	Ramleh	Ex RAF
Beer Menuha		Beer Menuha	IDF
Beit Daras	Faluja	Faluja	Ex RAF
Bir Gifgafa	Refidim	Bir Gifgafa	Ex EAF
Bir Hassana		Bir Hassana	Ex EAF
Bir Lahma	El Arish	El Arish	Ex EAF
Ein Shemer	–	Natanya	Ex RAF
Eitam	El Arish	El Arish	Built post-1970
Ekron	Aqir	Ramleh	See Aqir
El Bassa	Bezet, Betset	Betset	Ex RAF
El Mulayz	Mulayhis, El Mushash	El Mulayz	Built post-1967
El Sur	El Tor, El Tur	El Sur	Ex EAF
El Themada	Thamad	El Themada	Ex EAF
Etzion	–	Dahab	Built post-1967
Faluja	Beit Daras	Faluja	Ex RAF/EAF
Haifa	–	Haifa	Ex RAF
Hatzerim	–	Beersheba	IDF
Hatzor	–	Hatzor	IDF
Herzliya	Hertzlia	Herzlia	IDF
Jenin	–	Jenin	Ex RAF
Jericho	–	Jericho	Ex RAF LG
Livnat	–	Livnat	IDF strip
Lydda	Lod	Lydda (Lod)	–
Megiddo	–	Megiddo	Ex RAF
Natanya	–	Natanya	IDF strip
Nevatim	–	Beersheba	IDF strip
Niram	–	Gaza	IDF strip
Ovda	Ouvda, Uvdah	Eilat	US-funded
Petah Tiqva	Lydda Satellite	Tel Aviv	Ex RAF
Qalandiya	Kolundia, Atarot, Hebron	Jerusalem	Ex RAF
Qastina	Kfar Sirkin, Kastina	Qastina	Ex RAF
Ramon	Matred Ramon	Eilat	US-funded
Ramallah	–	Jerusalem	Ex RAF LG
Ramat David	–	Nazareth	Ex RAF
Ramleh	Rehovot	Ramleh	Ex RAF LG
Ras Nasrani	Ophir	Sharm el Sheikh	Ex EAF
Rosh Pinna	Mahanayim	Rosh Pinna	Ex RAF
Ruhama	–	Ruhama	IDF strip
St Jean	–	Acre	Ex RAF LG
Sde Dov	Ramat Aviv, Dov Hoss, Yafo	Tel Aviv	IDF
Sde Teyman		Beersheba	IDF
Sedom	–	Sedom	IDF
Urim	–	Gaza	IDF strip
Yavneel	–	Tiberias	IDF strip

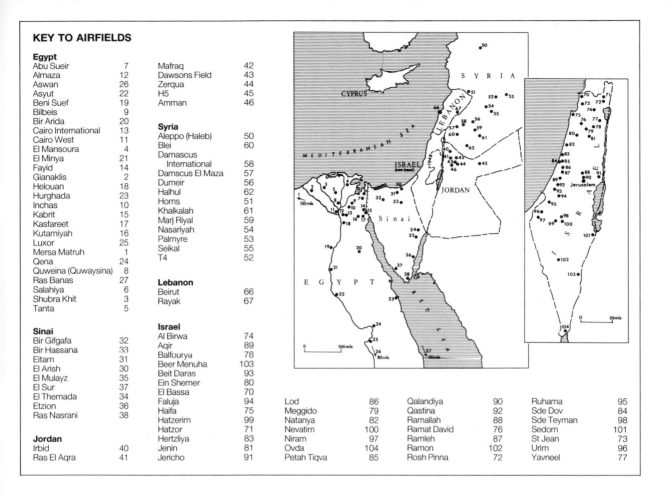

KEY TO AIRFIELDS

Egypt

Abu Sueir	7
Almaza	12
Aswan	26
Asyut	22
Beni Suef	19
Bilbeis	9
Bir Arida	20
Cairo International	13
Cairo West	11
El Mansoura	4
El Minya	21
Fayid	14
Gianaklis	2
Helouan	18
Hurghada	23
Inchas	10
Kabrit	15
Kasfareet	17
Kutamiyah	16
Luxor	25
Mersa Matruh	1
Qena	24
Quweina (Quwaysina)	8
Ras Banas	27
Salahiya	6
Shubra Khit	3
Tanta	5

Sinai

Bir Gifgafa	32
Bir Hassana	33
Eitam	31
El Arish	30
El Mulayz	35
El Sur	37
El Themada	34
Etzion	36
Ras Nasrani	38

Jordan

Irbid	40
Ras El Aqra	41
Mafraq	42
Dawsons Field	43
Zerqua	44
H5	45
Amman	46

Syria

Aleppo (Haleb)	50
Blei	60
Damascus International	58
Damscus El Maza	57
Dumeir	56
Halhul	62
Homs	51
Khalkalah	61
Marj Riyal	59
Nasariyah	54
Palmyre	53
Seikal	55
T4	52

Lebanon

Beirut	66
Rayak	67

Israel

Al Birwa	74
Aqir	89
Balfourya	78
Beer Menuha	103
Beit Daras	93
Ein Shemer	80
El Bassa	70
Faluja	94
Haifa	75
Hatzerim	99
Hatzor	71
Hertzliya	83
Jenin	81
Jericho	91
Lod	86
Meggido	79
Natanya	82
Nevatim	100
Niram	97
Ovda	104
Petah Tiqva	85
Qalandiya	90
Qastina	92
Ramallah	88
Ramat David	76
Ramleh	87
Ramon	102
Rosh Pinna	72
Ruhama	95
Sde Dov	84
Sde Teyman	98
Sedom	101
St Jean	73
Urim	96
Yavneel	77

2.1. Palestine, 1945–1948

After conquering Palestine from Turkey in the First World War, Britain was granted a mandate in 1920. The British Government supported the establishment of a Jewish State in principle, to the concern of Arabs. As the Jewish population rose from 4,000 in 1931 to 62,000 in 1935, with no sign of developments, illegal Jewish militia organizations were established. In 1936 serious fighting broke out, but the Second World War led to a cessation of violence. During the war Britain based troops in Palestine and began an extensive airfield construction programme. In general the Jews co-operated with the British, some serving with distinction. As the war drew to a close and many stateless and homeless Jews fled to Palestine from the concentration camps, impatience with the administration led to a resumption of fighting.

Most Jews in Palestine lived in settlements, and it was here that the Yishuv movement spawned the Irgun Haganah. Within or deriving from Haganah were the Chish, Rekhesh, Palmach and Aliyah Bet movements. All of these organizations benefited from having worked with the British and in general were committed to the protection of Jews actually or potentially in Palestine. There were those who wanted to see a more proactive stance taken, and these extremists formed the Irgun Zvai Leumi (IZL) and Lohamei Herut Israel (LHI). LHI opened the postwar offensive with the assassination of the British Minister of State, Lord Moyne, in Cairo in April 1945. No. 6 Sqn. RAF, with Hurricane IVs, was moved to Meggido and 208 Sqn., with Spitfire IXs, joined 32 Sqn. (Spitfire VCs) at Ramat David. As British attitudes to illegal immigration hardened, Irgun and LHI agreed with Haganah to work in concert as the Tenuat Humeri (TH).

A bombing campaign now began, concentrating initially on the railway system. As 32 Sqn. moved south to Petah Tiqva it was replaced at Ramat David by the Mustangs of 213 Sqn. By November, there was in addition 644 Sqn. with Halifaxes, a detachment of Dakotas of 78 Sqn. at Aqir, Warwick GR.5s of 621 Sqn. for anti-immigration patrols and, of great value in an anti-terrorist campaign, a flight of Austers of 651 Sqn. Survey work in the Eastern Mediterranean was conducted by Mosquitoes of 680 Sqn. at Aqir. By January 1946 there were 80,000 British troops in Palestine, and they were to be the target of the next offensive: on 22 January the RAF base at Aqir was raided and arms stolen; on 20 February the RAF radar station on Mount Carmel was attacked and damaged; and five days later seven Spitfires of 208 Sqn. were destroyed in a raid on Petah Tiqva. As incidents increased the security forces occupied the Jewish Agency offices on 29 June and swept the settlements; 2,700 arrests were made.

Within a month, Irgun retaliated by blowing up the King David Hotel in Jerusalem, and 91 people, mostly associated with the security forces, were killed. In September the 6th Airborne Division occupied Tel Aviv and RAF fighters flew constant armed reconnaissance patrols, reporting on traffic and curfew violations. At the end of 1946 the RAF transport force had increased and 38 Sqn. had replaced 620 and 621 Sqns. in the anti-smuggling/immigration patrol role, flying 'Sunburn' sorties. Nos. 6 and 213 Sqns. had meanwhile moved to Cyprus to re-equip with the Tempest F.6. Military strength had increased to 100,000 men, but this did nothing to stem the flow of extremist activities. At the end of March an oil refinery at Haifa was blown up and in May Irgun organized a breakout from Acre prison in which 271 escaped. Some of the organizers were caught and hanged, and on 30 July two British Intelligence Corps sergeants were hanged at Natanya in retaliation.

This event, together with the turning back of the refugee ship *Exodus*, focused world opinion, and on 29 November the UN voted 33–13 in favour of the partition of Palestine west of the Jordan. As Britain prepared to withdraw there was no let-up in the watch on illegal immigration and arms smuggling. Operation 'Bobcat' replaced the earlier 'Sunburn' patrols in mid-September 1947, and Lancasters of 203 Sqn. were detached to Ein Shemer to supplement those of 37 Sqn. which had arrived earlier. On 15 November Lancasters spotted the steamer *Elia*, which, when intercepted and boarded by the destroyer HMS *Venus*, was found to have 800 illegal immigrants on board. In another interception on 22 December by Lancasters of 37 Sqn., 850 immigrants were caught on a small vessel off the coast.

In the autumn of 1947 the Jews created Shin Aleph, the air arm of Haganah. Initially equipped with flying-club aircraft, it acquired eight Taylorcrafts in July, while a further eighteen Auster AOP.5s were built from twenty-five surreptitiously bought from the RAF as scrap, many of the aircraft being given identical registrations to conceal their numbers from the British. During April the fledgeling Air Force, soon to become the Chel Ha'avir, lost several aircraft to groundfire, including Tiger Moths VQ-PAT and -PAU. The aircraft operated from Sde Dov in support of Jewish groups in Palestine, flying liaison, reconnaissance and supply sorties. By now civil war had broken out between Jew and Palestinian Arab, and the British were obliged to intervene in an often vain attempt to maintain order. The Jews organized the supply of arms from a number of sources: on 31 March, for example, an American-registered DC-4 delivered a consignment from Prague to Beit Daras, although further shipments were stopped by US intervention.

The Spitfires of 32 and 208 Sqn. were kept busy, and in April 1948 they supported an attack by the Life Guards and 4/7 Dragoon Guards on Jewish headquarters in the Gold Star brewery in Jaffa. The city was occupied by Arabs but surrounded by Jewish militia who were frustrating British attempts to evacuate through the port. The extent of fighting in the last few months of

To help police Palestine in the aftermath of the Second World War, the RAF deployed two Spitfire squadrons. Initially equipped with the Mk. VC, 32 Sqn. had re-equipped with the FR.18 by the time of independence in May 1948. Based at Ramat David, aircraft of the squadron were attacked by REAF Spitfires, probably in the mistaken belief that they were Israeli. Two RAF Spitfires were destroyed and several damaged. T2214/ GZ-J is seen during maintenance; note the cockpit canopy, resting against the rear fuselage. (RAF Museum)

TABLE OF UNITS: BRITISH OPERATIONS IN PALESTINE, 1945–1948

Unit	Aircraft (code)	Base	Role	Dates
RAF				
32 Sqn.	Spitfire VC/IX/FR.18 (GZ)	Ramat David, Petah Tiqva, Aqir, Ein Shemer, Nicosia	Day fighter	00/02/45 to 00/01/51
208 Sqn.	Spitfire VC/IXC (RG)	Ramat David, Petah Tiqva, Aqir	} Day fighter	00/07/45 to 00/06/46
	Spitfire FR.18E	Ein Shemer, Nicosia		00/06/46 to 00/11/48
6 Sqn.	Hurricane IV	Meggido, Petah Tiqva, Ramat David	} Day fighter, ground attack	07/07/45 to 00/06/46
	Spitfire IX, Tempest F.6 (JV)	Ein Shemer, Nicosia		00/06/46 to 00/07/47
213 Sqn.	Mustang III/IV, Tempest F.6 (AK)	Ramat David, Nicosia	Fighter, ground attack	00/09/45 to 00/07/47
680 Sqn.	Mosquito XVI, PR.34	Aqir, Ein Shemer	PR (to 13 Sqn.)	00/02/45 to 13/09/46
13 Sqn.	Mosquito XVI, PR.34	Ein Shemer, Kabrit, Fayid	PR (ex 680 Sqn.)	01/09/46 to 00/01/55
651 Sqn.	Auster AOP.5	Det. Haifa	Liaison, local recce	00/11/45 to 17/06/48
621 Sqn.	Warwick GR.5, Lancaster GR.3	Aqir, Ein Shemer	Coastal recce	00/11/45 to 01/09/46
644 Sqn.	Halifax VII/IX	Quastina	Transport, recce	00/11/45 to 00/09/46
620 Sqn.	Halifax VII (QS)	Aqir	Transport, MR (to 113 Sqn.)	00/06/46 to 01/09/46
113 Sqn.	Halifax VII, Dakota C.4	Aqir	Transport, MR (ex 620 Sqn.)	01/09/46 to 00/04/47
38 Sqn.	Lancaster ASR/GR.3 (RL)	Ein Shemer, Luqa	Coastal recce	14/09/46 to 18/05/48
37 Sqn.	Lancaster GR.3	Ein Shemer	Coastal recce	14/09/47 to 00/04/48
203 Sqn.	Lancaster GR.3 (CJ)	Det. Ein Shemer	Coastal recce	00/10/47 to 00/11/47
78 Sqn.		Kabrit, det. Aqir		00/09/45 to 00/02/51
216 Sqn.		Kabrit, Fayid, Kabrit		00/00/46 to 00/11/55
215 Sqn.	} Dakota C.4	Kabrit	} Transport	01/08/47 to 01/05/48
204 Sqn.		Kabrit		01/08/47 to 00/02/51
114 Sqn.		Kabrit		01/08/47 to 00/03/56
FAA				
800 NAS	Seafire XVII	} Triumph	} Fighter	} 00/06/47 to 30/05/48
827 NAS	Firefly FR.1		Strike fighter	

the mandate can be gauged from Jewish deaths alone, which numbered 1,200 between January and May 1948.

On 14 May 1948 the State of Israel was declared and the emergent nation was immediately attacked and invaded by all neighbouring Arab states. A number of British units remained in the country for a few weeks, and at dawn on 22 May Spitfire IXs of 2 Sqn. Royal Egyptian Air Force (REAF) attacked Ramat David airfield then occupied by 32 and 208 Sqns. Two Spitfire FR.18s of 32 Sqn., including TZ232, were destroyed, and in another attack two hours later seven aircraft of 208 Sqn. and a visiting Dakota were damaged. This time the RAF was prepared, and two REAF Spitfires were shot down by 208 Sqn. with a further two aircraft destroyed by RAF Regt. anti-aircraft fire. The following day the RAF left Ramat David, keeping 1909 Flt. of 651 Sqn. at Haifa until 18 June, when it departed for Amman. Policing Palestine from 1945 to independence cost the British security services 223 dead and 478 injured.

AIRCRAFT MARKINGS

RAF

Spitfire IX Silver overall, black anti-glare panel on nose, black serial and codes on rear fuselage: BS467/RG-C (208 Sqn.). Dark Green/Dark Sea Grey over, light grey under, Sky fuselage band and white codes; NH487/RG-R (208 Sqn.).

Spitfire FR.18 Dark Green/Dark Sea Grey over, light grey under, black serial, white codes on rear fuselage: TZ220/GZ-X (32 Sqn.); TP443/RG-V (208 Sqn.).

Mustang IV Bare metal overall, black anti-glare panel on nose, black serials and codes: KM348/AK-V (213 Sqn.).

Dakota IV Dark Green/Dark Sea Grey over, light grey under, black serial on rear fuselage: FL524 (216 Sqn.).

Halifax VII Dark Green/brown over, black under (extending up the fuselage sides), white serial and codes on fuselage, large underwing serials: PN295/FJ (620 Sqn.); PN309/F (644 Sqn.).

Lancaster GR.3 White overall, black serial and codes: SW336/V (38 Sqn.). Washed-out Dark Slate Grey/Extra Dark Sea Grey over, white under, black serials and codes: TX269/RL-N (38 Sqn.).

Halifax VII PN309/F of 644 Sqn. making a parachute drop. Aircraft of the squadron were based at Qastina from November 1945 to September 1946 and were committed to general support duties, including supplies movements and reconnaissance, until replaced by more specialized types. (Via A. S. Thomas)

2.2. Israel, 1948–1949

With independence scheduled from 15 May 1948, the Jews in Palestine began preparing for the inevitable war with Arab neighbours. As light aircraft were acquired, arrangements were made for the secret training of paratroopers in Czechoslovakia. The Shin Aleph had two each of the Polish RWD-8, -13 and -15 high-wing monoplanes which together with Auster Autocrats VQ-PAS and -PAT formed the Tel Aviv Squadron based at Sde Dov. The Negev Squadron based at Beit Daras operated three Taylorcraft J-2 Cubs (VQ-PAH, -PAI and -PAJ) while the third, Judean, Squadron was given the newly rebuilt ex-RAF Austers at Yavneel. In addition there was a miscellany of aircraft including two DH Dragon Rapides, one Noorduyn Norseman, three DH Tiger Moths, a Miles Falcon, a Beechcraft Bonanza, a Fairchild F-24R Argus, a Zlin XII, a Benes-Mraz Be550, three Short Scions and three C-47s. In all, the Sherut Avir, as Shin Aleph had become, possessed 54 aircraft at Independence.

Confronting Israel were Egypt, Syria, Jordan, Lebanon and Iraq. Of these, Egypt had fifteen Spitfire IXs, five C-47s and four Lysanders at El Arish; in addition, Hawker Fury demonstrator NX798 was commandeered on 27 April. Iraq had a flight of T-6 Harvards based in Jordan and Syria had ten. Jordan and Lebanon had no offensive aircraft. Fighting had started as early as January 1948 when Arab Liberation Army (ALA) forces attacked Kfar Szold. Further settlements were attacked, but more serious was the blockading of Jews in Jerusalem. Relief convoys from Tel Aviv needed British escorts after one convoy lost 21 out of 40 vehicles despatched.

On 9 April a joint Irgun/LHI force attacked the village of Deir Yassin astride the Tel Aviv–Jerusalem road and in a controversial action killed 254 Arabs including many women and children. Later in April the Jews established control in Haifa and Jaffa. On 14 May the Egyptian 3rd Division, supported by the Royal Egyptian Air Force (REAF), struck in the south to Gaza, Beersheba and Tel Aviv. The attacks came

as no surprise: the build-up of forces had been monitored by two South African pilots in Bonanza ZS-BWS. After an initial bombardment, Lebanese and Syrian forces advanced along the coast road to Ein Gev, and on the 15th the Arab Legion crossed the Jordan to safeguard Nablus and Ramallah. The Iraqi Army followed through in an attempt to cut Israel laterally, but they were forced to stop short just twelve miles from Natanya. REAF Spitfires of 2 Sqn. attacked Sde Dov airfield, causing some damage. Syrian Harvards were in action from the 16th to the south of Lake Tiberias in support of attacks, and it became imperative that the Israelis acquire combat aircraft.

Despite heavy fighting in the east, especially around Jerusalem, the Israelis were holding their lines and with newly delivered artillery were able to contain a new Syrian offensive at Degania on the 20th. The light aircraft squadrons had been used to bomb both Syrian and Egyptian positions with limited effect; by 22 May the position in the south was critical as the Egyptian 2nd Infantry Brigade reached Bethlehem. Compulsory military service was ordered on the 26th, and although the Jordanian border was stabilized the Egyptians had reached Ashdod by the 29th. An Israeli counterattack on 3 June was repulsed, and as further fighting broke out in the north the Israelis were grateful for the respite provided by a UN-inspired truce from 11 June.

Desperate for arms, the Israelis had concluded a number of deals with the Czechs, and the first deliveries of ammunition were made to Beit Daras in a chartered C-54 of Overseas American Airlines in April. On 23 April a contract for eleven Avia S.199s was signed at a unit cost of $190,000; the Czechs were glad to see the back of this locally developed version of the Messerschmitt Bf 109G with its appalling handling qualities. Meanwhile Israeli pilots were being trained at Urbe airport, Rome, by US instructors. At home the Sherut Avir drew on the experience of the Carmel Club, the Camel Flying Club and

The use of the ubiquitous Spitfire by the REAF, IDF and RAF in the Near East caused some confusion and accidental loss. Illustrated is a Mk. IX of 2 Sqn. REAF, which was based at El Arish throughout the War of Independence.

the Civilian Flying Club in addition to the Aviron Company (which bought and repaired aircraft) and Palestine Air Services Ltd.

The REAF used its Spitfires to bomb the Reading power station at Tel Aviv on 15 May, but one aircraft was damaged by anti-aircraft fire and crash-landed on the beach at Herzliya. It was later repaired and taken into Israeli service. The following day two C-46s were delivered to Ekron, and an Air Transport Command was formed on the 17th. The first of the Avias was delivered on the 20th to Ekron two days after REAF C-47s had bombed transport and fuel stores at Tel Aviv; several days later the first Israeli C-47 was operational, bombing Ramallah. The 29th saw the first operational use of the Avias when four aircraft of 101 Sqn. at Herzliya diverted from a planned attack on El Arish to strafe an Egyptian column approaching Tel Aviv. One was shot down and a second crash-landed on return to base. The following day a third Avia was lost in an attack on Iraq Suweidin fortress.

At the end of May the Haganah became the Tsvah Haganah le Israel and the air arm was renamed Heyl Ha'Avir. All eleven Avias had been delivered by a circuitous route from Prague via Campo Delloro, Corsica, to Ekron in Operation 'Balak'. Early in June a further deal was concluded with the Czechs, this time for 50 Spitfire IXs. The Israeli Defence Force/Air Force C-47s were carrying the attack into Arab territory with bombing raids on Amman on 1 June and Damascus on the 11th, and the Israelis were having some success in the air: on 3 June an Avia shot down a REAF C-47 bombing Tel Aviv and damaged a second. However, on the 4th yet another Avia was lost attacking an Iraqi column at Natanya and later in the day the Argus was lost at sea attacking a small Egyptian naval force which was threatening Tel Aviv. At Ashdod on the 7th Autocrat VQ-PAS was shot down by Sqn. Ldr. Abu Zaid of the REAF flying the Fury demonstrator. As the truce came into effect the REAF moved a Spitfire VC squadron up to El Arish.

The Israelis used the truce to good effect,

TABLE OF UNITS: ISRAEL, 1948–1949

Unit	Aircraft	Base	Role	From
Heyl Ha'Avir (IDF/AF)				
Tel Aviv Flt.	Autocrat, RWD-8/13/15	Sde Dov	Liaison, recce, light bombing	00/12/47
Negev Flt.	Taylorcraft J-2	Beit Daras	Liaison, recce, light bombing	00/03/48
Judean Flt.	Auster AOP.5	Yavneel	Liaison, recce, light bombing	00/04/48
101 Sqn.	Avia S.199, Spitfire V/IX	Herzliya, Ekron	Fighter, ground attack	00/05/48
	P-51D	Hatzor, Quastina		00/11/48
13 Sqn.	C-46, C-47, Norseman	Ekron	Transport	17/05/48
103 Sqn.	C-47, Beaufighter X	Sde Dov, Ramat David	Transport, bombing, ground attack	00/06/48
69 Sqn.	B-17	Ramat David	Bombing	16/07/48
105 Sqn.	Avia S.199, Spitfire IX	Herzliya	Fighter, ground attack	00/01/49
1 Sqn.	Auster, etc.	Sde Dov	Liaison, recce (ex flts. above)	00/11/48
35 Flt.	Harvard	?	Light bombing, training	00/11/48
REAF				
2 Sqn.	Spitfire IX		Fighter, ground attack	
4 Sqn.	C-47	El Arish	Transport, bombing	15/05/48
3 Sqn.	Lysander		Liaison, light bombing	
6 Sqn.	Spitfire VC		Fighter, ground attack	11/06/48
1 Sqn.	G.55B	El Hama	Fighter	00/11/48
RIAF				
? Sqn.	AT-6, Fury	Mafraq	Light ground attack	15/05/48
SAF				
? Sqn.	AT-6	El Maza (Damascus)	Light ground attack	15/05/48

bringing in a range of aircraft from various sources. Four British Beaufighters, bought for 'filming', were flown in during July; similarly, four P-51s destined for 101 Sqn. arrived at Ekron. The truce was broken as Israeli Avias attacked Egyptian concentrations on the Al Majdal–Beit Dibrin road with the loss of two aircraft, both in accidents, while a further Avia was lost at sea on the 9th chasing an REAF Lysander. Syrian positions were also attacked, and there was major fighting as the Israelis attempted to retake the historically important settlement of Mishmar Hayarden. Syrian Air Force (SAF) T-6 Harvards used in the bombing role caused serious Israeli casualties, although one was shot down by an

At independence, the Israelis were pleased to be able to acquire any fighters to defend the new state; the Czechs were equally pleased to dispose of a number of Avia S.199s, developments of the Messerschmitt Bf 109G powered by a Jumo 211 engine driving paddle-bladed propellers. In Czech service the type was dubbed 'Mezec' (Mule). Illustrated is aircraft 107, of 101 Sqn. IDF/AF, probably at Herzliya. (Via M. Schoeman)

Avia. The eighth Avia was lost chasing a T-6 into Syria.

Heavier air power for the IDF/AF arrived on 15 July in the form of three B-17s flown indirectly from the US via Czechoslovakia, where they were bombed up. The aircraft bombed Cairo, Gaza and El Arish en route. The first Spitfires also began to arrive, although the French, under US pressure, had banned the Corsica delivery route. Arrangements were made with the Yugoslav government for the use of the airfield at Podgorica (Titograd) for delivery to Ramat David in Operation 'Velvetta'. Further heavy bombers were delivered on the 19th in the shape of three Halifaxes from the UK. The previous day two REAF Spitfires engaged three Avias attacking positions at Beersheba and one was shot down by the leading Israeli pilot Modi Alon, who was killed when his aircraft crashed on landing. As a second truce began on the 19th it was clear that

the Israelis were making some progress towards consolidating their borders.

During this truce the IDF/AF began a major operation to resupply settlements cut off in the south, opening a new airstrip at Ruhama. Between 23 August and 9 September six C-46s, five C-47s and six Norsemen made 170 flights. The truce was punctuated by violence and combat. The UN mediator Count Folke Bernadotte was assassinated in Jerusalem by members of LHI on 17 September. Later in the month REAF Spitfires attempted to prevent Israeli forces from occupying high ground to the east of Faluja. As the second truce came to an end on 15 October, fighting was concentrated in the south where 5,000 Egyptian troops were bottled up in the Faluja pocket. A Beaufighter of 103 Sqn. was damaged attacking REAF aircraft on the ground at El Arish and on the 20th a second was shot down at Iraq Suweidin.

A series of bombing raids had brought fighting in the north to a virtual standstill when the third truce was declared on 31 October. These truces seem only to have had the effect of limiting fighting. On 8 November Iraq Suweidin fell to the Israelis and on the 19th the Egyptians attempted a breakthrough from Gaza and Khan Yunis to Faluja. On 20 November Mosquito PR.34 PF620 of 13 Sqn. RAF was shot down over Israel by a 101 Sqn. P-51 while on a reconnaissance sortie flying out of Fayid. The delivery of Spitfires to the IDF/AF was progressing slowly with many accidents en route, but by mid-December the position was improving to the point where on the 22nd, the day the third truce ended, twelve aircraft which had left Prague two days earlier all arrived intact.

The final offensive of the war began with an attempt to clear Israel of Egyptian forces: first El Auja, then Asluj, then Abu Ageila and finally, on the 30th, El Arish fell to Israeli forces. British pressure subsequently forced an Israeli withdrawal from Egyptian territory two days before

A Spitfire IX, also of 101 Sqn. IDF/AF. Large numbers of this famous fighter were acquired from Czechoslovakia. (M. Schoeman)

The IDF/AF operated the P-51D Mustang from November 1948, originally in the air defence role and latterly as a ground- attack fighter. No. 41 probably belonged to 101 Sqn., based at Ekron. (P. Coggan via J. Ethell)

an armistice was agreed on 6 January 1949. In the last two weeks of fighting the IDF/AF had lost eight aircraft, mainly to ground fire. The final act of the war, strangely, involved the RAF. On 7 January four Spitfire XVIIIs of 208 Sqn. were patrolling south of Faluja when they were attacked by two Spitfires of 101 Sqn. Three RAF aircraft were shot down and a fourth lost to ground fire. Later in the day, as Tempests and Mosquitoes searched for the missing aircraft, a Tempest 6 was also brought down. No explanation was forthcoming, but it is clear that the Israeli pilots knew they were attacking RAF aircraft. Later in the day two REAF Fiat G.55s were shot down by P-51s escorting Harvards bombing Deir el Ballah.

At the end of January the UK formally recognized the State of Israel, and armistices with Egypt, Lebanon, Jordan and Syria were agreed between 24 February and 20 July 1949. Air combat in the War of Independence had been intensive and conducted by a miscellany of aircraft pressed into uses for which they had not been designed. Perhaps most impressive was the

ability of the Israelis to secure aircraft from many sources and, against the odds, keep them maintained.

AIRCRAFT MARKINGS

IDF/AF
Israeli aircraft appeared in a range of markings, often as delivered.
Spitfire IX *Silver overall, black code on rear fuselage, black/red diagonal recognition stripes on the rudder: '64' (101 Sqn.). Dark Green/Dark Sea Grey over, light grey under, white code on rear fuselage: '42' (101 Sqn.).*
Avia S-199 *Pale grey overall, red/white diagonal recognition stripes on the rudder and small black codes and double white stripes on the rear fuselage: 108.T, 120.T, 427 (101 Sqn.).*

REAF
Spitfire IX *Dark Green/Dark Sea Grey over, medium grey under, serials in Arabic on rear fuselage.*

2.3. Sinai, 1956

After the uneasy armistices of 1949 Israel was troubled by Fedayeen raids: in 1955 alone, 260 Israeli citizens were killed by Arab groups based in Gaza or Jordan. There was also a serious military threat as the Egyptian Government turned to the Soviet bloc for arms. Significant quantities of Il-28 bombers and MiG-15 and -17 fighters, delivered from 1955, were beginning to replace Egypt's old Vampire and Meteor fighters, and the Egyptian Air Force had intruded into Israeli airspace from time to time, as noted elsewhere. Israel was pleased, therefore, to be brought covertly into Anglo-French planning for an invasion of Egypt to take place in the autumn of 1956. President Nasser had nationalized the Suez Canal on 26 July, and the French and British were not prepared to concede financial benefit or

a potential economic and military stranglehold on such an important route. To justify an invasion it would have to appear that the Canal was under threat, and the Israelis were encouraged to make a bold advance into the Sinai peninsula.

The IDF/AF was not well equipped for an offensive operation. By the summer of 1956 it had about 80 fighters operational, comprising sixteen Mystère IVAs, twenty Ouragans, ten Meteor F.8s, three Meteor NF.13s and 30 P-51D Mustangs; also operational were two B-17s, sixteen Mosquitoes, seventeen AT-6 Harvards, sixteen C-47s and three Noratlases. By comparison the EAF employed more and newer aircraft, with about 90 fighters operational comprising 50 MiG-15s, twelve MiG-17s, fifteen Vampire

FB.52s, twelve Meteor F.8s and four Meteor NF.13s. Perhaps even more worrying were the 40 Il-28 bombers of 8 and 9 Sqns. based at Cairo West. The EAF transport force comprised about twenty each of the C-46, C-47 and Il-14.

Israeli concern was that, although the IDF/AF had enough fighters to support an attack in Sinai, there were no reserves to protect Israeli cities against air attack; there was, moreover, a shortage of transports to maintain troops in the field, given the difficulty of overland routes of resupply. The problem was solved by the French offer of fighter cover and a squadron of Noratlas transports for the duration. While military planning went ahead the principles of the collusion were finally agreed at a secret tripartite meeting at Sévres on 22–24 October.

The British put pressure on Israel to ignore Jordan and in August had flown Venom FB.4s of 32 Sqn. RAF into Amman, where they were later joined by flights of Hunter F.5s from 1 and 34 Sqns. detached to Cyprus from the UK. The British were dismayed when on 10 October the IDF attacked a police post at Qalqilya in southern Jordan as a reprisal for yet another Fedayeen attack. On 23 October, 36 Mystère IVAs of EC 1/2 'Cigogne', EC 2/2 'Côte d'Or' and EC 3/2 'Alsace' arrived at Haifa from their base at St. Dizier. On the following day, eight Noratlases of ET 2/64 'Anjou' left Le Bourget for Haifa, and on the 25th 36 F-84F Thunderstreaks of EC 1 arrived at Lydda from Dijon. As final preparations were made for Operation 'Kadesh', the IDF/AF unit commanders were briefed at Haifa on the 27th for their part in the air element, Operation 'Machbesh' (Press). The Israelis planned a limited advance into Sinai with options for deeper penetration subject to progress. The potential objectives were to deal the Egyptians a military blow, to clean up the Fedayeen camps in Gaza and to occupy the important garrison at Sharm el Sheikh which commanded access to the Israeli port of Eilat through the Straits of Tiran.

There are three routes across Sinai. To the north is the coastal road from Gaza via Rafah and El Arish to El Qantara. Some 24 miles to the south is the Beersheba–Abu Ageila–Bir Gifgafa–Ismailia route. The southern route is through more difficult terrain from Kuntilla via Themed, Nakhle and the Mitla Pass to Suez. The IDF prepared to advance on all three routes, holding back some units to apply them where they would be most needed. The Egyptians occupied Sinai with one infantry division based on Gaza/Rafah, one infantry division based on El Arish/Abu Ageila, an armoured brigade based at Bir Gifgafa and an infantry brigade at the western end of the Mitla Pass; in addition, there was a light mobile frontier force. The IDF had available to it six infantry brigades, two mechanized brigades, one armoured brigade and 202 Parachute Brigade.

The campaign opened on 29 October with a paradrop on the eastern end of the Mitla Pass, some 156 miles from the Israeli border, when sixteen C-47s dropped a battalion of 202 Para Brigade at 1700hrs; two hours earlier, P-51Ds had attempted to inhibit Egyptian communications by cutting telephone wires to the west and north of Mitla. The vulnerable transports were escorted by ten Meteor F.8s on the way in and eight Ouragans on the return, while a total force of twelve Mystère IVAs maintained a two-aircraft standing patrol just to the east of the Canal. The drop went without significant incident, and at 2100hrs French Noratlases dropped eight jeeps, four 106mm recoilless guns, two 120mm mortars and ammunition. As the Mitla battalion dug in, the remaining two battalions moved through Kuntilla to work westwards to join up with the detached force. At 0700hrs on the 30th they had reached Themed, where they came under air attack by two EAF MiG-15s which caused 40 casualties and destroyed six vehicles.

At the same time the Egyptians had despatched an infantry brigade from Suez towards Mitla, and as the IDF/AF attacked the advancing column the Mitla force was subject to the first of a series of Egyptian air attacks. Two MiGs made the first attacks at 0730hrs, followed an hour later by four Vampires of 2 Sqn. from Fayid with a MiG escort. In the afternoon two EAF Meteors slipped in to attack while their MiG escort fought inconclusively with a Mystère patrol. In a second dogfight over the Canal between eight Mystères and twelve MiGs, two of the latter were claimed for no loss to the IDF/AF. By early afternoon 202 Brigade had reached Nakhle under fighter escort and at 1700hrs, despite concerted EAF attacks on the advancing Israelis, the town fell. At 2230hrs the two elements of the Brigade linked up at Mitla.

The strong Israeli position so close to the Canal was critical. At 1615hrs an Anglo-French ultimatum was issued, requiring both Israel and Egypt to withdraw ten miles either side of the Canal. The Israelis were not within ten miles of

This unidentified MiG-15 of the Egyptian Air Force was forced down by an IDF/AF Mystère IVA. It landed in shallow water on the edge of Lake Sirdon, from where it was recovered by the Israelis and subsequently displayed at Tel Aviv. Behind is a captured M-1C Sokol liaison aircraft, no. 322.

the Canal, while the Egyptians legitimately occupied most of Sinai and could not reasonably be expected to withdraw unless forced. During 31 October the EAF again attacked Israeli positions at Mitla, losing several Vampires, but the local Israeli commander, against orders, decided to improve his position by attacking Egyptian positions at the western end of the Pass, during which he suffered serious losses: 38 paratroopers died and 120 were injured, to be evacuated by C-47 in the afternoon. Mitla was now safe in Israeli hands, with a direct overland supply route, but EAF attacks continued into 1 November. The Israeli assault on the heavily defended Abu Ageila complex, including Um Katef, began at 1600hrs on 30 October, led by the 7th Armoured Brigade with two infantry brigades.

The initial approach was from the south via Kusseima, with a second assault the following day from the east. At 1700hrs on 31 October there were reports of an Egyptian armoured column, comprising a number of T-34 tanks and a company of SU-100 tank destroyers, plus motorized infantry, having left Bir Gifgafa for Abu Ageila. The column was supported by MiG-15s and Meteors, which did not deter the IDF/AF from pressing home napalm and rocket attacks throughout the day, eventually bringing the force to a halt. Israeli forces were making slow progress mopping up Egyptian defences around Abu Ageila. Air support was provided, but at 0800hrs on the 31st two of four AT-6s which attacked Um Katef were shot down having missed the target.

The IDF/AF also played a part in the capture of the Egyptian destroyer *Ibrahim el Awal*, which on 31 October was sailing off Haifa. Initially attacked by the French destroyer *Crescent*, the ship was pursued by two IDF frigates. At 0545hrs a C-47 vectored two Ouragans on to the vessel and their attacks succeeded in damaging its steering gear to the extent that surrender was inevitable.

The first RAF operations against Egyptian airfields began at 2000hrs on the 31st, after which the AA fighters in Israel were free to support the ground offensive; it is believed that the Mystères were given Israeli markings. The Israelis had begun their assault on Rafah just before midnight on 31 October, again using P-51s, Mosquitoes and Ouragans in support, and the breakthrough came on the morning of 1 November. The IDF then made for El Arish as an Egyptian brigade was reported to be advancing along the coast road from Suez. It was attacked by AA F-84s and stopped short of El Arish, which was secured on the 2nd. A total of 385 vehicles were captured, including 40 T-34 tanks. Gaza was surrendered at midday.

After 31 October there was no further air combat; during the day IDF/AF Mystères claimed a MiG-15 and a MiG-17 shot down over the Canal, and several Vampires were destroyed in

TABLE OF UNITS: SINAI, 1956

Unit	Aircraft	Base	Role	Dates
IDF/AF				
? Sqn.	AT-6	?	Light ground attack	
? Sqn.	P-51D	Ekron	Ground attack	
? Sqn.	Meteor F.8, NF.13		Air defence	
? Sqn.	Ouragan	?	Ground attack	Permanently based
? Sqn.	Mosquito FB.6, TR.33		Bombing, ground attack	
101 Sqn.	Mystère IVA		Air defence, ground attack	
? Sqn.	C-47, Noratlas	Ekron	Transport	
? Sqn.	Cub	Various	Liaison, light supply	
EAF				
2 Sqn.		Fayid	Ground attack	
? Sqn.	Vampire FB.52	Kasfareet	Ground attack	
? Sqn.		Cairo West	Ground attack	Permanently based
6 Sqn.	Meteor F.8	Fayid		
? Sqn.		Abu Sueir	Air defence	
? Sqn.	MiG-15	Abu Sueir		
? Sqn.		Almaza		
? Sqn.		Kabrit	Air defence, ground attack	Permanently based
? Sqn.	MiG-17	Kabrit	Air defence	Permanently based
8 Sqn.	Il-28	Cairo West	Bombing, ground attack	29/10/56 to 01/11/56
9 Sqn.				
4 Sqn.	C-47			
? Sqn.	C-46	Almaza	Transport	Permanently based
? Sqn.	Il-14			
AA				
EC 2	Mystère IVA	Haifa	Air defence	23/10/56 to 00/11/56
ET 2/64	Noratlas	Haifa	Transport	25/10/56 to 00/11/56
EC 1	F-84F	Lydda	Air defence, ground attack	25/10/56 to 00/11/56

the last EAF attacks on 202 Brigade at Mitla. With the EAF effectively neutralized and the northern and central objectives achieved, the IDF turned its attention to the final objective, the garrison at Sharm el Sheikh. At 1300hrs on 2 November the town was attacked by four rocket-firing Mystères, one of which was shot down by ground fire; later, Mystères rocketed HMS *Crane*, allegedly mistaking it for the Egyptian frigate *Domiat* and causing some damage. At 1700hrs two of the Mitla paratroop companies were parachuted into A-Tor, where they prepared an existing airstrip for the airlift of the 12th Infantry Brigade in 23 C-47 and Noratlas sorties. This force then struck south for Sharm el Sheikh. At 2300hrs the 9th Infantry Brigade set out to the west through Ras el Naqb. Ras Nasrini and

Sharm el Sheikh were subjected to P-51 and Ouragan rocket and napalm attacks throughout 3 November, and an Ouragan was downed. The two B-17s bombed Sharm el Sheikh on the 4th and the fighters also bombed Sanafis Island, on which were sited gun emplacements. The ground forces reached the garrison on the 5th and the town fell after heavy fighting at 0930hrs. By then, international pressure had forced the cessation of hostilities and over succeeding months the Israelis withdrew from Sinai, leaving Sharm el Sheikh under UN control in March 1957.

The short war cost the IDF/AF nine P-51s, three Cubs, two Harvards, three Ouragans and a Mystère. The EAF lost at least four MiG-15s, one of which landed intact to be evaluated by the Israelis, one MiG-17, five Vampires and two Meteors. The EAF lost many other aircraft to RAF bombing and a large part of the Il-28 force which had fled to Luxor on 1 November where it was attacked by Israeli-based French Air Force F-84s on the 4th. Arguably the IDF/AF would have had a much more difficult task without the RAF containment of the EAF and without French fighter cover releasing IDF fighter for offensive work. Deficiencies in aircraft indicated a clear need for modernization, but the organization worked well, providing support for rapidly moving ground forces.

AIRCRAFT MARKINGS

IDF/AF

At the time of the campaign, the IDF/AF was in a transitional stage in markings, and the earlier scheme of tan/dark green was giving way to a pale pinkish tan/slate blue scheme. Some newly delivered Mystères were flown in natural metal finish. All aircraft had three yellow and two black stripes applied crudely to the rear fuselage and the outer wings. In principle these were the same markings as those applied to French and British aircraft participating in the Suez campaign; in detail, however, they varied considerably, in many cases appearing as a wide yellow band with two thin black lines overpainted.

This underside view of an IDF/AF Ouragan clearly shows the crudely applied recognition markings, in this case apparently black and white six-inch bands. It was the use by the IDF/AF of these markings, ordered for French and British aircraft taking part in the Suez campaign, that led to accusations of collusion between the two NATO allies and Israel. Of interest are the rocket rails on either side of the bomb rack.

Ouragan *Tan/dark green over, pale grey under, black code on forward fuselage and fin: '29' (? unit). Pale sand/slate blue over, pale grey under, code white on forward fuselage, black on fin: '49' (? unit).*

Mystère IVA *Natural metal overall, black code on forward fuselage and fin, red lightning stripe down fuselage: '52' (101 Sqn.). Dark green/tan over, pale grey under, white code on forward fuselage: '09' (101 Sqn.). Pale sand/mid brown/dark green over, pale grey under, white code on forward fuselage: '62' (101 Sqn.).*

P-51D *Tan/dark green over, pale grey under, white code on rear fuselage: '19' (? unit). Pale sand/slate blue over, pale grey under, white code on rear fuselage: '146' (? unit).*

Meteor F.8 *Tan/dark green over, pale grey under, white code on rear fuselage: '11' (? unit).*

Mosquito TR.33 *Tan/dark green over, pale grey under, no apparent codes.*

Harvard *Pale tan/slate blue over, pale grey under, white code on forward fuselage and fin: '60' (? unit).*

C-47 *Pale tan/green over, pale grey under, small white code on rear fuselage: '04' (? unit).*

Noratlas *Pale tan/slate blue over, pale grey under, no apparent codes.*

The French provided direct support to Israel, both in respect of fighter cover against Egyptian air raids on towns and cities and with transports. ET 2/64 'Anjou' Noratlas 64-KC is seen at Haifa late in October; in the background are Mystère IVAs of EC 2. It is possible that the latter aircraft flew in Israeli markings during their stay in Israel: on their return to France, some machines were seen with the French roundel crudely applied over what was assumed to be the Star of David.

EAF

Egyptian fighters appear to have been flown in bare metal or silver finishes with no codes or serials. On MiG-15s two thin black bands were worn on the outer wings and the rear fuselage. Transport aircraft were also bare metal but three-numeral codes were carried on the rear fuselage.

AA

French aircraft were finished bare metal overall; they carried black/yellow stripes, but interestingly the fighters wore only 6in stripes, in keeping with those generally applied to IDF/AF

aircraft.
Noratlas *Properly applied 2ft black and yellow stripes around the rear boom and mid wing, white 'C' on fin in blue circle: 64-KC (ET 2/64 'Anjou').*
Mystère IVA *Properly applied 1ft black and yellow stripes around rear fuselage and mid wing, lightning flash along fuselage: 2-SF, red flash (EC 3/2 'Alsace'); 2-EG, yellow flash outlined in black (EC 1/2 'Cigognes').*
F-84F *Crudely applied 1ft stripes around rear fuselage and mid wing, American serial retained and last letter of code, both in black, on fin: 1-PX 29110/X (EC 1/1 'Corse').*

2.4. Suez, 1956

Having had a long-term interest in Egypt, the British withdrew forces in 1955, retaining stocks and an agreement for the use and defence of the critical Suez Canal. Under President Nasser Egypt looked to the West for arms; the West refused, so the Soviet Union via Czechoslovakia stepped in. The West withdrew financial support for the economically essential Aswan High Dam. Critically, on 26 July 1956, Nasser nationalized the Suez Canal. The Canal provided an economic route from Europe to the Far East both in terms of time and money; in the mid-1950s shipping was still the prime mover of men and *matériel*. On the day the Canal was nationalized the British Prime Minister, Anthony Eden, asked the Chiefs of Staff to plan for a military intervention; the first meeting at which the issue was considered was on the 27th. Not only had the UK to contemplate the loss of revenues, but Nasser might limit the Canal's use; in any event the Egyptians were considered technically incapable of operating and managing it.

The French Prime Minister, Guy Mollet, suggested to Eden a joint venture, and planning for an invasion of Egypt followed, the operation to be headed by General Sir Charles Keightley. On 2 August it was announced that Canberra squadrons would be flown to Malta, UK reservists were called up, and at Toulon the French invasion force began forming. Three days later troops of the 16th Parachute Brigade left Portsmouth for Cyprus on board the carrier HMS *Theseus*, and a further four days later two infantry battalions were despatched to Malta. No sooner had the Paras reached Cyprus than they were flown back to the UK for training, urgently needed by both the paratroopers and the transport pilots.

The original plan, requiring some 80,000 troops, was for an assault on Alexandria, followed by a drive to Cairo. Known initially by the code-name 'Hamilcar' and later 'Musketeer', a new, more realistic plan, 'Musketeer Revise' was offered in mid-August. This plan called for a seaborne and airborne assault on Port Said by the combined

French/British force, with a drive down the Canal to Ismailia. The assault would have to be preceded by the neutralization of the Egyptian Air Force (EAF) and interdiction missions to isolate the war zone. In August, 894 British civilians were evacuated from Egypt, many by Solent flying boats of Aquila Airways.

The Israeli Chief of Staff, General Moshe Dayan, first heard of the joint invasion plan on 1 September when French interests suggested that Israel join in. By 12 September the plans for 'Musketeer' were ready, although their implementation depended on the very slow process of requisitioning, loading and sailing the large numbers of merchant vessels required. The Israelis flew to Paris for a further planning meeting on the 29th, and on 3 October Eden told close advisers that Israel had offered to collaborate. The die was finally cast at a series of tripartite meetings at Sévres between 22 and 24 October; concurrently, the French reached a private agreement with Israel for defensive support involving warships and fighter aircraft. The final plan was for the Israelis to invade Sinai on 29 October. When the Israelis reached the Canal the British and French Governments would issue an ultimatum requiring the Israelis and Egyptians to stop fighting and withdraw their forces ten miles east and west respectively. It was confidently predicted that the ultimatum would be rejected by Egypt, which would give the Allies a justifiable excuse for military intervention.

That the British did not trust the Israelis was evident through the preparation of Operation 'Cordage', designed to neutralize IDF/AF air bases in the event that Israel attacked Jordan. One senior RAF commander is on record as having said that he did not know whether his aircraft were to bomb Egyptian or Israeli airfields until twenty-four hours before the operation began. The military intervention in Egypt would initially take the form of bombing and would be followed by a period of psychological warfare during which aircraft would be used to drop

Part of the vast Huckstep military depot under attack by 27 Sqn. Canberras. Clearly visible is the extensive rail network within the depot. In the bottom left-hand corner of the photograph may be seen exploding bombs, while craters made by weapons dropped on earlier strikes spread from left to right across the site. The buildings seem to have escaped damage; much RAF bombing was ineffective owing to the altitudes from which the Canberras and Valiants had to operate. (27 Sqn.).

leaflets and spurious radio broadcasts would deceive and confuse. The civilian population would also be warned of further impending bombing. RAF bombers from Malta and Cyprus would attack airfields and military installations, initially by night and from high altitude. Further targets would be attacked by carrier-based strike aircraft, which would later be used to cover the invasion proper. Once the Egyptian Air Force had been neutralized and the population confused, the invasion would begin with paradrops to the west of Port Said (British) and on Port Fuad to the east (French); these drops would be followed up by seaborne troops who would push south down the Canal with armoured support.

The French invasion convoy left its assembly port, Bône in Algeria, on 27 October. At 2200hrs on the 30th the British fleet, with a shorter sailing time, left Malta heading for Suez. The whole operation had nearly suffered a vital blow when the RAF Comet taking the Planning Group to Cyprus on 23 October lost all four engines at 45,000ft. Fortunately they relit at lower altitude. With the Israelis spreading across Sinai towards the Canal, the Allies issued their ultimatum at 1615hrs on 30 October. The order to the RAF to commit itself to the bombing of Egyptian airfields was given at 1500hrs.

The ultimatum required the combatants to retreat to positions ten miles either side of the Canal; understandably, the Egyptians did not accept the ultimatum, which also required Allied occupation and maintenance of the Canal Zone. The first task in the 'police' intervention was to deal with the EAF. The Allies were most concerned about the strength of the EAF, the fighting capability of its aircrew and especially the preparedness of Czech and Soviet 'advisers' to fight. Allied intelligence was based on aerial reconnaissance, while Israeli assessments were probably the result of more direct espionage.

The Israelis were thus aware that Egypt could at best use no more than 50 MiG-15s, about a dozen MiG-17s, 30 Vampire FB.52s, sixteen Meteors of several marks and 40 Il-28s. Allied estimates of Egyptian strength were roughly double those of the Israelis, while none of the parties could be confident of the role to be adopted by the 'advisers'. The British assessments almost certainly came directly from the American Central Intelligence Agency (CIA). A U-2A unit, WRS(P)-2, was formed in September 1956 at Incirlik Air Base, at Adana in Turkey, with three aircraft; for several months its aircraft overflew the eastern Mediterranean and especially Egypt. By the time of the invasion, relations between Britain and America were bad. The CIA, however, enjoyed a high degree of independence, and although informed had not advised President Eisenhower of the details of the Allied invasion plan. Throughout the Suez action the USAF's Strategic Air Command (SAC) was placed on alert, including the B-47-equipped 306 Bomb Wing (BW) at Ben Guerir in Morocco; on 26

October the RB-47s of 70 Strategic Reconnaissance Wing (SRW) arrived at Sidi Slimane, also in Morocco.

The destruction of the EAF became the responsibility of the Royal Air Force. Since August, Canberras from three units had been ferrying bombs to Malta and from September Canberra and Valiant units began moving out to Mediterranean bases. By 30 October there were five squadrons of Canberra B.6s and four squadrons of Valiant B.1s on Malta, and seven squadrons of the shorter-range Canberra B.2 in Cyprus. Also in Cyprus were four reserve crews and aircraft of 35 Sqn. By the beginning of the campaign there were no fewer than 112 aircraft at Akrotiri, 127 at Nicosia and 46 at Tymbou. The Israelis were expecting the RAF attacks to begin at dawn on 31 October but the first aircraft did not take off from Luqa until 1930hrs; two hours later the Cyprus-based aircraft began to take off. The targets were important air bases, including Abu Sueir, Almaza, Bilbeis, Cairo International, Cairo West, Dekheila, Deversoir, Fayid, Gamil, Inchas, Ismailia, Kabrit, Kasfareet, Luxor and Shallufa.

The first bombs were dropped on Almaza by Canberra WH853 of 12 Sqn. at about 2230hrs. The first wave of eight Valiants was recalled to Malta before reaching its target, Cairo West airfield. Late in the day the War Office had become aware that United States nationals were being evacuated through Cairo West and radioed Keightley to prevent an escalation of the ill-feeling between the Allies and the US. The Valiants landed at Malta amid the second wave taking off for other targets. The delay was important: during the following day a number of Egyptian aircraft escaped south, with further aircraft destined for Syria. They were flown by Soviet instructors.

Despite the bombers' having to operate from

45,000ft, their job was made easy by the absence of blackout, clear skies and the lack of an Egyptian air defence system. Conventional 500lb and 1,000lb bombs were used, proximity fused. Target marking was undertaken by 18, 109 and 139 Sqns. flying at low level and using two aircraft for illumination and two for marking. The first Valiant in action was XD814 of 148 Sqn. in an attack on Almaza airfield. During the night the British cruiser HMS *Newfoundland*, part of an Allied task force in the Red Sea, engaged and sank the Egyptian frigate *Domiat*, but not without a short, sharp battle.

Reconnaissance was ordered at dawn on 1 November, and Canberra PR.7s of 13 Sqn., supplemented by aircraft from 58 Sqn. plus RF-84Fs of EC 1/33 'Belfort', were despatched from Akrotiri. The results were disappointing, with much cratering but no evidence of substantial aircraft losses. It has subsequently been concluded that the total tonnage of bombs dropped on all the airfields by the bomber force would have been required to guarantee neutralizing just one of them. The Canberra bombers were to return that night, later to attack concentrated targets, but much of the precision bombing work was subsequently handled by the lighter attack aircraft from Cyprus and the carriers. Among subsequent targets were the group of 28 Il-28s that had fled south to Luxor. They were eventually destroyed on 4 November by F-84Fs of EC 1 based at Lydda, flying to the extremes of their range. Fitted with 450gal tanks, twenty aircraft made the long flight in two waves. This was not before eight Ilyushins had departed for the greater safety of Riyadh, Saudi Arabia, to join a number that had earlier flown direct. Twenty MiG-15s destined for the SAF had flown to Hama, Syria, after the initial bombing.

During the daylight hours the Cyprus Canber-

The scene at Nicosia during the early stages of the Suez action. Ten Canberras from unidentified units are seen taxying out prior to a strike on military targets in Egypt. To the left are Valettas, probably of 114 Sqn., while lined up on the right are Meteor NF.13s of 39 Sqn. The special recognition stripes were, generally, crudely applied in Cyprus, and when yellow paint ran out ground crews resorted to cream emulsion, normally used to decorate accommodation buildings. (27 Sqn.)

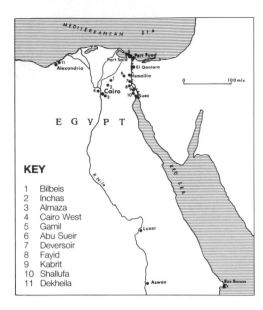

KEY

1 Bilbeis
2 Inchas
3 Almaza
4 Cairo West
5 Gamil
6 Abu Sueir
7 Deversoir
8 Fayid
9 Kabrit
10 Shallufa
11 Dekheila

ras, and for good measure the Hunters of 1 and 34 Sqns. and F-84Fs of EC 3, joined the fray. The Hunters quickly resorted to a defensive role. Without drop tanks, which had been damaged in firing practice, their range limited time over target to no more than ten minutes. The F-84Fs flew protective top cover.

The British carrier force had sailed from Malta on 26 October and was on station, 50 miles off the Egyptian coast, almost due north of Cairo, by the 31st. Sea Hawks supported by Sea Venoms attacked airfields at Dekheila, Bilbeis, Abu Sueir, Inchas, Almaza and, for the first time, Cairo West. The last four airfields were all MiG-15 bases and in due course 27 aircraft destined for Syria were destroyed at Abu Sueir. Some 500 sorties were flown on this first day of the air offensive without loss to the Allies. The naval pilots had not been briefed to avoid Cairo West, but fortunately spotted Pan Am airliners on the airfield before committing themselves.

Further photo-reconnaissance confirmed the effectiveness of the attacks, which were generally made with minimal civilian casualties. The British-run Sharq al Adna propaganda radio station had issued warnings to the Egyptian population well in advance of the raids. Control of this Cyprus-based organization was part of the remit of Brigadier Bernard Fergusson. His was also the task of organizing leaflet-dropping in Egyptian cities through the 'aeropsychological' phase of the operation. After several days of bombing it was clear that the British bomber force far exceeded the supply of suitable targets; this did not encourage volunteers for the task of leaflet dropping, traditionally seen as an unnecessary risking of resources.

It was also decided to bomb Cairo radio station, situated some 15 miles outside the city, in order that Sharq al Adna could broadcast

spurious messages on the same wavelength. The task fell to 27 Sqn., who flew with F-84Fs as top cover on the morning of the 2nd; the station was off the air for two days following the attack. On this second full day of air attacks, attention turned to concentrations of ground forces, especially at Almaza, Cairo and Huckstep, the last being attacked continuously for three days. As some indication of the intensity of flying, 6 Sqn's. Venoms flew eighteen sorties on the 1st, mainly against Dekheila airfield on the delta; 830 NAS's Wyverns flew a similar number of sorties on the same day against the same target. The day's activity was not without cost. A Canberra PR.7 of 13 Sqn. was damaged by anti-aircraft fire, as was Sea Venom FAW.21 WW284/O-095 of 893 Sqn. which crash-landed on HMS Eagle with a damaged undercarriage and injured observer.

The French carriers had joined the action on 2 November, and by the following day, while the airfields and army concentrations remained important targets, a further change of approach was indicated. From this day specific tactical targets around Port Said were attacked, critically the road-carrying Damietta bridge to the west of the town and the only northern road link from the delta to the Canal. While attacking the bridge, 830 NAS Wyvern WN330, piloted by Lt. McCarthy, was hit; the pilot ejected out at sea and was picked up by HMS Eagle's planeguard Whirlwind HAS.3. Targets of opportunity were also attacked, but with great care to avoid civilian casualties. During the day HMS Albion withdrew for refuelling. Mention should be made of the work of the carrier support aircraft, not only the planeguard Whirlwinds but also the Avengers and Skyraiders.

Each of the Royal Navy carriers had embarked a Whirlwind HAR.3 for rescue duties. The Skyraiders of 849 NAS flew airborne early warning (AEW) patrols over the task force; apart from

This photograph of F-84F Thunderstreaks of EC 3 clearly illustrates the peculiar way in which recognition stripes were applied to the type; Israel-based aircraft of EC 1 wore only six-inch wide stripes, in keeping with Israeli practice. The aircraft are undergoing maintenance at Akrotiri; (5)27300 has the rear fuselage removed for engine replacement. (ECPA)

Wyvern S.4s of 830 NAS taxy on the deck of HMS *Eagle* in preparation for a strike against military targets in the Port Said area. In this instance armed with bombs and carrying fuel tanks, the Wyverns also used rockets with great effect on pinpoint strikes. Of note are the Skyraider AEW.1 early warning aircraft on the stern of the carrier: much of their effort was spent keeping track of units of the US Sixth Fleet. Immediately behind the carrier is its destroyer plane-guard escort. (FAA Museum)

Allied aircraft, they must have identified much traffic from the US Sixth Fleet which was shadowing the carriers and flying numerous sorties perceived by the French and British as disruptive. The Avengers of *Bulwark*'s ship's flight were used on anti-submarine patrols. French naval Avengers of Flotille 9F were of the ASW TBM-3E and AEW TBM-3W variants. Based on *La Fayette*, they also contributed to the patrol tasks.

The Malta and Cyprus-based support units were also playing important roles. On Malta four Meteor FR.9s of 208 Sqn. were maintained at readiness until 10 November and during the critical period they made a number of intercepts. The other Malta support unit was 37 Sqn. with Shackleton MR.2s, which provided cover for the convoys with, at one stage, a detachment based in northern Libya. Also involved, flying nine operational sorties, was 28F of the French Navy flying the PB4Y-2 from Karouba, Tunisia. The Cyprus air defence units were 39 Sqn. with the Meteor NF.13 and 1 and 34 Sqns. detached from Tangmere flying the Hunter F.5, with flights at Amman, Jordan. Also in Jordan throughout the crisis was 32 Sqn. equipped with the Venom FB.4. At Akrotiri were the three RAF Venom units, 6, 8 and 249 Sqns., and the Canberra PR.7s of 13 Sqn. The French units at Akrotiri comprised EC 3 with F-84Fs and ER 1/33 with the RF-84F. It is understood that one other type was on Cyprus at the time. This was a Pembroke, believed to be WV700, released from the Kenyan emergency and used there for sky-shouting. It was required by Brigadier Fergusson for the aeropsychological

phase but the loudspeakers were removed en route, rendering the aircraft useless for its intended task.

Sunday 4 November saw no let-up in activity, and despite the fact that HMS *Eagle* was withdrawn for refuelling the Royal Navy flew no fewer than 355 sorties. The Cyprus squadrons also remained busy, and during the day 8 Sqn. lost a Venom. Much of the action was again in the vicinity of Port Said in preparation for the airborne assault due early the following morning. The third and final phase of the operation, the occupation of Egyptian territory, began formally on the morning of 5 November with a parachute drop of 600 men of the 3rd Battalion the Parachute Regiment, part of 16 Para Brigade. Only a few days earlier they had been actively pursuing EOKA terrorists on Cyprus; it was from their base at Nicosia that they flew out before dawn in Valettas drawn from 30, 84 and 114 Sqns. and Hastings of 70, 99 and 511 Sqns. In all, there were only 27 aircraft available: indeed, so short of transport aircraft was the RAF that Shackletons of 42 and 206 Sqns. were pressed into service to fly troops and RAF ground crews from the UK to Malta and Cyprus.

The target for 3 Para was Gamil airfield to the west of Port Said. The DZ had already been marked with flares by a Canberra B.2 from 115 Sqn. 'A' Company with sappers of 3 Troop, 9 Sqn., Royal Engineers, dropped first on the western edge of the airfield; the road link from Port Said to the delta had already been cut to the west of the airfield in attacks by FAA aircraft already described. 'C' Company then dropped near the control tower in the middle of the airfield, followed by 'B' company who had the unenviable task of holding the eastern edge of the airfield where it bordered a sewage farm. The opposition to Allied landings around Port Said had been assessed as one regular and two national guard battalions, with coastal and anti-aircraft artillery and with a few self-propelled guns in support.

In the event, the landing was totally successful, despite some resistance. This was both remarkable and fortunate. Such were the logistics problems suffered by the invasion force that the paras could not benefit from a softening-up of Egyptian positions by naval bombardment, while the minesweepers necessary to clear channels were still one day's sailing from the area. Further, for five hours the troops had to fight with a bare minimum of equipment and supplies. It was not until 1345hrs that a second drop of 100 reinforcements was made in addition to seven jeeps and six 106mm recoilless anti-tank guns borrowed from NATO stocks. These items were dropped from under the wings of the Hastings; Valettas carried smaller, 300lb loads under each wing. Despite their vulnerability, no transport aircraft were lost.

During the day the paras made excellent progress, though not without casualties. FAA units flew continuous 'cab-rank' patrols and were called on to specific targets by a liaison team dropped with the first wave of troops. During one such attack on the coastguard barracks between Gamil and Port Said proper, Wyvern WN328 was seriously damaged and was ditched in the sea, the pilot being rescued unharmed. Support throughout the day was provided by the aircraft of *Albion* and *Eagle*, as HMS *Bulwark* finally took time off to refuel, and in excess of 400 sorties were flown. While British troops were holding the airfield, their French counterparts had dropped at the same time to the east of the town to hold two key bridges and the waterworks. Five hundred men of the 2e Régiment de Parachutistes Coloniaux (RPC), including a handful of British sappers and reconnaissance troops of the Guards Independent Parachute Company, were flown from Tymbou in Cyprus in a combined force of Noratlas and C-47 aircraft from ET 61 and ET 63.

The paratroopers landed from low altitude and achieved most of their objectives although, again, not without resistance. One of the two bridges, carrying the north–south Canal road over a feeder canal at Raswa, was blown before it could be secured. With their basic objectives safe, the French used their second drop early in the afternoon to land a second battalion of 450 men of 2 RPC at Port Fuad. During the day they had had the benefit of their own air support from Corsairs of 14F and 15F from the carrier *Arromanches*, although one aircraft had been lost

TABLE OF UNITS: SUEZ, 1956

Unit	Aircraft (code)	Base	Role	Normal base
RAF				
21 Sqn.	Canberra B.2	Malta	Bomb transport (August)	Waddington
9 Sqn.		Luqa, Hal Far	Bombing	
12 Sqn.		Luqa, Hal Far	Bombing	
101 Sqn.	Canberra B.6	Luqa	Bombing	Binbrook
109 Sqn.		Luqa	Target marking	
139 Sqn.		Luqa	Target marking	
138 Sqn.				Wittering
148 Sqn.	Valiant B.1	Luqa	Heavy bombing	Marham
207 Sqn.				Marham
214 Sqn.				Marham
10 Sqn.			Bombing	Honington
15 Sqn.			Bombing, bomb transport (August)	Honington
27 Sqn.			Bombing	Waddington
44 Sqn.	Canberra B.2	Nicosia	Bombing, bomb transport (August)	Honington
115 Sqn.			Bombing	Marham
18 Sqn.			Target marking	Upwood
61 Sqn.			Target marking	Upwood
35 Sqn.			2 aircraft for 18 Sqn., 2 for 61 Sqn.	Upwood
1 Sqn.	Hunter F.5	Nicosia	Air defence, close support	Tangmere
34 Sqn.	Hunter F.5	Nicosia	Air defence, close support	Tangmere
6 Sqn.		Akrotiri		Akrotiri
249 Sqn.	Venom FB.4	Akrotiri	Close support	Akrotiri
8 Sqn.		Akrotiri		Khormaksar
32 Sqn.		Amman		Shaibah
39 Sqn.	Meteor NF.13	Nicosia	Air defence (all-weather)	Nicosia
208 Sqn.	Meteor FR.9	Ta Kali	Air defence, PR	Ta Kali
13 Sqn.	Canberra PR.7	Akrotiri	PR	Akrotiri
58 Sqn.	Canberra PR.7	Akrotiri	PR	Wyton
37 Sqn.	Shackleton MR.2	Luqa	MR, transport	Luqa
30 Sqn.	Valetta C.1		Medium transport	Dishforth
70 Sqn.	Hastings C.1		Transport	Nicosia
84 Sqn.	Valetta C.1	Nicosia	Medium transport	Nicosia
99 Sqn.	Hastings C.1		Transport	Lyneham
114 Sqn.	Valetta C.1		Medium transport	Khormaksar
511 Sqn.	Hastings C.1		Transport	Lyneham
JHU	Whirlwind HAR.2, Sycamore HC.14	*Ocean*	Light transport, rescue	Middle Wallop

with its pilot, destroyed by gunfire. Despite some heavy fighting, in terms of immediate military objectives the day must be judged a success. 3 Para suffered four killed and 36 wounded, while 2 RPC lost ten dead and 30 wounded. Possibly in excess of 200 Egyptians were killed.

During the day a French C-47 landed at Gamil and carrier-based helicopters were used for casualty evacuation. The Allied airborne troops effectively surrounded Port Said by nightfall; indeed, in the early evening, a tentative surrender had been organized but it was not to be formalized. Standing off the Egyptian coast were the invasion fleets of Britain and France. They were to begin landing at dawn but for political reasons were denied a preliminary naval bombardment. This directive did not prevent naval initiative from offering 'gunfire support', although with weapons of no more than 4.5in calibre. At 0500hrs on 6 November the first troops of 40 and 42 Commando, which had sailed from Malta, landed on the beach in front of Port Said; half an hour later, Centurion tanks of 'C' Squadron, 6th Royal Tank Regiment (RTR), were ashore. The Commandos and tanks made a concerted drive south through the town, often ignoring localized pockets of resistance.

42 Commando was on the right flank, due to join up with 3 Para, while 40 Commando on the

left flank was to press on down the Canal. 45 Commando had been held in reserve on HMS *Ocean* and *Theseus*. It was becoming evident that it would take time to clear the city, and after an attempt to land helicopters at the sports stadium – obviously still held by Egyptian forces – a landing ground in the square by de Lessep's statue was selected. Whirlwinds and Sycamores of the Joint Helicopter Unit (JHU) on board *Ocean* ferried the soldiers in waves from 0610hrs. This was the first time that helicopters had been used in this way, and on return journeys they were used most successfully to evacute the wounded. The task facing the 417 men of the Commando, landed in just 1½ hours, was to contain the city centre and link up with 3 Para, who had had a busy morning, having been strafed by a solitary MiG-15. The helicopters, numbering just six Whirlwind HAR.2s of JHU, six Sycamore HC.14s of JHU and seven Whirlwind HAR.22s of 845 NAS at the start of the action, made no fewer than 200 deck landings during the day.

40 Commando met stubborn resistance in its move south at Navy House, the previous head-quarters of the Royal Navy in Egypt. A strong Egyptian force resisted assault, and aircraft from the cab-rank were called in to assist. The post eventually fell after a concerted rocket and bomb attack, but a Sea Hawk from *Albion* was shot down in the process. Late in the afternoon the British and French back-up forced arrived by sea. The remainder of 16 Para Brigade, 2 Para, was landed with the balance of Centurions from 6 RTR. On the Port Fuad side a battalion of the 1e Régiment Étranger Parachutiste (REF), three naval commandos and a squadron of AMX light tanks of 7 Light Armoured Division were landed to consolidate positions on the eastern side of the Canal.

Time was running out, and the military leaders knew it: with increasing international pressure for a ceasefire, it was clear that further fighting was probably futile. Tanks of 6 RTR, carrying French paratroops from Raswa, pushed down the Canal road south to Quantara. In the course of the drive they moved through the forward position reached by the Guards the previous day. The

whole Canal could easily have been taken, with French paratroops of le Régiment de Chasseurs Parachutistes (RCP) standing by in Cyprus for a drop on Ismailia at the southern end. But it was not to be. A ceasefire was indeed ordered, with effect from 12 midnight GMT (0200hrs on 7

TABLE OF UNITS: SUEZ, 1956 (continued)

Unit	Aircraft (code)	Base	Role	Normal base
FAA				
800 NAS	Sea Hawk FGA.4/6	*Albion*	Ground attack	*Ark Royal*
802 NAS	Sea Hawk FB.3	*Albion*	Ground attack	*Albion*
804 NAS	Sea Hawk FGA.6	*Bulwark*	Ground attack	*Bulwark*
809 NAS	Sea Venom FAW.21	*Albion*	Air defence, close support	*Albion*
810 NAS	Sea Hawk FGA.4	*Bulwark*	Ground attack	*Bulwark*
830 NAS	Wyvern S.4	*Eagle*	Ground attack	*Eagle*
892 NAS	Sea Venom FAW.21	*Eagle*	Air defence, close support	*Eagle*
893 NAS	Sea Venom FAW.21	*Eagle*	Air defence, close support	*Ark Royal*
895 NAS	Sea Hawk FB.3	*Bulwark*	Ground attack	*Bulwark*
897 NAS	Sea Hawk FGA.6	*Eagle*	Ground attack	*Eagle*
899 NAS	Sea Hawk FGA.6	*Eagle*	Ground attack	*Eagle*
849 NAS	Skyraider AEW.1	*Eagle* (A Flt.) *Albion* (C Flt.)	AEW	*Eagle* *Albion*
845 NAS	Whirlwind HAS.22	*Theseus*	Light transport	*Ocean*
British Army				
1913 Flt.	Auster AOP.6	Akrotiri, Gamil	Liaison	Nicosia
AA				
EC 1/3	F-84F (3-H, 3-I)	Akrotiri	Air defence	Reims
EC 3/3	F-84F (3-V)	Akrotiri	Air defence	Reims
ER 4/33	RF-84F (33-C)	Akrotiri	PR (formed from 1/33)	Cognac
ET 1/61	Noratlas (61-N)		Medium transport	Algiers
ET 3/61	Noratlas (61-Q)	Tymbou	Medium transport	Algiers
ET 2/63	Noratlas, C-47 (63-L)		Medium transport	Orléans
ET 1/62	Noratlas (62-W)		Medium transport (det.)	Reims
ET 2/64	Breguet 761 (64-P)	Orléans	Heavy transport	Le Bourget
EC 1/2	Mystère IVA (2-E)	Haifa	Fighter, air defence	Dijon
EC 3/2	Mystère IVA (2-S)	Haifa	Fighter, air defence	Dijon
EC 1/1	F-84F (1-N)	Lydda	Air defence, ground attack	St. Dizier
EC 3/1	F-84F (1-P)	Lydda	Air defence, ground attack	St. Dizier
ET 2/64	Noratlas (64-K)	Haifa	Transport	Le Bourget
CEAM	HD-32	Tymbou	STOL transport (1 only)	Mont de Marsan
Aéronavale				
14F	F4U-7	*Arromanches*, *La Fayette*	Close support, air defence	*Arromanches*
9F	TBM-3S/W	*Arromanches*	AEW, ASW	*La Fayette*
15F	F4U-7	*La Fayette*	Close support, air defence	*Arromanches*
23S	HUP-2	*Arromanches*, *La Fayette*	SAR	*Arromanches*, *La Fayette*
28F	PB4Y-2	Karouba (Tunisia)	MR	Karouba
ALAT				
GH 3	Bell 47G	Gamil	Liaison	Algeria

Note: The Fleet Air Arm's 895 and 897 NAS exchanged aircraft just before the campaign and they were flown with the original unit's markings. The RAF bomber and transport units generally comprised between four and six aircraft drawn from each unit; the naval units generally had a complement of six to nine aircraft.

Primarily all-weather air defence fighters, the Fleet Air Arm's Sea Venoms were used for close-support work after early strikes clarified the level of Egyptian resistance to the Suez invasion. FAW.21 XG670/220Z of 809 NAS, based on HMS *Albion*, has immaculately applied recognition stripes in deep yellow and black.

November local time), when the leading units were at El Cap, just a couple of miles north of Quantara.

Apart from the Sea Hawk lost from *Albion*, another aircraft of the type from HMS *Eagle* was destroyed and two Whirlwinds are understood to have been damaged beyond repair. Canberra PR.7 WH799 of 58 Sqn., piloted by Flt. Lt. Hunter, was shot down off the coast of Syria on 6 November by a MiG-17, having photographed a cut oil pipeline in Syria. Another casualty on the 6th was Canberra B.6 WT371 of 139 Sqn., which crashed on landing at Nicosia, killing the crew of three, after having been shot up over Port Said. Finally, at some stage in the previous few days, an F-84F of EC 1 in Lydda had been reported missing.

Pressure for the ceasefire had come from several directions. A run on Sterling resulted in the need for a loan from the International Monetary Fund, in effect dominated by US interests. The Americans agreed to support a loan of $500 million – against a ceasefire. On 5 November the Soviet leader, Nikolai Bulganin, had threatened to destroy London and Paris with nuclear missiles.

On the home front, British politicians and people were divided, with the issue of collusion being aired for the first time. The plan was for a UN force to occupy Port Said and for French and British withdrawal, but components of the British 3rd Infantry Division continued to land. The Allied soldiers did their best to get things working again in Port Said, but by 15 November UN forces were beginning to arrive in DC-4 and DC-6 aircraft of Swissair at Abu Sueir. From 7 November a miscellany of aircraft flew in the Port Said area, wearing the now irrelevant stripes, including a Hurel-Dubois HD.321, PV-2 Har-

poons, and, reportedly, a Halifax and a Sea Vampire. Auster 6s of 1913 Light Liaison Flight (LLF) and Bell 47Gs of GH 2, French Army, were also in evidence.

On their island bases the bomber units were packing up to return home. The first to go on the 7th were the Valiants of 138 Sqn., followed by 10 Sqn's. Canberras on the 9th. Most units were home by Christmas but at least three – 15, 61 and 109 Sqns. – did not return until the New Year. The last troops left Egypt on 22 December. The total cost of the action to the British was estimated at £100 million. French distrust of the British was confirmed, and the 'special relationship' between Britain and the US had suffered badly. Middle East oil was cut off except by the long Cape route, Nasser having blocked the Canal with scuttled ships, and Syria had blown the land pipeline. The British suffered sixteen dead and 96 wounded, the French ten dead with 33 wounded. The total operational aircraft losses were one Canberra, one Venom, two Sea Hawks, two Wyverns, two Whirlwinds, one Corsair and one F-84F.

The Egyptians suffered considerably higher losses, with an estimated 650 dead in the Port

A fine photograph of Sea Hawk FGA.6 XE402/486J of 899 NAS being launched from HMS *Eagle*. The aircraft is armed with eight 3in rockets and fitted with auxiliary fuel tanks. The cockpit canopy remains open to enable the pilot to exit quickly in the event of an accident, while under the aircraft the catapult strop is seen dropping away. The FAA flew several thousand sorties in the campaign and gained a reputation for the accuracy of its close-support and ground-attack strikes. (FAA Museum)

Typical of the targets assigned to the FAA was Dekheila airfield, seen here under attack by Wyverns of 830 NAS from HMS *Eagle*. The EAF put up virtually no resistance in the air, allowing the French and British ground-attack pilots to concentrate on the target. Although the airfield appears deserted apart from several light aircraft, the bomb crater on the runway intersection indicates the precision of the FAA strikes.

Said area alone as well as 900 wounded. Their air force reportedly lost 260 aircraft on the ground, including a number destined for the Syrian Air Force. Canberra sorties totalled 72 from Malta and 206 from Cyprus, while Valiants flew 49. A total of 1,439 1,000lb bombs were dropped and 44 photo-reconnaissance sorties were flown by the RAF. As a measure of the tactical air activity, the figures for HMS *Eagle* are valuable. The carrier made 621 launches of aircraft, which carried and used a total of 72 1,000lb bombs, 157 500lb bombs, 1,448 3in rockets and 88,000 rounds of cannon ammunition.

AIRCRAFT MARKINGS

All aircraft operating in support of the Suez War were required to wear striped markings. It would appear that the original order was for two black on three yellow stripes on the rear fuselage and each wing outboard of the engines. The stripes were to have been 1ft wide in the case of smaller aircraft and 2ft wide for bombers, transports etc. Helicopters did not carry stripes, neither did the Valiants. In practice, there was considerable variety, indicating a degree of vagueness in the order. The Royal Navy applied the stripes meticulously, except that in some instances codes or serials were covered. The Malta Canberra units applied 1ft stripes. The Cyprus-based units applied stripes of the correct size, though crudely and often obliterating serials. On Cyprus there was no stock of yellow paint so cream emulsion, normally reserved for the interior decoration of quarters, was used.

RAF
Canberra B.2 *Silver overall, large black serial and light grey fin panel (Honington home-based aircraft carried a stylized pheasant in white on the fin): WK107 (15 Sqn.); WH907 (61 Sqn.). Small serial, Lincoln crest on fin, red fuselage flash: WH742 (27 Sqn.); WH178 (44 Sqn.). Medium Sea Grey/Light Slate Grey over, PR Blue under, white serial, squadron badge on silver tip tank: WH665 (10 Sqn.).*
Canberra B.6 *Badge on fin, red nose flash: WH995 (9 Sqn.); red fox on tail, 1ft stripes: WH958 (12 Sqn.). Badge on fin, 1ft stripes: WH951 (101 Sqn.). Yellow/black flash on fin, 1ft stripes: WJ772 (109 Sqn.). Badge on fin: WJ776 (139 Sqn.).*
Valiant B.1 *Aluminium overall, black serial, squadron badge on nose: WZ400 (138 Sqn.); XD816 (148 Sqn.); XD812 (207 Sqn.); WZ395 (214 Sqn.).*
Hunter F.5 *Dark Sea Grey/Dark Green over, aluminium under, black serial, unit markings on nose, code on fin and nosewheel door, fuselage stripes in front of roundel: WP180/F (1 Sqn.). Fuselage stripes behind roundel: WP136/N (34 Sqn.).*

Venom FB.4 *Dark Sea Grey/Dark Green over, PR Blue under, serial obliterated: WR476 (6 Sqn.). Serial obliterated, code white on rear boom: WR399/T (8 Sqn.). Serial cut around, white code on nose: WR398/H (249 Sqn.).*
Meteor NF.13 *Medium Sea Grey/Dark Green over, Medium Sea Grey under, black serial, white code on lower fin, squadron marking astride roundel: WM317/J (39 Sqn.).*
Meteor FR.9 *Dark Sea Grey/Dark Green over, PR Blue under, orange stripes on mid fuselage and engine nacelles, black serial, white code on lower fin, blue nose flash, no stripes: WX956/A (208 Sqn.).*
Canberra PR.7 *Aluminium overall, no unit markings, crude 2ft stripes covering serial: WE137 (13 Sqn.).*
Shackleton MR.2 *Dark or Medium Sea Grey overall, squadron number in red 54in figures on rear fuselage, code on nose: WR965/B (MSG), WL785/E (DSG) (both 37 Sqn.).*
Valetta C.1 *Bare metal, white upper fuselage decking, 2ft stripes (84 and 114 Sqn.) or 1ft stripes (30 Sqn.), black serial on rear fuselage and code on fin, green cheat line and spinners: VW850/850 (114 Sqn.).*
Hastings C.1 *Bare metal, white upper fuselage decking, 2ft stripes (70 Sqn.) or 1ft stripes (99 and 511 Sqns.), unit number in diamond on fin, black codes and serial on rear fuselage: TG604/604 GAC (511 Sqn.).*
Whirlwind HAR.2 *Dark Green/brown overall, white code and serial on rear fuselage, no stripes: XK968/9 (JHU).*
Sycamore HC.14 *Dark Green/brown overall, white code and serial on upper fuselage, no stripes: XG507/3 (JHU).*

FAA
Sea Hawk FB.3 *Extra Dark Sea Grey over, Sky under, unit badge or marking on nose, serial and nose codes in black, carrier code white on red fin panel: WM938/131Z (802 NAS); WM928/191J (895 NAS).*
Sea Hawk FGA.4 *Carrier codes white on red panels on fin and rudder: XE333/233ZB (810 NAS).*
Sea Hawk FB.5 *As FGA.4: WN115/466B (897 NAS).*

An anonymous Canberra B.2 of 27 Sqn. at Nicosia on 1 November 1956. The airfield was packed with no fewer than 127 aircraft, while neighbouring Tymbou, occupied by French transport units, held 46 aircraft at the height of the campaign. The squadron badge is on the nose, while the arms of the City of Lincoln appear on the fin. The fuselage lightning stripe is red. (27 Sqn.)

Sea Hawk FGA.6 *As FGA.4: XE391/109Z (800 NAS); XE365/1710 (804 NAS); XE364/485J (899 NAS).*

Sea Venom FAW.21 *Extra Dark Sea Grey over, Sky under, nose unit markings, carrier code on fin, black serials, code on lower fin, carrier code above white on red panel: XG673/227Z (809 NAS). Code on boom, carrier code black: WW286/452J (892 NAS). Code on nose, carrier code not displayed: WW265/094O (893 NAS).*

Wyvern S.4 *Extra Dark Sea Grey over, Sky under, rear fuselage codes in black obliterated by stripes, maroon spinner and finlets: WN325/373J (830 NAS).*

Skyraider AEW.1 *Sea Blue Gloss overall, white code and serial on fuselage, carrier code on fin , 2ft stripes: WJ954/417J (A Flt., 849 NAS); WT947/422Z (C Flt., 849 NAS).*

Avenger AS.4 *Sea Blue Gloss ('Midnite Blue') overall, white fuselage code and serial, carrier code on fin: XB373/981B (HMS Bulwark's Ship's Flt.).*

Whirlwind HAS.22 *Extra Dark Sea Grey over, Sky under, black serial, white code on nose, no stripes: WV204/P (845 NAS).*

British Army
Auster AOP.6 *Light stone/very light stone overall, black serial: WJ403 (1913 LLF).*

AA
F-84F *Bare metal overall, black code on nose, unit marking by cockpit, wide, angled, coloured stripe on mid fuselage, exceptionally angled black/yellow 1ft stripes immediately behind and crudely applied, blue band: 28947/3-IV (EC 2/3); yellow band: 28842/3-VW (EC 3/3).*

RF-84F *Bare metal overall, red wing tips, code in black and unit badge on front fuselage: 117019/33-CF (ER 1/33).*

Noratlas *Bare metal overall, 2ft stripes, unit codes on boom in black: 123/61-NF (ET 1/61); 09/61-QH (ET 3/61); !/63-LC (ET 63).*

Aéronavale
F4U-7 *Midnite Blue overall, unit marking on fin, white codes and serial on rear fuselage, neat stripes cut around codes: 133720 14.F.2 (14F); 133654 15.F.11 (15F).*

TBM-3W *White codes on fuselage, number on front fuselage and fin: 9.F.15 (9F).*

2.5. The Six-Day War, 1967

From the Sinai War of 1956, after a period of relative peace, Arab raids across Israel's borders increased. A United Nations peacekeeping force had been established in Sinai and the main attacks came from Syria and Jordan. There were spasmodic intrusions into Israeli airspace (these are dealt with elsewhere), and border fighting increased with IDF retaliatory raids on Jordan in November. During 1966 one Royal Jordanian Air Force (RJAF) Hunter, two Egyptian Air Force (EAF) MiG-19s and three Syrian Arab Air Force (SAAF) MiG-21s had been destroyed for no Israeli loss. On 7 April 1967 the IDF/AF attacked Syrian artillery positions on the Golan Heights which had been shelling settlements. The SAAF intercepted the Israeli fighters and in the ensuing dogfights lost at least four MiG-21s for the possible loss of a Mystère. The IDF/AF supported raids on Samu in Jordan in May, when an RJAF Hunter was claimed destroyed.

On 14 May the Egyptian Chief of Staff discussed in Damascus a reported build-up of Israeli troops on the Syrian border, and on the following day the Egyptian Army mobilized. The UN was asked to withdraw from Sinai, and after an initial refusal the withdrawal was agreed on the 17th. From the 21st IDF/AF Vautours and Mirages from Hatzerim began to fly a series of sorties designed to test EAF reaction times. By 22 May the Egyptians were in control of all posts in Sinai and the Gulf of Aqaba was closed to Israeli shipping. On 24 May Israeli intelligence learned of a stockpile of Soviet manufactured VR-55 nerve gas shells at Abu Ageila. Gas masks were purchased from the US and West Germany for immediate delivery. Despite limited international diplomatic action, by 4 June Iraqi armour was in Jordan, where Jordanian forces had been placed under Egyptian command.

The Israeli Government decided to take the initiative and strike first, the initial objective being the neutralization of the EAF. At the beginning of June, the IDF/AF had about three hundred combat aircraft, of which probably seventy per cent were operational at any given time. The total Arab combat aircraft strength was about 750, with lower serviceability but with the prospect of Algerian Air Force (AAF) reinforcement.

The IDF/AF struck at 0745hrs Israeli time on 5 June 1967 against at least ten Egyptian airfields. El Arish, Jebel Libni, Bir Gifgafa and Bir Themada, all in Sinai, were attacked by Ouragans and Mystères flying on a direct course from bases in southern Israeli, and airfields in the Canal Zone and along the Nile were attacked by Super Mystères and Mirage IIICJs flying from their normal bases out across the Mediterranean and then turning south-east to attack from the West. The airfields attacked in the first wave included Kabrit, Abu Sueir and Fayid on the Canal and Cairo West, Inchas and Beni Suef. All the attacks were made by flights of four aircraft operating in pairs, with follow-up attacks some minutes later. After the loss of surprise all flights were made direct, and added targets included radar and surface-to-air (SAM) missile sites. The Israeli aircraft flew with mixed stores, including fuel tanks, 500lb and 1,000lb bombs, rockets and, in some instances, a French-designed 1,200lb concrete-penetrating bomb, fitted with retro-firing rockets and parachute to enable accurate vertical penetration. Small, delayed-action bombs were also used to inhibit runway repair, and the attacking aircraft made full use of their guns against ground targets.

The timing of the raids was such that the maximum number of aircraft was on the ground. Only at Abu Sueir were significant numbers of EAF aircraft able to take off, and in the ensuing dogfight, involving twenty MiG-21s and sixteen Mirages, four of the MiGs were claimed destroyed. After re-arming and refuelling, the aircraft set out again, including in the second main strike airfields at Helouan, Almaza, El Mansoura and El Minya, all on the Nile. From midday the airfields at Ras Banas, Hurghada and Luxor were attacked by Vautours flying from Hatzerim and Ramat David. Finally the civil airport, Cairo International, was attacked at 1715hrs since a number of Tu-16s had escaped there from Cairo West. The IDF/AF counter-air strikes were totally successful, leaving Israel free from the threat of bombing and leaving Egyptian forces in Sinai with limited air cover. In excess of 500 sorties were flown against Egyptian targets and about 100 EAF aircraft were destroyed by midday.

Although the EAF was unable to mount raids on Israel, both Jordan and Syria did. At 1100hrs sixteen RJAF Hunters attacked Natanya, apparently mistaking it for Haifa, and the airfield at Kfar Sirkin, where at least one Noratlas was destroyed. At 1130hrs twelve SAAF MiG-17s and -21s attacked the oil refinery at Haifa and Megiddo airfield. Little damage was done, and two aircraft were shot down. The IDF/AF retaliated immediately, and Mystères were dispatched to attack the Syrian airfields of Damascus, Marj Riyal, Dumeir, Seikal and T4. Shortly afterwards, Jordanian bases at Amman and Mafraq were bombed; at Amman the British Air Attaché's Devon C.1 VP966 was destroyed in the raid. The Marconi 247 air defence radar at Ajlun was also attacked and destroyed.

The Israeli Army struck west into Sinai from 0815hrs on the 5th. The Egyptian Army had seven divisions with 950 tanks in Sinai, and against these the Israelis deployed three divisions with 700 tanks. The first was to attack in the north through Khan Yunis and El Arish to Suez; in the centre a force of mainly reservists was to make for Suez via Jebel Libni and Bir Lahfan; and to the south a third division, incorporating a paratroop element, was to move later in the day through Abu Ageila, Kuntilla and Nakhle. The northern division with 300 tanks reached Rafah in the afternoon, but called for IDF/AF support in the form of rocket-equipped Magisters. Two squadrons of these trainers had been formed for close support; they were also used at Bir Lahfan, where the first of several major tank battles developed.

By the end of Monday 5 June the IDF/AF claimed 240 Egyptian, 45 Syrian, sixteen Jordanian and seven Iraqi aircraft destroyed – 308 in total. Israeli losses comprised four Super Mystères, four Mystères, four Ouragans, four Magisters, two Mirages, one Noratlas, several communications aircraft and one Vautour, the last the only aircraft to fall in air combat. Such was the extent of the blow delivered to Arab air forces that on 6 June Egyptian President Nasser claimed that Britain, France and the US had participated on Israel's behalf. This could not be substantiated, but certainly reconnaissance aircraft were active in the area; in addition, from 3 June Lightning aircraft of 74 Sqn. RAF transited across Turkey and Iran from Leuchars in Scotland to Singapore, supported by seventeen Victor tankers based at Akrotiri, Cyprus. From preoccupation with counter-air activity on the 5th, the IDF/AF concentrated on supporting the Army from the 6th. At dawn paratroopers were landed by S-58 and Frelon helicopters at Abu Ageila to take out artillery positions at Um Katef.

The EAF also managed to get a few aircraft airborne. Two MiG-21s attacking Israeli positions at Bir Lahfan were claimed destroyed, as were two Su-7s which bombed El Arish. Later in the day six Algerian-manned MiG-21s landed at El Arish, now in Israeli hands, and all are believed to have been shipped to the US. Throughout the day the IDF/AF flew sorties in support of the Army, attacking armoured concentrations at Kusseima, Bir Themada, Bir Hasana, Bir Gifgafa and Jebel Libni in Sinai; interdiction sorties were also flown against supply columns and reinforcements. The Egyptians fought hard throughout the day, and by nightfall the Israelis had reached Jebel Libni and some 38 miles west of El Arish along the coast road. During the 6th a single IAF Tu-16 attacked Natanya, but it was shot down by anti-aircraft fire over the Jezreel valley on the return. The IDF/AF dispatched a number of Mirages to attack the Iraqi airfield at H3, where it

When Israel launched its pre-emptive strikes against Egyptian airfields on 5 June 1967, its Mirage IIICJs were committed to the Canal and Delta targets while the slower and older Ouragans and Mystères dealt with airfields in Sinai. About 100 Egyptian aircraft were claimed to have been destroyed by midday. The Mirages were uncamouflaged at the time. (IDF/AF)

is believed that as many as three Mirages were shot down by waiting Hunters, one of which was also destroyed. A Lebanese Air Force (FAL) Hunter on a reconnaissance sortie over northern Israel was shot down at lunchtime.

Israeli forces had moved on Jordan on the 5th at Latrun and Jenin, and on the 6th they moved on Jerusalem. The objective was to secure Jordan west of the Jordan valley. The Jordanian Army also fought hard, and the IDF/AF was in close-support action against artillery positions and Patton tank concentrations at Jenin. The important Damya bridge over the Jordan was also bombed. By the end of the second day a further 108 Arab aircraft were claimed destroyed. The 7th saw the Israelis push on towards Suez, and by nightfall they had reached Kantara on the Canal itself, Bir Gifgafa, where a major armoured battle took place, and the Mitla Pass, by now jammed with burning tanks and vehicles caught by Israeli aircraft.

Paratroopers were helicoptered into Sharm el Sheikh in the morning, to find the town deserted.

The main force was flown in by Noratlases, while an advance party flew on to El Tor. By now the IDF/AF was heavily committed to the supply of ground forces, and helicopters were stretched on search and rescue work and casualty evacuation. The Magisters were withdrawn from Sinai to concentrate on the Jordanian front, where the main strikes were against armour outside Nablus. Fighting continued on the Jordan front, but by mid-morning Jerusalem was occupied. There was heavy fighting around Kabatiya and Nablus, but with all three bridges over the Jordan in Israeli hands a UN-inspired ceasefire was agreed by both parties from 2000hrs. Occupation of west Jordan cost the IDF 550 dead and 2,500 wounded, indicating the ferocity of the battles. Jordanian losses were 6,000 dead, missing or wounded plus about 170 tanks and 29 aircraft destroyed.

Thursday 8 June saw the occupation by Israel of Sinai to the Canal. The IDF/AF did not have absolute control in the air, and EAF MiG-21 fighters attacked an Israeli column at Romani on the coast road, causing casualties. In four days,

This was the scene in the Mitla Pass after Egyptian reinforcements moving to the Sinai front were hit by IDF/AF strike fighters. Hundreds of tanks and vehicles were destroyed over several days. (IDF/AF)

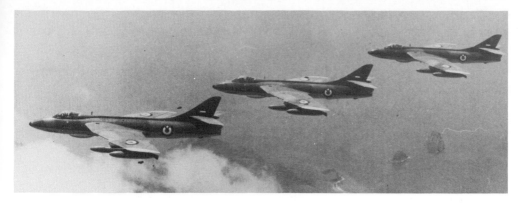

Israeli targets were subjected to air strikes by both Syrian and Jordanian fighters on the morning of 5 June. Illustrated are Hunter FGA.9s of 1 Sqn. RJAF, based at Mafraq. Aircraft of the squadron attacked Natanya and the airfield at Kfar Sirkin, where at least one Noratlas was destroyed. Most of the unit's aircraft were destroyed on the ground when the IDF/AF attacked Mafraq later in the day. (RAF Museum)

however, the IDF claimed to have destroyed 338 EAF aircraft, 23 radar sites and sixteen SAM sites. The Egyptians also lost 10,000 dead, 20,000 wounded and 5,500 captured, plus 500 tanks destroyed and 300 captured, 450 artillery pieces captured and in the order of 10,000 vehicles lost. The cost to Israel was 275 dead and 800 wounded.

A highly controversial incident was the Israeli attack on the US intelligence-gathering ship *Liberty*. On the 8th it was sailing 26 miles off El Arish when it was approached by three IDF fast patrol boats from Ashdod. At 1400hrs the ship was strafed by two IDF/AF Mystère IVAs and two Mirage IIICJs, apparently making a gun attack only. At 1500hrs several IDF attack craft engaged the vessel with machine guns and 20mm and

TABLE OF UNITS: THE SIX DAY WAR, 1967

Unit	Aircraft	Base	Role	Nos. (lost)
IDF/AF				
(3 sqns.)	Mirage IIICJ		Air defence, ground attack	72 (6)
(1 sqn.)	Super Mystère	?	Air defence, ground attack	24 (4)
(3 sqns.)	Mystère IVA		Ground attack, close support	60 (8)
(3 sqns.)	Ouragan		Ground attack, close support	40 (4)
(1 sqn.)	Vautour II	Hatzerim, Ramat David	Medium bombing	25 (5)
(2 sqns.)	Magister	?	Light close support	76 (6)
(1 sqn.)	Noratlas	Kfar Sirkin, ?	Medium transport	20 (2)
(1 sqn.)	Stratocruiser, C-47	?	Medium transport	15 (?)
(1 sqn.)	Frelon	?	Light transport, SAR, casevac	6 (?)
(1 sqn.)	S-55, S-58, Alouette	?	Light transport, SAR, casevac	18 (?)
EAF				
(6 sqns.)	MiG-21	El Arish, Bir Gifgafa, Abu Sueir, Fayid, Inchas, Hurghada	Air defence, ground attack	120 (90)
(4 sqns.)	MiG-19	Jebel Libni, Kabrit, Fayid, Bilbeis	Air defence, ground attack	80 (43)
(5 sqns.)	MiG-15, MiG-17	Jebel Libni, Bir Themada, Kabrit, El Mansoura, El Minya	Air defence, close support	150 (94)
(1 sqn.)	Su-7M	Fayid	Ground attack, close support	30 (17)
(3 sqns.)	Il-28	Abu Sueir, Cairo West, Helouan	Light bombing	40 (27)
(2 sqns.)	Tu-16	Cairo West, Beni Suef	Medium bomber	30 (30)
(2 sqns.)	Il-14	Almaza, ?	Medium transport	70 (23)
(1 sqn.)	An-12	Cairo International	Light transport, liaison	20 (6)
(1 sqn.)	C-47	?	Medium transport	8 (0)
(2 sqns.)	Mi-4, Mi-6, Mi-8	Various	Light transport, liaison, casevac	32 (8)
RJAF				
1 Sqn.	Hunter F.6, FGA.9	Amman	Day fighter, ground attack	21 (21)
2 Sqn.	Vampire FB.5	Mafraq	Ground attack	8 (8)
9 Sqn.	F-104A (forming)	Amman	Air defence	5 (0)
(2 sqns.)	Dove, Whirlwind, Alouette	Amman, Mafraq	Light transport, liaison, casevac	22 (6)
SAAF				
(2 sqns.)	MiG-21	Damascus, ?	Air defence, ground attack	36 (30)
(4 sqns.)	MiG-15, MiG-17	Damascus, Dumeir, Seikal Marj Riyal	Air defence, ground attack	100 (25)
(1 sqn.)	Il-28	T4	Light bombing	6 (2)
(1 sqn.)	Il-14, C-47	Damascus	Medium transport	16 (2)
(1 sqn.)	Mi-1, Mi-4	Various	Light transport, liaison, casevac	14 (2)
IAF				
(2 sqns.)	MiG-21	?	Air defence, ground attack	20 (12)
(1 sqn.)	MiG-19	?	Air defence, ground attack	15 (0)
(2 sqns.)	MiG-17	?	Air defence, close support	20 (2)
(3 sqns.)	Hunter F.6	H3, ?	Day fighter, ground attack	33 (5)
(1 sqn.)	Il-28	H3	Light bombing	10 (3)
(1 sqn.)	Tu-16	?	Medium bombing	12 (1)
(1 sqn.)	Il-14	Habbaniyah	Medium transport	10 (0)
(1 sqn.)	An-12	?	Light transport, communications	10 (0)
(2 sqns.)	Mi-1, Mi-4, Wessex	Various	Light transport, liaison, casevac	23 (0)
LAF				
(1 sqn.)	Hunter F.6	Beirut	Day fighter	12 (1)

40mm cannon, finally firing one torpedo which missed. Although *Liberty* had radioed to the Sixth Fleet for help, the US Navy did not respond and the damaged ship limped towards Malta with 34 dead and 164 injured. Israel later admitted the attack and apologized, but no sensible explanation for the event has been given.

On the northern front, the Syrians had been content to engage in an artillery duel from commanding positions on the heavily fortified Golan Heights overlooking northern Israel. At 0435hrs on 9 June, Egypt accepted a UN call for a ceasefire and with only residual fighting in Sinai and west Jordan the IDF was able to turn its attention to Syrian positions. The assault was made from 1130hrs at a number of points by three armoured and five infantry (two motorized) brigades, heavily supported by aircraft. The main armoured thrust was from Kfar Szold in the north via Mas'ada and Q'ala on Kuneitra. A Syrian armoured concentration at Q'ala was dealt with by the IDF/AF, which operated at constant readiness to deal with obstructions. Progress was slow in such difficult terrain, however, and by nightfall the penetration extended some 4 miles. Overnight the IDF/AF airlifted paratroops by helicopter to positions at El Al and later at Boutmiye to relieve pressure on the main force.

Throughout the morning of Saturday the 10th, the IDF fought against determined opposition, but as Israeli aircraft intensified their attacks against forces denied air cover or support the Syrians panicked and withdrew east, destroying installations and equipment in their wake. By 1400hrs Kuneitra was occupied and the Israeli perimeter in Syria consolidated before the acceptance of a ceasefire at 1630hrs. Losses in the 36 hours of fighting amounted to 2,500 Syrian troops dead and 5,000 wounded, plus 100 tanks and 200 artillery pieces lost. Israeli losses were remarkably light at 115 dead and 306 wounded.

The Six-Day War was particularly significant in two respects. First, it demonstrated the power of the pre-emptive strike when carefully planned, and its effectiveness was far better than might be expected in a European setting: the ratio of aircraft lost on the first day was 12 to 1 in favour of Israel. In all, 452 Arab aircraft were destroyed, 79 of them in the air, for the loss of 46 IDF/AF aircraft. Second, the Sinai front produced tank battles on a larger scale than at any time since the Second World War. As in the Sinai campaign of 1956, the IDF operated with flexible objectives and the territorial achievement extended Israel's borders, offering unprecedented security. But the relatively low cost of gains may have led to a degree of complacency that would cost Israel dearly in future years. No sooner had the fighting ceased than all parties began extensive re-equipment programmes.

Dispersals at an Egyptian airfield, probably Abu Sueir, with Il-28s under attack by Mirages. One aircraft is burning in the background, while five more remain unscathed. By the end of 5 June the Israelis claimed 240 EAF aircraft destroyed, nearly all on the ground. (IDF/AF)

S-58 351 of the IDF/AF. With Frelon helicopters, the S-58s were used to transport troops quickly, often behind Egyptian lines. On 8 June paratroopers were lifted by helicopter to Sharm el Sheikh (which was found to be deserted), completing the Israeli occupation of the Sinai peninsula. (IDF/AF)

AIRCRAFT MARKINGS

IDF/AF
Israeli aircraft were generally camouflaged sand/slate blue over, pale grey under, with white codes. The S-58 was camouflaged overall and the Ouragan wore a blue-green/tan camouflage over. Mirage IIICJs were silver overall with red on air intakes and black codes, Magisters wore blue-green/sand/brown over.
Mirage IIICJ '259', '741', '780', '942'.
Super Mystère '18', '705'.
Mystère IVA '09'.
Ouragan '29', '48'.
Vautour '210', '421'.
Magister '219', '242'.
Noratlas '4X-FAB'
S-58 '07', '20'.

EAF
Egyptian aircraft were finished in a range of schemes and with the exception of helicopters carried black nose codes.
MiG-21 *Bare metal overall:* '5202'.
MiG-19 *Brown/tan over, pale blue under.*
MiG-17F *Silver overall, red/white check rudder:* '022'. *Brown/tan over, pale blue under:* '1043', '2412'. *Dark green/light green/pale yellow over, pale blue under:* '2717'.
Su-7 *Tan/green over, light grey under:* '7664'.
Il-28 *Green/tan over, light grey under:* '1733'.
Tu-16 *Silver overall, code on rear fuselage:* '4378'.

RJAF
Hunter F.6 *Brown/sand over, light grey under, white code on rear fuselage:* '712' (1 Sqn.).

SAAF
Syrian aircraft were generally finished brown/tan over, sky blue under, with black nose codes.
MiG-21 '1073'.
MiG-19 '1103', '1118'.

IAF
MiG-21 *Bare metal overall, black nose codes:* '524', '570'.
Hunter F.6 *Brown/sand over, light grey under, white code on rear fuselage:* '405'.

FAL
Hunter F.6 *Dark Green/Dark Sea Grey over, light grey under, white codes on rear fuselage in Roman and Arabic:* 'L715'.

Super Mystères were operated by the IDF/AF from 1959; two of the type are seen here scrambling from their base in the south. During the Six-Day War the Super Mystère was used extensively in the close-support and ground-attack role. These aircraft are camouflaged slate blue and sand over and pale grey under; the censor has removed the 'serials' and unit markings on the print. (IDF/AF)

2.6. The War of Attrition, 1969–1970

The ceasefire at the end of the Six-Day War did not bring an end to fighting. On 1 July 1967 Egyptian forces ambushed an Israeli patrol on the eastern side of the Suez Canal, and ten days later there was firing across the Canal. Both air forces attacked artillery positions, and in ensuing fights the Israeli Defence Force/Air Force (IDF/AF) claimed four MiG-17s and three MiG-21s for no loss. The Syrian Arab Air Force (SAAF) also made raids into Israel, and in October four MiG-19s were claimed in a single attack. On 21 October the Egyptian Navy sank the IDF destroyer *Eilat* (ex-HMS *Zealous*) with 'Styx' missiles fired from an *Osa* Class patrol boat moored in Port Said harbour. Hit by three missiles at 1732hrs, the ship sank two hours later with the loss of 47 of the crew of 199, 90 of whom were wounded. On the 25th the Israelis retaliated by firing on the refinery at Suez, causing great damage.

On a continuous war footing, the IDF/AF now sought to make good the losses it had incurred in

the summer. The French had embargoed the supply of fifty Mirage 5 fighters, and initially the Fiat G.91Y was considered as an alternative. Eventually, in 1969, an order was placed for fifty F-4Es and six RF-4Es from the US. In the meantime, the US Government freed an earlier order for 48 A-4H and two TA-4H Skyhawks; a further 25 ex-US Navy A-4Es were delivered in 1969, and twenty or so Bell 205 helicopters were also delivered in 1968 to replace the ageing S-58. From September 1968 the Egyptians, with Soviet aid, began reconstructing their armed forces. Additional MiG-21s were supplied and 150,000 troops were deployed along the Canal.

On 8 September an extensive artillery duel took place across the Canal and in October the IDF began a series of deep-penetration commando raids. In March 1969, as the Israelis completed extensive fortifications in depth on the eastern bank of the Canal (the Bar Lev Line), President Nasser of Egypt announced a war of attrition.

TABLE OF UNITS: THE WAR OF ATTRITION, 1970

Unit	Aircraft	Base	Role	Nos.
IDF/AF				
(3 sqns.)	F-4E, RF-4E	⎱	Ground attack, air defence, recce	32
(3 sqns.)	Mirage IIICJ		Air defence, ground attack	55
(4 sqns.)	A-4E/H, TA-4H		Ground attack, close support	85
(1 sqn.)	Mystère IVA	} ?	Close support, ground attack	24
(1 sqn.)	Super Mystère		Air defence, ground attack	9
(1 sqn.)	Vautour		Bombing, ground attack	10
(1 sqn.)	Ouragan		Training, ground attack	25
(3 sqns.)	Magister	⎰	Training, close support	85
(1 sqn.)	Stratocruiser, C-97, C-47	Lod	Transport, ECM	15
(2 sqns.)	Noratlas	?	Medium transport	30
(1 sqn.)	S-65C-3, Super Frelon	Various	Transport	18
(2 sqns.)	Bell 205	Various	Transport, liaison, SAR	20
			Total	408 (325 combat, inc. trainers)
EAF				
(6 sqns.)	MiG-21F	Abu Sueir, Kabrit, Fayid, Bilbeis, Hurghada	Air defence	130
(5 sqns.)	MiG-15, MiG-17F	Kabrit, El Mansoura, Bilbeis, El Minya	Air defence, ground attack	150
(5 sqns.)	MiG-21MF	Inchas, Gianaklis, Aswan, El Mansoura, Beni Suef	Air defence (Soviet det.)	120
(1 sqn.)	Tu-16	Cairo West	Medium bombing	15
(1 sqn.)	Tu-16	El Mansoura	MR (Soviet det.)	12
(5 sqns.)	Su-7M	Fayid, Kabrit, Abu Sueir	Ground attack	90
(2 sqns.)	Il-28	Abu Sueir, Helouan	Light bombing	24
(2 sqns.)	Il-14	Almaza, Cairo	Medium transport	40
(1 sqn.)	An-12	?	Light transport, liaison	20
(2 sqns.)	Mi-4, Mi-6, Mi-8	Various	Light transport, casevac, SAR	55
			Total	524 (409 combat) plus 132 Soviet

The Egyptians had superiority in artillery, an area of weaponry neglected by the IDF. Attrition for the Egyptians meant causing more damage on the east bank of the Canal than the Israelis could return. Frustrated at the imbalance, the IDF/AF began a campaign of attacking Egyptian positions on the west bank from July, and within two months 1,000 sorties had been flown against artillery and radars. Three Israeli aircraft were lost, and 21 Egyptian.

The IDF/AF tactics during 1969 were threefold: first, to cause disruption through deep-penetration raids, during which elements of the air defence system were often targets; second, to learn more about the technical details of the air defence system and its components; and third, to destroy those components and the artillery they protected. The pressure was maintained throughout the year, and it appeared that the Israelis were retaining the initiative. On 9 September they mounted the largest operation since June 1967 with a major attack on an Egyptian training camp at Ras Abu-Daraj, supported by air strikes. In six months to November the EAF lost 51 aircraft, comprising 34 in air combat, nine to anti-aircraft fire and eight to Hawk SAMs. Eight of 30 SA-2 sites had been destroyed, and during the period the IDF/AF admitted losing five aircraft. The Soviet presence had grown (from May a squadron of Soviet Tu-16s was based in the delta region for reconnaissance duties in the Mediterranean), and in December a delegation went to Cairo to advise on anti-aircraft defences and tactics.

The IDF/AF appeared to be able to overfly Egypt with impunity; on Christmas Day the United Nations Treaty Supervisory Organization (UNTSO) noted eighteen A-4, three Mirage, three F-4 and two Vautour sorties, mostly intent on bombing. As part of their support, the Russians unsuccessfully attempted to steal a Mirage III from Beirut for evaluation against the MiG-21, but the IDF/AF was luckier in gaining intelligence when an Su-7M belly-landed intact near the Giddi Pass in November. The last straw for Egypt was the removal, intact, of a complete P-12 'Bar Lock' ground control and interception (GCI) radar from Ras Ghareb. The equipment was lifted out by two newly acquired S-65C-3s (essentially CH-53Ds) in a daring raid on 26 December.

The New Year began with Egypt revising her air defences and the IDF/AF changing its tactics and hitting military targets in the immediate vicinity of Cairo. This display of air superiority, designed to bring the war to the attention of the Egyptian public, had the effect of galvanizing the Soviet Union, and at least five squadrons of MiG-21MFs, with 150 'volunteer' pilots, were sent to Egypt for air defence. In addition the low-level SA-3 SAM and the powerful radar-directed ZSU-23/4 AA guns were delivered and installed in a new system defending not only the west bank of the Canal but also the major cities. In the first four months of 1970 the IDF/AF flew some 3,300 sorties over Egypt, dropping 8,000 tons of ordnance. The Israelis became increasingly aware of the role that Russian pilots were playing and from April the decision was taken to cease intrusions in order to avoid a confrontation.

During 1970 the Soviet Air Force (V-VS) flew a number of Yak-26 'Mandrake' high level photo-reconnaissance sorties over Israel from a base at Yerevan in Soviet Armenia.

From April the EAF then turned to the offensive and began a series of hit-and-run raids across the Canal; in one such raid three Su-7s were brought down. With a mounting casualty rate, Israel turned on to the offensive again from the end of May, dropping 4,000 bombs in a week. The Soviet/Egyptian air defence system was changed yet again as the IDF/AF became increasingly involved in dogfights with Soviet pilots. During this period the Israelis suffered significant losses, including at least five F-4s during July alone. Russian advisers now numbered 15,000 and they controlled the airfields at Inchas, Gianaklis, El Mansoura, Beni Suef, Cairo West and Aswan in addition to 37 SA-3 sites. On 30 July a flight of A-4s approached Inchas. MiG-21s were scrambled, only to be bounced by waiting Mirage and F-4 fighters. In the ensuing battle four MiG-21s were destroyed, two by the F-4s and two by Mirages. Three of the Soviet pilots were killed, and one A-4 was badly damaged by an 'Atoll' air-to-air missile (AAM).

Behind the scenes there had been diplomatic activity, and on 8 August 1970 both parties agreed to a ceasefire. The War of Attrition had cost the Egyptians and Syrians some 113 aircraft compared to an Israeli loss of about 35 fighters. Overflights did not cease completely: on 11 September an Su-7 on reconnaissance was shot down, and five days later an IDF/AF C-97 engaged on electronic warfare (EW) work was brought down by an SA-2 15 miles to the west of the Canal. On 28 September President Nasser died suddenly.

AIRCRAFT MARKINGS

IDF/AF

By 1970 most Israeli aircraft except the Mirage III were camouflaged in a three-tone scheme of pale beige, brown and green, with light grey undersurfaces. Codes were in black on nose and fin except where stated.

F-4E *'147', '153', '167' (tail only), '609', '693' (tail only).*

RF-4E *'188' (tail only).*

A-4E *'208', '218' (tail only), '228', '284'.*

A-4H *'882', '890'.*

TA-4E *'542' (nose only), '547'.*

Mirage IIICJ *Silver overall: '259' (red/white striped rudder), '703'.*

Vautour *White codes nose only: '126', '226'.*

Mystère IVA *White code nose only: '62'.*

Super Mystère *'70' (white, nose only), '821' (tail only).*

EAF

Generally camouflaged brown/sand over, pale grey-blue under. Black codes on nose.

MiG-17F *'2412'.*

MiG-21MF *'8312', '5203'.*

Su-7M *'7224'.*

The F-4 Phantom entered service with the IDF/AF in 1969 and has since been acquired in large numbers. The aircraft was used extensively in the latter stages of the War of Attrition, attacking targets on the Egyptian side of the Suez Canal. About a dozen were brought down before the ceasefire in August 1970. F-4E 601 appears to be carrying an ECM pod on the inboard pylon. (IDF/AF)

2.7. The Yom Kippur War, 1973

From August 1970 the Egyptian armed forces built up their defences on the west bank of the Suez Canal in contravention of the ceasefire terms. By the end of September 1970 there were reported to be 45 SAM sites in the Canal Zone, 30 of them placed within the month. After some immediate postwar clashes there was no fighting until June 1970 as described in section 2.12; there were then occasional air combats to the spring of 1973. Israel's Arab neighbours were loth to encourage Israeli readiness as they were now preparing a war to recover territory lost in 1967. Egypt and Syria had agreed to invade Israeli-held ground on two fronts simultaneously, and for a year meticulous planning and rehearsal had taken place. Both countries by now had a complex air defence system, in depth, immediately behind the 1967 ceasefire lines. The intention was to mount heavy armoured assaults supported by air attacks by fighters largely freed

from the need to defend against IDF/AF attack. The agreed date for the attack was 6 October, the Jewish Yom Kippur or Day of Atonement and also the tenth day of Ramadan.

In autumn 1973 the IDF/AF was still outnumbered by the local Arab air forces. Secrecy in the region has always been high, but never more so than then. Estimates of operational aircraft strengths vary considerably, but the IDF could probably have mustered 340 combat aircraft against 490 Egyptian and 265 Syrian. In addition the Arab air forces would be bolstered by 80 Iraqi fighters, 15 Algerian and 30 Libyan. The Egyptian air defence system was impressive, SA-2 and SA-3 fixed-site missiles on the west bank of the Canal being supplemented by the newly deployed and mobile SA-6, the man-portable SA-7 and radar-controlled ZSU-23-4 anti-aircraft guns.

The Egyptian Army struck across the Canal at 1405hrs on the 6th under a barrage from 2,000 artillery pieces. In all during the day, eleven crossing points were used, from south of El Cap to north of Port Tewfik. Most crossings were started with inflatable boats and consolidated using pontoon or Bailey bridges. The EAF flew 250 sorties in support, and within four hours each division had established a bridgehead four miles wide. Tanks began crossing from midnight. The Israelis were taken by surprise and scrambled fighters from Ras Nasrani but suffered early losses from the SAM cover. In the evening the EAF landed a large commando force at Mitla but lost fourteen Mi-8 helicopters, mainly to ground fire. Commandos were also dropped at Sudr Pass, where they held out for sixteen days.

The EAF attacked airfields in Sinai, including El Mulayz, Bir Themada and El Sur. Hawk missile sites and radars were also attacked, and Tu-16 bombers released some AS-5 'Kelt' missiles at more distant targets including Tel Aviv. Frogs (Free Rocket Over Ground) were launched against Bir Gifgafa and Tasa and the Umm Kusheiba command post. By 1600hrs the IDF/AF was striking back on an organized basis, but successes were achieved mainly against Egyptian aircraft operating beyond their air defence cover. By nightfall the IDF/AF had lost thirty aircraft, most on the Sinai front, and all the Egyptian objectives had been achieved with minimal loss. On the Golan Heights the Syrians attacked at 1400hrs with 900 tanks supported by Su-7s and MiG-17s. The Syrians penetrated twelve miles beyond the 1967 ceasefire line and outstripped their SAM cover, resulting in lighter IDF/AF casualties. The 82nd Commando Battalion was dropped by helicopter on Mount Hermon and succeeded in capturing the Israeli observation post.

At 0630hrs on the 7th the IDF/AF attacked Egyptian airfields at Beni Suef, Bir Arido, Tanta, El Mansoura, Shubra Hit, Gianaklis and Katamiya. The EAF airfields were well protected and the aircraft in hardened shelters, and little damage was done, although the Israelis lost at least five aircraft. The IDF/AF then turned to attacking the pontoon bridges but again little was achieved. Egyptian MiG-17s and Su-7s and Iraqi Hunters strafed Israeli columns, losing twelve aircraft during the day. The IDF is believed to have lost about twenty fighters. In tank battles the Israelis lost 170 tanks.

In the north, the Syrians had continued their armoured assault throughout the night and by the afternoon had pushed the Israelis back to the edge of the Heights. IDF/AF F-4s and Super Mystères flew hundreds of sorties, attacking missile batteries with the AGM-45 Shrike, but with advancing anti-aircraft defences losses were again high. At the end of the day the Syrians claimed 43 IDF/AF aircraft (the actual loss is believed to have been less) for a loss of nineteen.

The Israelis made a disastrous and uncoordinated counterattack on the 8th, using 170 tanks against 600 Egyptian tanks and losing 70, some to their own Air Force. A number of the losses were to AT-3 'Sagger' missiles and RPG-7 anti-tank rockets. The Air Force operated in support and again the Canal crossings were attacked, but with little damage caused. The EAF, with Iraqi support, pressed home ground-attack missions on the Israeli forces, losing fifteen aircraft in the day. It was reported that a squadron of Algerian Air Force Su-7s transferred to an Egyptian base. At the end of the day the Egyptians were in a strong position, having advanced to a line five miles east of the Canal.

On Golan the Israelis managed to stem the advancing Syrian armour, again with many close-support sorties flown: 28 aircraft were claimed destroyed, including two over Jordan attempting to fly around the anti-aircraft defences. On the 9th the Egyptians attempted to extend their advance beyond SAM cover and suffered heavier casualties to the IDF/AF, even though the latter was now more heavily committed in Syria. The EAF lost ten aircraft in attacks on airfields and command centres in Sinai, although some IDF helicopters were destroyed at Bir Themada. Over Golan 600 sorties were flown, but again the newly activated SA-6 missiles were taking a heavy toll of ground-attack F-4 and A-4 aircraft and the Israelis admitted having lost over fifty of both types. In retaliation for Frog attacks on Mahanaym airfield, the IDF/AF launched raids on Damascus and the Homs oil refinery.

Losses to both sides were now becoming critical, and from the 9th a major resupply operation was mounted. Eighty Soviet Air Force An-12 and An-22 transports, supported by twenty Aeroflot aircraft, flew from bases in the Ukraine and the Caucasus to Palmyra, Aleppo and Cairo with munitions and replacement missiles of all types. Tanks and MiG-21 fighters were delivered by sea, some diverted from WarPac units. In 556 sorties between now and the end of the war the United States delivered 22,345 tonnes in C-5 and C-141 transports, plus 5,500 tonnes in El Al Boeing 707 aircraft. Tanks, CH-53 helicopters and 36 A-4s were delivered by sea, and at least 32 F-4 fighters were delivered from Seymour-Johnson AFB and from USAF units in Europe. As the Egyptians moved their air defence screen forward there was limited air activity, with far fewer losses to both sides in Sinai.

Again on the 10th the major air fighting was in Syria as the Israelis pushed the Syrians back beyond their starting positions of five days earlier. The IDF/AF attacked SAF airfields including Damascus, Haleb, Halhul and Blei. Eighteen Syrian aircraft were destroyed for moderate Israeli losses as the IDF/AF developed new tactics and used US-supplied countermeasures equipment to combat the SAM defences. Chaff was increasingly used, and where purpose-designed pods were unavailable the material was packed into the airbrake recesses, while helicopters were used to spot SAM launches and warn overflying fighters. As launches were identified, the sites were noted for subsequent attack.

On Thursday 11 October both sides consolidated their positions in Sinai, but on the Golan Heights the IDF began an invasion of Syria. The Israelis had apparently decided to eliminate the Syrian threat before turning on the Egyptians. Airfields at Seikal, Dumeir, Nasiriyak and T4 were attacked in addition to those already bombed. During Friday fighting continued on the Sinai front, with both air forces attacking tank and troop concentrations. The major IDF activity was in Syria with the Israelis launching a determined push along the Qneitra–Damascus road. Sixteen Syrian and Iraqi aircraft were claimed against the loss of two IDF/AF aircraft. At the end of the first week of fighting the Israelis are believed to have lost 78 combat aircraft, including 30 A-4 Skyhawks; Syria lost 80 aircraft, plus some Mi-8 helicopters, Iraq six Hunters and Egypt 82 aircraft, including 49 MiG-21s and 17 Mi-8s. The Su7B appeared to fare relatively well. As both major powers continued the resupply operation, positions in Sinai were consolidated. The push into Syria continued with heavy armoured fighting and IDF/AF interdiction sorties. In one such strike, heliborne commandos succeeded in blowing a bridge to the north-east of Damascus.

Jordan formally entered the war with an armoured brigade, but by now the Syrian position was so desperate that pressure was applied on the Egyptians to open up the Sinai front. Sunday 14 October was to see the bloodiest tank warfare since the Second World War. The Egyptians fought towards the Khatmia, Giddi and Mitla Passes, pitting 1,000 tanks against the Israelis' 800. Artillery and close-support aircraft broke up the Egyptian assault, and in the day 250 tanks were destroyed to Israel's 40. The airfields at Salahieh, El Mansoura and Tanta were attacked to dissuade the EAF ground-attack aircraft based there from joining the fray. In Syria the IDF/AF flew sorties against Maza airfield.

On the 15th the war entered its final phase. In phase one the Arab forces were on the offensive and made valuable territorial gains until the reoccupation of the Golan positions by Israel; phase two saw fighting concentrated in Syria as Israel invaded towards Damascus. Now the Israelis were to exploit a gap between the Egyptian Second and Third Armies and cross the Canal at Deversoir. The Egyptians counterattacked fiercely, and many close-support sorties were flown in a desperate attempt to stem the Israeli advance, at least fifteen EAF fighters being destroyed for limited IDF losses. A priority target for the IDF ground forces was the SAM batteries on the west bank and a number of these were overrun. For the next few days the EAF attacked

TABLE OF UNITS: ISRAEL, 1973

Unit	Aircraft	Base	Role	Nos.
IDF/AF				
(6 sqns.)	F-4E	?	Ground attack, air defence	130
(3 sqns.)	Mirage IIICJ, Nesher	?	Air defence, ground attack	55
(6 sqns.)	A-4E/H	?	Ground attack, close support	135
(1 sqn.)	Super Mystère	Hatzor	Close attack, ground support	12
(1 sqn.)	Vautour	?	Light bombing, ground attack, ECM	10
(1 sqn.)	Super Frelon	?	Medium lift	8
(1 sqn.)	CH-53D	?	Heavy lift	12
(2 sqns.)	UH-1, AB.205	Various	Liaison, casevac, light transport	30
(2 sqns.)	Noratlas	?	Medium transport	38
EAF				
(10 sqns.)	MiG-21PF	Bir Arida, El Mansoura, Katamiyah, Inchas etc.	Air defence	180
(8 sqns.)	Su-7BM	?	Ground attack, close support	120
(6 sqns.)	MiG-17	Quweisina etc.	Close support, ground attack	110
(4 sqns.)	MiG-19	?	Close support	60
(1 sqn.)	Tu-16	Cairo West	Medium bombing	18
(1 sqn.)	Il-28	Helouan	Light bombing	5
(8 sqns.)	Mi-8, Mi-4, Mi-6	?	Light transport, casevac, liaison	160
(1 sqn.)	Mi-12	?	Heavy lift	12
SAAF				
(8 sqns.)	MiG-21PF	Dumeir, Seikal, T4 etc.	Air defence	120
(6 sqns.)	MiG 17	?	Ground attack	100
(3 sqns.)	Su-7BM	Dumeir, Blei etc.	Ground attack, close support	45
(2 sqns.)	Mi-8	?	Light transport, casevac, liaison	30

IDF forces, causing high losses. The IDF/AF attacked airfields, missile and radar sites and Egyptian tank formations on both sides of the Canal. There were extensive dogfights, some involving as many as 60 aircraft. There were reports of Libyan Mirage III fighters joining the fighting, and certainly from this time the IDF/AF marked its Mirages with yellow triangular panels outlined in black on wing tips and fins as a recognition feature.

By 20 October the Israelis had established a sound bridgehead on the west bank and had captured the airfields of Fayid, Kabrit and Kasfareet, using the last to fly in supplies. The EAF was still totally committed, attacking the Israeli-held pontoon bridges but daily losing more aircraft than since the first days of the war. Not only was the EAF flying ground-attack sorties; with gaps in the SAM system, MiG21 air defence fighters were having to fly up to 500 sorties a day as the IDF/AF pilots ranged over the Canal with relative impunity. From this stage in the war Egyptian sources suggest that US pilots were flying the newly supplied F-4 replacements, and certainly the Israeli pilots would have been inexperienced in using the range of ECM equipment and precision-guided munitions now being added to the IDF inventory. On the other side, it is believed that a number of North Korean pilots flew in Egyptian service.

On 22 October, following diplomatic moves, the UN Security Council passed Resolution 338, calling for a ceasefire the same evening. The Israelis were not inclined to halt without further consolidation and late in the day recaptured the Mount Hermon observation post with heliborne troops and a paradrop. On the 23rd fighting continued around Suez as the IDF pushed north and south along the west of the Canal, destroying Egyptian bases and missile batteries. The Egyptian Third Army on the east bank of the Canal had been completely encircled for several days and the EAF was active in trying to protect it from constant air and ground attack. The IDF/AF was also still active on the Syrian front, continuing raids on targets of strategic importance, and at least ten SAF aircraft were destroyed in the air or on the ground.

In a final attempt to cause maximum damage before the inevitable formal end to hostilities, the IDF flew hundreds of sorties with minimum loss; in contrast, the EAF lost fifteen aircraft on the last day of fighting as a second ceasefire came into effect at 1700hrs on the 24th. So tense was the situation that the US government put its forces on a full war footing. In the nineteen days of fighting, losses to both sides were formidable. In the early stages, with the benefit of surprise and with a high degree of commitment, planning and training, the Arab forces dictated the course of battle and caused high Israeli casualties. At one stage attrition was so high that without massive US support, and with better co-ordination of Arab tactics, the Israelis would have been in real danger of defeat. However, their pilots were quick to learn new lessons in dealing with the effective air defence system, and losses soon dropped to an acceptable level. In air combat the IDF/AF retained superiority at all times, and few Israeli aircraft were brought down in air fighting.

The true figures of losses are not available, but reliable US estimates put the final figures at 115 to Israel (in 11,233 sorties) against the figure of 328 claimed by Egypt on the Sinai front alone; included in this number are 35 F-4s, 55 A-4s, twelve Mirages and six Super Mystères. During and immediately after the war the US delivered 48 F-4s, including some F-4Js from Sixth Fleet carriers, and 80 A-4s, some from USN second-line units. Egyptian losses are reported to have totalled 242, Syrian 179 and Iraqi 21.

There were undoubtedly important lessons learned by both sides (and presumably transferred to their sponsors in return for material support). It became clear that however effective the air defences the war would have to be won beyond them: in other words, the Egyptian and Syrian Air Forces had to attack where they were no match for better equipped and trained Israeli forces. The necessity of a strategic airlift capability to sustain a war beyond even a week was clearly demonstrated. In 1973 the Arab forces acquitted themselves extremely well, and although their losses were higher the war un-

doubtedly paved the way for relative peace in the region and the eventual return for Egypt to pre-1967 borders. The war also made considerable impact in Europe: Arab states quadrupled the price of oil, leading to unprecedented inflation and a reduced manufacturing capability.

AIRCRAFT MARKINGS

IDF/AF
IDF aircraft, with the exception of the Mirage IIICJ and the locally built Nesher copy, were finished brown/green/sand over with pale grey undersurfaces. In general codes were carried on the fin only, in black.
F-4E '593'. Sharkmouth marking on nose: '187'. Ex-USAF machine: '616'. Orange rudder with blue stripe: '201'.
A-4N '215'.
Mirage IIICJ '776'. Purple/white diagonal rudder stripes: '758'. Some aircraft were painted with yellow triangles outlined in black on wings and fin.
CH-53D '961'.
Bell 205 White code on boom: '63'.

EAF
Most Egyptian aircraft were finished sand/dark green-brown over with sky undersurfaces; some additionally employed mauve/sand/dark green-brown over. Codes were in black on the nose and white or black on the fin.
MiG-21PF Mauve scheme: '8312'.
Su-7BM '6907', '7664'.
Aero L-29 Delfin '1555'.
Mi-8 Green/sand over, pale blue under: '1486'.

SAF
Syrian aircraft were finished similarly to those of Egypt.
MiG-21PF '1072'.
MiG-17 '1041', '1043'.

In the 1973 Yom Kippur War, the rugged and versatile A-4 Skyhawk bore the brunt of the air fighting. In several versions, about 135 were operated by six squadrons in the ground-attack and close-support roles, flying more sorties than all other types combined. Illustrated are three A-4Es with markings censored. By now camouflage had changed to brown, green and sand over, with pale grey under. In due course the IDF/AF bought over 300 Skyhawks in eight versions. (IDF/AF)

2.8. Lebanon, 1958

Lebanon had been an independent republic only since 1946 and comprised a range of Moslem and Christian factions. Early in 1958 opposition to the Maronite Christian President Camille Chamoun hardened from all quarters in response to his pro-Western stance over the Suez affair. In May, Muslims in Tripoli revolted and unrest soon spread to Sidon, Beirut and Baalbek; Syrian forces, in support of the opposition, crossed the border. Through June there was heavy fighting in Tripoli and Beirut, and with the overthrow of the monarchy in Iraq, Chamoun appealed to the US for military intervention on 14 July. The US Government response was immediate, ostensibly to protect the 2,500 US citizens in Lebanon, and 1,700 US Marines of 2 Bn. 2nd Regt. were landed at Beirut from units of the Sixth Fleet on the 15th.

The Sixth Fleet was composed of no fewer than seventy vessels, including the carriers *Essex* (CVA-9) and *Saratoga* (CVA-60), embarking Air Task Group (ATG) 201 and Carrier Air Group (CAG) 3 respectively. On the 16th, 3 Bn. 6th Marine Regt. was landed as Military Air Transport Service (MATS) C-124s and C-130s of 322 Air Division (AD) flew in 2,000 paratroops from bases in southern Germany. A minor diplomatic row broke out as the transports overflew neutral Austria without authority, in response to which the Austrian Air Force moved three Vampires to Innsbruck to intercept further transgressors. The final landings were on the 18th, when 1 Bn. 8th Marine Regt. beached at Beirut. By the 20th there were 10,000 US troops in Lebanon and SAC was on full alert status; as a further precaution, the USAF's Composite Air Strike Force (CASF) 'Bravo' was activated and detachments of tactical strike and reconnaissance aircraft flown to Turkey from the US.

Four squadrons of F-100Ds of the 354th TFW flew from their home base at Myrtle Beach, South Carolina, to Adana in Turkey, where troop reinforcements were held. A detachment of five RF-101Cs was sent from 18 Tactical Reconnaissance Squadron (TRS) at Shaw AFB to Incirlik, where they were joined by a detachment of B-57Bs from 345 Bomb Group (BG) from Langley AFB. All landings were covered by USN fighters, which at that time were of a variety of types as the Navy was in a transitional phase. The fighter units included VF-32 with F8U-1 Crusaders and VF-31 with F3H-2N Demons, both from USS *Saratoga*, and VF-13 with F4D-1 Skyrays and VF-62 with FJ-3M Furies from *Essex*. In addition,

TABLE OF UNITS: LEBANON, 1958

Unit	Aircraft	Base	Role	Dates
USN				
VF-13	F4D-1		Air defence	
VF-62	FJ-3M	*Essex*	Air defence	
VA-83	A4D-2		Ground attack	
VAH-7	AJ-2		Medium bombing, air refuelling	
VAW-33	AD-5Q	Dets. *Essex*, *Saratoga*	ECM	
VAW-12	AD-5W	Dets. *Essex*, *Saratoga*	AEW	4/07/58 to 23/08/58
VF-31	F3H-2N		Air defence	
VF-32	F8U-1		Air defence	
VA-34	A4D-1	*Saratoga*	Ground attack	
VA-35	AD-6		Ground attack	
VAH-9	A3D-2		Medium bombing	
VFP-61	F9F-6P		PR	
USAF				
322 AD	C-130A	Rhein-Main AB	Transport	15/07/58 to 00/10/58
63 TCW	C-124B	Rhein-Main AB	Heavy transport	15/07/58 to 00/10/58
CASF 'Bravo'				
354 TFW (352, 353, 356 TFS)	F-100D	Adana/Incirlik AB, ex Myrtle Beach AFB	Ground attack	20/07/58 to 00/10/58
345 BG	B-57B (det.)	Adana/Incirlik AB, ex Langley AFB	Light bombing	00/07/58 to 00/10/58
18 TRS (432 TRW)	RF-101C (det.)	Adana/Incirlik AB, ex Shaw AFB	PR	17/07/58 to 00/10/58

The American landings in Lebanon in 1958 were covered by Sixth Fleet units embarked on two carriers, *Essex* and *Saratoga*. Visiting HMS *Eagle* during the campaign was this AD-6 Skyraider, 139799/401AC 'Miss Rita Kay', of VA-35 from *Saratoga*. The US Navy units withdrew on 23 August, leaving the Turkey-based F-100Ds of 354 TFW to provide air support if needed. (Author's collection)

there were two squadrons of A4Ds of VA-34 and VA-83, a number of which were on standby armed with nuclear weapons. Later the A4Ds patrolled the Lebanese border, including that with Israel. The Sixth Fleet carriers withdrew on 23 August, leaving the Turkey-based CASF to cover the ground forces. As an indication of activity, VF-32 flew 533hrs in July and 762hrs by 23 August. During the course of a routine reconnaissance sortie one RF-101C was damaged by ground fire.

The US presence helped to stabilize the country, and on 31 July Gen. Fuad Chehab was elected President. The new government was formed on 15 October, and the last US troops left on the 25th. The Lebanon crisis demonstrated the ability of the United States to bring enormous power to bear in the eastern Mediterranean at very short notice. Order was restored without bloodshed in one of the more successful superpower interventions.

AIRCRAFT MARKINGS

All USN aircraft were finished Gull Gray over, extending down the fuselage, and white under. Serials were carried in full on the rear fuselage in 6in numbers, with (usually) the last four digits repeated larger on the lower fin. Individual codes were carried on the nose, wings and upper fin, and the unit code appeared in large letters on the mid-fin. All serials and codes were in black. Many units also carried bright unit markings on the fin and/or forward fuselage.

F8U-1 *143747/AC 201 (VF-32).*
F3H-2N *137018/AC 104 (VF-31).*
FJ-3M *139227/AP 00 (VF-62).*
F4D-1 *134949/AK 113 (VF-13).*
AD-6 *135279/AC 403 (VA-35).*
AD-5W *135180/GE 704 (VAW-12).*
A4D-1 *139963/AC 307 (VA-34).*
A4D-2 *142138/AJ 306 (VA-83).*

At the time of the Lebanon landings the US Navy's aircraft inventory was in a state of transition. The two carriers embarked no fewer than nine basically different types, including the FJ-3M Fury air superiority fighter, the naval version of the famous F-86 Sabre. Seen here at Akrotiri is 139238/211AP of VF-62 from Air Task Group 201, USS *Essex*, (C. Shepherdson)

2.9. Israel in Lebanon, 1978 to date

During early 1974 civil war broke out between factions in Lebanon. Initially between Muslim groups and Christian phalangist militia, the war, which saw no air action, involved the Syrian-backed Palestine Liberation Organization (PLO) fighting with the Muslims. Syria invaded Lebanon, ostensibly to maintain peace, from 31 May 1976 with the 3rd Armoured Division supported by Su-7 and MiG-21 aircraft and Mi-8 helicopters. Their forces thrust along the Damascus–Beirut road and in due course north and south up the Bekaa Valley. The IDF/AF kept a watch on Syrian activity over the next two years with RF-4E overflights, and there were occasional clashes.

On 11 March 1978 a PLO group landed by sea on the Israeli coast and hijacked a coach, killing 36 people. The Israeli reaction was to mount a limited invasion of Lebanon up to the Litani river with a view to taking out PLO camps across the border. Operation 'Litani' began on the 14th with 20,000 regular troops supported by the IDF/AF. Large numbers of cluster bombs were dropped on PLO targets, but international intervention prevented the Israelis from achieving all their objectives. A United Nations Interim Force In Lebanon (UNIFIL) was established on 22 March; included in it was an Italian AB.205 unit for communications work. The Israelis withdrew by mid-April.

In September 1978 the historic Camp David agreement was reached, and the Israel/Egypt peace treaty was signed the following April. Immediately the PLO stepped up its raids from south Lebanon into Israel. On 27 June IDF/AF F-4Es and A-4s attacked targets in Tyre and Sidon, with F-15 and Kfir top cover aided by airborne early warning (AEW) E-2Cs. Twelve Syrian Air Force MiG-21s attacked the strike aircraft, and five were downed by the protecting fighters.

The IDF/AF maintained its reconnaissance flights, and on 24 September four MiG-21s of a number attacking a single RF-4E were shot down by escorting F-15s. There was limited air activity during 1980, although two MiG-21s attacking an IDF/AF raid were destroyed on 31 December. On 13 March 1981 a MiG-25 attacking an IDF/AF RF-4E was claimed destroyed by an AIM-7 Sparrow missile fired from an escorting F-15, the reconnaissance having been prompted by an outbreak of fighting between Syrian forces and Christian Militia which continued into April. On 26 April the IDF/AF attacked PLO tanks north of Sidon, allegedly losing two aircraft to one Syrian fighter; the same day, a Syrian Air Force MiG-23U was shot down in error by an SA-7 missile fired by the PLO.

Two days later the Syrians were actively supporting the PLO in transporting soldiers to a Christian stronghold at El Matan in the Bekaa

Valley. The Israelis in general supported the Christians and sent F-4E fighters in support. Two Syrian Mi-8s and a Gazelle gunship were destroyed, crashing at the nearby Rayak airfield. The IDF/AF also attacked Syrian positions at Zahle. The following day the Syrians moved the first of a number of mobile SA-6 batteries into the Bekaa Valley, and the IDF/AF now mounted an intense reconnaissance operation along the Valley to keep track of installations and test radar frequencies. The RF-4Es were supported by Ryan Teledyne 1241 (AQM-34L) drones, three of which were shot down by 25 May. From July the IDF/AF also resumed its raids on PLO and Syrian positions along the coastal plain, especially on Damour, Sidon and Nabatiyeh. On 17 July, F-4Es escorted by F-16s made a heavy raid on PLO targets in Beirut. Reports put the number of dead and wounded, mainly civilians, at 300 and 800 respectively. After further attacks on a PLO post in Beaufort Castle (built by the Crusaders) and the Zahrani oil refinery, a ceasefire was agreed on the 24th.

The Bekaa Valley reconnaissance was maintained and a second MiG-25 shot down while attacking an RF-4E over Akura on 29 July, the fifteenth Syrian aircraft lost in two years. By the end of the year Syria had claimed eight drones destroyed and had deployed five SA-6 batteries in the Valley, with eight SA-2, -3 and -6 batteries along the Syria-Lebanon border. IDF/AF reconnaissance and strike sorties continued to be met by the Syrian Air Force. On 21 April 1982, as the PLO stepped up a shelling campaign into northern Israel, two MiG-23BMs were destroyed over the Bekaa Valley and a month later two MiG-21s were shot down over Beirut. As tension increased it was clear that the IDF was planning a second invasion of Lebanon. The event that triggered the invasion was the attempted assassination, on 3 June in London, of the Israeli ambassador. On the 4th at 1515hrs, seven waves of A-4s, F-4Es and F-16s attacked the PLO in Beirut, concentrating on an ammunition store in a football stadium. The following day the IDF/AF made 60 raids into Lebanon, including a leaflet raid on Sidon. In one strike at 0800hrs an A-4 was brought down by SA-7 near Nabatiyeh.

The invasion itself began at 1100hrs with 60,000 troops supported by 500 tanks and attack helicopters. Two routes were used, one up the coastal plain and the other to the east up the Bekaa Valley; in addition, attempts were made to land amphibious units up the coast at Sidon, and an IDF/AF helicopter supporting a landing was shot down by an SA-7 missile at the mouth of the Zahrani river. Fighting was heavy despite the relative strength of the IDF. A second attempt at landing near Sidon was made on the 8th, and in dogfights in the area during the day the IDF/AF claimed two Syrian MiG-21s and six ground-attack types. Syria claimed two Israeli aircraft.

CH-53D heavy lift helicopters moved an armoured unit up to the Shouf mountains, where it was promptly attacked by Syrian Gazelle anti-tank helicopters.

Although the Israelis had made good progress, they were hindered by the PLO post in Beaufort Castle and the denial of air supremacy through the Bekaa Valley. The Castle was stormed by the Golani Brigade after being softened by shelling and air strikes. At 1414hrs on 9 June a first wave of F-4Es and Kfirs, with F-15 and F-16 escorts, attacked the radars. Estimates of the size of the first wave range from 26 to 92. The details have not been released, but it is probable that the raid was initially protected by at least one stand-off Boeing 707 configured for jamming and using data on frequencies established through drone overflights. E-2C AEW aircraft were used to identify any Syrian response. The first targets were the ground control intercept (GCI) radars, in order to deny the SAAF its control facility. The second group of targets were the radars associated with the SAMs themselves. Weapons used are believed to have included the long-range AGM-78 Standard ARM and the AGM-45 Shrike, AGM-65 Maverick and GBU-15 guided bomb, and the aircraft involved were well equipped with warning, decoy and jamming devices. It is understood that a large number of decoy drones was released.

Ten of the nineteen SAM sites were inoperable after ten minutes and the Syrian GCI radars in the area destroyed. The follow-up attack dealt with the remaining radars, the missiles and other soft targets. Again, the size of the attack is in dispute, with estimates ranging from 40 to 96. It was certainly a larger attack, and the main weapons were conventional and cluster bombs; A-4s were added to the types used. With no effective radar cover, the SAAF had to send large numbers of fighters into the area on an unco-ordinated basis, and between 60 and 100 MiG-21s and MiG-23s met the second-wave attack.

An IDF/AF F-4E, 220, armed with an external gun pod and Sparrow missiles, banks over Lebanon. The armament is unusual since the F-4E was more commonly configured for the strike role, operating with an F-15 or F-16 escort. The Israelis carried out numerous bombing raids on what they claimed were PLO targets in the Lebanese capital. In one series, between June and August 1981 (at the time of the Israeli invasion), some 15,000 deaths are believed to have resulted in the city. The harbour is to the left, and the US embassy is seen by the coast road immediately above the fin of the aircraft. (IDF/AF via S. Katz)

There then followed extensive dogfights, with F-15s and F-16s engaging MiG-21s and MiG-23s. The initial Syrian claim was 26 aircraft for 16 lost, whereas the Israeli claim was for 29 without loss. These claims were later adjusted to 19 for 16 lost and 22 without loss respectively. Most Israeli kills were to AIM-9L or Shafrir 2 AAMs, although, overall, seven per cent were accounted for by cannon-fire and several by Sparrow missiles fired at visual range because of the congested state of the sky. The attacks were maintained on the 10th, again with significant air combat, Israel claiming a further 26 MiGs and three helicopters. The Syrians admitted losing five MiG-21s, two MiG-23s and six helicopters.

At 1200hrs on the 11th a ceasefire was called between Israel and Syria but excluding the PLO; by this time the IDF/AF had claimed a further eighteen Syrian fighters. In seven days of fighting the IDF/AF claimed to have destroyed no fewer than 80 MiG-21s, MiG-23s and Su-20s, plus five helicopters. Israeli losses are believed to have comprised at least thirteen aircraft, including an F-16, an F-4, two A-4s, an AH-1 and an AB.212. The ceasefire did not see an end to the fighting, however. The IDF now encircled Beirut from 13 June and began a campaign of artillery and air bombardment on PLO targets, and many deaths resulted from the use of phosphorous shells and Mk. 20 Rockeye cluster bombs with dartlets. The IDF/AF also resumed its air attacks on Syrian targets. On the 24th an RF-4E was shot down by an SA-6 over the Bekaa Valley, and in a follow-up attack on the site two SAAF MiG-23s were shot down. After dropping leaflets on Beirut advising civilians to evacuate the city, the Israelis began a blockade on 3 July, cutting off water and supplies. Bombing and shelling on a large scale continued without let-up until the Syrians and PLO agreed to withdraw after a fifteen-hour bombardment on 1 August.

The final IDF/AF attack took place on the 12th, by which time it was estimated that some 15,000 deaths had resulted since 4 June. The IDF/AF also continued to reconnoitre over the Bekaa Valley, losing an RF-4E to an SA-6 on 24 July. The aircraft is believed to have been High-Altitude Camera (HIAC) equipped, and later in the day, during a rocket attack on the aircraft to destroy equipment, eleven Soviet engineers engaged in dismantling it were killed.

Such was international concern over the ferocity of the Israeli bombardment of Beirut that a Multi-National Force (MNF) was organized to help stabilize the position. The first contingent of French paratroopers flew from Bastia, Corsica, in Transall C-160 transports of ET-64 on 19 August, and six days later the first US Marines landed. This force could not intervene in the fighting, and shortly after its arrival IDF troops stood by as Christian Militia massacred 1,000 Palestinians in the Sabra and Chatila camps. On 22 September, however, eight French Navy Super Étendard fighters from the carrier *Foch*, with two more flying top cover, attacked Syrian positions at Dahr al Baidar and Ain Dara. Early in 1983 Syria had received the first SA-5 missiles, based at Dumeir and Shamshar near Homs. These missiles had the range to deal with Israeli E-2C

Around 50 of the potent F-15 have been operated by the IDF/AF in two squadrons based in northern Israel. Much of their work has been flying as escorts to Kfir, A-4, F-4 or Mirage fighters conducting ground-attack sorties in Lebanon. During one escort mission, on 27 June 1978, five Syrian MiG-21s (out of a group of twelve attacking an Israeli strike force) were shot down by F-15 Eagles. (IDF/AF)

aircraft normally standing well off the combat zone. The IDF/AF maintained its reconnaissance of the Bekaa Valley, losing several drones. Around Beirut fighting broke out in August and in attacks on the Airport area on the 29th two US Marines were killed. The Americans responded with artillery and AH-1T SeaCobra gunships of HMM-169. The amphibious assault ship USS *Iwo Jima* (LPH-2), with the 24th Marine Amphibious Unit embarked, was standing off Beirut and as fighting continued the carrier *Dwight D. Eisenhower* (CVN-69) sailed into Lebanese waters.

Israeli forces began a gradual withdrawal from 4 September, and shortly afterwards further elements of the MNF moved into Beirut. The British Force in Lebanon (BRITFORLEB) was supported by Hercules transports into Cyprus, where Phantoms of 56 Sqn. on Armament Practice Camp (APC) were put on Quick-Reaction Alert (QRA). Flown in from the UK to RAF Akrotiri were six Buccaneer S.2Bs of 12 and 208 Sqns. and three Chinook HC.1 heavy-lift supply helicopters. The Buccaneers made low passes over Beirut on the 11th, while Super Étendards of the French Aéronavale were also active. The Lebanese Air Force (FAL) made its first contribution to the fighting on the 16th when three Hunter F.70s, operating from a temporary base north of Byblos, attacked Syrian and Druze anti-aircraft positions. One Hunter subsequently crashed in the sea while a second crash-landed on RAF Akrotiri.

On 23 October there were bomb attacks on US and French MNF forces in Beirut, during which 239 US Marines and 58 French paras were killed. The attackers were Muslim extremists supported by Iran, and on 17 November fourteen super Étendards from *Clemenceau* bombed Iranian troops at Baalbeck in retaliation. On 3 December the Syrians fired no fewer than ten SAMs at a pair of F-14As of VF-32 while flying on a reconnaissance mission; the following day 28 USN attack aircraft from the carriers *Independence* (CV-62) and *John F. Kennedy* (CV-67) attacked Syrian positions on the Damascus road. There is some evidence that laser-guided weapons were used against targets illuminated from the ground. One A-6E (1152915/556AC of VA-85) and an A-7E (160738/300AE of VA-15) were shot down, after which air attacks were limited, although the battleship *New Jersey* (BB-62) fired her 16in guns against Syrian targets around Beirut.

TABLE OF UNITS: ISRAEL IN LEBANON, 1978 TO DATE

Unit	Aircraft	Base	Role	Nos.
IDF/AF				
(2 sqns.)	F-15A/B	Ramat David, ?	Air defence	39
(3 sqns.)	F-16A/B	?	Air defence, ground attack	75
(5 sqns.)	Kfir C2	Hatzor, ?	Ground attack, air defence	150
(1 sqn.)	Mirage IIICJ	?	Ground attack, close support	30
(5 sqns.)	F-4E	Hatzor, Ovda, Matram	Ground attack	138
(4 sqns.)	A-4H/N	Ekron, ?	Close support, ground attack	130 + 116 stored
(1 sqn.)	RF-4E	?	Tactical recce	13
(1 unit)	OV-1E, RU-21J, EC-130E	Kastina	Intelligence-gathering	6
(1 unit)	EC-707, E-2C	?	AEW, EW	8
(3 sqns.)	AH-1G/Q/S	?	Anti-tank, close support	30
(1 sqn.)	Hughes 500MD	?	Anti-tank, close support	20
(3 sqns.)	C-47, C-130E/H	Lod	Transport	41
(1 sqn.)	AB.212	Bezet, ?	Casevac, liaison	18
(1 sqn.)	Bell 206A	Sde Dov	Liaison	20
SAAF				
(11 sqns.)	MiG-21PF/MF	Rayak, Dumeir, Nasariyah, Sikel, Homs, ?	Air defence	220
(1 sqn.)	MiG-25	Nasariyah	Air defence	24
(4 sqns.)	MiG-23BM	Rayak, El Maza, Dumeir, Sikel, T4, Homs, ?	Ground attack	70
(2 sqns.)	Su-20	?	Ground attack	40
(1 sqn.)	Su-7B	?	Ground attack	18
(5 sqns.)	MiG-17	Rayak, Nasariyah, ?	Close support, ground attack	84
(1 sqn.)	Mi-24	?	Anti-tank	12
(3 sqns.)	Gazelle	?	Anti-tank, liaison, recce	48
(4 sqns.)	Mi-8	?	Light transport, casevac	75
FAL				
(1 flt.)	Hunter F.70	Byblos	Ground attack	6

MULTI-NATIONAL FORCE

Unit	Aircraft	Base	Role	Dates
Great Britain (RAF)				
12 Sqn.	Buccaneer S.2B (3 aircraft)	Akrotiri	Strike	09/09/83 to 00/02/84
208 Sqn.	Buccaneer S.2B (3 aircraft)	Akrotiri	Strike	09/09/83 to 00/02/84
7 Sqn.	Chinook HC.1 (2 aircraft)	Akrotiri	Heavy lift resupply	09/09/83 to 00/02/84
18 Sqn.	Chinook HC.1 (1 aircraft)	Akrotiri	Heavy lift resupply	09/09/83 to 00/02/84
LTW	Hercules C.1/3	Lyneham/Akrotiri	Medium transport resupply (ex UK)	00/09/82 to 00/02/84
84 Sqn.	Wessex HC.2	Akrotiri	Light transport, SAR	Permanently based
56 Sqn.	Phantom FGR.2 (6 aircraft)	Akrotiri	Air defence	00/09/83 to 00/12/83

TABLE OF UNITS: ISRAEL IN LEBANON, 1978 TO DATE (continued)

MULTI-NATIONAL FORCE (continued)

Unit	Aircraft	Base	Role	Dates
Great Britain (FAA)				
846 NAS	Sea King HC.4	*Reliant*, Dekhelia	Light resupply	00/09/83 to 00/02/84
France (AA)				
ET 61	Transall C.160	Bastia/Larnaca	Medium transport	00/08/82 to 00/02/84
ET 64				
France (Aéronavale)				
11F, 14F, 17F	Super Étendard	*Foch*	Ground attack, air defence	00/09/82 to 00/04/83
16F	Super Étendard		Recce	
12F	F-8E		Air defence	
11F, 14F, 17F	Super Étendard	*Clemenceau*	Ground attack, air defence	00/04/83 to 00/02/84
Italy (AMI)				
50° Gr	C-130H	Pisa/Larnaca	Medium transport	00/09/82 to 00/02/84
98° Gr	G.222			
United States (USN)				
CVW-3 (AC)				
VF-11	F-14A	*John F. Kennedy*	Air defence	00/07/83 to 00/02/84
VF-31	F-14A		Air defence	
VA-75	A-6E, KA-6D		Attack, refuelling	
VA-85	A-6E		Attack	
VAQ-137	EA-6B		EW	
VAW-126	E-2C		AEW	
VS-22	S-3A		ASW	
HS-7	SH-3H		SAR	
CVW-7 (AG)				
VF-142	F-14A	*Dwight D. Eisenhower*	Air defence	00/08/83 to 00/03/84
VF-143	F-14A		Air defence	
VA-65	A-6E, KA-6D		Attack, refuelling	
VA-12	A-7E		Light attack	
VA-66	A-7E		Light attack	
VAQ-136	EA-6B		EW	
VAW-121	E-2C		AEW	
VS-31	S-3A		ASW	
HS-5	SH-3H		SAR	
CVW-6 (AE)				
VF-14	F-14A	*Independence*	Air defence	00/12/83 to 00/06/84
VF-32	F-14A		Air defence	
VA-176	A-6E, KA-6D		Attack, refuelling	
VA-15	A-7E		Light attack	
VA-87	A-7E		Light attack	
VAQ-131	EA-6B		EW	
VAW-122	E-2C		AEW	
VS-28	S-3A		ASW	
HS-15	SH-3H		SAR	
United States (USMC)				
HMA-169	AH-1T (SN)	*Iwo Jima*	Attack	00/08/83 to 00/01/84
HMA-261	CH-46E (EM)	*Iwo Jima*	Transport	00/08/83 to 00/01/84
HMA-269	AH-1T (HF)	*Guam*	Attack	00/01/84 to 00/07/84
HMA-263	CH-46D (EG)	*Guam*	Transport	00/01/84 to 00/07/84

Note: It had been intended to base a small force of AMI F-104Ss on Cyprus, but the use of sovereign bases there is restricted.

The IDF/AF had continued its reconnaissance sorties with follow-up attacks where indicated. In an attack on Bhamdoun and Sofar on 20 November a Kfir was shot down, the pilot parachuting into British positions in Beirut. These two towns and Baalbeck were to remain targets for IDF/AF attacks through early 1984 as units based there harried the Israelis in their withdrawal. In February the MNF began leaving Beirut to the warring Christian and Muslim militia. The Israelis continued to attack Syrian and Shi'ite Muslim targets throughout the period of their withdrawal from Lebanon, and they also carried out reprisal raids, attacking re-established PLO camps at Tripoli on 10 July 1985 in response to car-bomb attacks at Hasbaya and Nabatiyeh.

From 1986 the IDF has continued to attack suspected PLO training camps, generally from the air, and undertake reprisal raids for PLO actions against Israel. In one air attack in October 1986 an F-4E crashed near Sidon after a faulty fuse on a bomb detonated it under the aircraft on release. During strikes against southern Lebanon on 19 November two SAAF MiG-23s were shot down. Further raids followed early in 1986 when AH-1 Cobra gunships were used; one was shot down at Srifa on 18 February. Several days earlier a UN AB.204B came under fire near Sidon and crashed. The next raid came on 8 May 1986 when a refugee camp at Ain al Hilweh, south of Sidon, was the target. This area has been regularly attacked by the IDF/AF, which lost an F-4E on 16 October to an SA-7. Internal conflict heightened in the summer of 1987 when on 1 June the pro-Syrian Prime Minister was killed by a bomb placed under the seat of his Lebanese Army Puma. The bomb was reported to have been placed by Christian Army officers. On 6

September the IDF again hit Ain al Hilweh, killing over 50.

To a reasonable extent, Israel had been protected since withdrawal by a ten-mile buffer zone occupied by the friendly South Lebanon Army (SLA), which it supports in several ways. But late on the night of 25 November 1987 Palestinian extremists crossed the border from Lebanon in two powered hang-gliders. One landed at Metlla and was killed, while the other, after landing, carried out an attack on Gibor Army Camp, killing six and wounding eight soldiers before being shot. On 25 May 1988 there were several helicopter attacks on Muslim guerrillas fighting the SLA in the buffer zone and camps near Sidon in which twenty were killed. Sidon was again the target for strikes on 9 and 25 August. On 21 October the IDF/AF began a series of raids against Hisbollah fundamentalist and PLO bases in southern Lebanon. The air strikes, by F-4s and AH-1 helicopters, were in retaliation for a car bomb attack in Israel in which eight Israeli soldiers were killed. The raids continued into November.

The war in Lebanon is complex and continues with no apparent sign of ending. The USSR, through its Syrian client, appears content to encourage instability in the area, although at the time of writing the Syrians were attempting to occupy the whole of Beirut. With the Iran-Iraq war apparently having drawn to a conclusion, it remains to be seen what Syria's position in Lebanon will be if attacked by Iraq. Meanwhile the SAAF is re-equipping with the MiG-29. Israel achieved, at considerable cost, her objective of dispersing the PLO. The IDF/AF also acquitted itself well in taking out the SAM sites in the Bekaa Valley and demonstrably maintained superiority in the air. Anti-tank helicopters were used with moderate success only, the IDF/AF preferring to use them in defence on 'clean' ground.

AIRCRAFT MARKINGS

IDF/AF

Israeli types used predominantly in ground attack were finished sand/brown/dark green (or in the case of the F-16 a pale emerald green) over and neutral grey under. F-15s and those Kfirs used primarily for air defence were finished in two-tone grey-blue. Codes were in black on the fin.

F-16A *'105', '107', '135', '232', '242', '248', '257', '265'.*

F-16B *'001', '100'.*

Kfir C2 *Camouflaged and with yellow triangles outlined in black on wings and fin, black/white diagonal checks on rudder: '718'. Others: '714', '824', '855'. Grey: '804', '837', '841', '864', '871', '876', '880', '884', '895', '987'.*

Nesher *'501', '524', '529'.*

F-4E *'151', '160', '175', '311', '317'.*

RF-4E *'198'.*

A-4N *Codes on nose and fin, white/red striped rudder: '307', '344'. Blue rudder: '291'.*

F-15A *'620' ('Storm'), '622', '669', '672', '678', '687' ('Sky Blazer'), '695'.*

C-130E *Sand/brown/green over, sand under: 4X-FBL.*

Boeing 707-329 *White over, bare metal under, wide blue cheat line, 'Israel Air Force' on fuselage in blue: 4X-JYL*

C-47 *Sand/green over, codes white on nose. '017', '032'.*

E-2C *Two-tone grey overall, code on nose: 946.*

OV-1A *Khaki-brown overall, code white on nose. '056'.*

CH-53D *Sand/brown/green overall, code on nose and rear fuselage: '542', '544'.*

AB.205 *Sand/green, code white on boom: '1069'.*

AB.212 *Khaki-brown overall, code on nose and fin: '059', '070'.*

Hughes 500MD *Khaki-brown overall, black code on engine fairing: '206', '209', '214', '220'.*

AH-1S *Khaki-brown overall, black code on engine fairing and fin: '326', '332', '335'.*

SAAF

MiG-21PF *Mauve/green/tan over, grey under, code on fin: '8312'.*

MiG-23BN *Tan/brown/green over, pale blue under: '712', '2407'. Brown/tan over, sky under: 2017.*

A Kfir C2 with its number painted out but allegedly belonging to 101 Sqn. Most C2s are finished in blue-grey air superiority paintwork, but this aircraft is in a two-tone brown and sand finish; its also wears the triangular, black-outlined, orange recognition panels on fin and wings which were originally designed to distinguish the type from Lebanese Mirages. Kfirs were used over Lebanon mainly in the ground-attack role, but the type has achieved a reputation as a dogfighter. (IDF/AF)

The IDF/AF bought four E-2C Hawkeyes in 1978 and they have been used extensively, directing and protecting strike and reconnaissance missions, especially in the Bekaa Valley. The Israelis were particularly concerned when in 1983 Syria deployed her first SA-5 SAMs, which had the range to deal with the E-2C standing off well outside the combat zone. (IDF/AF)

MiG-17 *Brown/tan over, sky under: '1041'.*
Gazelle *Sand/emerald green overall, black code on boom: '1222'.*

FAL
Hunter F.70 *Dark Sea Grey/Dark Green over, medium grey under, black code on rear fuselage: 281L.*

MNF – Great Britain

RAF
The standard RAF camouflage was Dark Sea Grey/Dark Green overall (Buccaneer), Dark Sea Grey/Dark Green over, Light Aircraft Grey under (Hercules), and black under (Chinook, Wessex). Resupply helicopters carried large Union flags on the rear engine cowling and under the ramp (Chinook) or on the rear fuselage and under the nose (Sea King).
Buccaneer S.2B *Black serial with numerals repeated larger on fin: XV359, XV361, XV530 (12 Sqn.); XX885, XX901, XZ430 (208 Sqn.).*
Hercules C.1 *Black serial, numerals repeated on fin and nose in white: XV184, XV223 (Lyneham Transport Wing).*
Chinook HC.1 *Black serial on fuselage, code on rear engine fairing: ZA705/EZ, ZA711/ET (7 Sqn.): ZA675/BB (18 Sqn.).*
Wessex HC.2 *White stripe around rear fuselage: XV719, XV721 (84 Sqn.).*
Phantom FGR.2 *Medium Sea Grey, Mixed Grey, Light Aircraft Grey overall, white serial on fuselage, red code on rudder: XV489/A, XV501/B (56 Sqn.).*

FAA
Sea King HC.4 *Matt olive drab overall, black serial and code: ZA293/VK (846 NAS).*

MNF – France

AA
Transall C-160 *Dark green/medium grey over, light grey under, black codes on rear fuselage: 64-GA (ET 64); 61-MB (ET 61).*

Aéronavale
Super Étendard *Blue-grey over, white under, white code on intake and fin: 18 (11F); 57 (17F).*
F-8E *Light blue-grey overall, extra dark grey serial on forward fuselage: 27 (17F).*

MNF – Italy

AMI
C-130H *Silver overall, black code on forward fuselage: MM61995/46-09 (50° Gruppo).*
G.222 *Dark green/dark slate grey over, medium grey under, white code on rear fuselage: MM62123/46-28 (98° Gruppo).*

MNF – United States

USN
The majority of US naval aircraft were finished mid-grey over, light grey under, with national markings, serials etc. in blue-grey and unit markings in light grey.
F-14A *159431/106AE (VF-14); 159201/105AC (VF-11); 160428/102AG (VF-143).*
A-6E *159178/500AE (VA-176); 160998/542AC (VA-85); 155703/505AG (VA-65).*
A-7E *160879/306AE (VA-15); 156863/404AG (VA-12)*
EA-6B *158801/605AC (VAQ-137).*
E-2C *160011/600AC (VAW-126).*

USMC
USMC helicopters were finished in dark Olive Drab, with codes and serials in matt black.

2.10. Jordan, 1958

From 1955 the Soviet Union gave military aid to both Egypt and Syria, including the supply of aircraft and, in the case of Syria, the building of new airfields during 1957 at Palmyre, El Rasafa and Hama. These airfields, in the west of the country, clearly threatened Lebanese and Jordanian integrity. In February 1958 the United Arab Republic (UAR) was formed between Egypt and Syria; simultaneously, Iraq and Jordan agreed to an anti-communist, anti-Nasser Federation, which would have led, *inter alia*, to a combined Air Force. The situation at the eastern end of the Mediterranean grew more tense with revolt in the Lebanon, and following the assassination of the Iraqi president, King Hussein of Jordan appealed to Britain for assistance in maintaining stability. The appeal, which came on 16 July, was immediately supported, and at dawn on the 17th 200 troops of the 2nd Bn. the Parachute Regt.

TABLE OF UNITS: JORDAN, 1958

Unit	Aircraft	Base	Role	Dates
RAF				
208 Sqn.	Hunter F.6	Akrotiri, to Amman	Day fighter	20/07/58 to 00/10/58
70 Sqn.	Hastings C.1/2	Nicosia	Transport (45 troops per aircraft)	17/07/58 to 02/11/58
99 Sqn.	Hastings C.1/2	Lyneham	Transport	
84 Sqn.	Beverley C.1	Khormaksar	Transport (80 troops per aircraft)	17/07/58 to 00/10/58
216 Sqn.	Comet C.2	Lyneham	Trooping (ex UK, 44 troops per aircraft)	18/07/58 to 00/08/58
?42 Sqn.	Shackleton MR.2	St. Mawgan	Trooping (ex UK, 31 troops per aircraft)	18/07/58 to 00/08/58
?204 Sqn.	Shackleton MR.2	Ballykelly	Trooping (ex UK)	
RJAF				
1 Sqn.	Vampire FB.52/9	Amman	Ground attack, air defence	Permanently based

were in Amman, having been flown in from Cyprus by Hastings of 70 Sqn. For a time they seemed to be isolated, since Israel temporarily refused permission for further overflights.

After pressure from the US Government, which was itself heavily involved in the Lebanon, the Israelis relented, and successive flights of RAF transport aircraft were escorted by American fighters from the Sixth Fleet; by the 18th, 2,200 troops of the 16th Independent Para Brigade were in Amman with light artillery support. Reinforcements had been flown into Cyprus from the UK by Comet C.2s of 216 Sqn. and Shackletons, possibly drawn from 42 and 204 Sqns.; Beverleys of 84 Sqn. flew in heavy equipment from Cyprus. In all, 1,000 tons of freight was flown in, plus 120 vehicles and 6,000gal of fuel. The troops were followed on the 20th by a detachment of Hunter F.6 fighters of 208 Sqn. from Akrotiri.

The Royal Jordanian Air Force (RJAF) was no match in terms of equipment for those of Syria or Iraq. The combat element comprised a total of nine Vampire FB.9s and seven Vampire FB.52s, the latter ironically a gift from Egypt. King Hussein secured a pledge of loyalty from the powerful Bedouin tribes on 11 August, and British troops began withdrawing after the UN resolution calling for an end to Western intervention later in the month. The last British troops left on 2 November 1958. Although the Jordanian position was not as volatile as that in Lebanon, the British presence helped to stabilize the area and mended relationships with Jordan, which had deteriorated from 1956.

AIRCRAFT MARKINGS

RAF

Transports were finished in silver with white upper fuselage and dark blue cheat line. Serials were in black.
Beverley C.1 *XM111 (84 Sqn.).*
Hastings C.1 *TG602 (70 Sqn.).*
Hunter F.6 *Dark Green/Dark Sea Grey over, silver under, black serial, squadron markings across fuselage roundel, code in white on upper fin: XJ694/D (208 Sqn.).*

RJAF

Vampire FB.9 *Brown/sand over, aluminium under, black serial on boom: F608 (1 Sqn.).*

Hunter F.6 XE579/A, of 208 Sqn., taxies out at Akrotiri in July 1958 prior to leaving for Amman to provide cover for 16th Independent Para Brigade. Cover for early trooping flights was provided by fighters of the US Sixth Fleet. At one stage Israel refused permission for overflights, leaving the initial contingent of British troops vulnerable for a time. (C. Shepherdson)

2.11. The Jordanian Civil War, 1970

From 1967 Palestinian refugees flocked across the Jordan to the East Bank. Many joined one or other of the liberation groups operating under the aegis of the Palestinian Liberation Organization (PLO) headed by Yasser Arafat of Al-Fatah. The most powerful was the Popular Front for the Liberation of Palestine (PFLP), which established camps and whose heavily armed members roamed freely throughout Jordan in contempt of authority. Indeed, in 1969 Arafat formed the Palestinian Armed Struggle Command (PASC) to act as the military police force of the PLO. Having

initially espoused the Palestinian cause, King Hussein came under increasing pressure from the West and his own army to deny the Palestinians a base. There was fighting in the streets of Amman in early June, and despite attempts at a peaceful resolution there were fresh outbreaks in late August.

Then, on 6 September, a Swissair DC-9, a TWA Boeing 707 and a Pan Am Boeing 747 were hijacked by the PFLP, which had by now developed a reputation for acts of aerial terrorism. The 747 was flown to Cairo where it was blown up the next day after the removal of the passengers and crew. The other aircraft were taken to Dawson's Field, a disused aerodrome outside Zerqa. They were joined there on the 9th by a BOAC VC-10, G-ASGN, hijacked en route from Bahrein to London. The Palestinians demanded the release of a number of terrorists held in West European jails. Although ringed by units of the Jordanian Army, the PFLP was allowed to remove the passengers and crews and the three aircraft were blown up on the 12th. The Army felt humiliated, and Hussein was advised that unless he took positive action to allow it to deal with the PLO components he could not rely on its continuing loyalty. But Hussein was worried about the possibility of Syrian intervention.

In June he had been advised that the US and Israel would support him in the event of a Syrian invasion, and on the 16th martial law was imposed after the PLO occupied several major towns. The following day there was heavy street fighting in Amman and around PFLP camps involving tanks and artillery. Heavy losses were sustained by the PLO groups, but it became clear that hand-to-hand fighting was the only way to deal with the problem without causing unacceptable civilian casualties.

On 20 September the Syrian 5th Division crossed into Jordan from Dera towards Irbid. Royal Jordanian Air Force Hunters temporarily based at H5 from Mafraq attacked the Syrians and they were halted about ten miles within the border. There was only part of an armoured brigade and dispersed infantry units between the Syrians and the main Palestinian groups to the south, and the RJAF contribution was critical. Fighting continued on the 21st, but after diplomatic activity between the US and the Soviet Union the Syrians withdrew, having lost 62

TABLE OF UNITS: THE ROYAL JORDANIAN AIR FORCE, 1970

Unit	Aircraft	Base	Role
1 Sqn.	Hunter F.6, FGA.9	Mafraq, H5	Ground attack, air defence
6 Sqn.	Hunter F.6, FGA.9	Mafraq, H5	Ground attack, air defence
9 Sqn.	F-104A	Amman, H5	Air defence
? Sqn.	C-47, Devon	Amman	Medium transport
? Sqn.	Alouette III, Whirlwind	Amman	Liaison, light transport

tanks, 60 armoured personnel carriers (APCs) and about 600 men.

A ceasefire was announced on the 23rd, but not until April 1971 did Hussein manage to oust the PFLP from Amman. The final push against the PFLP came in July 1971 when the Army, supported by the RJAF, attacked a stronghold at Ras el Agra. The civil war was of greater political than military significance, although estimates of casualties run as high as 25,000 dead.

In the wake of the Jordanian civil war in 1970, the British offered essential medical and related supplies. Typically they were flown into Amman in specially marked aircraft like this Argosy C.1, XN820 of 70 Sqn., based at Akrotiri. (Via A. S. Thomas)

AIRCRAFT MARKINGS

Hunter F.6 *Brown/sand over, light grey under, white serial on rear fuselage, code on fin, wolf's head squadron badge on nose: 704/E (1 Sqn.).*
F-104A *Bare metal overall, black code on fin.*

2.12. Miscellaneous conflicts and incidents

1. The Israeli Government organized the airlift of Jews from around the Middle East to Israel. In Operation 'Magic Carpet' in 1950, 45,000 were moved from the Yemen; in Operation 'Ali Baba' a year later, Iraqi Jews immigrated, while subsequent operations moved Jews from India and Persia. Israeli-registered C-46s were used, in spurious 'Alaskan Airlines', 'Near East Air Transport' and 'Cuban Airlines' markings.

2. On 15 October 1951, the Egyptian Government abrogated the treaty of 1936 providing for British forces to be based in the Canal Zone. As fighting broke out around the bases, 16 Independent Parachute Brigade was flown from Cyprus to Egypt in Valetta transports of 70, 78 and 204 Sqns. (Fayid) and 114 and 216 Sqns. (Kabrit). Fighting continued, and by January 1952, when riots broke out at Cairo Airport, some 40 British

servicemen had been killed. The situation improved, but there were further riots in 1953, and in 1954 agreement was reached for a British withdrawal. The last British forces left Egypt on 26 March 1956.

3. From the end of the War of Independence, the Israelis maintained a constant state of alert, intercepting any aircraft approaching the borders. On 17 July a DC-3 of Compagnie des Transportes, Lebanon, was attacked near the border and three passengers were killed. The aircraft landed safely at Beirut. On 12 April 1956 an IDF/AF Meteor F.8 shot down a Vampire FB.52 over the Negev. On 29 August 1956 two IDF/AF Meteors attacked four EAF Vampires at 15,000ft over the Negev, destroying one, and in a similar encounter two days later over Ashkelon two Vampires were shot down.

4. On 27 July 1955, El Al Constellation 4X-AKC, flying from Vienna to Tel Aviv, was shot down by Bulgarian Air Force (BAF) MiG-15 fighters after having been forced across the Bulgarian border. The aircraft crashed north of Petrich, killing the seven crew and 51 passengers.

5. Since the end of the 1956 Sinai War there have been numerous incursions into Israeli airspace, and numerous air combats between Israeli and Arab aircraft, and these are summarized in the accompanying table.

6. In September 1961 Syria left the United Arab Republic. Egypt decided to retaliate and on the 28th 120 paratroopers were dropped on Latakia airfield. Negotiations prevented the follow-up drop and the paratroopers surrendered.

7. In November 1962 the Royal Jordanian Air Force Chief of the Air Staff defected to Cairo in a Heron escorted by four Hunter F.6s of 1 Sqn.

8. The US carefully monitored Israeli military developments. In July 1963 two IDF/AF Mirages forced down a United States Air Force (USAF) RB-57A to Lod Airport. The aircraft was on an overflight from Saudi Arabia to Turkey, reviewing progress on the Dimona nuclear reactor in the Negev.

9. In 1964 Lebanon and Syria planned to divert the rivers flowing into the Jordan, thus denying Israel her main source of water. Israeli reaction was to bomb the engineering works in November, which had the effect of halting the scheme, but in the attacks an IDF/AF Mirage was lost, as was an SAAF MiG-21.

10. An SAAF MiG-17 pilot defected with his aircraft in 1965, but a richer prize the same year was a flight of six MiG-17s which landed at an Israeli airfield by mistake. Most were returned, but it is understood that at least one found its way to the US. On 16 August 1966 the prearranged defection of an Iraqi pilot with MiG-21F '524' resulted in the aircraft being shepherded into Ramat David AB for evaluation. It too finished up at Wright-Patterson AFB for US assessment.

11. After the Six-Day War, hostilities continued between Israel and her Arab neighbours. On 21 March 1968 the A-4 saw action for the first time with the IDF/AF. The IDF/AF attacked a PLO base at Karameh in Jordan, and while paratroops were landed behind the village to prevent escape, the A-4 was used to attack positions around the Damiya bridge and further to the rear of Karameh. The Israelis withdrew at 2100hrs, leaving the IDF/AF to attack the residual PLO position at Es Salt the following day. One A-4H was lost.

12. In August 1968 two Syrian MiG-17s were captured when they landed at Bezet airfield in error.

ARAB-ISRAEL AIR INCIDENTS, FROM 1956

Date	Location	Attacker	Victim
00/10/58	?	IDF	MiG-17
25/05/60	Negev	Super Mystère (IDF)	MiG-17 (EAF)
28/04/61	Negev	Super Mystère (IDF)	MiG-17 (EAF)
20/08/63	Galilee	Mirage (IDF)	MiG-17 (SAAF)
00/00/64	Nukheila	Mirage (101 Sqn. IDF)	MiG-21 (SAAF)
14/07/66	?	Mirage (101 Sqn. IDF)	MiG-21 (SAAF)
15/07/66	?	IDF	2 × MiG-17 (SAAF)
15/08/66	Galilee	Mirage (IDF)	2 × MiG-17 (SAAF)
03/11/68	Sinai	MiG-21 [EAF]	Mirage (IDF)
03/12/68	Jordan	?	Super Mystère (IDF)
10/12/68	Sharm el Sheikh	Mirage (IDF)	MiG-17 (EAF)
24/02/69	Damascus	Mirage (IDF)	2 × MiG-21 (SAAF)
13/06/72	Mediterranean	Mirages (IDF)	2 × MiG-21 (EAF)
09/11/72	?	Mirages (IDF)	2 × MiG-21 (SAAF)
21/11/72	Syria	Mirages (IDF)	6 × MiG-21 (SAAF)
02/01/73	N. Lebanon	Mirages (IDF)	MiG-21 (SAAF)
08/01/73	Syria	Mirages (IDF)	6 × MiG-21 (SAAF)
		MiG-21s (SAAF)	4 × Mirage (IDF)
15/02/73	Gulf of Suez	Mirages (IDF)	MiG-21 (EAF)
		MiG-21s (EAF)	Mirage (IDF)
13/09/73	Latakia	F-4E, Mirage (IDF)	13 × MiG-21 (SAAF)
		MiG-21s (SAAF)	F-4E (IDF)

13. On 31 October 1968, a dam at Qena and a hydro-station at Najh Hammadi, both in Egypt, were attacked by Israeli special forces flown in aboard three Super Frelons. During this period targets in Jordan were also attacked by the IDF/AF.

14. On 26 December 1968, passengers from an El Al Boeing 707 were attacked by the PLO at Athens Airport and one was killed. The predictable reprisal came on the 29th when four IDF/AF Super Frelons flew commandos into Beirut Airport. There they damaged installations and destroyed thirteen Arab airliners, including a VC-10, three Comet 4Cs and a Boeing 707.

15. In November 1972 King Hussein of Jordan was slightly injured when his helicopter was hit, while on the ground at Amman, by an RJAF F-104 from Mafraq. The F-104 is believed to have been shot down by other Jordanian fighters and a group of RJAF officers arrested.

16. A newly delivered Egyptian Boeing 707 was shot down in error by Egyptian forces south of Cairo on 6 December 1972.

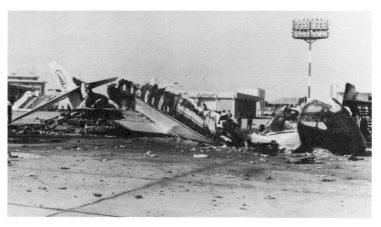

PLO terrorists attacked Israeli passengers at Athens airport on 26 December 1968, killing one. Israeli retribution was swift, and taken against Lebanon, from where the PLO operated. On 29 December, commandos were flown into Beirut Airport, where they destroyed installations and thirteen Arab airliners on the ground. Among them was this Middle East Airways Caravelle IVN, OD-AEF. (MEA via L. Pinzauti)

17. A Libyan Airlines Boeing 727, 5A-DAH, was shot down by an IDF/AF F-4E on 2 February 1973 near the northern tip of the Great Bitter Lakes. Of the 113 on board, 108 died in the resulting crash.

18. From the end of the Yom Kippur War to the Israeli invasion of Lebanon, there were occasional clashes in the air, including the following:

Date	Location	Attacker	Victim
06/12/73	Gulf of Suez	F-4E (IDF)	MiG-21 (EAF)
		MiG-21 (EAF)	F-4E (IDF)
27/06/77	Syria	F-15 (IDF)	4 × MiG-21 (SAAF)

19. In November 1973 Syrian radar sites were attacked by IDF F-4Es using AGM-45 Shrike anti-radiation missiles (ARM). Trouble flared again in early April 1974 when the IDF/AF attacked Syrian positions threatening the Israeli post on Mount Hermon. Syrian troops attacked the post on the 13th, and six days later a major air battle ensued as Israeli F-4Es clashed with Syrian MiG-21s. Syria claimed seven IDF/AF aircraft in combat and a further ten to AAA fire; the IDF/AF admitted the loss of two aircraft but claimed two SAAF aircraft brought down. Fighting continued until a ceasefire was signed on 30 May; on 29 April IDF/AF fighters had shot down four MiG-21s flying top cover to MiG-17 ground attack aircraft.

20. A Canadian Armed Forces Caribou attached to the UN was shot down by a Syrian SAM on 9 August 1974.

21. A Saudi Air Force C-130, with 36 on board, including three American crew, entered Israeli airspace on 12 April 1976. It was intercepted by IDF/AF fighters and forced to land at Ben Gurion airport, where it was held for 21hrs before being escorted on its way.

22. On 16 April 1981, Israeli AAA brought down a Palestinian-manned hot air balloon over the border with Lebanon. The crew were killed.

23. Early in November 1981 the IDF/AF began flying reconnaissance sorties over Saudi Arabia.

24. From July 1984 Soviet-made mines were laid in the Gulf of Suez and Red Sea, and within a month fifteen vessels were damaged. Four RH-53Ds of HM-14, USN, were flown to Egypt in a USAF C-5A to begin clearing operations in August, where they were joined by Royal Navy minehunters.

25. Late In August 1987 an IDF reconnaissance drone was shot down by the Egyptians while flying over Egyptian Army positions in southern Sinai.

26. In fighting between security forces and Arabs on the West Bank and in Gaza in summer 1988, IDF/AF helicopters have been used for moving troops and drooping CS gas.

3: North and West Africa

All wars are tragic, but those of Africa are singularly miserable. The majority have been colonial wars, involving well-equipped European troops fighting far from home in an alien environment and with no sign of prospective victory. A minority of wars in North and West Africa have been civil wars.

French interests in Africa have been in the north and centre, and two countries, Morocco and Tunisia, achieved independence without significant struggle. The position in Algeria, a part of metropolitan France, was different. Not only did the Muslim community hope to secure independence, but there was a complex civil war as European settlers fought for the *status quo*. At the peak of the war, France had at least 800 aircraft committed in a highly original organization. Some of these same aircraft were used to put down a revolt in Tunisia in 1961.

Independence was the issue in Portuguese Guinea. Waiting until neighbouring countries had secured independence, nationalists were able to operate most effectively from secure bases. The Portuguese Air Force was therefore committed defensively to supporting troops under attack or to hitting supply lines and camps across international borders.

The Nigerian Civil War resulted in part from the arbitrary boundaries drawn across Africa and Asia by conquering nations insensitive to tribal territories. The Biafran leader Ojukwu was able to capture widespread support for a war he could not win and which well-meaning aid agencies inadvertently prolonged. Mercenaries were well used, in particular in managing a small but effective air arm. The war gave interesting insights into the world of the arms dealer and the methods used to deliver weapons ranging from bullets to aircraft.

A complex civil war has been fought for twenty years in Chad, with leadership shifting confusingly. The French seem to have achieved an appropriate military presence in the area by having aircraft and troops available to send in from neighbouring territories without appearing provocative. Notwithstanding Libyan support for rebels in the north, at the time of writing there seems the prospect of peace at last.

Wider Libyan support for terrorism resulted in the sharp US surgical raids on military targets in 1986. These were an interesting illustration of superpower intervention: the care that went into avoiding Russian installations and the temporary removal of anti-submarine elements in the Sixth Fleet indicates a degree of collusion. For the immediate future, it seems that the application of air power in North Africa will revolve around Libyan aspirations.

3.1. Algeria, 1954–1962

From 1850 Algeria was effectively a part of metropolitan France. The country was inhabited mainly by nine million Arabs and Berbers, but there were also nearly one million European settlers or *colons* (also colloquially called '*pieds noirs*'). By the end of the Second World War there were three movements for independence from France. The most extreme was the Muslim Movement pour le Triomphe des Libertés Démocratiques (MTLD). On 8 May 1945, at a victory parade in Sétif, the MTLD demonstrated. Following shooting there was a sharp escalation of violence, during which 103 *colons* were killed. In the revenge that ensued several thousand Muslims were killed. Where settlements were inaccessible they were bombed or subjected to naval bombardment, and no fewer than forty villages were attacked by SBD-5 Dauntless dive-bombers of 3F flying from Algiers-Maison Blanche. Available in the event of further trouble were the Mosquitoes of GC 19.

There was relative peace for nine years, but after the administration twice rigged elections against the MTLD, conflict was inevitable. In 1951 an armed splinter group of the MTLD was formed; eventually, in October 1954, this became the Front de la Libération Nationale (FLN) and its armed wing the Armée de Libération Nationale (ALN). The ALN prepared for action against the Government by carefully organizing its forces. The country was divided into six regions or *Wilayas*, and initial attacks against gendarmeries, local administrative buildings and public utilities were planned for 1 November 1954. These attacks were not particularly successful and led to traditional search and cordon operations, especially in the Aures mountains. Troops were land-transported, and rebels often had enough notice to escape.

Air assets were few and not well suited to

B-26B 4322537 in typical black overall finish and displaying the markings of EB 3/91 on the nose. The Armée de l'Air used the B-26 extensively, both in Indo-China and Algeria, in the latter case with EB 91 and in the reconnaissance version with ER 1/32. Clearly visible are the HVARs under the wing. The Algerians had no effective anti-aircraft weapons, so losses were relatively light. (ECPA)

need. At Oran were the Mistrals of EC 6 operating primarily in the air defence role for Air Region 5. At Blida were the ACC.1s and C-47s of GT (later ET) 1/62, together with a Liaison Groupe, and at Lartigue there was a flight of P2V-6 Neptunes of 22F. The Mistrals were supplemented by those of EC 7 in Tunisia and EC 8 in Morocco. The Navy also provided land-based F4U-7 Corsairs from 12F. It soon became clear that the relatively delicate and fast Mistral was not ideal for attacking mountain targets, and in June 1955 the first four Escadrilles d'Aviation Légère d'Appui (EALA) were formed with the MS.500 and MS.733 Alcyon. The air units were operated within three Groupes Aériennes Tactiques (GATAC): GATAC 1 Constantine, to the east and covering Wilayas 1 and 2; GATAC 2 Oran, to the west and covering Wilaya 5 and GATAC 3 Algiers covering Wilayas 3, 4. and 6. With the acquisition of large numbers of T-6Gs from early 1956, there was an increase in the numbers of EALA and they were reorganized initially within one Groupe d'Aviation Légère d'Appui (GALA), 70; later this was split into three GALAs, one within each GATAC. Apart from regional air defence, the units were available for local development and this flexibility was one key to military success.

A large number of air command posts were established, and with good radio communications aircraft could report sightings to local Army units, while the Army could bring air power to bear at short notice. Operations during 1955 broke up a number of ALN units, forcing the organization to operate from within the main cities and in the Aures mountains where support could be channelled from neighbouring Tunisia. The light attack aircraft were used to flatten villages in the immediate neighbourhood of ALN activity, usually after the inhabitants had been warned to leave.

On 14 October 1956 a PB4Y-2 of 28F based at Lartigue spotted a blockade-running ship, the SS *Athos*, approaching the coast. Naval units were directed to the ship, which was found to be carrying a massive arms shipment for the FLN. At the time many French units were preparing

for the Suez expedition; French enthusiasm for an expedition into Egypt was in part encouraged by the knowledge that Egypt was a key supporter of the ALN. Within Algeria not only was the need for light attack aircraft recognized, but the early establishment of EH 2/57 with Bell 47Gs and H-19s gave operational experience of helicopters, particularly in the observation and troop transport roles. The first major use of helicopters in the assault transport role was between 23 and 26 May 1957 at Agounnenda, south of the Blida–L'Arba road. An important ALN battalion had been identified and a flexible ambush laid. The ALN initially held its own until two companies of paras were flown in by H-21C. The ALN force then dropped to the valley bottom, where it was strafed by aircraft. Notwithstanding the French supremacy and tactics, two-thirds of the ALN force escaped. Eventually helicopters were flown by all three services in large numbers: by June 1959 221 heavy helicopters were in use.

Through 1956 to 1958, much of the fighting was urban. The EALA had added Sipa S.111s and S.12s to their inventories, but from early 1956 the first of some 700 T-6G Harvards were delivered. These robust aircraft were the mainstay of operations until replaced from 1960. They were fitted to carry two 7.5mm pods, a 100-litre napalm tank, four 10kg bombs, six T10 rockets or two rocket packs. The Air Force was further strengthened by the addition of EB 91 with the B-26 light bomber and EC 20 with the F-47D.

The rural war was fought in the context of a system of *quadrillage*, where cities, towns and villages were protected by a static defence force in an attempt to deny the rebels support. In addition, an elaborate, 3,000km fence was constructed along the borders with Tunisia and Morocco, from where an increasing number of ALN attacks were launched. The fence was electrified and mined, and any identified breach resulted in prepositioned howitzer fire followed by air attack and heliborne commando response. Air surveillance of the fence was also organized and Aéronavale PB4Y-2s were detached from Karouba, Tunisia, since their endurance and night attack capability were particularly valuable. In the last six months of 1957 there were 80 major shooting incidents across the fence.

On 11 January a French patrol was ambushed by an FLN battalion which had crossed the wire, apparently from the Tunisian village of Sakiet, and some days later an aircraft was shot down during a reconnaissance flight over the village. On 8 February a second aircraft was shot at crash-landed within Tunisia. Three hours later Sakiet was heavily attacked by B-26 bombers of EB 91, which hit a school and hospital, killing 80 and presenting the FLN with a propaganda coup. The most significant attempt to breach the fence occurred on 27 April 1958 at Souk-Ahras when 800 men attacked the line, to be met almost immediately by airborne troops. Fighting continued for a week, with air strikes across into Tunisia, before the ALN withdrawal, leaving 600 dead or captured.

There was growing resentment by the *colons* of Government handling of the Algerian war. It appeared that the French Government might concede Algeria to the nationalists, and in May 1958 General de Gaulle was called back to power with a mandate, *inter alia*, to keep Algeria French.

Tension existed between the Government, the *colons* and the Muslim majority; as so often happens, the Army was placed between the three interests. The position was worsened by the Army's need for military success after defeat in Indo-China and the débâcle at Suez. In January 1959 Air Force General Maurice Challe was appointed commander of the French forces in Algeria. He immediately prepared for a new, mobile campaign to purge the Wilayas working from west to east. His objective was to destroy the ALN rather than to occupy territory. Forming

highly mobile groups of Foreign Legion infantry and paratroops, he relied on aerial reconnaissance for assessments of local situations. Any ALN concentration was first surrounded and the target then bombed. Napalm was used sparingly where mountainous conditions reduced the effect of anti-personnel bombs or rockets. Heliborne troops were then brought in while the surrounding forces moved in and any escapers were picked up by patrolling aircraft.

The first of the new operations, 'Oranie', was launched in February against ALN positions in the lightly wooded Ouarsenis mountains working from Saïda. Within three months 1,600 ALN had been killed, and from mid-April the French embarked on Operation 'Courroie' in Wilaya 4 north of Orléansville. This operation was again successful. The third major operation, 'Jumelles', was mounted from July and involved 25,000 troops. Now the area covered was the Kabylia mountains in Wilaya 3 to the east of Algiers. At an early stage a supplementary operation was mounted as intelligence reports indicated an ALN group in the Hodna mountains to the south. Operation 'Étincelle' was effective and left Wilaya 3 isolated with no hope of retreat to the south. The main operation in the Kabylia mountains ran into March 1960, by which time the ALN had lost a further 3,750 men.

By now the air forces were deploying over 700 aircraft in the theatre. In the attack role, EC 20 had acquired AD-4N Skyraiders, and the EALA were re-equipping with a French re-worked version of the T-28D Trojan, which in Armée de l'Air service became the Fennec. As the ALN gained access to more sophisticated weapons, replacing the vulnerable T-6 became overdue: in twenty months to August 1959, 65 pilots were killed and 31 injured flying the type, most being

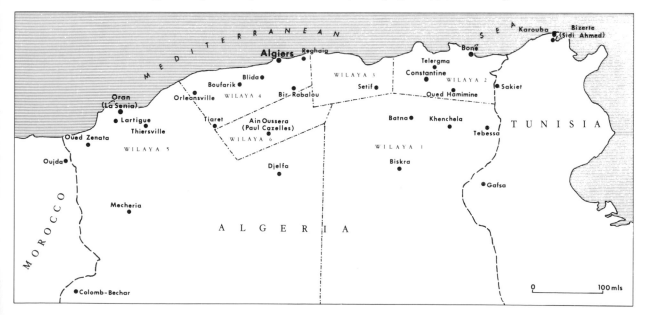

hit by ground fire. The GALAs were disbanded in 1959 and the EALA operated with a higher degree of independence and flexibility. The majority of air crews were drawn from European-based combat units on term secondment; they were required to make the transition from modern jet fighters to what were in reality slow piston-engined trainers.

The most important acquisitions were the licence-built H-34 helicopter operated by the Air Force and the twin-rotor H-21 operated by the Navy and Aviation Légère de l'Armée de Terre (ALAT). Both types entered service from 1957 and the H-21C, with its ability to transport twenty fully armed troops, was particularly valuable. The Army purchased 98 while the Navy operated ten in 31F, mainly to place marines who were now fighting with the Army. Large helicopters of all three services were available for the fast movement of troops, and a feature of the Algerian war was the excellent co-operation that developed between the services. Another characteristic of the war was organizational flexibility: the aircraft of regular, relatively fixed-base units were available for deployment within GATACs, the lighter, more mobile aircraft of the EALA were generally ascribed to zones, while observation aircraft worked within sectors. The Army commands were advised daily of the assets available to them, depending on the location and scale of operations.

In support of planned operations there were a number of Joint Operations Centres (JOC), while for spontaneous action widespread use was made of mobile command posts. A widespread network of VHF transmitters, receivers and repeaters

enabled air support to be applied with the maximum speed and effectiveness. From 1959 the F-100D Super Sabres of EC 1/3 attacked pre-planned targets from their home base at Rheims, refuelling at Istres on the return flight.

The last of Challe's operations was 'Pierres Précieuses', which began in November 1959. This was the most easterly of the operations covering the area north of Constantine and again it was successful, although further operations were frustrated following a revolt in Algiers. From September 1959 de Gaulle had made clear that he was prepared to treat with the FLN, and the same month they announced a government in exile, the Gouvernement Provisoire de la République Algérienne (GPRA). The *pieds noirs* were disgusted at the prospect of a 'sell out' and with help from some sympathetic members of the armed forces occupied the centre of Algiers in January 1960. Challe made no initial attempt to remove the barricades and was replaced in April. His planned Operation 'Trident' to mop up the remaining pocket of ALN activity in the Aures mountains was thus overtaken by events.

As the *pieds noirs* now formed their own paramilitary organization, the Front de l'Algérie Française (FAF), military operations recommenced around Algiers. However, the military were losing heart, and the FAF gained invaluable support from disillusioned officers. After a major speech by de Gaulle on 11 April 1961, Challe flew secretly to Algeria, where he led a mutiny on 24 April joined by many senior officers and based on the headquarters of the 1st Régiment Étranger Parachutiste (1e REP) at Zéralda.

Tanks rolled into the streets of Paris to guard

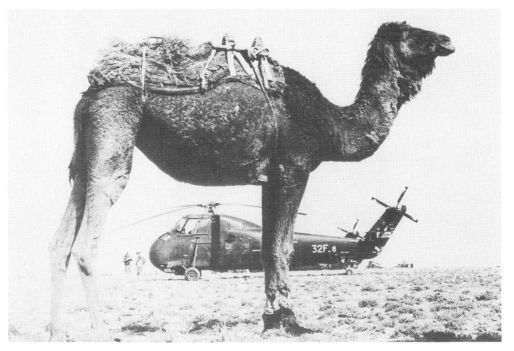

A French Navy HSS-1 in an obviously North African setting. The French services made extensive use of helicopters in the Algerian War; indeed, it was the first war in which significant troop movements depended on the helicopter. The AA used the Bell 47, S-55, H-34 and Alouette II, the Navy the H-19, H-21C and HSS-1 and the Army the Bell 47, H-19, H-21C, SO-1221 and Alouette II. By 1960 some 650 helicopters were operational in the theatre. Here 32F.8 (no. 58944) is shown in overall olive drab finish. (ECPA)

TABLE OF UNITS: ALGERIA, 1954—1962

Unit	Aircraft	Base	Role	Dates
AA				
GC 19	Mosquito	Maison Blanche	Air defence, ground attack	00/00/45 to 00/00/49
EC 1/6	Mistral	Oran	Air defence, ground attack (to EC 3/20)	01/10/52 to 01/12/60
EC 2/6	F-47D, Mistral, Vautour IIN	Oran	Night fighter (to ECTT 2/30)	11/12/51 to 00/02/62
EEOC 1/17	F-47D	Oran, Telergma	Ground attack (to EC 1/20)	00/00/54 to 01/04/56
EC 1/7	Vampire, Mistral, Mystère IVA	Sidi-Ahmed	⎫	17/11/51 to 00/11/61
EC 2/7	Mistral, Mystère IVA	Sidi-Ahmed	⎬ Air defence, ground attack	17/11/51 to 00/10/61
EC 1/8	F-47D, Mistral, Mystère IVA	Rabat, Oran	⎮	01/07/49 to 00/09/61
EC 2/8	Mistral, Mystère IVA	Rabat, Oran	⎭	01/07/55 to 00/09/61
EC 1/20	F-47D, Mistral, AD-4N	Oran, Boufarik, Bone	Ground attack, close support (ex EEOC 1/17)	01/04/56 to 30/09/63
EC 2/20	F-47D, AD-4N	Oran, Boufarik	Ground attack, close support	00/00/56 to 31/12/63
EC 3/20	AD-4N	Boufarik, Oran	Ground attack, close support (ex EC 1/6)	01/12/60 to 01/11/63
EC 1/3	F-100D	Rheims	Ground attack	00/00/60 to 00/00/61
ECN 1/71	MD.315, B-26N	Bone, Tebessa	Night support	00/11/59 to 31/08/62
EB 1/91	B-26B/C	Bone	Light bombing	00/09/56 to 00/00/62
EB 2/91	B-26B/C	Oran	Light bombing	00/12/56 to 00/00/62
EB 3/91	B-26B/C	Oran	Light bombing	00/12/56 to 00/00/62
ER 1/32	RB-32	Bone, Oran	Recce	00/09/56 to 01/12/63
ET 2/64	Noratlas	Blida	Transport (to ET 2/62)	00/00/55 to 00/00/56
ET 1/62	AAC.1, C-47, Noratlas	Maison Blanche, Blida	Transport	01/08/45 to 01/10/63
ET 2/62	Noratlas	Blida	Transport (ex ET 2/64)	00/00/56 to 07/12/61
ET 3/62	C-47, Noratlas	Maison Blanche, Oran	Transport	00/00/56 to 31/03/64
GLA 45	C-445, N.1002, N.1101, LeO 453, Martinet, C-47, MD.311	Boufarik	Liaison, light transport, rescue	00/00/45 to 31/03/64
ELO 2/45	Broussard	Oujda, Reghaia	Observation (ex EALA 2/70)	01/09/57 to 31/07/63
ELO 3/45	Broussard	Telergma, Boufarik, Oued Hamimine	Observation (to GALO 54)	00/05/56 to 00/00/59
ELO 4/45	Broussard	Oran	Observation	00/00/56 to 00/00/58
ELO 5/45	Broussard	Oued Zenata, Oran	Observation (ex EALA 3/70; to GALO 53)	01/02/58 to 00/00/59
ELA 46	C.445, Martinet, C-47	Rabat	Liaison	00/00/47 to 00/00/61
ELA 47	N.1101, C.445, LeO 453, C-47, Martinet	Bizerte	Liaison	00/00/47 to 00/00/61
ELA 53	N.1000, N.1100, Martinet, Broussard	Oran	Liaison (merged with ELO 5/45, 1959; to form GALO 53)	00/00/55 to 31/10/62
ELA 54	N.1101, Martinet, Broussard	Oued Hamimine	Liaison (merged with ELO 3/45, 1959; to form GALO 54)	00/00/55 to 31/10/62
GSRA 76	AAC.1, C-47, Broussard	Tunis, Ouargla	Light transport, rescue	00/00/55 to 31/01/63
GSRA 78	AAC.1, C-47, Broussard	Colomb-Bechar	Light transport, rescue	00/00/56 to 31/01/63
GOM 86	Martinet, MD.315/311	Blida	Utilty, communications (formed by merging EOM 86 and EOM 87)	00/00/55 to 31/07/63
Light attack units				
EALA 3/1	T-6G	Oued Zenata	(Ex 14/72, 20/72)	01/12/59 to 31/01/62
EALA 2/2	T-6G	Paul Cazelles, Blida	(Ex 1/72, 8/72)	01/12/59 to 00/01/62
EALA 3/4	T-6G, T-28D	Bone, Telergma	(Ex 17/72, 18/72)	01/12/59 to 09/07/62
EALA 3/5	T-6G, T-28D	Mecheria	(Ex 2/72, 9/72)	01/12/59 to 09/07/62
EALA 3/9	T-6G	Telergma, Bone, Blida	(Ex 7/72, 12/72)	01/12/59 to 09/07/62
EALA 3/10	T-6G	Batna, Kenchela	(Ex 3/72, 6/72)	01/12/59 to 09/07/62
EALA 3/12	T-6G	Blida, Paul Cazelles	(Ex 5/72, 15/72)	01/12/59 to 30/06/61
EALA 2/70	MS.500, Broussard	?	(To ELO 2/45)	01/03/56 to 01/09/57
EALA 3/70	MS.500	Oued Zenata	(To ELO 5/45)	01/03/56 to 01/02/58
EALA 4/70	MS.500	Thiersville		00/00/56 to 00/00/58
EALA 5/70	?	Bone	(Sponsored by 4 EC; to EALA 17/7)	01/03/56 to 01/07/57
EALA 6/70	MS.733	Tebessa	(Sponsored by 9 EC; to EALA 7/72)	01/03/56 to 01/07/57
EALA 7/70	MS.733	?	(Sponsored by 4 EC; to EALA 18/72)	01/09/56 to 01/07/57
EALA 1/71	Sipa 12A/111A	Gafsa	(Sponsored by 3 EC; to EALA 19/72)	06/04/56 to 01/07/57
EALA 2/71	Sipa 12A/111A	Tunisia	(Sponsored by 1 EC; to EALA 20/72)	15/04/56 to 01/07/57
EALA 3/71	Sipa 12A	Djelfa	(Sponsored by 11 EC; to EALA 21/72)	00/05/56 to 01/07/57
EALA 1/72 ⎫		Oued Zenata, Setif, Blida	(Sponsored by 2 EC; to EALA 2/2)	01/04/56 to 01/12/59
EALA 2/72 ⎮		Batna	(Sponsored by 5 EC; to EALA 3/5)	01/04/56 to 01/12/59
EALA 3/72 ⎮		Oujda, Batna	(Sponsored by 10 EC; to EALA 3/10)	01/04/56 to 01/12/59
EALA 4/72 ⎮		Marrakech, Mecheria, Tiaret, Tebessa	(Sponsored by 3 EC)	01/07/56 to 01/09/61
EALA 5/72 ⎮		Colomb-Bechar	(Sponsored by 12 EC; to EALA 3/12)	01/07/56 to 01/12/59
EALA 6/72 ⎮		Thiersville, Biskra, Khenchela, Batna	(Sponsored by 10 EC; to EALA 3/10)	01/07/56 to 01/12/59
EALA 7/72 ⎮ T-6G		Tebessa	(Ex EALA 6/70; to EALA 3/9)	01/07/57 to 01/12/59
EALA 8/72 ⎮		Tebessa	(Sponsored by 2 EC; to EALA 2/2)	00/00/56 to 01/12/59
EALA 9/72 ⎮		Mecheria	(Sponsored by 5 EC; to EALA 3/5)	15/08/56 to 01/12/59
EALA 10/72 ⎮		Orléansville, Setif	(Sponsored by 30 ECTT)	01/09/56 to 30/09/60
EALA 11/72 ⎮		Reghaia, Bir Rabalou	(Sponsored by 33 ER)	01/10/56 to 31/08/61
EALA 12/72 ⎮		Bone	(Sponsored by 9 EC; to EALA 3/9)	01/10/56 to 01/12/59
EALA 13/72 ⎮		Paul Cazelles, Bir Rabalou		01/10/56 to 30/06/60
EALA 14/72 ⎮		Thiersville	(Sponsored by 1 EC; to EALA 3/1)	15/11/56 to 01/12/59
EALA 15/72 ⎮		Paul Cazelles	(Sponsored by 12 EC; to EALA 3/12)	15/11/56 to 01/12/59
EALA 16/72 ⎭		Biskra	(Sponsored by 33 ER)	01/12/56 to 01/05/61

TABLE OF UNITS: ALGERIA, 1954–1962 (continued)

Unit	Aircraft	Base	Role	Dates
EALA 17/72		Bone	(Ex EALA 5/70; to EALA 3/4)	01/07/57 to 01/12/59
EALA 18/72		Oued Hamimine	(Ex EALA 7/70; to EALA 3/4)	01/07/57 to 01/12/59
EALA 19/72		Telergma, Setif	(Ex EALA 1/71)	01/07/57 to 01/09/61
EALA 20/72		Oujda, Oued Zenata	(Ex EALA 2/71; to EALA 3/1)	01/07/57 to 01/12/59
EALA 21/72	T-6G	Djelfa	(Ex EALA 3/71)	01/07/57 to 00/00/61
EALA 3/73		Mecheria, Paul Cazelles, Oued Zenata		00/00/57 to 31/10/60
EALA 4/73		Paul Cazelles	(Sponsored by 33 ER)	01/08/57 to 02/05/58
EALA 5/73		Djelfa, Blida		00/00/61 to 00/02/62

Helicopter units

Unit	Aircraft	Base	Role	Dates
GMH 57	Bell 47, S-55, H-34	Boufarik	(Ex ELA 57; to EH 1, EH 2)	01/04/55 to 01/10/56

EH 1 became EH 3 in 1957, EH 2 became 22 EH in 1961 and embraced the following Escadrilles:

Unit	Aircraft	Base	Role	Dates
EH 3/57	S-55, H-34	Boufarik, Oran		00/00/56 to 00/00/59
EH 4/57	Bell 47, H-34			
EH 2/58	S-55, H-34	Oran	(To EH 2/22, EH 3/22)	00/00/57 to 00/00/61
EH 1/57	Bell 47, Alouette II	Boufarik, Oran	(Ex EH 3; to EH 1/22)	00/00/58 to 00/00/61

EH 3 became 23 EH in 1961 and embraced the following Escadrilles:

Unit	Aircraft	Base	Role	Dates
EH 1/57	Bell 47		(To EH 2)	00/00/56 to 00/00/58
EH 2/57	S-55			00/00/56 to 00/03/60
EH 5/57	Alouette II	Boufarik	(To EH 1/23)	00/02/57 to 00/00/61
EH 6/57	Alouette II			00/00/57 to 00/00/59
EH 1/58	H-34		(To EH 2/23, 3/23)	00/00/57 to 00/00/61
EH 7/57	?			00/00/58 to 00/00/59
EH 1/22	Alouette II		(Ex EH 1/57)	
EH 2/22	Alouette II	Oran	(Ex EH 2/58)	
EH 3/22	H-34		(Ex EH 2/58)	00/00/61 to 00/00/62
EH 1/23	Alouette II		(Ex EH 5/57)	
EH 2/23	H-34	Reghaia	(Ex EH 1/58)	
EH 3/23	H-34		(Ex EH 1/58)	

Aéronavale

Unit	Aircraft	Base	Role	Dates
11F	F6F-5, Aquilon	Hyères, Karouba, Bizerte, Maison Blanche	Air defence, ground attack	00/00/53 to 00/09/59
12F	F4U-7	Karouba, Hyères		00/11/53 to 00/00/62
14F	F4U-7	Karouba, Hyères	Ground attack	00/00/56 to 00/00/62
15F	F4U-7, AU-1	Hyères, Karouba, Telergma		00/00/58 to 00/00/62
16F	Aquilon	Hyères, Karouba	Air defence, ground attack	00/08/58 to 00/00/59
17F	F4U-7	Karouba	Ground attack	00/00/58 to 00/00/60
8S	JRF-5	Maison Blanche	MR	00/00/53 to 00/00/54
21F	P2V-6	Lartigue	MR, SAR	00/00/53 to 00/00/61
22F	P2V-6	Lartigue	MR, SAR	00/00/53 to 00/00/61
23F	P2V-6/7	Port Lyautey (Morocco)		00/00/53 to 00/00/61
1S	PBY-5A, PB4Y-2	Lartigue	MR	00/10/54 to 00/11/54
15S	TBM-3	Lartigue		00/00/55 to 15/06/56
28F	PB4Y-2, P2V-6	Karouba, Lartigue		00/00/56 to 00/00/62
10S	H-19	Sétif	Trials det.	00/00/56 to 00/00/56
31F	H-21C, HSS-1	Sétif, Sidi Bel Abbès		00/06/56 to 00/02/60
32F	HSS-1	Lartigue	Assault transport	00/01/58 to 00/08/62
33F	H-19, HSS-1	Lartigue		00/00/59 to 00/00/62
GH 1	HSS-1	Headquarters for 31F, 32F and 33F from 00/00/59 to 00/00/62		
SL (GH 1)	SE.3130	Lartigue	Liaison	00/00/59 to 00/00/59
4S	Lancaster GR, SO.95	Lartigue, to Karouba / Lartigue	Operational training (to 5S)	00/01/55 to 31/03/55 / 00/00/56 to 00/00/60
5S	Lancaster GR, SO.95 / Ju 52, SNJ-5, TBM-3	Maison Blanche, Lartigue / Karouba	Operational training (ex 4S)	01/04/55 to 00/00/56 / 00/00/56 to 00/00/60
32S	SO.30P, SNB-5	Maison Blanche	Transport, liaison	00/00/54 to 00/00/62
SL Algers	PV-2, NC.702, SO.30P	Maison Blanche	Liaison	00/00/53 to 00/00/58

ALAT

Unit	Aircraft	Base	Role	Dates
GH 2	Bell 47G, H-19, H-21C	Sétif	Light transport, observation	22/11/54 to 00/00/62
GH 1	Bell 47, H-19	Sétif	Light transport, observation	00/03/55 to 00/00/62

Note: When 4S became 5S, a new 4S was formed at Algiers, then to Tunisia. The two units exchanged locations in 1956. From 1956, ALAT introduced organic air elements to Army ground units as Pelotons Divisionnaires (Platoons); by the end of the war these numbered 32 and were both highly mobile and widely dispersed. Types operated were Bell 47G, H-19, SO.1221, H-21C and Alouette II helicopters and Broussard, L-18, L-19, L-21, N.3400 and NC 856 aircraft; seventeen of the units used helicopters only. In 1960 the 700 aircraft and 400 helicopters of the platoons and GH 2 were organized within three Groupements ALAT for administrative purposes. These were: GA 101, at Sétif and Constantine (nine platoons and GH 2); GA 102, at Oran (seven platoons); and GA 105, at Algiers (fifteen platoons).

against a possible airborne coup from Algeria; indeed, two groups of paras, totalling 2,400, were waiting in woods outside Paris, but, deprived of their leaders and reinforcement from Algeria, they disbanded. Most of the 45 Noratlas transports in Algeria flew empty to airfields in southern France, but combat patrols were flown by Super Mystère fighters along the Rhône valley to force down any aircraft making for the capital. Without support in France itself the revolt was unsuccessful and the leaders fled to establish the Organisation Armée Secrète (OAS). The 1e REP was disbanded. The OAS maintained a terrorist campaign in Algeria and France. Attempts were made on the President's life, and on 26 April 1962, the anniversary of the collapse of the revolt, Air France Constellation F-BAZE was blown up at Algiers.

A ceasefire was announced in March 1962, with independence following in July. The cost in human terms was enormous: 3,200 *colons*, 17,456 French military, 141,000 FLN and 16,000 Muslims dead and vast numbers wounded or missing. At independence most settlers left Algeria and many loyal Muslims were executed. The total death toll has been estimated at one million.

The French military, recovering from defeat in Indo-China and humiliation at Suez, performed superbly in Algeria. Both strategy and tactics were sound, and the extensive operational use of helicopters was especially remarkable. The ALAT was formed at the beginning of the war, when it included only a handful of aircraft, but it rapidly grew to a service operating over 1,000 aircraft and helicopters, most of them in Algeria.

AIRCRAFT MARKINGS

AA

Most Armée de l'Air aircraft were finished in bare metal, with serials and codes in black.
F-47D Code LS on forward fuselage (EC 20).
Broussard Olive drab overall with white top decking, 1521M:N°010 in black on rudder, code ZB in white on rear fuselage (GLS 3/45).
T-6G Code on fuselage, serial on two parts on fin and rudder, scorpion unit badge on cockpit side: 149-19/DH (EALA 19/72); 114-475/K (EALA 3/72); 012-93/A (EALA 1/40).
T-28D-52 Ladybird unit badge on cockpit side: 1194/18 (EALA?).

AD-4N Serial on fin, codes on rear fuselage: 125719/20-LL (EC 1/20); 123797/20-QT (EC 2/20).
B-26B Black overall, white top decking, red serials: 4139358 (GB 1/91).
B-26C Black overall, white top decking, red serials and codes: 4435926 (ECN 1/71); 4435607/L (GB 2/91); 711-C/I, 201-B/V (GB 1/91).
Vautour IIN Serial on fin top, code on forward fuselage: 306/6-QA (EC 2/6).
F-100D Serial on lower fin, code mid-fuselage: 42171/3-IS (EC 1/3).
S-55 Olive drab overall, white serial and code on upper fuselage: 55937 MS (EH 2/57).
H-34 Olive drab overall, white serial and code on mid-upper fuselage: 58637 DY; 58593 LR (EH 1/58).
Flamant Serial on rudder, code on fin: 70/FC (GLS 45).

Aéronavale

F4U-7 Midnite blue overall, white serial and code on rear fuselage: 133703/12F.12 (12F).

ALAT

L-18C Olive drab overall, small black serial on rudder top, white code on fuselage, three white identification stripes on upper wing: 185374/ATI (7ème DMR).
L-19 Silver overall, orange panels on upper wing, black code on fuselage: 30A.
Bell 47G Olive drab overall, white code on fuel tank: AZN.
SO.1221 Djinn Olive drab overall, small white serial and larger code on lower fuselage: FR-33/WO.
H-21C Olive drab overall, serial in yellow, code white on fin: 40/AAR, 72/AAB (GH 2). Code on forward fuselage: ?/AAY (GH 2).

3.2. Morocco in the Spanish Sahara, 1975 to date

Morocco, previously administered by the French and Spanish, achieved independence in 1956. In 1955 there had been nationalist rioting in major towns, to which the French military had reacted. Bedouins then massacred Europeans in Oued Zem, following which the retreating column was attacked by Mistrals of EC 1/8 flying from Rabat-Sale. Also involved, albeit in a peripheral role, was 23F of the Aéronavale with the P2V-6 based at Port Lyautey. There was further unrest in December 1956 when a Spanish parachute group was dropped at Tiliuin, in the Ifni enclave, to seize control of the airfield there. In an unrelated incident a company of French paratroopers was dropped at Ameillag in Mauretania on 24 January 1957 after localized attacks.

In 1965, after disturbances, a royal dictatorship was determined by King Hassan II. Civil unrest

continued, however, and on 16 August 1972 there was an attempt on the King's life. Three Royal Moroccan Air Force (FARM) F-5A fighters based at Kenitra attacked his Boeing 727 on a return flight from France. The aircraft was severely damaged, but it made an emergency landing on one engine at Rabat-Sale with the King unharmed. One of the F-5As then strafed airport buildings, and later in the day four more attacked the Royal Palace but without injuring the monarch. Two of the senior officers involved in the attempted coup commandeered a helicopter from Kenitra and fled to Gibraltar seeking asylum. From 1974 Spain announced that she would withdraw from neighbouring Spanish Sahara, Mauretania and Morocco agreeing on partition when the Spanish withdrew.

The Spanish government had held talks with

the Algerian-backed Popular Front for the Liberation of Saguiet el-Hamra and Rio de Oro (Polisario), and from 27 January 1976 there were clashes between Moroccan and Algerian troops at Amgala Oasis. On 26 February Spain withdrew from the disputed territory: Mauretania and Morocco now occupied south and north Spanish Sahara respectively, and Polisario fighters of the Armée de Libération Polpulaire Sahraoui (ALPS) began attacking regular forces. The Mauretanian Islamic Air Force (FAIM) operated six Britten-Norman Defenders in the counter-insurgency (coin) role, but two of these were early casualties to ground fire. The FARM had one squadron of fifteen F-5As, three F-5Bs and two RF-5As at Kenitra, together with a light attack squadron of 24 Magisters based at Meknes. Tactical transport was provided by six C-130Hs, also based at Kenitra. The French supported the Moroccans, and when the ALPS held eight French civilians hostage in Algeria in late 1977 the French Air Force moved eight Jaguars of EC 3/11 into Dakar, Senegal. They were supported by two Transall C-160 transports of ET 61 and a single Atlantique of 24F.

On 15 December Polisario forces based in Algeria attacked the Zouerate–Nouadhibou railway. French Jaguars operating from Mauretania attacked the column, allegedly with napalm and phosphorous bombs, destroying 25 vehicles. Early in 1978 Jaguars of EC 1/11 joined those of EC 3/11 and attacked Polisario units in support of Moroccan forces. On the fourth major strike on 3 May, one Jaguar was shot down by SA-7; it was one of three aircraft to be lost during French involvement. In July 1978 there was a coup in Mauretania and a ceasefire was agreed with the Polisario, who were now able to operate out of southern Spanish Sahara. Fighting intensified, and the FARM lost several F-5As to SA-7 missiles.

In October 1979 Operation 'Uhud' was launched against Polisario forces at Djebel Ouarksis with

full air and artillery support. The following month the FARM was heavily committed to attacks on Polisario bases along the border with Mauretania and Algeria, during which F-5A 97099 was shot down. In autumn 1980 a start was made on building a fortified 'wall' from Djebel Ouarksis in the north to Cap Bojador; it was completed in May 1982. The FARM was now in need of new combat aircraft, and the first of 24 F-5Es and 50 Mirage F.1CHs were delivered; also received were six OV-10As for intelligence-gathering, but two were soon lost to SAMs. Polisario strength was such that on 12 October 1981 it was able to mount an attack supported by tanks on the Moroccan base at Guelta Zemmour; it had been supplied with T-54 and T-55 tanks, and SA-6, SA-7 and SA-8 SAMs from Algeria and Libya. The FARM flew supply and attack sorties, during one of which, on 12 October 1981, C-130H CNA-OH/4717 was lost to SA-7 attack and, more significantly, a Mirage F.1CH flying at 30,000ft was shot down by an SA-8 launched from Algeria. The Polisario also claimed a further Mirage on 12 January 1985, an F-5, an SA.330 Puma helicopter, an OV-10A on 21 January 1985 and an F-5E on 21 August 1987.

Civil aviation has also suffered in the fighting.

TABLE OF UNITS: MOROCCO, 1975 TO DATE

Unit	Aircraft	Base	Role	Nos./dates
MIAF, 1977				
(1 flt.)	Defender	Nouakchott	Ground attack, light transport	4
FARM, 1982				
(1 sqn.)	F-5A/B, RF-5A	Kenitra	Close support, recce	17
(1 sqn.)	F-5E	Kenitra	Close support, air defence	24
(2 sqns.)	Mirage F.1CH/EH	Sidi Slimane, El Aïoun	Ground attack, air defence	38
(1 flt.)	OV-10A	Kenitra	Recce	4
(1 sqn.)	Alpha Jet	Meknes	Ground attack	24
(1 sqn.)	C-47, C-130H, KC-130H, 707-138B	Kenitra	Transport, refuelling	19
	AB.205, 206, 212	Various	Light transport, casevac, liaison	27
	SA.330 Puma	?	Transport	35
AA				
EC 1/8	Mistral	Rabat-Sale	Air defence, ground attack	00/00/55 to 00/00/60
EC 3/11	Jaguar A/E	Dakar	Ground attack	00/11/77 to 00/06/78
EC 1/11	Jaguar A/E	Dakar	Ground attack	00/01/78 to 00/06/78
ET 61	Transall C.160	Dakar	Transport	00/11/77 to 00/06/78
Aéronavale				
24F	Atlantique	Dakar	Recce	00/11/77 to 00/06/78

On 8 December 1988 five Americans were killed when their DC-7, under contract to the US Agency for International Development, was shot down by a SAM over the western Sahara. A second aircraft was damaged. The aircraft were among a number supporting crop-spraying operations against locusts.

The war continues, with the FARM flying a high level of attack and supply sorties against an increasingly well-equipped Polisario. Further C-130Hs have been delivered, with two converted to carry side-looking airborne radar (SLAR) for surveillance along the border; 24 Alpha Jets have replaced the Magisters in the light attack role. Saudi Arabia provides finanical support to meet the cost of munitions and attrition. At the time of writing, the cost of the war to Morocco is estimated at $1bn annually, and with relations re-established with Algeria in May 1988, peace now looks to be a distinct prospect.

AIRCRAFT MARKINGS

FARM

FARM aircraft markings are unusual in that the national insignia are normally carried on the rudder. Codes and serials are in 'Western' rather than Arabic numerals.
F-5A Sand/green over, pale grey under, serial on fin in black: (6)97094.
F-5E Tan/sand/green over, pale grey under, serial presentation as F-5A: (7)91921; (7)91934.

Mirage F.1CH Tan/sand over, sky under, serial on fin in black: 146, 162.
Mirage F.1EH Green/sand over, sky under, serial on fin in black: 171, 172.
Alpha Jet Medium grey overall, unit badge on forward fuselage, serial on fin: 235.
C-130H Tan/sand over, pale grey under, serial on fin, last two on forward fuselage: 4742/42. Registration on fin, last two letters on nose: CNA-OQ/OQ.
Boeing 707 White over, bare metal under, blue/white/red cheat line, registration on rear fuselage: CN-ANR.

MIAF

Defender Tan/sand overall, white registration on rear fuselage: 5T-MAS.

AA

Jaguar E Dark green/dark grey over, silver-grey under, code on intake, serial on rudder: 11-RF/E31 (EC 3/11).

The Moroccan Air Force operates one squadron of Alpha Jets in the ground-attack role, based at Meknes and detached to temporary bases up-country. The type has been used to supplement the F-5 and Mirage F.1CH in attacking Polisario targets in the long war. (Via B. Wheeler)

3.3. Tunisia, 1961

A French protectorate since 1881, Tunisia saw clashes between nationalists and the French during the Algerian war. On 8 February 1958, President Bourguiba demanded the evacuation of the French from bases at Bizerta following French Air Force attacks on the village of Sakiet; he agreed to suspend the demand until after the war with Algeria ended. In July 1961 he protested at the extension of the runway at Karouba naval airfield and on the 17th announced a blockade. The French parachuted 7,000 reinforcements into the base, and from the 19th there were battles with the Tunisians using artillery, mortar and machine-gun fire against French bases in Bizerta.

The French responded by bringing the cruisers *Chevalier Paul*, *Colbert* and *Bouvet* into the harbour area; in addition, Mystère IVAs of EC 7 based at Sidi Ahmed airfield and Aquilon fighters of 16F flying from *Arromanches* attacked Tunisian positions with rockets and cannon fire. UN pressure forced a ceasefire from the 22nd, and later in the year the French began their withdrawal, leaving Bizerta in Tunisian hands from 30 June 1962. It is estimated that in the three days of fighting 1,300 Tunisians and 21 French died.

AIRCRAFT MARKINGS

Mistral 532 Bare metal overall, number and first letter of code green outlined in black: 7-CO (EC 1/7).
Mystère IVA Bare metal overall, red lightning stripe on fuselage, black code on forward fuselage: 7-AP (EC 2/7), 7-CH (EC 1/7).
Aquilon 20 Midnite blue overall, white codes: 27 (16F).

TABLE OF UNITS: TUNISIA, 1961

Unit	Aircraft	Base	Role
AA			
EC 7	Mistral 532/535, Mystère IVA	Sidi Ahmed	Ground attack
Aéronavale			
12F	F4U-7		Ground attack
14F	F4U-7		Ground attack
16F	Aquilon 20	Karouba	Ground attack, air defence
28F	PB4Y-2		MR
5S	SO.95		Communications

3.4. Libya, 1971 to date

Muammar al-Qadhafi assumed control of Libya in September 1969; earlier, in 1967, Britain and the US had been asked to vacate their air bases at El Adem and Wheelus Field respectively. In 1971 links with the Soviet Union were forged, and in 1972 British oil interests nationalized. By 1973 Libya was being supplied with Soviet arms, and in October territorial waters were unilaterally extended when the 3,200 square miles of the Gulf of Sirte (Sidra) to latitude 32° 30' N were declared Libyan. Shortly afterwards a USAF C-130 was attacked by Libyan fighters in the area.

Qadhafi's first act of military aggression was directed against Egypt. Perhaps to threaten Egypt over peace initiatives with Israel, in July 1977 Libyan artillery fired on Egyptian settlements along the coast at Sollum. On 21 July Egyptian forces, including tank elements, attacked the Libyan village of Musaid, while radar sites were attacked by Egyptian Air Force Su-20s and MiG-21s. On the first day of fighting a Libyan Arab Republic Air Force (LARAF) Mirage and an Egyptian Air Force (EAF) MiG were claimed destroyed, both to SA-7 fire. On the 22nd the EAF bombed Gamal Abdul Nasser Air Base (El Adem) in retaliation for LARAF air strikes on border villages; several aircraft were claimed destroyed on the ground. Fighting continued to the 24th, when President Sadat ordered an end to Egyptian operations. By this time the two sides had lost at least six aircraft apiece, but the EAF had destroyed numerous radar and control sites across the border and had also attacked the airstrip at Al Kufra. In January 1980 Libyan-backed rebels attacked Gafsa in Tunisia, and the US responded by supplying immediately to the Tunisian Air Force six Bell UH-1 helicopters and a C-130 and confirming an order for twelve F-5E fighters.

Meanwhile the US Sixth Fleet pointedly continued to exercise within the Gulf of Sirte. In one exercise on 19 August 1981, involving USS *Nimitz* and USS *Forrestal*, an E-2C of VAW-124 picked up a pair of LARAF fighters approaching the Carrier Group and directed two F-14A Tom-cats of VF-41 from *Nimitz*. The Libyan fighters, later identified as Su-22 'Fitter-Js', assumed aggressive attitudes and one fired an AA-2 'Atoll' IR-seeking missile. This was successfully evaded by the Tomcats, the pilots of which in turn – and apparently exercising their own discretion – fired at least two AIM-9L Sidewinders. The result was the destruction of both LARAF aircraft and the loss of one pilot.

The Palestine Liberation Organization (PLO) extended its terrorist activities through the early 1980s. Perhaps frustrated by his inability to deal with the US militarily, Qadhafi had decided to increase pressure through subsidising terrorism. In the autumn of 1985 the Italian-registered cruise liner *Achille Lauro* was hijacked and an American Jew killed. In October the Israeli Air Force demonstrated its ability to hit the PLO by attacking its headquarters at Borj Cedria outside Tunis with a force of F-15 or F-16 fighters flying a 3,000-mile round trip from Hatzor and Tel Nof Air Bases. Both conventional 1,000lb 'iron' bombs and heavier, laser-guided munitions were used and the building was wrecked, with many dead. Minutes before the attack the PLO leader, Yasser Arafat, had delayed his arrival at the HQ and thereby survived. The Americans also decided not to allow the PLO to go unpunished. Four of the terrorists who had taken part in the hijack were to be transferred from a military airfield outside Cairo on an Egyptair Boeing 737 to an unspecified destination.

The aircraft was picked up by a waiting E-2C of VAW-125 from the USS *Saratoga* (CV-60) and then intercepted south of Crete by two F-14As believed to be from VF-74. The F-14As subsequently handed the Boeing into the care of a second pair of Tomcats and it was forced to land at the NATO air base at Sigonella. The terrorists were then handed over to the Italian Government to stand trial. The PLO retaliated with two attacks on civilians at Rome and Vienna Airports on 27 December: nineteen people were killed, including five American citizens.

Washington declared that any PLO terrorism

A Libyan Mirage F.1ED intercepted by US Navy F-14A Tomcats from USS *Saratoga*. The LARAF operates a mix of French and Soviet equipment, the French fighters flying in the air defence role from Gamal Abdul Nasser airfield. (USN)

An F/A-18A Hornet of VFA-132 is prepared for launch from USS *Coral Sea*. Six Hornets from two CVW-13 squadrons provided strike support cover for A-6Es and A-7Es in attacks on Libyan air defences. The strikes were well co-ordinated with those conducted by UK-based F-111F bombers, and the Navy's objectives were achieved. (USN)

TABLE OF UNITS: LIBYA, 1971 TO DATE

Unit	Aircraft	Base	Role	Dates
USN, 1981				
VF-41	F-14A	*Nimitz*	Air defence	00/07/81 to 00/10/81
VAW-124	E-2C	*Nimitz*	AEW	00/07/81 to 00/10/81
LARAF, 1981				
(1 sqn.)	Su-22	Ukba Bin Naf'i	Ground attack, air defence	Permanently based
USN, 1986				
CVW-17 (AC)				
VF-74	F-14A		Air defence	
VF-103	F-14A		Air defence	
VMA-533	A-6E		Attack	
VA-81	A-7E		Attack	
VA-83	A-7E	*Saratoga*	Attack	00/11/85 to 00/03/86
VMAQ-2	EA-6B		EW	
VAW-125	E-2C		AEW	
HS-3	SH-3H		SAR	
CVW-13 (AB)				
VF-33	F-14A		Air defence	
VF-102	F-14A		Air defence	
VA-34	A-6E		Attack	
VA-46	A-7E		Attack	
VA-72	A-7E	*America*	Attack	00/03/86 to 00/07/86
VAQ-135	EA-6B		EW	
VAW-125	E-2C		AEW	
HS-11	SH-3H		SAR	
CVW-13 (AK)				
VF-21	F-14A		Air defence	
VF-154	F-14A		Air defence	
VA-196	A-6E		Attack	
VFA-131	F/A-18		Air defence, attack	
VFA-132	F/A-18	*Coral Sea*	Air defence, attack	00/02/86 to 00/06/86
VMFA-314	F/A-18		Air defence, attack	
VMFA-323	F/A-18		Air defence, attack	
VAQ-?	EA-6B		EW	
VAW-127	E-2C		AEW	
HS-17	SH-3H		SAR	
VAQ-2	EA-3B, EP-3E	Rota AB	Intelligence-gathering	Permanently based
USAF, 1986				
48 TFW	F-111F	Lakenheath	Strike	
42 ECS	EF-111A	Upper Heyford	EW	
9 SRS	U-2R, TR-1A	Akrotiri (Det. 3)	Recce	
55 SRW	RC-135V/W	Hellenikon AB (922 SS)	Recce	Permanently based
9 SRW	SR-71A	Mildenhall (Det. 4)	Recce	
4950 TW	C-135C	Andrews AFB (Det. 1)	Support	
7 ACCS	EC-135E	?	Tactical control	10/04/86 to 16/04/86
960 AWCS	E-3A	?	AEW	10/04/86 to 16/04/86
LARAF, 1986				
(2 sqns.)	MiG-23	Benina	Ground attack, air defence	
(1 sqn.)	MiG-23	Ghurdabiyah	Ground attack, air defence	
(1 sqn.)	Mirage 5D	Gamal Abdul Nasser	Air defence	
(1 sqn.)	Mirage F.1AD/DR	Gamal Abdul Nasser	Air defence, recce	
(2 sqns.)	SF.260W	Sabha	Light attack	Permanently based
(1 sqn.)	Tu-22	Ukba Bin Naf'i	Strike (V-VS)	
(1 sqn.)	Su-20, Su-22	Ukba Bin Naf'i	Ground attack, air defence (V-VS)	
(2 sqns.)	MiG-25	Ukba Bin Naf'i	Air defence, recce (V-VS)	

would be met with a 'strong US military reaction'. At the time, the Sixth Fleet comprised two Carrier Groups (CVW). Between Italy and Libya was CVW-13, based on the USS *Coral Sea* (CV-43), and further to the east was CVW-17, structured around *Saratoga*. Both carriers were operating two squadrons of F-14As and one of A-6Bs, together with support, but whereas *Saratoga* had two A-7E squadrons embarked, *Coral Sea* was operating the new F/A-18 in two squadrons, one USN and one USMC.

Qadhafi, who was now maintaining no fewer than twenty-two terrorist training camps, responded by announcing a 'line of death' enclosing the Gulf of Sirte. The LARAF appeared to be one of the strongest air forces in the Mediterranean, but most aircraft were in storage in early 1986. The Soviet Union had built up large stockpiles in Libya and the Soviet Air Force – Voenno-Vozdushney Sily (V-Vs) – maintained Frontal Aviation (Frontovaya Aviatsiya) units to protect its interests. At least one squadron of Tu-22 'Blinder-A's, one squadron of Su-20/22 'Fitter-H's and 'F's and perhaps a regiment of MiG-25 'Foxbat-A's, 'B's and 'R's were operated from Ukba Bin Naf'i (Wheelus) airfield.

Of the LARAF assets proper, transport and helicopter units were focused on Tripoli Airport, with one or two squadrons of MiG-23 'Flogger-Fs' at Benina (Benghazi). Two squadrons of Mirage 5Ds, F.1ADs and F.1EDs operated from Gamal Abdul Nasser airfield outside Tobruk, while a small number of MiG-23 'Flogger-Es' were based at Ghurdabiyah near Sirte. Although the air defence fighters were inadequate, the anti-aircraft equipment was formidable. For point defence there were ZSU-23-4 quad 24mm radar-controlled cannon, M-53/59 twin cannon and Swedish 40mm L/70 cannon. Sixty Crotale and 300 SA-2, -3 and -6 surface-to-air missiles were deployed with the recently sited 185-mile range SA-5 'Gammon' radar-homing missile at several sites around the coastline.

On 24 March 1986, CVW-17 was exercising in the Gulf of Sirte. At 1252hrs GMT an SA-5 missile from a site near Sirte was fired at USN aircraft from *Saratoga* after two F-14As had turned away a pair of MiG-25s. The Carrier Group made immediate preparations to retaliate, and after two more SA-5s were launched the site was attacked by A-7E aircraft of VA-83 using AGM-88A HARM anti-radiation missiles. At least two radars were hit. USN surface units were also threatened by Libyan Navy attack vessels. USS *America* (CV-66), as part of CVW-13, was on station to relieve CVW-17, and two A-6Es of VA-34 were launched to attack a French-built Combattante-II, Otomat-equipped patrol boat. It was sunk by direct hits with AGM-84 Harpoon missiles. Later in the evening several A-6Es attacked and sank a Nanuchka-II Class corvette. During the 25th there was continuing action, A-

TABLE OF UNITS: LIBYA, 1971 TO DATE (continued)

USAF TANKER UNITS, 11–17 APRIL 1986

Unit	Type	Temporary base	Normal base
2 BW	KC-10A	Mildenhall, Fairford	Barksdale AFB
22 ARW	KC-10A	Mildenhall, Fairford	March AFB
68 ARG	KC-10A	Mildenhall	Seymour Johnson AFB
2 BW		Mildenhall, Fairford	Barksdale AFB
5 BW		Mildenhall	Minot AFB
7 BW		Fairford	Carswell AFB
42 BW		Fairford	Loring AFB
92 BW		Mildenhall, Fairford	Fairchild AFB
96 BW		Mildenhall	Dyess AFB
97 BW	KC-135A	Mildenhall, Fairford	Blytheville AFB
379 BW		Mildenhall	Wurtsmith AFB
410 BW		Mildenhall, Fairford	Sawyer AFB
416 BW		Mildenhall	Griffiss AFB
509 BW		Fairford	Pease AFB
19 ARW		Fairford	Robbins AFB
22 ARW		Fairford	March AFB
305 ARW		Fairford	Grissom AFB
116 ARS	KC-135E	Mildenhall	Fairchild AFB
9 SRW	KC-135Q	Mildenhall	Beale AFB
380 ARW	KC-135Q	Mildenhall, Fairford	Plattsburgh AFB

7Es again attacking SA-5 sites and causing more damage without loss, despite a further three missiles being launched in addition to at least one SA-2 from the Benghazi area. The cruiser USS *Yorktown* sank a further patrol boat, and a third was destroyed in an attack by A-6Es of VMA-533 from *Saratoga*. Action ended at 0730hrs GMT.

On 5 April the La Belle discotheque in Berlin was blown up and a US serviceman was killed. There was evidence of Libyan complicity and the US Government decided to act 'in exercise of the inherent right of self-defense recognized in Article 51 of the Charter of the United Nations'.

RAF Mildenhall was to be home to C-135C 612669 of the 4950th Test Wing (TW), USAF Systems Command, from 10 April. At about the same time, several 55 SRW RC-135Ws and a sole RC-135V flew through, presumably bound for

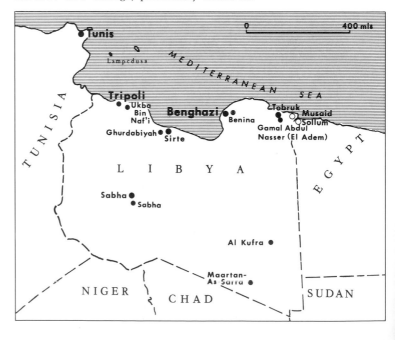

Hellenikon AB, Greece, and the 922nd Support Squadron (SS). These aircraft, together with the EP-3Es and EA-3Bs of VQ-2 at Rota, Spain, were to pursue intelligence-gathering while the U-2Rs and TR-1As of Det. 3, 9 SRS, 99 SRW, at RAF Akrotiri on Cyprus and SR-71As of 1 SRW's Det. 4 from Mildenhall were involved in the reconnaissance of possible target areas in Libya. It had been decided to mount an attack on Libyan military and terrorist targets, in an operation named 'El Dorado Canyon'.

Tanker aircraft also began arriving in the UK from bases and units across the United States. KC-10As of three units went to RAF Fairford (eight aircraft) and RAF Mildenhall (sixteen aircraft) between 11 and 13 April. RAF Fairford was also home to fourteen KC-135s, mainly -As, and Mildenhall hosted twenty of the type, including six -Qs. At Lakenheath, 24 F-111Fs of the 48th Tactical Fighter Wing (TFW) were also preparing to depart on what was to be a 5,500-mile round trip, France and Spain having denied the US the right to overfly their countries.

Included in the F-111F force, which took off from 1836hrs*, were six back-up aircraft which returned to their base after the first refuelling in the Bay of Biscay some time after 1940hrs. Also involved in the USAF attack force were five EF-111As of the 42nd Electronic Combat Squadron (ECS), 20th TFW, from RAF Upper Heyford. Of the five, two were standby aircraft, one of which returned to base after refuelling once while the second apparently completed the trip.

The plan was for a joint USAF/USN attack. The specific targets for the UK-based USAF aircraft were the military side of Tripoli Airport (occupied by the Il-76 'Candids' used to transport terrorists and their equipment around the world, often under diplomatic cover), the Al Aziziyah Barracks, a command and control centre and Qadhafi's home, and Sidi Bilal, a training area which included a terrorist marine sabotage camp. The Sixth Fleet's targets in the eastern zone were the Al Jamahiriyah Barracks – an alternative to Al Azaziyah – and Benina air base. Exact coordination was not of paramount importance, but it is believed that an EC-135E, possibly of the 7th Airborne Control and Command Squadron (ACCS), acted as a tactical command centre. Airborne early warning was provided for the F-111F force by an E-3A of the 960th Airborne Warning and Control Squadron (AWCS) of the 552nd AWCW and for the naval aircraft by E-2Cs of VAW-123 (USS *America*) and VAW-127 (USS *Coral Sea*). EA-3Bs of VQ-2 from Rota are also believed to have been involved, with F-14A

protection; these aircraft would have been on station by about 2230hrs. As the F-111F force approached Libya after a total of four air refuellings, the naval aircraft began taking off.

At 2320hrs USS *Coral Sea* launched six F/A-18s of VFA-132 and VMFA-323 for strike support; the ship also launched eight A-6Es of VA-196 and a single EA-6B. USS *America* launched six A-7Es of VA-46 and VA-72 equipped with AGM-88A HARM and AGM-45 Shrike anti-radiation missiles for defence suppression, six A-6Es of VA-34 and a single EA-6B of VAQ-135. The force from *Coral Sea*, with its EA-6B electronic countermeasures (ECM) support, attacked the airfield at Benina after AGM-88A HARM-equipped F/A-18s and *America*'s A-7Es had attacked air defence radars. The A-6Es used their Norden AN/APQ-148 multi-mode search radars to acquire their targets, with data transfer to the AN/AAS-33 Target Recognition Attack Multisensor (TRAM) system for weapon release.

At least four MiG-23s were destroyed and many more damaged in the airfield strike; also destroyed were two Fokker F-27s (5A-DLP and -DLY) and two Mi-8 helicopters. Meanwhile, the A-6Es from *America* attacked Al Jamahiriyah Barracks, causing much damage. Both the airfield and barracks attacks were made at midnight, reportedly using conventional 500lb and 750lb bombs, although the A-6E is equipped to use both the 500lb Snakeye retarded delivery and CBU Rockeye Mk. 20 cluster bomb. By 0013hrs on the 15th all naval aircraft reported returning

On 24 March 1986 US Navy units were threatened by Libyan surface vessels. An Otomat-equipped patrol boat was sunk, and then, in the evening, A-6Es of VA-34 attacked and damaged this *Nanuchka* Class corvette in the Gulf of Sirte; it was probably hit by an AGM-84 Harpoon missile. Two more boats were sunk the following day by USS *Yorktown* and A-6E Intruders of VMA-533. (USN)

An F-111F of 493 TFS, 48 TFW, based at Lakenheath. The aircraft is equipped with the AN/ AVQ-26 Pave Tack designator and four Paveway GBU-10 Mk. 84 2,000lb laser-guided bombs. The F-111 force was well equipped for the task of attacking precise targets in Libya, and reliability was such that most aircraft reached their targets after four in-flight refuellings. One aircraft hit the sea north of Tripoli on the way back. (USAF)

---

* Throughout this section, except where stated, the author has used British Summer Time (BST). At the time BST was one hour ahead of Greenwich Mean Time (GMT), two hours behind local Libyan time and five hours ahead of US Eastern Standard Time (EST).

and all had recovered by 0153hrs. Two of the fourteen A-6Es launched aborted for unspecified reasons.

Meanwhile, the F-111Fs had crossed the Libyan coast under the protection of the EF-111As to the west of Tripoli. They split into two groups, approaching their targets at 200ft and 400kts from the south. At midnight one group, by now comprising only eight out of an intended twelve aircraft, attacked Qadhafi's headquarters at Al Aziziyah barracks and the Sidi Bilal training camp.

The aircraft used their AN/AVQ-26 Pave Tack marking system to confirm targets and guide GBU-10 Mk. 84 2,000lb Paveway II bombs. Despite the normal efficiency of the equipment, there was considerable collateral damage south of the barracks to the embassies of Austria, Finland, France, Iran and Switzerland. The US claimed that the damage was caused by SAM boosters, but subsequently admitted a degree of responsibility. The second group, of five aircraft, attacked the military side of Tripoli Airport with Mk. 82 500lb Snakeye retarded bombs, resulting in six Il-76s, a Boeing 727 and a G.222 destroyed. The Soviet-controlled airfield at Ukba Bin Naf'i was carefully avoided. Shortly after the attack, at 0010hrs, an F-111F hit the sea 20 miles north of Tripoli. From the lack of radio transmissions it is assumed that the aircraft was not hit by anti-aircraft weapons; both crew members were killed, the only US casualties of the entire operation. At about 0315hrs a returning F-111F diverted to Rota AB with an overheating engine; it returned to the UK on 16 April.

After more refuellings, the F-111 bombers and their tanker support started landing at their UK home bases of Lakenheath, Upper Heyford, Fairford and Mildenhall from 0545hrs. Before the first aircraft touched down, however, an SR-71A departed Mildenhall for post-strike survey. On its return, the C-135C of the 4950th TW flew off to Washington with evidence of the damage. The KC-10As and KC-135s also began the return trip to the US from 15 April.

Technically, Operation 'El Dorado Canyon' must be judged a qualified success, especially with no apparent loss of aircraft to Libyan defences. However, five of the F-111F force of eighteen aborted, as did two of the A-6Es. There was, moreover, significant collateral damage within half a mile of the main Tripoli target.

US Navy fighters were in action again on 4 January 1989. Two LARAF MiG-23s made a threatening approach to a pair of F-14As from the carrier *John F. Kennedy*, then steaming eastwards, north of Tobruk. Deciding that the MiGs were intent on attack, the lead Tomcat fired an AIM-7 and an AIM-9, destroying both the LARAF fighters. The F-14As were from VF-32 and the action, which took place at midday, was over in three minutes.

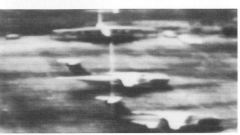

This unusual sequence of photographs was taken via the F-111F Pave Tack laser-guided delivery system. It shows a line of Il-76 transports at Tripoli Airport, immediately before and during the attack with 500lb bombs. From the third frame, the seeker has swivelled so that the aircraft are viewed as the bomber exits. Buildings presented less distinct targets and some mistakes were made in identification. (USAF)

AIRCRAFT MARKINGS

LARAF

Su-22 *Brown/tan/sand over, pale grey under, no evident serial.*

MiG-23 *Brown/green/sand over, blue-grey under, serial on forward fuselage and fin: 712, 6915.*

MiG-25 *Bare metal overall, code on fin in black: 127.*

Mirage F.1ED *Sand/khaki over, pale grey under, no serial apparent.*

USAF

F-111F *Tan/medium green/dark green over, black under, serial on fin: 721448/LN (CO's aircraft, 48 TFW).*

EF-111A *Mid-grey over, grey under, serials etc. in Insignia Gray: 660039 (42 ECS, 20 TFW).*

KC-135A *Medium grey overall, serial in black on fin, red vertical stripes on fin tip: 638884 (410 BW). 'Fairchild' on blue band on fin: 580056 (92 BW).*

KC-10A *White over, medium grey under, dark blue cheat line: 830075 (2 BW). Charcoal grey/green/olive drab over, pale grey under ('European 1' camouflage): 850027 (22 ARW).*

USN

Naval finishes were in a transitional stage. Some aircraft retained the Gull Gray/white scheme with colourful fin and fuselage markings, while others had been finished in low-visibility, counter-shaded Compass Gray with Insignia

Gray national and unit markings. Examples given are in the new scheme except where stated.

F-14A *Gull Gray over, white under: 159446/212AB (VF-33); 159006/103AB (VF-102).*

A-6E *161681/502AK (VA-55); 151548/511AB (VA-34). Gull Gray over, white under: 151789/521AB (VA-34).*

A-7E *160613/302AB (VA-46); 160549/401AB (VA-72).*

F/A-18A *161987/210AK (VFA-132); 162435/411AK (VMFA-323).*

E-2C *Gull Gray over, white under: 160987/603AK (VAW-127).*

The Libyan raids were followed up by reconnaissance sorties flown by a US Air Force SR-71. This post-strike photograph shows damage inflicted by USN aircraft on the airfield at Benina: destroyed and damaged Mi-8 helicopters may be seen at the bottom of the print, while left centre is a destroyed F.27 Friendship. Quite why the latter was singled out for attention is not clear. (USAF)

3.5. Chad, 1968 to date

Chad gained independence from France in 1960. French troops remained to support a minority Christian government, although the majority of the population, focused in the north, is Muslim. Through the early 1960s rebel groups banded as the Front de Liberation Nationale de Tchad (FROLINAT) and operated with increasing effectiveness against Government forces. France was asked for military assistance, and in August 1968 French forces returned. The initial air component was a flight of AD-4N Skyraiders of 1/21 Escadron d'Appui Aérien (EAA) 'Aures Nemenchas', detached from Djibouti and based at N'Djamena (Fort Lamy). From the beginning of March 1969 the flight was expanded as EAA 1/22 'Ain', and from July was supported by Groupe de Marche du Tchad (GMT) 59 'Orleans', with Noratlases, Alouette IIs, Broussards and the Détachement Permanent d'Hélicoptères (DPH) 02/67 with H-34s.

The situation worsened, and with FROLINAT rebels threatening N'Djamena France was asked for further help, which arrived in October as five companies of the 2nd Foreign Legion Parachute Regt. and one company of the 2nd Foreign Legion Infantry Regt. These units were formed into two motorized commands and began operating with immediate effectiveness, taking the fight into the rebel bases. One company parachuted into strongholds in the Guera mountains in the Tiberti region. The units were assigned their own helicopter support, and the AD-4s flying from advance bases suffered no threat from poorly armed irregulars. By 1972 there were only isolated pockets of resistance and the French formally ended their active support, although troops remained. The following year Libya annexed the disputed Aouzou strip in the extreme north, an area believed to be rich in mineral deposits.

The Government was powerless to deal with the intervention; for some time the Libyan administration had been backing the rebels. In April 1975 there was a coup, and from October the French were asked to withdraw, leaving at least four AD-4s as the nucleus of the Escadrille Nationale Tchadienne (ENT). From 1976, with Libyan troops now occupying the Aouzou strip, the French lent three Noratlases of Escadrille de

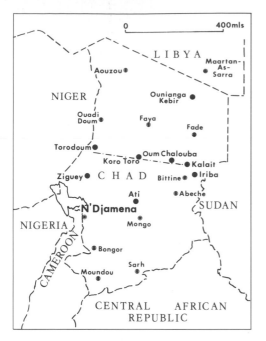

Transport d'Outre Mer (ETOM) 55 from Senegal. As the situation deteriorated France was again asked for help, and in February 1978 elements of the Foreign Legion with light tanks together with two companies of Marines arrived at N'Djamena. A flight of Jaguar fighters of Escadre de Chasse (EC) 11 transferred from Senegal in time to support the relief of Ati on 4 April: an important town, taken by well-armed irregulars, it was recaptured by the French after Jaguar and Alouette sorties.

The Government of Chad, although in the hands of Muslims, was precarious and complex, and during this period shared by Goukouni Oueddei and Hissene Habré. In March 1980 civil war raged in N'Djamena, and as the French prepared to leave, Habré was ousted by Oueddei; he fled to the Sudan border, where he formed the Forces Armées du Nord (FAN). The Libyans were effectively invited in by Oueddei and from summer 1981 began a bombing campaign of FAN bases, some inside Sudan. On 16 September a 'bomber' was shot down by Sudanese defences over Al-Geneina and the crew of two killed. The main type used in these attacks was the SF.260WL. Relationships between Libya and the West were generally very bad with Colonel Qadhafi supporting a wide range of terrorist organizations. Worried by a potential threat to Egypt and the Sudan, the United States despatched two E-3A Airborne Warning and Control System (AWACS) aircraft to Cairo West from 21 October.

A scandal now broke when it was confirmed that a number of ex-Central Intelligence Agency (CIA) operatives headed by Edwin Wilson had been recruiting pilots and engineers for Libyans through a London office. The pilots flew transport and support sorties into Chad and were particularly needed for the CH-47C helicopters and C-130 Hercules, some of which Wilson had supplied despite an embargo. The Organization of African Unity (OAU) had been trying to bring about a peaceful settlement to the long civil war in Chad, and in November 1981 a peacekeeping force of Zaïrean, Nigerian and Senegalese troops replaced the Libyans in N'Djamena. By now Habré's FAN had gained control in the eastern central region, and on 7 June it occupied the capital. As Oueddei fled to the north to raise a Libyan-backed Armée de Libération Nationale (ALN), the FAN became the Forces Armées Nationales Tchadiennes (FANT).

The OAU force remained, supported in the air by three Zaïrean Air Force (FAZ) MB.326GBs; the ENT had added some Pilatus Turbo-Porters to its inventory, but if these were used offensively they were almost certainly flown by mercenaries. The French also provided some civilian instructors to the Chad Army. As Oueddei built up his base in the north with Libyan aid, an attack on Chad came from another direction: after a dispute in April 1983 over fishing on Lake Chad, Nigerian forces attacked several lakeside villages with artillery and MiG-21s, leaving 90 dead and many wounded. Far more serious, however, was an attack on the northern oasis town of Faya-Largeau by rebels with Libyan air support on 23 June. The FANT held out, but on 6 July Oum-Chalouba fell. Six days later, as Zaïre agreed to send another 1,750 troops and three Mirage 5M fighters, the rebels were outside Abeche.

By 31 July Faya-Largeau had changed hands twice and the Libyan Air Force (LARAF) flew several MiG-23 sorties, dropping phosphorous bombs. The town was subjected to repeated LARAF attacks in early August and the US agreed to a major aid programme, including the supply of Stinger and Redeye SAMs. The French provided more instructors but held back from full military involvement. The LARAF strikes were flown by Su-22s, MiG-23s and Tu-22s normally based at Sabha but detached to Aouzou; armed helicopters were also used, probably Mi-8s. The leader of one twelve-aircraft strike was captured when his Su-22 was brought down on 4 August. The constant bombing caused many casualties, who were ferried out to N'Djamena at night by mercenary pilots flying light aircraft and several DC-4 and C-54 transports. French involvement gradually expanded, and on 5 August two Puma helicopters of the Aviation Légère de l'Armée de Terre (ALAT), 5 Régiment d'Hélicoptères de Combat (RHC), were flown into N'Djamena. Later, Gazelles of 1 and 2 RHC and three L-19s were to join them.

The US was now maintaining a regular C-141 supply operation, and in addition on the 9th sent two E-3As and two KC-10s, escorted by eight F-

TABLE OF UNITS: CHAD, 1968 TO DATE

Unit	Aircraft	Base	Role	Dates
AA, 1968–1975				
EAA 1/21	AD-4	N'Djamena	Ground attack, recce	00/08/68 to 00/03/69
EAA 1/22	AD-4	N'Djamena	Ground attack, recce	00/03/69 to 00/10/75
GMT 59	Noratlas, Alouette II, Broussard	N'Djamena, Mongo	Transport, liaison	00/07/69 to 00/10/75
DPH 02/67	H-34	N'Djamena	Transport	00/00/69 to 00/00/75
ENT, 1968–1975				
–	Broussard, C-47	N'Djamena	Transport, liaison	00/01/65 to date
AA, 1978–1980				
EC 11	Jaguar A	N'Djamena	Ground attack	00/04/78 to 00/05/80
ETOM 55	Noratlas, Alouette II	N'Djamena	Transport, liaison	00/07/77 to 00/05/80
ENT, 1978–1980				
–	AD-4	N'Djamena	Ground attack, recce	00/10/75 to 00/00/81
–	Broussard, C-47, DC-4, C-54, Turbo-Porter, Cessna 337	N'Djamena, Moundou, Mongo	Transport, liaison, casevac, coin	00/00/75 to date
AA, 1981 to date				
EC 11	Jaguar A/E	N'Djamena, Bangui, Libreville	Ground attack, recce	21/08/83 to date
EC 7	Jaguar A	Bangui	Ground attack	00/02/86 to 00/04/86
EC 5	Mirage F.1C		Air defence, ground attack	21/08/83 to date
ER 33	Mirage F.1CR	N'Djamena, Bangui	PR	00/11/85 to date
ET 1/63	Transall C.160NG		Medium transport	00/07/83 to date
ERV 93	KC-135F		Air refuelling	21/08/83 to 00/02/86
Aéronavale, 1981 to date				
22F	Atlantique	N'Djamena, Bangui, Dakar	Airborne command, sigint, recce	21/08/83 to 00/02/86
ALAT, 1981 to date				
5 RHC	Puma	N'Djamena, Abeche	Light transport, attack	05/08/83 to 00/00/85
1 RHC	Gazelle	N'Djamena etc.	Liaison, casevac	08/08/83 to 00/00/85
2 RHC	Gazelle	N'Djamena etc.	Liaison, casevac	08/08/83 to 00/00/85
–	L-19	N'Djamena etc.	Liaison	00/08/83 to 00/00/85
ENT, 1981 to date				
–	PC-7	N'Djamena	Light attack	00/00/85 to date
–	Broussard, C-47, DC-4, C-54, Turbo Porter, Cessna 337, C-130A, Aviocar	N'Djamena, Moundou, Mongo	Transport, liaison, casevac	00/00/82 to date
–	Gazelle, Puma	N'Djamena etc.	Light transport, liaison, casevac	00/00/77 to date
FAZ, 1981 to date				
21 Wing	Mirage 5M, MB.326GB	Kamina, N'Djamena	Ground attack, close support	00/11/81 to 00/11/83
LARAF, 1981 to date				
–	SF.260WL	Sabha, Aouzou, Ouadi Doum, Faya-Largeau	Ground attack	
–	Mirage 5, MiG-21, MiG-23, Su-22	Sabha, Aouzou, Sara, Ouadi Doum	Ground attack	00/06/81 to date
–	Tu-22	Okba Ben Nafi, Sabha	Strike	
–	C-130H	Sabha, Aouzou	Transport	
–	CH-47C, Mi-8, Mi-25	Sabha, Aouzou, Sara, Faya-Largeau, Ouadi Doum	Transport, attack, casevac	

15s, to Khartoum, although the help was not early enough to prevent the final overrun of Faya-Largeau on the 11th. French paratroops were now arriving in Operation 'Manta' and they quickly moved up to positions around Abeche. At least four Jaguars of EC 11 arrived in Bangui in the Central African Republic from Libreville, Gabon, as fighting came to a temporary halt on the 14th. The French also redisposed a number of units of the Force d'Assistance Rapide (FAR) to bring them within easy reach of Chad.

On 21 August a small force comprising six Jaguars of EC 3/11 'Corse', four Mirage F.1Cs of EC 1/5 'Vendée', two C-135Fs of Escadre de Revitailement en Vol (ERV) 93 and two Atlantiques of 22F flew to N'Djamena. The Jaguars were in action on 2 September, buzzing a rebel force attacking Oum Chalouba; their presence was enough to deter the attackers. French forces established and held a 'red line' roughly along the 15th parallel from Torodoum to Oum Chalouba, and from early September there were few major attacks. On 24 January, however, a strong force attacked Ziguey. A pair of Jaguars with two

Mirage F.1Cs and a KC-135F in support were despatched to identify the aggressors, with instructions to attack only if fired upon. One Jaguar of EC 4/11 'Jura' was shot down, probably by SA-7, after which the column, which was north of Torodoum, was destroyed. A second Jaguar was lost on 16 April when it flew into sand dunes near Faya-Largeau.

In autumn 1984 France and Libya agreed to withdraw from Chad. The French air component departed to Bangui in Operation 'Silure' at the beginning of October, but Libyan forces made a token withdrawal only – indeed a large new air base was now built at Ouadi Doum. On 10 February 1986 the ALN, supported by aircraft flying from Ouadi Doum, crossed the red line and threatened Government positions. The French responded by preparing and implementing Operation 'Épervier' (Sparrowhawk). Eight Jaguars with four to six Mirage F.1C escorts, several C-135Fs and an Atlantique signals intelligence (sigint) aircraft flew from Bangui to take out Ouadi Doum on 16 February. Most of the attackers were armed with BAP-100 anti-runway weapons in addition to ECM equipment, while several carried 400kg (880lb) retarded bombs. The attack was successful, but on 24 February a LARAF Tu-22 bombed N'Djamena Airport, putting it out of commission for two days.

The attack was carried out from an altitude beyond the range of the Crotale missiles deployed at the airport, and the French chartered USAF C-5 Galaxies to airlift in Hawk SAMs capable of preventing further high-level incursions. For a short time Mirage F.1Cs were based at N'Djamena, but these were withdrawn to neighbouring states.

There was renewed fighting in the Tibesti mountains in December 1986, and on 4 January 1987 four LARAF MiG-21s or MiG-23s bombed Arada and Oum Chalouba, apparently in retaliation for French 'interference' in the fighting farther north; certainly, two Transall C-160s had parachuted supplies to a group of pro-Government forces in the north. The French response was fast. On 7 January a major air strike was mounted against installations at Ouadi Doum involving Jaguars of EC 4/11 and Mirage 5Fs of EC 13, supported by C-135Fs and Atlantiques and escorted by Mirage F.1Cs of EC 5; pre- and post-strike reconnaissance was carried out by Mirages of ER 33. Martel AS-37s were used, and the attack was successful in destroying radars at the base. At the same time three USAF C-5s brought a number of personnel carriers from Nantes to N'Djamena as preparations were made for extending the war against the rebels.

As fighting intensified from the 10th around Faya-Largeau, the LARAF conducted more bombing raids against Government-held towns. Then on 19 March, with French support, Government troops attacked positions around Ouadi Doum airfield, which was captured after bloody fighting on the 22nd. A large amount of important equipment was captured, including 70 T-55 tanks, SA-6 batteries, eleven L-39s, two SF.260s and three Mi-25s. Much of the material was transferred to France, and possibly the US, for evaluation.

In the fighting from January, some 3,655 Libyans were killed and 800 captured. The airfield was subjected to LARAF air attacks following its capture. On 8 August the Government recaptured Aouzou after fourteen years. Their successes were due not only to French backing: for some time Government forces had been strengthened by Zaïrean troops and instructors, and the US supplied arms and equipment. Libyan air strikes against Chadian positions were continuous from 8 August, and on 24 August a LARAF Mirage was claimed to have been shot down over Ounianga Kebir. Under constant pressure, the Chadians had to concede Aouzou after several weeks of sustained Libyan attacks, but in an effort to prevent further air strikes Chad invaded Libya on 5 September and destroyed

some 22 aircraft, including MiG-21s, MiG-23s, Su-22s, Mirages and Mi-25s, together with installations at Sara (Maartan-As-Sarra) airfield, before withdrawing. Two days later French forces brought down a LARAF Tu-22 over N'Djamena with Hawk SAMs of the 403rd AAA Régiment. Shortly afterwards, both sides accepted a ceasefire called by the OAU, although the Libyans continue to conduct frequent overflights. With the war apparently at an end, the French are building an air base at Faya, and they retain a handful of aircraft in the country. In April 1988 a Jaguar A of EC 2/11 crashed near N'Djamena, while early in December 1988 a LARAF SF.260 was shot down by Chadian Forces in northern Chad.

AIRCRAFT MARKINGS

ENT
AD-4 *Aluminium overall, black anti-glare panel, black serial on fin: 126949, 126998.*
Broussard *Dark olive green overall, white top decking, grey serial on rudder: TT-KAB.*
C-130A *Bare metal overall, black serial on rear fuselage: TT-PAA.*
Turbo-Porter *Pale grey overall, last three of serial on rear fuselage: TT-KAA.*

AA
AD-4 *Bare metal overall, black anti-glare panel, code on rear fuselage on white panel, serial in black on fin: 127888/21-LE (EAA 1/21).*
Noratlas *Bare metal overall, white tope decking, code on boom, serial on fin: 59-CT/51 (GMT-59).*
Jaguar A *Sand/brown over, pale blue grey under, unit marking on fin, code on intake, serial on rudder: 11-MO/A-139 (EC 2/11); 11-RM/A-147 (EC 3/11); 11-YJ/A-86 (EC 4-11).*

Chadian Government forces took Ouadi Doum airfield with French help and after heavy fighting in March 1987. A large amount of equipment was captured intact, including this Mi-24 attack helicopter; much of the captured *matériel* is believed to have found its way to the USA via France. LARAF aircraft continued to attack Chadian positions in the north, so on 5 September Chadian troops mounted a limited invasion to Sara airfield, where 22 aircraft were destroyed on the ground. (Via L. Pinzauti)

Mirage F.1C Grey-blue over, white under, unit marking on fin, code on forward fuselage, serial on fin: 5-OD/220 (EC 2/5).
Mirage F.1CR Sand/brown over, pale blue-grey under, unit marking on fin, code on forward fuselage, serial on fin: 33-CP/607 (ER 1/33).
Transall C-160NG Dark green/grey over, light grey under, code on rear fuslage, serial on fin top: 64-GC/F203 (ET 64).
C-135F Light grey overall, code on lower rear fuselage, serial on fin: CL/312740 (ERV 93).

Aéronavale
Atlantique Blue-grey over, white under, black serial on rear fuselage and fin: 66 (22F).

FAZ
Mirage 5M Purple/apple green over, pale grey under, serial on rear fuselage: M402 (21 Wing).
MB.326GB Tan/green/dark green over, grey-white under, white code on rear fuselage: FG-463 (21 Wing).

LARAF
MiG-23MF Sand/brown/dark green over, blue-grey under, black serial on fin: 617, 712, 6915.
Tu-22 Tan/green over, pale grey under, no serial evident.
Su-22 Sand/tan/brown over, pale grey under, no serial evident.

3.6. Cameroons, 1960–1961

The Cameroons were a United Nations trust territory administered by the British in the north and the French in the much larger southern region. There was a revolt in the south in December 1956, and on the 20th French paratroopers were dropped at Eseka to help restore order. The French granted independence in 1960, and in the British-administered territory the constitutional position was due to be determined by plebiscite in 1961. It was anticipated that there would be local disturbances, and accordingly 1 Bn. The King's Own Royal Border Regt. were flown to the Cameroons in September 1960 where they were supported by a detachment of three Twin Pioneer light transports from 230 Sqn. based at nearby Mamfi in Nigeria. Order

was maintained, but the Twin Pioneers were involved in combating smuggling as well as resupplying army outposts. The wishes of the people were respected, and in June and October 1961 respectively the northern region was ceded to Nigeria and the southern part joined the new republic. The 1st Bn. Grenadier Guards took over internal security responsibilities in May 1961, but in September British forces left, having enabled a peaceful transition to take place.

AIRCRAFT MARKINGS

Twin Pioneer CC.1 Silver overall, white fuselage top decking, black serial on rear fuselage, code on fin: XM961/D (230 Sqn.).

3.7. Portuguese Guinea, 1963–1974

Guinea was the poorest and least settled of Portugal's African colonies, with 40 per cent of the land uninhabited, and dissatisfaction with conditions led to the formation of the Partido Africano de Independencia da Guiné e Capo Verde (PAIGC) from 1956. In August 1959 members staged a dock strike at Bissau and the police opened fire on the strikers, killing fifty. From then PAIGC was committed to an armed struggle, but the first guerrilla attacks were not made until January 1963 against police and Army targets at Buba, Tite and Fulacunda. At this time the Portuguese had just two infantry companies in Guinea and were coping with wars in Angola and Mozambique. The PAIGC revolutionaries were trained in Algeria, Cuba, Russia and China and operated from neighbouring Guinea Republic and Senegal, where there were camps at Kindia and Kolda respectively. At the outset the Portuguese Air Force (FAP) had a few lightly armed T-6 trainers at Bissau, but these are believed to have been supplemented by some F-84G fighters in 1963.

The guerrillas worked in small, self-sufficient groups and moved easily on land and along the vast east–west running rivers. After an unsuccessful attempt to retake the island of Como in February 1964, the Portuguese forces remained in

fire bases protected by howitzers. Attempts were made to resettle villagers in order to discourage or deny support from the static population, but these efforts met with little success. By 1967 the PAIGC could claim to have launched 142 attacks on barracks or camps and 22 against airfields or ports, and to have set 476 ambushes in the year. Their equipment was becoming more sophisticated, and some operations were mounted by larger groups.

The FAP at Bissalanca near Bissau, Base Aérea (BA) 12, had expanded to include 121 Sqn. of West German-supplied Fiat G.91R-4 fighters, additional T-6s and some Do 27 communications aircraft. Their main task was the support of troops under attack, and interdiction along the many incursion routes from Guinea and Senegal. All FAP aircraft were based at Bissalanca but operated from forward airstrips during the day, refuelling and re-arming as near as possible to the scene of action.

In May 1968 General Antonio de Spinola was appointed Governor, with full military and civil authority. He began a 'hearts and minds' campaign, with a massive home, school, hospital and road building programme, and ordered the delivery of twelve Alouette III helicopters, which arrived in 1969. These were essential for communications in a land which, despite its compactness, has so much marsh and water. Spinola also began a much more vigorous campaign of taking the fight to the guerrillas. From 1970 napalm was used, as were defoliants and herbicides to destroy crops and clear roadsides to make ambush more difficult. A flight of Noratlas transports of the Esquadra de Transporte Médio was permanently based at BA 12 for local supply flights. Troops and *matériel* from Portugal were flown in by hard-pressed and overworked DC-6 of Transportes Aéreos Militares (TAM). Initially Spinola attempted unsuccessfully to negotiate with President Sekou Touré of Guinea of dissuade him from allowing Guinea to be used as a base and to secure the release of a number of prisoners held in Conakry. There followed attacks on border villages in Guinea and Senegal, and on 22 November 1972 a seaborne invasion around Conakry of about 400 Guineans led by Portuguese officers. The invasion did not encourage a popular uprising as had been hoped, but a number of prisoners, including FAP air crews, were released.

Because they were operating from secure bases, the PAIGC made use of aircraft exceptionally. In 1969 a Guinea Republic Air Force (FAG) An-14 light transport, apparently carrying supplies for a guerrilla unit, landed by mistake at Bissalanca. From 1971 Nigerian Air Force (NAF) MiG-17s based at Conakry made regular reconnaissance overflights, while two Soviet-marked Mi-4 helicopters were operated from clearings in the extreme east. The PAIGC was also equipped with Chinese-supplied 12.7mm AA cannon and SA-7 missiles, both of which were deployed extensively along the border with Guinea. It was reported that an embryo air force was forming at Conakry, serviced initially by East Europeans and equipped with the ubiquitous MiG-17. As FAP strikes were stepped up, so losses increased, especially to ground fire: on 23 March 1973 two Fiat G.91s were shot down by SA-7s and a third aircraft of the type was lost six weeks later. In seven years the PAIGC claimed 21 aircraft shot down.

In September 1973 the PAIGC declared on independent republic but clearly was not in a position to govern. The wars in Africa, however, were costing the Portuguese heavily, and a coup in Portugal in April 1974 therefore opened the door to independence for her African colonies. Independence was granted on 10 September, and the last troops withdrew on 15 October. Civilians and the military departed in an extensive airlift organized by TAM and using large numbers of civil aircraft. In all, 1,875 Portuguese soldiers had been killed and the PAIGC lost at least 6,000 dead. Little military equipment was returned to Portugal, and several Do 27s and Alouette IIIs formed the nucleus around which the air force of Guinea-Bissau was formed.

AIRCRAFT MARKINGS

Fiat G.91R-4 *Dark green/medium sea grey over, blue-grey under, sharkmouth around intake, black serial on fin: 5403, 5423 (121 Esq.).*

Alouette III *Olive drab overall, black serial on lower fuselage: 9303.*

T-6G *Bare metal overall, black serial on fin and upper wing surface: 1605, 1534.*

TABLE OF UNITS: PORTUGUESE GUINEA, 1963–1974

Unit	Aircraft	Base	Role	Dates
FAP				
Esq. 121	Fiat G.91R-4		Ground attack, air defence	00/00/67 to 00/10/74
–	T-6G		Light attack, recce	00/00/62 to 00/10/74
–	Alouette III	BA12 Bissalanca	Liaison, light transport, recce	00/03/69 to 00/10/74
–	Do 27		Communications, light transport	00/00/61 to 00/10/74
–	Noratlas		Medium transport	00/00/62 to 15/10/74
NAF				
–	MiG-17	Conakry	Recce, air defence, ground attack	00/00/70 to 00/00/73

3.8. The Nigerian Civil War, 1967–1970

The British colony of Nigeria achieved Federal Republic status in 1963. The country comprised four regions, the richest of which was in the east primarily peopled by Ibos and where oil had been discovered. After a coup in 1966 involving Ibo army officers there were massacres of Ibos living in the north, and the Governor of the Eastern Region, Lt. Col. Ojukwu, announced secession as the State of Biafra on 30 May 1967. Ojukwu had been preparing for some time and had transferred Nigerian Government funds into Swiss banks in order to fund his adventure. A Nigerian Air Force (NAF) had been formed in August 1963 with West German and Indian help, initially equipped with twenty Do 27 liaison aircraft, fourteen Piaggio P.149D trainers and ten Noratlas transports. Although he was not confronting an air force equipped with combat aircraft, Ojukwu recognized the need for air power from the beginning.

On 23 April 1967 Nigerian Airways Fokker G.27 5N-AAV was hijacked en route from Benin City to Lagos and flown to Enugu. It was there converted for use as a makeshift bomber. A second commercial aircraft, DC-3 9G-AAD of Ghana Airways, was reported as hijacked on 15 June at Port Harcourt, but there seems some doubt. It was several weeks before fighting started after the Federal Army was mobilized on 6 July. Federal forces attacked and secured Ogoja, Nsukka and the important oil terminal at Bonny. On 9 August Biafran forces crossed the Niger at Asaba and soon reached Benin, eventually stopping at Ore. During this period numerous sorties using a range of aircraft were flown on behalf of the Biafrans. The acquisition and operation of these machines remain unclear, but it has been possible to construct a partial picture from contemporary reports.

Apart from the F.27 and possibly the DC-3, both of which were flown from Port Harcourt, there was also reported to be at least one B-25 Mitchell at the airport flown by an ex-Luftwaffe pilot, 'Fred Herz'*, while a Douglas B-26 was operating from Enugu from early July. This last machine is believed to have been 4139539 bought by 'Pierre Follorey/Pierre Lorez' from ex-French Air Force stock at Brétigny in May 1967. It was subsequently registered to 'Ernest Koenig' of Luxembourg as N12756 and on 15 June was spotted at Courtrai in Belgium where it had gone for radio fitting. It was then flown to Lisbon by a Belgian pilot and on to Biafra by 'Jean Zumbach' (otherwise known as 'Johnny Brown' or 'Kamikaze Braun') via Dakar and Abidjan, landing at Port Harcourt, then Enugu, on 29 June. The pilot was paid £4,000 for delivery, and the aircraft was operational by 10 July when it bombed the airfield at Makurdi, damaging several civilian-flown DC-3s involved in supply flights for Federal troops.

Several days earlier, an American-registered Riley Dove, N477PM, flew into Port Harcourt from Switzerland piloted by 'André Juillard/Girard/Gerard', an arms dealer. The purpose of the trip was probably to deliver 2,000 Hungarian-manufactured rifles, and the aircraft appeared to make several reconnaissance sorties in the area before leaving the country. On 13 July it was seized at Hassi-Messaoud in Algeria and the crew was arrested for spying; the aircraft was subsequently impressed into the Algerian Air

---

* Mercenaries and arms dealers are often understandably coy about their identities. Throughout this section the author has used names in quotes since popular spellings are at variance or aliases are known or believed to have been used.

A unique photograph of a Biafran B-26, believed to be 4134531, at Enugu in 1967. Together with a second B-26, this aircraft was used for several attacks on Federal targets until both were destroyed by the end of the year. The aircraft was flown by Jean Zumbach under contract to the Biafrans. For some time the Biafrans were without any offensive air power, but in 1969 Count Carl Gustav von Rosen formed a flight of five MFI.9B Minicon sporting aircraft adapted for firing rockets. (J. Zumbach via M. Robson)

Force. Ojukwu not only received arms dealers: he also operated an apparently corrupt purchasing organization, the Biafra Historical Society, from 33 Rue Galilée, Paris. Certainly he was required to pay heavily for the miscellany of arms and equipment delivered.

The sole B-26 was operated extensively through early July in raids on Lagos and Kano. After crash-landing at Enugu on the 12th it was supplemented to some extent by the DC-3 and a Dove, 5N-AGF, requisitioned from Bristows at Port Harcourt. On 26 July the B-26 and DC-3 were used in an attempt to damage or drive off the destroyer *Nigeria* which was blockading Port Harcourt. In early August it was joined by a second aircraft, a B-26C, to be piloted by 'Jean Bonnel'. The aircraft was possibly 4434531 seen in Belgium in July and apparently also registered N12756. Both bombers operated together on 12 August in an attack on Lokoja, destroying the ferry across the Niger.

The Federal forces were now in desperate need of combat aircraft, both in close support and, critically, in the counter-air role to take out the Biafran aircraft on the ground. Both Britain and the Soviet Union were supporting the Federal position, and it was from the latter that aircraft were forthcoming. From 13 August Kano Airport was closed to all commercial traffic as Aeroflot An-12 transports unloaded sixteen L-29 Delfin armed trainers and six MiG-17s; further MiG-17s and MiG-15UTI trainers were delivered to Lagos in a Polish vessel. In addition, Sudan had lent two armed Jet Provosts, but these were unserviceable by the time fighting started. The British Government turned a blind eye to the recruiting activities of the mercenary John Peters, who was advertising for pilots at £1,000 a month, and in due course British, Australian, South African, Rhodesian and Egyptian pilots flew in the Federal cause. Airwork Ltd. provided contract ground crew. The United States remained neutral, although it was rumoured that the CIA actively supported the Biafrans. The French certainly supported Ojukwu and opened an arms supply line through Fort Lamy (Chad), Cotonou (Dahomey) and Libreville (Gabon).

The covert supply of arms was directed through Lisbon or Faro and then to Port Harcourt via Bissau (Portuguese Guinea) and São Tomé or Fernando Poo. Some arms are also believed to have been supplied by South Africa, probably flown in by DC-7s of Air TransAfrica. Soon some eighteen aircraft were operating out of Lisbon, many in the name of 'Henry Wharton' (Heinrich Wartski). In October 1966 Wharton had crashed a DC-4M Argonaut spuriously registered I-ACOA at Garoua in Cameroun, implying early plans for a Biafran secession. The aircraft was registered to Royal Air Burundi and was flying arms loaded in Rotterdam. Wharton lost a second aircraft when Super Constellation 5T-TAF (c/n 4618) made an emergency landing at Malta where it was impounded. The Super Constellation had been operated by Transportes Aereos Portugueses (TAP) as CS-TLC and was sold to International Aerodyne in September 1967 with two identical aircraft. It was also operated by Phoenix Air Transport, whose aircraft bore the bogus Nigerian registrations (perhaps based on US registrations) 5N83H, 5N84H and 5N86H.

Also involved in covert flights was Ernest Koenig using DC-7C VP-WBO, alias ZP-WBO (? of Air Trans-Africa) possibly shipping money to Switzerland; others included the Rhodesian Jack Malloch and the mercenary Alistair Wickes with Air Trans-Africa. The aircraft used were generally time-expired Constellations, DC-4s, DC-6s and DC-7s. Wharton made a charge of £22,000 per flight.

On 19 and 20 August the B-26 Invaders attacked Kano and claimed several of the newly delivered MiG-17s destroyed. The first operational use of the MiG-17 was on the 30th of that month in an attack on Onitsha airfield. Eleven days later one of the B-26s was destroyed in a MiG attack on Enugu airfield.

The Biafrans were now being pushed back into the Eastern Region as Benin City was retaken on 22 September; on 4 October Enugu fell and Ojukwu was forced to move his capital to Umuahia. On 7 October the Biafrans lost their F.27 over Lagos. Without access to conventional bombs, Biafran armourers improvised. It appears that the air crew departed from Port Harcourt with alcohol and girlfriends on board and inadvertently triggered the home-made and internally carried bomb over Lagos. Federal troops claimed the aircraft to anti-aircraft fire. The pilot, 'Jacques (Paul) Langhiaume', had earlier crash-landed Constellation 5N-07G at Enugu, bringing in Czech arms.

Fighting continued through the winter, with Calabar falling and then Onitsha. There was little air activity, both because of the weather and because of the unavailability of spares, and with the capture of Port Harcourt on 18 May 1968 the Biafrans lost their DC-3 and B-25. In

Nigerian Air Force Do 28 NAF174. The Nigerians had purchased five of the type by 1970 and they were used for light transport and communications work. (M. Robson)

February a Widgeon impressed from Bristow Helicopters had been lost in a crash at Uzuakoli. Desperate again for aircraft, Ojukwu suffered another setback in May when a charter aircraft carrying the wings of a pair of Magister armed trainers was sabotaged at Bissau, leaving the useless fuselages of the ex-Austrian aircraft, 4D-YF and 4D-YI, at Lisbon.

On 16 June Awgu fell, leaving Biafra with just one airstrip, a stretch of straightened road, at Uli-Ihialia, code-named 'Annabelle'. The Red Cross was constructing a second strip at Afikpo, but by now the NAF was operating six Il-28 bombers out of Calabar and Port Harcourt, flown by Egyptian and Czech crews, and these aircraft mounted an indiscriminate bombing campaign from May, killed an estimated 2,000 people by October.

Early in the war Ojukwu had hired a Swiss public relations consultancy, Markpress, to represent Biafra to the world. In the summer of 1968 the company focused on the plight of the starving in a contracting and blockaded Biafra, and the Federal Government was portrayed as committing genocide against the Ibos. Thus began the relief flights into Uli, which, sadly, had the effect only of prolonging the agony of defeat by over a year. So harrowing were the filmed scenes from Biafra that some were moved to contribute directly.

In 1968 the RAF had retired the last of its Avro Anson communications aircraft, and at least six were bought by organizations with the intention of using them to haul medical supplies around Biafra. G-AWML was registered to the Save the Children Fund, while -AWMG and -AWMH were registered to Mercy Missions. 'ML did not leave the country, 'MG reached Biafra only to crash at Uzuakoli near Umuahia on 3 September, and 'MH crash-landed at Port Etienne in Mauretania.

By November there were twenty tons each of ammunition and relief supplies being flown into Uli every night, for by now daytime landings were hazardous, the NAF having complete command of the skies. The increased flow of arms enabled the Biafrans, strengthened by the mercenary-led

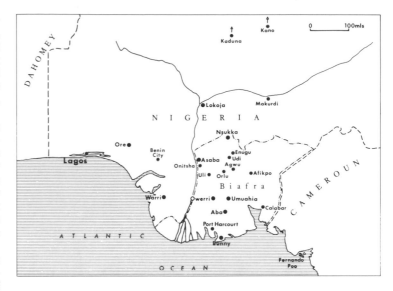

4th Commando Brigade, to begin an offensive on Onitsha. DC-3 transports of Nigeria Airways impressed by the NAF were used in February 1969 to drop supplies to the surrounded 3rd Commando Division at Owerri, but the Biafrans eventually recaptured the town in May. Aware of the international image of Nigeria, General Gowon gave instructions not to bomb civilian targets and attempted to find ways of enabling relief aircraft to operate safely while filtering in the arms supplies.

To the end of the war there was no solution to the problem, and arms continued to flow while relief aircraft were shot down. The relief flights were handled by various organization contracted by the International and national Red Crosses, JointChurchAid and the World Council of Churches. Balair chartered two DC-6As to the Swiss Red Cross and four C-97Gs to the International Red Cross. The French Red Cross chartered a DC-4 and the Swedish Red Cross a Swedish Air Force C-130E registered as SE-XBT. The International Red Cross also chartered DC-7C PH-DST from Martinair and DC-6B OH-KDA from Kar Air. The West German Government

A Nigerian Air force Il-28 photographed at Lagos after the war. The Air Force is believed to have taken delivery of six of the Russian bombers, and they became a prime target for Col. Ojukwu's air arm. Operating from Port Harcourt and Calabar, and flown by Czech and Egyptian crews, they caused heavy damage in the bombing campaign, which began in May 1968. The Minicons of Count von Rosen claimed at least three damaged or destroyed on the ground. (M. Robson)

released the third prototype Transall C-160 to Balair as HB-ILN. It flew 198 missions from Cotonou, Dahomey, to July 1969.

JointChurchAid chartered four KC-97Gs direct from the Utah ANG. The national markings were overpainted by the Christian sign of the fish and the serials converted to civil registrations by prefixing an 'N'. The World Council of Churches used several DC-7Bs of Transair, one being piloted by Count Carl Gustav von Rosen, the company's senior pilot. Von Rosen had led an adventurous life, flying against the Russians briefly for Finland and before the war for the Red Cross in Ethiopia at the time of the Italian invasion. He was greatly concerned by the plight of the Biafrans and on his release from Transair at the age of sixty returned to Sweden to form an air force for Biafra. He purchased five MFI-9Bs as sporting aircraft and shipped them to France for the fitting of rocket launchers by Matra. From there they were shipped to Libreville, where they were assembled and camouflaged. They were not given markings or serials.

The first strike by the light aircraft, popularly called 'Minicons', was on 22 May 1969 against the airfield at Port Harcourt: flying from Orlu, four aircraft claimed two MiG-17s and two Il-28s damaged or destroyed. On the 24th they attacked the airfield at Benin City, claiming damage to one MiG and one Il-28. On the 27th the airfield at Enugu was the target, and on the 28th some damage was caused to the oil facilities at Port Harcourt. The Minicons transferred operations

to Uli and continued to sting the Federal forces, who by now were surrounding a much contracted Biafra with a view to starving the country into submission. Von Rosen returned to Europe, where he purchased more MFI-9 aircraft from private owners, allegedly for the Abidjan Flying Club but transferring them to Biafra in October. The main task of the Minicons was to inhibit the oil industry, which they did to some effect.

It appears that Ernest Koenig also bought two ex-West German Air Force C-47s for Biafra and early in November Fred Herz flew in two, possibly four, AT-6s. On 9 November an AT-6 attacked Port Harcourt airfield and claimed a DC-4 of Pan African Airways. The NAF subsequently claimed the destruction of the AT-6 by a MiG-17. The NAF had been reinforced and

Relief flights were frequently hazardous. This DC-6 of Fred Olsen Line, LN-FOM, crashed at Uli in November 1969, presumably while attempting to land at night on the small strip. Many civil types, including C-46s, DC-6s, DC-7s, Constellations and Super Constellations, were used to fly in both aid and arms to the Biafrans. (B. Haugh via M. Robson)

TABLE OF AIRCRAFT: THE NIGERIAN CIVIL WAR, 1967–1970

No. of aircraft	Type	Base	Role	Serials/registrations
NAF (aircraft delivered by 1970)				
26	Piaggio P.149D	Kaduna	Training	201–214
20	Do 27	Benin City, Kaduna, Kano	Communications, liaison	150–169
5	Do 28	Benin City	Light transport	170–174
4	MiG-15UTI	Kano	Training	627
2	Jet Provost	Lagos, Benin City	Light attack (ex Sudan)	?
9	Whirlwind 2/3	Kaduna	Communications (ex Austria)	?
16	L-29	Benin City, Kaduna	Light attack	401–416
24 +	MiG-17	Benin City, Lagos, Enugu, Kaduna, Port Harcourt	Air defence, ground attack	601–624
6	Il-28	Port Harcourt, Calabar, Benin City	Light bomber (ex USSR, Egypt)	015, 158
9	DC-3	Benin City	Transport (Nigerian Airways, Sabena)	5N-AAK-N, P, 303-306
2	DC-4	Benin City, Lagos	Transport (Pan African Airways)	311, 501
10	Noratlas	Benin City, Lagos	Transport	301-310
1	Aztec	Benin City	Liaison	001
Biafran Air Arm (aircraft purchased or requisitioned)				
1	DC-3	Port Harcourt	Transport, bombing (ex Ghana Airways)	9G-AAD (5N-41G)
2	Riley Dove	Port Harcourt	Recce (1 ex Bristows)	5N-AGF, N477PM
1	F.27	Port Harcourt	Bombing (ex Nigerian Airways)	5N-AAV
1	HS.125	São Tomé	Not delivered	5N-AER
1 (?2)	B-25	Port Harcourt	Bombing	?
2	B-26	Enugu, Port Harcourt	Bombing, ground attack	N12756 (4139539), N12756 (sic) (4434531)
3 (?6)	Alouette II	Udi	Liaison	F-OCJS, T, 5N-ACI
3	Widgeon	Udi	Liaison, recce (ex Bristow)	5N-ABV, GA, GL
2	Hiller UH-12E	Udi	Liaison (ex Bristow, Shell)	5N-ABY, GE
12 +	MFI.9B Minicon	Orlu, Uli	Light attack, recce (five delivered, ex SE-EUE, L, N, WE, F)	5N-71H (not carried)
4	AT-6	Uli	Light attack (ex AA)	14810, 114798, 114873, 115051
2	Meteor NF.14	Bissau	Not delivered	G-AXNE, SLW

Note: The Biafran HS.125, UH-12Es and Meteors were either not used or not delivered. In addition, there have been reports of the following attempted purchases or deliveries (source refers to location rather than any government involvement): twelve more AT-6s (Portugal); two Vampire T.11s (Portugal); three DC-3s (Phoenix Air Transport); six Provosts (West Germany); Vautours (?); Vikings (?); Mirage 5s or IIIs (?); B-26s (?); T-28s (?).

DC-6B LN-SUD of Braathens-SAFE, chartered by the Red Cross and painted white overall. The aircraft was photographed in September 1968 at Fernando Poo, which was one regular staging post for flights originating in Europe. (Via M. Robson)

night sorties were now being flown over Uli to harass the supply flights. Early in June Captain David Brown was killed crossing the coast at Eket in a Red Cross DC-7 when it was attacked by a MiG-17 flown by a contract pilot, allegedly British. Biafra was now searching for a jet night fighter. Initially an attempt was made to purchase two Swedish-registered Meteor NF.11s but export proved impossible. The answer came in the form of two Meteor NF.14s released for sale by the Ministry of Defence (MoD).

The aircraft were the ex-Rolls Royce G-ASLW and ex-RAE Bedford WS804 registered as G-AXNE. They were registered to the Target Towing Aircraft Co. Ltd. and hired to 'Enterprise Films'. G-AXNE departed from Exeter for Bordeaux on 6 September and flew to Bissau via Faro. It appears to have been allowed no further. The second aircraft was reported missing off the Cape Verde Islands on 10 November, the Dutch pilot being rescued. The brokers were reportedly Templewood Aviation, and in April 1970 four men appeared in court in England charged with attempting to export jet aircraft illegally.

The war in Biafra was now reaching a conclusion. Federal forces launched a final offensive on 22 December, cutting the territory in two and forcing a surrender on 13 January 1970. Ojukwu left Uli in Super Constellation 5N-86H for Abidjan. With so many starving, however, the need for emergency help remained. A large number of flights were made into Lagos, and when the British contribution ended on 2 February, 63 had been completed, mainly by chartered C-130s and all from Manston.

AIRCRAFT MARKINGS

Nigerian Air Force
All serials in black and generally in 24–36in characters. Communications and training types were finished medium grey overall, usually with red rudders and nose panels.
Piaggio P.149D Serial on rear fuselage: NAF⊙202.

Do 28 Serial on fuselage: NAF⊙170.
Piper Aztec D Serial on fuselage: ⊙NAF001.

Fighters were finished bare metal with roundels on fin and a large serial, or a fin flash and smaller serial.
L-29 Delfin Serial on forward fuselage: NAF401.
MiG-17 Roundel on fin, serial on rear fuselage: NAF 612. Fin flash, smaller serial on rear fuselage: NAF⊙615.
Il-28 Mottled very dark green/emerald green overall, no serial evident.

Biafran Air Arm
In general, aircraft were flown in markings as delivered. The B-25 and B-26 were delivered in a bare metal finish. One B-26 was subsequently painted green over, medium blue under, and had shark's teeth applied. The Minicons were originally finished glossy medium grey/glossy dark grey-green overall, without registration or serial. Machines delivered later appear to have retained their civilian colour schemes, normally white gloss overall with a bronze cheat line.

Relief aircraft
Most aircraft used for genuine relief flights were painted white or cream overall with a large red cross on the wings and fin or fuselage. Some were painted a dull medium blue-green over to simulate the jungle cover.

Super Constellation 5T-TAK at Lisbon after the war. With several other aircraft of the type, it was operated by Henry Wharton in arms supplies flights from Lisbon to Enugu; 5T-TAF was 'lost' when it made an emergency landing at Malta and was impounded. (M. Robson)

3.9. Miscellaneous conflicts and incidents

1. On 19 February 1964 French paratroopers were dropped at Libreville, Gabon, to aid the Government in the face of an attempted coup.

2. At the request of the Sierra Leone Prime Minister, troops, a Bell 47 helicopter and three MiG-17s of the Guinea Republic were flown into Freetown on 28 March 1971 to help maintain order at a time of political unrest. In September a MiG-15UTI and a MiG-17 of the Guinea Republic were lost in the Ivory Coast. On 30 July 1972 a South African Twin Comanche crashed in the sea off Guinea, reportedly shot down.

3. A Mali Air Force MiG-17 crashed in November 1974 at a time when it appeared that there might be border fighting between Mali and Upper Volta (now Burkina Faso).

4. In January 1976 VP-49 of the USN, equipped with the P-3C, was detached to Ascension Island as part of Task Group 84.2.5 for surveillance duties. The target was 'high interest units' off the coast of West Africa. On the 27th a Soviet Aeroflot An-30 fitted for photo-reconnaissance and intelligence-gathering was held for 24hrs at Libreville, Gabon.

5. There have been several attempts at overthrowing African governments on the part of mercenaries and involving the use of aircraft. On 16 January 1977 Bob Denard flew to Benin in Air Trans Africa DC-7CF TR-LNZ with 90 men to mount a coup against the Marxist government. On arrival at the Presidential palace the President was not found in residence and the group returned to the airport, unsuccessful in their endeavour. After a firefight, in which eight died, the DC-7 flew back to Gabon.

6. There was border fighting between Mali and Burkina Faso from 25 December 1985, possibly involving the use of aircraft. An Ivory Coast Alouette III crashed at Kouni on 14 January 1986 while helping to supervise a ceasefire.

7. Late in September 1986 the French Government sent 150 paratroopers and four Jaguar As of EC 4/11 from Libreville, Gabon, to Togo. On the 24th about 50 rebels, possibly based in Ghana, had attacked the military headquarters, but they were soon killed or captured. The French troops returned on 5 October, the Jaguars a week later.

4: Central and Southern Africa

So many of the problems of Africa seem to stem from the imposition of arbitrary boundaries determined by colonizers and taking no account of tribal territories. Surprisingly, Central and Southern Africa were remarkably quiet for the first fifteen years following the Second World War, and most of the conflicts have arisen to hasten independence, as civil wars post-independence or, in several cases, against white minority rule. The Portuguese Empire in Africa was challenged in Guinea (q.v.), Angola and Mozambique. In the latter cases civil war followed, in Angola with extensive third-party intervention. Angola also witnessed the use of mercenaries, whose widespread employment in Africa is indicative of the unreliability of indigenous troops whose tribal loyalties extend beyond national boundaries. Angola was also to become the springboard for Cuban troops fighting a proxy war for the Soviet Union across Africa from 1975.

Belgium decided to relinquish control of the Congo without ensuring that adequate preparations were made for the country's post-independence government. The result was a vicious civil war in which the major powers played important parts. Mercenaries were used by both major factions, and some eventually became powerful enough to see themselves as local warlords acting independently. It is barely surprising that many whites were used by local parties as bargaining pieces. The appalling circumstances of the fates of many inevitably led to retribution and escalation, but in fairness it has to be said that mercenaries were often instrumental in saving the lives of hostages. It was in the Congo that maximum ingenuity was used to locate and operate aircraft in fighting roles for which few were originally designed. The ubiquitous T-6 played a major part, and the B-26, a hallmark of covert US activity, surfaced yet again.

France seems to have managed to find a role in Africa which legitimizes intervention without involvement. Thus she was able to deploy forces without hesitation to rescue hostages at Kolwezi in 1978, withdrawing as quickly and with as little fuss as she had entered.

White minority rule in Rhodesia highlighted dilemmas for the West which continue to obtain in respect of South Africa but which create little concern for the Soviet Union and Eastern Bloc countries who continue to trade where it suits them. The British response to unilateral independence in Rhodesia was to impose sanctions and a physical blockade. Having just announced the scrapping of the carrier fleet the Government was embarrassed to have to rely on a succession of carrier-borne units to impose the futile blockade while arrangments were made for a land-based operation. The Government of Ian Smith found ways around the sanctions, and the security services dealt effectively with the emerging nationalists. The fight was taken into neighbouring countries in surgical raids of the type for which the Israelis are renowned. This is also a characteristic of the South African war against nationalist movements – not surprising, given the close relationship between the two countries, especially in respect of covert arms supplies. Paradoxically, a major contribution to the end of white rule in Rhodesia was pressure from South Africa, which wished to see a stable buffer between herself and more extreme neighbours.

In South Africa there seems no end in sight to what amounts to civil war on two fronts. The West depends upon raw materials from the country and cannot afford to see the essential Cape sea lanes become dominated by communist interests. If the whites are considered as a minority (but governing) tribe, then the position is little different from that in many other parts of Africa. What makes the South African position unique and indefensible in the eyes of the rest of the world is the maintenance of apartheid.

The transfer of troops to Swaziland in 1963 was an example of the value of air transport in bringing force to bear speedily, although in this instance the transports were able to overfly friendly colonies. The despatch of troops to distant places is nowadays impeded by lengthy administration and is often only effectively solved by the deployment of commando carriers or by in-flight refuelling.

4.1. The Congo, 1960–1964

In 1959, with little preparation and in the wake of British and French withdrawal from their African colonies, Belgium decided to grant independence to the Belgian Congo. Nearly the size of Western Europe but with a population of only 14 million from 200 tribes, the country produced significant quantities of gold, diamonds, copper, uranium and a range of other minerals, mainly in Katanga province. Independence was declared on 30 June 1960 with Joseph Kasavubu as President and the radical Patrice Lumumba as Prime Minister. Belgian forces were temporarily reinforced as the new Nationalist Army mutinied in Leopoldville, critically at the continuing appointment of Belgians in all senior posts. The local military presence was the Force Publique (FP) which operated aircraft in the shape of two S-55 and three Alouette II helicopters, a Heron and ten Doves. Most of these aircraft were based at either Leopoldville or Kamina.

From the beginning the new Government was destabilized, and many Europeans left in what rapidly became an exodus. Colonel Joseph-Désiré Mobutu was foremost in attempting to control the Army and seek out likely Congolese NCOs to promote in place of Belgian officers. No. 15 Wing of the Force Aérienne Belge (FAB), equipped with the C-47, C-54, DC-6 and C-119G, began repatriating civilians while moving Belgian forces to centres of trouble, while several Alouette II helicopters of 16ème Escadrille Légère from Germany supplemented three of the type already in Ruanda to retrieve civilians from remote homesteads. Sixteen T-6G Harvards and four Magisters of the Flying School (Vervolmakings VliegSchool, VVS) at Kamina had been fitted with machine guns and rockets for escort duty. The VVS Harvards were in action on armed reconnaissance and escort missions and soon suffered losses. H-202 was shot down over Matadi on 11 July and on 18 July H-210 was brought down with the loss of the pilot over Inkisi while escorting an Alouette. Two more crashed in the period. A more serious loss was that of C-119F CP-36 of 15 Wing which crashed on 19 July. Two of the Army's Alouettes, A-1 and A-2, were also lost.

The Belgians maintained their bases in the south, partly to protect their considerable financial interests in the Union Minière du Haut-Katanga, in which British, French and South African parties also had substantial holdings. An Armée Nationale Congolaise (ANC) revolt in Elisabethville, the Katangese capital, was put down by Belgians on 9 July. On the 10th, at the request of the Katangese leader, Moise Tshombe, a Belgian parachute company was dropped into Kongolo from Kamina to restore order. The following day, with the full support of the Union Minière and the Belgian Government, Tshombe announced the secession of Katanga from the Congo and began to hire white mercenaries to lead his gendarmerie; Lumumba recognized his inability to control events and sought help from the UN. On 14 July the UN agreed to the formation of the Force de l'Organisation des Nations Unies au Congo (ONUC), to comprise troops from neutral countries.

RAF Comets (216 Sqn.), Britannias (99 and 511 Sqns.) and Beverleys (30 Sqn.) began moving Ghanaian troops and equipment from Accra, while 132 USAF C-130 and C-124 transports had brought in 4,000 troops from across Africa by 18 July. Irish troops were flown in by C-130As of 322 Air Division, and by the end of the month their were 10,000 UN troops in the Congo. The UN resolution called for the withdrawal of Belgian forces, and by 15 August all but 600, in Katanga, had left. The FAB removed a number of Magisters to Belgium but left five Doves, eight T-6s, a Heron, an Alouette II, an L-18C and an S-55 as the nucleus of the Force Aérienne Katangaise (FAK). In August Kasai was declared an independent mining state and, notwithstanding the UN presence, from 6 September the Soviet Union 'lent' Lumumba at least nine Il-14 transports to lift ANC troops to Bakwanga to persuade the local population to remain loyal to the Congo. Included in the Soviet support were 100 GAZ-63 trucks and more than 200 'technicians'.

The US now became concerned at Russian intervention and, as the CIA plotted the overthrow of Lumumba, Mobutu seized control on 14 September; Lumumba was placed under UN-supervised house arrest. Mobutu ejected the Russians. The CIA enabled Lumumba to escape from Leopoldville on 27 November and he made for Stanleyville; he was recaptured by the ANC several days later. On 12 December his vice-premier, Antoine Gizenga, established a pro-communist regime in Stanleyville. On 17 January 1961 Lumumba was to be flown to Bakwanga for imprisonment; in fact the runway was blocked, so the aircraft flew on to Elisabethville, where his future would be equally certain. He was beaten up on the aircraft, and shortly after landing was believed to have been killed but there remains controversy about the exact circumstances of his death, which was not announced until 12 February. If the CIA was not directly involved in Lumumba's assassination, it was certainly authorized to kill him.

Meanwhile civil aircraft, mainly operated by Sabena, had evacuated civilians (34,484 by the

In 1959 the Belgians began arming some Harvards to form a Fire Assistance Flight at Kamina. H210, photographed here with rockets and machine-gun pod, was shot down by small-arms fire over Inkisi on 17 July 1960 while escorting an Alouette which was evacuating civilians for repatriation. The Belgian Air Force also had at its disposal twenty Fouga Magisters and miscellaneous helicopters, transport and liaison types. (Via K. Valentijn)

One of three Fouga Magisters operated by the Katanga Air Force and flown by mercenaries. The aircraft were delivered by air from Toulouse in February 1961 and were soon in action. No. 92 was the last Magister in service and was immobilized at Kisenge in December 1961 during a strike on the airfield by Indian Air Force Canberras. (J. Hedges via D. Becker)

end of July) through Leopoldville. In addition, many more civilians had departed on military aircraft: Dakotas of 3 Sqn. Royal Rhodesian Air Force (RRAF) evacuated many from Ndola to Salisbury, while many Italian nationals were flown out in C-119Gs. Two Hastings of 114 Sqn. RAF supported the Ghanaian ONUC force. To control the wide range of transport flights within the country – many operated by Transair on UN charter – the UN Air Division was formed in August. Additionally, the Swedish Voluntary Air Component was established to handle liaison flying for the UN with Otters, Beavers and several helicopters. The first UN losses were suffered on 9 November when a ten-man Irish patrol was ambushed at Niemba by Baluba 'Jeunesse' (Young Fighters) and massacred.

Pro-Gizenga forces now threatened Kasai and northern Katanga, and sporadic fighting broke out between them and Katangese troops despite the UN presence. Desperate for more potent aircraft than the Harvards, Tshombe had shopped abroad and on 15 February YC-97 N9045C of Seven Seas delivered three Magisters from Toulouse; these were operated from Kolwezi using mercenary pilots. By now, apart from the UN, there were four major forces in conflict within the Congo: the ANC, generally from Leopoldville and Equateur, numbered 7,500; Gizenga's Kivu and Orientale pro-communists were 7,000 strong; the Kasai Balubas – Katanga's arch enemies – numbered 3,000; and the Katangese gendarmerie comprised 5,000, led by up to 500 white mercenaries. On 24 February Luluabourg fell to Gizenga, and henceforth ONUC forces appeared to pursue objectives which have

TABLE OF UNITS: CONGO, 1960–1964

Unit	Aircraft	Base	Role	Dates
Force Publique, July 1960				
–	S-55, Alouette II, Heron, Dove	Leopoldville, Kamina	Liaison, observation, transport	
FAB, July 1960				
15 Wing	C-47, C-54, DC-6, C-119G	Leopoldville, Kamina	Transport	
VVS	T-6G, Magister, C-47	Kamina	Training, armed escort, transport	
16 EL	Alouette II	Kamina, Ruanda	Liaison, light transport	
Belgian Army				
–	Piper Super Cub	Leopoldville	Liaison, communications	
ONUC				
5 Sqn., IAF	Canberra B(I).58	Kamina	Medium bombing	09/10/62 to 00/03/63
F22, SAF	Saab J29B, S29C	Luluabourg, Kamina	Ground attack, recce	04/10/61 to 21/04/63
EAF	F-86F	Luluabourg, Kamina	Fighter, ground attack	00/09/61 to 00/12/62
46 AB, AMI	C-119G	Leopoldville, Kamina	Transport	00/01/61 to 00/07/62
4 AB, AMI	Sabre 4	Kamina Leopoldville	Fighter	14/01/63 to 00/00/63

FAC, June 1962
3 C-47/DC-3s, 1 DC-4, 1 Do 27, 2 T-6s, 1 S-55, 2 Doves and 2 Piper PA-20s, plus air Congo DC-3s. All based at Leopoldville.

FAK INVENTORY, 1960–1964

No. of aircraft	Type	Serials	No. of aircraft	Type	Serials
1	Heron	KAT-01 (ex OO-CGG)	1	Alouette II	KAT-53
3	DC-3	KAT-02–04	1	Piper 95 Super Cub	KAT-61
1	Piper PA-22	'7-4'	1	Piper Tripacer	'72'
9	Dove	14–22	3	Magister	91–93
3	T-6G	KA-22, -33, -34	1	Piper PA-24 Comanche	KA-119
1	Sikorsky S-55	KAT-42	5	Do 28	KA-3016–3020

In addition, impressed aircraft are believed to include C-54 KA-ADF, DC-4 KA-ADJ, DC-3s KA-ADN and -DFN and Heron KA-TUR. Bases included Kolwezi, Jadotville, Kisenge, Dilolo and Kipushi.

been the subject of controversy ever since. Instead of attempting to bring order across the country, they operated discriminately, primarily with a view to ending Katangase secession. The UAR contingent withdrew in February 1961 leaving, allegedly at Soviet request, 67 tons of arms for Gizenga.

On 4 April the airport at Elisabethville was liberated from Swedish control by local Katangese, and three days later at Manono there was the first clash between Katangese and ONUC, in which several Ethiopian troops were killed. On 14 April ONUC was authorized to use force in pursuit of its goals. At Coquilhatville, on 26 April, Tshombe was arrested while there for talks. He was released on 22 June, on conditions which he subsequently broke. In the meantime the FAK had been further strengthened by the delivery of five Piper Caribbeans from South Africa. Tshombe's growing band of mercenaries was also strengthened following the disbandment, in disgrace, of the French 1er REP in Algeria.

As clashes between ONUC and the Katangese increased, the UN began Operation 'Rumpunch', a sweep in Katanga to round up mercenaries. Of 512 whites supporting Tshombe, 400 were caught, but most slipped away and returned to the fight; foremost among these was a Belgian planter, Jean Schramme. As the situation worsened, fighting began in Elisabethville on 13 September when Indian troops seized key positions in the city. The UN Secretary-General, Dag Hammarskjold, flew into Leopoldville the same day. The Magisters had been operational for some time and two pilots, Joseph Deulin and one Magain, were particularly successful. On 15 September, while strafing UN positions at Elisabethville Airport, Deulin destroyed DC-4 OO-ADN, and two days later Starways Skymaster G-APIN, on charter to the UN, was written off at Kamina. On the 17th 500 Katangese surrounded the 158-man Irish garrison at Jadotville, and Deulin strafed a relief column.

Damaged at Elisabethville by machine-gun fire was DC-6B SE-BDY 'Albertina', of Transair, which received hits in one engine. After repair the aircraft was flown up to Leopoldville. There it picked up Hammarskjold to fly him to Ndola, just across the Northern Rhodesian border, for discussions with Tshombe. The aircraft, piloted by Captain Per-Erik Hallonquist, approached Ndola at around midnight but crashed just to the north at 0010hrs on the 18th, killing all on board. There was immediate speculation about the cause of the accident and those possibly behind it. Two accident theories emerged, one based on engine failure and one on instrument failure – the altimeter was found to be 37m adrift. A sabotage theory variously blamed the Soviet Union, Mobutu and Conor Cruise O'Brien, the Irish UN representative in the Congo. Then there

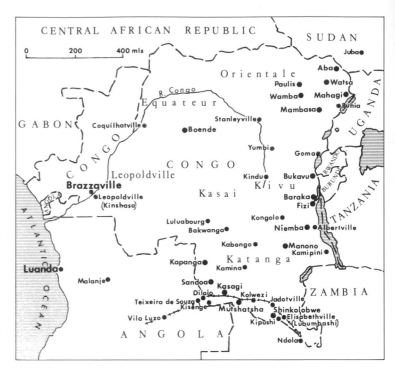

were the external attack theories, supported by the alleged sighting of a second aircraft in the vicinity. These suggested an RRAF Vampire, Deulin's FAK Magister or a FAK Dove bombing the DC-6B from above. Although the cause has never been satisfactorily established, the most likely reason for the loss is engine or instrument failure. In the light of Hammarskjold's death, a ceasefire was agreed on the 21st, but not before Deulin had attacked O'Brien's HQ in Katanga. The ceasefire did not last long as ONUC acquired air assets to begin the elimination of the FAK on the ground in Operation 'Morthor'. Late in September four Ethiopian Air Force (EAF) F-86Fs were sent to Leopoldville, where they were joined by six Indian Air Force (IAF) Canberra B(I).58s of 5 Sqn. on 9 October, ground crews being transported from Agra in four USAF C-124s. On 5 October five ex-F10 J29B fighters of F22 Swedish Air Force (SAF) arrived at Luluabourg, from where they flew on to Kamina.

In October 1961 the Swedish Air Force detached five Saab J29Bs of F22 to Kamina; they were later joined in the Congo by two reconnaissance S29Cs. The aircraft operated in support of United Nations forces for eighteen months, but most of the aircraft were blown up at Kamina by the Swedes since the remaining airframe hours were insufficient to merit their return to Sweden. Illustrated is 29475/J, in blue-grey/olive camouflage with clear UN markings; it was photographed from a Katangese C-47 en route from Kabongo to Kolwezi in November 1962. (J. Hedges via D. Becker)

On 20 October 5,000 ANC troops crossed into Katanga and FAK aircraft were kept busy attacking them, especially around Kabongo. The FAK obtained five Do 28As from Munich on the 21st. At the beginning of October UN-chartered aircraft lifted 1,500 Gizengist troops from Stanleyville into northern Katanga to join the fight, but on 11 November the UN was repaid for its trouble when Gizengist troops at Kindu caught and massacred, in the most brutal fashion, thirteen Italian airmen flying the C-119G with 46° Stormo, Italian Air Force (AMI). Throughout the month Indian troops held the airfields at Elisabethville and Kamina, supplies being delivered from Leopoldville in chartered C-46 transports of Seven Seas; based in Luxembourg, this company appears to have operated for both sides in the conflict. As Albertville, Niemba and Manono fell to the ONUC, preparations for a final offensive against Katanga were made.

Twenty-seven USAF C-124s of 63 Troop Carrier Wing (TCW) brought troops, arms and armoured cars into Elisabethville, where at least one was damaged by groundfire. From 5 December the IAF Canberras attacked the airfields at Jadotville and Kolwezi, destroying two Do 28s, a DC-3, a DC-4, a Dove and the sole remaining Magister. On the 7th the attacks turned to communications centres in Elisabethville, notably the post office and radio station. Daily the Canberras struck at Katangese troop concentrations and at buildings in the provincial capital. At Kolwezi a Union Minière fuel store was set ablaze and tragically, on the 12th, a hospital at Shinkolobwe was attacked.

As the ONUC attempted to force the integration of Katanga by military means there was an exodus of civilians, mainly white, to Northern Rhodesia. Tshombe refused to surrender, calling instead for a ceasefire, but as his forces were obliged to withdraw from the capital he retreated to Kipushi. By 18 December Elisabethville was under UN control, but heavy fighting continued around Kongolo to the north. On the 19th there was a suspension of hostilities as Tshombe flew to the UN base at Kitona in the US Presidential VC-121E 537885 'Columbine III' for talks with the Prime Minister Cyril Adoula. A ceasefire operated from 21 December, and on 8 January Gizenga was placed under house arrest. Tshombe had flown to Geneva where he now planned to resurrect his air force under mercenary leadership. Balubas were still active around Kongolo, where they had massacred nineteen missionaries in December. There was evidence of further threats to whites in the region which the UN appeared incapable of preventing. Six T-6Gs, ex-USAF stock in Belgium, were acquired, and after testing at Geneva were flown back to Antwerp, from where they were delivered to Luanda, Angola, via Lisbon in May 1962.

At Luanda the T-6s were assembled by Portuguese Air Force (FAP) technicians and then flown to Kolwezi via Malanje, Vila Luzo and Teixeira de Souza with a Dove escort. The aircraft were to be operated from airfields at Kipushi, Kolwezi, Jadotville, Kisenge and Dilolo, outside the UN control zones. The crews were to avoid the capital and were in Katanga ostensibly to help form a new airline.

In June the Dove, by now armed with a Hotchkiss machine gun and locally made bombs, carried out an armed reconnaissance in the Kongolo area. The FAK bought more aircraft in the form of a Lodestar, two Cessnas and four T-6s from Aero Services at Johannesburg and recovered a second Dove, a Comanche and a Tripacer. During September Albertville was occupied by Kivu ANC troops, and four T-6s, a Dove and the Comanche were flown up to meet with Schramme near Niembe. From there they attacked a local HQ. Conflict between the Katangese and the ANC extended, and between 11 and 16 November there was heavy fighting around Kongolo and Kabongo. The T-6Gs attacked ANC positions, and it is believed that Katangese casualties were evacuated by Rhodesian-registered DC-3s. The USAF brought in C-133s of 1607 Air Transport Wing (ATW) and C-118s of 1611 ATW in support of Irish troops in Elisabethville; the USAF also airlifted two reconnaissance S29Cs of the SAF to Leopoldville to join F22. As it became clear that Tshombe was not observing the ceasefire, Ethiopian troops were flown into Elisabethville and the UN began a fresh air offensive after he rejected an ultimatum. Although the Force Aérienne Congolaise (FAC) comprised only transport and liaison aircraft based at Leopoldville, the UN force at Kamina had been reinforced by the delivery of four more J29Bs, ex-F8, to replace the EAF F-86Fs which had played little part in operations. Four AMI Sabre Mk. 4s of 4 Aerobrigata arrived in Leopoldville on 14 January 1963.

The FAK aircraft were dispersed but were soon

Among the types operated by the Katangese was the Do 28. This aircraft is almost certainly KA-(3)016, which survived an Indian Air Force Canberra raid on Kolwezi but was destroyed in a flying accident in March 1962. The white overall finish was camouflaged except for the engine nacelles and undersurfaces by the application of green paint crudely daubed by hand. (J. Hedges via D. Becker)

A KAF T-6G photographed at Kongolo in November 1962. The aircraft was one of three operated by the Katangese, and the light bomb racks are clearly visible. The Harvards were used extensively to attack ANC positions from May 1962, flying from Kisenge and Kolwezi until destroyed early in January 1963. (J. Hedges via D. Becker)

taken out in air strikes by Canberras and J29s at Kipushi, Kabongo and Jadotville. Two Vampires of indeterminate origin and variety had been delivered via Johannesburg, but these were destroyed on the ground at Kolwezi before becoming operational. On 21 December the Lodestar and two remaining T-6Gs were flown to Dilolo and Kisenge respectively, from where the latter flew to a flying club strip at Kolwezi each day to mount air strikes. By the 15th full UN control was established and Tshombe's military commander swore an oath of allegiance to the Congo. Four J29Bs left for Sweden in April, the remainder being destroyed at Kamina. UN forces remained in the Congo, gradually withdrawing by 30 June 1964.

AIRCRAFT MARKINGS

FAK
Magister Bare metal overall, orange nose, tailband and wing tanks, black serial on forward fuselage: 93.
Do 28A White over, bare metal under, black cheat line, black serial on fin: KA3018, KA3020.
T-6 Dark green/dark brown over, medium blue under, white serial on rear fuselage: KA-33.
Alouette II Olive drab overall, white serial: KAT 53.

ONUC
Canberra B(I).58 Bare metal overall, black serial on fin, large black 'ONU' on rear fuselage: IF 961 (5 Sqn. IAF).
Sabre Mk. 4 Bare metal overall, black serial on fin, large black 'ONU' on forward fuselage: 13695 (4 Aerobrigata AMI).
Saab J29B Bare metal overall, small black serial on rear fuselage, large white code outlined in black on fin, 'UN' in black on white box on fuselage and upper wings: 29475/J (F22 SAF).
Saab S29C Blue-grey/olive with yellow streaks over, bare metal under, markings as J29B: 29944/A (F22 SAF).

4.2. The Congo, 1964–1967

With the UN withdrawal from the Congo, left-wing rebels under the leadership of Pierre Mulele became active in Kivu and Orientale provinces. In an apparent volte-face, Mobutu called Tshombe from exile on 10 July 1964 to act as Prime Minister and lead the operation against the rebels. He immediately recruited white mercenaries, who, under the command of 'Mike' Hoare, formed 5 Commando; in addition, he reached agreement with the US Government for the use of T-28B and B-26K aircraft detached from 602 Fighter Squadron (FS), 1 Air Commando Wing (ACW), at Hurlburt Field, with Cuban exile pilots. Established on 27 April 1962 to support covert operations, particularly in South-East Asia, this unit specialized in the use of counter-insurgency (coin) aircraft. Its motto was 'Any time, any place' and its aircraft were soon operating from Leopoldville. Tshombe also recruited pilots from his Katanga days to fly five Italian-supplied T-6Gs equipped with machine guns and rocket rails.

On 5 August Stanleyville was captured by Simbas (Lions) of the Mulele movement, and an independent State of Kivu and Orientale was proclaimed, with Chinese backing. Over 1,500 white hostages were taken, including, allegedly, a four-man CIA team. On the 13th, four C-130Es of 776 Troop Carrier Squadron (TCS) from Pope AFB carrying three Bell 47 helicopters flew into Leopoldville. By now the Belgian Air Force (FAB) was again operating in the Congo with eight C-47s based at Kamina, where 5 Cdo. was in training. The first 5 Cdo. attack was on Albertville on 30 August after soldiers of 51 Cdo. had been flown to Kamipini by FAB C-47. From there they had approached the city on water along Lake Tanganyika. No. 56 Cdo. moved north through Kongolo in October and captured Kindu on 5 November after a road block and the ferry landing stage had been attacked by T-28s based at Luluabourg.

As the commandos advanced they found dead or wounded hostages, and there was now major concern for the safety of the whites at Stanleyville. Tshombe sought help from the US and Belgium, and it was decided to launch a parachute assault, with 5 Cdo. attacking from the south the east and blocking withdrawal routes. A total of 543 Belgian paracommandos were flown in USAF C-130E transports to Ascension, from where, on 23 November, they flew to Kamina. Meanwhile 56 Cdo. was having difficulty holding a bridge over the Elela river and again advance was only possible after T-6 and T-28 strafing. The T-6s, based at Leopoldville, were also in action around Boende. The bulk of 5 Cdo. set out from Bukavu on the 23rd, making for Stanleyville via Yumbi, while other units approached from Mambasa. At 0600hrs on the 24th, 320 Belgian paras dropped on the golf course at Stanleyville in Operation 'Dragon Rouge'. Despite the speed of the attack, sadly 29 hostages were murdered by the Simbas and three paratroops killed. Over the next week 2,000 Europeans were evacuated from the area, including 143 by a Beverley of 84 Sqn. RAF and an Argosy of 105. Sqn. A Royal Army Medical Corps (RAMC) unit also flew in to provide medical aid.

The remaining paras turned their attention to Paulis, where over 200 hostages were being held. In Operation 'Dragon Noir' on the 26th they dropped from five USAF C-130Es to complete a successful operation. As the T-28s moved up to Stanleyville, a UN-chartered DC-4, OO-DEP of the Belgian International Air Service, crashed on take off on the 29th. The Soviet Union increased its supplies of arms to the rebels, and these were now coming in through Congo-Brazzaville in Algerian-marked An-12s and Ghanaian Il-18 transports.

Egyptian Air Force transports also kept open the main supply route from Cairo to Juba in Sudan via Khartoum; the arms were paid for in gold from the Moto mines. On 12 February 1965 DC-4 HP-925/CF-TFM was detained at Schipol, Amsterdam, with arms en route from the UK to the Congo. USAF C-130E Hercules remained in the Orientale region in support of 5 Cdo. as it attempted to clear up the province. Operating from Stanleyville, Bunia and Paulis, they were engaged in bringing up arms and evacuating the ever-increasing flow of rescued hostages: in December another 100 were released when Wamba was taken. In February the rebels were visited by the Latin American revolutionary Che Guevara, but his presence and that of some Cuban advisers did little to strengthen their resolve. No. 5 Cdo. with its excellent T-28 and B-26 air support was now making fast progress, and in March Mahagi, Aba and Watsa fell. The last pocket of resistance was at Fizi and Baraka on the

northern shore of Lake Tanganyika. Twelve T-28s and several helicopters moved into Albertville, from where the final attack would be launched.

The assault began on 27 September, but even with constant air cover and support the towns were not finally in Government hands until 5 November, by which time the Simba revolt was over. The same day Tshombe, having served his purpose, was exiled to Spain by Kasavubu, who was in turn deposed on 25 November by Mobutu. Hoare was also asked to leave the Congo, although remnants of 5 Cdo. under John Peters, the French 6 Cdo. under Bob Denard and 10 Cdo. under Jean Schramme remained. On 23 July 1966 Katangese gendarmes being disarmed at Stanleyville revolted. While the mercenaries sat on the fence, the ANC massacred large numbers.

The mercenaries were also demobilized but Schramme established himself at Yumbi. With a large force of Kansimbas from north Katanga, and in concert with other planters, he effectively developed a state within a state using captured Simbas as forced labour. When Mobutu demanded that he disarm and disband 10 Cdo., recalling the massacre at Stanleyville, he refused. On 23 June 1967 he received arms in a DC-4 together with reinforcements, and on 5 July occupied by force Stanleyville and Kindu. The latter town was quickly lost, and the USAF despatched three C-130s to help Mobutu get ANC troops into Stanleyville, which fell on the 12th. Meanwhile 30 men of Denard's 6 Cdo. were captured in Leopoldville and executed. A number of wounded mercenaries were flown in stolen DC-3 9Q-CUL to Rhodesia, from where Schramme hoped that Denard would open a second front in Katanga.

Schramme now turned his attention to Bukavu, which he invested on 9 August with 1,500 men. Unfortunately there was no airstrip in the town, and in one attempt to bring up arms from the south, Aztec 9Q-CQJ crashed on the lake. Arms were parachuted from a DC-3 and DC-4. The 10 Cdo. positions were subject to attack by FAZ T-28s and B-26s, but it was reported that the

In addition to the use of T-28s and B-26s of the USAF's 602nd Fighter Squadron, the Congolese bought five T-6Gs from Italy. Piloted by mercenaries, they were formed into 21 Sqn. and operated from Leopoldville in support of Mike Hoare's 5 Commando. Here 9T-P46 is seen flying 'clean' near Ndolo, late 1964. (J. Hedges via D. Becker)

Congolese pilots were unreliable and had to be replaced by a number employed through WIGMO, an alleged but previously unrecorded CIA proprietary. A fierce assault began on 28 October, possibly aided by Israeli advisers, and on 1 November 6 Cdo. moved into Katanga from Angola, taking Dilolo, Kisenge and Kasagi on the 2nd. By 4 November the fight was over as both mercenary units were subjected to continuous air attack. No. 10 Cdo. retreated into Ruanda, while 6 Cdo. withdrew to Angola. On 23 April 1968 two Red Cross-chartered DC-6s repatriated 115 white mercenaries to Italy, France, Switzerland and Belgium. Later in the year the Katangese of 10 Cdo. in Ruanda were promised repatriation and some 600 returned to the Congo. They were never heard of again.

Tshombe was not to live in freedom for long after his expulsion. On a flight from Ibiza to Majorca on 30 June 1967 his aircraft was hijacked by his own bodyguard, François Bodenan, who was believed to be in the pay of the CIA. Certainly Tshombe is likely to have had enough money is Swiss banks to have financed further revolution. The aircraft was flown on to Algiers, where Tshombe was imprisoned. Despite several reported mercenary attempts to release him, his death was announced on 30 June 1969.

AIRCRAFT MARKINGS

FAC
National markings comprised an adapted US 'star and bar' with yellow star and red bar on rear fuselage. Blue fin panel with red/yellow diagonal.
T-6 Aluminium overall, red wing tips, large black serial below cockpit: 9T-P46 (21 Sqn.).
T-28B Bare metal overall, black serial across star and bar: FG-289 (5146289).
B-26K Dark emerald green over, light grey under, grey serial on fin.

4.3. Zaïre, 1977–1978

From 10 March 1977 Zaïre (as the Congo had been renamed in 1972) was invaded by Lunda rebels of the Front de Liberation Nationale Congolaise (FLNC) in Shaba (Katanga) province. The invaders, many of whom had been members of the Katangese gendarmerie, received support from the Angolan Movimento Popular de Libertacao de Angol (MPLA) and included some Cubans. The towns of Mutshatsha, Kapanga, Sandoa and Kasagi were soon taken, and President Mobutu declared a state of emergency and appealed for help. In Operation 'Verveine' the French Air Force made available thirteen Transall C-160 transports of 61 Escadre de Transporte (ET) for the movement of 1,500 Moroccan troops to Kolwezi and Lubumbashi.

The operation began on 10 April, the US also providing financial and military aid. The rebel positions at Dilolo, Kasagi, Sandao and Kisenge were repeatedly attacked by Zaïrean Air Forze (FAZ) Mirage 5Ms based at Kamina and the Kolwezi-based MB.326GBs. Few attacks were accurate: on 22 March Angola complained of attacks on three villages, while on 13 April Zambia accused Zaïre of bombing two villages and a hospital. From the 19th the Congolese Army, strengthened by Moroccan troops, began to advance on rebel-held towns, while Egypt offered pilots to supplement those of the FAZ. By the end of April Mutshatsha had been retaken, followed by Kasagi on 12 May after heavy Mirage strikes. As the remaining eastern towns fell, the Moroccans announced the conclusion of their task on 22 May, and by the 26th the war was over.

The following year, 1978, the FLNC struck again from Angola, occupying Mutshatsha on 11 May. By the 13th they had taken Kolwezi after the Congolese Army had offered little resistance, and were holding over 2,000 Europeans hostage, including 400 French nationals. As the FLNC fought around the airfield at Kolwezi, some six MB.326s, several light aircraft, a Puma, an Alouette and a C-47 were damaged or destroyed on the ground. There was now international concern for the fate of the hostages and a recognition that if the slow processes of the UN were used to discuss intervention, many lives would be lost. On 16 May the Zaïrean 311st Parachute Regiment dropped on Kolwezi from C-130Hs of 19 Wing FAZ. The drop was a complete failure and as the troops landed they were annihilated, taking 60 per cent casualties. They did manage to take Kolwezi airfield, however.

The French ambassador requested French support, and at 0430hrs on the 17th, after guarantees of US backing, the 2ème Régiment Étrangère Parachutiste (2 REP) was brought to the alert at Calvi, Corsica. 61 ET was alerted at Orleans, and five DC-8s of UTA were requisitioned to move the paras to Kinshasa, where the first three companies arrived from 1300hrs on the 18th. They quickly transferred to four FAZ C-130Hs and a Transall, and at 1515hrs, in Operation 'Bonite-Léopard', the first of 400 paras dropped just to the north of the old town. After regrouping, the troops moved to predetermined objectives, all of which were reached by nightfall despite heavy fighting. Although the rebels were taken by surprise, they were to kill over 130 hostages before fighting ceased. The second echelon of 2 REP arrived over Kolwezi at 1755hrs, but the commander on the ground, rather than risk a night drop, directed the aircraft on to

TABLE OF UNITS: ZAÏRE, 1977–1978

Unit	Aircraft	Base	Role	Dates
FAZ				
21 Wing	Mirage 5M/DM	Kamina	Ground attack	
21 Wing	MB.326GB	Kinshasa, Kamina	Ground attack	
21 Wing	T-6G, T-28B, F.337 Milirole	Kamina	Ground attack, coin	
22 Wing	Caribou, Buffalo	Kinshasa	Transport	
19 Wing	C-130H	Kinshasa	Transport	Permanently based
11 Wing	C-46, C-47, C-54, DC-6	Kinshasa	Transport	
122 ES	Alouette III, Bell 47G	Kamina, Kinshasa, Kolwezi	SAR, liaison	
21 Wing	Puma	Kamina, Kinshasa	Transport	
AA				
61 ET	Transall C.160	Orléans, Kinshasa	Transport	10/04/77 to 30/05/77 19/05/78 to 07/06/78
UTA	DC-8	Calvi, Kinshasa	Transport	18/06/78 to 20/05/78
FAB				
20 Sqn.	C-130H	Melsbroek, Kamina	Transport	18/05/78 to 18/06/78
RAF				
LTW	Hercules C.1	Lyneham, Lusaka	Medical supply	18/05/78 to 30/05/78
10 Sqn.	VC-10 C.1	Brize Norton, Lusaka	Medical team and supply	
AMI				
50 Gr.	C-130H	Pisa, Lusaka	Medical and food supply	18/05/78 to 30/05/78
USAF				
437 MAW	C-141A	Charleston AFB		
438 MAW	C-141A	McGuire AFB	Transport	18/05/78 to 30/06/78
436 MAW	C-5A	Dover AFB		

Lubumbashi. They returned late the following afternoon.

Through the 20th the paras cleared the town of rebels, although to the north they encountered a strong counterattack by reinforcements. Air support was called for, and a Mirage 5, directed by an Alouette III, arrived on the scene but its guns apparently jammed. On 21 May their vehicles arrived and they made for Kapata to the south-west and Luilu to the north, where more rebels were rounded up. In the meantime a strong force of Belgian paras arrived at Kamina from Belgium in C-130Hs of 20 Sqn., while three RAF Hercules and a VC-10 of 10 Sqn. transported a medical team and supplies to Lusaka and an Italian Air Force (AMI) C-130H brought food supplies. The USAF committed 18 C-141As and C-5As to the task of bringing in French and Belgian equipment and shifting fuel and supplies from Kinshasa to the south.

By 25 May all the FLNC forces had been killed or captured or had retreated to Angola, having suffered many hundred dead. Over 2,000 hostages were released. The French withdrew to Lubumbashi and on 5 June began returning to Corsica as a 5,000-strong contingent of troops from African countries was brought in on USAF C-141A transports to help the Congolese Army maintain

peace; 2 REP losses were five dead and 20 wounded. The Belgians had arrived at Kolwezi by the 20th, but were restrained from taking part in fighting for political reasons; they delayed their return until 17 June. Determined action by Western powers, independent of the UN, no doubt prevented the carnage of the 1960s in the Congo.

AIRCRAFT MARKINGS

FAZ
Mirage 5M *Green/tan over, medium grey under, black serial on rear fuselage: M413 (21 Wing).*
MB.326GB *Green/tan over, pale grey under, white serial on rear fuselage: FG-463 (21 Wing).*
C-130H *Tan/mid-green/dark green over, pale grey under, white serial on fin: 9T-TCA (19 Wing).*

AA
Transall C-160 *Dark green/dark sea grey over, medium grey under, small yellow serial on fin, yellow code on rear fuselage: F4/61-MD (61ET).*

FAB
C-130H *Dark green/tan over, pale grey under, black serial on fin: CH-10 (20 Sqn.).*

4.4. Angola, 1961–1975

Angola was a Portuguese colony from 1655, and from 1955 an overseas province. Nationalist movements formed from 1956 but were denied external bases from which to operate until Britain and France gave independence to their colonies from the late 1950s. The Marxist Movimento Popular de Libertação de Angola (MPLA) was founded by Agostinho Neto in Luanda in 1956, while the more conservative União das Populações de Angola (UPA) was formed in 1958 by Holden Roberto. With the first signs of unrest in 1959, the Força Aérea Portuguesa (FAP) moved several C-47s and PV-2 Harpoons to Luanda.

The first tangible action against the Portuguese was on 4 February 1961 when a small group attacked the prison at São João to release political prisoners; attacks on the police station at Luanda and further raids on prisons followed. This initial action was dealt with harshly by the Portuguese. A revolt of a much larger scale began on 15 March 1961 when UPA groups occupied towns north of Luanda, starting with Quitexe, where 21 Europeans and several hundred Africans were massacred. Soon 48 towns and the city of Carmona were under siege. The authorities responded with difficulty since there were only three infantry companies in Angola at the time and a handful of utility aircraft. Direcção dos Transportes Aéreos (DTA) DC-3s and Beech 18s supplemented the FAP transports, and some were converted for use as light bombers. Light civil aircraft were formed into Formações Aéreas Voluntárias (FAV) 201 at Luanda to support the townships. Comprising Piper Cubs, Austers and Voyagers, the unit flew many supply sorties over the ensuing months and also operated in the light attack role, firing hand-held guns through the open cockpit windows at UPA rebels.

On 1 May two Portuguese Army battalions arrived at Luanda, and in June F-84G fighters from Esquadra 21 were transferred from Portugal to form Esq. 93; the Harpoons, which were fitted as bombers, formed Esq. 91. The FAP now indiscriminately attacked African groups in the Dembos Mountains with fragmentation bombs and napalm. The first paratroop operation was on 11 August, when a company was dropped at Quipedro, with a larger operation in the Serra de Coanda on the 25th. Both achieved limited objectives. By October all towns were relieved, but the UPA continued to operate in the area, setting ambushes and attacking isolated farms.

The FAP now expanded, purchasing its first batch of Noratlas transports and Do 27s together with Alouette II helicopters for use in African territories, while the transport fleet was further strengthened by the delivery of a number of DC-6As and -6Bs. On 1 June 1962 Base Aérea (BA) 9 was activated at Luanda as the headquarters of the FAP 2nd Air Region, with two smaller bases, Aérodromos-Base (AB) 3 at Negage and AB 4 at Henriques de Carvalho. Grupo Operacional (GO) 901 was formed to control the growing air force, which now included Esq. 92 with the Noratlas and Esq. 94 with the Alouette II.

During the year the UPA became the Frente Naçional de Libertação de Angola (FNLA), with support from the US through the Congo and from the Chinese. The Kennedy administration wanted to ensure that as Angola inevitably achieved independence, the dominant force was pro-Western rather than the Soviet-backed MPLA now operating from Cabinda. Both the MPLA and FNLA confined their activities mainly to the Dembos Mountains between 1963 and 1966, and

the FAP countered with air strikes and paradrops on suspected positions.

The Noratlases operated form BA 9, AB 3 and Maquela do Zombo, dropping men of 21 Battalion Regimento de Caçadores Paraquedistas (RCP) on trouble spots and supplying outlying garrisons. Many villagers fled the area and were captured or killed as assumed collaborators. Much of the action was in the Ambriz, Damba and Bembe areas. During the first three years of operations the FAP lost five F-84Gs, all in accidents.

Despite the initial US position maintaining an embargo of arms to support Portuguese action in Africa, seven B-26 light bombers were supplied to the FAP in 1965. Sold by Aero Associates of Tucson, they were delivered by an ex-RAF pilot, John R. Hawke. On one occasion he inadvertently flew low in the vicinity of the White House and after landing at Washington was detained, but he was released after FBI intervention. He was arrested in September 1965 in Miami and tried for illegally exporting arms, but he was acquitted in 1966. The MPLA was also acquiring more arms from Soviet sources, and several hundred members went to Eastern Europe for training. The arms were shipped to Dar-es-Salaam and transported to Zambia, where the MPLA had operational bases. On 18 March 1966 it carried

out its first attacks against the Portuguese in the east in Moxico. During the year a third rebel force emerged in the form of the FNLA breakaway movement União Naçional para a Independência Total de Angola (UNITA), headed by Jonas Savimbi. UNITA drew its strength from tribes in the south, although its centre of operations was the eastern section of the Benguela railway. Disruption of this important rail link angered both the Congolese and Zambians, who relied on it for transporting copper to the coast. The rebels were now as active against each other as against the Portuguese.

With the war extended to the east, the Portuguese relied increasingly on helicopters for transport, setting up important bases at Gago Coutinho and Cuito Cuanavale. They also introduced horse cavalry, which was able to move more quickly and safely away from frequently mined roads. In April 1968 a large offensive was mounted in Zona Zil. As operations in Moxico increased, the MPLA claimed it first aircraft shot down – a Do 27 – on 9 June 1967, and several Alouettes were lost the following year as the MPLA began operating in Luanda. The FAP used its Alouettes, now including many of the more capacious IIIs, to place troops from garrisons wherever trouble was reported, and used the B-26s, T-6s and Do 27s to strike at identified targets; in September 1968 it attacked an MPLA hospital near Miué, inflicting many causalties. The shorter-range F-84Gs were operated form BA 9 in the northern areas. The Portuguese were now receiving support from white southern African countries, South African nationals, for example, allegedly guarding the Cassinga iron mines, supplied by helicopter from Namibia, and Rhodesia supplying helicopter pilots. The growing Alouette force was supplemented from 1969 by several Pumas.

Tactics now extended to the use of herbicides to deny crops to the rebels and the burning of large tracts of land along roads to make ambush difficult and the spotting of rebel units easy. Despite an extensive 'hearts and minds' policy and the movement of over one million Angolans to strategic or 'peace' villages, the rebel movements, especially the MPLA, were gaining ground and popular support. On 10 June 1970 the Portuguese launched Operation 'Zaga' to eliminate the MPLA from Moxico, especially around Miué. This operation and a second in July, 'Zumbo' in Bié, were not successful. The next major offensive was Operation 'Attila' in the Moxico region in February 1972, which again met with only limited success.

The Government forces in Angola, mainly conscripts, were becoming increasingly dejected, and as morale fell so did the will to take the fight to the enemy. In 1972, to boost the F-84G esquadra, a number of Fiat G.91R-4 ground-attack fighters were transferred to BA 9 from Esq. 707 in Mozambique, and although these were used to some effect the Portuguese economy could no longer cope with the strain of fighting in three territories so far from home. The FAP sustained more losses from accidents than action, but in 1972 two Alouettes were reported shot down, one by Congo-Brazzaville AAA. The remaining F-84Gs were supplemented in the summer of 1973 by six B-26s attached to Esq. 91 and finally released from duties in Portugal.

With little warning, the Armed Forces Movement (MFA), largely composed of left-wing offi-

With the first signs of nationalist unrest in Angola in 1959, the Portuguese transferred several C-47s and PV-2 Harpoons to Luanda. The Harpoons were fitted for bombing, and from May 1961 formed Esq. 91; much later, they were supplementcd by several B-26s. Illustrated is 4629, seen at Luanda in 1972. The aircraft was one of 24 supplied by the United States. (M. Robson)

Throughout its ex-colonies Portugal operated the ubiquitous C-47 for many years. About sixty were bought from a variety of sources, and 6153 was one of the last in use. The military transports were supported in Angola by DC-3s of DTA for routine supplies work and early paratroop operations. From 1961 the Noratlas was also introduced in the theatre.

TABLE OF UNITS: ANGOLA, 1961–1975

Unit	Aircraft	Base	Role	Dates
FAP (Grupo Operaçional 901)				
–	T-6	Luanda	Ground attack	00/00/59 to 11/11/75
–	C-47, Beech 18	Luanda	Transport	00/00/59 to 11/11/75
Esq. 91	PV-2, B-26B/C	Luanda, BA9	Light bombing	00/00/60 to 11/11/75
Esq. 93	F-84G	BA9	Ground attack	00/06/61 to 00/00/73
Esq. 93	G.91R-4	BA9	Ground attack	00/00/73 to 00/10/75
Esq. 92	C-54, Noratlas	BA9, Maguela, AB4	Transport	00/07/61 to 11/11/75
Esq. 94	{ Alouette II/III	Various	Transport, liaison	00/06/61 to 00/10/75
	{ Puma	BA9, Gago, Cuito	Transport	00/00/69 to 10/10/75
–	Auster D.5, Do 27A/Q	BA9, AB3, AB4	Liaison, light transport, coin	00/00/61 to 00/10/75
Gr. Trans.	DC-6A/B, Boeing 707	AB1 (Lisbon)	Transport	Permanently based
Civilian				
DTA	DC-3, Beech 18	Luanda	Transport, light bombing	00/04/61 to 00/09/61
FAV 201	Auster D.4, Cub, Super Cruiser, Voyager	Luanda	Liaison, light transport	00/04/61 to 00/00/62

cers, overturned Prime Minister Caetano in Lisbon on 25 April 1974 and replaced him with General Spinola. On 1 July Angola was offered independence. The nationalist movements began what was to become a civil war, and the major powers began a race to arm their protégés. The Portuguese seemed powerless to prevent the flow of arms, and the South Africans moved up to Ruacana to protect the important hydro-electric works.

As independence was set for 11 November 1975 the Europeans began an exodus, 300,000 leaving Luanda by the end of October. Many flew out on board Transportes Aéreos Portugueses (TAP) Boeing 707s, while 5,700 left in VC-10 C.1s of 10 Sqn. RAF. Portuguese troops left in the DC-6s and 707s of BA 1, and the more modern equipment was flown or airlifted to Portugal, though much was left behind. As independence dawned, Angola was already locked in a tripartite civil war.

AIRCRAFT MARKINGS

FAP
Most aircraft were finished in bare metal with a white fuselage decking. The exceptions were the F-84Gs and Fiat G.91R-4s, which were bare metal overall and light grey overall respectively. Black serials were carried on the fin and in some cases under the wings. Helicopters were finished olive drab overall.
PV-2 *4605, 4610, 4616 (Esq. 91).*
F-84G *Last three number of serial repeated large on forward fuselage, orange nose and wing tanks: 5141, 5164, 5195 (Esq. 93).*
G.91R *5440 (Esq. 93).*
B-26B *7104, 7105 (Esq. 91).*
Do 27A *3352, 3355.*
Do 27Q *3420, 3480 (BA 9).*
Noratlas *6402, 6411 (Esq. 92).*
C-47 *6166 (BA 9).*
Beech 18 *2520 (BA 9).*

4.5. Angola, 1975 to date

As independence drew near for Angola, the three nationalist movements prepared to fight for supremacy in government. During 1969 the MPLA leader Neto had agreed with the Soviet Union that base facilities would be granted in the event of MPLA victory; in return, arms were guaranteed. The FNLA eventually drew its support from the US via Zaïre, whereas UNITA was supported by South Africa, with bases in Zambia and some arms from China. From early 1975 Portuguese rule was token, and the nationalists vied for territorial control with open arms deliveries. Soviet arms flowed into Maya Maya AB, Brazzaville, where they were assembled by Cubans and shipped into Luanda. By March there were 250 Cubans in Angola and in July, with the help of Cuban advisers and Portuguese pilots flying reconnaissance sorties in Transportes Aéreos de Angola (TAAG) F.27s, MPLA forces pushed the FNLA from the capital.

The United States had by now decided covertly to back FNLA through the CIA, and it organized the first shipment of arms late in July. The arms, generally second-hand and untraceable, were taken from CIA warehouses at San Antonio, Texas, and flown in USAF C-130 transports to Charleston AFB in South Carolina. From here they were flown in C-141s of 437 Military Airlift Wing (MAW) to Kinshasa via Robertsfield, Monrovia. From Kinshasa the arms were broken down and sent into northern Angola by truck or flown into Ambriz by a miscellany of requistioned aircraft. For each C-141 flight the USAF billed the CIA $80,000. The CIA set up an Angola Task Force and committed $32m to the FNLA through Mobutu in Zaïre. It was reported that some arms were also flown to Negage from US bases in Germany on board C-54s or C-118s.

Limited support was also given to UNITA at Silva Porto, where the French Service de Documentation Extérieure et Contre-Espionage (SDECE) also maintained a presence. South Africa entered the picture initially by sending troops to protect the Cassinga iron mines and the shared hydro-electric works at Calueque and Ruacana on the Cunene river. On 11 September the 4th and 7th Commando Battalions of the Zaïrean Army were committed to FNLA support and flown to Ambriz in FAZ C-130s. On the 17th they supported the FNLA in retaking Caxito, and on the 24th a Fiat G.91 was claimed as shot down in the area.

By now armoured vehicles and tanks were being shipped into Pointe Noire, together with Cuban troops in ever-increasing numbers: by the end of September there were at least 1,500 Cubans in Angola. Meanwhile the Americans were struggling to get their arms from Kinshasa. Eventually, a small fleet of commandeered aircraft was operating into Negage and Ambriz. These included an Aztec, a Cessna 172, a Cessna 180, a Turbo Commander, an Alouette III, a Mooney, two F.27s and a Cessna 310. The last, which allegedly belonged to President Amin of Uganda and was stolen at Carmona, was used for leaflet dropping over Luanda. An F.27 and a Viscount were leased from Air Congo and Pearl Air respectively, and the FAZ also supported the deliveries with DC-4 and C-130 sorties. South African involvement with UNITA began on 21 September when a small group of advisers flew into Savimbi's headquarters at Silva Porto to set up a training camp. Based there was a Learjet loaned to UNITA from the British Lonrho company for Savimbi's personal use, while HS 125 G-BAZA of Trader Airways, a Lonrho subsidiary, was also a regular visitor, bringing arms from Zambia.

On 7 October fourteen South Africans with an FNLA column were involved in a skirmish with Cuban/MPLA troops at Norton de Matos. The MPLA unit included five T-34 tanks and it was supported by light spotter aircraft. Two days later South Africa decided to take a more active part in the civil war, and on 14 October Force Zulu crossed into Angola from Rundu. It comprised two battalions, one of Bushmen and one FNLA loyal to Daniel Chipenda who had broken from the MPLA earlier in the year and was operating in the south. Around this time 22 armoured cars were airlifted to Silva Porto in South African Air Force (SAAF) C-130s to support what was to become Force Foxbat. Zulu sped north through Pereira d'Eca (14th), Rocadas, where it was strengthened by armoured cars and 81mm mortars (20th), Joao de Almeida (22nd), Sa da Bandeira (24th) and Moçâmedes (27th). At each place the force captured the airfield first then cleared the town. At Moçâmedes a Portuguese corvette and a Noratlas belonging to the Frente de Libertação de Moçambique (Frelimo) evacuated MPLA troops as the South Africans attacked.

Cubans were now flooding directly into Angola, and it was clearly only a matter of time before Zulu would confront serious resistance. The South African columns were air-supplied, and on at least one occasion two unmarked SAAF C-130s had picked up arms from a C-141 flight at Kinshasa and flown them direct to Silva Porto. On 2 November both columns reached the outskirts of Catenque, where they were ambushed; after heavy fighting they moved to Benguela, which was taken on the 5th. Meanwhile an attempted invasion of the MPLA-controlled Cabinda enclave by Zaïrean troops and the Frente de Libertaçao de Enclave Cabinda (FLEC) on the 2nd had failed. Lobito was taken on 7 November, and the column now moved north to achieve maximum territorial gain by independence.

The decision was then taken, with US backing, that the South Africans would remain in Angola post-independence. On the 12th the columns had neared the outskirts of Novo Redondo when they came under sustained 122mm rocket fire, and only after a battery of 25pdr guns was flown in to Benguela and brought up was the town taken. The next major battle was at Santa Comba between 9 and 12 December, where an estimated 200 Cubans were killed. A fresh South African force, Orange, now occupied Quibala as a fourth group, X-Ray, supported an FNLA attack on Luso on the Benguela railway. They were aided by American pilots flying Do 27 aircraft of the FAZ. During the month the CIA had bought four Alouette IIs from France, and these were delivered by C-141 from Istres to Kinshasa, although there were no pilots to fly them nor ground crew to maintain them. On the MPLA/Cuban side, twelve MiG-21s and ten MIG-17s had been assembled at Brazzaville from October and flown to Luanda and Henriques de Carvalho, where large fuel stocks were now held.

As far as is known, no aircraft were used offensively in the fighting by either side, although the SAAF did lose a Cessna 185 on 25 October and a Puma to gunfire north-west of Cela on 21 December. The CIA had attempted to purchase two AC-47 gunships, at $200,000 each, which it was convinced would have enabled a comprehensive FNLA/UNITA victory. In putting most of its support behind the FNLA, the US had backed the wrong movement and in January 1976, with Negage airfield overrun, the Americans decided to pull out, leaving the South Africans in the lurch. On 29 January they began to withdraw, although CIA arms supplies to UNITA continued for several weeks through Gago Coutinho. The CIA also funded the recruitment of British mercenaries, who fought for the FNLA in the north; fortunately, their appalling record is outside the scope of this book. The FNLA effectively lost its position in Angola with the fall of São Salvador on 15 February.

The first use of Cuban air power was on 25 January 1976 at Novo Redondo, two days after the Angolan Air Force (FAPA) was formed with several Noratlases and C-47s, four G.91s, assorted helicopters and the first batch of MiG-17s and -21s. Huambo fell on 9 February, followed by Benguela, and by the 23rd SAAF C-130s were evacuating the last Portuguese nationals from Pereira d'Eca. On 13 March several MiG-21s attacked the airfield at Gago while an F.27 leased from Air Congo was unloading food supplies from Rhodesia. The aircraft was destroyed on the ground and the MiGs escaped, despite two SA-7 rounds being fired (both of which failed to operate). Fifty of these widely used missiles were delivered by Israel against the same number of traceable Redeye SAMs donated by the US. The CIA had to pay $600,000 compensation to Mobutu for the loss of the F.27. By 27 March the South Africans had left Angola and on the 31st were censured by the UN Security Council for their role. With at least 15,000 Cubans and up to 5,000 Nigerians supporting the MPLA, Angola was admitted to the UN in December 1976.

UNITA was now the only effective resistance to the MPLA, with its forces operating in the central and southern areas, and from July 1976 the MPLA launched a succession of operations designed to eliminate UNITA, although with limited success. Helicopter gunships were used in these actions, and several were claimed as shot down. In March 1977 Government forces launched a largely unsuccessful offensive around Huambo (Nova Lisboa). UNITA was operating on a guerrilla basis, and in July and November claimed the destruction of An-26 transports, on the latter occasion in an attack on Silva Porto airfield. Angola was rapidly becoming a base for Soviet adventures in other parts of Africa, through its Cuban puppet, and in December 1977 two Tu-95 'Bears' were operating out of Luanda.

In October two Boeing 707s had been purchased by TAAG from British Caledonian and flown by British and American crews. They were used to supplement the Cuban air bridge maintained by Cubana Britannias. The Cubans were also helping the FAPA to expand, and by 1978, in addition to types already mentioned, a number of Mi-4s and Mi-8s were being operated, some as gunships.

From May 1978 the South African Government decided to pursue South-West Africa People's Organization (SWAPO) guerrillas in Angola, where they were based. No doubt some of these actions, described separately, were co-ordinated with UNITA forces. Certainly UNITA needed support in contending with the increased use of air power deployed by the FAPA: in March 1978, for example, there were reports of MiGs using napalm against FNLA remnants in the north. By November 1980 FAPA strength consisted of eleven MiG-21MFs, seven MiG-17Fs, two Fiat G.91R-4s, ten Mi-8s, thirteen Alouette IIIs and three MiG-15UTIs; in addition, two F.27s, a C-130E, seven An-12s, ten An-22s, ten An-2s, three C-47s, six Islanders and four Nord 262s were operated by TAAG.

TABLE OF UNITS: ANGOLA, 1975 TO DATE

Unit	Aircraft	Base	Role	Nos./dates
FAPA, 1976				
?	MiG-21MF	Luanda, Henriques de Carvalho	Ground attack, air defence	12
?	MiG-17F	Luanda	Ground attack	10
?	G.91R-4	Luanda	Ground attack	4
?	F.27, C-47, An-26, An-2, Noratlas	Luanda	Transport	23
?	Alouette II/III	Various	Transport, liaison	13
FAPA, 1986				
?	MiG-23		Ground attack	23
?	Su-22	Various	Ground attack	24
?	MiG-21MF		Ground attack, air defence	70
?	An-26	Luanda	Transport	30
?	An-12	Luanda	Transport	12
?	Islander	Luanda, various	Light transport	16
?	Mi-25		Gunship	25
?	Mi-17		Gunship, transport	17
?	Alouette III	Various	Transport, liaison	30
?	Mi-8		Gunship, transport	52
?	PC-7	Luanda	Armed trainer	25
USAF				
437 MAW	C-141A	Charleston AFB, Kinshasa	Strategic transport	29/07/75 to 29/01/76
SAAF				
28 Sqn.	C-130B	Waterkloof	Transport	
FAZ				
19 Wing	C-130H	Kinshasa	Transport	

Note: FAPA fighters were based at Luanda, Henriques de Carvalho, Negage and Menongue, and helicopters were stationed at most bases, including Gago Coutinho and Cuito Cuanavale.

To the present, UNITA operates against the much stronger Força Arma Populaire de Liberaçione Angola (FAPLA), with covert South African and US support. From time to time FAPLA launches major offensives, such as that around Cangamba in September 1982 when SAAF fighters attacked FAPLA columns. A year later the town was besieged by UNITA forces, and despite being subjected to napalm and phosphorous bomb attacks the guerrillas took Cangamba, again after SAAF strikes. UNITA also began claiming success in destroying FAPA aircraft, both on the ground and with the SA7. On 8 June 1980 it claimed an An-26 shot down (in fact a TAAG Yak-40, D2-TYC, crashed on that date). During 1982 eleven helicopters were claimed, together with several fighters, and in the 1983 Cangamba battle five MiG-21s and four helicopters were claimed. On 10 November 1982 a Boeing 737 of TAAG was destroyed by an SA-7 while taking off from Lubango (Sa da Bandeira) Airport, with the loss of 126, including Cubans, and another 737 was claimed in February 1984 at Huambo. On 25 August 1983 an Angolan Government-chartered Trans America L-100-30 Hercules, N24ST, crashed near Dondo, shot down by UNITA forces while delivering food. In 1984 an ex-TAAG F.27 was flown to Omega base in South-West Africa, having allegedly been hidden from FAPLA since independence, but the aircraft suffered engine failure on landing. From 1 September there were major battles around the air-supplied FAPLA garrisons at Huambo and Menongue (Serpa Pinto). UNITA claimed eighteen aircraft destroyed in six weeks, including four MiG-21s, two MiG-23s and twelve helicopters.

Further to the north, a South African air-infiltrated sabotage team was caught attempting to destroy the Gulf Oil Malongo complex in Cabinda in May 1985. September saw yet another FAPLA offensive, this time focused on Mavinga. In fierce fighting SAAF Mirages and Impalas supported UNITA forces and destroyed several helicopters, including at least on Mi-25; two MiG-21s were also claimed as shot down. UNITA suffered serious losses again in October when bases at Jamba and Cazombo were attacked with tanks and armoured cars.

By the end of the year the FAPA inventory included 23 MiG-23s, ten Su-22s, 70 MiG-21s, 25 Mi-25s, 17 Mi-17s, 52 Mi-8s, 30 An-26s, twelve An-12s, eleven An-2s and 25 PC-7 trainers. On 7 December an An-26 was brought down near Mavinga with the loss of 21, including ten Russians. Although claimed by UNITA, FAPLA blamed the crash on SAAF fighters. FAPA may have lost another transport on 3 April 1986. It claimed an SAAF C-130 shot down and a second damaged on a UNITA supply fight near Andulo. The loss was denied by the SAAF, and it is believed that the aircraft was actually on contract to TAAG; certainly a C-130 with a damaged engine was reported at Dondo shortly afterwards. The main 1986 offensive against UNITA was a more mobile campaign in Moxico Province, launched from Menongue where the air base had received 23 MiG-21/MiG-23s and eight Su-22s. Additional helicopters were brought into Cuito Cuanavale. As FAPLA pursued UNITA groups, the latter prepared its own attack on Cuito Cuanavale, where 4,000 guerrillas struck on 9 August. The road to Menongue was cut and the airstrip destroyed with several helicopters on the 11th, and several fighters were shot down in the inevitable counterattack. By the end of August UNITA claimed to have destroyed 22 aircraft, including five MiG-23s, two MiG-21s and many helicopters.

At the end of the year UNITA was clearly in control of much of southern and central Angola, and there were no signs of early submission. In the north, however, the final FNLA unit surrendered at Uige on 14 March 1987. There have been further attempts to contain UNITA growth, with a large offensive around Mavinga in August 1987 and another operation from 9 November in the area of the source of the Chabinga and Hube rivers. Each involved a considerable build-up of arms and ammunition, flown into Luanda in a series of An-24 sorties, but each has resulted in heavy FAPLA losses. In the November offensive the Soviet Union based four Il-76s at Luanda to aid with the positioning of stores, and because of the difficulty for Government forces in using surface transport, one was fitted to carry fuel. UNITA remains in control of Mavinga, whose airport is essential for resupply from South Africa, Kamina (Zaïre) and Gabon.

During battles in the region, SAAF strike aircraft have ensured that UNITA is not denied air support, but more important are the G-5 155mm guns which provide long-range artillery support. This support was also provided during UNITA's January 1988 campaign, when Cuito Cuanavale was surrounded and the airfield put out of action by gunfire. FAPA MiG-21 and MiG-23 air strikes from Menongue did succeed in containing the siege, but these were limited, due both to the use of Stinger SAMs, which have claimed numerous aircraft since 1987, and to continuous heavy rain. At the time of writing South Africa appears to have withdrawn from Angola and the future for UNITA remains unclear.

AIRCRAFT MARKINGS

SAAF

C-130B *Olive drab/dark earth overall except underside of fuselage dark sea grey, no markings. (28 Sqn.).*

FAZ

C-130H *Tan/mid-green/dark green over, pale grey under, white serial on fin: 9T-TCA (19 Wing).*

FAPA

Few details available, but aircraft and helicopters believed to be finished tan/dark green over, pale blue under. Serials recorded include the following:
MiG-17F *721, 723.*
MiG-21F *C307.*
MiG-23 *C534.*
Su-22 *131.*
Mi-8 *H6–H12*
Mi-24 *H314, H318.*

4.6. Mozambique, 1962–1975

Mozambique was a Portuguese colony from 1498. Somewhat later than in the other Portuguese African colonies, a nationalist movement, the Frente de Libertação de Moçambique (FRELIMO), was formed in 1962, headed by Eduardo Mondlan. The Portuguese had moved a handful of T-6Gs and C-47s to Beira in late 1961 and conducted their first sorties in February 1962 in the extreme north, but the first significant FRELIMO forays were not made until 25 September 1964 in the Muende Plain, by which time there were 16,000 troops in the colony and airfields at Nampula and

Vila Cabral. The Força Aérea Portuguesa (FAP) inventory had been extended to include more T-6Gs, eight PV-2 Harpoons, a dozen Do 27s and some Alouette III helicopters.

FRELIMO depended for support on the Makonde tribe which straddled the border with Tanzania, in which country it was given bases, notably at Nachingwea. Opposition from other tribes confined FRELIMO operations to the north-east for several years, but by 1967, with a strength of about 7,000 men, the movement was operating in Niassa province. After Zambia achieved independence, it too provided bases for FRELIMO, and in 1968 the first attacks on the Cabora Bassa dam were made. The dam provided extensive irrigation, navigation and power and was guarded by 15,000 Portuguese troops. The nationalists were loth to cause complete disruption for fear of alienating the indigenous population, but supply routes were ambushed and barracks attacked with 122mm rockets fired at maximum range. FAP commitment in Mozambique was now higher than in Guinea or Angola.

Aircraft were generally attached to Bases Aéreas (BA), which were the main centres of operations, or Aérodromos-Bases (AB) rather than to Esquadras (Squadrons), although there were exceptions. Beira became BA 10 in 1961 and AB 5 was also formed there, moving to Nampula in August 1962 and Nacala in 1966. In the north-east, Vila Cabral was AB 6 until it moved to the rail junction at Nova Freixo in 1965. By 1966 the Harpoons and several T-6s were established as Esq. 101 at BA 10. AB 7 was formed at Tete in 1967 at the same time as AB 8 formed at Lourenço Marques in the south to provide a second transport base. The C-47s of Esquadrilha 801 were based here, while Noratlases operated from BA 10. There were additional airfields in regular use, especially in the north at Mueda and Porto Amelia, and about forty strips suitable for light aircraft. To the end of 1968 FAP tactics extended to spotting work and liaison, for which the Do 27 was ideal, to light ground attack on guerrilla groups with T-6s, and to flying up troops into identified areas of guerrilla activity in the ubiquitous Alouette, large numbers of which were based at Nacala. The Noratlases were ideal for dropping paratroopers in support of more extensive operations. With FRELIMO having extended its bases and using heavier equipment, however, the need for an attack aircraft more

The Portuguese obtained a total of thirty Noratlases, including eighteen from West Germany. The elephant marking of LTG 62 was retained on a number of aircraft and painted on some supplied from other sources. This N.2502, with wing-tip mounted auxiliary jet engines and the serial 6404, was bought from UAT and flown with the Esquadron Transportes in Mozambique. (M. Schoeman)

TABLE OF UNITS: MOZAMBIQUE, 1962—1975

Unit	Aircraft	Base	Role
FAP, 3rd Air Region, February 1962			
BA10	T-6G, C-47, PV-2, Alouette III	Beira	Ground attack, liaison, transport
FAP, 3rd Air Region, February 1973			
AB5	T-6G (9), Auster D.5 (5), Alouette III (32), Do 27 (16)	Nacala, Mueda, Porto Amelia	Ground attack, liaison, transport
Esq. 101	PV-2 (6), T-6G (4)	Beira (BA10)	Light bombing, reconnaissance
Esq. 502	Fiat G.91R-4 (8)	Nacala (AB5)	Ground attack
AB6	T-6G (6), Do 27 (12), Auster D.5 (4)	Nova Freixo	Ground attack, liaison, transport
AB7	T-6G (10), Do 27 (6), Auster D.5 (4), Alouette III (4)	Tete (AB7)	Ground attack, liaison, transport
Esq. 702	Fiat G.91R-4	Tete (AB7)	Ground attack
Esq. Trans.	Noratlas (10)	Beira (BA10)	Transport
Esq. 801	C-47 (10)	Lourenço Marques (AB8)	Transport

potent than the evergreen T-6 became apparent. In January 1969 Esq. 502 'Os Jaguares' formed with Fiat G.91R-4s at Nacala, and later in the year Esq. 702 'Os Escorpioes' formed at Tete. Napalm was added to the weapons inventory.

On 3 February 1969 Mondlane was killed by a book bomb at his base in Dar-es-Salaam and later in the year was succeeded by the less moderate Samora Machel. As FRELIMO became bolder in its attacks, Operation 'Gordian Knot' began on 10 June 1970 in the north. It was to last seven months, during which time 651 guerrillas were reported killed and 1,840 captured. Known FRELIMO bases within Mozambique were first subjected to artillery bombardment, then heliborne troops were flown in to surround and eliminate the guerrillas.

Fighter aircraft were on hand to attack any ensconced groups or escapers, but there were no attacks on the secure bases in neighbouring countries. Aircraft were used both for psychological and chemical warfare. In December 1971 and May 1972 unidentified aircraft dropped millions of leaflets over southern Tanzania, attacking President Nycrere and purporting to represent the views of internal opposition. On 30 April six South African-registered crop dusters flew to Mozambique from Johannesburg. From Lourenço Marques they flew on to Nacala, then to Mueda, from where they operated with FAP escort from 6 April. Their task was to deprive FRELIMO of food, especially in the border region, using the powerful 2,4-D-based herbicide Convolvotox. On 14 April an escorting T-6G was brought down by anti-aircraft fire from a village across the Rovuma river in Tanzania. Three days later the village was severely damaged after an attack by G.91s using 50kg and 100kg bombs. After a crop duster and T-6 were hit by small-arms fire on 17 April, the South Africans departed without completing their contract.

A new FRELIMO offensive was launched on 9

November in Tete province, which led to dramatic reprisals in villages thought to be supporting the guerrillas. Although a programme of civil development was now in hand, including the building of a number of 'strategic villages' connected by tarred roads (to make mining more difficult), FRELIMO spread its influence and by 1973 was operating in Beira and Zambezia provinces, threatening the railway line with Rhodesia. Rhodesian forces joined those of Portugal in several major pursuit operations. Guerrilla equipment was supplied mainly from China and now included the SA-7 missile.

As Government forces became increasingly demoralized fighting a war thousands of miles from home, there was a military coup in Lisbon leading to a left-wing government. Discussions were quickly in hand to agree terms for independence in Portugal's African colonies, and in Mozambique a ceasefire came into effect on 8 September 1974. The G.91R-4s of Esq. 702 were transferred to Angola, while those of Esq. 502 were shipped to Portugal. At independence on 25 June 1975 Machel became president with no apparent formalized opposition. The fledgeling state was given three Noratlases and several T-6s and Alouettes with which to form the nucleus of an air force.

The robust Do 27 was flown widely in Africa with many air forces. With the FAP, it was flown from AB6 and AB7 to support counter-insurgency Harvards and on general liaison and observation duties. With a range of 685 miles and a minimum speed of 30mph, the Do 27 needed only a 650ft strip from which to operate. Illustrated is 3472. (M. Schoeman)

The PV-2 was widely used abroad by the FAP, but never in its original maritime patrol role. In Mozambique, six of the type were flown by Esq. 101 at Beira. Early in 1966, after the Rhodesian declaration of independence and British reaction, they flew patrols ready to prevent British intervention in Mozambique. They were joined for a time at Beira by eight F-84Gs of Esq. 93. (M. Robson)

FAP
G.91R-4 *Light grey overall, black serial on fin: 5419.*
C-47 *White over, bare metal under, black serial*
on fin: 6161 (Esq 801).
Noratlas *Dark green/dark grey over, medium grey under, orange rudders, engine cowlings and wingtips, black serial on fin: 6420.*
Cherokee Six *Olive drab overall, black serial on fin: 3602 (AB 8).*

4.7. Mozambique, 1975 to date

A few months after independence in Mozambique there was an abortive coup in Lourenço Marques on 17 December 1975. Early the following year President Machel's left wing Government abolished the right of private property ownership, and shortly afterwards the border with Rhodesia was closed. For the next four years Rhodesian security forces pursued nationalist elements into Mozambique in a series of attacks, and both Cuba and Russia courted the country, offering weapons and advisers, especially in the area of air defence. The first MiG-21 fighters were reportedly delivered to Nacala in March 1977, and the following month the South African Government announced the building of a new air base at Hoedspruit near the Mozambique border.

By the time a Força Aérea Popular de Moçambique (FAPM) pilot defected to South Africa with his MiG-17 on 8 July 1981 the Air Force appeared still to rely on seven Noratlases and five C-47s from colonial days plus two An-26s, three Mi-8s and 24 MiG-17s, all based at Maputo. From about 1980 a resistance movement, supported by South Africa, had been growing: with bases in northern Transvaal, the Resistançia Naçional Moçambicana (RENAMO) infiltrated from early 1981, flown up to the border in SAAF transports and helicopters. The Força Popular de Libertação Moçambique (FPLM) became increasingly sensitive to suspicious activity and on 2 August 1981 brought down a French DC-3 on legitimate oil exploration work with the loss of the crew of six. During the preceding six years several civilian aircraft had been shot down over Mozambique.

Although a spotter aircraft was shot down by rebels on 11 October 1980, the first major RENAMO offensive began on 28 October 1981 when roads and railways between Beira and newly independent Zimbabwe were blown up. The FPLM was weak and attempted to destroy the guerrillas by the use of its MiG-17 ground attack force, but with little success. RENAMO rebels continued to attack sensitive communications targets and on 5 January 1983 blew up the Beira–Mutare (Umtali) oil pipeline. The FAPM now acquired more Mi-8s and an initial batch of Mi-25 gunships in an effort to establish tighter control, while the transport fleet was extended to eight An-26s and two An-12s to move troops to centres of disturbance. There was no evidence of the use of the reported MiG-21 fighters, which

TABLE OF UNITS: MOZAMBIQUE PEOPLE'S AIR FORCE, 1986

Unit	Aircraft	Base	Role	Nos.
?	MiG-23	Nacala	Ground attack	50
?	MiG-21	Beira	Air defence, ground attack	30
?	Mi-25	Maputo, Beira	Gunship, troop transport	15
?	Mi-8	} Maputo	Gunship, troop transport	8
?	An-26		Medium transport	8
?	An-12		Transport	2

On 8 July 1981 Lt. Bomba of the FAPM defected to South Africa in his MiG-17, serial 21. After independence the Mozambique Air Force relied on inherited Portuguese equipment and Soviet supplies, the main base being at Maputo. Twenty-four MiG-17 'Fresco-As' were delivered, but the type was almost useless fighting a counter-insurgency war. (M. Schoeman)

were thought to have numbered as many as 40 at one time.

In March 1984 Mozambique and South Africa reached an agreement whereby neither party would support rebel movements and RENAMO lost its bases and equipment from South Africa, although supply flights are alleged to have continued to August 1984. This merely seems to have had the effect of spreading the movement. The Mozambique Government secured considerable support from Zimbabwe in tracking down rebel groups, and on 28 August a large combined operation began against RENAMO headquarters at Gorongosa about 95 miles from Beira. Two thousand Zimbabwean paratroopers dropped behind the town while heliborne FPLM troops approached from the east with gunship and fighter support. After fierce fighting the rebels withdrew to centre their activities on Inhaminga, which has subsequently been the scene of repeated MiG-17 attacks. During the battle RENAMO claimed three AFZ helicopters, two Mi-25s, one MiG-17 and an Ethiopian Air Force (EAH) Mig-21, but these claims were almost certainly exaggerated since the rebels lacked anything in the way of anti-aircraft weapons apart from a few 14.5mm guns. The reference to Ethiopian aircraft is interesting, since Cubans regularly flew Ethiopian fighters and it is conceivable that some operated in support of Machel. There appeared to be some hope of South Africa and Mozambique reaching a long-term understanding, but on 19 October 1986 Machel was killed when his Tu-134A C9-CAA was destroyed in flight. The South African Government was blamed. By the end of 1986 RENAMO appeared to have little external support, while the Government arsenal grew to include the first of a reported 50 MiG-23 fighters. In April 1987 RENAMO lost it main base at Morrumbala, but in February the following year the MNR captured Muamba barracks. The civil war continues, with an estimated 150,000 killed to date.

AIRCRAFT MARKINGS

FAPM
MiG-17 *Medium cream-grey overall, red serial outlined in black on nose: 21.*
An-26 *Brown/sand over, medium grey under, black serial on rear fuselage: 030.*

4.8. Rhodesia, 1965–1980

In 1963 the Central African Federation, comprising Northern and Southern Rhodesia and Nyasaland, broke up and the following year Northern Rhodesia and Nyasaland achieved independence as Zambia and Malawi respectively. There were disturbances within (Southern) Rhodesia, and in September 1963 Rhodesian Special Air Service (SAS) troopers were dropped by Dakotas of 3 Sqn. Royal Rhodesian Air Force (RRAF) in the Melsetter area. The white minority in Rhodesia had no intention of conceding black majority rule and banned the two nationalist parties, the Zimbabwe African People's Union (ZAPU) and the Zimbabwe African National Union (ZANU), headed respectively by Joshua Nkomo/Robert Mugabe and Ndabaningi Sithole. The principals were detained while the British Government pressed for reform. The leader of the Rhodesian Front, Ian Smith, finally made a unilateral declaration of independence (UDI) on 11 November 1965, and Provost T.52s of 4 Sqn. were detached to Wankie and Kariba to help guard key installations against guerrilla attack.

The British response was to impose sanctions on imports and exports, a military solution committing British troops to fight whites being considered untenable by the Government. Rhodesia is landlocked, as is her northern neighbour Zambia, but unfortunately Zambia relied on the railway link from Mozambique via Bulawayo for trade since the line to Benguela via the Congo was blocked because of the Angolan civil war. The British, with Canadian help, decided to supplement Zambia's oil stocks by airlift from Dar-es-Salaam and Leopoldville respectively.

During mid-November HMS *Eagle* arrived off the Mozambique coast to provide air defence in the event of the RRAF attempting to disrupt the airlift. Embarked were 800 Naval Air Squadron with Buccaneer S.1s and Scimitar F.1s (for air refuelling), 820 NAS with Wessex HAS.1s, D. Flt. of 849 NAS with Gannet AEW.3s and 899 NAS with Sea Vixen FAW.2s which were to provide the air defence cover until relieved by 29 Sqn. Javelins from Akrotiri. The oil lift began on 19 December and involved Britannia C.1s of 99 and 511 Sqns., supported by Hastings C.1s of 36 Sqn. By 31 October 1966, when the airlift ended, the Britannias had flown 1,563 sorties in over 10,000 hours and had carried 3.5 million gallons of oil, much of it for the Javelins. The Canadian effort involved four CC-130Es of 437 Sqn RCAF. The British Government also decided to monitor Rhodesian communications and built a listening post/transmitter at Francistown in Botswana; ostensibly run by the BBC, it was used to transmit 'black' propaganda and was guarded by a company of 1 Bn. the Gloucester Regt., who were flown in aboard Hastings of 24 Sqn.

The RRAF was the strongest air force in the region apart from that of South Africa and represented a serious threat to the integrity of neighbouring states. At UDI the RRAF comprised 1 Sqn. (Hunter FGA.9), 2 Sqn. (Vampire FB.9) and 4 Sqn. (Provost T.52) at Thornhill (Gwelo) and 3 Sqn. (C-47), 5 Sqn. (Canberra B.2/T.4) and 7 Sqn. (Alouette III) at New Sarum (Salisbury); in addition, a number of Vampires and Canberras were held in reserve. From 3 December ten Javelin FAW.9s of 29 Sqn. were detached from Akrotiri to Ndola with a flight of four at Lusaka. Equipment was brought by Argosies of 114 and 267 Sqns. flying via the Middle East, where they picked up air defence radars. HMS *Eagle* departed for the Far East, but in January 1966 HMS *Ark Royal* and a supporting frigate took up station off the Mozambique port of Beira to begin a blockade to prevent the delivery of oil to the railhead. Embarked were 803 NAS (Scimitar F.1), 890 NAS (Sea Vixen FAW.1), 815 NAS (Wessex HAS.1) and C Flt. of 849 NAS (Gannet AEW.3).

Relations between Britain and Portugal deteriorated, and the Força Aérea Portugesa (FAP) transferred eight F-84Gs of Esq. 93 from Angola to Beira during late February. From there they flew standing patrols, and with the resident Esq. 101 equipped with the PV-2 and T-6 were prepared to counter any British intervention in Mozambique. On 2 March *Ark Royal* was relieved by HMS *Eagle*, which was at sea for a record 71 days, during which time her fixed-wing aircraft carried out 1,070 sorties observing 770 ships. On

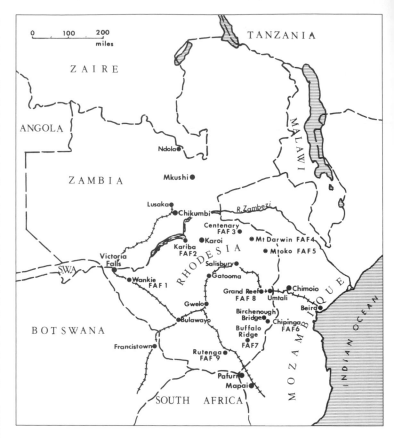

10 May *Ark Royal* was back on station, to be relieved by HMS *Victorious* shortly afterwards. Embarked on *Victorious* were Buccaneer S.2s (801 NAS), Sea Vixen FAW.2s (893 NAS), Wessex HAS.1s (814 NAS) and Gannet AEW.3s of A Flt., 849 NAS. The carrier departed for the Far East in early August, leaving the blockade to land-based aircraft. Coincident was the departure of 29 Sqn. to Cyprus.

Early in the year the British Government had begun negotiating with the French for the use of Majunga airfield on Malagasy, but it was not until March that the first detachment of Shackleton MR.2s of 37 Sqn. arrived from Luqa. They were followed by aircraft of 38 Sqn. later in the year and in February 1967 it was the turn of 42 Sqn. The futile blockade of a single port was maintained until February 1972, by which time 204 and 210 Sqns. had also sent detachments. The Royal Navy retained one frigate on station to August 1975. As Rhodesia made arrangements to beat the blockade she also took the precaution of securing provision for the dispersal of the RRAF in the event of a British military intervention. Facilities were given by the Portuguese at Lourenço Marques and South Africa at Mpacha in the Caprivi Strip. In April 1966 the first limited incursions by guerrillas of ZANU from Mozambique occurred, but these were quickly dealt with.

Late in 1966 the RRAF began co-operating with the Portuguese against Frente de Libertação de Moçambique (FRELIMO) guerrillas who were supporting ZANU in the border area. At the end of the year there were talks between the British and the Smith Government, but these were fruitless, as were a second round in October 1968. The first serious incursions from the north occurred in August 1967 around the Victoria Falls when a force of 90 ZAPU guerrillas was wiped out. In Operation 'Nickel', RRAF Alouettes and Provosts played an important role, as did light aircraft of the Police Reserve Air Wing (PRAW). On 22 August Hunters of 1 Sqn. flew their first operational sorties, strafing guerrillas. A more determined attack on Karoi on 21 March the following year resulted in the second significant offensive RRAF action when Vampires of 2 Sqn. strafed the intruders. For several years there were limited incursions, easily met by the Rhodesian armed services; the nationalists lost heart, and infighting resulted only in a few poorly organized raids.

On a wider front, diplomatic attempts at a solution to the Rhodesian problem successively failed, and on 2 March 1970 Rhodesia was declared a republic, the 'Royal' prefix to the Air Force being dropped. From August 1967 ten Aermacchi AL.60-F5 Trojans had joined the armed Provosts of 4 Sqn. and a single Beech Baron joined the C-47 transports of 3 Sqn. In 1971 ZANU decided on a planned offensive and secured bases in Tanzania; the Zimbabwe African National Liberation Army (ZANLA) was created with Chinese help, and incursion routes through Mozambique were established. Operations began in the north-east on 21 December 1972 and gradually escalated. In 1974 more than 500 guerrillas were killed for the loss of 58 members of the Security Forces, but there was now renewed pressure for a settlement.

With Portuguese provision for independence in Angola and Mozambique and the probability of Marxist governments in both, South Africa preferred the prospect of a stable black government in Rhodesia as a buffer. As 2,000 South African paramilitary troops were withdrawn from December, a ceasefire was agreed and the nationalists were persuaded to form a united front under Bishop Abel Muzorewa. The truce did not last long, however, and early in 1975 the Zimbabwe People's Revolutionary Army (ZIPRA) was formed as the fighting arm of ZAPU. Aid was forthcoming from the Soviet Union and bases were secured in Angola and Zambia. On the Government side, at least 50 SAAF helicopter air and ground crew remained after the South African withdrawal. Rhodesia now faced increasingly well organized guerrilla movements on three fronts.

As Mozambique achieved independence the RhAF began striking at ZANLA camps in the Country. By early 1976 the Air Force had been strengthened by the purchase of twelve Islanders for 3 Sqn., about 35 Alouette IIs and IIIs for 7 Sqn. and eighteen Reims-Cessna FTB.337Gs, named Lynx in Rhodesian service and operated by 4 Sqn. The Provosts formed 6 Sqn. and were used for training only. Rhodesia had little difficulty securing arms and support from South Africa, Israel, France and Italy. From 1976 there was a real intensification of guerrilla activity. The first significant RhAF cross-border strike was against Pafuri on 28 February 1976 when Hunters attacked a ZANLA base. Botswana added her support to the guerrillas, and on 6 May a group damaged the important Botswana–Bulawayo railway line. Later in the month there were raids in the Umtali district and the following month the RhAF struck at a ZIPRA arms depot in Mozambique. On 9 August Rhodesian Selous Scouts attacked a ZANLA camp in Mozambique, killing 600 personnel and causing the remainder to flee.

Rhodesia had by now defined four operational areas: 'Hurricane' in the north-east, 'Thrasher' in the east, 'Repulse' in the south-east and 'Tangent' in the south-west. Four Fireforces were also established, to provide rapid response to infiltration. The Fireforces used several types of aircraft to destroy guerrilla groups, either in response to intelligence reports or at short notice during an attack. In a planned mission a mixed force of a C-47, several Alouette III gunships (K-Cars), Alouette III transports (G-Cars) and a Lynx were used. Once the target was identified by the lead K-Car it was marked and up to twenty paratroops dropped as near as was reasonable. They were then lifted by G-Car to the target while the Lynx used a variety of weapons to keep the enemy's heads down. The use of paradrops was primarily to conserve the helicopter fleet. From 1972 a number of forward airfields (FAF) had been identified or newly constructed where fuel and ammunition stocks were maintained for quick refuelling and re-arming during missions. This approach to fighting groups of insurgents assumed more importance as the guerrillas mined roads on the approaches to attack sites.

As the war progressed, the RhAF developed new weapons, mainly for the Lynx, to counter guerrilla activity. Original napalm bombs were found to be difficult to place accurately, and 68-

The British maintained a futile blockade of Beira to prevent the delivery of oil to the railhead. Initially carried out by the Fleet Air Arm, from March 1966 until February 1972 the task was undertaken by Shackletons rotated into Majunga. 'Z' of 210 Sqn. is seen at the Malagasy base in December 1970. (D. Wildsmith via A. S. Thomas)

litre frangible tanks ('frantans') made of reinforced plastic and fitted with fins were found to be much more effective. Various types of anti-personnel bombs were tested to provide for detonation above ground. Eventually the standard 1,000lb bomb fitted with a 1.2m proboscis and improved fins was used by Hunters, with a scaled-down version carried by the Lynx. They were named 'Golf' and 'Mini-Golf' respectively.

Another anti-personnel bomb was the Alpha, which was designed for use by Hunters and Canberras. These small 155mm spherical bombs were delivered from carriers and detonated to explode about 3m above ground, giving a lethality of 45 per cent of the mass compared with only 8 per cent with conventional fragmentation bombs. Simple flechettes with plastic tails were also used. The standard weapons fit on the Lynx was two 0.303in MGs mounted above the cabin, plus (normally) two 18-tube SNEB 37mm rocket launchers on the inboard pylons. The outboard pylons were used for bombs or flares. Not only were the Lynx used for Fireforce work, they also acted as communications relays on 'Telstar' sorties, especially in support of cross-border attacks. In addition, they were employed to drop flares on areas being subjected to night attack, for forward air control (FAC) in support of strikes by jet fighters and for reconnaissance.

Rhodesia suffered a number of aircraft losses, both military and civil, over the next few years. A Vampire of 2 Sqn. crashed outside Umtali on 22 November 1977 after a strike, and on 28 July 1978 an Alouette was lost to an RPG7 hit over Mozambique. the RhAF had little to fear from neighbouring countries, which, although possessing aircraft capable of attacking at least the slower Rhodesian machines, lacked any air de-

fence system. Losses were to groundfire or SAMs. On 3 September 1978 Viscount VP-WAS of Air Rhodesia was brought down near Victoria Falls by a ZIPRA SA-7; of the 56 on board, 38 were killed in the crash and ten survivors murdered on the ground. Prior to this attack several aircraft had been the targets for SAMs but this was the first loss. On 19 September Rhodesia launched a series of mainly airborne attacks on ZANLA camps in Mozambique and on 18 October turned its attention on Zambia in retaliation for the Viscount loss.

In Operation 'Gatling', troops were dropped on Chikumbi, just 12 miles from Lusaka; other centres of attack were Rufunsa and Mkushi. The RhAF maintained total control of the air in the area for three days, during which 1,500 guerrillas were claimed to have been killed. In response to a plea from the Zambian Government Britain shipped out a Rapier-based air defence system. Rhodesia had added twelve SF.260W Warriors (Genet in RhAF service) and eleven AB.205 helicopters, delivered from Israel via South Africa, to its air force. The helicopters formed a new squadron, No. 8, while the Genets were used by 6 Sqn., especially for convoy protection. A DC-7C was added to 3 Sqn. Despite repainting its Viscounts in light-blue 'camouflage', a second aircraft of Air Rhodesia, VP-YND, was shot down by two SA-7s on 12 February 1979 near Kariba with the loss of 59 passengers and crew. A week later Salisbury Airport came under ZANLA mortar fire, although no aircraft were damaged. Again the Rhodesians struck back at targets in Zambia on 23 February, but the next raid was to be the most ambitious of the war.

Russian and Cuban advisers had supported a ZIPRA training camp at Vila de Boma south of

During the latter years of the war in Rhodesia, much use was made of the Cessna FTB.337G, named Lynx in Rhodesian service. In this view of an aircraft of 4 Sqn., the underwing rocket pods and overwing machine guns are apparent. The aircraft was extremely successful in the counter-insurgency role, and as far as is known none was lost to enemy action. (Via A. S. Thomas)

The Rhodesian Air Force had a total of eighteen Canberras, including three trainers. In addition to internal security flights, the medium bomber was used against targets in Angola and Mozambique, where at least two were brought down. By 1979, when this photograph was taken, RhAF aircraft were flying in camouflage, with no national markings or serials. The type was operated by 5 Sqn., based at New Sarum. (Rhodesian Air Force via A. S. Thomas)

Luso in Angola. On 26 February four Canberra B.2s of 5 Sqn. left Wankie for the long flight to bomb the camp. Angolan sources claimed that the raid was supported by five Mirage fighters 'given to Smith by South Africa', but this is unlikely. The bombers overflew western Zambia, avoiding the extensive missile belt in the south of Angola, and it is quite likely that SAAF Mirages operating from the Caprivi Strip at least co-ordinated their activities to give some protection to the Canberras. During the day ZIPRA guerrillas in Zambia scored their first SAM kill, a Zambian Air Force (ZAF) MB. 326. There were further Canberra and Hunter raids into Zambia and Mozambique throughout March and April.

Starting on 5 September, Rhodesian forces launched major offensives against guerrilla bases in Mozambique's Gaza province as Operation 'Uric'. Fighting was hard and far from one-sided: in the operation an Agusta-Bell 205 was brought down by an RPG7 on the 5th, as was an SAAF Puma on the 6th with twelve killed. On 27 September the security forces made a large-scale attack on a major ZANLA camp at Chimoio holding 6,000 guerrillas. Several hundred Rhodesian Light Infantry (RLI) were parachuted behind the camp to block retreat while 200 Selous Scouts made a frontal attack The fight lasted three days, during which time Canberras and Hunters repeatedly bombed and strafed guerrilla positions called in by Lynx acting as FACs. At the time of withdrawal most of the occupants of the camp were dead or wounded. During the operation the RhAF lost a Hunter and Canberra, both on 3 October.

The days of the Smith Government were now numbered, however. In April 1979, after universal pressure, elections were held in which Muzorewa's United African National Council won 50 of the 72 seats; he was sworn in as Prime Minister in June. The banned ZANU and ZAPU parties could not participate, and in September a fresh round of talks began in London. These resulted in an agreement in December, but not before Zambia was placed on a full war footing after Rhodesian forces isolated Lusaka from the south by blowing three main bridges. The RhAF bombed camps south of Lusaka on 25 November for the last time. Lord Soames arrived in Salisbury on 12 December as sanctions were lifted and almost immediately a five-nation Ceasefire Monitoring Force (CMF) was established to support the disarming and potential integration of guerrillas.

In Operation 'Agila', the RAF committed seven Hercules of 47 and 70 Sqns., together with six Pumas of 33 Sqn. Twelve Gazelles and Scouts of 656 Sqn. were flown into Salisbury in two C-5As and equipment and troops were transported in VC-10s of 10 Sqn. RAF and ten C-141s of 437 MAW, Sadly, one day before the ceasefire came into effect on 28 December, a Puma was lost when it hit telephone cables. During February 1980 three RCAF CC-115s of 440 Sqn. flew to Salisbury to join the CMF. The CMF left from 16 March, having supervised the acceptance of more than 50,000 guerrillas at assembly points. Elections were held in March in which ZANU took 63 per cent of the votes to form a government under Robert Mugabe.

Regrettably, peace was short-lived. Early in 1982 a large force of the Zimbabwe National Army (ZNA) moved into Matabeleland where Nkomo's ZAPU received major support. Arms caches were allegedly found and large numbers of Matabeles reportedly massacred. Then, on 25 July, in a series of explosions, seven Hunters, a newly delivered Hawk and a Lynx were destroyed at Gwelo (Thornhill), one Hunter and three Hawks being badly damaged. White officers of the Air Force of Zimbabwe (AFZ) were accused, but it is widely believed that South Africa was responsible in a supportive gesture to Nkomo. Zimbabwe continues to operate in support of the

Mozambique Government, and in April 1987 it was reported that the AFZ was to take delivery of twelve MiG-29s, although there must be doubt about its ability to operate such complex aircraft. The fourteen years of UDI cost the lives of 410 white and (officially) 691 black civilians; 954 members of the Security Force were killed, as were an estimated 8,250 guerrillas in Rhodesia with up to 30,000 possibly killed beyond Rhodesian borders.

The following is a list of known RhAF operational losses during the period 1965 to 1979:

Date	Type	Location	Cause
14/04/74	Trojan	Rushinga	RPG7
20/04/74	Trojan	Rushinga	RPG7
14/08/74	Alouette III	Madziwa	Shot down
12/01/77	Canberra B.2	Mozambique	Unknown
18/05/77	Alouette III	?	Shot down
02/06/77	Dakota	Mapai	RPG7
02/09/77	Lynx	?	Flew into ground
28/07/78	Alouette III	?	RPG7
22/10/78	Alouette III	Zambia	AAA
05/09/79	AB.205	Mozambique	RPG7
06/09/79	Puma (SAAF)	Mozambique	RPG7
03/10/79	Canberra B.2	Mozambique	?
03/10/79	Hunter FGA.9	Mozambique	?

The Rhodesian Government managed to circumvent sanctions in a number of ways, and what has been reported gives interesing insights into the arms trade. A purchasing office was set up in Geneva and from 1967 aircraft were imported in a variety of ways. Until 1976, when the South African Government responded to international pressure, most arms came into Rhodesia from South Africa aboard SAAF C-130s. In addition, from about 1969, the locally based charter line Affretair (otherwise Air Trans Africa) carried exports out of Rhodesia, invariably indicating some other country of origin, and also shipped arms in, either from the supplier or from a third-party country.

After 1978 the Rhodesians secured most of their arms via the Comoro Islands, to which end-user certificates were made out by the suppliers; once landed in the Comoros, Affretair freighters delivered direct to Salisbury. Affretair also operated as Air Gabon Cargo and CargOman, with offices at Libreville and Seeb respectively. The Oman connection was useful as a focal point for the purchase of Hunter spares, and at least ten Avon engines were delivered. As an indication of the complexity of the deals, the delivery of AB.205A helicopters is noteworthy. Thirteen AB.205s were ordered from Agusta by a customer in Kuwait. They were delivered, crated, to Beirut and off-loaded to be held in a Christian suburb. They were then handed to Israel by the Christians in exchange for arms. From Israel, eleven examples were flown to Salisbury, possibly bought by a Singapore purchaser, but on arrival the helicopters turned out to be worn ex-IDF/AF examples rather than the original order from Agusta.

The Affretair fleet comprised two CL-44s, three DC-8s and five DC-7s, at least one of which last also carried an RhAF serial. Most were registered in Gabon, and one in Oman. The aircraft also travelled the world searching for business to generate income, but they carefully avoided Britain and the USA. The main centre for European operations was Schipol. Aircraft imported, despite sanctions, included the following:

Year	Number	Type	Source
1967	10	Aermacchi AL.60	Italy, Delivered crated.
1968	4	Alouette III	?
1972	6	Alouette III	?
1974	3	Alouette III	?
1975	8	Alouette III	3 ex-Portuguese Air Force
1976	18	Cessna FTB.337G	France. Purchaser 'Canaries Fishing Co'. Flown out.
1976	6	Islander	Mozambique. Flown out.
1977	3	Cessna FTB.337G	France. Purchaser 'Panama Coast Guard'. Flown out.
1977	17	SF.260	Belgium. Delivered crated ex-Paris.
1978	11	AB.205A	Israel. Delivered crated.
1978	14	SF.260	?

Air Rhodesia civil aircraft were operated in the front line, two Viscounts, VP-WAS and VP-YND, being shot down by SA-7s near Victoria Falls (September 1978) and Kariba (February 1979) respectively. This view of VP-YTE shows the Viscount in its original markings. After the first loss the type was repainted pale blue overall. (M. Robson)

The Rhodesians were adept at beating sanctions against both arms supplies and trade. A first batch of SF.260 Genets was delivered from Belgium, while a second batch was delivered from the manufacturer via the Comoro Islands. An SF.260W, registered D6.ECD, is seen here before being airlifted to southern Africa. These aircraft were flown in the light attack role by 6 Sqn. (D. Binda via L. Pinzauti)

TABLE OF UNITS: RHODESIA, 1965–1980

OIL LIFT AND BLOCKADE

Unit	Aircraft	Base	Role	Nos./dates
FAA				
800 NAS	Buccaneer S.1, Scimitar F.1		Anti-ship, ground attack	
899 NAS	Sea Vixen FAW.2	Eagle	Air defence	00/11/65 to 05/12/65
820 NAS	Wessex HAS.1		ASW, liaison	02/03/66 to 10/05/66
849 NAS	Gannet AEW.3 (D Flt.)		AEW	
803 NAS	Scimitar F.1		Ground attack	
890 NAS	Sea Vixen FAW.1	Ark Royal	Air defence	00/01/66 to 03/03/66
815 NAS	Wessex HAS.1		ASW, liaison	10/05/66 to 00/06/66
849 NAS	Gannet AEW.3 (C Flt.)		AEW	
001 NAS	Buccaneer S.2		Anti-ship, ground attack	
893 NAS	Sea Vixen FAW.2	Victorious	Air defence	00/06/66 to 00/08/66
814 NAS	Wessex HAS.1		ASW, liaison	
849 NAS	Gannet AEW.3 (A Flt.)		AEW	
RAF				
29 Sqn.	Javelin FAW.9R	Ndola, Lusaka	Air defence	03/12/65 to 00/08/66
114/267 Sqns.	Argosy C.1	Benson	Transport of radar etc.	01/12/65 to 00/01/66
24 Sqn.	Hastings C.1	Colerne	Troop transport	00/12/65 to 00/12/65
99/511 Sqns.	Britannia C.1	Lusaka, Dar-es-Salaam	Oil transport	19/12/65 to 31/10/66
36 Sqn.	Hastings C.1A/2	Colerne, Lusaka	Support transport	00/12/65 to 00/01/66
37/38/42/204/ 210 Sqns.	Shackleton MR.2	Majunga	MR	00/03/66 to 00/02/72
RCAF				
437 Sqn.	CC-130E	Lusaka, Leopoldville	Oil transport	00/12/65 to 00/03/66
RRAF, 11 November 1965				
1 Sqn.	Hunter FGA.9	Thornhill	Ground attack, air defence	12
2 Sqn.	Vampire FB.9, T.11	Thornhill	Ground attack	25
5 Sqn.	Canberra B.2, T.4	New Sarum	Medium bombing	12
4 Sqn.	Provost T.52	Thornhill	Armed training	14
3 Sqn.	C-47	New Sarum	Transport	7
7 Sqn.	Alouette II	New Sarum	Light transport, liaison	8

CEASEFIRE PERIOD

Unit	Aircraft	Base	Role	Nos./dates
RRAF, 31 December 1979				
1 Sqn.	Hunter FGA.9	Thornhill	Ground attack, air defence	9
2 Sqn.	Vampire FB.9, T.11	Thornhill	Ground attack	20
5 Sqn.	Canberra B.2, T.4	New Sarum	Medium bombing	5
4 Sqn.	AL-60 Trojan, FTB. 337G Lynx	Thornhill	Coin, recce, FAC	21
6 Sqn.	SF. 260W, Genet	New Sarum	Armed training	26
7 Sqn.	Alouette II/III	New Sarum, Thornhill	Gunship, light transport, liaison	45
8 Sqn.	AB, 205 Cheetah	New Sarum	Transport	10
3 Sqn.	C-47, DC-7C, Cessna 402, Cessna 185, Islander	New Sarum	Transport	19
RAF (Ceasefire Monitoring Force)				
10 Sqn.	VC-10	Brize Norton	Strategic transport	12/12/79 to 00/03/80
47/70 Sqns.	Hercules C.1	Lyneham, Salisbury	Transport	12/12/79 to 00/04/80
33 Sqn.	Puma HC.1	Odiham, Salisbury	Transport	18/12/79 to 00/03/80
656 Sqn.	Gazelle AH.1, Scout AH.1	Various	Liaison, light transport	18/12/79 to 00/04/80
USAF (Ceasefire Monitoring Force)				
60 MAW	C-5A	Salisbury	UK equipment lift and return	16/12/79 to 00/04/80
437 MAW	C-141A	Salisbury	UK equipment lift and return	16/12/79 to 00/04/80
RAAF (Ceasefire Monitoring Force)				
37 Sqn.	C-130E	Richmond, Salisbury	Transport	25/12/79 to 00/02/80
RCAF (Ceasefire Monitoring Force)				
440 Sqn.	CC-115 Buffalo	Salisbury	Tactical transport	00/02/80 to 00/04/80

Note: The RRAF held additional Vampires and Canberras in store in 1965. There were reports of the RhAF flying four ex-Indonesian OV-10Fs and some T-28s, although this seems extremely unlikely.

AIRCRAFT MARKINGS

FAA, 1965–66
Royal Navy fixed-wing aircraft were finished Extra Dark Sea Grey over and white under. Codes were usually white.
Buccaneer S.1 *Black nose code: XN971/102E (800 NAS).*
Buccaneer S.2 *XN980/233V (801 NAS).*
Scimitar F.1 *Code on mid-fuselage, frothing tankard marking on fin: XD321/116E (800B NAS). Nose code: XD323/032R (803 NAS).*
Sea Vixen FAW.2 *XS576/125E (899 NAS).*
Gannet AEW.3 *Black nose and fin code: XL496/073E (849 NAS, D Flt.).*
Wessex HAS.1 *RAF blue-grey with yellow upper decking, white code on nose and 'last two' repeated mid-fuselage: XP117/273V (814 NAC); XP104/053R (815 NAS).*

RAF, 1965–66
Javelin FAW.9R *Dark Green/Dark Grey over, silver under, white serial on engine intake and code on fin: XH886/J, XH890/H (29 Sqn).*
Shackleton MR.2 *Extra Dark Sea Grey overall, white fuselage decking, red code on nose and squadron number on rear fuselage, both outlined in white: WL757/D (37 Sqn.): WL737/J (204 Sqn.).*

RRAF, 1965
At UDI the national marking was an RAF roundel with a narrow white element ('C' type), with a single assegai superimposed. Operational types were finished Dark Green/Dark Earth over, Sky under.
Hunter FGA.9 *White serial on rear fuselage: RRAF119 (1 Sqn.).*
Vampire FB.9 *White serial on rear boom: RRAF109 (2 Sqn.).*

Canberra B.2 *Black serial on rear fuselage: RRAF206 (5 Sqn.).*
Provost T.52 *Black serial on rear fuselage: RRAF306 (4 Sqn.).*
Alouette III *Dark Green/Dark Earth overall, black serial on lower fuselage: RRAF506 (7 Sqn.).*
C-47 *Natural metal overall, white fuselage decking, black serial on rear fuselage: RRAF180 (3 Sqn.).*

RhAF, 1979
By 1979, all aircraft wore camouflage, generally matt Dark Earth/Dark Green over and Dark Earth under, and as a rule no markings of any sort were carried. The C-47 camouflage was pale green/pale earth over, pale earth under, and the engine exhausts were ducted to reduce the infra-red signature.

CMF, RAF and British Army, 1979
Aircraft were finished in the standard tactical camouflage of the period. Large white crosses were marked in addition on the forward fuselage (Hercules C.1, e.g. XV213/213 LTW), on the cabin side (Puma HC.1, e.g. XW204/CA, 33 Sqn.) and on the cabin side and fin (Gazelle AH.1, e.g. XW912, 656 Sqn.).

The Hunter has proved to be a most capable ground-attack fighter in numerous postwar conflicts. The Rhodesians operated twelve ex-RAF Hunter FGA.9s with 1 Sqn. at Thornhill, three being lost, one in action over Mozambique. This brown and green camouflaged (but unidentifiable) Hunter is seen with four external fuel tanks, which were used on long-range navigation flights to South Africa. (Via A. S. Thomas)

4.9. South Africa, 1966 to date

South Africa has used aircraft in support of two distinct but related campaigns, both strictly concerned with internal security; in addition, her forces invaded Angola in 1975, but that campaign is dealt with separately. The more extensive action has been against nationalists in South-West Africa, the other against banned nationalists in South Africa itself. Both are dealt with in the same section because aircraft are switched around from base to base as the need is identified.

South-West Africa, or Namibia, was a German colony until 1915, when it was conquered by South Africa, which was given a mandate to administer the territory. After the Second World War the terms of administration were disputed, but for several reasons, primarily political rather than economic, South Africa has refused to relinquish control. In 1958 the South-West Africa

People's Organization (SWAPO) was formed, and two years later it spawned a military arm, the People's Liberation Army of Namibia (PLAN); secure bases were provided in newly independent Zambia. The first PLAN insurgents entered Namibia in September 1965, and the first clash occurred on 26 August 1966 when South African Air Force (SAAF) helicopters lifted police to a camp in Ovamboland. Activities were easily contained by the police until January 1973, when a police station in the Caprivi Strip was attacked. From then, responsibility for security passed to the armed services, and by August 1976 there were 12,800 combat troops and 5,000 reserves in the territory, with a supporting Air Commando of detachments from one Impala and one Mirage squadron plus a range of helicopters. Following the Angolan expedition of 1975–76 the South

Africans formed 32 Battalion, partly from Angolans, as a key counter-insurgency force.

The unit was to operate outside South Africa's borders, being infiltrated, exfiltrated and resupplied by helicopter but generally operating on foot. It was involved in a clash with the MPLA on the border on 18 February 1977 but more significantly in Operation 'Reindeer' which began on 4 May 1978. Two major PLAN camps had been identified in Angola, 'Moscow' at Cassinga, 155 miles into Angola, and 'Vietnam' at Chetequera just across the border. A small airborne battalion was dropped by eight SAAF C-130Bs and Transall C-160s at Casinga after a temporary helicopter base had been secured 15 miles to the east. Four Canberras dropped anti-personnel bombs on the base, followed by four Buccaneer sorties dropping conventional 1,000lb bombs on buildings. After the attack, in which an estimated 1,000 PLAN members were killed, the troops were lifted out by waiting Puma and Super Frelon helicopters while Mirage IIIs and Buccaneers strafed and rocketed an advancing Cuban column. The Chetequera base was dealt with by a mechanized column. In subsequent operations a Canberra was shot down on 14 March 1979, while a Mirage was lost on 6 July.

On 15 June 1979 the SAAF conducted a strike against Humbe, but the next major operation was into Zambia in August 1979 as Operation 'Safraan'. A barracks at Katima Mulilo had been attacked from Zambia with 122mm rockets and ten soldiers killed. In a swift raid ground forces were supported by Impalas based at Mpacha while Canberras and Buccaneers flew strike sorties. The security forces were extending their bases along the border, and it was claimed that several aircraft were destroyed in a PLAN mortar attack on Ondangwa in May 1980, although this seems unlikely. An Impala had been shot down

on 18 October 1979 while a Mirage F.1C took an SA-7 hit in June 1980.

By 1980 PLAN had recovered sufficiently from the 1978 raids on Angolan bases to have established new bases around an area in southern Angola code-named 'Smokeshell' by the South Africans. A mechanized force crossed the border on 9 June in Operation 'Sceptic' to eliminate the threat. The operation lasted three weeks, during which several hundred tons of equipment were captured or destroyed and 360 rebels killed for the loss of seventeen members of the security forces. Impalas again supported the operation, flying several close-support sorties, while helicopters were used extensively to ferry troops around the complex of bases. On 30 July there was a quick heliborne attack on a camp at Chitado. At any given time there were no more than a few hundred guerrillas operating in Namibia, and their activities were confined in the main to minelaying on key roads and limited attacks on politicians and police outposts.

To support the Army the South-West Africa Territory Force was formed on 1 August 1980, with three units working in the northern 'Operational Area'. Included was a light aviation squadron, No. 112, using civilian aircraft for liaison work. On 16 July there had been a cross-border rocket and mortar attack on installations at Ruacana, and Operation 'Klipkop', launched on 2 August, saw two infantry platoons lifted by helicopter to a PLAN base at Chitado which was destroyed. From now the SAAF regularly overflew southern Angola on reconnaissance sorties, and occasional strikes were made when a PLAN target was identified. As a result of these intrusions the Força Arma Populaire de Liberaçione Angola (FAPLA) began to establish an increasingly complex air defence system in the region.

The next major South African adventure into

A Mirage F.1CZ of 3 Sqn. SAAF. After considerable experience on the Mirage III, the SAAF introduced the F.1 into service in 1975. On escort tasks over Angola, the type shot down at least two MiG-21s in 1981–82, flying from a temporary base in Namibia. (Via A. S. Thomas)

Angola came on 24 August 1981 with Operation 'Protea', which began with an air strike on SA-3 and SA-6 sites and the radar station at Cahama, after which a mechanized column crossed the border at Ruacana. It raced north to Humbe both to block escape and prevent FAPLA interference. A second column crossed from Ondangwa to Xangongo, where it spread out to attack and destroy PLAN headquarters and bases. This group then worked south-east to Ngiva, which it reached on the 26th after heavy fighting en route. Throughout the operation the columns were supplied by helicopters, which also performed casualty evacuation (casevac) duties, and Impalas were on hand in the ground support and reconnaissance roles. On the 25th an SAAF Alouette III was brought down near Xangongo. The operation ended on 1 September with the capture of many vehicles and arms and the estimated loss of 1,000 guerrillas.

The deepest penetration of Angola since 1975 came with Operation 'Daisy', designed to destroy PLAN's north-eastern headquarters at Bambe following intelligence gathered in 'Protea'. From 1 November a mechanized column drove north to a tactical base at Ionde. After bases at Bambe and Cherequera had been subjected to bombing and strafing by Buccaneers, Canberras and Mirages on the 4th, the troops moved up to destroy the camps. PLAN guerrillas were being advised of incoming sorties through the FAPLA

air defence system, so the radar at Cahama was against bombed. On 6 November two MiG-21s were scrambled from Menongue to meet a pair of Mirage F1s; one MiG was shot down and the other allowed to return. In a brief incursion on 29 December 1981 troops were lifted by Puma up to Evale to destroy a PLAN camp; five Impalas covered the operation. The action lasted from 1155hrs to 1800hrs, during which time an Alouette III was lost to ground fire.

The next operation was 'Super' on 13 March 1982 against a PLAN base at Cambeno where there was a reported build-up of guerrillas ready for a major offensive into north-eastern Namibia. A total of 45 men of 32 Bn. were dropped by Puma and supported by a mortar group, also dropped by helicopter on a nearby hill, and 201 rebels were killed and several Mi-8 helicopters destroyed on the ground. SAAF strikes against Angolan targets continued, and in May an Impala was shot down with the loss of one of the Air Force's most experienced pilots. A more protracted operation, 'Mebos', began on 31 July with an attack on a PLAN HQ near Mupa. The guerrillas had warning and evacuated the base, but were pursued for some weeks, the South African forces following on foot and by helicopter. On 12 August a Puma was shot down, by ZSU-23-2 AAA, with the loss of fifteen troops and crew. The operation ended in mid-August.

There were few incursions for the next eighteen

months, but reconnaissance aircraft kept a close watch on movements and the developing air defence system. On 5 October 1982 a Canberra PR sortie escorted by two Mirage F.1s was intercepted by four MiG-21s from Menongue, and in the ensuing brief air battle one MiG was destroyed. By the end of 1983 PLAN had reorganized sufficiently to justify another major operation, named 'Askari' and designed to hit at a range of bases and arms depots deep in Angola. On 6 December four mechanized columns each of 500 men crossed the border to make for sites in the vicinities of Cahama, Mulando, Caiundo and Cuvelai. The SAAF played a major part in the operation, striking at targets at Lubango, Cassinga and Cahama as well as flying many close-support missions with the Impala. FAPLA had deployed newer SAMs and soon claimed four SAAF aircraft to the SA-8s sited around Cahama. On the 29th an Impala returned to Ondangwa with an SA-9 warhead embedded in its tail.

On 3 January 1984 there was heavy fighting at Cuvelai involving FAPLA's 11 Brigade reinforced by two Cuban battalions. Shortly afterwards the South Africans withdrew and began negotiations with the Angolan Government to proscribe PLAN activity in Angola. A Joint Monitoring Force (JMF) comprising FAPLA elements and 32 Battalion was established, based from Cuvelai and gradually working south. These arrangements appeared to work for some time and, indeed, the next indication of a PLAN threat was from Botswana in March 1984. It is likely that South African forces never completely withdrew from Angola, and towards the end of 1984 the SAAF flew air defence suppression sorties. During 1984 and 1985 a number of 'hot pursuit' raids were made into Angola following guerrilla attacks on military installations. These demanded full SAAF support, especially in tracking the rebels and in keeping units supplied by helicopter to enhance mobility. The Kudu and Bosbok were especially valuable in Namibia itself, where

there was little threat from the ground and where PLAN groups could find negligible cover.

FAPLA began a major offensive against UNITA groups around Mavinga in September 1985, and the SAAF operated extensively in support of UNITA. South African Defence Force (SADF) units also operated in the area with close support, and during the inconclusive fighting a MiG-21 and four MiG-17s were destroyed on the ground at Menongue while four Mi-25s and three Angolan Alouettes were claimed brought down by UNITA. The UN subsequently told South Africa to pay Angola $36 million compensation for damage caused during what it believed was unwarranted interference. The SAAF supported UNITA forces in fighting in the Mavinga and Cuito Cuanavale areas from July 1987, during which it was reported that the MiG-23 was introduced.

After a series of successful battles where UNITA held FAPLA forces with South African air and artillery support, South Africa withdrew some forces late in the year, although cross-border raids and air sorties continued. In a strike against Cuito Cuanavale and Lubango on 19 February 1988, allegedly in retaliation for a SWAPO bomb attack on a bank in Namibia, a Mirage was shot down. Shortly after this it was confirmed that the South African task force supporting UNITA was still in place around Cuito Cuanavale, and an important target was the airfield and radar complex there. By early 1988 the air defence system in Angola was the most sophisticated of Soviet origin outside the Warsaw Pact countries. It comprised 75 mobile radar sets, 40 MiG-21s and 40 MiG-23s, SA-2, SA-3, SA-6, SA-8, SA-9 and SA-13 SAMs, ZSU-23 AAA and the man-portable SA-7 and SA-14 missiles. This impressive range of equipment failed to deter the SAAF, which continued its strikes against SWAPO targets.

In May, by which time there were 10,000 South African troops in Angola, talks began between the protaganists with a view to ending

TABLE OF UNITS: SOUTH AFRICAN AIR FORCE, 1966 TO DATE

Unit	Aircraft	Base	Role	Dates
1 Sqn.	Sabre 6	Waterkloof	Air defence	00/09/56 to 00/02/67
	Sabre 6, Impala I	Pietersburg	Air defence, ground attack	00/01/67 to 00/10/75
	Mirage F.1AZ	Waterkloof	Air defence, ground attack	00/10/75 to 14/01/81
		Hoedspruit		14/01/81 to date
3 Sqn.	Mirage F.1CZ	Waterkloof	All-weather fighter, ground attack	00/02/75 to date
2 Sqn.	Mirage IIIAZ/BZ/CZ/DZ/RZ,	Waterkloof	Air defence, ground attack	00/00/63 to 00/02/75
	Vampire T.55	Hoedspruit		00/00/78 to date
85 AFS	Mirage IIIDZ/EZ, Impala II	Pietersburg	Advanced training, ground attack	00/03/75 to date
4 Sqn.	Harvard, Impala I	Swartkop	Ground attack, recce	01/11/61 to 00/12/72
	Impala I/II	Waterkloof, Lanseria		00/12/72 to date
5 Sqn.	Harvard, Impala I/II	Durban	Ground attack, recce	00/12/50 to 28/03/85
	Impala II	Louis Trichardt		00/03/88 to date
6 Sqn.	Harvard, Impala I/II	Port Elizabeth	Ground attack, recce	00/05/61 to date
7 Sqn.	Harvard, Impala I/II	Cape Town	Ground attack, recce	01/08/61 to 00/00/85
	Impala II	Langebaanweg		00/00/85 to date
8 Sqn.	Harvard, Impala I/II	Bloemspruit	Ground attack, recce	01/01/51 to date
24 Sqn.	Buccaneer S.50	Waterkloof	Light bomber, ground attack	00/10/65 to date
12 Sqn.	Canberra B(I).12, T.4	Waterkloof	Light bomber, recce	00/00/63 to date
40 Sqn.	Harvard	Dunnotar	Ground attack	01/01/51 to ?
41 Sqn.	Auster AOP.9, Cessna 185	Johannesburg	Army co-operation	00/01/63 to 00/05/73
	Bosbok, Kudu	Swartkop, Lanseria	Army co-operation, FAC	00/05/73 to date
42 Sqn.	Cessna 185	Potchefstroom	Army co-operation	00/05/62 to 00/00/74
	Bosbok, Kudu		Army co-operation, FAC	00/00/74 to date
17 Sqn.	Alouette II, III	Ysterplaat, Swartkop (flts. at	Transport, liaison, SAR	00/07/61 to ?
		Ysterplaat, Bloemspruit)		00/00/63 to ?
16 Sqn.	Alouette III, Puma	Ysterplaat, Durban (flts. at	Transport, liaison, SAR	01/02/68 to 05/07/72
		Bloemspruit, Port		05/07/72 to date
		Elizabeth, Ysterplaat)		
31 Sqn.	Alouette III, Puma	Hoedspruit	Transport, SAR	00/00/82 to date
19 Sqn.	Puma	Swartkop (flt. at Durban)	Transport, SAR	00/00/69 to date
15 Sqn.	Super Frelon, Puma	Swartkop, Bloemspruit	Transport, SAR	19/02/68 to 00/01/81
		Durban		00/01/81 to date
30 Sqn.	Super Frelon, Puma	Ysterplaat	Transport, SAR	06/01/81 to date
25 Sqn.	Dakota	Ysterplaat	Transport	00/02/68 to date
44 Sqn.	DC-4, Dakota	Swartkop	Transport	00/11/53 to date
28 Sqn.	C-130B, C-160Z	Waterkloof	Transport, paratrooping	00/01/63 to date
21 Sqn.	Dakota, Viscount,	Swartkop, Waterkloof	Transport, communications	00/02/68 to date
	Mercurius (HS.125),			
	Merlin			
11 Sqn.	Cessna 185	Potchefstroom	Liaison, communications	02/01/74 to date
43 Sqn.	Cessna 185	Durban	Army co-operation	00/00/74 to 00/00/80
27 Sqn.	Dakota, P-166S Albatross	Ysterplaat, Cape Town	Coastal recce	00/10/62 to date
35 Sqn.	Shackleton MR.3, C-47	Cape Town	MR	00/10/57 to date
60 Sqn.	Boeing 707 variant	Waterkloof	Elint	00/05/86 to date
22 Flt. Sqn.	Wasp HAS.1, Alouette III	Ysterplaat	Naval transport, utility	00/04/64 to date

Note: There are also thirteen Air Commando squadrons using civilian aircraft and numbered 101–112 and 114 (Women's).

---

the war. The conditions were independence for Namibia and the withdrawal of South African forces from Angola, against Cuban withdrawal of its 40,000 troops in Angola. Despite disagreements over the timings, South Africa claimed by August to have withdrawn, and at the time of writing withdrawals by both sides are confirmed.

In a country governed by a minority white population, the African National Congress (ANC) had been formed to represent black interests. After a demonstration at Sharpeville on 21 March 1960, during which police killed 69 blacks, the ANC was banned. During riots at Soweto in June 1976, in which 176 were killed, Alouette helicopters of 16 Sqn. were used to drop tear gas.

From this time ANC guerrillas attacked targets in South Africa from bases in Mozambique and later Zambia, Botswana, Lesotho and Zimbabwe. Training was undertaken by Soviet instructors in Angola. During 1980 a number of attacks on police stations and economic targets were made from Mozambique, culminating in a major raid on a SASOL coal-to-oil plant. The SADF decided

to destroy the ANC HQ in the Matola suburb of Maputo. Using captured vehicles of Russian origin, the attackers drove to the target, where they killed twelve ANC members, destroyed buildings and captured documents. The group was withdrawn by Puma without loss. Following this attack the Soviet Union offered increased aid to Mozambique, and for several weeks two warships stood off Maputo. A token of the Russian aid was delivered to the South Africans on 8 July 1981 when Lt. Adriano Bomba defected to Hoedspruit with his MiG-17; in a second defection, a Cessna of the Air Force of Zimbabwe (AFZ) was flown to South African on 17 August.

South African observation posts in the Caprivi Strip were hit by fire from the village of Sesheke, Zambia, in September. On the 11th the village was attacked by four Impalas, and the SAAF also bombed known ANC bases in the country. A year later three white officers of the SADF were killed on an apparently unauthorized foray into Zimbabwe. In December it was the turn of Lesotho when a security force unit attacked ANC bases, after which they were exfiltrated by

A Kudu 971, believed to be from 41 Sqn. This strong utility aircraft derives from a type built by Lockheed-Azcarate for use in rough country and produced in Mexico as the LASA-60, Aermacchi secured manufacturing rights outside the USA and supplied versions to Rhodesia (as the Trojan) and South Africa (Bosbok). Finally, an indigenous version was built by the Atlas Aircraft Corporation as the Kudu. (M. Schoeman)

Pumas of 19 Sqn. On 13 February 1983 a fuel dump in Lesotho was blown up. The SAAF was the next ANC target when a bomb was placed near its HQ in Pretoria on 20 May. Nineteen civilians were killed and 215 injured. Retribution was swift, although delayed over a weekend to minimize civilian casualties. At 0725hrs on Monday 23rd, Impalas attacked the ANC building in Maputo where the bombing had been planned. The strike was made by the slower aircraft to guarantee precision, and weapons were confined to rockets and cannon. An SA-3 site was also attacked. In the strike 41 ANC personnel, seventeen Mozambique soldiers and six civilians were killed, but the ANC was not to be cowed. On 17 October the SAAF supported a further strike against the ANC in Maputo in retaliation for the bombing of a fuel depot in northern Transvaal.

Shortly afterwards, South Africa and Mozambique reached an agreement whereby neither country would support guerrilla movements inimical to the other. As ANC operations continued, so the SADF struck at bases. On 19 May 1986 offices at Harare, Zimbabwe, were attacked, and the same day an ANC centre at Gaberones was blown up by an SADF unit brought in by Pumas with an Impala escort. The action was preceded by a leaflet drop, and aircraft fitted for sky-shouting warned the local Defence Force not to intervene. Later in the month, using intelligence gathered in the earlier raids, two SAAF fighters attacked an ANC centre at Makeni Plots in Zambia. South Africa is clearly intent on maintaining internal security by surgical operations against external bases, and no immediate political solution appears likely.

The powerful Puma flies with five units, partnering the Super Frelon in a variety of roles. The undercarriage fairings are squared off to enable flotation bags to be fitted for over-sea operation on search and rescue duties, but the type was also used for inserting troops into Angola. Seen here in brown/green overall camouflage is no. 156. (M. Schoeman)

AIRCRAFT MARKINGS

Before the mid-1970s most aircraft were finished natural metal overall, but from that time all but some trainers have been camouflaged. With the exceptions noted, light combat aircraft are generally olive drab/deep buff over, Light Admiralty Grey under, with black serials on the rear fuselage.

Mirage IIICZ *Squadron badge on fin: 802, 813 (2 Sqn.).*
Mirage IIID2Z: *849 (2 Sqn.).*
Mirage IIIEZ: *831 (85 AFS).*
Mirage F.1AZ *Squadron badge on fin: 231, 244 (1 Sqn.).*
Mirage F.1CZ: *204, 210 (3 Sqn.).*
Impala I *Silver overall, squadron badge on nose, black serial on rear fuselage, last two digits on nose: 490, 518 (5 Sqn.); 555 (8 Sqn.).*
Impala II *Squadron badge on nose, last two digits of serial on nose: 1027, 1037 (4 Sqn.).*
Canberra B(I).12 *PR Blue overall, black serial on rear fuselage: 453, 455 (12 Sqn.).*
Canberra T.4 *458 (12 Sqn.).*
Buccaneer S.50 *Dark Sea Grey over, PR Blue under, squadron badge on intake, black serial on rear fuselage: 416, 419 (24 Sqn.).*

Support aircraft are generally finished Olive Drab/Dark Earth overall.
Bosbok *Black serial on rear fuselage: 930 (42 Sqn.).*
Kudu *Black serial on rear fuselage: 961, 970 (42 Sqn.).*
Cessna 185 *Black serial on rear fuselage: 732, 738 (11 Sqn.).*
Alouette III *Black serial mid-fuselage: 639 (16 Sqn.).*
Puma *Black serial on rear boom: 146, 186 (19 Sqn.).*
Super Frelon *Black serial on rear boom: 305, 311 (15 Sqn.).*

Transport aircraft are finished Olive Drab/Dark Earth over and PR Blue under (C-47, DC-4) or overall Olive Drab with Dark Sea Grey under-fuselage (C-130B, C-160Z).
C-47 *Black serial on rear fuselage with last two digits in yellow on nose: 6857, 6892 (44 Sqn.).*
DC-4 *Black serial on rear fuselage: 6903, 6904 (44 Sqn.).*
C-130B *Black serial on rear fuselage: 401, 403 (28 Sqn.).*
C-160Z *Black serial on rear fuselage: 331, 333 (28 Sqn.).*

4.10. Miscellaneous conflicts and incidents

1. On 13 January 1949 there were local riots in Durban against the Indian population. Police were flown to the city to help restore order.

2. Shortly after the creation of the Federation of Rhodesia and Nyasaland there were riots at Cholo in Nyasaland. Southern Rhodesian Air Force (SRAF) Spitfire F.22s and several transport aircraft were sent to Blantyre in a show of force.

3. The Central African Federation (The Rhodesias and Nyasaland) did not develop as had been hoped. There were serious disturbances in Nyasaland early in 1959, and Royal Rhodesian Air Force (RRAF) armed Provosts of 4 Sqn. supported Dakotas of 3 Sqn. taking 1,200 troops to Blantyre. Within a month the emergency was over.

4. Disagreement between the British Government and that of Rhodesia led to the RAF transporting troops to Nairobi with the intention of enabling the secession of Northern Rhodesia from the Federation by force if necessary. In February 1961 an RRAF Canberra was sent to Nairobi to establish the extent of the British build-up and plans were made to block runways to prevent transport aircraft from landing. In the event the matter was settled by diplomacy.

5. On 20 May 1963 there was widespread unrest at the Havelock asbestos mine outside Mbabane, the capital of Swaziland; this was followed by a call for a national strike by nationalists seeking immediate independence from Britain. To maintain law and order in this most conservative of colonies, the 1st Bn. Gordon Highlanders was lifted, with equipment, from Kenya on 13 June. The aircraft involved, which operated out of Eastleigh, were Argosy C.ls of 105 Sqn., normally based in Aden, and Beverley C.1s of 30 Sqn. The position quickly stabilized without recourse to arms, and the troops withdrew on 20 June. Independence finally came in 1968.

6. A US satellite recorded what was assumed to be a low-yield nuclear explosion in the South Atlantic on 22 September 1979. A South African Navy task force was alleged to be in the area and apparently related SAAF activity was also reported.

7. A Piper Cherokee, ZS-JPP, was shot down by Botswana forces on 11 December 1982.

5: East Africa

As in West Africa, since 1945 much of the conflict in East Africa has arisen as a result of tribal differences and the artificiality of territorial boundaries drawn by reference only to lines of latitude and longitude. In the north-east, the so-called Horn of Africa, there has been constant fighting since 1947.

In this area there were originally three Somali-lands, French, British and Italian. The last two were under British mandate until 1950, during which time there were local troubles with Shifta (bandit) tribesman. The Royal Air Force, operating out of Aden, helped to maintain order through demonstrations and occasional raids. British and Italian Somaliland were united as the Somali Republic in 1960, from which time the Somalis attempted to extend their borders to incorporate parts of Kenya and Ethiopia peopled by Somali tribes. This led to wars with Kenya from 1963 and Ethiopia from 1977. In the process the Somali Government moved from a close relationship with the Soviet Union to looking towards the US for support. In the whole region alliances seem to be founded more on the basis of common enemies than on common causes.

Further north, Eritrea has attempted to maintain independence since being federated to Ethiopia in 1952. Again the rebels have found their supporters switching sides, but they have attempted to work in common with at least four other Ethiopian separatist movements. Their guerrilla war with Ethiopia continues.

While Sudan provides a haven for Eritrean rebels, it has problems of its own. Deep racial and religious differences between the north and south of the largest country in Africa have resulted in a continuous guerrilla war since 1955, the southern rebels getting much of their support from Uganda and Ethiopia. In the Horn of Africa the number of people lost in so much continuous fighting is eclipsed only by the number lost to disease and famine. With adverse climatic conditions leading to failed crops and ruined economies, the position seems only likely to get worse as guerrillas and govern-ments alike use famine as a weapon.

In the old British colonies of Kenya, Uganda and Tanganyika, only in Kenya was there a pre-independence war, officially described as an 'emergency'. Here the cause was land occupation and the targets local settlers rather than the British Government. The techniques employed by the Government were similar to those used successfully in Malaya, and as in Malaya it was troops on the ground, with air support, who succeeded in gradually mopping up guerrilla activity. In all three countries there were army mutinies shortly after independence, and in each case the British Government was invited to help in putting them down. Again the flexibility of naval air power was demonstrated to good effect.

In Uganda, the British later sowed a wind in helping Idi Amin gain power, and the Israelis were to reap the whirlwind in 1976. By then Uganda was formally a Muslim state with a PLO base and was happy to support terrorists when they diverted a hijacked aircraft to Entebbe. In a carefully planned and brilliantly executed raid on the airport, the Israelis recovered nearly all of the hostages. As he gradually lost support internally, Amin ordered a raid into neighbouring Tanzania in 1978. This was followed the next year by a full scale invasion of Uganda by Tanzanian troops and Ugandan exiles; Amin fled to Saudi Arabia, and one of the bloodiest regimes in Africa's bloody history came to an end. Internal differences have, however, resulted in a continuing civil war.

The islands off East Africa have not escaped war. In Madagascar from 1947 the French, in characteristically uncompromising fashion, put down a serious rebellion by nationalist groups seeking independence from colonial rule. Much later, in 1981, in a notorious fiasco, a group of mercenaries attempted unsuccessfully to topple the Government of the Seychelles. In neither case were aircraft used as machines of war, merely as a means of transporting ground forces.

5.1. Madagascar, 1947–1948

As the Second World War came to an end three local politicians in the French colony of Madagascar formed the Mouvement Democratique de la Rénovation Malagache (MDRM), which by the end of 1946 had an estimated 300,000 members bent on securing independence. On 29 March 1947, without warning, 1,200 MDRM members attacked a military base at Moramanga, killing twenty French and Senegalese troops. At the time the French were preoccupied with the

Unit	Aircraft	Base	Role	Dates
AA				
SLA 50	Martinet. AAC.1. Goeland. Criquet	Ivato	Liaison, transport	Permanently based
EOM 85	Martinet	Ivato	Communications	Permanently based
GT 2/61	ACC.1	Dakar	Transport	00/08/47 to 00/09/47
Aéronavale				
31S	AAC.1	Diego Suarez, ex Orly	Transport	09/04/47 to 03/05/47
32S	AAC.1	Diego Suarez, ex Algeria	Transport	09/04/47 to 03/05/47
SLS	AAC.1. C-47 (1/2 aircraft)	Diego Suarez	Transport, communications	00/05/47 to 00/00/58

war in Indo-China and had few units based in Madagascar; the only Armée de l'Air (AA) units were Secteur Liaison Air (SLA) 50 based at Ivato and comprising six AAC.1s, three Martinets, one Goeland and a Criquet, and Escadrille d'Outre Mer (EOM) 85, also at Ivato, with eight Martinets. These aircraft were basically liaison or transport types, there being no combat aircraft in the region.

There were simultaneous attacks at Farafangana, Antsirabe and Diego Suarez, and within a few days most of the east coast was in MDRM hands. From 9 April to 3 May nine AAC.1s of Escadrilles 31S and 32S of Aéronautique Navale flew in troops and supplies; the aircraft were then used to supplement those already in the colony. Although the French garrison was reinforced, the MDRM attacked the capital Tananarive on 3 July, but after fierce fighting they were beaten back. The French now flew Senegalese troops and Foreign Legion paratroopers in from Dakar in AAC.1s of Groupe de Transport (GT) 2/61. From then until operations ceased in January 1948 at the start of the rainy season, the French forces fought a succession of uncompromising battles with the MDRM and by April all resistance had collapsed.

The vicious fighting cost around 1,000 French troops and 200 civilians killed. The cost to the MDRM has never been reliably assessed, and estimates range from 11,000 to 90,000 dead and 558,000 surrendered. The ferocity of the fighting was such that international opinion resulted in diplomatic pressure being applied to the French; it was reported that, perhaps coincidentally, a squadron of Lincoln bombers of the RAF was detached to East Africa in the spring of 1948.

5.2. Somaliland, 1947—1950

Situated on the Horn of Africa, what is now the Somali Republic was once two colonies: the northern part, on the Gulf of Aden, was British Somaliland, while the eastern part, facing the Indian Ocean, was Somalia Italiana. The Italian territory was occupied by the British from 1941, and after the war there were tribal revolts, mainly on the part of the Shifta and revolving around land disputed with Ethiopia in the Ogaden. During the spring of 1947 Mosquito FB.6s of 8 Sqn. were to be seen at Hargeisa showing the flag, and in January 1948 Tempests of 6 Sqn. were detached to Mogadishu to fly demonstration sorties. From time to time they were supplemented by aircraft of 8 Sqn. from Aden which flew into Hargeisa when there was unrest, for example, in nearby Jijiga at the end of March 1948.

There was increased activity in June 1948 when it was announced that the disputed Ogaden territory was to be transferred to Ethiopia. The Somali Youth League (SYL) fomented unrest, and the RAF sent 213 Sqn. to Mogadishu; again, demonstration flights were often sufficient to stabilize the situation. On 23 September 1948 the last British troops left the Ogaden and in October 213 Sqn. returned to Deversoir. Tempests and then Brigands of 8 Sqn. were flown to Mogadishu throughout 1949 as the local situation demanded, until in February 1950 84 Sqn. sent a detachment of Brigands from Habbaniyah to coincide with the handing back of Somalia Italiana to Italian administration. In British Somaliland the RAF retained facilities at Hargeisa but with no aircraft permanently based; an RAF officer commanded the contingent of native

After the Second World War there was unrest in Somaliland, with revolts by Shifta tribesmen. When the British handed over Somalia Italia to Italian administration in 1950, 84 Sqn., based at Habbaniyah, detached a number of Brigands to Mogadishu. Illustrated is Brigand B.1 RH818. (RAF Museum)

scouts, and any potential local disturbances would have been contained through air policing.

AIRCRAFT MARKINGS

Tempest F.6 Silver overall, black serials on rear fuselage and under wings, unit badge on nose: NX147/JV-J, NX201/JV-U (6 Sqn.): NX169/C (8 Sqn.). Ocean Grey/Dark Green over, Medium Sea Grey under, black serial on rear fuselage, white code spanning roundels, red spinner, Sky band around rear fuselage: NX229/AK-R (213 Sqn.).

Brigand B.1 Medium Sea Grey over, black under, white serial on rear fuselage and under wings, code on mid-fuselage, white spinners: RH817/A, RH818/B (84 Sqn.).

TABLE OF UNITS: THE ROYAL AIR FORCE IN SOMALILAND, 1947–1950

Unit	Aircraft	Base	Role	Dates
6 Sqn.	Tempest F.6	Mogadishu, ex Fayid	Ground attack	00/01/48 to 00/05/48
8 Sqn.	Tempest F.6 (det.)	Hargeisa, ex Aden	Ground attack	00/03/48 to 00/03/48
213 Sqn.	Tempest F.6	Mogadishu, ex Deversoir	Ground attack	17/08/48 to 02/10/48 00/11/50 to 00/12/50
8 Sqn.	Brigand B.1 (det.)	Mogadishu, ex Aden	Light bombing	00/09/49 to 00/12/49 00/02/50 to 00/03/50
84 Sqn.	Brigand B.1 (det.)	Mogadishu, ex Habbaniyah	Light bombing	00/02/50 to 00/03/50
683 Sqn.	Lancaster GR.1 (det.)	Hargeisa	Survey	00/01/52 to 00/04/52

5.3. Eritrea, 1950–1952

Eritrea, on the Red Sea, was colonized by Italy from 1882 but occupied by Britain in 1941, after which it was subject to British administration. From time to time there was civil unrest and small British forces were deployed, although the main responsibility for order rested with the Eritrean Police Field Force (EPFF). To assist with the task a detachment of Mosquito PR.34s of 13 Sqn. was sent to Asmara in April 1947, primarily to provide the basis for mapping. Then in April 1948 a detachment of Tempest F.6s of 39 Sqn., recently re-formed at Nairobi, was sent to Asmara to support ground forces as rebel Shifta nomads made a number of guerrilla attacks. The Tempests were in action late in the year rocketing rebel positions.

Matters became worse from 1950 as there was discussion about the future of the territory. No. 1910 Flt., equipped with Auster AOP.6s, was sent from Tripoli to operate in a variety of roles. The unit sent permanent detachments to Agordat and Barentu and flew reconnaissance sorties, also providing liaison, light resupply and occasionally casualty evacuation services. Primarily the flight

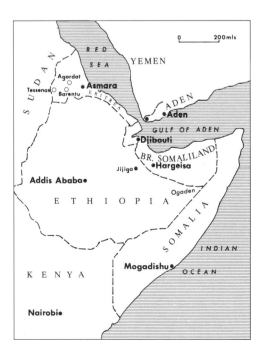

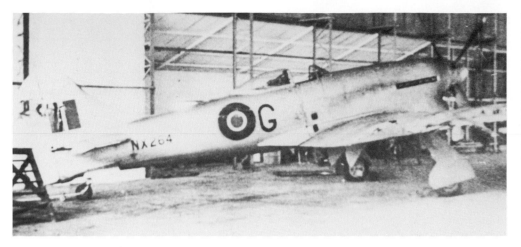

The Shifta did not confine their activities to Somaliland. In 1948 Tempests of 39 Sqn. were detached to Asmara, Eritrea, to support ground forces working with the Eritrean Police Field Force. Seen here at Khartoum is Tempest F.6 NX264/G after colliding with NX247 of the same unit. (M. D. Howley via A. S. Thomas)

kept mobile ground units in touch with base and acted to bring heavier air support to bear when required. To provide firepower, Brigand light bombers of 8 Sqn. and Spitfire FR.18s of 208 Sqn. from Aden and Fayid respectively were detached to Asmara from August. Detachments remained in Eritrea to contain guerrilla activity until summer 1951. The Spitfires of 208 Sqn. were retired in favour of the Meteor FR.9, and these aircraft maintained the fighter support role until late in the year.

By early 1952 it had been decided by the UN that Eritrea should become federated to Ethiopia, and before withdrawal the RAF deployed several Lancaster GR.1s of 683 Sqn. to Hargeisa for survey work. British forces generally left Eritrea in June 1952, although 1910 Flt. operated until September when it departed to join the parent 651 Sqn. at Ismailia.

AIRCRAFT MARKINGS

Brigand B.1 *Medium Sea Grey over, black under, white serials on rear fuselage and under wings, code on mid-fuselage: VS816/A (8 Sqn.).*
Tempest F.6 *Silver overall, black serial on rear fuselage, code mid-fuselage: NX264/G (39 Sqn.).*

TABLE OF UNITS: ERITREA, 1950–1952

Unit	Aircraft	Base	Role	Dates
RAF				
13 Sqn.	Mosquito PR.34 (det.)	Asmara. ex Fayid	PR	21/04/47 to 28/04/47
39 Sqn.	Tempest F.6	Asmara. ex Nairobi	Ground attack	00/04/48 to 00/11/48
208 Sqn.	Spitfire FR.18. Meteor FR.9	Asmara. ex Fayid	Ground attack	00/08/50 to 00/04/51
8 Sqn.	Brigand B.1 (det.)	Asmara. ex Aden	Light bombing	00/08/50 to 00/07/51
British Army				
1910 Flt.	Auster AOP.6	Asmara (dets. at Agordat. Barentu. Tessenas)	Recce. liaison. casevac. light supply	31/07/50 to 00/09/52

5.4. Kenya, 1952–1956

For many years before the Second World War there was dissension in Kenya on the part of the Kikuyu tribe in the central province to the north of Nairobi. Essentially it was felt, perhaps not without some justification, that Europeans had deprived them of their lands. After the war the Kenya African Union (KAU) was formed and from it sprang an extremist group, Mau Mau, otherwise calling itself the Kenya Land Freedom Party. As the population grew, pressure on the land was such that the indigenous peoples found themselves working on increasingly less advantageous terms for European farmers. In 1948 and 1949 there was discontent among the labour force and the local RAF Communications Flight was involved in leaflet dropping.

Through 1952 there were isolated attacks on white farmers. However, by no means all Kikuyu supported Mau Mau, and it was the murder of Chief Waruhiu, a close British ally, on 9 October 1952 that led to a state of emergency being declared on 21 October. That day the 1st Bn. Lancashire Fusiliers was flown into Nairobi on Hastings transports of 511 Sqn., joining four battalions of the King's African Rifles and the Kenya Regiment already in the country. The first operation, 'Jock Scott', was the rounding up and internment of 83 known Mau Mau leaders. A large region north of Nairobi was declared the operational area, and within that were two prohibited tracts within which the security forces could work freely on the assumption that anyone found within them could be deemed to be a terrorist. One area, of 820 square miles, was in the Aberdare Mountains, while the second, of 780 square miles, was around Mount Kenya. Without their leaders the Mau Mau were inactive for a few weeks, but on 1 January 1953 the first white farmers were killed.

At the time the strength of the RAF in Kenya amounted to six aircraft in a Communications Flight based at Eastleigh, and these included two Dakotas left by 82 Sqn. when it had returned to the UK in October following a survey. Plans were put in hand to improve the position, and as the Rhodesian Air Training Group (RATG) was being disbanded a number of its Harvard IIBs were formed into 1340 Flt. at Thornhill. The flight moved to Eastleigh on 23 March 1953 and it immediately began bombing operations using 20lb fragmentation bombs. There was one other air unit that was to prove of immense value to the security forces – the Kenya Police Reserve Air Wing (KPRAW), which had been formed in 1949. By 1953 it comprised several Austers and some Piper Pacers and Tri-Pacers, and these were soon put to work supporting police and army outposts and searching for signs of the elusive enemy.

There was an outrage on 26 March when 84 loyal Kikuyu were massacred at Lari only 20 miles out of Nairobi, and the same day guns were stolen from a police station at Naivasha. The military commander called for more units from Britain, and on 7 June HQ 39 Brigade, with a battalion from the Royal East Kent Regiment and one from the Devon Regiment, was flown in and a separate East Africa Command established. The security forces now began a series of intense operations in and around the prohibited areas. The KPRAW and 1340 Flt. moved up to Nyeri, then Mweiga, where a Joint Operations Centre (JOC) was established to co-ordinate bombing in support of ground forces. The KPRAW was invaluable in that its pilots were familiar with

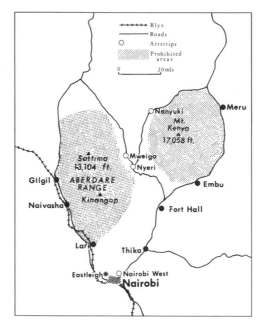

the local geography and were able to reconnoitre for the Harvards; so important was the unit that its CO, an RAF reserve officer, was given tactical command under the RAF Commander of Air Forces.

The situation became worse through the summer of 1953 with the Mau Mau building up a town-based infrastructure of support for operational groups in the mountains. Savage atrocities were committed against any loyal Kikuyu in order to ensure support and neutralize local opposition. A second brigade HQ and two more infantry battalions were flown into Kenya from 29 September 1953 on 41 RAF Hastings and civilian charter flights. In September the Harvards flew 332 sorties, dropping 2,555 bombs, but their limitations soon became apparent in attacking small, elusive Mau Mau groups working from mountain hideouts. From November 1953 Lin-

In Kenya, as in Malaya, the RAF used heavy bombers to strike at elusive guerrilla groups in dense jungle. Apart from any psychological value, the bombs did little damage to the Mau Mau. In all, five Lincoln squadrons were rotated through Eastleigh from the UK, 49 Sqn. completing two tours of duty. Seen here at Eastleigh in November 1953 is RF349 of 49 Sqn. (Flt. Lt. A. Clarke via A.S. Thomas)

TABLE OF UNITS: KENYA, 1952–1956

Unit	Aircraft	Base	Role	Dates
RAF				
Comms. Flt.	Anson C.21. Proctor IV. Valetta C.1. Dakota III Auster AOP.6. Pembroke C.1 Sycamore HR.14	Eastleigh	Communications. light transport Sky-shouting Casevac	Permanently based
82 Sqn.	Lancaster PR.1. Dakota III	Eastleigh	PR	01.07.52 to 31.10.52
1340 Flt.	Harvard IIB	Eastleigh. Nyeri. Mweiga	Light ground attack	23.03.53 to 30.09.55
49 Sqn.				11.11.53 to 00.01.54
100 Sqn.	Lincoln B.II	Eastleigh	Medium bombing	00.01.54 to 00.03.54
61 Sqn.				00.03.54 to 19.06.54
8 Sqn.	Vampire FB.9 (det.)		Ground attack	00.04.54 to 00.05.54
214 Sqn.	Lincoln B.II	Eastleigh	Medium bombing	12.06.54 to 10.12.54
13 Sqn.	Meteor PR.10 (det.)		PR	18.08.54 to 25.07.55
49 Sqn.	Lincoln B.II	Eastleigh	Medium bombing	30.11.54 to 28.07.55
21 Sqn.				00.03.55 to 00.04.55
KPRAW				
–	Pacer. Tri-Pacer. Cessna 180	Nairobi West. Nyeri. Mweiga	Liaison. recce. light supply. target-marking	Permanently based

coln bombers were rotated into Eastleigh to provide scope for pattern bombing of known terrorist camps, the first detachment being provided by 49 Sqn.

In January 1954 100 Sqn. took over from 49 Sqn. and in March it in turn was replaced by 61 Sqn., which lost RE297 when it crashed on a night operation on 22 March. The Lincolns normally worked early in the morning before clouds and turbulence had built up. Their loads generally comprised five 1,000lb and nine 500lb bombs, although on occasions 350lb cluster bombs were carried. The supply of bombs was a problem throughout the campaign and many were unreliable. Fuses were normally set at 25 seconds because of the low altitudes often required. On one urgent raid on 14 August 1954 three Lincolns of 214 Sqn. were required to bomb a concentration of Mau Mau near Nyeri. The aircraft were already bombed up, but the cloud ceiling meant that the weapons had to be released at only 900ft. The first bomb detonated on impact, and the shock waves set up sympathetic explosions among the succeeding bombs until one exploded just below the bomb bay of the third aircraft, causing great damage and killing the flight engineer. The KPRAW generally under-

took spotting and target marking as for the Harvards.

Early in the year Eastleigh acquired two Auster AOP.6s and a Pembroke fitted with loudspeakers for use in post-bombing sorties, to encourage surrender while the terrorists were still confused; in addition, a Sycamore was added to the Station Flight to enable the speedy recovery of casualties in terrain where surface transport could take many days to cover a few miles. As intelligence improved, the Mau Mau dependence on town-based supporters for supplies became clearer, and Operation 'Anvil' between 24 April and 7 May led to 16,538 suspects being detained in sweeps around Nairobi. Coincident with this operation, a detachment of Vampire FB.9s of 8 Sqn. was sent to Eastleigh from Aden.

One problem identified in early 1953 was the lack of photo-reconnaissance aircraft to provide post-attack information on the success of strikes. This was remedied from August when two Meteor PR.10s were detached from 13 Sqn. then based at Fayid in Egypt. From the end of 1954, by which time 49 Sqn. had begun its second Kenyan tour, the Mau Mau were demonstrably weaker. Operation 'Hammer' in January in the Aberdares and Operation 'First Flute' from February around

When a state of emergency was declared in Kenya in October 1952, the 1st Bn. Lancashire Fusiliers was flown to Nairobi in Hastings transports of 511 Sqn. Through the 1950s and 1960s the Hastings was the standard RAF medium-range transport, moving troops to trouble spots around the world. Units were based in the UK and in the Near and Far East. This is TG577 of 511 Sqn., at Malta. (C. Shepherdson)

Mount Kenya resulted in 161 and 277 Mau Mau dead respectively; during these sweeps, 49 Sqn. lost SX984 when it hit a police post during a demonstration. The terrorists were now effectively defeated, but the Lincolns did not depart until July 1955, and at the end of September 1340 Flt. was disbanded. During the emergency its aircraft had dropped 21,936 20lb bombs and lost eight aircraft out of nineteen in accidents. On 17 November 1956 the Army withdrew, and in December the operational phase ended. By then the war had cost the Mau Mau 10,527 dead and 2,633 captured; the security forces had lost 602 dead, of whom 534 were Africans. The British Government calculated the cost at precisely £55,585,424!

AIRCRAFT MARKINGS

Lincoln B.II Medium Sea Grey over, black under, large white serials on rear fuselage and under wings, white spinners: RF349, RF444 (49 Sqn.). White spinners: RE320 (100 Sqn.). Red serial, large white codes: RF507/HW-G (100 Sqn.); RF555, SX979 (61 Sqn.). Yellow spinners: RE299 (214 Sqn.).
Harvard IIB Yellow overall, black serial and code on rear fuselage: FT392/G. Later silver overall with black serial on rear fuselage: KF326, KF390, KF625 (all 1340 Flt.).
Vampire FB.9 Silver overall, black serial on boom and code (when carried) on rear boom: WL608/U, WL586 (8 Sqn.).

5.5. The East African Mutinies, 1964

Four East African British colonies, Kenya, Uganda, Tanganyika and Zanzibar, achieved independence in the period 1961–1963. Zanzibar was the last to gain independence, on 10 December 1963, but on 12 January 1964 the new government was overthrown and Britain was asked for help by the deposed ruler. This was refused, but the frigate HMS *Rhyl* was dispatched from Mombasa with a company of 1 Bn. The Staffordshire Regt. to protect and if necessary evacuate British nationals from the island. The survey ship HMS *Owen* and the RFA *Hebe* were also on the scene. In the event, the issue was resolved without recourse to arms.

On the mainland, trouble broke out when on 20 January men of 1 Bn. Tanganyika Rifles mutinied at Colito, detaining their British officers and NCOs. The next day men of 2 Bn. mutinied at Tabora, seized Dar-es-Salaam airport and captured the British High Commissioner. HMS *Rhyl* was ordered back on the 20th and the carrier HMS *Centaur* sailed from Aden with men of 45 RM Commando and 16/5 Lancers. Apart from her own aircraft complement *Centaur* embarked two Belvedere HC.1 helicopters of 26 Sqn. President Julius Nyere formally asked Britain to intervene on 24 January, by which time the British captives had been released. On the 25th a company of 45 RM was landed by helicopter at the Colito barracks and took the mutineers by surprise after a brief display of force; other marines rounded up mutineers in the neighbourhood. The barracks at Tabora, 700 miles inland, was the target for a Fleet Air Arm (FAA) strike on the afternoon of the 25th. A mixed force of Sea Vixen FAW.1s of 892 NAS and Buccaneer S.1s, probably of 801 NAS detached from HMS *Victorious*, were ten minutes from the target when the strike was aborted following the surrender of the mutineers.

The revolt was apparently a response to poor conditions and the continued employment of

The Presidents of newly independent Tanganyika, Uganda and Kenya sought British help when their troops mutinied early in 1964. The carrier HMS *Centaur* was to hand, and among her Fleet Air Arm complement were two Belvedere HC.1s of 26 Sqn. RAF. embarked at Aden. These were used to transport men of 45 Commando to barracks at Colito, which soon surrendered. Seen here at Dar-es-Salaam is Belvedere HC.1 XG461/G of 26 Sqn. (J. A. Pike)

British officers and NCOs, and on 23 January there were further mutinies for the same reasons in Uganda and Kenya. In Uganda men of 1 and 2 Bns. Uganda Rifles mutinied at Jinja, and the same day President Milton Obote asked Britain for help. In response, 450 men of 1 Bn. The Staffordshire Regt. and 2 Bn. The Scots Guards were flown into Entebbe in Beverley transports of 30 Sqn. from Eastleigh. While the Scots Guards held the airport, the 'Staffs' drove the 70 miles to Jinja and early on the morning of the 25th took the barracks without a fight.

In Kenya it was 250 men of 11 Bn. Kenya Rifles who mutinied at Lanet. Again Britain was asked to intervene, and at Gilgil a battery of 3 RHA was ordered to the scene. The 75 artillerymen were unable to clear the barracks completely, and on the 24th they were joined by more gunners, some engineers and men of the Gordon Highlanders. After negotiations the mutineers surrendered. HMS *Centaur* was relieved by HMS *Victorious* on 29 January, which brought men of 41 Commando who relieved those of 45 Commando; 41 Commando remained in Tanzania until April, when it was relieved by Nigerian troops. Early in April a squadron of T-28As of the Ethiopian Air Force (EAF) arrived at Dar-es-Salaam to help maintain internal stability.

TABLE OF UNITS: THE EAST AFRICAN MUTINIES, 1964

Unit	Aircraft	Base	Role
FAA			
892 NAS	Sea Vixen FAW.1		Air defence, ground attack
815 NAS	Wessex HAS.1	*Centaur*	ASW, transport, liaison
849 NAS	Gannet AEW.3 (B Flt.)		AEW, communications
893 NAS	Sea Vixen FAW.1		Air defence, ground attack
801 NAS	Buccaneer S.1	*Victorious*	Strike
814 NAS	Wessex HAS.1		ASW, transport, liaison
849 NAS	Gannet AEW.3		AEW, communications
RAF			
26 Sqn.	Belvedere HC.1 (det.)	*Centaur*	Transport
30 Sqn.	Beverley C.1	Eastleigh	Medium transport
British Army			
8 IRF	Alouette AH.2, Beaver AL.1	Eastleigh	Recce, liaison
EAF			
–	T-28A	Dar-es-Salaam	Patrol

AIRCRAFT MARKINGS

RAF

Belvedere HC.1 *Silver overall, white top fuselage decking and tail surfaces, squadron badge on rear engine mounting, black serial on rear fuselage, code mid-fuselage: XG461/G (26 Sqn.).*

EAF

T-28A *Light grey overall, black serial on fin: 551.*

5.6. Somalia and Kenya, 1963–1967

When the Italian Trust Territories and British Somaliland Protectorate achieved independence as the Somali Democratic Republic (SDR) on 1 July 1960, the new state immediately claimed rights to territory in north-east Kenya and French Somaliland (Djibouti). Prior to independence in Kenya a British commission was sent to the country to establish the views of Kenyans, mainly of Somali extraction, living in the north-east. Despite the people's wish to be merged into the SDR, their views were ignored, and in March 1963 diplomatic relations between SDR and Britain were broken off. Shifta tribesmen now crossed the border, supported by the Somali Government, making raids against villages and police posts. British troops and units of the King's African Rifles (KAR) were supported by Beverley transports of 30 Sqn. and Twin Pioneer utility aircraft of 21 Sqn., both operating out of Eastleigh. The Twin Pioneers were equipped with bomb racks and light machine guns to scatter raiding parties in the scrub.

Kenyan independence in December 1963 was followed by a mutiny in the fledgeling army, leaving the Government with no cohesive response to the continuing guerrilla war backing the SDR claims over the three provinces of Mandira, Wajir and Garissa. No. 21 Sqn. remained until 1965 while an embryo Air Force was established with Chipmunks, seven Beavers and four Caribou. Initially, the new Kenya Air Force (KAF) was largely manned by seconded RAF officers and men, and the Beavers were soon flying out of Wajir in support of company-strength units of the Kenya Rifles. In the arid conditions, the Kenyan policy was to control the wells and manage small-scale operations against units wherever they could be located.

No offensive sorties were flown, but the aircraft were invaluable in spotting guerrillas in the sparse scrub which provided no cover. The Caribou flew supply missions out of Eastleigh while the Beavers flew reconnaissance, resupply, casevac and redeployment sorties. Despite some damage caused by mined roads, the Shifta were making no progress, and following a conference at Kinshasa in October 1967 President Kenyatta offered an amnesty to any Shifta still carrying arms. The small local war ended.

AIRCRAFT MARKINGS

RAF

Twin Pioneer CC.1 *Silver overall, white fuselage top decking, black serial rear fuselage, code on fin: XM960/C (21 Sqn.).*

KAF

Beaver *Silver overall, large serial on rear fuselage in black: KAF102.*

Unit	Aircraft	Base	Role	Dates
RAF				
21 Sqn.	Twin Pioneer CC.1	Eastleigh, Wajir	Armed light transport	00/09/59 to 00/06/65
30 Sqn.	Beverley C.1	Eastleigh	Medium transport	00/10/59 to 00/10/64
British Army				
8 IRF	Alouette AH.2, Beaver AL.1	Eastleigh	Recce, liaison	00/00/59 to 00/00/66
KAF				
–	Beaver	Eastleigh, Wajir	Light transport, recce, casevac	
–	Caribou	Eastleigh	Medium transport	

5.7. The Ethiopian Wars

Ethiopia has been caught up in at least three distinct wars since 1961 involving Eritrea, the Somali Republic and the Sudan. In 1945 the country was an independent empire with strong western ties, the British having helped liberate it from the Italians in 1941. In 1952 Eritrea came under Ethiopian rule, and despite a harsh internal regime based on feudalism the Emperor, Haile Selassie, received significant American aid from 1953. A Military Assistance Advisory Group (MAAG), numbering at its peak about 300, was established, and by 1974 some 25,000 Ethiopians had been trained in the US and $400 million given in aid. An important communications post was established at Kagnew outside Asmara.

After a disastrous famine in 1973–74, and despite attempts at government reform, the Emperor was overthrown by junior army officers and imprisoned on 12 September 1974; many politicians were executed. For a time US support continued. In Eritrea, rebels seeking independence were being supplied and trained by Iraq, Libya and East Germany. The Eritrean Red Sea ports were considered strategically important to the West, as were the Indian Ocean ports of Somali already available to the Soviet Union. The Somali Republic was threatening to make good its territorial claims in the Ogaden, and Western support of a radical new regime seems to have been as much against communist domination of the Horn of Africa as it was for the Ethiopian Government. After a series of internal power struggles in the Dergue (Committee), and after opposition had been ruthlessly exterminated, Mengistu Haile Mariam took control in February 1977. The US Government now refused further aid on the grounds of human rights, and outstanding orders for aircraft and tanks were cancelled.

With the Somalis massing for an attack into the Ogaden, Ethiopia now turned to the Soviet Union for aid. The next twelve months saw a reversal of allegiances as Russian and Cuban advisers moved into Addis Ababa, Libya stopped support for Eritrean rebels in favour of the Government and the Somali Republic expelled Soviet advisers and troops from bases.

From 1945 the Imperial Ethiopian Air Force (IEAF) had been Swedish- and British-trained and equipped, and by the time of the revolution it comprised four Canberra B.52s, one squadron of F-86Fs, one squadron of F-5A/Bs and a flight each of T-28Ds and T-33As. Training was undertaken on Saab Safirs and T-28s, while several C-47s and C-54s served in the transport role. An order had been placed for twelve F-5Es, twelve A-37Bs and fifteen Cessna 310s, but these were embargoed. By 1978 combat aircraft are believed to have comprised about 50 MiG-21s, mainly flown by Russian or Cuban pilots, two Canberra B.52s, possibly as many as eighteen F-5A/Bs (twelve were reported as having been transferred from the Imperial Iranian Air Force) and six T-28Ds. The transport elements now included a number of An-12s and An-24s, five C-47s, two C-54s,

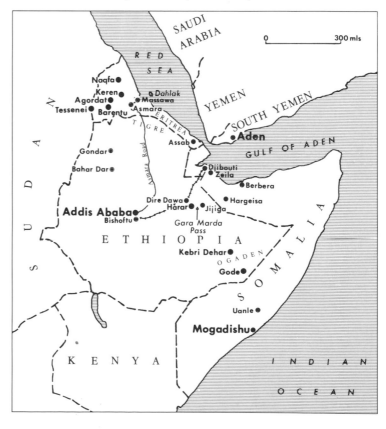

seven C-119Ks and an Il-14. Two L100-30 Hercules were delivered to Ethiopian Airlines for military use in July 1988. The growing helicopter force included six AB.204Bs and up to thirty Mi-8s. The Army flew six UH-1Hs, four Otters and three Twin Otters. In addition there were at least twelve and possibly twenty MiG-23s operated by Cubans and East Germans, ten Soviet Mi-6 heavy-lift helicopters and a squadron of South Yemeni MiG-21s. The Air Force has expanded steadily as Ethiopia has become a Soviet client state and at the time of writing is believed to fly as many as 180 MiG-21s, some MiG-23s and about 40 Mi-8s and Mi-24s. These aircraft are used on two fronts, making occasional raids into Somalia and regularly attacking Eritrean rebels.

AIRCRAFT MARKINGS

F-5A *Brown/sand/dark green over, light grey*

TABLE OF UNITS: THE ETHIOPIAN AIR FORCE, 1972–1978				
Unit	**Aircraft**	**Base**	**Role**	**Nos.**
(1 sqn.)	F-86F	Bishoftu	Air defence	12
(1 sqn.)	F-5A	Gondar	Ground attack	15
(1 flt.)	T-28D	Dire Dawa	Coin	6
(1 sqn.)	Canberra B.52	Bishoftu	Light bombing	4
(1 sqn.)	C-119K, C-47, C-54, Dove	Bishoftu	Transport	17
	Alouette III, Mi-8	Bishoftu, Gondar	Liaison, recce, transport	7
	T-33A	Bishoftu	Advanced training	8
	Saab 91B	Bishoftu	Training	25

under, black serial on fin and forward fuselage: 425, 430.

Canberra B.52 *Dark Green/Dark Sea Grey over, light grey under, black serial on fin: 351, 354.*

T-28D *Light grey overall, black serial on fin: 551.*

C-119K *Brown/sand over, light grey under, serial on fin: 913, 917.*

Colour schemes of Russian-supplied types are not known.

5.8. Eritrea, 1961 to date

In 1952 the United Nations granted government of Eritrea, on a federal basis, to Ethiopia, partly in response to its support in the Korean War. In 1962 Ethiopia annexed the state. Within Eritrea a movement for total independence evolved, becoming in 1960 the Eritrean Liberation Front (ELF). In September 1961 the ELF, supported by Iraq and Syria, began an armed struggle which initially made little impact as divisions within the organization diverted its energy. By 1970, however, a radical offshoot, the Eritrean People's Liberation Force (EPLF), began a military campaign in earnest, on 21 November 1970 ambushing and killing the commanding officer of the 2nd Division, and on 16 December a state of emergency was declared. Over the next few years the ELF/EPLF joined forces and gradually extended their control over the countryside, only the towns remaining in Government hands. During the period to 1974 the ELF claimed that the Ethiopian Air Force (EAF) had lost seven aircraft on operations.

Following rebel attacks within Asmara in January 1975, the Government declared all-out war on the ELF and created a large peasant militia, trained over the ensuing months. As the EAF struck at villages north of Asmara, the RAF, USAF and Italian Air Force (AMI) evacuated foreign nationals from Asmara. During the fighting the ELF claimed a light spotter aircraft and an F-86 shot down. On 13 September 1975 there was an ELF raid on the US listening post at Kagnew in which nine were killed and a number abducted. The militia, supported by F-5As flying from Gondar, did not begin operations until 18 May 1976, but it was quickly routed by a much smaller but better-disciplined guerrilla force which attacked assembly points.

At this stage the ELF was equipped with Soviet arms supplied from sympathetic Arab states, but captured Government arms became more important as the rebels grew in strength; of particular value were anti-aircraft weapons and ammunition. By early 1977 the only major towns in Government hands were Asmara, Massawa and Assab, plus Naqfa, Agordat, Barentu and Adi Caieh. Despite constant air strikes, Keren, on the Massawa–Khartoum railway, had been held by the rebels since 1975, while Barentu was now completely surrounded and had to be supplied, with difficulty, by air. The ELF/EPLF developed a social infrastructure embracing education and health provision which over the years has proved a major strength. In August the ELF took Agordat then Barentu, but by the end of the year the first deliveries of MiG-21s were being made; although these were for use against the Somalis in the Ogaden, the guerrillas had to revise their tactics, improve their air-raid warning system and plan for most movements taking place in darkness.

In late December the ELF/ELPF surrounded Massawa and planned an attack to take it. Although the rebels controlled three-quarters of the town, including the airport, they failed in an assault on the Government base on the 23rd. The attackers were subjected to strafing and bombing strikes by EAF F-5As, MiG-21s and a solitary Canberra. The rebels continued their attacks, but in early January 1978 they were allegedly subjected to shelling from Soviet destroyers lying eight miles offshore. The Eritrean nationalists were now as powerful as ever, comprising over 30,000 trained fighters, with tanks, artillery, large mortars and anti-aircraft artillery, but the Government was planning to recapture the towns as 1,500 Russian and 3,000 Cuban advisers freed troops from holding the Ogaden front. The EAF began a new bombing campaign in January 1978, concentrating on five towns between Asmara and Tessenei; napalm was used extensively.

On 15 May a new land offensive was launched, and gradually through the year the Eritrean-held towns fell. On 28 July the rebel grip on the Asmara road was broken after fierce fighting, although not until November was the Massawa road opened. By the end of 1978 only Naqfa and Keren remained in rebel hands. As the year went on the EAF began using MiG-21s and MiG-23s in increasing numbers against fixed rebel positions, and these attacks were instrumental in paving the way for limited Government successes. The war continued until 1982 with the Ethiopian armed forces managing to hold most of the towns and the EAF subjecting ELF/EPLF areas to constant bombing attacks. On the political front the ELF and EPLF worked hard at improving internal relationships, opened an office in Mogadishu and supported two Ethiopian dissident groups, the Tigre People's Liberation Front (TPLF) and the Oromo Liberation Front (OLF) in Bala province. The ELF/EPLF also acquired new weapons; on 16 May 1981 it claimed a MiG-21 shot down by SA-7 50 miles south of Asmara.

The Ethiopian Army began a further assault on the last significant ELF/EPLF stronghold, Naqfa, in April 1982 in the 'Red Star' campaign. There and at Helhal the rebels were subjected to unprecedented bombing raids, and phosphorous bombs and napalm were used extensively; there were also claims of nerve gas having been used. Soviet An-12 transports helped move some of the 100,000 Government troops, and the attacks were supported by air-dropped propaganda leaflets. Despite some of the most severe fighting to date the Government was unable to take Naqfa, the rebels being helped by TPLF attacks on communication lines and a flare-up in the Ogaden which distracted and stretched Ethiopian resources. At the same time Ethiopian troops crossed into Sudan, where ELF/EPLF guerrillas

had training camps.

The campaign cost the Government heavily for no gains: up to 100,000 lives may have been lost, and the rebels' grip on the countryside remained. On 14 January 1982 an An-26 was claimed shot down near Asmara, of increasing importance to the Russians as a base for Il-38 'May' reconnaissance aircraft. The Soviet Union had earlier lost its base at Berbera in Somali, and apart from access to Asmara it had gained the use of the Dahlak naval complex, which included a helicopter site. The base at Asmara has been subjected to at least one guerrilla commando attack. On the night of 20–21 May 1984 no fewer than 32 aircraft were claimed to have been destroyed, including sixteen MiG-23s, two An-26s, two 'bombers', four other aircraft and six Mi-8 and Mi-24 helicopters. A second raid was reported to have taken place on 14 January 1986 in which 42 aircraft were claimed as destroyed. In addition, the ELF has claimed aircraft shot down, including An-12 '1506' on 15 January 1984 at Tessenei and a MiG-23 on 16 April near Nafqa.

The year 1985 saw renewed fighting at Barentu, which in July fell to the ELF who captured large quantities of weapons including thirteen T-54 tanks. Later in the year, in the second week of October, there were major battles as Government forces tried in vain to take Naqfa and Helhal. The attacks were again supported by air strikes; by now the EAF fighter force was equipped exclusively with MiGs. In March 1988, after consolidating their position, the ELF again attacked Ethiopian forces in the Nafqa area, capturing large amounts of equipment including AAA. During April the EAF bombed targets in Tigre, by now almost completely held by rebels. In an attack on Axum airstrip on 2 May, DC-3 ET-AGT was destroyed in one MiG-23 strike. The Ethiopians were also accused of deliberately firing crops with napalm in an effort to defeat the TPLF. In July the ELF claimed that 600 were killed in an air strike conducted by four MiG-23s on Hawzwen.

5.9. Somalia, 1977 to date

With a large number of ethnic Somalis living beyond its borders, the Somali Democratic Republic (SDR) had long laid claim to territory in northern Kenya, eastern Ethiopia and the French colony of Djibouti. On 15 October 1969 the President was assassinated and replaced by Siad Barre, who proclaimed a socialist state a year later. Somalia then turned to the Soviet Union for aid, which was forthcoming in return for an agreement to permit the building and use of a port and airfield complex at Berbera. For the Somali Aeronautical Corps (SAC), the assistance was in the form of ten Il-28 bombers, 48 MiG-17s, twelve MiG-21s and several Mi-4 and Mi-8

helicopters, plus a few transports. The aircraft were based at Mogadishu, except for one squadron of MiG-17s and the MiG-21 unit, which were based at Hargeisa.

The Somali Government supported and sponsored the Western Somali Liberation Front (WSLF) which was formed in 1974 and was dedicated to securing 'Somali' territory beyond the borders and especially in the Ogaden region of Ethiopia. As the Somalis watched the internal strife within Ethiopia and the continuing commitment to the war with Eritrea, the WSLF decided on incursions into the Ogaden during May 1977; by the end of the month it claimed to control seven towns. The Government then determined covertly to support the guerrillas, having noted the entry of Cubans into Ethiopia from April and the concurrent closure of US facilities. The first major attack was launched on 12 July against Gode in the south. During the fighting Count von Rosen, who had been organizing famine relief flights, was killed. The town was finally captured on the 25th. At this early stage in the war, when the SAC was on roughly even terms with the EAF, Somali aircraft were involved in ground-attack sorties.

During the early fighting the EAF claimed four SAC MiG-21s, two near Kebri Dehar, and a MiG-17; for their part, the Somalis claimed a civilian DC-3, shot down by SA-7, and a military C-47. The Somalis were able to exploit their gains, however, and by 9 August the Ethiopian Government admitted that the Ogaden was in Somali hands. The same week the EAF began bombing towns in north-western Somalia, from where guerrillas and regular troops were grouping for an attack on the important military base at Jijiga. Two F-5s were brought down, but the SAC lost another precious MiG-21.

The Soviet Union came formally into the war on the side of Ethiopia when a contract was signed on 2 September for the delivery of arms, including 48 MiG-21s and SA-3 and SA-7 missiles. As Jijiga fell to the WSLF on 13 September, the EAF brought its Canberra and F-5 force up to Bhir air base at Dire Dawa in an attempt to hold the Somali advance. It was reported that Israeli pilots were flying for the EAF; certainly it was later admitted that Israel was supplying arms to the Ethiopians throughout the war. On the Somali side, Iraqi and Syrian troops were involved. By 29 September the Somalis controlled the Gara Marda pass between Jijiga and the regional capital Harar, which was the next objective before Dire Dawa. From 6 October Harar was surrounded and the Ethiopian 3rd Division trapped. Despite repeated attacks the Ethiopians held out, and on 1 November there was a Cuban led counterattack, with MiG-23 fighters committed.

With clear evidence of Soviet involvement on the side of Ethiopia, the SDR renounced its treaties and expelled 6,000 Russians from the country on 13 November. On the 25th the Russians began an intensive airlift of arms and ammunition stockpiled in Tashkent which required some 225 large transports including Il-18s, An-12s, An-22s and Il-76s, mostly flying in Aeroflot colours. The normal route was from Black Sea bases, with refuelling at Baghdad, then on down the Persian Gulf, round Oman for a second refuelling at Aden, before the final run to Addis Ababa. One An-22 unit operated out of Tbilisi in Georgia. The airlift was supplemented by ships sailing from Odessa and Sevastopol and smaller vessels bringing stockpiled material from

South Yemen to ports south of Massawa.

The SAC was now confined to the defence of the SDR, and the WSLF operated without air support while being subjected to constant and growing air strikes by the newly supplied MiG fighters. The Somalis made a concerted attack on Harar on 28 November as the EAF at Dire Dawa was grounded through unexpected rain but was unable to take the town. Although the SDR was receiving some aid from China and West Germany, the US was loth to offer military aid. By the year's end the Somalis were in clear danger of being evicted as the Ethiopians, supported by an influx of Cuban troops from Angola, prepared to recover lost ground. The Ethiopian offensive began on 3 February 1978 with repeated air strikes on Somali positions around Harar. The WSLF was pushed back, and by the 8th the Ethiopians claimed to be on the outskirts of Jijiga. In fact a two-pronged attack had been launched, and the signs were that the Ethiopians intended to invade the SDR to free the Berbera base, which with Hargeisa had been subjected to bombing; during the air raids two EAF MiG-21s had been claimed as shot down.

Another 6,000 Cubans were now on their way to Ethiopia and, anticipating an escalation, the French carrier *Clemenceau* was standing off Djibouti, while a US Task Force comprising a destroyer and two frigates was also in the area. On 9 February Somali civilians were called to military service, and some twenty Pakistani pilots began flying the remaining MiG-17s and MiG-21s out of Hargeisa.

Support was also coming to the SDR from Egypt. On 15 February an Egyptair Boeing 707 was forced down at Embakasi Airport, Nairobi, by two Kenya Air Force Hunters. The aircraft, one of four, had unofficially overflown Kenya while delivering nineteen tons of arms. The WSLF was spread along the road from Dire Dawa to Jijiga, and in early March up to 3,000 rebels are believed to have been killed in air strikes. From

TABLE OF UNITS: ETHIOPIA AND SOMALIA, 1977 TO DATE

Unit	Aircraft	Base	Role	Nos.
SAC, 1977				
(1 sqn.)	MiG-21	Hargeisa	Air defence, ground attack	12
(2 sqns.)	MiG-17, -15	Hargeisa, Mogadishu	Ground attack, air defence	42
(1 sqn.)	Il-28		Light bombing	10
(?)	An-2, An-24, C-47, C-45	Mogadishu	Transport	10
(?)	Mi-4, Mi-8		Liaison, recce, transport	9
(?)	Yak-11		Training	20
EAF, 1978				
(1 sqn.)	MiG-23	Asmara	Ground attack	20
(3 sqns.)	MiG-21	Dire Dawa, Bishoftu, Asmara	Ground attack, air defence	50
(1 sqn.)	MiG-17 (S. Yemen AF)	Dire Dawa	Ground attack	12
(1 sqn.)	F-5A/B	Gondar, Dire Dawa	Ground attack	6
(?)	Canberra B.52	Bishoftu	Light bombing	2
(1 flt.)	T-28D	Gondar	Coin	5
(?)	C-119K, C-47, C-54	Bishoftu	Transport	{14
(?)	An-12, An-22, An-24			{15
(?)	Mi-8, Alouette III, AB.204	Various	Liaison, recce, transport	45
(?)	Mi-6 (Sov. AF)	Dire Dawa	Heavy lift	10
(?)	T-33A	Bishoftu	Advanced training	11
(?)	Saab 91B, T-28A	Bishoftu	Training	23

the 5th there was furious fighting around Jijiga, with the WSLF completely surrounded. Russian and Cuban pilots had airlifted 70 tanks under Mi-6 helicopters to behind the Somali positions and the 60 or so MiG-21s were also supplemented by a squadron of South Yemeni MiG-17s. On 7 March Jijiga fell, and on the 9th, in an attempt to forestall an invasion, President Barre announced a complete withdrawal of Somali troops from Ethiopian territory.

In the event the Ethiopians did not invade, but numerous border villages occupied by the WSLF were attacked, several being completely destroyed by napalm. The war was now over, but from time to time, notably in August 1980, August 1982, September 1985 and February 1987, there have been Ethiopian ground or air attacks on towns and villages near the border. The USA has provided defensive military aid from 1981, and in October that year began occupying the Berbera complex, which is now a major Rapid Deployment Force (RDF) base.

5.10. Sudan, 1955 to date

The Sudan is the largest country in Africa, embracing many tribes and with a critical division between north and south: the north is essentially Arab, while the poorer south is peopled by black Christians or Animists. The country was ruled as an Anglo-Egyptian condominium from 1896 until 14 December 1955, when it achieved independence. In the period 1947–1949 the RAF based three Tempest squadrons at Khartoum, Nos. 6 and 213, as 324 Wing, from October 1947 to August 1948, then 39 Sqn. for a period in 1949. These units were on hand either to support Egyptian units or to assist ground forces dealing with dissidents in Somaliland or Eritrea. In the spring of 1955 there was unrest in the south, and the decision was taken to fly northern troops to quell the revolt rather than trust the local Equatoria Corps which was ordered to prepare for northern posting.

On 18 August the southern troops revolted and 8,000 Government troops were flown in from Khartoum in RAF Valettas drawn from 70 and 84 Sqns. based at Fayid and 114 and 216 Sqns. based at Kabrit. Although the revolt was put, down many Equatorian troops deserted into the bush with their weapons.

Over the next few years the new Government ignored the calls for a degree of southern autonomy while the rebels grew in strength. With British help the embryo Sudanese Air Force (SAF) was established from 1957 with four Provost T.53s, later supplemented by five ex-RAF aircraft, and four Gomhourias from Egypt. In 1962 the SAF acquired four Jet Provost T.51s and eight T.52 trainers. The southern rebels unified in 1963 as the Land Freedom Army, more popularly known as Anya-nya. From January 1964 Anya-nya, with support from Ethiopia, Uganda and Zaïre, began a series of attacks on Government posts.

As the position deteriorated there was civil unrest, leading to political chaos in the north and famine and the collapse of government in the south. After several changes in central government there was a coup in May 1969 which brought Colonel Jaafar Numeiri to power. As the SAF received five light strike BAC 145s the British withdrew their training teams and Numeiri looked to the Russians, then the Chinese, for military equipment; in contrast, Anya-nya was receiving support from the Israelis by September 1969, with regular weekly airdrops of arms flown via Uganda. By now international charities were concerned about famine and disease among the civilian population, and contact was made by mercenaries who were prepared to build an airstrip within the Sudan for relief supplies to be flown into.

By early 1970 there were three mercenary groups operating on a small scale, including a one-aircraft charter company, Southern Airmotive, which also dropped supplies en route to Uganda. Ethiopian airfields were also used to supply the rebels, and these were subjected to attack on several occasions by the SAF's newly acquired MiG-21s based at Wadi Seidma. The Numeiri government now began alienating local left-wing elements, and after covert British help in containing a counter-coup in July 1971 started to look again to the West while accepting a squadron of Shenyang F-4s (MiG-17s) from China. These aircraft were also based at Wadi Seidma, as were some of the ten Mi-8 helicopters received from the Soviet Union. The new fighters were in

In 1962 Sudan acquired four Jet Provost T.51s and eight T.52s for counter-insurgency tasks in the south of the country. Based at Khartoum, they were later supplemented by five BAC 145s in 1969 and three Strikemaster Mk. 90s in 1983. Jet Provost T.51 124 is shown, with practice rockets fitted.

action on 20 September 1972 when five Libyan C-130H transports, overflying the Sudan and carrying 399 troops and equipment to Uganda, were forced to land at Khartoum. In view of Sudanese relationships with Uganda the aircraft were allowed to leave only on the understanding that they returned to Libya via Cairo; in fact, after take-off the transports made for Entebbe.

In 1972 Numeiri reached a limited accommodation with the rebels, enabling the south to be self-governing to a degree. Gradually relationships with the West improved to the extent that late in 1975 elements of the British Army, including an Alouette detachment of 7 Regiment AAC, held Exercise 'Jowar' in the Sudan. In May 1977 Soviet advisers were expelled. Although the civil war was formally over, a new dissident group emerged in the south, the Sudan People's Liberation Army (SPLA), which included Anya-nya rebels. It has been reported that the RAF provided seconded air and ground crews to fly the Jet Provosts, which may have been further supplemented from RAF stocks.

Guerrilla fighting has been sporadic, but Sudan has had continuing problems with her neighbours. While Ethiopia gave support to the SPLA, Sudan aided Eritrean separatists and both countries have attacked camps across their borders. In 1980 Sudan added ten F-5Es and two F-5Fs to the SAF inventory, but these aircraft have been unable to prevent Ethiopian transports intruding into Sudanese airspace to supply the SPLA. To the north-west, Libya has on several occasions attacked border villages believed to have been harbouring Chadian rebels, notably in September 1981 when the target was Kolous and in 1983 when Egypt sent troops to help defend against an anticipated invasion.

In 1985 the SPLA was gaining strength, with active support from Libya, Ethiopia and Uganda and the offer from the Ugandans of the use of an airfield at Gulu; the SPLA was unable to secure aircraft, however, and in any event the offer was withdrawn after the overthrow of President Obote. In July the SPLA threatened to shoot down civilian aircraft in the south as it claimed that the Sudanese Government was resupplying troops in the area using non-military transports. The threat was made good on 16 August 1986 when F-27 ST-ADY was destroyed by ground fire with the loss of 57 passengers and crew while en route from Malakal to Khartoum. As Numeiri handed over to a civilian government in January 1986, the SPLA launched an offensive around Adok, and at the time of writing there is no end in sight to the escalating guerrilla war in the south, although diplomatic moves have resulted in a lessening of tension with neighbours.

AIRCRAFT MARKINGS

C-47 *White over, bare metal under, black serial on rear fuselage: 421.*
BAC.145 *Creamy grey overall with red dayglo on nose, rear fuselage and outer wings, black serial in English and Arabic on rear fuselage: 177, 187.*
DHC-5 Buffalo *Chocolate/sand overall, black serial on fin: 800.*

TABLE OF UNITS: SUDAN, 1975 TO DATE

Unit	Aircraft	Base	Role	Nos.
SAF, 1975				
(1 sqn.)	MiG-21PFM	Wadi Seidma	Air defence, ground attack	18
(1 sqn.)	Shenyang F-5	Wadi Seidma	Ground attack, air defence	15
(1 sqn.)	F-27, An-12, An-24	Khartoum	Transport	9
(?)	Mi-4, Mi-8	Khartoum, Wadi Seidma	Liaison, transport, casevac	12
(?)	Turbo-Porter	Khartoum	Light transport	4
(?)	BAC.145	Khartoum	Light strike	4
SAF, 1986				
(1 sqn.)	F-5E/F	Khartoum	Air defence, ground attack	12
(1 sqn.)	MiG-21PFM	Wadi Seidma	Air defence, ground attack	8
(1 sqn.)	Shenyang F-5	Wadi Seidma	Ground attack, air defence	9
(1 sqn.)	C-130H, DHC-5, An-24, F-27	Khartoum	Transport	17
(?)	Turbo-Porter	Khartoum	Light transport	8
(?)	Mi-4, Mi-8	Khartoum, Wadi Seidma	Liaison, transport, casevac	6
(?)	Bö-105, Puma	Various	Transport, liaison, attack	24
(?)	Jet Provost T.51/52, BAC.145	Khartoum	Training	9

AN-12 *Medium grey overall, white fuselage decking, black serial on fin: 911.*
MiG-21PFM *Olive/sand over, light blue under, black serial on fin: 344.*

C-130H *Olive/sand over, light grey under, serial white on fin, black on forward fuselage: 1101.*

5.11. Uganda, 1972 to date

After independence, Uganda's President, Milton Obote, moved his country, *inter alia*, towards the nationalization of foreign assets, mainly British. The British Government appears to have covertly supported the replacement of Obote on 25 January 1971 by Idi Amin Dada, a former army sergeant and Obote's right-hand man. Obote was given asylum in neighbouring Tanzania. Initially Amin, supported by Israel, protected British interests, but he soon began to display instability and in 1972 received his first supplies of MiG-17 fighters from Russia, which complemented the Ugandan Army Air Force (UAAF) Israeli-supplied Magisters. As he began purging the Army of elements perceived to be disloyal, exiles loyal to Obote in Tanzania prepared to launch an invasion. The plan was to mount an airborne commando raid on Entebbe Airport to disable the MiG force, and then invade.

The exiles stole a transport aircraft at Dar-es-Salaam on 15 September 1972 and flew it to Kilimanjaro to pick up the commando force. There it developed mechanical trouble and the plan was abandoned, although the land invasion went ahead on the 17th. The rebels reached Mbarara before they were pushed back; Amin kept his forces at Kampala and Jinja to prevent the threat of mutiny or civil uprising. At this stage the Libyan Government sent support via the Sudan, where five C-130Hs were forced to land, but after an interrupted flight they carried on to Entebbe. A Libya-Uganda accord had been signed in February, shortly after which the Israelis were expelled and their embassy given by Amin to the Palestine Liberation Organization (PLO). Fearing a counter-invasion, the Tanzanian Army moved 10,000 troops supported by heavy artillery up to the border.

On the 18th and 19th Bukoba was bombed by 'Ugandan aircraft', and on the 22nd Mwanza was hit. It was reported at the time that the Libyan Arab Republic Air Force (LARAF) had dispatched combat aircraft to Uganda, and it is possible that it was these aircraft, probably Mirage 5Ds, which carried out the bombings. It was at this time that Amin expelled Ugandan Asians and implicated Britain in the Ugandan exile attack. During the next few years Uganda received more Soviet equipment and Amin continued his racial and tribal purges, relying more heavily on mercenary and Muslim support at high levels in the Army, which by 1975 totally controlled the state. From 1976 the country was formally declared Muslim, and in July of that year the UAAF lost eleven

TABLE OF UNITS: UGANDA, 1972 TO DATE

Unit	Aircraft	Base	Role	Nos.
UAAF				
(1 sqn.)	MiG-17F	Entebbe	Ground attack. air defence	12
(1 sqn.)	MiG-21	Entebbe	Air defence. ground attack	10
(1 sqn.)	Magister	Jinja	Light attack. training	8
(?)	MiG-15UTI, L-29	Gulu	Training	7
Uganda Police Air Wing (UPAW)				
	Super Cub	Entebbe	Liaison. recce	10
	AB.205, AB.206	Entebbe, Jinja	Liaison. recce	10
	Twin Otter. DHC-4	Entebbe	Transport	2
LARAF				
—	Tu-22	Nakasongola	Bombing	2–3
TPDFAW				
(1 sqn.)	F-4	Mikumi	Ground attack. air defence	10
(1 sqn.)	F-6	Mikumi	Ground attack. air defence	8
(1 sqn.)	F-7	Ngerengere	Air defence. ground attack	15
(1 sqn.)	DHC-4, DHC-5. HS.748	Dar-es-Salaam	Transport	17
(?)	Cessna 310	Dar-es-Salaam	Liaison. training	6
(?)	Cherokee	Dar-es-Salaam	Training	5
Tanzanian Police Air Wing (TPAW)				
—	Bell 47G. AB.206	Dar-es-Salaam	Liaison. recce	6

fighters during the Israeli commando raid on Entebbe. The loss was soon made good by Russia. Shortly after the raid the LARAF is reported to have detached about 30 Mirage 5s to Entebbe and Jinja.

The brutal and erratic regime of Amin continued: after a threat to Americans in the country in February 1977, he turned the occasion into a banquet as the Americans brought USS *Enterprise* and her Air Group off the East African coast. Now fearing invasion again from Tanzania, where the number of exiles had grown and united as the Ugandan National Liberation Front (UNLF), Uganda prepared for a pre-emptive strike into Tanzania. On 10 October 1978 Ugandan MiG-17s dropped bombs in open country north of Bukoba; they struck the town itself on the 18th, causing little damage. On the morning of the 27th three waves of MiGs again attacked Bukoba with 250lb bombs, one of which landed near the hospital. The Tanzanians brought an SA-7 team up from Tabora, and the following day a Ugandan MiG-17 was brought down in a follow-up raid.

From the 27th Ugandan forces occupied the Kagera salient for several weeks until the Tanzanian Army forced withdrawal in November – but not before 8,000 Tanzanians had been massacred. During air strikes on a bridge at Kyaka several more Ugandan aircraft were reported shot down. On 3 November the Tanzanians apparently lost three Xian F-7 fighters brought up from Ngerengere to Mwanza when they were shot down in error by their own SA-7s over Musoma. On 20 January 1979 10,000 Tanzanian troops, accompanied by 1,000 UNLF rebels, invaded Uganda. They made a two-pronged thrust for Masaka, which was taken on 25 February, and Fort Portal via Mbarara. By the end of March the Tanzanians had reached Entebbe as the Libyans began flying in troops in support of Amin.

The Libyans airlifted some 3,000 troops and are also reported to have sent several Tu-22 bombers to the Ugandan base at Nakasongola, from where one bombed Mwanza on 1 April, missing the town and hitting a game reserve. Although the Tanzanian invasion was essentially an infantry operation, the Tanzanian People's Defence Force Air Wing (TPDFAW) used its Chinese-supplied F-6s (MiG-19s) and F-7s (MiG-21s) to attack Kampala, Jinja and Tororo on the 1st, Entebbe on the 3rd and Kampala again on the 10th. On the 7th, Tanzanian troops began their assault on Entebbe, and the following day some 30 or more escaping Libyans were killed in C-130H '116' of the LARAF when it was hit by RPG while taking off from the airport. On the 11th the Tanzanian Army occupied Kampala and Amin fled to Saudi Arabia. By May Tanzanian forces had captured Gulu and Nakasongola airfields, and on 3 June the war ended as Tanzanian tanks reached the Sudan border. Uganda's troubles were not over, however, for it proved impossible to create a stable successor government; after several attempts, Obote assumed control in 1980.

New opposition groups emerged, initially based in Zaïre, from where Obote feared an invasion. Purges followed, and by January 1982 the dissidents had formed a National Resistance Army (NRA) within the Ugandan Popular Front (UPF). In February 1982 there was a major NRA attack on Kampala, and in March 1983 a general NRA offensive was launched. The UAAF by now had no serviceable combat aircraft and was able to use only a handful of AB.206s to transport troops to trouble spots; one of these helicopters was shot down by rebels on 2 December 1983. From 1984 the NRA assumed power, but rival groups, primarily the Ugandan People's Democratic Army (UPDA), are now fighting the new government. The Ugandan Army now flies some ten assorted Agusta Bell helicopters and two SF.260WLs, a gift from Libya. At the time of writing the guerrilla war continues.

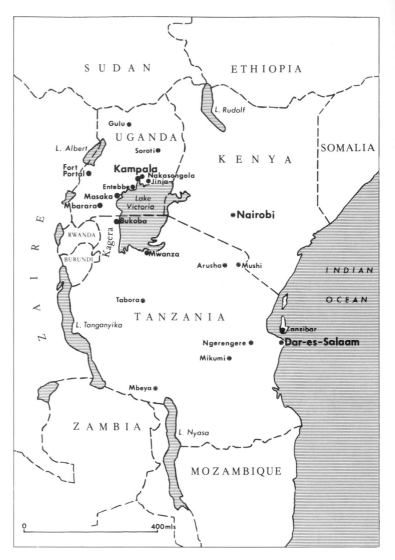

AIRCRAFT MARKINGS

Confirmed details of combat aircraft markings of both Air Wings have proved impossible to secure.

TPDFAW
DHC-4 *Pale grey overall, black serial on fin: 9013, 9014.*

5.12. The Israeli Raid on Entebbe, 1976

On 27 June 1976 Airbus A300B2 on Air France Flight 139 from Tel Aviv to Paris landed at Athens. There, four terrorists boarded, and after take-off the aircraft was hijacked and ordered to fly to Benghazi to refuel. From there the aircraft was directed to Entebbe, Uganda, where the terrorists could rely on support from the erratic President Idi Amin. The 256 passengers and twelve crew were taken off the aircraft and detained in the old airport terminal building. On 29 June the terrorists, whose number was increased to about sixteen, demanded over Uganda Radio the release of some 53 convicted terrorists, most of whom were detained in Israel, in exchange for the safe return of the hostages. The Israelis now bought time while consideration was given to a military solution.

A plan was devised for a group of paratroopers to fly into Entebbe at night, storm the terminal building and release the hostages. Intelligence was gathered over the next few days from non-Israeli passengers who were released on 1 July and from Israelis who had trained the Ugandan Army and been involved in the construction of the airport. It has been reported that IDF/AF RF-4E reconnaissance aircraft overflew the airport to gain up to the minute details of Ugandan dispositions. The main concerns were the number of Ugandans supporting the terrorists and the proximity of armoured units at nearby Kampala. The Israelis began rehearsing the finely balanced plan on Friday 2 July in northern Israel. The rescue force would fly into Uganda in four C-130s with one or two Boeing 707s in support. For the first part of their journey south down the Red Sea the Hercules were to be escorted by IDF/AF F-4Es, flying at very low level unless required to do otherwise.

The special forces now assembled to conduct the rescue attempt were divided into five groups and assigned separate roles. These were (a) to illuminate and secure the runway; (b) to occupy the old terminal building and release the hostages; (c) to control the new terminal; (d) to secure the airfield, defend it if necessary and destroy any fighter aircraft on the ground; and (e) to evacuate the hostages. Approval for the plan was given as the force took off from Sharm el Sheikh at 1530hrs.

It may be years before the full details of the rescue, called Operation 'Thunderbolt', are known: reports vary in their detail. According to one report, the first C-130, with the runway and release groups aboard, landed at 2301hrs behind a British charter aircraft which provided cover. The commander of the release group, who was subsequently killed (the only IDF casualty), led his men to the old terminal building in a black Mercedes saloon, similar to that used by Amin, in an elaborate deception plan. The hostages were released almost immediately, although in the short firefight three were killed, as were all the terrorists in the immediate vicinity. As the remaining Hercules landed the hostages were recovered and led out to the waiting aircraft. In the meantime Ugandan soldiers had been engaged and about twenty killed. Up to seven MiG-17PFs or MiG-21s were destroyed on the ground to prevent pursuit. The whole operation was allegedly controlled from a circling Boeing 707. Most reports refer to 33 doctors plus other medical staff being aboard the last C-130. Some claim that the Hercules were to be refuelled at Entebbe for the return flight, but no group was detailed with the task.

In the event the aircraft took off 53 minutes after landing and made for Nairobi, where they all refuelled. It is claimed that a second 707, fitted out as a hospital aircraft, was waiting at Nairobi, where casualties, numbering about ten, were transferred. The six aircraft then returned to Tel Aviv to a rapturous reception. Subsequently, the Israelis formally claimed that they had conducted the rescue with no external help, in effect forcing the Kenyans to assist them. In fact they must have had support, even passively, from Ethiopia, which they overflew at will, as well as from Kenya, but the denial of any external support would at least offer some protection to third parties against reprisals.

The highly successful raid has given rise to several myths. In a newspaper report a year later it was stated that a Canadian inventor had been honoured by the Israeli Government for producing an electronic 'ray' device that freezes equipment, including radars!

AIRCRAFT MARKINGS

C-130H Brown/sand/medium green overall, blue-grey under wings and tailplane, black serial on nose and civil registration on fin: 420/4X-FBQ, 428/4X-FBX.

After an Air France Airbus, en route from Tel Aviv to Paris and with many Jewish passengers on board, was hijacked to Entebbe, the Israelis refused to accept terms for the safe release of the hostages. Instead they planned, and then mounted, an audacious raid, details of which remain obscure. Certainly, at least four C-130 Hercules were used to transport commandos to the Ugandan capital for the successful rescue. The aircraft involved are believed to have included C-130H 428, seen here with its call-sign 4X-FBX. (Lockheed)

5.13. The Seychelles, 1981

The Seychelles, far out in the Indian Ocean, had been granted independence on 29 June 1976, but a year later the President, James Mancham, was deposed by his Prime Minister. The new President effectively evicted whites, a number of whom moved to South Africa. At the same time the new Government courted the Soviet Union and some base facilities were apparently agreed. Exiles contacted Mike Hoare, veteran of the Congo and Biafra, with a view to his managing a coup and reinstating Mancham. On 25 November 1981, with 44 men plus several already waiting in the Seychelles, he took off from Swaziland in Fellowship 3D-ALN of Royal Air Swazi; the group travelled as a party of 'The Ancient Order of Frothblowers' bent on a holiday in the island.

Each carried a holdall containing arms in a false base. After landing the group had mostly cleared customs when one bag was searched and the arms found.

Once the alarm was raised there was little hope of success and the mercenaries held off the Tanzanian Presidential Guard until an Air India Boeing 707-437, believed to be VT-DNY, was hijacked and flown to Durban, South Africa. The South African Government had supported the coup attempt – South African Military Intelligence had provided weapons, captured in Angola – and Hoare expected to be allowed to return home. He was, in fact, arrested and imprisoned for twenty years, to be released early on 6 May 1985.

5.14. Miscellaneous conflicts and incidents

1. On 26 January 1949 Alaska Airlines C-46F N1241N on lease from the USAF and also carrying the Israeli registration 4X-AQD crashed on take-off from Asmara, Eritrea. The aircraft was involved in smuggling Jews from Yemen to Israel in Operation 'Magic Carpet'.

2. There were riots in Djibouti on 19 March 1967, following which French troops were flown into the colony to maintain order. The French have maintained troops and air units in Djibouti. The Armée de l'Air has EC 3/10 with the Mirage IIIC, due to be replaced by EC 1/5 with the Mirage F.1C-200 in autumn 1988, and Groupe d'Outre Mer (GOM) 88 with Transall C-160s, Broussards, Pumas and Alouettes. The Aéronavale keeps one Atlantique of 24F in the Republic, while ALAT has the Peloton Djibouti with Pumas and Alouettes.

3. There was an uprising of the Hutu tribe in Burundi on 29 April 1972. There followed reprisals by the minority Tutsi tribe, which manned the Army, and many were killed or fled to neighbouring Rwanda. French pilots are understood to have flown Burundi Army Alouette helicopters on search and destroy operations against the Hutu. There was a repetition in August 1988, when it was claimed that Burundi SF.260s used napalm against Hutus and Alouette gunships to pursue fleeing tribesmen.

4. On 25 March 1977 two Somali Aeronautical Corps (SAC) MiG-17s flying from Hargeisa attacked a French Navy Atlantique flying over the Gulf of Aden.

5. Early in June 1988 the rebel Somali National Movement (SNM) claimed to have captured Hargeisa Airport after fighting with Government forces.

6: The Arabian Peninsula, Iraq and Iran

Most wars in the Gulf region have been one-sided in terms of air power. British involvement in South Arabia began as a policing exercise and built up to contain demands for independence from internally divided factions supported by external powers. Fighting spilled over into neighbouring Yemen until Government policy dictated the need for evacuation, leaving a power vacuum in the region.

Local instability was also reflected in the Yemen Civil War, in which Egypt, then acting as a Soviet proxy, supported the Republican cause while the British and Saudi Arabian Governments covertly backed the Royalists. After the withdrawal of the British and Egyptians there was fighting between the Yemen and the People's Republic in the south between 1972 and 1980; by now the People's Republic was a Soviet client state, providing important bases in the region.

In the Gulf itself the British also supported the Omani Government against Saudi Arabian forces in conflict over the mutual border. As so often happens in the region, local tribal dissatisfactions were exploited. The Saudis were in turn supported by US oil interests; oil has been a powerful factor in influencing territorial ambition in the Gulf area. Indeed, the Iraqi threat to Kuwait in 1961 was based on boundary considerations previously considered unimportant. The speed and extent of British reinforcement in the theatre clearly demonstrated the importance to the UK of protecting her oil interests in the Gulf and was probably instrumental in avoiding Iraqi invasion.

Britain further protected her Arabian interests by strongly supporting the Omani regime in the Dhofar War, critically by supplying equipment and large numbers of loaned and contract members of the armed forces. Support was also forthcoming from Jordan, Iran and Saudi Arabia; allegiances change fast in this volatile region.

Further to the north the Kurds have occupied the attention of Turkey, Iraq and Iran since the end of the Second World War. With little prospect of achieving autonomy they have successfully tied down large numbers of Iranian and Iraqi forces for some years. The Kurds seem to have increasing dissident support in Iran against the fundamentalist regime of the Ayatollahs. The US Government must have been banking on internal support from dissident factions in Iran in planning their fragile attempt to rescue hostages held by militant students. The attempt could also not have been mounted without external support from Saudi Arabia, Oman and, particularly, Egypt – again a reminder of how quickly loyalties can shift.

The Gulf War between Iraq and Iran finally drew to an end in 1988 after eight years of bitter fighting. No war has better served to illustrate

Two Hunter FGA.9s of 43 Sqn. RAF flying at low level along the Dhala road; the aircraft are fitted with 230gal drop tanks and rocket rails. During 1963 there were three Hunter squadrons in Aden, all equipped with the FGA.9, while 1417 Flt. operated the FR.10 on reconnaissance tasks. (RAF Museum)

the hypocrisy of the major arms-producing nations, both East and West, committed or neutral. The superpowers and their allies appear to be content to keep arms supplies and support at a level that allowed both parties to keep the war running with no clear outcome. The war between Muslim states began over religious differences and a minor territorial dispute, but that dispute affected oil rights and passage. Oil was then to become both the means of continuing the war at enormous human cost and the prime target for attack by both sides, and the 'Tanker War' was to bring major powers into the conflict to protect shipping.

The Gulf War was prosecuted incompetently by both sides, and particularly remarkable was

the Iraqi inability to use air power properly. Despite there being no real shortage of aircraft in the Gulf War there has been negligible air-to-air fighting and Iraq has made little effective use of her superior air force. It was for Israel to demonstrate the potency of air power in the carefully planned and executed raid on the Iraqi nuclear reactor outside Baghdad.

There have been persistent rumours of RAF involvement in the Iraqi reactor raid and alleged sightings of Jaguars marked with the Star of David. These rumours can safely be discounted, but they serve to illustrate the difficulty of reporting accurately in a region where there is limited access and where misinformation and 'disinformation' are endemic.

6.1. South Arabia, 1945–1967

Southern Arabia from the Red Sea to Dhofar was subject to British influence from 1839, with Aden becoming a Crown Colony in 1937. In the hinterland there were constant inter-tribal conflicts, and after the success of air control in Iraq the process was extended to the Aden Protectorates in 1927 with the posting of 8 Sqn. Problems were thus dealt with by a combination of air policing and expeditions of ground forces, including the Aden Protectorate Levies (APL). Although a singularly unpleasant environment, Aden was an important British base because of its location both on the route to India and between East Africa and the Gulf, both spheres of British influence.

During the Second World War little attention was paid to tribal disputes, but in May 1945 RAF armoured cars supported by Mosquitoes of 114 Sqn. dealt with hostilities within the Subeihi tribe. In 1946 there were further demonstrations of force after the Dathina tribe ambushed the local assistant political officer. In September 114 Sqn. was renumbered 8 Sqn., and the following year Sheikh Othman airfield was placed on a care and maintenance basis as Khormaksar was developed. In early February 1947 a dissident fort on Jebel Jihaf was attacked by a force of RAF armoured cars and APL and rocketed by 8 Sqn. Mosquitoes. In April, as 8 Sqn. was converting to the Tempest VI, a mixed flight of both types attacked the village of Al Husein after the political agent had been killed collecting fines.

Some 60 miles to the north of Aden, situated on the important Dhala road, the ancient trade route into the Yemen, is Thumier. The local Quteibi tribe had long practised the extraction of tolls for safe passage, but a series of lootings in 1947 led to complaints and demands for retaliation. Over the years various local leaders had sought British protection through formal agreement, and positive action in upholding the law was essential. Thumier was attacked by air in

October and the village substantially destroyed. Tempests of 8 Sqn. were supported by Lincoln bombers of 101 Sqn. on a 'Sunray' exercise: 66.7 tons of bombs and 247 rockets were expended, but advance notice was, as usual, given by leaflets dropped by Anson communications aircraft.

Action against dissident tribes continued through 1948: at Wadi Mirria, sixteen forts of the Mansuri tribe were attacked over three days, 468 60lb rockets being fired and resulting in the destruction of eleven of the forts. In 1949 8 Sqn. re-equipped with the Brigand B.1 light bomber, which it used to attack forts at Naqd Marqad in August and in the Wadi Hatib two years later. At the end of 1952 8 Sqn. began converting to the Vampire FB.9, and in January 1953 a detachment of 32 Sqn. from Deversoir was based at Khormaksar, undertaking several small operations. In May 8 Sqn. used its Vampires to attack a fort at Mariba. These local forts were very strongly

built, and armour-piercing rockets were often necessary to ensure their destruction. In November an airstrip was constructed at Am Ruseis in the Wadi Hatib to support the APL based in Nisab and Lodar engaged in keeping the trade routes open. Elements of the Shamsi tribe in the Wadi were bombed by Lincolns of 49 Sqn. in January 1954.

A more serious situation developed in May when troops had to be airlifted by Valettas of the Middle East Communications Squadron (MECS) to Am Ruseis to relieve the APL fort at Robat which was under constant attack. The relief column was protected by overflying Vampires, and an Air Control Post (ACP) was established to direct ground-attack strikes. The Vampires, in familiar territory, also target-marked for Lincolns of 49 Sqn. In June action continued with raids against the Rabizi tribe around Nisab, who with Yemeni support were striking daily at Government targets. Vampires used 500lb bombs, rockets and cannon fire in an attempt to force the dissidents into submission. In the month 8 Sqn. flew for 483 hours, dropping 316 500lb bombs and using 316 60lb rockets and 9,000 rounds of ammunition.

Air strikes were highly accurate but there was often confusion as to targets and the siting of some meant hazardous approaches or exits. From May 1955 the first RAF Intelligence Officers (RAFIO) were based upcountry to co-ordinate strikes, initially at Wadi Mirria where 169 sorties were flown. The RAFIOs were highly successful, developing networks of intelligence sources and ensuring that only appropriate targets were selected for economic attack. In June 8 Sqn. re-equipped yet again, this time with the Venom FB.1, which it changed a year later for the FB.4 fitted with ejection seats. These aircraft were in use in July in support of an operation from Ataq to relieve Robat yet again. Sycamore helicopters of the MECS (re-formed as the Aden Search and Rescue Flight in 1958) were used for the first time for casualty evacuation. During 1955 Lincolns of 7 Sqn. were detached to Khormaksar, and on 2 January 1956 the detachment became 1426 Flight. These were supplemented for a time by a detachment of Shackletons from 42 Sqn. based in the UK.

Also in 1956, 78 Sqn. was formed with six Twin Pioneer light transports to relieve the overworked Valettas and Pembrokes of the MECS. Target identification was always a problem in this desolate region and maps were invariably inaccurate, so to assist in the reconnaissance role four Meteor FR.9s formed the Arabian Peninsula Reconnaissance Flight (APRF) in 1957. Further support was added in January with the establishment of 37 Sqn. with four Shackleton MR.2 aircraft, which were to be used for bombing, reconnaissance, troop transporting, strafing, search and rescue and, lastly, the role for

which the aircraft were designed, maritime reconnaissance. Concurrently 1426 Flight disbanded. The Shackletons were used for the first time at Ghaniyah, strafing Yemeni attackers.

With very poor surface communications, the need for heavy transports capable of using short strips became pressing as attacks from the Yemen increased. No. 84 Sqn., long associated with the Middle East, formed with Beverleys at Khormaksar in June 1958. A month later a Venom crashed at Harib in the Yemen attacking field guns directed across the border. To support 8 Sqn., Vampires of 2 Sqn. Royal Rhodesian Air Force (RRAF) were detached from Salisbury in August. To strengthen the political framework, a Federation of Emirates of the South was established in February 1959, and later in the year Air Forces Middle East (AFME) was formed as part of a unified Middle East Command covering East Africa, Aden, the Gulf and the Indian Ocean. From 1960 use was also made of Royal Navy aircraft from carriers in Aden waters: in March Sea Venoms of 891 Naval Air Squadron from HMS *Centaur* participated in Operation 'Damen' against targets in the Yemen, while Sea Vixen FAW.1 fighters of 892 NAS from HMS *Hermes* were to be used in 1963.

Hunters were introduced in January 1960 with 8 Sqn., and as activity increased 208 Sqn., also with the Hunter, had a permanent detachment at Khormaksar, from Eastleigh in Kenya, from June. The transport force was further enhanced by the creation of 233 Sqn. with the Valetta C.1, taking over some aircraft used by 84 Sqn. The Army also introduced aircraft to the theatre in the form of the Auster AOP.9s of 16 Flight from April 1961. Army aircraft were based at Falaise airfield at Little Aden to lighten the now considerable load at Khormaksar, and another airstrip with a 1,400yd tarmac runway was constructed upcountry at Beihan in July. Eastern Aden Province was in part policed by the Hadrami Bedouin Legion (HBL), and on 19 July a post was attacked by dissidents, resulting in the death of sixteen HBL personnel. A force of Hunters, Meteors, Shackletons and Twin Pioneers was dispatched to Riyan to seek out and attack the culprits. Later

No. 8 Sqn. RAF operated the Tempest F. Mk. 6 in Aden from 1947 to 1949, when it converted to the Brigand. Its aircraft flew light strike sorties in support of ground forces in South Arabia until the British withdrawal in 1967. Seen here loaded with two 1,000lb bombs is Tempest F.6 NX237; the more normal load was rockets. (C. Thomas) in the year 208 Sqn. moved permamently to Khormaksar.

In May 1962 an attempt was made to build an airstrip at Hilyan. A reconnaissance Shackleton in the area was hit by small-arms fire, and a Beaver which subsequently landed was fired upon. Hunters were called in to strike, but the site was not developed. A further change in the transport force was now made: although ideal for local use, the Beverleys were slow and short ranged, and they were supplemented in June by the less robust but faster Argosies of 105 Sqn. for general theatre use.

In October there was a revolution in the Yemen, which then claimed South Arabia. Attacks from Yemen increased, and on 22 October MiG aircraft of the Egyptian Air Force (EAF) struck at Nuqab near Beihan. The RAF set up patrols along the border, and some days later Hunters destroyed a fort in the Yemen in retaliation. A show of strength was made when a Valiant of 90 Sqn. on a 'Lone Ranger' exercise flew low along the frontier. Canberra PR.7 aircraft of 13 and 58 Sqns. were detached to Khormaksar to track Egyptian arms supply vessels in the Red Sea. The year 1963 saw Aden merged into the Federation, which then became known as the Federation of South Arabia. Tension increased between the tribes in the Protectorates and the townspeople of Aden, where, in addition, political groups set on independence were growing in strength, some supported by the Egyptian-backed Yemen Republic. The security forces thus had dissident tribes, incursions from the Yemen and terrorist action within Aden to contend with.

Further RAF re-equipment in the year included the establishment of 1417 Flt. with the Hunter FR.10 and 26 Sqn. with the Belvedere medium-lift helicopter and the transfer of 43 Sqn. with the Hunter FGA.9 from Akrotiri, all in March. Khormaksar was now one of the busiest airfields in the world, sharing the single runway with civil movements. December saw a further temporary addition to the base in the form of an Il-14: on the 3rd the Yemen Air Force aircraft landed by mistake at Lodar, where its path was blocked to prevent it taking off. The aircraft was subsequently flown by an RAF crew to Khormaksar for evaluation.

A state of emergency was declared after a hand grenade was thrown at the High Commisioner at Khormaksar. He and 52 others were injured and two died in the attack, which was apparently the work of the People's Socialist Party (PSP) which in 1963 merged with the South Arabian League (SAL) to form the Organization for the Liberation of the Occupied South (OLOS). The other major terrorist group was the National Liberation Front (NLF), which in 1966 was to merge with OLOS to become the Front for the Liberation of Occupied South Yemen (FLOSY). Operations in 1964 were concentrated on the Radfan area to the east of

Thumier. The Quteibi rebelled against the centralized collection of tariffs, and with arms and training from Egyptians in the Yemen they extended their action against traffic using the Dhala road. Some of this traffic was almost certainly arms and British Government-sponsored mercenaries en route for the Yemen in support of the Royalist cause in the civil war.

Military action rather than air control was decided upon, and Operation 'Nutcracker' was launched on 4 January, its purpose to demonstrate the Government's ability to enter and control the Radfan at will. Three battalions of the Federal Regular Army (FRA), as the APL had now been renamed, were assembled at Thumier with armoured cars, some British Army tanks and J Battery 3rd Regiment Royal Horse Artillery. One FRA battalion was airlifted by Belvederes and four Wessex HU.5s of 815 NAS from HMS Centaur to ridges overlooking Wadi Rabwa. As pickets were established and 105mm howitzers lifted into position, a number came under attack, and the Hunters and Shackletons were called in for close support. The main force then worked along the Wadi, and engineers began the construction of a road to Wadi Taym. One battalion moved along the Bakri ridge to Jebel Haqla with helicopter support and Hunter cover.

The bulk of the forces then moved back on Thumier, and the Rabwa road was opened in February. By March it was clear that the area could be contained only at the expense of enabling more incursions from the Yemen, and the force withdrew, leaving Thumier garrisoned; shortly afterwards, the Rabwa road was closed by the Quteibi. A major raid across the border was launched on 13 March by armed helicopters supported by MiG-17 fighters, the targets being the village of Bulaq near Beihan and a Frontier Guard (FG) post. On the 28th eight Hunters retaliated by attacking and destroying Harib fort. There were also reports of a group of 700 well-trained dissidents operating in the Radfan, and attacks on convoys on the Dhala road increased. The Government decided that further military action in strength was required and the 'Radfan Force', abbreviated to 'Radforce', was established.

The force comprised 45 Commando Royal Marines, a company of 3 Para, two FRA battalions, a Royal Tank Regiment squadron with armoured cars, J battery 3 RHA, a Royal Engineer (RE) troop, 3 Troop 22 Special Air Service (SAS) Regiment and, in due course, a battalion of the East Anglian Regiment. All RAF units were available for support, although by now 233 Sqn. had disbanded. Initially no Navy helicopters were in the theatre, but the Army now had the first Scout helicopters with 13 Flt; in addition, the SAR Flight had re-equipped with the more powerful Whirlwind HAR.10. The objectives of the new initiative were to end the operations of dissidents in the area, to stop revolt spreading

From 1956, Shackletons of RAF Coastal Command were detached to Aden to provide extra firepower against dissidents. In January 1957 a locally based unit, 37 Sqn., was formed, but the detachments continued until the withdrawal. Illustrated at Khormaksar is Shackleton MR.1A WB831/T-Q of 220 Sqn. RAF. (R. B. Trevett via A. S. Thomas)

and to keep the Dhala road clear. The basic plan was for troops to dominate the Danaba basin and Wadi Taym, thought to be the centre of dissident occupation. Withdrawal to the Yemen would also be denied.

The Commando force could not be lifted quickly enough to the heights with the available helicopters, so a landing of 120 paras on a feature named 'Cap Badge' was planned, the target to be marked by the SAS lifted in by Scout at last light on 29 April. Unfortunately the SAS group was discovered and subjected to intense opposition throughout the 30th. Hunters of 43 and 208 Sqns. fired some 127 rockets and 7,131 rounds of ammunition in very close support, and the group withdrew at night, losing two members. During the 30th the marines had advanced along the Wadi Rabwa and branched north up the Wadi Boran to link up with the paras, but the latter could not now be dropped and the advance was halted. Some 105mm howitzers were moved up, under Hunter cover, to positions from where they could fire on 'Cap Badge'. The 1st East Anglians were now released to the operation, and they moved from Thumier to the marines' position, enabling the latter to take 'Cap Badge' on foot on the night of 4–5 May. 3 Para had also been brought up to Thumier and moved along through the marines' positions to the Wadi Taym.

Out of effective artillery range, the paras relied on Hunter support. Resupply was effected by the Belvederes, Scouts and, later, Beavers of 15 Flt. flying into a newly created airstrip at Danaba, 'Monk's Field'. Thus all the initial objectives were achieved by 5 May. The difficulties experienced demonstrated the need for a stronger force, and on 11 May a regular Brigade HQ, 39 Bde. from Northern Ireland, was established with additional infantry battalions, the balance of 3 Para, a second armoured car squadron, 170 Battery 7 RHA with 5.5in guns and a Centurion tank troop of the 16th/5th Queen's Royal Lancers.

From the 24th six Wessex helicopters of 815 NAS were available, and Thumier had been extended to take Beverleys. The Wessexes were a welcome addition as the Belvederes, although

essential for lifting large artillery pieces to otherwise inaccessible heights, were suffering from sand ingestion. In the relative lull a number of areas were identified for air attack, and the Hunter and Shackleton units carried out continuous air strikes. The Hunters worked by day and the pressure was maintained at night by the Shackletons of 37 Sqn. supplemented by two aircraft from 224 Sqn. from Gibraltar. The new focus of enemy activity was deemed to be the Bakri ridge and Wadi Misrah to the south, and an exploratory drive was begun along the ridge from the 18th by men of 3 Para after reconnaissance by Scout helicopters. The paras found little opposition until they reached Qudeishi.

Resistance at this highest point on the ridge was heavy, and it fell only after repeated strikes by the Hunters. By 24 May the paras were in control of the whole area. It was decided to push further south to occupy the dominant Jebel Huriyah, having first cleared the Wadis Misrah and Dhubsan. All stores were manhandled, and again the paras relied on Hunter close support to achieve their objectives. As they moved along the Wadi Dhubsan they were fired upon from a strong force of dissidents, and a Scout helicopter which had managed to support a reconnaissance was badly damaged by rifle and machine-gun fire. During this period the Scouts operated in threes, with one aircraft armed with three GPMGs and the other two carrying four soldiers, with a Wessex in support carrying up to fourteen men. Such groups could operate with a degree of independence, certainly until further support arrived.

By the end of May Radforce was in a position to attack Jebel Huriyah. The 1st East Anglians picketed the sides of Wadi Misrah while 4 RTR cleared the bed of the wadi. The advance continued to 4 June, by which time the foothills had been reached, and 2 FRA joined the assault force ready for the final attack. This began on 7 June, and the FRA was immediately pinned down by gunfire from a ridge. Despite concerted Hunter strikes and artillery assault, the dissidents held their position. The attack continued on the 8th, and it was found that the rebels had withdrawn, having suffered heavy losses. The final assault on the Jebel was made on the night of 10/11 June, the way being lighted by a succession of flares dropped by the Shackletons. The peak was reached before dawn.

All territorial objectives had now been met, but action continued until November. Air control was maintained, and gradually the tribes sued for peace. Hunters were directed by Beavers acting as forward air control (FAC) aircraft, and until retirement in September the Austers of 13 Flt. operated in their designated role spotting for the artillery. The Army Air Corps was now operating from four strips in the region. The Navy helicopters also performed magnificently in moving troops and supplies, often under fire. The Navy is also understood to have flown some strike sorties with the Buccaneers of 800 NAS from HMS *Eagle*. During May and June RAF Hunters flew 642 sorties, fired 2,508 rockets and used 183,900 cannon rounds. In the period the Belvederes flew 1,027 sorties, carrying 1,798 passengers and over 1,000,000lb of freight. During the year the Beavers of 15 Flt. AAC made nearly 10,000 landings, with an average sortie time of just under twenty minutes. These figures convey some idea of the intensity of flying during the Radfan operations.

In July 1964 the British Government announced its intention of granting independence by 1968, but with the retention of a military base. This resulted in fighting in and around Aden both between nationalist groups and with the security forces. During 1965 equipment changes included the introduction of the Wessex with 78 Sqn., which transferred its Twin Pioneers to 21 Sqn. which had moved up from Eastleigh, and the first AAC Sioux troop. In urban guerrilla warfare strike aircraft are of little use, but the Wessexes were able to place troops quickly where needed while the Sioux were used for a range of reconnaissance and resupply tasks around the town. Twin Pioneers were used to drop leaflets. During 1965 and 1966 operations continued up-country, and a mobile radar was set up at Mukeiras to warn of any air threat from the Yemen. On numerous occasions there were MiG attacks on villages in the Beihan area, although the RAF was now prevented from making retaliatory raids.

As the situation in Aden deteriorated the British Government announced in February 1966 that it would not retain a military presence after independence, and this only served to increase violence and lose all support for the British from hitherto friendly leaders. Those who remained loyal were attacked; several died when DC-3 VR-AAN of Aden Airways blew up on 22 November 130 miles east of Aden as a result of sabotage. As British forces prepared to leave in 1967, unrest spread from the mainland, and in March Beverleys flew to Riyan to lift an HBL force on to Socotra island to quell a local revolt. In June there were mutinies both by the South Arabian Army (SAA),

as the FRA had been renamed, and by the APL, which had become the South Arabian Police (SAP).

In July Wessex helicopters lifted a company of the Argyll and Sutherland Highlanders to the Crater district of Aden to regain control; earlier, on 20 June, Sioux XT173 was brought down in the area by rifle fire on a resupply sortie. From now on RAF units disbanded or moved to airfields in the Gulf. By October 21, 37 and 30 Sqns. had disbanded and 105 and 8 Sqns. had moved. The Beverleys of 84 Sqn. were active in pulling back into Aden forces from the hinterland, and on 6 October XM106 was destroyed at Thumier when it ran over an anti-tank mine. The RAF now prepared for its largest airlift since Berlin in 1948. Earlier in the year, over 9,000 dependants had been flown out to Gatwick in RAF transports and VC-10 airliners of British United Airways (BUA).

The military withdrawal was carefully planned, and from 1 November 5,800 men were flown out to Muharraq in stages on Hercules of 36 Sqn. and Britannias of 99 and 511 Sqns., with Belfasts of 53 Sqn. moving freight. The last Army units to move were the Argylls on the 26th, on which day 42 and 45 RMC moved into Khormaksar; 45 Commando was then airlifted to Muharraq. From Muharraq the men were flown directly to Lyneham by VC-10s of 10 Sqn., chartered VC-10s or Britannias. The final withdrawal was that of

The Shackletons of 37 Sqn. RAF saw a considerable amount of action over the inhospitable terrain of South Arabia. Not only did they drop leaflets and bombs, both by day and by night, but their two 20mm nose-mounted cannon were used to good effect in strafing runs. Photographed on a support sortie is WL752/ D. (Via A. S. Thomas)

TABLE OF UNITS: SOUTH ARABIA, 1945–1967

Unit	Aircraft	Base	Role	Dates
RAF				
114 Sqn.	Mosquito FB.VI	Khormaksar	Light bombing (to 8 Sqn.)	00/05/45 to 00/09/46
8 Sqn.	Mosquito FB.VI. Tempest F.VI. Brigand B.1. Vampire FB.9. Venom FB.1/4. Hunter FGA.9	Khormaksar	Light bombing. close support. ground attack. air defence	00/09/46 to 00/08/67
32 Sqn.	Vampire FB.9 (det.)	Khormaksar, ex Deversoir	Ground attack	00/01/53 to 00/02/53
208 Sqn.	Hunter FGA.9	Khormaksar	Close support. ground attack. air defence	00/11/61 to 00/06/64
43 Sqn.	Hunter FGA.9	Khormaksar		01/03/63 to 14/10/67
APRF	Meteor FR.9	Khormaksar		00/00/57 to 00/00/60
13 Sqn.	Canberra PR.9 (det.)	Khormaksar, ex Akrotiri	PR	23/10/62 to 00/11/62
58 Sqn.	Canberra PR.7. PR.9 (det.)	Khormaksar, ex Wyton		24/10/62 to 00/11/62
1417 Flt.	Hunter FR.10	Khormaksar	Fighter recce	00/03/57 to 00/08/67
37 Sqn.	Shackleton MR.2C	Khormaksar	Bombing. SAR. troop transport. MR	00/01/57 to 00/09/67
101 Sqn.	Lincoln B.2 (det.)	Khormaksar, ex Binbrook	Heavy bombing	00/10/47 to 00/11/47
138 Sqn.		Khormaksar, ex Wyton		00/11/47 to 00/12/47
57 Sqn.		Khormaksar, ex Waddington		00/02/48 to 00/03/48
49 Sqn.		Khormaksar, ex Upwood		00/01/54 to 00/07/54
7 Sqn.		Khormaksar, ex Upwood		00/02/55 to 02/01/56
1426 Flt.	Lincoln B.2	Khormaksar		02/01/56 to 16/01/57
42 Sqn.	Shackleton MR.2 (det.)	Khormaksar, ex St. Mawgan	MR. bombing. SAR. troop transport	00/00/56 to 00/01/57
224 Sqn.	Shackleton MR.2 (det.)	Khormaksar, ex Gibraltar	Bombing. SAR. MR	00/05/64 to 00/06/64
MECS	Dakota C.4. Valetta C.1. Pembroke C.1. Hastings C.1. Andover CC.2	Khormaksar	Communications. transport	00/00/53 to 00/09/67
30 Sqn.	Beverley C.1	Eastleigh. Muharraq	Heavy transport	00/04/57 to 06/09/67
84 Sqn.	Valetta. C.1. Beverley C.1	Khormaksar	Heavy transport	00/06/58 to 00/11/67
105 Sqn.	Argosy C.1	Khormaksar	Medium transport	17/06/62 to 00/08/67
233 Sqn.	Valetta C.1	Khormaksar	Transport	01/09/60 to 31/01/64
26 Sqn.	Belvedere HC.1	Khormaksar	Transport	00/03/63 to 30/11/65
21 Sqn.	Twin Pioneer CC.1	Khormaksar	Communications. light transport	00/06/65 to 00/07/67
78 Sqn.	Twin Pioneer CC.1. Wessex I IC.2	Khormaksar	Communications. light transport	00/07/56 to 00/11/67
SAR Flt.	Sycamore HR.14, Whirlwind HAR.10	Khormaksar	SAR. light transport	00/00/58 to 00/10/67
FAA				
891 NAS	Sea Venom FAW.22	*Centaur*	Ground attack	00/03/60 to 00/03/60
892 NAS	Sea Vixen FAW.1	*Hermes*	Air defence. ground attack	00/07/63 to 00/07/63
800 NAS	Buccaneer S.1/2	*Eagle*	Strike	00/06/64 to 00/06/64
				00/03/66 to 00/04/66
				00/10/67 to 00/11/67
899 NAS	Sea Vixen FAW.2	*Eagle*	Air defence	00/10/67 to 00/11/67
815 NAS	Wessex HAS.1	*Centaur*	Light transport	00/01/64 to 00/07/64
848 NAS	Wessex HU.5	*Albion*	Light transport	00/10/67 to 00/11/67
British Army 3 Wing, 653 Sqn.				
16 Flt.	Auster AOP.9	Falaise	Recce, liaison	00/04/61 to 00/09/61
15 Flt.	Beaver AL.1	Falaise	Light transport, FAC, recce	00/09/62 to 04/10/67
13 Flt.	Auster AOP.9, Scout AH1	Falaise	Recce, AOP, liaison	02/10/61 to 00/10/67
8 Flt.	Beaver AL.1, Scout AH1	Falaise	Light transport, recce, FAC	14/10/64 to 00/06/67
Air Troop 1 RHA			AOP, recce, liaison	00/03/65 to 00/09/67
Air Troop 10 Hussars			Recce, AOP, FAC, liaison, casevac	00/06/65 to 00/08/65
Air Troop 4/7 RDG	Sioux AH.1	Falaise	Recce, AOP, FAC, liaison, casevac	00/08/65 to 00/09/66
Air Platoon 1 RNF			Supply, liaison, recce, casevac	00/04/66 to 00/09/67
Air Troop QDG			Recce, AOP, FAC, liaison, casevac	00/09/66 to 00/00/67
Air Troop 45 RMC	Sioux AH.1	Falaise, Khormaksar	Liaison, recce, FAC, casevac	00/10/66 to 00/11/67
Air Platoon 1 IG/1 KOB	Sioux AH.1	Habilayn, Falaise	Supply, liaison, recce, casevac	00/02/67 to 00/08/67
Air Troop RAC/RA	Sioux AH.1	Falaise, Khormaksar	Supply, liaison, recce, casevac	00/08/67 to 00/10/67
RRAF				
2 Sqn.	Vampire FB.9	Khormaksar	Ground attack	00/08/58 to 00/10/58

42 Commando by Wessexes of 848 NAS to HMS *Albion*, covered by armed Wessexes of 78 Sqn. whose helicopters then embarked on assault ships and *Albion*. The final phase was supported by Buccaneers and Sea Vixens of 800 and 899 NAS respectively, from HMS *Eagle*. Although there had been contingency plans in the event of fighting, the withdrawal took place without incident.

Aden had been an important base until the British withdrawal of forces east of Suez, and a staging post was retained on the island of Gan. The security forces had fought what turned out to be a number of pointless battles over the years in a hostile environment, with a loss of 90 dead and 510 wounded.

AIRCRAFT MARKINGS

RAF

Combat aircraft were variously finished while transports were finished white over and painted aluminium or silver under. From 1964 Beverleys were camouflaged in Light Stone/Dark Earth over, black under, with white serials. Most transports carried the title 'Royal Air Force Middle East' along the upper fuselage.

Tempest F.VI *Silver overall, black serial and code on mid-fuselage: NX169/C (8 Sqn.).*
Brigand B.1 *Medium Sea Grey over, black under, black serials and code mid-fuselage: RH764/B. White serials: VS839 (8 Sqn.).*

Vampire FB.9 *Silver overall, black serials and code on rear boom: WL608/U (8 Sqn.).*

Venom FB.1 *Dark Green/Dark Sea Grey over, PRU Blue under, black serial, white code on rear boom: WE477, WK434/W (8 Sqn.).*

Venom FB.4 *Dark Green/Dark Sea Grey over, silver under, black serials and code on rear boom; WR548/F (8 Sqn.).*

Meteor FR.9 *Dark Green/Dark Sea Grey over, silver under, red nose, black serials: VZ604 (APRF).*

Hunter FGA.9 *Dark Green/Dark Sea Grey over, silver under, black serials, white codes on fin, squadron markings across roundel (208 Sqn. on nose): XK151/X (8 Sqn.). Chequered wingtips: XG154/B (43 Sqn.); XE607/F (208 Sqn.). White wing tips: XF460/KS (1417 Flt.).*

Lincoln B.2 *Medium Sea Grey over, black under, large white serials: RF444 (49 Sqn.); RF340, SX982 (1426 Flt.).*

Shackleton MR.2 *White over, Dark Sea Grey under, red code on nose, squadron number and serial on rear fuselage outlined in white: WR965/B, WL757/D (37 Sqn.).*

Valetta C.1 *Club marking and code on fin: VW141/141 (84 Sqn.); VW860/860, VW198/198 (233 Sqn.).*

Dakota C.4 *KN452 (MECS).*

Beverley C.1 *Playing card symbol on upper fin, black serials and code on lower fin: XH121/121 club. Camouflaged aircraft with medium grey codes on forward fuselage: XM103/V diamond, XM109/R spade, XM107/P club (all 84 Sqn.).*

Twin Pioneer CC.1 *XM958/A, XM963/B (21 Sqn.); XL993, XM284 (78 Sqn.).*

Belvedere HC.1 *Large black code mid-fuselage: XG463/B, XG458/E (26 Sqn.).*

Wessex HC.2 *Dark Green/Dark Sea Grey overall, code on fuselage side in grey: XR500/A, XR506/B (78 Sqn.).*

Sycamore HR.14 *Chrome yellow overall; XG504 (SAR Flt.).*

Whirlwind HAR.10 *Chrome yellow overall: XK970, XL111 (SAR Flt.).*

FAA

Wessex HAS.1 *Yellow over, blue-grey under, white code on fuselage and nose: XP106/300C (815 NAS).*

Wessex HU.5 *Sand/Dark Green over, sand*

Wessex HC.2 XR508/B of 78 Sqn. RAF lifts a 105mm lightweight pack howitzer into place on a picket in 1966. During Operation 'Nutcracker' in the Radfan in 1964, ground forces had had to rely on naval Wessex HU.5s of 815 NAS and Belvederes of 26 Sqn. to move men and equipment along the mountain ridges. (RAF Museum)

under, NAS badge on cowling, white code on mid-fuselage, ship code on tail: XS492/MA (848 NAS).

AAC

All aircraft and helicopters were camouflaged Dark Earth/Dark Green overall, generally with white serials.

Auster AOP.9 *XP240 (13 Flt.).*

Beaver AL.1 *White bands on mid-wing, black serial: XP773, XP827 (15 Flt.).*

Scout AH.1 *XR601, XV633 (13 Flt.).*

Sioux AH.1 *XT150/RM (1 RMC Air Troop).*

6.2. Yemen, 1962–1970

The Imam Ahmad, who had worked for links with Egypt in his fight against the British in the south, died on 19 September 1962, and his more progressive son, Badr, was deposed by an Egyptian-backed coup on the 26th. Badr fled to the mountains of the north as, within four hours, 150 Egyptian paratroops landed at Hodeida airfield. Royalists then effectively held the north and east

of the country bordering Saudi Arabia, while Republicans, with massive Egyptian support, held the centre and south. Attacks across the border into the Beihan area increased, and after the Amir's palace at As-Saylan was bombed in October the British brought in light anti-aircraft guns from Hong Kong. In November 240 Egyptian paratroops were dropped at Sirwah to reinforce

Republican units. The Egyptians also began attacking Royalist centres in the south-east, including Marib in December.

The British Government was most concerned with developments and, after a semi-official foray by a former Special Operations Executive (SOE) officer, the Cabinet is believed to have agreed to sponsor the Royalist cause. Support was organized in the form of recently retired Special Air Service (SAS) Regiment members, who also recruited French mercenaries. The first group of six flew into Aden from Paris in May 1963, whence they were flown up to Beihan before entering the Yemen by camel train. Their initial tasks were to assess training and supply needs for Royalist forces and to organize the supply sources and routes. By now the Egyptians had 30,000 troops in the Yemen, some 100 or so MiG-17s and about 30 Il-28 bombers. Some of these aircraft may have been Soviet-manned, as was an unreported type of Yak reconnaissance aircraft which crash-landed in May in a Royalist area.

A most disturbing development occurred on 8 June when it was reported that the village of El Kawma had been bombed with mustard gas (HN3), killing seven; evidence suggested that it had been manufactured in China. The Imperial Iranian Air Force (IIAF) is believed to have dropped arms to Royalists in August. It was also reported that French intermediaries bought arms from Bulgaria on the pretext that they were to be used by African nationalists against the French! They were then flown to the Yemen out of Djibouti in five flights by DC-4 of Rhodesian Air Services (Pvt.) Ltd. from 11 August. The problem of air supply was critical. With powerful Egyptian forces in the Yemen, Saudi Arabia, especially with Americans working across the country, could ill afford to receive aircraft and thus become the target for Egyptian aggression.

TABLE OF UNITS: YEMEN, 1962–1970				
Unit	Aircraft	Base	Role	Dates
EAF				
(5 sqns.)	MiG-15, MiG-17	Sana'a, Taiz, Hodeida	Ground attack	26/09/62 to 00/00/67
(2 sqns.)	Il-28	Sana'a, Hodeida	Light bomber	00/10/62 to 00/00/67
(1 sqn.)	Il-14	Sana'a	Transport	
RSAF				
3 Sqn.	Hunter FGA.9	?	Ground attack	00/06/66 to 00/08/67
6 Sqn.	Lightning F.53	Khamis Mushayt	Ground attack, air defence	00/12/67 to 00/04/70

The US Government had learnt from the Central Intelligence Agency (CIA) of Britain's covert involvement and Kennedy was applying pressure on the Prime Minister to desist just before he was assassinated on 22 November. In that month a Constellation of Aero Transport Flugbetriebsgesellschaft (ATF) of Austria was grounded at Djibouti when it was found that the aircraft was carrying arms. As Egyptian forces built up to 50,000 in 1964, new arrangements were made for arms supplies. Weapons were now bought across Europe and shipped either to Aden or perhaps Ethiopia. They were then flown by an undisclosed carrier across the Red Sea, crossing the coast well to the north of Hodeida where MiG-17s were based, to be dropped near the Imam's headquarters at Qara. With mercenary help, an Egyptian offensive towards Haradh was repulsed in October and armoured vehicles were destroyed. As the Royalists became better equipped and trained they sought to harass the Egyptians.

In April 1965 a convoy was attacked at Hazm and the road held, after which Egyptian garrisons in the south and east had to be supplied by air. Saudi Arabia had been supporting the Royalists with bases and funds but in August 1965 agreed a ceasefire with Egypt; all Egyptian troops were to leave the Yemen by September 1966. A UN observer team was dispatched, supported by 134 Air Transport Unit, Royal Canadian Air Force (RCAF), with Caribou and Otter transports. With the British announcement of its complete withdrawal from South Arabia by 1968, however, the Egyptians reversed their decision and built up their forces to about 50,000. Royal Saudi Air Force (RSAF) Hunters were operational from June against Egyptian incursions in the north, and in October Il-28 bombers attacked Royalist bases in Saudi Arabia at Jizan and Najrab and the RSAF base at Khamis Mushayt. The Royalist bases were again bombed in January 1967.

A new and much more extensive range of gas attacks was now reportedly begun, starting with the village of El Kitaf on 5 January. Two MiG-17 fighters dropped smoke markers to check wind drift, after which nine Il-28s each dropped three 500lb bombs. The gas is believed to have been a new, third-generation type, either chemical VR-55 or a biological T-toxin with mustard gas and phosgene (CG) added as a confusing overlay. Later the Egyptians are believed to have followed up attacks with napalm or high explosive (HE) to burn off residues. In the El Kitaf bombing 200 died, and there were five similar attacks by February, with 195 dead. From contemporary accounts it would appear that the Russians were using the Yemen as a proving ground for new chemical and biological (CB) weapons, and the precision of the attacks lends weight to the theory. The gas raids recommenced on 4 May with an attack on Bassi, and by 17 May, the last suspected gas bombing, a further 550 people are believed to have been killed in nine attacks.

On the 10th, at Gadafa, some bombs failed to explode and an attempt was made to recover them, but the site was subject to intensive bombing with HE, apparently destroying the evidence. The mercenaries now left the Yemen, and after the June war with Israel, Egypt also rapidly withdrew forces. In November the Royalists lost support through Aden, and while the President was in Egypt there was a bloodless coup, after which the Yemeni leadership turned to the Soviet Union for direct support. With increasing arms supplies from Iran and Saudi Arabia, the Royalists took Sana'a in December. The RSAF now used its new Khamis Mushayt-based Lightning fighters of 6 Sqn. in the ground

attack role, but fighting through 1968 was mainly on the ground, although Russia had some 30 aircraft in the Yemen. During the year Republican forces recaptured Sana'a and Hajjah, but through 1969 there were peace moves, leading to the establishment in April 1970 of a coalition government of the new Yemen Arab Republic.

The civil war had cost many lives, but it was remarkable for the introduction of CB warfare, played down at the time perhaps because of the Americans' use of chemical agents in South-East Asia.

AIRCRAFT MARKINGS

For Egyptian aircraft, see entry under the Six-Day War.

RSAF
Lightning F.53 *Bare metal overall, black serial on rear fuselage: 53-698 (6 Sqn.).*

UN
Caribou *White overall, black serial on fin and rear fuselage, 'United Nations' on nose, large 'UN' on rear fuselage: 9321 (134 ATU, RCAF).*

6.3. Oman, 1952–1959

Britain has long maintained close links with Oman through a succession of treaties to protect her oil interests and sea routes. For many years Saudi Arabia had contested the border at the key crossroads of Buraimi Oasis, but when the area was felt to have potential oil reserves a Saudi Arabian party of about 80 settled in the village of Hamasa on 31 August 1952. The British Government protested, and from 15 September a small force of Trucial Oman Levies (TOL) was dispatched to the village and three Vampire FB.5s of 6 Sqn., supported by a Valetta, were flown to Sharjah from Habbaniyah. After demonstrations and leaflet drops, talks began, and the aircraft returned to Iraq in October.

The talks dragged on, and in March 1953 it was decided to mount a blockade of the Saudi investment. The Vampires returned, but because of runway corruption through jet efflux from the small aircraft they were replaced by four Meteor FR.9s of 208 Sqn. These aircraft treated the runway no more kindly, and from the end of April two Lancaster GR.3s each from 37 and 38 Sqn. at Malta were detached to Habbaniyah to operate from Sharjah. The aircraft were used on reconnaissance duties but could barely be spared from NATO commitments in the Mediterranean. They were in turn replaced by Valettas from the Aden Communications Flight for a few weeks in July until two Lancaster PR.1s of 683 Sqn. took over. With the imminent disbandment of 683

Sqn., 1417 Flt. was formed on Ansons at Bahrein, and they supported the blockade until 15 August 1954 when the Saudi force withdrew.

Throughout the operation the use of offensive airpower was resisted as the Saudi party was almost certainly supported by US interests, critically the Arabian-American Oil Company (ARAMCO), which at the time operated not only C-46 transports but also B-26 light bombers. In addition, in June 1951 the US had concluded rights for the use of Dharan airfield for five years,

TABLE OF UNITS: OMAN, 1952—1959

Unit	Aircraft	Base	Role	Dates
RAF				
6 Sqn.	Vampire FB.5, Venom FB.1 (det.)	Sharjah, ex Habbaniyah	Close support, ground attack	15/09/52 to 00/12/55
208 Sqn.	Meteor FR.9 (det.)	Sharjah, ex Abu Sueir	Close support, recce	00/04/53 to 00/04/53
37 Sqn. 38 Sqn.	Lancaster GR.3 (det.)	Sharjah, ex Luqa	Recce, ground attack	00/04/53 to 00/07/53
ACF	Valetta C.1	Sharjah, ex Khormaksar	Recce, transport	00/07/53 to 00/07/53
683 Sqn.	Lancaster PR.1 (det.)	Sharjah, ex Habbaniyah	Recce, ground attack	00/07/53 to 30/11/53
1417 Flt.	Anson C.19, Pembroke C.1	Sharjah	Recce, communications	00/09/53 to 29/09/58
7 Sqn.	Lincoln B.2 (det.)	Khormaksar, ex Upwood	Recce, heavy bombing	23/01/55 to 00/10/55
1426 Flt.	Lincoln B.2 (det.)	Sharjah, ex Khormaksar	Recce, heavy bombing	00/02/56 to 00/12/56
249 Sqn.	Venom FB.4 (det.)	Sharjah, ex Akrotiri	Close support, ground attack	00/07/57 to 00/08/57
8 Sqn.	Venom FB.4 (det.)	Sharjah, ex Khormaksar	Close support, ground attack	00/07/57 to 09/02/59
37 Sqn.		Masirah, ex Khormaksar	Recce, ground support, bombing	
42 Sqn.	Shackleton MR.2 (det.)	Masirah, ex St. Mawgan		00/00/58 to 00/00/58
228 Sqn.		Masirah, ex Gibraltar	Recce, ground support	00/09/58 to 00/12/58
224 Sqn.		Masirah, ex Gibraltar		00/01/59 to 00/02/59
208 Sqn.	Meteor FR.9 (det.)	Sharjah, ex Ta Kali	Fighter recce	00/07/57 to 00/08/57
58 Sqn.?	Canberra PR.7 (det.)	Bahrein, ex Wyton	Recce	
84 Sqn.	Valetta C.1, Beverley C.1	Sharjah, Bahrein	Logistic air support	00/07/57 to 00/02/59
SAR Flt.	Sycamore HR.14 (det.)	Sharjah	SAR, light transport	
152 Sqn.	Pembroke C.1, Twin Pioneer CC.1	Sharjah	Light transport, communications	29/09/58 to 00/12/67
FAA				
801 NAS	Sea Hawk FGA.6		Ground attack	
891 NAS	Sea Venom FAW.22	Bulwark	Ground attack	00/09/58
849 NAS	Skyraider AEW.1 (D Flt.)		Recce	

renewed in 1956. In January 1955 there were reports of a Saudi Arabian group entering Oman in northern Dhofar. From 23 January Valettas from Aden, supported by two Lincoln B.2s of 7 Sqn., mounted reconnaissance sorties to no effect; they were called off in May. Then, in September, Saudi Arabian aircraft were sighted dropping 'civilians' at the airstrip at Buraimi. From 25 October a force of TOL, supported by Lincolns, Valettas, Ansons, Pembrokes and Venom FB.1s of 6 Sqn., surrounded the Saudi posts and removed the incumbents by Anson and Pembroke to Bahrein. To reinforce governmental authority, the Lincolns demonstrated over Hamasa. The operation ended on 27 October.

The Saudis next courted the Imam Ghalib bin Ali, based on Nizwa, who barely accepted the authority of Sultan Said bin Taimur. The Sultan decided to act, and on 15 December 1955 a force of Muscat and Oman Field Force (MOFF) and TOL occupied Nizwa, having been moved up by

Valetta, 1417 Flt. and 6 Sqn. again supporting the operation. The Imam's brother Talib escaped to Saudi Arabia, where, possibly with ARAMCO help, he formed the Omani Liberation Army (OLA). Through 1956 the Oasis area was kept under scrutiny by Lincolns, Ansons and Pembrokes, but it was not until 14 June 1957 that Talib landed near Muscat, joining the Imam and moving up to the Jebel Kaur. Within a month the OLA had occupied many villages in the area, and, with the potential loss of central Oman, the Sultan sought British help.

Venom FB.4s of 6 and 249 Sqns. moved to Sharjah, and Beverleys and a Valetta of 84 Sqn. and two Shackletons of 37 Sqn. were detached to Sharjah and Bahrein. From 24 July the Venoms began attacking forts at six locations, including Nizwa, Tanuf and Firq. Forty-eight hours before the attacks, Shackletons dropped warning leaflets. A large area was proscribed, and all daylight movement resulted in strafing or bombing from

Among the RAF units supporting the Oman Government in 1957 was 8 Sqn. RAF, then equipped with the Venom FB.4. Air contact teams, working with the SAF, called in fighters for strikes against rebel positions around the Jebel Akhdar, but, even with the heavier support from Shackletons of a succession of detached units and from Fleet Air Arm fighters, the rebels continued to maintain their hold on the Jebel. They were finally defeated after an SAS assault in February 1959. (Via A. S. Thomas)

patrolling aircraft. The peak of air activity was on the 30th when Meteor FR.9s of 208 Sqn. and a Canberra PR.7, probably from 58 Sqn., also participated. After the period of softening up from the air, ground forces moved into the area on 7 August and, with Venom support called in by Air Contact Teams (ACT), first Firq then Nizwa were occupied. The OLA now withdrew to the impenetrable Jebel Akhdar, a fertile plateau above 7,000ft with few easily guarded approaches. From here the OLA presented less of a threat, and most British forces withdrew, leaving detachments of 8 Sqn. and 1417 Flt. On 25 September the Trucial Oman Scouts (TOS), as the TOL had been renamed, made a probing reconnaissance of the lower slopes of Jebel Akhdar supported by a Shackleton.

The rebels soon took the initiative and in October nearly captured Tanuf. The Sultan's Armed Forces (SAF), with RAF help, attempted to force a route to Habib on the Jebel, but this failed and so a blockade was attempted, to halt the flow of arms, although the British Government was keen not to get drawn into a major confrontation. In February 1958 two 17,000yd-range 5.5in howitzers were set up and began shelling the summit villages while the RAF concentrated on attacking the water supply system in the hope of so disrupting the pattern of life that the villagers would deny support to the OLA.

Nevertheless, the supply of arms continued, and the rebels were able to mine approach tracks, making the prospect of assault virtually impossible. Clearly, air control alone would not contain let alone eliminate the OLA. From July the blockade was tightened, and, while plans for a paradrop or heliborne assault were considered (and rejected for a range of technical reasons), the RAF again increased their attacks. In one week in September Shackletons used 148 1,000lb bombs while Sea Hawk and Sea Venom fighters from HMS *Bulwark* joined the action for a few days, flying 77 sorties. It was now decided to bring in D Squadron, 22 SAS Regiment, from Malaya. As the unit settled down to probing the approaches and determining its tactics it was joined by A Squadron and a number of Kenyan trackers. The final assault was made on the night of 26–27 January 1959 and the plateau was reached before

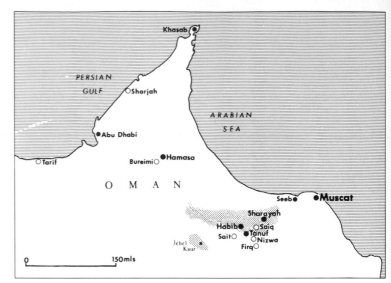

dawn after a magnificent climb during which ropes were used. By the 30th the key villages of Saiq, Habib and Sharayah were occupied.

From 9 February the SAS and RAF units were withdrawn, but 152 Sqn., which had formed from 1417 Flt. in September, remained at Muharraq to support the SAF. An airstrip was cleared near Saiq to help with the process of reconstruction.

AIRCRAFT MARKINGS

RAF

Vampire FB.5 *Silver overall, squadron badge on nose, motif on rudder, black serials and code on boom: VX981/K (6 Sqn.).*
Venom FB.1 *Dark Green/Dark Sea Grey over, PR Blue under, squadron badge on nose, bars flanking roundel on boom, black serial and code on rear of boom: WL435/T (6 Sqn.).*
Venom FB.4 *As FB.1: WR531/R (249 Sqn.).*
Twin Pioneer CC.1 *White over, silver under: XL996 (152 Sqn.).*
For other types involved see entry under South Arabia.

FAA

Sea Venom FAW.22 *Extra Dark Sea Grey over, Sky under, squadron badge on nose, black serial on boom, code on fin: XG701/B (891 NAS).*

6.4. Kuwait, 1961

Britain reached an exclusive agreement for protection with the Ruler of Kuwait in 1899 well before oil was discovered in the 1930s. By 1960 the agreement was dated and an Exchange of Notes was signed in June 1961 agreeing, *inter alia,* that Her Majesty's Government would assist the Ruler if requested. On 25 June the leader of Iraq, Abdul Qarim Qassem, declared

Kuwait a part of Iraq and troops began to move south from Baghdad. The following day all UK forces in the Middle East were placed on four-day standby. There were three frigates in the theatre and the commando carrier HMS *Bulwark*, with 42 RM Commando embarked, at Karachi. An amphibious warfare squadron was based on Bahrein, Army units were located at Sharjah,

Bahrein, Aden, Kenya and Cyprus, and the RAF had two Hunter ground-attack squadrons at Aden and Nairobi, light transport and communications aircraft at Bahrein and Aden and heavier transports at Aden. Equipment reserves were stocked at Bahrein and in Kenya.

A Reinforced Theatre Plan (RTP) for support to Kuwait had already been drafted as Plan 'Vantage'. The plan envisaged supplementing the locally available forces with those on Cyprus, plus UK-based transport squadrons and Germany-based Canberra units. Problems anticipated were the lack of any surface routes into the area, the absence of air defence radar and restrictions on overflying many countries, including Saudi Arabia and Somalia. On 29 June, in advance of a request for help, the first moves were made. Stockpiles at Bahrein were opened up and HMS *Bulwark* steamed from Karachi. The two Hunter squadrons, 8 and 208, were prepared and moved up to Bahrein on the 30th from Khormaksar and Eastleigh respectively; they were operational by the end of the day. Two Shackleton MR.2s of 37 Sqn. moved up to Bahrein for reconnaissance duties, and 88 Sqn. at Wildenrath was ordered to Sharjah. Five Britannias in the area were cleared to join with Comet 4 and Argonaut aircraft of East African Airways in transporting HQ 24 Brigade from Kenya to the Gulf. Argonauts of 3 Sqn. Royal Rhodesian Air Force (RRAF) also supported the transfer. The formal request for military support came late on the 30th, but early on the following day there was a setback when Turkey and Sudan refused permission for overflights. Both countries relaxed their positions later in the day.

The first unit to land in Kuwait on 1 July was 42 RM Commando, lifted from HMS *Bulwark* by Whirlwinds of 848 NAS. The Hunters landed at Kuwait New airfield at Farwania later in the morning; Britannias of 99 and 511 Sqns. began lifting 45 RM Commando and the 11th Hussars from Aden; four Canberras of 88 Sqn. landed at Sharjah, where they were joined on the 2nd by eight B(I).6s of 213 Sqn. from Bruggen; and Twin Pioneers of 78 Sqn. from Aden joined those of B Flight of 152 Sqn. at Bahrein, with elements operating from Kuwait New. The build-up continued with maximum RAF commitment by the 4th. By then Comets of 216 Sqn. were involved with fourteen Britannias in transporting elements of the 2nd Bn. Parachute Regiment from the UK and Cyprus. Their equipment was moved by 27 Hastings from three UK-based units and the Cyprus-based 70 Sqn., together with twelve Beverleys from 47 and 53 Sqns. The 1st Bn. Royal Inniskillings were transported from Kenya in chartered aircraft and Beverleys of 30 Sqn., and two companies of the Coldstream Guards moved up to Kuwait from Bahrein with the help of six Valettas of 233 Sqn. Finally, several Canberra PR.7s of 13 Sqn. flew into Bahrein from Akrotiri.

Once in Kuwait, the troops took up positons along the Moutla Ridge to the north-west of

TABLE OF UNITS: KUWAIT, 1961

Unit	Aircraft	Base	Role	Dates
RAF				
8 Sqn.	Hunter FGA.9	Khormaksar, Kuwait New	Ground attack, air defence	30/06/61 to 30/07/61
208 Sqn.	Hunter FGA.9	Eastleigh, Kuwait New	Ground attack, air defence	30/06/61 to 22/07/61
88 Sqn.	Canberra B(I).8	Wildenrath, Sharjah	Medium bombing	01/07/61 to 20/07/61
213 Sqn.	Canberra B(I).6	Bruggen, Sharjah	Medium bombing	02/07/61 to 20/07/61
37 Sqn.	Shackleton MR.2	Khormaksar, Bahrein	Recce, SAR	30/06/61 to 22/07/61
13 Sqn.	Canberra PR.7	Akrotiri, Bahrein	Recce	04/07/61 to 21/07/61
152 Sqn.	Twin Pioneer CC.1, Pembroke C.1	Bahrein, Kuwait New	Communications, light transport	30/06/61 to 00/09/61
78 Sqn.	Twin Pioneer CC.1	Khormaksar, Kuwait New	Communications, light transport	30/06/61 to 00/08/61
233 Sqn.	Valetta C.1	Khormaksar, Bahrein	Medium transport	30/06/61 to 00/08/61
84 Sqn.	Beverley C.1	Khormaksar	Heavy transport	
30 Sqn.	Beverley C.1	Eastleigh, Bahrein	Heavy transport	01/07/61 to 00/08/61
70 Sqn.	Hastings C.1	Akrotiri	Medium transport	03/07/61 to 00/08/61
24 Sqn. 36 Sqn. 114 Sqn.	Hastings C.1	Colerne	Medium transport	03/07/61 to 24/07/61
99 Sqn. 511 Sqn.	Britannia C.1	Lyneham	Troop transport	01/07/61 to 26/07/61
216 Sqn.	Comet C.4	Lyneham	Troop transport	03/07/61 to 09/07/61
47 Sqn. 53 Sqn.	Beverley C.1	Abingdon	Heavy transport	03/07/61 to 26/07/61
RRAF				
3 Sqn.	C-4 Argonaut	Salisbury	Troop transport	01/07/61 to 08/07/61
Chartered aircraft				
EAA	Comet 4, Argonaut	Nairobi	Troop transport	01/07/61 to 08/07/61
FAA				
848 NAS	Whirlwind HAS.7	*Bulwark*, Kuwait New	Light transport	01/07/61 to 20/07/61
803 NAS	Scimitar F.1	*Victorious*	Ground attack, air defence	09/07/61 to 31/07/61
892 NAS	Sea Vixen FAW.1		Air defence	
849B NAS	Gannet AEW.3		AEW	
807 NAS	Scimitar F.1	*Centaur*	Ground attack, air defence	31/07/61 to 24/08/61
893 NAS	Sea Vixen FAW.1		Air defence	
849D NAS	Gannet AEW.1		AEW	
824 NAS	Whirlwind HAS.7		ASW	

Kuwait town. Conditions were appalling, with daytime temperatures of 120°F and high winds creating sandstorms and a visibility often less than 400yds. During the emergency one Hunter of 208 Sqn. was lost when it flew into the Moutla Ridge after the pilot was presumed to have become disorientated. Most RAF ground crew were already from the theatre, and they were to some extent acclimatized, but the men were rotated on to HMS *Bulwark* for rest. The carrier also provided the only air defence radar, with an effective range of about 80 miles, and complex communications to the Hunter squadrons.

Communications as a whole were a major problem. The headquarters was established on HMS *Jufair* at Bahrein, some 300 miles from Kuwait. Distances were too great for the use of landlines and radio/telegraphy, and most signals were delivered by air letter using the AOC's Canberra between Aden and Bahrein and Pembrokes of A Flt., 152 Sqn., between Bahrein, Sharjah and Kuwait. A further problem was that RAF aircraft were fitted with VHF radio while those of the Fleet Air Arm (FAA) were UHF-equipped. Air defences were improved from 9 July with the arrival of HMS *Victorious* with AEW Gannets and Sea Vixen all-weather fighters. The carrier's Type 984 radar extended cover to 150 miles. It was not until the 18th that the RAF had its own radar unit, a 'portable' Type SC 787, set up, although that lacked a height-finding capability. If an attack was to be made it might have been expected on Iraq's national day, the 14th, but no moves were made beyond Basra. From the 20th it was felt safe to withdraw forces, and 42 Commando and 2 Para moved to Bahrein while 45 Commando returned to Aden.

The Canberras returned to Germany, although a Cyprus-based unit was earmarked to reinforce if necessary. No. 208 Sqn. Hunters withdrew to Bahrein. The UK-based transport aircraft were released late in July, and on the 31st HMS *Centaur* relieved HMS *Victorious*. By the end of September all units had returned to their more usual policing tasks. It is not possible to say whether the reinforcement averted a war in the area. The speed of relocation in difficult circumstances was remarkable, and several important lessons concerning communications and stockpiling were learnt and subsequently applied.

AIRCRAFT MARKINGS

RAF

Canberra B(I).6 *Dark Green/Dark Sea Grey over, light grey under, white serial, unit badge on fin: WT307 (213 Sqn.).*
Canberra B(I).8 *Dark Green/Dark Sea Grey over, black under, large white serial, unit badge on fin: WT332 (88 Sqn.).*
Pembroke C.1 *White over, silver under, black serial and code on fin: WV743/J (152 Sqn.). For other RAF types involved see entry under South Arabia.*

FAA

Sea Vixen FAW.1 *Extra Dark Sea Grey over, white under, white code on nose, ship's code on fin, unit badge on fin: XJ523/462C (892 NAS); XN650/456C (893 NAS).*
Scimitar F.1 *Extra Dark Sea Grey over, white under, white code on nose, ship's code on fin, unit badge on intake: XD236/150V (803 NAS).*
Gannet AEW.3 *Extra Dark Sea Grey over, Sky under, black markings, code on nose, ship's code on fin, black/yellow-striped finlets and spinner: XL481/428V (B Flt., 849 NAS); XL474/421C (A Flt.,849 NAS).*
Whirlwind HAS.7 *Light Stone overall, black markings, code on nose and rear fuselage, ship's code on nose: XN363/PB (848 NAS).*

6.5. Dhofar, 1965–1975

Oman was extremely conservatively ruled, and it was inevitable that frustration about relative taxation and deprivation would lead to rebellion. After the problems in the north the SAF had been strengthened and the Sultan of Oman's Air Force (SOAF) formed in 1959, based at Muscat. But trouble was now to come in the Dhofar region in the south, where the Sultan Said bin Taimur lived. In 1962 the Dhofar Liberation Front (DLF) was formed and with help from Egypt, Saudi Arabia and Iraq formally began operations against the regime from 9 June 1965, with bases at Hauf and Al Ghayda in East Aden Protectorate. Soon the mountains behind the narrow coastal plain were under DLF control, and by 1966 Salalah, the regional capital and RAF staging post, was protected by a ring of defences, including wire; it was virtually isolated by road.

Offensive air power was confined to five armed piston-engined Provost trainers flown by seconded RAF or direct-contract pilots. In the early days of the conflict there was no prospect of dealing with the situation through air control, especially when the population supported the DLF, whose base was better secured when Britain left Aden late in 1967. The following year it was absorbed into the People's Front for the Liberation of the Occupied Arabian Gulf (PFLOAG), sponsored by the People's Democratic Republic of the Yemen (PDRY). Britain was keen to retain influence and stability in the area, to guarantee the free flow of oil through the Straits of Hormuz.

With the withdrawal from Aden, several RAF

units moved up into the Gulf area, including the two Hunter squadrons. It is not clear whether any of these units operated against targets in Dhofar before their disbandment in 1971. Certainly an increasing number of RAF pilots were seconded to the SOAF, but throughout the operations Britain went to some lengths not to appear publicly to be involved in the internal affairs of Oman. The position deteriorated through 1968. On 7 August the rebels attacked the RAF camp at Salalah and a Provost was hit by groundfire, Baghdad Radio claiming 49 British servicemen killed and a Hunter shot down. In August 1969 the rebels captured the coastal town of Rakhyut. Also in 1969, the SAS Regiment saw action on the Musandam Peninsula overlooking the Straits of Hormuz. An Iraqi irregular group had infiltrated, and SAS soldiers were landed by sea and air to deal with the problem. To the many British military and administrative advisers it now became clear that, if the integrity of Oman was to be preserved, radical changes in governance and military response were essential.

On 23 July 1970 the Sultan was deposed by his son, the Sultan Qaboos bin Said. Almost immediately plans for social change and military action were formulated, and SAS units were moved to Salalah to form British Army Training Teams (BATT) to work in the Jebel on a 'hearts and minds' campaign. Leaflet drops encouraged surrender, and many rebel supporters were eventually formed into tribal 'firqats' (paramilitary groups) to fight in support of the Government. In February 1971, with Strikemaster support, the SAS and a local firqat liberated the eastern town of Sudh. The overall plan was to secure areas to the east of Salalah and then to prevent supplies flowing from South Yemen, all in the context of denying the PFLOAG popular support. In Operation 'Jaguar' from October to December 1971, key posts were established at Jibjat and Medinat al Haq and sustained by helicopter supply.

By now the SOAF could boast a squadron of Strikemaster light attack aircraft, a squadron of AB.205 and 206 helicopters and a large detachment of Skyvan light transports at Salalah. It was possibly the availability of these rugged and reliable short take-off and landing (STOL) aircraft that in the long term enabled the war to be won. They carted loads around the region using roughly and often hastily prepared strips only several hundred yards long. The AB.205 version of the ubiquitous UH-1 also come into its own to ensure the deployment of troops, their resupply and, most importantly, speedy casualty evacuation.

The rebels, numbering about 2,500 were very well supplied with modern Soviet weaponry, including rifles, machine guns, heavy mortars, 14.5mm anti-aircraft MGs and Katyusha rockets. They were extremely mobile and could bring their weapons to bear on Government forces

from easily protected positions on the Jebel. But the key to supply was a single route from South Yemen through the Wadi Sayq, overlooked by Sarfait. In April 1972 the town was taken by the Desert Regiment of the SAF in a heliborne assault. Initially the SAF was supplied by Skyvan, but constant shelling from across the border made this method too dangerous, so for the next four years resupply was by helicopter. In April and May Strikemasters attacked targets in South Yemen, critically at Hauf, Jaadib and Habarut. On 11 May the PDRY formally protested that British aircraft were violating Yemeni airspace and attacking towns and villages including Socotra island. During the summer months Dhofar is subject to monsoons during which air support is hazardous. In these conditions the PFLOAG prepared for a full-scale assault on the eastern coastal town of Mirbat, which was defended only by a small SAS unit, local gendarmerie and a firqat.

A force of 250 well-organized rebels attacked at dawn on 19 July 1972, having taken a small hill to the north of the town. The defenders held out through the initial attack and within several hours Strikemasters flew in below the cloud to strafe enemy positions while helicopters brought reinforcements and removed the injured. By mid-morning the battle was won, and the rebel forces not only lost face but were never able to mount a

The Sultan of Oman's Air Force was formed in 1959, based at Muscat and comprising five armed Provost T.52 trainers flown by RAF contract pilots. These aircraft were operated by 1 Sqn., which was later based at Salalah. Illustrated in 1966, with a British serial, is XF907. (Via A. S. Thomas)

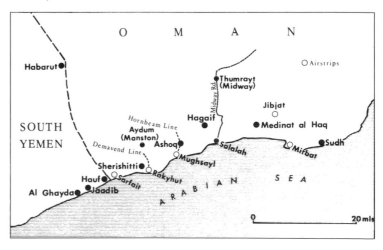

similar attack in the future. During 1972 Oman received tangible external support from Jordan (a Special Force Battalion), Pakistan (100 Baluchi NCOs and officers) and, most notably, Iran (which eventually contributed 2,400 troops and several squadrons of fighters and helicopters). All of these forces were under SAF control and made a vitally important contribution to winning the war; indeed, through 1973 the Iranian AB.205s supported the supply of the Sarfait garrison. The SOAF lost its first aircraft on 9 July 1973 when Strikemaster '413' was shot down over western Oman; the British pilot was killed. When PDRY aircraft bombed Omani territory on 18 November, Iran guaranteed the integrity of Omani airspace.

In 1973, in an effort to restrict supply trains, construction began of the 'Hornbeam' line. Completed in 1974, it ran inland from Mughsayl for some 33 miles and was constructed of barbed wire and mines. The Imperial Iranian Battle Group (IIBG) was based around Midway (later renamed Thumrayt) and had responsibility for the Midway Road from Salalah. Although rebels were still operating widely in the area behind Salalah, the Government's grip was tightening. In 1974 the PFLOAG assumed the less ambitious title of People's Front for the Liberation of Oman (PFLO). There were many contacts with small group of the PFLO through 1974, and plans were now drawn up to extend Government control in the west.

The IIBG evacuated Thumrayt in October, moving their main base of operations to Manston, from where they reoccupied Rakyhut on 5 January 1975 with Strikemaster cover. Development of a second supply filter, the 'Demavend' line, began. Operations were now focused on clearing rebel positions along the line. In each case the SAF would move on foot or by helicopter with Strikemaster support available at 15 minutes' notice; subject to location, resupply would be by helicopter or Skyvan. Fighting was often intense, with PFLO fighters making optimum use of the difficult terrain. In January fighting was concentrated around Sherishitti, followed in February by Operation 'Himaar', an attack on the 9 June Regiment's HQ north of Ashoq on the Hornbeam line.

By now the helicopters were flying a total of 600 hours a month, and several were lost in accidents and to groundfire; on 8 March an AB.206 was shot down near Hagaif. Preparations were now made to clear the area west of the Demavend line. In August a new threat emerged when on the 19th Strikemaster '406' was shot down near Sherishitti by SA-7. More rounds were fired at rescue helicopters and a circling Strikemaster, but no further hits were recorded and the pilot was picked up injured. In all, 23 SA-7 rounds would be fired for the loss of three aircraft, one being an IIAF gunship on 15 September. From now on, aircraft operating patterns changed, with the slow helicopters keeping to altitudes above 10,000ft. In October, what was to be the final major operation began as the plateau below Sarfait was invested. In order to counter the cross-border artillery fire, three 5.5in howitzers were flown in by IIAF CH-47C Chinooks and rapidly set up; in addition, newly delivered Hunters of 6 Sqn. from Thumrayt attacked targets in South Yemen from 17 October to 21 November, concentrating on Hauf and Jaadib.

Despite losing two more AB.205 helicopters on 1 November and 25 December, the SAF was in a sufficiently commanding position that on 11 December the war was declared won, although

The British gave covert support to Oman throughout the long Dhofar campaign. Camouflaged Beverley XM109/R, of 84 Sqn., is pictured here taking off from Bait al Falaj, with an SOAF Beaver, XR214 of 5 Sqn., in the foreground. Four Beavers were transferred from British Army stocks. (RAF Museum)

TABLE OF UNITS: DHOFAR, 1965–1975

Unit	Aircraft	Base	Role	Dates
RAF				
208 Sqn.	Hunter FGA.9	Muharraq	Ground attack	00/06/64 to 10/08/71
8 Sqn.	Hunter FGA.9/FR.10	Muharraq	Ground attack, recce	00/09/67 to 15/12/71
210 Sqn.	Shackleton MR.2	Sharjah	MR	00/11/70 to 15/11/71
84 Sqn.	Beverley C.1, Andover C.1	Sharjah, Muharraq	Transport	00/11/67 to 31/10/71
78 Sqn.	Wessex HC.2	Sharjah	Light transport, SAR	00/11/67 to 01/12/71
SOAF				
1 Sqn.	Strikemaster Mk.82	Salalah	Close support, ground attack	00/01/69 to 00/00/79
6 Sqn.	Hunter F.6/FGA.9/Mk.73	Thumrayt	Ground attack, close support	00/08/75 to 00/00/86
5 Sqn.	Beaver AL.1, Defender	Seeb (det. Salalah)	Liaison, recce, medevac	00/00/62 to 00/00/86
2 Sqn.	Skyvan 3M	Seeb (det. Salalah)	Light transport, medevac	00/08/70 to 00/00/86
4 Sqn.	Dakota, Caribou, Viscount, BAC.111, C-130H	Seeb	Transport	00/00/68 to 00/00/86
3 Sqn.	AB.205A, AB.206B	Salalah	Light transport, liaison, casevac	00/10/70 to 00/00/86
IIAF				
? Sqn.	F-5E	Thumrayt	Ground attack	00/00/74 to 00/00/74
? Sqn.	F-4E	Thumrayt	Ground attack	00/00/74 to 00/00/76
? Sqn.	C-130H	Thumrayt, Manston	Transport	00/00/73 to 00/00/76
? Sqn.	CH-47C	Manston	Heavy lift	00/09/75 to 00/12/75
? Sqn.	AB.205	Thumrayt, Manston	Light transport, casevac, gunship	00/09/73 to 00/00/76

the shelling of positions around Sarfait continued until a negotiated ceasefire in March 1976. There has been sporadic action since that time, and an IIAF F-4E was reported to have been shot down over eastern Yemen on 25 November 1976. The SAS Regiment, although formally withdrawn in March 1976, has retained a strong presence for 'training' purposes, and the SOAF continues to fly operational sorties against rebels.

AIRCRAFT MARKINGS

SOAF

Strikemaster Mk. 82 *Dark Green/Dark Earth over, Light Aircraft Grey under, serial in black on rear fuselage and under wings: 404, 408 (1 Sqn.).*

Hunter FGA.73 *Dark Green/Dark Sea Grey over, Light Aircraft Grey under, black serial on rear fuselage: 815, 842 (6 Sqn.).*
Skyvan 3M *Dark Green/Dark Earth overall, black serial on rear fuselage: 916 (2 Sqn.). Dark Green/Dark Earth over, Dark Green under: 904 (2 Sqn.).*
AB.205A *Dark green/light brown overall, black serial on boom: 718, 725 (3 Sqn.).*

IIAF

F-5E *Chocolate/medium brown/sand over, pale grey under, black serial on fin: 00933.*
F-4D *Chocolate/dark green/sand over, pale grey under, black serial on fin: 3-602.*
AB.205A *Sand/tan overall, black serial on fin.*
CH-47C *Pale grey/apple green overall, black serial on rear rotor mounting: 4-067.*

6.6. The Gulf War, 1980–1988

A characteristic of the war between Iraq and Iran has been probably the most inept use of aircraft in a modern major conflict. Gross exaggeration of achievement makes a precise and clear description of the course of events difficult to chart, except in a general way.

After agreement in 1975 on the boundary along the Shatt al Arab waterway, the Iraqi Government became concerned about Iranian intentions in 1980 after the Islamic Revolution. First, Iraq was worried about the declared Iranian intention to export the revolution to her neighbours; and second, she wanted Iranian withdrawal from islands in the Shatt. There was some desultory Iranian shelling early in September, and on the 22nd Iraq invaded Iran on several fronts towards Khorramshahr, Ahwaz, Susangerd and Qasr-e-Shirin.

The attacks were preceded by air strikes against ten airfields, including Ahwaz, Omdiya, Dezful, Meharabad, Sharokhi, Khatami, Tabriz, Shiraz and Busheir. These strikes, unlike those mounted by Israel against Egypt in 1967, had little impact because of the sloppiness of the Iraqi attack and the extent of hardened shelters. At this stage in the war the Iraqi Air Force (IAF) possessed about 350 operational combat aircraft plus 165 helicopters; Iran, already starved of spares, could field about 325 combat aircraft and 600 helicopters. Anticipating retaliation, Iraqi aircraft moved west to safer bases and transports were flown into Jordan. Strike aircraft continued to bomb targets in the south-west Khuzestan Province, while the Iranians bombed Baghdad and Kirkuk and airfields at Al Kut and Basra. By the 25th both sides were making extravagant claims of aircraft shot down. Iran may have lost several dozen of the 110 claimed by Iraq, which probably lost fifteen or so.

On the ground the fighting was fierce but

neither side gave its forces close support from the air, preferring to use small units of aircraft to attack targets behind the lines. The initial Iraqi objective, Khorramshahr, was taken on 13 October, after which Iraq increased pressure in the direction of Ahwaz and Dezful, gradually grinding to a halt. Part of the Iraqi assumption was that the Islamic Government of Iran was weak and did not enjoy the support of the armed forces; the original attack was expected to provoke another revolution. Once this did not materialize, it became clear that there would be no speedy outcome. Iran, relatively isolated, secured support from Syria, Libya and North Korea, while Iraq found friends in Kuwait, Jordan and Saudi Arabia; on 28 September, after bombing Tehran, eight Tu-22 'Blinders' had flown to the safety of Riyadh. Iran bombed targets in Iraqi Kurdestan with the intention not only of disrupting production in the Iraqi oilfields but also of fomenting unrest and rebellion among the Kurds.

Iraq was also treating oil as a major target, and on 14 October there were the first reported dogfights over Abadan. MiG-21 fighters covering bombing raids on the huge production facility fought F-4 Phantoms of the Islamic Republic of Iran Air Force (IRIAF), and one MiG was claimed shot down. The IRIAF began using its AH-1J gunships in support of troops, and F-4 Phantoms attacked an Iraqi pontoon bridge across the Karun river. Western powers, anxious to protect their oil interests, moved forces into the Gulf area. Britain dispatched the destroyer HMS *Coventry* and frigate HMS *Alacrity* to Oman to form the Armilla Patrol, while the US sent four E-3A AWACS aircraft to Dhahran. An early non-partisan casualty of the war was an 824 NAS Sea King, which ditched in the Gulf on 28 January 1981.

By mid-November a stalemate had been reached and the pattern of the next few years established. Aircraft of both sides made bombing raids on oil targets and cities, normally in single sorties or pairs. On 16 November, for example, Iran attacked oil installations at Abdali in Kuwait. Targets close to the front line were attacked by artillery and from Iraq by Frog rockets; later in the war Iran would use Syrian-supplied SS-1 'Scud-B' missiles. It is estimated that, as the rainy season set in at the end of the year, Iraq had 310 operational aircraft and Iran only 150, plus reserves for spares. The Iranians now counterat-

tacked at Susangerd, where in January 1981 a large tank battle ensued. Limited use was made by both sides of helicopter gunships, but again troops fought without the benefit of air support.

In the spring, the fighting was focused in the north around Qasr-e-Shirin, with several dog-fights reported and some Iraqi successes attributed to the mating of the French Matra Magic AAM with the MiG-21. In the fighting in this mountainous area Mi-24 'Hind-D' helicopters, probably crewed by Soviet advisers, were used for the first time. It was also reported that Iran was using its few serviceable F-14A Tomcats as radar pickets to pick up incoming raids, flying from Meharabad, Khatami and Shiraz. During 1981 the Iranians attacked Kuwaiti oil installations at Umm al-Aish in June and again on 1 October. Throughout the year the bombing of strategic targets, including power stations, continued, but with little real effect on the course of the war. Iran launched a major offensive in March 1982 from Dezful, soon gaining the upper hand despite appalling losses. The Islamic Revolutionary Guards Corps (IRGC) or *Pasradan* was receiving training in Russia and with death in battle perceived as a short cut to paradise, human wave attacks were now becoming a feature of the battles.

There were already attempts to reach a peaceful settlement, and related to one was the loss of Algerian Government Learjet 7T-VHB. With a group of fourteen Algerians aboard, it was reportedly shot down by Iraqi air defences on 3 May in the north-west of Iran, returning from Tehran. The Iranian forces now moved on the southern front, and with gunship support Khorramshahr was retaken on 24 May. In July the Iranians began an assault on Basra, which was contained after heavy fighting; both sides lost helicopters in the battles, but there is no evidence that they were used effectively in the anti-armour role. On 7 November the IAF attacked Iranian ships in the Gulf. Although causing little damage and initially not pressed home, such attacks by both sides were to become a unique feature of the war.

February 1983 saw the opening of yet another Iranian offensive across marshland against Iraqi fixed positions east of Al Amarah. Iraqi gunships took a toll of the lightly armed IRGC, and the IAF concentrated its attack aircraft in hitting airfields and military targets behind the front line. IRIAF tactics were improving as pilots imprisoned by the Revolutionary regime were freed to fight, although several defected in Phantoms to Turkey and Saudi Arabia; Iran is also believed to have improved its F-4 and F-5 availabilty with the help of, among others, Israel. Iraq had received its full quota of Mirage F.1EQs and, in addition, Egypt is believed to have supplied some F-6s (MiG-19s) and F-7s (MiG-21s) to make good attrition. The war had now clearly reached an impasse. The Iraqis, with superior air power, were not prepared to take the war to Iran on the

ground; the Iranians, with superior numbers but ill-equipped, were incapable of making any significant impact on Iraqi fixed positions.

Towards the end of the year there was renewed fighting on all fronts, and Iraq is believed to have used napalm and other chemical weapons for the first time; mustard gas was fired in artillery and mortar shells. International concern was heightened as Iraq secured the lease of five Super Étendard fighters from France. Equipped to fire the Exocet missile, their purpose could only be to extend the tentative anti-shipping war in the Gulf, and the USA moved an additional carrier group into the Indian Ocean. The war now broadened in scope. Anticipating another Iranian drive, the IAF began attacking towns, causing civilian casualties. This bombing was accompanied by long-range shelling and rocket attacks. The Iranians replied in kind, and towns and cities along the Tigris were bombed and rocketed. Thus began the so-called 'War of the Cities'. In March 1984 the Iranian offensive was launched across the Hawizah marsh, the intention being to separate the Iraq Fourth Army defending Al Amarah and the Third Army defending Basra. The Iranian forces, spearheaded by IRGC units, crossed the marshes by pontoons and small boats, initially catching the Iraqis off guard. It was not long, however, before the IAF gunships were causing heavy losses. Further to the south, Iranian gunships supported an attack on Majnoon Island in the Shatt.

During 1983 the IAF had made desultory raids on the main Iranian oil terminal at Kharg Island. On 22 November the 12,550-ton Greek cargo

At the outbreak of the Gulf War in 1980, the Iranian forces were extremely well equipped with the latest Western armaments, including the F-14A Tomcat. However, because of an embargo on the supply of spares, and owing to indifferent maintenance, few were to see the end of the war, and, from a delivery of 55, only five of these complex and expensive fighters were believed to be operational in 1988.

ship *Antigone* had been hit there by an Exocet fired from a Super Frelon. On 22 February 1984 Kharg Island was the target, and several days later the British bulk carrier *Charming* (30,000 tons) was hit. The 'Tanker War' proper began on 27 March when the Super Étendard was brought into action against a Greek tanker.

After several other tankers were attacked, the Iranians retaliated with strikes against tankers leaving Kuwaiti and Saudi Arabian ports. On 13 May the IRIAF hit the tanker *Umm Qasbah*, 55,400 tons, sailing from Kuwait to Bahrain, and three days later the Saudi-registered Supertanker *Yanbu Pride* was hit leaving the Saudi refining centre at Ras Tannurah. On the 24th Saudi F-15 fighters, directed by an E-3A, pursued an F-4E which had attacked the Liberian *Chemical Venture*. The Iranians are believed to have used two versions of the AGM-65 Maverick fired from the F-4 to make their attacks. In a further escalation, a number of Saudi F-15s were scrambled by AWACS on 5 June to meet an incoming IRIAF raid, and two F-4s were claimed to have been shot down. On 24 June the Greek tanker *Alexander the Great* (152,000 tons) was attacked at Kharg Island by the IAF and damaged. By the end of 1984 67 major vessels had been hit, with some loss of life, but loaded tankers are notoriously difficult targets to destroy. In addition, the Iranians were by now taking countermeasures, believed to be in the form of radar-reflective balloons towed behind barges.

The tempo quickened in 1985, the twenty-ninth attack of the year being made by Iraq on 12 February against the supertanker *Fellowship*. By the end of March a total of eleven tankers had had to be scrapped completely. During the year the IAF paid more attention to the terminal itself, forcing the Iranians to ship oil in smaller vessels to Sirri Island, where, out of range of Iraqi aircraft, it was transferred to tankers. The 'Tanker War' was to develop in 1986 when the Iranians began using helicopter-launched missiles from aircraft based on the Rostam platform in the lower Gulf. Fourteen strikes are understood to have been launched from the platform during the year.

There was great international concern at the continuing losses, and proposals were made to protect tankers sailing in the Gulf. One suggestion was for ships to be coated with a radar-absorbent paint and to tow radar reflectors on inflatable rafts (at a cost of £650,000 for a 300,000-ton vessel). Another idea for the 'low value' ships on the Kharg–Sirri shuttle was to increase the radar cross-section at the bow so that hits would be taken on non-critical parts of the ship.

On the mainland, attacks against the cities had continued through 1985 by aircraft and missiles, and from time to time strategic targets were attacked. On 9 June, for example, the IRIAF attacked Rashid airfield, while the IAF struck at

Ilam with ten aircraft. During the year the IAF claimed that it had flown 20,011 sorties, including 77 raids on Kharg Island. It was reported that the Iraqis had been supplied with a number of SS-12 medium-range missiles. The Iranians launched yet another offensive, 'Dawn 8', on 9 February 1986 across the Shatt al Arab to Al Faw, which was eventually taken despite the IAF's flying 1,200 sorties in four days. In March the Iranians moved into Iraq towards Sulamaniyah in Kurdestan. IAF ground-attack units bombed the Iranians, but most of their effort was directed towards a concentration of tanks of Dezful, which was attacked by upwards of 50 MiG-23s. The Iranians were now about to benefit from the covert US supply of arms, including large numbers of TOW and Hawk missiles and F-4 parts. The deliveries were made by the CIA using Boeing 707 freighters of Southern Air Transport; earlier deliveries via Israel had resulted in the Iranians receiving worn or redundant items. These arms supplies were intended to secure the release of American hostages, but the Israeli perfidy did little to improve relations.

The 'War of the Cities' was resumed in December 1986 with Iran hitting Baghdad with 'Scud-Bs' and Iraq retaliating with air strikes on a number of Iranian centres. Iran claimed ten Iraqi aircraft destroyed during the month. From 12 January 1987 there was a further round of attacks as the IAF flew 200 offensive sorties in the month, during which two Tu-16s were lost. There was another bout at the end of February 1988, Iraq using up to forty SS-12s on Tehran and Qom on this occasion.

The next Iranian offensive, 'Karbala 5' against Basra in January 1987, caused sufficient concern that both Jordan and Saudi Arabia offered help to Iraq in the form of F-5 fighters with crews. Iran opened a second-front attack on Sumar towards Baghdad but lacked the leadership or equipment to consolidate temporary gains. The IAF flew many sorties and admitted losing more than 45 aircraft in the fighting; one reason for the increased losses was the effectiveness of the Iranian air defences, especially in terms of SAMs. More attacks were launched against Iraqi Kurdestan in March and Basra in April, but after that there was little fighting in the year as the Iranians appeared to be preparing for an invasion in the rainy season in early 1988, a campaign which in the event never materialized. In April 1988 the Iraqis, using Kuwaiti bases, recaptured the Faw peninsula and then struck across the border in May, leaving both sides where they started in 1980.

For several years the Iranians had had no air force to speak of. Their operations were limited, and it was estimated at the end of 1986 that the IRIAF could only muster about 60 aircraft against about 500 flown by the IAF. A small number of F-6s were delivered by China, but these were used

TABLE OF UNITS: THE GULF WAR, 1980–1988

Unit	Aircraft	Base	Role	Nos.
IAF, 1980 (probable dispositions)				
(5 sqns.)	MiG-21MF/PFM	H2, Baghdad, Nasiriyah, Habbaniyah, Basra	Air defence, ground attack	90
(2 sqns.)	Mirage F.1EQ	Kirkuk	Air defence	36
(2 sqns.)	MiG-17	Kirkuk, Nasiriyah	} Ground attack	30
(3 sqns.)	Su-7	H2, Habbaniyah		40
(2 sqns.)	Su-20/22	Kirkuk, Mosul		30
(4 sqns.)	MiG-23, MiG-27	H2, Nasiriyah		80
(1 sqn.)	Jet Provost	Mosul	Light attack, coin	12
(1 sqn.)	Hunter FGA.9/FR.10	Habbaniyah	Ground attack, recce	15
(1 sqn.)	Il-28	Baghdad	Light bombing	8
(1 sqn.)	Tu-22	H2	Heavy bombing	10
(?)	Gazelle	Nasiriyah, Basra, Kut	Anti-tank, liaison	45
(?)	Alouette III	Baghdad, Basra etc.	Liaison, light transport, casevac	40
(?)	Mi-4, Mi-8	Basra, Habbaniyah etc.	Anti-tank, light transport	70
(?)	Super Frelon	Basra, Nasiriyah	Anti-shipping, transport	11
(?)	An-2, An-12, An-24, Il-14	Baghdad, Habbaniyah	} Transport	40
(?)	Tu-134, Il-76	Baghdad		7
IRIAF, 1980 (probable dispositions)				
(3 sqns.)	F-14A	Tehran, Shiraz, Khatami	Air defence, AEW	55
(10 sqns.)	F-4D/E	Busheir, Tehran, Shiraz, Khatami, Tabriz, Dezful, Bandar Abbas	Ground attack, air defence	150
(8 sqns.)	F-5E	Busheir, Tabriz, Chah Bahar	Ground attack	120
(1 sqn.)	RF-4E	?	Recce	8
(1 sqn.)	P-3F	Bandar Abbas	MR	5
(1 sqn.)	707-3J9C tanker	Tehran	Air refuelling	14
(2 sqns.)	C-130E/H	Tehran, Shiraz	Transport, EW	52
(1 sqn.)	F.27	Tehran, Shiraz	Transport	15
(1 sqn.)	747F	Tehran	Transport	6
(?)	AB.205, AB.206	Various	Liaison, light transport, casevac	100
(?)	AB.214C	Bandar Abbas, Dezful etc.	SAR	35
Iranian Army, 1980				
(?)	AH-1J	Isfahan, Dezful etc.	Anti-tank	160
(?)	CH-47C	Isfahan	Heavy lift	25
(?)	Bell 214A	Isfahan etc.	Liaison, light transport, casevac	230
Iranian Navy, 1980				
(?)	SH-3D	Bandar Abbas	ASW	16
(?)	AB.205, AB.206, AB.212	Kharg Island etc.	Liaison	13
(?)	RH-53D	Bandar Abbas	Minesweeping	4

In addition, all services operated small numbers of various liaison and light transport aircraft.

Unit	Aircraft	Base	Role	Nos.
IAF, 1985 (probable dispositions)				
(2 sqns.)	F-6 (MiG-19)	H2, Nasiriyah	Air defence	24
(5 sqns.)	MiG-21MF/PFM, F-7	H2, Baghdad, Nasiriyah, Habbaniyah, Rashid	Air defence, ground attack	90
(5 sqns.)	Mirage F.1EQ	Qarrayah, Nasiriyah, Kirkuk	Air defence	85
(1 sqn.)	MiG-25	Habbaniyah	} Strike	10
(1 sqn.)	Super Étendard	? Nasiriyah		5
(2 sqns.)	MiG-17	Kirkuk, Nasiriyah	} Ground attack	24
(3 sqns.)	Su-7	H2, Habbaniyah, Rashid		30
(2 sqns.)	Su-20/22	Kirkuk, Mosul		25
(4 sqns.)	MiG-23, MiG-27	H2, Nasiriyah, Qarrayah		65
(1 sqn.)	Jet Provost	Mosul	Light attack, coin	10
(1 sqn.)	Hunter FGA.9/FR.10	Habbaniyah	Ground attack, recce	12
(2 sqns.)	L-39ZO	Kirkuk, Mosul	Light attack	35
(1 sqn.)	Il-28	H2	Light bombing	8
(1 sqn.)	Tu-22	H2	Heavy bombing	7
(?)	Gazelle	Nasiriyah, Basra, Kut	Anti-tank, liaison	38
(?)	Alouette III	Baghdad, Basra etc.	Liaison, light transport, casevac	35
(?)	Mi-4, Mi-8	Basra, Habbaniyah etc.	Anti-tank, light transport	60
(?)	Bell 214B	Basra, various	Light transport	20
(?)	Super Frelon	Basra, Nasiriyah	Anti-shipping, transport	8
(?)	An-2, An-12, An-24, Il-14	Baghdad, Habbaniyah	} Transport	40
(?)	Tu-134, Il-76	Baghdad		7
IRIAF, 1985 (probable dispositions)				
(3 sqns.)	F-14A	Meherabad, Shiraz, Khatami, Busheir	Air defence, AEW	9
(1 sqn.)	F-6 (MiG-19)	Meherabad	Air defence	20
(7 sqns.)	F-4D/E	Khatami, Meherabad, Tabriz, Bandar Abbas, Shiraz, Hamadan, Dezful, Busheir	Ground attack, air defence	50
(5 sqns.)	F-5E	Busheir, Tabriz, Chah Bahar, Bandar Abbas, Hamadan, Dezful	Ground attack	50
(1 sqn.)	RF-4E	?	Recce	4
(1 sqn.)	P-3F	Bandar Abbas	MR	2
(1 sqn.)	707-3J9C tanker	Meherabad	Air refuelling	14
(2 sqns.)	C-130E/H	Meherabad, Shiraz, Tabriz	Transport, EW	35
(1 sqn.)	F.27	Meherabad, Shiraz	} Transport	9
(1 sqn.)	747F	Meherabad		3
(?)	AB.205, AB.206	Various	Liaison, light transport, casevac	60
(?)	AB.214C	Bandar Abbas, Dezful etc.	SAR	22

TABLE OF UNITS: THE GULF WAR, 1980–1988 (continued)

Unit	Aircraft	Base	Role	Nos.
Iranian Army, 1985				
(?)	AH-1J	Isfahan. Dezful etc.	Anti-tank	80
(?)	CH-47C	Isfahan	Heavy lift	12
(?)	Bell 214A	Isfahan. Kermanshah. Lali	Liaison. light transport. casevac	100
Iranian Navy, 1985				
(?)	SH-3D	Bandar Abbas	ASW	5
(?)	AB.205. AB.206. AB.212	Kharg Island etc.	Liaison	9
(?)	RH-53D	Bandar Abbas	Minesweeping	2

In addition. all services operated small numbers of various liaison and light transport aircraft. The term 'squadron' is used loosely: most could only muster 3–5 aircraft.

USN units, June 1987 on

CVW-14 (NK), Constellation, June–October 1987

VF-21	F-14A	VAQ-139	EA-6B
VF-154	F-14A	VAW-113	E-2C
VFA-25	F/A-18A	VS-37	S-3A
VFA-113	F/A-18A	HS-8	SH-3H
VA-196	A-6E. KA-6D		

CVW-2 (NE), Ranger, September–December 1987

VF-1	F-14A	VAQ-131	EA-6B
VF-2	F-14A	VAW-116	E-2C
VMA(AW)-121	A-6E	VS-38	S-3A
VA-145	A-6E. KA-6D	HS-14	SH-3H

CVW-5 (NF), Midway, December 1987–March 1988

VFA-195	F/A-18A	VAQ-136	EA-6B
VFA-151	F/A-18A	VAW-115	E-2C
VFA-192	F/A-18A	HS-12	SH-3F
VA-115	A-6E. KA-6D		

CVW-11 (NH), Enterprise, March–July 1988

VF-114	F-14A	VA-95	A-6E
VF-213	F-14A	VAW-117	E-2C
VA-22	A-7E	VS-21	S-3A
VA-94	A-7E	HS-6	SH-3H

Other US shipborne units

Guadalcanal embarked HMM-263 (code EG). with four AH-1Ts. four UH-1Ns. two CH-53Ds and two CH-46Cs. and HM-14 (code BJ). with RH-53Ds. from August to November 1987. *Okinawa* embarked helicopter units believed transferred from *Guadalcanal* from November 1987 to February 1988. Oilfield support barges. from July 1988. were equipped with AH-58Ds (unit unknown). USN frigates and destroyers embarked SH-2Fs or SH-60Bs.

Land-based USN units

VR-24 (JM)	C-2A	Bahrain
VP-46 (RC)	P-3C	Dhahran
HC-2 (NU)	SH-3F. SH-3G	? Bahrain
HM-12 (DH)	CH-53E	? Bahrain

US Army

?	MH-6A	? Bahrain

RN ships (Armilla Patrol), March 1987 on

Type 42	Type 22	Type 21	Leander	RFA	From
Nottingham			Andromeda	Orangeleaf	00/03/87
Cardiff	Broadsword	Active		Orangeleaf	00/06/87
Edinburgh	Brazen		Andromeda	Brambleleaf	00/08/87
York	Battleaxe		Scylla	Tidespring	00/01/88
Exeter				Tidespring	00/03/88
Manchester	Beaver			Tidespring	00/06/88

RN destroyers and frigates embarked Lynx HAS.2s of 815 NAS while the larger RFAs embarked Sea King HAS.5s of 824 NAS.

---

by the IRGC at Zahedan and were never in combat. Poor maintenance is believed to have resulted in many losses, including that of a C-130 at Zahedan on 2 November 1986.

The IAF acquired 24 MiG-29s from July 1987 and had also been flying some Su-25s for several years. The type most used, however, was the Mirage F.1EQ, 113 of which were delivered. Several of the Mirages were lost in the fighting early in 1987 and three more were lost in combat with F-4s over the northern Gulf of 9 February 1988. It appears that to the end of the war the IAF did not make full use of its aircraft in close support, preferring to spread their use among attacks on centres of population and on Kurdish villages, and in the 'Tanker War'.

The IAF made its first attack on Sirri Island terminal on 12 August 1986, using several Mirage F.1s refuelled by An-12s converted to the tanker role. The strike was in retaliation for an Iranian attack on the Al-Dowra refinery outside Baghdad and it forced the Iranians to move their terminal farther west to Larak. Attacks on shipping continued through 1986, and as a result

some merchantmen were armed with anti-aircraft guns. Larak was hit by IAF Mirages in November 1986, and shortly after this it was claimed that a unit of the IAF flying the long-range Gulf strikes was manned by mercenaries, the Iraqi pilots lacking the experience to fly air-refuelled sorties. It is quite possible that the sorties were not air-refuelled; on several occasions Iraqi Mirages were noted at Dhahran in Saudi Arabia. In March 1987 there were first reports of the basing of Chinese HY-2 'Silkworm' missiles near Bandar Abbas. As attacks on shipping and the oil terminals had increased, the US committed more warships to the area, and in March Britain added a Type 42 destroyer to the Armilla Patrol; the Soviet Union built up its naval forces in the Gulf after a Soviet freighter was attacked by Iran in May. The IRGC was now also involved in the 'Tanker War', using speedboats to place mines and rake tankers with MG and RPG fire. On 16 May a mine placed by the IRGC off Kuwait claimed its first victim.

The 'Tanker War' escalated further on 17 May when the USS *Stark* (FFG-31) was hit and

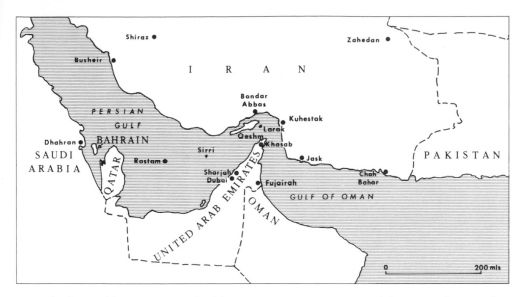

seriously damaged by two Exocets fired by IAF Mirages. The Iraqis apologized for the attack, claiming it had been aimed at a tanker; 37 crew were killed and damage was estimated at $142 million. By July the USS *Constellation* was on station in the Arabian Sea, having replaced *Kitty Hawk*. Together with P-3C Orions based at Dhahran, its aircraft were keeping a close eye on the 'Silkworm' sites which were now established at Kuhestak, Al Faw and Qeshm: there was real concern that the concentration of the missiles on the Strait of Hormuz could only mean that the Iranians intended to use them against shipping in the area. On 20 July the UN called for a ceasefire, but this was ignored by Iran. The Kuwaitis re-flagged a number of their tankers under US or Soviet registration and now sought American protection for ships moving to and from Kuwaiti ports. The first convoy under US protection left Fujairah on the Gulf of Oman on 22 July for Mina al Ahmadi in Operation 'Earnest Will'. On the 23rd, the convoy was approached by four IRIAF F-4s, which were warned off, but on the 25th, in

Kuwaiti waters, one of the supertankers, *Bridgeton*, struck a mine.

The United States now attempted to secure a base in Kuwait for RH-53D mine-clearing helicopters, but without success. The USS *Guadalcanal*, a helicopter landing ship, was therefore diverted to the Gulf, as was the battleship *Missouri*. By the end of July, 279 ships had been attacked in the Gulf in the war, and the Americans turned to Britain for support with mine detection and clearance, an area given a low priority in the US Navy. Both Britain and France placed more warships in the region. The IRIAF transferred most of its dwindling stock of F-4s and F-14s from Nowshahr to Bandar Abbas and again relocated some of the 'Silkworms'.

In the first of several helicopter accidents, the USN lost an SH-3G of HC-2 while it was trying to land on the command ship USS *La Salle* on 30 July. During August the *Guadalcanal* arrived in the Gulf, embarking a mixed group of helicopters as HMM-263 and RH-53Ds of HM-14, one of whose helicopters was lost on 9 September. The

As the threat to shipping in the Persian Gulf increased, so the nations with a commercial interest kept a watch on events. The Indian Government, which had been among the first to arm its merchant vessels, committed the Indian Navy to maritime reconnaissance flights by its newly acquired Tu-142M 'Bear-Fs'. This aircraft, one of five belonging to 312 INAS at Goa, was 'intercepted' by French Navy Crusaders in spring 1988. (French Navy)

RH-53Ds had been flown from Norfolk, Virginia, to Diego Garcia in C-5As before being assembled and embarked. The British agreed to send four *Hunt* Class mine-countermeasures ships to the Gulf, where they arrived in September, and the Italians also decided to escort their merchantmen in the Gulf. On 8 August a US Navy F-14A fired two AIM-7 AAMs at Iranian aircraft closing on a P-3C but no hits were recorded. The IAF resumed its air strikes on ships and terminals, and through the month the 'Tanker War' escalated. USAF reconnaissance aircraft of 9 SRW, both U-2Rs and SR-71s, made several overflights of the region late in the month.

The Iranian IRGC was caught red-handed laying mines of North Korean origin on 21 September. Helicopters, believed to be MH-6As of the US Army and based on the frigate *Jarrett*, spotted a small vessel, the *Iran Ajr*, dropping mines and attacked it. While towing the disabled boat, the frigate fired on Iranian hovercraft. On 5 October the world's largest tanker, *Seawise Giant*, 564,739 tons, which had been chartered by Iran as a shuttle tanker, was hit by the IAF at Larak. Three days later USN AH-1Ts sank three patrol boats which had fired a Stinger SAM at an investigating MH-6A. On the 19th the USN shelled two Iranian oil platforms in retaliation for a 'Silkworm' attack on a US-registered tanker. The air strikes by the IAF and missile attacks by the IRGC continued, and on 22 December Larak was again struck by IAF Mirages, two supertankers taking hits. In 1987, 178 ships had been hit, twice the number for 1986.

Late in 1987 the US vessels *Ranger*, *Guadalcanal* and *Missouri* were replaced by *Midway*, *Okinawa* and *Iowa* respectively, but by February it was felt safe to withdraw the last two ships, leaving *Midway*, which was in turn replaced by *Enterprise* in March. On 7 February the IRIAF made its first air attack on shipping since it used AS-12-equipped AB.212s in August 1985: two

F-4s attacked a ship with missiles in retaliation for an IAF strike on Kharg Island. The USMC lost an AH-1T of HMM-263 on 15 April when it was shot down off Sharjah by the IRGC. Three days later the frigate USS *Samuel B. Roberts* was damaged when it hit a mine.

Tension in the Gulf remained high and resulted in a major tragedy when on 3 July 1988 Iran Airbus A300 EP-IBU was shot down in error by the cruiser USS *Vincennes*. The aircraft had left Bandar Abbas for Dubai and was allegedly taken to be an F-14. The cruiser's powerful radars and computerized weapons systems tracked and interrogated the aircraft, which was flying at about 12,000ft, and when it did not respond launched two Standard SAMs. All 290 people on board were killed.

By now the US was operating two oil support barges manned by SEALs and equipped with AH-58D helicopters in an attempt to survey and deal with IRGC units intent on reprisals, but the war was drawing to a close: without notice, on 19 July, the Iranians accepted UN Resolution 598 calling for a ceasefire. The IAF continued to fly reconnaissance sorties for several weeks, and on the last day of the war it claimed two Iranian

In the 'War of the Cities', both Iran and Iraq made indiscriminate attacks on towns and cities with rockets and air strikes. The Iranians relied on the F-4 for its air strikes. This Iranian F-4E was photographed early in the war, releasing its bombs on an Iraqi pontoon bridge on the Karun river north of Abadan.

A two-seat Mirage F.1BQ, 177, in dark brown/tan camouflage. The Iraqis operated around 80 Mirage F.1s in five squadrons, primarily in the air defence role. They also operated the Mirage's stable-mate, the Super Étendard, on lease from the French: five were flown on anti-shipping strikes in the Gulf. (Dassault via B. Wheeler)

F-14As shot down in the northern Gulf. At the time of writing the peace looks like holding, but the prospect of an Iraqi attack on Syria seems real.

POSTSCRIPT
On 21 December 1988 Pan American Boeing 747-121 N739PA on Flight PA103 from Heathrow to New York exploded over Lockerbie, Scotland; 258 occupants were killed. It has been suggested that an extremist Palestinian organization planted a bomb on board under contract to Iranian revolutionary elements and in revenge for the destruction of Airbus EP-IBU.

AIRCRAFT MARKINGS

IAF
Hunter FGA.9 *Dark Green/Dark Sea Grey over, medium grey under, white serial on rear fuselage: 575.*
MiG-21MF *Dark brown/tan over, pale grey under, black serial on nose: 4902.*

L-39ZO *Dark brown/tan over, pale grey under, black serial on rear fuselage: 1275.*
Mirage F.1EQ *Dark brown/tan over, pale grey under, black serial on nose: 4014.*
Tu-22 *Dark green/dark grey over, pale grey under.*
Super Étendard *Blue-grey over, white under, white serial on intake and fin: 66.*
Mi-24 *Dark brown/mid-brown over, blue grey under, black serial on boom: 2119.*
Gazelle *Dark brown/tan over, pale grey under, black serial on boom: 4237.*

IRIAF
Air Force aircraft were camouflaged dark brown/sand/brown-green over, pale grey under. Serials, if carried, were on the fin in black and were those applied before the Revolution.
F-4D *3-620/6714870.*
F-5E *00947/7300947.*
F-14A *3-866/160302.*
C-130E *5-122.*
P-3F *Brown/grey-brown/sand over, off-white under: 5-256/159347.*

6.7. Kurdestan, 1945 to date

The Kurds are a national group numbering 17 million and living in an area of 250,000 square miles in south-east Turkey, Syria, northern Iraq, north-west Iran and Russia. They have long sought independence, and autonomy was promised by the Allies in 1920 but did not materialize. Inter-tribal conflict has made unity of purpose impossible, and most of the fighting has occurred in Iraq. In 1942 the Democratic Party of Kurdestan (DPK) was formed, and at the end of the Second World War the Kurds in Iraq revolted. The Royal Iraqi Air Force (RIAF) used its Gladiators, flying from Mosul against the rebels, and by 1947 the fighting had died down. After the overthrow of the Iraqi monarchy in 1958, the Kurds began negotiating with the new government, but in 1961 Kurdish landlords around Sulaymaniyah revolted, following which the Iraqi administration launched a major offensive. From September over 500 villages between Sulaymaniyah and Zakho were bombed and 270 destroyed by Vampires, Venoms and Furies of the now republican IAF. The Kurdish rebels now adopted the name Peshmerga (literally, 'Forward to Death').

The Iraqi Government launched an offensive in June 1963 in which 167 villages were bombed; a ceasefire was agreed in February 1964, but further offensives began in June 1964 and April 1965. By now the IAF was operating three squadrons of Hunters and one of MiG-17s and up to twenty armed Jet Provost T.52s from Habbaniyah, Rashid, Mosul and Kirkuk. Despite committing large ground forces, the Government was unable to contain the Kurds and losses were high. In

January 1966 fighting broke out around Penjwin, and May saw another Government offensive in the area of Chouman, the rebel HQ. The addition of another Hunter squadron and one of MiG-19s did not prevent a rout at Mount Hardrin on 11 May, after which peace terms were agreed.

Negotiations continued over three years, but in January 1969 there was renewed fighting around Penjwin and the Kurds later claimed that in attacks on 57 villages nitric acid bombs and napalm were dropped. The IAF now operated a squadron of Tu-16 bombers in addition to MiG-17 and MiG-21 air defence fighters. Operations were stepped up in August, when no fewer than 70,000 troops, supported by T-54 and T-55 tanks and major elements of the IAF, fought 12,000 Peshmerga, again without conclusion. Peace terms were agreed in March 1970.

Fighting again broke out on the Turkish border around Zakho on 12 March 1974, and the IAF was soon in action. The IAF ground-attack and

Iraq must have been the last country to use the Gladiator operationally. Nine Mk. Is and five Mk. IIs were transferred from RAF stocks between 1940 and 1944 and used against Kurdish dissidents until around 1949. Flying from Mosul, the biplane fighters were adequate to the task until maintenance became a problem. Seen at Habbaniyah in 1941 is K7957 of 94 Sqn. RAF, whose aircraft were distributed around the Middle East when the unit converted to the Hurricane. (RAF Museum) bomber inventory now included one squadron each of Tu-22s (Soviet crewed), Tu-16s and Il-28s, plus three each of Hunters, MiG-17s and Su-7s and one of Jet Provost T.52s; an increasing number of helicopters were also taken into service. This force was brought to bear on the Kurds in August when the Government launched its largest offensive since 1961, in the Ranya area.

After 130,000 Iraqi Kurds fled to Iran, the Peshmerga was given material support from Iran in the form of troops, 130mm guns and Hawk missiles, and in six months the rebels claimed the destruction of eighteen Iraqi aircraft, including two Tu-16s. The Iranians had their own reasons for helping the Kurds: they wished to conclude a border agreement with Iraq. Once agreement was reached early in 1975, Iran immediately withdrew support and in March the Iraqi Government began yet another offensive. The following year the Peshmerga began operations in Iran and the Imperial Iranian Air Force (IIAF) used F-4 Phantoms and armed AH-1J helicopters against the rebels in Kordestan province. Fighting along the border continued unabated for three years until subsumed in the Gulf War.

Iraq persuaded the Kurds to press the fight into Iran while Syria, supporting Iran, encouraged Syrian Kurds to move into Iraq and foment against the revolutionary regime, and in November 1983 Iraq concluded another ceasefire. Talks broke down, however, and in September 1984 the Iraqis had to commit 250,000 troops with air support to contain fighting in the Qasr-i-Shirin area. At the same time the People's Mujahideen Organization (PMO) was formed in Iran with 2,000 men under arms. In a year the PMO was involved in 320 clashes with Government forces and claimed twenty combat aircraft put out of action, plus the destruction of 540 military vehicles. In Iraq the

Kurds were similarly active under the auspices of the Kurdish Patriotic Union (KPU).

The IAF attacked a Kurdish village in Iran on 9 June 1985, and through 1986 the Kurds intensified their attacks on Iraqi military installations in the north and power stations at Dukan and Dahok. Significantly, under Iranian guidance, the DPK and KPU merged in 1986. Towards the end of the year, Iraqi Kurds were also active in southern Turkey, and after a bomb attack early in 1987 the Turkish Air Force (TAF), with Iraqi agreement, launched air strikes against Kurdish bases in northern Iraq in March; the aircraft involved are believed to have been F-100C/Ds of 181 and 182 Sqns. flying from Diyarbakir. To prevent infiltration, the Turkish Army flew commando units to the border. The dissidents were by now receiving considerable support with arms from Iran, and the Iraqi response was to begin using chemical weapons, both air-dropped and artillery, against Kurdish villages either side of the border

The Fury was a most potent fighter, the last piston-engined design from Hawker and with a pedigree stretching back to the Sopwith fighters of the First World War. As the Sea Fury, the type fought with distinction in the Korean War, and it was used in operations by the air arms of Burma, Egypt, Cuba and Pakistan in addition to that of Iraq. Aircraft 312 is seen in pristine condition on delivery. (G. Jenks via C. Thomas)

with Iran. By mid-May at least twenty villages had been bombed.

A fresh campaign against the Kurds began in September when the Kirkuk oilfield and the pipeline to Turkey were threatened. Several hundred villages were razed and Kurds were moved to desert areas in the south. In their air strikes the IAF inadvertently bombed the Turkish village of Narli on the 23rd. The pattern of air raids continued into 1988, and after Iranian forces had taken Halabja in March the IAF bombed the town, allegedly with cyanide and mustard gas, killing 3,000. From May there was further fighting on the Turkish border, with more IAF incursions. As Iraqi chemical attacks on the Kurds mounted, refugees began flooding into Turkey in September. Equipped only with small arms, the rebels are unable to pursue their demands for autonomy, and, with the Gulf War apparently ended, the Iraqis may be expected to press their fight against them.

AIRCRAFT MARKINGS

Gladiator II *Dark Green/Dark Earth over, grey under.*
Fury *Sand/medium brown over, pale grey under, black serial on rear fuselage: 231 (1 Sqn.); 254 (7 Sqn.).*
Jet Provost T.52 *Pale grey overall, black serial on rear fuselage: 612.*
Vampire FB.52 *Dark Green/Dark Sea Grey*

over, medium grey under, black serial on boom: 337, 342 (5 Sqn.).
Venom FB.50 *Dark Green/Dark Sea Grey over, medium grey under, black serial on boom: 354, 360 (6 Sqn.).*
Hunter F.6 *Dark Green/Dark Sea Grey over, silver under, black serial on rear fuselage: 396 (1 Sqn.).*
Hunter FGA.59 *Dark Green/Dark Sea Grey over, silver under, white serial on rear fuselage: 571 (4 Sqn.).*

TABLE OF UNITS: THE KURDS, 1946 TO DATE

Unit	Aircraft	Base	Role	Nos.
RIAF, 1946				
1 Sqn.	Gladiator II	Mosul	Ground attack	
IAF, 1961				
4 Sqn.	Fury	Kirkuk		
5 Sqn.	Vampire FB.52	Habbaniyah		
6 Sqn.	Venom FB.50	Habbaniyah	Ground attack	
1 Sqn.	Hunter F.6	Habbaniyah		
? Sqn.	Il-28	Rashid	Light bombing	
IAF, 1974				
(1 sqn.)	Jet Provost T.52	Mosul	Coin. light attack	16
(2 sqns.)	Hunter FGA.59	Habbaniyah, Kirkuk	Ground attack	36
(3 sqns.)	MiG-17	Habbaniyah, Rashid, Mosul	Ground attack	35
(3 sqns.)	Su-7	Habbaniyah, Rashid	Ground attack	50
(1 sqn.)	Il-28	Habbaniyah	Light bombing	8
(1 sqn.)	Tu-16	Habbaniyah	Medium bombing	9
(1 sqn.)	Tu-22 (Soviet-crewed)	H3	Heavy bombing	10
(1 sqn.)	Wessex	Baghdad	Light bombing	8
(2 sqns.)	Mi-4	Various	Light transport. casevac	35
(2 sqns.)	Mi-8	Various	Assault transport	25
(2 sqns.)	Alouette III	Various	Liaison. casevac	24

Note: For later IAF status see Gulf War entry. In addition. the IAF operates about 24 PC-7 trainers in the coin role.

6.8. The Iranian Hostage Rescue Attempt, 1980

On 4 November 1979 militant Islamic students invaded the US embassy in Tehran in retaliation for the United States' position in harbouring the exiled Shah, and 66 occupants were taken hostage. While diplomatic moves began, military options for the rescue of the hostages were considered in great secrecy. Planning was helped when, later in November, thirteen hostages were released, providing valuable intelligence. The eventual recovery plan, code-named 'Ricebowl', called for the placing of special forces near Tehran by helicopter, after which they would storm the embassy building, to be evacuated by air. The full details of the plan have undoubtedly not been published: the official version of how the plan would have worked is described, although certain aspects seem implausible.

First, an élite unit from Fort Bragg, Delta Force, would be lifted to a remote airstrip (Desert One) south-east of Tehran by three MC-130Es. Accompanying the transports would be three EC-130Hs with additional fuel bladders on board. This force would be met by eight RH-53D helicopters from the carrier USS *Nimitz* sailing in the Gulf. The helicopters would refuel from the EC-130H, then transport the special force to a

hideout at Garmsar (Desert Two) nearer Tehran. The troops would move into the capital in trucks apparently to be secured by local agents. They would storm the embassy and foreign affairs building (where a small number of hostages were kept separately) and recover to a nearby football stadium. From here the hostages and rescuers would be lifted by helicopter to the disused airbase at Manzariyeh (Desert Three) south-west of Tehran, which would have been taken by a Ranger unit flown in aboard two C-141As. The hostages, Delta Force and the Rangers were then to be evacuated in the transports, perhaps to Dhahran, where a waiting C-9A would fly any casualties out to Germany. Two AC-130E gunships would be available to fly over the embassy building and Mehrabad air base to suppress groundfire and destroy F-4E attack aircraft on the ground. After the evacuation they were to destroy the building. As far as is known, the actual operation, code-named 'Eagle Claw', progressed as follows.

Late in 1979 six RH-53Ds, drawn principally from HM-16, were flown to Diego Garcia from where they embarked on board USS *Kitty Hawk* (CV-63); in January 1980 they transferred to USS

Nimitz to join four more of the type. The RH-53D version was selected for its avionics and because the Iranian Navy operated the version. Stripped of its minesweeping gear, the aircraft could carry 30 fully equipped troops and extra fuel. Meanwhile training progressed in the Nevada Desert, with Marine Corps pilots, unfamiliar with the RH-53D version, replacing Navy pilots. Apparently all parts of the operation were rehearsed separately but, for reasons of security, never as a complete operation.

On 31 March 1980 a STOL aircraft, possibly a Caribou, landed at Desert One at Posht-e-Badam near Tabas. The strip, which had been prepared by the Americans in 1975 in connection with earthquake relief, was surveyed, and beacons, or perhaps landing lights, were left. On 11 April it was decided that diplomatic solutions were exhausted and the rescue attempt was set in motion. On the 20th Delta Force flew from Pope AFB to Frankfurt in C-141A transports. Here they were joined by the 13-man team which would handle the foreign affairs building rescue.

On the 21st the whole group flew on to Wadi Qena air base in Egypt, from where the mission would be controlled; the base was selected because of its extensive satellite communications facilities. At this time the USS *Coral Sea* replaced *Kitty Hawk* in the Gulf area. The rescue team now moved on to Masirah in Oman, from where the operation was launched. Already at the island airfield were the C-130 support aircraft – AC-130Es from 1 Special Operations Squadron (SOS), MC-130Es from 8 SOS and EC-130Hs from 7 Airborne Command and Control Squadron (ACCS). On board *Nimitz* the helicopters were painted sand overall and all markings were covered. During the 24th five RH-53Ds in the carrier's hangars were inadvertently soaked by the sprinkler system; they were immediately washed down. At dusk eight of the helicopters lifted off to begin the long flight, in pairs, to Desert One. They crossed the Iranian coast west of Chah Bahar. Meanwhile the rescue group of 132 men and equipment left Masirah in six C-130s.

The first arrival at Desert One at 1807hrs GMT* was an MC-130 with a road block team. This unit was soon in action as it stopped a loaded bus passing the airstrip. Shortly after a tanker was flagged down, but after it refused to stop it was fired on, the driver escaping in a following car. With the operation potentially blown, all the C-130s were down by 1915hrs GMT. By now the helicopters should have arrived, but the RH-53Ds ran into difficulties at an early stage. First, No. 6 suffered a blade spar malfunction. It landed in the desert and the crew transferred to No. 8. Shortly afterwards, No. 5

* Throughout this section GMT has been applied; local time was four hours behind GMT.

TABLE OF UNITS: THE IRAN HOSTAGE RESCUE ATTEMPT, 1980

Unit	Aircraft	Base	Role
USN (Mission)			
HM-16	RH-53D	*Nimitz*	Force and hostage transport around Tehran
USAF (Mission)			
8 SOS	MC-130E	} Masirah	Force placement on Desert One
1 SOS	AC-130E		Fire suppression and support over Tehran
7 ACCS	EC-130H		Heli-refuelling and communications. Desert One
? MAW	C-141A	? Dharan	Hostage and force evacuation. Manzariyeh AB
435 TAW	C-9A	Masirah	Medical support
USN (Support)			

CVW-8 (AJ). *Nimitz*: VF-41, -84 (F-14A): VA-82, -86 (A-7E). VA-35 (A-6E. KA-6D): VAW-124 (E-2C): VQ-2 (EA-3B): HS-9 (SH-3H).
CVW-14 (NK). *Coral Sea*: VMFA-323, -531 (F-4N): VA-97, -27 (A-7E): VA-196 (A-6E. KA-6D): VAW-113 (E-2B): HS-? (SH-3).

had a major instrument failure and the aircraft returned to *Nimitz*. The remaining helicopters then ran into a massive dust storm, which made flying both hazardous and extremely wearing. At 2010hrs GMT, nearly 90 minutes late, the first RH-53D, No. 3, landed at Desert One.

The remaining five were down by 2110hrs, but No. 2 had a hydraulic malfunction which could not be repaired. The minimum number of helicopters required for completion was six. Radio silence, which had hitherto been maintained at considerable cost, was broken to report the situation and the mission was aborted. As the aircraft had kept their engines running, fuel was now at a premium, and the five serviceable RH-53Ds began refuelling from the EC-130H tankers. As No. 3 lifted off the ground to make way for No. 4 in front of EC-130H 621809, the rotors hit the rear fuselage of the Hercules. Fire broke out immediately and as crew members were dragged out of the two aircraft ammunition began cooking. Nearby helicopters were evacuated as they were damaged by shrapnel and eventually all were shut down, the crews transferring to the remaining Hercules. All five lifted off safely at 2255hrs GMT, leaving eight dead behind. The Hercules then either returned to Masirah or perhaps Dharan to rendezvous with the C-9A so

Two RH-53Ds of HM-16 aboard USS *Nimitz* prior to the Iranian hostage rescue attempt; the helicopters are completely unmarked and finished in a pinkish-sand overall camouflage scheme. The loss of several of the aircraft resulted in the attempt being aborted, and full details of how it might have progressed have never been made public. (USN)

that the injured – some badly burned – could be attended to.

At the expense of seven RH-53Ds, one EC-130H, eight dead and many wounded, the operation was a costly failure. Contributory factors must have included poor intelligence, a complex but fragile plan, lack of comprehensive training and the demand for radio silence. There must have been some local collusion, and it was reported that the MC-130Es with their Fulton recovery systems were to be used to recover agents. It was also reported that a senior Iranian Air Force officer was charged with supporting the operation after the abandoned helicopters and Desert One had been bombed by the Air Force, allegedly to destroy evidence. The hostages were released in 1981.

AIRCRAFT MARKINGS

USN

RH-53D *Sand overall, all markings obliterated (although two aircraft are reported to have carried outline national markings).*
A-7 and F-4 attack aircraft on both carriers had special wing markings applied, suggesting that they were prepared to support the operation over Iran. These markings comprised 3ft red bands on upper and lower wing surfaces outboard of the wing-fold. Either side of the main bands were narrower bands of white, in turn outlined in black.
A-7E *Gull Gray over, white under, codes in black: 156872/300NK (VA-97); 156838/414NK (VA-27). Aircraft on Nimitz coded AJ in the 300 series (VA-82) and 400 series (VA-86).*
F-4N *Gull Gray over, white under, codes in*

black: 150480/100NK (VMFA-323); 153023/206NK (VMFA-531).

USAF

AC-130E *Medium blue-grey (Gunship Gray) overall: serials not known.*
EC-130H *Shadow green/medium green/dark grey over, pale grey under: 621818 (7 ACCS).*
MC-130E *Dark green/medium green overall: 640572 (8 SOS).*

6.9. Israel and Iraq, 1981

The volatile nature of international relations in the Middle East is such that the prospect of any power having access to nuclear weapons is unthinkable. It is, however, widely believed that the Israelis have a nuclear capability, derived from their facility at Dimona in the Negev. From the Israeli viewpoint, the possession of such weapons by a major protaganist could not be tolerated. They had known that from 1976 the Iraqi Government had invested heavily in a nuclear 'research' facility that made no economic sense in a country where oil is a cheap source of energy: with French and Italian technology, the Osirak plant was being constructed at Taimatha, twelve miles south-east of Baghdad. The production of enriched uranium and the separation of weapons-grade plutonium was believed to be planned from September 1981. The Israeli secret service is suspected of having been behind the sabotage of key components at Toulon in April

1979 and the murder of a contracted Egyptian physicist in Paris in June 1980.

On 30 September 1980 two anonymous F-4 Phantoms had attacked the plant without causing damage; it is believed that the aircraft were Iranian. With start-up only months away, after which a raid would be unthinkable because of the release of radioactive fallout, the Israelis prepared for an air attack. On Sunday 6 June 1981 eight F-16As and six F-15As took off from Etzion air base. The F-16As were tasked with the attack, and each is believed to have carried two 1,000kg bombs and presumably drop tanks for the long flight; the F-15s would have carried tanks and a full load of defensive missiles.

The route followed is understood to have been across the waist of Jordan and north-west Saudi Arabia, then across Iraq to the target, all flying being conducted at low level and avoiding a USAF E-3A AWACS aircraft known to be patrolling the Gulf area. The aircraft bombed the target after an 80-minute flight at 1837hrs local time, just before dusk and with the sun behind. Local defences were taken by surprise, although there was some anti-aircraft gunfire. All sixteen bombs are reported to have hit the target, although one failed to detonate.The aircraft then returned by the most direct route and without being intercepted.

The damage caused, although its full extent was not revealed, was considerable and may have enabled the French Government to re-think its position in any renegotiated contract. The precision of the attack was remarkable and must have been highly disciplined and extremely well rehearsed; some reports suggest that a mock-up of the target was built in the Negev. The outcome indicates the use of precision-guided or 'smart' bombs, but with the speed of the one-pass attack, target designation would have been a problem unless the marker was ground-based. No information has been released about the units involved or of any particular markings or camouflage worn by the aircraft.

6.10. Miscellaneous conflicts and incidents

1. During the Second World War Iran was occupied by Britain and the Soviet Union, both to keep Germany out and to provide a supply line to Russia. After the war the Russians refused to evacuate the north-western part of the country, actively supporting anti-Government elements. It is understood that the Soviets moved several air units to Tabriz, while the Imperial Iranian Air Force (IIAF) flew Hurricane armed reconnaissance sorties from Mehrabad. The issue was resolved diplomatically, and Russia finally withdrew in May 1946.

2. In May 1948 a USAF B-29, based in Germany, exploded over Saudi Arabia.

3. In June 1951 Iran nationalized her oil industry. Following unrest some 900 civilians were evacuated from Abadan by BOAC between the 7th and 27th of the month.

4. In August 1969 border fighting broke out between the Yemen Arab Republic and Saudi Arabia. RSAF Lightnings flew offensive sorties into the Yemen, and in January 1970 forced down an Iraqi Air Force (IAF) An-12. In February a Lightning was lost over the Yemen.

5. From 1970 Saudi Arabia gave support and bases to exiles from the People's Democratic Republic of the Yemen (PDRY); in addition, a number of refugees fled to the Yemen Arab Republic (YAR) in the north. Inevitably fighting broke out on the borders around Dhala, following which PDRY forces supported by MiG-17 fighters attacked towns and villages in southern YAR, focusing on Qa'tabah and Marib. Fighting continued to 28 October, when a second ceasefire took effect. At the time the PDRY had one squadron of MiG-17s and one of Il-28s at Aden, while the YAR had no effective air force.

6. In May 1971 the Iranian Government threatened that it would fire on any British aircraft overflying its ships or islands, after what were described as 'provocative and threatening flights'.

7. During 1973 the Dubai Defence Minister was shot down by hostile tribesmen while flying a Bell 205A of the Dubai Police Air Wing (DPAW).

8. From January 1973 the V-VS began flying regular MiG-25 reconnaissance sorties over Iran.

9. The Iraqi security chief led an abortive coup on 30 June 1973. He fled with supporters in a column of armoured vehicles which was spotted by helicopter while fifteen miles away from the Iranian border. The column was strafed by IAF Hunters and stopped.

10. The Iraqi Air Force lost two fighters to Iranian Hawk SAMs on 14 and 15 December 1974. The Iraqi aircraft were engaged on armed reconnaissance, searching for an Iranian artillery battery.

Although dissident elements in Oman have been formally contained, the police and armed forces operate a range of aircraft and helicopters to maintain peace. At the first hint of trouble, troops are moved up by helicopters in the difficult terrain, typically illustrated in this photograph of an Omani Police AB.205A, A40-GB. (Author's collection)

11. With the revolution in Iran under way, two USAF C-5As of 436 MAW evacuated military dependants from Tehran in December 1978. In January 1979 RAF VC-10s of 10 Sqn. and Hercules of the Lyneham Wing evacuated British nationals.

12. Political moves to unite the two Yemens came to nothing and fighting again broke out on 25 February 1979. Saudi Arabia mobilized its forces as, with air support, PDRY troops invaded the YAR around Qa'tabah, only to withdraw on 13 March after Syrian and Iraqi mediation. By now the YAR Air Force comprised twelve MiG-17s, fourteen Il-28s and several Il-14 and C-47 transports based at Sana'a, Taiz and Hodeida. The PDRY Air Force had twelve MiG-21s, fifteen MiG-17s, six Il-28s, eleven transports and eight Mi-4/8 helicopters based at Aden, Beihan and Socotra. The USAF flew two E-3As from Okinawa to Riyadh to monitor events.

13. On 13 January 1986 there was an effective coup within the Yemeni Socialist Party (YSP). The militia and Air Force supported the embattled President, as a result of which the air bases at Aden (Khormaksar) and Al Halt were attacked both by rocket and by unidentified aircraft believed to have operated from Socotra or Ar-Rayan (Riyan). An estimated 75 per cent of the Air Force was destroyed, but the fifteen or so Mi-24 helicopter gunships are understood to have escaped damage. Their location and, therefore, affiliation is unknown, but with YAR backing the ex-President is fighting a guerrilla war from the east of the country. It was reported that at least two MiG-21 fighters operating against the President's supporters were shot down while attacking the town of Zinjibar. At the time of the coup the Air Force of the PDRY operated two squadrons of MiG-17s, one of MiG-21s, one of MiG-25s (presumably Soviet flown) and two of Su-20/22s in addition to the Mi-24s and a range of transports.

14. There has been a continuing dispute involving Qatar and Bahrain over the ownership of islands situated between the two states. On 26 April 1986 four Qatari helicopter gunships attacked Fasht el Debel coral reef and later took construction workers captive. Ironically the island was being reclaimed and prepared for the building of a radar station funded by the Gulf Co-operation Council (GCC), of which both countries are members. The workers were later released.

15. During 1987 several Syrian Air Force (SAF) aircraft were shot down over Iraq by Iraqi fighters, including a MiG-21 in July.

7: The Indian Sub-Continent

Pressure for independence from British rule occupied India for several years after the defeat of Japan, but no sooner had Hindu India and Muslim Pakistan achieved self-determination than they were at war over disputed areas of Jammu and Kashmir. Both new air forces were actively involved in the fighting, using equipment left by the British for the fledgeling Indian Air Force. There were many superb feats of flying in the Himalayas, where air operations were conducted in one of the most inhospitable areas known to man. Officers and men of both air forces had been trained together, and for both services these early operations were to stand them in good stead for the future.

Pakistan was also involved in assuming the traditionally British role of dealing with dissidents in the North-West Frontier region, thus having to divide its meagre resources between two fronts. After a tentative settlement to the Kashmir dispute, both air forces concentrated on development, the Indian Air Force with British and French equipment, the Pakistani Air Force with British and then American aircraft. In the early 1960s India also turned to the Soviet Union for aircraft.

Although the Kashmir settlement was not to Pakistan's liking, the next conflict in the region was further south in the Rann of Kutch. Early in 1965 Indian forces overran a police post and occupied territory claimed by Pakistan. Fighting broke out but, quite remarkably, personal relationships between Indian and Pakistani air commanders ensured that fighting in the air was limited.

The Pakistanis had their eyes on other opportunities, however. In August 1965 they launched attacks on Indian positions in Jammu and Kashmir and soon the two countries were locked in combat. Although the IAF was larger than the Pakistani Air Force, IAF air strikes were held off and the Indians suffered defeat in the air in the short war. Pakistani flying and discipline seems to have been better, although the Indian Gnat light-weight fighters did achieve some notable kills against more sophisticated aircraft. The result of the war was inconclusive and led to acceptance by both parties of the prewar boundaries.

After the war both countries again concentrated on rebuilding their air forces and in 1971 it was India which re-opened the war with support for East Pakistan against the Karachi government. Fighting took place on two fronts, and the PAF was soon defeated in the east; in the west there were large tank battles, this time with effective Indian close support. Having achieved its objectives, India declared a ceasefire in December, and both countries again retired to the prewar borders. In the 1971 war it was the PAF which suffered defeat. The two countries still face each other high up in the Karakoram mountains, where their dispute simmers.

Pakistan has been affected by the continuing war in Afghanistan, acting as home for hundreds of thousands of refugees and mujahideen. The war started in 1979 with a Soviet invasion, but it was clear from the early stages that the Russians would be incapable of occupying the country; rather they propped up the Government, helping to retain some degree of control in the cities. As in Vietnam, helicopters have been used in great numbers, but losses have been heavy as the rebels have acquired increasingly powerful weaponry from the USA. As the Russians now withdraw, it is difficult to see the prospect of stable government in this important buffer state, especially given the ever-changing scene in neighbouring Iran.

Far away from Afghanistan, there has been civil war in Sri Lanka, at first localized, in 1971, but more recently on a far larger scale with Tamil uprisings. The Tamils initially gained support from mainland India, but it was India that sent a peacekeeping force in 1987 when the Sri Lankan Government could not control the fighting. The Indians have suffered for their intervention, but at the time of writing seem to have the revolt under control.

7.1. Kashmir, 1947–1949

With the partition of Indian into India (Hindu) and East and West Pakistan (Muslim), a number of Princely States were given the option of transferring to either country or remaining independent. One of the largest, Jammu and Kashmir, was 80 per cent Muslim but ruled by the Hindu Maharajah, Sir Hari Singh, who prevaricated, hoping to create an independent state. After partition on 15 August 1947, the Pakistanis attempted to persuade Singh to accede to Pakistan, and after his refusal began to plan to force the issue. Muslim Azad (Free) Kashmiris were armed to carry out an insurrection, and Pathans from the North-West Frontier province also organized to effect a tribal invasion. After a rebellion in Poonch in September was put down, the Pathans invaded on 24 October, soon reaching a position near Srinagar.

The Indian Government was quickly alerted but was powerless to intervene. Late in the day the Maharajah asked for help to defeat the invasion, but it was first necessary to confirm accession to India, a process completed on the 26th. The following day three Dakotas of 12 Sqn. Royal Indian Air Force (RIAF) flew the first troops into Srinagar, 1 Bn. The Sikh Regt. Because of the distances involved, land communications were impossible, and the sixteen aircraft of 12 Sqn. were quickly supplemented by nearly one hundred commercial airliners, mainly Dakotas. For three weeks the transports maintained an air bridge between Delhi (Palam) and Srinagar, many supplies having to be brought up from Jubbulpore in the south. On the first day 22 RIAF and six civilian sorties were flown into Srinagar, each taking in fifteen fully equipped troops. The invaders had spent time around Baramulla, looting and killing, and would not respond to Pakistani urging to advance on Srinagar.

The delay gave the Indians time to bring in the reinforcements necessary for the town's defence. The Indians then advanced on Baramulla, with fighter cover from aircraft based at Ambala, but were forced to withdraw as the tribesmen advanced to surround Srinagar. The fighters were unable to spend more than a few minutes over their targets, flying as they were from bases in India. On the 30th, therefore, the RIAF flew in to the airfield at Srinagar two Spitfire F.XIIIs of the Advanced Flying School, shortly afterwards to be replaced by aircraft of 7 Sqn., which was in the process of converting to the Tempest. The Spitfires soon began attacking convoys on the Uri–Baramulla road to some effect, while Harvards flew reconnaissance sorties. The Tempests of 10 Sqn. were also moved to Ambala, from where they began attacking troop concentrations on the 29th.

By 31 October, 1,527 troops had been flown into the Kashmir Valley, and they prepared for a counterattack while Tempests maintained continuous strafing runs on the tribesmen. On 3 November a large force attacked Indian troops defending the airfield and were only driven off after repeated close-support sorties flown by the locally based Spitfires. The fighters maintained their close support for several days while further supplies and reinforcements arrived by air. On the 5th, Tempests of 7 Sqn. were detached to Srinagar. Also on the way was an armoured car unit and other ground forces, which arrived under air cover on the 6th having travelled over

the tortuous 9,000ft Banihal Pass. The following day Indian forces broke out towards Baramulla, which fell on the 8th. After consolidating their positions, and after more strikes flown by Tempests of 10 Sqn., now moved up to Amritsar, the Indians captured Uri on the border on the 13th. The first stage of the Kashmir War was over.

Pakistan was not overtly involved in the war at this stage, and its aircraft took no part in flying close-support sorties, leaving its ground forces exposed to constant Indian attack. The Muslims had, however, been able to make considerable gains in Jammu from Bhimbar to Poonch from early October, but the Indians first concentrated on the relief of Srinagar. With that sector safe, attention now turned to Jammu, where in several centres State troops were surrounded. Supplies were dropped to the beleaguered garrisons while reconnaissance sorties were flown to estimate enemy strength and disposition. On 3 November positions around Kotli were struck by Spitfires, and on the 5th Tempests from Amritsar also flew offensive sorties in the area, attacking with 250lb bombs, rockets and cannon fire. The garrisons at Mirpur and Kotli were supplied by airdrop, but Rawalkot and Bagh had to be evacuated. On the 12th Rajauri fell to the Muslims and the garrison at Beripatten was also captured.

The 50,000 or so Azad Kashmiris were backed

After the partition of India, there was immediate fighting over the disputed territories of Jammu and Kashmir. The Royal Indian Air Force's assets had been divided between India and Pakistan, so that both had similar equipment and organization, albeit the Royal Pakistan Air Force was by far the smaller. Five Indian units flew the Tempest II, large numbers of which were transferred from RAF stocks in the theatre. HA626 (ex MW391) is seen here in typical silver finish. (Via C. Thomas)

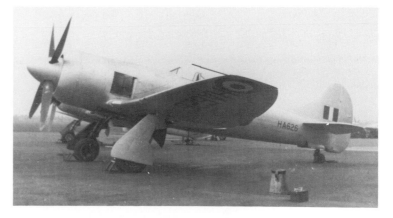

Pakistani Tempests were finished in Dark Earth and Middle Stone over. While both India and Pakistan were fighting over Kashmir, the RPAF also supported ground forces in the North-West Frontier region, where dissidents were causing trouble. No. 5 Sqn. moved to Peshawar in December 1947, from where it flew 47 offensive sorties in the month. (Via C. Thomas)

by the Pakistan 7th Division, which generally remained behind the border but provided artillery support and stiffening. With Srinagar held, the Indians moved a column north from Jammu under air escort on the 16th. It successively relieved towns held or surrounded by the enemy, until by the 27th only Bhimbar and Poonch remained in Muslim control. Attempts to relieve Poonch by a column from Uri failed, and the town was kept supplied with food and ammunition by the Dakotas of 12 Sqn. There was no airfield at Poonch, but because many supply drops were lost, a strip was constructed; this was first used on 8 December. Within six days, 73 sorties were flown, taking in supplies and evacuating refugees. Meanwhile the fighters flew offensive strikes, the Spitfires working in the Srinagar-Uri sector while the Tempests from Amritsar attacked targets widely over the Jammu sector.

Winter had now set in, and during a period when the fighters were grounded, Jhangar, on the border, was taken by the Muslims. Through the spring of 1948 the Indians gradually recaptured towns in Jammu after fierce fighting. On 18 March Janghar was recaptured, followed shortly by Rajauri, and the Indians then turned their attention to Tithwal, where a bridge across the

Kishanganga gave easy access to the Kashmir Valley from the Muslim headquarters at Muzaffarabad. The bridge was demolished in a strike by Tempests on 24 April despite being heavily defended by Pakistani AA artillery. Tithwal itself was captured on 23 May. Further south, Poonch was still surrounded, and plans were made to relieve the town. Supplies were regularly flown in from Jammu, including an artillery battery which forced the Muslims to retreat some distance. At its peak the air supply effort resulted in 35 sorties a day being flown into the small airstrip. When the Muslims brought up heavy artillery pieces and began shelling the airstrip, two 25pdr guns were flown in at night, while Dakotas converted for bombing dropped 250lb bombs on enemy positions. Poonch was not relieved until the last week of November 1948.

Much further to the north, Pakistan had been developing its bases in the Gilgit Agency in the Himalayan foothills. Outposts at Skardu, Astor, Chilas and Gilgit were kept supplied by air, Dakotas of 6 Sqn. flying up the Indus from Chaklala. The Valley flights followed the course of the Indus between towering mountains twice as high as the Dakota's ceiling, using branch valleys to the drop point. Eventually airfields

TABLE OF UNITS: KASHMIR, 1947–1949

Unit	Aircraft	Base	Role	Dates
RIAF				
2 Sqn.	Spitfire FR.XIV, XVII	Cawnpore	Air defence, ground attack	
3 Sqn.	Tempest II	Kolar	Ground attack, air defence	
4 Sqn.	Tempest II	Cawnpore	Ground attack, air defence	
7 Sqn.	Spitfire FR.XIV, Tempest II	Poona, Srinagar	Air defence, ground attack	15/08/47 to post-1949
8 Sqn.	Spitfire FR.XIV, Tempest II	Poona	Air defence, ground attack	
10 Sqn.	Tempest II	Amritsar	Ground attack, air defence	
AFS	Spitfire FR.XIV	Srinagar	Ground attack, advanced training	00/10/47 to 00/00/48
5 Sqn.	B-24J Liberator	Cawnpore, Poona	Bomber-recce	17/11/48 to post-1949
12 Sqn.	C-47	Agra, Palam	Transport	15/08/47 to post-1949
1 AOP Flt.	Auster AOP.V/VI	Adampur	Observation, liaison	15/08/47 to post-1949
101 Flt.	Spitfire PR.XIX	?	PR	00/01/48 to post-1949
RPAF				
5 Sqn.				15/08/47 to post-1949
9 Sqn.	Tempest II, Sea Fury Mk.60	Peshawar, Miranshah	Ground attack	15/08/47 to post-1949
14 Sqn.				00/04/49 to post-1949
6 Sqn.	C-47, Bristol Freighter 21	Mauripur, Chaklali	Transport	15/08/47 to post-1949
12 Sqn.	Halifax B.VI	Mauripur	Transport, bomber	00/09/49 to post-1949
1 AOP Flt.	Auster AOP.V/VI	Peshawar	Observation, liaison	15/08/47 to post-1949

were constructed at most of the Agency's towns, but after an RIAF reconnaissance sortie on 23 April those at Gilgit and Chilas were bombed, causing some damage to buildings and radio installations.

In the spring a Pakistani column moved from Gilgit towards Leh high up at the southern end of the Karakorm range and well to the east of Srinagar; Kargil and Dras were taken en route. The Indians, having spotted the column, flew a reconnaissance group up to Leh on 24 May and then constructed a rough airstrip at 11,554ft. Supplies and two companies of Gurkhas were then flown into Leh in order to repulse the attack, which came on 11 July. The Muslims were beaten back but Indian troops were unable to force a break in the Pakistani line of communications despite sending columns out from Srinagar towards Kargil and, after eventually opening the Zojila Pass in November, they retook both Dras and Kargil, linking up with a column from Leh.

The Pakistanis also occupied the area south from Gilgit to Gurais about sixty miles north of Srinagar, but in June the Indians pushed them back on Astor. At this time the RIAF also began searching out the Royal Pakistani Air Force (RPAF) Valley flights which flew without the benefit of fighter cover. On 4 November Tempests attacked and damaged a Dakota over Chilas; the Dakota crew was late taking evasive action, thinking that the familiar Tempests were friendly. The RPAF now improved radio links with the Agency towns to give early warning of the presence of Indian fighters, introduced the Halifax to the operation and began night flying along what was already an extrememly hazardous route. In the year the RPAF flew 437 supply sorties along the Valley, dropping just 500 tons of supplies. With a stalemate in the region, the Indians took the case to the UN, and fighting ended on 31 December with a ceasefire operative from 31 January 1949. The ceasefire line was drawn leaving the Gilgit Agency area with Pakistan. Although the line has since been recognized as the boundary between the two countries, the region was again to see fighting in 1965.

AIRCRAFT MARKINGS

RIAF

Spitfire FR.XIV *Dark Green/Dark Sea Grey over, pale grey under, white bands on wing and across fin, black serial on rear fuselage: MV304 (6 Sqn.).*
Spitfire FR.XVII *NH848 (9 Sqn.).*
Tempest II *Silver overall, black serial on rear fuselage: HA554 (3 Sqn.). Orange spinner: HA729 (7 Sqn.).*

RPAF

Halifax B.VI *Dark Earth/Middle Stone over, black under, red serial on rear fuselage: Q1277 (12 Sqn.).*
For other types see section on North-West Frontier.

7.2. The North-West Frontier, 1947

While Pakistan and India were fighting over Kashmir, tribes on the North-West frontier with Afghanistan were encouraged to revolt by the Faqir of Ipi. The newly created Royal Pakistani Air Force (RPAF) now had to assume the policing role previously managed for so many years by the RAF. In December 1947 the Tempest II fighters of 5 Sqn. were moved up to Peshawar, and they were soon in action in the Khyber Pass area, flying 47 offensive sorties in the month in support of ground troops. The Dakotas of 6 Sqn. were meanwhile busy airlifting troops based at Razmak from Miranshah to Peshawar. The aircraft are believed to have been supplemented by Dakotas from 10 and 31 Sqns. RAF, which remained at Mauripur and Chaklala after partition.

Fighting continued into 1948, and in June it was the turn of 9 Sqn. to fly its Tempests up to Peshawar. The squadron flew in support of a unit of Tochi Scouts who became involved in fierce fighting at Isha, just south of the Pass, and in the course of three days from 18 June the aircraft flew 119 sorties. From the summer the fighting diminished considerably, but continuing skirmishes obliged the RPAF to maintain a squadron of piston-engined fighters in the area. A third unit, 14 Sqn., was formed with the Tempest in 1949, and in September of that year a second transport squadron was formed at Mauripur with the Halifax B.VI, which also flew in a secondary bombing role. The fighter squadrons exchanged their Tempests for the Sea Fury FB.60 from 1950, and 9 Sqn. retained the type until 1960 because of its suitability for anti-insurgency work.

AIRCRAFT MARKINGS

Tempest II *Sand/olive green over, Sky under, red spinner, black serial on rear fuselage: A141 (9 Sqn.); A145 (14 Sqn.). Silver over, Sky under, red spinner, black serial on rear fuselage: A160 (5 Sqn.).*
Sea Fury FB.60 *Dark Earth/sand over, Sky under, red spinner, black serial on rear fuselage: L967, L974 (9 Sqn.).*
C-47 *Light olive drab over, Sky under, black serial and code on rear fuselage: H705 (6 Sqn.).*

TABLE OF UNITS: THE NORTH-WEST FRONTIER, 1947—1950

Unit	Aircraft	Base	Role	Dates
PAF				
5 Sqn.	⎫			⎧15/08/47 to post-1950
9 Sqn.	Tempest II. Sea Fury Mk.60	Peshawar, Miranshah	Ground attack	⎨15/08/47 to post-1950
14 Sqn.	⎭			⎩00/00/49 to post-1950
6 Sqn.	C-47. Bristol Freighter 21	Mauripur. Chaklala	Transport	15/08/47 to post-1950
12 Sqn.	Halifax B.VI	Mauripur	Transport, bombing	00/09/49 to post-1950
1 AOP Flt.	Auster AOP.V/VI	Peshawar	Observation. liaison	15/08/47 to post-1950

7.3. The Rann of Kutch, 1965

To the east of the Indus is a large uninhabitable area known as the Rann of Kutch; under water for much of the year, the precise border between India and Pakistan has never been settled. About 3,500 square miles north of the 24th parallel was policed by Pakistan. During February 1965 Indian troops overran the police post at Chhad Bet; the action coincided with Indian exploration in the area, during which some indications of the presence of oil may have been found. In Operation 'Arrow-Head' Indian forces built up during March, and the Pakistani response was to put the 8th Infantry Division on alert; on 6 April the division was ordered to assert the Pakistani position in the Rann of Kutch. Fighting was sporadic until 26 April, when the Pakistanis launched Operation 'Desert Hawk' against the Indian post at Biar Bet. After heavy fighting the post was captured early on the 27th, but the same day an informal ceasefire was ordered. The ceasefire took formal effect on 1 July.

The use of aircraft in the brief battle was limited. Light observation aircraft were used up to the front line by both air forces, and combat aircraft were alerted. The Pakistani Air Force (PAF) also used its H-13A helicopters for casevac duties. Both air force commanders had served together in the Royal Indian Air Force (RIAF), and it seems probable that they had informally agreed to restrict air activity in order to limit hostilities. On 24 April an armed Ouragan of 51 Sqn. Indian Air Force (IAF) from Jamnagar was brought down by PAF F-86s at Jangshashi, but the aircraft proved to be lost.

AIRCRAFT MARKINGS

For notes on aircraft markings see section on the 1965 War.

7.4. India and Pakistan, 1965

In 1957 Kashmir was integrated into the Indian Union despite protests from Pakistan, which were supported by the UN. Talks were held, aimed at finding a more equitable solution, but these broke down in May 1963, following which Pakistan considered a military solution. In May 1965, after fighting in the Rann of Kutch, Pakistan began arming and training 5,000 irregulars at Murree, their task being to infiltrate Kashmir and provoke a revolution; at the same time, Indian forces were mobilized in the Punjab. On 5 August the Muslim irregulars, known as Gibraltar Force, crossed the border and soon held Mandi near Punch. Two days later, the Indians committed three infantry divisions and a brigade. On 15 August the Pakistanis began artillery fire across the border, giving the Indian XV Corps the excuse to cross the ceasefire line. On the 18th the Pakistanis implemented their War Readiness Plan. Awan Sharif, near Sialkot, was shelled by Indian artillery on the 23rd, and the following day the Haji Pass near Muzaffarabad was captured. As full hostilities seemed inevitable, the Pakistani Air Force (PAF) closed its training schools and sent their pilots to operational units.

The Pakistani Army launched a large attack against four Indian battalions in the Chhamb salient in Operation 'Grand Slam'. The Indians were soon overwhelmed, and the Pakistanis quickly reached the west bank of the Munawar Tawi river. The Indian Air Force (IAF) flew 28 sorties in support of the Army, but a Vampire mission mistakenly attacked Indian forces. The IAF claimed fourteen Pakistani tanks and 30 other vehicles destroyed but lost four Vampires of 45 Sqn. to PAF fighters. The PAF flew combat air patrols (CAP) of two F-86Fs with an F-104A flying top cover, and this was the pattern for the next month, the purpose being the defence of the important airfield at Sargodha.

At the start of the war the IAF comprised about 775 aircraft, of which 500 were combat types; against this force the PAF could field 140 first-line aircraft. Both air forces flew the Canberra, the PAF in the B-57 form. The IAF operated Hunters and Gnats in the air superiority role while the PAF had a smaller number of F-86F Sabres, about 25 of which were equipped to use the Sidewinder missile. Both air forces had one squadron of supersonic fighters, but whereas the Indian MiG-21 was not operational, the Pakistani F-104As equipping 9 Sqn. were fully worked up.

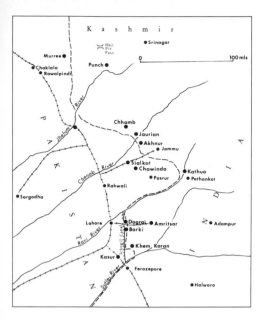

The IAF also operated a large number of Vampires, Ouragans and Mystères, but the first two types were withdrawn after the Vampire losses of the first day. The Pakistanis captured Chhamb on the 2nd, with 11 Sqn. F-86Fs armed with 2.75in rockets flying close-support sorties. The IAF apparently flew no sorties during the day but the PAF CAPs continued. The Sabres of 17 Sqn. were detached from Mauripur to Sargodha during the day; they were followed on the 3rd by 18 Sqn.

Akhnur was the next Pakistani target, but the Indians held on, bringing two more infantry battalions to the front. There were several dogfights over the battle area, and one F-86 was damaged by a Gnat. In return a Gnat was forced down by an F-104A at the small disused airfield at Pasrur, from where it was later flown to Sargodha. At the end of the day the IAF claimed three F-86Fs shot down by Hunters and one to AAA fire over Halwara. The fighting around Akhnur continued on the 4th, during which the PAF flew 34 CAP sorties. Several ground attack sorties were flown by 15 Sqn., in the course of which one aircraft was lost to a Gnat. The IAF, flying 30 sorties in the day, claimed a second F-86 destroyed: the PAF did lose an F-86 in East Pakistan when an aircraft of 14 Sqn., the only operational unit in the east, suffered a bird-strike.

On the 5th the Pakistanis captured Jaurian and the Indians claimed that the PAF had bombed Amritsar. It appears, however, that the only damage was caused by a sonic boom from an overflying F-104. The 6th saw the war escalate as the Indians crossed the border and advanced on the Ichogil Canal in Operation 'Riddle'. The defenders blew some 70 bridges on the canal and the Indians were held up. The IAF flew numerous ground-attack sorties, but both sides were ham-pered by their inability to fly true close-support missions owing to a lack of direct communications with ground units. No. 19 Sqn. PAF flew several missions, in which it claimed seven tanks and twenty vehicles. In all, the PAF flew about 80 ground-attack sorties, some of them against airfields.

As the war intensified the Pakistanis became increasingly concerned that the IAF would neutralize its air force on the ground. Detachments of Sidewinder-armed F-86Fs were sent from Sargodha to Mauripur and Peshawar for local air defence, and attacks were planned against the nearer Indian airfields. No. 19 Sqn. attacked Pathankot, claiming seven MiG-21s, five Mystères and one C-119G, although the MiG claim was confused and the IAF probably lost only one of the type. No. 11 Sqn. made for Adampur, but the Sabres were intercepted by Hunters, and in the ensuing fight two Hunters were claimed destroyed and three damaged. The airfield escaped unscathed. The third airfield strike was costly for the PAF. Two out of three 5 Sqn. F-86s attacking Halwara were shot down, although the PAF claimed the destruction of four or five Indian Hunters. The PAF also struck at a control centre at Bhuj airfield, using armed T-33 trainers, but a proposed strike on the important radar at Amritsar was aborted. In addition to the losses already mentioned, an IAF Mystère was shot down by a 9 Sqn. F-104A over the canal.

The Pakistanis decided to continue their strikes against the Indian airfields at night, using B-57 bombers, and by dawn on the 7th 89 tons of bombs had been dropped in 28 sorties against Jamnagar, Adampur, Pathankot and Halwara. Little damage was done, however, and one B-57 was brought down by AAA fire at Adampur. The day started with early raids on Sargodha airfield by IAF Mystères at 0530hrs. No damage was done, and two Mystères on the first raid were shot down, one by F-104s. Shortly afterwards the position was reversed when a Mystère destroyed a defending F-104. The second Indian raid on the airfield was expensive for the IAF: of six Hunters in the strike, five were shot down in the space of a few minutes by the CO of 11 Sqn., Sqn. Ldr. M. M. Alam, and the sixth was reported to have

When India and Pakistan again went to war in 1965, the Indian Air Force was equipped with a mixture of French and British types and had the MiG-21 just entering service. Mystères were used in the ground-attack role, and the type equipped four squadrons, at least three of which were based at Pathankot. Remarkably, a Mystère IVA was responsible for bringing down a PAF F-104A. (C. Shepherdson)

crashed in India. In a third raid at 0947hrs by four Mystères, an F-86 was destroyed on the ground, and in a fourth, carried out by four Mystères, at least one of the IAF aircraft was shot down.

On the ground the Indians crossed the border into the Chawinda salient in Operation 'Nepal', in which one armoured, one infantry and one mountain division employing 300 Centurion and Sherman tanks forced a Pakistani retreat. Further to the south the Indian attacks of the previous day were repulsed and the Indians pushed back on Khem Karan. Pakistani Army units were supported by Sabres from Peshawar which were also involved in strikes on the airfields at Srinagar (where two C-47s and a UN Caribou were destroyed) and Pathankot. Although there was little fighting on the ground in the east, the 7th also saw the first air attacks in the region. At 0630hrs Sabres of 14 Sqn. struck at Kalaikunda, and a second raid was mounted at 1100hrs.

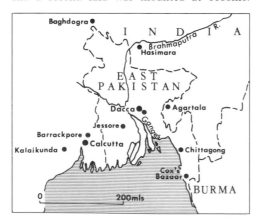

Twelve Canberras were claimed destroyed, plus seven Canberras and two Hunters damaged, but in the second strike an F-86F was shot down by a 37 Sqn. Hunter.

These claims were almost certainly exaggerated, for later in the day Dacca civil airport and Chittagong were bombed by IAF Hunters and Canberras. Little damage was done, but a defending F-86 flew into the ground. Both sides continued the airfield attacks in the evening, Mauripur, Rawalpindi and Sargodha being attacked by Canberras from Poona and Agra. One F-86 crashed while taking off from Mauripur, killing the pilot. The Pakistanis now adopted a novel but expensive tactic. Three 60 Commando paradrops were made by C-130s on Adampur, Halwara and Pathankot, but all were off target and most of the paratroopers were killed or captured. Early in the morning on the 8th there was a fiasco at Sargodha. Fearing Indian paradrops on their own airfields, the Pakistani defenders were involved in a serious firefight with Pakistani Army Scouts brought in to help defend the airfield against such an attack, believing them to be Indians. Fortunately, casualties were light.

Yet another front was opened on the day when an Indian battalion crossed the border at Gadro in Sind province. The Indians were held, and up to the 17th PAF T-33s of 2 Sqn. flew 27 sorties in close support. In the Kasur sector, Pakistani AAA brought down a Hunter, one of a number attacking tanks in the area, but also claimed one of the PAF's Sabres. During the night both air forces continued attacks against the airfields, the PAF aiming further afield to Jodphur and Ambala, although the latter was missed. On the ninth full day of the war the PAF tried again to destroy the Amritsar radar. It had been located by an RB-57F of 24 Sqn., on loan from the USAF and almost certainly partly American-crewed. Using napalm, four Sabres flew the mission, but they missed the target through early morning haze. IAF Hunters were also busy, maintaining pressure on Pakistani positions around Khem Karan.

The next day the Indians captured Barki on the canal, and further south at Asal Uttar captured or destroyed 40 tanks. At Samba, F-86Fs of 17 and 18 Sqn. attacked Indian tank concentrations, claiming nineteen vehicles destroyed, while over Khem Karan four Sabres claimed two Gnats shot down. Again the PAF hit Amritsar radar, this time with rockets, but after the first salvo the target was obscured by smoke and again it escaped. In the east, the PAF had more success when Sabres of 14 Sqn. bombed Baghdogra airield: one C-119, a Hunter, a Vampire trainer and an Mi-4 were destroyed on the ground. Amritsar radar was finally hit on the 11th and put off the air for several hours. This time four Sabres of 5 Sqn. used guns only, but at least one aircraft was brought down by Indian AAA. Earlier in the day, a PAF RB-57B was shot down by Pakistani AAA at Rahwali while practising its part in the radar strike. The following day the radar was hit by 1,000lb bombs dropped by four B-57s with F-86 and F-104 escort. Before dawn on the 11th a C-130 of 6 Sqn. had dropped eighteen 1,000lb bombs on Kathua bridge to hold up Indian movements in the area.

There were several dogfights over the battle-field on the 13th, during which at least one F-86 and one Gnat were shot down. Airfields at Srinagar and Jammu were also attacked and several transport aircraft destroyed, including a second UN Caribou. Early on the morning of the 13th, IAF Canberras attacked the airfields at Sargodha, where no damage was recorded, and Peshawar, where the B-57 fleet escaped damage by a hair's breadth: 4,000lb bombs were used, and at least one dropped close to parked aircraft but failed to detonate. Later in the day six B-57s were detached to Risalpur. The pattern of the air war continued through the next week.

On the 14th the Indians launched an armoured assault in the Chawinda sector which was repulsed by the Pakistan Army with ground attack support from the PAF. In fighting over the front the PAF lost an F-86, while they claimed a Hunter plus two Mystères lost to AAA fire. On the 15th the IAF Canberras were used for the only time in daylight in support of ground forces. Escorted by Gnats, they bombed Pakistani positions at Kasur, while PAF C-130s bombed tank and gun concentrations in the Lahore and Sialkot sectors at night. The battle of the airfields also continued, with Peshawar and the disued airield at Kohat attacked by Canberras while Sirsa and Halwara were the targets for PAF B-57 raids. In

TABLE OF UNITS: INDIA AND PAKISTAN, 1965

Unit	Aircraft	Base	Role	Nos.
IAF				
28 Sqn.	MiG-21F	Chandigarh, Pathankot	Air defence	10
7 Sqn.	}	Halwara	}	
14 Sqn.		Baghdogra		
17 Sqn.	Hunter Mk.56	Adampur	Ground attack, air defence	118
20 Sqn.		Adampur		
27 Sqn.		Halwara		
37 Sqn.	}	Kalaikunda	}	
2 Sqn.	}	Halwara, Adampur	}	
9 Sqn.	Gnat	Halwara, Srinagar	Air defence, ground attack	80
18 Sqn.		?		
23 Sqn.	}	Halwara, Srinagar	}	
1 Sqn.	}	Pathankot	}	
3 Sqn.	Mystère IVA	Pathankot	Ground attack	80
31 Sqn.		Pathankot		
32 Sqn.	}	?	}	
4 Sqn.	}	Jodphur	}	
29 Sqn.	Ouragan	Gahauti	Ground attack	56
51 Sqn.	}	Jamnagar	}	
15 Sqn.	}	Poona	}	
24 Sqn.		Poona		
45 Sqn	Vampire FB.52	Jammu	Ground attack	132
132 Sqn.		Jamnagar		
210 Sqn.		?		
220 Sqn.	}	?	}	
5 Sqn.	}	Ambala	}	
16 Sqn.	Canberra B(I).58	Kalaikunda	Light bombing	53
35 Sqn.	}	Ambala, Poona	}	
106 Sqn.	Canberra PR.57	?	PR	7
6 Sqn.	B-24J Liberator, L.1049G	Poona	MR	15
11 Sqn.	}	Palam, Srinagar	}	
43 Sqn.	C-47	?	Medium transport	55
49 Sqn.	}	?	}	
12 Sqn.	}	?	Medium transport	48
19 Sqn.	C-119G			
42 Sqn.	Il-14	Palam	Transport	24
25 Sqn.	}	Chandigarh	Medium transport	34
44 Sqn.	An-12B			
41 Sqn.	}	?	Light transport	20
59 Sqn.	Otter			
33 Sqn.	Caribou	?	STOL transport	8
109 HU	Mi-4	?	Transport	40
Indian Navy				
300 INAS	Sea Hawk FGA.6	Jamnagar, Santa Cruz	Fighter, ground attack	30
310 INAS	Alizé	Santa Cruz	MR, ASW	12
Indian Army				
—	Krishak, Auster AOP.9	Various	Observation, liaison	50
PAF				
9 Sqn.	F-104A/B	Sargodha	Air defence	12
5 Sqn.	}	Sargodha	Air defence, ground attack	}
11 Sqn.		Sargodha	Air defence, ground attack	
15 Sqn.		Sargodha, Peshawar	Ground attack, air defence	
19 Sqn.	F-86F	Peshawar	Ground attack, air defence	100
16 Sqn.		Mauripur	Air defence, ground attack	
17 Sqn.		Mauripur, Sargodha	Ground attack, air defence	
18 Sqn.		Mauripur, Sargodha	Ground attack, air defence	
14 Sqn.	}	Tezgaon (Dacca)	Air defence, ground attack	}
7 Sqn.	} B-57B	Mauripur	Light bombing	} 25
8 Sqn.		Mauripur, Sargodha	Light bombing	
24 Sqn.	RB-57B/F	Peshawar	PR, elint	5
20 Sqn.	T-33A, RT-33A	Mauripur, Sargodha	Light ground attack, PR	} 12
2 Sqn.	T-33A	Mauripur	Fighter conversion, ground attack	
6 Sqn.	C-130B	Chaklala	Transport	5
12 Sqn.	Bristol Freighter 31	Chaklala	Transport	4
4 Sqn.	H-19A, HH-43B, SA-16A	Drigh Road	SAR	14
Army				
—	OH-13A, L-19E	Various	Observation, liaison	80

Note: In addition, the PAF Academy at Risalpur flew the T-37C and T-6G.

the Peshawar raid 57 civilians in the cantonment were killed. In the east, Indian airfields at Barrackpore and Argatala were strafed by 14 Sqn.; several aircraft were claimed as destroyed at

The C-119G was the mainstay of the IAF transport force for many years. Fitted with an over-fuselage Orpheus jet engine, the type was used for resupply high up in the Himalayas. By the time of the 1965 war, the An-12B was beginning to assume the responsibilty for flights up to the highest airfields in the world. (C. Shepherdson)

Barrackpore, Agartala being used only at night by C-119 transports. The Indian radar at Rampurhat was also strafed.

The IAF is believed to have lost a Canberra in the first F-104 night interception on the 14th and another to the F-86/Sidewinder combination the next day. Ambala was bombed on the 16th, but the Indians claimed that a hospital was hit. Sirsa was again hit on the 17th, but the PAF lost two aircraft early in the morning while landing in dust storms. An F-104 crashed at Sargodha and a B-57 at Risalpur; the crew of the latter aircraft was killed. The ground fighting became more intense and both air forces were fully committed to support. For some time armed Harvards had been strafing convoys on the Pathankot–Amritsar road by moonlight, but from the 16th they were obliged to stop as the new moon did not provide adequate illumination.

In a major tank battle in the Chawinda–Jassoran Gap, 32 Wing Sabres claimed 18 tanks, 12 guns and 26 vehicles destroyed while PAF Sabres of 11 Sqn. claimed two more Hunters shot down on the way to attacking Halwara; one of the F-86Fs was shot down in the dogfight. On the 17th, F-86s knocked out a convoy on the way to the front at Sialkot. The Indians launched their final assault on Chawinda on the 18th but were beaten back. There were several dogfights over the front and a Gnat was shot down near Chawinda; meanwhile the IAF claimed a Sabre destroyed by a Gnat over Pakistan. In the south, an Indian transport was shot down by an F-86 of 16 Sqn. when it apparently strayed off course. As the position on the ground reached a stalemate, aircraft from both sides continued to attack troop and tank concentrations: Sabres attacking armour at Alhar in the Sialkot sector were intercepted by Gnats, one of which was brought down, although an F-86 crashed on landing at Sargodha, and the IAF also claimed two F-86s shot down by Gnats escorting Mystères in the Chawinda sector.

Aircraft of 19 Sqn. were committed to further attacks on Indian radars. That at Ferozepore had been moved, but the unit at Jammu was destroyed. In dogfights on the 20th four F-86s were intercepted by four Hunters and four Gnats. Two Hunters were claimed by the PAF, which lost a Sabre over Lahore. The next day the Indians launched their last offensive of the war, shelling

The PAF relied on the C-130B Hercules as its standard transport aircraft, supplemented by a handful of Bristol Freighters. Flying with 6 Sqn. at Chaklala, the Hercules were also fitted for night bombing, their load being a respectable eighteen 1,000lb bombs. (Via Air-Britain)

Lahore. PAF Sabres were called in to take out the guns and claimed fifteen medium and five heavy pieces destroyed. Early in the morning of the 21st an F-104 of 9 Sqn. on night CAP intercepted a Canberra at 33,000ft and shot it down over Fazilka: using a Sidewinder, the improvised night fighter had achieved the third successful night interception of the war.

In the south, Canberras from Poona, with a Gnat escort, attacked the Pakistani radar at Badin, destroying the FPS-6 height-finding system. Although most of the fighting had taken place in the north, the armed T-33s of 2 and 20 Sqns. flew 68 close-support sorties in daylight, destroying 62 guns and 16 railway wagons, while 16 Sqn. F-86Fs flew 160 CAP and 33 ground-attack sorties, destroying 30 tanks and 150 vehicles. The last day of the war was 22 September. During the day the PAF flew 68 close-support sorties, a number of them by B-57s, and an IAF Hunter was claimed shot down by AAA fire over Khem Karan. From the summer, however, the British and US Governments had imposed an arms embargo, and both sides were exhausted and desperately short of ammunition and arms. The Indians had lost 2,763 killed and about 375 tanks to Pakistan's 6,917 killed (mostly Muslim guerrillas) and 350 tanks. The last sortie of the war was flown by the PAF at 2302hrs, and a ceasefire came into effect at midnight.

In just over three weeks the PAF had flown 481 ground-attack and 1,188 air defence sorties; of the latter, 9 Sqn. F-104s flew 246 sorties, of which 42 were at night. The PAF fired 33 Sidewinder AAMs, claiming nine aircraft destroyed. Both India and Pakistan flew just under 200 Canberra and B-57 sorties, most at night, and each air force is believed to have lost three bombers in operations. In air combat it appears that the PAF fared better than the IAF. Reliable details are not available, but it is believed that the Pakistanis lost nineteen aircraft, seven in air combat, while the IAF lost around 50, including 22 in air combat. In January 1966 the Soviet Union hosted peace talks in Tashkent, as a result of which both sides agreed to recognize the prewar border in Kashmir.

AIRCRAFT MARKINGS

IAF

MiG-21F *Bare metal overall, black serial on fin: BC821 (28 Sqn.).*
Hunter F.56 *Dark Green/Dark Sea Grey over, silver under, black serial on rear fuselage, squadron badge on nose: BA360 (7 Sqn.), BA341 (14 Sqn.).*
Gnat *Bare metal overall, black serial on rear fuselage: IE1083 (2 Sqn.); IE113, IE1203, IE1246 (? unit).*
Mystère IVA *Bare metal overall, black serial on rear fuselage: IA1007 (1 Sqn.).*

Ouragan *Bare metal overall, black serial on rear fuselage, scorpion squadron marking on nose: IC692 (29 Sqn.); IC554 (4 Sqn.); IC698 (51 Sqn.).*
Vampire FB.52 *Bare metal overall, black serial on boom: BB445 (45 Sqn.); IB420, IB354/G (? unit).*
Canberra B(I).58 *Bare metal overall, black serial on fin and under wings: IF961 (5 Sqn.); IF919 (16 Sqn.).*
B-24J *Bare metal overall, black serial on fin, code on rear fuselage: HE924/L, HE346/T (6 Sqn.).*
C-119 *Bare metal overall, black serial on fin: IK446 (12 Sqn.).*
Caribou *Olive drab overall, white serial on fin, code on rear fuselage: BM775/G (33 Sqn.).*
Il-14 *Bare metal overall, white fuselage top decking, black serial on fin: IL860 (42 Sqn.).*

PAF

F-104A *Bare metal overall, black serial on fin and forward fuselage: 56-804, 56-879.*
F-104B *57-1309 (9 Sqn.).*
F-86F *Bare metal overall, black serial on rear fuselage, last three digits on forward fuselage: (5)45987, (5)54021 (? unit); (5)25026 (11 Sqn.); (5) 54029 (14 Sqn.); 531076 (17 Sqn.); (5)25384 (19 Sqn.).*
B-57B *Bare metal overall, black serial on fin: (5) 33948 (31 Wing). Black overall, dark red serial on fin: (5)33961 (31 Wing).*
T-33A *Bare metal overall, black serial on rear fuselage, unit code on fin top: 561746/SA, 535533/SA (2 Sqn.).*
C-130B *Bare metal overall, black serial on fin, code on nose: (6)24141/F, (6)24143/G (6 Sqn.).*
SA-16A *Light grey overall, black serial on fin: (5)17225 (4 Sqn.).*
HH-43B *Silver overall, black serial on rear boom and fin: (6)24554 (4 Sqn.).*

Pakistani Army

OH-13B *Olive drab overall, yellow serial on rear boom: 145.*
L-19A *Olive drab overall, white serial on fin: 503-04.*

Both sides in the 1965 war used versions of the Canberra as their standard light bomber. Whereas the Pakistanis used the American-supplied B-57B, the IAF flew the British B(I).58 version, which had a fighter-type cockpit canopy. Three squadrons were deployed in the war, and three aircraft were lost in action, several more being damaged in air strikes on airfields. IF900, camouflaged, is from 5 Sqn. (Via A. S. Thomas)

7.5. India and Pakistan, 1971

Apart from being Muslim, East and West Pakistan had little in common. Over time there was increased resentment in Dacca to rule from Islamabad, while most foreign earnings were derived from agriculture in the East. When elections were held in December to end military rule, the Eastern Awami League won an overall majority, but the Western-based People's Party refused to join the National Assembly. On 1 March 1971 the President decided to postpone the opening of the Assembly indefinitely; the following day, the Awami leader, Sheikh Mujibar Rehman, called a general strike, and later in the month the East declared iteself independent as Bangla Desh. India began helping to train Mukti Bahini (People's Army) irregulars, while Pakistan used the Pakistan International Airlines (PIA) fleet of Boeing 707s to ferry three divisions to Dacca via Colombo. The airlift was reportedly supported by C-130 Hercules of the Turkish and Iranian Air Forces. As civil war took a hold, millions of refugees fled to India.

It appears that India contemplated military action in May but decided to wait until its Army was trained to fight in the flat conditions of East Pakistan. Moreover, by delaying, the high Himalaya passes would be blocked off, preventing Chinese intervention. On 9 August India signed a defence pact with the Soviet Union. As the Pakistani Army began a systematic massacre of the educated classes in East Pakistan, the Mukti Bahini waged a guerrilla war and by October had temporarily taken over airstrips at Lalmonirhat and Shalutikar. On 16 October Indian Air Force Canberras penetrated West Pakistan, and on 3 November IAF interceptors were scrambled as four Pakistani Air Force (PAF) F-86s were reported heading for a western air base.

Fighting broke out when Indian forces probed the East Pakistan border at Boyra; the Pakistani Army lost thirteen Chaffee light tanks in the skirmish. The next day, as the Indian units were attacked by Sabres of 14 Sqn. PAF, Gnats of 22 Sqn. were scrambled. In the ensuing dogfight the IAF claimed three Sabres brought down for no loss, while Pakistan claimed a draw at two aircraft each. On 23 November Pakistan declared a state of emergency.

At the end of November the IAF was far larger than the PAF. Of an inventory of 735 combat aircraft, about 625 were operational, compared with the PAF inventory of around 240, of which some 210 were available. Since the 1965 war both sides had re-equipped. The Indians had acquired 175 MiG-21s and 150 Su-7BMs from Russia and had manufactured about 50 of the indigenous HF-24 fighter, plus more Gnats, of which about 160 were in service. Of the older types 100 Hunters, 60 Canberras and about 40 Mystères remained.

Pakistan, notionally cut off from Western supplies, looked to the Chinese, from whom it bought 70 F-6 (MiG-19) fighters, and France, which supplied 20 Mirage IIIEs. The residue of the F-86F Sabres was complemented by 90 Canadair Sabre Mk. 6s bought from West Germany via Iran without a US end-user certificate but probably with American connivance. The PAF had also built new airfields or extended existing ones at Mianwali, Chandar, Risalewala, Shorkot, Jacobabad and Murid.

At 1745hrs on 3 December the PAF launched a pre-emptive strike by Sabres and B-57s against Indian airfields in north-western India, perhaps hoping to emulate the Israeli strikes of 1967. The PAF failed: the strikes were spread too thinly, causing little damage, and coming as they did at dusk they gave the Indians the night to repair the runways. The airfields attacked included Agra, Ambala, Amritsar, Avantipur, Faridkot, Pathankot, Srinagar and Uttarlai; radars at Amritsar and Barnala were also attacked. The only serious damage caused was at Amritsar, where the runway was damaged and a radar destroyed; the PAF reportedly lost four aircraft. The IAF hit back at airfields at Chandar, Changa Manga, Masroor, Mianwali, Murid, Pasrur, Peshawar,

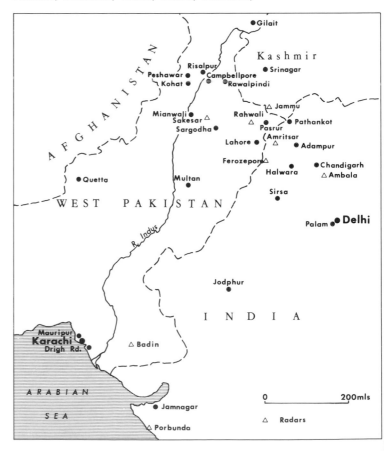

By the time of the 1971 war, India had added the Canberra B.66 to its Air Force inventory. No. 16 Sqn. was particularly active in the campaign: the unit flew 97 sorties on the eastern front, before transferring to the west on 8 December. With no effective opposition, the Canberras were able to make each strike tell. (Via A. S. Thomas)

Risalewala, Sargodha and Sialkot and Tezgaon in East Pakistan. At sea the Pakistani submarine *Ghazi*, in, reality the USS *Diablo* informally leased from the United States, was sunk off the Indian naval base at Vizakhapatnam. She had been waiting for the carrier *Vikrant* to leave port and was destroyed in a depth-charge attack by the destroyer *Rajput*. The loss was important in that the submarine was the only one with the range to operate in the Bay of Bengal.

For several days the Pakistanis had been bringing forward troops in the west prior to mounting attacks along the border, while in Bengal and Assam Indian units were prepared for the invasion of East Pakistan. As Pakistan had opened the war with counter-air strikes, so the IAF attempted to eliminate the PAF to give Indian troops freedom from air attack. In the morning of 4 December MiG-21s (30 Sqn.) escorted Hunters (14 Sqn.) and Su-7s (221 Sqn.) in raids on the sole PAF air base at Tezgaon outside Dacca; later, escorted by MiG-21s of 28 Sqn., Hunters of 17 and 37 Sqns. compounded the damage. In the raids the PAF claimed eight aircraft shot down for the loss of three Sabres, while the IAF admitted the loss of five aircraft while claiming three Sabres in combat and four on the ground. The runway was severely damaged. The Indian Navy maintained a task force in the Bay of Bengal centred on the carrier *Vikrant*, with Sea Hawks and Alizés of, respectively, 300 and 310 INAS embarked. Primarily there to effect a blockade, the naval aircraft were also used extensively to bomb targets south of the 21st parallel.

Eight Sea Hawks took off from *Vikrant* at 1100hrs armed with 5in rockets and 500lb bombs to attack the airfield at Cox's Bazaar; later in the day they flew sorties against installations at Chittagong. Throughout the war, in the east, the Navy flew 160 sorties, mainly against coastal and shipping targets. On the ground, the Indian plan was to isolate Dacca. The confluence of the rivers Madhumati, Ganga, Jamuna and Meghna made attack difficult and gave enormous advantage to the defenders. In effect East Pakistan comprised four major islands intersected by waterways, all of which had to be crossed by the attacking armies. From the west, II Corps was to strike through Jessore while in the north-west

XXXIII Corps was to attack through Bogra. In the east, IV Corps had perhaps the most difficult task in terms of river obstacles and the breadth of its front from Sylhet to Comilla. Notionally the easiest axis, from the north through Tangail, was assigned to the 95th Mountain Brigade. All the corps included armoured formations.

The Pakistani 14th Division, with four brigades, had been reinforced by a further 28 battalions but they had little artillery or armour. Their strategy was to hold defensively a number of border towns, while the Indian approach was to bypass and isolate, cutting off units as they advanced. The Indian attack was launched on 5 December with extensive close support; so successful had been the bombing of the PAF base at Tezgaon that the Sabres of 14 Sqn. managed just one sortie in the day. In the west the Pakistani Army had crossed the ceasefire line in Kashmir towards Poonch and Chhamb from the 3rd; further south, they moved on Longewala in Rajasthan on the 4th. IAF HF-24s of 10 Sqn. were used for the first time to bomb airfields, and during the day the IAF claimed nineteeen aircraft for the loss of six while the PAF counter-claimed 26 Indian aircraft for a loss of only two Sabres.

The Indian Navy attacked Pakistani vessels at Karachi using 'Styx'-equipped 'Osa-II' Class attack boats, sinking the destroyer *Khaibar*, a minesweeper and two merchant ships. The loss was partly avenged when an Indian frigate was sunk by submarine. The Indian Navy also initiated air patrols from Bombay, where light aircraft of the Juhu Flying Club were requisitioned to fly patrols along the many creeks up the coast; similarly, the PAF impressed a number of civilian aircraft for observation and liaison work, including Beavers of Plant Protection Ltd. On the 5th both sides maintained their counter-air strikes and there were numerous dogfights as attackers met CAPs. The IAF also bombed and strafed the fuel depot at Karachi, setting it on fire, and attacked T-59 and Sherman tanks which were attacking in open country in Rajasthan. They claimed 37 destroyed, and also brought down an F-104 over Amritsar. The PAF claimed 61 Indian aircraft destroyed to date, while the Indians claimed 47 for the loss of fourteen.

Whatever the Pakistani losses, they received

aid in the form of ten (some reports say sixteen) F-104As of 9 Sqn. Royal Jordanian Air Force (RJAF), which landed at Masroor on the 5th. It is not clear whether they were flown by Jordanians but some were certainly lost in action since at the end of the war only six returned to Jordan. Throughout conflict the battle of the airfields continued by day and night, both sides suffering losses in combat and to AAA fire. The United States finally decided to apply pressure on India in support of Pakistan. On the 6th a naval task force centred on the carrier *Enterprise* and the amphibious assault ship *Tripoli* sailed for the Bay of Bengal from Indo-Chinese waters; ostensibly there to evacuate US nationals from Dacca, their task was to distract and disrupt Indian Navy and Air Force operations. However, despite being subjected to attack by Sabres of 14 Sqn. from reopened Tezgaon, the Indians were making good progress.

In close support, the IAF flew about 200 sorties in the day; they also continued to bomb a range of targets. Gnats of 22 Sqn. attacked the airstrip at Barisal, which, although unable to take fighters, could have been used by transports. Kurmitola civil airport at Dacca was strafed by MiG-21s early in the morning, but at 1000hrs a local ceasefire was called in order to allow United Nations evacuation of foreign nationals. A Canadian Armed Forces (CAF) C-130 was attacked, presumably in error, and although damaged it landed safely at Bangkok. After the airfield at Jessore had been attacked by Su-7s of 221 Sqn. and the bomb dump destroyed, the city was taken by the Indians on 7 December; with no air opposition in the east IN Sea Hawks again attacked the airfields at Cox's Bazaar and Chittagong. The 7th was also the day on which the Bangla Desh Air Force was formed and began its first operations. Equipped with three Otters, the new air wing flew light transport and liaison sorties for the rest of the war.

In the Sylhet sector, Mi-4s of 110 Helicopter Unit (HU) were used for the first time to transport troops to the front when a battalion of 254 men was lifted from Kailashahr to Sylhet with Alouette gunship support. The feat was repeated the next day when 279 troops were airlifted at night from Kalaura. Airfields and shipping were attacked, a Greek freighter was sunk, and by the 9th the Indian grip on Dacca was tightening. No. 110 HU lifted 584 troops to reinforce those at Sylhet, carrying casualties on the return trip. Troops of IV Corps were now facing the Meghna river, and the small helicopter force prepared for the task of airlifting the force across the river on Narsingdi. With the defeat of the PAF in the east, a number of IAF units moved to the western battlefront around this time, including 16, 30 and 221 Sqns.

In the west, both sides had made some territorial gains. Pakistani forces had penetrated five

miles into Kashmir by the 7th, while the Indians struck into the Akhnur salient to prevent the capture of Chhamb from the rear. From the 6th the Indians had launched an attack on Shakargarh to strengthen the defences around Pathankot, and in the south they had moved on Naya Chor. In all sectors the air forces flew close-support and interdiction sorties, and Pakistan claimed that IAF bombing in Naya Chor had killed 112 civilians, although both sides made efforts to avoid civilian casualties throughout the war. During the attack on Islamabad a CAF Caribou of the UN and a USAF U-8 were destroyed. By the end of the day Pakistan claimed 52 Indian aircraft destroyed to date for the loss of 22, including a helicopter. In the Rajasthan sector an F-86 was shot down by an HF-24, while the IAF lost two Su-7s and a Hunter.

On 8 December the IAF flew numerous sorties in the Chhamb area, attacking troop concentrations and convoys, and two more Su-7s were brought down over Risalewala airfield. The next day the IAF flew concerted attack missions against targets around Karachi, during one of which a British freighter, the *Harmattan*, was bombed with the loss of seven lives. At Longewala many tanks of the Pakistani 27th Cavalry Regiment were destroyed by Hunters and HF-24s. Both air forces were losing aircraft at a steady rate.

During IAF attacks on airfields the Pakistanis noticed that a high-flying aircraft flew sorties at an altitude and on a track suggesting that it was on airborne control duty. The Pakistanis claimed that the Soviet Union had provided the IAF with support in the shape of a Tu114 AWACS aircraft, which they code-named 'Spider'. After the war the Indian explanation was that the aircraft was a MiG-21 working as a radio relay between control centres and low-flying attack aircraft. This would seem unlikely, given the limited range and equipment capacity of the MiG-21; certainly the Indian strike aircraft were able to take evasive action in advance of meeting Pakistan CAPS.

The Indian Navy suffered its first loss on 10 December when an Alizé was shot down by an RJAF F-104 off Karachi. In an effort to reduce the effectiveness of the IAF, Pakistani Mirages, F-86s and F-104s bombed Indian airfields close to the border during the day but with limited success; frequently the raiders were intercepted before reaching the target. On the 11th a Mirage was claimed by a Gnat pilot of 18 Sqn. The next day, over Jamnagar, several MiG-21s of 47 Sqn. fought attacking F-104s of 9 Sqn. and shot down one of the less manoeuvrable Pakistani fighters. On the 13th the PAF claimed two Su-7s in a dogfight over Pathankot, while IAF Hunters strafed and damaged a petrochemical plant at Khairpur.

With the war in the east drawing to a conclusion, both sides made concerted efforts to secure territorial gains in the west. On the 14th both air

TABLE OF UNITS: INDIA AND PAKISTAN, 1971

Unit	Aircraft	Base	Role	Remarks
IAF				
Jessore Sector				
30 Sqn.	MiG-21FL	Kalaikunda	Air defence, ground attack	102 sorties
22 Sqn.	Gnat	Dum Dum (Calcutta)	Escort, close support	248 sorties
221 Sqn.	Su-7BM	Kalaikunda	Ground attack, recce	
14 Sqn.	Hunter Mk.56	Kalaikunda, Jessore	Air support, light strike	225 sorties
37 Sqn.	Hunter Mk.56A	Kalaikunda	Air support, light strike	
16 Sqn.	Canberra B(I).58, B.66	Kalaikunda	Light bombing	97 sorties
112 HU	Mi-4	Dum Dum	Transport, casevac	
Sylhet-Comilla Sector				
1 Sqn.	MiG-21FL	Gahauti	Air defence, ground attack	
28 Sqn.	MiG-21FL		Air defence, ground attack	
15 Sqn.	Gnat		Escort, close support	10–15/12/71 only
24 Sqn.	Gnat		Escort, close support	
17 Sqn.	Hunter Mk.56	Agartala	Air support, light strike	
105 HU	Mi-4		Transport, casevac	
110 HU	Mi-4		Transport, casevac	
Western Front				
29 Sqn.	MiG-21FL	Uttarlai	Air defence, ground attack	
47 Sqn.	MiG-21FL	Jamnagar	Air defence, ground attack	
30 Sqn.	MiG-21FL	?, ex Kalaikunda	Air defence	From 08/12/71; 191 sorties
18 Sqn.	Gnat	Srinagar	Escort, close support	
26 Sqn.	Su-7BM	Pathankot	Ground attack	
32 Sqn.	Su-7BM	Pathankot	Ground attack	
101 Sqn.	Su-7BM	Faridkot	Ground attack, recce	
221 Sqn.	Su-7BM	Faridkot, ex Kalaikunda	Ground attack	From 12/12/71
222 Sqn.	Su-7BM	Uttarlai	Ground attack	
10 Sqn.	HF-24	Uttarlai	Ground attack	
20 Sqn.	Hunter Mk.56A	Faridkot	Air support, light strike	
27 Sqn.	Hunter Mk.56A	Uttarlai	Air support, light strike	
5 Sqn.	Canberra B(I).58, B.66	Jodhpur	Light bombing	
16 Sqn.	Canberra B(I).58, B.66	?	Light bombing	From 08/12/71
Balance				
4 Sqn.				
8 Sqn.	MiG-21FL	?	Air defence, ground attack	
45 Sqn.				
2 Sqn.				
9 Sqn.				
21 Sqn.	Gnat	?	Escort, close support	
23 Sqn.				
108 Sqn.	Su-7BM	?	Ground attack	
220 Sqn.	HF-24	?	Ground attack	
7 Sqn.	Hunter Mk.56	?	Air support, light strike	
3 Sqn.	Mystère IVA	?	Ground attack	
31 Sqn.				
35 Sqn.	Canberra B(I).58, B.66	Agra	Light bombing	
106 Sqn.	Canberra PR.57	Agra	PR	
6 Sqn.	L-1049G Constellation	Poona	MR	
11 Sqn.	HS.748	Palam	Transport	
43 Sqn.	C-47	?	Transport	
49 Sqn.				
12 Sqn.		Chandigarh		
19 Sqn.	C-119G	Chandigarh	Medium transport	
48 Sqn.		Tezpur		
42 Sqn.	Il-14	Palam	Transport	
25 Sqn.	An-12B	Chandigarh	Medium transport	
44 Sqn.				
41 Sqn.	Otter	?	Light transport	
59 Sqn.				
33 Sqn.	Caribou	Tezpur	STOL transport	
104 HU	Alouette III	?	Observation, liaison, gunship	
121 HU				
107 HU		?		
109 HU	Mi-4	Goa	Transport, casevac	
111 HU		?		

forces flew numerous close-support, interdiction and counter-air sorties. Several MiG-21s were shot down, and after taking evasive action for 15 minutes a Krishak of 660 Sqn. flying in the southern sector finally fell to the guns of an F-86. In Dacca, rather belatedly, the radio station was put off the air by MiG-21s of 28 Sqn. on 9 December, while on the 11th II Corps reached the Madhumati river, although a heliborne assault at Khulna was repulsed. In the north the Indians were held up at Mymesingh, so they gathered a large number of transport aircraft at Dum Dum (Calcutta) and launched a battalion strength paradrop on Tangail, to the south of Mymesingh, to cut off the defenders.

Dacca was now surrounded, and on the 12th, as Hunters of 14 Sqn. IAF began operating out of Jessore, RAF Hercules of the Near East Air Force (NEAF) began evacuating Britons from Dacca to Singapore. The task was completed, with 409

Unit	Aircraft	Base	Role	Remarks
Indian Navy				
300 INAS	Sea Hawk FGA.6, Mk.100/101	*Vikrant*	Ground attack	
310 INAS	Alizé	*Vikrant*, Bombay	ASW, MR, minelaying	
330 INAS	Sea King HAS.42	Bombay	ASW, MR	
Indian Army				
659 Sqn.		?		
660 Sqn.	Krishak, Auster AOP.9	Sind sector	Observation, liaison	
661 Sqn.		?		
662 Sqn.		?		
Bangla Desh Air Wing				
	Otter	Jessore	Liaison	
PAF				
14 Sqn.	F-86 Mk.6	Tezgaon	Air defence, ground attack	
5 Sqn.	Mirage IIIEP/RP/DP	Sargodha	Light strike, air defence	
9 Sqn.	F-104A/B	Mianwali	Air defence	
15 Sqn.		Sargodha		
16 Sqn.		?		
17 Sqn.	F-86 Mk.6	?	Air defence, ground attack	
18 Sqn.		Masroor		
19 Sqn.		Masroor		
11 Sqn.		Peshawar		
23 Sqn.	F-6	Rafiqui	Ground attack	
25 Sqn.		Masroor		
7 Sqn.	B-57B/C	Sargodha	Light bombing	
2 Sqn.	T-33A, RT-33A	Masroor	Combat training, recce	
6 Sqn.	C-130B/E, Hercules L-300	Masroor, Tezgaon Chaklala	Medium transport	
LARAF				
–	F-5A	Masroor	Believed training	
RJAF				
9 Sqn.	F-104A	Masroor	Air defence	From 05/12/71

evacuated, just before the runway was finally put out of commission. The RAF also lifted 925 evacuees from West Pakistan. On 14 December Indian forces entered the outskirts of Dacca while MiG-21s of 1 Sqn. bombed the Governor's house. The next day a ceasefire was announced in the east and preparations began for a transfer of power to a new Bangla Desh Government. On 16 December the commando carrier HMS *Albion*, with 848 NAS embarked, left the Bay of Bengal with her escorts, having been in the region since the end of November.

The war was to continue for a few days in the west. On 16 December Shakargah was the site of the biggest armoured battle of the conflict. Both air forces flew concerted strikes and many tanks were lost. By 2000hrs the next day, when a ceasefire was called by the Indians, aircraft losses included two F-104s shot down by a MiG-21 CAP of 29 Sqn. while attacking Uttarlai airfield. With the fighting over, both sides withdrew to the original borders and began counting the cost. In East Pakistan the PAF flew no more than about 30 sorties, while the IAF conducted 1,978, 1,178 of which were in close support of ground forces. No. 300 Sqn. IN flew 160 sorties without loss, all by day, against airfields, shipping and harbour installations. In the west the PAF flew 2,840 sorties, relatively few of them by the F-6, while the IAF flew about 4,000 sorties, of which about half were ground support, a quarter interdiction, including counter-air missions, and a quarter CAP.

India claimed 94 Pakistani aircraft, including

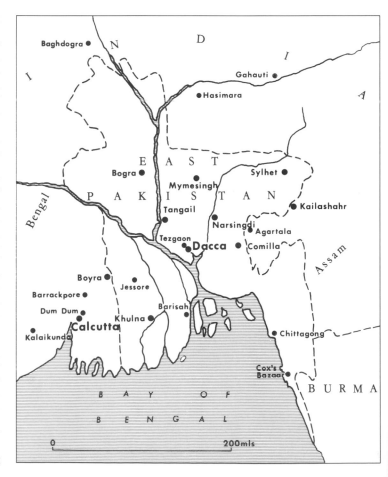

54 F-86s (eleven of which the PAF destroyed at Tezgaon to avoid capture), nine F-104s, six Mirages and five B-57s, against 54 lost; Pakistan claimed 106 Indian aircraft, including 32 Hunters, 32 Su-7s, ten Canberras, nine MiG-21s, five Mystères, five HF-24s, three Gnats, one Alizé, one Mi-4 and one Krishak, for the loss of 25 aircraft. The Hunters certainly bore the brunt of the daylight strikes, sometimes penetrating as deep as 230 miles, and the Su-7 proved to be vulnerable both to ground fire and in combat. Actual losses were probably around 65 for the IAF and 40 for the PAF.

Most aircraft lost in combat fell to guns, although the PAF claimed nine aircraft to AIM-9 missiles. At least one PAF B-57 was brought down by SA-2, while attacking Halwara airfield at night. The IAF emulated the PAF and converted a number of An-12 transports as bombers; they were used to attack troop concentrations and fuel and ammunition dumps close to the border in Kashmir. Indian forces claimed 220 Pakistani tanks while admitting the loss of 83. In human terms, Pakistan suffered the heaviest losses, with around 8,000 killed and 25,000 wounded, while India counted about 3,000 dead and 12,000 wounded.

AIRCRAFT MARKINGS

IAF

MiG-21PF Tiger-striped dark green/light grey-brown overall, light grey under flying surfaces, black serial on fin: C992 (? unit). Chocolate-brown/olive drab overall, light grey under flying surfaces: C746 (? unit). Bare metal overall, black serial on fin. C1128 (1 Sqn.); C776 (8 Sqn.); C1111 (28 Sqn.).

Gnat F.1 Bare metal overall, black serial on rear fuselage: E255, E256 (? unit).

Hunter F.56 Dark Green/Dark Sea Grey over, silver under, black serial on rear fuselage: BA341 (14 Sqn.).

Su-7BM Dark green/light brown-grey overall, light grey under flying surfaces, serial overpainted: (? unit). Cerulean blue overall, with chocolate/dark green/ochre on upper surfaces, black serial on fin: B817 (222 Sqn.).

HF-24 Bare metal overall, black serial on rear

fuselage: D-1224, D-1702 (31 Sqn.).

Canberra B(I).58 Dark Green/Dark Sea Grey over, silver under, black code on fin: IF976 (5 Sqn.). Silver overall, black serial on fin: IF919 (16 Sqn.).

Canberra B(I).66 Dark Green/Dark Sea Grey over, light grey under, black serial on fin: F1029 (5 Sqn.).

Canberra PR.57 Silver overall, black serial on fin: P1099 (106 Sqn.).

Indian Navy

Sea Hawk FGA.6 Extra Dark Sea Grey over, white under, black serial on lower fin and under wings, code on nose and fin: IN157/077W (300 INAS).

Alizé Extra Dark Sea Grey over, white under, black serial on rear fuselage and under wing, code on forward fuselage and fin: IN206/06W (310 INAS).

Sea King HAS.42 White over, glossy sea blue under, white serial and code on rear fuselage: IN502/W (330 INAS).

PAF

Mirage IIIEP Dark green/dark grey over, light blue under, black serial on rudder, last three digits on rear fuselage, pale grey fin tip: 67-101, 67-108, 67-114 (5 Sqn.).

Sabre Mk. 6 (F-86E) Dark green/dark grey over, silver-grey under, black serial on rear fuselage, last three digits in white on forward fuselage: 1739 (? unit); 1777 (17 Sqn.).

F-86F Light grey overall, black serial on rear fuselage: (5)54987 (? unit).

F-6 Silver overall, black serial on rear fuselage, last three digits on nose, squadron badge on fin: 47-1620, 47-1817, 3812 (? unit); 47-1710, 47-1819 (25 Sqn.). Dull brown/stone/blue-green over, pale blue under: 47-1423, 47-1425 (11 Sqn.).

B-57B Black overall, red serial on rear fuselage: BA-951, BA957.

RT-33A Green over, light blue under, black serial on rear fuselage, last three digits on nose: 535090 (2 Sqn.).

Pakistani Army

O-1E Light stone overall, yellow serial on fin and rudder: (5)76012.

Alouette III Olive drab overall, yellow serial on cabin: 1898.

Still equipping six squadrons in 1971, the Hunter was the most reliable and effective of the IAF ground-attack fighters. No. 14 Sqn., on the eastern front, flew 225 sorties in the close-support or light strike role, with the nimble Gnats of 22 Sqn. flying escort. Very much a pilot's aircraft, the Hunter was one of the great fighters of the postwar years. Illustrated is F.56 BA360. (Via A. S. Thomas)

7.6. Afghanistan, 1979 to date

The location and geography of Afghanistan combine to make it one of the most sensitive yet unruly areas in the world. During the nineteenth century both the Russians and British experienced setbacks in the country at the hands of fiercely independent tribesmen, and central government has always been a fiction. Although Muslim, there are many ethnic groups, and the primary allegiance is to the village or tribe; inter-tribal conflict has always been rife. The RAF undertook the first major airlift, out of Kabul into what was then India, when the monarchy and British Legation were threatened by rebels in late 1928. In 1973 the monarchy was overthrown and the successor Government turned increasingly to the Soviet Union, on its northern border, for assistance. A coup on 27 April 1978 by Army and Air Force officers brought to power a left-wing Government formed by the People's Democratic Party of Afghanistan (PDPA), headed by Nur Muhammed Taraki. During the fighting, MiG-21s of 322 Air Regt. (AR) strafed barracks and the Presidential Palace in Kabul.

The PDPA soon split into two factions, based primarily on the rate, rather than the extent, of social and economic change. Through 1979 Hafizullah Amin gradually assumed power, displacing Taraki. Amin, however, had been educated in the US and was distrusted by the Russians, who are believed to have suspected him of being in the pay of the CIA. There was widespread resistance to government changes, especially in respect of land reforms, and from early 1979 there were armed uprisings, although, significantly, these uprisings were locally based and completely unco-ordinated. The most serious was at Herat, where from 15 March virtually the entire 17th Division of the Army defected to the rebels with their arms. About 50 Soviet advisers and their families were killed, and Il-28s of 355 AR at Shindand bombed the city, concentrating on the barracks, until a task force from Pol-e-Charkhi could regain control. It was estimated that 5,000 were killed in the fighting. Afghanistan had signed a military aid agreement with the Soviet Union in 1955, from which date the Royal Afghan Air Force began to receive Soviet equipment to replace its Ansons and prewar Hinds. Airfields at Bagram, north of Kabul, and Mazar-i-Sharif were rebuilt, and first MiG-17 fighters then An-2s and Mi-1s were supplied. By 1979 the Democratic Republic of Afghanistan Air Force (DRAAF) comprised 35 MiG-21s, 12 MiG-19s, 80 MiG-17s, 24 Su-7BMs and 30 Il-28s; helicopters and transports included 19 Mi-4s, 22 Mi-8s, 10 An-2s and 10 Il-14s. In June Pathans claimed three MiG-21s shot down, and a further MiG-21 and two helicopters were allegedly destroyed in Ghazni province in July. As resistance to the Government increased, the Soviet Union supplied additional arms including T-62 tanks, twelve MiG-21s and twelve Mi-25s. By August the number of Russian advisers was 5,000.

Throughout 1979 the Army suffered a number of serious defections: in May, for example, a brigade of the 7th Division went over to rebels in Paktia. Fighting extended, and from May the town of Asmar in the Kunar valley was under siege. In August it was taken, and the 5th Brigade of 9 Division joined with guerrillas in a move on Chugha Serai further down the valley. Despite outnumbering the defenders, the combined rebel force was unable to take the town, primarily because of infighting. The friction arose out of the distribution of spoils, not only to sustain further fighting but also to sell in Pakistan. This incident was important in that it illustrated the inability of the rebel factions to co-ordinate their activities against a common threat: disunity was to characterize the resistance against Soviet occupation.

It was now clear to the Russians that the Kabul Government would need considerable support, and from September 1979 plans were made for an invasion. A Soviet-Afghan Friendship Treaty had been signed in December 1978 which provided, *inter alia*, that 'when the security of contracting parties was endangered they would take appropriate measures'. The Treaty was registered with the UN in September 1979. Soviet advisers now toured the country to 'help with ideas on anti-guerrilla warfare' but in reality to plan from within the impending invasion.

The reasons for invasion were complex. First, the Soviet Union could not tolerate the prospect of Muslim fundamentalism spreading into the homeland, given that some 40 million Soviet citizens are Muslim. Second, access to warm-water ports in the Arabian Sea would become easier. Third, pressure could be applied to Iran, the Gulf oilfields and China. Fourth, the United Stated could be embarrassed by being forced to counter by embracing the military dictatorship in Pakistan. Last, the Russians did not trust Amin. Taraki visited Moscow in early September and on his return attempted to assassinate Amin. The attempt failed and Taraki was 'retired' as President; his death was announced on 9 October, and Amin assumed the roles of Prime Minister and President.

The Soviet 40th Army established a headquarters at Termez on the border and began its planning. The invasion force was to comprise units from the much under-strength Turkestan and Central Asian Military Districts and was centred on the 105th Guards Airborne Assault Division (GAAD). The first component, a regiment transferred from the 103rd GAAD, was flown into Bagram on 6 and 7 December in An-12 and An-22 transports, and from the 19th this unit was deployed along the road into Kabul from the north.

The main force of the 105th GAAD, about 5,000 men, was then flown into Bagram and Kabul between 22 and 26 December with their heavy equipment, which included ASU-85 air-borne assault guns. Some 350 sorties were flown by An-12s, An-22s and Il-76s of the Air Transport Command (V-TA), accompanied by MiG-21 and MiG-23 escorts. Mi-8 and Mi-24 helicopters were also flown south, including requisitioned Mi-8s of Aeroflot. The Russians struck against the Kabul Government on 27 December. Advisers used a range of ploys to immobilize vehicles and confine loyal army officers, communications were cut and key installations were occupied with little resistance. In the occupation of the Presidential Palace, Amin was killed and 'Kabul Radio', in fact broadcasting from Termez, announced that the exiled former deputy Prime Minister, Babrak Karmal, had taken over and had requested Soviet military assistance. The same day the land-based invasion began. Pontoon bridges were placed across the Oxus river and the 360th and 201st Motor Rifle Divisions (MRD) moved south from Termez for Mazar-i-Sharif, then Kabul. In the west, the 66th and 357th MRDs invaded from Kushka to Herat and then Kandahar. Both forces were equipped with BMD and BMP tracked and BTR-60 wheeled armoured personnel carriers and were supported by T-55 and T-62 tanks. Ancillary

units included artillery and SA-4 brigades, the latter suggesting that the Russians were perhaps prepared for external intervention. By the 31st, 360 MRD was established on the outskirts of Kabul. The initial Soviet divisions were quickly supplemented by 5, 10, 16 and 54 MRDs, which were soon involved in fighting guerrilla mujahideen. The resistance groups declared a jihad, or holy war, against the invaders.

The United States' response to the invasion was immediate. Publicly, there were accusations of the use of chemical weapons (first reported in June 1979) although the claim has never been substantiated; less publicly the CIA began a covert operation to supply the rebels with arms of Soviet origin purchased through Egypt and supplied via Pakistan. The Russians had never intended to establish comprehensive control over Afghanistan: they were determined to maintain control in the towns and cities and along the main roads, but to leave the Afghan Army to fight the in-country war, although 201 MRD and elements of 105 GAAD were deployed to Nangarhar province to contain rebels operating between Kabul and the Khyber Pass, the main route into Afghanistan from Pakistan. There were further large-scale desertions from the Afghan Army, and the vulnerability of the lines of communication was soon exposed as convoys were subjected to ambush. Heavy fighting broke out in most major centres. The most important

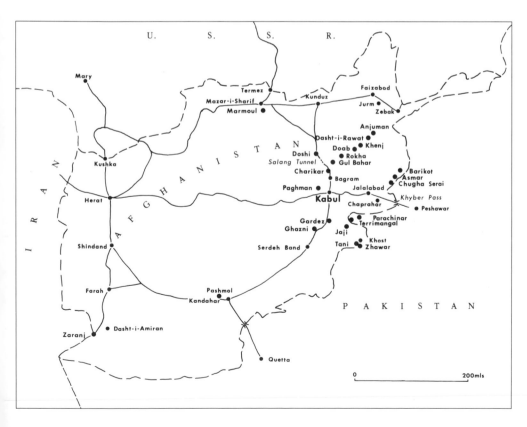

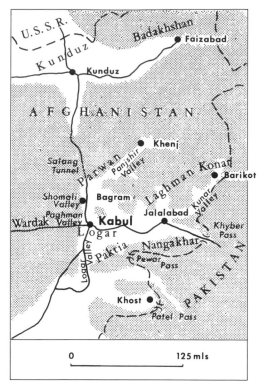

Map showing key locations in Afghanistan including U.S.S.R., Badakhshan, Faizabad, Kunduz, Khenj, Salang Tunnel, Parwan, Panjshir Valley, Laghman, Konar, Barikot, Shomali Valley, Bagram, Kunar Valley, Paghman Valley, Jalalabad, Wardak Valley, Kabul, Logar, Khyber Pass, Paktia, Nangakhar, Pewar Pass, Khost, Patel Pass, PAKISTAN. Scale 0 to 125 mls.

In the initial stages of the occupation, the 27th Fighter Air Regiment (FAR) was deployed to Bagram with the 50th Independent Com-posite Air Regiment (ICAR), while the 262nd Independent Reconnaissance Helicopter Squadron (IRHS) operated out of Kabul. There was now a need for more helicopters, both in the gunship and transport roles, to move forces rapidly in greater co-operation with the Army, and additional helicopter units were flown in, the number rising from 60 in June to 300 by early 1981. Ground-attack units were also moved into Shindand, Herat and Kandahar to provide rapid response to trouble, while longer-range aircraft were retained at Soviet bases for planned strikes.

Early in September Soviet and Afghan forces mounted what later became known as 'Panjshir 1' against rebels in the Panjshir valley. In a limited operation, assault troops were landed by helicopter, but the rebels claimed to have shot down ten in an inconclusive exercise. 'Panjshir 2' followed in October, prompted by repeated ambushes on the Salang road, and late in November a major offensive was launched in the Logar valley. For the first time helicopters were used in some numbers to drop assault troops in cordon and search operations. By the end of 1980, the Soviet Union had committed 100,000 men and 400 aircraft to Afghanistan.

By 1982, the rebels had gained control over much of Kandahar and were still setting ambushes from bases in the Panjshir. In February, the Russians began a bombing campaign – which resulted in the deaths of many civilians – in an endeavour to destroy guerrilla hideouts. In March, 'Panjshir 3' was launched, following a raid on Bagram air base in which an An-22 was destroyed, while on 26 April a DRAAF Mi-8 pilot defected with his helicopter, landing at Quetta after a 180-mile flight. Aircraft losses gradually mounted: in June a MiG-21 and Mi-24 were claimed shot down and five MiG-21s destroyed on the ground at Bagram when petrol was poured into drainage channels and fired. On 4 July a force from 108 MRD was airlifted from Jalalabad to attack guerrilla bases around Sarobi, the Russians achieving some success.

A battalion of Government troops then defected at Charikar, and rebels confirmed their dominance in the Panjshir when they murdered 70 Government sympathizers at Gul Bahar at the mouth of the valley. This event led to 'Panjshir 4': in the course of this disruptive operation the Soviets established a base at Anjuman at the top of the valley and Gul Bahar was again in Government hands. Between 5 and 15 September an operation was mounted in Farah, during which many sorties were flown by ground-attack aircraft from Shindand, and in October Herat was the centre of search and destroy sweeps. Simultaneously, an operation was being mounted against another resistance group based to the

rebel bases from which attacks were launched were the Logar valley along the road from Kabul to Kandahar, the Paghman valley immediately to the west of Kabul, the Kunar valley running north-east from Jalalabad and, most importantly, the Panjshir valley running north-east from Bagram. It was from the last that many early ambushes were sprung on the key Salang road into Kabul from the north.

In the centre of Afghanistan, in the Hazara Jat, the resistance operated with impunity but well away from major roads. The first significant Soviet operation began in March in the Kunar valley. After heavy preparatory shelling, 201 MRD, with armour, pushed up the valley, reaching Barikot by the 15th. It then withdrew, leaving the guerrillas to return. Many refugees fled to Pakistan, and in April there were first reports of DRAAF MiG-21s and Mi-25s attacking refugee camps at Gilgit in Pakistan.

In June a Soviet battalion was ambushed and destroyed on the Gardez–Khost road: the ill-trained conscripts stayed firm in their APCs until overwhelmed. It was now clear to the Russians that they would have to rethink tactics for their Limited Contingent of Soviet Forces in Afghanistan (LCSFA). They returned a number of Muslim conscripts to the USSR after some Tadjiks had defected and restructured their ground forces to provide more flexibilty and mobility. Over time, reservists were replaced by better-trained soldiers drawn from a range of established units. The use of air power was also reconsidered.

south of Mazar-i-Sharif in the Marmoul gorge. A squadron of Il-28s of 355 Air Regiment (AR) joined the resident MiG-17s of 393 AR at Dehdadi (Mazar-i-Sharif) airfield, from where a series of heavy bombing raids, supported by Soviet-based Su-24s, was launched against targets in the Marmoul area.

After a week of softening-up, an Afghan battalion from the 20th Division was helilifted to a site behind the village, from where it was supposed to drive the guerrillas out of the valley into the hands of units of the 18th Division, but in the event the troops had to be recovered by air when unable to fight their way out of the narrow valley. Pakistani frontier posts were attacked by DRAAF MiG-17 fighters on 5 September, and around this time the US resumed arms supplies to Pakistan after a long embargo. In November DRAAF Mi-25s attacked refugee camps at Parachinar, Basso and Matasangar with rockets and machine guns, and thousands of anti-personnel PFM-1 'butterfly' mines were dropped. The year closed with a concerted attempt to disrupt the flow of supplies entering Afghanistan through the Khyber Pass. By the end of their second year in Afghanistan the Russians were beginning to demonstrate revised tactics in tackling the mujahideen. First, they concentrated air power and used it to soften targets. Second, helicopters were used much more to drop troops to prevent withdrawal, then mobile 'hammer' forces were used to drive the resistance against the 'anvil' of the helicopter-landed group.

In the west, guerrillas were operating with impunity in Herat, and during January 1982 the Russians mounted numerous sweeps in support of DRA attempts to destroy the rebels. These operations were fully supported with strikes from DRAAF and Soviet fighters which in the open country were highly effective; the campaign represented a serious defeat for the resistance. In the Kandahar area the guerrillas were now using CIA-supplied SA-7 SAMs with limited success, and a Soviet general was killed in a helicopter crash in Paktia province.

Against a background of increasing ambushes on the Salang road, preparations were made at Bagram and Kabul for the biggest operation yet, 'Panjshir 5'. The most successful resistance leader by now was Ahmad Shah Massud, who had organized a number of company-sized mobile units prepared to fight away from their home villages for extended periods. His groups were based in the Panjshir. Learning of the impending operation, he mounted a battalion-sized offensive against Bagram air base on 25 April, and in a rocket and mortar attack from within the perimeter he claimed to have destroyed some 23 aircraft. The attack did little to postpone the advance, however. On 10 May DRA soldiers of the 8th Division and 38th Commando Brigade were posted around Gul Bahar at the entrance to

the valley, and there followed a week of day bombing conducted by an An-12 command post aircraft. The resistance escaped loss by taking to the mountains in daylight, and they mounted a number of attacks on Government forces. These air strikes witnessed the operational début of the Su-25, which equipped the 200th Independent Guards Attack Aviation Squadron based at Shindand but detached to Bagram.

On 17 May a battalion of 103 Air Assault Division was lifted by helicopter to Khenj at the head of the valley, and as these Soviet troops came under attack a regiment of 108 MRD advanced up the valley in BTR-60 APCs with T-62 and Mi-24 support. The first ambush, after the column had surmounted landslides started by the resistance, was at Bazerak, where three T-62s were destroyed by mines and rockets. There was a second, more costly, ambush at Doab, after which the column was protected by Mi-24 gunships. Hovering in a slow, six-aircraft 'circle of death', they were called down one at a time by forward air controllers (FAC) as targets were pinpointed.

By 20 May the main group linked up with Khenj battalion, and elements of both struck north-east to meet up with a battalion of 201 MRD from the Anjuman Pass. By early June the whole valley floor was in Government hands for the first time since 1978, but at a cost of 300 Russians and 700 DRA troops killed. The guerrillas also claimed 60 vehicles, including tanks, thirteen helicopters and three aircraft. In all, some 15,000 Soviet and Afghan troops were committed, plus about 190 helicopters, but within weeks the communist forces began to withdraw under fire from Massud's fighters, who had taken to the higher ground. The failure to make any real impact against Massud led to 'Panjshir 6', which began on 25 August with sustained bombing against suspected guerrilla targets. On the 30th assault troops were helilifted to Khenj while a mechanized column left Rokha. This time the offensive was brisker and subject to fewer ambushes: within two days the valley floor was occupied and the Russians began a series of strikes up into subsidiary valleys, traditionally resistance strongholds.

Using airlifted troops to block the heads of the valleys, the 'hammer and anvil' tactics forced the mujahideen fighters even higher up the mountains, from where they were ineffective. The Russians then withdrew, destroying houses, crops and irrigation systems and causing many of the inhabitants to flee the area, thus denying the resistance shelter and food. Several helicopters were claimed shot down, and total casualties in the valley through the year mounted to 600 Russian, 500 DRA, 1,200 civilian and 180 resistance fighters dead. The Russians maintained a reputation for callousness following reports that 105 civilians had been massacred at Padkhwab-e-

Shana, south of Kabul, on 19 September: found hiding in an irrigation channel, they were burned alive after petrol was poured in and ignited.

In general, however, the Soviet troops were well disciplined and excesses were rare. The Russians themselves suffered a setback on 10 November when there was an accident in the Salang tunnel: two lorries carrying aviation fuel are believed to have collided and exploded. Fearing a guerrilla attack, the Soviets blocked the entrances in the two-mile tunnel containing two convoys, but, in the fires, some 700 Russians and up to 2,000 civilians were reportedly killed. A defecting DRAAF pilot was killed when his MiG-17 crashed on landing at a Pakistani airfield on 18 October, and the final loss of the year is reported to have occurred on 27 December when a guerrilla raid, led by DRAAF defectors, destroyed twelve helicopters of 355 Independent Helicopter Regiment (IHR) at Jalalabad.

The garrison at Khost came under increasing pressure, and by January 1983 it was supplied completely by air, involving some 150 sorties a week from Kabul. Being close to the border with Pakistan, the local resistance was well equipped, and during an attack on an outpost some Government troops mutinied, resulting in its loss to the mujahideen; a series of MiG-21 and MiG-23 sorties followed, causing some loss. North of Kabul there was a respite for the guerrillas when a ceasefire was agreed in the Panjshir. This secured the Salang road from attack and freed Government and Soviet troops for operations elsewhere while allowing Massud time to regroup and recover.

The Russians now carried out operations up the Shomali valley north of Kabul, from where rebel groups had mounted attacks on the road. By May, after repeated gunship and fighter-bomber sorties, some 2,000 civilians were reported killed. The roads were still insecure and more helicopters were brought into service, including about 40 of the large Mi-6. More lorries were supplied to make good losses and new weapons and fittings used on vehicles to allow greater elevation in defence against attacks from hillsides. More effective air-dropped armaments were also brought into use, including parachute-retarded and cluster bombs, and napalm was also used against difficult hillside targets. As the threat of SAMs became real, the air forces made increasing use of flares as infra-red decoys. Through 1983 Khost remained under siege by a growing number of rebels who, if unified, could have taken the city. The Russians continued their operations in the Shomali, Kunar and Logar valleys.

Aircraft losses mounted both in the air and on the ground. By now the rebels had acquired a large number of anti-aircraft artillery pieces, and in the summer an An-12 was brought down at Jalalabad with the loss of fifty soldiers and crew, while at Ghazni a MiG-23 was shot down. In two separate rocket and mortar attacks on Kabul airfield some 21 fighters and helicopters were claimed as destroyed, together with a DC-10 of the national airline Ariana. At Mazar-i-Sharif two MiG-19s and three Mi-8s were destroyed and an ammunition dump blown up on 5 September. Somewhat safer were several Il-76s allegedly converted to the bomber role and used to attack isolated hill forts in the Hindu Kush, where Massud was now believed to be operating. Further to the south, the Khost siege continued, and the airfield there became difficult to use: in October three Mi-8s and two An-12s were claimed to have been destroyed in the area. Security in Kabul was stepped up in 1983, so guerrilla attacks were confined mainly to areas around the city. These finally resulted in one of the larger Russian offensives of the year when, with heavy air support, operations were mounted up three valleys leading off the Bagram road.

After initial bombing raids on 8–9 November, the main strikes followed on the 27th and a number of mujahideen were reported to have been killed. In the middle of the operation a DRAAF pilot defected to Pakistan with his Su-7. The Russians spent the early weeks of 1984 pursuing Massued around Zebak in the Hindu Kush, operating helicopters out of the new airfield built near the town. Likely hideouts in the area were bombed. Not only did Massud evade his pursuers, he also refused to extend the Panjshir ceasefire, resulting in numerous ambushes along the Salang road.

In March, after skirmishes along the road, a major operation was launched in which some 120 Mi-8s were used to transport 28 commando groups to positions in the lower Panjshir valley. Garrisons were reinforced, but after the Mattock bridge over the Ghorband river was destroyed by guerrillas on 15 March attention turned to the Paghman valley, where MiG-23s attacked rebel bases. Major operations with the now customary helicopter and figher-bomber support were also carried out against guerrilla groups around Kunduz and at Andkhoy near the Soviet border. As the Salang road became untenable, 'Panjshir 7' was initiated in April. New tactics were developed based on experience, but the operation was to begin with 'softening up' by high-level bombing by a regiment of 36 Tu-16s based in the Soviet Union. Massud anticipated the assault and mined roads into the valley. He also launched two pre-emptive strikes on the 19th and 20th. The first of these, against troop concentrations on the Salang road, met with an instant response from heliborne commandos and the rebels suffered heavy losses. The second was against Anawa in the valley mouth, and it prompted the Russians to begin their carpet-bombing of the valley floor. Two columns then advanced up the valley behind rolling bombing, and by the 24th they had reached Rokha.

One of the enduring images of the Afghanistan war, as it reached into millions of living rooms through the medium of television, was the Mi-24 gunship. This Soviet 'Hind-E', yellow 40, carries rocket pods on the inner pylons and four AT-6 'Spiral' missiles on the outer pylons. Large numbers of 'Hinds' were deployed to Afghanistan with the Soviet and Afghan Air Forces, and many were lost to guerrilla action.

A force was then airlifted to Dasht-e-Rawat high up in the valley, while early in May passes leading out of subsidiary valleys at Alishang and Kantiwar were blocked; a large force also moved to the head of the Andarab valley to the north, to block off all the escape routes. Having forced the guerrillas to break up in numerous hideouts, the attackers built a series of forts in the valley floor and withdrew. The action involved 10,000 Soviet and 5,000 DRA troops and marked the introduction of special Air Assault Forces (VDV) and Spetsnaz reconnaissance teams. Helicopter sorties were extensive, with as many as 2,000 soliders moved in single operations. For the rest of the year the pressure on the Salang road was relieved as the mujahideen concentrated their efforts on the forts and garrisons in the valley.

Goverment forces now turned their attention to guerrilla bases on the border with Pakistan, where large stocks of arms and ammunition were accruing. In August, elements of the 104th GAAD were flown directly from the Soviet Union to Kabul, from where they mounted attacks on rebels laying seige to Jaji near the border. Heavy air support was on hand, and during the operation a mujahideen camp at Terrimangal in Pakistan was bombed with the loss of 54 lives, an action which had the effect of relieving the pressure on the garrison and disrupting guerrilla activity in the area. In September, as Massud kept up attacks on the Panjshir forts, 'Panjshir 8' was embarked upon. Soviet-based bombers were again used extensively, and smaller forces than hitherto pursued rebels with limited success. There was also extensive high-level bombing around Herat. The increasing use of Russian-based Su-24s and Tu-16s may have been in response to the growing threat to slow or low aircraft from the wider use of SA-7s by the guerrillas.

On 22 September two An-12s were claimed to have been brought down in Paktia province and numerous helicopters were destroyed. On 28 October an Aeroflot An-22 was shot down on the approach to Kabul and as many as 240 troops are believed to have been killed; shortly afterwards, an Ariana DC-10 was hit, but it landed safely. On 18 November a major offensive began near Khost, involving no fewer than five Mi-6 squadrons, and in December 17,500 troops moved up the Kunar valley to relieve pressure on the garrisons at Asmar and Barikot. At the end of the year the Russians had around 115,000 troops in Afghanistan, with probably 40,000 committed at bases in the Soviet Union. The DRA Army was becoming more effective, playing a bigger part in operations. The mujahideen groups were no more cohesive, but they were making more use of heavy weapons, with American aid estimated at $250 million annually.

Government garrisons in the east remained under siege into 1985 and there was no let-up in resistance attacks on major supply routes, especially the Salang road. Guerrilla bases in the Paghman valley were bombed early in January. Rebels attacked airfields at Kandahar on the 14th and Bagram, where ten helicopters and six tanks were claimed destroyed, on the 16th. On the 27th, a heliborne force of commandos was dropped in Nangarhar province to eliminate a local resistance leader, who was killed in the fighting, and in February an operation was conducted against rebels in the Logar valley. Sweeps were maintained with full air support, especially in Laghman province where helicopter gunships were much in evidence, and in the lower Panjshir there were reports of an armoured task force having been destroyed later in March. Losses of aircraft mounted, with helicopters claimed in the Salang Pass (14 April), in Deobandi (15 April) and on the Pakistan border (19 April). A DRAAF MiG-17 was shot down at Jaji on the 17th.

In May a major offensive was initiated up the Kunar valley to relieve Barikot and from the 14th Jalalabad airfield was closed to all traffic to enable 10,000 troops to be flown in from Kabul in An-12s. Villages in the valley were bombed and by 10 June it had been temporarily cleared of mujahideen. In the Panjshir, Massud was still attacking Government forts, and on 16 June a force of 500 guerrillas captured 460 prisoners and much *matériel* from the garrison at Pechgur low in the valley. The prisoners were taken up the valley, and to recapture them 'Panjshir 9' was launched, Rebel bases in the valley were bombed and a heliborne unit dropped at the head of the valley to intercept the column of prisoners, who were promptly killed. In August a large operation was mounted to mop up guerrilla bases in the south-east, between Kabul and the Pakistan border; 20,000 troops were committed to the offensive, which began on the 20th.

Making great use of helicopters both for transport and fire support, one group struck out from besieged Khost north towards the rebel base at Jaji, then south to the stronghold at Zhawar. A second force moved from Kabul down the Logar valley, then east to the Nawa river, where it met up with a third task force from Jalalabad. For the Government, the exercise went smoothly, with many objectives achieved and large quantities of arms captured; only the base at Zhawar escaped after heavy fighting. This large operation to deprive the rebels both of bases and arms did not prevent the introduction of a new weapon. A number of Stinger SAMs had been supplied, and the first use of the missile resulted in the loss of an An-26 of the internal airline Bakhtar near Kandahar on 5 September while flying at about 9,000ft; 52 people on board were killed. Earlier, on 12 June, twenty DRAAF MiG-21s were destroyed at Shindand, where they had been moved from the less secure airfields at Herat and Kandahar. The loss is believed to have been the result of sabotage from within the base. A further loss occurred on 13 July when two DRAAF pilots defected to Miranshah with their Mi-25 helicopters; one of these machines was subsequently evaluated in the UK.

Aircraft losses mounted in the autumn: no fewer than fifteen Soviet aircraft were claimed to have been shot down in a two-day period while supporting a minor offensive in the Panjshir, four helicopters were claimed on 13 November at Kandahar, and a senior Soviet officer was lost when his MiG-21 was brought down en route to Bagram and Kandahar. On 14 January 1986 the Pakistani Air Force (PAF) shot down a MiG-21 over the border. At the time the DRA Army was committed to fighting in the border area, and during operations on 27 January two DRAAF Mi-25s rocketed Parachinar in Pakistan. Government efforts turned again to Herat province in late January: 120 rebels were killed during sweeps in the region and at least 200 civilians killed in the intense bombing which preceded ground operations. However, the scene of major activity remained the border area south-east of Kabul. On 19 March Pakistani border posts were strafed, and on 30 March a V-VS An-26 was shot down by two PAF F-16s.

The build-up now began of a major DRA force, with limited Russian support, for an attack on the resistance stronghold at Zhawar. From late March 10,000 men from many units were readied, and the offensive was launched on 2 April from Khost. To protect transport aircraft flying out of Kabul for Khost, each was accompanied immediately after take-off by two Mi-24s firing decoy flares. The column of over 10,000 troops made its way slowly from Khost towards Tani, led by a large number of tanks in the initial stages and with constant air support by Mi-24s, MiG-21s, MiG-23s, Su-17s and Su-25s.

Guerrillas rocketed the airfield at Khost to disrupt the flow of helicopter resupply sorties, but Tani was reached by 10 April and the column continued to the fortified stronghold. The base was subjected to constant air attack, and despite heavy AA fire aircraft losses were slight since supplies of SAMs were quickly exhausted and the mujahideen soon burnt out the barrels of their artillery pieces. A MiG-21 was shot down over Pakistan by PAF F-16 fighters on the 16th. Su-25s employed laser-guided bombs against caves, and many rebels were killed in the constant air strikes. Zhawar fell on the 22nd. The cost to the DRA Army was about 600 dead, while the mujahideen lost around 1,000 killed and vast amounts of arms and ammunition.

Karmal was retired on 4 May as General Secretary of the PDPA and replaced by the head of the KHAD secret police, Mohammed Najeebollah. The new Secretary had begun to succeed in bringing together a number of disillusioned tribal chiefs, especially from among refugee groups in Pakistan, and he set about bringing a new vigour to attacking resistance bases. An operation was mounted in the Jaji area in May, during which a DRAAF Su-22 was shot down by an F-16 of 9 Sqn. PAF over Parachinar. To the

TABLE OF UNITS: AFGHANISTAN, 1979–1988

Unit	Aircraft	Base	Role	Nos.
DRAAF, 1980				
322 AR	MiG-21L	Bagram, Kandahar	Air defence, ground attack	40
393 AR	MiG-17, MiG-19	Mazar-i-Sharif	Air defence, ground attack	60
321 AR	Su-7BM	Shindand	Ground attack	24
355 AR	Il-28	Shindand	Light bombing	40
232 AR	Mi-4, Mi-8, Mi-25	Kabul, Jalalabad	Army support	45
? AR	An-2, Il-14, An-26, Il-18	Kabul	Transport	35
DRAAF, 1982				
322 AR	MiG-21L	Bagram	Ground attack	40
393 AR	MiG-17, MiG-19	Mazar-i-Sharif, Kandahar	Ground attack	50
321 AR	Su-7BM, Su-22	Shindand	Ground attack	35
355 AR	Il-28	Shindand	Light bombing	30
232 AR	Mi-4, Mi-8, Mi-25	Kabul, various	Army support	20
? AR	Mi-8, Mi-25	Kabul, various	Army support	40
? AR	An-2, Il-14, An-26/30, Il-18	Kabul	Transport	35
DRAAF, 1986				
393 AR	MiG-21L/N	Mazar-i-Sharif	Ground attack	50
322 AR	MiG-23	Bagram	Ground attack, air defence	40
321 AR	Su-17	Bagram	Ground attack	40
355 AR	Il-28, MiG-17	Shindand	Light bombing, ground attack	30
232 AR	Mi-4, Mi-6, Mi-8	Kabul, Shindand	Army support	20
377 AR	Mi-17, Mi-25	Kabul, Kandahar	Army support	30
? AR	Mi-25	Kabul, Jalalabad	Army support	30
? AR	An-2, Il-14, An-26/30, Il-18	Kabul	Transport	35

north, Massud had left the Panjshir for Badakshan province, where Soviet troops set about destroying his force of 2,000 guerrillas. Up to 70 Mi-8 and Mi-17 helicopters were brought into Kunduz for the exercise, and in fighting in the Khejob valley the Russians are believed, for the first time, to have used helicopter pickets, landed on high ground in advance of units working up the valley floor. One such picket was ambushed and its two Mi-17s destroyed. Massud escaped capture. At the end of July, with the political situation looking optimistic and with the Russians believed to be losing 150 killed or seriously wounded each month, Soviet General Secretary Mikhail Gorbachev announced a limited withdrawal.

This offer made no impact on the resistance, who stepped up their attacks on targets around Kabul and on the airfield at Bagram. From 10 September, Su-25s pounded rebel bases in the Paghman valley, and there was heavy fighting in the area. An increasing number of aircraft were lost as the rebels began to receive the first of over 300 Blowpipe missiles supplied by the UK via the CIA, the first batch of 30 allegedly delivered from Nigerian stocks in the spring. The importance of this missile lay in the fact that, unlike the IR-seeking Stinger and SA-7, it was command-controlled and hence not susceptible to decoy flares.

The Russian withdrawal began in October, by which time some 500 helicopters had been lost and between 5,000 and 10,000 troops killed, DRAAF and V-VS aircraft were now being claimed by the resistance at the rate of one a day and were probably actually lost at about a third of that rate. V-VS and DRAAF helicopters in Afghanistan now numbered 900. Among losses late in the year were a MiG-23 at Bagram, an An-12 at Khost (19 November), a Soviet Il-18 at Mohipur (29 November) and an An-12 at Kabul (19 December). Fighters involved in a bombing campaign around Kandahar from 8 December were also attacked, and several are believed to have been lost. There were no major operations mounted by the Government in the early part of 1987, but as local actions continued the loss of aircraft mounted. The mujahideen now claimed some 50 aircraft a month as the use of aircraft on interdiction strikes increased. There were several large-scale attacks on rebel sanctuaries across the border in Pakistan, notably on 23 March when twelve MiG-21s attacked camps at Terrimangal and Angoor Adda and on 16 April when the PAF claimed a fighter shot down north of Miramshah. For the first time the PAF lost an aircraft, shot down near Khost on 29 April.

Notable substantiated losses to the DRAAF or V-VS included an An-12 (3 March), an An-26 en route from Kabul to Bagram (29 May), a civilian An-26 at Kandahar (11 June), another An-26 (13 August), an unspecified type near Kabul (4 September) and a DRAAF An-26 at Kunduz (13

TABLE OF UNITS: AFGHANISTAN, 1979–1988 (continued)

Unit	Aircraft	Base	Role	Nos.
V-VS, 1980				
27 FAR	MiG-21L/N	Bagram	Ground attack	36
50 ICAR	An-26, Mi-8C, Mi-24D	Bagram	Army support	40
262 IRHS	Mi-8, Mi-24D	Kabul	Army support	15
V-VS, 1982 (Afghanistan)				
27 FAR	MiG-21L/N	Bagram, Kandahar	Ground attack (ex Kaka)	24
115 FAR	MiG-21L/N	Kandahar	Ground attack	24
217 FBR	Su-17B	Shindand	Ground attack (ex Kizyl Arvat)	12
200 IGAAS	Su-25, Su-17C/D	Shindand, Bagram	Close support	13
263 ITRS	MiG-21R	Kabul	PR	9
50 ICAR	An-26, Mi-8C, Mi-24D	Bagram	Army support	50
262 IRHS	Mi-8C/E, Mi-24D	Bagram	Armed observation	15
280 IHR	Mi-6, Mi-8C	Kandahar, Shindand	Army support	55
355 IHR	Mi-8C, Mi-24D/E	Jalalabad	Army support	40
181 IHR	Mi-6, Mi-8C	Kunduz, Faizabad	Army support	60
302 IHS	Mi-2, Mi-8, Mi-24D	Shindand	Army support	15
254 IHS	Mi-24D	Kunduz	Army support	8
V-VS, 1982 (Soviet Union)				
? BR	Tu-16	Mary	Medium bombing	36
V-VS, 1986 (Afghanistan)				
27 FAR	MiG-21L/N, Su-17	Bagram	Ground attack	50
? FAR	MiG-23BN, Su-25	Bagram	Ground attack, close support	60
? FAR	MiG-21L/N	Shindand	Ground attack	24
200 IGAAS	Su-25	Shindand	Close support	10
115 FAR	MiG-21L/N, Su-17	Kandahar	Ground attack	60
263 ITRS	MiG-21R	Kabul	PR	15
? ITRS	MiG-25R	Shindand	PR	10
50 ICAR	An-26, Mi-8, Mi-24D	Bagram	Army support	50
262 IRHS	Mi-2, Mi-8/17, Mi-24	Bagram	Armed observation	15
? IHR	Mi-2, Mi-6, Mi-8/17, Mi-24	Shindand	\} Army support	60
280 IHR	Mi-2, Mi-6, Mi-8	Kandahar		30
355 IHR	Mi-8/17, Mi-24	Jalalabad		30
181 IHR	Mi-6, Mi-8/17, Mi-24	Kunduz		30
V-VS, 1986 (Soviet Union)				
? FAR	Su-24	Termez	Interdiction	50
? FAR	Su-24	Kushka	Interdiction	50
? BR	Tu-16	Mary	Medium bombing	36

Note: In addition, throughout the war An-12, An-22, An-26 and Il-76 transport aircraft of V-TA and Aeroflot have operated from Soviet bases into Afghanistan, mainly to Bagram and Kabul; 262 IRHS helicopters were supplemented by Mi-8s from Aeroflot in the 1980 entry. DRAAF helicopters have operated regularly from Faizabad, Farah, Herat, Jalalabad, Jurm, Kabul, Kandahar and Shindand.

September). The Soviet news agency Tass complained that rebels were being trained by the US in the use of SAMs in Nevada; certainly at this time several US companies were producing Mi-24 and Su-25 scale targets for AA practice. In June there was an offensive around Kandahar, with some suburban areas subjected to heavy bombing and several fighters shot down by Stingers. In September there was renewed fighting in the Panjshir, and on 3 October the garrison at Pechgur was evacuated. The rebels had also re-established themselves in the border area after the defeat at Zhawar, and yet another offensive was mounted from 17 October in the Logar valley. The Russians brought into use the BM-27 rocket launcher, but losses on both sides were heavy. The mujahideen tightened their grip on Khost yet again, and in December no fewer than 25,000 troops were reported to be massing to open the road to the garrison. The operation took six weeks, after which the town was once more relieved although the airfield remained subject to rocket and mortar fire.

The year 1988 saw the Russians beginning their withdrawal. In March there were reports of massive arms shipments being flown into Kabul, with troops being taken back to the USSR on the return flights. The DRAAF acquired its own tactical transport force in the form of An-12s. The garrison at Barikot was evacuated to Jalalabad on 22 April, and from 9 May the town, now in resistance hands, was heavily bombed. A UN mission was set up at Kabul, and the withdrawal proper began on 15 May.

The resistance was in control of the Jaji area, where a main base was again established, and the evacuation of Russian soldiers was disrupted, especially through the use of large numbers of Chinese manufactured rockets. The Russian withdrawal began from the south-east, and garrisons and towns were handed over to Government troops. Many were soon in mujahideen hands. By 15 August the target of a 50 per cent withdrawal had been completed, and all Soviet troops are expected to have left the country by February 1989. The DRAAF is being left with a large amount of equipment, although at the time of writing its status is not clear: throughout the war many Soviet aircraft flew in Afghan markings.

By August 1988 only Herat province in the west and the area around the road north from Kabul in the east were still in Government hands. Jalalabad and Kandahar had been evacuated. Pressure during the withdrawal has remained intense, and on 24 June eight DRAAF Su-25s were destroyed in a rocket attack on Kabul. Late in August rebels made successful attacks on several targets, including Kabul Airport and a barracks at Kalagay, while on the 15th a DRAAF transport was shot down while taking Government troops to Kunduz.

The DRAAF also lost aircraft on the Pakistani border. An Su-25 was shot down on 4 August and a MiG-23 on 7 September; also early in September five MiG-17 pilots defected. Another MiG-23 was shot down over Pakistan on 3 November. Under increasing pressure in Kabul the Russians brought in SS-1 missiles in November for use against mujahideen concentrations.

As the Russians withdraw it is assumed that they will want to see the strongest Government grip retained on the buffer zones in Herat and at Mazar-i-Sharif, and to this end extensive minefields are believed to have been sown. At the end of May the Russians announced that they had lost 13,310 dead, 35,478 wounded and 311 missing. The Afghan Government admitted the deaths of 243,900 soldiers and civilians.

POSTSCRIPT
The Russian withdrawal was completed in February 1989, leaving the country in a state of civil war.

AIRCRAFT MARKINGS

V-VS

MiG-21 'Fishbed' Olive/dark brown/sand over, light grey under, red code on nose: '17' (? unit).
MiG-23BN Olive/dark brown/sand over, light grey under, yellow code on nose: '43' (? Fighter Av. Regt., Kabul).
Su-25 Olive/sand over, light grey under, yellow code on nose: '04' (200 Ind. Guards Attack Av. Sqn.).
Mi-8 Olive/sand over, light grey under, yellow code on mid-fuselage: '71' (355 Ind. Hel. Regt.).
Mi-24 'Hind-D' Olive/sand over, light grey under, yellow code on rear fuselage: '55' (50 Ind. Composite Av. Regt.).
An-22 White over, bare metal under, red code on nose: '31' (? unit).

Aeroflot

Il-76 White over, bare metal under, blue cheat line, black registration on upper wing and lower fin: CCCP 76502.

DRAAF

MiG-17 Bare metal overall, black serial on nose: '46', '102', '136' (393 Av. Regt.).
Su-25 Stone/sand/green over, pale grey under, black serial on nose, green fin tip: '23' (? unit).
Mi-4 Olive drab overall, black serial on mid-fuselage: '241' (232 Av. Regt.).
Mi-8 'Hip-C' Olive/sand over, light grey under, black serial on mid fuselage: '378' (232 Av. Regt., Kabul).
Mi-25 'Hind-D' Olive/sand over, light grey under, black serial on rear fuselage: '317' (? Attack Hel. Sqn., Kabul).
An-26 Olive/sand/stone over, light grey under, no serial evident (? Av. Regt., Kabul).

7.7. Ceylon, 1971

Ceylon achieved independence in 1948 and among the armed forces the Royal Ceylon Air Force (RCyAF) was set up with British assistance. From 1958 there were riots involving the Tamil minority, but the first major insurgency in the country, in the light of economic difficulty and price increases, came from a Sinhalese group in March 1971. The scale of events took the Government by surprise, and elements of the RCyAF, spread across the country, were rapidly recalled to the main base at Katunayake. On 5 April a police station at Wellawaya was attacked and the following day more than 50 installations, including many more police stations, were attacked.

The first unit to be involved was 4 Sqn., equipped with three JetRanger helicopters, which immediately flew resupply missions to ground forces over a wide area to the east and north of

Colombo. By 11 April the squadron had flown 73 sorties. The only other units then operational were 3 Sqn. equipped with Doves and 2 Sqn. with Herons, both of which also flew supply and reconnaissance sorties from Katunayake. In the light of a deteriorating situation, several Jet Provost T.51s were recovered from storage and moved to Katunayake, where they were armed and formed into 6 Sqn. on the 9th. With its resources stretched, Ceylon appealed to other countries for help. On 12 April the Pakistan Air Force (PAF) provided two Alouette IIIs, and the following day the Indian Air Force (IAF) dispatched a further six of the type; on the 14th six Bell 47G-2s arrived in RAF Argosies, having been purchased in the US, and these were formed into 5 Sqn.

The most controversial source of aid was the Soviet Union, which from the 22nd flew in a MiG-15UTI, five MiG-17Fs and two Ka-26s in several An-22 flights. The helicopters went to 2 Sqn. while the fighters joined the Jet Provosts of 6 Sqn. The helicopters, armed with light automatic weapons and grenades, and the Jet Provosts, fitted for 60lb rockets and light bombs, were in great demand across the island for attacks on identified ambushes, road blocks and insurgent vehicles. Although based at Katunayake, the helicopters flew from Mannar, Anuradhapura, Kurunegala and Puttalam. The MiGs are believed to have flown some sorties, perhaps piloted by Russians, before the rebellion was crushed in May. The state of emergency continued until 1977.

Ceylon suffered from limited insurgency in 1971, but was unable to exercise immediate control. Aid came from several sources, including the Soviet Union, which supplied five MiG-17Fs, flown by Russian pilots with 6 Sqn. at Katunayake. They were not as effective as the Jet Provosts of the squadron, which were able to operate close-support sorties in familiar territory. Seen here after the uprising is CF906. (M. Robson)

AIRCRAFT MARKINGS

MiG-17F *Bare metal overall, black serial on upper fin: CF903 (6 Sqn.).*
Jet Provost T.51 *Silver overall, black serial on rear fuselage: CJ701, CJ711 (6 Sqn.).*
Heron *White over, silver under, red cheat line, black serial on rear fuselage: CR801 (3 Sqn.).*

TABLE OF UNITS: CEYLON, 1971

Unit	Aircraft	Base	Role
RCyAF			
6 Sqn.	Jet Provost T.51, MiG-17F	Katunayake, Puttalam, Kurunegala, Anuradhapura	Coin, ground attack
4 Sqn.	JetRanger	Katunayake	Supply, light gunship
2 Sqn.	Heron, Ka-26	Katunayake	Transport
3 Sqn.	Dove	Katunayake, Mannar	Communications, recce
5 Sqn.	Bell 47G-2	Katunayake, Puttalam, Kurunegala, Anuradhapura, Mannar	Liaison, supply
Pakistani Army			
?	Alouette III	Katunayake	Liaison, supply
IAF			
104 HU	Alouette III	Katunayake, various	Liaison, supply, light gunship

7.8. Sri Lanka, 1978 to date

From shortly after independence in 1948, Ceylon introduced legislation effectively discriminating against the Hindu Tamil minority. In May 1972, coincident with the declaration of the new Sri Lanka Republic, the Tamils formed a United Front (TUF) and proposed a separate Tamil state. The Front became the Tamil United Liberation Front (TULF) in May 1976, and from this date there was increasing anti-Tamil rioting by the predominantly Buddhist population. From the TULF sprang a militant wing, the Liberation Tigers of Tamil Eelam (LTTE), which was banned in May 1978 after several attacks by Tamils on the police. Although the Tamils lived mainly in the east and to the north around Jaffna, their terrorist activities were widespread; on 7 September 1978, they blew up an Air Ceylon HS.748 at Katunayake.

By July 1979 the number of attacks by rebels had increased to the extent that the Government committed four battalions to operations in the Jaffna area. From now there were more Sinhalese attacks on Tamils, and on 2 June 1981 a state of emergency was declared after serious rioting; this was rescinded in 1982. The LTTE was now being supplied with arms on a large scale from mainland India, and in December 1984 several vessels shipping men and arms to Jaffna were strafed by JetRangers from Mannar. Earlier in the year, on 18 May, a state of emergency had again been declared, and ten days later a Sri Lanka Air Force (SLAF) Bell 212 crashed in Batticaloa lagoon, possibly as a result of sabotage. In February 1985 a second helicopter was shot down by rebels on the north coast. Later in the year, at the suggestion of an Israeli advisory group, more aircraft were ordered from abroad to cope with the worsening situation, including six SF.260TPs from Italy and twenty Bell 206s and six Bell 212s through Singapore.

The main SLAF base was moved from Katunayake to Ratmalana, just south of the capital. From early in 1986, amid claims that British and Pakistani pilots were flying for the SLAF, there were several strikes on rebel bases in the Jaffna peninsula; the aircraft involved were reported to be Cessnas and Bell 212 helicopters. In March there was a temporary halt to air attacks on LTTE targets, but when there was serious fighting in January 1987 a Tamil ammunition dump near Jaffna was bombed and destroyed. The situation deteriorated rapidly, and on 20 April 105 civilians were killed in a bomb blast at Colombo bus station; two days later air strikes were resumed from China Bay. On 25 May Tamil targets at Maripay were again attacked from the air. In June the Government turned to Pakistan for assistance with air defence in the light of air drops to Tamils from sympathizers on the mainland, but two months later the Indian Government stepped in to provide a peace-keeping force (IPKF) in Operation 'Pawan': 6,000 men were flown into

TABLE OF UNITS: SRI LANKA, 1986–1987

Unit	Aircraft	Base	Role
SLAF, 1986			
4 Sqn.	Bell 206/212, JetRanger, SA.365	Ratmalana, China Bay	Supply, light gunship, recce
3 Sqn.	Dove, Cessna 150	China Bay	Communications, recce training
2 Sqn.	Cessna 206/337/421, HS.748, DC-3, Heron	Ratmalana	Transport, recce liaison, coin
IAF, 1987			
–	An-32	} Bangalore	Transport (drawn from 12, 19, 33, 48 Sqns.)
25 Sqn.	An-12B		Transport
44 Sqn.	Il-76		Transport
–	Mi-8	Ratmalana, China Bay, Jaffna	Transport, casevac, gunship (drawn from 109, 110, 118, 119 HUs)

Sri Lanka aboard 30 An-32s, six An-12s and four Il-76s of the recently re-formed 44 Sqn.

Troops were flown from a range of bases to the airhead at Bangalore and then to Colombo or Jaffna, and a large number of Mi-8 helicopters also joined the Force. The Indians had secured a fragile peace treaty, but within weeks this had broken down and in mid-October Indian troops were lifted by helicopter to a Tamil base at Wasama outside Jaffna, where there was heavy fighting. There was a second airborne strike on the base on 3 November. The Indians were now involved in heavy fighting in the north and east and suffered severe casualties. By late November the IPKF stood at 25,000 in two divisions, of whom 262 had been killed and 927 wounded, By May 1988 the number in the Force had risen to 50,322, but after more peace talks some troops were withdrawn in June.

The Sri Lankan Government is now totally dependent on India to contain the Tamils and to maintain order among the Sinhalese majority. A major part of the IPKF's work is in eliminating the local production of weapons and maintaining patrols over the sea to prevent the import of arms and ammunition from the mainland.

AIRCRAFT MARKINGS

SLAF
JetRanger *Sand/medium grey overall, black serial on fin: CH556 (4 Sqn.).*
Cessna 337 *White overall, silver lower fuselage, black serial on fin: CC653 (2 Sqn.).*
DC-3 *White over, silver under, red cheat line, black serial on fin: CR-822 (2 Sqn.).*
Riley Skyliner Heron *White over, silver under, red cheat line, black serial on fin: CR-804 (2 Sqn.).*

IAF
Mi-8 *Grey-green/pale grey-green overall, black serial on boom: Z1383 (? HU).*
An-32 *White over, light grey under, black serial on fin: K2711 (? unit).*
Il-76 *White over, light grey under, black serial on fin: K2663 (44 Sqn.).*

When the Tamil separatists began terrorist operations in Sri Lanka (Ceylon) from 1978, the Government responded with military action. The Air Force played a part in supplying ground forces, and helicopters were used for reconnaissance and coastal patrols. This work was of great importance, with the Tamils receiving support and supplies from India by boat. In December 1984 several vessels were strafed by JetRanger helicopters while shipping men and arms to Jaffna. (M. Robson)

7.9. Miscellaneous conflicts and incidents

1. In August 1959 a company of the 1st Bn. Cheshire Regt. was flown to the Maldives from Singapore in Hastings of 48 Sqn. to help an RAF Regt. unit quell local rioting.

2. Since 1960 the IAF has supported Indian Army units fighting Chinese-backed insurgency in Mizoram and Nagaland. Helicopter units have been used to transport commando teams and evacuate wounded, while C-47s and other transports have flown supply sorties. On 3 January 1960 Indian Airlines C-47A VT-CGG was shot down six miles from Taksing.

3. There were three established Portuguese enclaves on the west coast of India, at Diu, Damao and Goa. From Independence, the Indians at-tempted to negotiate a Portuguese withdrawal without success. Non-violent protesters began crossing into Goa from 1955, from where they were first deported, then imprisoned. With elections due in 1962, India decided to conclude the issue by force. In Operation 'Vijay' two brigades of the 17th Division and the 50th Parachute Brigade invaded Goa on 16 December 1961. Resistance from the four Portuguese battalions was light, and within 26 hours the Indians were in occupation. Portugal had asked Britain for transit facilities to support reinforcements but these were denied. Indian Air Force (IAF) units were placed on alert to support ground forces if necessary, and 109 Helicopter Unit (HU) equipped with the Mi-4 was used extensively to evacuate wounded and for liaison. They newly commissioned carrier *Vikrant* was also involved, with 310 INAS flying reconnaissance sorties in the area. The Indian suffered 75 casualties, the Portuguese 51; the latter also lost a frigate. Diu and Damao were occupied without resistance.

4. From 1973 the PAF has flown sorties against insurgents in Baluchistan. F-86 sorties were flown from May that year, and ground forces were supported by Mi-8 and C-130 supply drops; Imperial Iranian Air Force (IIAF) CH-47s were also used in operations. Lacking suitable aircraft for coin operations, the PAF purchased 45 Saab Supporters, which were used operationally from late 1975.

5. After the war of 1971, India and Pakistan agreed on a ceasefire line between Jammu and Kashmir and Baltistan. The line left the Siachen glacier, 100 miles to the west of the Karakoram Pass, as part of Pakistan. In mid-1982 an Indian force was ejected from the area, but in 1984 an Indian brigade dug in at the northern end of the glacier, since when there have been numerous clashes, the most serious of which was in late 1987. Both sides rely heavily on air supply, and helicopters are used to move artillery and stores locally. In June 1986 Pakistani forces fired a Stinger missile at an IAF Cheetah helicopter, which took evasive action. The IAF maintains a significant helicopter force in the region and other fixed-wing units are committed to maintaining Indian integrity. Units based in the region or committed to operations there include 126 HU with Mi-26s, 125 HU with Mi-25s, and Mi-17 and Cheetah units at Ladakh; 25 and 44 Sqns. with Il-76MDs at Palam; and 20 Sqn. with MiG-27Ms. In addition, several Jaguar and MiG-23BM and MF units are based in the region.

6. A Pakistan Air Force C-130 carrying President Zia and the US Ambassador to Pakistan blew up shortly after take-off from Bahawalpur on 18 August 1988, killing all 37 on board. At the time of writing the cause of the crash is not known, but it is believed to have been the result of either a bomb placed on board or a SAM hit.

7. On 3 November 1988, 400 Tamil mercenaries staged a coup in the Maldives, the third attempt to overthrow the Government there in ten years. The Indian Government responded to a request for help and sent 1,600 paratroopers by Il-76s of 44 Sqn. to Hulhule Airport. Three naval vessels were also involved. Further troops were flown in by An-12 and An-32 transports from Trivandrum and by the 4th a flight of Mi-8 helicopters was operating from the airport. Some mercenaries escaped on the ship *Progress Light* with hostages. The vessel was tracked by IAF Tu-142Ms and Il-38s from Goa and was finally boarded on the 6th.

8: China, Korea and Japan

The Chinese Civil War began well before the Second World War, but was interrupted by the Japanese occupation. It broke out again at the end of the war, with vicious fighting between Nationalists and Communists. The Nationalists, with American help, deployed large numbers of aircraft, although details of the air fighting are hard to come by. In this particular war the use of air power made no difference to the outcome, and by 1950 the Nationalists had been forced off the mainland. Many, however, fled to Burma, from which troubled country they made several unsuccessful attempts to invade China. Burma has had internal problems since 1948 and United States involvement with the Kuomintang in the north did nothing to help stabilize the country; indeed, there is clear evidence that the Chinese in Burma have a substantial investment in the drugs trade.

In the Korean peninsula, the North Korean attempt in 1950 to unify the country by military means almost succeeded, but the United Nations – essentially the United States – managed to turn near-defeat to near-victory through the landings at Inchon. Instead of settling for the postwar border of the 38th parallel, however, the United Nations commander, MacArthur, decided to move into the north; the North Koreans appeared totally demoralized, and staggering territorial gains were made within weeks. Rather than consolidate, the United Nations forces pushed on to the Yalu river, but this action was perceived as a threat by the Chinese, who suddenly swarmed across the river in support of the North Koreans at the beginning of November. Days later, the degree of Soviet support was demonstrated when the first MiG-15s appeared, flying from the sanctuary of Manchurian bases.

There is little publicly available evidence of any Sino-Soviet master plan to occupy Korea, and warnings of Chinese concern at North Korea being used as a springboard for an invasion of Manchuria were given in October. The Korean War eventually reached stalemate in July 1953 after both sides had suffered large casualties. There remains only an uneasy armistice, and from time to time there are incidents, any one of which might herald the start of the threatened unification of the country from the north. The Russians and Chinese are sufficiently uncertain of the North Koreans that they both now limit arms sales.

Notwithstanding its commitment in Korea, in October 1950 the new People's Republic (PRC) also turned its attention to Tibet, which it claimed as Chinese. Again the Americans indulged in covert operations using bases in Formosa and Thailand before finally withdrawing

The flexibility provided by naval air power was of enormous importance to the United Nations forces in Korea, and there were rarely fewer than three carriers off the coast. Towards the end of the war, the F2H-2P version of the Banshee saw active duty with VC-61. These aircraft are almost certainly from Detachment G on board USS Oriskany. The nearest machine is 128857/917PL. (USN via R. F. Dorr)

support for rebel tribesmen in 1970.

With the end of the Korean War the PRC turned its attention once again to the Nationalist stronghold on Formosa. From 1954 bases on offshore islands were shelled, and in the summer of 1958 the Chinese People's Armed Forces Air Force quadrupled the number of fighters on bases across the Formosa Straits. Air fighting began in August, and over six weeks many CPAFAF MiGs were destroyed, including some by Sidewinder air-to-air missile, the first time that such weapons had been used in anger. Eventually the temperature cooled, until in January 1979 the United States broke off diplomatic relations with Taiwan, having reached a new accord with China.

The deterioration of Sino-Soviet relations no doubt contributed to the change of American policy. In 1962 China invaded India at several disputed points on their extensive common border. The battles were fought high up in mountainous terrain, and the Indians were forced to concede important passes. The Russians were concerned at the Chinese action since there were numerous sections of the Sino-Soviet border which were also in dispute; in addition, the USSR saw India as an ally in the region, and had supplied many of India's aircraft. The Russians thus withdrew support from China, which critically affected the latter's arms supplies, and through to the end of the Cultural Revolution the indigenous aircraft industry failed to meet the needs of the Air Force.

Fighting between China and the Soviet Union finally broke out in 1969 but fortunately was limited, although both sides still maintain a careful watch on each other, especially at key border posts. China's last major military excursion was the invasion of North Vietnam in 1979. Again the cause involved the Soviet Union, which had concluded a treaty with North Vietnam in 1978 after which, with implied Soviet support, North Vietnam had invaded China's ally Kampuchea. The Chinese suffered a bloodied nose and were soon forced to withdraw, having met initial objectives only before the North Vietnamese rallied. With the opening up of China to trade with the West in recent years, it may be that the greatest threat posed over the next decade will be economic rather than military.

8.1. The Chinese Civil War, 1945–1949

Strictly speaking, the Chinese Civil War began on 1 August 1927 when the Chinese Communist Party led by Mao Tse-tung revolted against the Nationalist Kuomintang (KMT) Government of Chiang Kai-shek. In 1937 Japan invaded, and to some extent the two Chinese elements co-operated against the common enemy. Much of Manchuria plus the coastal region was occupied, and the Japanese sponsored two air forces to support their own Army Air Force, the Manchoukuoan Air Force in 1938 and the Cochin China Air Force in 1940. Both were equipped with second-line Japanese aircraft and charged primarily with air defence. With her sea ports cut off, China was dependent on supplies from India and Burma, and to protect the supply routes and harass the enemy Major Claire L. Chennault was invited to reorganize what was left of the Chinese Air Force. He formed the American Volunteer Group (AVG), equipped with three squadrons of P-40B fighters.

In July 1942 the AVG was incorporated into the 14th Air Force as the 23rd Fighter Group, and over the next two years the United States Army Air Force (USAAF) built a number of airfields to accommodate B-29 bombers and transports. As the war drew to a close, the Soviet Union liberated Manchuria and handed over arms and some captured aircraft to the Communist Party, which formed the People's Liberation Army (PLA) in May 1946. The National Air Force was equipped with a range of inherited American types, including the B-25, P-51B and D and P-40N, and some Tachikawa Ki-55 trainers.

At the Japanese surrender the United States airlifted over 500,000 KMT troops to key ports and to the north in an attempt to prevent an immediate communist takeover. Then, in direct support, Marines of III Amphibious Corps landed at Tientsin on 30 September 1945. Five infantry and two artillery regiments were supported by 12 and 24 Marine Air Groups (MAG), equipped mainly with F4U-4 Corsairs and based outside Peking; also in support were MAG-32 with F4U-4s at Tsangkon and MAG-25 with R4D transports at Tsingtao. The task of the Marines was to enable the Nationalists to stabilize the area while disarming the Japanese. Much of their work involved escorting trains or convoys of essential materials, during which the Corsairs flew cover against communist ambush. The marines departed from June 1946, having made relatively little use of their aircraft.

Through early 1946 there were talks aimed at reaching a settlement, but as these broke down the fighting extended through Manchuria and in Anhwei and Kiangsu provinces around the Yangtze river. Initially the Nationalist forces seemed to be dominating events, but from 1947 the PLA gradually extended its grip. By now the KMT Air Force operated a consolidated range of aircraft, including a Wing of 40 P-47Ds, three Wings of P-51C/Ds, one Wing each of 40 B-25Cs and 40 B-24Js and two Wings of 70 C-46s and C-47s. These aircraft were concentrated around Peking and along the coast. With poor communications and long distances, they were to make little impact on the outcome of the war, and only transport aircraft played any significant part.

Chennault returned to China and formed the China Nationalist Relief and Rehabilitation Administration Air Transport (CNRRAAT), which contracted with the United Nations Relief and Rehabilitation Agency (UNRRA), initially using fifteen C-46s, four C-47s and a Piper Cub floatplane. The first operations were flown on 3 February 1947. With roads, railways and waterways destroyed and a vast population to sustain, aircraft were the only means of transporting food and raw materials. Over time the loads were increasingly military in nature. The airline supported KMT troops with massive airlifts, notably at Hsuchow, Weihsien and Taiyuan. When the UNRRA contract ran out in 1948 the service became known as Civil Air Transport (CAT); two million ton-miles a month were now being flown. Apart from small-arms fire and latterly some effective anti-aircraft artillery, there was no opposition to concern CAT; rather it was fuel and maintenance problems that caused most difficulty. As the PLA took more towns and cities, KMT bases were overrun and CAT pulled more of its fleet back to its HQ at Kunming.

By late 1948 the PLA controlled most of eastern and central China with a Nationalist pocket around Peking and Tientsin, both of which cities fell in January 1949. Caught up in the civil war was the British frig-ate HMS *Amethyst*. The ship had been shelled by the communists from the north bank of the Yangtze between Shanghai and Chinkiang on 20 April 1949. Many crew were dead or injured, and medical supplies and a doctor were flown in aboard a Sunderland of 88 Sqn. from Hong Kong on the 21st. The eventual escape of the frigate in July is outside the scope of this book. On 11 May the RAF moved 28 Sqn. equipped with the Spitfire FR.18 from Malaya to Hong Kong. With the outcome of the war now inevitable CAT and its competitors, Central Air Transport Company (CATC) and China National Aviation Corporation (CNAC), flew their aircraft to sanctuary at Hong Kong, Hainan and Formosa, but while CAT established itself at Kaohsiung on Formosa its rivals found 73 of their aircraft held in Hong Kong in a legal wrangle. Seven did, however, flee to Communist China to join the 134 KMT aircraft captured by the PLA.

From the summer of 1948 the newly established CIA began using CAT and in September 1949 agreed a formal contract for support, particularly in the infiltration and exfiltration of agents. The CIA helped Chennault buy out CNAC and CATC, and eventually, in 1952, he secured the release of what were now his aircraft. The relationship of CAT with the CIA was to have great significance in the future.

The Chinese People's Republic was founded on

TABLE OF UNITS: THE CHINESE CIVIL WAR, 1945—1949

Unit	Aircraft	Base	Role	Dates
USMC				
MAW-1				
MAW-1 HQ	OY-1	Peking	Liaison	06/10/45 to 00/06/46
MAG-12				
VMF-323	F4U-4	Peking, Tsingtao	Ground attack	} 23/10/45 to 00/09/46
VMF-542	F4U-5N	Peking, Tsingtao	Night fighter	
MAG-24				
VMF-115	F4U-4	} Peking, Tsingtao	Ground attack	} 23/10/45 to 00/04/47
VMF-211	F4U-4		Ground attack	
VMF-533	F7F-2N		Night fighter	
MAG-32				
VMF-224	F4U-4	} Tsangkon	Ground attack	} 21/10/45 to 00/06/46
VMF-311	F4U-4		Ground attack	
VMSB-343	SB2C		Recce	
MAG-25				
VMR-152	R4D	} Tsingtao	Transport	28/10/45 to 00/06/46
VMR-153	R5C			
VMR-253	R4D			
CNAF, 1948				
3 FG				
4 FG	} P-51C/D	Various	Ground attack, air defence	
5 FG				
11 FG	P-47D	Various	Ground attack	
1 BG	B-25C	Various	Medium bombing	
8 BG	B-24J	Kunming	Heavy bombing	
1 ATG	C-46A/D	Various	Transport	
2 ATG	C-46A/D, C-47	Various	Transport	
12 RS	F-5E	?	PR	
6 Comp G	AT-6, AT-11, Mosquito FB.26	Various	Training, liaison, observation	

1 October 1949 and initially its air force consisted of captured aircraft, including a number of P-51Ds which were used briefly in Korea in 1950. The Soviet Union had refurbished two Japanese aircraft factories at Mukden and Harbin and now began supplying piston-engined fighters. In February 1950, when the Russians agreed to provide the MiG-15 against payment in gold, the Chinese People's Armed Forces Air Force (CPAFAF) comprised about 150 aircraft including F-51Ds, B-25Cs, C-46s, C-47s, La-11s and Yak-9s. Meanwhile the Nationalist Government had established itself on Formosa in December. The Chinese Nationalist Air Force (CNAF) comprised about 200 aircraft, including 110 F-51Ds and some F-47Ds; two further squadrons of F-47s were delivered from the USA. Both sides now set about building up their armed forces, but with the CPAF occupied elsewhere there would be no significant fighting between the two until 1958.

AIRCRAFT MARKINGS

Few photographs or records of Nationalist aircraft of the period are available, but it seems that most aircraft were finished olive drab over and pale blue or grey under. The current style of national marking was worn. Some P-51Ds were finished bare metal overall with blue/white striped rudders and US serials across the fin. One camouflaged P-38L Lightning had blue/white striped fins and rudders, with the serial number 424082.

8.2. Burma, 1948 to date

Burma became an independent state on 4 January 1948. Almost immediately civil war broke out, first between Communist and Government forces and then from August through a revolt of the powerful Karen tribe. An early aircraft loss was Peacock Airlines Norseman XY-ABB, which was destroyed at Rangoon. The Government was thus preoccupied when the final stages of the Chinese Civil War resulted in large numbers of nationalist Kuomintang (KMT) troops crossing into Burma for sanctuary. The CIA decided to support the nationalists, who formed the anti-communist National Salvation Army (NSA) in the Shan states to the north. They were regularly supplied by unmarked aircraft, mainly Civil Air Transport (CAT) C-46s flying from Formosa via Bangkok. In April 1950, 4,000 NSA troops made a two-pronged attack into China's Yunnan province but were defeated when the expected popular uprising failed to materialize. A second invasion attempt shortly afterwards also failed.

The KMT was now fortified by 700 troops from Formosa and the recruitment of local tribesmen, and the CIA renewed its supply effort with arms being routed through the Sea Supply Company in Bangkok. The Second World War airfield at Myitkyina was opened up as a main base, and CAT flights increased as preparations were made for a third invasion. Comprising a force of 12,000 men, this was launched in August 1952, but again it was unsuccessful. It is understood that the CPAFAF used piston-engined fighters of Soviet origin in pushing back the NSA.

Frustrated at their attempts to occupy Chinese territory, the KMT turned its attention to settling in northern Burma. The area included part of the infamous 'Golden Triangle' on the Burma-Thailand-Laos borders, where vast amounts of opium were grown and refined as heroin. The Chinese fought with the local hill tribes for control of the lucrative market and the right to exact tolls. By now the Union of Burma had established an air force (UBAF), initially comprising a flight each of Spitfire F.18s and Mosquito FB.6s, and these were used in support of ground forces flying against Communist, Karen and KMT groups. They operated out of Mingaladon and Meiktila with limited success, although several thousand KMT were forced to evacuate to Formosa in 1954. During 1955 a number of ex-Israeli Spitfire F.IXs were purchased.

Eventually the KMT problem was resolved through joint action with the Chinese Communists. By 1960 the KMT had established a secure base with a large airfield on the Mekong where China, Burma and Laos meet. There was considerable evidence of continuing CIA support, and the plans for attack were made in secret. Three divisions of the People's Liberation Army (PLA) and 5,000 Burmese troops, supported by Spitfire LF.9 and Sea Fury fighters, attacked the 10,000 defenders, who were finally beaten on 26 January 1961. CAT aircraft were then employed evacuating 4,200 KMT to Taiwan and 6,000 to Laos. A month later an unmarked B-24 carrying arms was shot down over Burma, reportedly by a Sea Fury. The Government now turned its attention again to the Karens, Communists and other tribal groups in revolt. The UBAF had received 24 Provost T.53s from Britain in 1959 and, armed with two 0.303 machine guns and a light underwing bomb load, these were used extensively for the next few years. Flying from Meiktila and up-country strips, they were ideal for use against lightly armed groups of guerrillas, but only when targets were identified.

The various rebel groups have never effectively collaborated, and their strategy appears to be the denial of areas to Government forces rather than offensives against key centres of administration. Without sound intelligence and good co-operation between ground and air forces, aircraft are relatively ineffective. The UBAF has subsequently updated its inventory with limited US aid, primarily to help Burma deal with the narcotics trade. The first helicopters were six Bell 47Gs delivered in 1960, and these were reportedly supplemented by thirteen HH-43Bs around 1970. Eighteen Bell 205As and seven 206Bs were delivered from 1975, and these have seen extensive service on the Laotian border, at least five having been lost. The US supplied eight AT-33As in 1967 and some remain in service, but these aircraft proved to be of limited value. Five were lost when they struck a mountain near Rangoon in 1974. The Air Force needed a more robust and versatile aircraft that could combine training and fighting roles, and so at least twenty SF.260MBs and WBs were purchased from 1975, while sixteen PC-7s have been added more recently.

During 1978 an SF.260 was shot down, and in June 1982 Karens succeeded in bringing down two helicopters. A Bell 205A was brought down on 12 February 1984. The civil war continues with sporadic low-key action, and without total co-operation from her neighbours Burma will never be capable of dealing with the opium warlords.

AIRCRAFT MARKINGS

Spitfire LF.9 *Dark Sea Grey/Medium Sea Grey over, Sky under, white serial on rear fuselage: UB439, UB442, UB450.*
Beech D18S *Bare metal overall, white fuselage decking, black serial on rear fuselage: UB377.*
Provost T.53 *Light grey overall, black serial on rear fuselage: UB208.*
Sea Fury FB.11 *Bare metal overall, black serial on rear fuselage: UB458.*

8.3. Tibet, 1950–1970

The Chinese province of Xizang Zizhiou, better known in the West as Tibet, lies to the north of the Himalayas. It has long been claimed by China, and on 16 October 1950 a force of 120,000 Chinese troops, supported by light bombers, invaded, soon occupying Chamdo in the east. The teenage national ruler, the Dalai Lama, fled south to the border with Bhutan, but by May 1951 the fighting was over and he returned to Lhasa as the puppet of the Chinese in August. Not all the population was easily subdued, and Khamba tribesmen who maintained resistance pockets were attacked by CPAFAF Il-2s and Il-10s from late 1951 after the Chinese had entered the capital. In the light of pressure on the economy as a result of the occupation, Golok Khamsa tribesmen revolted in March 1956, following which the Chinese again began a bombing campaign.

The United States now took an interest, and from 1957 began secretly training Khambas at Camp Hale, Colorado, returning them to Tibet in C-130s from Taiwan via Chiang Mai, Thailand. For resupplying the guerrillas the CIA relied on CAT, flying C-46s and C-47s out of Formosa. In March 1959 the Dalai Lama fled to Nepal as the Chinese People's Liberation Army Air Force (CPLAAF) built bases at Nagchuka, Kampa Zhong and Tingri further to establish their grip on the province. By May 1960 the CIA was supporting 14,000 guerrillas in Tibet from bases in Okinawa, Taiwan, Thailand and Laos, notwithstanding Tibetan casualties estimated at 90,000 in nine years. Despite further CIA attempts to maintain a force in the field through a further air proprietary, Air Ventures Inc., support was eventually withdrawn in 1970.

8.4. Korea, 1950–1953

At the end of the Second World War, the Japanese occupied Korea. The Soviet Union was given responsibility for disarming the Japanese north of the 38th parallel, while the United States had a similar task in the south. It was then assumed that the two Koreas would unify but this did not happen. Instead, a communist regime developed in the north, and Kim Il Sung was proclaimed President of the Democratic People's Republic of Korea in September 1948, just three months before the Russians departed; in the south, Dr. Syngman Rhee became President at the same time. For the next two years there were incidents across the parallel but the Americans, who retained an advisory group in the south, underestimated the military strength of the north and the degree of anti-Rhee feeling in the south, where no progress was being made to rebuilding and reform.

Without warning, the North Koreans invaded the south at 0400hrs on 25 June 1950, quickly reaching Kaesong. The United Nations met, and in the absence of the Soviet Union adopted a resolution calling for the withdrawal of North Korean forces. Two days later, as the US agreed to give support to South Korea, the UN called on member nations to give aid in repelling the invasion. That day USAF B-29s bombed targets on the Han river outside Seoul, but this did not prevent the capital falling on the 29th. The North Korean People's Army (NKPA) pushed south relentlessly. The first US troops of the 24th Infantry Division had landed at Pusan on 1 July, and when they met the NKPA on the 4th at Osan the leading elements were routed.

By 2 August the Americans, now forced back to the Naktong river, had reinforced the initial division with three more and the First Marines Brigade. They now held a perimeter roughly forty miles around Pusan, and as the British 27th Brigade arrived from Hong Kong, plans were already in hand for relieving the position. It was decided to mount an invasion way behind enemy lines at Inchon, the gateway to Seoul. Involving no fewer than 230 allied ships and risking high tides, the invasion was successful, and by the 26th X Corps led by the Marines had retaken Seoul; at the same time UN forces broke out of the Pusan pocket. Whereas it was the UN intention to stabilize the borders at the 38th parallel, the Supreme UN Commander, General MacArthur, thought otherwise, and South Korean Republic of Korea (ROK) troops crossed the parallel on 1 October, followed a week later by US forces. UN troops now advanced at a very fast rate: on the 19th Pyongyang fell as the 187th Regimental Combat Team was parachuted into positions north of the city to cut supply lines and escape routes, and on 25 October the ROK 6th Division reached Chosan on the Yalu river, where they were suddenly confronted by counterattacking Chinese troops of the Chinese People's Volunteer Army (CPVA).

The entry of the Chinese into the war came as a total surprise, and within days the UN forces were forced to retreat. The next surprise for the UN came on 1 November, when for the first time Chinese MiG-15 fighters appeared over North Korea; the first major air battle followed on the 8th. After a lull in the fighting as diplomatic moves were made, MacArthur launched an offensive on the 24th, which was followed by a Chinese counterattack on the 26th. On the east coast, the UN was forced to evacuate Hungnam and Wonsan by sea and air, and on Christmas Day the Chinese crossed the 38th parallel. A fresh communist offensive began on New Year's Day, and within three days Seoul was once more in communist hands. By the middle of the month the Chinese were halted at a line from Suwon to Wonju.

The UN Eighth Army in turn counterattacked, retaking Seoul on 13 March and recrossing the parallel on the 22nd. On 11 April MacArthur was relieved of his command after public criticism of President Truman's concept of limited war, and General Ridgway was appointed to succeed him. The Chinese then began their spring offensive, and after the Battle of Imjin River the Eighth Army was pushed back to a position north of Seoul. The front line now stabilized as UN Air Forces began Operation 'Strangle' in an endeavour to cut the Chinese supply routes, but without a committed ground offensive the CPVA was able to conserve its stocks and the operation failed to meet its objectives through no fault of the Air Forces.

Moves were now made to arrange a ceasefire, and armistice negotiations began at Kaesong on 10 July, discussions which were to drag on for two years. Henceforward, much of the air effort would be directed to forcing the Chinese to maintain the negotiations. The first sticking point came over the repatriation of prisoners-of-war. Nearly half of those taken by UN forces did not wish to return, but the Chinese rejected the idea of voluntary repatriation. By May 1952 the talks were at a stalemate, so to concentrate the communist mind major air strikes on the North Korean power system began on 23 June. Then on 11 July, and again on 29 August, Pyongyang was subjected to the heaviest air raids of the war. In October an indefinite recess in the talks was announced, but at the end of March 1953 the Chinese agreed to the voluntary exchange of sick and wounded prisoners. On 26 April armistice talks resumed at Panmunjom, but UN forces maintained pressure. On 13 May the North Korean irrigation dams were breached, and the following week the American National Security Council determined that, if conditions dictated, the war would be pursued into China.

The prisoner-of-war problem was finally resolved on 8 June, but two days later the Chinese launched yet another offensive at Kumsong, primarily for reasons of 'face' and to establish the most favourable ceasefire line. The armistice was signed on 27 July and became effective at 2200hrs.

This brief summary of events and the details of the air war that follow necessarily make little reference to the war on the ground, which was as vicious as any in modern times. South Korean military casualties were put at 415,000 dead and 249,000 wounded, while the Americans, who bore the brunt of the fighting, lost 33,629 men

with 105,785 wounded. The other UN participants lost over 3,000 dead and nearly 12,000 wounded; estimates of Chinese and North Korean dead range from 1 to 1½ million. UN Air Forces flew 1,040,708 sorties for the loss of 2,670 aircraft on operations, while North Korean and Chinese losses certainly exceeded 2,200 aircraft. North and South Korea remain technically at war, and from time to time there have been border incidents.

USAF COMBAT AIRCRAFT MARKINGS
During the period of the Korean War the USAF was using a system of 'buzz' markings to identify aircraft flying at low level in peacetime; strangely, this practice was retained throughout the war. The markings comprised a two-letter code identifying the type, followed by the last three numbers of the serial; where the last three numbers were duplicated, they were followed by a suffix letter. The markings were applied prominently on the fuselage, normally in front of or behind the wing. Letter codes used by aircraft of the Korean War are set out below.

BC	B-26	FQ	F-82	LTA	T-6
BE	B-45	FS	F-84	RF	RF-51
FA	F-94	FT	F-80	TA	T-6
FF	F-51	FU	F-86	TR	T-33

AIRFIELDS
The United Nations applied numbers with a 'K' prefix to South Korean airfields, and to certain North Korean airfields from which UN aircraft operated. Those identified are set out below.

Number	Name	Number	Name
K1	Pusan (West)	K16	Seoul
K2	Taegu	K18	Kangnung
K3	Pohang	K24	Pyongyang
K4	Sachon	K27	Yonpo
K5	Taejon	K37	Taegu West
K6	Pyongtaek	K40	Cheju
K8	Kunsan	K41	Chongiu
K9	Pusan (East)	K46	Hoengsong
K10	Chinhae	K47	Chunchon
K13	Suwon	K55	Osan
K14	Kimpo		

8.4.1. AIR SUPERIORITY
At the outbreak of the war the North Korean Air Force (NKAF) possessed a fighter regiment with about 70 Yak-9s and La-7s and -11s and a ground-attack regiment with 65 Il-2s and -10s, plus about 30 Yak-18 and Po-2 trainers. The Republic of Korea Air Force (ROKAF) comprised a handful of trainers. The NKAF fighters were soon in action against the airfields being used to evacuate civilians, destroying a C-54 on the ground at Kimpo on 25 June. Three F-82G squadrons, the 4th, 68th and 339th, based at Naha, Itazuke and Yokota respectively, were ordered to cover the evacuation. There were also two F-80C Wings based in Japan, and of these 8 FBG at Itazuke was committed since 35 FIG at Johnson AB was

effectively out of range. Both Wings retained some of the F-51s from which they were in the process of converting.

Three NKAF fighters, including at least one Yak-9, were shot down over Seoul on the 27th, the first enemy loss of the war being claimed by Lt. W.G. Hudson of 68 F(AW)S. Later in the day four Il-10s were shot down by four F-80Cs of 8 FBG. With demonstrable supremacy in the sky, UN air effort was directed at ground-support and interdiction, although the USMC's VMF(N)-513, a night fighter unit, was placed under 8 FBG's control for a six-week period from 3 August. In September 8 FBG relinquished its air defence role, which was assumed by 51 FIG with the F-80Cs based at Kimpo after the Inchon landings. At the beginning of November, the UN received a shock with the introduction into combat of the first MiG-15 of the CPAFAF, based at Antung across the Yalu river. On the 1st several MiGs attacked a T-6 and its F-51 escort, while on the 8th Lt. R. Brown of 16 FIS brought down the first MiG-15 of the war while escorting B-29 bombers on a raid against Sinuiju.

However, it was clear that the F-80 was no match for the faster MiG, and on 11 November the US-based 4 FIW, equipped with F-86A, was directed to the Korean theatre. Unfortunately the aircraft were not adequately protected for their sea transit, and many suffered corrosion damage by the time they reached Japan. Even so, sufficient aircraft were made airworthy to equip 336 FIS, which began operations from K14 on 15 December. The first F-86 MiG kill came on the 17th, to Lt. Col. B. Hinton flying F-86A 491236 while he was leading a flight of four aircraft. No sooner had 4 FIW arrived in Korea, however, than it had to vacate K14 for the safety of Japan as the Chinese advance overran the airfield. At this stage in the war there were few airfields capable of handling jets, and for the time being 27 Fighter Escort Group (FEG) took over air defence work flying from K2. Despite being equipped with the F-84E, on 21 and 23 January the 523rd FES destroyed, respectively, one and four MiGs while supporting an attack on Sinuiju.

The 336th FIS of 4 FIW returned to Korea on 22 February, but being based at K2 its aircraft could patrol no further than Pyongyang until it moved on 6 March to K13, where the Wing was to remain for the rest of the war. Three MiG-15s were shot down in March, fourteen in April and five in May, during which latter month Capt. J. Jabarra became the first jet 'ace' (five kills) when he brought down two aircraft on the 20th. His 334 FIS was part of a 28-aircraft group which fought 50 MiGs over the Yalu river. The Chinese fighters, also flown by Soviet instructors from June, were all based around Antung and generally only ventured south as far as Sinanju, retreating to sanctuary in the Manchurian bases which were placed strictly out of bounds to UN pilots.

The triangular area from Antung along the Yalu to Suiho and south to Sinanju became known as 'MiG Alley'.

Large numbers of MiG-15s would patrol at heights in excess of 45,000ft, where they had a distinct advantage over the slower F-86A, diving down to fight when it suited them. In contrast, the NKAF began night nuisance raids on UN airfields using Yak-18 or Po-2 trainers with the second crew member throwing hand grenades from the cockpit. Dubbed 'Bedcheck Charlies', these raiders were disproportionately troublesome. On 17 June the first F-86A was lost to a Po-2 raid at K13 and a second aircraft seriously damaged. These raids continued throughout the war and there was no satisfactory answer to them. One attacker was shot down by a B-26 which happened to cross the aircraft, while another was flown through by a pursuing F-94B of 68 FIS. The AT-6, F-82G, F7F-5N, F4U-4N and F3D-2 were all tried without success, although towards the end of the war Lt. G. Bordelon USN

achieved ace status: flying an F4U-5N with VC-3, but attached to the 5th AF, he brought down five of the night intruders.

The first dogfights involving Soviet instructors occurred in mid-June, but in three days ten MiGs were lost to two F-86s. By the end of June the F-86 had brought down 42 of the aircraft for the loss of three Sabres and the expenditure of 1,024 0.50in-calibre rounds per aircraft engaged successfully. By the end of August there were three regiments of MiG-15s, based at Fencheng, Antung, Uiju, Takushan, Tatunkou and Suiho and with a major rear base and servicing facility at Mukden. The MiG pilots developed new tactics to take advantage of the aircraft's greater speed and practical endurance. These included working in 'trains' – flying staggered parallel tracks at varied heights – enabling later 'trains' to pounce on exhausted Sabres returning from dogfights. However, the new tactics did little to shift the balance from the much better trained American pilots.

Following the airfield attacks by B-29 bombers in October, during which many were destroyed or damaged, the decision was taken to re-equip the 51st FIW with the newer F-86E and return it to the air superiority role based at K14. The re-equipment was also necessary to respond to the introduction of the more powerful MiG-15bis, which had entered service in the summer. On 13 December the Chinese ventured south in force, sending out 145 MiGs against the two Sabre Wings. Thirteen MiG-15s were shot down for no loss. Other types were also destroyed occasionally. In June, light bombers had set out to attack the UN-held Cho-do island base, but they were beaten off by F-51s. In November, sixteen La-9s escorted 12 Tu-2s in a second raid, and in the ensuing fighting 4 FIW F-86As destroyed three La-9s and eight Tu-2s.

By the end of 1951 it was estimated that total communist aircraft losses were 339 destroyed with another 100 probables, but a new pattern of MiG activity was now being identified. Large groups of aircraft, apparently flown by novice pilots under supervision, operated at maximum

height, keeping well clear of the F-86 patrols. Over a six-week period the communists gradually became more adventurous until the cycle started again as a new 'course' was introduced to air warfare. The Chinese thus dictated the pace of the air war, but not the outcomes once combat was joined: through 1952, an average of one MiG-15 a day was destroyed, for the loss of one F-86 a week. In terms of equipment it was clear that the F-86E was enabling 51 FIW to score most of the kills, and the later mark was evenly spread between the two Wings to maintain morale. On 10 March, 319 FIS arrived at K13 from Moses Lake AFB with its F-94Bs, to replace the detachment of 68 FIS from Itazuke.

So successful was the Fifth Air Force in its attacks on the North Korean airfields that the MiG-15 never operated from bases south of the Yalu. By April 1952 the NKAF Yak-9s had moved back to Sinuiju, while on the complex of airfields around Antung no fewer than 400 MiGs were seen at one time. In May the communists began using ground control intercept (GCI) radars, enabling the MiGs to position themselves optimally to handle F-86 patrols; at the same time, the USAF set up its own GCI radar on Cho-do island. The Sabres flew 5,190 sorties in the month, the highest in the year, to claim 27 MiG-15s for the loss of one F-51, three F-84s and five F-86s. July saw the arrival of the more powerful F-86F, which went first to 39 FIS, newly transferred from the fighter-bomber role with 18 FBG to 51 FIW.

During September the US Air Force began bombing targets in MiG Alley to draw the MiGs down to fight. In the toughest month of the year, 63 MiG-15s were destroyed for the loss of nine F-86s. Many novice pilots lost their MiGs when turning too tightly, which induced a spin for which the aircraft was notorious. After this, the communist pilots stayed at heights beyond the reach of the F-86, but further advances were to bring near equality in aircraft performance by the spring of 1953. Despite the overall picture of success in combat, it was felt that the six 0.50-calibre machine guns of the F-86 were inadequate

Unit	Aircraft	Base	Squadrons	Dates
4 F(AW)S	F-82G	Naha	Attached to 51 FIW	25/06/50 to 00/06/51
68 F(AW)S	F-82G, F-94B	Itazuke (det. K13)	Attached to 8 FBW	26/06/50 to 22/03/52
339 F(AW)S	F-82G	Yokota	Attached to 35 FIW	26/06/50 to 00/06/51
8 FBW	F-51D, F-80C	Itazuke	35, 36, 80 FBS	26/06/50 to 00/07/50
35 FIG	F-51D	Johnson, K2	39 FIS; trans. to 18 FBG 00/12/50	26/06/50 to 00/12/50
35 FIG	F-51D, F-80C	Johnson, K1, K3, K13	40, 41 FIS	26/06/50 to 00/01/51
4 FIG	F-86A/E	K14, Japan, K2, K13	334, 335, 336 FIS	12/12/50 to 31/07/53
51 FIG	F-86E/F	K13, K14	16, 25, 39 FIS	00/09/51 to 31/07/53
319 FIS	F-94B	K13	Replaced 68 F(AW)S	22/03/52 to 31/07/53

compared to the two 23mm and one 37mm cannon of the MiG-15, and in Project 'Gunval' four F-86Es and six F-86Fs were fitted with four 20mm T-160 cannon in their place. After some initial problems, and given the limited number of rounds carried, the arrangement was judged a success, though not before the war had come to an end.

A more widely applied development was the '6–3' wing for the F-86F, which did away with the leading-edge slat and added six inches and three inches to the chord at the wing root and tip respectively. This modification gave the model improved manoeuvrability at height and in the final months of the war gave US pilots a weapon equal to the enemy, although the MiG always retained a height advantage. Even given the disparity in pilot quality, the Chinese suffered high losses as the war came to an end – 56 in May and 77 in June 1953. On 22 July the last MiG-15 to be brought down fell to 51 FIW, while Capt. R. Parr of 335 FIS, 4 FIG, shot down the last aircraft of the war, an Il-12. Despite the early availability of the superior MiG-15, the Chinese were never able to capitalize on its performance and heavier cannon armament, even with Soviet support, and the air war properly belonged to the better-handled F-86 Sabre. From February 1950 the CPAFAF was supplied with 4,000 MiG-15s, most of which were based behind the Yalu; of these, it is estimated that only 2,000 were available by the end of the war, many having been damaged beyond repair or lost in accidents.

Both sides are believed to have had access to examples of the other's principal fighter, but evaluation made little impact on tactics or redesign: in July 1951 the Royal Navy recovered an early MiG-15 which had crashed in seventeen feet of water off the north-east coast of Korean, while on 3 and 4 February 1952 an F-86 spotted across the Yalu and behaving in a hostile fashion was assumed to be a captured example. According to official US sources, a total of 954 enemy aircraft were destroyed in combat by the American services; of these, 810, including 792 MiG-15s, were claimed by the F-86. The war produced 39 F-86 aces who between them claimed 305 aircraft destroyed in combat. USAF fighters completed 341,269 sorties, and 605 aircraft were lost to enemy action, including 78 F-86s in air combat. A total of 968 USAF fighter pilots were killed or reported missing, of whom 112 were F-86 pilots.

AIRCRAFT MARKINGS

USAF

In general, fighters were left in natural metal finish, although for a short period several F 86As of 4 FIG were finished Olive Drab over, but the paint reduced the aircraft's top speed by 20mph. The exception was the F-82G, which was finished black overall with red markings. Because of the basic similarity in outline between the F-86 and MiG-15, the former were marked with large fuselage and wing bands from shortly after their introduction. Initially these took the form of three black and two white bands of equal width, but from mid-1951 the bands were yellow, outlined thinly in black.

Photographs of Chinese aircraft are rare, but this well-known example shows a line-up of MiG-15s at an airfield across the Yalu river. The colour scheme is believed to have been two shades of green over, with light stone ripples, and medium blue under. The entry of the Soviet-built fighters into the war came as a great surprise to the Americans, who lacked a locally based fighter capable of countering the MiG.

F-82G White spinners: (4)6403, (4)6351, 'Double Trouble' (4 FS); (4)6383, (4)6401 (68 FS); (4)6367 'Lover Boy' (339 FS).

F-80C Code on nose, fuselage lightning stripe and fin/rudder stripe all in yellow: (4)9819/45 'Baby Doll II' (41 FIS). Red nose and fin/rudder stripe, unit badge on fin: (4)9700 (25 FIS).

F-86 Aircraft of 4 FIG marked with yellow horizontal fin/rudder band outlined in black. Machines of 51 FIG had black/white fin/rudder checks. Squadron insignia were carried below the cockpit on 4 FIG aircraft.

F-86A (4)91281 (334 FIS); (4)91110 'Miss Kumsum Mo' (335 FIS); (4)91236 (336 FIS).

F-86E (5)12738, (5)12756 'Hell-er Bent' (16 FIS); (5)12738 (25 FIS); (5)12821, (5)12857 (334 FIS); (5)00623 'Mary and the J's' (335 FIS); (5)12747 'Honest John' (336 FIS).

F-86F (5)24584 'MiG Mad Marine' (25 FIS); (5)12897 'The Huff' (39 FIS); (5)112972 'Billie' (335 FIS).

F-94B Unit badge on nose, blue fuselage stripe, mid-fuselage buzz number: (5)15353 (68 FS). Unit badge on nose, yellow fin/rudder stripe: (5)15449, (5)15428 (319 FIS).

NKAF

Yak-9P Bare metal overall, black serial on fin: 32.

MiG-15 Bare metal overall, red serial outlined in white on forward fuselage: 2057. Red intake and rear fuselage/tail assembly, white serial outlined in blue: 4115.

CPAFAF

MiG-15 Bare metal with red wings, tailplane, upper fin/rudder and lower nose and black serial on nose: 1177. Dark green/light green/pale grey 'wave' pattern over, grey/blue under: no serial.

8.4.2. FIGHTER-BOMBERS

From late 1949 the US Far East Air Force (FEAF) F-51D fighter Wings began re-equipping with the F-80C. At the time of the North Korean invasion, however, few crews were proficient in the new fighter, and the decision was taken to retain one F-80 squadron in each Group while taking the familiar F-51D out of storage for the remaining squadrons. Crews were then to work their way through the F-80 unit until there were sufficient to re-form on the jet type. This process continued until the spring of 1951. For some months there was no clear distinction between the air defence and ground-attack roles since the FEAF had complete domination of Korean skies until the introduction of the MiG-15 into the conflict in November.

At the end of June 1950 the 8th Fighter Bomber Group (FBG) was based at Itazuke with two F-51D squadrons and one of F-80Cs. The 35th Fighter Interceptor Group (FIG) based at Johnson AB operated the same mix; 18 FBG was based at Clark AB on the Philippines, where 44 FBS was retained for air defence with the F-80 while 12 and 67 FBS with the F-51D were sent to Korea. The F-80 units generally operated from Japan while the F-51 squadrons flew from South Korean bases, moving to keep near the front line. The first F-51D unit to operate from Korea was 40 FBS, which moved to Pohang on 16 July. A fourth F-80 Wing, 49 FBG, based in Japan, retained its jets, and two squadrons were dispatched to Taegu while one was retained at Misawa. The immediate task of the war, local air defence, was handled by 8 FBG, but by the end of June all four Wings were supporting ground forces. Many of the missions flown through July and August were against armour and the supply lines.

The F-51D was excellent in the close-support role, and typical loads included one 500lb bomb and six 5in high-velocity aircraft rockets (HVAR), although napalm was also used. After the Inchon landings the Mustangs moved up from Chinhae to Kimpo, and such was their value that large numbers were shipped across from the USA to cover attrition. The F-80 was limited in range when carrying a useful weapon load, and local modifications to the wing-tip tanks were made, increasing their capacity from 165 to 265 gallons, although even then the radius of action was little more than 250 miles compared with 850 for the F-84. The close-support force was expanded from early July with the addition of 77 Sqn. Royal Australian Air Force (RAAF), who took their F-51Ds to Iwakuni where they came under the control of 35 FBG. In early November the South African Air Force (SAAF) committed 2 Sqn., also equipped with the F-51D, and its aircraft initially operated from Pyongyang in support of retreating UN forces. The squadron came under the control of 18 FBG.

The Republic of Korea Air Force (ROKAF) comprised only a few trainers, half of which were destroyed on the ground in the early fighting. From July, in Project 'Bout One', the United States supplied a squadron of F-51Ds with instructors, and by 1952 the ROKAF was operating a Wing of the type from a permanent base at Kangnung. As the war settled down the ground-attack units flew primarily against supply lines, but for many months target intelligence was poor. Until well into 1951 the main routes only were attacked, whereas the Chinese quickly took to using minor routes or moved only at night. From the introduction into combat of the MiG-15, the piston-engined types were confined to close support along the front line or flying combat air patrol (CAP) missions covering downed airmen until the search and rescue (SAR) helicopters arrived.

The first ever jet-versus-jet air combat occurred on 8 November. During an attack on Sinuiju airfield, a flight of four F-80Cs of 51 FIW got between a group of MiG-15s and the Yalu river. In the ensuing combat, one F-80, flown by Lt. R. J. Brown, managed to turn within its adversary and put in a quick burst of 0.5in machine-gun fire; the MiG exploded. The following day a second MiG was brought down by a naval pilot flying an F9F Panther, but the Russian fighter demonstrated its potency in bringing down an RB-29 and a B-29 on the 10th. The jets available in the theatre were also vulnerable, so the Fifth Air Force called for more modern types. The 27th Fighter Escort Group, equipped with the F-84E, was transferred from Bergstrom AFB to Taegu, with a rear base at Itazuke. The F-84 was faster than the F-80 and could carry a heavier weapon load. Its first operations began on 7 December 1950 with an armed reconnaissance by four rocket-equipped aircraft south of Pyongyang. The Group flew mainly armed reconnaissance and close-support sorties, although it had been trained as an escort Group, this function being borne in Korea by the F-86. The priorities for the 27th were established as follows:

1. The destruction of enemy air power.
2. Close support to ground forces.
3. Armed reconnaissance and related strikes.
4. Interdiction of supply lines and communications.
5. Escort for air, naval or ground units.
6. Air defence of military installations.
7. Other missions as required.

In the first full month of operations, the Group flew 2,076 sorties, amounting to more than 6,000 flying hours. Most were in close-support or armed reconnaissance roles.

At the end of January the Group was withdrawn to Itazuke because of the damage done to the airfield at Taegu through overcrowding, but the F-84 pilots had met the MiG-15, three being shot down between 21 and 23 January. From the spring of 1951 there were a number of changes in the deployment of units as the front line became static. In January, 35 FIG was withdrawn to Johnson AB, where it remained in the air defence role, although its 39 FIS was handed over to 18 FBG which was one squadron light, having left its F-80 squadron at Clark AB. In April, 18 FBG moved its units to Chinhae as the sole USAF F-51D Wing, while 8 FBG, now fully operational on the F-80, transferred to Suwon. In the same month, 77 Sqn RAAF was withdrawn to Iwakuni to begin conversion on to the Meteor F.8, with which it returned to Kimpo on 12 July.

The Meteor was soon engaged in fighter sweeps in 'MiG Alley' and in escorting the B-29 raids. In an eight-aircraft sweep on 29 August the first Meteor was lost, but in successive months the type continued probing, claiming several damaged MiG-15s. On 1 December the squadron claimed its first MiG kill, but in this combat three Meteors were lost, and the type was now confined to the ground-attack work for which it was more

suitable. In all, the Meteors were to fly over 15,000 sorties, of a total of 18,872 flown by 77 Sqn, during the course of which 41 pilots were lost. The unit pioneered the use of an Australian-designed weapon, the napalm rocket with an incendiary rather than high-explosive (HE) warhead; although much lighter than the conventional napalm tank, it was extremely accurate. In June, 27 FEG assisted 49 FBG to re-equip with the F-84E while itself being replaced by the 136 FBW, the first Air National Guard (ANG) fighter unit committed to the conflict.

A second ANG F-84 Wing, the 116th FBG, arrived in Japan in August, primarily for air defence although its pilots flew many combat support missions over Korea in the ensuing months. Thus by the summer of 1951 the USAF had one F-51D, one F-80C and two F-84E Wings in Korea, with a third F-84 Wing in Japan in reserve. Talks began at Kaesong on 10 July with a view to ending the war by negotiation, but with stalemate on the ground, pressure on the Chinese

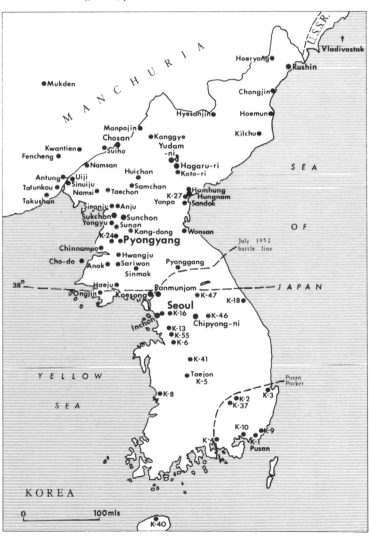

was maintained from the air. Operation 'Strangle' was designed to choke the forward Chinese positions of supplies by hitting at the road and rail links from the north, working within a strip between 38°15'N and 39°15'N. The USAF was allocated the well-defended western sector, the carrier-borne aircraft of Task Force 77 the centre and the ground-based USMC units the eastern sector. Because of the Chinese ability to fight on low levels of supplies and their use of unskilled labour for porterage and road repairs, the effort failed. Had it been associated with a committed drive on the part of the ground forces, demanding the consumption of much higher levels of supply, the strategy might have paid off, but as it was the UN had by now decided to settle for the 1950 borders rather than seek unification.

From September the air forces switched their attention to railways further north, as a result of which the Chinese moved a third MiG-15 regiment on to the Yalu airfields. Through the latter part of 1951 the ground-attack units put in a large number of sorties for very limited returns. To give an indication of the problem in choking the Chinese of supplies, there were sixty divisions in North Korea, each consuming about 45 tons daily – compared with the equivalent American consumption of 610 tons daily. The Chinese requirement demanded the daily use of 6,000 trucks, apart from the limited use of forward rail lines. However, the trucks and road repair gangs only worked at night, and by day all that could be found to attack were the rail links. As local air defence became more effective, the fighter-bombers were forced to drop their bombs from greater altitudes and therefore with less accuracy. On 19 September, 49 FBG put up 48 aircraft carrying a total load of ninety-six 500lb bombs just to cut an exposed section of line south of Sukchon. The formation was bounced by MiGs and the entire bomb load had to be jettisoned. In December the three squadrons of 116 FBG flew some ground-attack missions from Taegu in rotation. The main target was a rail complex at Wonsan. Between 2 and 6 December 159 FBS flew 92 sorties; from the 12th to the 19th 158 FBS made 114 sorties, some being flown by 136 FBS pilots. For this effort the reward was twelve rail cuts, 23 buildings destroyed and one MiG-15. The supply strikes were maintained until the

TABLE OF UNITS: THE KOREAN WAR—FIGHTER-BOMBERS

Unit	Aircraft	Base	Squadrons	Dates
USAF, 1950				
8 FBG[1]	F-51D, F-80C	Itazuke, K2	35, 36, 80 (F-80) FBS	25/06/50 to 00/03/51
35 FIG[2]	F-51D, F-80C	Johnson AB, K1, K2, K3	39, 40, 41 (F-80) FIS	25/06/50 to 00/01/51
18 FBG[3]	F-80C	Clark AB	44 FBS	25/06/50 to 31/07/53
	F-51D	K2, K24, K10	12, 67 FBS plus 39 FBS from Jan. 1951	25/06/50 to 00/01/53
49 FBG	F-80C	K2, Misawa	7, 8 FBS	00/06/50 to 00/07/51
51 FIW[4]	F-80C	K14, K13	16, 25 FIS	00/09/50 to 00/09/51
27 FEG[5]	F-84E/G	Itazuke, K2	522, 523, 524, FES	06/12/50 to 31/05/51
ROKAF, 1950				
1 Sqn.	F-51D	K18	Expanded to Wing by 1952	00/07/50 to 31/07/53
RAAF, 1950				
77 Sqn.	F-51D	Iwakuni, K3, K2	Controlled by 35 FIG	11/08/50 to 00/04/51
SAAF, 1950				
2 Sqn.	F-51D	Pyongyang, K10	Controlled by 18 FBG	22/11/50 to 31/07/53
USAF, 1951–1953				
8 FBG[6]	F-80C, F-86F	K13	35, 36, 80 FBS	00/04/51 to 31/07/53
18 FBG[7]	F-51D, F-86F	K10, K55	12, 39, 67 FBS	25/06/50 to 31/07/53
27 FEG[8]	F-84E/G	Itazuke, K2	522, 523, 524, FES	06/12/50 to 31/05/51
49 FBG[9]	F-80C, F-84E/G	K2, K8	7, 8, 9 FBS	00/06/50 to 31/07/53
136 FBW[10]	F-84E/D	K2	111, 154, 182 FBS	00/06/51 to 00/07/52
116 FBG[11]	F-84E/G	Misawa, Chitose	158, 159, 196 FBS	06/08/51 to 10/07/52
474 FBW[12]	F-84E/G	K8	428, 429, 430 FBS	10/07/52 to 31/07/53
58 FBW[13]	F-84E/G	K2	69, 310, 311 FBS	00/07/52 to 31/07/53
ROKAF, 1951–1953				
1 Wing	F-51D	K18	1, 2, 3 Sqns.	00/07/50 to 31/07/53
RAAF, 1951–1953				
77 Sqn.	Meteor F.8	K14		30/06/51 to 31/07/53
SAAF, 1951–1953				
2 Sqn.	F-51D, F-86F	K10, K55	Under control of 18 FBG	22/11/50 to 31/07/53

Notes:
1. Fully equipped with F-80 by April 1951 and moved to Suwon (K13).
2. Handed over 39 FIS to 18 FBG; remaining units returned to Johnson in air defence role.
3. Retained F-51D until replaced by F-86F January 1953, but 39 FBS transferred to 51 FIG February 1952.
4. Changed to air defence role September 1951; 39 FBS transferred from 18 FBG February 1952.
5. Replaced by 136 FBW.
6. Re-equipped with F-86F from April 1953.
7. Lost 39 FBS to 51 FIW February 1952; 2 Sqn. SAAF under control as third unit.
8. Replaced by 136 FBW.
9. Re-equipped with F-84 July 1951; 'paper' switch with 474 FBW April 1953.
10. ANG unit replaced 27 FEG; renumbered 58 FBG July 1952.
11. ANG unit for air defence. Ground attack sorties flown from K2. Renumbered 474 FBG July 1952.
12. Renumbered from 116 FBG; 'paper' switch with 49 FBG April 1953.
13. 136 FBW renumbered.

summer of 1952, by which time the fighter-bomber units had lost many aircraft to ground fire and a shortage of spares for weary machines had resulted in a much lower sortie rate.

With more unit changes impending, there was also to be a change of tactics. The Japanese-based 116th FBG had begun practising air-to-air refuelling from December 1951 in Operation 'Hi Tide'. From May to early July a number of missions were flown direct from Japan to targets in North Korea, but by July the facilities at Kunsan had been developed to accommodate another F-84 Wing. Since both 136 and 116 FBGs were ANG units, they were statutorily required to return to the US, so their aircraft were handed over to the 58th and 474th FBWs respectively. It was thus the 474th FBW that took up residence in Korea too late to share in the most effective attacks of the war.

Several potential strategies had been developed but, for political reasons, not applied. One of these was the destruction of the North Korean power system. Policy changed in the summer of 1952 to force the pace of negotiations, and plans were put in hand to attack the hydroelectric plants. On 23 June the Suiho, Fusen and Chosen dams were bombed: 124 F-84s and F-80s, plus 70 naval aircraft, dropped 145 tons of bombs on the main Suiho plant just 15 miles from the MiG base at Antung, with 84 F-86s flying top cover, and simultaneously an F-51 force attacked Fusen, USMC Corsairs bombed Chosen and more naval fighters attacked secondary plants at Fusen. In four days 1,276 sorties were flown for the loss of two aircraft; 90 per cent of North Korea's power potential was destroyed and a complete blackout

followed, resulting in an industrial standstill. Operation 'Strangle' was replaced by the follow-on operation, 'Saturate', and by December so limited were the number of targets that some F-84 units turned to night sorties along the rail lines.

The venerable F-51D had performed sterling work with 18 FBG but it was beginning to show its age, and from January 1953 the Group re-equipped at Osan with the new Sabre version, the F-86F with a more powerful engine and wing hardpoints. For some time the F-86s of the air superiority Wings had flown strafing attacks on targets of opportunity while returning from conventional missions, and some aircrew now transferred to the fighter-bomber units. The last F-51D sortie was flown by 67 FBS on 23 January. During the war the F-51D fired 183,034 rockets in 62,607 sorties, with 194 aircraft lost to enemy action. In March it was the turn of 8 FBG to trade in its F-80s for the F-86F at Suwon. At the time of withdrawal from service the F-80 had flown 98,515 sorties for the loss of 143 aircraft; 33,266 tons of bombs and 8,327 tons of napalm had been dropped and 37 enemy aircraft destroyed in the air.

The new aircraft of both Wings joined in an attack on the radio station at Pyongyang on 1 May in retaliation for continuing reports that the Fifth Air Force was bombing civilian targets. The station was put off the air, and, despite advance notice, no MiGs were encountered. May 1953 saw another change of policy when the North Korean irrigation system was attacked for the first time. Starting on 13 May, dams at Toksan, Chosen and Kuwonga were destroyed in concerted

A fine study of a pair of F-86F fighter-bombers of 2 Sqn. SAAF, taking off from Osan and loaded with bombs. The Commonwealth unit was an integral part of 18 FBW and had been equipped with the P-51D until 1952. The nearest aircraft is 602/J 'Imp VIII', while 6??/K is 'Black Dick'. The Sabre was responsible for 792 MiG kills; 110 of these US fighters were lost to enemy action. (Via R. F. Dorr) strikes, the intention being to ruin the rice crop and flood roads and railways. All the dams were destroyed, but that at Kuwonga was drained before the strikes, so flood damage was minimal. In total, five miles of railway line were flooded, as was the airfield at Sunan. There is no doubt that the attacks encouraged the North Koreans to conclude peace talks, but the fighter-bombers maintained the pace of their strikes until the war ended two months later.

In over 250,000 ground-attack sorties, FEAF fighter-bombers dropped a total of 105,454 tons of bombs and 29,256 tons of napalm and fired 288,285 rockets. The average number of operational aircraft available was about 650.

AIRCRAFT MARKINGS

Fighter-bomber aircraft of all air forces were finished bare metal. Buzz numbers were carried, but not by Commonwealth aircraft. Many of the F-51Ds bore irrelevant unit badges carried over from previous service, especially with ANG units. F-84 unit markings are especially difficult to confirm as aircraft changed units on paper, or were redistributed.

F-51D Black serial below cockpit, large K on fin: 28, 39, 40 (1 Sqn. ROKAF). Black serial on rear fuselage: 330, 332 (2 Sqn. SAAF). Red/white/blue spinner, black serial on rear fuselage: A68-781, A68-753 (77 Sqn. RAAF). Serial on fin: (4)484647 'Mouse Meat', blue/yellow spinner and fin, shark mouth, and (4)511736 (both 12 FBS). No buzz number: 474 'Eight Ball' (35 FBS); (4)484910, (4)473888 (39 FBS). Red fin tip: (4)484936 (40 FIS) and (4)472278 'Shoot You're Faded' (41 FIS). Red diagonal stripes on fuselage, red fin tip, serial not displayed: (4)475728 (67 FBS).

F-80C Aircraft of 8 FBG wore coloured 'sunburst' markings on the fin and diagonal stripes on tip tanks in blue (35 FBS), red (36 FBS) or yellow (80 FBS); 49 FBG had coloured noses and a single horizontal fin stripe in blue (7 FBS), yellow (8 FBS) or red (9 FBS); and 51 FIW wore two horizontal fin stripes with coloured noses in blue (16 FIS) or red (25 FIS). Buzz numbers were carried on the mid-fuselage: (4)9550, (4)9181 (7 FBS); (4)9489, (4)9767 (9 FBS); (4)9795 'Kansas Tornado', (4)9650 'Saggin Dragon' (both 16 FIS); (4)9805 (25 FIS). Buzz number on nose: (4)9705 'Ramblin Reck Tew' (35 FBS); (4)8675, (4)9489 (36 FBS); (4)9722, (4)9670 (80 FBS).

Meteor F.8 Black serial on rear fuselage, last three on nose: A77-734, A77-859, A77-881 (77 Sqn. RAAF).

F-84E/G Coloured noses (all units), coloured arrows on tip tanks (except 49 FBG/474 FBW), and coloured tail markings. Buzz number on nose, often suffixed. Tail markings were single diagonal fin stripe (27 FEG, then 136 FBW, then 58 FBW); two horizontal fin/rudder stripes,

single rear fuselage band (116 FBG, then 474 FBW, then 49 FBG); vertical chevrons on fin and rudder and tip tanks (49 FBG, then 474 FBW) in blue/white (7 FBS), black/yellow (8 FBS) or red/white (9 FBS). Some 9 FBS aircraft carried a unit badge on the nose, while some 111 FBS aircraft wore a Star of Texas unit badge on the fin. Known colours used in markings as described are blue (69 FBS/111 FBS, 523 FES), yellow (310 FBS/429 FBS, 524 FES), red (311 FBS, 522 FES). Examples: (5)110306, (5)10393 (7 FBS); (48)613 FS-613-A 'Lois K', (5)1655 FS-655-B (8 FBS); (5)01119 FS-119-A (9 FBS); (50)1111 FS-111-B (69 FBS); (4)92398 (111 FBS); (5)110530 FS-530-B, (5)110459 (310 FBS); (5)1511 FS-511-B 'Ace High' (429 FBS); (5)1745 FS-745-A (430 FBS); (4)92333 (522 FBS); (5110)490 FS-490-B (523 FES); (51)1424 FS-424-A (524 FES).

F-86F Carried yellow fuselage and wing bands as air superiority units. 8 FBG fin markings were sunburst in blue (35 FBS), red (36 FBS) or yellow (80 FBS); 18 FBG fin markings were initially a large fin/rudder band in blue outlined yellow with four white stars (this changed by May 1953 to a large red/white/blue fin flash or, in the case of 2 Sqn. SAAF, orange/white/blue). Noses were coloured yellow (12 FBS) or red (67 FBS). SAAF aircraft carried large codes mid-fuselage and serial on rear fuselage. Examples: 603/B 'Ruth', 607/D 'Just Joan' (2 Sqn. SAAF); (5)24369 (12 FBS); (5)24425 (35 FBS); (5)24413, (5)24405 (36 FBS); (5)24341 (67 FBS); (5)24437, (5)24488 (80 FBS).

8.4.3. BOMBER OPERATIONS

At the outbreak of the war there were two bomber units in the theatre available for immediate action. At Johnson AB in Japan was the depleted 3 BG (Light) with a mixture of B-26B and C models. At Andersen AFB, Guam was the only non-Strategic Air Command (SAC) B-29 unit, the 19 BG (Medium); this Group was brought up to Kadena on 27 June 1950, from where it flew the first bomber sorties of the war against rail and bridge targets around Seoul. The following day the B-26 Invader Wing was in action against similar targets, and on 1 July it moved to Iwakuni to reduce flying time. As the North Korean advance continued, two more B-29 Wings, 22 and 92 BG, were prepared for overseas service and were in action against the port and marshalling yards at Wonsan on 12 July.

With limited fighter-bomber resources, the heavy bombers were used tactically against troop and tank concentrations and supply dumps until August, by which time two further B-29 Wings, 98 and 307 BG, had arrived from the US. Most of Korea's industry was in the north, and the 100-strong B-29 force now turned its attention to destroying manufacturing potential and transportation systems. Steel plants, oil depots, rail-

TABLE OF UNITS: THE KOREAN WAR—BOMBERS

Unit	Aircraft	Base	Squadrons	Dates
USAF				
3 BG(L)	B-26B/C	Iwakuni, K8, K16	8, 13, 90 BS; 731 BS from 27/10/50	25/06/50 to 31/07/53
19 BG(M)		Kadena	28, 30, 93 BS	25/06/50 to 31/07/53
22 BG(M)		Kadena, ex March AFB	2, 19, 33, 408 BS	10/07/50 to 05/11/50
92 BG(M)	B-29A	Yokota, ex Fairchild AFB	325, 326, 327 BS	10/07/50 to 00/11/50
98 BG(M)		Yokota, ex Fairchild AFB	343, 344 BS	06/08/50 to 31/07/53
307 BG(M)		Kadena, ex MacDill AFB	370, 371, 372 BS	06/08/50 to 31/07/53
452 BG(L)	B-26B/C	Miho, K1	728, 729, 730 BS	27/10/50 to 10/05/52
17 BG(L)	B-26B/C	K1	34, 37, 95 BS (ex 452 BG)	10/05/52 to 31/07/53
USN				
VC-6	AJ-1	K3, K6		00/05/52 to 00/00/53

way yards and harbour facilities were all hit extensively during August, after which there was little still operating effectively. A total of eighteen key strategic targets were destroyed by September. Large raids included one by 47 aircraft against the Cho-Sen nitrogen explosives plant at Konan, a 39-aircraft attack on Bogun chemical works and a raid on Pyongyang arsenal. The bombers then reverted to tactical bombing, and after the landings at Inchon plans were put in hand for the return of 22 and 92 BG to the USA.

In October the 452nd BG(L), a reserve B-26 unit activated on 30 July, flew into Miho with four squadrons, one of which was transferred to 3 BG to bring it up to strength. The B-26 units concentrated on night interdiction, often of supply columns or trains, for which the crews developed a range of techniques. The normal weapons load for this work was four 500lb general-purpose (GP) bombs on wing racks and fourteen 250lb fragmentation bombs in the bomb bay; for daylight work, 5in rockets and napalm were often used, especially against rail targets. Night flying was particularly hazardous in the mountainous Korean terrain, and the North Korean People's Army (NKPA) made matters worse by stringing heavy cables across the valleys, which accounted for many aircraft losses. As UN forces moved up the peninsula, the B-29 effort was directed to the many bridges on the NKPA supply routes. Once the Chinese intervened, the bridges across the Yalu river were added, although UN protocol forbade the overflying of Manchuria, making approaches both difficult and relatively ineffective.

No. 19 Group began using the guided 1,000lb range and azimuth only (RAZON) bombs with some success, although only fifteen bridges were totally destroyed between October and December for the expenditure of 489 bombs. Daylight bombing was made much more dangerous with the appearance on 1 November of the first MiG-15 fighters flying out of Antung: just nine days later the first B-29 fell to the newly deployed jets, and, in future, missions were flown with escorts. In January 1951, 19 BG began using the much more powerful 12,000lb TARZON guided bomb against bridges, the first such flight being against Kanggye bridge on the 13th. In the programme, which lasted until 12 April, 30 TARZONs were

launched, six bridges totally destroyed and one damaged; nineteen bombs missed, and two failed to detonate.

As the position on the ground consolidated, the two B-26 Wings transferred to Korea, 452 BG moving to Pusan in May and 3 BG to Kunsan in August 1951. They assumed responsibility for all interdiction work in the east and west respectively, and in recognition of the fact that most flying was now done at night the squadrons were redesignated BS (Light, Night Intruder). The units ran trials with powerful searchlights against targets but only drew increased AAA fire. They turned to hunter-killer tactics where two aircraft flew in line and between one and three miles apart. After the first B-26 had overflown, for example, a convoy, lights would be turned on in time for the second aircraft to register hits; when the second aircraft's ammunition was expended, the roles were reversed. These tactics proved very effective against moving targets where radar navigational aids like short-range navigational radar (SHORAN) were of no use.

The MiG-15s were now being used in greater numbers and with more determination: on 12 April 1951, 48 B-29s attacking a railway bridge over the Yalu near Antung were bounced by about 75 MiGs, with the loss of three bombers and their crews. The raids continued, however: 68 aircraft attacked military targets at Pyongyang on 14 August, only two days after the first SHORAN attack on Rashin docks just 17 miles from the Manchurian border. The first Rashin raid was followed up with a second on 22 August (diverted through bad weather) and a third on the 25th when fighters from USS *Essex* provided an escort for 35 bombers. Bombing was normally from a height of 20,000ft, although individual targets like bridges made a lower ceiling necessary. By now a third MiG-15 regiment was operating, with the more powerful MiG-15bis.

The biggest air battle of the war was fought on 23 October when B-29s attacked four newly constructed airfields at Samchan, Taechon, Uiju and Namsi. The ten aircraft on the Namsi attack were escorted by no fewer than 55 F-84Es and 34 F-86Es. Over the target the escort was engaged by about 100 MiG-15s while a further 50 attacked the bombers. Of the bomber force, three were shot down, four crash-landed in South Korea and three made it to Kadena where their damage was so extensive that they were scrapped. Six MiGs were claimed destroyed, including three to the bombers, for the loss of one F-84. Five B-29s were lost in attacks on Uiju, and after that the B-29 was confined to night bombing with SHORAN. In February 1952 attention turned again to the bridges, although, using conventional 1,000lb bombs, several hits were required to do any significant damage. During May 66 spans were dropped on ten bridges from low level, and then it was the turn of the airfields, which were attacked throughout the summer. At about this time a squadron of AJ-1 Savage bombers of VC-6, equipped with nuclear bombs, was detached to Pohang and Pyongtaek, where they remained for some months although they appear to have flown no operational sorties.

On 10 May the 452nd BG was redesignated 17 BW(L) and its squadrons renumbered. The Wing had spent its maximum 21 months in the war zone and, as it was a reserve unit, it was by law required to return to the United States. In fact, crews and aircraft were simply redesignated. Through the latter part of 1952 the bombers concentrated on industrial targets, ports and marshalling yards. This pattern continued into 1953, but as the armistice talks came to a conclusion the ten major airfields in North Korea came under repeated attack to deny them to aircraft which might move up at short notice. The last B-29 raid, on 27 July 1953, was against Samchan and Taechon airfields.

The light bomber force flew over 55,000 sorties, of which some 80 per cent were at night. The B-26s destroyed 38,500 vehicles, 3,700 railway wagons, 406 locomotives, 168 bridges and seven aircraft. The last sortie of the war was flown by a B-26 of 3 BG, just 24 minutes before the truce was signed. The B-29 force flew on all days of the 37-month war except 26 and, in 21,000 sorties, 167,100 tons of bombs were dropped and 33 enemy aircraft claimed shot down, of which sixteen were MiG-15s. At least sixteen bombers were shot down by fighters or AAA fire over North Korea, but many times that number were lost on the return journey or in crash-landings.

AIRCRAFT MARKINGS

The B-26s were finished bare metal overall then, increasingly, black overall with red markings to reflect their role. Aircraft came from many sources, and a small number were finished Olive Drab over, light grey under. Many aircraft carried red trim regardless of unit, but it is believed that 452 BG used coloured trim as follows: green, 728 BS; red, 729 BS; yellow, 730 BS; and white 731 BS.

The B-29s were finished bare metal overall, although many were painted with black undersides extending up the fuselage in a wavy line. A few were finished black overall. The aircraft carried Group markings on the fin as follows: Indian head or figure in circle, 19 BG; E in circle, 22 BG; W in circle, 92 BG; H in square, 98 BG; and Y in square, 307 BG. In addition, aircraft of 19 BG carried fin trim: green, 28 BS; blue, 30 BS; or red, 93 BS.

B-26B *Black overall, red trim, white code on fin: (4)434582/M (13 BS). Olive Drab over, light grey under, white serial: (4)434547 (90 BS). Bare metal: (4)434553 'Hollywood Hangover' (728 BS); (4)434571 'KTTV Channel 11' (729 BS). Olive Drab over, light grey under, yellow serials: (4)434552 (730 BS).*

B-26C *Black overall, yellow trim and code: (4)435754/K (8 BS). Bare metal: (4)434517/P (34 BS).*

B-29A *Bare metal: (4)462060 'Spirit of Freeport' (19 BS); (4)4224616 (325 BS); (4)486335 'TDY Widow' (343 BS). Bare metal, large A-667 on rear fuselage in black: (4)469667 'Snugglebunny' (343 BS). Black under: (4)224748 (371 BS). Black under, green trim: (4)484657 'Command Decision' (28 BS).*

8.4.4. NAVAL AIRCRAFT

When North Korean forces invaded the South there were two Allied aircraft carriers in the region: USS *Valley Forge* was at Subic Bay in the Philippines, while HMS *Triumph* was en route to Hong Kong from Japanese waters. Both carriers were immediately stocked with emergency provisions, *Triumph* at Kure in Japan, and they sailed on 29 June for the Korean west coast. *Valley Forge*, an *Essex* Class carrier, embarked Carrier Air Group (CAG) 5 comprising no fewer than five full squadrons and a photo-reconnaissance detachment. The mix of units, typical of the first two years of operations, comprised VF-51 and -52 with the F9F-2 Panther, VF-53 and -54 with the F4U-4 Corsair and VA-55 with the AD-2 Skyraider; the PR detachment of VC-61 flew the F4U-5P. *Triumph* was a *Colossus* Class carrier and embarked CAG-13 with just two units, 800 NAS with the Seafire 47 and 827 NAS with the Firefly FR.1, although the Royal Navy squadron inventory was greater. The US and British carrier were 890ft and 690ft in overall length and their displacements 33,250 and 13,350 tons respectively.

On station the ships joined Task Force (TF) 77 as Task Group (TG) 77.4 and began operations on 3 July, initially against North Korean airfields and troop movements along coastal roads. The first strikes were against airfields at Pyongyang and Onjong-ni (CAG-5) and Haeju and Ongjin (CAG-13) and saw the first use of naval jet aircraft in combat. At least ten aircraft were destroyed on the ground and two Yak-9s were shot down by F9F-2 pilots flying cover for the strikes. Throughout early July the pace was

AD-2 Skyraiders of VA-55 firing 5in rockets at a tactical target in North Korea in October 1950. The unit was part of CAG-5 on board *Valley Forge*, the first US carrier to sail operationally in Korean waters. The AD Skyraider was a rugged and potent attack aircraft, built in large numbers to 1957 and remaining in service through much of the Vietnam War. (Via J. Winton)

maintained, but as the North Koreans advanced, TG.77.4 demonstrated the flexibility of naval air power by covering, on the 15th, an amphibious landing at Pohang.

The purpose of the landing was to secure the eastern end of the Pusan pocket, and as soon as the landing was completed the carrier units returned to attacking the eastern airfields, including Yonpo, Sandok and Hamhung. Altogether 32 NKAF aircraft were destroyed and 13 damaged in two days, after which the NKAF retreated to bases further north. Significantly, North Korean operations around the Pusan perimeter were made with very limited air cover after the first few days. On 18 July CAG-5 units hit the Wonsan oil refinery with considerable success, and shortly after this TF.77 was given a free area around south-west Korea in which to operate independently, in order to maintain pressure on North Korean forces pending the Inchon landings. The TF was joined by USS *Philippine Sea* at the end of July and USS *Boxer* from mid-September; the carriers joined the TF after having delivered 145 F-51Ds to Japan.

The whole Task Force gathered off the west coast in September to support the Inchon landings on the 15th, where TG.90.51, comprising USMC units on the escort carriers USS *Badoeng Strait* and *Sicily*, was also stationed for close support; TF.77 units were in indirect support again, attacking airfields and hitting supply lines and bridges. Aircraft from *Triumph* (TF.91) were also committed to bombardment spotting for the cruisers *Jamaica* and *Kenya* and flying combat air patrol (CAP) sorties. Patrol and reconnaissance was the function of TF.99 comprising VP-6 (P2V) and 88 and 209 Sqns. RAF (Sunderland) as TG.99.1, and VP-42 and VP-47 (PBM-5) as TG.99.2. The ships were subjected to what is believed to be the only attack on vessels during the war when on the 17th two Yak-3s bombed USS *Rochester*, one aircraft being shot down by *Jamaica*. By the end of September the scale of flying had been such that CAG-13 had only two Fireflies and one Seafire operational. Only one aircraft had been lost in action however – a Seafire shot down by a B-29 in error.

On 10 October *Triumph* was relieved by HMS *Theseus* with CAG-17 on board. CAG-17 comprised 807 NAS with the Sea Fury FB.11 and 810 NAS equipped with the Firefly FR.5, and this combination was to be deployed for the remainder of the war by Commonwealth carriers. Together with the escort carrier USS *Bataan*, *Theseus* formed TG.95.11 in November to effect a blockade of the Yalu estuary. The remit of the Group was set out as comprising:

1. Daily reconnaissance of the coast for enemy shipping.
2. Combat air patrol (CAP) and anti-submarine (AS) patrols over the Group.
3. Bombardment spotting.
4. Airfield surveillance.
5. Indirect close support to land forces.

The first strikes were against airfields at Chinnampo and Haeju, and in thirteen days of the first operational period for the carrier 384 sorties were flown, two-thirds of them by Sea Furies. On the first day of operations a Sea Fury was shot down, but the injured pilot was rescued from behind enemy lines by a USAF H-5A of 3 Air Rescue Squadron (ARS), giving the Royal Navy a foretaste of the versatility of the helicopter in this role; at that time the British carriers flew a single Sea Otter amphibian for air–sea rescue. As UN forces moved into North Korea they were supported by naval aircraft, which by November had turned their attention to the Yalu river bridges as the Chinese invaded. During one such attack on 9 November the strike aircraft of CAG-11 from *Philippine Sea* were met by a number of MiG-15s. The covering F9F pilots were soon in combat, during which Lt. Cdr. W. T. Amen, the CO of VF-111, became the first pilot to bring down a victim in an all-jet dogfight.

Two more MiGs were shot down by naval pilots from *Valley Forge* on the 18th. From 9 to 21 November AD and F4U strike aircraft flew 593 sorties against the bridges, dropping 232 tons of bombs, and all but one was destroyed, but by now the river was freezing to the extent that rail lines could be laid over it. Naval aicraft then joined with those of the USMC to support the Marines' breakout from Chosen and generally harass the advancing Chinese. As the land position stabilized, the Task Force was assigned the role of interdiction and attacking troop movements along the eastern coast. The carrier strength was maintained at four ships (three USN, one Commonwealth), but this demand initially stretched American resources. At the outbreak of the war there were only nine CAGs constituted, and on 20 July fourteen Naval Air Reserve squadrons were mobilized, with a further 28 being called up from September.

The first reserve CAG entered the war zone as CAG-101 embarked on USS *Boxer* on 27 March 1950, in time to take part in Operation 'Strangle' designed to choke the Chinese supply system. Almost immediately the reserve units were in action, the AD-2s of VA-702 hitting the bridge at Toko-ri, which had been under repeated attack since 2 March. The bridge was regularly repaired and required constant attention to prevent its rebuilding, but when the Chinese launched a fresh attack on 22 April the carrier squadrons were once again employed on close-support work. At this time the F9F was used in the ground-attack role for the first time when VF-191, operating the F9F-2B version with extra wing points, attacked a bridge at Songjin on 2 April.

The AD Skyraider was a powerful aircraft, brought into service too late to see combat in the Second World War. It carried a formidable weapons load of up to 5,000lb, typically in the form of two 500lb or 1,000lb bombs plus up to twelve 6in rockets or flares. The F4U carried up to 2,000lb of weapons, normally in the form of rockets or small bombs. When HMS *Theseus* was relieved by *Glory* in May, her aircraft had flown 3,489 sorties, averaging 2½ hours, off both coasts. Although not possessing the firepower of their American counterparts, the British aircraft

were operated efficiently and on one occasion a flight returning to HMS *Ocean* was landed on at 16-second intervals. The Sea Fury normally flew with eight 60lb rockets or two 500lb bombs, while the Firefly typically carried two 1,000lb bombs or rockets and smaller bombs, depending on the required range. In general, the Commonwealth carriers operated off the west coast, where 30ft tides and numerous islands, coupled with the risk of mining, made bombardment spotting largely unnecessary, especially when there were few coastal tactical targets. The American Seventh Fleet carriers sailed in the Sea of Japan with virtually no tide and a straighter coastline, with important coastal communications systems offering valuable targets.

From May to October the US attack carrier strength was reduced to two, but from early 1952 there were never fewer than four US carriers in the theatre. In the year TG.96.7 based on the escort carrier *Bairoko* was formed, to counter a possible submarine threat. Between embarking USMC units, the escort carriers turned to anti-submarine work, and in August 1952 the AF-2W was introduced into the theatre by VS-931 on board *Badoeng Strait*.

From the end of 1951 there was also a technical change in formations as *Valley Forge* embarked Air Task Group (ATG) 1. The *Essex* Class carriers had for some time been established at not more than four squadrons, although more were usually carried. ATGs were non-commissioned formations designed to enable the operation of the surplus squadrons. An important preamble to Operation 'Strangle' was an attack on the Hwachon dam on 1 May 1951 by eight AD-4 Skyraiders of VA-105. Using torpedoes, and escorted by eight F4U-4s, they made an unopposed strike and scored six hits to breach the dam, thus denying the North Koreans the ability to control

The dock area at Chinnampo, under attack by Fireflies of 810 NAS from HMS *Theseus*. The Royal Navy and Royal Australian Navy carriers were smaller than those of the US Navy and operated only piston-engined aircraft, but the embarked squadrons had a slightly larger complement. (Via J. Winton)

TABLE OF UNITS: THE KOREAN WAR—NAVAL AIRCRAFT

CARRIER AIR GROUPS

CAG 13 (P), Triumph, 3 July 1950–9 October 1950

800 NAS	827 NAS
Seafire 47	Firefly FR.1

CAG 5 (S), Valley Forge, 3 July 1950–23 November 1950

VF-51	VF-52	VF-53	VF-54	VA-55	VC-61
F9F-2	F9F-2	F4U-4B	F4U-4B	AD-2/4Q	F4U-5P

CAG 11 (V), Philippine Sea, 1 August 1950–28 March 1951

VF-111	VF-112	VF-113	VF-114	VA-115	VC-61
F9F-2	F9F-2	F4U-4B	F4U-4B	AD-4	F4U-5P

CAG 2 (M), Boxer, 15 September 1950–22 October 1950

VF-21	VF-22	VF-63	VF-64	VA-65
F4U-4	F4U-4	F4U-4	F4U-4	AD-4

CAG 3 (K), Leyte, 9 October 1950–19 January 1951

VF-31	VF-32	VF-33	VF-34	VA-35	VC-61	VC-62
F9F-2	F9F-2	F4U-4	F4U-4	AD-2	F2H-2P	F4U-5P

CAG 17 (T), Theseus, 10 October 1950–19 April 1951

807 NAS	810 NAS
Sea Fury FB.11	Firefly FR.5

CAG 19 (B), Princeton, 5 December 1950–29 May 1951

VF-191	VF-192	VF-193	VA-195	VC-61 Det.E
F9F-2	F4U-4	F4U-4	AD-4	F9F-2P

CAG 2 (M), Valley Forge, 16 December 1950–28 March 1951

VF-24	VF-63	VF-64	VA-65
F4U-4	F4U-4	F4U-4	AD-2

CAG 101 (A), Boxer, 27 March 1951–2 June 1951

VF-721	VF-791	VF-884	VA-702	VC-3	VX-1
F9F-2B	F4U-4	F4U-4	AD-2/3	F4U-5NL	AD-3E

CAG 2 (M), Philippine Sea, 28 March 1951–2 June 1951

VF-24	VF-63	VF-64	VA-65
F4U-4	F4U-4	F4U-4	AD-2

CAG 14 (R), Glory, 3 May 1951–4 October 1951

804 NAS	812 NAS
Sea Fury FB.11	Firefly FR.5

CAG 102 (D), Bonne Homme Richard, 30 May 1951–30 November 1951

VF-781	VF-783	VF-874	VA-923	VC-3	VC-11	VC-35
F9F-2	F4U-4	F4U-4	AD-2/3	F4U-5NL	AD-4	AD-4

CAG 19 (B), Princeton, 2 June 1951–10 August 1951

VF-23	VF-821	VF-871	VF-34	VA-195	VC-61
F9F-2	F4U-4	F4U-4	F4U-4	AD-3	F9F-2P

CAG 5 (S), Essex, 22 August 1951–5 March 1952

VF-51	VF-172	VF-53	VF-54	VC-61 Det.B
F9F-2	F2H-2	F4U-4	AD-4N	F9F-2P

CAG 21 (K), Sydney, 4 October 1951–25 January 1952

805 NAS	808 NAS	817 NAS
Sea Fury FB.11	Sea Fury FB.11	Firefly FR.5

CAG 15 (H), Antietam, 15 October 1951–22 March 1952

VF-713	VF-831	VF-837	VA-728	VC-61 Det.D
F4U-4	F9F-2	F9F-2	AD-4L	F9F-2P

CAG 19 (B) ATG 1, Valley Forge, 12 December 1951–13 June 1952

VF-111	VF-52	VF-653	VF-194	VC-61 Det.H
F9F-2	F9F-2	F4U-4	AD-4	F9F-2P

CAG 11 (V), Philippine Sea, 30 January 1952–8 July 1952

VF-112	VF-113	VF-114	VA-65	VC-61 Det.C
F9F-2	F9F-2	F4U-4	AD-3	F9F-2P

CAG 2 (M), Boxer, 10 March 1952–6 September 1952

VF-63	VF-64	VF-24	VA-65	GMU-90	VC-35	VC-3
F4U-4	F4U-4	F9F-6	AD-4B	F6F-5K	AD-4N	F4U-4NL

CAG 14 (R), Glory, 1 April 1951–11 May 1952

804 NAS	812 NAS
Sea Fury FB.11	Firefly FR.5

CAG 19 (B), Princeton, 14 April 52–18 October 1952

VF-191	VF-192	VF-193	VA-195	VC-61 Det.E
F9F-2	F4U-4	F4U-4	AD-4	F9F-2P

CAG 17 (O), Ocean, 11 May 1952–30 October 1952

802 NAS	825 NAS
Sea Fury FB.11	Firefly AS.5

CAG 7 (L), Bonne Homme Richard, 21 June 1952–18 December 1952

VF-71	VF-72	VF-74	VF-75	VC-61
F9F-2	F9F-2	F4U-4	AD-4	F9F-2P

ATG 2 (W), Essex, 18 July 1952–13 January 1953

VF-23	VF-821	VF-871	VA-55	VC-61
F9F-5	F9F-5	F4U-4	AD-4N	F9F-2P

TABLE OF UNITS: THE KOREAN WAR—NAVAL AIRCRAFT (continued)

CARRIER AIR GROUPS (continued)

CAG 101 (A), Kearsage, 14 September 1952–22 February 1953

VF-11	VF-721	VF-884	VA-702	VC-61 Det.F
F2H-2	F9F-2B	F4U-4	AD-4	F2H-2P

CAG 102 (D), Oriskany, 28 October 1952–2 May 1953

VF-781	VF-783	VF-874	VA-923	VC-61 Det.G
F9F-5	F9F-5	F4U-4	AD-4	F2H-2P

CAG 14 (R), Glory, 1 November 1952–15 July 1953

801 NAS	821 NAS
Sea Fury FB.11	Firefly FR.5

CAG 5 (S), Valley Forge, 30 December 1952–10 June 1953

VF-51	VF-52	VF-92	VF-54	VC-61 Det.B
F9F-5	F9F-5	F4U-4	AD-4N	F9F-5P

CAG 9 (N), Philippine Sea, 29 January 1953–31 July 1953

VF-91	VF-93	VF-94	VA-95	VC-61 Det.M
F9F-2	F9F-2	F4U-4	AD-4NA	F9F-5P

CAG 15 (H), Princeton, 13 March 1953–27 June 1953

VF-152	VF-153	VF-154	VA-155	VC-61
F4U-4	F9F-5	F9F-5	AD-4	F9F-5P

ATG 1 (V), Boxer, 12 May 1953–31 July 1953

VF-52	VF-111	VF-151	VF-44	VF-194	VC-61 Det.H	VC-33
F9F-5	F9F-5	F4U-4	AD-4N	F2H-2P	AD-4Q	

CAG 4 (F), Lake Champlain, 10 June 1953–31 July 1953

VF-22	VF-62	VF-44	VA-45	VC-12	VC-33	VC-62
F2H-2	F2H-2	F4U-4	AD-4B	AD-4W	AD-4N	F2H-2P

CAG 17 (O), Ocean, 15 July 1953–31 July 1953

807 NAS	810 NAS
Sea Fury FB.11	Firefly FR.5

MISCELLANEOUS NAVAL UNITS

Unit	Aircraft (code)	Base	Role	Dates
VC-3	F4U-5N, F3D-2, F2H-3 (NP)	Various carriers	Composite night fighter	27/03/51 to 31/07/53
VC-33	AD-3, -4E/N/Q, TBM-3N (SS)	Various carriers	Composite night attack	00/00/52 to 31/07/53
VX-1	AD-3E (XA)	Boxer	EW	27/03/51 to 02/06/51
VC-11	TBM-3W/Q, AD-3W/Q, -4W (ND)	Various carriers	AEW, EW	00/03/51 to 31/07/53
VC-35	AD-4D/N/Q (NR)	Boxer	Guided missile (F6F-5K) control	10/03/52 to 06/09/52
GMU-90	F6F-5K	Boxer	Pilotless guided bomb	10/03/52 to 06/09/52
VC-61	F4U-5P, F9F-2P, F2H-2P (PP)	Various carriers	PR	03/07/50 to 31/07/53
VC-62	F4U-5P, F9F-2P, F2H-2P (PL)	Various carriers	PR	19/01/51 to 31/07/53
VS-931	AF-2W (SV)	Badoeng Strait	ASW	00/07/52 to ?
VR-3	R5D-3 (RT)	Japan	Transport	00/08/50 to 31/07/53
VR-23	P2V-3Z (RC)	Japan	Staff transport	Not known
HU-1	HO3S-1, HUP-1 (UP)	Various carriers	SAR	00/01/51 to 31/07/53
FASRON 120	SNB-3	?	Maintenance-related liaison	00/06/50 to 31/07/53
VU-5	TBM-3 (UE)	?	General utility	00/00/50 to 31/07/53

Note: Light carriers embarking USMC or anti-submarine units were: *Sicily* (15/08/50 to 31/07/53); *Badoeng Strait* (15/08/50 to 31/07/53); *Bataan* (00/12/50 to 31/07/53); and *Bairoko* (12/02/52 to 31/07/53). Many of the miscellaneous naval units listed were based on Japanese airfields between embarking, sometimes for short periods, on carriers of TF.77; some were trials units, and may have had more than one detachment in the theatre.

---

the river levels. However, the strikes on the two major central routes allocated to TF.77 proved largely ineffective. Despite the use of delayed-action bombs and 'butterfly' anti-personnel bomblets, the communists used their labour relentlessly in rebuilding or re-routing roads and railways. The strikes were not off target, but mobile anti-aircraft defences were widely extended, making the attacks a demoralizing business.

In its first three months of operations, CAG-5, flying from *Essex*, lost 27 aircraft and eleven pilots. The Group introduced the F2H-2 Banshee into combat with VF-172: less powerful than the F9F, and with no better weapons capability, the aircraft nevertheless had a far greater range. Another change came in October, when HMAS *Sydney* relieved *Glory* and began a tour of duty in the war zone. Slightly larger than the *Colossus* Class ships, she embarked two Sea Fury squadrons and one of Fireflies. From 15 January 1952 the

naval fighters turned to night attacks on communications in Operations 'Moonlight Sonata' and latterly 'Insomnia', but results were poor and from March the roads and railways were again the main target. Then, in June, a switch was made to industrial targets.

The attack on the North Korean power system on 23 June 1952 required a maximum effort, and units from three CAGs were involved in the strikes on the Suiho dam, 40 miles east of Antung, the two plants at Fusen and the plant at Kyosen. Thirty-five Skyraiders, each fitted with two 2,000lb and one 1,000lb bombs, made for Suiho with an escort of 35 F9F-2s. It was to be the first occasion for nearly two years on which naval fighters had entered 'MiG Alley'. Ninety TF.77 aircraft then hit Fusen, while Kyosen was attacked by 70 aircraft. There were follow-up raids the next day, and in the two days aircraft from the Task Force completed 546 sorties against a total of thirteen power plants. The details and results are described elsewhere. On 11 July TF.77 units, together with those of the FEAF and USMC, were engaged in major attacks on military targets around the now heavily defended city of Pyongyang. In 1,254 sorties, 23,000 gallons of napalm and 1,400 tons of bombs were dropped on the city, causing major damage. A second raid took place on 29 August in which 1,403 sorties were flown.

In late August aircraft from ATG.2 on *Boxer* were committed to a unique operation. Six F6F-5K Hellcats of Guided Missile Unit (GMU) 90 were flown against high-value targets. The aircraft were pilotless drones fitted with a television camera and a 2,000lb bomb, flown off the carrier and guided on to their targets by AD-4 aircraft of VC-35. The first strike was against a bridge at Hungnam on 28 August, and by the end of September all six drones had been successfully expended.

HMS *Ocean* began her tour on 11 May, during which her aircraft set several notable records. On 17 May the ship put up 123 sorties in a day to claim the record for the war. Then, on 9 August, when a flight of Sea Furies of 802 NAS was attacked by a number of MiG-15s north of Chinnampo, Lt. P. Carmichael was able to put in several bursts on one machine to bring it down. By the end of the next day, several more MiGs were claimed as probables or damaged, and almost certainly at least one more was destroyed, although there was no third-party witness. By 30 October, when *Ocean* withdrew, she had flown off more than 1,900 sorties, each averaging about 1 hour 40 minutes. No. 802 NAS which included pilots from 1832 NAS Royal Naval Reserve, used 420 1,000lb and 3,358 500lb bombs, plus half a million rounds of cannon ammunition; 825 NAS used mainly rockets, firing nearly 16,000. The Force's effectiveness was reduced from 16 September, however, when an F2H-2 missed the wire on *Essex* and crashed into aircraft parked forward. Four machines were destroyed, eight men killed and 27 wounded. It speaks highly of the crew and the organization that the ship was back on station on 3 October after repairs in Japan.

Night strikes against military installations on the east coast began again in October as the targets became too heavily defended for the slow B-29 bombers. Then, in November, matters became potentially complicated when there was an incident involving the Russians. USS *Oriskany* embarked CAG-102, which included VF-781 equipped with the more powerful -5 version of the Panther. During a bombardment south of Vladivostok on the 18th, four F9F-5s were attacked by seven MiG-15s of the Soviet Air Force, during which at least one of the latter was shot down. Fortunately there were no repercussions.

The pace continued through early 1953 but began to intensify from May when up to five

carriers operated simultaneously. Interdiction and close-support sorties were stepped up, and towards the end of the war the naval units were called upon to deal with the continuing threat posed by the night-time Po-2 and Yak-18 'Bedcheck Charlie' flights, during which these slow aircraft dropped 25lb fragmentation bombs on parked aircraft and similar soft targets. A detachment of F4U-5Ns of VC-3 was flown from *Princeton* to Osan, and Lt. G.P. Bordelon became the US Navy's only ace by bringing down three Po-2s and two Yak-18s between 30 June and 16 July. A flight of Fireflies from the newly arrived 810 NAS was also detached, but without success.

In the last two months of the war the fighting intensified and the Air Groups were flying about one-third of their sorties in close-support as the communists mounted their final offensives. When the war ended there were five carriers on station, and on the last full day of operations around 700 sorties were flown, over four times the average rate for May. After three years of constant combat the naval record was impressive: TF.77 had flown 167,552 sorties and dropped 120,000 tons of bombs; fourteen enemy aircraft had been shot down, including seven MiG-15s, and around 50 destroyed on the ground. The roles were essentially attack, however, and 37,000 buildings and 4,500 trucks were among the final tally. The cost to the Task Force was 814 aircraft lost on operations and 354 men.

AIRCRAFT MARKINGS

USN
American naval aircraft of the period were almost invariably finished in Sea Blue Gloss, otherwise referred to as 'midnite blue'. Lettering was in white, with the serial on the rear fuselage, unit code on the forward fuselage and top starboard wing and CAG code on the fin.
F4U-4 *97503/310S (VF-53, CAG-5); 80109/109M*

TF.77 assumed the responsibility for the eastern side of North Korea, which included many of the important road and rail links, and thus bridges became an important target for the carrier-borne strike aircraft. This bridge has been damaged by Fireflies of 810 NAS, and preparations are being made for relaying the track across the river bed. Bridges were repaired almost as fast as they were taken out. (Via. J. Winton)

(VF-64, CAG-2); 81975/411L (VF-74, CAG-7); 62924/309V (VF-113, CAG-11); 81624/204D (VF-783, CAG-102); 81972/211A (VF-791, CAG-101); 80788/413A (VF-884, CAG-101).
F4U-5N 124713/6NP (VC-3).
F4U-5P 12977/S (VC-61, CAG-5).
F9F-2 123824/124B (VF-23, CAG-19); 123490/116K (VF-31, CAG-3); 123468/101L (VF-71, CAG-7); 123484/206L (VF-72, CAG-7); 123592/108N (VF-91, CAG-9); 123600/115B (VF-191, CAG-19); 123713/123A (VF-721, CAG-101); 127129/112D (VF-781, CAG-102).
F9F-2P 123???/50PP (VC-61).
F9F-5 127210/401M (VF-24, CAG-2); 123487/ 308H (VF-153, CAG-15); 126034/109D (VF-781, CAG-102).
F2H-2 125019/210F (VF-62, CAG-4).
F2H-2P 128863/28PP 'Look See' (VC-61).
AD-1 09174/511A (VA-702, CAG-101).
AD-2 122310/406A (VA-702, CAG-101); 122248/515D (VA-923, CAG-102).
AD-3 122907/12XA (VX-1); 122875/SS (VC-33); 122737/504D (VA-923, CAG-102).
AD-4 125721/409S (VF-54, CAG-5); 124047/ 501S (VA-55, CAG-5); 123244/513M (VA-65, CAG-2); 123934/515L (VA-75, CAG-7); 127003/515N (VA-95, CAG-9); 123841/518V (VA-115, CAG-11); 123811/411B (VF-194, CAG-19); 123936/517B (VA-195, CAG-19); 124741/02NR (VC-35).
AF-2W 124877/17SV (VS-931).

Commonwealth Navies
Aircraft of the Royal and Royal Australian Navies were finished in Extra Dark Sea Grey over and Sky under. Lettering was in black, with the serial on the rear fuselage and under the wings, the unit code on the mid-rear fuselage and the ship letter code on the fin. The types flown were unfamiliar to US servicemen, and to avoid confusion with enemy types two black and three white one-foot stripes were painted around the rear fuselage and wings. There is no evidence of unit badges being worn.
Seafire FR.47 *Two white and one black fuselage stripes only:* VP461/178P, VP492/180P, VR965/177P (800 NAS).
Firefly FR.1 PP488/272P (827 NAS).
Firefly FR.5 WB338/239T (810 NAS); VT500/201K, VX372/207K (817 NAS RAN); VT368/207R (821 NAS); WB409/2920 (825 NAS).
Sea Fury FB.11 WJ238/1040 (802 NAS); WF610/100R, VW551/108R (804 NAS); VX730/109K (805 NAS RAN); VW577/113T, TF956/123T (807 NAS); VX752/131K (808 NAS RAN).

8.4.5. US MARINE CORPS OPERATIONS
For the USMC the war started on 2 August when the 1st Provisional Marine Brigade, comprising the 5th Regiment and Marine Air Group (MAG) 33, landed at Pusan. The brigade had left San Diego on 12 July in transports and the escort carrier USS *Badoeng Strait* (CVE-116), and the MAG consisted of VMF-214 and -323 equipped with F4U-4 and AU-1 Corsairs, VMF(N)-513 with F7F-3Ns and F4U-5Ns and VMO-6 with OY-2 light aircraft and HO3S-1 helicopters. By the time of the landings, the night fighter unit had been disembarked at Itazuke, where it remained for a time under the control of 8 FBW. Having sailed from Guam, the escort carrier *Sicily* (CVE-118), now embarking VMF-214, also joined what was now Task Group (TG) 96.8. Corsairs of VMF-214 were in action from Pusan on 3 August against targets at Chinju and Simban-ni, and for the next few weeks they maintained close-support sorties around the Pusan perimeter. On 10 August an HO3S-1 of VMO-6 was involved in the first rescue by helicopter of the war.

In late August the USMC squadrons were withdrawn to Japan to prepare for the forthcoming landings at Inchon, and at the same time the 1st Marine Air Wing, including MAG-12, left El Toro MCAS for Japan; MAG-12 comprised VMF-212 and -312 with Corsairs and VMF(N)-542 equipped with F7F-3Ns and F4U-4Ns. As the USMC units assembled for the invasion, the communists launched fresh offensives around Pusan and VMF-323 was flown back to that town to support the ground forces. By the eve of the Inchon invasion the three fighter squadrons of MAG-33 had flown 1,511 sorties, including 995 in close support, and 1 Prov. Marine Brigade was awarded the first Presidential unit citation of the war.

The USMC carrier units involved at Inchon comprised TG.90.51 and included the day fighter squadrons of MAG-33 on *Sicily* and those of MAG-12 in reserve on *Badoeng Strait*. The carriers were in position by 10 September, and aircraft from MAG-33 units attacked targets on Wolmi-do island outside Inchon with napalm, the whole area being subjected to bombing and bombardment for several days before the landings at 0633hrs on the 15th. As the Marines of the 5th Regiment landed they were supported by their own aircraft, often firing at the enemy only fifty yards ahead of the fighting; throughout the war, close air support for their own men was the priority for the USMC squadrons. The landings at Inchon took the North Koreans by surprise, but they rallied and the fighting on the outskirts of the city soon intensified.

On the 16th the Corsairs were called in to deal with a group of T-34 tanks, which were stopped by accurate napalm attacks but with the loss of one aircraft. On the 18th Kimpo airfield was taken; the helicopters of VMO-6 were the first aircraft to land, followed by the night fighters of VMF(N)-542 from Itami. At this stage the two Air Groups exchanged units, thus the less ex-

perienced VMF-212 and -312 flew ashore as
MAG-33 while VMF-214 and -323 remained on
the carriers as MAG-12. Operations continued,
and on 24 September 1 and 5 Regiments marched
into Seoul. By 9 October, when all the local
objectives had been met, the four day fighter
squadrons had flown 2,163 sorties while VMF(N)-
542 achieved 573; VMO-6 helicopters had lifted
139 wounded to safety. MacArthur now turned
his attention on Wonsan on the east coast, which
was being softened up prior to invasion. On 14
October MAG-12, now consisting of VMF-312
and VMF(N)-513, arrived at Wonsan airfield prior
to the landings on the 26th. By the end of the
month three regiments had reached Chosen.

The Marine division consolidated its positions,
but late on 27 November up to 100,000 Chinese
'volunteers' attacked the perimeter. By now
MAG-12 had VMF-312 and VMF(N)-542 at Yonpo,
some fifty miles distant, with VMF-212 and
VMF(N)-513 at Wonsan, while the two Corsair
squadrons of MAG-33 were on the escort carriers
off the coast. On 2 December, surrounded, the
Marines broke out from Yudam-ni to Hagaru-ri,
where an airstrip had been built for resupply.
Notwithstanding the most appalling weather, as
the Marines withdrew they were constantly
covered by an umbrella of aircraft from the Task
Force which attacked any likely target: on 4
December alone, 239 close-support sorties were
flown, 111 by the USMC and the remainder by
the USN. As related elsewhere, the supply operation was considerable and included the dropping
of a sectioned bridge in order to enable the troops
to cross a gorge. On 10 December VMF-311, the
first USMC jet squadron, landed at Yonpo, where
it was to remain for just one week before flying
south to Pusan East.

During the withdrawal to Hungnam, the

Marines lost 730 dead and 3,670 wounded, but
they reached the coast as a fighting unit with
their wounded, their weapons and equipment.
The evacuation by sea and air was completed on
24 December, by which time 105,000 soldiers
had been taken off, together with 17,500 vehicles.
As the Chinese moved south the Marines regrouped. By March, after the F9F Panthers had
been grounded for a period, MAG-33 at Pohang
comprised VMF-311 and -212, while at Pusan
West MAG-12 included VMF-214, -312 and -323
and VMF(N)-513. The carriers returned to the
United States for a time, but USS *Bataan* (CVL-
29) joined the Task Force, embarking VMF-312,
which remained carrier-borne until relieved by
VMA-332 in June 1953. The USMC now became
involved in Operation 'Strangle', assuming the
responsibility for the Korean east coast supply
routes.

The Chinese launched a fresh offensive towards
Seoul on 22 April 1951 and the Marines were
particularly active in the Hwachon reservoir
area. VMO6 helicopters were busy lifting out
wounded troops, moving 77 in one day late in the
month, but the Marines were anxious to get a
helicopter with greater capacity and on 2 September HMR-161 unloaded fifteen HRS-1s at
Pusan. The unit moved to Kangnung, where
operations began on the 21st when troops were
inserted to relieve a surrounded ROK group. The
helicopters worked on troop movement for the
remainder of the war, but their aircraft were
occasionally used for rescue work where extra
lifting capacity was required.

The USMC night fighter units were particularly
successful at night interdiction, working in
partnership with USN Privateer flareships and
managing 24 sorties a night in the summer of
1951. By the end of the year the piston-engined

United States Marine
Corps organic air power
was a critical factor in
facilitating the
withdrawal to Hungnam
in the winter of 1950. The
first USMC jet-equipped
squadron, VMF-311, with
the F9F Panther, operated
from Yonpo for just one
week. Early in 1951,
VMF-115 joined MAG-12
at K3 with the F9F-2B.
Aircraft 123063/6AE is
illustrated. (USMC via R.
F. Dorr)

TABLE OF UNITS: THE KOREAN WAR—THE UNITED STATES MARINE CORPS

Unit	Aircraft (code)	Base	Role	Dates
MAG-33, summer 1950				
VMF-214	F4U-4 (WE)	K9, Ashiya, K9, *Sicily*	Close-support fighter	02/08/50 to 31/07/53
VMF-323	F4U-4 (MS)	K9, Ashiya, *Sicily*	Close-support fighter	02/08/50 to 05/07/53
VMF-513	F7F-3N, F4U-5N (WS)	Itazuke	Night fighter	01/08/50 to 31/07/53
VMO-6	HO3S-1, OY-2, OE-1	K9, *Sicily*, K14	Observation, liaison	02/08/50 to 31/07/53
MAG-12, summer 1950				
VMF-212	F4U-4 (LD)	*Badoeng Strait*, K14	Close-support fighter	10/09/50 to 31/07/53
VMF-312	F4U-4 (WR)	*Badoeng Strait*, K14	Close-support fighter	10/09/50 to 08/06/53
VMF-542	F4U-4N, F7F-3N (WH)	K14	Night fighter	18/09/50 to 00/01/52
MAG-33, autumn/winter 1950				
VMF-214	F4U-4	*Sicily*	Close-support fighter	
VMF-323	F4U-4	*Badoeng Strait*	Close-support fighter	
MAG-12, autumn/winter 1950				
VMF-212	F4U-4	Wonsan	Close-support fighter	
VMF-312	F4U-4	Wonsan, K27	Close-support fighter	
VMF-513	F7F-3N, F4U-5N	Wonsan	Night fighter	
VMF-542	F7F-3N, F4U-5N	Wonsan, K27	Night fighter	
VMF-311	F9F-2B (WL)	K27, K9	Fighter	10/12/50 to 31/07/53
VMO-6	HO3S-1, OY-2, OE-1	Wonsan, K27		
MAG-33, spring 1951 on				
VMF-311	F9F-2B/5	K3	Fighter	
VMF-212	F4U-4, AU-1	K3	Close-support fighter	
VMF-542	F7F-3N, F4U-5N	K8	Night fighter	
VMA-121	AD-3 (AK)	K3	Attack	21/10/51 to 31/07/53
MAG-12, spring 1951 on				
VMF-214	F4U-4	K1, K6	Close-support fighter	
VMF-312	F4U-4	K1, various carriers	Close-support fighter	
VMF-323	F4U-4, AU-1	K1, K6	Close-support fighter	
VMF-513	F7F-3N, F4U-5N, F3D-2N	K1, K6	Night fighter	
VMF-115	F9F-2B/4 (AE)	K3, K6	Fighter	10/02/51 to 31/07/53
VMA-332	F4U-4 (MR)	*Bairoko*	Close support (rel. VMF-312)	08/06/53 to 31/07/53
VMA-251	AD-3 (AL)	K6	Attack (rel. VMF-323)	05/07/53 to 31/07/53
Miscellaneous units				
VMO-6	HO3S-1, HTL-4, HO5S-1, OY-2, OE-1, L-17, L-20	Various	Various	
HMR-161	HRS-1 (HR)	K18	Troop transport, rescue	21/09/51 to 31/07/53
VMC-1	AD-4N/W (RM)	K16, Itami	AEW	00/09/52 to 31/07/53
VMJ-1	F2H-2P (MW)	K3, K14	PR	25/02/52 to 31/07/53
VMJ-3	F9F-5P (MU)	Itami	PR	? to 31/07/53
VMR-152	R4D-1, R5D-1 (WC)	Itami	Transport	00/08/50 to 31/07/53
VMR-253	R4Q-1 (AD)	Itami	Transport	00/08/50 to 31/07/53
VMR-252	R5C-1 (LH)	Itami	Transport	00/09/50 to ?
MAMS 12	AD-2, TBM-3E (WA)	K6	Engineer support	? to 31/07/53
MAMS 33	HO3S-1, F9F-4, AD-2Q (WM)	K3, K14, K27	Engineer support	? to 31/07/53
HEDRON 1	R4D-1, F7F-3P (AZ)	Itami, K3	HQ squadron	00/08/50 to 31/07/53

equipment was exhausted and crews in short supply, so VMF(N)-513 took over the aircraft of VMF(N)-542. More modern equipment in the form of the F3D-2N was not available until November 1952, but with these machines the unit was to bring down one Po-2, one Yak-15 and five MiG-15s by the end of the war. Further changes of equipment included the arrival in October 1951 of the first AD-2 squadron, VMA-121, to MAG-33, and in February 1952 the second F9F unit, VMF-115, joined the Group from MCAS Cherry Point. The USMC also acquired its own theatre photo-reconnaissance unit in March when VMJ-1, equipped with the F2H-2P, began operations under Fifth Air Force control. The following month MAG-12 moved from Pusan to Pyongtaek, and in June VMF-311 and -323 were redesignated attack squadrons (VMA). These squadrons played an important part in the strikes on the dams on 23 June and appropriately were given the Chosen 3 and 4 stations as targets.

As mentioned elsewhere, there were two mas-sive raids on Pyongyang on 11 July and 29 August 1952 in an attempt to force the Chinese to hasten the pace of negotiations. In Operation 'Pressure Pump', the USMC contributed a significant number of sorties, and by the autumn 1 MAW was flying a minimum of 100 a day. This level gradually rose in the last year of the war as the Air Wing continued to fly both interdiction and close air support sorties against continuing Chinese offensives. Late in the war there were several further changes in the order of battle when the veteran VMF-312 was replaced on *Bairoko* by VMA-332 on 8 June, and on 5 July VMA-251, with the AD-3, relieved VMA-323 at Pyongtaek. On 27 July 1 MAW flew 222 sorties before the last jet mission of the war by an F9F-5 of VMF-311 at 1635hrs. In two and a half years, VMF-311 flew a total of 18,851 sorties.

Before the Korean War the future of the US Marine Corps had looked bleak, but by concen-trating on the task of providing immediate support for its own forces 1 MAW, together with the 'mud' Marines, demonstrated the value of a closely knit and well trained force able to operate flexibly and in all conditions. Marine Corps aircraft flew 127,496 sorties, of which nearly one-third were in close support; 8,200 tons of bombs were dropped and twenty enemy aircraft shot down, including a MiG-15 destroyed by Capt. J. G. Folmar of VMF-312 while flying an F4U-4B off *Sicily* on 10 September 1952. Its splendid record in Korea cost the Marine Corps 368 aircraft in combat.

AIRCRAFT MARKINGS

USMC combat aircraft were finished similarly to those of the USN except for the difference in service identification, with 'Marines' replacing 'Navy' on the rear fuselage. One- or two-digit individual numeric codes were carried on the forward fuselage and two-letter unit codes on the fin.

F4U-4 *White/Sea Blue Gloss checks on nose: 97201/9WR (VMF-312); 82166/11WS (VMF-323).*

F4U-5N *134667/13WF (VMF(N)-513).*

AU-1 *133843/LD (VMF-212).*

F9F-2B *123063/6AE (VMF-115); 123451/2WL, 123464/6WL (VMF-311).*

F3D-2N *12!!!!/2WH (VMF(N)-542).*

F2H-2P *125687/3MW (VMJ-1).*

F7F-3N *80454/AZ (HEDRON 1).*

AD-2 *122225/5WA (MAMS-12).*

AD-4N *125723/3RM (VMC-1).*

AD-4W *126840/24RM (VMC-1).*

HRS-1 *127801/2RH (HMR-161).*

HO3S-1 *123120/11WM (MAMS-33).*

OY-2 *(5)03928/5WB (VMO-6).*

R4D-6 *Bare metal, last three of serial on mid-fuselage: 17257/257AZ (HEDRON 1).*

R4Q-1 *Bare metal overall: 126735/AD (VMR-253).*

8.4.6. RECONNAISSANCE AND OBSERVATION AIRCRAFT

At the outbreak of the war there were two reconnaissance units in the area, one strategic, one tactical and both based at Yokota. The 6204th Photo Mapping Flight operated the ageing RB-17G, while the 8th Tactical Reconnaissance Squadron (TRS) flew the RF-80A. For several months all strategic reconnaissance was flown by 6204 PMF, but it was soon clear that the RB-17 was inadequate for the task of mapping and target reconnaissance in a hostile environment. During August the 31st Strategic Reconnaissance Squadron (SRS), equipped with the RB-29, replaced the flight, but this unit returned to the USA on 16 November as it was realized that more versatility was required: the RB-29 was not suited to the task of Manchurian and Russian overflights, essential in order to alert UN forces to any further surprises like the Chinese invasion.

The replacement unit was the 91st SRS, destined to remain in Japan for the rest of the war. Not only did the squadron operate its own aircraft, it was also the parent unit for aircraft of other detached units on temporary duty (TDY). The squadron used six types of aircraft in four main roles. For strategic reconnaissance along or near the communist borders the large RB-29 and later the RB-50 and RB-36 were used, for weather reconnaissance over the Sea of Japan and Yellow Sea the WB-26 was operated (TDY), while for long-range reconnaissance over the Yalu and into Manchuria the RB-45C was used. Three aircraft from 84 Bomb Squadron (Light) (BS(L)) were detached from November 1950, but one crashed on Midway during transit; a second was shot down over North Korea by a MiG-15 on 4 December, but not before the type had brought back the first Western pictures of the fighter at Chinese bases. The RB-45C was no match for the MiG-15, and the problem of reconnaissance over the Chinese bases was not satisfactorily resolved until late in the war.

The fourth role assumed by 91 SRS was that of air-to-air refuelling. Detachment 4 operated the KB-29 from the 43rd Air Refueling Squadron (ARS) from June 1951, conducting the first operational sorties in July when three RF-80As of the 67th Tactical Reconnaissance Wing (TRW) were refuelled en route to the Yalu river. Later in the year the tankers began supporting ground-attack F-84 Thunderjets of 116 Fighter Bomber Group (FBG). Tactical reconnaissance was initially a poorly co-ordinated activity. In August 1950 the RF-80 was joined by the 162nd TRS (Night Photo) with the RB-26, which was transferred from Langley AFB to Itazuke. In September 45 TRS with the F-6D (RF-51D) was activated, although it did not begin operations until December, by which time it was based at Taegu.

Concern over the duplication of targets and poor planning led to the tactical units' being reorganized in early 1951 under the 543rd Tactical Support Group (TSG) at Itazuke, with a forward base at Taegu. The basic problems were not resolved, however, so the organization was disbanded and rebuilt. From April 1951 the 67th Tactical Reconnaissance Wing (TRW) was activated at Taegu, which from now on would be the base for all USAF tactical reconnaissance in Korea. The 8th TRS and 162nd TRS were inactivated and replaced by 12 and 15 TRS flying the RB-26 and RF-80A respectively; the third component was the 45th TRS. With better film supplies and a single centre for co-ordination, much better results were obtained, and the Wing kept a close watch on supply routes and forward troop concentrations, although the problem of PR over the Manchurian bases remained. In mid-1952 45 TRS exchanged its F-6Ds for the RF-80C, but F-86 escort was still essential.

The answer to the problem was the conversion of the F-86 to a reconnaissance vehicle, and in

1952, in Project 'Ashtray', seven F-86As were modified to RF-86A configuration by incorporating one K25 and two K24 cameras in the lower gun bay, the aircraft retaining two machine guns with limited ammunition. In practice they were not distinctively marked and were flown among the standard fighter type. Early in 1953, in Project 'Haymaker', seven F-86Fs were converted for the reconnaissance role with the installation of one K17 and two K22 cameras, and these were operated successfully by 67 TRW until the end of the war. The unit suffered few losses and from June 1952 to the end of the war produced 736,684 negatives. The last operational sortie of the war was carried out by an RB-26 which set out at 2000hrs on a final check on North Korean dispositions.

Early on in the war, forward air control (FAC) sorties to pinpoint targets for close-support aircraft were flown by US Army L-4s and L-5s, sometimes with USAF crews, but from August 1950 the USAF established its own FAC unit equipped with the AT and LT-6G Texan. The 6148th Tactical Control Squadron (TCS) was later joined by 6149 TCS within 6149 TCW, based at K47 Chunchon. The aircraft maintained a constant airborne vigil, and on identifying a front-line target they would contact the Joint Operations Center (JOC) at Seoul; from there, the nearest available fighter-bombers would be directed to the target, which would be marked by the waiting Texan. When the T-6 was operating at a distance from base, a radio relay aircraft in the form of a C-47B supported the sorties. The JOC also operated a number of USN SNJ-5s.

USMC and USN tactical reconnaissance and observation activities are dealt with separately, but other air arms flew aircraft in the FAC or observer role. The ROKAF flew L-19A FAC aircraft, while the British and Turkish Armies operated the L-18B and Auster AOP.6 for artillery spotting along the front line. In addition to one heavy reconnaissance squadron, VJ-61 flying the AJ-2P Savage, the USN also committed a number of maritime patrol aircraft to the war. VP-47, equipped with the PBM-5 Mariner flying boat, was already at Yokosuka when the war began, and early in July it was joined by the land-based P2V-3 Neptunes of VP-6. VP-28, equipped with the P4Y-2 Privateer, followed a few days later, and from then on there were never fewer than three maritime patrol squadrons operating in the theatre. Many of the units involved carried out tasks in addition to their assigned roles of searching for enemy vessels and seaborne infiltrators: some aircraft acted as flareships for USMC ground attack units flying night sorties, for example, and they also assisted in the air–sea rescue task. Most units spent some time before or after their Japanese deployments operating from bases on Formosa, and by February 1951 such was the burden that reserve units were brought into action, the first being VP-772.

The RAF also contributed flying boats to maritime patrol operations, the aircraft coming under the control of Fleet Air Wing (FAW) 6 and being drawn from 88, 205 and 209 Sqns. at Hong Kong and Singapore. The aircraft were committed from the start of the war and flew their first operational sortie over the Yellow Sea early in July. A flight was constantly on hand at Iwakuni, which base the aircraft shared with the USN Mariner squadrons. They flew weather reconnaissance and minefield spotting sorties and also provided a transport service in support of British forces.

AIRCRAFT MARKINGS

USAF
RF-80A *Bare metal overall, no buzz number, black serial, yellow fin stripe and tip-tank flash: (4)58374 'Mary Lou' (15 TRS). Olive Drab overall, yellow serial (experimental scheme): (4)58310 (15 TRS).*

After the first year of fighting in Korea, the war settled to a fixed front line, roughly along the 38th parallel. Both the Americans and British maintained observation units along the Front, flying liaison and spotting sorties from small strips. While the British used the Auster for these tasks, the US Army relied on the robust L-19A Bird Dog. (US Army via R. F. Dorr)

F-6D *Bare metal overall, black serial, white polka dots on dark blue on spinner and wing tips, yellow fin tip: (4)484853 'Oh-Kaye Baby', (4)414547 'Symon's Lemon' (45 TRS).*

RB-26C *Black overall, red serial: (4)435456, (4)435555 (12 TRS).*

RB-45C *Bare metal overall, red nose flash and arrow on tip tanks, black I in square on fin: (4)8039, (4)8033 (91 SRS).*

RB-29A *Bare metal overall, black serial, X in circle on fin: (4)461815 'Moon's Moonbeam', (4)484000 'Tiger Lil' (91 SRS).*

AT-6G *Grey overall, green mottle over, red nose, fin and rudder, no serial: TA-533 (6149 TCS). Bare metal overall, black/white nose checks, black/yellow/black wing stripes,*

red/yellow/blue fin tip: (4)294216 (6149 TCS).

LT-6G *Bare metal overall, red fin tip: (4)93550/LTA-550, (4)483542 (6148 TCS).*

US Army

L-5E *Grey overall, Olive Drab mottle over: A(4)417377.*

L-19A *Olive Drab overall, light green mottle over, yellow serial: (5)01653.*

USN

As far as is known, all USN patrol and reconnaissance aircraft operated in the Korean theatre wore Sea Blue Gloss camouflage overall with white lettering. Code letters were applied large on the fin, and the individual aircraft

TABLE OF UNITS: THE KOREAN WAR—RECONNAISSANCE UNITS

Unit	Aircraft (code)	Base	Role(s)	Dates
USAF				
6204 PMF	RB-17G	Yokota	Photographic mapping, recce	25/06/50 to 00/09/50
8 TRS	RF-80A	Yokota, Itazuke	Tactical recce	25/06/50 to 00/04/51
162 TRS	RB-26C	Itazuke, K2	Night recce	00/08/50 to 00/04/51
31 SRS	RB-29A	Yokota	Strategic recce	00/08/50 to 16/11/50
45 TRS	F-6D (RF-51D), RF-80C	Itazuke, K2	Tactical recce	00/12/50 to 31/07/53
12 TRS	RB-26C	K2	Night recce (ex 162 TRS)	00/04/51 to 31/07/53
15 TRS	RF-80A	K2	Tactical recce (ex 8 TRS)	00/04/51 to 31/07/53
91 SRS	RB-29A, RB-50A, RB-36A	Yokota	Strategic recce (ex 31 SRS)	15/11/50 to 31/07/53
	WB-26	Yokota	Weather recce	00/11/50 to 31/07/53
	RB-45C	Misawa, Yokota	Fast strategic recce (84 BS TDY)	15/11/50 to 00/00/52
	KB-29A	Yokota	Air refuelling (43 ARS TDY)	00/06/51 to 31/07/53
6148 TCS	AT-6G, LT-6G	K16, K47	FAC	00/09/50 to 31/07/53
6149 TCS	AT-6G, LT-6G	K47	FAC	00/00/51 to 31/07/53
US Army				
–	L-4A, L-5E, L-19A	Various	Air observation, FAC	25/06/50 to 31/07/53
British Army				
1903 Flt.	Auster AOP.6	HQ Commonwealth Div.	Air observation	00/08/51 to 31/07/53
ROK Army				
–	L-19A	Various	FAC	00/00/51 to 31/07/53
Turkish Army				
–	L-18A	K13	Air observation	00/10/50 to 31/07/53
USN				
VP-47	PBM-5 (BA)	Yokosuka, Iwakuni		25/06/50 to 28/12/50
VP-6	P2V-3 (BE)	Johnson AB, Atsugi		07/07/50 to 11/02/51
VP-28	P4Y-2S (CF)	Naha		14/07/50 to 07/08/50
VP-1	P2V-3/5 (CD)	Naha	Maritime patrol	07/08/50 to 14/11/50
VP-42	PBM-5S (SA)	Iwakuni		21/08/50 to 10/04/51
JOC	SNJ-5	K16	FAC	00/11/50 to 31/07/53
VP-22	P2V-3/4/5 (CE)	Naha		14/11/50 to 02/05/51
VP-772	P4Y-2 (BH)	Atsugi		11/02/51 to 07/08/51
VP-28	P4Y-2 (CF)	Itami, Atsugi, K1		05/04/51 to 14/12/51
VP-892	PBM-5 (SE)	Iwakuni		01/05/51 to 09/06/51
VP-1	P2V-3/5 (CD)	Naha		02/05/51 to 01/09/51
VP-40	PBM-5 (CA)	Iwakuni		01/06/51 to 15/12/51
VP-6	P2V-3 (BE)	Johnson AB, Atsugi	Maritime patrol	30/07/51 to 15/01/52
VP-2	P2V-4 (SB)	Naha		01/09/51 to 01/12/51
VP-46	PBM-5 (BD)	Iwakuni		30/09/51 to 04/04/52
VP-22	P2V-3/4/5 (CE)	Naha		01/12/51 to 01/06/52
VP-42	PBM-5S (SA)	Iwakuni		08/12/51 to 02/06/52
VP-871	P4Y-2 (CW)	Atsugi, K1, K14		10/12/51 to 04/07/52
VJ-61	AJ-2P (PB)	?	PR	00/00/52 to 31/07/53
VP-1	P2V-5 (CD)	Atsugi, Kadena		28/03/52 to 01/10/52
VP-28	P4Y-2S (CF)	Naha		30/05/52 to 30/11/52
VP-731	PBM-5 (SF)	Iwakuni		01/06/52 to 08/12/52
VP-9	P4Y-2 (CB)	Iwakuni		29/06/52 to 05/01/53
VP-47	PBM-5 (BA)	Yokosuka, Iwakuni		29/11/52 to 01/06/53
VP-22	P2V-3/4/5 (CE)	Kadena	Maritime patrol	30/11/52 to 30/05/53
VP-17	P2V-6 (BH)	Iwakuni		29/12/52 to 30/06/53
VP-57	P2V-5 (?)	Atsugi		29/03/53 to 31/07/53
VP-1	P2V-5 (CD)	Atsugi, Kadena		30/05/53 to 27/07/53
VP-50	PBM-5 (MB)	Iwakuni		05/06/53 to 31/07/53
VP-7	P2V-5 (HE)	Iwakuni		30/06/53 to 31/07/53
RAF				
88 Sqn.				25/06/50 to 31/07/53
209 Sqn.	Sunderland GR.5	Hong Kong, Iwakuni	Maritime patrol	25/06/50 to 31/07/53
205 Sqn.				00/00/51 to 31/07/53

Throughout the Korean War, the RAF was stretched elsewhere, especially in Malaya, and its contribution was confined to the provision of rotated Sunderlands from three squadrons attached to TF.99 and based at Iwakuni in Japan. Illustrated is RN277/D of 209 Sqn. (Via A. S. Thomas)

number codes were painted on the forward fuselage except in the case of the PBM-5 Mariner, where they were applied on the mid-fuselage.
P4Y-2 *59900/8CB (VP-9); !/5CW (VP-871).*
PBM-5 *!/8BD (VP-46).*
P2V-5 *131548/1BH (VP-17).*
P2V-6 *127720/6CF (VP-28).*
AJ-2P *129185/6PB (VJ-61).*
SNJ-5 *Bare metal overall, black lettering, 'JOC Korea' on fin and below cockpit, 'last three' on nose: 51683/683 (JOC).*

British Army

Auster AOP.6 *Brown/green overall, white serial on rear fuselage and under wings: VF582 (1903 AOP Flt.).*

Turkish Army

L-18B *Olive Drab overall, black US serial on fin: (492)792.*

RAF

Sunderland GR.5 *White overall, black serial and code mid-fuselage: RN282/C (88 Sqn.).*

8.4.7. TRANSPORT OPERATIONS

At the time of the North Korean invasion there was one transport unit in the theatre, the 374th TCW with C-54As based at Tachikawa in Japan. Aircraft were rushed to Kimpo and Seoul to begin evacuating American civilians, but at noon North Korean Air Force (NKAF) Yak-7 fighters strafed the airfields and destroyed a C-54 at Kimpo. This was the first aircraft loss of the war, and fighters were rushed across from Japan to provide cover. Because of the need for more transports, 21 TCS was brought up from Clark AFB and the region scoured for spare C-47 aircraft. As the North Koreans closed on Pusan the C-47s were desperately flying supplies and ammunition into Taegu or Pusan, and in August the first C-119 of 314 TCG joined them. Casualties were flown out on the return trip to Japan.

Transport strength was increased by the addition of 1 Provisional Group flying C-46s from Japan and then, after the Inchon landings, Seoul. The C-46s were particularly valuable in the casevac role, having a greater capacity than the C-47. In December 1 PG's aircraft were absorbed into 437 TCW, the first reserve unit to be activated. As the United Nations forces fought their way north through the autumn, the airlift of supplies was maintained, and in October C-47s and C-119s were involved in the first parachute operation of the war. The 187th Regimental Combat Team (RCT) was a new élite unit of the 11th Airborne Division and had been prepared for duties in Korea. On 20th October 3,000 men of 187 RCT, with over 300 tons of equipment, were dropped at Sukchon and Sunchon north of Pyongyang by 75 C-119s and 40 C-47s. Their task was to secure the area and cut off supplies to Pyongyang which was under attack by the US Eighth Army. The operation was totally successful.

Such was the impetus of the UN advance that supply was a major problem. Recently evacuated North Korean airfields were put to immediate use, and on 26 October alone over 2,000 tons of supplies were moved forward from Seoul and Kimpo to Pyongyang and Wonsan; Sinanju was later also used as a supply base. The Chinese intervention caught the UN forces unawares, and the 1st Marine and 7th Infantry Divisions were effectively surrounded at Chosen. At the time they were being resupplied by USMC R4D-1s of VMR-252 and C-47s of 21 TCS, but a much greater effort was now needed, so 314 TCG C-119s from Ashiya dropped routine requirements while a small detachment based on Yonpo handled emergencies.

The position of the troops rapidly deteriorated and, with mounting casualties, bulldozers and crews were dropped near Hagaru-ri, where a 2,300ft airstrip was quickly completed. By 6 December 4,000 wounded had been evacuated to Yonpo by 21 TCS C-47s. On that date a second airstrip was built near Koto-ri and more wounded lifted out. The retreating troops made for the safety of Hungnam but were stopped by a deep gorge, the bridge over which had been blown by the Chinese. On 8 December, in one of the most remarkable episodes of the war, a sixteen-ton Bailey bridge was dropped in eight sections from a height of 800ft by eight C-119s flying from Yonpo. It was hurriedly assembled, and the next day the Marines linked up with the relief column from the 3rd Infantry Division. Combat Cargo Command now concentrated on airlifting out the supplies it had only a month earlier taken into North Korea, 437 TCW and 314 TCG running a non-stop evacuation from Yonpo with as many as 30 aircraft on the ground at one time. When the Chinese were within range, everything that could not be taken out was destroyed and the last aircraft departed. The scene was to be repeated at Seoul, Kimpo and Suwon.

In one humane mission in late December over 1,000 Korean children were airlifted from Seoul away from the combat zone to Chejudo island, where an orphanage had been established. A further important airdrop took place between 14 and 16 February 1951 when a French battalion was surrounded at Chipyong-ni: 400 tons were dropped, mainly at night and in appalling weather, enabling the French to fight their way out. As United Nations forces eventually held the Chinese advance, the C-119 continued to bear the brunt of supplying ground forces, with many drops to front-line units. 374 TCW C-54s were supplemented by the arrival of aircraft of 61 TCG at Ashiya in December for the movement of men and materials between Korea and Japan. Combat Cargo Command was replaced by 315 Air Division (AD) on 25 February 1951, and the airlift effort again increased in preparation for the UN counteroffensive.

So hard had the C-119 force been operating that in April it was grounded for a few weeks for urgent overhaul. During late 1950, 13 Flt. of the Royal Hellenic Air Force (RHAF) had begun operations in Korea and now with 61 Sqn. of the Royal Thai Air Force (RTAF) added their C-47s to 21 TCS. CAT was contracted to provide an intra-Japan transport service to relieve more aircraft for the combat zone. In September the first C-124A, which was able to carry twice the load of the C-54, visited Korea for trials, but it was not

until May 1952 that 374 TCW began re-equipping on an operational scale. As the war settled to one of attrition on a static front, the main supply base became Hoengsong and casualty evacuation flights steadily increased. There was now a regular shuttle of men to and from Japan on rest and recuperation (R&R), 750 soldiers being airlifted out of the combat zone each day. Hastings C.1s of 53 Sqn. RAF ran regular flights from Iwakuni to the UK repatriating wounded troops.

The transport flying settled down to routine for the rest of the war, although restrictions on passenger flights aboard the C-119 placed an increased burden on the ageing but reliable C-46. In June 1952 the 437 TCW became the 315th TCW, but only as a paper exercise. Reserve units were limited in the amount of time they were allowed to spend in war theatres, and the renumbering was merely a device to meet the demands of bureaucracy: the crews and aircraft in fact remained. At the same time, the C-119 units were reorganized to create an additional Wing, 403 TCW, and in a final reorganization, and as a result of the arrival of the C-124, 61 TCG returned to the US late in the year, although its 14 TCS was redesignated 21 TCS, which unit in turn became 6461 TCS at Ashiya. By the end of the war Combat Cargo Command/315 Air Division had airlifted no fewer than 2,650,000 passengers, evacuated 314,500 wounded, carried 697,000 tons and airdropped 18,000 tons. Sadly, on 18 June 1953, just days before the end of the war, a C-124A lost power on take-off from Tachikawa and crashed, killing all 129 aboard in the worst air disaster to date.

AIRCRAFT MARKINGS

In general, USAF transports were finished bare metal overall, but many C-46s, which were drawn from stocks across the US, were painted Olive Drab over/sky under. C-119 units used coloured fin markings believed to have been as follows. Plain tips (314 TCG): green (61 TCS), blue (62 TCS) or red (50 TCS). Diagonally striped tips (403 TCW): blue (37 TCS), green (65 TCS) or red (63 TCS).

C-46D *Bare metal overall, red trim, black serial*

As the war continued, with no signs of an early settlement, the USAF built up an extensive airlift operation. Supplies were flown in direct from the US to Japan and Korea, from where they were distributed by the locally based units. A C-124A belonging to 6 TCS, 374 TCW, is seen at Seoul in 1952, waiting to evacuate wounded. (J. Carreras)

TABLE OF UNITS: THE KOREAN WAR—TRANSPORT UNITS

Unit	Aircraft	Base	Squadrons	Dates
USAF				
374 TCW	C-54A, C-124A	Tachikawa	6, 22 TCS	25/06/50 to 31/07/53
374 TCW	C-47, C-54A	Tachikawa, K2, Itazuke	21 TCS (became 6461 TCS 01/12/52)	25/06/50 to 31/07/53
314 TCG	C-119B/C/G	Tachikawa, Ashiya, K27, K1	61, 62 TCS (50 TCS from 10/4/52)	00/08/50 to 31/07/53
1 PG	C-46A/D	K14, Brady AFB	Absorbed into 437 TCW	19/10/50 to 00/12/50
437 TCW	C-46A/D	Brady AFB	344 TCS, plus 3 other	19/10/50 to 10/06/52
61 TCG	C-54A	Ashiya	14, 15, 53 TCS	00/12/50 to 21/11/52
403 TCG	C-119B/C/G	Ashiya	37, 65 TCS; 63 TCS from 8/52	10/04/52 to 31/07/53
315 TCW	C-46A/D	Brady AFB	Renumbered from 437 TCW	10/06/52 to 31/07/53
374 TCW	C-54A	Tachikawa	21 TCS (ex 14 TCS)	01/12/52 to 31/07/53
374 TCW	C-47, C-54A	Ashiya	6461 TCS (ex 21 TCS)	01/12/52 to 31/07/53
CAT	C-46	Various Japanese		00/03/51 to 31/07/53
RAAF				
30 Sqn.	C-47	As 21 TCS	Attached to 21 TCS, USAF	00/08/50 to 31/07/53
RHAF				
13 Flt.	C-47	As 21 TCS	Attached to 21 TCS, USAF	00/11/50 to 31/07/53
RTAF				
61 Sqn.	C-47	As 21 TCS	Attached to 21 TCS, USAF	24/06/51 to 31/07/53
RAF				
53 Sqn.	Hastings C.1	Iwakuni, K-16	Wounded evacuation only	00/09/50 to 31/07/53

on fin: (4)477966 (344 TCS). Bare metal, white fuselage decking, dark blue cheat lines, registration on fin: B-870 (CAT).

C-47A Bare metal overall, red trim, black serial on fin: (4)476323, (4)224326 'Little Miss Carriage' (21 TCS). Serial on rear fuselage, code on fin: 92630/F 'Mars' (13 Flt. RHAF).

C-54A Bare metal overall, black serial on fin: (4)317204 'Tarheel State' (6 TCS).

C-119B Bare metal overall, green trim, black serial on fin, last three digits on forward fuselage: (4)9113/113 'Carolina Baby', (4)8146/146 (61 TCS).

C-119C Red trim: (5)12572/572 (63 TCS).

C-124A Bare metal overall, black serial on fin: (5)1116 (6 TCS).

8.4.8. SUPPORT OPERATIONS

To support the combat units and ground forces, a number of important support units functioned from bases in Japan and Korea. Perhaps foremost among these was the Air Rescue Service, which was already well established in the theatre at the outbreak of war. In June the Service relied on fixed-wing aircraft specially fitted for search and rescue, carrying stores, emergency equipment and, in the case of the SB-17G, a lifeboat. On 22 July, Detachment F of 3 Air Rescue Squadron (ARS) was formed with the H-5A and established at forward bases. Such were the weather conditions in Korea for much of the time that a fast rescue was essential to survival. From the beginning, SB-17 or SB-29 aircraft accompanied B-29 raids on their long hauls over the sea to North Korean targets.

Whereas over the sea it was the cold that was the enemy, over land it was Chinese or North Korean forces, and Detachment F helicopters moved up from Pusan via Seoul and Pyongyang to Sinanju in order to remain as close as possible to the scene of any intended rescue attempt. Over enemy territory the helicopters were supported by any conveniently based fighters, but from November 1950 the F-51s of 18 FBW were assigned the primary responsibility for the task of protection and for suppressing anti-aircraft fire and enemy intervention during the rescue process. The ARS conducted many extremely daring rescues many miles into enemy territory, often in appalling weather and at night. On occasions the SA-16 amphibian, which carried a medical

TABLE OF UNITS: THE KOREAN WAR—SUPPORT UNITS

Unit	Aircraft	Base	Role	Dates
US Army				
MASH	H-13, H-23A	Various	Casevac	00/00/51 to 31/07/53
–	L-5E, L-17B	Various	Liaison	00/10/50 to 31/07/53
THC-6	H-19C	Various	Transport, liaison	00/03/53 to 31/07/53
USAF				
1 ARS	SC-47	Cho-do	Rescue	? to 31/07/53
3 ARS	SB-17G, SB-29A, H-5A/G, H-19, L-5, SA-16A, SC-46, SC-47	Japan, K14, K96, Cho-do	Rescue	25/06/50 to 31/07/53
3 ARS	VB-17G, H-19A	Japan, Cho-do	Agent insertion and exfiltration	00/02/52 to 31/07/53
10 LS	L-5A	Various	Liaison	00/00/51 to 31/07/53
ROKAF				
–	Tachikawa 95, T-6	K14, K2	Training	25/06/50 to 31/07/53
British Army				
1913 LLF	Auster AOP.6, L-19A	HQ Comm. Div.	Liaison	00/10/51 to 31/07/53

team, was used to alight on rivers as well as at sea. The probability of rescue in the event of being downed was most important for morale, especially given the harsh treatment meted out to prisoners.

The ARS also evacuated troops from difficult situations and appeared to work flexibly with other units regardless of service; a number of British naval flyers owe their lives to the ARS. From the summer of 1951 the ARS operated out of Cho-do island up the west coast of Korea, some way north of the 38th parallel. Later, a ground control intercept radar station was built on the island, and it is remarkable that the North Koreans allowed the base to remain although several attempts to bomb it were made without success. From February 1952 the Cho-do Detachment received the larger H-19, which facilitated the internal carriage of the rescued and the prospect of early treatment. By the end of the war the ARS had recovered a staggering 996 UN personnel from behind enemy lines and evacuated 8,598 front-line casualties.

A special unit of 3 ARS was used to infiltrate and exfiltrate CIA agents into North Korea, Manchuria and, possibly, Russia. Flying from Japan, the unit used the VB-17 to parachute agents behind enemy lines while locally based H-19s were used to pick up returning agents from predetermined positions.

Essential to the conduct of the war were the liaison units which often operated on the front line. These units were used to move staff officers around the battlefield and for carrying light supplies. They used small strips along the front, and their ground crews became used to aiding combat aircraft making emergency landings at the nearest strips in friendly hands. Introduced into service in Korea in 1952 was the L-20A Beaver, which proved particularly effective, but the bulk of the work was carried out by the L-5, L-19 and Auster AOP.6.

Last, mention must be made of the second-line ROKAF training units in the south. Based initially at Seoul and then Taegu, the training organization prepared pilots for F-51 combat units. Among the types still in use in 1950 was the Tachikawa Type 95 left by the Japanese after the war, although these aircraft were soon replaced by the T-6.

AIRCRAFT MARKINGS

US Army
H-13C Olive Drab overall, code on plexiglass: WB-31 (MASH).
L-17B Grey overall, Olive Drab mottle over: A(4)81035.
H-19C Olive Drab overall, yellow lettering, serial on mid-boom: (5)114273 (THC 6).

USAF
L-5E Aluminium dope overall, black serial: (4)417609 (HQ FEAF).
SC-47 Bare metal overall, yellow bands outlined black on mid- and rear fuselage and wings: (4)348957 (1 ARS).
SB-17G Bare metal overall, yellow bands outlined black on rear fuselage and outer wings: (4)483511 (3 ARS).
SB-29A As SB-17 with extra band around fuselage: (4)484078 (3 ARS).
SA-16A Light grey overall, yellow bands outlined in black on rear fuselage and wings: (4)9095 (3 ARS).
H-5G Olive Drab overall, yellow lettering: (4)8541, (4)8557 (3 ARS).
H-19A Olive Drab overall, yellow lettering: (4)92014. Bare metal overall, black lettering: (5)13858 (3 ARS).

British Army
Auster AOP.6 Dark Green/Dark Earth overall, white lettering: VF516, VF564/T-TS, VF622 (1913 LLF).
L-19A Olive Drab overall, black lettering: (5)14754 (1913 LLF).

ROKAF
T-6 Bare metal overall, serial in black on fin: 101.

8.5. North and South Korea, 1953 to date

In July 1953 the war between communist and United Nations forces in Korea did not end; rather there was a ceasefire, which has remained tenuously intact ever since. Included in the terms of the armistice was an agreement that no new arms would be deployed, but that provision has been ignored. In the south, most of the Allied units had withdrawn by the end of 1954, by which time the USAF had reduced its commitment to two F-86F Wings, which re-equipped with the F-100D by 1958; the ROKAF was building up its strength from two fighter-bomber Wings of F-51Ds in 1953 to an additional F-86F Wing by 1956, while from 1958 the USAF increased its strength in South Korea through Temporary Duty (TDY) detachments of F-100Cs, B-57s, B-66Bs and RF-101As. To the north, the Korean People's Armed Forces Air Corps (KPAFAC), which became the KPAFAF in 1955, consolidated its position. On 21 September 1953 Lt. Noh Keun Suk of the KPAFAC landed his MiG-15 intact at Kimpo from Pyongyang, the first of several defections. His information was that communist forces committed to the Korean

War included 400 Soviet, 400 Chinese and 125 North Korean MiG-15s.

Late in 1953 there was the first of a number of incidents when a USAF RB-45C was attacked by MiG-15s over the Demilitarized Zone (DMZ); escorting F-86Fs of the 67th FBS shot down four of the attackers. In February 1955 two MiG-15s were shot down after making attacking passes on an RB-45C off the North Korean coast, and in the same year an RB-29 was attacked. By 1955 the NKAFAF had 400 combat aircraft in five divisions, comprising mainly MiG-15s and MiG-17s but also including 60 Il-28 bombers. In both North and South Korea, air force inventories changed as the F-100 was replaced in service from 1965 by the F-105D while the NKAFAF received a number of J-6s and Su-7s.

The US Air Force continued its offshore reconnaissance activities – on 27 April 1965 an RB-47 was attacked by two NKAFAF MiG-17s – but, with an increasing commitment in Vietnam, the USAF in Korea was run down. The Americans were apparently taken by surprise when, on 23 January, 1968 the intelligence-gathering ship USS *Pueblo* (AGER-2) was boarded from North Korean gunboats and taken to Wonsan; this occurred two days after 31 North Korean commandos had crossed the DMZ into Seoul to carry out an assassination attempt on the South Korean President. On 25 January eleven Air National Guard (ANG) squadrons were mobilized and the twelve locally based F-105Ds of 18 TFW were reinforced by an F-4D Wing at Osan from the USA, plus further F-105Ds from 18 TFW to

Kimpo, in Operation 'Combat Fox'. For air defence, 16 FIS, equipped with the F-102A, was sent from Okinawa to Suwon, and in addition the nuclear carrier USS *Enterprise* (CVAN-65), embarking CVW-9, and *Ticonderoga* (CVA-14) were deployed, together with an anti-submarine group in USS *Yorktown* (CVS-10). Early in March both Carrier Wings were briefed for attacks on North Korean airfields and the strikes only cancelled one hour before launch.

There were several shooting incidents in the DMZ in February, so further reinforcements were brought in from July, when the first ANG units arrived in the theatre. Two F-100C squadrons, 127 and 166 TFS, arrived at Kunsan on 4 July and the first RF-101G squadron, 154 TRS, began its TDY at Itazuke. In November, the latter unit was relieved by 192 TRS, which in turn was relieved by 165 TRS in February 1969. The remaining ANG units mobilized to Federal control remained in the USA to take pressure off the regular units, but they were eventually stood down in June 1969 after the crew of *Pueblo* was released in December – although not before a second serious incident.

On 15 April an EC-121M of VQ-1 operating in the Sea of Japan was shot down by two MiG-17s of the 2nd Air Division flying from East Tongchongni, with the loss of 31 crew. During 1969 there was also fighting across the DMZ, during which 21 Americans were killed. On 13 October a North Korean vessel intent on infiltration was caught by a South Korean destroyer and several F-5As and sunk. There was a similar incident on

TABLE OF UNITS: NORTH AND SOUTH KOREA, 1968 TO DATE

Unit	Aircraft		Base	Role	Dates
USAF, 1968 Emergency (Operation 'Combat Fox')					
18 FBW (12, 44, 67 TFS)	F-105D		Kimpo, Kadena	Fighter-bomber	00/01/68 to 00/03/69
? FBW	F-4D		Osan	Fighter-bomber	00/02/68 to ?
16 FIS	F-102A		Suwon	Air defence	00/02/68 to ?
127 TFS	F-100C		Kunsan	Ground attack	04/07/68 to 18/06/69
166 TFS	F-100C		Kunsan	Ground attack	04/07/68 to 18/06/69
154 TRS					24/07/68 to 18/11/68
192 TRS	RF-101G		Itazuke	PR	18/11/68 to 03/02/69
165 TRS					03/02/69 to 24/04/69

USN, 1968 Emergency

CVW-9 (NG), Enterprise, January–March 1968				*CVSG-55 (NU), Yorktown*			
VF-92	F-4B	VAH-2	KA-3B	VS-23	S-2E/F	HS-4	3H-3A
VF-96	F-4B	RVAH-1	RA-5C	VS-25	S-2D/F	VAW-11 (det.)	EA-1E
VA-35	A-6A	VAQW-13	EKA-3B				
VA-56	A-4E	VAW-112	E-2A				
VA-113	A-4F						

CVW-19 (NM), Ticonderoga, February–April 1968			
VF-191	F-8E	VA-195	A-4C
VF-194	F-8E	VAQW-33	EA-1F
VA-23	A-4E	VFP-63	RF-8G
VA-192	A-4E	VAW-111	E-1B

Unit	Aircraft	Base	Role	Nos.
ROKAF, 1968 Emergency				
(1 Wing)	F-5A/B	?	Ground attack	54
(1 Wing)	F-86D	?	All-weather air defence	36
(2 Wings)	F-86F	Osan	Air defence	95
(1 sqn.)	RF-86F	?	Recce	10
(1 Wing)	C-46, C-47	Kimpo	Transport	30
(1 flt.)	H-19	Kimpo	Transport/liaison	6

NKAFAF, 1968
The NKAFAF in 1968 comprised 30 MiG-21s, 50 MiG-19s, 450 MiG-15s/MiG-17s, 60 Il-28s, 40 An-2s, 10 Li-2s and 24 Mi-4s.

TABLE OF UNITS: NORTH AND SOUTH KOREA, 1968 TO DATE (continued)

Unit	Aircraft	Base	Role	Nos.
USAF, 1988 (314 Air Division, Seventh Air Force)				
8 TFW (35, 80 TFS)	F-16C/D	Kunsan	Air superiority, strike	
51 TFW				
36 TFS	F-4E	Osan	Ground attack	
497 TFS	F-4E	Taegu	Ground attack	
25 TFS	A-10A	Suwon	Anti-tank	
19 TASS	OV-10A	Osan	FAC/coin	
18 TFW	F-15C	Osan (det. ex Kadena)	Air defence	
15 TRS	RF-4C	Osan (det. ex Kadena)	PR	
9 SRW	U-2R	Osan (det. ex Kadena)	Sigint (Det. 2)	
38 ARRS	HH-3E	Osan	Rescue (Det. 13)	
USMC, 1988				
13 MAS	UC-12F	Osan (det.)	Communications	
HMS-36	OV-10D	Suwon (det. ex Futenma MCAS)	Coin, recce	
US Army, 1988				
?	RU-21H, RV-1D	?	Intelligence-gathering	
2 Inf. Div.	AH-1S, OH-58	Various	Anti-tank, observation	
ROKAF, 1988				
(1 Wing)	F-16C/D	Taegu	Air superiority, strike	36
(3 Wings)	F-5A/E/F	Taejon, Chongjin, Kwangju, Suwon	Ground attack	150
(2 Wings)	F-4D/E	Kangnung, Taegu	Ground attack	65
(1 sqn.)	A-37B	?	Close support	24
ROK Army, 1988				
—	Hughes 500MD	Various	Anti-tank, observation, liaison	200
KPAFAF, 1988				
(?)	Su-7, Su-9		Ground attack	120
(?)	MiG-15, MiG-17, MiG-23BM		Ground attack	290
(13 sqns.)	MiG-19, J-5		Ground attack	100
(?)	MiG-23		Air defence	32
(?)	MiG-21, J-7		Interception	160
(12 sqns.)	MiG-19, J-6	?	Interception	100
(3 sqns.)	Il-28, H-5		Light bombing	70
(?)	An-2		Light transport	250
(?)	An-24		Transport	10
(?)	Il-14, Il-18, Tu-154		Transport	10
(?)	Mi-4, Mi-8		Transport, gunship	60

1 June 1971, during which an ROKAF C-46 dropping flares was reportedly shot down and a T-33 damaged. From 1971 the US withdrew from behind the DMZ, leaving one infantry division in Korea. The US Army lost a CH-47 over the DMZ on 14 July 1977 when it inadvertently strayed into North Korean airspace. The Americans kept a close eye on North Korea, and in 1978 they made a comprehensive assessment of the country's capability. Their intelligence estimate showed the North Koreans to have 800 combat aircraft and 2,200 tanks: in short, they had the ability to invade the South without external assistance.

As the only comprehensive communist dictatorship, and with high internal security, North Korea represents a singular threat to world stability. Of particular concern in the South is the number of special forces troops who are trained to infiltrate using the large fleet of aged but versatile An-2 biplanes that is still operated, and the ROKAF has a real need for air defence systems capable of detecting and eliminating these elusive aircraft. The Air Force operates a unit of OV-10Gs to counter the threat, and Japan-based USMC OV-10Ds are also frequently deployed. Since 1978 the USAF has made regular SR-71 overflights of North Korea from Kadena in order to ensure that any potential attack is detected well in advance and reinforcements brought to bear in time to contain an invasion. On 26 August 1981 an SA-2 burst near an overflying Blackbird off the east coast. In 1985 the North Koreans complained of 140 overflights and in 1986 170. In addition, a U-2R detachment of 9 SRW is maintained at Osan AB and various USAF and Army reconnaissance aircraft are permanently deployed. The USAF has two fighter Wings in Korea and can also draw on Japan-based assets at short notice. Since 1985 the North Koreans have made considerable improvements to their air defences and now operate the MiG-23 and SA-5 SAM. The South maintains a high state of alert, and many strategists believe that if there is to be a Third World War it will start in Korea.

8.6. Formosa, 1954 to date

As Chinese Nationalist forces consolidated on Formosa after the civil war, the People's Republic of China (PRC) turned its attention to Korea, and in June 1950 the United States deemed it wise to send USS *Valley Forge* to the area to prevent the Nationalists attempting an invasion of the mainland. US involvement in the Korean War encouraged their recognition of the Nationalists, and from May 1951 a Mutual Assistance Advisory Group (MAAG) began work aiding the reconstruction of the armed forces. By 1954 the Chinese Nationalist Air Force (CNAF) comprised two F-84G Wings, two of F-47Ds and one of F-51Ds, and a bomber Wing operated a mix of B-24s and B-25s. The Americans also used Formosa as a base for various covert activities: between 1951 and 1954, 106 US citizens were killed and 124 captured on or over mainland China, and several SC-17s and SC-29s were brought down.

In addition to Formosa, the Nationalists occupied four offshore islands, the most distant and untenable of which, Tachen and Nanchi, were evacuated in January 1954 with the support of the US Seventh Fleet; the remaining islands are strategically placed, Quemoy opposite the port of Amoy and Matsu outside Fuchow. In 1954 these islands were used as bases from which to fire on communist positions, and artillery duels were fought, commando raids launched and many reconnaissance overflights made. On 3 September the PRC began a massive bombardment of Quemoy in retaliation, but the situation relaxed as the American Government applied pressure on the Nationalists, sending the carriers *Yorktown* and *Essex* to the area from December 1954 and transferring the F-86F-equipped 18th Fighter Bomber Wing (FBW) in February 1955. Forces were built up over the next few years, and it was planned to base Matador missiles there from 1958.

The PRC again applied pressure and built up its forces on the mainland through 1958. The USN maintained units of the Seventh Fleet in the area, and in July the Marine Corps sent Marine Air Group (MAG) 11 to Tainan after a CNAF F-86 was brought down by four MiG-17s. In August, CNAF RF-84F reconnaissance flights brought back evidence of a build-up of MiG-17 units on Chenghai and Liencheng airfields, and on the 18th a new shelling campaign began; at the same time, CNAF F-86Fs on patrol over the straits met MiG-15s in combat and on 14 August the first MiG was brought down. By now the United States had mobilized its newly established Composite Air Strike Force (CASF), 'X-Ray' of Tactical Air Command (TAC), and the first units were on Okinawa by the end of August. The CNAF had re-equipped and it now comprised three F-86F Wings and two of F-84Gs, and a squadron of RF-84Fs. In addition, the USAF maintained a Tenth Air Force F-100D Wing on the island on Temporary Duty (TDY) under Thirteenth Air Force control, and by the end of August the Seventh Fleet had no fewer than four carriers in the area with two more on the way. The ships' primary function was to deter the PRC from invading, a threat it announced on 29 August.

The CNAF extended its patrols, and with four air divisions (12 regiments each of three squadrons) now based in the Fuchow Military Region, more MiGs were encountered. Fighting increased, until on 24 September fourteen F-86Fs of 3 Wing claimed ten MiG-15s and MiG-17s destroyed in the air, including four from Sidewinder missile strikes; this was the first time that air-to-air missiles had been used in combat. There was no further fighting for the time: in just six weeks 31 MiG-15s and -17s were claimed to have been shot down, for the loss of two F-86Fs. Not all the fighting took place over the sea, and at least one F-86 crashed on the Chinese mainland. The USN task force provided air defence and freed the CNAF for offensive sorties.

The Nationalists remained alert, and the following year, on 5 July, five MiG-17s were claimed destroyed in another skirmish. The CPAFAF moved a whole air division on to airfields opposite Quemoy late in December 1959, but there was no further fighting of consequence. On 12 January 1960 a defecting CPAFAF MiG-15 pilot died on landing at Taipeh, having been pursued from the mainland.

From late 1958 American strategic reconnaissance aircraft were based on Formosa, normally operating out of Taoyuan AB. Initially RB-57Ds of 4028 SRS, recently withdrawn from Yokota, were used to keep a check on PRC military intentions, although the aircraft bore CNAF markings and were flown by Chinese pilots. The B-57 was developing wing fatigue problems, and after one was shot down over China on 7 October 1959 the CIA engineered the sale of two U-2As from Lockheed to the CNAF and the first pilots began training. For the U-2 programme, however, the CIA was interested in the Lop Nor nuclear development site in Sinkiang province and the Chiuchuan missile range in Kansu province: overflights of some 3,000 miles began in early 1960, and these continued at a rate of about three per month for many years.

The first CNAF U-2 was lost over Nanching on 9 September 1962, and when the second aircraft was brought down over Shanghai in November 1963 both were replaced. The first nuclear test in October 1964 was monitored, and although at least eleven U-2 variants were to be lost over

TABLE OF UNITS: FORMOSA, 1954–1959

Unit	Aircraft	Base	Role	Dates
USAF, 1954–1955				
18 FBW	F-86F	Taipeh	Air defence	From 00/07/55

USN 1954–1955							
CVG-15 (H), Yorktown				*CVG-2 (M), Essex*			
VF-151	F9F-8B	VA-154	F9F-5	VF-23	F9F-6	VF-64	F2H-3
VF-152	F2H-3	VA-155	AD-6/7	VF-24	F9F-6	VA-65	AD-6
VA-153	F9F-6	VA-156	F9F-6/8	VA-63	F9F-8	VA-26	F9F-8/8B

Unit	Aircraft	Base	Role	Dates
CNAF, 1958				
1 FW		Taipeh		
2 FW	F-86F	Taipeh	Air defence	
3 FW		Tainan		
5 FBW	F-84G	?	Ground attack	
TRS	RF-84F	Taipeh	Recce	
TW	C-46D, C-47, SA-16A	Taipeh	Transport, liaison	
USAF, 1958				
511 TFS	F-100D	Ching Chuan	Air defence, ground attack	TDY
83 FIS	F-104A	Ching Chuan	Air defence	00/09/58 to 00/12/58
354 TFW (2 sqns.)	F-100D	Kadena (ex Myrtle Beach AFB)	Ground attack	00/09/58 to 00/12/58
27 TFW (522 TFS)	F-101C	Kadena (ex Bergstrom AFB)	Ground attack	07/09/58 to 08/12/58
363 TRW (20 or 29 TRS)	RF-101C	Kadena (ex Shaw AFB)	Recce	00/09/58 to 00/02/59
345 BG (499 BS)	B-57B	Kadena (ex Langley AFB)	Light bombing	29/08/58 to 00/12/58
314 TCW (1 sqn.)	C-130A	Ashiya	Transport	00/08/58 to 00/12/58
? ARS	KB-50J	? Japan	Air refuelling	00/08/58 to 00/12/58
USMC (MAG-11), 1958				
VMF(AW)-115	F4D-1	Tainan	Close support	00/00/58 to 00/12/58
VMF(AW)-314	F4D-1	Tainan	Close support	30/09/58 to 18/03/59

USN, 1958–1959							
CVG-9 (NG), Ticonderoga, October 1957–April 1958				*ATG-1 (NA), Ticonderoga, October 1958–February 1959*			
VF-91	FJ-3	VA-95	AD-6/7	VF-112	F3H-2M	VA-35 (det.)	AD-5N
VF-122	F3H-2M	VAH-2 (det.)	A3D-2	VF-52	F2H-3	VAW-11 (det.)	AD-5W
VA-93	A4D-1			VA-151	FJ-4B	VFP-61	F9F-8P
				VA-196	AD-6	HU-1	HUP-2
CVG-15 (NL), Hancock, February–October 1958				VAH-2 (det.)	A3D-2		
VF-23	F4D-1	VA-155	AD-6				
VF-154	F8U-1	VAH-4 (det.)	A3D-2	*CVG-19 (NM), Bon Homme Richard, November 1958–April 1959*			
VA-153	A4D-1			VF-191	F11F-1	VA-35 (det.)	AD-5N
				VF-192	FJ-4B	VAW-11 (det.)	AD-5W
CVG-11 (NH), Shangri-La March–November 1958				VF-193	F3H-2	VFP-61	F9F-8P
VF-114	F3H-2	VA-156/VF-111	F11F	VA-195	AD-6	HU-1	HUP-2
VA-113	A4D-1	VAH-4 (det.)	A3D-2	VAH-2 (det.)	A3D-2		
VA-115	AD-6						
				Princeton			
CVG-21 (NP), Lexington, August–November 1958				VS-23	S2F		
VF-24	F3H-2M	VA-212	FJ-4B	HS-4	HSS		
VF-213	F4D-1	VA-215	AD-6				
CVG-2 (NE), Midway, September 1958–January 1959							
VF-64	F3H-2	VA-35 (det.)	AD-5N				
VF-211	F8U-1	VAW-11 (det.)	AD-5W				
VA-63	FJ-4B	VFP-61	F8U-1P				
VA-65	AD-6	HU-1	HUP-2				
VAH-8	A3D-2						
ATG-201 (AP), Essex, September–December 1958							
VF-11	F2H-3	VAH-7 (det.)	AJ-2				
VF-62	FJ-3M	VA-33 (det.)	AD-5N				
VA-83	A4D-2	VAW-12	AD-5W				
VA-105	AD-6	HU-2	HUP-2				
VA-36	F9F-8						

Unit	Aircraft	Base	Role	Dates
CIA				
–	RB-57D, U-2A/B/R	Taoyuan	Strategic recce	00/12/58 to 00/10/74

CPAFAF
By September 1958 four air divisions each comprising nine squadrons of MiG-15s or MiG-17s were deployed on bases in Fuchow Military Region. These included Amoy, Longhai, Anhai, Huian, Putian, Minhow, Nantai, Nanping and Liancheng. A further division is believed to have been based on airfields around Swatow, including Chenghai and Kaochi.

China by 1974 the Agency made good the attrition. The flights were finally halted in October 1974 after a US-China accord was reached. The CNAF also flew hit-and-run strikes over the mainland, the PRC complaining of a total of 399 such attacks between 1963 and 1969.

The United States continued to support the Nationalists until January 1979, when, after having at last recognized the Peking Government, it broke off diplomatic relations with Formosa (by now called Taiwan). Since then, the CNAF has had to look to its own aircraft industry or further afield for new combat aircraft, its most modern units being three Wings of F-5Es. The peculiarities of international relations are such that by June 1981 the US was manning a listening post near Lop Nor, co-operating with the PRC in spying on the USSR.

AIRCRAFT MARKINGS

F-86F *Bare metal overall, black serials on fin and 'last three' on rear fuselage: F-86098/ (5)12894/098 (1 FW CNAF). Red nose, single yellow fuselage and wing stripe outlined in red,* *unit badge on fin: F-86141/(5)24545/141 (2 FW CNAF). Red/white fin checks, shark's mouth over intake, double yellow fuselage and wing stripes outlined in black: F-86152/(5)112976/152 (3 FW CNAF).*

F-84G *Bare metal overall, black serial on fin and code on forward fuselage: (5)28392/070 (5 FW CNAF).*

RF-84F *Bare metal overall, black serials on fin and CNAF serial repeated on forward fuselage: 5607/(5)117036, 5611/(5)27446 (TRS CNAF).*

RB-57D *White over, black under and fin and rudder, red serials on fin, CNAF serial repeated on rear fuselage: 5544/(5)33981 (CIA/CNAF).*

When fighting began between Communist and Nationalist forces in 1958, the CNAF was equipped with three Wings of F-86Fs. The aircraft were widely used in the air superiority role over the Formosa Straits, and in six weeks 31 MiG-15s and MiG-17S were claimed as having been shot down, some by AIM-9 Sidewinder missiles.

8.7. China and India, 1962 to date

The boundary between India and Tibet had been settled in 1914 along the McMahon Line, but after the Chinese occupation of Tibet from 1950 the border was disputed. To supply Tibet from Xinjiang, the Chinese built a road through eastern Aksai Chin to which the Indians belatedly took exception in 1958, The other disputed boundary was in the North-East Frontier Agency (NEFA) region north of Burma. The first significant border clash occurred at Longju on 25 August 1959 when there were exchanges of fire, the Indian troops being supported by S-55 helicopters of 104 Helicopter Unit.

Relations between the two countries deteriorated when the Dalai Lama was forced to flee Tibet and India began occupying forward positions during the summer of 1962. After crossing the McMahon Line on 8 September 1962, China launched a massive attack against India on two fronts on 20 October. The NEFA area was held by the Indian 4th Division, which because of the inhospitable terrain and isolation was completely supplied by airdrop by Il-14s of 14 Sqn. Indian Air Force (IAF). The two forward battalions of the division were hopelessly outnumbered by the 20,000 attacking Chinese, and forward positions were soon conceded: 7 Brigade, based around Tawang to the west, was destroyed as the town was evacuated after a day of fighting.

In a desperate position, the Indian troops were supported by two helicopter units. The Tezpur-based 110 Helicopter Unit, equipped with Mi-4s, flew from Darang at the foot of the hills to the advance base at Lumpu situated at 7,200ft, bringing in supplies and ammunition and returning with casualties. By 26 October a detachment was also operating from Walong in the east, where 11 Brigade was under attack. From 15 November the whole unit moved to Tezu, where it lost a helicopter to groundfire near Walong. As the Chinese pressed forward, 105 Helicopter Unit with Bell 47Gs and Mi-4s also operated between Tezpur and Lumpu, losing at least four machines to ground fire in the course of flying 716 sorties each averaging just under one hour in duration. Walong was eventually abandoned on 16 November, but on the 21st the Chinese announced a unilateral ceasefire and withdrew to ten miles from the disputed border. It had been decided by the Indian Government not to use aircraft in offensive roles for fear of retaliation, but it is understood that at least one photo-reconnaissance sortie was flown on the first afternoon, probably by a Canberra PR.57 of 106 Sqn. The units fighting in the east were supplied throughout by Il-14s flying into Tezpur and Jorhat.

In the north-west, the Chinese attack was directed against a line of Indian posts along the bank of the Pangong Tso in front of the forward airfield at Chushul. From 1959 India had built up four advanced airfields, at Chushul (14,000ft), Leh (11,554ft), Thoise (11,500ft) and Fukche (14,000ft), all capable of taking the transport aircraft then in service; there was, in addition, a strip at Daulet Beg Oldi at 16,800ft, probably the highest in the world. The 3rd Infantry Division was already established at Leh, but as soon as fighting started the 114th Brigade was airlifted to Chushul to support the defence, by means of the Orpheus jet boosted C-119Gs of 12 and 19 Sqns. and the newer An-12 of 44 Sqn. based at Chandigarh. By 13 November 150 sorties had been completed, and the two troops of AMX-13 tanks of the 20th Lancers flown up were critical in defending the airfield until the ceasefire. From January 1963 the US Air Force detached twelve C-130s to the IAF, and these were used to supplement the transport fleet in taking supplies up to the Aksai Chin front.

In the north-west, the Indians suffered relatively light casualties, but in NEFA some 1,383 died, with many more missing or wounded. The border remains disputed, and in the NEFA area it has in practice moved south to embrace the eastern end of the Himalaya range. There is continuing tension in Aksai Chin.

TABLE OF UNITS: CHINA AND INDIA, 1962 TO DATE

Unit	Aircraft	Base	Role	Dates
IAF				
104 HU	S-55	Tezpur	Transport	25/08/59 to 00/10/59
106 Sqn.	Canberra PR.57	?	PR	
14 Sqn.	Il-14	Chandigarh		
12 Sqn.	C-119F/G	?	Transport	Permanently based
19 Sqn.	C-119F/G	?		
44 Sqn.	An-12	Chandigarh		
110 HU	Mi-4	Tezpur	Transport, casevac, liaison	20/10/62 to 00/04/63
105 HU	Mi-4, Bell 47G			26/10/62 to 00/04/63
USAF				
? TCS	C-130A	?, Chushul	Transport	00/01/63 to 00/04/63

AIRCRAFT MARKINGS

C-119F/G *Bare metal overall, black serial on fin, code on nose: IK454/O, IK464Y (12 Sqn.); IK465 (19 Sqn.).*
An-12 *Light grey overall, white cockpit top, black serial on fin: BL734 (44 Sqn.).*
Mi-4 *Light grey overall, black serial on boom: Z1017.*

8.8. China and Vietnam, 1979 to date

During the Vietnam War, China backed North Vietnam; on 21 August 1967, for example, two US Navy A-6 Intruders were destroyed by a flight of Shenyang J-6s from the Air Force of the People's Liberation Army (AFPLA) over the Gulf of Tonkin. Relationships soured, however, after President Nixon visited China in 1972. In November 1978 the Soviet Union and the now unified Vietnam concluded a treaty, and in December that year Vietnam invaded China's ally, Kampuchea, at the same time as US-Taiwan relations were broken. Following a series of border incidents, China invaded Vietnam on 17 February 1979, primarily to relieve the pressure on Kampuchea.

The PLA crossed the border at 26 points with 85,000 troops and a further 200,000 in reserve, the main targets being Lao Cai, Cao Bang and Lang Son, with Hanoi as the eventual objective. By early March the PLA had accomplished its initial aims and the towns were razed, but by then Vietnamese forces had rallied and the PLA was forced to retire behind the border. It has been reported that Vietnam used an unnamed chemical weapon, probably artillery shells containing a nerve gas.

In the brief but bloody fighting, the PLA lost 62,500 troops killed or wounded, 280 tanks and, most importantly, face. The AFPLA played little part in the war, although some 700 fighter aircraft, mainly A-5s and J-6s (Chinese built MiG-19s), with some J-7s (MiG-21s), were deployed in the area. The aircraft were drawn from the Guangzhou and Kunming Military Regions and were based at Nanning, Bose, Debao, Guangnan and Mengzi. They were poorly flown, and bad weather meant that the few ground-support sorties flown achieved no results. The aircraft did not meet the better-organized Vietnamese Air Force (VAF) in action, but several were shot down by SA-6 and SA-7 missiles. The VAF operated a mix of Soviet-supplied MiG-21s and MiG-23s and captured Northrop F-5s, mainly based around Hanoi.

AIRCRAFT MARKINGS

AFPLA
J-6 *Dark tan distemper over dark green overall, serial in red on nose: 5065.*

8.9. Miscellaneous conflicts and incidents

1. The US Air Force went on the alert in Alaska in March 1948. On 13 April the 82nd Fighter Group arrived at Ladd Field, from where its F-51Hs flew armed sorties until June.

2. During 1952, Chinese Communist MiG-15s made several attacks on US Navy patrol aircraft, on for example 16 and 31 July, 20 September and 23 November. On 29 November a CAT aircraft was shot down over Manchuria. In June and July 1953 there were further attacks on USN patrol aircraft by Chinese ships and shore batteries.

3. After an incident between a Chinese Communist gunboat and a Royal Navy launch in September 1953, 28 Sqn. Vampires flew regular armed sorties for some years. In October 1956, Venoms of the squadron made low passes over rioters in Kowloon.

4. A Cathay Pacific DC-4 was shot down off Hainan on 23 July 1954. USN Corsairs and Skyraiders from USS *Philippine Sea*, searching for survivors, were bounced by two La-7s, and both Chinese aircraft were shot down by the AD-4 Skyraiders.

5. From August 1958 to April 1964 the USAF detached one squadron of the 3rd Bomb Wing in rotation to Kunsan AB in Korea. These aircraft were armed with Mk. 7 nuclear bombs for a potential nuclear strike into China (the USAF was prohibited from storing nuclear weapons in Japan).

6. CAT C-46 B-908 crashed after take-off from Suinam airfield, Taiwan, on 20 June 1964 in suspicious circumstances. All 57 on board were killed.

7. On 10 January 1966 a CNAF HU-16A was flying three important defectors from Matsu to Taiwan for a press conference when it was ambushed by CPAFAF J-6 fighters. The aircraft was shot down and those aboard killed.

8. During 1967 the Cultural Revolution was in full swing in China. In the year there was reportedly a PLAAF paratroop drop to quell anti-Mao demonstrations.

9. In July 1960 the Soviet Union stopped aid to China, and from then onwards relations between the two countries deteriorated. The Russians had expressed particular concern over Chinese incursions into disputed territory in India in 1959. At the beginning of March 1969 there was limited fighting over Damansky (Chenpao) Island on the Ussuri river, which forms the north-eastern border of the two nations. This first incident was provoked by China and was followed by a number of Soviet attacks over the next few months. Later in March, 3,000 Soviet and 2,000 Chinese troops were involved in major fighting, in which tanks, artillery and helicopters were used, at Chuguchak and Yu-Min, 2,500 miles to the west in Sinkiang. Between May and July there were further incidents near Khabarovsk. Although combat aircraft were not used during the incidents, helicopters were deployed for liaison work and to move troops to reinforce vulnerable border points. J-6 and J-7 fighters were used in mock raids on Chinese cities in the east in association with air-raid drills, which included

defence against chemical weapons. The Soviet Air Force in the region was reinforced and the Army grew from 40 divisions on the Chinese border in 1969 to 52 in 1984, although it has now been reduced to about 40.

10. Japan has long-standing disputes with the Soviet Union and has laid claim to Sakhalin Island and the southern islands of the Kuriles chain. These important areas are heavily defended by Soviet sea and air installations, especially to allow free access to the Pacific for the Soviet Eastern Fleet. Since 1953, even before they possessed an air arm, the Japanese have had to counter Soviet penetrations of their airspace. Reportedly on 6 February that year two Japanese pilots flying USAF F-84s intercepted two Russian fighters over Hokkaido, damaging one. In 1968, after the installation of the air defence system, there were numerous incursions, all intercepted by Japanese Air Self Defence Force (JASDF) F-104Js. By 1972 the number of intercepts was running at 380 a year, and early in 1973 there was a particularly high level of activity associated with the Nike SAM system. In 1978 the number of intercepts was 798, in 1979 636, in 1980 783 and in 1981 939, most of them against probing flights by Tu-16s, Tu-95s, Tu-142s and Il-38s. From 1958 to 1988 the JASDF flew over 53,000 air defence sorties to intercept aircraft flying along, or occasionally over, Japanese territory. The high level of sorties is a reflection of the denial to the JASDF of an in-flight refuelling capability, requiring relays of fighters to monitor intruders.

In 1988 the JASDF and USAF air defence units in Japan were as follows:

JASDF

2 Wing	F-15J	Chitose
3 Wing	F-1, E-2C	Misawa
5 Wing	F-4EJ, F-15J	Nyutabaru
7 Wing	F-4EJ, F-15J	Hyakuri
8 Wing	F-1, F-4EJ	Tsuiki
83 Group	F-4EJ	Naha

USAF

432 TFW	F-16A	Misawa
18 TFW	F-15C	Kadena

In addition, the USS *Midway* is home-ported at Yokosuka and embarks four F/A-18 and one A-6E squadrons. When docked, the aircraft fly from Atsugi.

11. A Soviet MiG-25 pilot defected with his aircraft to Hakodate airport on 6 September 1976. The aircraft was stripped and examined before being returned.

12. From late 1987, Soviet Tu-95s from Vietnam and Vladivostok began intruding into Taiwanese airspace. The flights are regularly intercepted.

9: Indo-China

Until the final months of the Second World War, Indo-China was ruled by the French as they had ruled it for decades, albeit latterly under Japanese occupation. As the war ended, the British assumed responsibility for disarming the Japanese and maintaining control until the French were again able to govern the colonies (Tonkin, Annam, Cochin-China, Cambodia and Laos), but the British were soon having to use Japanese troops to help them maintain order as Viet Minh elements rioted. When the French returned in late 1945 they already had a war in the making to contend with.

Under the leadership of Ho Chi Minh and the generalship of Vo Nguyen Giap, the Viet Minh gradually built up a guerrilla army, concentrating in Tonkin but operating throughout Vietnam. In 1954, after the massive defeat at Dien Bien Phu, the French began to withdraw: for the first time in modern history, a major power had been defeated by a peasant army. The Geneva Accords left Laos and Cambodia independent and neutral, while it was agreed that the French would withdraw to the south of the 17th parallel while the Viet Minh withdrew to the north; it was further agreed that in Vietnam there would be free elections to determine the future shape of government. However, the Americans filled the vacuum left by the departing French and effectively ensured that the elections would not be held, in order to prevent communist domination; indeed, it was in April 1954 that President Eisenhower first espoused the 'domino' theory, which predicated that once one country fell to communist control, so would neighbouring countries in succession, as a row of dominoes inevitably falls one by one.

The Americans propped up successive corrupt governments in South Vietnam, and, denied the promised free elections, the North Vietnamese supported the Viet Cong in the South until there was open warfare, albeit with covert American participation, by 1961. When North Vietnamese patrol boats opened fire on US destroyers in the Gulf of Tonkin in August 1964, it gave Congress the excuse to pursue the war overtly, although there remains doubt about North Vietnamese intentions: there is some uncertainty as to whether a second attack on the destroyers actually took place. The war soon escalated, but it was one the Americans could not hope to win. In 1970 they began a programme of 'Vietnamization', and withdrew following peace talks in early 1973

after the 'Linebacker II' bombing raids brought the North Vietnamese back to negotiations. Two years later the North invaded South Vietnam, which quickly fell.

The Americans also intervened in Laos to counter illegal incursions into the country by North Vietnamese forces supporting the communist Pathet Lao movement and using trails along the border with South Vietnam to supply the Viet Cong and infiltrate their own forces. In practice, the USA supported two anti-communist factions: the State Department, representing official policy, backed the Royalist neutralists, while the CIA, more pragmatically, backed the right-wing military, exemplified by the Meo tribesmen who took the war to the Pathet Lao. It is ironic that the CIA necessarily colluded with drug-traffickers, whose products finished up in South Vietnam where drug abuse became a major problem among American troops. Eventually the Americans were obliged to evacuate Laos, leaving the Meo to annihilation by the North Vietnamese and Pathet Lao.

Involvement in Cambodia began somewhat later for the United States, the first significant action being the blanket bombing of North Vietnamese depots and Khmer Rouge concentrations by B-52 bombers from March 1969. The bombing was carried out with great secrecy: the B-52s hardly differentiated between the enemy and peaceful villagers, and a significant proportion of the population was wiped out. After the Government was defeated by the Khmer Rouge in 1975, there began one of the most tyrannical regimes of modern times.

For three years the Khmer Rouge emptied the cities and attempted to create a new closed and ultimately socialist order, and at least a million

The Aéronavale played an important part in the war in Indo-China, its carrier-based fighters often operating for protracted periods from shore. Illustrated is an F6F-5, 841/12.F3, of 12F, which flew numerous close-support missions between 1952 and 1955. The potent American fighter also saw service with three Armée de l'Air squadrons. (IWM)

people died or were executed in major re-education programmes. Then, in 1978, the Vietnamese, at one time cautious allies of the Khmer Rouge, invaded and occupied the country. The Khmer Rouge are now the refugees, although they work in a coalition of parties to free what is now Kampuchea from Vietnamese control. In the Alice in Wonderland world of Indo-China, it is of interest to note that the coalition gets support from China and the West and is recognized as the legitimate government of Kampuchea at the United Nations.

Fighting continues in Laos and Kampuchea. Since 1945, the cost of a succession of wars in Indo-China cannot be counted, but suffice it to say that this part of South-East Asia has witnessed every misery that modern warfare can bring. Sadly, none of the major powers see it to be in their interests to search for a framework for ending conflict in the region.

9.1. Indo-China, 1945–1954

Indo-China comprised the five French colonies or protectorates of Tonkin, Annam and Cochin-China (Vietnam), Laos and Cambodia. During the Second World War it was occupied by the Japanese, but until March 1945 the Vichy French colonial government was allowed to continue to administer the territory. By then France had been liberated and a new French Government installed, after which British, American and French agents were infiltrated into Indo-China to support nationalists against the Japanese. The Viet Nam Doc Lap Dong Minh Hoi, abbreviated to Viet Minh, had been founded in China in May 1941 to link nationalist movements. Its postwar aim was to achieve independence for Vietnam and its leader was the communist Nguyen Ai Quoc (Nguyen the Patriot), better known as Ho Chi Minh (He Who Enlightens). Vo Nguyen Giap was appointed to form guerrilla bands around Cao Bang, but there were few operations during the war.

On 9 March 1945 the Emperor Bao Dai, on the instructions of the Japanese, proclaimed the independence of Vietnam and the French were disarmed and interned. There followed four months of sporadic fighting. At the Potsdam conference in July 1945 it was agreed that China would accept the Japanese surrender north of the 16th parallel while the British were to occupy the south. It was understood that the country would eventually be handed over to the French, although the Americans were keen to see the disbandment of the British, Dutch and French empires, especially in Asia. The war in the Far East ended suddenly in mid-August following the dropping of the atomic bombs at Hiroshima and Nagasaki, but the Supreme Allied Commander, MacArthur, was slow to accept the surrender of the Japanese.

In the intervening period, Giap ensured that the Viet Minh filled a vacuum, and it quickly established control around Hanoi and Saigon, and on 2 September, as the surrender was accepted, Ho Chi Minh declared the independence of Vietnam as a republic; in the north, the Chinese began disarming the Japanese, transferring many of their weapons to the Viet Minh. On 11 September Dakotas of 62 Sqn. brought the first troops of the 80th Brigade, 20th Indian

Division, to Saigon, and the following day 150 French troops arrived in C-47s of the Escadrille de Marche d'Extrême-Orient (EMEO). The British then, in effect, allowed the French to deal with the Viet Minh while themselves disarming the Japanese. Rioting around Saigon made it clear that the Viet Minh could not control a number of nationalist groups, and there was soon serious fighting around the capital. After a fragile truce fighting again broke out, and on 13 October Tan Son Nhut airfield came under heavy attack. The British were now required to use the Japanese to assist in containing the Viet Minh.

No. 273 Sqn. RAF, equipped with Spitfire IXs, had flown into Tan Son Nhut on 19 September, and the aircraft were now involved in armed reconnaissance flights in the south. By the date of the attack on the airfield, 267 Sqn. with Dakotas and a flight of Mosquito PR.34s of 684 Sqn. were also present, together with a unique outfit called the Gremlin Task Force. This was a unit of Japanese pilots under British command formed to fly and maintain Japanese transport aircraft in support of British and French forces, and by the end of January 1946, when the unit was disbanded, it had flown over 2,000 sorties. French aircraft were also operational from October: the 9th Division d'Infantrie Coloniale (DIC) brought several L-4Bs to Saigon, and Groupe de Chasse (GC) I/7 flew some captured Ki-43 fighters for a short time from Phnom Penh. In France, the Aéronavale had established the Groupement Aéronavale Indochine (GANI) on 24 August, the first unit of which, 8F, equipped with the PBY-5 Catalina flying boat, began arriving at Saigon on 27 October. Already operating in the theatre was 8S, which had formed during September at Cat Lai on locally available aircraft, including captured Japanese types.

Two further brigades of the 20th Division were flown into Saigon, and through November there was continuing fighting. The targets were mainly French troops or settlers, and on 11 December the Spitfires of 273 Sqn. fired their guns in anger against Viet Minh guerrillas surrounding a French force at Ban Me Thuot. Leaflets were dropped in advance. Two days later the first Armée de l'Air (AA) fighter unit proper, GC II/7, was formed at

Tan Son Nhut with Spitfire VIII fighters borrowed from the RAF pending delivery of Spitfire IXs, which arrived in January. Gradually, control of Saigon was handed over to the French, and the last British troops left on 30 March 1946. No. 273 Sqn. was disbanded on 31 January, and the 267 Sqn. element returned to Burma; the Mosquito detachment had completed its mapping task on 12 January. During the phase of British occupation, forty Allied troops were killed, against 2,700 Viet Minh dead.

During March the French entered the north, having formally recognized the Republic of Vietnam. AA strength now stood at 30 Spitfires (GC 7), 23 C-47s (GMTEO) and eighteen AAC.1s (GT I/34). By the end of the month Haiphong and Hanoi were occupied. The C-47s of what was now the Groupe de Marche de Transport d'Extrême-Orient (GMTEO) had flown 4,000hrs and had dropped 15 tons of 50kg and 100kg bombs, while Spitfires of GC I/7 and GC II/7 had flown 600 sorties, dropping 28 tons of bombs and firing 150,000 rounds of ammunition.

During the summer of 1946, talks were held in France to try amicably to settle the future of Indo-China, and there was agreement in principle to the autonomy of Laos and Cambodia within a federation, itself within the French Union. Ho Chi Minh accepted, but he was unable to effect compliance. Isolated fighting had occurred in Laos in September when paratroopers were dropped at Luang Prabang, and the next paratroop action was on 25 November when four hundred men were dropped north of Haiphong to recapture the airfield at Cat Bi and contain Viet Minh forces after serious fighting had broken out. Three days later, with no let-up in sight, the French commander gave a two-hour ultimatum to the Viet Minh to stop fighting. When they refused, the sloop *Savorgnan de Brazza*, standing off the port, opened fire on the Indo-Chinese suburbs of the city, reportedly killing over 6,000 during the course of an intensive bombardment.

The Viet Minh began a series of attacks on French garrisons from 19 December and soon gained a measure of control in the northern towns and cities. Early in 1947 the French regained the initiative, and by March the Viet Minh had withdrawn its main fighting forces to the Chinese border. The air forces were now reinforced by the arrival in the South China Sea of the carrier *Dixmude* with 3F (SBD-5) embarked; the Dauntlesses were first in action from Tan Son Nhut on 16 March. A feature of the Indo-China war was the close co-operation between the AA and the Aéronavale; the inter-service rivalries that have dogged the British and Americans were totally absent. In April, Operation 'Papillon' was launched to free Hoa Binh: 500 paratroopers were dropped from C-47s of GT II/15 (ex-GMTEO) and Ju 52/3M of GT I/34, which latter had been formed in February 1946 to

supplement the C-47s. They took control of the city and linked with a column of relieving Moroccan troops from Hanoi.

In October the French forces launched Operation 'Lea' to contain the Viet Minh in the Viet Bac region north-west of Hanoi. Several paradrops of 300 troops near the Chinese border were covered by SBD-5s of 4F from *Dixmude*, which was now in the Gulf of Tonkin. During the operation, aircraft of 4F flew 200 sorties and dropped 65 tons of bombs. Despite the commitment of over 15,000 troops, the operation was inconclusive, although 6,000 guerrillas were claimed to have been killed and several ammunition caches destroyed. During 1948 the French attempted a process of pacification and the guerrilla war continued on a limited basis, although there was further use of paratroops at Vien Tri, just west of Hanoi. Towards the end of the year the carrier *Arromanches* brought 4F with the SBD-5 into the war. Mention might also be made of the use of seaplane tenders. The

Commandant Robert Giraud was in operation from October 1947 supporting the Loire 130s of 8S. By 1948 naval aviation operated under Air Force control, and the following year *Robert Giraud* was replaced by *Paul Goffeny*, which was in turn replaced by *Marcel le Bihan* in 1951. By then, 8S was operating the Sea Otter and JRF-5.

During 1949 the French established a number of key garrisons along Route Coloniale (RC) 4 north at Lang Son, That Khe, Dong Khe and Cao Bang, but the Viet Minh, now being supplied by the newly established People's Republic of China (PRC), simply took control of the road to deny resupply. The Chinese position, however, also benefited the French since the United States was now prepared to offer material support in the fight against communism; hitherto, with the exception of the ubiquitous C-47, the French had to retain US-supplied equipment for commitment to Europe. The original Spitfires had changed hands several times as fresh GCs were brought into the theatre, but by early 1950 there were only enough to equip one unit, GC 1/6.

From July 1949, the USA supplied a number of P-63C Kingcobras to equip four Groupes, and these were followed by a number of F6F-5 Hellcats as an interim measure pending the delivery of an initial batch of 60 F8F-1 Bearcats from 1951. One outcome of Chinese support for the Viet Minh was the delivery of anti-aircraft artillery (AAA). Although by 1950 three aircraft had been lost and some 25 damaged by small-arms fire, the first to be shot down by AAA was a P-63C of GC 2/5 on 19 January 1950. It was now that Giap announced the end of the guerrilla war stage. On 25 May the Viet Minh 308th Division embarked on the first of a series of actions designed to give them control over RC4 north of Hanoi when they attacked the outpost at Dong Khe. The Viet Minh were now more substantially armed and possessed considerable mortar and artillery pieces, which were used to good effect to soften up the post. Dong Khe was evacuated as bad weather prevented the French from flying in reinforcements. On the 27th, however, a paratroop battalion was dropped from 30 AAC.1s just to the north of the garrison, which was recaptured by the paras and a relief force from That Khe.

At this stage the French might have been wise to evacuate the outposts along the road, which itself was under communist control, but the ease with which Dong Khe was recaptured encouraged them to stay. The summer rainy season delayed further attacks until September, when Dong Khe was again the target. After two days of shelling from the 18th, the garrison again fell, with half the defenders dead or wounded. Cao Bang was now isolated and Operation 'Therese' was launched in an endeavour to support the evacuation of the garrison. A column from Lang Son was ordered to move up RC4 through That Khe and Dong Khe to link up with the retreating legionnaires from Cao Bang, but, unknown to the column's commander, Dong Khe was now in enemy hands.

The relief column reached That Khe on the 19th and remained there until the 30th. It was then ordered to take Dong Khe and link up with the retreating Cao Bang garrison, but in the event the column suffered heavy casualties against a vastly superior enemy force: Dong Khe was held, and the remnants of the French force were ordered to skirt the post and link up with the Cao Bang garrison at Namsang. The latter had departed south on 3 October but were ordered off the road to meet up with the relief force now pinned down in the jungle. The columns met on the 7th but were wiped out by Viet Minh attacks. In the retreat from the Cao Bang ridge, the French lost over 6,000 men; only 23 walked out of the jungle to That Khe. During the disastrous operation to withdraw from the ridge the air forces were hampered in their efforts to support the Army by poor weather and a lack of adequate intelligence. Nevertheless, in 5,480 hours of flying, 391 fighter, 326 transport, 78 reconnaissance and 49 AAC.1 'bombing' sorties were flown, two P-63Cs and several MS.500s being lost. During the withdrawal, two battalion-size paradrops, one of which suffered heavy casualties, were made on the road, but the Viet Minh was now so strong that these drops had no influence.

The next set of objectives for Giap was in the Red River Delta embracing Hanoi and Haiphong. The first objective was Vinh Yen, just 35 miles north-west of Hanoi. On 13 January 1951 the 308th and 312th Divisions attacked and destroyed the fort at Bao Chuc, but Giap's preparations had been made openly, and the French had sufficient

It was not until 1949 that the Armée de l'Air deployed a dedicated reconnaissance unit, EROM 1/80. The types selected for the task were the NC.701 (Siebel Si 204D) and F8F-1P Bearcat, the latter also in service in the ground-attack role with several squadrons. Seen at Bach Mai are several aircraft of the unit.

troops in the area to contain the communist attacks, although only with concentrated air support. By now the Army MS.500s were playing an increasingly important role as fighter directors and in artillery spotting, and it was often due to their tenacity that fighter strikes were effective.

The AA was ordered to provide maximum support to Groupements Mobiles (GM) 1 and 3 which were disposed to hold Vinh Yen. All available aircraft were committed and napalm was used, with AAC.1 and C-47 transports being employed as bombers. By the 17th the Viet Minh had been driven off with the loss of 6,000 dead. While several communist divisions were withdrawn to divert French attention, Giap now prepared for an offensive at Dong Trieu. The first assault was on the outpost at Mao Khe on 23 March, and this would have fallen had it not been for a naval barrage from five warships off the Ba Dac river and concentrated air support. In February the first B-26 light bombers operated by Groupe de Bombardement had arrived at Tourane and these, together with F6F-5s of GC 1/6 and 2/6, flew 138 sorties; one F6F-5, one P-63C and two MS.500s were brought down. This was the first significant occasion on which dedicated bombers were used; in 1947 GC 1/3 had operated the wooden-construction Mosquito from Tan Son Nhut, but the aircraft were unsuited to the climate and were soon withdrawn.

The communists now decided to turn their attention to the south-west, along the Day river. On 28 May the 308th Division attacked outposts near Ninh Binh, but the French rapidly moved three GMs, an armoured group and a paratroop battalion to the scene. The Army and Navy co-operated in using a mix of vessels on the river, and convoys were covered by Sea Otters of 8S flying from Cat Bi. Also committed were eight B-26s, 48 F6F-5s, 23 P-63Cs, 29 AAC.1s and eleven C-47s. The fighters dropped 55 tons of bombs and 216 napalm tanks in 381 sorties, while the B-26s dropped 130 tons of bombs. The transports flew in 31 tons of ammunition while 117 wounded were evacuated by MS.500s.

By 18 June the communist lines of communication had been cut and, having suffered an estimated 11,000 casualties, the Viet Minh withdrew. For the Viet Minh the Day river battles had amounted to a 'meatgrinder', and the French were now determined to draw them into another. A strong defensive line had been constructed along the Red River Delta, running from Phat Diem, along the Day river to Viet Tri and then east past Tien Yen to the coast. The site chosen for the French offensive was Hoa Binh on RC6 to the west of Hanoi. On 14 November 1951 three parachute battalions were dropped on the town by AAC.1s in their last combat action, while fifteen infantry battalions and seven artillery battalions with support advanced up the Black river. The Viet Minh observed and waited, and

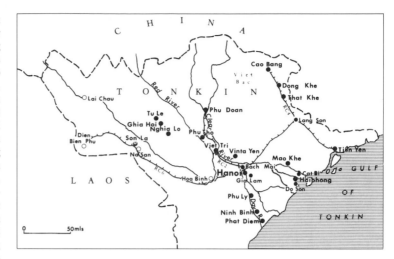

then attacked the lines of communication. During December the French position became serious and GMs 1, 4 and 7 were sent in to reinforce the town which was now under fire from Viet Minh units in the surrounding hills.

Soon the river route alone was untenable and RC6 was used instead; to keep them open the French had to commit no fewer than twelve infantry battalions and three artillery groups in a series of forts. One of the river forts at Tu Vu was the scene of a vicious battle on 10–11 December during which, despite air support, 400 French troops were killed before the communists disengaged. The cost of maintaining the air-head at Hoa Binh was now prohibitive. In December alone 586 offensive sorties were flown by naval fighters, 414 by F6F-5s of 1F and 172 by SB2C-5s of 3F, both flying off *Arromanches*, which had arrived in Vietnamese waters on 24 September; 400 transport sorties were flown, in which 550 tons of supplies and 1,600 troops were moved in and 700 paratroopers dropped. By January 1952 the twelve route protection battalions and air and surface transport elements were serving to supply just five battalions at Hoa Binh.

After a number of successful local attacks by the communists around Hoa Binh in early January, including one in which a river convoy was wiped out, the French decided to withdraw. As Operation 'Amarante', the process began on 22 February. The casualties suffered during the withdrawal, which lasted a week, were enormous, for absolutely no benefit. During the occupation six aircraft were lost at Hoa Binh either on the ground or on the confined approach to the airfield. At the end of the rainy season the Viet Minh launched their next offensive along the Nghia Lo ridge between the Black and Red rivers. The 312th Division surrounded Ghia Hoi on 15 October 1952, the French responding by dropping paratroopers at Tu Le 15 miles away. The paras relieved the garrison, which was then evacuated to Tu Le. On the 17th Nghia Lo was attacked by

the 308th Division and evacuated by the 20th under heavy air cover. Having lost the ridge, the French reinforced by airlift the garrisons at Lai Chau, Son La and Na San to prevent an invasion of Laos.

Notwithstanding the defeat at Hoa Binh, the French clung to the idea of maintaining *Iles Aéro-Terrestres* as fortified centres into which supplies and men could be flown and from which offensives could be launched. Na San was such a base, and despite heavy communist attacks it held out. Up to 84 C-47 sorties a day were flown into the base by aircraft of GT 1/64 and 2/62 from Bach Mai. AAA deployed around the base made these flights increasingly hazardous and escorting F8F-1 Bearcats flew flak-suppression sorties, but with little success. In an effort to relieve the pressure, cut the communist supply lines and force a set-piece battle, the French now launched Operation 'Lorraine', committing 30,000 troops, the largest number ever in the war. The objective was to move up RC2 from Viet Tri.

Beginning on 29 October, two columns set off to link up at Phu Tho, which they reached on 5 November. The operation was supported by the whole C-47 force plus civilian aircraft, full fighter and bomber support being available from Tourane and Gia Lam. On 9 November 2,354 paratroopers were dropped on Phu Doan and met by the column working north from Phu Tho. By the 14th the French had reached Phu Yen Bink, 100 miles from Viet Tri. Giap was not prepared to confront the French incursion into communist-held territory, preferring to retain his forces north of Laos: instead, he detached two regiments to harry the extended French line while two divisions were committed to attacks in the Delta, thus forcing a withdrawal, which was completed by the 24th. In the inconclusive operation the French lost 1,200 troops, although they did capture arms and supplies. During the fighting, helicopters of Escadrille d'Hélicoptères Légère (EHL) 1/65 were used to evacuate wounded from Phu Doan, while naval air support came from F6F-5s of 12F and SB2C-5s of 9F off *Arromanches* on her third cruise. When the carrier left in February the two units remained based at Cat Bi.

Through the winter the Viet Minh prepared for the invasion of Laos, which began in March 1953. The French again decided to establish what were now called *Bases Aéro-Terrestres* (BAT) at Luang Prabang, Chieng Khouang, Plaine des Jarres, Muong Sai and Muong Khoua. The communist invasion by three divisions was supported by 4,000 Pathet Lao irregulars, and they forced an early retreat by the mainly Laotian Government troops. The main BAT at Plaine des Jarres was rapidly reinforced from Hanoi, 500 miles away, and although that at Chieng Khouang was abandoned on 19 April the French held out. During April the transport fleet flew 4,480hrs, against an average of 2,400; bombers flew 390hrs and liaison aircraft 1,800, while the fighters put in 1,840 sorties.

The Viet Minh were unable to secure an adequate foothold in Laos and withdrew into west Tonkin. The next French operation, code-named 'Hirondelle', was against communist supply dumps around Lang Son, evacuated in the 1950 fighting. The plan was to drop a large force on Lang Son itself, capture and destroy supplies and withdraw to the coast. At 0810hrs on 17 July, after a fifteen-minute period during which all identified enemy positions were strafed by F8F-1s of GCs 1/22 and 3/6 and B-26s of GB 1/25, two battalions of paratroopers were dropped at Lang Son by 56 C-47s from Gia Lam and Bach Mai, a third battalion, including engineers, being dropped at Loc Binh by 29 C-47s to cover the withdrawal once supplies had been captured. The operation was a total success, and vast amounts of weapons and supplies were found and destroyed. Casualties were slight, mainly as a result of a forced march in intense heat. The paras linked up with a ground force from Tien Yen and were taken by sea to Haiphong on the 20th. Helicopters evacuated 21 wounded during the operation.

The BAT at Na San was evacuated covertly from 15 July to provide a reserve in the Delta, 9,000 men being airlifted out by 13 August without the Viet Minh realizing what was happening. During August, the flying hours for all services numbered 9,060, of which the C-47 flew 3,860. On 7, 8 and 9 August, 75 movements a day were flown out of the air-head. The ease with which the French had been able to evacuate Na San encouraged them to believe that the BAT concept was sound, a view reinforced in December 1953 when they were able to reinforce the air-head at Seno when it came under communist attack. They now decided to create a BAT at Dien Bien Phu in a wide valley near the Laotian border. On 20 November they began Operation 'Castor', designed to provide a base from which to mount attacks against the Viet Minh, which had five divisions preparing for another offensive into Laos.

The French had just signed a mutual defence treaty with Laos, and it was hoped that the Viet Minh could be drawn from their continuing war of movement into a static battle where French firepower would triumph. The village had the remains of an airfield built by the Japanese, and in the 7 × 2-mile valley were a number of small hills considered ideal for local defence. However,

Following the French resumption of control in Indo-China in 1946, transport duties were shared between the C-47 and the distinctive tri-motor Junkers Ju 52. The first unit equipped with the latter type, GT 1/34, used captured German aircraft, but later units used the AAC.1, the postwar, French-built version. AAC.1 88/V is from GT 2/62 at Bach Mai.

the site was surrounded by heavily overgrown hills, enjoyed a very high rainfall and was subject to fog. The operation began with the dropping of three parachute battalions on the airstrip. These battalions, flown in aboard 64 C-47s, were reinforced by a further two battalions and support units. They soon cleared the immediate area of communists, and by the 24th the airfield was in use. The first surprise was the amount of locally sited AAA; in two weeks from 24 November, of the 51 aircraft involved in strafing and bombing 45 had been hit and three brought down.

On 7 December Operation 'Pollux', the evacuation of the remote BAT at Lai Chau, began, involving 183 C-47 sorties. This was the T'ai provincial capital, which was now to be removed to Dien Bien Phu, but many of the T'ai soldiers ordered to make for the new capital disappeared into the hills.

Over the next few months the French brought in supplies and ammunition to Dien Bien Phu, including ten Chaffee light tanks which were flown in dismantled and assembled on site. Each tank required five C-47 and two Bristol Freighter flights; the latter aircraft were provided by Air-Vietnam. For their part, the Viet Minh had moved four infantry and one artillery division to surround Dien Bien Phu. In an incredible logistics exercise, they moved a large number of artillery pieces and ammunition stocks into the surrounding hills without French knowledge, and by 13 March 1954, when the siege began, the force comprised 70,000 troops and 60,000 auxiliaries. They had no fewer than 48 105mm and 48 75mm guns, plus 48 120mm mortars with 130,000

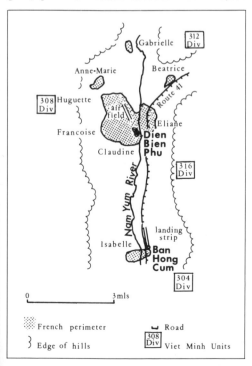

artillery rounds. These guns had been carefully dug into the hillsides under cover of the dense vegetation which not only hid them but protected them from the worst effects of napalm strikes, the jungle also making French spotting extremely difficult. There were, additionally, more than 180 AA pieces from 12.7mm upwards, many placed on the only approaches to the airstrip.

In contrast, the French forces comprised 10,133 men, with four 155mm and 24 105mm guns, ten Chaffee tanks and 127 vehicles. Situated on the airstrip was a flight of F8F-1s from GC 1/22, four C-47s of GT 2/62 and several H-19Bs of Escadrille d'Hélicoptères Moyen (EHM) 2/65. Some years earlier the air units had been ascribed to one of three Groupes Aériennes Tactiques (GATAC), Nord covering Tonkin having a major call on available aircraft. For air support were 40 F8F-1s of GCs 1/21 and 1/22, 30 B-26s of GB 1/25 and Aéronavale F6F-5s of 11F and SB2C-5s of 3F (both from *Arromanches*) and, as heavy bombers, six PB4Y-2s of 28F now at Bach Mai, supplemented from May by crews in training from 24F. In all, GATAC Nord could call on 107 combat aircraft out of a total of 128 in Vietnam. Transports comprised C-47s from GTs 1/64, 2/64, 2/62 and 2/63, plus civilian aircraft.

With the Korean War now over, the United States committed additional but indirect support. From November 1953 the first five C-119 transports were made available from aircraft operated by 314 and 403 TCGs but re-marked and flown under contract by Civil Air Transport (CAT) crews. By March the number of C-119s had increased to 29. The need for additional aircraft had been emphasized when, on 7 March, Viet Minh guerrillas had crawled through sewers to attack aircraft on the ground at Cat Bi and Gia Lam. At least 38 were destroyed and more damaged. The Americans also made good F8F-1 and B-26 losses, the latter from locally held stocks.

On 13 March the siege began in earnest and the strongpoint 'Beatrice' was overrun. There were a number of strongpoints, mostly on hills, but all were exposed through the defenders' having stripped the valley of wood for defence works: two miles to the north of the village was 'Gabrielle', to the east 'Beatrice', 'Dominique' and 'Eliane' and to the west 'Anne-Marie', 'Huguette' and 'Françoise', while three miles to the south was 'Isabelle' with its own newly prepared airstrip. On 14 March a reinforcing battalion was dropped, but resupply was now extremely hazardous. A C-119 had been lost on the approach on the 11th, two MS.500s on the 12th and an F6F-5 of 11F on the 13th. On the 14th, six F8F-1s of GC 1/22 were destroyed on the ground by artillery fire. On the 15th 'Gabrielle' fell, and two nights later Thai troops left their posts on 'Anne-Marie'. The Viet Minh 367 Regiment now installed 37mm AAA on these captured positions directly in line with the final approach to the airstrip.

It was now possible to use the airstrip only at night, but over the next few weeks 223 wounded were evacuated, plus a further 101 by helicopter. Supplies were dropped, but at great risk to the crews who were forced to fly higher. On 23 March, in a desperate attempt to contain the Viet Minh AAA, C-119s were used as bombers, dropping six-ton loads of napalm on gun positions, but in the rain-soaked forest little damage was done. From 31 March parts of 'Dominique' and 'Eliane' were overrun and 'Isabelle' was isolated.

From 1 April a second reinforcing battalion was dropped in by parachute and on the 10th another was dropped, bringing the total strength of the defenders to 3,300 in the centre and 1,600 at 'Isabelle'. Sadly, many men were to be lost in counterattacks to relieve pressure on 'Huguette', 'Dominique' and 'Eliane'. The fate of Dien Bien Phu was now sealed.

The United States drew up a plan, code-named 'Vulture', to bomb the perimeter with a massive force of B-29s, and it has been reported that

TABLE OF UNITS: INDO CHINA, 1945–1954

Unit	Aircraft	Base	Role	Dates
RAF				
GTF	Various Japanese		Transport	00/10/46 to 31/01/46
62 Sqn.	Dakota III		Transport	12/09/45 to 00/10/45
273 Sqn.	Spitfire IX	Tan Son Nhut	Fighter, ground attack	19/09/45 to 31/01/46
267 Sqn.	Dakota III		Transport	00/10/45 to 00/01/46
684 Sqn.	Mosquito PR.34		PR	12/10/45 to 12/01/46
AA[1]				
9 DIC	L-4B, MS.500	Tan Son Nhut	Liaison (to 3 GAOA)	00/09/45 to 00/04/47
1 GAOA	MS.500	Tan Son Nhut		00/02/46 to 31/10/49
2 GAOA	MS.500, L-19A	Nha Trang	AOP, FAC, liaison	? to 31/10/49
3 GAOA	?			00/04/47 to 31/10/49
1 CHES	H-23B	Hanoi		00/00/53 to 00/00/54
GFH	H-19B, H-23B	Hanoi, Dien Bien Phu	Medevac	00/02/54 to 00/00/55
GAOA 21		Ta Son Nhut, Cat Bai		
GAOA 22	MS.500, L-19A	Tan Son Nhut, Nha Trang	AOP, FAC, liaison	01/01/54 to 00/00/55
GAOA 21		Tan Son Nhut, Gia Lam		
GAOA 21		Tourane		
GC I/7[2]	Ki-43, Spitfire LF.IX	Phnom Penh, Tan Son Nhut	Ground attack (became GC I/2)	26/11/45 to 00/07/46
GC I/2	Spitfire LF.IX	Tan Son Nhut, Lang Son	Ground attack (became GC 1/4)	00/07/46 to 00/10/47
GC 1/4	Spitfire LF.IX	Nha Trang	Ground attack (became GC 1/3)	00/10/47 to 00/11/48
GC 1/3	Spitfire LF.IX	Gia Lam, Nha Trang	Ground attack (became GC 1/6)	00/11/48 to 00/04/50
GC 1/6	Spitfire LF.IX, F6F-5, F8F-1	Nha Trang, Tourane	Ground attack (became GM 1/8)	00/04/50 to 00/09/51
GM 1/8	F8F-1	Tourane	Ground attack (became GC 1/22)	00/09/51 to 00/10/53
GC 1/22	F8F-1	Dien Bien Phu	Ground attack	00/10/53 to 00/02/55
GC II/7	Spitfire VIII, LF.IX	Tan Son Nhut	Ground attack (became GC II/2)	13/12/45 to 00/07/46
GC II/2	Spitfire LF.IX	Tan Son Nhut, Lang Son	Ground attack (became GC 2/4)	00/07/46 to 00/10/47
GC 2/4	Spitfire LF.IX	Nha Trang, Tourane	Ground attack (became GC 2/3)	00/10/47 to 00/11/48
GC 2/3	Spitfire LF.IX	Gia Lam, Nha Trang	Ground attack (became GC 2/6)	00/11/48 to 00/04/50
GC 2/6	P-63C	Tan Son Nhut, Tourane	Ground attack (became GM 2/9)	30/10/49 to 00/00/50
GM 2/9	F6F-5, F8F-1	Tan Son Nhut	Ground attack (became GC 2/21)	00/00/50 to 00/10/53
GC 2/21	F8F-1	Tan Son Nhut	Ground attack	00/10/53 to 00/03/55
GC III/2	Spitfire LF.IX	Tan Son Nhut, Lang Son	Ground attack	00/07/46 to 00/10/47
GC/GM 1/9	P-63C, F6F-5, F8F-1	Tan Son Nhut	Ground attack (became GM 2/8)	00/07/49 to 00/02/52
GM 2/8	F8F-1	Tan Son Nhut	Ground attack	00/02/52 to ?
GC 1/5	P-63C	?	Ground attack	31/08/49 to 00/00/50
GC 2/5	P-63C	?	Ground attack	31/08/49 to 00/00/50
GC 3/6	P-63C, F8F-1	Gia Lam	Ground attack	00/08/50 to 00/04/54
GM 1/21	F8F-1	Nha Trang, Dong Hoi	Ground attack (became GC 2/22)	00/09/52 to 00/06/54
GC 2/22	F8F-1	Nha Trang	Ground attack	00/06/54 to ?
GC I/3	Mosquito VI/XVI	Tan Son Nhut	Light bombing	00/01/47 to 00/07/47
GB 1/19	B-26B/C	Saigon, Tourane, Tan Son Nhut, Cap St. Jacques, Cat Bi	Light bombing	01/01/51 to 00/11/55
GB1/25	B-26B/C	Cat Bi	Light bombing	00/03/52 to 00/08/55
EROM 1/80	NC.701, F8F-1P	Bach Mai	Recce (to ER B-26)	00/00/49 to 00/11/51
ER 'B-26'	RB-26C, F8F-1B	Tourane	PR (to ERP 2/19)	00/11/51 to 00/01/54
ERP 2/19	RB-26C, F8F-1B	Tourane	PR	00/01/54 to 00/08/55
GB 1/91	B-26B/C	Tourane	Light bombing	00/06/54 to 00/11/54
EMEO	C-47B	Tan Son Nhut	Transport (to GMTEO)	12/09/45 to 00/11/45
GMTEO	C-47B	Tan Son Nhut, Gia Lam	Transport, bombing (to GT II/15)	00/11/45 to 00/08/46
GT II/15	C-47B	Tan Son Nhut	Transport, bombing (to GT 2/64)	00/08/46 to 00/07/47
GT 2/64	C-47B, Noratlas	Tan Son Nhut	Transport	00/07/47 to 00/06/55
GT I/34	Ju 52/3M, ex JAAF types	Bien Hoa, Nha Trang, Tan Son Nhut	Transport, bombing (to GT 1/64)	00/02/46 to 00/07/47
GT 1/64	Ju 52/3M, AAC.1, C-47B	Tan Son Nhut, Bach Mai		00/07/47 to 00/07/55
GT III/64	AAC.1	Bach Mai	Transport, bombing	00/10/47 to 00/07/48
GT 2/62	AAC.1, C-47B	Tan Son Nhut, Bach Mai		00/08/49 to 00/11/55
GT 2/63	C-47B	Tan Son Nhut, Gia Lam, Tourane, Cat Bi	Transport	00/11/53 to 00/05/55
SSI	Hiller 360	Tan Son Nhut	Casevac, liaison	16/05/50 to 00/00/52
EHL 1/65	Hiller 360, S-51, S-55	Tan Son Nhut, Bien Hoa	Liaison, casevac, transport	00/06/52 to 00/00/56
EHM 2/65	S-55	Tan Son Nhut	Transport, casevac, liaison	00/00/54 to 00/00/56
ELA 52	NC.701, MS.500, Goeland, N.1001/1002, Hiller 360	Tan Son Nhut	Liaison, communications (to ETLA 52)	00/00/46 to 00/00/55
ETLA 52	L-20A, C-47B	Cap St. Jacques	Liaison, transport	00/00/55 to 31/07/56
ELA 53	NC.701, MS.500, L-20A, Hiller 360	Bach Mai	Liaison, communications, medevac	00/03/54 to ?

consideration was given to the use of three tactical nuclear weapons on Viet Minh concentrations, but the Americans feared that their involvement would lead to escalation with Chinese intervention, so in the event the French were left to their own devices. The air forces were hopelessly stretched trying to meet the ground force's rate of consumption. Combat aircraft were fully committed to flak-suppression, but with little success and with high losses. PB4Y-2 28F24 was shot down on 12 April, on 6 May a C-119 was brought down, and on 8 May a second PB4Y-2, 28F26, was shot down over the valley. On 25 April the Aéronavale committed 14F, based at Bach Mai with pilots transferred from Tunisia and newly equipped with 25 AU-1 Corsairs, but the new unit was able to make little impact. Despite a brave attempt to break the communist grip by a relief force from Laos in Operation 'Condor', the base finally surrendered on 7 May. The following day 'Isabelle' was overrun and the war in Indo-China was effectively at an end. Only 73 men walked out.

The battle for Dien Bien Phu cost the French

TABLE OF UNITS: INDO CHINA, 1945—1954 (continued)

Unit	Aircraft	Base	Role	Dates
EIA 54	NC.701, MS.500, N.1001, Hiller 360	Hue, Tourane. Dong Hoi	Liaison, communications	? to ?
ELA 57	NC.701, MS.500, N.1001	?	Liaison, communications	? to ?
GAOA 21	⎧	Tan Son Nhut, Cat Bai	⎫	⎧ 01/11/49 to 31/12/53
GAOA 22	MS.500, L-19A	Tan Son Nhut, Nha Trang	AOP, FAC, liaison	01/11/49 to 31/12/53
GAOA 23		Tan Son Nhut, Gia Lam	⎭	01/11/49 to 31/12/53
GAOA 24	⎩	Tourane		⎩ 00/00/51 to 31/12/53
Aéronavale				
Land-based				
BM1/SLI	C-47, MS.500, Loire 130, AAC.1, L-19	Tan Son Nhut	Base communications	00/10/45 to 00/01/56
8F	PBY-5A, PB4Y-2	Tan Son Nhut. Cat Lai, Cat Bi, Tourane	Ground support, recce (renumbered 28F)	27/10/45 to 00/07/53
28F	PB4Y-2	Tan Son Nhut, Tourane (det.), Cat Bi (det.)	Ground support, recce (ex 8F)	00/07/53 to 00/01/56
	MS.500	Cat Bi	Autonomous liaison flt. of 28F	00/00/52 to 00/00/54
8S	Loire 130, Aichi E13A1, Nakajima A6M2-N, Sea Otter, PBY-5A, JRF-5, MS.500	Cat Lai, Can Tho, Cat Bi, Pleiku (det.). Nha Trang (det.)	Recce, communications, training	00/09/45 to 00/00/56
9S	Sea Otter	Cat Lai, Can Tho (det.)	Communications, recce (air crews to 8S)	01/10/50 to 00/03/52
24F	PB4Y-2	Tan Son Nhut	Training only	00/04/54 to 00/06/54
14F	AU-1	Tourane, Bach Mai, Tan Son Nhut (embarked on *Bois Belleau* during 10/54)	Close support	25/04/54 to 00/06/55
Carrier-based				
3F	⎫ SBD-5	*Dixmude*	Ground attack	⎧ 03/03/47 to 14/04/47
4F	⎭			⎩ 21/10/47 to 03/04/48
4F	SBD-5, Seafire III	*Arromanches*	Ground attack	02/12/48 to 04/01/49
1F	F6F-5	⎫ *Arromanches*	⎧ Ground support	⎫ 24/09/51 to 17/05/52
3F	SB2C-5		⎩ Ground attack	
12F	F6F-5	⎫	⎧ Ground support	⎫
9F	SB2C-5	*Arromanches*	Ground attack	29/09/52 to 27/02/53
58S (det.)	S-51		⎩ Plane-guard	
12F[3]	F6F-5	⎫ *La Fayette*	⎧ Ground support	⎫ 09/04/53 to 00/05/53
9F[3]	SB2C-5		⎩ Ground attack	
11F	F6F-5	⎫	⎧ Ground support	⎫
3F	SB2C-5	*Arromanches*	Ground attack	29/09/53 to 00/03/54
58S (det.)[4]	S-51		⎩ Plane-guard	
11F[5]	F6F-5	*Arromanches*	Ground support	00/04/54 to 13/07/54
3F[5]	SB2C-5		Ground attack	30/04/54 to 09/10/54
11F	F6F-5	⎫ *Bois Belleau*	⎧ Ground support	13/07/54 to 09/10/54
12F	F6F-5		Ground support	13/07/54 to 09/10/54
14F	AU-1	⎩	⎩ Close support	01/10/54 to 09/10/54
12F	F6F-5	*La Fayette*	Ground support	01/06/55 to 00/10/55
VNAF				
312SMS	C-47, Beech 18S, Seabee	Nha Trang, Tan Son Nhut	Liaison, support, transport	01/08/51 to 30/06/55
1 GAOA	MS.500	Tan Son Nhut	Liaison, recce	01/10/53 to 30/06/55
2 GAOA	MS.500	Nha Trang	Liaison, recce	01/10/53 to 30/06/55
ELA	MD.315, C-47, AAC.1	Nha Trang	Liaison, transport (ex GT 2/63)	00/00/54 to 30/06/55
USN				
MAAG	JRB-4	Tan Son Nhut	Communications	00/00/54 to ?

Notes:
1. The AA GAOAs were transferred to AA control from 1 November 1949 to 31 December 1953 and renumbered GAOA 21 to 23. They reverted to Army control on 1 January 1954.
2. It is the practice in the AA to name units after French *départements*. Names in use during the Indo-China war were: GC I/2 Cigognes; GC II/2 Alsace; GC I/7 Provence; GC II/7 Nice; GC 1/3 Corse; GC 1/3 Navarre; GC 2/3 Champagne; GC 1/4 Dauphiné; GC 2/4 La Fayette; GC 1/5 Vendée; GC 1/6 Corse; GC 2/6 Normandie-Niémen; GC 3/6 Roussillon; GM 1/8 Saintonge; GM 2/8 Languedoc; GC/GM 1/9 Limousin; GM 2/9 Auvergne; GM 1/21 Artois; GC 2/21 Auvergne; GC 1/22 Saintonge; GC 2/22 Artois; GB 1/19 Gascogne; ERP 2/19 Armagnac; GB 1/25 Tunisie; GB 1/91 Bourgogne; GT II/15 Anjou; GT I/34 Bearn; GT III/64 Tonkin; GT 2/62 Franche-Comté; GT 2/63 Sénégal; GT 1/64 Bearn; GT 2/64 Anjou.
3. 12F and 9F remained shore-based at Cat Bi until embarked on *La Fayette*.
4. Guard helicopters were initially S-51s detached from 58S, but from 1954 they were replaced by carrier HUP-2 flights of 58S.
5. 11F and 3F remained shore-based at Cat Bi and Bach Mai respectively until embarked on carriers as shown. The two units were shore-based at Tourane during August and September 1954.
   Transport aircraft belonging to airlines or the USAF were used extensively, especially towards the end of the war when there was a need to bring in reinforcements from France. Among others, the following were involved: Air Viet-Nam (DC-3, DC-4, Bristol Freighter); Air Outre-Mer (DC-3); Aigle Azur (DC-3, Boeing Stratoliner); Autrex (Dragon Rapide); CAT (314 and 403 TCGs, USAF) (C-119); Air France (DC-4, Constellation); SAGETA (Armagnac); and 62 TCW USAF (C-124A).

2,293 dead and 5,134 wounded, some 885 of whom were allowed to be evacuated by helicopter and light aircraft over the next few days; 9,000 were taken prisoner-of-war, but in an enforced march to camps in the north two-thirds of them died. The Viet Minh lost an estimated 23,000 dead and wounded. Transport aircraft flew in 6,410 tons of supplies in 6,700 sorties, while the combat aircraft flew 3,700 sorties. In all, 48 aircraft were shot down, 167 damaged and fourteen destroyed on the ground.

Talks on the future of Indo-China began at Geneva on 8 May, and on 21 July a ceasefire came into effect. It was agreed that Cambodia and Laos would achieve full independence while Vietnam would be split on the 17th parallel. As the French began to withdraw from the north the Viet Minh withdrew from the south. The United States had set up a Military Assistance Advisory Group (MAAG) at Saigon in 1950, and it now turned its attention to the creation of an independent South Vietnam Air Force (VNAF), which was formally established on 1 July 1955. An embryo Vietnamese Air Force had been developed by the French but with little enthusiasm and with no combat aircraft; this now formed the nucleus of the new arm. Gradually the French withdrew from South Vietnam, the last AA units leaving in July 1956. The nine-year war had cost the French and their colonial units 75,000 dead and the Viet Minh twice that number.

The war was the first in modern times in which a great Western power had been defeated by a peasant army – it was also one of the few wars lost by a regular rather than conscript army – but it is unlikely that, even with much greater resources, especially in terms of air power, the French could have won. The Viet Minh were highly motivated and exceptionally well organized, and, in the north especially, the French were unpopular. The defeat was not only French, for by the end of the war the Americans, who were by then committed to making a stand against communism in Asia, were meeting about 80 per cent of the cost. Peace was not to last.

AIRCRAFT MARKINGS

AA

Nakajima Ki-43 *Silver overall, no serial, black code on rear fuselage: A (GC I/7).*
Spitfire IX *Dark Green/Ocean Grey over, medium grey under, Sky band, white code, black serial on rear fuselage: PV2??/E (GC II/4).*
P-63C *Bare metal overall, black serial on fin: (4)4037 (GC 2/6).*
F6F-5 *Glossy Sea Blue overall, white serial on rear fuselage, code on fin: ?/S (GC 2/9).*
F8F-1 *Glossy Sea Blue overall, white serial on fin, white code in red circle on fin and nose: (9)5172/G (GC 1/21). White serial on rear fuselage, code on fin, unit badge on nose: (95)195/P, (94)780/D, (94)890/R (GC 2/21). White code and unit badge on nose: (9)5128/R (GC 1/22).*
B-26B *Bare metal overall, black nose and engine cowlings, black serial and code on fin, USAF buzz number on rear fuselage: (4)434564/K BC-564 (GB 1/19).*
B-26C *Bare metal overall, black serial and code on fin: (4)434105/Q (GB1-19), (4)435774/C (GB 1/25).*
AAC.1 *Bare metal overall, black serial on nose, white code in black circle on fin: 88/V (GT 2/62); 334/G (GT 1/64).*
C-47 *Olive Drab overall, black serial on fin: (4)476356 (GMTEO). Bare metal overall, black serial, white code on black circle on fin: (4)476352/F (GT 2/61). Bare metal over, black under, black serial, white code in black circle on fin: (4)476675/Q (GT ?).*
C-119C *Bare metal overall, black serial on fin, 'last three' on forward fuselage: (4)9165/165, (4)9185/185 (CAT for 403 TCG, USAF).*
H-23A *Olive Drab overall, white serial and code on boom: (51)16094/VE (? unit).*
WS.51 *Olive Drab overall, white serial on mid boom: Z-111 (EHL 1/65).*
S-55 *Bare metal overall, black serial on forward boom and nose: N-592 (EHM 2/65).*
MS.500 *Olive Drab overall, black serial on*

From 1949, the French received considerable US support with the supply of aircraft, but generally of obsolescent types no longer suitable for use in a hostile environment like Korea, where more modern equipment was essential. An exception was the robust B-26, which served with distinction in both theatres. B-26B 4434538 is seen at the Mitsubishi Aircraft plant in Japan, prior to delivery from US stocks. (USAF via R. F. Dorr) rudder, white code on rear fuselage: 376/T (ELA 53).

L-19A Olive Drab overall, white serial on fin, code on rear fuselage: (5)112850/VI (22 GAOA); (5)112694/MM (? unit).

L-20A Bare metal overall, black serial on fin: (5)26151 (ELA 52); (5)26147 (ELA 53).

Aéronavale

PBY-5A Gull Gray over, white under, black serial on nose: 70 (8F) (later marked as 8F.1).

Loire 130 Bare metal overall, black unit and code on rear fuselage: 8.S.15 (8S).

SBD-5 Sea Blue and Intermediate Blue over, Gull Gray under, white unit and code on mid-fuselage: 3.F.3 (3F); 4.F.17 (4F).

F6F-5 Glossy Sea Blue overall, white unit and code on mid fuselage, code repeated on nose and rear fuselage, serial on rear fuselage: 70387/1.F.23 (1F); 78802/11.F.22 (11F).

SB2C-5 Glossy Sea Blue overall, white unit and code on mid fuselage, serial on rear fuselage: (89)403/3.F.3 (3F).

AU-1 Glossy Sea Blue overall, white serial on rear fuselage: 129340 (14F).

JRF-5 Glossy Sea Blue overall, white serial on rear fuselage, red cross on white circle on fin, mid fuselage and mid wing: 37784 (8S).

PB4Y-2 Glossy Sea Blue overall, white unit and code on rear fuselage, code repeated on fin: 59774/28F4 (28F).

HUP-2 Glossy Sea Blue overall, white serial on rear fuselage, unit and code on tail surfaces: 130083/58S.21 (58S).

9.2. Vietnam, 1954–1975

The scale of the Vietnam War was such that it can be covered only in summary form in the present volume. The approach taken by the author is to give an overall introduction, then to highlight aspects of the air war by reference to example and detailed tables. A separate glossary covering the wars in Vietnam, Cambodia and Laos between 1960 and 1975 should enable the reader to secure a clear understanding of the flow of the war and undertake more detailed study. Particular aspects of the war have been well documented, and although full details of units are given, only representative markings are offered for reasons of space.

After having provided technical and training support to the South Vietnamese since 1954 the United States was drawn formally into war with North Vietnam and the Viet Cong (VC) in 1964. In summary, the VC was the military wing of the South Vietnamese Communist Party, which was supported and strengthened by the North Vietnamese Army (NVA). On 2 August North Vietnamese torpedo boats attacked two destroyers, leading to the Tonkin Gulf Resolution. For a period the war was concentrated in the South, but after attacks on US installations first 'Flaming Dart' then 'Rolling Thunder' strike operations were approved from late 1964. By this time there were 23,000 US servicemen in the South. In March 1965 the first ground forces, US Marines, arrived at Da Nang, and by the end of the year the number of servicemen had risen to 181,000. There was a bombing lull over Christmas and New Year aimed at encouraging peace talks, but it did not last long. In March the VC and NVA captured a Special Forces camp in the A Shau valley, and in April B-52 bombers attacked targets in the North for the first time.

By now the United States was supported by South Korea, the Philippines, Australia, New Zealand and Thailand, and by December 1966 its strength had increased to 385,000 men. Early 1967 saw major operations in the Iron Triangle, north of Saigon, with 'Cedar Falls' and 'Junction City'. Early in 1968, by which time there were 486,000 Americans in South Vietnam and Thailand, the Marine post at Khe Sanh was besieged by the VC and NVA. By March the post had been relieved, but at great cost, and shortly afterwards it was abandoned. The siege coincided with the new year, or Tet, offensive, with attacks throughout South Vietnam. At the end of March President Johnson called a halt to the bombing in southern North Vietnam, a directive which was extended to the whole of the North in November. The halt lasted to December 1971, and preliminary peace talks began in Paris in May. Reconnaissance flights continued, but when any aircraft were attacked retaliatory raids followed. By the end of 1968 American forces were at a peak of 536,100.

The architect of Vietnamese integrity, Ho Chi Minh, died on 4 September 1969, shortly after the US Government announced the reduction of forces in South-East Asia. A process of 'Vietnamization' now began as arms and equipment were transferred to the South Vietnamese, who were to be increasingly responsible for their own security. US strength was down to 474,000 by the end of 1969. North Vietnam was supplying the VC and placing elements of the NVA in the South via the Ho Chi Minh Trail. The Trail, which was a network of roads and tracks, actually ran through Laos, while another supply line from Kampot ran through Cambodia. Both routes gave the Americans justification for extending the war into Laos and Cambodia, and by 1970 an enormous effort went into sensing movement and interdiction both on land and in the air.

On 29 April 1970, US forces joined South Vietnamese in an invasion of Cambodia and several days later major demonstrations broke out across the US, leading to the deaths of four students at Kent University. The US withdrew and later in the year Congress banned the further use of ground forces in Laos and Cambodia. The Tonkin Gulf Resolution was also repealed. At the end of the year reconnaissance had indicated a build-up of NVA troops in Laos and across the DMZ, so Operation 'Lam Son 719' was launched into Laos, aimed at cutting the Trail and destroying the NVA concentrations. The Army of the Republic of Vietnam (ARVN) made the assault with US Army helicopter support, but although it served to slow the NVA it was a disaster.

At the end of the year the build-up had regained momentum and there was a concomitant increase in US air strikes against targets in the North and Laos. On 30 March 1972 North Vietnamese forces invaded the South and the now depleted air units were rapidly reinforced in the 'Constant Guard' programme. In May Quang Tri fell to the communists, but a month later the siege of An Loc was broken. Also in May, the full-scale bombing of the North recommenced in Operation 'Linebacker', which lasted to October. Since the North Vietnamese continued to delay peace negotiations the bombing was restarted as 'Linebacker II' in December, and eleven days of

concentrated bombing brought talks to a conclusion.

The war ended formally on 23 January 1973, after which the final US troop withdrawals began. The last ground troops left on 29 March, by which time some POWs had been released; the fate of many remains unknown at the time of writing. However, the war continued without US manpower commitment, and in the spring of 1975 the NVA launched a fast offensive towards Saigon, which fell on 30 April.

In terms of aircraft, the war was incredibly expensive. From 1962 to 1973, no fewer than 2,561 aircraft and 2,587 helicopters were lost in combat, with a further 1,158 and 2,282, respectively, lost in accidents. The total, of probably in excess of 20,000 airframes committed, was 8,588. Altogether, 2,118 USAF airmen were killed and 3,460 wounded; the Navy lost 317 air crew killed, the USMC 579 and the Army at least 3,000, mainly helicopter crews. Of 1,175 air crew captured or missing, only 512 were returned as prisoners-of-war.

Between 1961 and 1975, the US lost around 50,000 dead in Indo-China and at least 300,000 wounded. The South Vietnamese lost 184,000 dead and the North and VC an estimated 900,000. Perhaps of all wars in the twentieth century, as the first 'television' war the Vietnam conflict is remarkable for its outcome having been confirmed through public opinion at home. There could never have been any question of American and South Vietnamese forces winning: it was simply a matter of how long they were prepared not to lose.

9.2.1. VIETNAM, 1954–1964

The United States established a Military Assistance Advisory Group (MAAG) in Indo-China in the summer of 1950 to help the French combat the Viet Minh. After the French defeat at Dien Bien Phu, Vietnam was partitioned at the 17th parallel and the French departed by 1956. The understanding was that both North and South Vietnam would hold general elections to determine the future of the country, but these were not forthcoming. When the French had departed they left a small number of aircraft flown by the VNAF, which was formally established on 1 July 1955. The first combat unit was formed with F8F-1 Bearcats on 1 June 1956. The Americans stayed on to support the South Vietnamese and by 1957 had established a training centre at Nha Trang for the fledgeling Vietnamese Air Force (VNAF).

From mid-1957, communists in the South began carrying out attacks on a range of targets and the civil war began. The attacks increased through 1958, and in April 1959 the South Vietnamese Communist Party (Lao Dong) was formed. Its members involved in the subsequent armed struggle were the Viet Cong (VC), who

from May of 1959 received overt support from the North when Ho Chi Minh announced that he sought the unification of Vietnam – and perhaps implicitly the whole of Indo-China – by force. The same month the US sent more advisors. Sadly, the regime in the South under President Ngo Dinh Diem was repressive and insurgents found considerable local support for their ambitions, and, to make matters worse, there was a three-way civil war developing in Laos in which the US was secretly involved. The North Vietnamese Army (NVA) made incursions into northern Laos partly to secure free passage for supplies to the South, skirting the demilitarized zone.

The range of routes running down the eastern border of 'neutral' Laos became known as the Ho Chi Minh Trail, and throughout the war the route remained open despite great and continuing efforts to close it off. As insurgency in the South was fuelled, so the American support to the Diem Government increased. Initially this was in the form of equipment and advisers and, for the NVAF, supplies including helicopters to improve mobility in difficult terrain and A-1H attack aircraft to replace the ageing Bearcats. From 1961, after President Kennedy's inauguration, US units began covert operations, ostensibly in an advisory capacity under Army of the Republic of Vietnam (ARVN) control – but in reality the US was determining the shape of the South Vietnamese response to the civil war.

Late in 1961, as concern about the extent of North Vietnamese action increased, the USAF sent a flight of RF-101Cs of the 15th TRS to Tan Son Nhut as Project 'Pipe Stem'; later, these duties were extended under Project 'Able Mabel' and shared by the 15th and 45th TRS on a six-monthly basis. In December two United States Army helicopter companies, the 8th and 57th, began operations with the ARVN, supplementing the local H-19 and H-34 unit; at the same time,

The A-1 was in continuous use by the Vietnamese Air Force throughout the long Vietnam War. The first deliveries began in 1960, and for five years the aircraft flew in Gull Gray overall camouflage, betraying their naval origins. By the time this photograph was taken, dark green/medium green/tan camouflage was in widespread use. The aircraft are A-1Hs (1)35355 and (1)39762, of the 514th Fighter Squadron. (Via J. Ethell)

TABLE OF UNITS: VIETNAM, 1954–1964

Unit	Aircraft	Base	Role	Dates
VNAF				
1 FS	F8F-1, AD-6	Bien Hoa	Fighter, ground attack (to 514 FS)	01/06/56 to 31/12/62
514 FS	A-1H	Bien Hoa	Ground attack	01/01/63 to 00/04/75
2 FS	T-28D	Nha Trang	Ground attack (to 516 FS)	00/12/61 to 00/01/63
516 FS	T-28D, A-1H	Nha Trang, Da Nang	Ground attack	00/12/61 to 00/00/68
518 FS	A-1H	Bien Hoa	Ground attack	15/10/63 to 00/04/75
520 FS	A-1H	Bien Hoa		16/06/64 to 00/03/75
522 FS	A-1H	Tan Son Nhut		01/06/65 to 00/09/66
716 RS	RT-28D, C-47	Tan Son Nhut	Recce	00/12/63 to 00/06/64
312 SMS	C-47		Transport (to 314 SMS)	01/07/55 to 00/00/56
314 SMS	C-47, Beech 18, RT-28D		Transport	00/00/56 to 00/04/75
1 TS	C-47	Tan Son Nhut	Transport (to 413 TS)	01/07/55 to 31/12/62
413 TS	C-47		Transport	01/01/63 to 00/09/67
2 TS	C-47		Transport (to 415 TS)	00/07/56 to 31/12/62
415 TS	C-47		Transport	01/01/63 to 00/00/73
1 HS	H-19A/B, H-13A	Tan Son Nhut	Airlift, SAR (to 211 HS)	00/06/57 to 31/12/62
211 HS	H-19B, UH-34A	Tan Son Nhut	Airlift, SAR	01/01/63 to 00/00/69
2 HS	H-19B, UH-34A	Da Nang	Airlift, SAR (to 213 HS)	01/10/61 to 31/12/62
293 HS	UH-34A	Tan Son Nhut	Airlift	00/12/62 to 00/08/64
213 HS	UH-34A	Da Nang	Airlift, SAR	01/01/63 to 00/00/69
215 HS	UH-34A	Bien Hoa, Nha Trang	Airlift, SAR	00/00/64 to 00/00/69
217 HS	UH-34A	Da Nang, Tan Son Nhut	Airlift, SAR	01/05/64 to 00/00/69
1 GAO	MS.500, L-19A	Da Nang	Liaison (to 110 OS)	01/07/55 to 31/12/62
110 OS	L-19A	Da Nang	Recce, liaison, FAC	01/01/63 to 00/03/75
2 GAO	MS.500, L-19A	Nha Trang, Tan Son Nhut	Liaison (to 112 OS)	01/07/55 to 31/12/62
112 OS	L-19A	Tan Son Nhut, Bien Hoa	Recce, liaison, FAC	01/01/63 to 00/04/75
3 OS	L-19A	Da Nang	Recce, liaison, FAC (to 114 OS)	00/12/61 to 31/12/62
114 OS	L-19A	Da Nang, Pleiku	Recce, liaison, FAC	01/01/63 to 00/03/75
116 OS	L-19A	Nha Trang	Recce, liaison, FAC	00/06/64 to 00/03/75
ELA	MS.500, C-47	Tan Son Nhut	Communications	01/07/55 to ?
USAF				
Project 'Pipe Stem'				
15 TRS	RF-101C	Tan Son Nhut, ex Kadena	Tactical recce	18/10/61 to 19/11/61
Project 'Able Mabel'				
45 TRS	RF-101C	Don Muang, Tan Son Nhut, ex Misawa	Tactical recce (shared with 15 TRS at 6-month intervals)	07/11/61 to 31/01/65
Project 'Farm Gate'				
4400 CCTS	T-28B, SC-47, B-26B, RB-26C; U-10A, RB-26L (Det. 2A)	Bien Hoa	Training, ground support (to 1ACS)	26/12/61 to 07/07/63
4410 CCTS	T-28B	Bien Hoa	Training, ground support (to 1 ACS)	00/00/62 to 07/07/63
1 ACS	T-28B, SC-47, B-26B, RB-26C/L U-10A, A-1E	Bien Hoa, Pleiku (Det. 1) So Trang (Det. 2)	Training, ground support (became 602 ACS)	08/07/63 to 00/10/64
19 TASS	O-1E	Bien Hoa, Can Tho	Tactical support, liaison	00/07/63 to 00/11/68
Project 'Mule Train' [1]				
346 TCS		Tan Son Nhut, Da Nang	Tactical transport (to 776 TCS)	02/01/62 to 00/06/62
776 TCS		Tan Son Nhut	Tactical transport (to 310 TCS)	00/06/62 to 00/07/63
310 TCS	C-123B	Tan Son Nhut	Tactical transport	00/07/63 to 00/00/72
309 TCS		Tan Son Nhut	Tactical transport	00/07/63 to 00/07/70
777 TCS		Da Nang, Don Muang	Tactical transport (to 311 TCS)	00/06/62 to 00/07/63
311 TCS		Da Nang, Don Muang	Tactical transport (ex 777 TCS)	00/07/63 to 00/00/70
Project 'Ranch Hand' [1]				
SASF	UC-123B/K	Tan Son Nhut	Defoliation	10/01/62 to 00/07/64
Project 'Water Glass'				
509 FIS	F-102A, TF-102A	Tan Son Nhut, ex Clark	Air defence	21/03/62 to 00/05/63
VAW-35	AD-5Q	Tan Son Nhut	Air defence	00/04/62 to 00/05/63
Project 'Candy Machine'				
509 FIS	F-102A	Tan Son Nhut, Da Nang	Air defence	00/05/63 to 00/06/64

as Project 'Farm Gate', Detachment 2A of the 4400th Combat Crew Training Squadron (CCTS) took up residence at Bien Hoa to provide a much-needed offensive boost. The Geneva Accord forbade jet equipment to the Vietnamese air forces, so the unit comprised piston-engined types. The next USAF contribution came from the 346th Troop Carrier Squadron (TCS) under Project 'Mule Train'. Also early in 1962, under Project 'Ranch Hand', UC-123Bs of the Special Aerial Spray Flight arrived at Tan Son Nhut to begin the controversial defoliation sorties using Agent Orange to clear growth in areas of Viet Cong operations.

When the flights became public in 1963 it was claimed that their sole purpose was to keep power lines free. On 2 February 1962 one of the 'Ranch Hand' C-123 Providers crashed, killing the crew – the first USAF casualties in the war. As the C-123 force built up it was consolidated as the Tactical Air Force Transport Squadron (Provisional) 2 (TAFTS(P)-2), then the increased number of squadrons became the 315th Troop Carrier Group (TCG) from July 1963. Airmobility was further developed from April 1962 with the USMC Operation 'ShuFly', whereby UH-34D helicopters were rotated into Da Nang. More Army transportation companies were deployed

Unit	Aircraft	Base	Role	Dates
Project 'Patricia Lynn'				
33 TG	RB-57E	Tan Son Nhut	Recce (to 6250 CSG)	07/05/63 to 00/08/64
Project 'Dragon Lady'				
4080 SRW	U-2A/C	Bien Hoa (OL 20)	Recce	00/12/63 to 11/02/66
Miscellaneous				
–	EC-54 (single aircraft)	Tan Son Nhut	EW	20/04/62 to 00/02/63
–	EC-97G (single aircraft)	Tan Son Nhut	EW	00/02/63 to ?
6091 RS	RB-57D (det.)	Tan Son Nhut, ex Yokota	Recce	00/05/63 to 00/07/63
556 RS	RC-130A (det.)	Don Muang, ex Yokota	Recce	00/07/64 to 00/00/71
3960 SW	KC-135A (det.)	Tan Son Nhut, ex Clark	Air refuelling	09/06/64 to 00/08/64
511 TFS	F-100D	Da Nang, ex Clark	Ground attack	09/06/64 to 00/00/65
?	U-8A	Tan Son Nhut	Communications	00/01/64 to ?
US Army				
8 Tr. Co.	CH-21B, OH-13E	Qui Nhon	Troop transport (to 117 AHC)	11/12/61 to 24/06/63
117 Av. Co.	UH-1A/B	Qui Nhon	Supply, medevac, liaison, gunship	25/06/63 to 00/00/65
57 Tr. Co.	CH-21B, OH-13E	Can Tho	Troop transport (to 120 AC)	11/12/61 to 24/06/63
120 Av. Co.	UH-1B	Tan Son Nhut	Gunship, transport	25/06/63 to 00/10/72
93 Tr. Co.	CH-21B	Da Nang, Soc Trang	Troop transport (to 121 AHC)	25/01/62 to 24/06/63
121 AHC	CH-21B, UH-1B	Soc Trang	Gunship, transport	25/06/63 to 10/12/70
18 Av. Co.	U-1A	Tan Son Nhut	Supply, support, liaison	07/02/62 to 16/04/71
57 M Det.	UH-1A	Nha Trang, Qui Nhon	Casevac	02/05/62 to 00/00/73
33 Tr. Co.	CH-21B	Ta Son Nhut	Troop transport (to 118 AHC)	00/05/62 to 24/06/63
73 Av. Co.	O-1F	Vung Tau	Liaison, recce	31/05/62 to 29/04/72
118 AHC	UH-1B	Bien Hoa, Ninh Long	Gunship, transport	25/06/63 to 31/08/71
81 Tr. Co.	CH-21B	Pleiku	Troop transport (to 119 AC)	07/09/62 to 13/06/63
119 Av. Co.	UH-1B	Pleiku	Gunship, transport	14/06/63 to 14/12/70
UTTC	UH-1A/B	Tan Son Nhut	Transport, liaison (to 68 Av. Co.)	16/10/62 to 00/08/64
68 Av. Co.	UH-1A/B	Tan Son Nhut	Gunship, transport	15/08/64 to 01/03/65
1 Av. Co.	C-7A	Thailand, Vung Tau	STOL transport	31/02/62 to 09/12/66
56 Tr. Co.	CH-37B	Tan Son Nhut	Heavy lift transport	00/05/63 to ?
61 Av. Co.	C-7A	Vung Tau	STOL transport	27/06/63 to 31/12/66
23 SWADet.	OV-1A	Tan Son Nhut	Reconnaissance	00/09/62 to ?
114 AHC	UH-1B	Vinh Long	Gunship, transport	10/05/63 to 29/02/72
USMC 'Shufly'[2]				
HMM-362	UH-34D	Soc Trang, Da Nang	Troop transport	15/04/62 to 31/07/62
HMM-163				01/08/62 to 11/01/63
HMM-162				12/01/63 to 07/06/63
HMM-261				08/06/63 to 01/10/63
HMM-361	UH-34D	Da Nang	Troop transport	02/10/63 to 31/01/64
HMM-364				01/02/64 to 21/06/64
HMM-162				17/06/64 to 07/10/64
HMM-365				08/10/64 to 31/12/64
H&MS-12	C-117D, OV-10A, O-1B	Chu Lai	Support	00/04/62 to 00/00/70
VMO-2	O-1B		Liaison	00/04/62 to 00/00/72

USN							
CVW-19 (NM), Bonne Homme Richard, 28 January–21 November 1964				*CVW-5 (NF), Ticonderoga, May–December 1964*			
VF-191	F-8E	VA-196	A-1H/J	VF-51	F-8E	VA-55	A-4E
VA-192	A-4C	VAW-11	E-1B	VF-53	F-8E	VAW-11	E-1B
VF-194	F-8C	VFP-63	RF-8A	VA-52	A-1H/J	VFP-63	RF-8A
VA-195	A-4C	VAH-4	A-3B	VA-56	A-4E	VAH-4	A-3B
CVW-14 (NK), Constellation, 3 May 1964–1 February 1965							
VF-142	F-4B	VA-146	A-4C				
VF-143	F-4B	VAW-11	E-1B				
VA-144	A-4C	VFP-63	RF-8A				
VA-145	A-1H/J	VAH-10	A-3B				

Notes:
1. 'Mule Train' and 'Ranch Hand' C-123s became TAFTS(P)-2, May 1962 to July 1963, then 309, 310 and 311 TCS under 315 TCG.
2. USMC 'Shufly' comprised Task Unit 79.3.5 until 6 November 1962, and then Task Element 79.3.3.6.

in 1962, during which year the machine that was to become synonomous with the Vietnam War, the UH-1, or 'Huey', arrived. It was initially operated by the Utility Tactical Transportation Company (UTTC) at Tan Son Nhut.

The USAF reacted to the worsening situation by deploying a flight of F-102A interceptors to Tan Son Nhut in March 1962 as Operation 'Water Glass', the air defence task then being shared on a six-weekly basis with Navy AD-5Q Skyraiders. From May 1963, as Operation 'Candy Machine', the responsibility fell on 509 FIS alone. Intelligence-gathering assumed an increasing importance and led to detachments of RB-57Ds and Es from 1962, and as Operation 'Dragon Lady' a U-2 of 4080 SRW was flown from Bien Hoa from late 1963. In addition, first an EC-54 then an EC-97 was flown from Tan Son Nhut, equipped to track down the sources of Viet Cong radio traffic. In February 1962 the United States had established the Military Assistance Command Vietnam (MACV) to co-ordinate support to the Vietnamese, who were now facing a well-organized guerrilla army. By the end of 1962 there were around 10,000 US military personnel in Vietnam, against just 875 in 1960.

At the beginning of 1963 the ARVN suffered a severe setback at Ap Bac in the Plain of Reeds. In a helicopter lift, the assault force found itself confronted by a VC regular battalion which, exceptionally, did not melt into the undergrowth. Five helicopters were lost and 65 ARVN killed, mainly by friendly forces. The operation highlighted the need for air support for helicopter insertions and helped to speed the concept of the helicopter gunship. On the political front, Diem was overthrown on 1 November 1963 and shot in a military coup inspired by the CIA. By the end of 1963, the last year before formal American participation, there were 117 USAF aircraft under the 2nd Air Division, Thirteenth Air Force, in Vietnam and 325 Army helicopters; eighteen aircraft and 58 helicopters had now been lost. The VNAF boasted three A-1 squadrons, a reconnaissance unit, two C-47 squadrons and three helicopter units, the last now equipped with the UH-34A. USAF sorties in the year were 6,929, against 2,334 in 1962, while personnel numbered 16,263.

The 'Farm Gate' detachment had been redesignated 1 Air Commando Squadron in June 1963, and in early 1964 it suffered setbacks in having its B-26 force grounded, together with the T-28 Trojans, as a result of accidents. New equipment was forthcoming in the shape of the A-1E. The Viet Cong continued to make progress, capturing the town of Kien Long in April and in May sinking the USS *Card* in Saigon Docks with underwater munitions. The NVA had invaded Laos, and 'Yankee Team' reconnaissance flights were flown by both USN and USAF aircraft.

On 6 June an RF-8A of VFP-63 on a flight over Xieng Khouang was shot down by AAA, which both the NVA and VC were employing in increasing numbers. The following day an F-8D on escort duty in the same area was also shot down, and the United States decided to retaliate. The 'Yankee Team' effort was stepped up and the 511th TFS sent to Da Nang from Clark AB, together with four Temporary Duty (TDY) KC-135As of the 3960th Strategic Wing (SW). On 9 June the F-100D Super Sabres made the first of a series of strikes against AAA targets in Laos, and to all intents and purposes the US was now at war with North Vietnam. As part of the intelligence-gathering effort, the US Navy deployed warships in the Gulf of Tonkin from the early spring of 1964 in the 'Desoto' project. On 2 August the destroyer *Maddox* (DD-731) was attacked by North Vietnamese torpedo-boats, one of which was subsequently sunk by F-8 Crusaders from USS *Ticonderoga*. Two days later, in poor weather and atmospheric conditions which caused electronic equipment to malfunction, the destroyer, in company with the USS *C. Turner Joy* (DD-951), believed that she was under attack a second time. As a result, Congress passed a resolution on 7 August authorizing President Johnson 'to take all necessary steps, including the use of armed force, to assist any member or protocol state' of the South-East Asia Treaty Organization (SEATO).

AIRCRAFT MARKINGS

VNAF

F8F-1 Silver overall, black serial and code on fin: (9)5338/E (1 FS).

A-1H Light grey overall, black code and serial on fin: (1)39703/N, (1)34479/E, (1)37551/B (514 FS). Dark green/chocolate over, light grey under, 83 SOG marking on fuselage in place of national marking, serial in light grey panel on lower fin, code in black on fin and rudder: (1)35298/UG, (1)35392/US (522 FS).

T-28D Gull Gray over, white under, black code and serial on fin: (1)38367, 140457/C, 140556/J (2 FS).

C-47 Bare metal overall, white fuselage decking, black code on yellow circle and serial on fin: (4)348387/MN (1 TS), (4)348874/O (2 TS).

H-34A Olive Drab overall, yellow serial on rear fuselage: (5)34486 (2 HS).

L-19A Olive Drab overall, white serial on fin, code on rear fuselage: (5)112829/DM (112 OS).

USAF

B-26B Light grey overall, black engine nacelles, black serial on fin: (44)35703, (44)35813 (4400 CCTS).

T-28D Dark green/medium green/dark brown over, light grey under, no national markings, white serial on fin: 0-(4)91604 (4410 CCTS).

A-1G Silver overall, black serial on fin, code on nose: (1)34989/2 (1 ACS).

UC-123B Light grey overall, black serial on fin: (5)54548 (SASF); 0-(5)40701 (315 TCG).

O-1E Light grey overall, black serial on fin: (5)62062 (19 TASS).

F-102A Light grey overall, black serial and unit badge on fin: (5)61165 (509 FIS).

US Army

CH-21B Olive Drab overall, yellow serial on fin: (5)28642 (33 Tr. Co.).

Seen in its revetment at Ubon, Thailand, is F-4D (6)67766/FG of 433 TFS, 8 TFW. The Phantom joined the war in April 1965 with 12 TFW, and it served with distinction with the USAF, USN and USMC. This particular aircraft is fitted with the AVQ-10 Pave Knife pod. This incorporated a laser designator and low light-level television, which allowed the crew to use LGBs at night. The armament comprises two Mk. 84 LGBs. (J. Ethell)

CH-21C *Olive Drab mottled dark green overall:* *(5)54143 (57 Tr. Co.).*
CH-37B *Olive Drab overall, yellow serial on rear fuselage: (5)50636 (56 Tr. Co.).*
UH-1A *Olive Drab overall, yellow serial on vertical tail surface: 591673/2 (UTTC).*

USMC
UH-34D *Olive Drab overall, white serial on rear fuselage, code on mid fuselage, tail and nose: (14)5770/YZ65 (HMM-363).*

9.2.2. OFFENSIVE OPERATIONS

Immediately after the Tonkin Gulf incident, the United States deployed a number of additional fighter and bomber units to Vietnam. The initial response to the formal opening of the war was left to the US Navy's carrier-borne strike aircraft, and until 1965 the US Air Force operated only in support of the ARVN and covertly in Laos. Two squadrons of B-57Bs were stationed at Bien Hoa from Clark AB, while fighter squadrons from Japan, the Philippines and the USA were sent to bases in Thailand. The 18th TFW, with the F-105, moved to Korat with the similarly equipped 4 TFW, while the sole 405 TFW F-100 unit, 511 Sqn., was transferred to Takhli; 35 TFW, with three F-100 squadrons, was established at Phan Rang. By September 1964 there were nine ground-attack and two light bomber squadrons in the theatre. The sole air defence assets were the F-102s of 509 FIS at Da Nang, which seemed reasonable given the lack of offensive aircraft in the NVAF inventory. However, the USAF suffered its first combat losses on the ground, at Bien Hoa, when five B-57s were destroyed by a VC mortar attack on 1 November.

A number of units were withdrawn to Pacific Air Force (PACAF) bases and safety. As the VC grew in strength, regularly supplied down the Ho Chi Minh Trail, Operation 'Barrel Roll' was authorized from 14 December 1964, allowing armed reconnaissance sorties over eastern Laos. Following a VC mortar attack on Pleiku on 2 February 1965 which destroyed and damaged eighteen helicopters and seven aircraft, 'Flaming Dart' was authorized. This operation took the form of joint VNAF, USAF and USN strikes against the Chap Le barracks and Vinh in North Vietnam. Vinh was bombed again on the 11th following further VC attacks.

It was now clear that the North Vietnamese would not heed the warning, and a longer-term offensive programme against the North, 'Rolling Thunder', was approved on 13 February. The Joint Chiefs of Staff (JCS) had drawn up a list of 94 strategic targets, mainly connected with supply and storage. Rules of engagement (RE) were drawn up which gave little local discretion and which were to remain controversial throughout the war: ports were not to be attacked in case neutral shipping was damaged; the two main centres of population, Hanoi and Haiphong, were also prohibited, to avoid civilian casualties; and North Vietnamese fighter aircraft were only to be engaged after they had attacked. The first 'Rolling Thunder' raids were carried out by 111 aircraft on 2 March against the naval base at Quang Khe and an ammunition depot at Xom Bang. Four strike aircraft were lost to AAA fire.

Over the next month the North Vietnamese air defence system improved and on 3 April the first MiG-17s were encountered. The following day two F-105s engaged on a strike against the Ham Rung (Dragon's Jaw) road and rail bridge at Thanh Hoa were attacked and brought down before the escorting F-100 Super Sabres could intervene. Immediately 45 TFS was sent to Ubon with the first F-4 Phantoms in the theatre, to provide enhanced support to the strike aircraft. There was a short break in May between Phases I and II of 'Rolling Thunder', and in Phase II, which ended with a Christmas truce at the end of the year, additional targets north of the 20th parallel were added.

By the end of 1965 the North Vietnamese had deployed some 2,000 heavy, radar-directed AAA pieces. The AAA was most dangerous up to 4,500ft, but the heavier 57mm and 85mm pieces were effective to about 15,000ft. It was decided to confine attacks to a single pass at about 5,000ft, to avoid the worst of the flak while retaining bombing accuracy. To jam the fire control radars, the RB-66Cs of 41 TRS began operating from Tan Son Nhut. From April the first SA-2 sites were identified from photo-reconnaissance pictures, but they were ruled off limits to attack in case Soviet technicians were killed or injured. The first aircraft to be brought down by a SAM was an F-4C of 45 TFS outside Hanoi on 24 July.

From its experience in Cuba and Vietnam, the USAF set about developing a new series of weapons systems, based around aircraft, to identify and destroy the SAM sites. Under the code-name 'Ferret', shortly changed to 'Wild Weasel' to avoid confusion with a Second World War operation, four F-100Fs were prepared. They were fitted with the APR-25 radar homing and warning (RHAW) system, which gave 360-degree warning of radars in three bands, an IR-133 signal analyzer and an APR-26 launch warning receiver (LWR). These four aircraft operated from 26 November with 388 TFW at Korat, and after losing one aircraft on 20 December the Wild Weasel's claimed their first SA-2 site destroyed on the 22nd. Initially the weapons used to take out the sites were rockets in LAU-3 canisters plus 20mm cannon, but from May 1966 the F-100 was plumbed for the AGM-45 Shrike anti-radiation missile (ARM). Between May and August 1966 the F-100 was replaced by the F-105F, which had similar equipment but also an azimuth and elevation bearing system. Known informally as the EF-105F, the aircraft were first flown by a flight of 13 TFS, 388 TFW, at Korat. By the end of 1966, over 100 SA-2 sites had been identified and the number of dedicated Wild Weasel aircraft increased accordingly; by the end of 1967, 89 SA-2 sites had been destroyed, and many more damaged or forced off the air at a critical point in a raid. Over the next few years the equipment was improved, and from March 1968 the much longer-range Standard ARM was used by 357 TFS.

A developed Wild Weasel type, the F-105G, was introduced into service in September 1970 by 6010 TFS, which became 17 WWS within 388 TFW. The unit was the last to operate the F-105 in Vietnam, departing in November 1974. The final Wild Weasel type in the theatre was the F-4C, which was flown by 67 TFS from October 1972 in support of 'Linebacker' operations, during which 460 sorties were flown. On sorties, the Wild Weasels normally led a flight of fighters armed for SAM suppression, and the dedicated aircraft, having identified a target, would lead the attack, also marking the target for the remainder. In these 'Iron Hand' missions two F-100Fs and 46 F-105s were lost in action, while two Medals of Honor were won by crew members.

In November 1965, to simplify planning and to capitalize on aircraft availability, North Vietnam had been described in terms of Route Packages (or Packs). RPs I to the extreme south, V to the west of Hanoi and VIA to the north of Hanoi were allocated to the USAF; targets were within striking distance of bases in South Vietnam and Thailand. The USN was allocated RPs II, III and IV to the south of Hanoi and VIB to the east. All presented coastal targets and again minimized flight times over hostile territory. During 1956 the strike force was also expanded. From April two squadrons of F-105s with 23 TFW were deployed on TDY to Da Nang, while 474 TFW sent two squadrons of F-100s to South Vietnam. On a more permanent basis, 3 TFW was formed at Bien Hoa with the F-100 while 12 TFW was established at Cam Ranh Bay with the F-4C. During October 1965, 4503 TFS took its F-5As to Vietnam to operate within 3 TFW in Operation 'Skoshi Tiger'. The F-5 was found to be extremely agile, but its range and load-carrying capability were inadequate and the aircraft were turned over to the VNAF, which subsequently used the type extensively in close support.

In Thailand, 355 TFW was formed with the F-105 at Takhli, replacing the TDY aircraft of 4 TFW, while 388 TFW at Korat, with the same aircraft, replaced 18 TFW. A second F-4 Wing, 8 TFW, was formed at Ubon, and early in 1966 366 TFW was established with the F-4 at Phan Rang. By now the F-100 was limited to fighting the in-country war and a further Wing, 31 TFW, was formed at Tuy Hoa. From July the F-104Cs of 479 TFW, which had earlier served in the air defence role, were deployed to Da Nang for escort work and incountry strikes, while the two B-57 units which had earlier operated from Clark AB on TDY were now attached to 35 TFW at Da Nang. In summary, therefore, by mid-1966 there were three F-100, two F-4, one F-105 and one F-104 Wings in South Vietnam, with two F-105 and one F-4 Wings in Thailand. In general, the South Vietnamese units fought the in-country war and attacked targets in RP I, while the Thai-based units struck targets in RPs V and VIA.

In addition to its theatre-based units, the US Air Force was able to call on a large number of Strategic Air Command's B-52s, based initially at Andersen AFB in Guam, where the holding Wing for TDY units was the 3960 Strategic Wing (SW), established in 1955. In February 1966, 3960 SW was redesignated 4133 Bomb Wing (Provisional), and in 1970 it was again redesignated 43 SW. In June 1966 the first B-52s were sent to U-Tapao in Thailand, where they were controlled by 4258 SW, redesignated 307 SW in 1970. Later, in 1968, 4252 SW at Kadena would be formed to provide a third operating base for the large bombers as the facilities at Andersen became overcrowded. The first B-52 unit deployed, in April 1965, was 22 BW, with the B-52B. In June it was replaced by 2 and 7 BWs with the B-52F, which was locally modified to enable the carriage of external ordnance, taking the bomb load up to fifty-one 750lb bombs.

B-52 missions were flown under the code-name 'Arc Light', and the first of the war was on 18 June against VC bases in Binh Duong province. Sadly, two aircraft collided during refuelling and were lost, with eight of the twelve crew members killed. Over the next few months techniques improved, and the B-52 flew close-support missions from 15 November when attacks were made against the VC at Ia Drang. In December, 320 and 454 BW crews took over the aircraft of 2 and 7 BWs, and they were relieved in turn by 28 and 484 BWs with the B-52D in April 1966. In September that year, 91 and 306 BWs were deployed, and by now the older B-52D had been modified to carry a staggering load of ninety 750lb bombs. The return journey to Vietnamese targets was 5,500 miles, which took up to 15 hours to complete; with a fully laden aircraft the crew's workload was extremely heavy.

In January 1966, Phase III of 'Rolling Thunder' began, with targets confined to southern North Vietnam in the hope of encouraging peace talks. These did not materialize, and at the end of March Phase IV began, with few targets off limits and with petrol, oil and lubricants (POL) added to the objectives. The next pause in the campaign was in January 1967. From 1966 bombing accuracy was improved and a night and bad-weather bombing capability conferred with the introduction of a blind-bombing system by triangulation under Project 'Combat Proof' (later called 'Combat Skyspot'). This relied on MSQ-77 ground radars. Targets in the north were bombed consistently through 1967 in Phase V, a brief halt being called in August to support a new peace initiative. Although this pattern of bombing halts provided a well-earned rest for the air crews, it also enabled the North Vietnamese to regroup. However, the halt only lasted ten days on this occasion, and afterwards all North Vietnamese airfields except Gia Lam International were released as targets.

Phase V ended with a Christmas halt, but on 30 January 1968 the North Vietnamese and VC launched the Tet offensive into South Vietnam; this achieved little in the way of territorial gain, but it cost the NVA and VC 37,000 killed or wounded. The final phase of 'Rolling Thunder' began in January 1968, but the United States announced a ban on bombing north of the 20th parallel from 31 March in an attempt to bring the North to negotiate; when Hanoi accepted the invitation, the bombing ban was extended to the 19th parallel. During 1967 yet another F-100 Wing, 37 TFW, had been formed at the newly opened airfield at Phu Cat, and 2 Sqn. RAAF began operations with its Canberra B.20s within 35 TFW. In 1968, fighter units were added to 432 TRW at Udorn, increasing the F-4 force. In the same year 12 TFW returned to the US, leaving only 366 TFW with the F-4 in Vietnam, and four ANG F-100 squadrons deployed to Vietnam from May 1968 to May 1969. More sophisticated equipment arrived in the theatre in March 1968 when six F-111As of 428 TFS were flown to Takhli for evaluation under Project 'Combat Lancer'. After a disastrous introduction into the theatre, during which three aircraft were lost within a month, the remainder completed 51 sorties without loss to October 1968.

At the end of October a total halt was called to the bombing of North Vietnam, air strikes now being confined to the South. One target in the 1968 Tet offensive was the combat base at Khe Sanh, just 20 miles south of the Demilitarized Zone (DMZ), manned by Marines. US Marine Corps helicopter units had operated in Vietnam since 1962 in support of the ARVN, but fixed-wing aircraft were not deployed until spring 1965. The USMC had provided the first troops to operate in South Vietnam when they landed on Da Nang on 8 March 1965 to assume responsibility for guarding the air base from the ARVN. Already established at the base since March was Marine Air Group (MAG) 11 with one F-8 and two F-4B squadrons, plus the Headquarters and Maintenance Squadron responsible for tactical co-ordination. In late 1966 the potent A-6A arrived with VMA-242 to provide a night and all-weather strike potential. The Marines flew local sorties initially, but as the troops went on the offensive close-support missions were flown. On 1 June 1965 a second Group, MAG-12, was

formed at Chu Lai south of Da Nang, this time equipped with the A-4C, which was ideal for close-support work. The A-4 operated almost exclusively with MAG-12, with five squadrons based at Chu Lai until the end of 1966. The Group also acquired an A-6A unit in early 1967. The third Group, MAG-13, was established in January 1966 with the F-4Bs of VMFA-323, also at Chu Lai; later, an F-8E squadron was added.

Towards the end of 1967, as intelligence reports indicated that a substantial enemy force was massing for an assault on Khe Sanh, planning went ahead for aerial support. In the autumn of 1967, in Operation 'Neutralize', air power had been used effectively in support of the combat post at Con Thien. Now Operation 'Niagara', the aerial bombardment of Khe Sanh's besiegers, was planned. Defending the base were three battalions of the 26th Marines, and during the battle a further two battalions were added. In the early weeks of January, reconnaissance patrols identified numerous North Vietnamese bases from which, it was clear, a large-scale attack was about to be launched. Each base located was destroyed by artillery fire or air strike. The attack came early on 21 January, and from now there was continuous air activity in the immediate vicinity as USMC, USAF and USN aircraft attacked North Vietnamese positions, many very close to the perimeter. On the 22nd, B-52s bombed four targets in the area. At the same time, transport aircraft were bringing in supplies

The F-105 Thunderchief served with three Wings, initially with 23 TFW at Da Nang from April 1965 and finally with 388 TFW, Korat, until the aircraft's withdrawal in August 1973. Illustrated is a fully armed F-105D, (6)24336 of 355 TFW, on its way to a target in the North. In later years the aircraft served in the Wild Weasel role, attacking enemy air defence systems. (Via R. F. Dorr)

An unusual photograph of an SA-2 launch from a site north-west of Hanoi, taken by an RF-101C Voodoo. As the war developed, the air defences in the North became increasingly formidable, but casualties to the SA-2, with its distinctive exhaust plume, were remarkably light. (USAF via J. Ethell)

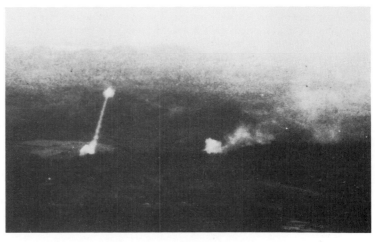

to the airstrip while USMC helicopters brought in the 1st Battalion, 9th Marines, as reinforcements. The USMC was also committed to battle in defence of Hue and Da Nang, and all available close-support units were fully stretched.

All services remained committed: in February, for example, the carrier-borne aircraft of TF.77 flew 2,800 sorties of a total 3,672 in the month in the general area of Khe Sanh. Importantly, all the air forces were united under a single command, with clear limits of discretion. It was now that the B-52 force was expanded, with an additional Wing deployed to Kadena in response to the *Pueblo* crisis in Korea. Under 'Bugle Note' procedures, target areas around Khe Sanh were divided into 1 × 2km boxes, each to be saturated by a three-aircraft cell at 90-minute intervals using 'Skyspot' techniques. Forty-eight sorties a day were flown, and from late February the aircraft bombed as close as 1,000yds from the perimeter. During March, no fewer than 444 close-support sorties were flown by 3rd Air Division B-52s.

In all, 2,548 sorties were flown, with 59,542 tons of bombs dropped; 274 North Vietnamese defensive positions were destroyed, and 1,382 secondary explosions and 108 secondary fires were reported. By 6 April the siege was over, and in June the combat post was dismantled and abandoned. NVAF fighters never ventured South, and in the North the attack aircraft had contended initially with the nimble MiG-17, but an additional hazard was encountered from November 1965 when the first MiG-21s were supplied to the NVAF. The first dogfight occurred on 10 July 1965 when F-4Cs of 45 TFS escorting an F-105 strike on the Bac Giang bridge outside Hanoi engaged a number of MiG-17s, two of which were brought down by AIM-9 Sidewinder missiles.

The F-4C was limited in having no gun armament. During the year there were several engagements, and by the end of June 1966 fifteen NVAF fighters, mainly MiG-17s, had been shot down for the loss of two USAF F-4Cs. By the end of the year the USAF pilots were frustrated at the few opportunities they got for air combat, especially since the MiG bases were prohibited targets for bombing. Operation 'Bolo' was therefore conceived to provoke the NVAF into combat. On 2 January 1967 a large force of F-4Cs of 366 and 8 TFW took off from Phan Rang and Ubon respectively, together with six flights of F-105 Wild Weasels and EB-66 jammers and an escort of F-104Cs of 479 TFW from Da Nang. Critically, the 8 TFW aircraft were configured to emulate the F-105 which, normally bomb-laden, were attractive targets for the MiGs. The Phantoms used F-105 communications and refuelling procedures, relying on the highly efficient North Vietnamese air defence system to identify the massive strike as comprising mainly F-105

Thunderchiefs. The 366th TFW was to cover the east over Kep and Cat Bai airfields and provide a barrier combat air patrol (BARCAP) to prevent MiGs escaping to Chinese sanctuary, while 8 TFW covered Gia Lam and Phuc Yen airfields. The ruse was a total success, and seven MiG-21s were shot down for no loss; at the time, this represented almost half the MiG-21 force. On 6 January two more MiG-21s were brought down when several F-4Cs simulated an unarmed RF-4 run. Bad weather prevented further combat for several months, but in April nine NVAF fighters were brought down for a loss of seven. The MiG-21 airfields at Kep and Hoa Lac were now authorized for attack, and by the end of May, 26 fighters had been destroyed on the ground. By the time the NVAF stood down on 5 June it had lost 54 aircraft in the air compared to the US loss to fighters of eleven machines.

The F-4D was introduced into service in May with 555 TFS, 8 TFW; significantly, the new version was armed with the M61A1 20mm Vulcan cannon, and within a month three MiGs were shot down with the new weapon. After remaining inactive for several months, the NVAF used a new tactic from late August. On the 23rd, several F-4Ds escorting a strike on Yen Vien railyard were shot down by MiG-21s which had remained low to avoid detection, then being directed by GCI to a steep, climbing attack from astern. In the resulting dogfight two MiG-17s were shot down by gunfire. In October permission was given for attacks on the air defence centre and airfield at Phuc Yen, and in a joint strike on the 25th USAF and USN fighters destroyed four MiG-21s and four MiG-17s on the ground with a fifth MiG-21 destroyed in the air. The North Vietnamese defences were further strengthened with new electro-optical tracking for the SA-2 batteries which was not susceptible to jamming.

The VNAF also introduced new air fighting tactics which co-ordinated MiG-17 and MiG-21 attacks from many headings. Between August and the bombing halt in March 1968 the United States lost eighteen aircraft to MiGs while shooting down five MiG-21 and seventeen MiG-17 fighters. By the time of the 1968 bombing halt, the USAF claimed 86 NVAF fighters brought down in air-to-air combat, roughly one-third to the F-105 and the remainder to the F-4. A total of 41 USAF fighters had been destroyed, giving a kill ratio of 2.1:1. During this period 442 AAMs had been fired, to score 52 kills. The early AIM-9 suffered from heat-return problems, while the AIM-7 was affected by clutter at low altitude.

Throughout the war there were several targets which for years defied attempts at destruction. Foremost among these were the Paul Doumer bridge west of Hanoi and the Ham Rung (Dragon's Jaw) bridge at Thanh Hoa. The first strike on the 540ft Dragon's Jaw was on 3 April 1965. Seventy-nine aircraft were involved, mainly F-105s from

18 TFW and 4 TFW with F-100 escorts. The weapons used on this first attempt were the AGM-12 Bullpup and 750lb 'iron' bombs. Little damage was done to the structure, but two aircraft were shot down by heavy AAA fire; a second strike was ordered for the following day. This time only bombs were used and severe damage was caused for the loss of one F-105 to 57mm AAA fire; in addition, two F-105s were lost to MiG-17 attacks as already described. The bridge was closed for some time for repairs. There were two further attempts on 7 and 30 May, now with F-4C protection, but despite 26 bridge targets of a total of 27 having been destroyed the Ham Rung, though scarred, remained intact. After the introduction of the RP system the bridge became the 'property' of the USN, which tried unsuccessfully for three years to destroy it; the first attempt was on 17 June 1965.

In the meantime, a novel approach was tried on 30 May 1966 with Project 'Carolina Moon'. A C-130 was prepared to drop a mass-focus weapon 8ft in diameter into the Song Ma waterway. The mine was intended to float downstream to detonate when magnetic sensors detected the bridge's metal structure, but despite the fact that four out of five weapons used hit the bridge, again little damage was done, while a second C-130 flying a follow-up mission the next day also failed to do any significant damage and was itself brought down by AAA fire. The first of a new family of weapons was used against the bridge on 12 March 1967 when A-4 Skyhawks dropped AGM-62 Walleye electro-optical guided bombs (EOGB). All the missiles hit the aim point to within five feet of each other, but still the bridge stood. The last attack before the bombing halt was an unsuccessful joint effort between the USN and USAF on 28 January 1968.

The Paul Doumer bridge was a restricted target until the summer of 1967, but on 11 August F-105s of 355 and 388 TFWs, escorted by F-4Ds of 8 TFW, attacked it with 3,000lb bombs, causing considerable damage; 94 tons of bombs were dropped on the target, for no loss. After repairs were confirmed there were further raids on 14 and 18 December. Although several spans were down the bridge was judged reparable, but bad weather prevented further strikes before the bombing halt. After the bombing halt, offensive operations were not resumed until 6 April 1972 with the North Vietnamese invasion. The Ham Rung bridge had been completely repaired in the interim, but it was now a prime target, and on 27 April it was attacked by F-4Ds of 8 TFW using 2,000lb EOGBs. The bridge was badly damaged at no loss to the attackers, and in a second strike on 13 May the structure was wrecked by a combination of 3,000lb bombs and 2,000lb laser-guided bombs (LGB). As determined repair work went ahead, the bridge was attacked eleven more

FLOATING CRANE

REPLACED SPANS ←

times by the USN and twice by the USAF before 23 October, when bombing was again halted.

The Paul Doumer bridge was struck on 10 May by 8 TFW F-4Es using 2,000 LGBs and EOGBs; despite intense AAA fire and the launching of 160 SAMs, not a single aircraft was lost. The structure was severely damaged, and it was completely destroyed on a follow-up raid the next day in which the 3,000lb M118 LGB was used. The bridge was attacked just once more, on 10 September, to ensure that it could not be used for some time. During the bombing halt from October 1968, the United States started the process of 'Vietnamization' and began to withdraw its forces. In 1969 the short-lived 37 TFW disbanded; then, in 1970, 3 and 31 TFWs with the F-100 were deactivated and 355 TFW handed the last of its F-105s to 388 TFW at Korat.

The interdiction of the trails in Laos and the in-country war continued, and 13 TBS, now flying B-57Gs fitted with low light-level television (LLLTV) and forward-looking infra-red (FLIR) equipment, joined 8 TFW in September; the two B-57 units within 35 TFW had disbanded between 1968 and 1969. In 1971 the final F-100 Wing, 35 TFW, returned to the USA, leaving 8 TFW, 388 TFW and 432 TRW with the F-4 and some F-105G squadrons in Thailand and 366 TFW with the F-4E at Da Nang. Meanwhile MAG-12 and MAG-13 left Chu Lai, their squadrons being dispersed. Although the South Vietnamese had assumed responsibility for their own ground defence and close-support air power, the Americans kept a close watch on the North. During late 1971, US aerial reconnaissance indicated a massive build-up of North Vietnamese forces north of the DMZ. It appeared that an offensive was in preparation, but despite this the withdrawal of American troops continued.

The blow fell early on 30 March 1972 with a rocket, artillery and mortar attack pounding across the DMZ, followed by an invasion by some 40,000 troops who quickly linked up with

The Paul Doumer bridge over the Red river near Hanoi was a continuing target for US air strikes. This reconnaissance photo was taken in May 1968 and clearly shows the extent of the damage following an attack. The ruptured spans were soon replaced, but the bridge was finally destroyed in May 1972. (USAF)

TABLE OF UNITS: THE VIETNAM WAR—OFFENSIVE OPERATIONS

Unit	Aircraft (code)	Base	Role	Dates
USAF (SAC)				
3960 SW	B-52D	⎫	Holding Wing for TDY B-52D units	01/04/55 to 01/02/66
4133 BW(P)	B-52D/F	⎬ Andersen AFB	Replaced 3960 SW	01/02/66 to 01/04/70
43 SW	B-52D	⎪	Replaced 4133 BW(P)	01/04/70 to ?
72 SW(P)	B-52G	⎭	Holding Wing for TDY B-52G units	01/06/72 to 15/11/73
4252 SW	B-52D	⎫ Kadena AB	Holding Wing for TDY B-52D units	01/01/68 to 01/04/70
376 SW	B-52D	⎭	Replaced 4252 SW	01/04/70 to 01/09/70
4258 SW	B-52D	⎫	Holding Wing for TDY B-52D units	02/06/66 to 01/04/70
307 SW	B-52D	⎬ U-Tapao	Replaced 4258 SW	01/04/70 to 30/09/75
310 SW(P)	B-52D	⎭	Holding Wing for TDY B-52D units	01/06/72 to 01/07/74

Among TDY Bomb Wings contributing to TDY attachments in the period 1964–1966 were 22 BW (B-52B); 28 BW, 91 BW, 96 BW, 306 BW, 484 BW (B-52D); and 2 BW, 7 BW, 320 BW, 454 BW (B-52F). In addition, KC-135 tankers were detached to the three bases on TDY.

Unit	Aircraft (code)	Base	Role	Dates
USAF (PACAF and TAC)				
4 TFW (August 1964 to 1965 TDY ex Yokota)				
36 TFS	⎱ F-105D	Takhli, Korat	⎱ Strike	14/08/64 to 00/00/65
80 TFS	⎰	Korat	⎰	00/08/64 to 00/00/65
18 TFW (August 1964 to May 1965 TDY ex Kadena)				
12 TFS	⎱		Strike (to 388 TFW)	00/08/64 to ?
44 TFS	⎬ F-105D	Korat	Strike (to 388 TFW)	00/08/64 to 00/05/65
67 TFS	⎰		Strike	00/08/64 to 00/05/65
405 TFW (August 1964 to 1965 TDY ex Clark AB)				
511 TFS	F-100D	Takhli	Strike	00/08/64 to 00/00/65
405 TBW (August 1964 to June 1966; became 6252 TFW June 1965 TDY ex Clark AB)				
8 TBS	B-57B	Bien Hoa, Tan Son Nhut, Da Nang	Light bombing (to 35 TFW)	04/08/64 to 00/06/66
13 TBS	B-57B	Bien Hoa, Tan Son Nhut, Da Nang	Light bombing (to 35 TFW)	04/08/64 to 00/06/66
35 TFW (August 1964 to June 1971)				
612 TFS	F-100D/F (VS)	⎫	⎫	00/08/64 to 26/06/71
614 TFS	F-100D/F (VP)	⎬ Phan Rang	⎬ Strike	00/08/64 to 26/06/71
615 TFS	F-100D/F (VZ)	⎪	⎪	00/08/64 to 26/06/71
352 TFS	F-100D/F (VM)	⎭	⎭	00/06/66 to 26/06/71
8 TBS	B-57B/C/E (PQ)	⎱ Da Nang, Phan Rang	Interdiction (ex 405 TBW)	00/06/66 to 06/10/69
13 TBS	B-57B/C/E (PV)	⎰		00/06/66 to 15/01/68
2 Sqn.	Canberra B.20	Phan Rang	Light bombing (RAAF)	23/04/67 to 00/06/71
120 TFS	F-100D/F (VS)	Tuy Hoa, Phan Rang	Strike (Co. ANG)	05/05/68 to 30/04/69
23 TFW (April 1965 to 1966 TDY ex McConnell AFB)				
562 TFS	⎱ F-105D	Da Nang	Strike	00/04/65 to 00/00/66
563 TFS	⎰			
12 TFW (April 1965 to 1968)				
45 TFS	⎱ F-4C	Ubon	⎱ Strike	00/04/65 to 00/00/68
43 TFS	⎰	Cam Ranh Bay	⎰	00/11/65 to 00/00/68
557 TFS	F-4C (XC, XT)	Cam Ranh Bay, Udorn	⎫	
558 TFS	F-4C (XD)	Cam Ranh Bay	⎬ Strike	00/11/65 to 00/00/68
559 TFS	F-4C (XN)	Cam Ranh Bay	⎭	
389 TFS	F-4D (HB)	⎱ Phu Cat, Udorn	Strike (ex 366 TFW)	00/00/70 to 00/08/73
480 TFS	F-4D (HK)	⎰		
474 TFW (June 1965 to December 1965)				
429 TFS	F-100D	Bien Hoa	Strike	00/06/65 to 00/12/65
481 TFS	F-100D	Tan Son Nhut	Strike	00/06/65 to 00/11/65

regular forces already placed in the South. The first attacks were against Quang Tri and Hue, then by a second force against Pleiku, while a third attack came from Cambodia via Loc Ninh towards Saigon. By now the VNAF comprised some 1,300 aircraft transferred from US stocks, but USAF forces were confined to one F-4 Wing at Da Nang with three further Wings in Thailand. The B-52 force had declined over the previous years, but in February 1972 five Stratofortress units were deployed to Andersen AFB. Immediately after the invasion, 35 TFS of 3 TFW was sent from Kunsan, Korea, to join 366 TFW at Da Nang. Soon the four F-4 squadrons of 49 TFW at Holloman AFB were alerted for overseas duty, and the first, 8 TFS, was operating with 432 TRW within a few weeks.

These deployments were initiated under the 'Constant Guard' programme and were quickly followed by two squadrons of 4 TFW from Seymour Johnson AFB (8 TFW), the remaining three squadrons of 49 TFW (366 TFW), three squadrons of F-4s of 31 TFS from Homestead AFB (432 TRW) and the F-105Gs of 561 TFS, 23 TFW, McConnell AFB (388 TFW); at the same time, two squadrons of 347 TFW with the F-111A were sent to Takhli from where they made numerous successful 'one aircraft, one target' sorties. A massive airlift supported the transfer of units from the continental United States (CONUS), involving large numbers of strategic transports; two squadrons of C-130s were also transferred. The B-52 force was built up under the 'Bullet Shot' programme to a total of 63 D models and 98 Gs, the latter coming under the control of the newly formed 72 SW(P) at Andersen AFB. The bombers were supported by the considerable tanker force of 168 KC-135s. The USMC sent

TABLE OF UNITS: THE VIETNAM WAR—OFFENSIVE OPERATIONS (continued)

Unit	Aircraft (code)	Base	Role	Dates
3 TFW *(October 1965 to 1970)*				
307 TFS	F-100D		Strike	00/10/65 to 00/00/67
308 TFS	F-100D		Strike (to 31 TFW)	00/10/65 to 00/00/66
510 TFS	F-100D (CE)		Strike	00/10/65 to 00/00/69
531 TFS	F-100D/F (CP)	Bien Hoa	Strike	00/10/65 to 00/00/67
90 TFS	F-100D/F (CB)		Strike (to 90 AS)	00/10/65 to 00/00/69
4503 TFS	F-5A		Light strike (Skoshi Tiger)	23/10/65 to 00/02/66
8 AS	A-37B		Light strike	00/11/69 to 00/00/70
90 AS	A-37B		Light strike	00/00/69 to 00/00/70
355 TFW *(November 1965 to October 1970)*				
333 TFS	F-105D/F (RK)		Strike, Wild Weasel	
334 TFS	F-105D		Strike	
335 TFS	F-105D		Strike	00/11/65 to 06/10/70
354 TFS	F-105F (RM)	Takhli	Strike, Wild Weasel (to 388 TFW)	
357 TFS	F-105D/F (RU)		Strike, Wild Weasel	
428 TFS	F-111A		Strike (Combat Lancer, 474 TFW)	15/03/68 to 19/12/68
44 TFS	F-105D/F (RE)		Strike, Wild Weasel (ex 388 TFW)	10/10/69 to 06/10/70
388 TFW *(November 1965 to 1975)*				
421 TFS	F-105D		Strike	00/11/65 to 00/09/68
13 TFS	F-105D/F		Strike, Wild Weasel	00/11/65 to ?
469 TFS	F-105D, F-4E (JV)		Strike	14/03/66 to 00/00/73
561 TFS	F-100F, F-105F/G (WW)		Wild Weasel	14/03/66 to 00/00/71
44 TFS	F-105F (JE)		Strike, ECM (ex 18 TFW, to 355 TFW)	00/00/68 to 10/10/69
12 TFS	F-105D/F (ZA)		Strike (ex 18 TFW)	00/00/68 to 00/00/69
34 TFS	F-105D/F, F-4D/E (JJ)		Strike	00/00/69 to 00/11/74
6010 TFS	F-105F/G (ZB)	Korat	Wild Weasel (to 17 TFS)	24/09/70 to 12/01/71
17 TFS	F-105G (ZB, JB)		Wild Weasel (from 6010 TFS)	12/01/71 to 00/11/74
44 TFS	F-105F (RE)		Strike, Wild Weasel (ex 355 TFW)	06/10/70 to 30/04/71
354 TFS	F-105F (RM)		Strike, Wild Weasel (ex 355 TFW)	
67 TFS	F-4C (ZG)		Wild Weasel (ex 18 TFW)	00/10/72 to 00/02/73
25 TFS	F-4E (JJ)		Strike	00/11/72 to 00/11/74
561 TFS	F-105G (MD, WW)		Wild Weasel (TDY 23 TFW)	11/06/72 to 00/08/73
3 TFS	A-7D (JH)		Light strike	00/00/74 to 00/09/75
8 TFW *(December 1965 to 1974, also Holding Wing for TDY units spring 1972)*				
433 TFS	F-4C/D (FG, WP)		Strike, air superiority	00/12/65 to 00/00/74
497 TFS	F-4C/D (FP, WP)	Ubon, Korat	Strike, night fighter	
25 TFS	F-4D (FA, WP)		Strike, sensor dropping (to 388 TFW)	00/12/65 to 00/11/72
555 TFS	F-4C/D (FY)	Ubon	Strike, air superiority (to 432 TRW)	00/05/67 to 00/00/68
435 TFS	F-4D (FO, WP)	Ubon, Korat	Strike, air superiority	00/00/68 to 00/00/74
13 TBS	B-57G (FK)		Night interdiction	15/09/70 to 12/04/72
35 TFS	F-4D/E (UP)	Ubon	Strike (TDY 3 TFW; ex 366 TFW)	00/00/72 to ?
336 TFS	F-4E (SC)		Strike (TDY 4 TFW)	00/05/72 to ?
334 TFS	F-4E (SA)		Strike (TDY 4 TFW)	11/04/73 to ?
366 TFW *(March 1966 to December 1972; also holding Wing for TDY units spring 1972)*				
389 TFS	F-4C/D (A)		Strike (to 12 TFW)	00/03/66 to 00/00/70
390 TFS	F-4C/D (B, LF)	Phan Rang, Da Nang	Strike	00/03/66 to 00/00/72
480 TFS	F-4C/D (C)		Strike (to 12 TFW)	00/03/66 to 00/00/72
4 TFS	F-4E (LA)		Strike	00/00/70 to 00/00/72
421 TFS	F-4E (LC)	Da Nang	Strike	
35 TFS	F-4D/E (UP)		Strike (TDY 3 TFW; to 8 TFW)	03/04/72 to 00/00/72
7 TFS	F-4E (HO)		Strike (TDY 49 TFW)	
9 TFS	F-4E (HO)	Takhli	Strike (TDY 49 TFW)	13/05/72 to 00/12/72
417 TFS	F-4E (HO)		Strike (TDY 49 TFW)	

two F-4 units to Da Nang under MAG-15, but these were soon transferred to the new airfield at Nam Phong in Thailand, where they joined an A-6A squadron. Two A-4E squadrons went to Bien Hoa under MAG-11.

For the next few months the air strikes were mainly confined to the South, initially in defence of positions in Military Region 1 around Hue. By the end of June 55,803 sorties had been flown, nearly one-third by the VNAF; B-52 sorties, nearly all in close support, ran at around 2,000 a month. The Paris peace talks were abandoned on 4 May, and North Vietnamese ports were mined for the first time from 8 May; on the same date, Operation 'Linebacker I', the resumption of bombing in the North, began. Within three days 1,800 sorties had been flown for the loss of seven aircraft, against eleven MiG-17s and -21s shot down. There were now about 170 MiG-17s and 80 MiG-21s in the North, together with 300 SAM sites and a huge concentration of AAA covering all the targets of importance.

Hanoi and Haiphong were the best defended areas in the world against air attack, and the Americans adopted new tactics to enable strikes to be pressed home with minimum cost. Essentially, air crews specialized in particular roles, with perhaps 20 strike aircraft being led by sixteen SAM-suppression and ECM aircraft with sixteen escorts. Increasingly, 'smart' bombs with a limited stand-off capability were used against high-value targets. From 19 June over 300 sorties a day were being flown, many against the supply system, and by July the position in South Vietnam had stabilized. The peace talks resumed on 13 July, but the pace of bombing continued unabated, and in October the attacks turned to the MiG airfields. The first phase of 'Linebacker'

TABLE OF UNITS: THE VIETNAM WAR—OFFENSIVE OPERATIONS (continued)

Unit	Aircraft (code)	Base	Role	Dates
479 TFW (July 1966 to July 1967)				
435 TFS	F-104C	Da Nang	Light strike	00/07/66 to 00/07/67
476 TFS	F-104C			
31 TFW (1966 to 1970)				
306 TFS	F-100D/F (SD)		Strike	
308 TFS	F-100D/F (SM)		Strike (ex 3 TFW)	00/00/66 to 00/00/70
309 TFS	F-100D/F (SS)		Strike	
355 TFS	F-100D/F (SP)	Tuy Hoa	Strike (to 37 TFW)	00/00/66 to 00/00/67
416 TFS	F-100D/F (SE)		Strike (to 37 TFW)	
136 TFS	F-100D/F (SG)		Strike (NY ANG)	00/05/68 to 11/06/69
188 TFS	F-100D/F (SK)		Strke (NM ANG)	
37 TFW (1967 to 1969)				
612 TFS	F-100D/F (HS)		Strike	
355 TFS	F-100D/F (HP)	Phu Cat	Strike (ex 31 TFW)	00/00/67 to 00/00/69
416 TFS	F-100D/F (HE)		Strike (ex 31 TFW)	
174 TFS	F-100C/F (HA)		Strike (Ia ANG)	00/05/68 to 28/05/69
432 TRW (Mixed recce and fighter Wing, 1968 to 1973; also Holding Wing for TDY units spring 1972)				
13 TFS	F-4D (OC, UD)		Strike	00/00/68 to 00/08/73
555 TFS	F-4D (OY)		Strike (ex 8 TFW)	00/00/68 to 00/01/73
524 TFS	F-4E (ZF)		Strike (TDY 31 TFW)	00/04/72 to ?
8 TFS	F-4D (HO)		Strike (TDY 49 TFW)	00/04/72 to ?
308 TFS	F-4E (ZF)	Udorn	Strike (TDY 31 TFW)	00/05/72 to ?
307 TFS	F-4C (ZF)		Strike (TDY 31 TFW)	00/09/72 to 00/00/73
58 TFS	F-4E (ED)		Strike (TDY 33 TFW)	00/11/72 to 15/08/73
523 TFS	F-4D (PN)		Strike (TDY 3 TFW)	08/02/73 to ?
4 TFS	F-4D/E (UD)		Strike	00/08/73 to 00/00/74
347 TFW (May 1972 to August 1973)				
429 TFS	F-111A (HG)	Takhli, Korat	Strike	00/05/72 to 15/08/73
430 TFS	F-111A (NA. HG)			
354 TFW (October 1972 to April 1974)				
353 TFS				15/10/72 to 00/04/74
355 TFS	A-7D (MB)	Korat	Light strike	14/10/72 to 22/04/74
356 TFS				10/10/72 to 00/04/74
USMC				
MAG-11 (March 1965 to June 1971)				
H&MS-11	TF-9J, TA-4F (TM)		Tac. co-ordination, FAC	00/00/65 to 00/06/71
VMF-235	F-8E (DB)		Close support	00/00/65 to 00/05/68
VMFA-542	F-4BJ (WH)	Da Nang	Close support	00/03/65 to 00/02/70
VMFA-531	F-4B (EC)		Close support	11/04/65 to 00/00/66
VMA-242	A-6A (DT)		Strike	00/11/66 to 00/09/70
VMO-2	OV-10A (UV)	Marble Mountain	FAC, light strike	06/07/68 to 00/00/71
VMA-225	A-6A (CE)	Da Nang	Strike	00/02/69 to 00/04/71
VMA-311	A-4E (WL)	Da Nang	Close support	00/07/70 to 00/05/71
MAG-12 (June 1965 to November 1970, May 1972 to January 1973)				
VMA-224	A-4C (WK)			00/00/65 to 00/00/66
VMA-225	A-4C (CE)			01/06/65 to 00/00/66
VMA-311	A-4E (WL, WT)			01/06/65 to 00/07/70
VMA-214	A-4C (WE)	Chu Lai	Close support	00/06/65 to 00/04/67
VMA-223	A-4E (WP)			00/12/65 to 00/01/70
VMA-211	A-4E (CF)			00/12/65 to 00/11/70
VMA-533	A-6A (ED)	Chu Lai	Strike	00/04/67 to 00/11/69
VMA-121	A-4E (VK)	Chu Lai	Close support	00/11/66 to 00/10/68
VMA-311	A-4E (WL)	Bien Hoa	Close support	00/05/72 to 00/01/73
VMA-211	A-4E (CF)			
MAG-13 (January 1966 to September 1970)				
VMFA-323	F-4B (WS)	Chu Lai	Close support	00/01/66 to 00/00/69
VMF-232	F-8E (WT)	Da Nang, Chu Lai	Close support	00/12/66 to 00/09/67
VMFA-115	F-4B (VE)			00/00/68 to 00/07/70
VMFA-232	F-4J (WT)	Chu Lai	Close support	00/03/68 to 00/00/69
VMFA-122	F-4B (DC)			00/00/69 to 00/09/70
MAG-15 (April 1972 to September 1973)				
VMFA-115	F-4B (VE)	Da Nang, Nam Phong	Close support	00/04/72 to 00/08/73
VMFA-232	F-4J (WT)			06/04/72 to 00/09/73
VMA-533	A-6A (ED)	Nam Phong	Strike	00/06/72 to 00/08/73

ended on 22 October with the prospect of an early settlement at Paris, but the North Vietnamese walked out on 13 December; 'Linebacker II' was thus ordered from the 15th. By now three squadrons from 354 TFW with the A-7D were based at Korat and the B-52 force had grown to over 200, about 50 of which operated from U-Tapao and the remainder from Andersen AFB. The B-52G, which was new to the theatre, carried fewer bombs and an inferior ECM suite to that on the B-52D but had a superior range.

The scene was now set for the most intense bombing raids since the Second World War. The purpose of the strikes was to halt the communist supply effort and deal such a blow that the North Vietnamese would be forced back to the negotiations. The first strikes on the 18th proceeded in three waves, but strong tailwinds denied the bombers protection against the SAMs when chaff was blown adrift. During the day over two hundred missiles were fired and three B-52s lost; no aircraft were lost on the 19th, but on the 20th six were shot down and on the 21st two more.

Since six of the eleven bombers lost were the B-52G version with an inferior ECM fit, immediate field modifications were put in hand to improve the aircraft's equipment, and the tactics were changed to spread the bombers within waves. Between 22 and 24 December the bombers again attacked airfields, POL targets and railway yards with no loss, downing two MiG-21s. There was then a break for Christmas while planning continued. On the eighth day of the campaign no fewer than 120 bombers struck targets around Hanoi. Two B-52s were lost, one on landing at U-Tapao, and the next day two more went down to SAMs, despite many of the missile sites having been destroyed in the raids. The short campaign, known subsequently as the 'Eleven-Day War', ended on the 29th, by which time 729 B-52 sorties had been flown, 15,000 tons of bombs dropped and 1,242 SAMs recorded as having been fired. The North Vietnamese returned to negotiations, and by 23 January 1973 a ceasefire was signed, marking the end of US military operations in the whole of Vietnam.

The 8th and 388th TFWs remained in Thailand until 1974, while the 432nd TRW at Udorn and the 366th TFW at Takhli were deactivated. MAG-12 left South Vietnam in January 1972, MAG-15 following in August, when the F-111As of 347 TFW also returned to the USA. The A-7Ds

of 354 TFW remained at Korat, where they were joined by a fourth squadron (within 388 TFW) in early 1974. The B-52 Wings at U-Tapao were disbanded by 1975.

AIRCRAFT MARKINGS

USAF
Initially USAF fighters and attack aircraft were finished bare metal (BM) overall, often with bright unit markings. From August 1965 camouflage (C) was applied, and from May 1967 Wing or squadron codes appeared. Camouflage on fighters was dark green/medium green/tan over, light grey under, while the B-52 was finished dark green/blue-green/tan over and black (B), grey (G) or white (W) under. From about 1966 the standard form of presentation of the serial numbers was the first two digits in small black numerals followed by the last three in larger white or light grey numerals; there were many local exceptions.
B-52D *B, black fin and rudder: (5)50069.*
B-52F *Silver-grey over, black under, red horizontal stripe and black serial on fin: (5)70162, (5)70181/2 (320 BW).*
B-52G *G: (5)76515.*
B-57B *BM, black serial on fin, buzz number on rear fuselage: (5)33833/BA-833 (405 TBW).*
B-57E *C, black under, white serial and code on fin: 0(5)54282/PQ (8 TBS).*
B-57G *(521)588/FK (13 TBS).*
F-100C *C, serial and code in white: (54)1741/SK (188 TFS ANG).*
F-100D *BM: (5)63097 (481 TFS); (5)63397 (307 TFS); (5)53797 (416 TFS). C: (5)63025/VP (120 TFS); 0-(5)62910/SM 'Jeanne Kay' (208 TFS).*
F-100F *C: 563775/VM (352 TFS).*
F-104C *C: (5)70928 (435 TFS).*
F-105D *BM: (5)91723 (334 TFS); (6)10169/FH-169 (562 TFS). C: 61(O)152/JJ (34 TFS); 58(1)172/RU (357 TFS).*
F-105F *C: (6)38285/JE (44 TFS).*
F-105G *C: (6)38321/WW (561 TFS).*
F-4C *C: (6)40665 (389 TFS).*
F-4D *C: (6)60234/FO (435 TFS). C, black under: (6)60239/FP (497 TFS).*
F-4E *C, code and serial white: 229/ED (58 TFS); 69(0)288/SA (334 TFS).*
F-111A *Dark green/green/tan overall, white serial and code on fin: 67065/NA (430 TFS); 67113/HG (429 TFS).*
A-7D *C, white serial and code on fin: 70967/MB (354 TFW).*

USMC
USMC fighters were finished as USN fighters; for details see notes on markings in Section 9.2.3 on carrier operations.
A-4E *(15)1046/15WL (VMA-311).*
A-4F *(15)1125/01CF (VMA-211).*

One of the more controversial aspects of the Vietnam War was the widespread use of the B-52 strategic bomber. Vast areas were laid waste by indiscriminate carpet bombing, especially in Cambodia. However, the Stratofortresses were also used in a tactical role, for example in the defence of the beleaguered base at Khe Sanh. These B-52Ds are seen bombing at medium altitude near what appears to be a built-up area. (USAF via J. Ethell)

TA-4F *(15)3489/7TM (H&MS-11).*
A-6A *152595/10DT (VMA-242); 155616/06DT*
(VMA-255).
F-4B *(15)1453/4WS (VMFA-323); (14)8431/17VE*
(VMFA-115).
F-4J *(15)5811/6WT (VMFA-232).*
F-8E *150316/17WT (VMF-232); (15)0328/DB*
(VMF-235).

RAAF
Canberra B.20 *Dark Green/Medium Sea Grey*
over, light grey under, red lightning flash on fin,
black serial on rear fuselage: (A84-)240 (2 Sqn.).

9.2.3. CARRIER OPERATIONS

When the destroyers *Maddox* and *C. Turner Joy*
reported being attacked by North Vietnamese
patrol boats the US Navy had three aircraft
carriers in the South China Sea: USS *Bonne
Homme Richard* (CVA-31) embarked Air Wing
(CVW) 19, *Constellation* (CVA-64) had CVW-14,
while *Ticonderoga* (CVA-14) embarked CVW-5.
Each Wing comprised two A-4 and one A-1
attack squadrons while the fighter units were
equipped with the F-8E or, in the case of those on
board *Constellation*, the F-4B; in addition, each
had one heavy attack squadron equipped with
the A-3B, one RF-8A detachment of VFP-63, and
early warning E-1B detachments. On 5 August
1964, in Operation 'Pierce Arrow', *Ticonderoga*
and *Constellation* launched 64 aircraft to attack
patrol boat bases in North Vietnam in retaliation
for the alleged attacks on the destroyers. The
same day USS *Ranger* with CVW-9, also with
F-4B units, sailed for South-East Asia and on the
7th the United States put its forces on a war
footing. *Ranger* also brought to the theatre the
RA-5C heavy reconnaissance aircraft. Originally
built as a bomber but with low-level speed
restrictions, the A-5 was developed as a fast and
powerful reconnaissance platform and during the
war the production line was re-opened to provide
an extra forty airframes.

The four carriers maintained their presence off
North Vietnam, but by the end of the year *Coral
Sea* and *Hancock*, with CVW-15 and CVW-21
respectively, had replaced *Bonne Homme Richard*
and *Ticonderoga*. When the North Vietnamese
attacked US military installations in South
Vietnam early in 1965, the replacement carriers
were to hand to launch two retaliatory strikes.

On 7 February 1965, 49 aircraft attacked
the Dong Hoi barracks in Operation 'Flaming
Dart', and four days later, in 'Flaming Dart II',
CVW-15 and -21 were joined by aircraft from
Ranger in a 99-aircraft strike on Chanh Hoa
barracks. From 3 March 'Blue Tree' medium-
level photo-reconnaissance sorties were flown
from the carriers over North Vietnam, and just a
month later the first SA-2 sites were spotted. The
USN flew its first 'Rolling Thunder' missions of
the war on 18 March when aircraft from *Coral
Sea* and *Hancock* attacked supply depots at Phu
Van and Vinh Son. On 9 April the Navy fought
its first combat of the war when VF-96 from
Ranger lost a stray F-4B to Chinese MiG-17
fighters over Hainan, although one of the latter
was claimed. Surprisingly, a MiG-17 was brought
down by an A-1H of VA-25 on 20 June. On 17
July there was more fighting when two F-4Bs of
VF-21 from *Midway* brought down two MiG-17s.

By now the US Navy was playing a major part
in the 'Rolling Thunder' campaign against strategic and communications targets and from July
the potent A-6A joined Task Force (TF) 77. With
advanced electronics, this bomber could hit
targets with a wide range of ordnance in all
weathers and at night, although the type suffered
many teething problems and it was two years
before its full potential was realized. On 22
December 100 aircraft, from *Enterprise*, *Kitty
Hawk* and *Ticonderoga*, bombed the thermal
power plant at Uong Bi. Although the plant was
damaged, it was not put out of action until 18
April 1966, when two A-6As destroyed it with
just thirteen 1,000lb bombs. In February 1966 the
Route Package system was introduced, the USN

From May 1972, the
United States began the
mining of North
Vietnamese ports by
carrier-borne strike
aircraft in Operation
'Pocket Money'. Here,
Mk. 19 mines are being
loaded on the wing pylons
of an A-7E Corsair II of
VA-94. The squadron was
then operating from USS
Coral Sea as part of CVW-
15. (USN via J. Ethell)

being allotted RPs II, III, IV and VIB. The latter two areas, to the south and east of Hanoi, were increasingly well defended and new types of mission were required for successful penetrations.

Beginning in March 1966, the Navy flew 'Alpha' strikes, each employing about 30 aircraft. A core bomber force was protected by specifically assigned escorts, led by SAM-suppression aircraft and supported by jamming and detection aircraft offshore. Tankers were also required to top up returning aircraft low on fuel, and airborne early warning types gave notice of NVAF fighter reaction. The original E-1 AEW aircraft was supplanted by the much more powerful E-2 from November 1965 when the new type was introduced by VAW-11 on *Kitty Hawk*. Whereas 'Rolling Thunder' sorties required a continuous stream of aircraft taking off from and landing on the carriers, the 'Alpha' missions were flown off at the rate of three a day, making handling somewhat easier.

On 9 October 1966 the USN claimed its first MiG-21 kill, to an F-8E of VF-162 from *Oriskany*. Embarking CVW-16, the carrier was the second Atlantic Fleet ship brought in to supplement those of the Seventh Fleet. In October its tour was abbreviated following a serious fire caused by a flare, which caused the death of 44 crewmen

TABLE OF UNITS: THE VIETNAM WAR—USN CARRIERS, 1964–1975

CVW-19 (NM), Bonne Homme Richard,
January–November 1964

VF-191	F-8E	VAH-4	A-3B
VF-194	F-8C	VFP-63	RF-8A
VA-192	A-4C	VAW-11	E-1B
VA-195	A-4C	HU-1	UH-2A
VA-196	A-1H/J		

CVW-14 (NK), Constellation, May 1964–February 1965

VF-142	F-4B	VAH-10	A-3B
VF-143	F-4B	VFP-63	RF-8A
VA-144	A-4C	VAW-11	E-1B
VA-145	A-1I/J	HU-1	UH-2A
VA-146	A-4C		

CVW-5 (NF), Ticonderoga, May–December 1964

VF-51	F-8E	VA-56	A-4E
VF-53	F-8E	VAH-4	A-3B
VA-52	A-1H/J	VFP-63	RF-8A
VA-55	A-4B	VAW-11	E-1B

CVW-9 (NG), Ranger, August 1964–May 1965

VF-92	F-4B	VAH-2	KA-3B
VF-96	F-4B	RVAH-5	RA-5C
VA-93	A-4C	VFP-63	RF-8A
VA-94	A-4C	VAW-11	E-1B
VA-95	A-1H/J		

CVW-15 (NL), Coral Sea, October 1964–May 1965

VF-151	F-4B	VA-165	A-1H/J
VF-154	F-8D	VAH-2	A-3B
VA-153	A-4C	VFP-63	RF-8A
VA-155	A-4E	VAW-11	E-1B

CVW-21 (NP), Hancock, November 1964–May 1965

VF-24	F-8C	VA-216	A-4C
VF-211	F-8E	VAH-4	A-3B
VA-212	A-4E	VFP-63	RF-8A
VA-215	A-1H/J	VAW-11	E-1B

CVW-2 (NE), Midway, March 1965–November 1965

VF-21	F-4B	VA-25	A-1H
VF-111	F-8C	VAH-8	KA-3B
VA-22	A-4C	VFP-63	RF-8A
VA-23	A-4E	VAW-11	E-1B

CVW-19 (NM), Bonne Homme Richard, April 1965–January 1966

VF-191	F-8E	VAH-4	A-3B
VF-194	F-8E	VFP-63	RF-8G
VA-192	A-4C	VAW-11	E-1B
VA-195	A-4C	HU-1	UH-2A/B
VA-196	A-1H/J		

CVW-7 (AG), Independence, May 1965–December 1965

VF-41	F-4B	VAH-4	A-3B
VF-84	F-4B	RVAH-1	RA-5C
VA-72	A-4E	VAW-12	E-1B
VA-75	A-6A/B	HS-2	SH-3A
VA-86	A-4E		

CVW-16 (AH), Oriskany, May–December 1965

VF-162	F-8E	VAH-4	A-3B
VMF-211	F-8E	VAQW-13	EA-1F
VA-163	A-4E	VFP-63	RF-8A
VA-164	A-4E	VAW-11	E-1B
VA-165	A-1H/J		

CVW-5 (NF), Ticonderoga, September 1965–May 1966

VF-51	F-8E	VAH-4	A-3B
VF-53	F-8E	VFP-63	RF-8A
VA-52	A-1H/J	VAW-11	E-1B
VA-56	A-4E	HC-1	UH-2A/B
VA-144	A-4C		

CVW-9 (NG), Enterprise, October 1965–June 1966

VF-92	F-4B	VA-94	A-4C
VF-96	F-4B	VAH-4	KA-3B
VA-36	A-4C	RVAH-7	RA-5C
VA-76	A-4C	VFP-63	RF-8A
VA-93	A-4C	VAW-11	E-1B

CVW-11 (NH), Kitty Hawk, November 1965–June 1966

VF-114	F-4B	VA-115	A-1H/J
VF-213	F-4B/G	VAH-4	KA-3B
VA-85	A-6A	RVAH-13	RA-5C
VA-113	A-4C	VAW-11	E-2A

CVW-21 (NP), Hancock, December 1965–August 1966

VF-24	F-8C	VAH-4	KA-3B
VF-211	F-8E	VAQW-13	EA-1F
VA-212	A-4E	VFP-63	RF-8G
VA-215	A-1H/J	VAW-111	E-1B
VA-216	A-4C		

CVW-14 (NK), Ranger, December 1965–August 1966

VF-142	F-4B	VA-146	A-4C
VF-143	F-4B	VAH-2	KA-3B
VA-55	A-4E	RVAH-9	RA-5C
VA-145	A-1H/J	VAW-11	E-2A

CVW-10 (AK), Intrepid, April–November 1966

| VA-15 | A-4B | VA-165 | A-1H/J |
| VA-95 | A-4B | VA-176 | A-1H/J |

CVW-15 (NL), Constellation, May–December 1966

VF-151	F-4B	VA-155	A-4E
VF-161	F-4B	VAH-2	KA-3B
VA-65	A-6A	RVAH-6	RA-5C
VA-153	A-4C	VAW-11	E-1B

CVW-16 (AH), Oriskany, May–November 1966

VF-111	F-8E	VA-164	A-4E
VF-162	F-8E	VAH-4	A-3B
VA-152	A-1H/J	VFP-63	RF-8G
VA-163	A-4E	VAW-11	E-1B

CVW-1 (AB), Franklin D. Roosevelt, June 1966–February 1967

VF-14	F-4B	VAH-10	KA-3B
VF-32	F-4B	VFP-62	RF-8G
VA-12	A-4E	VQ-2	EA-3B
VA-72	A-4E	VAW-12	E-1B
VA-172	A-4C		

CVW-2 (NE), Coral Sea, July 1966–February 1967

VF-21	F-4B	VA-25	A-1H
VF-154	F-4B	VAH-2	KA-3B
VA-22	A-4C	VFP-63	RF-8G
VA-23	A-4E	VAW-11	E-2A

CVW-19 (NM), Ticonderoga, October 1966–May 1967

VF-191	F-8E	VA-195	A-4C
VF-194	F-8E	VAH-4	A-3B
VA-52	A-1H/J	VFP-63	RF-8G
VA-192	A-4E	VAW-111	E-1B

CVW-11 (NH), Kitty Hawk, November 1966–June 1967

VF-114	F-4B	VA-144	A-4C
VF-213	F-4B	VAH-4	KA-3B
VA-85	A-6A	RVAH-13	RA-5C
VA-112	A-4C	VAW-11	E-2A

CVW-9 (NG), Enterprise, December 1966–July 1967

VF-92	F-4B	VA-113	A-4C
VF-96	F-4B	VAH-2	KA-3B
VA-35	A-6A	RVAH-6	RA-5C
VA-56	A-4C	VAW-112	E-2A

CVW-5 (NF), Hancock, January–July 1967

VF-51	F-8E	VA-115	A-1H/J
VF-53	F-8E	VAH-4	KA-3B
VA-93	A-4E	VFP-63	RF-8G
VA-94	A-4C	VAW-11	E-1B

CVW-21 (NP), Bonne Homme Richard, January–August 1967

VF-24	F-8C	VAH-4	KA-3B
VF-211	F-8E	VAQW-13	EA-1F
VA-76	A-4C	VFP-63	RF-8G
VA-212	A-4E	VAW-111	E-1B
VA-215	A-1H/J	HC-1	UH-2E

CVW-14 (NK), Constellation, April–December 1967

VF-142	F-4B	VA-196	A-6A
VF-143	F-4B	VAH-8	KA-3B
VA-55	A-4E	RVAH-12	RA-5C
VA-146	A-4C	VAW-113	E-2A

CVW-10 (AK), Intrepid, May–December 1967

VF-111	F-8C	VA-145	A-1H/J
VSF-3	A-4B	VAQW-33	EA-1F
VA-15	A-4C	VFP-63	RF-8G
VA-34	A-4C	VAW-121	E-1B

CVW-17 (AA), Forrestal, June–September 1967

VF-11	F-4B	VAH-10	KA-3B
VF-74	F-4B	RVAH-11	RA-5C
VA-46	A-4E	VAW-123	E-2A
VA-65	A-6A	HS-2	SH-3A
VA-106	A-4E		

CVW-16 (AH), Oriskany, July 1967–January 1968

VF-111	F-8C	VA-164	A-4E
VF-162	F-8E	VAH-4	KA-3B
VA-152	A-1H/J	VFP-63	RF-8G
VA-163	A-4E	VAW-111	E-1B

CVW-15 (NL), Coral Sea, August 1967–March 1968

VF-151	F-4B	VA-155	A-4E
VF-161	F-4B	VAH-2	KA-3B
VA-25	A-1H/J	VAQW-13	EA-1F
VA-153	A-4C	VAW-116	E-2A

CVW-2 (NE), Ranger, November 1967–May 1968

VF-21	F-4B	VAH-2	KA-3B
VF-154	F-4B	RVAH-6	RA-5C
VA-22	A-4C	VAH-13	EKA-3B
VA-147	A-7A	VAW-115	E-2A
VA-165	A-6A		

CVW-19 (NM), Ticonderoga, December 1967–July 1968

VF-191	F-8E	VA-195	A-4C
VF-194	F-8E	VAQW-33	EA-1F
VA-23	A-4F	VFP-63	RF-8G
VA-192	A-4E	VAW-111	E-1B

CVW-11 (NH), Kitty Hawk, December 1967–August 1968

VF-114	F-4B	VAH-4	KA-3B
VF-213	F-4B	RVAH-11	RA-5C
VA-75	A-6A/B	VAQW-13	EA-1F
VA-112	A-4C	VAW-114	E-2A
VA-144	A-4E		

CVW-9 (NG), Enterprise, January–July 1968

VF-92	F-4B	VAH-2	KA-3B
VF-96	F-4B	RVAH-1	RA-5C
VA-35	A-6A	VAQW-13	EKA-3B
VA-56	A-4E	VAW-112	E-2A
VA-113	A-4F		

CVW-5 (NF), Bonne Homme Richard, January–October 1968

VF-51	F-8H	VAQW-13	EKA-3B
VF-53	F-8E	VFP-63	RF-8G
VA-93	A-4F	VAW-111	E-1B
VA-94	A-4E	HC-1	UH-2C
VA-212	A-4F		

CVW-21 (NP), Hancock, March–December 1968

VF-24	F-8H	VA-164	A-4E
VF-211	F-8J	VAQ-130	EKA-3B
VA-55	A-4F	VFP-63	RF-8G
VA-163	A-4E	VAW-111	E-1B

CVW-6 (AE), America, April–December 1968

VF-33	F-4J	VAH-10	KA-3B
VF-102	F-4J	RVAH-13	RA-5C
VA-82	A-7A	VAQ-130	EKA-3B
VA-85	A-6A/B	VAW-122	E-2A
VA-86	A-7A	HC-2	UH-2A/B

CVW-14 (NK), Constellation, May 1968–January 1969

VF-142	F-4B	VAH-2	KA-3B
VF-143	F-4B	RVAH-5	RA-5C
VA-27	A-7A	VAQW-13	EKA-3B
VA-97	A-7A	VAW-113	E-2A
VA-196	A-6A/B		

CVW-10 (AK), Intrepid, June 1968–February 1969

VF-111	F-8C	VAQW-33	EA-1F
VA-36	A-4C	VFP-63	RF-8G
VA-66	A-4C	VAW-121	E-1B
VA-106	A-4F		

CVW-15 (NL), Coral Sea, September 1968–March 1969

VF-151	F-4B	VAH-10	KA-3B
VF-161	F-4B	VAQ-130	EKA-3B
VA-52	A-6A	VFP-63	RF-8G
VA-153	A-4F	VAW-116	E-2A
VA-216	A-4C		

CVW-2 (NE), Ranger, October 1968–May 1969

VF-21	F-4J	VAH-10	KA-3B
VF-154	F-4J	RVAH-9	RA-5C
VA-147	A-7A	VAQ-130	EKA-3B
VA-155	A-4E	VAW-115	E-2A
VA-165	A-6A		

CVW-11 (NH), Kitty Hawk, December 1968–July 1969

VF-114	F-4B	VA-105	A-7A
VF-213	F-4B	RVAH-11	RA-5C
VA-37	A-7A	VAQ-131	EKA-3B
VA-65	A-6A	VAW-114	E-2A

CVW-16 (AH), Ticonderoga, February–September 1969

VF-111	F-8H	VA-112	A-4C
VF-162	F-8J	VAQ-130	EKA-3B
VA-25	A-7B	VFP-63	RF-8G
VA-87	A-7B	VAW-111	E-1B

CVW-9 (NG), Enterprise, March–August 1969

VF-92	F-4J	VAH-2	KA-3B
VF-96	F-4J	RVAH-6	RA-5C
VA-145	A-6A	VAQ-132	EKA-3B
VA-146	A-7B	VAW-112	E-2A
VA-215	A-7B		

CVW-19 (NM), Oriskany, April–November 1969

VF-191	F-8J	VA-195	A-4E
VF-194	F-8J	VAQ-130	EKA-3B
VA-23	A-4F	VFP-63	RF-8G
VA-192	A-4F	VAW-111	E-1B

CVW-5 (NF), Bonne Homme Richard, May–October 1969

VF-51	F-8J	VAQ-130	EKA-3B
VF-53	F-8J	VFP-63	RF-8G
VA-22	A-4F	VAW-111	E-1B
VA-94	A-4E	HC-1	UH-2C
VA-144	A-4E		

CVW-21 (NP), Hancock, September 1969–April 1970

VF-24	F-8H	VA-212	A-4F
VF-211	F-8J	VAH-10	EKA-3B
VA-55	A-4F	VFP-63	RF-8G
VA-164	A-4F	VAW-111	E-1B

CVW-14 (NK), Constellation, October 1969–May 1970

VF-142	F-4J	VA-97	A-7A
VF-143	F-4J	RVAH-7	RA-5C
VA-27	A-7A	VAQ-133	EKA-3B
VA-85	A-6A/B	VAW-113	E-2A

CVW-15 (NL), Coral Sea, October 1969–April 1970

VF-151	F-4B	VA-86	A-7A
VF-161	F-4B	VAQ-135	EKA-3B
VA-35	A-6A	VFP-63	RF-8G
VA-82	A-7A	VAW-116	E-2A

and aviators. In December the rules of engagement (RE) were relaxed and Hanoi was bombed for the first time, while on 26 February 1967 waterways were mined, although shipping bringing in war *matériel* to Haiphong and other major ports sailed unhindered for American fear of damaging neutral vessels. The Song Ca and Song Giang waterways were mined by A-6As of VA-35 from the nuclear-powered *Enterprise* to deny their use to small boats moving supplies down the coast. The carrier fleet continued to fly 'Rolling Thunder' missions within the same constraints applied to the USAF and described elsewhere. TF.77 suffered a major loss on 29 July 1967 when *Forrestal* was seriously damaged in a fire: a Zuni rocket was inadvertently fired from an F-4 on the flight deck, and in the ensuing conflagration 134 were killed; 21 aircraft were destroyed and 43 damaged. The carrier returned to the United States for repairs which cost $72 million.

Further new equipment reached the Task Force in December in the form of the A-7A attack aircraft of VA-147. The A-7A eventually replaced the A-4 on the larger ships, able to carry twice the payload of the older machine. The Navy was particularly active during the Tet offensive, but from the March 1968 bombing halt

operations were limited to support in the South, even though five carriers remained in the region. Three, *Enterprise*, *Ticonderoga* and *Ranger*, were dispatched to Korea in April following the North Korean capture of the intelligence-gathering ship *Pueblo*. On 10 April the last A-1H attack sortie was flown by VA-25 from *Coral Sea*, but the last operational sortie by the type was flown in July by an EA-1F of VAQ-33. For the next three years reconnaissance sorties only were flown over the North, but the Task Force suffered its third major blow on 14 January 1969 when a fire was started on *Enterprise* while it was working up off Hawaii: 28 personnel were killed and fifteen aircraft destroyed when yet again a Zuni rocket was accidentally fired from an F-4. The repair bill this time was $56 million.

The reconnaissance sorties identified a new build-up of North Vietnamese forces and supplies late in 1971, and on 26 December Operation 'Proud Deep' was launched. Aircraft from *Constellation* and *Coral Sea* flew 423 sorties in just five days, against a range of military targets. When the Paris peace talks were abandoned in May 1972 the bombing campaign resumed and the CVWs operated in full support of the 'Linebacker' raids. In addition, from 8 May, in Operation 'Pocket Money', the ports of Haiphong,

TABLE OF UNITS: THE VIETNAM WAR—USN CARRIERS, 1964–1975 (continued)

CVW-2 (NE), Ranger, January–July 1970

VF-21	F-4J	VAH-?	KA-3B
VF-154	F-4J	RVAH-5	RA-5C
VA-56	A-7B	VAQ-134	EKA-3B
VA-93	A-7A	VAW-115	E-2A
VA-196	A-6A		

CVW-8 (AJ), Shangri-La, March–December 1970

VF-111	F-8H	VA-172	A-4C
VF-162	F-8H	VAH-10	KA-3B
VA-12	A-4C	VFP-63	RF-8G
VA-152	A-4E	VAW-121	E-1B

CVW-5 (NF), Bonne Homme Richard, April–November 1970

VF-51	F-8J	VAQ-130	EKA-3B
VF-53	F-8J	VFP-63	RF-8G
VA-22	A-4F	VAW-111	E-1B
VA-94	A-4E	HC-1	UH-2C
VA-144	A-4E		

CVW-9 (NG), America, May–November 1970

VF-92	F-4J	RVAH-12	RA-5C
VF-96	F-4J	VAQ-132	EKA-3B
VA-146	A-7E	VAW-124	E-2A
VA-147	A-7E	HC-2	UH-2C
VA-165	A-6C		

CVW-19 (NM), Oriskany, July–December 1970

VF-191	F-8J	VAQ-130	EKA-3B
VF-194	F-8J	VFP-63	RF-8G
VA-153	A-7A	VAW-111	E-1B
VA-155	A-7B		

CVW-2 (NE), Ranger, October 1970–June 1971

VF-21	F-4J	VA-145	A-6A/B/C
VF-154	F-4J	RVAH-1	RA-5C
VA-25	A-7E	VAQ-134	EKA-3B
VA-113	A-7E	VAW-111	E-1B

CVW-21 (NP), Hancock, November 1970–June 1971

VF-24	F-8J	VA-212	A-4F
VF-211	F-8J	VAQ-129	EKA-3B
VA-55	A-4F	VFP-63	RF-8G
VA-164	A-4F	VAW-111	E-1B

CVW-11 (NH), Kitty Hawk, November 1970–July 1971

VF-114	F-4J	VA-195	A-7E
VF-213	F-4J	RVAH-7	RA-5C
VA-52	A-6A/B	VAQ-133	EKA-3B
VA-192	A-7E	VAW-114	E-2A

CVW-5 (NF), Midway, April–November 1971

VF-151	F-4B	VA-115	A-6A
VF-161	F-4B	VAQ-130	EKA-3B
VA-56	A-7B	VFP-63	RF-8G
VA-93	A-7B	VAW-115	E-2B

CVW-19 (NM), Oriskany, May 1971–January 1972

VF-191	F-8J	VA-215	A-7B
VF-194	F-8J	VAQ-130	EKA-3B
VA-153	A-7A	VFP-63	RF-8G
VA-155	A-7B	VAW-111	E-1B

CVW-14 (NK), Enterprise, June 1971–February 1972

VF-142	F-4J	VA-196	A-6A/B
VF-143	F-4J	RVAH-5	RA-5C
VA-27	A-7E	VAQ-130	EKA-3B
VA-97	A-7E	VAW-113	E-2B

CVW-9 (NG), Constellation, October 1971–June 1972

VF-92	F-4J	VA-165	A-6A/B
VF-96	F-4J	RVAH-11	RA-5C
VA-146	A-7E	VAQ-130	EKA-3B
VA-147	A-7E	VAW-116	E-2B

CVW-15 (NL), Coral Sea, November 1971–July 1972

VF-51	F-4B	VMA-224	A-6A/B
VF-111	F-4B	VAQ-135	EKA-3B
VA-22	A-7E	VFP-63	RF-8G
VA-94	A-7E	VAW-111	E-1B

CVW-21 (NP), Hancock, January–September 1972

VF-24	F-8J	VA-212	A-4F
VF-211	F-8J	VAQ-135	EKA-3B
VA-55	A-4F	VFP-63	RF-8G
VA-164	A-4F	VAW-111	E-1B

CVW-11 (NH), Kitty Hawk, February–November 1972

VF-114	F-4J	VA-195	A-7E
VF-213	F-4J	RVAH-7	RA-5C
VA-52	A-6A	VAQ-135	EKA-3B
VA-192	A-7E	VAW-114	E-2B

CVW-5 (NF), Midway, April 1972–March 1973

VF-151	F-4B	VA-115	A-6A
VF-161	F-4B	VAQ-130	EKA-3B
VA-56	A-7B	VFP-63	RF-8G
VA-93	A-7B	VAW-115	E-2B

CVW-3 (AC), Saratoga, April 1972–February 1973

VF-31	F-4J	RVAH-1	RA-5C
VF-103	F-4J	VMCJ-2	EA-6A
VA-37	A-7A	VAW-123	E-2B
VA-75	A-6A	HS-7	SH-3D
VA-105	A-7A		

CVW-8 (AJ), America, June 1972–March 1973

VF-74	F-4J	RVAH-6	RA-5C
VMFA-333	F-4J	VAQ-132	EA-6B
VA-35	A-6A	VAW-121	E-2B
VA-82	A-7C	HC-2	SH-3G
VA-86	A-7C		

CVW-19 (NM), Oriskany, June 1972–March 1973

VF-191	F-8J	VA-215	A-7B
VF-194	F-8J	VAQ-130	EKA-3B
VA-153	A-7A	VFP-63	RF-8G
VA-155	A-7B	VAW-111	E-1B

CVW-14 (NK), Enterprise, September 1972–June 1973

VF-142	F-4J	RVAH-13	RA-5C
VF-143	F-4J	VAQ-131	EA-6B
VA-27	A-7E	VAW-113	E-2B
VA-97	A-7E	HS-2	SH-3D
VA-196	A-6A/B		

CVW-2 (NE), Ranger, November 1972–June 1973

VF-21	F-4J	VA-145	A-6A/B
VF-154	F-4J	RVAH-5	RA-5C
VA-25	A-7E	VAQ-130	EKA-3B
VA-113	A-7E		

CVW-9 (NG), Constellation, January–September 1973

VF-92	F-4J	VA-165	A-6A
VF-96	F-4J	RVAH-12	RA-5C
VA-146	A-7E	VAQ-134	EA-6B
VA-147	A-7E	VAW-116	E-2B

CVW-15 (NL), Coral Sea, March–November 1973

VF-51	F-4B	VA-95	A-6A/B
VF-111	F-4B	VAQ-135	EKA-3B
VA-22	A-7E	VFP-63	RF-8G
VA-94	A-7E	VAW-112	E-2B

CVW-21 (NP), Hancock, June 1973–February 1974

VF-24	F-8J	VA-212	A-4F
VF-211	F-8J	VAQ-135	EKA-3B
VA-55	A-4F	VFP-63	RF-8G
VA-164	A-4F	VAW-111	E-1B

CVW-5 (NF), Midway, September 1973–1974

VF-151	F-4B	VA-115	A-6A/B
VF-161	F-4B	VMCJ-1	EA-6A, RF-4B
VA-56	A-7A	VFP-63	RF-8G
VA-93	A-7A	VAW-115	E-2B

CVW-19 (NM), Oriskany, November 1973–June 1974

VF-191	F-8J	VA-215	A-7B
VF-194	F-8J	VFP-63	RF-8G
VA-153	A-7A	VAW-111	E-1B
VA-155	A-7B		

CVW-11 (NH), Kitty Hawk, November 1973–July 1974

VF-114	F-4J	VAQ-134	EA-6B
VF-213	F-4J	VS-37	S-2G
VA-52	A-6A	VS-38	S-2G
VA-192	A-7E	VAW-114	E-2B
VA-195	A-7E	HS-4	SH-3D
RVAH-7	RA-5C		

CVW-2 (NE), Ranger, April–October 1974

VF-21	F-4J	VA-113	A-7E
VF-154	F-4J	VA-145	A-6A
VA-25	A-7E	RVAH-13	RA-5C

CVW-9 (NG), Constellation, June–December 1974

VF-92	F-4J	VA-165	A-6A
VF-96	F-4J	RVAH-5	RA-5C
VA-146	A-7E	VAQ-131	EA-6B
VA-147	A-7E	VAW-116	E-2B

CVW-14 (NK), Enterprise, September 1974–May 1975

VF-1	F-14A	VA-196	A-6A
VF-2	F-14A	RVAH-12	RA-5C
VMFA-115	F-4B	VAQ-137	EA-6B
VA-27	A-7E	VAW-113	E-2B
VA-97	A-7E	HS-2	SH-3D

CVW-15 (NL), Coral Sea, December 1974–July 1975

VF-51	F-4N	VA-94	A-7E
VF-111	F-4N	VA-95	A-6A
VA-22	A-7E	VFP-63	RF-8G

Mine clearance (Operation 'End Sweep'), February 1973
TF.78, New Orleans

HM-12	CH-53A	HMH-463	RH-53D

Unit	Aircraft (code)	Base
Carrier support units (COD and vertrep)		
VR-21	C-1A, C-2A (RZ)	Cubi Point
VRC-51	C-1A, C-2A (RG)	Cubi Point
HC-1	UH-25C, UH-46A (UP)	Various
SAR and plane-guard helicopter units		
HS-2	SH-3A (NU)	Attached to carriers 1965–1967
HS-4	SH-3A (TA)	Attached to carriers 1966–1967
HC-1	UH-2A/B, HH-2C (UP)	Carrier plane-guard from 1965
HC-4 (Det 36)	UH-2A/B (HT)	Land-based. South Vietnam SAR
HC-7	UH-2A/B/C, HH-2C, SH-3A, HH-3A, UH-46D (VH)	Based on escort ships SAR

Note: In general, aircraft operating from carriers applied the CVW code on the fin and wing; exceptions were RVAH-5 (GK): VFP-63 (PP): VFP-62 (GA): VAQW-13 (VR): VAQ-33 (GD): VQ-2 (JQ): VAW-11 (RR): VAW-12 (GE): HM-12 (DH); and HMH-463 (YH). HSs operating in the anti-submarine role based on CVSs were also available for SAR.

Hon Gai, Cam Pha, Quang Khe, Dong Hoi and Thanh Hoa were mined by A-6 and A-7 aircraft from the six carriers now on station. So severe was the effect of this action that within ten days the North Vietnamese shore batteries were silent through lack of ammunition. In all, 11,000 mines were sown.

On 10 May, in a series of raids, US Navy fighters claimed eight MiG fighters, while the Air Force shot down three more. Strikes continued through 1972 with a break from October to December. The last of 61 MiG fighters to fall to carrier-based aircraft was destroyed on 12 January 1973 by an F-4B of VF-161 off *Midway*, and the Navy now turned to the task of clearing the mines from North Vietnamese ports in Operation 'Endsweep'. As part of TF.78, CH-53As and RH-53Ds of HM-12 and HMH-463 were embarked on the helicopter landing platform *New Orleans*. Helicopters had served with the Navy in a number of roles. From early in the war anti-submarine carriers had patrolled in the South China Sea, and SH-3As of the HS units, notably HS-2, were attached to carriers as search and rescue (SAR) aircraft, while HC-1, equipped with the smaller UH-2, provided the carriers with plane-guard detachments. From 1 September 1967, HC-7, equipped with a range of helicopters, took over SAR responsibilities from the HS units until 25 September 1973, by which time it had effected 140 rescues, many over land. The helicopters were based on carriers and a range of escort vessels close to the North Vietnamese coast: aviators in difficulty invariably tried to reach the sea, where rescue was certain.

Throughout the war seventeen carriers completed 73 cruises with a total of 8,248 days on line. A total of 538 aircraft and thirteen helicopters were lost in combat, sixteen to enemy fighters, and 316 aircraft and 35 helicopters were lost for operational reasons. Of the 2,430 Navy personnel killed, 317 were air crew. Between April 1965 and March 1973 US Navy aircraft flew 275,000 sorties over North Vietnam, 52 per cent of the total.

AIRCRAFT MARKINGS

Unless otherwise stated, US Navy aircraft were finished Gull Gray over, white under, with the black serial number on the lower rear fuselage or lower fin and with the aircraft code on the fin and forward fuselage and the Air Wing code on the fin. Most aircraft wore colourful unit markings throughout the war.

F-4B 150468/204NL (VF-111); (15)3006/401NE (VF-154); (15)3011/104NH (VF-213).

F-4G (15)0636/107NH (VF-213).

F-4J (15)3832/212NG (VF-92); (15)3819/112NG (VF-96).

F-8C 147056/452NE (VF-111).

F-8E 150927/401NM (VF-194); 149158/206NF (VF-53).

F-8J 150863/106NM (VF-194).

F-14A 158986/206NK (VF-2).

A-1H (1)39768/577NE (VA-25); (1)39728/514AH (VA-152).

A-1J (1)42058/502NK (VA-145).

A-3B 142657/9ZB (VAH-4).

A-4E (15)0001/413AB (VA-12); (15)1105/313NF (VA-93).

A-6A 154155/412NK (VA-196); 155645/505NG (VA-165).

A-7A (15)3247/401NL (VA-86).

A-7E 158833/400NG (VA-147).

RA-5C 149297/125NK, 156624/603NG (RVAH-5).

RF-8A 146830/909PP (VFP-63).

RF-8G 144613/600NP (VFP-63).

EA-1F 135051/708VR (VAQW-13).

EKA-3B 142638/613NE (VAQ-130).

E-1B (14)7212/011NE (VAW-111).

E-2B (15)1714/706RR (VAW-11); (15)1715/703NL (VAW-116).

S-2B (15)2343/13NS (VP-21).

UH-2B *Sea grey overall, white codes etc.: (15)0186/38UP (HC-1).*

SH-3A *Gloss Sea Blue overall, serial and codes*
etc. in white: (14)8967/61NT (HS-8); (14)9920/52NV (HS-2).

UH-46A *Sea Blue overall, white serial and code: 151903/51VH (HC-7).*

Note *The USN experimented with camouflage in 1966, but the trials were short-lived as the dark tones made aircraft handling at night hazardous. Examples of schemes used are as follows.*

F-4G *Dark green over, white under, black serial on fin: 150642/102. (VF-213).*

F-4J *Medium green/Olive Drab over, white under: (15)5761/112 (VF-114).*

A-1H *Medium green over, white under, black serial on fin, white code on nose: (1)37527/507 (VA-?).*

KA-3B *Medium green over, white under, white serial on fin: 1?????/1 (VAH-4).*

A-4C *Medium green/Olive Drab/sand over, white under, black serial on fin, code on nose: (14)8593/306 (VA-113).*

RA-5C *Medium green/Olive Drab over, white under, dark grey serial on fin, code on nose: 149313/702 (RVAH-6). Dark green/green/tan over, light grey under, black serial on fin: 150834/601 (RVAH-13).*

A-6A *Dark green/green over, white under, black serial on fin, white code on nose: 151586/407 (VA-65).*

9.2.4. RECONNAISSANCE AND ELECTRONIC WARFARE

When the United States formally entered the war there were already several US Air Force reconnaissance units operating in the theatre.* The RB-57Es of 33 TG continued to fly infra-red (IR)

The US Navy suffered three major fires aboard carriers, all the results of accidents; in two instances, Zuni rockets were inadvertently fired from F-4 Phantoms while on deck. USS *Enterprise* was severely damaged off Hawaii on 14 January 1969, with the loss of 28 crew and fifteen aircraft. In the foreground is an F-4J of VF-96. (USN via J. Winton)

---

* Army observation operations and USN carrier-borne reconnaissance and EW missions are dealt with separately in the appropriate sections.

reconnaissance sorties, mainly in-country, until 1971 with constantly upgraded equipment. Pre- and post-strike sorties were flown by the RF-101Cs of 15 TRS until April 1966 and by 45 TRS until late 1970. The RF-101C force was increased with the addition of 20 TRS in 1965 and in 1966 by 12 TRS, both units operating within 460 TRW at Tan Son Nhut. Well after the introduction of the RF-4C, the Voodoo bore the brunt of deep-penetration sorties, and 39 were brought down, mainly over the North. Twelve RF-101 pilots were killed in action and ten taken prisoner; for a time the loss rate was one a week.

The RF-4C was a technical improvement over the RF-101C but it lacked the latter's range and speed. The first RF-4 squadron was 6461 TRS, deployed from Shaw AFB to Udorn (432 TRW) in July 1965. In 1966 it became 11 TRS and was later joined at Udorn by 14 and 15 TRS. At Tan Son Nhut the RF-4 was operated by 16 and 12 TRS from October 1965. Tactical reconnaissance sorties were also flown by two heavy attack and photographic squadrons of the US Navy, VAP-61 and VAP-62 from Da Nang and Bangkok; in addition, the VNAF operated several reconnaissance units, although the RF-5A was received late in the war and little use was made of it. Local photo-reconnaissance sorties were flown by several USMC Headquarters and Maintenance squadrons (H&MS) flying the two-seat TF-9J. As the importance of the supply routes from the North, collectively the Ho Chi Minh Trail, was appreciated, Project 'Practice Nine', later to become better known as 'Igloo White', was established.

Initially, tactical aircraft were used to drop air-delivered seismic detection (ADSID), Acoubuoy and Spikebuoy sensors. For a time this task was taken over by a naval unit, VO-67, but a high loss rate led to the work being transferred to F-4D Phantoms of 25 TFS. The sensors, variously camouflaged, transmitted data on movements along the Trail which were monitored by EC-121s of 553 RW and from 1968 relayed to the 'Dutch Mill' Infiltration Surveillance Center at Nakhon Phanom from where the operation was co-ordinated. For a period in 1970 to 1971 the relay task was assumed by the much smaller, remotely controlled QU-22B of 554 RS, developed under the 'Pave Eagle' programme, but the type was soon withdrawn. The programme was a success – albeit hugely expensive – and attack aircraft could be directed to targets with precision and within minutes of identification.

The US Army Security Agency (USASA) managed its own intelligence-gathering operations. The 224th Aviation Battalion handled electronic intelligence work through the 1st Aviation Company, which specialized in sigint and the 1st Radio Research Company which flew the AP-2E (and possibly RP-2E) version of the Neptune. These aircraft were equipped for transmitter location and elint work and mainly operated in the Mekong Delta region. In contrast, the 1st (Special Aircraft) Aviation Company flew the ultra-quiet YO-3A observation aircraft for surveillance, target-acquisition and night observation (STANO). The aircraft had been developed after earlier trials with the QT-2PC quiet-observation 'Prize Crew' project and was reported to be silent at only 50ft. The USASA also operated at least four companies of the OV-1 Mohawk within 225 Aviation Battalion in the tactical photo-reconnaissance and radar-reconnaissance roles.

Strategic intelligence-gathering had begun in December 1963 with the deployment of the U-2 to Bien Hoa. The US Air Force and Navy had long had units in the Far East based at Yokota and Kadena, and it was not long before first the RB-47H then versions of the RC-135 were flying around Vietnam. The aircraft were operated under the control of 4252 Strategic Wing (SW), later to become 376 SW, on a range of elint and sigint work. An early task under Project 'Big Team' was the identification of SA-2 fire-control radars and missile-fusing details, carried out by RB-47Hs of 55 SRW and drones. Elint tasks were also carried out by 6091 RS (later 556 RS) using highly classified EB-57D and C-130A-II aircraft based at Don Muang, while the Kadena-based detachment of 1 SRS, 9 SRW, flew occasional SR-71A photo-reconnaissance sorties from 1967.

One of the most fascinating units in the theatre was 4025 RS, which operated a range of AQM-34 and AQM-91 drones. The drones were flown from DC-130A and E control aircraft on a very wide range of missions, including elint, sigint, jamming, photo-reconnaissance (especially at low level), real-time televised reconnaissance and leaflet-dropping (the last known as 'Litter Bug' sorties). The drones were pre-programmed, but after release progress was monitored and the 'pilot' could override the programme manually if necessary. On their return to the South, the drones deployed a parachute and were snared by CH-3 or CH-53 recovery helicopters. Altogether 3,435 missions were flown and 578 drones lost.

Operation 'Market Time' was the USN maritime patrol task involving both flying boats and land-based aircraft. The sorties began in February 1965 and their purpose was to monitor small vessels off the South Vietnamese coast in order to prevent infiltration and seaborne supplies deliveries. The patrol units were deployed on rotation, coming under the control of Fleet Air Wings 8 and 10, and they also provided anti-submarine cover for TF.77. The SP-5 Marlin squadrons operated from seaplane tenders moored off Cam Ranh Bay, where the P-2 and later P-3 units were based. When Cam Ranh Bay was vacated in the run-down from December 1971, the Orions continued to fly ASW sorties from the Philippines.

TABLE OF UNITS: THE VIETNAM WAR – RECONNAISSANCE AND ELECTRONIC WARFARE

Unit	Aircraft (code)	Base	Role	Dates
TACTICAL RECONNAISSANCE[1]				
USAF				
33 TG[2]	RB-57E	Tan Son Nhut	In-country IR PR	07/05/63 to 00/08/71
45 TRS	RF-101C (AH)	Tan Son Nhut (460 TRW)	PR	01/02/65 to 16/11/70
16 TRS	RF-4C (AE)	Tan Son Nhut (460 TRW)	PR	30/10/65 to 00/08/71
20 TRS	RF-101C	Tan Son Nhut, Udorn (460 TRW)	PR (replaced by 14 TRS)	00/12/65 to 31/10/67
12 TRS	RF-101C, RF-4C (AC)	Tan Son Nhut (460 TRW)	PR	00/00/66 to 00/08/71
15 TRS	RF-101C	Udorn (460 TRW)	PR	01/04/65 to 02/04/66
15 TRS	RF-4C (ZZ)	Udorn (432 TRW)	PR	? to 00/08/71
6461 TRS	RF-4C	Udorn (460 TRW)	PR (to 11 TRS)	00/07/65 to 00/00/66
11 TRS	RF-4C (OO)	Udorn (432 TRW)	PR	00/00/66 to ?
14 TRS	RF-4C (OZ, UD)	Udorn (432 TRW)	PR	01/11/67 to 00/00/73
VNAF				
716 RS	RT-28D, EC-47, RF-5A (M)	Tan Son Nhut (33 TW)	⎱ Tactical recce	⎰ 00/07/66 to 00/04/75
522 FS	RF-5 (HJ)	Bien Hoa (63 TW)	⎰	⎱ 00/00/72 to 00/04/75
'IGLOO WHITE' HO CHI MINH TRAIL MONITORING PROJECT				
USAF				
553 RW	EC-121R	Nakhon Phanom	⎱ Sensor monitoring and relay	⎰ 00/10/66 to 00/12/70
553 RS	EC-121R	Nakhon Phanom (388 TFW)	⎰	00/12/70 to 00/00/72
554 RS	QU-22B ('Pave Eagle')	Nakhon Phanom (388 TFW)		⎱ 00/12/70 to 00/08/71
25 TFS	F-4D (FA)	Ubon (8 TFW)	Sensor dropping	00/08/68 to 00/00/72
USN				
VO-67	OP-2E (MR)	Nakhon Phanom	Sensor dropping (replaced by 25 TFS)	00/11/67 to 00/07/68
US ARMY SECURITY AGENCY				
224 Aviation Battalion				
1 Av. Co.	RU-1A, RU-6A, RU-8A, RU-21D	Cam Ranh Bay	Sigint ('Left Foot')	00/07/66 to 00/01/73
1 RRC	AP-2E	Cam Ranh Bay, Pleiku	Elint, transmitter location	00/00/67 to ?
1 (SA)AC	YO-3A	Long Than North	STANO	00/03/70 to 00/00/71
225 Aviation Battalion				
138 AC	OV-1B/C	Tuy Hoa	⎱	⎰ 00/00/64 to ?
144 AC	OV-1B/C	?	⎰ PR, radar recce	? to ?
146 AC	OV-1B/C	?	⎰	? to ?
156 AC	OV-1B/C	?	⎰	⎱ ? to ?
STRATEGIC INTELLIGENCE-GATHERING				
USAF[3]				
4028 SRS	U-2A/C/F	Bien Hoa (4080 SRW)	Sigint, PR (to 349 SRS)	00/12/63 to 11/02/66
349 SRS	U-2C/F/R	Bien Hoa, U-Tapao	Sigint, PR (100 SRW) ('Giant Dragon')	11/02/66 to 00/03/76
6091 RS	RB-57D, C-130A-II	Don Muang	Elint (to 556 RS)	00/07/64 to 00/06/67
556 RS	EB-57E, C-130B-II (GT)	Yokota, Don Muang	Elint (347 TFW)	00/06/67 to 00/00/70
4025 RS	DC-130A, CH-3E, AQM-34	Bien Hoa (4080 SRW)	Drone ops. (to 350 SRS)	20/08/64 to 00/02/66
350 SRS	DC-130A/E, CH-53A, AQM-34	Bien Hoa, U-Tapao	Drone ops. (100 SRW)	00/02/66 to 30/04/75
1 SRS	SR-71A	Kadena	PR, Elint ('Giant Scale')	10/04/68 to 00/00/75
55 SRW	RB-47H, KC-135R, RC-135C	Kadena	Elint ('Big Team')	00/09/64 to 00/00/67
82 SRS	RC-135M/U	Kadena, ex Yokota	Elint ('Combat Apple', 'Combat Sent')	27/09/67 to 00/00/74
6 SW	RC-135D ('Rivet Brass')	Kadena, ex Eielson	Elint (supplemented 82 SRS)	00/00/67 to 00/00/74
CIA				
–	A-12	Kadena	PR, elint	00/00/66 to 00/06/68
USN				
VQ-1	EC-121K/M, EKA-3B, EP-3B (PR)	Atsugi, Da Nang	Elint, comint	00/08/64 to 00/00/74

Maritime Patrol ('Market Time')
USN units involved used three types of aircraft. Those flying the P-5 Marlin operated from tenders off the coast, while landplane units operated from Cam Ranh Bay. Identified units (with codes in brackets) include: VP-31 (RP), VP-40 (QE), VP-48 (SE), VP-50 (SG) – SP-5B/M; VP-1 (YB), VP-17 (ZE) – SP-2H; and VP-50 (SG) – P-3A

Notes:
1. At various times USN Heavy Attack and Photographic Squadrons VAP-61 (SS) and VAP-62 (GB), equipped with RA-3B, were based at Da Nang and Don Muang respectively.
2. Project 'Patricia Lynn', transferred to 6250 CSG August 1965, 460 TRW February 1966.
3. The RC-135 operations were managed by 4252 SW until 1971, when it became 376 SW.

As the anti-aircraft system rapidly improved in the North, so the need for electronic support measures (ESM) and electronic countermeasures (ECM) became of paramount importance. Initially the USAF used its own A-1E Skyraiders, but the piston-engined aircraft were unable to keep up with jet fighters so the Air Force increasingly relied on USMC composite squadron VMCJ-1 for jamming support. The unit flew old but reliable EF-10B Skyknights until 1969, by which time they were replaced by EA-6A Prowlers. The USAF acquired its own jammers in the form of the RB-66, later designated EB-66, initially from 41 TRS. The aircraft had been modified in the 'Rivet Racer' programme and equipped two squadrons, leading strikes of 355 TFW at Takhi and 388 TFW at Korat. The proliferation of the SAM defences, especially around Hanoi, led to the 'Wild Weasel' programme, as described in Section 9.2.2. The Navy flew similar missions, using the

EA-6Bs of VAQ-132 from June 1972, AEW support to strikes being provided by two versions of the EC-121D and M from various airfields. Command, control and communications (C³) was the responsibility of 7 ACCS flying the C-130E-II out of Udorn until as late as 1975. The protection of TF.77 was the task of carrier-borne units.

The co-ordination of strikes and, especially, rescue operations required sound communications, and, to ensure these, several units provided relay services. Initially they were flown by KC-135A tankers appropriately modified, but from 1969 specialized equipment appeared as the EC-135L, operated by 70 ARS from U-Tapao. A variation of the relay service was provided by the Navy, which flew several EC-121J aircraft equipped to transmit or relay radio and television programmes to ground forces in Project 'Jenny'. After the use of the P-2 by VO-67 in the 'Igloo White' programme, VAH-21 flew another variant, the AP-2H, on Trail and Road Interdiction, Multisensor (TRIM) sorties or in-country work for seven months to June 1969. Also confined to

the South were the EC-47 aircraft operated by 460 TRW in the 'Hawk Eye' programme, aimed at locating, identifying and jamming Viet Cong transmitters. The only other unit known to have been involved in jamming work was 44 TFS, equipped with modified F-105Fs: under the 'Combat Martin' programme, the aircraft were fitted with QRC-128 VHF jammers to black North Vietnamese fighter control.

The Vietnam conflict was the first truly 'electronic' war, and vast sums were spent on a wide range of reconnaissance and EW systems. Some proved unsuccessful, but many paved the way for revised tactical thinking, perhaps none more so than the Wild Weasel concept.

AIRCRAFT MARKINGS

Tactical aircraft were generally camouflaged (C) as described in the section on offensive operations, unless otherwise stated.

VNAF
EC-47Q (C), light grey under, black serial on fin: (43)49029/MF (718 RS).

TABLE OF UNITS: THE VIETNAM WAR – RECONNAISSANCE AND ELECTRONIC WARFARE (continued)

Unit	Aircraft (code)	Base	Role	Dates
ELECTRONIC WARFARE				
USAF				
41 TRS	RB-66B/C ('Rivet Racer')	Tan Son Nhut (363 TRW)	ESM, ECM (became 41 TEWS)	00/04/65 to 00/00/68
41 TEWS	EB-66C/E (RC)	Takhli (355 TFW)	ESM, ECM (ex 41 TRS)	00/00/68 to 00/11/70
6460 TRS	RB-66B	Takhli (355 TFW)	ESM, ECM (to 42 TEWS)	00/09/65 to 00/00/68
42 TEWS	EB-66B/E (RH)	Takhli (355 TFW)	ESM, ECM (ex 6460 TRS; to 388 TFW)	00/00/68 to 00/11/70
42 TEWS	EB-66B/E (JW)	Korat (388 TFW)	ESM, ECM	00/11/70 to 31/12/73
39 TEWS	EB-66E	Korat (388 TFW)	ESM, ECM	11/04/73 to ?
USMC				
VMCJ-1	EF-10B, EA-6A, RF-8A, RF-4B (RM)	Da Nang	ESM, ECM, PR ('Fogbound')	12/04/65 to 00/01/73
VMCJ-2	EA-6A (CY)	Da Nang	ESM, ECM (supplemented VMCJ-1)	00/03/72 to 00/01/73
SAM identification and suppression (Wild Weasel)				
561 TFS	F-100F, F-105F/G (WW, MD)	Korat (388 TFW)	Wild Weasel	26/11/65 to 00/08/73
357 TFS	F-105F (RU)	Takhli (355 TFW)	Wild Weasel	00/06/66 to ?
6010 TFS	F-105F/G (ZB)	Korat (388 TFW)	Wild Weasel (to 17 TFS)	00/00/67 to 00/00/69
17 TFS	F-105G (JB, ZB)	Korat (388 TFW)	Wild Weasel (ex 6010 TFS)	00/00/69 to 00/11/74
67 TFS	F-4C (ZG)	Korat (388 TFW)	Wild Weasel	00/00/72 to 00/00/73
VAQ-132	EA-6B	Cam Ranh Bay	SAM suppression	00/06/72 to 00/02/73
AIRBORNE WARNING AND CONTROL ('BIG EYE', 'COLLEGE EYE')				
USAF				
522 AEWCW	EC-121D/M ('Rivet Top')	Tainan, Tan Son Nhut, Ubon, Udorn, Korat	AEW and control	00/04/65 to 00/06/74
7 ACCS	C-130E-II (JC)	Udorn (432 TRW)	Command, control, communications	00/00/65 to 00/00/75
USN				
VW-1	EC-121K (TE)	Da Nang	AEW	00/09/64 to ?
MISCELLANEOUS				
USAF				
–	KC-135A, EC-135L	Kadena, Taiwan	Comms. relay ('Combat Lightning')	00/00/66 to 00/00/73
70 ARS	EC-135L	U-Tapao	Comms. relay	00/00/69 to 00/00/74
–	EC-121J	Cam Ranh Bay	Entertainment relay ('Jenny')	00/02/66 to 00/09/70
44 TFS	F-105F (JE)	Korat (388 TFW)	VHF jammer ('Combat Martin')	00/00/68 to 00/00/71
USN				
VAH-21	AP-2H (SL)	Cam Ranh Bay	Trim	00/11/68 to 00/06/69
USMC				
H&MS-11	TF-9J, TA-4F (TM)	Da Nang	} Local PR and FAC	{ 00/00/65 to 00/06/71
H&MS-13	TF-9J (YU)	Chu Lai		{ 00/09/66 to 00/10/69
H&MS-17	TF-9J (SZ)	Da Nang		{ 00/00/67 to 00/00/70
'HAWK EYE' OPERATIONS CONTROLLED BY 460 TRW THEN 483 TAW				
USAF				
360 TEWS	EC-47N/P (AJ)	Pleiku, Tan Son Nhut	} Transmitter location	{ 00/00/65 to 00/08/71
361 TEWS	EC-47N/P (AL)	Nha Trang, TSN, Phu Cat		{ ? to 00/08/71
362 TEWS	EC-47N/P (AN)	Pleiku, Da Nang		{ ? to 00/08/71
VNAF				
718 RS	EC-47 (M)	Tan Son Nhut (33 TW)	Transmitter location	00/08/72 to 00/04/75

USAF

RF-101A *Dark green/green/light green/grey-brown over, light grey under, white 'last three' on fin: (54)512 (45 TRS).*

RF-101C *C, black serial on fin: O-(5)60211 (45 TRS). C, white serial and code on fin: 56(0)071/AH (45 TRS). Pale grey overall, black serial on fin: (5)60083 (20 TRS).*

RF-4C *Light grey over, white under, black serial on fin, buzz number on rear fuselage: (6)41054/FJ-054 (6461 TRS). C, white serial and code on fin: 68(0)609/OZ (14 TRS). Dark green/green/tan/light grey over, light grey under, white serial and code: 66(0)398/AE (16 TRS).*

RB-47H *Bare metal overall, black serial on fin and nose: O-(5)36248 (55 SRW).*

RB-57E *Black overall, red serial on fin: O-(5)54264 (6250 CSG).*

DC-130A *BM, black serial on fin, 'last three' on forward fuselage: (5)60527 (4025 RS).*

KC-135A *Light grey overall, black serial on fin: (6)10271 (Combat Lightning).*

RC-135M *Light grey overall, black serial on fin and nose: (6)24131 (82 SRS).*

RC-135U *(64)14847 (82 SRS).*

U-2C *Matt black overall, red serial on fin: (5)66952 (4028 SRS).*

SR-71A *Matt black overall, white serial on fin: (64)17972 (1 SRS).*

EC-121D *Light grey overall, black serial on fin: (5)30543, O-(5)30537 (522 AEWCW).*

RB-66B *Bare metal overall, black serial on fin, buzz number on rear fuselage: (5)30415/BB-415 (6460 TRS).*

EB-66E *C, white serial and code: 54(0)533/RH (42 TEWS).*

EC-47N *C, white serial and code on fin: 42(??)645/AN (362 TEWS).*

YQU-22A *Light grey overall, black serial on fin: (68)10532 (554 RS).*

USN

SP-5B *Glossy Sea Blue overall, white top fuselage decking, white serial and code on fin, black aircraft code on nose: (13)5482/3SE (VP-48).*

SP-5M *(14)1252/7QE (VP-42).*

SP-2H *Glossy Sea Blue overall, white top fuselage decking, white serial and unit code on fin, aircraft code on nose: 135553/10ZE (VP-17). Light grey overall, white fuselage top decking, black serial and code on fin: 150281/1YC(VP-?); 140964/5YB (VP-1); 131408/43RP (VP-31).*

OP-2E *Medium green over, light grey under, black serial and code on fin, aircraft code on nose: (5)131525/9MR.*

AP-2H *Light Gull Gray/dark Gull Gray/sea grey overall, black serial and code on fin, aircraft code on nose: 145903/SL4 (VAH-21).*

P-3A *Light grey overall, white fuselage top decking, black serial on fin, code on nose: 152185/1SG (VP-50); 152146/1ZE (VP-17).*

USMC

Aircraft were finished in standard Navy Gull Gray and white.

EF-10B *(12)5849/5RM, (12)7060/5RM (VMCJ-1).*

EA-6A *156986/6RM (VMCJ-1).*

US Army

AP-2E *Light grey overall, black serial on fin: 131531 (1RRC).*

YO-3A *Green/tan overall, black serial on fin: (69)18006 (1SA/AC).*

9.2.5. SUPPORT AND RESCUE OPERATIONS

In 1964 the US Air Force provided a limited air defence capability in South Vietnam in the 'Candy Machine' programme. In August, 16 FIS at Naha sent F-102 fighters to Tan Son Nhut, where they were supplemented by aircraft from 509 FIS, 405 TFW, at Clark AB. The latter unit was to provide air defence for the South, with its sister squadron, 64 FIS, until September 1968, when these duties were taken over by non-dedicated F-4 units. During 1966, 82 FIS was based for several months at Da Nang, where in 1965 two F-104C squadrons of 479 TFW were based. The Starfighters, however, were short-legged, and at no time was there a real threat of North Vietnamese air attack from the limited force of Il-28 bombers. The F-104C returned in 1966 for escort work but were generally unsuited to the theatre. Local air defence in Thailand was provided by two Sabre units, 11 Sqn. RTAF with the F-86F and L and 79 Sqn. RAAF with the Sabre 32, the latter until 1968.

The original Project 'Farm Gate' Air Commando Squadron, 1 ACS, was joined by a second, 602 ACS, with the A-1, at Bien Hoa in November 1964. Initially, the two-seat A-1E was used since it could accommodate a South Vietnamese navigator to legitimize the purely 'advisory' role of the American pilots, but once there was no need for the pretence the single-seat A-1H was widely used. As a diverse range of aircraft came into service with the Air Commando squadrons, the

One of the most remarkable developments to emerge from the Vietnam War was the gunship. Initially, C-47s were converted to fire heavy guns at a fixed aiming point, maintained by the pilot flying a tightly banked circuit around the target. Subsequently, C-119s, C-123s and C-130s were adapted, the last fitted with an extensive range of sensors and weapons. Aircraft 533129, shown, was the first production C-130A and was converted in 1968; named 'First Lady', it was still flying in 1986. (Lockheed)

organization was changed: from 8 March 1966 two Air Commando Wings were formed, 14 SOW at Bien Hoa and 56 SOW at Nakhon Phanom, and in 1968 the squadrons were redesignated Special Operations squadrons. In the close-support role, 606 SOS was formed in 1966 with the final version of the Invader, the B-26K, now designated A-26A. The aircraft was specifically reworked for the counter-insurgency (coin) role with fuselage turrets removed and improved avionics; it operated along the Ho Chi Minh Trail, latterly with 609 SOS, until November 1969. Two more A-1 squadrons were formed, 6 SOS in 1968 and 22 SOS in 1969. In the meantime, 3 TFW at Bien Hoa had introduced two new light close-support types into service. The 1965 'Skoshi Tiger' F-5A evaluation programme saw 4503 TFS locally redesignated 10 Fighter Commando Squadron (FCS) before the aircraft were handed over to the VNAF. The A-37A/B was first assigned to 604 ACS, which from 1968 became 604 SOS within 14 SOW. Two more 3 TFW squadrons formed on the A-37 in 1969, one of which became 8 SOS. The successful introduction of the Dragonfly resulted in the type being supplied in large numbers to the VNAF, where it eventually equipped ten squadrons. The close-support USAF units were employed on a range of missions where fast response was essential and the ability accurately to lay down a range of munitions critical. The Skyraiders played a crucial role, particularly in support of rescue operations, and they were not withdrawn until 1972.

One of the most important developments in air warfare to come out of the Vietnam conflict was the gunship. For some time engineers had been excited at the prospect of mounting side-firing guns on aircraft in order to bring continuous fire against a fixed target by flying around it in a banked turn. After trials in a C-131 in the United States, a C-47 was fitted with three GE SUU-11A/A 7.62mm Miniguns. The gunship project was now rushed into service, and 4 SOS formed at Bien Hoa in November 1965, building up to sixteen aircraft in 1966. The first daylight mission was flown on 15 December, the first night sortie on 23 December. The new type was initially designated FC-47 but shortly changed to AC-47 and given the call-sign 'Spooky'.

Gunship operations were immediately successful, and the aircraft were in great demand by ground-force commanders; a second unit, 14 ACS (later redesignated 3 ACS), formed at Nha Trang in January 1968. Another role undertaken by 14 SOW was psychological warfare. In November 1965 5 SOS was formed with the C-47 and U-10A for loudspeaker and leaflet work. In due course the 'psywar' C-47 worked in concert with the gunship AC-47D. Flying at night, the loudspeaker aircraft would orbit suspected VC camps, warning them to surrender and not fire on the aircraft. The inevitable groundfire would result in the

AC-47, following the orbit, opening fire with devastating results. The U-10As were mainly used for leaflet drops. A second 'psywar' unit, 9 SOS, was formed at Tan Son Nhut in 1968.

A purely heliborne special operations unit, 20 HS (later 20 SOS), was formed at Tan Son Nhut in 1966, subsequently moving to Nha Trang. The CH-3A and UH-1B and P were fitted for local base defence and psychological warfare. This relatively unknown squadron disbanded at Cam Ranh Bay in 1968. Meanwhile, in Project 'Gunship II', work was going ahead on a heavier aircraft, the AC-130. Fitted with an advanced night observation sight and LLLTV, it was equipped with four Miniguns and four 20mm Vulcan cannon. The type entered service with 16 SOS in October 1968 and again was an immediate success. Whereas the AC-47 was essentially used for local defence, the AC-130A was employed on search and destroy missions, mainly along the Trail. Later AC-130A versions incorporated a searchlight, FLIR, two 40mm Bofors cannon ('Surprise Package') and a 'Black Crow' low-level electronic emission detector ('Pave Pronto'). The 16th SOS transferred to 8 TFW at Ubon in 1969, where it acquired later versions of the AC-130.

The AC-130E 'Pave Spectre' incorporated additional armour and a rear observation blister and could carry extra fuel and ammunition. The armour was an important addition since aircraft 541629 was written off after being badly damaged by groundfire on 24 May 1969 and 541625 was shot down on 21 April 1970. Of the remaining four AC-130s lost in action – all in 1972 – three were AC-130As. There was also a need for a longer-range gun for heavily defended targets, and after tests the 105mm howitzer was fitted in place of the rear 40mm cannon in the 'Pave Aegis' programme. When the AC-130E was re-engined it became the AC-130H.

The final gunship type was the Project 'Gunship III' AC-119. The demand for aircraft to supplement both the AC-47 on in-country operations and the AC-130 for truck-hunting work on the Trail led to the choice of the C-119 airframe, since production C-130s were desperately required in the transport role. The AC-119G, fitted with four 20mm Miniguns, entered service in November 1968 with 71 SOS, manned by reservists. Used on in-country work, the AC-119G acquired the call-sign 'Shadow', while the heavier-armed AC-119K, which was equipped with two additional 20mm Vulcan cannon, became 'Stinger'. The latter type, used on the Trail, entered service in December 1969 with 18 SOS. With the exception of the AC-130, all gunships were deployed at bases across South Vietnam with the AC-47 (3 and 4 ACS) main base at Nha Trang and the AC-119 (17 and 18 SOS) main base at Phan Rang. The AC-47s were withdrawn from 1969 with the disbandment of 3 SOS. With the Vietnamization programme, aircraft of 4 ACS

TABLE OF UNITS: THE VIETNAM WAR — SUPPORT OPERATIONS

Unit	Aircraft (code)	Base	Role	Dates
AIR DEFENCE				
RTAF				
11 Sqn.	F-86F/L	Don Muang	Local air defence	00/00/62 to 00/00/75
RAAF				
79 Sqn.	Sabre Mk. 32	Ubon	Local air defence	00/05/62 to 00/08/68
USAF[1]				
16 FIS	F-102A	Tan Son Nhut	TDY ex Naha AB	00/08/64 to 00/12/64
509 FIS	F-102A, TF-102A (PK)	Tan Son Nhut, Bien Hoa	TDY ex 405 TFW, Clark AB	00/08/64 to 00/09/68
64 FIS	F-102A, TF-102A (PE)	Bien Hoa	TDY ex 405 TFW, Clark AB	00/00/66 to 00/09/68
82 FIS	F-102A		TDY ex CONUS	00/04/66 to 00/00/66
435 TFS	F-104C	} Da Nang	TDY 479 TFW	} 00/04/65 to 00/12/65
476 TFS	F-104C		TDY 479 TFW	
SPECIAL OPERATIONS AND RESCUE SUPPORT				
USAF[2]				
14 ACW/SOW				
1 SOS	T-28D, A-1E/G (EC)	Bien Hoa, Pleiku	Strike, rescue support (to 56 SOW)	00/02/64 to 00/00/68
6 SOS	A-1E/H (ET)	Pleiku	Strike, rescue support	00/05/68 to 00/00/72
8 SOS	A-37B (EK)	Bien Hoa	Close support (ex 3 TFW)	00/09/69 to 00/00/72
604 SOS	A-37A/B (CK)	Bien Hoa	Close support (ex 3 TFW)	00/08/68 to 00/00/71
4 SOS	AC-47D (EN)	Bien Hoa, Nha Trang, Tan Son Nhut, Da Nang	Gunship (to 817 AS VNAF)	00/11/65 to 15/12/69
14 ACS	AC-47D	Nha Trang	Gunship (to 3 SOS)	15/01/68 to 30/04/68
3 SOS	AC-47D (EL)	Pleiku	Gunship (ex 14 ACS)	01/05/68 to 00/09/69
16 SOS	AC-130A, NC-123K (EA)	Ubon, Nha Trang	Gunship (to 8 TFW)	00/10/68 to 00/00/69
71 SOS	AC-119G	Nha Trang	Gunship (to 17 SOS)	00/11/68 to 31/05/69
17 SOS	AC-119G	Phu Cat	Gunship (ex 71 SOS to 819 AS VNAF)	01/06/69 to 30/09/71
18 SOS	AC-119G/K (EH)	Phan Rang	Gunship (to 56 SOW)	21/12/69 to 25/08/71
5 SOS	AC-47D, U-10A (EO)	Nha Trang	Psychological warfare	00/11/65 to 00/00/71
9 SOS	AC-47D, O-2B (ER)	Tan Son Nhut	Psychological warfare	00/00/68 to 29/02/72
20 SOS	UH-1B/F/P, CH-3C (EV)	Tuy Hoa, Nha Trang, Cam Ranh Bay, Nakhon Phanom	Psychological warfare, infiltration	00/00/66 to 31/07/68
15 SOS	C-130E-I	Nha Trang	Special Forces support (to 318 SOS)	00/08/67 to 00/00/73
56 SOW				
602 SOS	A-1E/G/H/J (TT)	Bien Hoa, Nakhon Phanom	Rescue support	00/11/64 to 31/12/70
1 SOS	A-1E/G/H/J (TC)		Rescue support (ex 14 SOW)	00/00/68 to 00/12/72
22 SOS	A-1E/G/H/J (TS)		Rescue support	00/00/69 to 00/00/72
606 SOS	T-28D, C-123K, A-26A (TO)	} Nakhon Phanom	Close support, flareship, interdiction (to 609 SOS)	00/01/66 to 00/08/66
609 SOS	T-28D, A-26A (TA)		Close support, interdiction	00/08/66 to 09/11/69
21 SOS	CH-3C/E		Support, infiltration	00/00/68 to 00/00/73
18 SOS	AC-119K		Gunship (ex 14 SOW, to 821 AS VNAF)	25/08/71 to 31/12/72
8 TFW, 388 TFW				
16 SOS	AC-130A/E/H (FT)	Ubon, Korat	Gunship (ex 14 SOW)	00/00/69 to 00/00/75
318 SOS	MC-130E	Nha Trang, Korat	Special Forces support (ex 15 SOS)	00/00/72 to 00/00/74
432 TRW				
4 SOS	AC-47D (OS)	Udorn	Gunship base defence (ex 14 SOW)	00/12/69 to 00/06/70
315 TCW/ACW/TAW ('Ranch Hand')				
12 SOS	UC-123B/K	Bien Hoa	Defoliation (ex SASF)	00/07/64 to 31/07/70
310 TAS	UC-123K (WM)	Tan Son Nhut (A Flt.)	Defoliation (ex 12 SOS)	01/08/70 to 28/01/71
VNAF				
817 AS	AC-47D (K)	Tan Son Nhut, Nha Trang	Gunship (ex 4 ACS; 33, 62 TW)	00/06/69 to 00/04/75
819 AS	AC-119G (HR)	Tan Son Nhut	Gunship (ex 17 SOS; 53 TW)	00/09/71 to 00/04/75
821 AS	AC-119K (F)	Tan Son Nhut, Da Nang	Gunship (ex 18 SOS; 53 TW)	00/12/72 to 00/04/75
314 SMS	C-47, U-6A (C,M)	Tan Son Nhut	Special missions (33 TW)	00/00/56 to 00/04/75
SUPPORT AND STRIKE				
VNAF				
514 FS	A-1H (FF)	} Bien Hoa	Close support (23 TW)	01/01/63 to 00/04/75
518 FS	A-1H (KW)			15/10/63 to 00/04/75
522 FS	F-5A/B, RF-5A (HJ)			19/06/67 to 00/04/75
516 FS	T-28D, A-1H (L,P)	Nha Trang, Da Nang	Close support (41 TW to 74 TW)	00/01/63 to 00/00/68
615 Flt.	B-57B	Da Nang	Light bombing (41 TW)	00/08/65 to 20/04/66
522 FS	A-1H (U)	Tan Son Nhut	Close support (83 SOG to 23 TW)	01/04/65 to 00/09/66
528 FS	A-37B			01/12/70 to 00/03/75
550 FS	A-37B	} Da Nang	Close support (61 TW)	00/00/72 to 00/03/75
538 FS	F-5A			00/00/72 to 00/03/75
524 FS	A-1H	Nha Trang	Close support (62 TW to 74 TW)	15/09/65 to 31/12/67
516 FS	A-37B	Da Nang	Close support (74 TW ex 41 TW)	00/07/69 to 00/03/75
520 FS	A-1H (V), A-37B	Bien Hoa, Binh Thuy	Close support (74 TW)	14/06/64 to 00/03/75
524 FS	A-37B	Nha Trang, Phan Rang	Close support (74 TW ex 62 TW)	19/04/69 to 00/03/75
526 FS	} A-37B	Binh Thuy	Close support (74 TW)	00/08/69 to 00/03/75
546 FS				00/00/73 to 00/03/75
530 FS	A-1H	Pleiku	Close support (72 TW)	01/12/70 to 00/03/75
532 FS	A-37B	Phu Cat, Pleiku	Close support (82 TW)	01/10/72 to 00/03/75
534 FS	} A-37B	Phan Rang	Close support (92 TW)	01/11/72 to 00/03/75
548 FS				00/00/73 to 00/03/75
536 FS	F-5A/E (HQ)			00/12/72 to 00/04/75
540 FS	} F-5A	} Bien Hoa	Close support (63 TW)	00/00/73 to 00/04/75
542 FS				00/00/73 to 00/00/74
544 FS				00/00/73 to 00/04/75

TABLE OF UNITS: THE VIETNAM WAR — SUPPORT OPERATIONS (continued)

Unit	Aircraft (code)	Base	Role	Dates
FAC AND LIGHT STRIKE UNITS				
USAF				
19 TASS	O-1E/G, O-2A, OV-10A	Bien Hoa	⎫	⎧ 00/07/63 to 00/11/68
20 TASS	O-1E/F, O-2A	Da Nang	⎪	? to ?
21 TASS	O-1E/F, O-2A	Phu Cat, Tan Son Nhut	⎬ FAC	? to 00/00/73
22 TASS	O-1E/F, O-2A	?	⎪	? to 00/05/71
23 TASS	O-2A, OV-10A	Nakhon Phanom	⎭	⎩ ? to 15/08/73
3 TFW				
10 FCS	F-5A (4503 TFS)		⎧ Ground attack (Skoshi Tiger)	23/10/65 to 16/04/66
604 ACS	A-37A/B (CK)	⎫	⎪ Close support (to 604 SOS 1968)	26/07/67 to 00/00/71
8 AS	A-37B (CF)	⎬ Bien Hoa	⎨ Close support (to 8 SOS)	00/00/69 to 00/09/69
90 AS	A-37B (CG)	⎭	⎩ Close support	00/00/69 to 00/00/71
USMC				
VMO-6	OV-10A (WB)	Quang Tri, Chu Lai	FAC, light strike (MAG-36)	00/00/65 to 00/11/69
VMO-2	OV-10A, YOV-10D (UV)	Marble Mountain	FAC, light strike (MAG-11)	06/07/68 to 00/00/71
USN (TF-116)				
HC-1	UH-1B	Vung Tau	Support (to HAL-3)	00/09/66 to 31/03/67
HAL-3	UH-1B/C/L/M	Vung Tau, Binh Thuy	Support (ex HC-1)	01/04/67 to 26/01/72
VAL-4	OV-10A (UM)	Vung Tau, Binh Thuy	Observation, light strike	00/03/69 to 10/04/72
VNAF				
110 OS	O-1E/F, U-17A, O-2A (B,G,X)	Da Nang	FAC (41 TW)	00/01/63 to 00/03/75
120 OS	O-1E/F, U-17A	Da Nang	FAC (41 TW)	00/05/71 to 00/03/75
112 OS	O-1E/F	Tan Son Nhut, Bien Hoa	FAC (23 TW)	00/01/63 to 00/04/75
124 OS	O-1E/F	Bien Hoa	FAC (23 TW)	00/00/72 to 00/04/75
114 OS	O-1E/F, U-17A	Da Nang, Pleiku, Nha Trang	FAC (62 TW)	00/01/63 to 00/03/75
116 OS	O-1E/F, U-17A (E)	Nha Trang, Binh Thuy	FAC (74 TW)	00/06/64 to 00/03/75
122 OS	O-1E/F, U-17A	Binh Thuy	FAC (74 TW)	01/08/72 to 00/03/75
118 OS	O-1E/F, U-17A, O-2A	Pleiku	FAC (72 TW)	00/04/71 to 00/03/75
MISCELLANEOUS				
USAF				
1 WG	WC-130B	Tan Son Nhut	Rain seeding	00/00/67 to 00/00/72
Rescue (3 ARRG)				
33 ARRS	HH-43B/F, HU-16B, CH-3C	Bien Hoa, Nakhon Phanom, Korat, Takhli, Udorn, Da Nang, Pleiku	SAR, local airbase rescue	00/06/64 to 00/09/67
37 ARRS	HH-43B/F, HU-16B, HH-3E, HH-53B/C	Da Nang, Udorn	SAR, local airbase rescue	00/08/64 to 30/06/73
38 ARRS	HH-43B/F, HC-54, HC-130H, HH-3E	Tan Son Nhut, Da Nang, Bien Hoa, Korat	SAR, local airbase rescue	00/11/65 to 00/08/73
39 ARRS	HC-130P	Tuy Hoa	SAR, helicopter refuelling	00/09/67 to 00/08/73
40 ARRS	HH-43B, HH-3E, HH-53C	Nakhon Phanom, Udorn	SAR, local airbase rescue	00/11/67 to 31/01/76
56 ARRS	HC-130P	Korat	SAR, helicopter refuelling	00/00/70 to 00/08/73
31 ARRS	HC-54, HC-130H	Clark AB	⎫	
36 ARRS	HH-43B, HC-54, HC-130H	Tachikawa AB	⎬ SAR	00/00/64 to 00/00/75
79 ARRS	HC-54, HC-130H	Andersen AFB	⎭	
EVACUATION OF SAIGON ('FREQUENT WIND'), APRIL 1975				
USMC				
HMM-165	CH-46D (YW)	⎫		
HMM-365	CH-46D (YM)	⎪		
HML-367	UH-1E (VT)	⎪		
HMA-369	AH-1J (SM)	⎬ *Hancock*		
HMH-462	CH-53A (YF)	⎪		
HMH-463	CH-53A (YH)	⎭		
USAF				
37 ARRS	HH-53C	*Midway*		
21 SOS	CH-53B	*Midway*		
Air America	UH-1	Tan Son Nhut		

Notes:
1. Both F-104C units returned in 1966 for escort and limited ground attack tasks.
2. Initially Air Commando squadrons, from 8 March 1966 within 14 Air Commando Wing, then from 1 August 1968 as Special Operations squadrons within 14 or 56 Special Operations Wing.

were transferred to 817 Attack Squadron (AS) VNAF, a few aircraft being retained for local defence by 432 TRW at Udorn. In 1971 17 SOS handed its AC-119Gs to 819 AS VNAF and the following year 821 AS acquired the AC-119Ks of 18 SOS.

The gunship programme was parallelled by a 'mini-gunship' project. This culminated in the 'Credible Chase' Fairchild AU-23A Peacemaker and Helio AU-24A Stallion, neither of which served with US forces. Both were fitted with a 20mm Gatling-type cannon, and the fifteen of each type built were sold to the RTAF and the Khmer AF respectively. The 16th SOS also operated two NC-123K Project 'Black Spot' aircraft, which were fitted with advanced sensor and tracking equipment; flown from Ubon on truck-hunting sorties, they were equipped to drop bomblet clusters and operated between 1968 and 1971. Another unusual version of a transport type to be flown by the Special Operations units was the Project 'Combat Talon' C-130E-I, later redesignated MC-130E. Initially operated by 15 SOS, then 318 SOS, the aircraft was fitted with Fulton recovery gear and terrain-following radar and was used in support of Special Forces, especially in covert infiltration and exfiltration. The VNAF also managed covert operations supported by 314 Special Missions Squadron (SMS) flying the C-47 and U-6A.

The ubiquitous Hercules was also operated, in its WC-130B version, by 1 Weather Group (WG) at Tan Son Nhut. In another covert programme, 'Pop Eye', the aircraft were used between 1967 and 1972 to hamper the North Vietnamese supply effort by seeding rain clouds with silver iodide. This was only one form of chemical warfare applied by the USAF. The 'Ranch Hand' UC-123B defoliant sprayers of the SASF were absorbed into 310 TAS within 315 TCW. It then became 12 ACS/SOS while the TCW was redesignated an Air Commando Wing. Finally, in 1970, the remaining aircraft were incorporated into 310 TAS. The last sortie was flown on 28 January 1971, by which time 6.2 million acres had been sprayed with 100,000,000lb of herbicides. The main defoliant was Agent Orange, a concoction of 2,4-D and 2,4,5-T, but at least three other types were used. Agent Orange produces a lethal by-product, dioxin, which has resulted in disease in the civilian population and the 'Ranch Hand' crews; furthermore, the defoliated and deforested areas of Vietnam and Cambodia will remain so for a hundred years. In a less long-term operation, 'Banish Beach', C-130s were used to drop fused fuel drums on forest areas to burn off the trees; in a similar operation, 'Pink Rose', B-52 bombers used incendiaries to set fire to the jungle on the Ho Chi Minh Trail in 1970.

Ground attack against pre-planned targets in South Vietnam was the responsibility of the F-100 Wings working with forward air control (FAC) aircraft of the Tactical Air Support squadrons. The job of the slow FAC aircraft was to identify and then mark targets, normally with white phosphorous, and the aircraft type used for this dangerous work were first the O-1, then the O-2A and finally the armed OV-10A. In parts of southern North Vietnam, where the AAA defences were strongest, 'fast mover' FAC was provided by two-seat F-100Fs and TF-102As of 509 FIS under the 'Commando Sabre' project. The VNAF began the war with three fighter squadrons (FS) but gradually built up its close-support strength to four A-1H, six F-5A/E and ten A-37B squadrons within seven Tactical Wings (TW). From 1971 the full establishment of squadrons was notional since many existed on paper only because of shortages of aircraft. For a short period several B-57Bs were loaned from 405 TBW to form 615 Flight, but the project was abandoned after eight months, during which one aircraft was lost. In the FAC role the VNAF flew the O-1 and U-17, finally operating eight squadrons. The USMC brought its own FAC to Vietnam, first with VMO-6 and then VMO-2, both of which

were equipped with the OV-10A, which the Marines also used in the light strike role. In 1970 VMO-2 also operated several YOV-10D night observation gunships (NOGS) for night attack sorties.

The US Navy also managed air support operations in South Vietnam. TF.116 was charged with patrolling the vast lengths of the Mekong Delta to deny the VC their supply routes from Cambodia. These 'Game Warden' riverine operations were initially handled by fast patrol boats and hovercraft, but it soon became clear that they were hindered without helicopter support, especially for reconnaissance. The first such support was provided by UH-1Bs of HC-1, flying out of Vung Tau, from September 1966 to March 1967, but HC-1 was primarily responsible for ship-related work and on 1 April 1967 HAL-3 was formed with detachments at Vung Tau and Binh Thuy. The need for faster-reacting aircraft with a strike capability was met from March 1969 with the formation of VAL-4, equipped with the OV-10A. Riverine operations ceased from April 1972.

A range of aircraft from many units was engaged from time to time in rescue activities. In June 1964, 33 Air Rescue Squadron (ARS) sent HH-43B helicopters for local rescue to Nakhon Phanom. (The ARS designation was changed to Air Rescue and Recovery Squadron on 8 January 1966 to avoid confusion with Air Refueling squadrons.) HU-16B amphibians were also deployed. Although operating near base, the HH-43B was vulnerable to ground fire, so the HH-43F, with armour and a machine gun for defence, was introduced. In August 1964, 37 ARS sent the same HH-43/HU-16 mix to Da Nang, and in March 1966 39 ARS provided the rescue service from Tan Son Nhut, where it also based HC-54 long-range search aircraft, later to be replaced by the HC-130H. The HH-43 was valuable but very short-ranged, so, from the autumn of 1965, 38 ARS was equipped with the HH-3E, quickly nicknamed the 'Jolly Green Giant'. Later, in 1967, Detachment 2 of 37 ARRS flew the much more powerful CH-53 'Super Jolly', which also joined 40 ARRS in Thailand.

US Air Force helicopters were confined to rescue and support duties, including the covert infiltration of agents. The first rescue type available was the short-range HH-43 Huskie; in January 1965 there were five detachments, two with the improved, combat-modified version which was soon seen in camouflage, like this HH-43F of 33 ARRS. In 1966 the Huskie was replaced by the HH-3 (Via R. F. Dorr)

To permit long loiter times and to facilitate the coverage of the whole of Indo-China, the HC-130P was introduced into service with 39 ARRS, providing not only a search capability but also in-flight refuelling for the helicopters. To maintain morale among air crews, who when captured were treated extremely badly, a dedicated rescue service was critical. Rescues from enemy-held territory were perilous and, at their most complex, could involve many aircraft. The basic unit was an HH-3 or CH-53 supported by two A-1Hs, call-sign 'Sandy', of one of the SOSs, with a second trio in the air as back-up. The downed air crew were located by FAC O-2A or, more normally, an OV-10A or ARRS HC-130 homing in on the survivors' PRC-90 transmitters. The first A-1 would troll the area for gunfire while the second acted as escort for the helicopter. All the time the rescue was co-ordinated by the HC-130. The 'Sandies' were normally fitted with rocket and gun pods, cluster bombs, phosphorous rockets and extra fuel tanks to give them long loiter times and armament for precision attacks. Once the groundfire was identified, the second A-1 was called in by the FAC for a strike; if necessary, aircraft from the back-up unit could be called in.

The 'Sandies' orbited some distance from the downed crewmen in order not to give away their positions to the enemy. In particularly strongly defended areas, any nearby 'fast-movers' would be called in by FAC for further strike support – rescue missions were always given priority. Gunships were also used where extra fire-suppression was necessary, and in some circumstances flights of smoke-laying Skyraiders were called in to create a barrier between the enemy and survivor to give added protection to the helicopter. It would be unusual for the helicopter to be able to land, in which case a weighted line was dropped through the 300ft jungle canopy, and if the survivor was injured, a para-jumper was dropped to aid the attempt. Occasionally the HC-130 was used to blast a jungle clearing for helicopter landing, using a specially prepared 15,000lb 'bomb'. The bomb was constructed on a pallet, fitted with a probe to ensure detonation above the ground, and rolled out of the aircraft. Throughout the war 3,833 personnel were rescued from death or captivity by the Aerospace Rescue and Recovery Service.

The culmination of the rescue missions would have been the attempt, on 21 November 1970, to free 100 prisoners-of-war from Son Tay prison just 23 miles from Hanoi. At about 0200hrs a nearby military school was marked by two MC-130Es of 318 SOS, and one HH-3E of 37 ARRS deliberately crash-landed in the prison compound while five CH-53Cs of 40 ARRS landed nearby. US Rangers quickly worked through the prison, but, sadly, intelligence had failed to reveal that the prisoners had been removed some months earlier. The damaged HH-3E was destroyed and

the helicopters returned to Udorn. The effort involved a fixed-wing escort of five A-1Es, five F-105Gs and ten F-4Ds. One F-105 was downed on the return and the pilot rescued. The attempt also involved HC-130Ps, KC-135Ms, EC-121Ds and several Air America C-123 aircraft for evacuating the prisoners.

The final evacuation from Saigon in April 1975 saw large numbers of helicopters in action for the last time. USAF and USMC machines were hurriedly embarked on the carriers *Midway* and *Hancock* in the Philippines and rushed to South Vietnam. With the support of a number of Air America UH-1s, the helicopter force lifted out 6,968 people on 29–30 April to the waiting ships in what was to become known as 'the night of the helicopters'. The last American casualties of the war were the pilot and co-pilot of a CH-46D of HMM-365 which crashed in the sea off *Hancock* in the dark.

AIRCRAFT MARKINGS

For general notes on camouflage schemes see section on offensive operations.

VNAF

A-1G *C: (1)32487/KWB (518 FS).*

A-1H *C, no markings of any sort: (83 SOG). C: (1)42034 (516 FS).*

A-37B *C: (67)14796 (62 TW); (67)22488 (516 FS); (67)14804 (524 FS).*

F-5A *Dark green/brown/tan over, light grey under, black serial on fin: (6)21213 (? unit, ex-Iranian AF). C, grey serial on fin: (65)10514 (522 FS).*

AC-47 *C, black under, white serial on fin: (43)49517 (817 AS).*

AC-119G *C, black under, red serial on fin: O-(5)25938 (819 AS).*

O-1E *Light grey overall: (5)112236/DP.*

U-17A *Light grey overall, grey serial, black code on fin and rudder: 63-13020/WF (116 OS).*

USAF

F-102A *Light grey overall, black serial on fin, buzz number on rear fuselage: (5)61165/FC-165 (509 FIS). C, white serial and code on fin: 56(1)113/PK (509 FIS).*

A-1E *C, no national markings, 'last three' and code in white on fin: (1)39577/TT (602 SOS). Light grey overall, black serial on fin: (1)32606 (1 ACS). C: (1)34555/TS (22 SOS).*

A-1H *C, black serial and code on fin: (1)34608/TC 'Blood, Sweat and Tears' (1 SOS); (1)35242/ET (6 SOS).*

A-26A *C, black under, black serial and code on fin: 64(17)645/TA (609 SOS).*

A-37A *Light grey overall, black serial on fin: (67)14517 (640 ACS). C, grey serial on fin: (67)14516 (640 ACS). C, white serial and code on fin: (67)14509/CK (604 ACS).*

AC-47 Chocolate/grey-brown/tan over, light grey under, white serial and code on fin: (4)49274 (4 ACS). Green/black/tan over, black under, white serial and code on fin: 43(??)010/OS (432 TRW).

C-47 Chocolate/grey/brown/tan over, light grey under, white serial and code on fin: (44)76558/ER (9 SOS).

AC-119G C, black under, red serial on fin: O-(5)25892 'Charlie Chasers' (17 SOS).

AC-119K C, black under, red serial on fin: O-(5)33154 'Pea-nut Special' (18 SOS).

C-123B C, black under, black serial and code on fin: (55)4577/TO (606 SOS).

UC-123B BM, black serial on fin: (5)6362 (12 SOS).

NC-123K Dark green/medium green/light green/black over, black under, red serial on fin: O-(5)40691 (16 SOS).

AC-130A Dark green/green/desert drab over, black under and on fuselage sides, red serial on fin: (5)50040/FT (16 SOS). White serial and code on fin: (54)1626/EA (16 SOS).

AC-130H Black overall, red serial and code on fin: 69(6)573/FT (16 SOS). Aircraft grey overall, yellow serial on fin: 69(6)575 (16 SOS).

UH-1F Dark green/tan over, light grey under, black serial on fin: (6)57930 (20 SOS).

CH-3C C, black serial on boom: (6)55690 (20 SOS).

O-1E Light grey overall, black serial on fin: (5)76026 (19 TASS).

O-2A Light grey overall, white top wing surfaces, black serial on fin: (67)21436 (22 TASS). Black overall, red serial on fin: (6721)418 (23 TASS). Green/tan/pale grey over, pale grey under, black serial on fin: (67)21450 (9 SOS).

OV-10A Light grey overall, black serial and yellow lightning flash on fin: (67)14650 (23 TASS).

U-10B C: 6313111, 66(14)374/EO (5 SOS).

HH-43B BM: (6)39714 (37 ARRS).BM, national markings removable, no other marks: (38 ARRS).

HH-43F C, black serial on fin: (6)39714 (38 ARRS).

HH-3E C, tan under, black serial on boom: (66)13290 (37 ARRS).

HH-53C C, tan under, black serial on boom: (68)10364, (68)10360 (37 ARRS).

HC-130P C, white serial on fin: 66216 (56 ARRS).

USN

OV-10A Medium green over, light grey under, black serial and unit code on fin, aircraft code on forward fuselage in white: (1)55471/6UM (VAL-4).

USMC

YOV-10D Gull Gray/dark Gull Gray/sea grey overall, black serial on fin: (1)52660 (VMO-2).

CH-46D Olive Drab overall, black serial on rear engine mounting: 154808/00/YW (HMM-165).

RAAF

Sabre 32 BM, black serial on rear fuselage: A94-964, A94-982 (79 Sqn.).

RTAF

F-86L BM, black serial on fin, code on mid fuselage, unit marking on fin: (5)30843/1221 (11 Sqn.).

Air America

UH-1 Bare metal overall, navy blue upper boom and fin, black registration on door: N8514F.

9.2.6. ARMY AND MARINE CORPS HELICOPTER OPERATIONS

It quickly became clear that the helicopter was to be a vital tool and weapon in the type of war being fought in Vietnam. The original seven US Army UH-1 Aviation Companies had developed tactics for deploying troops speedily into landing zones (LZ), whether in friendly hands ('cold') or defended ('hot'). The gunship was firmly established as an important component, and throughout the war new weapons fits and equipment were introduced as the NVA and VC used more sophisticated tactics and arms. The concept of airmobility was widely accepted both by the Army and Marine Corps, and troop insertion by parachute was soon abandoned in favour of faster and more concentrated deployment by helicopter. Eventually, a wide range of units would use helicopters as they had jeeps or trucks in earlier wars.

Typically, the Aviation Companies, later renamed Assault Helicopter Companies (AHC), flew about 25 UH-1s, about one-third of which were gunships. 'Eagle' flights were maintained at readiness, with sufficient helicopters to lift sixty or so troops, supported by five gunships, a command machine and one for casualty evacuation (casevac). The Companies were operated within 145 Aviation Battalion (AB) at bases around the country. In December 1964 two additional Companies were formed, and the organization was changed to comprise three ABs, mainly supporting operations in the south, leaving two Companies and the USMC 'Shufly' detachments in the north. Gradually, more Companies were deployed, and typically they included OH-13 or OH-23 light helicopters for reconnaissance as well as the ubiquitous UH-1. The AHCs were available to support operations in their Corps area, but from spring 1965, as the war escalated and infantry formations were committed, they brought their own integral Companies.

The USMC 'Shufly' detachments ceased from April as first Marine Air Group (MAG) 16 and then MAG-36 were established to support operations in the North. The Marines operated three squadrons of UH-34Ds as transports, with HMM-461 flying the CH-37C for heavy-lift work. From early 1966 CH-46Ds began to replace the UH-34s, but the new helicopters were lightly armed and separate units flew the armed UH-1E gunship, though never in large numbers. The Army relied on the CH-37B for heavy lift until September 1965 when the first CH-54A, of 478 Av. Co., arrived at Da Nang. The CH-54A, with a payload of ten tons, was capable of lifting a range of equipment over considerable distances, including earth-movers, artillery pieces and aircraft, although the type rarely entered combat zones. In the 'Combat Trap' programme, the CH-54 was used to drop with precision M121 10,000lb proximity-fused bombs to clear helicopter landing sites. From November, the CH-54s were supplemented by the first CH-47 Chinooks, each of which could carry 33 fully equipped troops compared with the Huey's twelve. From 1965, Cavalry Troops were also sent to Vietnam for armed reconnaissance and pursuit. Their equipment was similar to that of the Aviation Companies and they were attached to a range of formations.

In the United States, 11 Air Assault Division (Test) had proved the merit of basing a large formation around the helicopter, and from September 1965 components of the Division were used to create the 1st Cavalry Division (Airmobile), which began operations out of An Khe from October. The Division was equipped with 428 helicopters, most of them operated by three battalions within 11 Aviation Group. Two of these battalions had the UH-1 (each with three companies with transports, one with gunships) and the third was equipped with the CH-47.

Helicopters also served with the Support Command, the integral Artillery Battalion (Aerial Rocket) and the attached Cavalry Squadron. The first major commitment was to support a besieged camp at Plei Me, south-west of Pleiku, from 19 October, and for 35 days through the battle of Ia Drang the 1st Cavalry succeeded in pushing the NVA back into Cambodia. There were now four kinds of US Army helicopter organization in addition to VNAF and USMC commitments. First was the Airmobile Division (1st Cavalry and later 101 Airborne), then there were the infantry divisions (battalion strength with several companies and attached cavalry troops); third were the large number of AHCs within ABs available to Military Assistance Command Vietnam (MACV) for attachment to formations as and when required, and, last, there were the generally non-combatant support groups (signals, engineers etc). This organization was cumbersome, however, and, from May 1966, 1 Aviation Division was formed to control and co-ordinate the non-organic units. Four Aviation Groups were created, one for each Corps zone, and all air

assets, including the fixed-wing liaison and reconnaissance companies, were organized within battalions; training and maintenance was standardized and more flexible deployment facilitated. The last formation to arrive in Vietnam for combat was 101 Airborne Division (Airmobile), which was organized similarly to 1 Cavalry Division.

The workhorse of the helicopter war was the UH-1. The troop transport versions were the UH-1D and later the UH-1H with an uprated engine. The gunship UH-1B and later UH-1C were equipped with a formidable range of weapons, including fixed 7.62 machine guns (M6 and M60 systems), 2.75in rockets (XM157, XM158, XM3), 40mm grenade launcher (M5) and AGM-22B missile (M22). The most common armament subsystems were the M16 (four 7.62 M60 MGs and two rocket launchers) and later, from 1967, the M21 (two 7.62mm M134 Miniguns and two rocket launchers). Because of their cluttered appearance and relatively slow performance, the gunships were commonly called 'Hogs' ('Heavy Hogs' when fitted with grenade launchers), while the cleaner, faster transports were nicknamed 'Slicks'. Between May 1966 and February 1968

Typical of the hill-top forts in Vietnam was this well-equipped base. Such sites required helicopter resupply, for which the capable CH-47 Chinook was ideally suited. This CH-47A is believed to be a machine of A Company, 228th Assault Support Helicopter Battalion; enthusiasts will recognize the unit emblem on the panel in the foreground as that of the 1st Cavalry Division. (Boeing-Vertol)

TABLE OF UNITS: THE VIETNAM WAR — ARMY AND MARINE CORPS HELICOPTER OPERATIONS

Unit	Aircraft	Base	Wing	Dates	Remarks
VNAF					
211 HS	UH-34A	Tan Son Nhut, Soc Trang	33 TW	01/01/63 to 00/00/69	To 84 TW
213 HS	UH-34A (J)	Da Nang	41 TW	01/01/63 to 00/00/69	To 51 TW
215 HS	UH-34A	Bien Hoa	23 TW	00/00/64 to 00/00/69	To 62 TW
217 HS	UH-34A (R)	Da Nang, Tan Son Nhut		01/05/64 to 00/00/69	To 84 TW
225 HS	UH-1H	Soc Trang	74 TW	11/12/70 to 00/00/73	Ex 121 AC, US Army; to 84 TW
227 HS	UH-1H	Soc Trang		16/03/71 to 00/00/73	Ex 336 AC, US Army; to 84 TW
219 TW	UH-34A			00/00/66 to 00/00/73	To 62 TW
213 HS	UH-1H			00/00/69 to 00/03/75	Ex 41 TW
233 HS	UH-1H			01/02/72 to 00/03/75	Ex 282 AC, US Army
239 HS	UH-1H	Da Nang	51 TW	00/02/72 to 00/03/75	
247 HS	CH-47B/C			00/12/72 to 00/03/75	
253 HS	UH-1H			00/00/73 to 00/03/75	
257 HS	IH-1H			00/00/74 to 00/03/75	
211 HS	UH-1H	Binh Thuy	84 TW	00/00/69 to 00/03/75	Ex 33 TW
217 HS		Binh Thuy, Can Tho,		00/00/69 to 00/00/72	To 64 TW
225 HS		Soc Trang		00/00/73 to 00/04/75	Ex 74 TW
227 HS		Soc Trang		00/00/73 to 00/04/75	Ex 74 TW
215 HS	UH-1H	Nha Trang	62 TW	00/00/69 to 00/04/75	Ex 23 TW
219 HS				00/00/73 to 00/03/75	Ex 51 TW
223 HS	UH-1H			11/12/70 to 00/04/75	Ex 190 AC, US Army
221 HS	UH-1H			01/04/71 to 00/04/75	Ex 68 AC, US Army
231 HS	UH-1H	Bien Hoa	43 TW	01/09/71 to 00/04/75	Ex 118 AC, US Army
237 HS	CH-47B/C			00/09/70 to 00/04/75	
245 HS	UH-1H			00/12/71 to 00/04/75	
251 HS	UH-1H			00/00/73 to 00/04/75	
229 HS	UH-1H	Pleiku	72 TW	16/03/71 to 00/03/75	Ex 189 AC, US Army
235 HS				01/05/71 to 00/03/75	Ex 170 AC, US Army
217 HS	UH-1H	Can Tho	64 TW	00/00/72 to 00/04/75	Ex 84 TW
249 HS	CH-47B/C			00/12/72 to 00/04/75	
255 HS	UH-1H			00/00/74 to 00/04/75	
243 HS	UH-1H	Nha Trang, Phu Cat	82 TW	00/11/71 to 00/03/75	
241 HS	CH-47B/C	Phu Cat	82 TW	00/05/72 to 00/03/75	
259 HS	UH-1H	Various (medevac)		00/00/74 to 00/04/75	

heavier gunships in the form of several ACH-47As also operated in Vietnam. These Chinooks, referred to as 'Go-Go Birds', carried a devastating range of weapons, including a grenade launcher, rocket pods, 7.62mm Miniguns and 20mm M24 cannon giving a 360-degree field of fire. Extra armour afforded added protection to the crew, and the aircraft could carry a much greater ammunition load. Three of the four conversions were lost in operations and the type was replaced by the AH-1G HueyCobra. The AH-1G was based on the UH-1 but with a redesigned fuselage only 38in in width compared to the 100in of the UH-1. The armament fit included a chin turret mounting 7.62mm Miniguns or a 40mm grenade launcher. Stub wings accommodated a range of rocket and gun armament.

Gunships were used for four main tasks. As troop lift escorts, they attacked any enemy gunners detected en route to the LZ and then cleared the LZ in advance of the drop, remaining to provide fire support if necessary. Convoys and patrol boats were also escorted. In troop support missions, the gunships were on hand to give support fire during the advance and protect medevac helicopters. For reconnaissance, a wide range of equipment was used to provide round-the-clock cover. The Cavalry developed the 'Pink Team' approach, where a light reconnaissance helicopter (initially OH-13s or OH-23s and from 1967 the OH-6A) was supported by an escorting gunship. In the direct fire-support role the gunships were on hand to provide very close air support either in place of or complementing artillery fire.

The USMC helicopters operated in a broadly

A scene for ever associated with the Vietnam War. Troops scramble from a UH-1D in open ground; unusually the helicopter appears to be operating solo, although perhaps it is the last in a stream. As the war progressed and more landing grounds became 'hot', the troop-carrying 'slicks' were accompanied by heavily armed 'hog' gunships. (Bell Textron)

similar way to the Army's, but there was less reliance on gunships, those machines so equipped being capable of easy conversion to other roles. Close air support was provided by fixed-wing types. From 1967 the CH-46 was supplemented by the CH-53A, one unit of which operated with both Air Groups, but the UH-34D continued in service until 1969. The Marines had departed from Vietnam by May 1971, but two helicopter units returned in 1972 in response to the threatened invasion. Six squadrons supported Operation

'Frequent Wind' the final evacuation of Saigon, from USS *Hancock* and Thailand.

The VNAF operated the UH-34A in four squadrons until 1970, when the process of Vietnamization began in earnest. As the US Army wound down its operations, helicopters were transferred to the VNAF, which eventually had 21 UH-1H squadrons and four equipped with the CH-47. Serviceabilty was a considerable problem, and the peak operational strength was no more than half the notional level. Two other air arms

---

TABLE OF UNITS: THE VIETNAM WAR — ARMY AND MARINE CORPS HELICOPTER OPERATIONS (continued)

US Army

In August 1964 there were seven UH-1B companies operating within 145 Av. Bn., as follows: 68 (Tan Son Nhut), 114 (Vinh Long), 117 (Qhi Nhon), 118 (Bien Hoa, Vinh Long), 119 (Pleiku), 120 (Tan Son Nhut) and 121 (Soc Trang), plus A Flt., 19 Av. Co., with CH-37Bs, helicopters attached to 339 and 611 Trans. Co. To these were added A Co., 501 Av. Bn. (Bien Hoa, from 14/12/64) and A Co., 502 Av. Bn. (Vinh Long, from 14/12/64). By the end of 1964 the Aviation Companies were organized within three battalions, as follows: 52 Av. Bn. (I and II Corps), Pleiku (117, 119); 145 Av. Bn. (III Corps), Tan Son Nhut (68, 118, 120, A/501); and 13 Av. Bn. (IV Corps), Can Tho (114, 121, A/502). From January 1965 until the formation of 1 Aviation Brigade (23 May 1966), the following Aviation Companies were established:

Company	Aircraft	Base	From
197	UH-1B	Bien Hoa (ex 68 Av. Co.)	01/03/65
335	UH-1B/D	Bien Hoa, Kontum (ex A Co., 82 Av. Bn.)	00/04/65
336	UH-1B/D	Soc Trang (ex A Co., 101 Av. Bn.)	00/05/65
48	UH-1B/D	Cam Ranh Bay, Phan Rang, Ninh Hoa	06/11/65
162	UH-1B/D	Phuoc Vinh, Dong Tam	07/03/66
478	CH-54A	Da Nang	15/09/65 (replaced CH-37B of 19 Av. Co.)
116	UH-1B/D	Vung Tau, Bien Hoa, Phu Loi, Cu Chi	20/10/65
128	UH-1B/D	Phu Loi	20/10/65
129	UH-1B/D	Dong Ba Thin, An Son	21/10/65
147	CH-47A	Vung Tau	28/11/65
155	UH-1B/D	Ban Me Thuot	07/10/65
161	UH-1B/D	Chu Lai, Qui Nhon	23/12/65
170	UH-1C/D	Qhi Nhon, Pleiku	23/12/65
173	UH-1C/D	Vung Tau, Lai Khe	10/03/66
174	UH-1C/D	Phu Loi, Duc Pho	07/04/66

The UH-1 Companies also operated the OH-13E/S or OH-23G in the reconnaissance role. From the spring of 1965 the following formations operated the UH-1B/C/D/H or AH-1G and OH-13 or OH-6A:

Formation	Unit(s)	Base	Dates
173 Airborne Bde.	A Co., 82 Av. Bn.	Bien Hoa	From 00/05/65
1 Inf. Div.	A/B Cos., 1 Av. Bn., 162/173 Av. Cos.	Ban Me Thuot, Phu Loi	16/10/65 to 15/04/70
25 Inf. Div.	A/B Co., 25 Av. Bn.	Cu Chi	30/04/66 to 07/12/70
4 Inf. Div.	A/B Cos., 4 Av. Bn.	Pleiku	25/04/66 to 01/12/70
9 Inf. Div.	A/B Cos., 9 Av. Bn.		30/01/67 to 23/08/69
23 Inf. Div.	14 Av. Bn.; A Co., 123 Av. Bn.	Chu Lai	00/10/67 to 07/11/71

Some infantry units also had cavalry troops attached.

The Cavalry Troops were attached to a range of formations. Initially they flew the UH-1C and D models, and later the UH-1H and AH-1G. For armed reconnaissance, the OH-13S, and later the OH-6A, were operated. Troops known to have operated are as follows:

Troop(s)	Sqn.	Regt.	Attachments	Dates
D	1	4	1 Inf. Div.	00/04/65 to 05/02/70
A/B/C/D/E	1	9	11 Av. Gp., 1 Cav. Div.	15/09/65 to 28/06/71
D	1	10	4 Inf. Div.	04/10/66 to 08/11/71
Air	–	11	11 Arm. Cav., 25 Inf.	08/09/66 to 05/03/71
D	3	4	Div.	00/11/66 to 08/12/70
D	3	5	25 Inf. Div.	02/02/67 to 08/11/71
D	1	1	91 Inf. Div., 101 Air. Div.	00/08/67 to 10/05/72
F	–	8	23 Inf. Div., 101 Air. Div.	00/10/67 to 26/02/73
A/B/C	3	17	23 Inf. Div., 196 Inf. Bde.	30/10/67 to 30/04/72
A/B/C	7	17	12 Av. Gp., 1 Air Bde.	28/10/67 to 18/04/72
A/B/C/D	2	17	17 Av. Gp., 1 Air Bde.	12/12/67 to 08/02/72
A/B/C	7	1	160 Av. Gp., 101 Air Div.	00/02/68 to 07/04/72
C	–	16	164 Av. Gp., 1 Air Bde.	20/03/70 to 26/02/73
F	3	4 (ex D 3/4)	164 Av. Gp., 1 Air Bde.	08/12/70 to 00/04/72
H	–	10 (ex C 7/17)	12 Av. Gp., 1 Air Bde. 17 Av. Gp., 1 Air Bde.	30/04/72 to 26/02/73

1 Cavalry Division (Airmobile) (ex 11 Air Assault Division (Test)), An Khe, October 1965 to 14 March 1973, comprised three brigades, each with two UH-1Bs and six OH-13Es; 1 Sqn., 9 Cav Regt., with UH-1B/Ds and OH-13Es; and 2 Battalion, 20 Artillery (Aerial Rocket), with UH-1Bs and OH-13Es. 11 Aviation Group comprised 227 Av. Bn., A–C Cos. with UH-1Ds and OH-13Es and D Co. with UH-1Bs; 229 Av. Bn., A–C Cos. with UH-1Ds and OH-13Es and D Co. with UH-1Bs; 228 Av. Bn., A–C Cos. with CH-47As and OH-13Es and 53 Av. Det. with ACH-47As; and 11 Av. Co., with OV-1Bs, UH-1Ds and OH-13Es. Support Command comprised 17 Av. Co., with C-7As; 478 Av. Co., with CH-54s; 15 Med. Bn., with UH-1Ds; 15 Maint. Bn., with UH-1Ds and OH-13Es; and 17 Maint. Bn., with UH-1Ds and OH-13Es.

1 Aviation Division (which handled Aviation Companies from 23 May 1966 to 28 March 1973, based Tan Son Nhut then Long Binh) included the following Groups: 12 (11, 145, 165, 210, 214, 222, 269 and 308 Av. Bns.), III Corps area; 16 (14, 212 Av. Bns.), I Corps area; 17 (10, 52, 223, 268 Av. Bns.), II Corps area; and 164 (13, 307 Av. Bns.), IV Corps area.

flew helicopters in Vietnam. The Korean Capital Division's Aviation Section operated the UH-1D, while the RAAF's 9 Sqn., with the UH-1D and H, flew out of Vung Tau. The Australians also provided crews for 135 AHC also at Vung Tau.

The US Army maintained the traditions of the Korean War with its widespread use of the helicopter for casevac work. Recovery of the injured was critical both for practical reasons and to keep morale high, and from the original 57 Medical Detachment (Helicopter Ambulance) with detachments in each Corps zone the service expanded to at least twelve units, all operating the UH-1D or UH-1H. The casevac helicopters were invariably referred to as 'Dust-Offs', after the call-sign of the commanding officer of the 57th.

Despite carrying red crosses, the helicopters were key targets for the communists and the work was highly dangerous, and from an early date various weapons were carried for protection. More than 900,000 men were evacuated by

TABLE OF UNITS: THE VIETNAM WAR — ARMY AND MARINE CORPS HELICOPTER OPERATIONS (continued)

At various times the following Aviation Companies served with Battalions as indicated (unless otherwise noted, equipment comprised the UH-1):

Company	Base	Battalion	Dates	Remarks
17	Bien Hoa, Bao Loc, Long Binh	214	25/09/67 to 01/07/68	
48	Cam Ranh Bay, Phan Rang, Ninh Hoa	10	06/11/65 to 00/00/70	
	Tuy Hoa	268	00/00/68 to 23/08/72	
57	Kontum	52	08/02/67 to 13/03/73	Ex 236 Av. Co.
60	Pleiku	17	31/08/71 to 13/03/73	
61	An Son	10	From 21/11/67	
	Bong Son	268	28/02/68 to 20/03/72	
68	Vung Tau, Bien Hoa	145	28/11/65 to 01/04/71	To 221 HS, VNAF
71	Cu Chi, Bien Hoa, Chu Lai	14	02/09/66 to 01/10/71	Ex A Co., 501 Av. Bn.
92	Dong Ba Thin	10	08/02/67 to 01/01/72	
114	Vinh Long	13, 214	01/01/65 to 29/02/72	
116	Phu Loi, Chu Lai, Cu Chi	269	20/10/65 to 26/12/71	
117	Dong Ba Thin	10	From 00/12/65	
	Bien Hoa	145, 214, 222, 308	31/12/65 to 26/03/72	
118	Bien Hoa	145	00/00/65 to 31/08/71	To 231 HS, VNAF
119	Pleiku	52	00/00/65 to 14/12/70	
120	Tan Son Nhut	145, 210	From 01/01/65	
	Bien Hoa	165	00/00/69 to 00/10/72	
121	Soc Trang	13	00/00/67 to 10/12/70	To 225 HS, VNAF
128	Phu Loi	145, 11	20/10/65 to 30/01/72	
129	Dong Ba Thin	10	From 21/10/65	
	An Son	268	00/00/67 to 08/03/73	
132	An Khe	14	00/08/65 to 25/04/66	CH-47A/C
	Chu Lai	14	23/05/68 to 08/11/71	
134	Phu Hiep	268	22/11/67 to 29/12/71	
135	Vung Tau	145	From 03/10/67	
	Bear Cat	222, 214	From 00/10/68	
	Di An	11	00/00/71 to 14/02/72	
147	Vung Tau	222	28/11/65 to 17/03/72	CH-47A/C
155	Ban Me Thuot	52, 10	27/10/65 to 15/03/71	Ex A Co., 1 Av. Bn., 1 Inf. Div.
161	Qui Nhon	52, 14	23/12/65 to 08/12/67	
162	Phuoc Vinh	11	From 01/09/65	
	Dong Tam	214	From 1969	
	Can Tho	13	00/00/69 to 03/04/72	
163	Gia Le	10	00/01/71 to 18/01/72	CH-47A/C
170	Qui Nhon	10	From 22/12/65	
	Pleiku	52	00/00/67 to 30/04/71	To 235 HS, VNAF
173	Vung Tau, Lai Khe	11	10/03/66 to 31/03/72	
174	Phu Tai, Ninh Hoa, Duc Pho	52, 14	07/04/66 to 08/11/71	
175	Vinh Long	14, 13, 214	10/11/66 to 20/02/72	
176	Phu Hiep, Marble Mountain	14	20/02/67 to 10/11/71	
178	Chu Lai	14	06/03/66 to 05/03/72	CH-47A/B/C
179	Pleiku	52	25/06/66 to 23/08/71	CH-47A/C
180	Phu Hiep	268	10/11/66 to 29/03/73	CH-47A/C
187	Tay Ninh	269, 11	15/03/67 to 14/02/72	
188	Bien Hoa	269	04/05/67 to 01/07/68	
189	Pleiku	52	07/05/67 to 15/03/71	To 229 HS, VNAF
190	Bien Hoa	145	12/08/67 to 10/12/70	To 223 HS, VNAF
191	Bear Cat, Dong Tam, Can Tho	214	24/05/67 to 01/10/71	
192	Phu Hiep	268	From 30/10/67	
	Phan Thiet, Phan Rang	10	00/00/68 to 20/01/71	
195	Long Binh	214, 222	21/11/67 to 14/12/70	
196	An Son	10, 223, 268	21/01/67 to 23/12/70	CH-47A/C
197	Bien Hoa	145	01/03/65 to 01/09/66	To 334 Av. Co.
200	Bear Cat	214, 308	15/03/67 to 01/07/68	CH-47A/C
201	Tan Son Nhut, Nha Trang	17 Av. Gp.	26/10/67 to 13/03/73	Ex 58 Av. Det.
203	Da Nang	212	31/08/71 to 30/04/72	CH-47C
205	Phu Loi	222	30/05/67 to 15/04/71	CH-47A/C
213	Phu Loi	11	13/01/67 to 31/03/72	CH-47C
235	Can Tho	307	16/10/67 to 31/08/71	
236	Kontum	52	18/11/66 to 23/10/67	To 57 Av. Co.
238	An Khe, Tuy Hoa	268	20/03/69 to 23/12/71	
240	Bear Cat	214, 222	24/05/67 to 26/12/71	

Company	Base	Battalion	Dates	Remarks
242	Cu Chi	269	12/08/67 to 01/10/71	CH-47C
243	Dong Ba Thin	10	30/10/67 to 24/09/71	CH-47C
244	Bear Cat	52	31/08/71 to 26/12/71	
271	Can Tho	13	26/02/68 to 26/09/71	CH-47C
272	Cu Chi	269, 308	21/05/68 to 01/07/68	CH-47C
273	Long Binh	222	22/12/67 to 29/02/72	CH-54A
281	Nha Trang	10	09/06/66 to 10/12/70	
282	Da Nang	14	From 10/06/66	
	Marble Mountain	223, 212	25/03/67 to 31/01/72	To 233 HS, VNAF
334	Bien Hoa	145	10/11/66 to 01/03/72	Ex 197 Av. Co.
	Bien Hoa, Kontum	145	From 00/04/65	
335	Phu Hiep	214	From 00/08/67	
	Bear Cat. Vinh Long	214	00/00/69 to 18/11/71	
336	Soc Trang	13	00/05/65 to 15/03/71	To 227 HS, VNAF
355	Phu Hiep	52	18/01/68 to 28/12/70	CH-54A
361	Cu Chi, Di An	269	From 06/04/68	
	Pleiku	52	23/05/68 to 20/08/72	
362	Bien Hoa	229	30/06/71 to 20/08/72	CH-47C
478	Gia Le	11, 164, 223. 12	15/09/65 to 12/10/72	CH-54A

The 101st Airborne Division (Airmobile), at Camp Evans from December 1967, comprised three brigades each with UH-1s and OH-6As; 2 Sqn., 17 Cav. Regt. with UH-1Ds. AH-1Gs and OH-6As; and 4 Bn., 77 Artillery Regt. (Aerial Rocket), with UH-1Bs. AH-1Gs, OH-13Ss and OH-6As. The 160th Aviation Group (later 101 Aviation Group) comprised 101 Av. Bn. A–C Cos.. 158 Av. Bn. A–C Cos. and 159 Av. Bn. A–C Cos.. all with UH-1C/Ds, AH-1Gs and OH-6As, plus 158 Av. Co. with CH-47Bs.

UH-1 Av. Cos. operated the UH-1B/C in the gunship role and the UH-1D as a troopship; these types were replaced from 1968 with the AH-1G and UH-1H respectively. In the observation/reconnaissance role, these units operated the OH-13E (later OH-13S) or OH-23G, which began to be replaced by the OH-6A from 1967 and, to a limited extent, by the OH-58A from 1969.

The Medical Detachments (Helicopter Ambulance) started with 57 MD, which formed in May 1962. The type used was the UH-1A, then the UH-1D and H models. Units known to have operated are 57 MD (Nha Trang and Qui Nhon, 02/05/62 to 11/03/73); 82 MD (Soc Trang, from 11/11/64); 254 MD (Nha Trang, from 1965); 283 MD (from 1965); 498 MCo. (Qui Nhon, Nha Trang, from 1965); 159 MD (Cu Chi, from 1967); 54 MD (Chu Lai, from 1967); 571 MD (Nha Trang, from 1967); 50 MD (Phu Hiep, from 1967); 45 MD (from 00/07/67); 237 MD (from 1968); and 68 MD (from 1968).

Miscellaneous units that operated the UH-1, OH-6A or OH-58A included 1 Signals Brigade; 16 Signals Co.. 58 Av. Det.: 20 Engineer Brigade: 15 Maintenance Battalion; 17 Maintenance Battalion; and 82 Av. Det. (82 Airborne Div.).

Unit	Aircraft (code)	Base	Dates
USMC, 1964–1971			
Shufly			
HMM-162	UH-34D (YS)	Da Nang	17/06/64 to 07/10/64
HMM-365	UH-34D (YM)	Da Nang	08/10/64 to 31/12/64
HMM-163	UH-34D (YP)	Da Nang	01/01/65 to 00/03/65
MAG-16			
VMO-2	UH-1E (UV, VS)	Marble Mountain	00/05/65 to 00/00/71
HMM-161	UH-34D (YR)	Phu Bai	00/04/65 to 00/00/65
HMM-263	UH-34D (EG)	Da Nang	00/04/65 to 00/00/67
HMM-361	UH-34D (YN)	Da Nang	00/04/65 to 00/00/66
HMM-461	CH-37C (CJ)	Marble Mountain	00/06/65 to 00/00/67
HMM-163	UH-34D (YP)	Phu Bai	00/00/66 to 00/00/67
HMM-164	CH-46D (YT)	Marble Mountain	08/03/66 to 00/00/68
HMM-265	CH-46D (EP)	Marble Mountain	22/06/66 to 00/00/68
HMM-463	CH-53A (YH)	Marble Mountain	08/01/67 to 26/05/71
HMM-363	UH-34D (YZ)	Chu Lai	00/00/67 to 00/00/68 (ex MAG-36)
HMM-263	CH-46D (EG)	Marble Mountain	00/00/68 to 26/05/71
HMM-161	CH-46D (YR)	Phu Bai	00/00/68 to 26/05/71
HML-267	UH-1E (VS, UV)	Da Nang	00/00/68 to 00/00/70 (ex VMO-5)
HMM-361	CH-46D (YN)	Da Nang	00/00/69 to 26/05/71
HMM-364	CH-46D	Da Nang	00/00/69 to 26/05/71 (ex MAG-36)
HML-367	UH-1E, AH-1J (VT)	Da Nang	00/00/69 to 26/05/71
HML-167	UH-1E (TV)	Da Nang	00/00/70 to 26/05/71
MAG-36			
H&MS-36	CH-46D, CH-53D (WX)	Futema	?
VMO-6	UH-1E (WB)	Ky Ha	00/00/65 to 00/11/69
HMM-362	UH-34D (YL)	Chu Lai, Phu Bai	00/00/65 to 00/06/66
HMM-363	UH-34D (YZ)	Qui Nhon	00/00/65 to 00/00/67 (to MAG-16)
HMM-165	CH-46D, CH-53D, UH-1E (YW)	Ky Ha, Chu Lai	00/10/66 to 00/00/68
HMM-262	CH-46D (ET)	Ky Ha, Chu Lai	00/10/66 to 00/06/67
HMM-362	UH-34D (YL)	Phu Bai	00/00/67 to 18/08/69
HMM-364	UH-34D. CH-46D	Phu Bai	00/00/67 to 00/00/69 (to MAG-16)
HMM-367	UH-1E, AH-1J (VT)	Phu Bai	00/12/67 to 00/00/69
HMM-262	CH-46D (ET)	Phu Bai	00/01/68 to 00/00/69
USMC, 1972			
HMM-165	CH-46D (YW)	Da Nang	
HMM-463	CH-53A (YH)	Da Nang	
RAAF			
9 Sqn.	UH-1D/H	Vung Tau	12/06/66 to 08/12/71
Korean Army			
Capital Division Aviation Section	UH-1D/H		

helicopter by March 1973, just under half of whom were Americans. Of 1,400 pilots flying these missions, nearly 90 were killed and 400 injured. During the Vietnam War more than 10,000 helicopters were committed, and of these the Army lost 2,249. At its peak strength in July 1969, 1 Aviation Brigade employed 3,589 helicopters comprising 2,202 UH-1s, 441 AH-1Gs, 635 OH-6As and 311 CH-47s.

AIRCRAFT MARKINGS

VNAF

CH-34A *Olive Drab overall, yellow serial on fuselage: (5)40891/JE (213 HS).*
UH-1B *Olive Drab overall, white serial on boom: (6202)059 (211 HS).*
UH-1H *Olive Drab overall, white serial on fin: (69)15618 (215 HS).*

US Army

Unless otherwise stated Army helicopters were finished Olive Drab overall.
UH-1A *Gloss finish, yellow band around boom: (5)91679/2 (UTTCO).*
UH-1B *Gloss finish, yellow band around boom: (6)21878 (UTTCO). Medium green/black/Olive Drab: (64)13914 (A Co., 1 Av. Bn.); (6)38630 (120 AHC).*
UH-1C *659549 (118 AHC); (65)15045/32 'Lucky Leita' (175 AHC).*
UH-1D *6413806 (498 Med. Co.); (6)51806 (114 AHC).*
UH-1H *(68)15297/92 (92 AHC); (67)17831 (A Co., 25 Av. Bn.).*
AH-1G *Dark green/tan over, white under: (6)615259 (NET); (6515)189 (D Troop, 3 Sqn., 4 Cav.); (66)15399 (334 AHC).*
OH-13S *(64)15420 (1 Cav. Div.)*
OH-6A *Black serial on engine housing: (67)16346 'El Gato' (11 Armored Cav. Regt.); (67)16306 (C Troop, 7 Sqn., 17 Air Cav.).*
OH-58A *Black serial above cockpit: (68)16779 (120 AHC); (68)16801 (20 Eng. Bde.).*
CH-47A *(6)57985 (179 MHC); (6)58004 (180 MHC).*
CH-54A *(68)18418 (355 HHC); (68)18441 (478 HHC).*

USMC

Unless otherwise stated, USMC helicopters were finished medium green overall with black codes and serials.
UH-34D *White serial and codes: (15)7150/41YL (HMM-362).*
CH-46A *152504/169EP (HMM-265); 151960/16YT (HMM-164).*
CH-53A *154873/14YF (HMM-462).*
UH-1E *Yellow band around boom, white serial on boom, code on fin, unit code on door: 151852/185WB6 (VMO-6).*

9.2.7. TRANSPORT AND REFUELLING OPERATIONS

Early US support to the South Vietnamese Government had included a strong transport component in the 'Mule Train' programme, involving three squadrons of C-123s under 315 Troop Carrier Group (TCG); in addition, the US Army had six Aviation Companies of CV-2As (C-7As) based around Vung Tau. The C-7A had the same 3-ton payload as the C-47 but a much better short-field performance. USAF transport units in the region were under the control of 315 Air Division (AD), and throughout the war some units continued to report directly. At the start, 315 AD had four C-130A units, three on Okinawa and one in Japan, plus 22 Troop Carrier Squadron (TCS) equipped with the C-124 in Japan. In the early stages it was these units that bore the brunt of the supply and personnel work from Japan, Okinawa and the Philippines.

Initially, the USAF pressed for the conventional movement of troops by fixed-wing aircraft under its control, but there were few significant operations involving paradrops, the last of these being in September 1966 in Operation 'Thayer' when five battalions of the 101st Airborne Division were dropped in the Cay Giep mountains by C-123. The Army preferred to fly its troops to battle in its own C-7A, which unlike the C-123, could use small strips (of which there were many in Vietnam). By 1966 most troop placements were managed by the Army's helicopter units, and after some wrangling the C-7s were handed over to the USAF at the end of 1966, when they formed six squadrons within 483 Tactical Airlift Wing (TAW) under 834 AD, which had earlier been established to control inter-theatre transport operations.

In April 1966, by which time it comprised five squadrons of C-123Bs, 315 TCG was redesignated 315 Air Commando Wing (ACW). The aircraft were supplemented by the C-123K from May 1967. The K model was fitted with two GE J85 auxiliary turbojets of 2,850lb static thrust to improve short-field performance and increase payload. The C-123 operated in the transport role with the USAF in Vietnam until 1970, after which sufficient aircraft were handed over to the VNAF to form three squadrons. Gradually, the

Organic air support was a key feature of the war in Vietnam, the US Army using vast numbers of fixed-wing aircraft and helicopters. C-7A STOL transports were operated from 1962 to the end of 1966, when they were transferred to the Air Force, but the Army retained its helicopters, both troopships and gunships, throughout. This sharkmouthed AH-1G HueyCobra is from D Troop, 3rd Squadron, 4th Cavalry Regiment, attached to the 25th Infantry Division. The 'Centaurs' were based at Cu Chi. (US Army via R. F. Dorr)

TABLE OF UNITS: THE VIETNAM WAR — TRANSPORT OPERATIONS

Unit	Aircraft (code)	Base	Role	Dates
INTRA-THEATRE UNITS				
VNAF				
413 TS	C-47 (N)	Tan Son Nhut	Transport (33 TW)	01/01/63 to 00/09/67
415 TS	C-47 (E)	Tan Son Nhut	Transport (33 TW)	01/01/63 to 00/00/73
429 TS	C-7A (P)	Phu Cat, Da Nang, Tan Son Nhut	STOL transport (33 TW)	00/07/72 to 00/04/75
431 TS	C-7A (Y)	Phu Cat. Tan Son Nhut	STOL transport (33 TW)	00/08/72 to 00/06/74
413 TS	C-119G (N)		Transport (53 TW)	00/09/67 to 00/00/73
417 TS	C-47 (H)	Tan Son Nhut	Transport (53 TW to 817 AS)	01/01/67 to 00/06/69
419 TS	C-47 (PG)		Transport (53 TW)	00/00/67 to 00/00/70
421 TS	C-123K (Q)			00/05/71 to 00/01/73
423 TS	C-123K (R)	Tan Son Nhut	Short-field transport (53 TW)	00/07/71 to 00/01/73
425 TS	C-123K (X)			00/12/71 to 00/01/73
435 TW	C-130A (HC)	Tan Son Nhut	Transport (53 TW)	00/01/73 to 00/04/75
437 TS	C-130A (GZ)			
427 TS	C-7A	Phu Cat. Da Nang	STOL transport (41 TW)	00/03/72 to 00/06/74
US Army[1]				
1 Av. Co.		Vung Tau		31/12/62 to 31/12/66
61 Av. Co.		Vung Tau		27/06/63 to 31/12/66
92 Av. Co.		Qui Nhon		15/01/64 to 31/12/66
17 Av. Co.	C-7A	An Khe	STOL transport	15/09/65 to 31/12/66
57 Av. Co.		Vung Tau		31/12/65 to 31/12/66
134 Av. Co.		Can Tho		31/12/65 to 31/12/66
135 Av. Co.		Dong Ba Thin		31/12/65 to 31/12/66
USAF[2]				
315 Air Division units reporting directly[3]				
6485 OS	C-118A	Clark AB, Tachikawa	General transport (to 20 OS)	00/00/57 to 00/00/70
21 TCS	C-130A	Naha	Transport (to 374 TAW)	00/01/58 to 00/00/65
817 TCS	C-130A	Naha	Transport (to 374 TAW)	00/02/58 to 00/00/65
815 TCS	C-130A (MA)	Tachikawa	Transport	00/02/58 to 00/00/65
22 TCS	C-124A	Tachikawa	Transport (became 22 MAS)	00/00/62 to 00/00/69
35 TCS	C-130A	Naha	Transport (to 374 TAW)	00/00/63 to 00/00/65
20 OS	C-118A, C-124A, C-9A	Clark AB (405 FW)	General transport (ex 6485 OS)	00/00/70 to 00/00/75
315 TCG, 315 Air Division[4]				
309 TCS	C-123B/K (WH)	Tan Son Nhut, Phan Rang	Short-field transport	00/07/63 to 00/07/70
310 TCS	C-123B/K (WM)	Tan Son Nhut, Phan Rang	Short-field transport	00/07/63 to 00/00/72
311 TCS	C-123B/K (WV)	Da Nang, Phan Rang	Short-field transport	00/07/63 to 00/00/70
12 ACS	UC-123B/K	Bien Hoa	Defoliation (to 12 SOS, 14 SOW)	00/07/64 to 07/03/66
19 TCS	C-123B/K (WE)	Phan Rang	Short-field transport	00/00/66 to 00/00/70
483 TAW, 834 AD (ex US Army)[5]				
457 TAS	C-7A (KA)	Cam Ranh Bay		01/01/67 to 25/03/72
458 TAS	C-7A (KC)	Cam Ranh Bay		01/01/67 to 00/00/71
459 TAS	C-7A (KE)	Phu Cat, Cam Ranh Bay	STOL transport	01/01/67 to 00/06/70
535 TAS	C-7A (KH)	Vung Tau, Cam Ranh Bay		01/01/67 to 00/00/70
536 TAS	C-7A (KL)	Vung Tau, Cam Ranh Bay		01/01/67 to 00/00/71
537 TAS	C-7A (KN)	Phu Cat		01/01/67 to 00/00/71
374 TAW, 315 AD				
21 TAS	C-130A (YD)		Transport	00/00/65 to 00/00/70
35 TAS	C-130A (YJ)	Naha, Tan Son Nhut,	Transport	00/00/65 to 00/00/70
817 TAS	C-130A (YU)	Cam Ranh Bay	Transport	00/00/65 to 00/00/70
41 TAS	C-130A (YP)		Transport (ex 437 MAW)	00/u0/66 to 00/00/70
463 TAW, 315 AD				
772 TAS	C-130B (QF)	Mactan, Cam Ranh Bay		
774 TAS	C-130B (QW)	Mactan	Transport	00/03/66 to 00/03/72
29 TAS	C-130B (QB)	Clark AB, Cam Ranh Bay		
773 TAS	C-130B (QG)	Clark AB		
314 TAW, 315 AD				
50 TAS	C-130E (DE)		Transport (to 374 TAW)	
345 TAS	C-130E (DH)	Ching Chuan Kang AB	Transport (to 374 TAW)	00/03/66 to 00/05/72
776 TAS	C-130E (DL)		Transport (ex 464 TAW, to 374 TAW)	
374 TAW, 315 AD[6]				
21 TAS	C-130E (DY)		Transport	
50 TAS	C-130E (DE)	Ching Chuan Kang AB	Transport (ex 314 TAW)	00/05/72 to 00/00/75
345 TAS	C-130E (DH)		Transport (ex 314 TAW)	
776 TAS	C-130E (DL)		Transport (ex 314 TAW)	
USMC				
H&MS-12	C-117D, OV-10A (WA)	Chu Lai	General transport (MAG-12)	00/00/64 to 00/09/70
H&MS-13	C-117D, TF-9J (YU)	Chu Lai	General transport (MAG-13)	00/09/66 to 00/10/69
H&MS-17	TF-9J, US-2B, C-117D, C-54A (SZ)	Da Nang	General transport (MAW-1)	00/00/67 to 00/00/70
RAAF				
35 Sqn.[7]	Caribou	Vung Tau	STOL transport	08/08/64 to 00/02/72
161 I Flt.	Sioux, Cessna 180	Vung Tau, Ba Ria, Nui Dat	Liaison, recce (Independent Flt.)	00/10/65 to 00/00/71
RTAF				
61 Sqn.	C-47, Avro 748	Don Muang	Transport	00/08/64 to 00/00/75

Unit	Aircraft (code)	Base	Role	Dates
Miscellaneous operators				

Air America (Pilatus Porter, Turbo-Porter, U-1A, U-6A, U-10A, C-46, C-47, C-7A, Beech 18, Volpar Turboliner, C-123, C-130, S-51, UH-1, H-34); Air Vietnam (C-46, C-47, DC-4); and Birdair (C-130B). The International Control Commission (ICCS) used aircraft of Air America and Air Vietnam, including Volpar Turboliners, C-7As and Boeing 307s.

INTER-THEATRE UNITS
USAF/MAC
Aircraft types flown were the C-97G (including 109 MAS and 191 MAS ANG); C-124C (including 62 ATW/62 MAW, 63 TCW/63 MAW, 1501 ATW/60 MAW, 1502 ATW/61 MAW, 1607 ATW/436 MAW and 1608 ATW/437 MAW); C-130E (including 1501 ATW/60 MAW and 1608 ATW/437 MAW); C-133A (including 1607 ATW/436 MAW and 1501 ATW/60 MAW); C-135A (including 1501 ATW/60 MAW and 1611 ATW/438 MAW); C-141A (including 60 MAW, 62 MAW, 63 MAW, 436 MAW and 437 MAW); C-5A (including 437 MAW and 475 MAW); and C-118 and C-9A (375 AMAW, medical evacuation).

RAAF				
36 Sqn.	C-130A	} Richmond	Transport	{ 00/08/64 to 00/02/72
37 Sqn.	C-130E			{ 00/09/66 to 00/02/72
RNZAF				
40 Sqn.	Hastings C.3, C-130H	Whenuapai	} Transport	00/08/64 to 00/00/72
41 Sqn.	Bristol Freighter 31	Changi		

Civilian operators
Among the airlines operating under Government contract into South Vietnam were Alaska Airways, Eraniff, Continental, Pan American and World Airways.

AIR REFUELLING
USAF
The 421st ARS, equipped with the KC-50J and based at Yokota, operated from 1960 until October 1964. From August 1964, the USAF sent more than thirty KC-135A Air Refueling Squadrons to South-East Asia. These TDY units were based at Andersen AFB (3960 SW; 43 SW), Kadena and Clark ABs (4252 SW; 376 SW), Takhli, U-Tapao and Korat (all 4258 SW; 307 SW) and Ching Chuan Kang (4220 ARS, 4252 SW). From June 1972 the holding units were 4101 ARS(P) at Takhli; 4102 ARS(P) at Clark AB and Ching Chuan Kang; 4103 ARS(P) at Don Muang; 4104 ARS(P) at Korat; 72 SW(P) at Andersen AFB; and 310 SW(P) at U-Tapao.

USMC
The Marines flew KC-130Fs with VMGR-152 (QD) at Futema and Da Nang from 1964 to 1965 and with VMGR-352 (QB) at El Toro, Futema and Da Nang from 1966 to 1970.

Notes:
1. Control of the US Army C-7A units was transferred to the USAF on 1 January 1967. In addition to the C-7A, a large number of Army units operated fixed-wing light transport and liaison aircraft. The types involved were U-1s, U-6s, U-8s and U-21s.
2. In addition, the USAF operated the U-3A, U-10B and T-39A on courier and liaison work and the C-140A (1867 FCS) for facilities checking from Tan Son Nhut.
3. With the exception of 22 TCS and the OSs, TCSs became TASs on 1 July 1967. TDY units attached to 315 AD included 38 TAS (316 TAW), 346 TAS (516 TAW) and 779 TAS (464 TAW), all with C-130E.
4. 315 TCG became 315 Air Commando Wing on 1 April 1966 under the control of 834 AD, with TCGs becoming ACSs. By 1972 the remaining ACS, 310, was under the control of 377 Air Base Wing.
5. Aircraft handed over to VNAF from 1971. Wing inactivated on 25 March 1972.
6. TDY units attached to 374 TAW included 35, 61, 346 and 347 TASs.
7. Flight status only to May 1966, then within 315 AD USAF.

bulk of the transport work within Vietnam was handled by C-130 units detached from Wings in Japan, the Philippines or Taiwan. The first new Wing was 374 TAW, equipped with the C-130A and comprising three squadrons previously under direct 315 AD control. They were based at Naha but regularly operated out of Tan Son Nhut and later Cam Ranh Bay. In 1966, 463 TAW was formed in the Philippines with four C-130B squadrons, and these were primarily used for intra-theatre work. The third Wing to be established was 314 TAW at Ching Chuan Kang AB on Taiwan; with its proximity to South Vietnam, and since it flew the more powerful C-130E, the Wing provided detachments for in-country work.

Apart from conventional supply or assault flights, the USAF developed a number of C-130 delivery systems to cope with all situations in Vietnam. The Low-Altitude Parachute Extraction System (LAPES) involved reinforced containers being extracted by large parachute as the aircraft flew slowly a few feet from the ground. In the Ground Proximity Extraction System (GPES), the loads were extracted by hook and cable. In poor weather conditions the Adverse Weather Aerial Delivery System (AWADS) provided for blind drops, while the Container Delivery System (CDS) permitted accurate parachute drops from relatively low level.

A major test of the transport units came in January 1968 with the siege of Khe Sanh. The combat base was completely surrounded by the NVA and encircled by heavy AAA, making any approach to the airstrip hazardous in the extreme; once landed, the aircraft were subject to mortar fire. The available transports were 81 C-7As in six squadrons, 58 C-123s in four squadrons and 72 C-130s from three TDY squadrons. By March the number of C-130s available had increased to 96, and, in addition, the KC-130Fs of USMC VMGR-152 at Da Nang were available. Control of the transport operation was through the AirLift Control Center (ALCC) at Tan Son Nhut and handling was managed by units of the 2nd Aerial Port Group. Although most of the supplies were stored at Da Nang, the C-130 missions originated from Tan Son Nhut (463 TAW TDY squadrons), Cam Ranh Bay (374 and 314 TAW

TDY squadrons) and Tuy Hoa and Nha Trang (314 TAW TDY squadrons).

Many of the supplies landed at Khe Sanh were brought in by C-123K, the aircraft adopting a steep approach from the east to avoid a long taxi run to the off-loading point. The average time from touchdown to take-off was three minutes, but even then several aircraft were lost on the ground or on the approach. To reduce the risk of groundfire, many sorties were preceded by fighter strikes on likely AAA sites, although poor weather often limited the effectiveness of this support. The C-130 drops usually relied on CDS, with each aircraft dropping fourteen to sixteen one-ton loads. In five sorties on 25 and 28 January, 67 tons were delivered in this fashion. The safer but less accurate AWADS was unacceptable in the tightly confined area of Khe Sanh because of dispersal problems: the small size of the drop zone (300yds long) led to radar-controlled approach then instrument-dictated drops. The teamwork necessary required each crew to make one training flight over the airstrip to save precious supplies from reaching the enemy. Poor weather in mid-February saw the first use of the improvised system, and on the 17th and 18th 279 tons were dropped in eighteen sorties, each from an altitude of about 500ft. Although the ground radar was destroyed on the 19th, other ground aids were improved and by the end of the siege some 496 such C-130 sorties had been completed with a circular error average of 110yds. The last flights were made by 1500hrs each day to allow site clearance by nightfall, since the NVA or VC used the cover of night to mine or booby-trap the drop zones.

For large or difficult loads not easily broken down, LAPES was used to deposit them with precision. This was important since ground handling equipment was limited and drops had to be sequentially cleared. The continued use of LAPES did result in considerable damage to the last 700ft of the 3,900ft aluminium matting runway. The equipment used to unfurl the parachute was in extremely short supply, so the GPES was introduced in March. This had the advantage of ensuring that the pallet was under complete control, since the point of extraction was predetermined by the placement of the arrester cable. Supplies off-loaded from landed aircraft were the responsibility of the Marines, while a USAF combat control team handled all parachute drops, including marking, controlling the approach and recovery. Stacked supplies were then airlifted to outposts by USMC helicopters operating out of Quang Tri via Dong Ha.

The Khe Sanh airlift saw more supply drops in two months than in the whole of the war to the end of 1967. Between 21 January and 15 March, 8,120 tons were parachuted into the base in 601 sorties; 4,310 tons and 2,676 passengers were flown in aboard 179 C-123K, 273 C-130 and eight C-7 landings, and 1,574 people were evacuated. Fifteen GPES and 52 LAPES missions were flown. Miraculously, only one C-123 was brought down and two destroyed on the ground and a USMC KC-130F shot down, although many aircraft were seriously damaged. In delivering 4,661 tons of cargo and 14,562 passengers to the outposts around Khe Sanh, several dozen USMC helicopters were destroyed.

From 1970, the process of Vietnamization began, and the last USAF inter-theatre C-130 sortie was flown on 27 December 1970. The VNAF had flown several squadrons of C-47s from the beginning of the war, and in 1967 it acquired a squadron of C-119Gs. In 1971, three squadrons of C-123Ks were formed with ex-USAF aircraft, and the following year three C-7 squadrons were formed from USAF stocks. Finally, in 1973, two C-130A units were formed at Tan Son Nhut, the main VNAF transport base. The USAF C-130 units continued to fly into South Vietnam, however, and in February 1973 into North Vietnam in Operation 'Homecoming'. Between 12 February and 29 March, 591 prisoners-of-war were flown out in C-130Es of the re-formed 374 TAW, now based in Taiwan. During the war various units flew the U-3A, U-10B and T-39A on liaison and courier work, while the C-140A was flown on VIP work and for facilities checking.

The USMC also operated its own transport aircraft, with the Headquarters and Maintenance squadrons (H&MS) and the KC-130Fs of VMGR-152. Although USAF in-country operations ceased in 1970, several 'airlines' continued to fly transports on military missions, including Air America, Air Vietnam and Birdair. The International Control Commission (ICC) leased aircraft from Air America and Air Vietnam. Mention must also be made of the Australian contribution. No. 35 Sqn., with the Caribou (C-7A), operated from Vung Tau in support of Australian ground forces from August 1964 through to 1972, while 161 Independent Flight flew liaison and observation sorties for six years from 1965. C-47s and Avro 748s of 61 Sqn. RTAF also supported operations in Thailand.

The Vietnam War consumed an enormous volume of supplies, mainly flown in from CONUS. In the early stages of the war the bulk of this work was handled by the C-124C, C-133A and C-135A, but as the war progressed the C-130E and C-141A supplanted these types and from 1971 the huge C-5A of 475 MAW played a major part in the air bridge. Throughout the war ANG units supplemented the efforts of the regular airlift wings, mainly operating the C-97. Such was the effort that large numbers of civil contractors were also used, primarily on trooping flights. The C-141A was used extensively to evacuate wounded on return flights, although aircraft of 375 AeroMedical Airlift Wing (AMAW) were also involved. The RNZAF and RAAF also flew inter-

The siege of the combat base at Khe Sanh from January to March 1968 was a glorious episode in the annals of Military Airlift Command. In under two months the base, totally surrounded, was resupplied by air alone: 601 parachute sorties were flown, using a range of techniques, and 460 landings were made, mainly by C-123Ks and C-130s. To minimize the risk of being struck by 'incoming', aircraft were unloaded on the move. Only two aircraft were shot down and two destroyed on the strip. (Lockheed)

theatre supplies missions using the Hastings, Bristol Freighter and C-130H and the C-130A and E respectively.

The final involvement came in April 1975 with the evacuation of US personnel and of South Vietnamese who had overtly supported the Americans. Operation 'Frequent Wind' began on 1 April with the opening of the Evacuation Control Center (ECC) at Tan Son Nhut. Initially, the evacuation was carried out by sea from Saigon and Vung Tau, but gradually C-130E, C-141A and C-5A flights played a greater part, covered by the carriers *Midway, Enterprise, Coral Sea, Hancock* and *Kitty Hawk*. US Navy escort helicopters operated from USS *Okinawa*.

During the evacuation, the F-14A made its combat début, flying from *Enterprise* with VF-1 and -2. Protection and support was also given by Thai-based USAF units. In all, Military Airlift Command (MAC) flew 201 C-141, 174 C-130E and several C-5A sorties in April and, in addition, at least eight flights were made by civilian contractors and many by Air America to Thailand and Taiwan or latterly by UH-1 to the carriers. At first the payloads were restricted to peacetime limits, but from 20 April, as the position became more desperate with the communist encirclement of Saigon, the restrictions were lifted. By now the C-5A was grounded after a crash in which 155 people (mainly Vietnamese orphans) were killed. Passenger loads were by this time remarkable, perhaps none more so than in the case of the VNAF C-130A which carried out no fewer than 452 people, including, it was reported, eighteen in the cockpit. C-141 flights ceased from 27 April, leaving the C-130 to shoulder the burden day and night until the 29th.

From late on the 29th it was left to USAF CH-53s and HH-53s and USMC CH-53s and CH-46s to evacuate the last 7,014 people from the US Embassy and ECC to the carriers waiting off-shore. In the whole operation, over 51,000 were evacuated by air in 19,000 sorties. In the last two days 662 helicopter sorties were flown, and 173 USN and 127 USAF fighter sorties and 85 USAF support sorties were made. Many VNAF aircraft flew to Thailand, while helicopters and two O-1s landed on or near *Midway*.

With the build-up of US air power in South-East Asia, the need for air-to-air refuelling grew rapidly. In 1964 there was just one KB-50 unit at Yokota and several TDY KC-135As at Clark AB. After the KB-50 was grounded from October 1964, many more KC-135As were deployed to a range of new bases, starting with 4252 SW, Clark AB ('Foreign Legion'), in 1964. The KC-135A then went to 4252 SW, Kadena ('Young Tiger'), in January 1965, Don Muang ('Tiger Cub'), in March, 4258 SW, Takhli ('King Cobra'), in September and 4258 SW, U-Tapao ('Giant Cobra'), in August 1966. The aircraft operating from Andersen AFB, Clark AB and Kadena generally supported the B-52 'Arc Light' programme and reconnaissance missions, while those in Thailand also gave support to tactical types based in Thailand or South Vietnam. Twelve colour-coded tracks were flown, with links controlled from the ground control stations; for the tactical missions, it was usual to refuel aircraft twice on the outbound leg and once on their return.

From 1970, the tanker force was reduced, but it increased quickly from 1972 with the impending North Vietnamese invasion. 'Young Tiger' deployments were made to 4101 Air Refueling Squadron (Provisional) (ARS(P)) at Takhli, 4103 ARS(P) at Don Muang, 4104 ARS(P) at Korat, 4102 ARS(P) at Clark AB and Ching Chuan Kang AB, 310 SW(P) at U-Tapao and 72 SW(P) at Andersen AFB. That year saw the peak number of sorties flown. The tankers rarely flew over North

Vietnam and operated at 26,000ft for the B-52 and at 15–20,000ft for the fighters, well above the reach of ground fire. In all, five aircraft were lost in a total of 194,687 sorties, three-fifths of which were in support of tactical units, with 8,969 million pounds of fuel transferred in 813,878 refuellings.

AIRCRAFT MARKINGS

VNAF

C-47 *Dark green/grey-green/light tan over, light grey under, black serial on fin, code in coloured circle on fin: 4348491/EY (415 TS).*
C-123K *C, grey serial and code on fin: 54(00)590/XD (425 TS).*
C-130A *C, yellow serial, white code on fin: 56(00)482/HCK (435 TS).*
U-6A *Olive Drab overall, white serial on fin, code on rear fuselage: (5)37941/B (314 SMS).*

USAF

Transport aircraft were originally finished bare metal (BM) overall, then from August 1965 camouflage (C) was applied. This scheme was dark green/medium green/desert drab over, grey under.

C-123B *BM: (5)40655 (309 TCS).*
C-123K *C, white upper outer wing and tail surfaces, white serial and code on fin: 54593/WE (19 TAS). C: 54579/WV (311 TAS).*
C-130A *C, white serial and code: 56(0)489/YD (21 TAS).*
C-130B *BM: (5)95957 (463 TAW). C, white serial and code on fin: 61(2)643/QB (29 TAS).*
C-130E *BM: (6)21841 (314 TAW).*
C-7A *C, white serial and code on fin: 61(2)391/KE (459 TAS).*
C-118A *White over, silver under, red cheat line: O-(5)33238 (6485 OS).*
C-124C *O-(5)20992 (62 ATW).*
C-133A *BM: (5)62010 (1670 ATW); (5)40135 (436 MAW).*
C-135B *Silver-grey overall, black serial on fin: (6)24127, (6)24130 (438 MAW).*
C-141A *(6)40640. Red cross on fin: (6)50238 (60 MAW).*
C-5A *White fuselage top decking: (6)80212 (437 MAW).*
C-9A *White fuselage top decking: (7)10877 (375 AMAW).*
KB-50J *Bare metal overall, black serial on fin: O-(4)90358 (421 ARS).*
KC-135A *Light grey overall, black serial on fin: (5)71481 'Ark-La-Tex' (? BW); (6)14839 (? BW), (6)23572 (99 ARS).*

US Army

V-7B *Olive Drab overall, white serial and unit badge on fin: (6)39764 (57 Trans. Co.).*

USMC

C-117D *17152/1WW (H&MS-16).*
KC-130F *White over, light grey under, black serial and code on fin, 'last three' on forward fuselage: 148246/QD (VMGR-152).*

RAAF

Caribou *Semi-gloss olive overall, white serial on rear fuselage: A-171 (35 Sqn.).*

Air Vietnam

C-46 *Bare metal overall, white fuselage decking, registration on fin: B-1515 (leased from Air China).*

Air America

C-46 *Bare metal overall, black registration on rear fuselage: N67984.*
Caribou *Bare metal overall, black registration on fin: N544Y. White fuselage decking and fin and rudder, dark blue cheat line: N580PA.*
Turbo-Porter (U-23A) *White overall, dark blue upper fuselage band and fin and rudder, black serial on rear fuselage: N152L.*
Volpar-Beech 18 *Bare metal overall, white top fuselage decking, dark blue cheat line and tail assembly, white registration on rear fuselage: N9157Z, N8154U.*

9.2.8. THE NORTH VIETNAMESE AIR FORCE, 1954–1975

The North Vietnamese inherited from the French valuable airfields at Bac Mai and Gia Lam in Hanoi and Cat Bi in Haiphong, together with numerous strips, but no aircraft. Early equipment supplied by the Soviet Union and China included An-2, An-12 and Li-2 transports, plus Yak-11 trainers, the transports being used from 1960 to supply the Pathet Lao, some being flown by Russian crews. Shortly after the formal entry of the United States into the war in 1964, China supplied 36 MiG-15 and MiG-17 fighters which were based at Phuc Yen while air crews were

Two NVAF MiG-17s on Phuc Yen airfield in 1966. The MiG-17 was in action throughout the war and for two years operated without fear of counterstrike since airfields were barred as targets for US attack. Airfields were released as targets in October 1967, except for Gia Lam International, where civil aircraft were operated. (USAF)

hurriedly trained in the Soviet Union; at the same time, work on an air defence system began.

The Vietnam People's Air Force (VPAF) went into action on 3 April 1965, bringing down an F-8E, but thereafter losing aircraft in combat. Because of the risk of killing Soviet or Chinese instructors, the MiG bases were not bombed by the Americans, and in August the VPAF effectively stood down to retrain after its initial losses. Bases were developed at Phuc Yen, Hoa Lac, Kien An and Kep in addition to those already mentioned. Eight Il-28 bombers were supplied and based at Gia Lam but apparently never used. The MiG-21 entered North Vietnamese service in April 1966, but the first of six to be destroyed that year was brought down by an F-4C of 480 TFS. In January 1967 nine were brought down in three days over Phuc Yen in Operation 'Bold' (described elsewhere) and the VPAF was obliged to take stock: losing 75 MiGs of all types during 1967, the VPAF was only able to maintain its strength at about 30 MiG-15/MiG-17s and fifteen MiG-21s. It was reported that at this time North Korean pilots were flying airfield combat air patrol (CAP) sorties.

During the long bombing halt from 1968 the Air Force was rebuilt, and in addition to acquiring many more MiG-21s, including the PF version, about 25 F-6s (Chinese built MiG-19s) were supplied; the MiG-17 inventory was built up to about 80 aircraft. As US bombing was resumed in April 1972, losses mounted yet again, and by October over 60 aircraft had been brought down, although to some extent this attrition was made good by Chinese supplies. The last VPAF fighter loss in combat was a MiG-17, shot down on 12 January 1973.

After the ceasefire the Air Forces again consolidated and airfields in southern North Vietnam,

TABLE OF UNITS: THE NORTH VIETNAMESE AIR FORCE, 1964–1972			
Aircraft	Base	Role	Nos.
December 1964			
MiG-15, MiG-17	Gia Lam	Air defence	36
An-2, An-12, Li-2	Gia Lam, Cat Bi, Bac Mai	Transport	20
July 1966			
MiG-21	Phuc Yen	Air defence	15
MiG-15, MiG-17	Gia Lam, Hoa Lac	Air defence	50
Il-28	Phuc Yen	Light bombing	8
An-2, An-12, An-14, Li-2	Gia Lam, Cat Bi, Bac Mai	Transport	30
April 1972			
MiG-21F/PF	Phuc Yen, Kep	Air defence	90
MiG-19 (F-6)	Phuc Yen, Kien An	Air defence, ground attack	25
MiG-17, MiG-15	Gia Lam, Phuc Yen	Air defence	90
An-2, An-14, Li-2, An-24	Gia Lam, Cat Bi, Bac Mai	Transport	36
Mi-4, Mi-6	Various	Transport, liaison	24

notably at Ban Loi, Khe Phat and Dong Hoi, were reconstructed in anticipation of the 1975 offensive. In the event, there are no recorded MiG ground-attack sorties in support of the NVA, but on 28 April three captured A-37Bs of 532 FS VNAF were flown by North Vietnamese pilots in a strike on Tan Son Nhut airfield. From 1964 to 1973 the US lost 79 aircraft to MiG fighters while the VPAF lost 169 aircraft shot down.

AIRCRAFT MARKINGS

VPAF

MiG-17 Bare metal overall, black serial on nose: 102, 2533. Camouflaged brown/tan/green/grey-green mottle overall, red serial on nose: 2019. Grey-green/light brown mottle over, light grey under, red serial on nose: 3020.

MiG-21 Bare metal overall, black serial on nose: 4227, 4229, 4320, 5005, 5006, 5031, 5066, 5073.

F-5B Dark green/green/tan over, light grey under, grey serial on nose: 3502.

9.3. Laos, 1954–1975

The Geneva Accords of 1954 left Laos neutral in principle but with three factions ready to seek power through civil war. In the north, the Pathet Lao (Lao State) movement, headed by Prince Souphanouvong, was supported by the Viet Minh; from the capital, Vientiane, Prince Souvanna Phouma headed the Royalist-Neutralist Government; and there were, in addition, latent anti-communist forces headed by the military establishment. The Pathet Lao strengthened their grip from 1954 to November 1957 when a coalition government was established. At this stage the Laotian Army Aviation Service (LAAS) had received some help from the USA and comprised some twenty L-19s, ten C-47s, three L-20s and four Aero Commanders, as well as a handful of MS.500s from France. The coalition lasted to July 1958, when there was a right-wing coup through

which General Phoumi Nosavan emerged as head of state.

In 1959 heavy fighting broke out in the north and Government troops were flown up to Sam Neua to combat the Pathet Lao, and the CIA, who backed Nosavan, began covert operations in support of Meo (Hmong) tribesmen loyal to the anti-communists. A Military Assistance Advisory Group (MAAG) was established by the US, and a total of ten T-6s converted for light attack were supplied and pilots trained in Thailand; two were soon lost on operations. In August 1960 the Royalist-Neutralist Government was restored after a coup led by Capt. Kong Le, but when Nosavan regained power in December, Kong Le went north to link with the Pathet Lao. Now the US supported the Government by committing limited air assets, and the first reconnaissance flights were undertaken using the Air Attache's VC-47A, which flew two sorties on 21 and 27 December. These brought back evidence of Soviet Il-14 transports dropping supplies to the Pathet Lao. The SC-47 was damaged on its second sortie and was replaced from 11 January 1962 by an SC-47D which flew 38 sorties until it was shot down on 24 March. This was in turn replaced by an RT-33A, based at Udorn under Project 'Field Goal', which flew 33 sorties from 24 April until the ceasefire of 10 May. When the ceasefire was broken in October, the reconnaissance sorties were resumed, but as the situation worsened the USAF transferred four RF-101Cs of 45 TRS to Don Muang on 7 November in Project 'Able Mabel'. As a precautionary measure, the USAF deployed 510 TFS with the F-100D to Don Muang in December 1960 in Project 'Bell Tone'; this unit was replaced by 509 FIS with the F-102A in April 1961, and it remained until early 1964. As the war developed so did the CIA's involvement, and to aid the movement of Government forces, sixteen USMC HUS-1 (H-34) helicopters were flown in March 1961 to Udorn for transfer to the CIA properietary Air America. At the same time USAF C-130s and C-124s began delivering arms via Bangkok.

By now the LAAS had become the Royal Lao Air Force (RLAF), and early in 1962 the Soviet Union delivered nine Li-2s to aid Pathet Lao supplies while the US began its 'White Star' Special Forces Training Team programme. Early in 1962 the Pathet Lao began an all-out offensive towards Vientiane, and the South-East Asia Treaty Organization (SEATO) set up Joint Task Force (JTF) 116 in Thailand in May, ostensibly to protect Thailand against North Vietnamese or Pathet Lao incursion. Two USAF F-100D squadrons went to Takhli, while the USMC contributed HMM-261, equipped with the UH-34D, and VMA-332, with the A-4A, to support a 5,000-strong Marine contingent. The Commonwealth provided support in the form of 20 Sqn. RAF with the Hunter FGA.9 and 79 Sqn. RAAF with the Sabre 32.

Tactical transport was available, including 36 Sqn. RAAF and 41 Sqn. RNZAF, and from June a detachment from 777 TCS USAF with C-123B moved to Don Muang. After talks in Geneva aimed at finding a lasting settlement, the Royalist-Neutralist Government again assumed power as the Soviet Union and United States agreed to withdraw their support for the Pathet Lao and anti-communist forces respectively. Laos was now recognized as a neutral state, and the formal postion of the US State Department was one of total backing for the new government. However, as the North Vietnamese continued to back the Pathet Lao, the CIA decided to continue its covert and illegal support of the generals. From 1960 the CIA had established a large number of landing strips ('Lima Sites') to support their

secret war; in due course the number of such landing strips exceeded 200.

The MAAG was withdrawn in October 1962 and JTF 116 was deactivated in December. The RAF was involved in a second deployment to Thailand in June 1963 when Hunters of 20 Sqn. were again detached to Chieng Mai. The CIA and Air America continued operations out of Vientiane with a main base at Udorn, while the USAF maintained a close watch on northern Laos. In the 'Class A' programme, CIA pilots flew T-28 missions out of Udorn. On 16 March 1964 the Pathet Lao launched a sweeping attack across the Plain des Jarres, and three days later, at the invitation of Souvanna Phouma, the United States began its 'Yankee Team' armed reconnaissance sorties using USAF RF-101Cs and USN RF-8As and RA-3Bs. At the same time, the US initiated the 'Water Pump' programme, whereby T-28D coin aircraft were supplied to the RLAF and pilots trained by Detachment 6, 1 ACW, at Udorn. The T-28 force eventually numbered about 50, but since there were rarely enough trained Lao pilots, the aircraft were often flown by Air America or Thai personnel.

The first T-28D attack sortie was on 17 May against Pathet Lao positions. By now Air America was running a major operation, with many aircraft, including Helio Couriers, Beavers, Otters, C-123Bs, C-46s, O-1s and the remnants of the original H-34s which were used to move troops and provide a search and rescue (SAR) service for air crews. The Air America SAR capability was used for the first time by the military when an RF-8A of VFP-63 was shot down over Laos on 6 June 1964. The pilot was not recovered, but the pilot of an escort F-8D brought down the following day was rescued. The US attempted to suppress information about the controversial armed reconnaissance sorties.

The Air America H-34 fleet was now down to four helicopters, and the US Marine Corps was directed to transfer four more. In July a Control and Reporting Post and Air Operations Center was set up at Udorn to support Laotian operations, and in retaliation for the F-8 losses the USAF launched an attack on an AAA site at Xieng Khouang. Covert operations continued through the year, and RLAF T-28 main bases were established at Pakse, Luang Prabang and Savannakhet.

By the end of 1964, when it became obvious that the NVA was using routes through Laos to supply forces in South Vietnam, the US began its 'Barrel Roll' programme of 'armed reconnaissance' sorties over Laos, although in fact the programme provided cover for a range of strike sorties in support of Laotian Government forces against the Pathet Lao. To be effective, however, the strikes needed locally based FAC, and these were recruited from the USAF via the CIA. Initially working to the 'Butterfly' call-sign, as demand increased the pilots were recruited under the 'Steve Canyon' programme to fly highly dangerous O-1 and sometimes T-28 sorties in unmarked aircraft. So sensitive was the programme that the pilots were removed from the Air Force lists and bought their aircraft from USAF stocks at $1 apiece. Adopting the call-sign 'Raven', they were accountable to the Air Attaché in Vientiane. From 3 April 1965 the 'Steel Tiger' programme provided for strikes against infiltration routes in southern Laos, and within that 'Tiger Hound' sorties were conducted south of the 17th parallel under FAC guidance.

By 1966 the US was covertly supporting a major war in Laos through a range of devices. Air America and Continental Air Services provided a wide range of logistic support and search and rescue, while the Ravens provided local FAC from various secret locations. Air America and CAS used several 'sanitized' C-130 Hercules with all identification obliterated; these are likely to have included C-130B 612641 and C-130E 640506 and '507. The 56th Special Operations Wing (SOW) at Nakhon Phanom provided support and training, and in due course 40 ARRS supplemented the Air America rescue effort.

Strike aircraft in Thailand and South Vietnam were available on demand, ostensibly through 'Barrel Roll' and 'Steel Tiger' sorties, to attack any target offered by FAC, and by 1966 they were flying 1,000 offensive missions a month over Laos. There are also reports, unconfirmed, of 90 SOW comprising 20 SOS, 318 SOS, a C-123B squadron manned by foreign nationals and 219 HS VNAF, operating in support of the war; certainly the helicopters of 20 SOS and later 21 SOS played a part in the Laotian war. Last, there was the RLAF, which was stiffened informally with US air crews. The RLAF was still primarily equipped with the T-28, but a significant proportion of its strength was lost when twelve T-28s were blown up by the Pathet Lao at Luang Prabang on 16 July 1966.

Inevitably, the covert air units became involved in the vast opium trade in the area. In the 1950s, Air Lao Commerciale was one 'airline' operating purely in support of the drug trade, but the operation was closed down before the war. The Hmong general, Vang Pao, who was sponsored by the CIA with an extensive secret base at Long Tieng, was given assistance in setting up a local air operation, Xieng Khouang Air Transport, primarily for the purpose of shifting raw opium. Two C-47s came from Air America and CAS. In 1967 RLAF T-28s attacked an opium caravan on the Mekong, not on the part of Government but to capture the consignment for the personal benefit of warlord generals. On many occasions Air America flights were used by Lao officers moving opium around the country.

On 10 March 1968 the North Vietnamese Army managed to capture an important USAF radar and tacan beacon on Phou Pha Thi mountain in northern Laos, just 160 miles from Hanoi. The site had been established in 1966 and improved in 1967 in the 'Pony Express' programme, with equipment placed by 20 SOS CH-3Cs. On 12 January 1968 it had been attacked by three NVAF An-2s dropping mortar shells and firing machine-guns. Air America UH-1s were on the scene, and one An-2 was brought down by light machine-gun fire while the others crashed later. After those civilian and USAF technicians not killed or captured were rescued by Air America, the site was bombed heavily to deny the equipment to the communists. With this loss the CIA also lost the nearby LS-85, leaving LS-36 at Na Khang as the most northerly airstrip. Na Khang in turn fell on 1 March 1969.

The 'Steel Tiger' programme became 'Commando Hunt' from 15 November 1968, and with the bombing halt over North Vietnam many more aircraft were available for sorties in Laos. In the first month alone, 12,821 tactical and 661 B-52 sorties were flown, mainly against the Ho Chi Minh Trail. During 1969 the pace increased to a peak of 300 sorties daily, a level with which the forward air controllers were unable to cope. The USAF often armed its aircraft inappropriately for close-support work with the Hmong, now leading the fight against the Pathet Lao in northern Laos. The errors were compounded through using 'fast-mover' USAF FAC with inexperienced crews who lacked local knowledge and guided attack aircraft to the wrong target.

By now the Pathet Lao and North Vietnamese had a formidable range of mobile air defences in the north, and losses were heavy. As in North Vietnam, downed air crews were used as bait for rescuers, and many Air America and Raven personnel were killed or injured in covert rescue operations while the USAF was obliged to act with caution. Among the most effective aircraft to operate on interdiction work against the Trail was the A-26A, which flew for only four months from August 1966 with 606 SOS before being withdrawn. A suitable replacement was not available until September 1970, when the B-57Gs of 13 TBS began operations from Ubon; one was lost in December 1970 when it collided with an FAC O-1.

By this time some 2.2 million tons of bombs had been dropped on Laos, including a large tonnage by B-52s, which had begun sorties against Pathet Lao and NVA elements on 17 February 1970. These raids were from high altitude and largely ineffectual, because of dated or inadequate target intelligence. In contrast, Air America Caribou were dropping loads of fourteen 'Hot Soup' home-made napalm tanks on enemy positions identified by FAC. The RLAF had been supplied with five ex-VNAF AC-47s in early 1969, and these were put to use in the defence of LS-32 at Phon Nok Kok in May.

TABLE OF UNITS: LAOS, 1954—1975

Unit	Aircraft (code)	Base	Role	Nos./dates
LAAS (May 1954–August 1960)				
	L-19	Vientiane, Luang Prabang	Liaison, observation	20
	L-20	Vientiane	Liaison	3
	C-47	Vientiane	Transport	10
	Aero Commander	Vientiane	Transport	4
	MS.500	Vientiane, Luang Prabang	Liaison	15
RLAF				
	T-6	Vientiane, Luang Prabang	Light attack	10
	T-28D	Vientiane, Luang Prabang, Pakse, Long Tieng, Savannakhet	Light attack	60
	U-17	Vientiane, Luang Prabang	Liaison, light transport	10
	AC-47D	Vientiane	Gunship	5
	C-47	Vientiane	Transport	15
	C-123	Vientiane	Transport	12
	UH-34D, UH-1B	Various	Transport	30
USAF				
Project 'Bell Tone'				
510 TFS	F-100D (det.)	Don Muang	Air defence, ground attack	00/12/60 to 00/04/61
509 FIS	F-102A (det.)	Don Muang	Air defence	00/04/61 to 00/00/64
JTF 116 (MAY–DECEMBER 1962)				
USAF				
510 TFS	} F-100D	{ Takhli, ex England AFB	} Ground attack, air defence	00/05/62 to 00/12/62
? TFS		{ Takhli, ex Cannon AFB		
777 TCS	} C-123B	Don Muang	{ Tactical transport (to 311 TCS)	00/06/62 to 00/07/63
311 TCS			{ Tactical transport (ex 777 TCS)	00/08/63 to ?
USMC				
VMA-332	A-4A	Udorn, ex ?	Ground attack	00/06/62 to 00/10/62
HMM-261	UH-34D	Udorn, ex ?	Transport	15/04/62 to 00/10/62
RAF				
20 Sqn.	Hunter FGA.9	Chieng Mai	Ground attack, air defence	00/05/62 to 00/10/62
RAAF				
79 Sqn.	Sabre Mk.32	Ubon	Air defence	00/05/62 to 00/10/62
36 Sqn.	C-130A	Ubon, Butterworth	Tactical transport	00/05/62 to 00/10/62
RNZAF				
41 Sqn.	Bristol Freighter	? Chieng Mai	Transport	00/06/62 to 00/09/62
USAF reconnaissance units				
–	VC-47A, SC-47D, RT-33A	Vientiane, Udorn	PR ('Field Goal')	
45 TRS	RF-101C ('Able Mabel')	Don Muang, ex Misawa	Tactical recce	07/11/61 to 00/05/62
15 TRS	RF-101C ('Able Mabel')	Don Muang	Tactical recce	00/05/62 to 00/11/62
6091 RS	RC-130A (det.), RB-57D	Don Muang, ex Yokota	Recce (to 556 RS)	00/07/64 to 00/06/67
556 RS	EB-57E, C-130B-II	Don Muang	Recce (ex 6091 RS)	00/06/67 to 00/00/70
35 TG, 1 ACW (later 56 SOW)				
Det. 6	T-28D	Udorn	Training ('Water Pump')	00/03/64 to 00/00/72
Det. 1	O-1	Udorn and Laos	FAC ('Butterfly', 'Raven')	00/00/64 to 00/00/73
USAF Special Operations units				
56 SOW				
602 SOS	A-1E/G/H/J (TT)	Bien Hoa, Nakhon Phanom	Rescue support	00/11/64 to 31/12/70
1 SOS	A-1E/G/H/J (TC)	}	{ Rescue support (ex 14 SOW)	00/00/68 to 00/12/72
22 SOS	A-1E/G/H/J (TS)		Rescue support	00/00/69 to 00/00/72
606 SOS	T-28D, C-123K, A-26A (TO)	} Nakhon Phanom	Close support, flareship, interdiction (to 609 SOS)	00/01/66 to 00/08/66
609 SOS	T-28D, A-26A (TA)		Close support, interdiction	00/08/66 to 09/11/69
21 SOS	CH-3C/E		Support, infiltration	00/00/68 to 00/00/73
18 SOS	AC-119K	}	{ Gunship (ex 14 SOW, to 821 AS VNAF)	25/08/71 to 31/12/72

Note: Project 'Bell Tone' units became Det. 4, 405 FW, from July 1963. Air America, based at Udorn but operating across Laos, flew the following types: HUS-1/UH-34D, Bell 204, Bell 205 and CH-47; O-1, U-1, U-6, U-10, U-17, Volpar Turbo 18, C-45, Turbo Porter and Do 28; and C-46, C-47, C-123, C-130, Caribou. A. Bird & Sons/Continental Air Services, based at Bangkok but operating across Thailand and Laos, flew (from April 1965) the C-130/L.382B, Do 28, C-46, C-47 and Twin Pioneer. For details of USAF and USN strike units available for use in Laos, see appropriate sections.

The Pathet Lao/NVA advanced further each dry season (October to April), and on 18 March 1970 the important forward base at Sam Thong (LS-20) fell. Some 500 Thai troops were brought up by Air America C-123s to Long Tieng (LS-20 Alternate), which was now threatened with being overrun. Many non-combatants from the ultra-secret base had been evacuated by CH-53s of 21 SOS, three of which were stationed there, in January, and the base held out; indeed, at the end of March Sam Thong was retaken at a cost of three T-28s, two O-1s and one U-17. By late 1970 the NVA had 18,000 men in three divisions in Laos, and the US prepared for a pre-emptive strike, but on 22 December 1970 the US Congress prohibited the further use of US forces in Laos and Cambodia.

Operation 'Lam Son 719'/'Dewey Canyon II' was aimed at cutting the North Vietnamese infiltration routes in Laos by driving across the

Trail to Tchepone. From the beginning the operation was a disaster. The attack was launched by the ARVN with US Air Cavalry support, and because of the need for all plans to be translated, full details had been made available by the translators to the North Vietnamese, who were thus able to prepare their defences. In addition, the ARVN had to fight across valleys and ridges, while the NVA counterattacked along the valleys over ground with which it was familiar. The operation began on 8 February 1971 and ended prematurely on 25 March, by which time about 10,000 ARVN were dead and 107 US Army helicopters had been lost, with another 600 damaged. Sufficient damage was inflicted on the NVA, which lost 100 tanks in the fighting, to force it to defer its invasion plans.

In southern Laos the NVA drove Government forces from the Bolovens Plateau on 16 May 1971. Through the rainy season the NVA built up to seven divisions, but in November 1971 1,000 Thai troops were flown in to retake the region. Within a month the plateau was again in Government hands, but Saravane was under siege. The city remained under attack throughout 1972, the Lao Army being supplied almost exclusively by Air America.

On the Vietnamese border, near the DMZ, there was further fighting in September 1971 when the ARVN, with US air support, launched 'Lam Son 810'. In the north, the Pathet Lao steadily made territorial gains. After the January 1973 ceasefire in Vietnam, the USAF turned its attention again to Laos and in the month flew 4,000 tactical sorties in addition to 4,482 flown by the RLAF. Terms were now discussed in Paris for a ceasefire, which became effective on 22 February. It was agreed that all foreign troops would withdraw from the country, and although the US honoured the agreement the North Vietnamese did not. As Pathet Lao forces violated the ceasefire, capturing Paksong, the USAF flew some further B-52 sorties, the last strike of the war being on 17 April. A provisional administr-ation was determined on 14 September, and on 5 April 1974 a new coalition government was formed under Souvanna Phouma. The Pathet Lao gradually assumed control, however, and on 14 May 1975 Vang Pao and his entourage were evacuated from Long Tieng by a CIA-organized mission comprising a C-130, two C-46s, a Turbo Porter and a Bell 205. In December 1975 the King abdicated.

AIRCRAFT MARKINGS

RLAF

T-28D Light grey overall, no national markings, serial on fin in black: O-(4)91600, O-(4)91627, O-(4)91716, O-(1)38305 (ex-USN).
C-47 Light grey overall, black serial on fin: 24718.
AC-47 Chocolate brown/tan over, black under, serial on fin, 'last three' in white: 043263.

Air America

C-46 White over, bare metal under, black registration on rear fuselage and numbers only on nose: N335CA. Silver overall, black registration on rear fuselage: N8458Z, B-154, B-858.
Volpar Turbo Beech 18 White over, bare metal under, dark blue cheat line, rear fuselage and fin and rudder, black registration on rear fuselage: N9956Z.
Caribou Bare metal overall, black registration on rear fuselage: N544Y.
Bell 205A Light grey overall, dark blue top of boom and fin, registration on rear door: XW-PFJ.
Turbo-Porter Bare metal overall, dark blue cheat line and fin and rudder, black registration on rear fuselage: N393R.

Continental Air Services

C-46A Bare metal overall, white upper fuselage, fin and rudder, black registration on rear fuselage: XW-PHN.

9.4. Laos, 1975 to date

The Pathet Lao, having achieved supremacy within government by 1975, continued their persecution of the independent Meo (Hmong). In 1977 a treaty of friendship was signed with the Democratic Republic of Vietnam, and Vietnamese forces now joined the fighting. There is substantial evidence that from May 1977 the Meo were systematically killed in air strikes using chemical weapons, and it is widely believed that Soviet trials were being conducted using live subjects. T-toxins were established as the material involved, specifically trichothecane mycotoxins, dropped by 'MiG' fighters after reconnaissance by 'L-19s'. Witnesses spoke of canisters of blue and red smoke being dropped, followed by bags of yellow powder. It has been estimated that at least 20,000 Meo were killed by this means by 1982.

Many Meo fled to neighbouring Thailand, where in early 1987 border fighting broke out between Thai and Laotian/Vietnamese forces over disputed territory around Botene and on the Thai-Laos-Kampuchea border. By now the Thai Government was also using F-5 fighters against drug traffickers in the north. OV-10C light attack aircraft were withdrawn from that battle when it was reported that the traffickers were equipped with SA-7 missiles. In the border fighting, Thai F-5Es armed with napalm supported ground forces to prevent Laotian incursions. It was also alleged by Laos that the Thais fired chemical shells at Sayaboury, west of the Mekong, in fighting early in 1988. On 4 February an F-5E on a strike was brought down by SA-7 in the area, and it was followed a week later by a reconnaissance aircraft. Both countries agreed to a ceasefire in late February 1988.

TABLE OF UNITS: LAOS, 1988

Unit	Aircraft	Base	Role	Nos.
AFPLA, 1988				
?	MiG-21	Vientiane	Ground attack, air defence	50
	Yak-40, An-24, An-26, An-2, C-47, DC-4		Transport	20
	UH-34D, Mi-6, Mi-8		Liaison, transport	18
RTAF, 1988				
14 Sqn.	F-5E/F	Udorn, Ubon	Ground attack, air defence	36
13 Sqn.	F-5A/B	Don Muang	Air defence, ground attack	12
12 Sqn.	OV-10C	Nakhon Phanom, Udorn	Coin	24
73 Sqn.	A-37B, AU-23A	Prachuab, Satahip, Chieng Mai, Nakhon Phanom	Coin	36
11 Sqn.	RT-33A, RF-5A, EC-47	Don Muang	Recce	9
61 Sqn.	C-47, Nomad, HS.748	Don Muang	Transport	32
62 Sqn.	C-130H, C-123B/K	Don Muang	Transport	15
63 Sqn.	UH-1H/N, UH-34D, Bell 412	Various	Liaison, transport	35
Laotian Army, 1988				
?	O-1E	Various	Liaison, observation	24
?	UH-1B/D	Various	Liaison, transport	70
?	CH-47A	Don Muang	Transport	3
Laotian Navy, 1988				
?	S-2F, HU-16B, CL-215	Satahip	Maritime patrol, SAR	12
?	UH-1N	Satahip	Liaison	8

9.5. Cambodia, 1964 to date

For a time after independence from French rule, the neutral Cambodian Government, led by pro-communist Prince Norodom Sihanouk, looked to the France for arms and to the USA for support, but from 1963 the country turned to China and in August 1964 broke off relations with Washington and South Vietnam as a result of the ARVN and its US advisers intruding into Cambodia to strike at North Vietnamese sanctuaries. The Royal Khmer Aviation (RKA) flew a range of aircraft by 1966, including French-supplied AD-4 Skyraiders, Soviet MiG-17s and US T-28A/Ds, with a main base at Pochentong, Phnom Penh. One of the T-28s brought down a USAF O-1E of 19 TASS on 19 March 1964. From early on in the Vietnam War the Vietnamese had moved supplies from the port at Sihanoukville to strongholds in eastern Cambodia with, initially, some degree of Cambodian connivance. Antipathy to the Vietnamese, however, gradually shifted Sihanouk towards the United States, and he made it clear that he would accept American incursions into Cambodia to take out North Vietnamese camps.

The US started a secret bombing campaign, Operation 'Menu', on 18 March 1969, when 48 B-52 bombers struck at NVA positions in the 'Fish Hook' salient west of An Loc. The bombing continued for over a year, during which time Sihanouk was deposed while visiting Moscow by General Lon Nol on 18 March 1970. Lon Nol, concerned about the misery caused by the bombing (3,630 B-52 strikes to date) and violently opposed to the use of Cambodian territory as a springboard for North Vietnamese infiltration of the South, closed the 'Sihanouk Trail' and encouraged a US attack on Vietnamese positions. On 26 May the bombing was extended as Operation 'Freedom Deal', and it continued until March 1973. Most of the strikes were marked by FAC aircraft, which logged co-ordinates for attacks in South Vietnam but altered them in flight to Cambodian targets. The US also conducted tactical strikes: the first USAF loss in the campaign occurred on 2 May when an F-4D of 480 TFS was shot down.

The Americans also set in train operations by ground forces with air support to take out the NVA camps. These began with an ARVN invasion into the 'Parrots Beak' salient on 29 April 1970, followed two days later by a combined ARVN/US operation into 'Fish Hook' ('Toan Thang 43'), aimed at locating and destroying the HQ from which it was believed the NVA was directing the war. The attack was from the south-east, with air cavalry support from the north-east. Troops from 1 Cavalry Division were airlifted in from Tay Ninh and Quan Loi and supported by the Air Troop of 11 Armored Regt. and 1 Sqn. 9th Cavalry. The HQ was not located, but subsequent operations during May did uncover significant arms dumps. The invasions led to protests in the USA, and the ground forces withdrew on 29 June. On 22 December Congress prohibited the further use of US ground forces in Cambodia and Laos.

On the night of 21 January 1971, a North Vietnamese sabotage raid on Pochentong destroyed many of the newly renamed Khmer Air

Force's (KAF) aircraft. The US now began Project 'Flycatcher', the supply of aircraft to the KAF. This took the form of T-41A trainers, U-6, C-47 and C-123K transports, T-28D, A-37B and AU-24A light attack aircraft, and O-1 observation aircraft. The project ended on 30 June 1974, by which time about 160 aircraft had been delivered. The B-52 bombing continued against NVA targets east of the Mekong and on behalf of Lon Nol against communist Khmer Rouge guerrillas north of Phnom Penh. Following the Vietnam ceasefire in January 1973, the Khmer Rouge continued its struggle against the Government.

The United States' support of the Government continued as the 'Support Cambodia out of Thailand' (SCOOT) programme, and as Khmer Rouge forces sealed the Mekong and surrounded Phnom Penh they were subjected to heavy air attack. In the event, the last US bombing of Cambodia took place on 15 August 1973, after which there was financial and logistic aid. It has been estimated that as many as one million people died as a result of the bombing. Civilian contractors were now brought in by the CIA in the form of Bird Air and Continental Air Services, the former operating five loaned USAF C-130Es out of U-Tapao from August 1974. The Khmer Rouge maintained their grip on Phnom Penh, and on 1 April Lon Nol left the capital, which fell on the 17th.

The US mounted Operation 'Eagle Pull' to evacuate American and other foreign nationals from 11 April, using two USMC heavy helicopter units based on board USS Okinawa. About 100 aircraft of the KAF, together with many civil types, fled to Thailand. The 'reconstruction' of what became Kampuchea now began in earnest as the cities were emptied and all property confiscated under the harshest regime of the twentieth century. So revolutionary was the process that the first year of ultimate socialism became year zero, and over the next three years more than one million Cambodians were killed by the Khmer Rouge. However, the new regime was to find itself in direct conflict with the US just once more.

On 12 May 1975 the US-registered SS *Mayaguez*, a 10,776-ton container ship, was boarded by Kampuchean troops in international waters in the Gulf of Thailand. The ship radioed for help and was spotted by a Thai-based USN P-3A near Koh Tang island, where it was assumed that the Kampucheans had taken the crew. A rescue attempt was now authorized, and various units were alerted and moved to U-Tapao in Thailand. Two hundred and thirty Marines from the 3rd Marine Division were airlifted by C-141A from Okinawa to Thailand and a naval task force based on USS *Coral Sea*, with CVW-15 embarked, and three destroyers set sail. The following USAF units were readied for the rescue:

Unit	Aircraft	Unit	Aircraft
40 ARRS	HH-53C	347 TFS	F-111A
21 SOS	CH-53C	16 SOS	AC-130E
23 TASS	OV-10A	56 ARRS	HC-130P
388 TFW	A-7D	374 TAW	C-130E
432 TRW	F-4E	310 SW(P)	KC-135A

The complement of CVW-15 comprised VF 51 and VF-111 (F-4N); VA-22 and VA-94 (A-7E); VA-95 (A-6A); and VFP-63 (RF-8G).

During the 13th, the *Mayaguez* and Kampuchean gunboats were tracked by AC-130E, and when an attempt was made to move the ship to the mainland, the AC-130 attacked the escorting gunboats, preventing the move; A-7Ds also attacked the gunboats on the 14th, sinking five. Eleven H-53s of the two units lifted Marines to Koh Tang for the rescue attempt at 0700hrs local time on the 15th, three helicopters dropping their troops on the destroyer USS *Harold E. Holt* which was to recover the crewless ship. The Marines dropped on the island immediately came under heavy fire from Kampuchean forces, and several helicopters were lost to gunfire. Air

The Khmer Air Force operated one squadron of eight MiG-17s at Pochentong, although there is no evidence of their having been flown operationally. In the background of this photograph are several C-47s, AT-6s and U-6s. (Via L. Pinzauti)

TABLE OF UNITS: CAMBODIA, 1966–1975

Unit	Aircraft	Base	Role	Nos.
ARK, 1966				
?	A-4D		Close support	9
	T-28A/D		Close support	15
	MiG-17	Pochentong	Air defence, ground attack	8
	C-47, Flamant, Il-14, DHC-2		Transport	18
	S-58, Alouette II		Helicopter support	5
KAF, 1974				
?	T-28D	Pochentong, Ream	Close support	30
	AU-24	Pochentong	Coin, light gunship	24
	A-37B	Pochentong	Light attack	15
	C-47, C-123B/K	Pochentong	Transport	28
	U-6, O-1E	Various	Light transport, liaison	42
	UH-1C/D	Various	Transport, support	36
USMC, April 1975 ('Eagle Pull')				
HMH-464	CH-53D (YF)	*Okinawa*	Heavy transport	
HMH-463	CH-53D (YH)	*Okinawa*	Heavy transport	

cover was available but withheld for fear of wounding or killing the captive crew. As more Marines were landed, more helicopters were hit, and by the end of the day no fewer than eight out of eleven were destroyed or seriously damaged. To prevent Kampuchean air units becoming involved, the airfield at Ream was attacked at 0845hrs by A-6As and A-7Es, with F-4N cover from CVW-15, seventeen T-28s being destroyed. An oil depot at Kompong Som was also attacked. By now the deserted *Mayaguez* had been taken in tow by *Holt*, releasing more Marines for the rescue, and at 0945hrs a Thai fishing boat approached the destroyer *Henry B. Wilson*, carrying the 39 crew members of *Mayaguez*, who had in fact been transferred from Koh Tang on the 14th.

The Americans were now concerned only to recover the Marines on Koh Tang and, with the *Mayaguez*'s crew known to be safe, were free to provide close-support air power. Two recovery attempts were made, at 1215hrs and at 1430hrs, but both were beaten back by the Kampucheans. From 1600hrs OV-10A FACs were operating over the island, directing strikes by the A-7Ds, F-4Es and F-111As and the devastating firepower of the AC-130. A final recovery attempt was made at 1745hrs using the remaining helicopters, and

this time a 15,000lb bomb was dropped by C-130 to disorientate the Kampucheans. The third attempt was successful, and the remaining Marines were lifted out to *Coral Sea*. The cost of the operation was fifteen killed and three missing, plus 50 wounded.

As the Khmer Rouge exercised a total grip on the country, they also began to move into Thailand around Aranyaprathet in the south. There was heavy fighting in July 1977, during which the RTAF committed F-5s and armed helicopters. The KAF by now operated some 25 UH-1 helicopters but had few operational aircraft. In 1976, however, as links with China strengthened, a squadron of F-6s (MiG-19s) was delivered and based at Kompong Chang. Relations with the Vietnamese had long been strained, and in late 1977 border fighting broke out. Throughout 1978 there were skirmishes, and then, on 27 December that year, the Vietnamese invaded. Within two weeks Phnom Penh had fallen and the Khmer Rouge withdrew to prepared positions in the hills to continue a guerrilla war against the Vietnamese occupation. Much of the resistance centred around the southern end of the Thai border, and in March 1981 there were reports of Vietnamese An-2 aircraft spraying isolated Khmer

When many of the Khmer Air Force's aircraft were destroyed on the ground in a guerrilla attack on Pochentong on 21 January 1971, the US began a supply operation named 'Flycatcher'. Included in the deal were O-1 (L-19) observation aircraft such as O-313/(5)11699, seen here during an engine run. (Via L. Pinzauti)

positions with gas. In early 1985 the Vietnamese improved the airfields at Kompong Chang and Battambang to accommodate MiG-23s, and by July the guerrillas were using SA-7 missiles to counter air strikes. In September 1985 the Vietnamese Air Force attacked Khmer camps at Ban Sung and Ban Anrommiang, using An-26 transports converted to carry bombs and Mi-8 gunships operating out of Battambang.

On numerous occasions the Khmer have been pushed into Thailand, and there has been sporadic fighting between Thai and Vietnamese forces along the border. By summer 1986 the resistance was considerably reduced and the Vietnamese built a new helicopter base near Ban Nimit to back up their ground forces. Most of the Khmer had fled to refugee camps in Thailand, where they joined their former victims. The picture is further confused by the Vietnamese turning on their own puppet régime, and it was reported that the towns of Battambang and Chamka Chek were subjected to chemical shelling in November 1986.

Five armies are involved in the war, but only that of Vietnam (PAVN) has the use of air power. The PAVN is supported by the puppet People's Republic of Kampuchea Armed Forces (PRKAF). In opposition, but by no means working together, are the National Army of Democratic Kampuchea (NADK), the Khmer People's National Liberation Front (KPNLF, mainly Khmer Rouge) and the National Sihanoukist Army (ANS). In pursuit of the resistance forces, the Kampuchean Government shot down a Thai L-19 in early January 1987; Thai aircraft were charged with having violated Kampuchean airspace 33 times in the month. Early in February the NADK claimed to have shot down an Mi-8 near Phnum Priel, while

Thai F-5s are alleged to have used napalm against Vietnamese troops in the tri-border area. This region has seen continuing fighting, with daily Thai overflights by UH-1s, L-19s, F-5s and A-37s. At the time of writing, the civil war continues, but the Vietnamese have indicated a willingness to pull out of Kampuchea if a stable government can be formed.

Also included in Operation 'Flycatcher' was the supply of C-47 and C-123 transports. Both types are seen here at Phnom Penh in February 1980, apparently still in service. (Via L. Pinzauti)

AIRCRAFT MARKINGS

KAF
MiG-17 Bare metal overall, black serial on fin and nose: 1022, 1024, 1413, 7205.
T-28D Light grey overall, black serial on fin: O-(5)17823, O-(5)17833.
AU-24A Brown overall, white serial on fin: (7)21325.

USMC ('Eagle Pull')
CH-53D Dark green overall, white codes etc.: 157134/2YF (HMH-462).

9.6. Miscellaneous conflicts and incidents

1. There has been continuous fighting across the whole area covered since 1945, and there have been serious conflicts over the Spratly and Paracel groups of islands off the east coast of Vietnam since early 1988. China and Vietnam lay claim to the Paracels, and both countries are understood to have helicopters based on the islands. The Spratlies are claimed by China, Malaysia, the Philippines, Taiwan and Malaysia, and all these countries are building bases on the islands.

2. A Royal Navy Lynx HAS.3 of 815 NAS from the frigate *Sirius* was fired at by Chinese troops on 23 August 1988. The incident occurred near Triton Island in the Paracels, 300 miles south of Hainan in the South China Sea. There was no plausible explanation as to why the frigate was in the area, many hundreds of miles from its assumed position.

10: Indonesia, Malaysia and the Philippines

When the Second World War came to an end there were numerous communist or nationalist groups which had taken to arms on behalf of the Allies to fight the Japanese during the latter's occupation of the region. These groups then turned their attention either to the spread of communism or to independence from colonial rule. Throughout the area the United States made little effort to help the colonial powers to defeat the new threat, being determined to support the dismantling of the European empires. The British were initially involved in fighting in the Netherlands East Indies in an effort to stabilize the country, primarily to enable the orderly repatriation of Allied prisoners-of-war and internees. They then transferred control to the Dutch, who struggled against nationalists for several years until handing over government in 1950.

The new Indonesian Government soon encountered opposition and for years was involved in staving off revolution. Ironically, the US became involved in one unsuccessful attempt at revolution in 1958 from bases in the Philippines. In the meantime, the British had begun the fight against communist insurgency in Malaya. They were slow at first to recognize the seriousness of the threat, but after two years of poorly co-ordinated military action they embarked on a course which eventually cleared the peninsula of terrorists. Two factors combined to effect this achievement. First, through civil action, the rebels were isolated from potential support from sympathizers through a genuine 'hearts and minds' campaign coupled with an extensive psychological warfare programme. Second, a sound command structure was organized which placed an emphasis on the role of the police, especially the Special Branch and its intelligence-gathering role. The victory, albeit over a numerically far smaller force, was remarkable in that it was conducted largely by a conscript army fighting far from home in the most inhospitable conditions.

The lessons learned were to prove invaluable through the confrontation in Borneo with Indonesia. Bent on territorial gain, Indonesia's President Soekarno pursued the war into the Malaysian mainland. Sound tactics by the British and Malaysian Governments ensured that the insurgency was put down within four years and also cost Soekarno his presidency. Indonesia had already applied pressure on the last remaining Dutch foothold in the East Indies in 1962 when it attempted an invasion of Dutch New Guinea. Although the Dutch kept the Indonesians at bay, the possession was transferred after diplomatic moves. Indonesia also lay claim to East Timor, formerly a Portuguese colony, and, despite filling a power vacuum in 1975, fighting continues.

The Philippines, comprising 7,100 islands, have also been an area subject to continuous fighting for over forty years. In this case, the country has been supported by the United States throughout, primarily because of the importance of the bases leased there. The Huk revolt was successfully put down by 1954, but it was not long before there was insurgency both in the south from Muslims and in north from communists remustered as the New People's Army. The Government has been slow to deal with both groups through a combination of corruption and incompetence. The new Government of Mrs. Aquino has a hard task ahead, the constant prospect of a coup diverting energy from overdue reforms. Separating the police from the armed forces will help.

10.1. The Netherlands East Indies, 1945–1950

In April 1945 the Australian 9th Division landed at Tarakan in Borneo to begin the process of retaking the Netherlands East Indies from the Japanese. As the Japanese Empire collapsed, Field Marshal Hisaichi Terauchi promised the Indonesians independence, but on 14 August the Japanese surrendered. Significantly, the whole of the Indies was placed under South-East Asia Command (SEAC), a British area of operations. On the 16th, the leading nationalist, Achmed Soekarno, was advised by the Japanese that as they were now agents of the Allies there could be no independence from Dutch colonial rule. The same day the Recovery of Allied Prisoners-of-War and Internees (RAPWI) programme was established, and in September 28 Sqn. with the Spitfire FR.XIV was dispatched to Medan, Sumatra, to cover the evacuation of Allied de-

tainees. On the 17th, Soekarno declared independence, and it was anticipated that nationalists
would attempt to disrupt the evacuation.

During September, Air Headquarters Netherlands East Indies (AHQNEI) was formed from HQ
221 Group RAF in Burma; 904 Wing, comprising
60 and 81 Sqns., both equipped with the Thunderbolt II, was the air component. On 15 September,
HMS *Cumberland* docked at Tandjoeng with a
RAPWI control unit which linked up with a
reconnaissance group which had been parachuted
into Batavia (Djakarta) on the 8th; later in the
month, 23 Division arrived at Batavia. Meanwhile
A Flt., 656 Sqn., became operational at Soerabaya,
and on the 31st a flight of Mosquito FB.6s of 110
Sqn. arrived at Kemajoram, Batavia, from Seletar
to provide cover pending the arrival of 904 Wing.
The task of the British was to return the Japanese
and repatriate APWI before handing the NEI over
to civilian control.

The British made it clear that they recognized
the new Republic, which the growing number of
Dutch troops and re-armed internees found un-
satisfactory, especially since the Republicans had
aided the Japanese during their occupation. The
first sign of trouble came on 10 October when a
British patrol was ambushed. From then on there
were regular clashes; the Indonesians did not
trust the British to support their claim against
another colonial power. On 17 October, 904
Wing, including two squadrons of the RAF
Regiment, landed at Batavia and immediately set
about preparing Kemajoram to support operations. On the 19th, both Thunderbolt squadrons
were operational and within hours were in
action. SEAC forces had landed at Semarang and
worked south to free APWI. A company of 3/10
Gurkhas was cut off and required air support and
resupply by Dakotas of 31 Sqn.

By the 24th, British bridgeheads were established at Batavia, Semarang and Soerabaya and
on the 25th the Thunderbolts made round trips
of 900 miles to cover the landing of 49 Brigade
at Soerabaya. There was heavy fighting, and
six Thunderbolts of 60 Sqn. were detached to
Soerabaya to provide immediate support to ground
forces. The Republicans were strongest in the
east and were well armed from Japanese stocks.
They had also captured a number of assorted
Japanese aircraft in the vicinity of Soerabaya and
Djokjakarta and first flew one, a Yokosuka K5YI
trainer, on 27 October from Tajikmalaya; later,
numbers of these aircraft were flown against
Dutch forces. The fighting around Soerabaya
continued, despite the fact that Soekarno was
flown in by the British to calm the local
population. On the 30th, Brigadier A.W.S. Mallaby
was killed while attempting to negotiate a ceasefire, after which fighting spread to the west
around Batavia.

There was now considerable difficulty in repatriating the prisoners-of-war. No. 31 Sqn, now

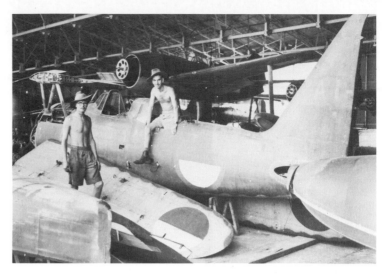

based at Kemajoram, was stretched supplying
RAPWI teams after several road convoys and
trains had been ambushed, but during November
10,000 internees were freed, many lifted out by
air. On 9 November, two Brigades of 5 Indian
Division arrived at Soerabaya to reinforce 49
Brigade, which was confined to the dock area.
Mosquitoes of 84 and 110 Sqns. from Seletar
were busy on leaflet-dropping sorties, exhorting
the Republicans to lay down their arms. The
following day eight Thunderbolts of 60 Sqn. and
two Mosquitoes of 110 Sqn. were detached to
Soerabaya, where they attacked buildings; ten
direct hits were confirmed. The aircraft continued
bombing sorties for several days, and it was
decided to strengthen 904 Wing by sending more
aircraft to Batavia.

Elements of 47, 84 and 110 Sqns., all with
Mosquito FB.6s, were available for close support,
the 47 Sqn. aircraft being equipped to fire rockets;
in addition, Spitfire PR.19s of 681 Sqn. for photo-
reconnaissance and Beaufighter Xs for rescue support were detached. For some time the Semarang–
Magelang road had been closed, and on 20
November Indonesian positions were bombed in
an attempt to re-open it. Three days later Dakota
III KG520 crash-landed five miles south-east of
Kemajoram; tragically, 21 sepoys and the crew of
five were killed on the ground by terrorists. The
same day Thunderbolt II KJ226 of 81 Sqn. crashed
into the sea on a strafing run against a gun-
running ship off Djokjakarta. On the 24th, radio
stations at Soerakarta and Djokjakarta were
bombed and destroyed by 47 Sqn. after Beaufighters of 27 Sqn. had dropped warning leaflets.
By the end of November the first Dutch unit, 321
Sqn. Marine Luchtvaart Dienst (MLD), equipped
with Catalinas and Liberators, was also based at
Kemajoram, which was by now becoming overcrowded.

As the flow of freed APWI increased, Sunderland flying boats of 230 Sqn. began repatriation

NCOs of 80 Sqn. RAF
examining the remains of
Japanese aircraft at the
seaplane base at
Sourabaya. Of great
interest are the markings
evident on the fuselage
and wing of this partially
dismantled Mitsubishi
F1M2 'Pete' observation
floatplane. The
Indonesian nationalists
prepared many Japanese
aircraft for flight and
marked them in
Indonesian colours by
simply painting white
over the lower half of the
Japanese red 'sun disc'. In
the background are at
least four Kawanishi
N1K1 'Rex' floatplane
fighters. (IWM)

flights to Malaya from Batavia. Operating conditions at Kemajoram were appalling, the short runways breaking up through use and floods, and to ease congestion and spread support the balance of 60 Sqn. went to Soerabaya on 1 December. Maintenance was very difficult, and 390 MU at Seletar acquired three Dakotas to fly spares throughout the theatre. No. 31 Sqn was now delivering 425 tons a week in Java, and the importance of air transport was underlined when a road convoy was ambushed at Soekaboemi on the 9th. Despite heavy fighter escort, there were numerous casualties, including two RAF controllers. In the new year the fighting diminished, but the convoy and train escort work was maintained.

In January 1946 the RAF organization changed. Soerabaya was brought into full use with 60 Sqn and detachments of 47 and 656 Sqns. Also at the station were the Catalinas of 321 Sqn. MLD, the Liberators having been returned to the United States. No. 904 Wing at Kemajoram comprised 81 and 84 Sqns. plus a detachment of 110 Sqn. and the Dakotas of 31 Sqn. No. 27 Sqn. returned to Malaya to disband, but, on the 15th, 18 NEI Sqn. RAAF was transferred back to the Royal Dutch Indies Army – Army Aviation (KNIL-ML); equipped with the B-25, this unit was the first to be based at Tjililitan. The 681 Sqn. detachment returned to Malaya, but its duties were taken over by Mosquito PR.34s of 684 Sqn. based at Seletar. To cover RAPWI work in Sumatra, 155 Sqn. with the Spitfire FR.XIV replaced the 28 Sqn. detachment at Medan, where it was supported by aircraft of 152 Sqn. operating out of Tengah. From March, as the Dutch gradually trickled back, the situation deteriorated and convoy escorts were stepped up, especially from Bandoeng.

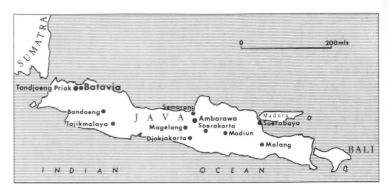

Around Soerabaya the position was improved and Dutch forces replaced British. No. 120 Sqn. ML replaced 60 Sqn., which returned to Kemajoram, from where both 47 and 84 Sqns. had departed for Malaya by April. Local negotiations brought about the recognition of an Indonesian Republic with authority in Java and Sumatra, while the Dutch, who had re-occupied the remaining major islands, would share the task of helping to bring the remainder of the East Indies into a federation. In the Netherlands, however, the more formal talks broke down. As the Dutch assumed greater control and their units began to replace RAF squadrons, the Indonesians also formed an embryo air force. On 9 April the Aviation Division of the People's Security Force was formed, with about fifty ex-Japanese aircraft in flying condition. The nationalists effectively controlled large areas of Sumatra and Java and their main stronghold was at Djokjakarta.

During May one of a flight of six Ki-9 trainers en route from Sumatra to Djokjakarta crashed, killing the pilot – the first Indonesian Air Division casualty. On 20 May two Dakotas of 31

Mosquito FB.6s of 110 Sqn., which was the second RAF unit to arrive at Kemajoram. The Mosquito was not well suited to operations in the humid climate of the Netherland East Indies, and maintenance was a continuing problem. Three squadrons were detached from Singapore between September 1945 and April 1946, primarily for escort duties. (Via A. S. Thomas)

Sqn. landed at Solo airfield, Soerakarta, to begin the final evacuation of 10,000 APWI. In June, 81 Sqn. disbanded, leaving just 60 Sqn. in Java and 155 Sqn. in Sumatra; in July, the Dutch assumed control of affairs in the NEI and there was a flare-up of anti-British feeling. The two RAF Regiment squadrons, 2962 at Kemajoram and 2739 at Medan, were fully committed to defending the bases from attack. By the end of August, only 60 and 31 Sqns. RAF remained in the NEI, with the Austers of 656 Sqn. From September 1945 the British had lost 556 dead (507 of whom were Indian troops) and 1,393 (1,259) wounded. The Dutch formally assumed responsibility for air support on 19 September, and by the end of 1946 the following units were operational:

Squadron	Aircraft	Base
KNIL-ML		
18	B-25D	Tjililitan
121	P-51D	Tjililitan
20	TB-25D, C-47	Tjililitan, Bandoeng
120	P-40N	Soerabaya
16	B-25D	Palembang
122	P-51D	Medan, Palembang
17	L-4J	Various
MLD		
321	PBY-5A	Morokrebangan
860	Firefly 1	Soerabaya

During September, 31 Sqn. disbanded at Kemajoram: in one year and six days, its Dakotas had flown over 11,000 sorties, carrying 127,800 passengers (many repatriated APWI) and 26,000 tons of freight, and two aircraft with their crews had been lost in crashes. No. 656 Sqn. returned to Malaya in November, and on the 28th 904 Wing and AHQNEI were disbanded; the Thunderbolts of 60 Sqn were broken up as the unit left for Singapore to re-equip.

The last British troops left NEI at the end of November, at a time when agreement appeared to have been reached on the future of Indonesia as a group of Federal United States with Dutch allegiance. A ceasefire agreement had been reached, but through early 1947 there were numerous breaches. There were, moreover, many misunderstandings on both sides about the exact nature and authority of the new Republic, which the Dutch attempted to control from enclaves around Batavia and Soerabaya in Java and Medan, Padang and Palembang in Sumatra. The Republic was banned from importing arms, but its Air Division urgently needed aircraft to replace those of Japanese origin, which by mid-1947 were mostly unserviceable. On 2 June a Dakota piloted by an American landed at Tajikmalaya from the Philippines; in Indonesian service it became RI-002. As ceasefire violations increased, the Dutch Governor-General ordered a police action on 20 July. Armed columns were sent out from Batavia, Bandoeng and Soerabaya. Aircraft attacked airfields around the Republican capital, Djokjakarta, destroying eight aircraft on the ground. The Fireflies of 860 Sqn. were particularly effective in

the ground-attack role, although three were lost to AA fire. On the 29th, a sole Republican Ki-51b attacked Semarang; Dutch P-40Ns of 120 Sqn. sent out to intercept the Mitsubishi instead shot down an Indian C-47 (VT-CLA) delivering medical supplies to Djokjakarta.

In the 'police action', three divisions were employed in Java and three brigades in Sumatra, but in general the Indonesians, who outnumbered the Dutch, withdrew to the hills without engaging, and casualties on both sides were light. The Dutch soon gained control of most towns and cities, except in central Java, and all the ports. For several months the Indonesians launched guerrilla attacks from the hills, where they were subjected to air strikes, but the scale of the attacks diminished as the Dutch blockade effectively starved the Republicans of weapons and ammunition. In July, twenty crated Spitfire IXs arrived at Tandjoeng for use by 322 Sqn. Dutch Air Force (LSK), although delays in the arrival of the unit from the Netherlands meant that it was not declared operational until 22 December at Semarang.

Meanwhile a ceasefire was agreed, effective from 5 August. The Dutch continued mopping-up operations and consolidated their positions; through late 1947 there was diplomatic activity in the UN; and on 19 January 1948 a precarious settlement was reached aboard the USS *Renville* anchored off Batavia. The Dutch continued to exercise a strong grip, however, maintaining their blockade of Republican areas. There was now a need for reconnaissance aircraft, and early in 1948 an ML photo-reconnaissance unit, PVA, was formed at Tjililitan with a mixture of aircraft; in June, the MLD also formed a mixed photo-reconnaissance/transport unit, OVTS, at Morokrebangan. On the Republican side there were divisions, and on 18 September the communist party (PKI) staged a coup at Madiun. The revolt was soon put down by Soekarno and the leader killed. The Republic was gradually acquiring aircraft, but on 1 October Dakota RI-002 was lost in south Sumatra. There were rumours that

By the spring of 1946, conditions at Kemajoram were vastly improved after the appalling state of the airfield in the early days of RAF occupation, when mud made operations hazardous and maintenance near-impossible. This Thunderbolt, with drop tanks, is being refuelled prior to a strike on nationalists at Soerabaya. (IWM)

there was gold on board and that the aircraft had been forced down by the Dutch at Palembang and the crew of seven killed.

The Dutch began a second police action on 19 December. Paratroops landed on the Republican airfield at Magoewo, capturing intact Dakota RI-001, Anson RI-004 and Catalinas RI-005 and -006, together with DH-86B G-ADYH, which was allegedly en route from Darwin to Penang. Most of the aircraft had been supplied through Australian sources, which were generally sympathetic to the Republicans. The Indonesian leader Soekarno and many members of the cabinet were captured and interned in the attack. Most Republican towns were in Dutch hands within days, but the action was widely condemned, and although a ceasefire was called from 1 January 1949 in Java the Dutch refused to release Soekarno. There was considerble guerrilla activity, and soon Djokjakarta was surrounded.

It was now only a matter of time before the Dutch would have to succumb to international pressure. With the threat of American aid being cut off, agreement was finally reached for a full transfer of sovereignty. A formal ceasefire was agreed for 11 August in Java and for 15 August in Sumatra. Soekarno was released, and the United States of Indonesia was formed on 27 December 1949. It was estimated that Dutch casualties in the four-year war were 25,000, while the Republicans suffered 80,000 killed and wounded.

There was now an orderly transfer of government, and as some Dutch air units returned to the Netherlands or disbanded, several handed

TABLE OF UNITS: NETHERLANDS EAST INDIES, 1945–1950

Unit	Aircraft (code)	Base	Role	Dates
RAF				
28 Sqn.	Spitfire FR.XIV	Tengah. Medan		00 09 45 to 00 00 46
155 Sqn.	Spitfire FR.XIV	Medan	Armed recce	00 01 46 to 31 08 46
152 Sqn.	Spitfire FR.XIV	Tengah		00 01 46 to 10 03 46
60 Sqn.	Thunderbolt II (MU)	Kemajoram. Soerabaya	Escort fighter. ground attack	19 10 45 to 28 11 46
81 Sqn.	Thunderbolt II (FL)	Kemajoram	Escort fighter. ground attack	19 10 45 to 00 06 46
110 Sqn.	Mosquito FB.VI	Kemajoram	Fighter-bomber	31 09 45 to 28 11 45
84 Sqn.	Mosquito FB.VI (PY)			20 10 45 to 00 04 46
47 Sqn.	Mosquito FB.VI (KU)	Kemajoram. Soerabaya	Fighter-bomber	15 11 45 to 12 03 46
27 Sqn.	Beaufighter X	Kemajoram	SAR	15 11 45 to 00 01 46
681 Sqn.	Spitfire PR.XIX		PR	
684 Sqn.	Mosquito PR.34	Seletar	Mapping	00 01 46 to 00 03 46
31 Sqn.	Dakota C.4	Kemajoram	Transport	30 10 45 to 00 09 46
230 Sqn.	Sunderland GR.V	Batavia	Repatriation	00 12 45 to 00 03 46
656 Sqn.	Auster AOP.V	Batavia. Soerabaya (A Flt.): Semarang (B Flt.): Bandoeng (C Flt.)	Liaison. observation	00 09 45 to 00 11 46
390 MU	Dakota C.4	Seletar	Stores transport	00 12 45 to 00 09 46
KNIL-ML				
18 Sqn.	B-25D.J	Tjililitan. Kemajoram	Medium bombing	15 01 46 to 26 07 50
120 Sqn.	P-40N. P-51D/K	Semarang. Soerabaya	Fighter. ground attack	06 04 46 to 25 07 50
121 Sqn.	P-51D.K	Tjililitan. Andir. Semarang. Palembang	Fighter. ground attack	01 05 46 to 21 02 49
16 Sqn.	B-25D.J	Palembang	Medium bombing (aircraft to 18 Sqn.)	00 10 46 to 31 07 48
122 Sqn.	P-51D.K	Medan. Padang	Fighter. ground attack	00 11 46 to 00 06 50
PVA	B-25D. L-4J. L-12A. P-51D	Tjililitan	PR	00 00 48 to 00 00 50
20 Sqn.	TB-25D. C-47	Tjililitan	Transport (ex 220 Sqn.)	01 11 46 to 27 06 50
19 Sqn.	C-47. L-12A. C-54B	Kemajoram	Transport (aircraft to 20 Sqn.)	00 04 47 to 00 03 48
17 Sqn.	L-4J	Medan. Palembang. Padang. Batavia. Bandoeng. Semarang	Liaison. observation	10 07 46 to 00 02 50
LSK				
322 Sqn.	Spitfire IX	Semarang	Fighter	22 12 47 to 01 09 49
6 ARVA	Auster III	Batavia. Soerabaya (A Flt.): Semarang (B Flt.): Andir (C Flt.): Semplak (D Flt.)	Liaison. observation	12 11 47 to 20 03 50
MLD				
321 Sqn.	PBY-5A. B-24D. C-47A	Kemajoram. Soerabaya. Morokrebangan	Bombing. recce	00 11 45 to 01 05 49
860 Sqn.	Firefly I	*Karel Doorman*. Soerabaya	Fighter. ground attack	00 06 46 to 00 10 47
OVTS	PBY-5A. C-47A	Morokrebangan	Recce. transport	00 06 48 to 01 05 49
8 Sqn.	C-47A	Soerabaya	Transport	01 02 50 to 15 12 50

Indonesia
From 1945. Indonesian rebels acquired various ex-Japanese aircraft. Among these were Ki.9s (4). Ki.21 (1). Ki.36s (4). Ki.43s (6). Ki.46s (4). Ki.49s (2). Ki.51s (8). Ki.61s (6). K6K5 'Mavis' (1) and K5Y1 'Willows' (70). Most of the aircraft were at Klutan. Malang and Soerabaya: the first flight of these was a K5Y1 from Tajikmalaya. Also flown. from Kalidjati. was a Blenheim fitted with Nakajima Sakae engines: it crashed on its first flight. Through 1946. many of the Japanese aircraft were made serviceable and flown on various missions. but many were lost to accidents.

Aviation Division, People's Security Force
From 1948 the new Government operated examples of the C-47. L-5A. PBY-5. De Havilland DH 86 and Anson from Tajikmalaya and Maguwo.

over their aircraft to Indonesia. The Spitfire in Dutch service in the NEI had not proved particularly effective and 322 Sqn. had disbanded in September 1949, its remaining aircraft being returned to the Netherlands. There were many accidents, and the unit flew a mere 800 sorties in 1948 and 685 in 1949. But the new air force acquired the Mustangs of 120, 121 and 122 Sqns., the Mitchells of 18 Sqn., the L-4Js of 17 Sqn. and the Dakotas of 20 Sqn.

AIRCRAFT MARKINGS

RAF
Thunderbolt II *Dark Green/Dark Sea Grey over, medium grey under, white bands around nose and on wings, tailplane and fin, white serial and code on rear fuselage: KL187/MU-M, KL266-MU-S (60 Sqn.); HD185/FL-D (81 Sqn.). Bare metal overall, dark blue bands, black serial and code on rear fuselage: KL317/MU-H (60 Sqn.).*
Spitfire FR.XIV *Dark Green/Ocean Grey over, Medium Sea Grey under, white serial and code on rear fuselage: MV320/X (28 Sqn.).*
Mosquito FB.VI *Silver overall, black serial and code on rear fuselage: TE650/KU-Y, RF942/ KU-H (47 Sqn.). Code in medium grey: PZ464/PY-P (84 Sqn.); HR438/A (110 Sqn.).*
Spitfire PR.XIX *PR Blue overall, white serial and code on rear fuselage: PA935/R (681 Sqn.).*
Dakota IV *Olive Drab over, pale blue under,*

black serial on rear fuselage, white code across nose: KP229/UC (31 Sqn.).
Sunderland V *Extra Dark Sea Grey over, white under, black serial, Dull Red code on rear fuselage: RN294/R (230 Sqn.).*

KNIL-ML
P-40N *Silver overall, black serial on rear fuselage: 326, 352 (120 Sqn.).*
P-51D *Bare metal overall, black serial on engine cowling: N3-609 (121 Sqn.). Black serial on rear fuselage: H-322, H-325 (122 Sqn.).*
B-25D *Olive Drab overall, white serial on nose: N5-256 (18 Sqn.). Black serial on rear fuselage: M-433 (18 Sqn.). Bare metal overall, black serial on rear fuselage: M-366 (20 Sqn.).*
L-4J *Olive Drab overall, white serial on rear fuselage: R-373 (17 Sqn.).*

LSK
Spitfire F.IX *Dark Green/Ocean Grey over, medium grey under, white serial on fuselage: H-50, H-68 (322 Sqn.).*

MLD
Firefly FR.1 *Extra Dark Sea Grey/Dark Slate Grey over, Sky under, white serial on rear fuselage: 11-23, 11-28 (860 Sqn.).*

The absence of distinguishing unit markings makes the squadron identification of this flight of P-51D Mustangs impossible. The aircraft are seen over Java in 1949, and are probably from 120 or 122 Sqn. The Mustang remained in service with the Indonesian Air Force after the Dutch withdrawal in 1950. (Netherlands Air Force Museum)

10.2. Indonesia, 1950–1962

From achieving full independence in December 1949, Indonesia has suffered numerous rebellions as minority groups, sometimes very large, have attempted to break away from the Republic. For the Government, the problem is that the country comprises well over 10,000 islands and a population of 100 million with a range of ethnic and religious backgrounds. The Indonesian Air Force (AURI) was originally equipped with Dutch aircraft left after independence: No. 1 Sqn. comprised P-51D and K fighters and B-25D and J bombers, while the transport squadron, No. 2, was equipped with the C-47. Early in 1950, 1 Sqn. was in action against rebels on the island of Ambon, who were strafed prior to Government troops landing to restore order. The aircraft were

again in action in 1953 to deal with a rebellion by dissident Muslims in the southern Celebes.

President Achmed Soekarno was essentially a Nationalist, but the Americans saw his tolerance of the communist party, the PKI, as a threat to stability in the region and they attempted to influence him towards the West, without success. There was particular concern when, early in 1957, reconnaissance aircraft photographed what appeared to be a new military airfield under construction at Natuna Besar north of Borneo – an airfield there could be an important staging post for Soviet aircraft in the region. The 3rd US Marine Regiment was placed on standby while the CIA gave its support to a group of politicians and senior officers who, on 15 February 1958,

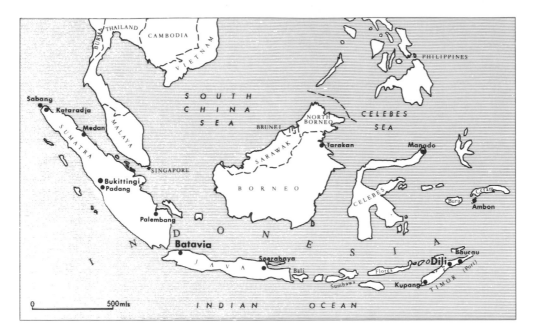

declared independence in Sumatra. There was a simultaneous rebellion in the Celebes, and many Dutch settlers were evacuated by air to Europe. On 31 December C-54D G-APID of Air Charter was forced down in Albania en route to Djakarta.

The CIA had established a support organization in 1957 with its HQ at Singapore, and had recruited mercenaries from the USA, Taiwan and the Philippines. Aircraft were procured from ex-USAF stocks, including fifteen B-26Bs, a C-54, several C-46s and C-47s and, reportedly, a B-29. The aircraft were flown via Clark AB to Manado on the northern tip of Celebes, from where they operated against Government forces trying to stem the rebellion. On Sumatra the rebels based their activities around Padang and set up an American-run radio station at nearby Bukittingi. On 12 March Soekarno announced a plan to drop paratroops on Padang airfield, and the drop was actually made on 18 April by eighteen C-47s in concert with an amphibious landing. Earlier, P-51s and B-25s had bombed and strafed both the airfield at Padang, destroying several aircraft, and the radio station. Many of the rebels fled to Celebes, from where they continued their campaign.

The CIA-backed rebel air force was operating from Manado in the general area of Celebes, and in a bombing raid on Ambon on 18 May an American pilot, Allen L. Pope, was shot down by light AA fire. Pope parachuted to safety but gave Soekarno evidence of US complicity; the latter used that evidence to apply pressure on the United States for financial assistance, although by now he had ordered a significant quantity of arms, especially aircraft, from the Soviet Union. The B-26 must have made some impact, for in 1960 eight were delivered to the AURI. Inter-estingly, in Operation 'Strongback', Marine Air Control Squadron 1, normally based at Atsugi in Japan, was shipped out to the southern Philippines in October 1957 in anticipation of an invasion of Borneo. Through the spring of 1958 the unit was temporarily based at Corregidor. The Government continued the fight against the rebels until 1961, when a political amnesty was offered.

AIRCRAFT MARKINGS

P-51D *Bare metal overall, black serial on rear fuselage: H-322, H-324 (1 Sqn.).*
B-25D *Bare metal overall, black serial on rear fuselage: M-433, M-439 (1 Sqn.).*

The P-51D Mustang served with 3 Sqn. Indonesian Air Force until well into the 1970s. When CIA-backed rebels began operations from Sumatra in 1957, paratroops were dropped on Padang airfield in April after strikes by Mitchells, escorted by Mustangs which strafed targets in the area. (USAF via J. Ethell)

TABLE OF UNITS: AIR FORCE OF THE REPUBLIC OF INDONESIA, 1950–1961

Unit	Aircraft	Base	Role
AURI			
1 Sqn.	P-51D/K, B-25D/J, PBY-5A	Kemajoram	Fighter, light bombing, recce
2 Sqn.	C-47	Djakarta	Transport
3 Sqn.	L-4	Various	Liaison, recce

10.3. West Irian (Dutch New Guinea), 1962

From 1957, President Soekarno had laid claim to Dutch New Guinea, on the basis that all Dutch colonies forming part of the Netherlands East Indies should have been ceded to Indonesia. Ethnically, the inhabitants of New Guinea are quite different from those of the remainder of Indonesia, and there would appear to have been little logic in the claim. As threats to take the colony by force were made in 1960, the Dutch sent 322 Sqn. RNethAF, equipped with twelve Hunter F.4s and two Alouette IIs, to the island of Biak. There they were based at Boeroekoe naval air station, where several C-47s and twelve P2V-7 Neptunes of 321 Sqn. already shared the base with the Firefly AS.4s of 6 Sqn. Dutch naval vessels also operated in the area.

On 15 January 1962 an Indonesian invasion fleet was spotted by a patrolling P2V-7, and warships rushed to intercept. The landings were covered by AURI P-51Ds, which also gave support to a paratroop drop. Apparently the AURI did not make use of its growing fleet of Russian-supplied fighters in the invasion. One landing ship was sunk by a Dutch warship, but it appears that the two air forces did not meet in combat; rather, the two countries began negotiations, which resulted in West Irian being handed over to Indonesia in May 1963.

TABLE OF UNITS: WEST IRIAN, 1962			
Unit	**Aircraft**	**Base**	**Role**
RNethAF			
322 Sqn.	Hunter F.4	Boeroekoe	Air defence, ground attack
MLD			
321 Sqn.	P2V-7	Boeroekoe	MR
6 Sqn.	Firefly AS.4		ASW, ground attack
AURI			
See section on Borneo 1962–1966.			

AIRCRAFT MARKINGS

RNethAF
Hunter F.4 *Dark Green/Dark Sea Grey over, silver under, white serial on nose and fin: N-110, N-232 (322 Sqn.).*

MLD
P2V-7 *Engine Grey overall, white fuselage top decking, white serial on nose and under wing, code on fin: 203/B (321 Sqn.).*
Firefly AS.4 *Extra Dark Sea Grey over, Sky under, black serial on rear fuselage, last two digits on nose: 16-69 (6 Sqn.).*

Indonesia laid claim to West Irian in 1957, and when, in 1960, it appeared that the claim would be realized through military action, the Dutch sent Hunters of 322 Sqn. to Boeroekoe. Naval air units were already based there. Landings were subsequently made, but there was no air combat. (Netherlands Air Force Museum)

10.4. East Timor, 1975 to date

The coup in Portugal in 1974 resulted in rapid de-colonization throughout the former Portuguese Empire but whereas in Africa there were established nationalist groups ready to assume power, there was a relative vacuum in East Timor. The local parties were divided on whether to maintain a relationship with Portugal (UDT), look for association with Indonesia, which included neighbouring West Timor (Apodeti), or seek total independence (Fretilin). On 12 August 1975, UDT staged a coup in the capital, Dili, after which civil war broke out between Fretilin (well-armed from Portuguese stocks) and the rest. Fretilin was soon in control of the capital, and a Republic was proclaimed on 28 November.

By now Indonesia had drafted troops and aircraft into Kupang, West Timor, and on 7 December they invaded. Marines were landed near Dili, and 1,000 paratroopers were dropped by C-130Bs of 31 Sqn. and C-47s of 2 Sqn., supported by 1 Sqn. F-51Ds. The Soviet-supplied aircraft were now mainly unserviceable and held in stock. Fretilin reaction was strong, and a second wave of Indonesians was landed on 25 December before the capital was secured. Anti-Fretilin parties declared a provisional government, and by May 1976 the country was incorporated into Indonesia. There has been sporadic fighting since Fretilin guerrillas took to the hills, especially after August 1983 when Government troops were ambushed. Over the years, the Indonesian Air Force, now the TNI-AU, has re-equipped with predominantly American types and, from 1980, 3 Sqn., with the OV-10F, has been operating against Timorese guerrillas from Baucau.

AIRCRAFT MARKINGS

OV-10F Dark green/sand over, white under, black serial on boom: S-105 (3 Sqn.).

TABLE OF UNITS: INDONESIAN ARMED FORCES — AIR FORCE, 1975 TO DATE

Unit	Aircraft	Base	Role	Dates
1 Sqn.	F-51D	Kemajoram	Fighter, ground attack	
14 Sqn.	Sabre Mk. 32	Soerabaya	Air defence	
2 Sqn.	C-47	Halim	Transport	1975
31 Sqn.	C-130B	Halim	Transport	
4 Sqn.	Alouette III	Various	Liaison, observation	
3 Sqn.	OV-10F	Baucau	Coin	
14 Sqn.	F-5E	Soerabaya	Air defence, ground attack	From 1980
6 Sqn.	Puma	Halim	Transport	
11 Sqn.	Hawk Mk. 53	Soerabaya	Light ground attack	From 1981
11 Sqn.	A-4E	Medan	Ground attack	From 1983
12 Sqn.	A-4E	Pakanbaru	Ground attack	From 1983

10.5. The Philippines, 1946–1954

Although the United States exercised strong control over the Philippines, the latter were notionally independent when invaded by the Japanese in 1941. During the Second World War a People's Anti-Japanese Army (Hukbalahap) had been formed, and until 1946 it was aided by the Chinese Hwa Chi 48th Unit. After the war, with full independence promised, the Huk movement, under a Democratic Alliance label, took six seats, one of which was won by the Huk leader, Luis Taruc, but the ruling party found the situation intolerable and denied the Huks their seats, accusing the party of fraud. The Huks took to the hills after clashes with Civil Guards, and it was not long before their positions were under attack by 75mm artillery fire, mortar fire and air strikes by P-51D Mustangs based in Manila.

The Republic was declared on 4 July 1946, and the new government prepared for an all-out offensive. The first major action was in the Mount Arayat area in March 1947 when 2,500 Huk irregulars were surrounded, but Government forces were indifferently led and the guerrillas slipped the net. Subsequent actions were equally ineffective. The Philippine Air Force (PAF) was established with Command status on 3 July 1947, initially comprising a squadron of P-51Ds and several C-47 transports. The Mustangs were formed into 6 Fighter Squadron (FS), and later 7 and 8 FS were also formed with the type. All the units were based at Manila but operated from other airfields as the need arose. The Huks gradually assumed control of central Luzon, and

by 1950 their numbers were estimated at 15,000, with 150,000 active supporters.

With the Americans heavily committed to the Korean War, the US bases on the Philippines assumed a new importance, especially Clark Field AB near Manila. Their security was critical, especially after the US had been required in 1949 to replace Chinese guards with locals. On 5 May 1949, Philippine Air Lines DC-3 PI-C-98 was sabotaged at Manila, with the loss of thirteen passengers and crew. At the beginning of 1950 the Huks renamed their organization the People's Liberation Army (PLA), and at the end of March began a new offensive, with full-scale attacks on San Mateo, San Simon, Los Banos and Montalban. Government forces were taken by surprise, as they were when Santa Cruz was attacked on 28 August. To combat the new guerrilla offensive, Ramon Magsaysay was appointed Secretary of National Defence in September, and he looked first to capture the support of peasants through land reform policies. This approach was soon rewarded when, in October, 105 senior communists were betrayed, including the party's secretary-general.

From November, a joint US Military Advisory Group (MAG) was set up under the CIA's Col. Ed Lansdale. The Army was re-formed into 26 combat battalions, each with integral artillery. The Air Force acquired new liaison and observation aircraft in the form of T-6s, L-4s and L-5s, all from US stocks, and on 23 December the Air Force assumed full service status. Through a

TABLE OF UNITS: THE PHILIPPINES AIR FORCE, 1946–1954

Unit	Aircraft	Base	Role	Dates
6 FS	P-51D		Fighter, ground attack	00/00/46 to post 1954
7 FS	F-51D		Fighter, ground attack	00/00/48 to post 1954
8 FS	F-51D	Manila	Fighter, ground attack	00/00/49 to post 1954
? 2 TS	C-47		Transport	00/00/46 to post 1954
?	L-4, L-5, T-6		Liaison, observation, light supply	00/10/50 to post 1954

combination of political initiatives and military action, Huk resistance was gradually broken. The F-51D Mustangs were frequently in action, and the aircraft were often detached to airfields around Luzon, away from the relative safety of Manila. The C-47s kept the detached combat battalions supplied, while the spotter aircraft kept watch on movements and identified guerrilla targets. The distance from the Asian mainland and the Chinese pre-occupation with the war in Korea probably combined to lead to the collapse of the Huk, and, starved of the supplies essential to the maintenance of a guerrilla war, Taruc surrendered on 17 September 1954. The war cost the Huks 9,695 dead, 1,635 wounded, 4,269

captured and 15,866 surrendered. In contrast, Government losses were 1,578 dead and 1,416 wounded.

AIRCRAFT MARKINGS

P-51D Bare metal overall, black serial on fin, code mid fuselage, squadron badge on fin and rudder: (47)3733/001; 473622/4?? (7 FS).
C-47 Bare metal overall, white fuselage top decking, black serial on fin: (4)292257 (? 2 TS).
L-5 Olive Drab overall, yellow serial on fin: (4)417091 (? 3 Sqn.).
T-6 Bare metal overall, black serial on fin, code mid fuselage: (4)150162/162 (? unit).

After the end of the Second World War, the anti-Japanese Army, the Huks, expected to assume some responsibility on independence. In fact, the organization was outlawed, and Government forces began to pursue guerrillas in the rural areas from which they operated. Three squadrons of P-51D Mustangs were formed at Manila. (R. Beseeber via J. Ethell)

10.6. The Philippines, 1964 to date

Just ten years after effectively removing the Huk threat, the Government of the Philippines again faced internal war, this time on two fronts. In February 1964, the 1st Special Forces Company (Airborne) was in action against Muslim separatists in the Sulu archipelago. The Muslims, ethnically Malaysian rather than Filipino, and sensing themselves under threat from Christian settlers in Mindanao, formed the Moro National Liberation Front (MNLF) in 1965. At the time the Philippines Air Force (PAF) was not equipped with aircraft of value in a guerrilla war – its F-51D Mustangs had given way to F-86D and F Sabres, primarily equipped for air defence – and only the C-47 transports were relevant to supporting an army fighting an elusive enemy.

For several years there were clashes between Muslim and Christian gangs and skirmishes with elements of the Armed Forces of the Philippines (AFP), which included the police force, the Philippines Constabulary (PC). In the meantime, the second threat emerged with the formation in 1968 of the Maoist Communist Party of the Philippines (PKP), composed of just fifty members. On 28 March 1969 the military wing, the New People's Army (NPA), was created; it operated from a base in Tarlac province, formerly

a Huk bastion. The NPA committed terrorist acts while building up its strength, and early targets included aircraft, several of which were damaged or destroyed by bombs over the years. On 8 March 1968, Air Manila F.27 PI-C-871 broke up off Panay Island with the loss of eighteen passengers and crew. On 21 April 1970 Philippines Air Lines HS.748 PI-C-1022 crashed with 36 killed, and six weeks later a bomb was placed on a PAL F.27, PI-C-507.

By 1971, the NPA had 2,000 men and women bearing arms, although counter-insurgency activities by the AFP had forced them to Isabela province. The PAF now began a reorganization and expansion programme to enable it to support ground forces against both the MNLF and NPA. Nos. 16 and 17 Fighter Squadrons were formed at Sangley Point with the T-28D fitted for the counter-insurgency (coin) role and tasked specifically with backing the Army and PC against the MNLF in the south, while the F-86 was beginning to be phased out as the F-5A entered service. Surprisingly, despite the potential for their use in the ground-attack role, neither the F-5 nor the T-28 was equipped with radio enabling direct contact with ground units. At the time of writing this deficiency remains, and it has severely

TABLE OF UNITS: THE PHILIPPINES, 1964 TO DATE

Unit	Aircraft	Base	Role	Nos.
PAF, 1964				
6 FS	⎫			⎧16
7 FS	⎬ F-86F	Basa AB	Air defence	16
8 FS	⎭			⎩16
9 FS	F-86D	Basa AB	Night fighter	14
21 TS	C-47	⎫		⎧15
22 TS	C-47, F.27-100	⎬ Mactan AB	Transport	⎩20
?	H-19A	?	Transport, rescue	5
?	SA-16A	?	SAR	5
?	T-34A	Basa AB	Tactical training	20
?	T-6, T-28A, T-33A, BT-13A	Manila	Training	50
PAF, 1972				
6 FS	F-5A/B	Basa AB	Fighter, ground attack	20
7 FS	⎫	Basa AB	Air defence	⎧14
8 FS	⎬ F-86F			⎩14
16 AS	⎫ T-28D	Sangley Point AB	Coin	⎧8
17 AS	⎭			⎩8
204 TS	F.27-100	⎫		⎧4
206 TS	C-47	⎬ Mactan AB	Medium transport	30
221 TS	C-123B/K	⎭		⎩15
?	UH-1H, H-19A	?	Transport, SAR	14
?	T-6, T-33A, T-34A, T-41D	Manila	Training	45
PAF, 1980				
5 Fighter Wing				
6 FS	F-5A/B	⎫	⎧Fighter, ground attack	22
7 FS	F-86F (converting to F-8H)	⎬ Basa AB	Air defence	20
9 TFS	T-34A		Tactical training	25
105 CCTS	T-33A, RT-33A	⎭	⎩Combat training, recce	13
18 Strike Wing				
16 AS	T-28D	Sangley Point AB		⎧12
25 AS	T-28D	Sangley Point AB, Zamboanga	⎬ Coin	12
17 AS	SF.260WP	Sangley Point AB		⎩16
27 SARS	HU-16B	Sangley Point AB	SAR	5
240 Composite Wing				
291 SAMS	Beaver	⎫	⎧Liaison, supply	8
303 ARS	AC-47	⎬ Sangley Point, Nichols AB	Recce, gunship	11
601 LS	U-17A/B		Liaison	6
901 WS	Cessna 210	Sangley Point	⎩Rain-seeding, weather recce	5
205 Tactical Airlift Wing				
204 TAS	F.27-100	⎫	⎧Medium transport	7
206 TAS	C-47	⎬ Nichols AB	Medium transport	15
207 TAS	C-47		Medium transport	15
505 ARS	UH-1H, Bö 105C	⎭	⎩Rescue	15
222 Heavy Airlift Wing				
221 HAS	C-123B/K	⎫		⎧15
222 HAS	C-130H, L-100-20	⎬ Mactan AB	Transport	5
223 HAS	GAF Nomad	⎭		⎩12
700 Special Missions Wing				
702 SMS	707, BAC.111, F.27, UH-1H	Nichols AB	Transport, special missions	9
100 Training Wing				
101 TS	T-41D	⎫ Fernando AB	⎧Advanced training	12
102 TS	SF.260MP	⎭	⎩Basic training	32
533 Airbase Sqn.	–	Zamboanga		None
Navy, 1980				
–	Defender, Bö 105C		MR, SAR	15
PAF, 1988				
6 TFS	F-5A/B	Basa AB	Fighter, ground attack	12
16 AS	S-76	⎫ Sangley Point AB	⎧Helicopter transport, coin	10
17 AS	SF.260WP	⎭	⎩Coin	10
9 TS	T-34A	Basa AB	Tactical training	12
204 ATS	C-47, AC-47	Nichols AB	Medium transport	7
222 HAS	L.100-20	⎫ Mactan AB	Transport	⎧3
223 HAS	GAF Nomad	⎭		⎩4
702 SMS	F.27, UH-1H, ? BAC-111	Nichols AB	Transport, special missions	8
27 SARS	F.27MP, Bö 105C, S-76	Sangley Point AB	MR, SAR	8
601 LS	U-17A/B	Sangley Point AB	Liaison, observation	15
210 HS	⎫	Nichols AB	Transport, gunship	⎧15
211 HS	⎬ UH-1H/N, Bell 205			⎩15
Police Force, 1988				
–	Bö 105C	Manila	Observation	2

Note: In addition, there were, in 1988, various PAF light aircraft and transports in dubious states of repair.

impaired the PAF in support of ground operations. In addition, new transport units were created with the Fokker F.27 and C-123, while the first UH-1H helicopters were acquired, permitting the rapid movement of troops to trouble spots. There is no doubt that the Government received considerable help from the United States, but corruption and incompetence negated much of the effort.

So serious was the position by 1972 that martial law was introduced on 21 September. A month later the Bangra Moro Army was formed as the military wing of the MNLF, and by March 1973 the MNLF, with 58,000 members and supported by Sabah and Libya, controlled Cotabato province and the Sulu archipelago. In February 1974 the town of Jolo was occupied and subjected to intense naval gunfire and to air attack by the T-28 units. Several attempts at a political solution were made, but a ceasefire was broken in early 1976 when 36 members of the AFP were killed in Jolo. AFP reprisals followed, and tracks were mined and camps subjected to further air strikes. In December 1977 the MNLF HQ north of Zamboanga was located and destroyed.

Peace talks were held, and a combination of moves towards some limited regional autonomy and internal divisions within the MNLF resulted in containment. The AFP now turned its attention again to the NPA, which was slowly growing, gaining support from peasant communities. The communists suffered some reverses between 1975 and 1978 when they lost Chinese support, and in 1978 the NPA was driven from Luzon province.

By 1980 the PAF was at its peak strength. The Fighter Wing in the north was changing its last Sabres for the F-8H; the Wing played little part in the internal wars, however, its aircraft being committed to the air defence role despite there being no obvious external threat to the country's integrity. The Strike Wing at Sangley Point now had a squadron of SF.260WPs in the ground-attack role, and a Composite Wing had been formed, split between Nichols AB and Sangley. This Wing operated various types in support roles, including the AC-47 gunship. The ubiquitous C-47 soldiered on in the transport role, but

GAF Nomads and Hercules of several variants now supplemented the older aircraft. More helicopters were available, including the Bö 105C, and an Air Base Squadron had been formed at Zamboanga to enable the efficient operation of detached aircraft.

On 15 January 1982, PAF fighters strafed a Japanese tanker off Mindanao which was claimed to be delivering arms for the rebels. The PAF now had to increase its maritime patrol force to cope not only with prospective gun-running but also with the growing number of pirates, some of whom were no doubt funding the guerrilla war. Three F.27MP surveillance aircraft were ordered.

In the middle of 1982 the AFP began a new offensive against the NPA, and on 15 July helicopter-borne troops attacked 100 rebels at Agusan del Norte. In late February 1983, 600 guerrillas in northern Mindanao were pursued. On 21 August that year an event that is likely to have lasting impact on the Philippines took place. The opposition leader, Benigno Aquino, was shot as he left his aircraft at Manila Airport after three years' self-imposed exile. The Government of President Marcos was widely exposed as totally corrupt, and this led to a revolution in 1986 in which Aquino's wife, Corazon, came to power. She has had a difficult time introducing reforms to cope with a range of threats to the Philippines' stability. On 26 September 1985, for example, four gunboats and three helicopters attacked the Maranas islet in the Sibutu Islands. Initially Malaysia was blamed, it being suggested that the attack was in retaliation for a pirate raid

In the guerrilla war from 1946 to 1954, the Philippine Air Force relied on the ubiquitous C-47 as its sole transport type. Illustrated is (4)347964 of 2 Transport Squadron. (Air-Britain)

From 1964, the Philippine Government has been fighting guerrillas on two fronts across a vast geographical area. The ageing Mustangs were replaced by F-86 Sabres, then F-5 Freedom Fighters, which equipped 6 Fighter Squadron at Basa. (Via B. Wheeler)

on Lahad Datu, Sabah. The Malaysians protested their innocence, and it was subsequently felt most likely that the raid came from Vietnam in an attempt to spoil relations between the two countries.

Despite attempts to reach an accommodation with the NPA, the many factions within Government ensure that Mrs. Aquino's rule is precarious and reforms are slow in their implementation. The PAF is in a sorry state at the time of writing: the F-8 Crusaders have been permanently grounded because the air defence radar system is inoperable; the F-5As and T-28Ds have been withdrawn to have FM radio fitted to enable them to communicate directly with ground forces; and the three C-130Hs have been grounded for deep overhaul. Attrition has taken a toll of other types: although some seventeen S-76/AUH-76s have been delivered, mainly for coin work, only ten were serviceable in early 1988, while of the remaining types the 28 UH-1H/Ns are the most important in support of the continuing war against the NPA.

AIRCRAFT MARKINGS

F-86F *Bare metal overall, black serial on fin, buzz number on rear fuselage: (5)24524/FU-542 (6 FS); (5)24843/843 (7 FS); (5)24317/317 (5 FW).*
F-86D *Bare metal overall, black serial on fin,*

buzz number on rear fuselage: (5)18406/FU-406 (9 FS).
T-28D *Light grey overall, black serial and squadron badge on fin: (5)13782 (17 AS). Olive Drab overall, no serial displayed: (16 AS).*
F-5A *Bare metal overall, black serial on fin, last three digits on mid fuselage: (6)13320/FA-320 (6 FS).*
F-5B *(6)10589/589 (6 FS).*
F-8H *Pale blue-grey over, white under, black serial on fin, code on nose and fin top, squadron badge on fin. (1)48661/301, (1)48649/304 (7 FS).*
RT-33A *Medium grey overall, black serial on fin, last three digits repeated on mid fuselage in red: (5)35457/457 (105 CCTS).*
AC-47 *Blue green/Olive Drab/sand over, light grey under, black serial on fin: (4)330717 (204 ATS).*
C-47 *Bare metal overall, white top fuselage decking, black serial on fin: (4)292257 (204 TAS).*
Islander *Medium grey overall, black serial on fin: 568, 552 (291 SAMS).*
HU-16B *White overall, large diagonal orange bands around forward fuselage and wings, orange panels on fin and tailplane: (5)17184 (27 SARS).*
S-76 *White overall, black serial on nose, orange band around fuselage: 216 (27 SARS).*
Bö 105C *Olive Drab overall, black serial on boom: 168 (? unit).*

10.7. Malaya, 1948–1960

Although the Malayan Communist Party (MCP) was formed in 1929, mainly from among the 38 per cent of the Malayan population who were ethnic Chinese, during the Second World War its members supported the Allies against Japan. In 1942 the Malayan Peoples' Anti-Japanese Army (MPAJA) was formed from among MCP members, who were armed by the British in order to harass the enemy and provide intelligence, and from 1943 the MPAJA worked with the British covert Force 136. When the war ended, the MPAJA was disbanded and expected to surrender its weapons, and although the majority were recovered, several hundred committed and armed members of the MCP took to the jungle to prepare for a guerrilla war against the British. A Malayan Union was introduced in April 1946, but this was unpopular because the Malays resented representation of Chinese and Indians while the communists opposed any central government.

There were demonstrations through 1946, and in 1947 over 300 strikes were called. By early 1948 serious riots had begun, and these increased after strikes were made unlawful in the spring. In June the Malayan Peoples' Anti-British Army (MPABA) was formed out of elements of the defunct MPAJA and the MCP. As the position deteriorated a state of

emergency was declared on 17 June, and on 23 July the MCP was banned. Operation 'Firedog', which was to last for twelve years, had begun. At the start of the emergency there were two British, five Gurkha and three Malay battalions in Malaya, and some 9,000 police. Intelligence was poor, despite the fact that the communists operated widely in the populated coastal plain. On 1 February 1949, the Malayan Races Liberation Army (MRLA) was formed from MCP and MPABA elements.

In June 1948 the RAF presence in Malaya was limited. Elements of two air defence squadrons, Nos. 28 and 60, both equipped with the Spitfire FR.18, moved up to Kuala Lumpur from Tengah. No. 84 Sqn. at Changi, with the Beaufighter X, was the only available strike unit, although the Sunderlands of 209 Sqn. could be called on for heavy support. In the reconnaissance role, 81 Sqn. with Spitfire FR.18s and PR.19s and Mosquito PR.34s was also at Changi. The transport units were based at Changi and comprised 48, 52 and 110 Sqns., all equipped with the Dakota. They were supplemented by a variety of aircraft of the Far East Communications Squadron (FECS). Last, there were the Austers of 1914 Flt., which was soon expanded to form 656 Sqn.

The war in Malaya went through three phases,

the first of which, the defensive phase, lasted from 1948 to 1951. During this period the population was subjected to attack by guerrillas, who then simply disappeared into the jungle. The ground forces were inexperienced at handling this type of fighting and, as already indicated, were poorly served with intelligence. The first RAF strike against communist terrorists (CT) was on 6 July, when a CT camp near Ayer Karah in Perak was attacked by Spitfires of 60 Sqn. A second strike was mounted on the 15th and a third the following day against a camp situated in swamps at Telok Anson, where ten CT were killed. The strikes continued into August, but the accidental firing of a rocket on the ground which killed a civilian brought a temporary ban on the use of underwing stores on the ageing Spitfires. Two Beaufighters of 84 Sqn. were brought up to Kuala Lumpur from Tengah, from where they continued to mount offensive sorties, being supplemented by a trio detached from 45 Sqn. based in Ceylon.

Throughout the war the RAF mounted two types of air strike. When intelligence indicated the precise location of a camp or other known target, pinpoint attacks were made, but with the prevailing weather conditions, which meant that the early mist did not clear until mid-morning, these operations were limited. Most of the successful strikes were made early in the war before the CT realized the potential of air power; by the end of 1948 they reduced the size of their camps, camouflaged them and became more mobile. The second type of air strike was the use of area bombing in regions believed to be occupied by the CT. Throughout the war an enormous tonnage of bombs was used to relatively little effect against the jungle. The guerrillas employed only hit-and-run tactics, never gaining sufficient strength to stand and fight set-piece battles. For this reason, close-support strikes were rarely flown, since by the time aircraft were alerted the enemy would have vanished. Escort patrols were flown, however, as in the early stages of the emergency the CT set many ambushes on road and rail convoys.

In October 84 Sqn. departed for Iraq, where it re-equipped with the Brigand; it was replaced by 45 Sqn., which was fully operational by May 1949. After August there was a lull in operations as the guerrillas re-formed after initial setbacks, but as the civilian authorities began a resettlement programme, intelligence improved and on 28 February 1949 one of the most successful strikes of the campaign was mounted. To date, operations had been hampered by the CT having advance warning of strikes by reconnaissance flights, and especially by the noise of troops setting up ambushes. The strike against a target in Mengkuang by eight Spitfires using fragmentation bombs and four Beaufighters killed nine out of a total of fifteen in the combined operation.

The first jet to serve in the Far East was the Vampire FB.5. It equipped 60 Sqn. and then (in the FB.9. version) 45 Sqn. from 1950 until replaced by the Venom. Serviceability was never high, and the nature of the campaign was such that piston-engined aircraft were better suited for most tasks. Seen here off Singapore Island are FB.5s of 60 Sqn., including WG827/B. (D. Goult)

The Sunderlands also occasionally took to bombing the jungle, but they spent most of their time on maritime reconnaissance, searching for vessels bringing arms up the coast. The apparently indiscriminate area bombing based on dated intelligence did have the effect of keeping the guerrillas on the move, however. The pattern bombing required larger aircraft than those permanently based in the theatre, and in January 1947 Lancasters of 7 Sqn. had detached to Changi from the UK in Operation 'Red Lion'; in 'Red Lion II', Lincolns of 97 Sqn. also gained experience of detaching. On 28 November 1949, in Operation 'Centipede', Lancasters of 210 Sqn. spent two weeks at Tengah where, it is understood, they dropped bombs on areas believed to be occupied by CT. These early detachments paved the way for a series of operations from March 1950 involving detached Lincolns (Operations 'Musgrave' and 'Bold') and then Canberras (Operation 'Mileage'). From 1957, Valiant and Vulcan bombers from the V-force also flew sorties from Changi. On a more permanent basis, the Lincolns of 1 Sqn. RAAF arrived at Tengah in July 1950, from which base they were to operate until 1958.

The fighters had been depleted when 28 Sqn. departed for Hong Kong, along with 656 Sqn.'s 1903 Flight, as the position in China worsened. Reinforcement came in August 1949 in the shape of Tempests of 33 Sqn., shipped from Germany aboard HMS Ocean. Over the next 21 months these aircraft flew nearly 2,000 sorties. There was further (albeit temporary) support when the Seafires of 800 NAS and Fireflies of 827 NAS disembarked from HMS Triumph in October. Throughout the emergency, Royal Navy carriers stopped off at Singapore, enabling their aircraft to add to the RAF and Commonwealth Air Forces in the theatre.

The mistakes made by the Government in the

early stages were soon recognized and gradually rectified. In April 1950, Sir Harold Briggs was appointed Director of Operations in Malaya, a distinct appointment from that of High Commissioner held by Sir Henry Gurney. The Director of Operations was responsible for all security forces, including the police, the Army and the air forces, and had authority to co-ordinate the work of those civil agencies whose actions affected the outcome of the war. Briggs recognized two problems. The first was the need for co-ordination between agencies, especially in the area of intelligence, and the second was the vulnerability of displaced Chinese villagers as communist tools. Thus a three-tier committee system was set up. At the top a War Council was established, with the Director of Operations in the chair and consisting of the Secretary of the Malayan Federation and police, Army and air force commanders. Next were the State War Executive Committees, comprising the State Prime Minister and police and Army representatives. At local level, District War Executive Committees were established, comprising the District Officer and local police and Army representatvies. While at each level civilians took the chair, the most important contribution came from the police, who were responsible for intelligence.

There was a further development from February 1951. Sir Henry Gurney was killed in a road ambush in October 1950, and shortly afterwards Sir Harold Briggs died. It was decided to combine the posts of High Commissioner and Director of Operations, and Sir Gerald Templar was the first appointee. From this date the situation improved rapidly: by the end of 1952, civilian deaths from CT raids were down from 90 a month to 15, and the CT strength was reduced from 8,000 to 2,800. The communists withdrew to the hills, where they pressed aboriginals to supply them with food.

The RAF, meanwhile, had received new equipment. No. 45 Sqn. had re-equipped with the Brigand from 6 December 1949, and in April 1950 84 Sqn., similarly equipped, had returned from Iraq in Operation 'Tireless'. Early in 1951, 60 Sqn. lost its Spitfires for the first jet in the theatre, the Vampire FB.5, although the squadron's primary function was air defence and the commitment of the unit to 'Firedog' was limited. The last Spitfire fighter sortie of over 1,800 in the campaign was flown against a target in Johore on 1 January. Through 1951 the Brigand was plagued with troubles and grounded on several occasions. No. 33 Sqn. exchanged its Tempests for the long-range Hornet in mid-1951, the type having gone out of service in Fighter Command. At the end of January 1952, 45 Sqn. also received Hornets, transferring its remaining Brigands to 84 Sqn.

The number of equipment changes, coupled with weapons problems on the Brigands, Vampires and Hornets, had a serious effect on availability through 1950 and 1951, and Harvard communications aircraft of the station flights and fighter squadrons were fitted with bomb racks and pressed into service as dive-bombers. The onset of the Korean War also reduced the availability of Sunderlands, which had played their part in the pattern bombing. Then, in March 1951, the Air Ministry blocked further detachments of Lincolns under Operation 'Musgrave' after 61 Sqn. departed. It was the view of Bomber Command that the detachments provided little in the way of proper training for the crews, and the number of squadrons available to NATO was to be reduced temporarily as the Command converted to the Washington. In any event, the cost of the bombing campaign was extremely high with little tangible result, and there was a shortage of 1,000lb bombs.

To a limited extent, the loss was made good by an increase in the establishment of 1 Sqn. RAAF. The Lincolns generally operated from Tengah, which was acceptable given that they usually took part in planned operations. The lighter units were based at Tengah but operated from Kuala Lumpur and Butterworth with aircraft held on two-hour standby, primarily to provide relief to police posts under attack and with the Brigands covering the south and the longer-range Hornets the north. The Hornets were particularly valuable in convoy support. The main weapons employed, apart from guns, were 1,000lb and 500lb high-explosive (HE) and 20lb fragmentation bombs. Rockets were generally ineffective, except when used against a specific hard target. Features of the main weapons used are set out below.

Weapon	MAE[1]	Usage (1951)	Unit cost[2]
1,000lb bomb (nose-fused)	75,000		£125 0s.
1,000lb bomb (tail-fused)	6,000	5,080	
500lb bomb (nose-fused)	15,000		£56 0s.
500lb bomb (tail-fused)	3,000	14,309	
20lb fragmentation bomb (fb)	1,000	34,618	£4 10s.
350lb clusters of 19lb fb	27,500	384	£90 0s. £18 10s.
60lb rocket	1,500	19,961	
20mm cannon shell	400	60,000	
0.5in ammunition	4	550,000	
0.303in ammunition	4	700,000	

1. Mean area of effectiveness in square feet.
2. Costs at 1951 prices.

The most effective way of achieving a mean area of effectiveness was to use one Lincoln

Among the most powerful – and perhaps the most beautiful – of piston-engined fighters was the Hornet, which flew ground-attack missions in Malaya with 33 and 45 Sqns. WB911/OB-B was a Hornet F.3 of 45 Sqn. The underwing rocket rails are clearly visible in this photograph. In 45 Sqn., the type was replaced by the Vampire FB.9. (D. Goult)

bomber loaded with fourteen nose-fused (and therefore air-bursting in the jungle) 1,000lb bombs. The total cost was £2,500, comprising £750 per sortie operating costs plus ammunition. In contrast, using tail-fused 500lb bombs, 80 Brigand sorties would be needed to cover the same area, at a cost in excess of £32,000. Other types of weapons were tried and rejected. Napalm was tested in 200lb canisters in 1950, but it was ineffective in the jungle, and depth charges also proved of little value. From 1953, 4,000lb HE bombs were used very occasionally, and smoke markers were dropped to move aborigines without causing lasting damage. From around 1954, 'screamers' in the form of empty beer bottles were dropped with conventional weapons, to economize on cost while still creating fear.

Initially, targets were passed through the RAF command chain from local ground forces, but this time-wasting procedure soon changed so that targets were allocated through a Joint Operations Centre. This procedure facilitated the speedy preparation of the best aircraft and weapons combination for the task and took full account of the need for care in minimizing the risk to civilians or ground forces. Occasionally local ground commanders were authorized to call for direct air support in conjunction with planned full-scale operations. As a result, accidents were few. It is a fact, however, that piston-engined aircraft were more suitable for attacking targets in the conditions of Malaya, where there was no effective anti-aircraft opposition, than the faster and less accurate jets. In the early days of the campaign, Army cars equipped with radios directed strike aircraft to the target, with Dakotas acting as relays, but by 1950 this method was rarely used as the cars had difficulty reaching the sites of attacks.

Working from aerial reconnaissance photos, from early on in the campaign the strike aircraft were guided by Austers of 656 Sqn. flown by pilots with local knowledge. Targets were then marked by the Austers using phosphorous grenades or flares. Over the years numerous other methods and devices were tried, but although some increased accuracy, they often meant moving heavy equipment in the jungle near to the scene of action. In a sizeable operation, the area to be attacked was first bombed by medium bombers using 500lb or 1,000lb bombs. This strike, of perhaps six to ten aircraft, would be followed immediately by fighters using lighter bombs, rockets and guns. Precise timing was important, to preserve the element of surprise. Raids would then be followed up by Sunderlands dropping fragmentation bombs over the next 24 to 48 hours to keep the CT in a state of shock and to inhibit the removal of the wounded.

The first major operation involving the Lincolns was 'Jackpot', mounted between 15 March and May 1950 in south-east Selangor. On 14–16

April 98 sorties were made, and after a further series of raids later in the month involving 108 sorties, 44 CT were eliminated. In 1950, 687 strikes were made, involving 4,938 sorties. The largest operation of 1951 was 'Warbler', mounted in Johore. The air forces were employed in harassing the CT and denying escape routes and assembly points and by attacking clearings and camps away from the area of operations of the ground forces. During two months 145 strikes involving 610 sorties were flown, despite the RAF Lincolns' having returned to the UK. Major strikes continued through the year, but the results were out of proportion to the effort involved. Particularly disappointing were the attempts to cut off and round up the CT responsible for the murder of the High Commissioner.

The year 1952 saw a change in the nature of targets as intelligence and reconnaissance photos indicated CT camps and cultivation clearings.

The Brigand was flown with some success by both 45 and 84 Sqns. in Malaya, but unfortunately it was unreliable and both units suffered fatal accidents when aircraft broke up in the air. WB236/J of 84 Sqn. is here fitted with rocket rails and shows to advantage the colour scheme of Medium Sea Grey over and black under, with the playing card 'heart' symbol on the fin. (D. Goult)

Thus the air forces turned to a higher level of pinpoint attack. In February, in Operation 'Puma', the first air-only attack was carried out against up to 400 CT in western Pahang, who could not be approached by ground forces. Eighteen Lincoln and 35 Brigand sorties were flown, with 132 1,000lb and 216 500lb bombs dropped and 6,800 rounds of 20mm ammunition expended in six days from 13 February, but because of the absence of ground forces in the area no evaluation of the strikes was possible. By the end of 1952, 676 targets had been attacked in 3,699 sorties.

When the campaign began, the transport force comprised three Dakota squadrons, 48, 52 and 110. They were all based at Changi, but one squadron was detached to Kuala Lumpur to provide direct support for ground operations on a rotational basis. As necessary, the detached aircraft were supplemented by Dakotas from Changi which were otherwise involved in flying the trunk routes. The RAF units were supported by aircraft from 41 Sqn. RNZAF and 38 Sqn. RAAF from December 1949 and June 1950 respectively. The plan devised by Briggs for defeating the CT was to clear areas from the south northwards while dealing with any local problems anywhere in the Federation. As areas were deemed to be clear, they were described as 'white'; thus many early operations were conducted within reach of the airfields on Singapore. As the campaign developed and the CT took to the mountainous jungle, they applied pressure on aboriginals to give them support, so from 1953 a series of hill forts, usually with their own airstrips, was constructed and the transport force not only supplied patrols in the jungle but also kept the hill forts supplied.

The importance of air supply in Malaya cannot be overstated. Without fresh stocks of food and ammunition the patrols would have been limited to four days' duration, while air drops allowed patrols lasting up to three months. The conditions for drops were far from ideal. Many were made into small clearings among 200ft trees or swamps, where a margin of error of more than 50ft could mean the loss of the supplies. Weather added to the problems, and it is remarkable that no more than 1.5 per cent of all supplies were not retrieved. The work of packing and dispatching fell to 55 Coy. Royal Army Service Corps (RASC). The average weight of the packs was 270lb, and it was usual for crews to lose over 3lb in body weight through perspiration on a single sortie. Parachutes used were the 18ft 'Irvin' costing £15 (weight limit 180lb) and the 24ft 'R' type costing £32 (weight limit 450lb); each could be used up to three times and were to some extent replaced by a 28ft 'Utility' disposable parachute costing £25. As 18,000 parachutes a year were used, the introduction of the later type resulted in savings.

The first drops were made in support of Operation 'Haystack' in northern Perak between 25 April and 27 May 1948, during which time a Dakota of 110 Sqn. detached to Taiping dropped 222 containers in fifteen sorties. The work was dangerous, and several Dakotas were lost early on in the war. KJ962 of 110 Sqn. crashed near Batu Melintang on 19 August 1948, followed on 12 November by KM633 of the same unit in which the CO was killed; 52 Sqn. lost KN536 on 7 September 1949 and KN630, in which twelve were killed, on 25 August 1950. Activity increased steadily to August 1951, when the number of patrols dropped and certain posts were supplied by road, but in January 1952 flooding resulted in a temporary increase. In February the Valetta, with a 50 per cent increase in payload over the Dakota, was used for the first time on supply drops.

The construction of hill forts from 1953 placed an extra burden on the transport units since all equipment, including tractors for clearing airstrips, was dropped by air. Moreover, from July 1953 to March 1954, two battalions of infantry operated continuously in southern Kedah in Operation 'Sword', while from October to December 1953, in Operation 'Valiant', a further four battalions were deployed in north-west Pahang. Both operations were completely supplied by air. To the end of 1954 the annual air supply activity is set out below.

Year	Sorties	Weight dropped (lb × 1,000)	Amount per sortie (lb)
1948	46	c. 62	1,348
1949	875	2,045	2,337
1950	1,421	3,724	2,637
1951	1,289	3,465	2,688
1952	988	3,013	3,050
1953	1,346	4,462	3,315
1954	2,080	6,793	3,266

The medium-range transport units were also employed on communications work, especially in moving troops and police around the country but also in evacuating wounded personnel and providing a courier service. They also played an important part in several operations where paratroops were deployed. Members of 22 Regt. Special Air Service (SAS) were dropped on several occasions, the first being during Operation 'Helsby' in February 1952 when 54 men of B Squadron were dropped near the Thai border. Because of local conditions, the four Dakotas employed dropped 44 paratroopers beyond the drop zone into 150ft trees, but all recovered. Thought was now given to the provision of improved equip-

As in so many postwar conflicts, the T-6 Harvard played an important part in Malaya. The type was flown by Malay Auxiliary Air Force squadrons on unarmed reconnaissance sorties from 1950 to 1958.

ment for paratroops dropping into and recovering from trees. Eventually several forms of abseiling gear were developed and used with success, although there were several fatalities during Operation 'Sword'. Operations were halted for a time while improvements were made, then, in the largest operation of the campaign, 'Termite', 180 men of 22 SAS Regt. were dropped into the Kinta and Raia valleys east of Ipoh. The paratroops took in equipment for cutting trees to make clearings for helicopter leandings, by which means many additional troops were brought in. After 'Termite' there were relatively few paradrops as the helicopter became available in greater numbers, although there were occasions when they were made from helicopters hovering at 750ft over particularly small and difficult drop zones.

The first helicopters in the theatre were three S-51 Dragonflies of the newly formed Far East Casualty Air Evacuation Flight. They became operational on 1 April 1950 at Seletar, soon moving to Changi, and the first casualty to be evacuated by helicopter was a policeman flown to Johore hosptital on 6 June. By the end of 1950, 26 casualties had been evacuated; although the initial numbers were small, the improvement in morale resulting from the knowledge that medical treatment was never far away was important. Fifty-five evacuations were made in 1951, but with more helicopters available from 1952 the number increased to 144, although one Dragonfly was lost in a crash. Late in 1952 it was decided to disband the Evacuation Flight and replace it with 194 Sqn., which, equipped with twelve aircraft, was to operate in a range of roles, including troop movement. The unit shared this task with 848 NAS, which brought its S-55 helicopters to Sembawang from the UK aboard HMS *Perseus* in January 1953. Both units operated within 303 (Helicopter) Wing, with detachments at Kuala Lumpur but with helicopters positioned at other bases as necessary.

Serviceability problems with the S-51 resulted in the type being progressively replaced by the Sycamore with 194 Sqn. Gradually the restrictions on the use of helicopters for work other than casevac were relaxed, and the units available undertook an increasing share of troop movements. The Fleet Air Arm's 848 NAS carried out its first trooplift on 16 February 1953 when three machines transferred twelve men of the Worcestershire Regiment to a hideout near Port Swettenham in search of a local CT commander. Nearly 12,000 troops were moved into operational areas by helicopter during 1953, but the small numbers of machines available placed heavy demands on aircraft and crews and at one stage in August 1954 only one S-55 and one S-51 were serviceable. To some extent the position was rectified by the establishment of 155 Sqn. with the Whirlwind, an inadequate licence-built version of the S-55 which was plagued with problems during its career in Malaya.

Although 848 NAS had been due to return to the UK in August 1954, it was retained in the theatre until the RAF was able to meet all the demands; the unit was disestablished on 10 December 1956. As the range of work undertaken by the helicopters increased, the rules for their use were again tightened, and from 1953 the first Pioneer short take-off and landing (STOL) light transports appeared in the theatre. Able to carry four passengers and with a take-off run of only 75yds, they were able to assume some of the roles hitherto reserved for the helicopters, especially in reinforcing and supplying the chain of hill forts. From 1955, as areas were declared clear, the helicopters were mainly confined to work in the north and south of Malaya. It was planned to replace the early Whirlwinds with Sycamores but problems with the rotors of the latter led to both types remaining in service, 155 and 194 Sqns. being merged into 110 Sqn. in June 1959. The peak month for trooplifting was October 1958, when, in support of Operation 'Tiger' in South Johore, 4,133 fully equipped troops were airlifted in and out of jungle clearings, 60 per cent of them by Sycamore.

Another important role carried out by the helicopter was crop-spraying. As the CT were denied access to the coastal towns and villages under the Briggs Plan, they lost much of the support from their Min Yuen (Peoples' Movement) civilian branch and therefore of their supplies of food. As they took to the hills they were obliged to cultivate crops in jungle clearings only identifiable from the air, and it was these clearings that were the target of the crop-spraying effort. Development work was undertaken in the UK using Auster Autocar J/5G G-ANVN, registered with the Secretary of State for the Colonies. The aircraft was subsequently brought into service with the RAF as XJ941 and sent to Malaya in 1956. Austers of 656 Sqn. were also used to spray verges of roads to reduce cover to CT preparing to ambush vehicles. Initially sodium arsenite was used, but since this was poisonous and might affect the indigenous population a change was made to a mixture of trioxene and diesolene which killed all vegetation and was non-poisonous but effective over a long period. The first operation was 'Cyclone 1', mounted on 31 August 1953 in the Kluang and Labis areas. Ten noted cultivation

Helicopters played a crucial role in the campaign in Malaya, where they were used initially to recover wounded troops from small jungle clearings and latterly for troop placement. These ex-USN HO4S Sikorsky S-55s were flown by 848 NAS as Whirlwind HAR.21s from January 1953. Nearest the camera is WV191.

sites were sprayed after being marked by Austers of 656 Sqn., and over several days two S-55s and one S-51 had destroyed 30 cultivations. Operation 'Cyclone II' followed shortly after this, and by the end of 1953, 88 cultivations had been sprayed. Work carried on into 1954, but the shortage of helicopters led to the work being taken over by aircraft of 267 Sqn. Helicopter operations through the period of the Emergency are summarized below.

Year	Casevacs	Troops	Passengers	Freight (lb × 1,000)
1950	26	–	–	–
1951	55	–	–	–
1952	144	–	–	–
1953	518	10,098	–	164
1954	743	8,829	3,033	238
1955	793	27,887	4,387	593
1956	701	25,890	3,769	439
1957	632	19,752	2,875	415
1958	752	26,767	2,709	629
1959	136	2,397	324	76
1960	173	4,033	369	92

In the early years of the campaign the brunt of liaison work was borne by the Austers of 656 Sqn. Originally based at Sembawang, the squadron comprised four Flights, 1902 at Taiping, 1903 at Seramban, 1914 at Kluang and the RAF Communications Flight at Kuala Lumpur. The last was disbanded in July 1948 and replaced by 1907 Flt. at the end of August. Then, in July 1949, 1903 Flt. was sent to Hong Kong, to be replaced in July 1950 by 1911 Flt. at Changi. The squadron now comprised about 30 Austers, mostly in the observation role, but in May 1952 Nos. 1902 and 1914 Flts. remained designated AOP while Nos. 1907 and 1911 became Light Liaison Flights to reflect the balance of work undertaken. The Austers were used extensively for a range of work, often in direct support of Army units, and their value was limited only by their payload.

No. 656 Sqn. was one of the few flying units to be continuously employed throughout the Emergency, being equipped for most of the time with the Auster AOP.5 and 6. Its roles included communications, reconnaissance, target-marking, supply-dropping, leaflet-dropping, AOP and liaison, and at the peak of the campaign it was flying nearly 23,000 sorties a year. The first Pioneers reached Malaya in early 1953, and by October they formed 1311 Transport Flight of 303 (Helicopter) Wing; they then formed part of the original equipment of 267 Sqn. As already mentioned, the Pioneers fulfilled some of the tasks previously undertaken by helicopters, especially in resupplying the forts. In 1954 the costs of flying the S-55 and S-51 were £73 and £53 per hour respectively, whereas the cost of operating the Pioneer and Auster were £35 and £15 per hour. As the short-range transport unit in Malaya and because it was based at Kuala Lumpur, 267 Sqn. was required to handle as wide a range of tasks as 656 Sqn. One of the new roles it assumed was leaflet-dropping and broadcasting.

Throughout the conflict an extensive campaign of psychological warfare was mounted. The objective was to encourage the surrender of CT through disaffection, especially at junior ranks, and to win the hearts and minds of the uncommitted population. In the first instance the leaflet-drops were of a strategic nature, advising the population of the emergency, but the emphasis quickly turned to tactical drops, often in association with operations, and the majority called for the surrender of CT, often naming individuals. Surrendered CT were used to draft the leaflets. As an indication of the effort involved, during the peak month for leaflet-dropping, October 1953, 19,536,000 leaflets were dispersed in 51 sorties, many in association with Operation 'Bison I'. Loud-hailer aircraft were also used in this operation.

The use of broadcasts from aircraft was first tested in October 1952 using a borrowed US Army C-47. From these trials and similar experiments with two 100-watt speakers tested on Auster J/1 Autocrat G-AJIZ, the RAF fitted equipment in two Valettas, which were used from early 1953. The Valetta suffered from excessive engine noise, however, limiting the range of broadcasts, so the RAF turned to the Dakota, three of which were fitted with a battery of speakers. Whereas the Valetta had to fly at 1,500ft to be heard over a 1,500yd range, the Dakota could fly at 2,500ft and be heard over 2,500yds. Flying on a creeping, left-handed, square circuit at little over stalling speed, the Dakota could remain within earshot for the 30 seconds necessary to get its message across. The Austers, with their shorter broadcast range, were used for known pinpoint targets. Initially they covered nearly half of the all sorties flown, but gradually, as the war drew to a close, they were used less and less and in 1958 were removed from the role.

The psychological warfare tasks were shared between the theatre transport units and first the FECS and then 267 Sqn. until, in 1958, it was renumbered 209 Sqn. The Voice Flight of 267 Sqn. only comprised at its peak three Dakotas and two Austers, which were normally based at Kuala Lumpur, but when 267 Sqn. was renumbered the Dakotas operated from Bayan Lepas, Penang, to be within reach of the remaining CT enclaves. A summary of psychological warfare sorties throughout the campaign to 1958 is set out below, bearing in mind that only dedicated leaflet-dropping sorties are listed; many leaflet

The Valetta was not as reliable as the Dakota it eventually replaced, but its climb rate enabled it to operate more safely in tight valleys, and from 1954 the type served with three squadrons. Illustrated is Valetta C.1 WJ497/U of 52 Sqn. on what looks like a leaflet-dropping sortie.

drops were made in conjunction with other tasks.

Year	Leaflet sorties	Broadcast sorties
1948	10	–
1949	69	–
1950	168	–
1951	261	–
1952	53	–
1953	184	327
1954	240	666
1955	365	922
1956	331	777
1957	348	821
1958	314	686

The psychological warfare campaign was most successful in complementing the war on the ground. Intensive leaflet operations offering rewards for information resulted in significant increases in valuable intelligence, and there is no doubt that the effort played a major part in isolating and demoralizing the CT.

Another important contribution to the intelligence war was the work of 81 Sqn. in its reconnaissance task. Initially the unit comprised two Spitfire PR.19s and nine Mosquitoes. One Spitfire was detached to Taiping in support of police operations in northern Perak in May 1948, but the Mosquitoes remained in Singapore throughout the campaign until their replacement in 1955. For a time, from March 1950, the Spitfires were transferred to 60 Sqn. at Tengah, but they returned to 81 Sqn. in November. The role of the PR squadron was both strategic and tactical. In the former role, maps had to be produced and revised while, tactically, photographs were required for intelligence and briefing purposes. No 81 Sqn. worked in close concert with the Army, both in the production of maps and in briefing; detailed photographs could highlight paths otherwise unseen and save ground forces much time in reaching targets. Regular PR flights were flown from July 1948 by the Spitfires, while the Mosquitoes maintained the task of completing the survey of Malaya. In the target and briefing work the aircraft took obliques at low level, while the mapping was carried out at around 16,000ft. Both aircraft types suffered from maintenance problems, but by the end of December 1950 the monthly output of photographs was 83,000.

The Spitfires flew on until 1954, the last sortie being flown in PS888 on 1 April of that year. The type was replaced by the Meteor PR.10 from late 1953, and when the Mosquitoes retired in 1955 they were replaced by four Pembroke C(PR).1s. Because of the limited availability of aircraft and the conflicting demands of the survey and tactical reconnaissance, from 1955 PR Canberras from 3 Group Bomber Command were detached from the UK in Operation 'Planter's Punch'. The detachments were maintained to October 1956; from then, two UK-based Canberras were detached for two-month periods twice a year. The total of PR sorties flown by 81 Sqn. to 1958 is set out below.

Year	Sorties	Year	Sorties
1948	271	1954	945
1949	612	1955	833
1950	642	1956	974
1951	1135	1957	709
1952	1172	1958	725
1953	1335		

As important as photo-reconnaissance in Malaya was visual reconnaissance, normally conducted by the Austers of 656 Sqn. The work was demanding and expert, for the pilots had to identify and interpret while trying not to arouse suspicion by circling. The squadron also provided contact reconnaissance support for the ground forces by confirming locations and bearings accurately in the featureless jungle. There were occasions when the Austers acted in their primary role of artillery spotting, both for field artillery and naval guns. As an indication of the value of visual reconnaissance, between March and August 1955 the Austers of 656 Sqn. located 155 CT camps, 77 possible camps, 313 cultivations, 31 re-cultivations, 194 man-made clearings and 21 aboriginal farms under CT control. At the other end of the scale, to about 1952 the Sunder-

The British Army has participated in virtually all the postwar British military actions, and until the advent of the helicopter in the observation role Austers were a common feature of operations abroad. This Auster AOP.6, VX129, is in silver finish overall and is from 656 Sqn. The pierced steel planking (PSP) suggests that the airfield may be Kuala Lumpur. (D. Goult)

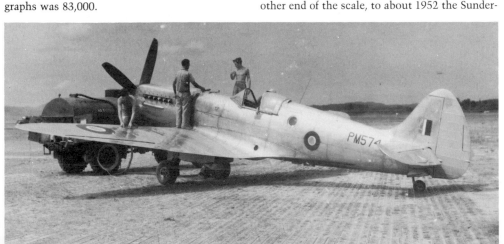

While the RAF in Europe was equipped with modern aircraft, the FEAF was required to fly obsolete types in an environment where there was no effective opposition to air power; not a single aircraft was brought down by enemy action. This Spitfire PR.19, PM574, is finished bare metal overall and was photographed at Kuala Lumpur with 81 Sqn.

land squadrons, in conjunction with naval vessels, conducted maritime reconnaissance patrols along the eastern coast to Malaya to prevent illegal immigration or arms-smuggling.

The defensive period for the security services ended in July 1951, which year saw a peak of violence. The next three years were the offensive period. By July 1954 the crisis was over and the CT confined to jungle along the central spine of Malaya, but the Emergency was far from finished, and for the next six years the security services methodically eliminated the threat during the consolidation period. A table showing the CT strength, incidents and casualties is set out below.

Year	MRLA	Incidents	Losses		
			MRLA	SF	Civilian
1948	2,300	1,274	693	360	554
1949	2,550	1,442	1,207	476	694
1950	3,923	4,739	942	889	1,161
1951	7,292	6,082	1,399	1,195	1,024
1952	5,765	3,727	1,527	664	632
1953	4,373	1,170	1,392	209	143
1954	3,402	1,077	971	241	185
1955	2,798	781	709	182	143
1956	2,566	435	473	126	92
1957	2,066				
1958	1,681				
1959	868				
1960	623				

Note Figures for losses from 1957 to 1960 are not available.

During the offensive period there was some reduction in the number of air strikes but an increase in their effectiveness. The period also saw further re-equipping and changes in units committed to the Emergency. No. 84 Sqn. disbanded on 20 February 1953, having completed 2,038 sorties and dropped 1,883 tons of bombs. The RAF said goodbye to the Brigand with few regrets and the unit was not replaced. On 31 March 1955, 33 and 45 Sqns. amalgamated, losing their Hornets at the same time to the Venom FB.1; when the dual-numbered squadron was again operational by October, it was renumbered 45 Sqn. To make good the loss of 33 Sqn., the Venoms of 14 Sqn. RNZAF entered the campaign, flying from Tengah. Finally 60 Sqn, having progressed to the Vampire FB.9, also changed to the Venom in May 1955, and with the exception of the Lincoln, the air strike capability was now all-jet. There were also changes with the Sunderland squadrons: 88 Sqn. disbanded in October 1954, and in December 205 and 209 were merged, the unit remaining dual-numbered until 1958.

Although the Lincolns of 1 Sqn. RAAF remained in the theatre until 1958, the RAF began to deploy Canberras from 1955 in Operation 'Mileage'. The first unit detached was 101 Sqn., which arrived at Butterworth in March. The Canberras were never as successful as the Lincolns in Malaya. Their range at operating height was limited, navigation

was more difficult and the weapons load was less; in addition, they were unable to operate at night. During 1955, because of the introduction of new equipment, training demands and the need for economy, the number of strike sorties dropped significantly. Intelligence remained a problem on occasions; in Operation 'Beehive' for example, against an alleged concentration of 200 CT in the Bukit-Resam Ambat area on 4 April, eleven Lincolns, four Canberras and twelve Hornets bombed and strafed the target, but the follow-up paratroopers found no evidence of the enemy.

From 1956 the air offensive was confined to promising targets where hard-core CT were likely to be located. On 21 February Operation 'Kingly Pile' was mounted by 1 Sqn. RAAF and 12 Sqn. Canberras. The target was a camp near Kluang, Johore, which was known to be occupied. In the attack twenty CT were killed by accurate bombing, including a notorious local commander. For the remainder of the year sorties were flown in support of ground operations, and the pattern continued through 1957. No. 1 Sqn. achieved another success on 15 May when four CT, again including an important local leader, were killed in the Jelebu district. During the year 45 Sqn. re-equipped with the Canberra. As the CT units were gradually eliminated and those remaining became more elusive, the number of pinpoint targets became fewer. No. 1 Sqn. RAAF finally left Malaya on 30 June 1958 after eight years of continuous flying, having made a superb contribution to the war. In that time the unit had flown over 3,000 strikes, dropping 33,000,000lb of bombs.

No. 1 Sqn. RAAF was replaced by 2 Sqn., flying the Canberra B.20 from Butterworth, and the strike force became all-Canberra when 75 Sqn. RNZAF replaced 14 Sqn. in July. Later in 1958, 3 Sqn. RAAF deployed to Butterworth with its Sabres; it was joined early in 1959 by the

Until 1 Sqn. RAAF took up to residence at Tengah in 1950, there was no theatre heavy bomber unit available. Squadrons were detached from the UK, first in Operation 'Red Lion' and then in 'Musgrave'. Seen here at Tengah is Lincoln B.2 DX-L of 57 Sqn., normally based at Waddington and sent to Malaya twice between March 1950 and July 1951.

TABLE OF UNITS: MALAYA, 1948–1960

Unit	Aircraft (code)	Base	Role	Dates
RAF				
28 Sqn.	Spitfire F.14, FR.18	Tengah, Sembawang	Ground attack, fighter-recce	01/01/48 to 11/05/48
60 Sqn.	Spitfire FR.18, Vampire FB.5/9, Venom FB.1/4	Tengah, Sembawang, Kuala Lumpur	Fighter, ground attack	01/01/48 to 30/09/59
60 Sqn.	Meteor NF.14	Tengah	Night fighter	01/10/59 to post-1960
45 Sqn.	Beaufighter X, Brigand B.1, Hornet F.3/4, Vampire FB.9, Venom FB.1, Canberra B.2 (Hornet coded OB)	Kuala Lumpur, Tengah, Butterworth	Light bombing, ground attack	01/05/49 to post-1960 (merged with 33 Sqn. 31/03/55 to 15/10/55)
33 Sqn.	Tempest II, Hornet F.3/4 (5R)	Changi, Kuala Lumpur, Tengah, Butterworth	Ground attack, fighter-recce	08/08/49 to 31/03/55 (merged with 45 Sqn.)
84 Sqn.	Beaufighter X	Changi, Tengah, Kuala Lumpur	Light bombing	01/01/48 to 11/10/48
84 Sqn.	Brigand B.1	Tengah, Kuala Lumpur	Light bombing	09/04/50 to 20/02/53
81 Sqn.	Spitfire F.18, PR.19, Mosquito PR.34, Harvard 2B, Anson C.19, Meteor PR.10, Pembroke C(PR).1, Canberra PR.7	Changi, Tengah, Seletar, Kuala Lumpur	PR	01/01/48 to post-1960
209 Sqn.	Sunderland GR.5	Seletar		01/01/48 to 31/12/54 (merged with 205 Sqn. 01/01/55 to 31/10/58)
205 Sqn.	Sunderland GR.5, Shackleton MR.1	Seletar, Changi	General/maritime recce	15/09/49 to post-1960 (merged with 209 Sqn. 01/10/55 to 31/01/58)
88 Sqn.	Sunderland GR.5	Seletar		01/10/50 to 05/04/54
656 Sqn.	Auster AOP.5/6/9, T.7	Sembawang, Kuala Lumpur, Taiping, Seremban, Kluang, Changi, Temerloh, Benta, Ipoh, Port Dickson	Observation, light liaison	15/07/48 to post-1960
1325 Flt.	Dakota C.4	Seletar	Medium-range transport	00/06/48 to 00/00/48
48 Sqn.	Dakota C.4, Valetta C.1, Hastings C.1/2, Beverley C.1	Changi, Kuala Lumpur	Medium-range transport	01/01/48 to post-1960
52 Sqn.	Dakota C.4, Valetta C.1	Changi, Kuala Lumpur	Medium-range transport	01/01/48 to post-1960
110 Sqn.	Dakota C.4, Valetta C.1	Changi, Kuala Lumpur	Medium-range transport	01/01/48 to 31/12/57
FECS	Dakota C.4, Valetta C.1/2, York C.1, Hastings C.1/4, Devon C.1, Pembroke C.1, Anson C.19, Harvard 2B, Auster AOP.6/T.7, Vampire FB.9, Venom FB.1, Meteor T.7	Changi, Kuala Lumpur, Butterworth	Communications	01/01/48 to post-1960
HQ FETW	Valetta C.1	Changi, Kuala Lumpur	Transport, psywar (to 267 Sqn.)	01/07/53 to 20/03/54
1311 Flt.	Pioneer CC.1	Kuala Lumpur	STOL transport (to 267 Sqn.)	01/09/53 to 15/02/54
267 Sqn.	Pioneer CC.1, Pembroke C.1, Auster AOP.6/T.7, Harvard 2B, Dakota C.4	Kuala Lumpur	Short-range transport (renumbered 209 Sqn.)	15/02/54 to 31/10/58
209 Sqn.	Pioneer CC.1, Twin Pioneer CC.1, Pembroke C.1, Dakota C.4, Auster AOP.6/T.7	Kuala Lumpur, Seletar, Bayan Lepas	Short-range transport	01/11/58 to post-1960
CEF	Dragonfly HC.2/4	Changi, Kuala Lumpur	Casevac (to 194 Sqn.)	01/05/50 to 02/02/53
194 Sqn.	Dragonfly HC.2/4, Sycamore HR.14	Sembawang, Kuala Lumpur, Ipoh, Kluang, Benta	Transport, casevac (renumbered 110 Sqn.)	02/02/53 to 03/06/59
155 Sqn.	Whirlwind HAR.2/4	Kuala Lumpur, Kluang, Seletar	Transport (to 194 Sqn.)	01/09/55 to 03/06/59
110 Sqn.	Whirlwind HAR.4, Sycamore HR.14	Butterworth, Kuala Lumpur	Transport (ex 194 Sqn.)	03/06/59 to post-1960

Temporary RAF dets., ex UK

Operation 'Red Lion'/'Red Lion II'

7 Sqn.	Lancaster B.1FE (MG)	Changi, ex Upwood	Medium bombing	00/01/47 to 00/02/47
97 Sqn.	Lincoln B.2 (OF)	Tengah, ex Hemswell		30/04/48 to 15/06/48

Operation 'Musgrave'

57 Sqn.	Lincoln B.2B (DX)			20/03/50 to 00/07/51
100 sqn.	Lincoln B.2B (HW)	Tengah, ex Waddington	Medium bombing	30/06/50 to 00/12/50
61 Sqn.	Lincoln B.2B (QR)			00/12/50 to 00/04/51

Operation 'Bold'

83 Sqn.		Tengah, ex Hemswell		23/08/53 to 07/01/54
7 Sqn.	Lincoln B.2B	Tengah, ex Upwood	Medium bombing	00/01/54 to 00/04/54, 15/07/54 to 00/10/54
148 Sqn.		Tengah, ex Upwood		00/04/54 to 00/07/54, 15/10/54 to 28/02/55

Operation 'Mileage'

101 Sqn.				01/03/55 to 00/07/55
617 Sqn.	Canberra B.6	Butterworth, ex Binbrook	Light bombing	00/07/55 to 00/11/55
12 Sqn.				00/10/55 to 00/03/56
9 Sqn.				00/03/56 to 00/07/56

Operation 'Profiteer'
Detachments of Valiants or Vulcans for two-week periods to Changi (31 October 1957 to 27 March 1958) or Butterworth (6 June 1958 to 26 June 1960). Units involved included 214, 90, 148 Sqns.).

Operation 'Planters Punch'

542 Sqn.				13/05/55 to 00/10/55
540 Sqn.	Canberra PR.7	Changi, ex Wyton	PR	00/11/55 to 00/03/56
82 Sqn.				00/03/56 to 00/07/56
58 Sqn.				00/08/56 to 00/10/56

Exercise 'Centipede'

210 Sqn.	Lancaster GR.3 (OZ)	Tengah, ex St. Eval	ASW	28/11/49 to 12/12/49

FAA				
848 NAS	Whirlwind HAR.21	Sembawang, Kuala Lumpur, Kluang	Transport	23/01/53 to 12/11/56

TABLE OF UNITS: MALAYA, 1948—1960 (continued)

Royal Navy carriers in Malayan waters or berthed at Singapore (between 1950 and 1953, en route to Korea), and whose aircraft are understood to have participated, were as follows:

Ship	Units	Aircraft type	Shore base	From
Triumph	800 NAS / 827 NAS	Seafire FR.47 / Firefly FR.1	Sembawang	00/10/49
Theseus	807 NAS / 810 NAS	Sea Fury FB.11 / Firefly FR.5	Sembawang	00/09/50
Glory	804 NAS / 812 NAS	Sea Fury FB.11 / Firefly FR.5	Sembawang	00/07/51
Ocean	802 NAS / 825 NAS	Sea Fury FB.11 / Firefly FR.5	Sembawang	00/10/52
Warrior	811 NAS / 825 NAS	Sea Fury FB.11 / Firefly FR.5	Sembawang	00/09/54
Centaur	801 NAS / 811 NAS	Sea Hawk FGA.4 / Sea Hawk FB.3	Tengah	00/04/56
Albion	804 NAS / 809 NAS	Sea Hawk FGA.6 / Sea Venom FAW.21	Seletar	00/03/59
Centaur	891 NAS / 810 NAS	Sea Venom FAW.22 / Gannet AS.4	Seletar	00/09/59 to 00/02/60

Unit	Aircraft	Base	Role	Dates
MAAF				
Malaya/Penang Sqn.	DH82A, Harvard 2B, Chipmunk	Butterworth	Light liaison, recce	01/03/50 to 31/12/58
Singapore Sqn.	DH82A, Harvard 2B, Spitfire F.24, Chipmunk	Tengah, Seletar	Light liaison, recce	01/03/50 to post-1960
Kuala Lumpur Sqn.	DH82A, Harvard 2B, Chipmunk	Kuala Lumpur	Light liaison, recce	01/03/50 to 31/12/58
RMAF				
1 Sqn.	Pioneer, Twin Pioneer, Chipmunk	Kuala Lumpur	Light transport	00/04/58 to post-1960
RAAF				
3 Sqn. / 77 Sqn.	Sabre 32	Butterworth	Fighter, ground attack	11/11/58 to post-1960 / 11/02/59 to post-1960
1 Sqn.	Lincoln B.30	Tengah	Medium bombing	16/07/50 to 30/06/58
2 Sqn.	Canberra B.20	Butterworth	Light bombing	01/07/58 to post-1960
38 Sqn.	Dakota	Changi, Kuala Lumpur	Medium-range transport	01/06/50 to 30/11/52
RNZAF				
14 Sqn.	Venom FB.1	Tengah	Fighter, ground attack	10/04/55 to 01/09/58
75 Sqn.	Canberra B.2	Tengah	Light bombing	01/07/58 to post-1960
41 Sqn.	Dakota C.3, Bristol Freighter	Changi, Kuala Lumpur	Medium-range transport	01/09/49 to post-1960
USAF				

In July 1953, at the end of the Korean War, three Thirteenth Air Force B-29s spent several weeks at Butterworth, from where they flew bombing sorties.

similarly equipped 77 Sqn. Only 47 strikes were ordered in 1958, by the end of which it was clear that mopping-up operations could be achieved without air support. The only two strikes of 1959 were on 13 and 17 August when camps at Bentong (Pahang) and Bukit Tapah (Perak) respectively were attacked, giving the Sabres their only taste of action. Throughout the campaign 23,004 sorties were flown in 4,063 strikes, during which 34,500 tons of bombs were dropped and 74,000 rockets and 9.8 million rounds of ammunition fired.

The transport units maintained a high rate of activity throughout the Emergency. From 1955 there was an increasing amount of work associated with the dropping of SAS units and their resupply, and each year the number of hill forts increased. The transport squadrons remained based at Changi, and through 1956 and 1957 only three Valettas and one or two Bristol Freighters of 41 Sqn. RNZAF were available for supply-dropping at Kuala Lumpur. In 1958 the transport force was stretched when the Pioneers had to be withdrawn from their resupply work through serviceability problems, but from 1959 there was relief as the fledgeling Royal Malayan Air Force (RMAF) took over this work.

The reliability of the Valetta was never as good as that of the Dakota, although its climb rate was better, allowing its use in valleys where the American aircraft would have been in difficulty. After 110 Sqn. disbanded in December 1957, although its aircraft went to 52 Sqn., the latter unit took two Dakotas on strength in 1960. Other changes in equipment towards the end of the campaign were the introduction of the Hastings by 48 Sqn. from May 1957 and the Beverley by the same unit from June 1959. Both types offered considerable increases in payload and were used in support of operations in the north after the Emergency had ended. The transport units made perhaps the most significant contribution to the prosecution of the anti-terrorist campaign, enabling ground forces to operate in inhospitable regions independent of normal supply lines. When the need for air support diminished the demand for air supply did not.

No account of Operation 'Firedog' would be complete without reference to the locally raised air forces. The Malayan Auxiliary Air Force (MAAF) was formed in 1950 with a view to augmenting the RAF air defence units. Four squadrons were formed, but they were unable to progress to fighters in a reasonable time. Using Tiger Moths and Harvards, the squadrons did, however, participate in a limited amount of leaflet-dropping and visual reconnaissance. Malaya achieved independence on 31 August 1957 and the MAAF paved the way for the establishment of the Royal Malayan Air Force (RMAF) from 1958. Initially equipped with four Twin Pioneers, four Pioneers and four Chipmunks, the RMAF assumed the responsibility for resupplying the hill forts from March 1959, relieving the RAF short-range transport force. Although it made a valuable contribution to the war effort, the RMAF found difficulty in meeting all the demands placed upon it.

The end of the Emergency was declared from 31 July 1960, by which time about 500 CT were still operating from a salient within Thailand. Policing continued, as did mopping-up operations, but the armed services were gradually withdrawn. Throughout the twelve-year war, the security forces lost 1,865 killed and 2,560 wounded, while 2,473 civilians were killed, 1,385 wounded and 810 missing. Of the estimated 12,000 members of the MRLA, 6,698 were killed, 2,819 wounded, 1,286 captured and 2,696 surrendered.

From a British point of view, the campaign was a total success, but many hard lessons were learnt. The war was, probably, unnecessarily extended because of the slow initial response and the lack of sound intelligence. Many comparisons have been made with Vietnam, but although in the early stages of the latter war British advisers were employed, the situation was fundamentally different.

AIRCRAFT MARKINGS

RAF

Spitfire FR.18 Dark Green/Dark Sea Grey over, Medium Sea Grey under, black serial, white code on rear fuselage: TP372/W, TP406/N, TP433/M (28 Sqn.); SM997, TP202/P, TP197 (60 Sqn.).

Beaufighter X Dark Green/Dark Sea Grey over, Medium Sea Grey under, black serial and code on rear fuselage: RD824/OB-K, RD805 (45 Sqn.).

Tempest II Silver overall, black serial and code on rear fuselage: PR774/D, PR852/5R-N (33 Sqn.).

Hornet F.3 Silver overall, black serial and code on rear fuselage, rear of spinners striped blue/red/blue/ silver/blue: WB876/OB-O, WB908/OB-L (45 Sqn.): WB871/5R-P, WB875/R (33 Sqn.). Dark Green/Dark Sea Grey over, PR Blue under, black serial on rear fuselage, white codes and squadron marking across roundel: PX298/5R-Q (33 Sqn.).

Hornet F.4 Silver overall, black serial and code on rear fuselage: WF966/OB-N (45 Sqn.).

Vampire FB.5 Aluminium overall, black serial on boom: WA238, WA241 (60 Sqn.).

Vampire FB.9 Aluminium overall, black serial on boom, code on forward fuselage, squadron marking and blue band on boom: WG872/W, WG882/D, WL555/E (60 Sqn.)

Venom FB.1 Dark Green/Dark Sea Grey over, PR Blue under, blue tip tanks with white stripe: WE469/O, WR350/Q, WR359/V (45 Sqn.).

Venom FB.4 Dark Green/Dark Sea Grey over, PR Blue under, black serial on boom, white code on fin, red tip tanks and rudders, squadron marking on boom: WR535/F, WR496/N (60 Sqn.).

Meteor NF.14 Dark Green/Medium Sea Grey over, light grey under, white serial on rear fuselage, code on lower fin, squadron marking across roundel: WS755/C, WS810/F, WS828/J (60 Sqn.).

Lincoln B.2 Medium Sea Grey over, black under, small white serial on rear fuselage, code on mid fuselage: RF386/DX-N (57 Sqn.); RF476/HW-A (100 Sqn.); RF502/QR-R (61 Sqn.). Large white serial on rear fuselage, no codes: RE415, RA662 (83 Sqn.); RE301, SX982 (7 Sqn.); RE347, SX958 (148 Sqn.).

Brigand B.1 Medium Sea Grey over, black under, white serial and code on rear fuselage, playing card symbol on lower fin: 'Hearts' RH831/H and VS854/G, 'Clubs' VS868/A, VS861/B and VS836/D, 'Diamonds' RH785/E, 'Spades' RH776/K (84 Sqn.). White code on rear fuselage: VS859/OB-V (45 Sqn.).

Canberra B.2 Silver overall, light grey fin panel, black serial on rear fuselage, squadron badge on fin: WJ630, WH667 (45 Sqn.); WJ758 (101 Sqn.).

Spitfire PR.19 Bare metal overall, black serial on rear fuselage: PM 574. Extra Dark Sea Grey overall, white fuselage top decking, orange/grey spinner, black serial on rear fuselage: PS836, PS888 (81 Sqn.).

Mosquito PR.34 Silver overall, black serial on rear fuselage: RG255/P, RG239/M (81 Sqn.).

Pembroke C(PR).1 Silver overall, black serial on rear fuselage: XF796 (81 Sqn.).

Sunderland GR.5 White overall, black serial on rear fuselage, code on mid fuselage: DP198/W, PP127/L, RN270/K (205 Sqn.); DP154/X, VB888/Z (209 Sqn.).

Shackleton MR.1 Medium Sea Grey overall, black serial on rear fuselage, squadron number in red on rear fuselage, code on nose: VP288/K, WB818/A (205 Sqn.).

Dakota C.4 Silver overall, black serial on rear fuselage, blue nose: KN569 (110 Sqn.). White top fuselage decking: KN525 (110 Sqn.); KN592/N (48 Sqn.). Dark blue cheat line with white serial to rear: KP277 (loud-hailing aircraft, 209 Sqn.).

Valetta C.1 Silver overall, white fuselage top decking, dark blue spinners and cheat line, black serial on rear fuselage, code on fin: WJ497/U (52 Sqn.); VX508/K (110 Sqn.).

Hastings C.1 Silver overall, white top fuselage decking, black serial and code on rear fuselage, last three digits of serial repeated on fin: TG516/GP-L, TG569/GP-D (48 Sqn.).
Beverley C.1 Silver overall, black serial on boom, code on nose: XB260/U (48 Sqn.).
Pioneer C.C1 Silver overall, white fuselage top decking, black serial on rear fuselage: XJ465 (267 Sqn.); XL706, XJ466 (209 Sqn.).
Dragonfly HC.2 Dark Green/dark brown overall, black serial on boom: WF311 (FECAEF); WF315 (194 Sqn.).
Whirlwind HC.4 Dark Green/Dark Earth overall, five yellow-orange stripes on rear boom, black serial on boom, white code mid fuselage: XD165/B, XJ421/T (155 Sqn.).
Sycamore HR.14 Dark Green/Dark Earth overall, black serial on boom: XE310, XF266 (110 Sqn.); XE322, XF267 (194 Sqn.).

FAA
S-55 Glossy Sea Blue overall, white serial on boom, code on rear fuselage: WV194/F, WV198/K (848 NAS).
Seafire FR.47 Extra Dark Sea Grey over, Sky under, black serial and code on rear fuselage, ship code on fin: VR965/177P, VP461/178P (800 NAS).
Sea Fury FB.11 Extra Dark Sea Grey over, Sky under, black serial on rear fuselage, code on mid fuselage, ship code on fin: WJ221/106J, WZ631/101J (811 NAS).

British Army
Auster AOP.6 Dark Green/Dark Earth overall, black serial on rear fuselage: TW535. Aluminium overall, black serial on rear fuselage: VF610, VX129 (656 Sqn.).
Auster AOP.9 Dark Green/Dark Earth overall, white serial on rear fuselage and under wings: WZ668 (656 Sqn).

RAAF
Lincoln B.30A Silver overall, black serial on rear fuselage: A73-34, A73-39, A73-46 (1 Sqn.).
Canberra B.20 Silver overall, black serial on rear fuselage, red lightning flash on fin: (A84-)203 (2 Sqn.).
Dakota Silver overall, black serial on rear fuselage, 'No 86 Transport Wing RAAF' along fuselage: A65-103 (38 Sqn.).

RNZAF
Venom FB.1 Dark Green/Dark Sea Grey over, PR Blue under, black serial on boom, grey code on tip tank, red/white checks on rudders: WE434/L, WR371/F (14 Sqn.).
Canberra B.2 Silver overall, black serial on rear fuselage: WF915, WJ605 (75 Sqn.).
Freighter Mk.31 Silver overall, white top fuselage decking, pale blue trim, black serial on rear fuselage: NZ5904 (41 Sqn.).

10.8. Borneo, 1962–1966

It was the ambition of Indonesia's President Soekarno to unite Malaysia, the Philippines and Indonesia within an Indonesian empire; a glance at the map shows how the territories are interrelated. Following the proposal in 1962 for a Malaysian Federation comprising Malaya, Singapore, Sarawak, Brunei and Sabah (North Borneo), Indonesia determined to prevent the development. One weak link in the prospective Federation was Brunei, which was autocratically ruled by a Sultan and was proportionately far richer, through oil revenues, than the other partners. Soekarno encouraged the local North Kalimantan National Army (TNKU) to revolt. With 4,000 members, 1,000 of whom were under arms, the TNKU struck on 8 December 1962. The initial targets were the power station and Sultan's palace in Brunei Town, police posts and other administrative centres at Limbang, Bangar, Tutong and Lawas and the oilfields at Seria.

Although the attacks were carried out on a Saturday, the British had some forewarning and by midday a battalion of Gurkhas was forming up at Seletar, Singapore, while transport aircraft were readied. A prepared plan was put into action as Operation 'Ale', later changed to Operation

'Borneo Territories'. From 1400hrs three Beverley transports of 34 Sqn. and a conveniently located Britannia flew the battalion into Brunei Town and Labuan respectively, the former's runways being too short to take the Britannia; further reinforcements were flown in by a Bristol Freighter of 41 Sqn. RNZAF, C-130As of 36 Sqn. RAAF, Valettas of 52 Sqn., Hastings of 48 Sqn. and Shackletons of 205 Sqn. RAF. By late afternoon control had been restored in Brunei Town as more aircraft flew into Brunei and Labuan.

Twin Pioneers of 209 Sqn. and Belvedere HC.1s of 66 Sqn. were available for local transport work, and Hunter FGA.9s of 20 Sqn. and Canberra B.15s of 45 Sqn. were detached to Labuan for close air support if necessary. More troops arrived on 9 December, as did Auster AOP.9s and Beaver AL.1s of 14 Liaison Flight, 656 Sqn. On the 10th several Twin Pioneers landed at a grass strip at Panaga, where the police station was soon recaptured, and later in the day a Beverley took rebels by surprise when it landed at Anduki with a full load of men of the Queen's Own Cameron Highlanders and their equipment. The airstrip was soon in British hands, and after more men were flown in the oilfield was retaken the following day. With men of 42 Commando Royal Marines also in action, Tutong had been retaken and Limbang and Lawas fell on the 12th. The commando carrier HMS *Albion* was now on the scene, and from the 14th Whirlwind HAS.7s of 846 NAS and Wessexes of 845 NAS were flown ashore to provide a muchneeded supplement to the RAF Belvederes.

Although there were some airstrips in the region, the interior generally comprised heavy jungle with few tracks (rivers were primarily used for transport) and helicopters were essential for the rapid movement of troops. HMS *Hermes* with her Air Wing embarked was also in the area as mopping-up operations continued, and by the 17th the rebellion had been squashed and most of the rebels captured. On the 18th, Major-General W.C. Walker arrived as Commander British Forces Borneo Territories, and operations continued for several months to pursue the remaining rebels. Some air units returned to Singapore, but as concern grew about Indonesian intentions in Sarawak and Sabah the ground forces were consolidated and men of 22 Regt. SAS brought in to provide a much-needed intelligence resource.

The first sign of further trouble came on 12 April 1963 with an Indonesian attack on a police station at Tebedu; although the attackers were dressed as guerrillas, they were believed to have been regular Indonesian soldiers. The raid was repulsed, but it set a pattern of activity for the next three years along the difficult 970-mile-long border. More helicopters were available as Whirlwinds and Sycamores of 110 Sqn. had detached from Seletar, but on 4 May a Belvedere HC.1, XG473 of 66 Sqn., crashed after taking off from Ba Kelalan, killing all on board, including three SAS men. Two days later a Sycamore was lost in an accident. In August, preceding the proclamation of the State of Malaysia on 16 September, there was an attack on Seng. The proclamation led to riots in Djakarta, and on 19 September three Argosies of the newly formed 215 Sqn. and a Hastings flew to the Indonesian capital to evacuate Britons. Indonesia had not

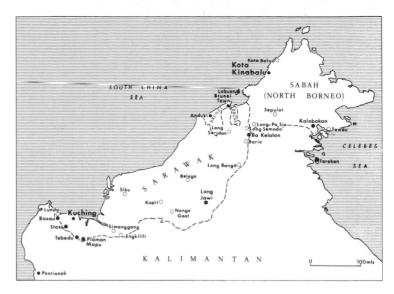

declared war with Malaysia and Britain, and throughout the campaign all parties were careful to refer to events as a 'confrontation'.

Late in September, Indonesians attacked an outpost at Long Jawi, which they overran, killing five defenders, including several Gurkhas. The retreating raiders were ambushed by helicopter-borne troops and paid heavily for the raid, the largest to date. Indonesia also began overflying Sarawak with B-25s, escorted by P-51s, from Pontianak, and during November nine incursions were reported although no attacks made. Nevertheless, from December four Hunters of 20 Sqn. and two Javelin FAW.9s of 60 Sqn. were permanently detached both to Kuching and Labuan. On 18 December an Auster AOP.9 became the first aircraft lost to enemy action when it was shot down in Sarawak with the loss of the passenger, a padre. Cross-border raids increased, and on 28 December there was a concerted attack on Kalabakan in Sabah.

The Kalabakan attack resulted in more troops being airlifted into East Malaysia, and from February 1964 the Herald transports of 4 Sqn.

When there was a revolt in Brunei in December 1962, troops were hurriedly flown into Brunei Town from Singapore in Beverley transports of 34 Sqn. With Hastings of 48 Sqn., the aircraft maintained a steady flow of supplies and men from Singapore to Borneo throughout the period of confrontation with Indonesia. Seen at Changi, this is Beverley XM104. (RAF Museum)

Royal Malayan Air Force (RMAF) began playing their part in the operation; RMAF Pioneers and Twin Pioneers of 1 Sqn. were also detached. During January, 60 Sqn. had been reinforced to counter the possibility of air strikes by Indonesia's force of Il-28 and Tu-16 bombers and MiG-17 and -19 fighters: four Javelins were flown out from the UK in the markings of 23 Sqn. to confuse Indonesian intelligence. On 26 February an Air Defence Intercept Zone (ADIZ) was established around Borneo, but only limited Indonesian air strikes were encountered, late in 1965.

Towards the end of June the first confirmed attack by Indonesian regulars was launched at Rasau, during which five Gurkhas were killed, and in July there were 34 similar attacks along the border. There was a clue to the next significant move during June, however, when a bomb, placed by an infiltrator, damaged a 205 Sqn. Shackleton at Changi on Singapore. On 17 August Indonesia launched the first of a number of raids on West Malaysia with the landing of 100 men at three sites on the west coast of Johore. Army units soon mopped up the infiltrators with the help of Army Air Corps (AAC) helicopters, but on 27 August an Esso bunkering station in Singapore was attacked. The most serious threat came on 2 September when 96 Indonesian paratroopers were dropped at Labis, West Malaysia, from a C-130B in Operation 'Dwikova'. Two aircraft left Djakarta and refuelled at Medan, but one was forced to return; the second aircraft which dropped the paras was lost on the return flight to causes unknown. Fourteen Hunter sorties were flown in the day, and concentrations of Indonesian troops were wiped out in rocket attacks. As the Army again began to mop up the remnants, a state of emergency was declared on the 2nd.

The Indonesians had penetrated Malaysian airspace in a radar gap between Bukit Gombak and Butterworth, and HMS *Kent*, a *County* Class destroyer, was stationed in the Straits of Malacca to fill the gap. From now the Gannet AEW.3s of 849 NAS flights from the carriers on station were critical to the maintenance of effective air defence. On 14 September a section of Bloodhound IIs of 65 Sqn. was brought to readiness at Seletar, and extra 20mm anti-aircraft guns were brought out of stock. Javelins of 64 Sqn. were flown out from the UK to join those of 60 Sqn., RAAF Sabres were detached to Alor Star and Kuantan, and Meteor F.8s of 1574 Flt. at Changi were alerted for local air defence. Finally, two extra Canberra squadrons were committed, 32 Sqn. RAF and 14 Sqn. RNZAF with the B(I).12. On 28 November a major air defence exercise involving the RAF, RN and RAAF was held and Gong Kedah airfield near the Thai border reopened. During October there was another seaborne infiltration, this time at Pontian opposite Singapore, but again the insurgents were quickly rounded up with helicopter support. A further infiltration on 23 December was attacked by Hunters and Canberras, with Sycamores of 103 Sqn. acting as forward air control (FAC) aircraft, in Operation 'Birdsong'.

Meanwhile, in Borneo, the helicopter force had been further strengthened by four Belvederes of 26 Sqn., Whirlwinds of 225 Sqn. and Alouette IIIs of 5 Sqn. RMAF, while 847 NAS provided Whirlwinds at Sembawang to supplement the depleted units in West Malaysia. The UH-1Bs of 5 Sqn. RAAF also moved to Butterworth. In October a million leaflets were dropped over Indonesia by Argosies and Hastings, but the incursions continued. During the year British Army tactics changed and pursuits into Kalimantan, known as 'Claret' operations, were allowed on a deniable basis up to 3,000yds, later extended to 10,000 and finally 20,000yds.

The conflict was beginning to take a toll of the aircraft in the theatre; to the end of 1964 one Pioneer, three Twin Pioneers, two Whirlwinds, one Sycamore, one Scout, one Auster AOP.9 and a Hunter had been lost in accidents. A new form of transport entered service on 23 March 1965 with the formation of the Joint Services Hovercraft Unit equipped with the SR.N5 at Tawau in Sabah, and these vehicles were extremely valuable in negotiating the miles of river and coastline in the area, but still more helicopters were needed, and on 2 March the Whirlwinds of 230 Sqn. arrived at Labuan, followed in April by the Wessexes of 848 NAS. They were soon in action when, on 27 April, there was a serious attack on an outpost at Plaman Mapu manned by 2 Para. The attackers were held off and reinforcements were brought up by helicopter. Thirty Indonesian regulars from a company of 150 were killed for the loss of two British soldiers.

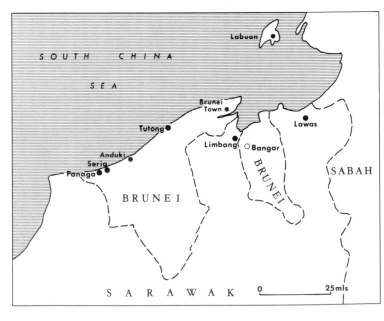

Helicopters were of great importance in the Borneo conflict. The first to arrive were Belvederes of 66 Sqn., supplemented by four aircraft of 26 Sqn. in 1964. The RAF also operated four squadrons of Whirlwinds at one time, while the Royal Navy contributed four squadrons of Whirlwinds and Wessexes and the Army deployed five Scout and five Sioux flights to numerous jungle sites. Seen here in typical terrain is Belvedere HC.1 XG456/A, of 66 Sqn. (P. H. T. Green via A. S. Thomas)

Later in the year, from 1 September, there was a series of hit-and-run attacks on isolated kampongs by Indonesian Air Force (AURI) B-25s and B-26s. These raids highlighted the inadequacy of the air defence system in East Malaysia: the Javelins could not react fast enough, and in any event would have been far too cumbersome trying to attack slower aircraft at low level. Fortunately little damage was done. Only once did the Javelins make an intercept in East Malaysia, when by chance they confronted a C-130 which turned tail and escaped. The Javelins were in their element around Singapore, however, and on 21 September an AURI Tu-16 was intercepted and escorted away from the area. The Indonesians did manage to establish a series of AAA posts along the border, and on 17 November 1965 a Whirlwind HAR.10, XR480 of 103 Sqn., was shot down near Stass. Several more Whirlwinds were lost in accidents during the year.

In West Malaysia the incursions continued unabated. To the end of March 1965, 41 landings has been reported, with 142 Indonesians killed and the remaining 309 captured. A new threat presented itself from 29 March when Indonesian AAA on the Riau Islands, just south of Singapore, began firing indiscriminately on aircraft approaching the civilian airport. Aircraft had to be rerouted, and fortunately none was damaged. On 30 May, 25 regulars landed at Tanjong Pen-Gelih, East Johore, where they occupied an old Japanese fort. The following day they were dislodged by four Hunters firing armour-piercing rockets.

On 9 August Singapore left the Federation and only weeks later, on 30 September, there was an attempted communist coup in Djakarta; the military counter-coup essentially ended Soekarno's rule. Although cross-border attacks continued in East Malaysia, incursions in the peninsula soon slowed, and the prospect of peace seemed likely. At the end of the year there were

14,000 British troops in Borneo, from a peak of 17,000. They were supported by over 100 helicopters, and the Beverleys were dropping supplies at the rate of 1,000,000lb a month.

During 1966 the pace slowed and peace talks began in Bangkok. Finally, on 11 August, the conflict ended with the signing of a peace treaty. Slowly forces were withdrawn, and RAAF Sabres were detached to Labuan to replace the Javelins of 60 Sqn. while a section of Bloodhound SAMs was deployed to Kuching. The confrontation in Borneo and Malaya had cost the Indonesians around 600 dead and the British 114, many of the latter Gurkhas. On 22 October a Beverley made the last airdrop of the conflict, 34 Sqn. having lifted 40,000,000lb in less than four years.

AIRCRAFT MARKINGS

RAF

Hunter FGA.9 *Dark Green/Dark Sea Grey over, silver under, white serial on rear fuselage, code on fin: XG272/H, XK142/P (20 Sqn.).*

Javelin FAW.9 *Dark Green/Dark Sea Grey over, silver under, squadron markings on fin, white*

The STOL Twin Pioneer light transport was a great asset to the RAF in its overseas operations. It could operate from 900ft strips and carried eleven fully equipped troops, and it had a range of 400 miles. Six squadrons flew the type through the 1960s in the UK, Bahrein, Kenya, Aden, Malaya and Borneo. XN319 is a CC.2 of 209 Sqn. and is marked with red fins and outer wing panels. (G. A. Heather via A. S. Thomas)

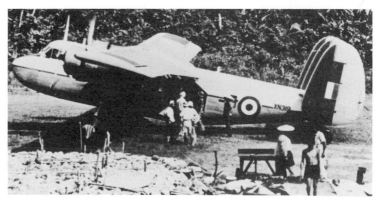

TABLE OF UNITS: BORNEO, 1962–1966

Unit	Aircraft	Base	Role	Dates
RAF				
20 Sqn.[1]	Hunter FGA.9	⎫	Ground attack, air defence	13/12/62 to 31/12/66
60 Sqn.	Javelin FAW.9	⎬ Labuan, Kuching, Tengah	Air defence	00/09/63 to 31/12/66
64 Sqn.	Javelin FAW.9R	⎭	Air defence	10/12/64 to ?
1574 Flt.	Meteor F.8	Changi	Local air defence	
45 Sqn.[2]	Canberra B.15	Tengah, Labuan, Kuching	Light bombing	13/12/62 to 31/12/66
32 Sqn.	Canberra B.15	Tengah, Kuantan	Light bombing	00/10/64 to 00/01/65
205 Sqn.[3]	Shackleton MR.2C	Labuan, Changi	Maritime/general recce	08/12/62 to 31/12/66
81 Sqn.	Canberra PR.7	Labuan, Tengah	PR	00/03/63 to 31/12/66
209 Sqn.	Pioneer C.1, Twin Pioneer CC.1	Labuan, Kuching, Brunei	Light STOL transport	08/12/62 to 31/12/66
66 Sqn.	Belvedere HC.1	Labuan, Kuching, Seletar	Transport	09/12/62 to 00/02/67
26 Sqn.	Belvedere HC.1	Seletar, ex Odiham	Transport (four aircraft absorbed into 66 Sqn.)	00/00/64 to 30/11/65
110 Sqn.	Sycamore HC.14, Whirlwind HAR.10	Seletar[4]	⎧	24/12/62 to 04/11/67
103 Sqn.	Sycamore HC.14, Whirlwind HAR.10	Seletar[4]	⎬ Transport, liaison, casevac	01/08/63 to 31/12/66
225 Sqn.	Whirlwind HAR.10	Kuching[4]	⎬	00/00/64 to 01/11/65
230 Sqn.	Whirlwind HAR.10	Labuan[4]	⎭	02/03/65 to 00/10/66
34 Sqn.	Beverley C.1	Labuan, Kuching, Seletar	⎫ Heavy transport	08/12/62 to 22/10/66
48 Sqn.	Hastings C.2	Labuan, Kuching, Seletar	⎬ Transport	08/12/62 to 31/12/66
52 Sqn.	Valetta C.1	Labuan, Kuching, Butterworth		
99 Sqn.	Britannia C.1	UK, Seletar	Transport (99 and 511 Sqn. crews)	08/12/62 to 31/12/62
215 Sqn.	Argosy C.1	Changi	Transport	00/08/63 to 00/10/67
65 Sqn.	Bloodhound II	Seletar	Air defence	14/09/64 to 31/12/66
FAA				
845 NAS	Wessex HAS.1, Whirlwind HAS.7, Hiller HT.2	*Albion, Bulwark* (dets. at Kuching, Labuan, Sibu, Belaga, Nanga Gaat, Simanggang)	Transport, liaison, casevac	14/12/62 to 00/08/65
846 NAS	Whirlwind HAS.7	*Albion* (dets. at Kuching, Labuan, Brunei, Tawau)	Transport, liaison, casevac	15/12/62 to 19/10/64
847 NAS	Whirlwind HAS.7	*Bulwark*, Sembawang	Transport, liaison	00/03/64 to 02/12/64
848 NAS	Whirlwind HAS.7, Wessex HU.5	*Albion* (dets. at Sibu, Nanga Gaat, Bario, Labuan, Kota Balud, Sepulot)	Transport, liaison, casevac	00/04/65 to 05/08/66

Royal Navy carriers[5]

Hermes (December 1962 to June 1963)
892 NAS (Sea Vixen FAW.1), 803 NAS (Scimitar F.1), 814 NAS (Wessex HAS.1), 849 NAS/B Flt. (Gannet AEW.3).

Ark Royal (June 1963 to November 1963)
890 NAS (Sea Vixen FAW.1), 800 NAS (Scimitar F.1), 815 NAS (Wessex HAS.1), 849 NAS/C Flt. (Gannet AEW.3).

Victorious (September 1963 to July 1965)
893 NAS (Sea Vixen FAW.1), 801 NAS (Buccaneer S.1), 814 NAS (Wessex HAS.1), 849 NAS/A Flt. (Gannet AEW.3).

Centaur (January 1964 to September 1964)
892 NAS (Sea Vixen FAW.1), 815 NAS (Wessex HAS.1), 849 NAS/B Flt. (Gannet AEW.3).

Eagle (January 1965 to April 1965)
899 NAS (Sea Vixen FAW.2), 820 NAS (Wessex HAS.1), 849 NAS/D Flt. (Gannet AEW.3).

Ark Royal (July 1965 to April 1966)
890 NAS (Sea Vixen FAW.1), 803 NAS (Scimitar F.1), 815 NAS (Wessex HAS.1), 849 NAS/C Flt. (Gannet AEW.3).

Eagle (September 1965 to July 1966)
899 NAS (Sea Vixen FAW.2), 800 NAS (Buccaneer S.1), 800B NAS (Scimitar F.1), 820 NAS (Wessex HAS.1), 849 NAS/D Flt. (Gannet AEW.3).

Flight/troop	Aircraft	Dates
British Army (656 Sqn.)[6]		
3 Recce Flt.	Scout AH.1	00/10/65 to 00/00/65
7 Recce Flt.	Auster AOP.9, Scout AH.1	24/12/62 to 31/12/66
10 Recce Flt.	Scout AH.1	00/00/64 to 00/12/65
11 Liaison Flt. (became 30 Flt. RASC)	Auster AOP.9, Beaver AL.1, Scout AH.1	00/05/63 to 00/05/64
14 Liaison Flt.	Auster AOP.9, Beaver AL.1, Scout AH.1	00/12/62 to 00/08/66
16 Recce Flt. (became Air Tp. 4RTR)	Auster AOP.9	30/09/64 to 01/10/64
30 Flt. RASC (from 11 Flt.)	Beaver AL.1	00/05/64 to 00/00/66
Air Tp., 4RTR (from 16 Flt.)	Auster AOP.9, Sioux AH.1	01/10/64 to ?
Air Tp., B Sqn., 1st Queens Dragoon Guards	Auster AOP.9	00/03/65 to 00/09/65
AOP Tp., 45 Light Regt. RA	Sioux AH.1	01/04/65 to 00/07/65
AOP Tp., 6 Light Regt. RA	Sioux AH.1	00/01/66 to ?
Air Pl., 1 Bn. Scots Guards	Sioux AH.1	08/03/65 to ?
Air Pl., 2 Gurkha Rifles	Sioux AH.1	00/06/66 to ?

COMMONWEALTH AIR FORCES (INVOLVED THROUGHOUT UNLESS OTHERWISE STATED)

Unit	Aircraft	Base	Role	Dates
RNZAF				
14 Sqn.	Canberra B(I).12	Tengah	Light bombing	00/09/64 to 00/11/66
41 Sqn.	Bristol Freighter Mk. 31	Kuching, Changi	Transport	
RAAF				
3 Sqn.	Sabre 32	Butterworth, Labuan	Air defence	
75 Sqn.	Sabre 32	Butterworth, Labuan	Air defence	
2 Sqn.	Canberra B.20	Butterworth	Light bombing	
5 Sqn.	UH-1B Iroquois	Butterworth	Transport, casevac	From 00/06/64
36 Sqn.	C-130A	Australia, Changi	Transport	

Unit	Aircraft (code)	Base	Role	Dates
RMAF				
5 Sqn.	Alouette III	Tawau, Labuan	Liaison, recce, casevac	From 00/06/64
1 Sqn.	Pioneer, Twin Pioneer	Kuala Lumpur, Labuan	Light transport	From 00/12/63
4 Sqn.	Herald	Kuala Lumpur, Labuan	Transport	From 00/02/64
8 Sqn.	Caribou	Kuala Lumpur, Labuan	Transport	From 00/08/64
Trooping				
Britannias of 99 and 511 Sqn. RAF, British Eagle and British United, Comet C.4s of 216 Sqn. RAF and Belfast C.1s of 53 Sqn. RAF (from 1966) were involved in trooping or freight flights to and from the UK.				
AURI				
1 Sqn.	P-51D/K, B-25D/J, B-26B	Pontianak, Taranak	Ground attack	
3 Sqn.	P-51D/K	Kemajoram	Ground attack	
11 Sqn.	MiG-17	Iswahjudi	Air defence	
12 Sqn.	MiG-19	Iswahjudi	Ground attack	
14 Sqn.	MiG-21	Kemajoram	Air defence	
1 Sqn.	Il-28	Kemajoram	Light bombing	
21 Sqn.	B-25D/J, B-26B	Pontianak	Light bombing	
41 Sqn.	Tu-16	Kemajoram	Bombing	
42 Sqn.	Tu-16	Iswahjudi	Bombing	
2 Sqn.	Il-14	Halim	Transport	
31 Sqn.	C-130B, An-12	Halim	Transport	
5 Sqn.	Mi-4, Mi-6	Various	Transport, liaison	

Notes:

1. 20 Sqn. Hunters are understood to have been supplemented by aircraft from 28 Sqn. (Kai Tak) from time to time.
2. In addition, detachments of heavy bombers in the form of Victor B.1As of 55 or 57 Sqns. were based at Tengah from 1963.
3. No. 205 Sqn. Shackletons were supplemented by detachments from UK-based squadrons (including 203, 204 and 210).
4. Light helicopter units in addition had detachments based at Brunei, Kuching, Labuan, Long Semado, Nanga Gaat, Sibu, Simanggang and Tawau.
5. In addition, Wasp HAS.1s of 829 NAS embarked on a range of frigates were active from 1963.
6. Army aircraft and helicopters were based on airfields at Kuching and Brunei Town. In addition, the following airstrips were used by detachments of Army aircraft: Bario, Kapit, Long Banga, Long Pa Sia, Long Semado, Long Seridan, Lundu, Nanga Gaat, Sepulot, Sibu, Simanggang, Tawau, Terendak. No. 656 Sqn. flights were rotated between West and East Malaysia and between Brigade Districts within East Malaysia.

serial on engine intake, black serial under wing, white code on fin and nose: XH841/D, XH885/R, XH390/O (60 Sqn.).

Javelin FAW.9R XH896/J (64 Sqn.).

Canberra PR.7 Dark Green/Dark Sea Grey over, silver under, squadron badge on fin, black serial on rear fuselage and nosewheel doors: WJ822 (81 Sqn.).

Canberra B.15 Camouflaged as PR.7: WH961, WH968 (45 Sqn.); WH947, WT303 (32 Sqn.).

Shackleton MR.2 Dark Sea Grey overall, white fuselage top decking, red serial and squadron number on rear fuselage, code on nose: WR965/K (203 Sqn.); WG555/K, WR966/O (204 Sqn.). White bands along wing fuel tanks, black serial, white squadron number on rear fuselage, code on nose: WG530/G, WL745/A (205 Sqn.).

Victor B.1A Dark Green/Medium Sea Grey over, white under, black serial on rear fuselage: XH588, XH621 (57 Sqn.).

Belvedere HC.1 White over, silver under, black serial on rear fuselage, code on mid fuselage: XG475/A, XG476/F (66 Sqn.). Dark Green/Dark Sea Grey over, silver under, white serial on rear fuselage, black code on nose: XG451/E (66 Sqn.).

Whirlwind HAR.10 Dark Green/Dark Sea Grey over, silver under, white serial on boom, code on rear fuselage and nose: XR481/J (110 Sqn.); XP393/O (225 Sqn.); XP 357/J, XS412/Y (230 Sqn.). Silver overall, black serial on boom, code on rear fuselage: XR479/G, XR483/X (103 Sqn.).

Sycamore HC.14 Silver overall, black serial on boom, code on fuselage: XE310/A (110 Sqn.).

Twin Pioneer CC.1 White over, silver under, red dayglo patches on fin and wing-tips, black serial on rear fuselage, serial digits on nose:

XL969, XM962, XN319, XP293 (209 Sqn.). Dark Green/Dark Sea Grey over, silver under, white serial on rear fuselage, serial digits on nose: XL995 (209 Sqn.).

Pioneer CC.1 White over, silver under, black serial on rear fuselage: XJ465, XL704 (209 Sqn.). Dark Green/Dark Sea Grey over, silver under, white serial on rear fuselage: XL517, XL969 (209 Sqn.).

Beverley C.1 White over, silver under, squadron number in diamond on fin, black serial on rear fuselage, serial digits on nose and fin: XB262, XB289, XH116, XM112 (34 Sqn.).

Hastings C.2 White over, silver under, squadron number in diamond on fin, black serial on rear fuselage, serial digits on fin: TG569, WD481, WJ337 (48 Sqn.).

Valetta C.1 White over, silver under, squadron number in diamond on fin, black serial on rear fuselage, serial digits on fin: VW150, VX512 (52 Sqn.).

Argosy C.1 White over, silver under, black serial on rear boom, serial digits on fin: XP444, XP447, XR107 (215 Sqn.).

FAA

Sea Vixen FAW.2 Extra Dark Sea Grey over, white under, white serial on rear fuselage, codes on nose and fin: XP924/492E (899 NAS).

Gannet AEW.3 Extra Dark Sea Grey over, Sky under, black serial on rear fuselage, codes on nose and fin: XL480/436E (D Flt., 849 NAS); XL498/040R (C Flt., 849 NAS)

Whirlwind HAS.7 Silver overall, black serial on boom, code on fuselage: XN384/HA (848 NAS).

Wessex HAS.1 Light Stone/olive green over,

Light Stone under, black serial on rear fuselage, white codes on mid fuselage and fin: XM868/MA (845 NAS). RAF blue-grey overall, yellow top decking, white serial on rear fuselage, code on mid fuselage and nose: XP117/273V (814 NAS).
Wessex HU.5 Light Stone/olive green over, Light Stone under, black serial on rear fuselage, white codes on mid fuselage and fin: XS495/QA (848 NAS).
Wasp HAS.1 Dark Sea Grey overall, white serial and codes: XS537/460AJ (829 NAS, HMS Ajax).

British Army
Auster AOP.9 Dark Green/brown overall, white serial on rear fuselage: XR622 (7 Flt.).
Beaver AL.1 Dark Green/brown overall, blue spinner, red square on fin, white serial on rear fuselage: XP779 (30 Flt.).
Scout AH.1 Dark Green/brown overall, white serial on boom: XP850 (3 Flt.); XP901 (7 Flt.); XP904 (10 Flt.); XP905 (14 Flt.).
Sioux AH.1 Dark Green/brown overall, white serial on fin: XT103 (4 RTR).

RAAF
UH-1B Olive overall, white serial on door: (A2-)484 (5 Sqn.).

RNZAF
Bristol Freighter White over, silver under, blue cheat line, squadron badge on fin, black serial on rear fuselage: NZ5904, NZ5910 (41 Sqn.).
Canberra B(I).12 Dark Green/Dark Sea Grey over, silver under, black serial on rear fuselage: NZ6105 (14 Sqn.).

RMAF
Alouette III Dark green-brown overall, white serial on boom: FM 1087, FM 1089 (3 Sqn.).
Pioneer Bare metal overall, white fuselage top decking, black serial on rear fuselage: FM 012, FM 016 (1 Sqn.).
Twin Pioneer Bare metal overall, white fuselage top decking, black serial on rear fuselage: FM 1001, FM 1002 (1 Sqn.).
Herald White overall, medium blue under fuselage, dark blue cheat line, white serial on rear fueslage: FM 1024 (4 Sqn).
Caribou Dark green-brown overall, white serial on rear fuselage: FM 1100, FM 1104 (8 Sqn.).

AURI
MiG-17F Bare metal overall, black serial on nose, code on rear fuselage: 1153/F, 1182/F (11 Sqn.).
MiG-21 Bare metal overall, black serial on nose: 2156 (14 Sqn.).
Tu-16 Bare metal overall, black serial on nose, code on rear fuselage: 1601/M (41 Sqn.).
Il-28 Bare metal overall, black serial on nose: 842, 847 (1 Sqn.).
B-25D Bare metal overall, red fins, black serial on rear fuselage: M-459 (1 Sqn.).
B-26B Bare metal overall, shark's teeth, black serial on rear fuselage: M-267, M-268 (1 Sqn.).
C-130B Bare metal overall, orange panels on upper wing, fuselage and fin, black serial on fin, constructor's code on nose: T-1307/3599 (31 Sqn.).

10.9. Miscellaneous operations, conflicts and incidents

1. Nuclear weapons tests have been carried out in Australia and the Pacific. The first American tests in the area were at Bikini Atoll and involved B-29s of the 509th Bomb Group; later tests in 1951 at Eniwetok involved B-50Ds, then B-36s and B-47s. British tests were initially conducted at Maralinga, the first on 3 October 1952, the weapon for which is believed to have been transported by a Sunderland of 88 Sqn. The first air-dropped test was at Maralinga on 11 October 1956 when the weapon was released by a Valiant of 49 Sqn. in Operation 'Totem'. Supporting the 1956 British tests was 269 Sqn. (Shackleton MR.1A). The first H-bomb tests were carried out at Christmas Island, a Valiant of 49 Sqn. dropping the weapon on 15 May in Operation 'Grapple'. Other units supporting the 1957 tests were 206 and 240 Sqns. (Shackleton MR.1A), 22 Sqn. (Whirlwind HAR.2), 76 Sqn. (Canberra B.6 Mod.), 100 Sqn. (Canberra PR.7) and a Station Flight (Auster AOP.9 and Dakota C.4). Royal Navy involvement included HMS *Warrior* with a Ship's Flight of Whirlwind HAR.3s and Avenger AS.5s. Later British tests were also conducted at Monte Bello Island, off the north-west coast of Australia.

2. Air India Constellation VT-DEP, carrying a Chinese Communist delegation to Bandoeng, blew up and crashed in the sea off Sarawak, killing around sixteen on board. A bomb had been planted by Chinese Nationalists at Hong Kong.

3. There were minor uprisings on West Irian in March 1984. Indonesian fighters overflew Papua New Guinea in their search for insurgents, and on 26 March a missionary Cessna 185, PK-RCH, was seized on landing at Yurup and two of the occupants were killed. The aircraft was later burnt.

11: The Caribbean and Central America

Wars in Central America spring primarily from the desire of the United States to keep its own 'back yard' free of communism. In pursuit of this cause, the Americans often work covertly, primarily through the Central Intelligence Agency.

In 1954, the US supported the overthrow of the left-wing Arbenz Government in Guatemala, felt to be the last potential 'domino' to fall before Mexico. A counter-revolution was foiled in 1961 by US forces in training in neighbouring Nicaragua. The training was in preparation for the ill-fated 'Cuban exile' invasion of Cuba, the infamous Bay of Pigs episode. Poor intelligence and political indecision led to inevitable failure, and international humiliation for the newly appointed President Kennedy. It is possible that before this event the United States might have found some accommodation with Fidel Castro, but after April 1961 his attitude hardened to the extent that Cuban troops are now to be found fighting for the Soviet cause across the world.

The Russians were not slow to capitalize on the Cuban position, and the siting of strategic missiles in Cuba in 1962 brought the world as close to the Third World War as it has ever been. This time, by exercising political will backed up by full mobilization, Kennedy was able to avert disaster. The wide range, scale and competence of the reconnaissance forces was vital in maintaining accurate intelligence during this crisis.

The next US intervention was in the Dominican Republic in 1965, when the perceived threat to US citizens was the pretext for American invasion. The same pretext was to be used in the invasion of Grenada in 1983, and in both instances the USAF and the USN carrier force were used.

A characteristic of Latin American air wars is the use of vintage warplanes, often left over from the Second World War. Types such as the P-47, P-51, F4U and ubiquitous B-26 figured in the civil war in Costa Rica from 1948 to 1955 and in the wars fought by Honduras against Nicaragua in 1957 and El Salvador in 1969 (the so-called 'Football War'). In these wars and in internal unrest in Haiti in 1963, the US appears to have played no role.

In the murderous civil wars in Nicaragua and El Salvador from 1979 and 1980 respectively, America has operated extensively, again primarily through the CIA. In El Salvador it is the Government which is supported, while it is the exiled 'Contras' who benefit from patronage in Nicaragua, apparently regardless of the wishes of Congress. The Honduran Government seems happy to provide extensive bases, while covert operations are also managed from within El Salvador.

British involvement in the region has been confined to over-reaction to events in Anguilla in 1969 and the maintenance of forces in Belize to counter territorial ambition by neighbouring Guatemala.

11.1. The Bay of Pigs, 1961

From 1959, with Castro firmly established in their country, many Cubans fled for nearby Florida as he purged the nation's establishment. The Americans saw the anti-Batista revolution as developing to embrace communism, and decided to support exile groups in a counter-revolution. On 29 November 1959, leaflets were dropped over Havana by unmarked C-46 transports. The first plan to train 30 guerrillas in Panama was sketched out by the CIA in January 1960. The plan soon developed, and from February a powerful radio transmitter was operating on Swan Island off Honduras as Radio Free Cuba. On 4 March the French ship *Le Coubre*, which was carrying munitions, was blown up in Havana harbour as the US National Security Agency (NSA) was debating how to change the Cuban Government. The CIA plan was embraced and

extended, and soon agents were negotiating for a training base in Guatemala. A site was identified at Retalhuleu and a training organization set up as Camp Trax, which by August had its own large airfield. Cuban dissidents were recruited in the Miami area, and initial training was carried out near Homestead AFB.

Pilots were at a premium, and the first group was assembled at Opa-Locka, an ex-naval air station (NAS) in Miami. From here they were transported by C-54 to San José in Guatemala, and then to Retalhuleu to begin training on the B-26, C-46 and C-54. The CIA hoped to replicate its Guatemalan operation of 1954 by building up an invasion force supported by its own air force, flying aircraft of the type operated in the invaded country. The aircraft were to carry Cuban markings. Once the invasion force had landed, it was assessed that there would be an internal revolution, supported by pre-placed saboteurs.

The FAR, as the Cuban Air Force had become, operated out of three main bases, Camp Libertad on the outskirts of Havana, San Antonio de los Baños 20 miles to the south, and Antonio Maceo airport at Santiago de Cuba. From these airfields the FAR flew up to eight T-33 armed trainers, twelve B-26C Invaders and twelve Sea Fury FB.11 fighters, although serviceability was not high. MiG-15 and -17 fighters were on order from Poland. The transport fleet included ten C-47s and eight Bell 47 helicopters. The Army operated a range of newly supplied Soviet equipment, including IS-II and T-34 tanks and 105mm guns, offset against Soviet sugar purchases after a US-imposed embargo in June 1960.

To function effectively in covert operations, the CIA works through a series of cover organizations, many of them highly profitable through conducting legitimate business. The earliest of these was Civil Air Transport (CAT), formed by Claire Chennault in 1946 and later reorganized under a holding company called Pacific Corporation. CAT was used widely throughout the 1950s in support of US operations against Communist China (q.v.). During this period, CAT was split to form, in addition, Air America and Air Asia, operating in South-East Asia and Taiwan respectively. In 1960, Southern Air Transport (SAT) was acquired, to support operations in Latin America from bases in Florida.

For the Cuban venture the CIA used a number of proprietaries. A large number of US citizens were engaged to train the Cuban pilots through the Double-Chek Corporation, and in October 1960 this company sought help from General Reid Doster, Commanding Officer of the Alabama Air National Guard (ANG), which included the 117th Tactical Reconnaissance Wing (TRW). This unit had flown the B-26 until 1957, and Wing members were familiar with the type. By December, Doster had assembled 80 personnel, including experts from other states' ANG units. All were paid through Double-Chek, as were the dependants of those subsequently killed. At least twenty ex-USAF B-26Bs were purchased from stocks at Tucson, Arizona, by Intermountain

Aviation. They were subsequently operated for the CIA by the Caribbean Marine Aero Corporation (CARAMAR), which also paid the Cuban air crews; Zenith Technical Enterprises Inc. was responsible for conversion work on the aircraft. Transport aircraft were provided by SAT, working out of Opa-Locka and Clewiston; some of the C-46 transports are believed to have been ex-CAT machines. Small arms were bought from Interarms, a major arms dealer run by Samuel Cummings, an ex-CIA employee, while the radio operation on Swan Island was managed by the Gibraltar Steamship Corporation.

Five ships were hired from the Garcia Line to transport the invasion force from Nicaragua. Each of about 5,000 tons, they were the *Atlantico, Caribe, Houston, La Playa* and *Rio Escondido*. The CIA operated two landing craft infantry (LCI), the *Barbara J.* and *Blagar*, from Key West, under cover of Mineral Carriers Ltd., and the 450ft landing ship dock (LSD) USS *San Marcos* was, in effect, requisitioned from the US Navy to transport a range of smaller, unmarked landing craft to the beaches. In November the ANG crews began training at the municipal airport at Fort Lauderdale, Miami, and after a few weeks they flew on to Guatemala via Opa-Locka to support the training of Cuban air and ground crews.

By now the more experienced Cubans were flying supply sorties to dissidents in Cuba from the advanced airfield at Puerto Cabezas ('Happy Valley') in Nicaragua. There were several accidents, and few of the missions were successful on account of poor radio communications and badly marked drop zones. By March 1961, 68 such sorties, each involving a round trip in excess of 1,200 miles, had been flown. During November, some crews were diverted from their supply task to help suppress a revolution in Guatemala City. On 11 March an AT-11 on a leaflet dropping sortie was shot down and the crew rescued by a USN destroyer.

John F. Kennedy was sworn in as President in January 1961, and he was quickly briefed on the Cuban operation. Although sympathetic in principle – he had been briefed in outline in August 1960 – he was concerned about explicit US

The Brigade operated several C-46 Commandos, purchased by the CIA from ex-USAF stocks. This bare metal example, anonymous apart from the number 857, was photographed at Miami before flying south to the base at Retalhuleu in Guatemala.

involvement. The CIA managers had promised the Cuban invasion force, now named Brigade 2506, total air cover, implicity by units of the US Navy, but it was now clear that Kennedy would not sanction such cover. The USN commitment extended to maintaining the carrier USS *Essex* (CVS-9) on station, escorted by the destroyers *Eaton*, *Conway*, *Cony*, *Murray* and *Waller*. Aboard *Essex* was VA-34 equipped with the A4D-2N, VS-34 with the S2F, VAW-12 Det. 45 with the AD-5W, and HS-9 with HSS-1 helicopters.

On 3 April, briefing staff for the operation, named 'Pluto', arrived at Puerto Cabezas from Washington. By now Kennedy had stated categorically that there would be no intervention by the United States with US forces, but still the Brigade was not advised. Kennedy also felt that the original plan to take out Castro's air force on the ground by sixteen B-26s would create too much 'noise'. The initial strike was reduced in scale to just six aircraft, and from this point the invasion was doomed.

From 0228hrs on Saturday 15 April, six B-26s in spurious FAR markings but with blue fuselage bands took off from Puerto Cabezas. In three flights of two, they were code-named 'Gorilla', 'Puma' and 'Linda' and were destined for the airfields at Santiago de Cuba, Camp Libertad and San Antonio de los Baños respectively. Each armed with two 500lb and ten 260lb fragmentation bombs, the aircraft struck at dawn, their targets the operational aircraft of the FAR. 'Gorilla' flight, comprising aircraft '929' and '933', destroyed Cubana DC-3 CU-T172, a C-47 and a Sea Fury but claimed three B-26s; aircraft '933' crash-landed at Puerto Cabezas on its return. 'Puma' flight was less successful but may have damaged a T-33. One of the attacking aircraft, 'Puma 3' was hit by AA fire and crashed into the sea, while the other suffered engine trouble and flew to Boca Chica NAS on Key West. 'Linda' flight claimed a T-33, a DC-3, a C-47 and an AT-6; one of the attacking aircraft, short of fuel, landed on Grand Cayman island.

At 0400hrs, Mario Zuñiga had taken off from Puerto Cabezas in a B-26B, also numbered '933' and painted in FAR markings. The aircraft landed at Miami International Airport at 0821hrs, purporting to have been part of a group of aircraft that had defected after having shot up Cuban airfields. Zuñiga was not in a flying suit or uniform, and suspicious reporters soon noticed that the B-26 was a solid-nosed B-26B whereas the FAR operated the B-26C; in addition, the guns had obviously not been fired.

U-2 reconnaissance photographs indicated that no more than five aircraft had been destroyed, with more damaged, and it now became clear that without air cover the landing would be at the mercy of the FAR's remaining aircraft. Permission was sought from Washington for another air strike on Sunday, but this was denied on the

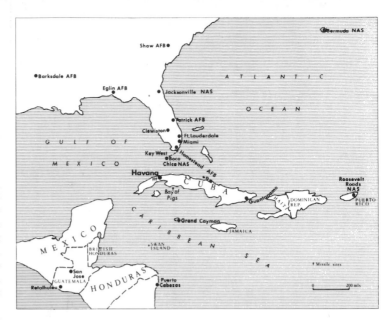

grounds that the aircraft could not possibly be operating from Cuba. Further attacks were ruled out until the Brigade Air Force could operate out of the airstrip at the proposed beach-head.

Just after midnight on Sunday, the invasion fleet prepared for the landings at two sites about fifteen miles apart. Blue beach was at Girón, where the airstrip was located, while Red beach, fifteen miles away, was at Playa Larga at the head of the Bahia de Cochinos (Bay of Pigs). The *Blagar* led the Red beach assault with an advance party, while *Barbara J.* headed the Blue beach attack. They were followed by the USS *San Marcos* with seven assorted landing craft, some of which foundered on coral reefs at Playa Larga. Successfully landed were five M41 tanks. Initially the landings went fairly smoothly, with the Brigade facing only local militia, but, by dawn, regular troops were in the area and the FAR had been alerted. At 0650hrs Sea Fury 541 flown by Capt. Enrique Carrerras and operating out of San

The scene at Santiago de Cuba airport after the attack by B-26 Invaders of 'Gorilla' Flight. Totally destroyed and burning out is Cubana DC-3 CU-T172; two other aircraft were also reported to have been destroyed in the raid. One of the attacking Invaders crashed on its return.

Antonio attacked the *Houston* standing off Playa Larga. The rocket strike destroyed the ship with her load of medical and radio equipment; some of the troops waiting to disembark were also lost.

Sea Furies returned three hours later and this time attacked and blew up the *Rio Escondido* off Girón, although one was shot down. The Brigade was now in need of ammunition, and as a number of landing craft led by the *Blagar* headed out to the *Altantico* and *Caribe* they were attacked by an FAR B-26, which was shot down. Later, the group was attacked by a Sea Fury. At dawn, six Brigade C-46 transports flew over the landing area to drop 177 paratroops three miles north-east of Playa Larga, their task to hold the road inland. The slow C-46s were attacked by a Sea Fury and several B-26s, and one was brought down in the sea.

The sole Brigade air strike of the day was at 1000hrs, when two B-26s attacked a Cuban column outside Pálpite; it was estimated that half a battalion was put out of action. After their passes, both B-26s were attacked by two FAR T-33s and a single Sea Fury. One was shot down by T-33 711 flown by Rafael del Pino, while the second, flown by José Crespo, was damaged by a Sea Fury and ditched en route to Nicaragua with the loss of the crew. During the fighting the A4D-2s from *Essex*, under strict orders not to fire, flew between FAR and Brigade aircraft in a futile attempt to protect the vulnerable B-26 bombers. The FAR claimed three further B-26s shot down in the day, two (including '935') by T-33 and one by a Sea Fury. Despite pressure, Washington refused to sanction overt US involvement, leaving the Brigade to its fate. By now many Cuban pilots, tired and demoralized through the limitations placed on their initial strikes and realizing that the promised air umbrella had been denied, refused to fly further sorties.

One pilot, Eduardo Ferrer, who had already flown a paradrop sortie in the morning, agreed to fly a heavily laden C-46 on to Girón airstrip. His B-26 escort soon turned back, but he pressed on until attacked by a T-33. At this stage he was warned off any attempt to land, and he returned

with his precious load of ammunition. Despite their reservations, six Cuban Brigade crews flew an attack mission against Cuban positions at 1400hrs on Tuesday 18 April. This strike was successful and no aircraft were lost. From Washington, *Essex* was ordered to put up a reconnaissance flight at dawn the following day and to obliterate all markings on her strike aircraft in preparation for possible action. At Kelly AFB, Texas, a squadron of C-130 transports of the USAF had their markings painted out in preparation for a pre-dawn supply drop over the beach-head, but agreement to their use was refused when delays meant a daylight drop. In Florida eight B-26s and four T-33s were prepared to reinforce the Brigade Air Force in Nicaragua, but without crews they were of no use.

The Brigade's position by the end of Tuesday was desperate. The *Atlantico* and *Caribe* had departed the battle zone with their loads of ammunition for the safety of the high seas. At Puerto Cabezas it had been decided to mount one more air strike at dawn on Wednesday. With a shortage of willing Cuban crews and on the understanding that the strike would be covered by VA-34's Skyhawks, the decision was taken locally to use American volunteer pilots, the Brigade's PBY-5 amphibian attempting to remain in the area to recover any air crews forced to ditch. At 0330hrs on the 19th, five B-26s took off from Puerto Cabezas for the final mission. They were flown by one Cuban, Gonzalo Herrera, and four American training advisers, William Goodwin, Thomas Ray, Riley Shamburger and Joe Shannon. As the five aircraft approached the Cuban coastline they saw four Skyhawks overflying: they were, in fact, the reconnaissance

There were apparently two Invaders marked in spurious FAR colours as '933'. One was involved in the 'Gorilla' flight attack on Antonio Maceo airport, Santiago de Cuba, but crashed on its return to Puerto Cabezas. One of the two is pictured in Nicaragua. (Via L. Pinzauti)

The second fake FAR Invader '933', seen at Miami International after having allegedly defected from Cuba following a bombing raid. Sharp-eyed observers soon noticed that the Invader was a B-26B with a solid nose, whereas the FAR flew the glazed-nose B-26C. The starboard propellers are feathered, the pilot having made a single-engined landing since the other had been 'damaged by ground fire'.

TABLE OF UNITS: THE BAY OF PIGS, 1961

Unit	Aircraft	Base(s)
FAR		
Esc. de Caza	Sea Fury FB.11, T-33	Camp Libertad, San Antonio de Los Baños, Santiago de Cuba
Esc. de Caza-Bomb	B-26C	San Antonio de Los Baños, Santiago de Cuba
Esc. de Transportes	C-46, C-47, Bell 47	Camp Libertad, Cienfuegos, Santiago de Cuba
Brigade		
–	B-26B	Puerto Cabezas
–	C-46, C-54	Retalhuleu, Puerto Cabezas
–	PBY-5A	Puerto Cabezas
USN		
CVSG-60 (AW), Essex		
VA-34 A4D-2	VAW-12 (det.) AD-5W	
VS-34 S2F	HS-9 HSS-1	

flight ordered the previous day, and to the surprise of the Brigade pilots the aircraft withdrew from the scene. The VA-34 escort agreed by Kennedy missed the rendezvous because of a communications failure, leaving the B-26 bombers exposed. Ray's aircraft attacked Castro's headquarters at the Central Australia sugar mill and was brought down by AA fire. Although the pilot and co-pilot, Leo F. Baker, survived the crash, the two men were subsequently shot.

The other bombers made their attacks and departed at low level. Shamburger's aircraft was pursued by a T-33 and brought down over the sea with the loss of the crew, and the remaining aircraft returned to Puerto Cabezas. The battle was now over, and most of the Brigade's troops were captured, although some escaped through the swamps. Propaganda guidance issued by the CIA on the 19th stated that there had been 'a mission to resupply insurgents in the Escambray Mountains'.

On 23 April, 50 Cuban pilots and ground crewmen were returned to Miami on a C-54 and the bases closed down. Of the original members of the Brigade, 114 were killed, 1,189 were captured and 150 escaped or never landed. The intended invasion failed for two reasons. First, there was faulty intelligence in respect both of forces and of popular support for Castro: there was no uprising. Second, the limitations on the use of air power left the Brigade and its supply ships exposed to air attack without cover. The CIA plan escalated over time, but with many aspects kept from Kennedy. At the last minute, when he became aware of the detailed proposals for overt US involvement, he refused (probably wisely), to the surprise of the CIA managers. Later, the CIA was reorganized, with a greater emphasis placed on intelligence-gathering and less on covert operations.

AIRCRAFT MARKINGS

FAR

Sea Fury FB.11 *Mottled green overall, yellow serial on rear fuselage repeated small on fin: 541.*
B-26C *Bare metal overall, serial on nose and fin: 917.*
T-33 *Bare metal overall, serial on nose and fin: 703, 709, 711.*
C-46 *White over, bare metal under, 'Escuadron de Transporte' on fuselage, serial on nose and fin: 610.*
C-47 *As C-46: 210.*

Brigade

B-26B *Bare metal overall, marked as FAR aircraft but with medium blue mid fuselage band: 929, 933, 935.*
C-46 *Bare metal overall, spurious serial on fin: 857.*
PBY-5A *White over, natural metal under, registration on fin: HP289.*

11.2. The Cuban Missile Crisis, 1962

Following the United States' humiliation over the Bay of Pigs incident and stalemate over Berlin, President Kennedy faced his toughest trial. Cuba had requested more arms from Russia to protect herself against the continuing threat of US interference, and by August 1962 the CIA was aware of significant arms shipments. On the 22nd of that month, the President was advised of the presence of large missiles on the island. Agency U-2 flights over Cuba were stepped up, and US Navy and US Air Force patrol and reconnaissance aircraft paid special attention to Soviet shipping.

On 29 August, a U-2 flight from McCoy Operating Location (OL), Florida, photographed two SA-2 sites on Cuba and six more under construction. Photo-interpreters became anxious when it was realized that the layout was similar to surface-to-air missile (SAM) sites associated with the protection of strategic missile bases in the Soviet Union. On 4 September Kennedy warned Khrushchev that the United States would not tolerate the siting of offensive weapons on Cuba, and Khrushchev replied by saying that the Soviet Union had no need to place such weapons in the Caribbean. Just four days later, however, a

The US Navy deployed three attack and four anti-submarine Air Groups to the Caribbean during the Cuban Missile Crisis. On board two of the attack carriers were detachments from VFP-62, equipped with the RF-8A Crusader. The USN, USMC and USAF all contributed to the constant tactical reconnaissance task. (Via A. Jones)

P-2 Neptune of VP-44 photographed the freighter *Omsk* heading for Havana with large, oblong canisters on the decks. U-2 flights were again stepped up. On 19 September, the US Intelligence Board reported its view that Russia would not deploy nuclear weapons in Cuba, although four days ealier a second shipment of missiles had arrived in Havana. Further reconnaissance flights showed more construction work, and on 10 October the US Air Force's 4080th Strategic Reconnaissance Wing (SRW) formally assumed responsibility for overflights from the CIA. The 4080th used CIA U-2E variants equipped with electronic countermeasures (ECM) equipment, and sorties were flown from McCoy, Barksdale and Laughlin AFBs.

The primary reason for the transfer of responsibility to the USAF was the threat from SA-2 missiles. The first USAF flights were flown on 10 October by Major Rudolph Anderson and highway construction was noted, but the flights were then halted for three days because of poor weather conditions associated with hurricane 'Ella'. Then, on 14 October, Major Steve Heyser flew a U-2E out of Patrick AFB, Florida. His route took him over Cuba for just six minutes, during which time he took 928 photographs of two sites at San Cristobal and Sagua la Grande; processed the following day, they were rushed to President Kennedy on the 16th. They clearly showed SS-4 'Sandal' medium-range ballistic missile (MRBM) sites in an advanced state of preparation and with missiles deployed, and what was to become known as the Cuban Missile Crisis had begun. A high-level Executive Committee was formed and low-level reconnaissance flights by RF-101Cs of the 29th Tactical Reconnaissance Squadron (TRS) from Shaw AFB in South Carolina were ordered. The following day what appeared to be intermediate-range ballistic missile (IRBM) sites were photographed at Guanajay and Remedios.

On Thursday 18 October, Kennedy kept a pre-arranged meeting with the Soviet Foreign Secretary Gromyko, but, when warned of the perceived threat to US security, Gromyko told the President that defensive arms only were in Cuba. Meanwhile the Executive Committee was analyzing Soviet intentions and debating res-

ponses. It seemed most likely that Russia was applying pressure to gain concessions over Berlin, and possibly the removal of 45 Jupiter and 60 Thor IRBMs from Italy, Turkey and England. The responses considered included invasion, air attack, ultimatum and blockade. On Monday the 22nd a quarantine (blockade) was announced, and 3,190 civilians were evacuated from the US Navy base at Guantanamo on Cuba.

B-52 bombers of Strategic Air Command (SAC) were put on full alert and dispersed to civilian airports, while naval vessels raced to the Caribbean to enforce the blockade. Air Defence and Tactical Air Commands moved units south to Florida. Guantanamo was reinforced with a garrison of 8,000 Marines and sailors, and Task Force 135 was established to defend the base; ships in the force included the carriers *Enterprise* (CVN-65) and *Independence* (CVA-62) with a total of eight attack, four fighter and two photo-reconnaissance squadrons embarked. The quarantine was enforced by units of Task Force 136, which comprised 180 vessels, including the carriers *Essex* (CVS-9), *Lake Champlain* (CVS-39), *Randolph* (CVS-15), *Shangri-La* (CVS-38) and *Wasp* (CVS-18).

The quarantine was signed on the 23rd, creating a barrier 800 miles distant but reducing to 500 miles to give the Russians more time to signal their ships in transit. By Wednesday some vessels

A tactical reconnaissance Voodoo photograph of the MRBM site at San Cristobal. The theodolite station, close to the missile erector, was essential for the launch and guidance of the 1,100-mile-range missiles. The blatant siting of equipment in the open with little attempt at camouflage can only have been considered provocative. (USAF)

were stopping, only to restart the following day. During this time the RF-101Cs of 29 TRS and the RF-8As of VFP-62 and VMJC-2 remained busy, and US Navy and Marine Corps aircraft flocked to the area: on the 20th there had been 109 fighters, 69 attack aircraft and 30 patrol types available, but by the 28th there were 336, 218 and 78 respectively excluding carrier-based machines. On Friday, after the freighter *Marucla* had been stopped and searched, Khrushchev accepted the American terms for the removal of offensive weapons (which by now included 44 Il-28s under construction at San Julian), but only in exchange for the Americans' removal of the Jupiter missiles, which had previously been ordered. Tension increased on the 27th as Major Anderson was killed during an overflight of naval installations at Banes, his pressure suit having ruptured after his aircraft was hit by an SA-2 missile.

Early the following day, Soviet intercontinental missiles (ICBMs) were readied as another U-2 inadvertently but embarrassingly overflew the Chukotka peninsula. At 1000hrs on the 28th the crisis ended as the Russians agreed to dismantle the missiles, under inspection. The freighter *Divinogorsk* sailed from Mariel with four SS-4s on 5 November, eight more missiles left on the 7th on the *Metallurg Anosov*, and six on the 9th on board the *Bratsk*. The Il-28s, however, were still under construction, and the quarantine was not lifted until 20 November, by which time the Russians had agreed to their removal. The first aircraft left Cuba in crates on 15 December aboard the *Kasimov*.

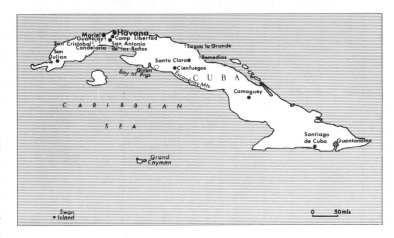

The USN moved large numbers of aircraft to bases in the south-eastern states and the Caribbean, and by 28 October it had 336 fighters, 218 attack aircraft and 78 patrol aircraft in the region. Illustrated is P-2H Neptune 148352/LQ5 of VP-56, which operated out of NAS Norfolk, Virginia. (USN)

TABLE OF UNITS: THE CUBAN MISSILE CRISIS, 1962

Unit		Aircraft	Base	Role
CIA (August–10 October 1962)				
–		U-2E	McCoy	Recce
USAF[1]				
29 TRS		RF-101C	Shaw AFB	PR
4028 SRS		U-2C/E	Barksdale AFB	Recce

USN (21 October–November 1962)

CVG-7 (AG), Independence				*CVSG-52 (AS), Wasp*			
VF-41	F-4B	VFP-62 (det.)	RF-8A	VA-64	A-4C	VAW-33 (det.)	EA-1E
VF-84	F-8C	VAW-12 (det.)	E-1B	VS-28	S-2A	HS-11	SH-34J
VA-72	A-4C	VAW-33	EA-1E	VS-31	S-2A		
VA-86	A-4C	HU-2	UH-2A				
VAH-1	A-5A			*CVSG-54 (AT), Lake Champlain*			
				VS-22	S-2A	VAW-12 (det.)	E-1B
CVG-6 (AF), Enterprise				VS-32	S-2A	HS-5	SH-34J
VF-102	F-4B	VMCJ-2	RF-8A				
VF-132	F-8C	VAW-12 (det.)	E-1B	*CVSG-58 (AV), Randolph*			
VA-94	A-4C	VAW-33	EA-1E	VS-26	S-2A	VAW-12 (det.)	E-1B
VMA-225	A-4C	HU-2	UH-2B	VS-36	S-2A	HS-7	SH-34J
VAH-7	A-5A						
				CVSG-60 (AW), Essex			
CVG-10 (AK), Shangri-La				VA-81	A-4C	VAW-33 (det.)	EA-1E
VF-13	F-6A	VA-176	A-1H	VS-24	S-2A	HS-9	SH-34H
VF-62	F-8E	VFP-62 (det.)	RF-8A	VS-27	S-2A		
VA-46	A-4C	VAW-12 (det.)	E-1B				
VA-106	A-4C	HU-2	UH-2B				

Shore based patrol aircraft were heavily involved from 21 October 1962, including the following: VP-8 (P-3A, NAS Bermuda), VP-44 (P-3A, NAS Bermuda) and VP-56 (P-2H,[2] NAS Norfolk).

Notes:
1. Tactical fighters were re-deployed to the south-eastern states; B-47 strategic bombers were dispersed to a number of civil and military airfields, while B-52 Wings went on alert status.
2. Other P-2H units operated from NAS Jacksonville, NAS Key West, NAS Guantanamo and NAS Roosevelt Roads; PR (two squadrons).

Although the crisis centred around missiles, it was conventionally equipped aircraft that gave Kennedy a range of response options. Large numbers of machines were deployed by all services, and the whole Soviet withdrawal was monitored by aircraft. During the period 14 October to 6 December, the USAF flew 102 U-2 sorties over Cuba, but low-flying aircraft were able to supervise the operation with a versatility unmatched by more remote observation. The following year the superpowers agreed to install the 'hot line' telephone link, and as further evidence of the thaw in relations a nuclear test ban agreement was signed in August.

The Soviet vessel *Kasimov* at sea, with fifteen crated Il-28 'Beagles' aboard. The ship is seen after the Russian decision to withdraw missiles and bombers from Cuba, and part of the packing has been removed to enable monitoring USN reconnaissance aircraft to confirm the contents. (USN)

AIRCRAFT MARKINGS

USN
Navy carrier-based, fixed-wing aircraft were painted Gull Gray over, white under.
F-4B *150438/104AE (VF-102).*
F-8E *145460/207AK (VMF-251).*
RF-8A *146871/926AF (VFP-62).*
A-4C *144903/311AK (VA-106); 147726/502AK (VA-46).*

EA-1E *133773/705GE (VAW-12, Lake Champlain).*
S-2A *Chequered rudder: 153582/115AT (VS-22).*
P-2H *Dark blue-grey overall, white upper fuselage decking: 148352/5LQ (VP-56).*
P-3A *Dark blue-grey overall, white upper fuselage decking: 150497/4LM (VP-44).*

USAF
RF-101C *Bare metal overall: 560166/FB-166 (29 TRS).*

11.3. Haiti, 1963

As one of the most impoverished states in a poor region, Haiti ran its air force, the Corps d'Aviation d'Haiti (CAH), on a shoestring, and thus, when rebels struck across the border from the Dominican Republic at Mont Organize on 15 August 1963, they were fairly safe from air attack. In fact, the CAH's six F-51D fighters, bought from the United States in 1952, were all unserviceable, although the following day one was brought into service at Bowen Field and was soon strafing reported rebel positions. On the 17th, troops were flown into the nearest airfield at Hinche in several C-47 transports and C-45 and C-78 communications aircraft, and with a second F-51D operational on the 18th the rebels soon retreated. In July 1964 the Haitian Government requested the import of fifteen T-28 Fennecs from the USA, but the request was rejected by the US Office of Munitions. Two months later, two of the type (513570 and 517618) were smuggled into the country, although the culprits were arrested in the United States. At the command of the life President, 'Papa Doc', the propellers were removed to prevent any chance of the aircraft being used in a revolt. Late in 1966 there was a plan by dissidents to liberate Haiti using US-based

A poor quality but extremely rare photograph of a Corps d'Aviation d'Haiti P-51D Mustang, with a Mitchell behind. The Mustangs, when serviceable, were used to strafe rebel positions in 1963. The fighter appears to be finished light grey overall, with a three-digit serial on the fin and a red fin-tip and spinner. (J. J. Suarez via M. Robson)

F-51D, B-25 and B-26 aircraft, and then to use the country as a springboard for an invasion of Cuba. The ringleaders were arrested while training in Florida in January 1967.

AIRCRAFT MARKINGS

F-51D *Bare metal overall, black US serial on fin: (44)15655.*
C-47 *Bare metal overall, black serial on fin: 4262.*

Unit	Aircraft	Base	Role
TABLE OF UNITS: THE HAITIAN AIR FORCE, 1963			
Composite	P-51D, PT-17, PT-19, T-6	Bowen Field (Port au Prince)	Ground attack, training
Composite	C-45, C-47, C-78, Boeing 307	Bowen Field	Transport, liaison

11.4. The Dominican Republic, 1965

The United States has always been sensitive to the policies of Caribbean nations close to her shores, and has from time to time intervened in the internal affairs of independent nations to protect her own interests. In 1955 the US arms dealers Interarms supplied 26 Vampire F.1s and FB.50s to the right-wing Government of the Dominican Republic, and some of these aircraft were used to repulse an attack by Cuban-backed rebels who landed at Puerto Plata in June 1959. Then, in December 1962, a left-wing President was elected following the assassination of President Trujillo eighteen months earlier. The new Government lasted only until July 1963, when a military coup took place and a right-wing civil junta was appointed. By December 1963, guerrillas were operating in the hills around Monte Gallo, and the Dominican Air Force (FAD) was operating rocket-armed F-51D fighters from Santiago in support of ground forces.

In 1964, the FAD acquired five B-26C light bombers to add to its inventory of four. These new aircraft 'force-landed' at San Isidro en route from Miami to Santiago in Chile; they were impounded, sold to private operators, and then purchased by the FAD. The junta was overthrown

by a military revolt in the capital, San Domingo, on 20 April 1965. Opposition to the revolt was led by Brigadier Wessin y Wessin from San Isidro air base, and F-51Ds, Vampires and B-26s were used to launch attacks on the capital just twelve miles away. During one strike, a Mustang was shot down by the rebels. As fighting developed, the US Caribbean Ready Amphibious Squadron of the Atlantic Fleet was ordered into Dominican waters on the 25th, to help prevent a perceived communist take-over.

The USS *Boxer* (LPH-4), with twenty UH-34As and two UH-1Es of HMM-264 on board, arrived off Dominica on 27 April and began evacuating civilians; 558 were lifted to the ship during the day. On the 28th, the US ambassador requested a Marine Corps landing to protect US citizens.

TABLE OF UNITS: THE DOMINICAN REPUBLIC, 1965

Unit	Aircraft (code)	Base	Role	Dates/sqns.
FAD				
Esc. de Caza	P-51D	San Isidoro. Santiago	Ground attack	
Esc. de Caza-Bomb	Vampire F.1/FB.50. B-26C	San Isidoro	Ground attack. light bombing	
Esc. de Transporte	C-46. C-47	San Isidoro. Hinche	Transport	
USMC				
HMM-264	UH-34A. UH-1E (EG)	*Boxer*	Utility helicopter	27/04/65 to 09/06/65
HMM-263	UH-34A (EG)		Utility helicopter	
HMM-461	CH-37C (CJ)	*Okinawa*	Utility helicopter	04/05/65 to 26/05/65
VMO-1	UH-1E (ER)		Observation helicopter	
USAF				
Transports (drawn from the following TAC and MATS Wings)				
313 TCW	C-130B	Forbes AFB		29. 47. 48 TCS
314 TCW	C-130B/C	Sewart AFB		18. 50. 61. 62 TCS
317 TCW	C-130B	Lockbourne AFB		39. 40. 41 TCS
463 TCW	C-130B	Langley AFB		772. 773. 774 TCS
464 TCW	C-130E	Pope AFB		776. 777. 778 TCS
516 TCW	C-130E	Dyess AFB		345. 346. 347 TCS
62 ATW	C-124C	McChord AFB / Kelly AFB		4. 8 ATS: 7 TCS / 19 ATS
63 TCW	C-124C	Hunter AFB / Robins AFB		14. 15. 52. 53. 54 TCS
1607 ATW	C-124C	Dover AFB		7 ATS
1608 ATW	C-124C / C-130E	Charleston AFB / Charleston AFB		9. 20 TCS: 31 ATS / 3. 17 ATS
1707 ATW	C-124C	Tinker AFB		41. 76 ATS / 1740 ATS
ANG				
185 ATS	C-97E	Ramey AFB	Communications relay (ex Oklahoma City)	
198 FIS	F-86H	San Juan	Air defence	
Fighters from the following TAC units are believed to have been brought to alert status:				
3 TFW	F-100D/F	England AFB		
4 TFW	F-105D	Seymour-Johnson AFB		
12 TFW	F-4C	McDill AFB		
15 TFW	F-4C	McDill AFB		
31 TFW	F-100D/F	Homestead AFB		
354 TFW	F-100D/F	Myrtle Beach AFB		
363 TRW	RF-101C. RF-4C	Shaw AFB		

The USMC helicopters then worked a two-way shuttle, taking Marines in and civilians out. By the following day, two battalions had landed on the western edge of the capital, and two battalions of the 82nd Airborne Division had emplaned and moved from North Carolina to Puerto Rico. The Organization of American States (OAS) called for a ceasefire on the 30th, with a proposed international neutral zone in the embassy area. At the same time, battalions of the 4th Marine Expeditionary Brigade began landing and the 101st Airborne Division was placed on alert. The two 82nd battalions in the theatre were flown into San Isidro in C-130 and C-124 transports.

By 1 May, 90 per cent of the US Air Force's US-based transport fleet was tied up in the operation and the USS *Okinawa* (LPH-3) had joined *Boxer*. The next day, further Airborne battalions were landed to hold a corridor linking the Marines to the west of San Domingo with the original Airborne troops to the east. The build-up of forces continued, and by the end of the month 32,000 US servicemen were committed. Fighting resumed after an interim ceasefire broke down on 7 May, and Vampires and F-51Ds again attacked rebel positions, including a radio station. One F-51D was brought down by US troops when it attacked tanks adjacent to the US embassy. In the meantime, the OAS called for an international peace-keeping force, and this began moving into place from 23 May. Fighting continued sporadically, and in mid-June rebels attacked US positions in the east of San Domingo.

Discussions between factions through August led to the formation of a provisional government in September, and on 20 September 1966 the OAS peace-keeping force HQ was closed after free elections in June. In the fighting, 2,000 civilians were killed and 3,000 injured, in addition to 800 Dominican troops; the United States lost 24 dead and 164 wounded.

AIRCRAFT MARKINGS

FAD
Vampire F.1 *Dark green over, pale blue under, unit badge on nose, black serial on boom and under wings: 2711 (Escuadron de Caza-Bombardero).*
F-51D *Light grey overall, unit badge below cockpit, black serial on mid fuselage and under wings: 1907, 1900 (Escuadron de Caza).*

USMC
UH-34A *Olive Drab overall, white aircraft code on mid upper fuselage, squadron code on fin: 86/EH (HMM-264).*

USAF
C-124C *Bare metal overall: O-(5)20962 (63 TCW).*
C-130E *Bare metal overall, 'MATS' on black band across fin and rudder: 637872 (1608 ATW).*

Fitted with rocket rails for ground attack missions, P-51D Mustang 1919 was flown by Escuadron de Caza, FAD. When rebels overthrew the civil junta in 1965, the Air Force remained loyal, and Vampires and Mustangs were used to attack rebel positions in the capital, flying from San Isidro airbase. (Via J. Ethell)

11.5. Anguilla, 1969

With a population of 6,000, Anguilla has been linked with St. Kitts and Nevis since 1822. From June 1967 there were negotiations with Britain after a local declaration of independence, but on 11 March 1969 the Parliamentary Under-Secretary responsible visited the island and was besieged by a crowd, some of whom discharged small arms. The British Government reacted by flying two companies of 2 Para to Anguilla – a total of 315 men – plus 47 policemen to restore order. Five Hercules of 24 and 36 Sqns. left Lyneham at 0235hrs on 18 March, refuelling at Gander and landing at Antigua. They carried nine Land Rovers, six trailers, and signals equipment. The main force was flown in three VC-10s of 10 Sqn., a Comet C.4 of 216 Sqn. and a Britannia of 99 Sqn., all of which made the non-stop flight from Brize Norton to Antigua later in the day. Also flown from the UK were two Andover C.1s of 46 Sqn., which flew from Abingdon for Antigua via Keflavik, Gander and Bermuda; they were joined by a third already in the Caribbean.

The men were landed on Anguilla at 0315hrs on the 19th from the frigates HMS *Rothesay* and *Minerva*. The ships' Wasps were busy from first light, dropping leaflets and later personnel. The heavy equipment was dropped on Wall Blake Airport by Hercules; an Andover later used the

TABLE OF UNITS: ANGUILLA, 1969

Unit	Aircraft	Base	Role	Dates
RAF				
24 Sqn. 36 Sqn.	Hercules C.1	Lyneham	Transport	18/03/69
99 Sqn.	Britannia C.1			
10 Sqn.	VC-10 C.1	Brize Norton	Troop transport	18/03/69
216 Sqn.	Comet C.4			
46 Sqn.	Andover C.1	Abingdon	Tactical transport	18/03/69
FAA				
829 NAS	Wasp HAS.1	*Minerva, Rothesay*	Communications	19/03/69

Note: RAF squadrons listed are those from which transport aircraft were drawn.

airport, which was too small for larger aircraft. Order had never been seriously threatened and the troops left in September, although some Royal Engineers remained until 1971, undertaking civil projects on the neglected island.

11.6. Grenada, 1983

Grenada, a former British colony, is situated 100 miles north of the Venezuelan coast. From March 1969 the Marxist premier, Maurice Bishop, turned to Cuba for aid, and military advisers were soon helping to train the 2,000-strong People's Revolution Army (PRA). Plans were drawn up for the construction of a new, large airport at Point Salines 'to cncourage tourism', and the contract was let to a British company, Plessey Airports, with most of the work to be undertaken by Cuban labour. About 1,400 American citizens were also on the island, most of them students at the University and Medical School. After a visit to the United States in June 1983, Bishop was placed under house arrest by his military commander, and on 19 October he and a number of supporters were killed in what the Americans saw as a Cuban-inspired coup.

The location of Grenada meant that it was an ideal refuelling site for Soviet flights to Latin America and a potential base for terrorism, and the CIA was aware that a small number of Soviet Spetsnaz (*Spetsialnoye Natznachenye*, or Special Purpose) officers were on the island. The National Security Agency (NSA) met on the 20th to consider its options for the evacuation of US citizens or intervention. On the 21st, two days before the Organization of Eastern Caribbean States (OECS) appealed for American support, US diplomats and planners moved into Bridgetown, Barbados, to effect a pre-arranged intervention rehearsed as 'Ocean Venture 81' in August 1981. D-Day for the invasion was set for the 25th, and forces on their way to the Mediterranean were diverted to the area. On Sunday the 23rd President Reagan authorized the execution of Operation 'Urgent Fury', Joint Task Force 120 (JTF-120) being established under the Navy's command.

Naval units included the carrier USS *Independence* (CV-62), with Carrier Air Wing 6 (CVW-6) embarked, and USS *Guam* (LPH-9), with the Marines of the 22nd Marine Amphibious Unit (MAU) and helicopters of HMM-261 on board. The proposed plan was for Marine units to land near Pearls Airport to the east and for US Rangers to take the Point Salines airfield to the south; a number of reconnaissance missions and special raids would be carried out by USN SEAL (Sea, Air and Land) units.

In the early hours of Monday the 24th, detachments of SEALs and Delta Force members were parachuted into Grenada using HALO (High Altitude, Low Opening) techniques. They are

AIRCRAFT MARKINGS

Andover C.1 *Gloss sand/dark brown over, black under, white serial under wing and on fuselage, digits repeated on fin: XS609 (46 Sqn.).*

understood to have been airlifted from Bridgetown in MC-130E Hercules of 8 SOS and were dropped to reconnoitre the landing areas, especially around Pearls Airport. Near midnight, MC-130E tranports also lifted the 1/75th and 2/75th Rangers from Hunter Army airfield in Georgia. At 0500hrs on D-Day the 25th, Marines from *Guam* departed for Pearls aboard CH-46Es escorted by four AH-1Ts of HML-167 after an earlier start was delayed by heavy rain. Twenty minutes later, the Marines landed with little opposition at Pearls and Grenville. By 0725hrs Pearls Airport was secured, as was Grenville two hours later.

Meanwhile, just after 0530hrs, the two Ranger battalions dropped on Point Salines, escorted by

CH-53D '22' of HM-261 warms up on the deck of USS *Guam* prior to lifting off Marines for Grenada on 25 October. The Marines were landed at Pearls Airport and Grenville, from where they made for the capital. The big 'Super Jollies' were also used to recover crashed helicopters.

AC-130H gunships. Opposition was relatively light as the Cubans had expected a seaborne landing. The runway was found to be blocked, but it was quickly cleared under light fire in preparation for the subsequent landing of the Rangers' heavy equipment. The 82nd Airborne Division flew out from Pope AFB on board C-141 Starlifters and C-130Es from 1000hrs, landing at Point Salines from 1405hrs. The Rangers had by this time moved out from the perimeter towards a Cuban camp, which was taken mid-morning. They were supported by strikes from the A-6E and A-7E attack aircraft from *Independence*. Three special raids were planned. The first, against Radio Free Grenada, was successfully carried out by SEALs at 0615hrs, but not before militia mobilization had been announced. The second, against Richmond Hill prison, was handled by Delta Force using 101st Airborne UH-60A helicopters from *Guam*. The helicopters were driven off by heavy AA fire, and one was shot down before the attempt was abandoned. The third raid, again by SEALs, was an attempt to rescue the Governor-General from Government House on the edge of St. George's. The 22-man team was trapped, and two AH-1Ts were launched to relieve the pressure on the surrounded group. One AH-1T was brought down to crash-land in a football field, while a second AH-1T escorting a casevac CH-46E helicopter was also shot down over the sea with the loss of the crew.

By now AC-130Hs had been brought into the battle area as the SEALs, lacking heavy weapons to fend off PRA attacks using armoured vehicles, became desperate. Strikes by A-7Es followed against nearby defences at Forts Frederick and Rupert, although unfortunately Fort Matthew, now converted to a psychiatric hospital, was hit and a number of patients were killed. At 0300hrs a company of 2/8 Marines was helilifted to a landing zone adjacent to Grand Mal Bay, north of St. George's. An hour later a second company was landed by sea on the beach, in armoured personnel carriers and with M60A1 tank escorts. By 0700hrs they had relieved the SEALs. Later in the day, Fort Rupert and then Fort George were captured.

Attention now turned to rescuing the American students. One campus had been secured the previous day, but that at Grand Anse was taken by a combined Marine and Rangers group flown in from *Guam* in twelve CH-46Es. One of the helicopters was brought down in the surf on the approach, and again AC-130H and Navy strikes were called for. The Grand Anse students were evacuated by helicopter, while those from True Blue campus were removed to point Salines and flown out directly to the USA. With the airfield under pressure, heavy equipment was flown into Bridge-town in C-5A Galaxies, including UH-60A helicopters of the 82nd Combat Air Battalion. These aircraft, with three of the 57th Medical Detachment and several OH-58s and UH-1s, flew from Barbados at 0300hrs on the 27th for Point Salines, where in due course they began the process of casualty evacuation and troop movement around the island. By the 27th, three battalions of the 82nd had landed and were advancing through Frequente to St. George's. Sixteen were wounded when an A-7E strike hit a misidentified target.

The final significant action was against military barracks at Calvigny. Eight 82 CAB UH-60As transported Rangers to the installation, which had been shelled by naval gunfire and artillery and then hit by air strikes from *Independence*. As the helicopters landed, some were hit, and when two collided on the ground a third flipped over while avoiding the debris, killing three Rangers; a fourth helicopter was damaged, but it struggled back to *Guam*. In a subsequent recovery operation by CH-53Ds, two of the damaged helicopters were dropped and written off. Mopping-up operations continued for several days, during which the prison was secured and all the students were recovered. The Marine units evacuated the island on 2 November, to continue their interrupted journey to the Lebanon, and the Rangers returned to their base, leaving the 82nd Airborne in control of the situation.

Earlier, on 30 October, F-15As of 33 TFW had

Although potent attack helicopters, at least two AH-1T SeaCobras were brought down to enemy ground fire off St. George's. This anonymous SeaCobra of HML-167 is refuelling on board USS *Guam* between sorties on 25 October. (USN)

These UH-60A Blackhawks of 101 Combat Air Battalion are seen at Point Salines disembarking airborne troops; an AH-1 appears to be hovering in the background. The Blackhawks, with their ability to lift eleven fully equipped troops, were extremely valuable, but one was shot down and four lost in accidents during the Grenada campaign.

moved into Puerto Rico, while the A-10As of 23 TFW deployed from Eglin AFB to Bridgetown, both these moves being in anticipation of the imminent departure of *Independence* and her Air Wing. The cost of the operation was high, with nineteen US servicemen killed and 116 wounded; in addition 70 Cubans and Grenadians were killed and 410, mainly civilians, wounded. All the US citizens were rescued and evacuated. Captured equipment and records revealed that Grenada was indeed established as a terrorist base, a fact which Eastern Bloc connections confirmed, and as a result Cuba suffered a loss of prestige in many Caribbean countries. For the invasion, the United States deployed extensive and varied resources on a scale not significantly smaller than those used by Britain in recovering the Falklands. Losses and the sometimes fierce defence probably justified the investment; certainly the Cuban reaction could not have been underestimated, although in the event there was no intervention from Havana.

AIRCRAFT MARKINGS

USN

A-6E Counter-shaded Compass Gray with Insignia Gray national and unit markings: 159178/500AE (VA-176).
A-7E As A-6E: 158819/312AE (VA-15); 157570/407AE (VA-87).

The scene at Pearls Airport on 26 October. A C-130E keeps its engines running in the foreground, having presumably just turned off the main runway. Behind is an HMM-261 CH-46E, and behind that is evidence of Soviet Bloc support in the shape of an An-26 and a venerable An-2.

TABLE OF UNITS: GRENADA, 1983

Unit	Aircraft (code)	Base	Role	Dates
USN (CVW-6 – code AE)				
VF-14	F-14A		Air defence	
VF-32	F-14A		Air defence	
VA-15	A-7E		Ground attack	
VA-87	A-7E		Ground attack	
VA-176	A-6E	*Independence*	Attack	22/10/83 to 03/11/83
VAQ-131	EA-6B		EW	
VAW-122	E-2C		AEW	
VS-28	S-3A		ASW	
HS-15	SH-3G		ASW	
Other USN units				
VR-56	C-9B (JU)	NAS Norfolk	Logistics, casevac	23/10/83 to 00/11/83
VR-58	C-9B (JV)	NAS Jacksonville		
USMC				
HML-167	AH-1T (TV)	*Guam*	Attack	22/10/83 to 00/11/83
HMM-261	CH-46E, CH-53D, AH-1T, UH-1N (EM)		Heavy lift	
US Army				
?	OH-58C, OH-6A, Hughes 500MD		Light attack, observation	
57.Med. Det.	UH-60A	*Grenada*	Casevac	24/10/83 to 00/11/83
82 CAB	UH-60A		Troop transport	
101 CAB	UH-60A		Troop transport	
(2 units)	AH-1S		Attack helicopter	02/11/83 to 00/11/83
USAF				
314 TAW	C-130E/H	Little Rock AFB		
317 TAW	C-130E	Pope AFB		
459 TAW	C-130E	Andrews AFB		
463 TAW	C-130H	Dyess AFB		
60 MAW	C-141B, C-5A	Travis AFB		
62 MAW	C-141B	McChord AFB	Transport	23/10/83 to 00/11/83
63 MAW	C-141B	Norton AFB		
315 MAW	C-141B	Charleston AFB		
437 MAW	C-141B	Charleston AFB		
438 MAW	C-141B	McGuire AFB		
514 MAW	C-141B	McGuire AFB		
436 MAW 512 MAW	C-5A	Dover AFB	Transport	25/10/83 to 00/11/83
8 SOS	MC-130E	Hurlburt Field	Paratroop transport	25/10/83 to 27/10/83
16 SOS	AC-130H	Bridgetown, ex Hurlburt Field	Fire-suppression	23/10/83 to 30/10/83
193 ECS	EC-130E	?	Communications monitoring	23/10/83 to 30/10/83
552 AWCW	E-3A	Tinker AFB	Airborne warning and control	24/10/83 to 30/10/83
71 ARS	KC-10A	Barksdale AFB	Air refuelling	25/10/83 to 00/11/83
33 TFW	F-15A	NAS Roosevelt Roads, ex Eglin AFB	Air defence	30/10/83 to 00/11/83
23 TFW	A-10A	Bridgetown, ex Eglin AFB	Ground attack	

USMC
AH-1T *Olive Drab overall, black serial on fin: 160801 (HML-167).*
CH-46E *Olive Drab overall, green-black low-visibility markings, ship code and serial on rear engine casing: 156423/16EM, 157654/01EM (HMM-261).*

USAF
AC-130H *Gunship Gray overall, serial on fin and nose: 696567, 696574 (16 SOS).*

C-130E *Shadow Green/medium green/dark grey overall, small black serial on fin and nose: 6810941 (317 TAW).*
C-141B *White over, bare metal under, large black serial on fin with 'MAC' in white on black band: 6138079 (437 MAW).*

US Army
UH-60A *Olive Drab overall, red cross in white square on fuselage side: 8123735 (57 Med. Det.).*

11.7. Costa Rica, 1948–1955

For several years after the 1948 civil war there was peace in Costa Rica, but on 11 January 1955 Nicaraguan-backed rebels invaded the country, supported by an F-47D, two C-47s and two AT-6s serviced by the Nicaraguan Air Force. These aircraft operated from Managua and were sold to the attackers by Interarms, who also sold small arms to the Costa Rican Government. The only response of which the Government was capable – it had dismantled its military forces after 1948 – was to borrow a DC-3 of LACSA again and arm it with two 0.30in machine guns. This was hardly adequate, however, so the Organization of American States asked the US for help, and four F-51Ds were sold to the Government for a nominal $1 each. They were transferred from the 182nd FS, Texas ANG, and are believed to have operated from Las Cañas, almost certainly flown by mercenary pilots in the ground-attack role. Aircraft 4473339 was written off on the 19th in an accident, and a second machine, 4511386, was lost on 22 January 1956 in a celebration flypast.

AIRCRAFT MARKINGS

F-51D *Bare metal overall, Costa Rican flag on fuselage and wings, local serial (range 1–4) on fuselage, US serial on fin: 4474978.*

11.8. Guatemala, 1954

The US Government fears the spread of communism in Central America and, applying the 'domino' theory, sees Guatemala as the last country to fall before Mexico. In the early 1950s, consideration was given to overthrowing the left-wing Government of President Jacobo Arbenz Guzman. In June 1954 a freighter, mistaken for a Soviet vessel believed to be delivering arms to the Government but in fact a British ship carrying coffee and cotton, was bombed by the Central Intelligence Agency (CIA) at Puerto Barrios. One bomb exploded. The aircraft, a B-26, was flown from Nicaragua, where a rebel force, led by Col. Carlos Castillo Armas, was being trained by the CIA. This group, initially made up of 150 exiles, was originally trained at a CIA barracks at the ex-naval air station at Opa-Locka on the outskirts of Miami.

On 18 June the rebels invaded from Honduras around Zacapa. They were supported by four B-26s, three F-47Ds and two C-47s operated by

American and Nationalist Chinese crews from Managua International Airport in Nicaragua. It has been reported that the aircraft flew in Guatemalan Air Force (FAG) markings. They

dropped leaflets over Guatemala City and bombed military installations in the capital and airfields at San José and Cobán. There was no opposition, since the FAG comprised only two P-26s at the time. One rebel F-47 crashed in the sea and another landed in Mexico short of fuel, but replacements, in the form of two F-51Ds, were transferred to the CIA from US Government stocks. On the 27th Arbenz resigned, and the following day the radio station at Guatamala City was bombed by F-47s, as was the Army HQ at Fort Matamoros. With little resistance, Armas

was flown into the capital on 2 July in the US ambassador's aircraft. He was assassinated three years later. There have been at least two further rebellions.

AIRCRAFT MARKINGS
Both FAG and CIA aircraft were bare metal overall. FAG F-51Ds carried serials in the range 24–30, C-47s in the range 500–590 and B-26Bs in the range 400–428. CIA aircraft carried false serials within these ranges, including 420.

11.9. Honduras and Nicaragua, 1957

North of the Coco river separating Honduras from Nicaragua is the inhospitable Mosquito Coast area, long disputed by both countries. From January 1956 C-47 aircraft of the Fuerza Aérea Hondureña (FAH) began flying in settlers and troops. On 21 February 1957 Honduras officially annexed the Mosquito Coast as the new department of Gracias a Dios, but within two months the Nicaraguan Army had crossed the Coco and occupied the town of Morocon. On 1 May a battalion of the Honduran Army retook the town, supported by five P-63 and P-38 fighters. C-47 transports stood by at Tocontin airfield to fly in reserves, but the following day, after a reconnaissance by F-51D aircraft of the Fuerza Aérea de Nicaragua (FAN), Nicaraguan forces counterattacked. By the 3rd they had again occupied Morocon.

After inconclusive fighting, a ceasefire was agreed for 1930hrs on the 5th, leaving the boundary at the Coco river. During this operation C-47 300 of the FAH crashed at Puerto Libertad in El Salvador while allegedly evacuating wounded.

By the end of 1958 the transports had airlifted 1,305 settlers, plus supplies, in 218 sorties. The relationship between the two countries improved, and Honduras effectively prevented armed incursion in 1958. A group of Nicaraguan revolutionaries hijacked a C-46 of Lineas Aéreas de Nicaragua (LANICA) at Miami Airport on 25 May. The aircraft was flown to the Lepaguara valley in Honduras, where a base had been prepared for the invasion of Nicaragua. FAH fighters overflew the base until the Army was able to occupy the area.

AIRCRAFT MARKINGS

FAH
P-38L *Bare metal overall, black serial on boom: 506.*
P-63E *Bare metal overall, black serial on rear fuselage: 404.*
C-47 *White over, bare metal under, black serial on rear fuselage: 304.*

11.10. Honduras and El Salvador, 1969

By 1969, over 300,000 Salvadorans were living in relatively underpopulated Honduras. In the run-up to the 1969 Football World Cup, in which the two countries were to play each other, increasing anti-Salvador propaganda was broadcast from Radio Honduras. The first game, played at Tegucigalpa, was won by Honduras and the second, played in San Salvador on 15 June, was won by El Salvador; rioting and anti-immigrant fighting followed in Honduras. The deciding match was played in Mexico City, and again El Salvador won. Tension increased, and shortly afterwards, on 4 July, Honduras complained of Fuerza Aérea Salvadoreña (FAS) aircraft violating her airspace. The following day diplomatic relations were terminated and troops were rushed to the border.

A mixed flight of FAS aircraft, including three F-51s, a B-26, a C-47 and a DC-3, flew from Ilopango airfield on the 10th, bound for the main

Fuerza Aérea Hondureña (FAH) base at Tocontin outside Tegucigalpa. They attacked the airfield and destroyed several aircraft on the ground; at the same time, 12,000 Salvadoran troops crossed the border at El Poy and El Amatillo. Over the next few days the Salvadoran Army advanced slowly on two fronts. In support, the FAS bombed targets at Santa Rosa de Copan, Gracias and

A line-up of Honduran Corsairs at Tocontin in 1969. At least four Corsairs were shot down on strikes against Ilopango airfield and the Standard Oil Company refinery at Acajutla. The nearest aircraft is 615. (M. Robson)

The Salvadoran Air Force also used the Corsair in its FG-1D form: pictured at San Miguel is a hastily camouflaged aircraft of the Escuadron de Caza. The FAS fighters supported ground forces in their cross-border advance in July 1969. (N. Waters via J. Ethell)

Nueva Ocotopeque in the north and at Nacaome, San Lorenzo, Ampala and Choluteca. On the 15th the FAH used its F4U fighters to attack Ilopango airfield and the Standard Oil Company refinery at Acajutla, losing four aircraft to ground fire. There were several occasions on which aircraft met in combat, and two FAS F-51Ds were shot down by F4U Corsairs.

The towns of Nueva Ocotopeque and Nacaome were captured by Salvadoran forces on the 16th after heavy fighting, but on the 18th the Organization of American States called for a ceasefire. Despite this there was sporadic fighting, and on 27 July the FAH bombed five Salvadoran border towns. This was the last action in the short but bitter war, and by 5 August all Salvadoran forces had withdrawn from Honduras. Total losses were between 500 and 2,000 dead and up to 100,000 wounded. The FAS lost four aircraft, including at least two F-51s, while FAH lost eight, including at least three F4Us and two C-47s.

AIRCRAFT MARKINGS

FAS
F-51D *Bare metal overall with hastily daubed green camouflage on upper surfaces, white serial on fin: 402, 403.*

FAH
F4U-4 *Midnite Blue overall, white serial on nose cowling: 604.*

TABLE OF UNITS: HONDURAS AND EL SALVADOR, 1969

Unit	Aircraft	Base	Role	Nos.
FAS				
Esc. de Caza	F-51D, FG-1D	San Miguel	Ground attack, air defence	10
Esc. de Caza-Bomb	B-26B	Ilopango	Light bombing	5
Esc. de Transporte	C-47	Ilopango	Transport	4
FAH				
Esc. de Caza	F4U-4	Tocontin (Tegucigalpa)	Ground attack, air defence	12
Esc. de Transporte	C-47, C-46, PB4Y-2	Tocontin	Transport	8

11.11. Belize, 1975 to date

The former colony of British Honduras has long been threatened by neighbouring Guatemala, which claims rights to the territory. In February 1948 it appeared that the Guatemalans might invade, and the cruisers HMS *Sheffield* and *Devonshire* were dispatched with the 2nd Battalion The Gloucester Regiment; from that time, a company of infantry was deployed. In October 1961 the country was devastated by hurricane 'Hattie', and additional troops were flown in from the UK via Kingston, Jamaica, in Operation 'Sky Help'; also taking part were two Shackletons of 204 Sqn. and two Valiant B(PR)K.1s of 543 Sqn. for survey work.

Although from 1962 the People's United Party (PUP) sought independence, it was committed to freedom from Guatemalan domination, and from 1964 internal self-government was obtained. A renewed threat developed in January 1972 with a concentration of Guatemalan troops on the border. The carrier HMS *Ark Royal* was diverted from an American cruise, and Buccaneer aircraft of 891 NAS demonstrated along the border. In February the carrier returned, leading a task force, and the 2nd Battalion The Grenadier Guards reinforced the garrison. In 1973 the country was renamed Belize.

Negotiations between Britain and Guatemala in 1975 ended in deadlock, and in October Guatemalan troops massed on the border. From 11 October, three Puma helicopters of 33 Sqn. were flown into Belize Airport by Belfast transports of 53 Sqn., and the garrison was again reinforced to 1,000 men. The frigate HMS *Zulu* was also dispatched. Teeth for the Belize force were provided by six Harrier GR.1A fighters of 1 Sqn., flown out from the UK via Goose Bay and Nassau between 6 and 8 November. The aircraft were refuelled in flight by Victor tankers. During this first major investment, operational and training routines were established.

The threat was perceived to have diminished

TABLE OF UNITS: BELIZE, 1975 TO DATE

Unit	Aircraft	Base	Role	Dates
RAF				
204 Sqn.	Shackleton MR.2	Kingston, ex Ballykelly	SAR, recce	00/10/61 to 00/11/62
543 Sqn.	Valiant B(PR)K.1	Kingston, ex Wyton	Recce	00/10/61 to 00/11/61
1 Sqn.	Harrier GR.1A		Ground attack	10/11/75 to 19/04/76
33 Sqn.	Puma HC.1		Support	15/11/75 to 00/03/81
1/3/4 Sqns.	Harrier GR.3	Belize International	Ground attack	09/07/77 to 00/03/81
1417 Flt.	Harrier GR.3		Ground attack	00/03/81 to date
1563 Flt.	Puma HC.1		Support	00/03/81 to date
FAA				
891 NAS	Buccaneer S.1	*Ark Royal*	Strike	00/01/72 to 00/02/72
829 NAS	Wasp HAS.1	Various ships	Liaison, communications	00/11/75 to 00/00/83
815 NAS	Lynx HAS.1			00/00/82 to date
British Army				
656/664 Sqns.	Scout AH.1	Belize	FAC, liaison, supply,	00/11/75 to 00/04/80
656 Sqn./25 Flt.	Gazelle AH.1		recce	00/04/80 to 00/00/82

sufficiently by April 1976 that the Harriers were dismantled and flown home in Belfasts. Further negotiations led nowhere, however, and after Guatemalan mobilization in June 1977 the garrison was again reinforced. The 3rd Battalion The Queen's Regiment was flown from the UK in VC-10 C.1 transports of 10 Sqn., and six Harrier GR.3s of 1 Sqn. again made the Atlantic crossing, flying direct on 7 July. They were accompanied by twelve Victor K.2 tankers, each being refuelled eight times. The frigate HMS *Achilles* took up station off the coast. The prospective invasion did not materialize, but the British Force in Belize (BRITFORBEL) has remained. Four Harrier GR.3s are operated by crews from 1, 3 and 4 Sqns. on rotation, under the auspices of 1417 Flt. based at Belize International Airport and able to deploy to some three dozen strips. Three Puma helicopters, operated by 1563 Flt. and flown by crews from 33 and 230 Sqns. on rotation, are also based at Belize.

A second helicopter component is provided by the Army. Four Scout AH.1s were operated by 656 or 664 Sqn. until 1979, when they were replaced by four Gazelles flown by 25 Flt. A Lynx HAS.1 of 815 NAS is normally available from the locally stationed frigate. Airfield defence at Belize is provided by the RAF Regiment, with Rapier detachments from 25 or 26 Sqns. and Bofors L40/70 anti-aircraft gun units from 58 or 66 Sqns. The Special Air Service (SAS) Regiment is known to have operated in Belize, possibly infiltrating Guatemala, and the Pumas are fitted for night flying in difficult terrain.

For as long as a British presence remains in Belize, Guatemala is unlikely to take military action to pursue her claims. The Belize Government maintains two Britten-Norman Defenders for search and rescue (SAR), medevac, liaison and anti-drug trafficking duties. On the other side of the border, the Fuerza Aérea Guatemalteca (FAG) operates a fighter-bomber squadron, including about ten A-37Bs and four T-33s, and a transport squadron, which flies several C-47s and about seven Aravas.

AIRCRAFT MARKINGS

RAF
Harrier GR.1A *Dark Green/Dark Sea Grey over, light grey under, black serial on rear fuselage, pale blue code on fin: XZ998/G (1417 Flt.).*
Puma HC.1 *Dark Green/Dark Sea Grey over, black under, black serial and code on boom: XW227/DN (230 Sqn.).*

British Army
Scout AH.1 *Dark Green/black overall, black serial on boom: XV131 (664 Sqn.).*
Gazelle AH.1 *Dark Green/black overall, black serial on boom: ZA735 (25 Flt.).*

Although there has been no fighting in Belize, Guatemalan threats have been taken seriously and Harriers detached to the country since November 1975. Initially, the aircraft were drawn from squadrons in the UK or Germany, but in March 1981 1417 Flt. was formed. The fighters are supported by Pumas of 1563 Flt. Nearest the camera is GR.3 XW923/N. (Via A. S. Thomas)

11.12. Nicaragua, 1979 to date

Nicaragua had been ruled by the Somoza family, with limited support from the United States, since 1933. In 1962, opposition became more focused with the creation of the Frente Sandinista de Liberación Naciónal (FSLN), named after Augusto Sandino who led resistence to the US between 1927 and 1933. The FSLN received arms through Costa Rica, and the first attempted use of aircraft by the Government against the rebels was on 14 October 1977, when an unidentified ship on the Rio Frio was attacked by two Aviocars in Costa Rican waters on the assumption that it was gun-running; in fact the Costa Rican Minister of Public Security was on board.

In October, the FSLN attacked a number of National Guard posts in major cities, but activity increased the following year when the leader of the opposition Union Democratica Liberación (UDEL), Pedro Chamorro, was killed on the orders of President Anastasio Somoza Debayle. The civil war escalated, and in June 1979 the FSLN occupied the slum quarter of Managua. The National Guard bombarded the area from 23 June, causing up to 12,000 civilian casualties. The Fuerza Aérea de Nicaragua (FAN) flew its Cessna 337D and T-28D light attack aircraft against rebel positions in the Matagalpa mountains, using napalm and defoliants indiscriminately. As the position worsened, Somoza fled to Miami on 17 July, and many members of the feared National Guard escaped to Honduras, some flying out in FAN aircraft. The following day a Sandinista junta was established. When President Reagan took office in January 1981, his Government, fearing total destabilization in the region, decided to support the growing number of contrarevolucionarios, or 'Contras', operating against the new left-wing Government.

There was particular concern that the Sandinistas were supplying arms to rebels in El Salvador, and late in 1981 there were reports of up to 70 Nicaraguans being trained to fly the MiG-21 in Bulgaria. Despite repeated rumours of the supply of fighters, the only aircraft received have been support types, notably Mi-8 and Mi-25 helicopters and several An-2 light transports, although a wide range of anti-aircraft weaponry, including SA-7 missiles, has been supplied. In January 1982, in support of its policy of giving aid to the Contras, the US Government displayed U-2R photographs showing improvements to the airfields at Managua, Bluefields, Puerto Cabezas and Montelimar. During the year the US built or extended airfields at La Mesa, Goloson, Palmerola and Durzana in Honduras, to support both the Honduran armed forces and the Contras. The rebel groups comprised the Fuerza Democratica Nicaraguense (FDN), consisting mainly of ex-National Guards and operating from Honduras; indigenous Miskito, Sumo and Rama (MISURA) Indians along the Atlantic coast; and the Alianza Revolucionaria Democratica (ARDE), led by an ex-Sandinista, Eden Pastora, and operating from Costa Rica. There was one major Contra clash in 1982 on the Honduran border in July, in which at least 100 were killed.

US energy through 1982 went into checking the flow of arms from Nicaragua into El Salvador with the US Navy operating outside the Gulf of Fonseca. In March, Nicaraguan coastguard ships claimed a Honduran Air Force aircraft shot down when it harassed them while they were arresting two fishing vessels in the Gulf. During the month a Fuerza Aérea Sandinista (FAS) aircraft defected to Honduras. The FDN claimed its first aircraft in January 1983 when an Mi-8 was brought down in the north.

From their bases in Honduras, the Contras attacked Government troops around Jalapa early in the year, with limited success but losing a helicopter piloted by a Canadian mercenary on 19 April. The supply of arms, both to Nicaragua and, through that country, to El Salvador, continued to exercise the United States. On 21 April three Il-76s and a C-130 from Libya and bound for Nicaragua were stopped in Brazil and searched. They were carrying arms and parachutes, and it is believed that many of the crews were terrorists due to remain in El Salvador. The US Air Force and the Army Security Agency (ASA) stepped up their intelligence-gathering efforts: 55 Strategic Reconnaissance Wing (SRW) RC-135s and 552 Airborne Warning and Control Wing (AWCW) E-3As, with KC-135 support, are believed to have operated from Howard AFB in Panama and SR-71As and U-2Rs flew directly from Beale AFB, while 114 ASA Aviation Company RU-21H communications monitoring operations were flown from Honduran airfields.

On 27 April the Panamanian-registered vessel *Lewbi*, bound for Corinto, put into the Costa Rican port of Puntarenas with engine trouble. She was found to have a cargo of explosives. A month later, the US Government produced U-2R photographs of two Soviet ships berthed at Corinto and allegedly unloading arms. Having held one joint exercise with the Hondurans in February, 'Big Pine', the Americans now planned a second for the autumn; in the meantime, they continued to develop facilities in Honduras, including a radar complex outside Tegucigalpa to manage reconnaissance flights and another manned by Marines on Tiger Island in the Gulf of Fonseca. On 9 September, Corinto was reportedly attacked, possibly by aircraft of the Fuerza Aérea Hondureña (FAH); in August, the US Navy had carried out a blockade exercise off the Pacific

In the civil war in Nicaragua, Government forces have relied heavily on Mi-8 helicopters supplied by the Soviet Union in moving troops to pursue American-backed rebels. These troops are disembarking in Jinotega province in Operation 'Victorious December' in 1984. (Via L. Pinzauti)

coast involving the carriers *Ranger* and *Coral Sea*.

From 23 September, 3,200 US servicemen were airlifted to Honduras in C-141, C-5A and C-130 transports. The headquarters for the exercise was Palmerola, and runways were extended at Trujillo and San Pedro Sula, where Tactical Air Command (TAC) staff trained Honduran air crews; airstrips capable of operating the C-130 were built at San Lorenzo and El Aguacate. The 101st Aviation Battalion brought with them 30 UH-60s, CH-47s and OH-58s, and there is little doubt that these aircraft, which regularly overflew Nicaragua, were used to support CIA and Contra activity. On 11 January 1984, an OH-58 was forced down on the border and the pilot shot and killed on the ground; his passengers, two US sabotage experts, escaped uninjured.

Air intrusion was not the sole preserve of the United States. On 8 September 1983, a T-28 flown for ARDE from Costa Rica attacked Managua Airport, where it was shot down after having destroyed a C-47, and a second aircraft attacked the home of the Foreign Minister and is believed to have crashed in Rio San Juan province. Although receiving little external support, the ARDE operated several aircraft; in November it was announced that 1,000 US engineers would operate in Costa Rica on civil projects.

The CIA's involvement in Nicaragua was developing in respect of intelligence and direct action, and in support of the Contras. On 10 October, oil storage tanks at Corinto were sabotaged and a high proportion of the country's oil reserves was destroyed; shortly after this, an oil pipeline at Puerto Sandino was sabotaged. These raids originated from the Gulf of Fonseca, and the boats carrying the saboteurs were accompanied by FAH helicopter gunships. During October an unmarked DC-3 supplying the Contras was shot down near Matagalpa; its crew of seven survived and reported that the flight had originated from a Honduran CIA base.

The first formal reports of the CIA's mining of Nicaraguan ports came early in April 1984 with the admission that Corinto, Puerto Sandino and El Bluff had been mined. By this time ten vessels had been damaged, and it was the controversy over this action that was probably responsible for the Congressional denial in June of further funding for the CIA's activities in Nicaragua. The check on the flow of arms to El Salvador was further enhanced from March 1984 with the deployment to Palmerola of OV-1D observation aircraft of 224 Military Intelligence Battalion, US Army. The Contras were active throughout the year, supported by aircraft of the FAH or their own air assets. During February an A-37 and five helicopters attacked Nicaraguan positions, and on 28 August another supply aircraft was lost at Jinotega together with its eight crew members. During September, in fighting around Jalapa, an

O-2A and a Hughes 500, both flown by contract pilots, were brought down. In the south, the ARDE was now operating twelve aircraft from Costa Rica, including helicopters and several unmarked DC-3s, one of which latter crashed in Costa Rica in April bound for El Salvador.

Intelligence reports indicated the building of a large new airfield at Punta Huete, north-east of Managua, and it was presumed by the Americans that the expected MiG-21 fighters were due for delivery. In November the Soviet cargo ship *Bakuriani* was reported to be making for Corinto, and the vessel was repeatedly overflown at low level by US reconnaissance aircraft. The SR-71 flights were stepped up, and three USN ships, including the cruiser USS *Paul*, sailed off the

An American-supplied UH-1H lies on its side after having force-landed following mechanical trouble. Over 60 Hueys have served with the FAS, at Ilopango and San Miguel. (Via L. Pinzauti)

TABLE OF UNITS: NICARAGUA, 1978 TO DATE

Unit	Aircraft	Base	Role	Nos.
FAN, 1978				
(Esc.)	Cessna 337D, T-28, T-33	Managua	Light attack	13
(Esc.)	C-47, C-45, Arava	Managua	Transport	13
(?)	OH-6A, S-58, Cessna 185	Various	Liaison, light transport	16
FAS, 1986				
(?)	Mi-8	Managua, Puerto Cabezas, Bluefields, Bocay	Gunship, transport, casevac	32
(?)	Mi-25	Managua, Bocay	Gunship	12
(?)	T-33, T-28, SF.260, Cessna 337	Managua, Puerto Cabezas	Light attack	16
(?)	OH-6A, S-58 (CH-34)	Managua	Communications, light transport	5
(?)	Aviocar, C-47, Arava, An-2	Managua, Puerto Cabezas	Transport	12
FAH, 1986				
(Esc.)	F-86E	Palmerola	Air defence, ground attack	8
(Esc.)	A-37B	San Pedro Sula	Coin	15
(Esc.)	Super Mystère	La Ceiba	Air defence, ground attack	9
(Esc.)	C-47, C-130, C-54	Tegucigalpa	Transport	14
(?)	Arava, Cessna 180, Westwind	Tegucigalpa	Liaison, light transport	16
(?)	UH-1B/H, S-76	Various	Gunship, transport, casevac	40
(?)	T-28, O-2, Commander 114, Tucano	Various	FAC, attack	18
ARDE, 1984				
–	C-47, Hughes 500, T-28 etc.	Northern Costa Rica	Transport, light attack	12
FDN/CIA, 1986				
–	C-47, Caribou, C-123K, C-54	El Aguacate	Transport	9
–	Hughes 500, Maule Rocket	El Aguacate	Light attack	8
USAF, 1985				
552 AWCW	E-3A	Howard AFB	AEW	
9 SRW	U-2R, SR-71A	Beale AFB	Recce	
55 SRW	RC-135	Howard AFB	Intelligence-gathering	
US Army, 1985				
101 AB	UH-60A, CH-47B, OH-58A	Puerto Lempira, El Aguacate, Palmerola	Transport, infiltration	
114 AC	RU-21H	San Lorenzo	Communications intelligence	
224 MIB	OV-1D	Palmerola	Recce	

coast, but the ship was in fact delivering parts for Mi-25 helicopters. The FAS had received a total of twelve Mi-8s, most of them operating as gunships and two of which were lost in 1984. The Mi-25 was a potent but reasonable addition to the FAS armoury in fighting a guerrilla war. The Russian helicopters were supplemented by two Alouette IIs, four OH-6As and two S-58s.

During November the Nicaraguan forces again went on the alert as the US 82nd Airborne Division held exercises, parachuting into Palmerola. An invasion was assumed imminent, but it did not materialize. There were regular clashes through 1985, a large battle taking place around Jalapa on 13 September and involving 700 FDN guerrillas. After an attack by Mi-8s and Mi-25s, the FAH supported the Contras with A-37 and F-86 sorties, claiming one helicopter destroyed. In January 1986 the ARDE was active in the south, shooting down two Mi-8s on the San Juan river. The Contras were now operating twelve aircraft, including two helicopters, two C-47s, four Maule Rockets and a C-54; a second C-54 had been lost in operations over Nicaragua in 1984. The FAS had on its inventory a handful of inherited types, plus five Mi-25s, ten Mi-8s and six An-2s, the Mi-25s operating from up-country bases, including San José de Bocay. The Contras suffered material losses in 1986 when, in July, the Panamanian Government seized an arms shipment marked for El Salvador and believed to have included SA-7 and Blowpipe SAMs; then, in September,

the Costa Rican police took control of an airfield on the border, including warehouses and barracks.

Despite the US Congressional limits on CIA action, the Agency was still operating in support of the Contras. On 5 October 1986 a C-123K was shot down by an SA-7 near La Flor in the southeast of Nicaragua. The crew of four, of whom three were killed, were employed by Southern Air Transport, which had earlier operated the aircraft out of Miami. The flight originated from Ilopango, El Salvador, and the cargo consisted of Soviet-made arms destined for the ARDE. It was also reported at the time that white Zimbabweans were flying helicopters on contract to the CIA from Honduran bases. That at El Aguacate was a main supply base, from where, at the end of 1986, the C-54, a Caribou and a Lockheed 18 operated.

Late in 1986 the United States began building yet another airstrip near the border, presumably to support the Contras, who continued to bring down helicopters through 1987 at the rate of about one a month, some, it was claimed, by US-supplied SAMs. In October 1987, against a background of doubt over future US support for the Contras, the Nicaraguan Government declared a ceasefire, but this resulted in a renewed Contra offensive. During the fighting the Contras fired a Redeye SAM at a DC-6 of Aeronica, causing it to make an emergency landing in Costa Rica. In January 1988 the FAH took delivery of its first F-5Es to replace the Super Mystères, and they may have been used in March when Nicaraguan

Army positions near the border at San Andres de Bocay were bombed. The attacks were in response to a Nicaraguan incursion after rebels. The Americans also responded by deploying 3,200 men to Honduras in 'Golden Pheasant'. In April the Government again announced a ceasefire, but the conflict continues.

AIRCRAFT MARKINGS

FAN

CASA 212 Aviocar *Tan/dark green over, off-white under, black serial on fin: 421.*
C-47 *White over, bare metal under, black code on fin: 418.*

FAS
Mi-8 *Tan/dark green over, sky under, black serial on nose: 274.*
Mi-25 *Tan/medium green over, sky under, black serial on nose: 338, 340, 355.*

FAH
A-37B *Tan/brown/green over, off-white under, black serial on fin: FAH 1005.*
F-86E *Pale grey overall, black serial on fin: FAH 3004.*
UH-1H *Olive Drab overall, black serial on fin: FAH 918.*

11.13. El Salvador, 1980 to date

The repression of the peasant class in El Salvador by a military-based right-wing Government led to the formation of numerous anti-Government groups. A reformist coup in late 1979 failed to develop, there were calls for a popular armed uprising, and a massacre of civilian demonstrators on the steps of San Salvador Cathedral on 22 January 1980 was followed two months later by the murder, by a Government-condoned 'Death Squad', of Archbishop Romero as he celebrated Mass. These events resulted in the merger of the opposition groups as the Frente Farabundo Marti de Liberación Naciónal (FFMLN). The United States believed the Nicaraguan and Cuban Governments to be behind the revolt, and offered limited support to El Salvador as civil war broke out. In 1980 the Salvadoran Air Force (FAS) operated one squadron of Ouragan fighters supplied by Israel, one squadron of Magister light attack aircraft and a mixed transport squadron; in addition, six helicopters were flown.

The US aid included up to fourteen UH-1H helicopters, used mainly against rebels in the Morazan province during early fighting in 1981. By May the rebels had gained control over much of four provinces to the east of the country and were receiving arms from Nicaragua. In fact, arms had probably been stocked from about 1978. On 23 June 1979, Ecuadorian-registered C-47 HC-SJI made an emergency landing at El Tamarindo, and, on inspection, the aircraft was found to be loaded with arms and confiscated. In May 1981 the rebels captured an Army communications centre at Chichontepec Volcano, and on the 11th they shot down a UH-1H. The United States supplied a further eight, and from 8 July the Government launched a counteroffensive in the Cabanas area, bombing targets on the Honduran border.

By November the rebels were embarked on a widespread campaign of disruption of the economy, pulling down power pylons and blowing up bridges on main roads. Their biggest success came on 27 January 1982, when a group of 100 infiltrated the main airfield at Ilopango and destroyed five Ouragans, six UH-1Hs and three C-47s and damaging a further five aircraft, although within a week the US had delivered twelve more UH-1Hs, eight A-37B light attack aircraft, four O-2s and three C-123s to make good the losses. The Government faced another severe blow on 17 June when the Minister of Defence was among fourteen people killed as a UH-1H crashed near Perquin. The utilization of the helicopters, both as troop transports and gunships, was high. A major battle developed in early February 1983 at Berlin. Rebels captured the town, which was recaptured only after their positions were strafed by A-37Bs and a battalion-strength attack. From May, the Government's image began to improve, following the election of the relatively moderate Napoleón Duarte as President.

The US extended its training of troops in Honduras and began flying AC-130H sorties, using aircraft of 16 Special Operations Squadron (SOS) based at Howard AFB, Panama. These sorties were intended to track down arms and guerrilla movements and destroy them, and the

TABLE OF UNITS: EL SALVADOR, 1985 TO DATE

Unit	Aircraft	Base	Role
FAS			
Esc. de Caza	Ouragan	Ilopango	Ground attack
Esc. de Ataque	Magister, A-37B	San Miguel	Light ground attack
Esc. de Transporte	C-47, Arava, DC-6B, C-123, C-130	Ilopango, San Miguel	Transport
–	UH-1H, Hughes 500MD	Ilopango, San Miguel	Light transport, gunship, casevac
–	AC-47	Ilopango	Attack, recce
–	O-2	Ilopango	Observation, liaison
USAF			
16 SOS	AC-130H	Howard AFB	Gunship, recce

aircraft were flown by crews without military identification. Panama was also used as a staging post for arms supplies flown into El Salvador by C-130 and distributed by FAS C-47s and C-123s, while the CIA used Ilopango AB as a centre for supplying Contra rebels in Nicaragua, using unmarked C-47 aircraft.

A new process of pacification began from 10 June 1983 in San Vincente province, but this was soon disrupted when rebels isolated the town of Suchitoto after blowing up the Las Guaras road bridge. A-37Bs were heavily committed to attacking rebel positions just eighteen miles from capital while 2,000 Government troops moved up to clear the road. During the year, the FAS carried out 227 strikes, mainly by UH-1H and A-37B, as the guerrillas gained strength. In March 1984 the Americans supplied yet more aircraft – fourteen UH-1Hs, ten A-37Bs, two O-2s and a C-130, the last to replace a C-123 which was written off when it hit a mine while landing at San Miguel on the 20th. Despite these deliveries, attrition was high, and in April the UH-1H force still comprised only 22 aircraft, of which eighteen were gunships. These had been used to relieve an ambush at Tecoluca on 25 March in which 32 soldiers were killed. They were in evidence again on 29 June when two companies of the élite Atlacatl Battalion were flown up to the Caroon Grande dam, which had been taken by rebels a day earlier. The next major Government offensive came in October against groups at Perquin and La Laguna, duing which a UH-1H was brought down with fourteen killed. Three more UH-1Hs were lost and four damaged in an attempt to regain Suchitoto after it had been captured on 9 November.

During 1984 the FAS received at least two C-47s converted as gunships and fitted with two 12.7mm heavy machine guns. The rebels were reported as having received SA-7 missiles from Libya, but there is as yet no evidence of their use. The CIA was active throughout the year. On 1 May the FAS had been persuaded to bomb a guerrilla communications base in Nicaragua on the understanding that the Agency would arrange for Contras to take responsibility. Then, on 19 October, an unmarked CIA aircraft, possibly a C-47, crashed north of San Salvador, killing the crew of four. The aircraft, which is believed to have operated from Honduras, was allegedly chasing an aircraft bringing in arms from Nicaragua.

More overt US help was given in June 1985 when a CH-47E of 101 Aviation Battalion based in Honduras was used to recover a lightly damaged UH-1H which had landed in a remote part of Morazan province; escorted by UH-1H gunships and a Hughes 500, the CH-47 removed the helicopter to Ilopango AB. Government control extended through 1985, although 100 troops were killed in a guerrilla attack on a training base at La Union in October. The US continued to supply aircraft, and no fewer than 63 UH-1Hs were in FAS service in 1986. Hughes (MD) 500s, possibly in their UH-6A form, are used as gunships, and in late 1987 the AC-47s, fitted with three 0.50in machine guns, were still operational. At the time of writing the guerrilla war continues.

AIRCRAFT MARKINGS

FAS

UH-1H *Olive Drab overall, black serial on boom: 250, 254.*

A-37B *Sand/brown/mid green over, pale grey under: 426.*

C-47 *White over, bare metal under, black serial on fin: 108.*

AC-47 *Light blue-grey overall, no markings.*

11.14. Miscellaneous conflicts and incidents

1. During 1947 a group of Dominican Republic exiles formed an air arm in Cuba to support an intended invasion. Based at Rancho Boyeros near Havana, the aircraft comprised a total of eleven P-38s, B-24s and C-46s. They were notionally included on the Cuban Air Force inventory and formally taken on charge when the Cuban Government stopped its support for the rebels in September.

2. Civil war broke out in Costa Rica in March 1948 when presidential elections were annulled. Anti-Government forces, led by Col. José Figueras Ferrer, took control of San Isidro to the south of the capital. With a very small standing army and no air force, the Government used three LACSA DC-3 transports hastily fitted with machine guns to attack the rebels. After several sorties, the aircraft, TI-1005, -1006 and -1007, were flown to safety in Nicaragua. By 20 April the rebels had occupied Cartago, and then San José on the 24th. Around La Cruz, as the army was being disbanded, there was a limited invasion by ex-Government supporters from Nicaragua on 10 December. It was driven back.

3. The Dominican rebels found a new base in Guatemala, from where they mounted a small invasion of the Republic on 18 June 1949. Six aircraft left Guatemala, but four were forced to land in Mexico through poor weather. A PBY-5A did land off Puerto Plata, where it was promptly attacked by naval craft and FAD Mosquitoes and Beaufighters.

4. Dominican F-51D fighters flew armed reconnaissance sorties over Haiti late in 1949 in a display of force intended to dissuade the Haitian Government from supporting rebels.

5. There was an abortive coup in Haiti in 1956 during which, it is believed, F-51Ds and T-6s demonstrated over the capital, Port au Prince.

6. In December 1956 Fidel Castro and a small group of revolutionaries landed in eastern Cuba from Mexico. Although attacked by F-47Ns of the Cuban Air Force (FAEC), the group soon established itself and over three years, with popular support, fought to assume control of the country from the dictatorship of Fulgencio Batista. The FAEC also used B-26s and DHC-2 Beavers, converted for coin tasks, against the insurgents but with no success. The rebels purchased at least five F-51Ds with help from Venezuela, but two were never delivered; they were probably operated from Manzanilla. Castro's forces also captured several FAEC aircraft (including an OS2U-3, two C-47s, a Beech C-45, a B-26 and a B-25) and flew them in action.

7. In July 1957 three Dominican F-51Ds intercepted a US Navy R4D-1 and forced it to land. In March 1959 several FAD F-51Ds attempted to shoot down a second aircraft of the type.

8. In April 1959 Dominican rebels landed at Constanza in a C-46 marked with spurious FAD insignia. Two boats supporting this insurgency were destroyed by F-47, F-51 and Vampire strikes. On 4 June the same year a second group invaded the Republic from Cuba, but the attackers were met by FAD F-51Ds and Vampires and the attempt was foiled.

9. On November 1960 B-26 bombers belonging to the CIA and based at Puerto Cabezas, Nicara-

gua, attacked rebel officer bases in Guatemala City. CIA C-46 transports based at Retalhuleu in Guatemala were used to fly troops into Puerto Barrios; the aircraft were in Central America as part of a force preparing for the invasion of Cuba. The FAG remained loyal, and F-51Ds flew attack sorties against Zacapa base and Puerto Barrios airfield. The rebels surrendered on the 18th.

10. From 1962 Guatemalan Air Force F-51s operated on strike missions against insurgents in the east of the country.

11. It was reported that a Constellation bombed Port au Prince, Haiti, on 4 June 1969. In April 1970 the crews of two cutters rebelled and shelled the Presidential palace. The Air Force, which had been relieved of its bombs for fear of revolution, dropped 55gal drums of gasoline on the ships from C-47, but to no effect. The vessels escaped and were given haven at the US naval base at Guantanamo, Cuba.

12. On 8 August 1983 President Montt of Guatemala was overthrown by right-wing elements in the armed forces and A-37B aircraft and helicopters of the FAG overflew the capital in a show of force. A major US military exercise in neighbouring Honduras began the same day.

In 1960, CIA B-26 Invaders based in Nicaragua prior to the Bay of Pigs operation were used to help suppress a rebellion in Guatemala. After the Cuban adventure, several surviving Invaders were transferred to the Nicaraguan Air Force, including 601, seen here minus engines.

Castro's insurgent force purchased several F-51D Mustangs through Venezuela. They were operated from 1959, probably from Manzanilla. This example, 401, is preserved at Havana. (M. Robson)

12: South America

By comparison with the countries of Central America, those of South America appear relatively stable. Aircraft are known to have been used in relation to a number of attempted revolutions, but only in the cases of Argentina (1955) and Chile (1973) was the revolution successful. In the latter case, no doubt due, in part, to covert American intervention, FAC Hunters were involved in just one strike on the Presidential palace.

Unrest in British Guiana led to a British military presence for four years in the mid-1960s, but the major British involvement in the region came in 1982 with the Argentinian invasion of the Falklands Islands. Since 1945 there have been few true air wars involving combat, but the Falklands War was an important exception. Operating in circumstances and conditions in which no other type could have flown, the Sea Harriers of the British Task Force provided an effective defensive screen around ships 8,000 miles from their home bases. Despite their presence, and partly through the absence of airborne early warning, Argentinian air attacks succeeded in sinking six ships and damaging many more. Large aircraft carriers embarking conventional aircraft would have been unable to launch their machines on many occasions when the Sea Harriers flew, regardless of wind direction or visibility, while the relatively poor performance of SAMs would have made such capital ships vulnerable indeed.

12.1. British Guiana, 1962–1966

In 1953, elections in British Guiana brought a result that, it was feared by the Governor, might lead to a communist government. The constitution was suspended, and two companies of the 1st Battalion Royal Welch Fusiliers were dispatched in Royal Navy frigates. There was continuing unrest, essentially between ethnic groups since the majority People's Progressive Party (PPP) represented the Indian minority. In February 1962 a general strike was called, and further Army units were sent to Georgetown from Jamaica and the UK. A detachment of Shackleton MR.2 aircraft was sent from Jamaica in a show of force. Rioting was contained but broke out again a year later. In addition to ground forces, a small Royal Navy Wessex flight was based at Atkinson Field near Georgetown for support duties.

In September 1964 these aircraft were replaced by three Whirlwind HC.10s of 1310 Flt. RAF. In October they were joined by Auster AOP.9 aircraft of 24 Recce Flt. for reconnaissance and liaison work under the overall control of 2 Wing AAC at Middle Wallop; at the same time, two Canberra PR.7s of 58 Sqn. were detached from Piarco Airport, Trinidad, for survey work. The colony became independent of Britain as Guyana in May 1966 under a coalition government. Most British servicemen left, a few remaining in order to train local forces. Minimal military intervention over thirteen years prevented local insurrection and enabled the colony to progress to maturity.

12.2. Venezuela, 1958

One of the more stable Latin American states, Venezuela witnessed several attempted revolutions from 1958. On 1 January that year, 200 paratroopers of the Fuerza Aérea Venezolana (FAV) occupied bases at Palo Negro and Boca del Rio, both near Maracay. Their action was in response to the arrest the previous day of the Army commander and his deputy chief of staff Col. Jesus Maria Castro Leon for allegedly plotting to over-throw the Government of Brig. Gen. Marcos Perez Jimenez. It appears that neither the Army nor the Navy was initially keen to follow the example of the FAV; in an effort to gain

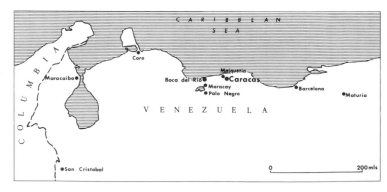

support for a military uprising, a total of fourteen aircraft of various types overflew Caracas at 1100hrs. There was still no response from the other services, so shortly afterwards Vampires of Escuadron de Caza (EC) 35 and F-86Fs of EC 36 strafed the Miraflores Presidential palace and the Ministry of Defence building. One Vampire and one F-86F were hit by anti-aircraft fire.

F-86F fighters then bombed the National Security headquarters, but few bombs exploded and there was little damage. It was now felt that there could be no general uprising, and the leaders of the attempted coup flew to Colombia in the Presidential C-54; other participants flew their aircraft to Maiquetia and surrendered. In fact, the Navy and elements of the Army continued the revolt, and on 23 January the President stood down and flew to the Dominican Republic. Leon was released and fled to Colombia, from where he led an incursion on 20 April 1960. San Cristobal and its airfield were occupied, and a headquarters was established. Canberra B.2s of Escuadron de Bombardeo (EB) 39 at Barcelona were dispatched to attack the rebels, who subsequently surrendered.

The Canberras were in action a year later when, on 26 June 1961, they attacked a mutinous garrison at Barcelona. There was further trouble on 4 May 1962 when a Marines battalion revolted at Carupano. Air Force Canberras again attacked

TABLE OF UNITS: THE VENEZUELAN AIR FORCE, 1958			
Unit	Aircraft	Base	Role
EC 34	Venom FB.54	Maiquetia	Ground attack, air defence
EC 35	Vampire FB.5	Maiquetia	Ground attack
EC 36	F-86F	Maracay	Air defence
EB 39	Canberra B.2, B(I).8	Barcelona	Light bombing
EB 40	B-25J	Palo Negro	Light bombing
ET 1	C-45, C-47, C-54	Maiquetia	Transport, communications
ET 2	C-123	Maiquetia	Transport

the rebels, and Government forces were brought up to Cumana from Maiquetia in Air Force C-47s and C-123Bs on the 5th. The next day the rebels capitulated. There was yet another rebellion on 2 June by elements within the Navy. The FAV flew reconnaissance sorties and Vampires strafed naval buildings at Puerto Cabello, and two frigates manned by loyal naval crews then shelled the Marines barracks. On the 3rd the FAV carried out more strikes using machine guns and rockets, and the rebellion was mopped up by the 4th.

AIRCRAFT MARKINGS

Vampire FB.5 *Bare metal overall, red lightning stripe and black serial on forward fuselage: 2-A35, 3-A35 (EC 35).*
F-86F *Bare metal overall, black serial on nose: 4B36 (EC 36).*
Canberra B.2 *Bare metal overall, black serial on nose: 2B39 (EB 39).*

12.3. Argentina, 1955

From 1946 Argentina was ruled by Juan Domingo Perón, essentially as a right-wing dictatorship. After the death of his wife, Eva, he lost popular support, especially through the Church, and in 1955 there was a succession of uprisings. On 16 June the Navy fought against the Government, supported by some other elements of the armed forces. The rebels captured the airfields at Ezeiza and Moron, Punta Indio having come under Army attack. Naval aircraft bombed Government House but with little effect, and by late afternoon the revolt had collapsed.

The Navy led a second revolt on 16 September. This time the rebels captured Cordoba, where they found at least three Meteor F.4 fighters of the Fighter School under repair. These were hastily put to use against advancing Government forces, flown by seven disaffected FAA pilots. An early target was the railway station, where some 2,000 troops were detraining.

During the 16th, Fuerza Aérea Argentina (FAA) Meteors of VII Brigada Aérea (BA) were flown against rebels in the naval base at Rio Santiago and against two destroyers standing off the capital; both ships were damaged, and, during strafing, one aircraft was shot down by anti-aircraft fire. Navy aircraft from Commandante Espora also made attack sorties, flying a miscel-

lany of types including PBY-5s, SNJ-4s, AT-11s and J2F-5s. One of the last was shot down by AAA while attacking a tank column on the 18th, and a Meteor was also reported to have shot down a Navy SNJ-4. On the 18th the rebels began shelling targets along the coast and several units switched their loyalty. During this period Lincoln bombers of V BA made demonstration flights, but it is understood that they were not used offensively.

Fighting continued in the Cordoba area, and the rebels were either forced to use petrol in their aircraft or the fuel supply was sabotaged. Without a significant proportion of oil mixed, serious damage results from such abuse, and on 19 June Meteor I-079 blew up, killing the pilot, who was named as Lt. Morandini. Within a few days the fighting was over and Perón was forced into exile. A military junta was established and in June the following year a Perónista officer revolt easily crushed.

AIRCRAFT MARKINGS

FAA
Meteor F.4 *Silver overall, black serial on nose*

and rear fuselage: I-058 (I Grupo de Caza, VII BA).

Lincoln B.2 *Medium grey over, black under, white serial on rear fuselage: B-017 (I Grupo de Bombardeo, V BA).*

Rebels
Meteor F.4 *Silver overall, marked as FAA aircraft but with the addition of a cross over a 'V' on the engine nacelles and rear fuselage, probably in pale red: I-066.*

TABLE OF UNITS: ARGENTINA, 1955

Unit	Aircraft	Base	Role
FAA			
BA I	C-47. C-54. Viking. Dove. Bristol Freighter	El Palomar	Transport. communications
BA II	I.Ae-24 Calquin	Paraná	Ground attack
BA III	Lancaster B.1. I.Ae-24	Moron	Bombing. ground attack
BA IV	I.Ae-24	Mendoza	Ground attack
BA V	Lincoln B.2	Villa Reynolds	Bombing
BA VII	Meteor F.4	Moron. El Palomar. Tandil	Air defence. ground attack
AA			
2 EC	F6F-5	Bahia Blanca	Air defence
1 EE	PBM-5A	Puerto Belgrano	MR. SAR
2 EE	PBY-5A	Punta del Indio	
1 EH	Bell-47D	Ezeiza	Liaison
1 EPG	JRF. J2F-5. AT-11. SNJ-4	Various	SAR. communications. training
1 ESL	C-39. C-47. C-54	Ezeiza	Transport

12.4. The Falkland Islands, 1982

Sovereignty over the Falklands has been disputed by Argentina and the United Kingdom since 1833 when a British sloop evicted Argentinian settlers and formally claimed the islands for Britain. From time to time discussions were held, but despite a resolution at the United Nations (2065) in 1965 reminding members of a pledge to end colonialism, little progress was made. A military government took power in Argentina in 1976, and the following year the British Government sent a small naval task force to the South Atlantic following intelligence reports that an occupation of the South Georgia dependency seemed imminent. The invasion came five years later with the landing of demolition workers on the island from the Argentinian fleet transport *Bahia Buen Suceso* on 19 March 1982. The task of the workers was to dismantle the derelict whaling station.

Four days later the polar vessel *Bahia Paraiso* was diverted from routine tasks to support the South Georgia civilians. The first tangible British response was the landing of a small observation post on South Georgia from the ice patrol vessel HMS *Endurance* on 23 March and the landing of a Royal Marine detachment on the 31st. From the 25th, nuclear submarines were dispatched to the South Atlantic. Meanwhile, on 23 March, the decision to invade the Falklands was taken in Buenos Aires, and five days later Argentinian Task Groups 40 (landing force) and 20 (covering

force) sailed from mainland ports bound for invasion in Operation 'Rosario'.

With clear evidence of Argentinian intentions, the British decided on 31 March to assemble a task force capable of retaking the Falklands if necessary, and Operation 'Corporate' was set in train. There were actually two naval task forces, TF.317 and TF.324, the latter comprising the submarine element. On 1 April seven RAF Hercules flew into Gibraltar with essential naval supplies for ships assembled for Exercise 'Springtrain'; the aircraft also brought air traffic control staff and equipment for use on Ascension Island, which was to become a critical staging post. Although the island is British, Wideawake airfield had been built by the United States to support its tracking station and was managed by Pan American Airways; from its normal three movements a week, the airfield was to handle 400 movements a day at the height of the war.

The first Argentinian landings on the Falklands came at 0430hrs on 2 April as 150 men arrived to the west of Port Stanley. The British Royal Marine garrison (Naval Party 8901) comprised 68 men, a number larger than usual due to the fact that the invasion coincided with a 24hr handover period; in addition, there were twelve sailors from HMS *Endurance*. The two COs were advised of the impending invasion on the 1st and ordered to make their dispositions accordingly. They chose to defend the airfield area to the east of

Port Stanley. As news came through of the size of the invasion force, the Marines regrouped around Government House and some brisk fighting ensued.

From daybreak it was clear that the position was untenable, and at 0925hrs, with 2,800 Argentinians ashore, the Governor, Rex Hunt, ordered the garrison to surrender. Later in the day the first Pucarás of Grupo 3 de Ataque (G3A) of the Fuerza Aérea Argentina (FAA) landed at the airfield, and a C-130H brought in an AN/ TPS-43F surveillance radar. South Georgia was captured the following day by Argentinian Task Group 60 after being stoutly defended by the small Royal Marine detachment from *Endurance*. During the landings the first aircraft casualty of the war occurred when Puma AE-504 of Batallon de Aviacion de Combate (CAB) 601 was hit by machine-gun fire and two Argentinian Marines were killed.

On the British side, Rear-Admiral John Woodward, who had been appointed Task Force commander, sailed from Gibraltar on board HMS *Glamorgan* for Ascension on 2 April. In company were four destroyers, five frigates and three support ships. A naval party was flown into Ascension to become the basis of British Forces Support Unit Ascension Island (BFSUAI). In Britain, major elements of the Task Force were assembled at Portsmouth and Devonport. After a hectic weekend, during which Parliament sat on a Saturday for the first time since the Suez crisis in 1956, the Task Force departed from the 5th. The key components were HMS *Hermes*, with 800 NAS Sea Harriers, supplemented by aircraft from 899 NAS, plus 826 NAS (Sea King HAS.5), 846 NAS (Sea King HC.4) and A Coy. 42 Commando; and HMS *Invincible*, with 801 NAS (Sea Harrier), again supplemented by aircraft and crews from 899 NAS, and 820 NAS (Sea King HAS.5).

HMS *Fearless* left on the 6th with an element of 846 NAS (Sea King HC.4) embarked, and two Sea King HAS.2As of 824 NAS departed on the RFA *Olmeda*; two frigates provided an escort, and three support ships and four landing ships logistic (LSL) completed the initial fleet. The requisitioned liner *Canberra* sailed from Southampton on the 9th with 2,000 troops of 40 and 42 Commando and 3 Para aboard. The first RAF detachment to Ascension was made on the 6th when two Nimrod MR.1s of 42 Sqn. arrived to provide maritime reconnaissance cover for the Task Force. Meanwhile, in the South Atlantic, the Argentinians had established an Information and Control Centre (ICC) at Port Stanley, and a new FAA command structure was set up to provide for integrated air defence. In anticipation of the British military response, the Teatro de Operaciones del Atlantico Sur (TOAS) was established, with its headquarters at Comodoro Rivadavia.

On 7 April Britain declared a 200-mile Maritime Exclusion Zone (MEZ) around the Falklands, to become effective from 0400hrs GMT on the 12th. Some time shortly after the 10th, it is believed that Canberra PR.9 aircraft of 39 Sqn. began operating from Punta Arenas in Chile, having been given Fuerza Aérea de Chile (FAC) markings en route at Belize; it is possible that Nimrod R.1 intelligence-gathering aircraft of 51 Sqn. also operated from Punta Arenas. The UK- and Gibraltar-based ships of the Task Force began assembling at Ascension from the 10th as the cruise liner *Uganda* was requisitioned to serve as a hospital ship. Meanwhile aircraft had been repainted in low-visibility schemes and many markings obliterated. For some ships the stay at Ascension was short. The destroyer *Antrim*, the frigate *Plymouth* and the tanker RFA *Tidespring* picked up equipment and a small force comprising M Coy. 42 Commando, D Sqn. 22 SAS and a Special Boat Squadron (SBS) detachment; also embarked were a Wessex HAS.3 of 737 NAS (*Antrim*), two Wessex HU.5s of 845 NAS (*Tidespring*) and a Wasp HAS.1 of 829 NAS (*Plymouth*). As TF.317.9, they were to rendezvous with HMS *Endurance* in the South Atlantic on the 12th for Operation 'Paraquat', the retaking of South Georgia.

At Ascension, hurriedly stored supplies were reorganized on the assembling ships and additional equipment was flown in from Britain and the United States for incorporation, VC-10 transports of 10 Sqn. joining the Lyneham Wing Hercules and chartered civil aircraft in a constant airlift. The anti-submarine Sea Kings of 820 and 826 NAS performed with the HC.4s of 846 NAS, the Wessex HU.5s of 845 NAS and the Ship's Flights' Wasps and Lynx of 829 and 815 NAS respectively in a continuing job of vertical replenishment (vertrep) and cross-shipping.

Vertrep tasks continued at sea after the Task Force had left Ascension, and on one such sortie, at night on 23 April, Sea King HC.4 ZA311 of 846 NAS ditched off *Hermes* with the loss of an air crewman. The assembly of the Task Force required maximum security, and on the 12th the more capable Nimrod MR.2s of 120, 201 and 206 Sqns. replaced the aircraft of 42 Sqn. Later, on the 18th, the first Victor tankers arrived, including aircraft equipped for radar reconnaissance.

On the Falklands, the Fuerza Aérea Argentina had commissioned Port Stanley airfield as Base Aérea Militar (BAM) Malvinas and BAM Condor at Goose Green, and the Commando Aviacion Naval Argentina (CANA) had established a base at Pebble Island as Estacion Aéronaval (EAN) Calderon. By late April, 24 Pucarás of G3A were operating from Stanley and Goose Green, six MB.339As of 1 Escuadrilla de Ataque (CANA) were based at Stanley and four T-43Cs of 4 Escuadrilla de Ataque (CANA) were flying from Stanley and Pebble Island. In addition, a search and rescue element of Grupo 7 de Coin Escuadron Helicopters (G7CEH), with two Bell 212s and two CH-47Cs, was operating from Goose Green and a range of Ejercito helicopters of CAB601 was headquartered at Moody Brook. Finally, two Skyvans and a Puma of the Prefectura Naval Argentina (PN) were based at Port Stanley. FAA and CANA transports were operating freely into Port Stanley. The two East Falklands airfields were heavily defended with 20mm and 35mm anti-aircraft guns and Tigercat and Roland SAMs, two companies of FAA officer cadets having been drafted on to the islands to handle airfield defence. On the mainland bases, within striking distance of the Falklands, were the following combat units:

Unit	Equipment
BAN Trelew	
Grupo 2 de Bombardeo (G2B)	8 Canberra B62
BAM Comodoro Rivadavia	
Grupo 8 de Caza (G8C) (det.)	Mirage IIIEA
Grupo 4 de Ataque (G4A)	8 Pucará
San Julian	
Grupo 6 de Caza (G6C) Esc II	10 Dagger
Grupo 4 de Caza (G4C)	15 A-4C
BAM Rio Gallegos	
Grupo 5 de Caza (G5C)	26 A-4B
Grupo 8 de Caza (G8C)	10 Mirage IIIEA
BAN Rio Grande	
Grupo 6 de Caza (G6C) Esc III	10 Dagger
2 Escuadrilla de Caza y Ataque (2ECA)	5 Super Etendard
3 Escuadrilla de Caza y Ataque (3ECA)	8 A-4Q

Although there were limited reserve aircraft, the total number of combat machines available to the FAA was about 110, including mainland-based Pucarás. The CANA could call on just twelve since one Super Étendard was used as a source of spares.

In preparation for Operation 'Paraquat', Victor XL192 of 57 Sqn. flew the first of three long-range maritime radar reconnaissance (MRR) sorties on the night of 20-21 April. It covered over 7,000 miles, conducting a 150 square mile search in a record 14hr 45min sortie. The flight was supported by four tankers in each direction.

The first move in South Georgia was the placing of Special Forces on Fortuna Glacier by the Wessex HAS.3 of 737 NAS and two Wessex HU.5s of 845 NAS on 21 April, but weather conditions deteriorated to such an extent that the SAS called for withdrawal early the next morning. In quick succession, the two HU.5s were lost when they crashed in white-out conditions, fortunately without serious injury, and the troops and crews were recovered by the remaining Wessex. On the 23rd the Argentinian submarine Santa Fe was detected in the vicinity, and HMS Brilliant joined TF.317.9, bringing with her two Lynx HAS.2s. The submarine HMS Conqueror was also in the area. Contact with the Santa Fe was made by Antrim's Wessex, which dropped depth charges near the vessel. Damaged, she returned to Grytviken but en route was subjected to a torpedo attack by Brilliant's Lynx

and then to several AS.12 attacks by Wasps from Plymouth and Endurance. The now disabled submarine was beached alongside the jetty.

It was decided to launch an invasion at short notice to take advantage of the shock created by the British action, and H-Hour was set for 1445hrs, despite the Royal Marine component's being aboard Tidespring some 200 miles away. A naval gunfire support (NGS) officer was flown to a suitable observation site in advance of a bombardment, and 30 SAS men went ashore nearby. The 235-round naval bombardment began shortly afterwards, bracketing Argentinian positions, and more troops were landed from Endurance and Plymouth. Without a fight, the Argentinian garrison surrendered at 1715hrs, and the small garrison at Leith surrendered the following day.

The Task Force had left Ascension from the 18th, and shortly after this 5 Infantry Brigade, now comprising 2nd Scots Guards, 1st Welsh Guards and 7th Gurkha Rifles, began training in the Brecon Beacons. This follow-up force was to leave the UK early in May. The main Task Force was located on 21 April by an FAA Boeing 707, which was intercepted by a Sea Harrier of 800 NAS. By the 27th the fleet had reached a position north-east of the Falklands, and two days later the FAA stopped daylight transport flights into the Islands. On the 30th, as diplomatic attempts to find an accommodation failed, the United States formally took the British position, and with 70 British ships now committed the MEZ became a total exclusion zone (TEZ). A third operational Sea Harrier squadron, 809 NAS, had been formed at Yeovilton from development and reserve aircraft, and the first six machines made the long flight to Ascension via Banjul, involving no fewer than fourteen air refuellings each. They were to be loaded on Atlantic Conveyor on 5 May. The Sea Harriers of 800 and 801 NAS were by this time flying regular combat air patrols (CAPs) over the Task Force, which now prepared for action.

The war began in earnest early on the morning of 1 May when a Vulcan B.2 of 101 Sqn. made the first 'Black Buck' bombing raid from Ascension. This involved a round trip of 14hrs 50mins and required fifteen Victor sorties and eighteen in-flight refuellings to get the single aircraft to the target. Twenty-one 1,000lb bombs were dropped from 10,000ft across the runway of Port Stanley airfield, which was cratered by one bomb; others caused damage to aircraft and installations. Twelve Sea Harriers of 800 NAS took off from Hermes from 0748hrs to follow up the raid on Port Stanley and to attack the airfield at Goose Green. Nine aircraft bombed Port Stanley from three directions, applying a combination of toss-bombing and conventional bombing techniques and delivering 1,000lb direct action (DA) and variable timed (VT) bombs and BL.755 cluster bomb units (CBUs). Little damage was done, but the airfield remained unsafe for some time. The Goose Green attack was more successful, and three Pucarás were put out of action for the duration, one pilot being killed as he waited to take off.

From midday, *Glamorgan*, *Alacrity* and *Arrow* began a naval bombardment of Argentinian positions in Port Stanley. Task Force helicopters were also busy around the island, and it is probable that the Argentinian command saw the morning's activity as a prelude to imminent invasion. From 1000hrs, a series of FAA sorties was launched against the British ships but few targets were found. The A-4 Skyhawks of Grupos 4 and 5 and the Canberras of Grupo 2 were provided with top cover from the Mirages and Daggers of Grupos 8 and 6. Later in the day Grupo 8 lost two aircraft in quick succession to AIM-9L AAMs fired by 801 NAS Sea Harriers. A flight of Daggers found and attacked the vessels bombarding Stanley and caused some damage. A Dagger from a separate flight was brought down by a Sea Harrier of 800 NAS, and 801 NAS completed its hattrick by destroying a Canberra 150 miles north-west of Port Stanley. The Sea Harrier force had had a highly successful day with no loss, and the aircraft/AIM-9L missile combination was proven in combat.

The Task Force's helicopters had also been busy, and, in a search for the submarine *San Luis*, Sea King HAS.5 XZ577 of 826 NAS claimed a record operational sortie: with a spare crew aboard and refuelling in flight from the frigates *Brilliant* and *Yarmouth*, the aircraft remained aloft for 10hrs 20mins. Early the next morning, the Sea King HC.4s of 846 NAS installed men of G Sqn. 22 SAS on the Falklands. On 2 May the Argentinians sufferred a more serious loss with the sinking of the cruiser *General Belgrano*, torpedoed by HMS *Conqueror*; her Alouette III was lost with her. Some time in the day a CANA Lynx HAS.23 was destroyed when it collided with the destroyer *Santisima Trinidad*. The Lynx of *Glasgow* and *Coventry* enjoyed more success when, early the next morning, using Sea Skua anti-ship missiles, they attacked and damaged the patrol craft *Alferez Sobel*; she had been detected by a Sea King of 826 NAS while searching for the missing Canberra crew.

The Argentinians lost two aircraft on 3 May: an MB.339A of 1EA crashed on the approach to Port Stanley, where a Skyvan of the PN was destroyed by naval gunfire. To add a dedicated ground-attack capability to the Task Force, the first Harrier GR.3 of 1 Sqn. departed St. Mawgan on 4 May for a non-stop, 4,600-mile, 9¼hr flight to Ascension. Over the next few days more aircraft followed, and by 6 May they were embarked on *Atlantic Conveyor* with the Sea Harriers of 809 NAS; they were to join the Force's carriers on 18 May. On the night of 3–4

May the second 'Black Buck' raid was made by Vulcan B.2 XM607 of 50 Sqn., but on this occasion the runway was not hit. May 4 saw the first Argentinian success, when two Super Étendards of 2ECA attacked warships on picket duty to the west of the Task Force, which for several days had been shadowed by an SP-2H of the Escuadrilla de Exploracion (EE). Two aircraft flying from Rio Grande launched one Exocet ASM each, one missile hitting HMS *Sheffield* at 1058hrs. The warhead failed to explode, but in the ensuing fire 21 men died; the second Exocet failed to find its target. The crippled destroyer sank under tow six days later, the loss demonstrating the vulnerability of the Task Force, which was denied early warning of impending air attacks.

The Royal Navy was to suffer a further loss that day. Lt. N. Taylor of 800 NAS was killed when his Sea Harrier was shot down by AA fire on a raid on Goose Green airfield. At 0900hrs the following morning, two senior pilots of 801 NAS were lost, presumed to have collided in mist while searching for a contact near the hulk of *Sheffield*. On the positive side, the Argentinian carrier *25 de Mayo* returned to port, there to remain throughout the conflict, her Skyhawks transferring to Rio Grande.

Poor weather slowed activity for several days, although the Sea Harriers maintained their CAPs. To the north, *Canberra* sailed from Ascension on the 8th, and from the 11th extended MR cover for the Task Force was provided by the Nimrod MR.2Ps of 206 Sqn., newly adapted for in-flight refuelling. Grupo 4 dispatched several A-4C sorties against the warships on 9 May, but suffered its first losses when two aircraft crashed en route in bad weather. A Puma of CAB601 was shot down by a Sea Dart fired from HMS *Coventry* over Choiseul Sound, and a UH-1H was seriously damaged at Moody Brook by naval gunfire. The intelligence-gathering trawler

On 2 May 1982, when this photograph was taken, 3 Escuadrilla of the Argentine Navy was still operating from the carrier *25 de Mayo*. This A-4Q, 3-A-305, is seen being prepared for a strike against HMS *Invincible* – always assuming that the British carrier could be located. (Via J. Ethell)

Narwal was attacked by Sea Harriers from 800 NAS and boarded by SBS men dropped by Sea Kings. The bombardment of Port Stanley had continued, but on 12 May *Glasgow* and *Brilliant* were attacked by A-4Bs of Grupo 5. *Glasgow* was effectively put out of action after being hit by a 500lb bomb which failed to explode.

The attackers paid a high price, losing two aircraft to Seawolf SAMs fired from *Brilliant*, while a third aircraft crashed into the sea and a fourth was brought down by Argentinian 35mm AA fire. At the same time, a Sea King of 826 NAS was lost when it ditched following engine failure. In the UK the requisitioned liner *Queen Elizabeth 2* sailed from Southampton with 5 Brigade direct for South Georgia, where the troops would be transferred to less vulnerable ships. On 13 May 'Black Buck 3' was aborted due to adverse winds. Late on the 14th, SAS troops were inserted into Pebble Island by 846 NAS Sea Kings. Before dawn the following day they attacked the airfield and damaged or destroyed six Pucarás, four Mentors of 4EA and one Skyvan. They withdrew without loss. From Ascension, Nimrod MR.2P XV232 set a new operational reconnaissance sortie record, flying 8,300 miles in 19hrs 5mins while checking Argentinian naval dispositions.

As the time for invasion approached, the Sea Harriers attacked vessels around the Falklands coast, damaging the *Rio Carcarana* and *Bahia Buen Suceso* on the 16th. On the 17th, two Sea Kings were lost: an HAS.5 of 826 NAS ditched during a sonar search when its radio altimeter failed, while HC.4 ZA290 of 846 NAS was burnt by its crew at Agua Fresca near Punta Arenas in Chile after a one-way sortie associated with the insertion of Special Forces to sabotage or report on aircraft, probably the Super Étendards at Rio Grande. As the weather continued to inhibit operations, Sea King HC.4 ZA294 of 846 NAS was lost after a bird-strike while transferring SAS troopers from *Hermes* to *Intrepid*, and 21 died in the accident. As the amphibious group joined the battle group north-west of the Falklands, the Argentinian TOAS became the Centro de Operaciones Conjuntas (CEOPECON). The invasion was now set for Friday 21 May at San Carlos, and in softening-up operations 1 Sqn. Harriers flew their first sorties against installations at Goose Green, destroying a fuel dump.

The Task Force entered the TEZ on the 20th, and after a redistribution of troops the first landings of Operation 'Sutton' were made at San Carlos by 2 Para just before dawn. The invasion force had moved into the protected San Carlos Water under cover of mist but had been spotted by an FAA Canberra. A Nimrod of 206 Sqn. set off from Ascension in the early hours of the 21st on yet another record-breaking sortie, covering 8,453 miles to monitor any Argentinian naval countermoves, and SAS and SBS units made diversionary attacks on the nearby Goose Green and

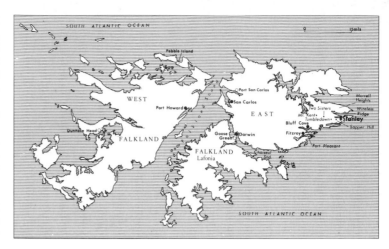

Darwin garrisons. The landings went smoothly, but there was an urgency to establish effective defensive and AAA positions ashore before the inevitable air strikes began.

While the Sea Harriers flew their CAPs, the Harriers attacked a helicopter concentration on Mount Kent, from where reinforcements could have been flown to the beach-head. A Puma and a CH-47C were destroyed by gunfire at 0800hrs. Soon after this Flt. Lt. J. Glover ejected from his Harrier when it was shot down by a Blowpipe SAM while on an armed reconnaissance sortie over Port Howard. Near the beach-head, 3CBAS lost two Gazelles in quick succession in support of a Sea King sortie; both pilots were killed, and the vulnerability of the type to small-arms fire was quickly apparent. The invasion fleet was spotted by a Pucará at about 1000hrs after one of the type had been shot down by a Stinger SAM fired by an SAS NCO. Shortly afterwards, a sole MB.339A attacked HMS *Argonaut*, causing superficial damage. The first mainland-based attacks followed at 1025hrs, by A-4Bs of Grupo 5 and Daggers of Grupo 6. The aircraft came in undetected and disabled *Antrim* and *Argonaut*. One Dagger crashed into the sea after having been hit by a Seawolf from HMS *Brilliant*.

The Sea Harriers had little time to spend over the landings since the carriers had withdrawn well to the east, out of range of attack. Without airborne early warning (AEW) and 'look-down' radars, they were dependent on radar pickets for

The indigenous Pucará coin aircraft was flown by Grupo 3 from Santa Cruz and bases in the Falklands, including Port Stanley. Although Pucarás were used at the time of the British landings, they did little damage, and those not destroyed on the ground or shot down were immobilized by Argentine forces at Port Stanley. A-512 is seen here, with a centreline fuel tank and armed with rocket lauchers. (Via J. Ethell)

warning of raids. Around midday HMS *Ardent* was attacked by Pucarás of Grupo 3, one of which was destroyed over Lafonia by cannon fire from an 801 NAS Sea Harrier.

The next strike on the ships came at 1300hrs, by A-4s of Grupos 4 and 5. The carriers had increased their CAPs, and although one aircraft caused some damage to *Ardent*, two were brought down at low level by AIM-9Ls fired by 800 NAS Sea Harriers. The third mainland strike came at 1435hrs as Daggers of Grupo 6 darted in at low level. One was destroyed on its run-in by a Sea Harrier of 800 NAS; another further damaged *Ardent* and wrote off her Lynx. Fifteen minutes later a second flight was bounced by 801 NAS, and all three aircraft were destroyed by AIM-9L. Despite a series of attacks pressed home with determination, the FAA sorties achieved little, owing the use of old or inadequately fused bombs which did not explode. The CANA now joined the fray with a raid at 1510hrs by A-4Qs of 3ECA. Using retarded bombs, the aircraft again made for *Ardent*, which was fatally damaged and sank the following day. Two Skyhawks were shot down by 801 NAS pilots, who also damaged a third which was abandoned by the pilot after an abortive attempt to land at Port Stanley. By the end of the day the FAA and CANA had lost twelve combat aircraft and two helicopters, with four pilots killed, while British losses were one Harrier, three helicopters and two pilots. For their efforts, the Argentinians had destroyed one frigate, disabled a destroyer and damaged three more frigates. Saturday saw the Argentianians frustrated from making further attacks when the weather again favoured the British as they landed more men and supplies. Harriers again struck the airfield at Goose Green.

First blood on Sunday in the air war was drawn at 1030hrs when the Sea Harrier CAP spotted helicopters delivering supplies on West Falkland. In several passes, two Pumas and an A.109A were shot up by 801 NAS pilots. The first strikes on the shipping in Falklands Sound came just before 1400hrs. A-4s of Grupo 5 hit HMS *Antelope*, which was subsequently destroyed when an unexploded bomb blew up while being defused. One A-4B was destroyed by a SAM, while in a later attack a Dagger was shot down by an 800 NAS Sea Harrier. Early in the evening a Sea Harrier of 800 NAS was lost when it hit the sea and exploded shortly after taking off for a toss-bombing sortie.

By 27 May the beach-head was secure and 2 Para prepared to break out towards Goose Green. In the meantime, shipping had been subjected to further attacks. On the 24th three Daggers and an A-4C were destroyed, the former all to 800 NAS, the latter to naval gunfire. On the 25th HMS *Coventry* was attacked by Grupos 4 and 5 while on picket duty to the west of the islands. She brought down an A-4B and an A-4C with Sea

Dart SAMs before being hit and sinking shortly afterwards. A third A-4 was destroyed by naval gunfire in San Carlos Water. The British suffered another serious loss with the destruction of *Atlantic Conveyor* loaded with Chinook and Wessex helicopters plus many essential materials and spares. The ship was hit at 1636hrs by an Exocet fired by a Super Étendard. A second missile failed, leaving the CANA with just one round available. The loss of helicopters was critical, causing a major transport problem for the British troops.

Shortly before the breakout, men of the Ejercito's 12 Regt. had been airlifted from Mount Kent to Goose Green, and the fighting from the 27th was hard, with only limited support from the Harriers. During one sortie, Sqn. Ldr. R. Iveson was hit over Goose Green and ejected; he hid up for three days, to be rescued by 3 CBAS Gazelle on the 30th. One A-4B (to gunfire), two Pucarás (small-arms fire) and an MB.339A (Blowpipe) were lost while attacking shipping and troop positions. Napalm was dropped unsuccessfully by Pucarás on the 28th – the only occasion on which the weapon was used – and a Scout AH.1 of 3CBAS was shot down by a Pucará during a casevac sortie. Further afield, two Vulcans fitted for firing the AGM-45 Shrike anti-radiation missile (ARM) deployed to Ascension, and 'Black Buck 4' was aborted five hours into the sortie when a one of the refuelling Victors' hose drum units (HDU) failed.

On the ground, 45 Commando and 3 Para made their epic march towards Port Stanley, initially to Teal Inlet, and air support consisted of Harrier sorties, mainly around Mount Kent, which were, however, limited by appalling weather; in addition, the depleted helicopter force was busy ferrying supplies and casualties. The Sea Harriers maintained the CAPs to protect the Task Force but saw little action. One of the type was lost in an accident on the 29th, and a second was shot down over Port Stanley by a Roland SAM on 1 June. The pilot ejected but spent many hours in the sea before being recovered by a Sea King of 820 NAS. A C-130E of Grupo 1 de Transporte Aereo (G1TA) was claimed by 801 NAS on 1 June after the aircraft had climbed out of Port Stanley to observe British shipping. In attacks on warships, a Dagger was destroyed by a Rapier on the

Of ten Canberra B.62s of 2 Grupo. one was unserviceable and two were shot down, one by the Sea Harrier/ Sidewinder combination and one by Sea Dart. Thirty-five sorties were flown, most of them by night. B-111 is seen here at Rio Gallegos, without wing-tip tanks but with 1,000lb bombs on wing pylons. (Via J. Ethell)

29th, and Sea Darts fired by HMS *Exeter* cost Grupo 4 two A-4Cs the following day. They were supporting the last Exocet strike against HMS *Invincible*, but the missile appears to have burnt out after having been decoyed.

Argentina was searching desperately for a further source of Exocets, but despite large arms shipments from Israel in Ecuadorian, Peruvian and Uruguayan aircraft none was forthcoming. There were no further attacks on ships until 8 June due to the continuing bad weather, which also hampered Harrier sorties. The Harriers pressed home strikes and armed reconnaissance sorties when possible, but they suffered damage from small-arms fire as a result of the heights at which they were required to fly. XZ963 was lost on the 30th when fuel line damage necessitated the pilot ejecting short of *Hermes*. Fortunately,

the forward operating base (FOB) at Port San Carlos was completed by 2 June, allowing longer time in target areas. The first Vulcan anti-radar raid, 'Black Buck 5' on 31 May, caused little damage. 'Black Buck 6', on 3 June, was more successful, damaging a Skyguard radar, but after the refuelling probe broke the aircraft was forced to divert to Rio de Janiero, where it was detained.

By the beginning of June, 5 Brigade was landing at San Carlos and preparations began to move elements of 2 Para to Fitzroy and Bluff Cove, just south-west of Port Stanley. With only one Chinook available, plans were made to bring up the Scots and Welsh Guards by ship, but in two sorties the Chinook lifted 156 men of 2 Para on 2 June. The weather continued to impede air activity, but the Sea Kings maintained a constant vigil around the Task Force, while on the island a

TABLE OF UNITS: THE FALKLAND ISLANDS, 1982

Unit	Aircraft	Base	Role	Dates
RAF				
51 Sqn.	Nimrod R.1	Ascension. ? Chile (ex Wyton)	Elint	00/04/82 to 00/06/82
39 Sqn.	Canberra PR.9	? Punta Arenas	Photo-recce	00/04/82 to 00/06/82
24 Sqn.				
30 Sqn.				
47 Sqn.	Hercules C.1/3	Ascension. Stanley (ex Lyneham)	Transport	02/04/82 to 19/08/83
70 Sqn.				
10 Sqn.	VC-10 C.1	Ascension. Stanley (ex Brize Norton)	Personnel transport	03/04/82 to 31/07/82
18 Sqn.	Chinook HC.1	Culdrose. Ascension. Port San Carlos (ex Odiham)	Heavy lift	06/04/82 to 19/10/83
42 Sqn.	Nimrod MR.1	Ascension (ex St. Mawgan)	MR. SAR	06/04/82 to 05/11/82
120 Sqn.				
201 Sqn.	Nimrod MR.2	Ascension (ex Kinloss)	MR. SAR. aerial relay	13/04/82 to 19/08/82
206 Sqn.				
55 Sqn.	Victor K.2	Ascension. Stanley (ex Marham)	Air refuelling / MRR. PR. air refuelling	18/04/82 to 12/03/85
57 Sqn.				
44 Sqn.				
50 Sqn.	Vulcan B.2	Ascension (ex Waddington)	Bombing	29/04/82 to 14/06/82
101 Sqn.				
1 Sqn.	Harrier GR.3	Ascension. *Hermes.* Stanley (ex Wittering)	Ground attack	03/05/82 to 10/11/82
202 Sqn.	Sea King HAR.3	Ascension (ex Lossiemouth)	Transport. SAR. casevac	09/05/82 to 07/09/82
29 Sqn.	Phantom FGR.2	Ascension (ex Coningsby)	Air defence	25/05/82 to 14/07/82
FAA				
800 NAS		*Hermes.* Port San Carlos. Stanley		05/04/82 to 03/07/82
801 NAS	Sea Harrier FRS.1	*Invincible.* Port San Carlos. Stanley	Air defence. ground attack	05/04/82 to 28/08/82
809 NAS		*Hermes. Invincible. Illustrious*		18/05/82 to 21/10/82
820 NAS	Sea King HAS.5	*Invincible.* Ascension. Stanley	Transport. ASW. SAR	05/04/82 to 28/08/82
824 NAS. A Flt.	Sea King HAS.2A	*Olmeda.* Port San Carlos	ASW. transport	05/04/82 to 21/06/82
824 NAS. C Flt.	Sea King HAS.2A	*Fort Grange*	Transport. ASW	03/06/82 to 17/09/82
825 NAS	Sea King HAS.2/2A	*Queen Elizabeth 2. Atlantic Causeway.* Port San Carlos	Transport	27/05/82 to 13/07/82
826 NAS	Sea King HAS.5	*Hermes.* Port San Carlos	ASW. SAR. casevac	05/04/82 to 03/07/82
846 NAS	Sea King HC.4	*Hermes. Fearless. Intrepid. Canberra. Elk. Norland.* various on Falklands	Troop transport	05/04/82 to 02/07/82
737 NAS	Wessex HAS.3	*Antrim, Glamorgan*	ASW. transport. casevac	14/04/82 to 28/06/82
845 NAS. A Flt.		*Resource.* Stanley	Troop transport	30/04/82 to 26/06/82
845 NAS. B Flt.		*Fort Austin.* Port San Carlos. Stanley	Troop transport. gunship	03/05/82 to 03/07/82
845 NAS. C Flt.		*Tidespring.* Port San Carlos	Transport	21/04/82 to 03/07/82
845 NAS. D Flt.		Ascension	Transport	11/04/82 to 00/10/82
845 NAS. E Flt.		*Tidepool.* various on Falklands	Transport. casevac	05/05/82 to 12/07/82
847 NAS	Wessex HU5	*Engadine. Atlantic Causeway.* Port San Carlos. various on Falklands	Transport. casevac	01/06/82 to 10/07/82
848 NAS. A Flt.		*Endurance. Regent*		01/05/82 to 10/07/82
848 NAS. B Flt.		*Olna.* Port San Carlos	Transport	30/05/82 to 31/08/82
848 NAS. C Flt.		*Fort Austin. Olwen*		28/06/82 to 16/10/82
848 NAS. D Flt.		*Atlantic Conveyor. Astronomer*		18/05/82 to 25/05/82. 27/06/82 to 02/09/82
815 NAS	Lynx HAS.2	Yeovilton. *Sheffield/Broadsword/Amazon* Class ships	ASW. EW. vertrep	
829 NAS	Wasp HAS.1	Portland. *Leander/Rothesay* Class ships	ASW. vertrep. liaison	
Royal Marines				
3 CBAS	Scout AH.1. Gazelle AH.1	Various on Falklands	Recce. liaison. gunship. casevac	16/05/82 to 22/06/82
British Army				
656 Sqn.	Scout AH.1. Gazelle AH.1	Various on Falklands	Recce. liaison. gunship. casevac	19/05/82 to 02/08/82

range of helicopters kept up a regular flow of supplies and casevac sorties as the Paras and Commandos pressed relentlessly on towards Port Stanley. These trips were not without risk: in the early hours of 6 June, a Gazelle of 656 Sqn. was shot down, possibly by British naval fire, while delivering supplies to Mount Pleasant.

RAF Hercules dropped essential supplies around ships of the Task Force in extended, air-refuelled flights from Ascension, and additional Harriers for 1 Sqn. made the long flight from Ascension direct to HMS *Hermes*. The FAA conducted several Canberra night bombing sorties on Port San Carlos, and on 7 June a Learjet reconnaissance aircraft was brought down over Pebble Island by a Sea Dart from HMS *Exeter*. In moving the Guards to Fitzroy by ship, the vessels were exposed without adequate air defence or natural cover and, further, the anchorage at Port Pleasant was within sight of Argentinian positions. The two assault ships *Fearless* and *Intrepid* were initially used, together with the LSLs *Sir Galahad* and *Sir Tristram*. Their positions were reported and, perhaps not surprisingly, they were subjected to heavy air attacks on 8 June. The weather had cleared, and on the mainland urgent plans were put in hand to mount a series of raids.

In the first strike, Grupo 5 was to put up eight aircraft to attack the ships, supported by six Daggers of Grupo 6 and with four Mirages of Grupo 8 making a raid on San Carlos to distract the waiting Sea Harriers. Refuelling problems reduced the A-4B force to five aircraft, but all got through to Port Pleasant at 1350hrs, where they bombed the two LSLs. *Sir Galahad* was hit, and in the explosions and ensuing fire 43 Welsh Guardsmen and seven seamen were killed, with many more suffering serious injury. *Sir Tristram* was also seriously damaged. In subsequent rescue attempts, the Sea Kings of 825 NAS, involved in off-loading stores, played a major part. The unit had been commissioned on 7 May at Culdrose with the HAS.2 model rapidly converted to transports, and it had arrived in the Falklands only days earlier to support the overworked HC.4s of 846 NAS. While crossing Falklands Sound, the Daggers spotted HMS *Plymouth* in an exposed position and turned to attack her, causing disabling damage. The Mirages did indeed draw the Sea Harriers in their strike on San Carlos, but they dashed off before the naval fighters could close. All the aircraft returned safely to their bases.

The second strike was planned for 1645hrs, this time by sending four Grupo 5 aircraft against shipping with four Grupo 4 machines armed with anti-personnel weapons while Mirages flew top cover. The defences were now prepared, however, and after one A-4B had attacked and destroyed a landing craft from *Fearless* between Fitzroy and Goose Green, the Sea Harriers of 800 NAS brought down three aircraft in as many

minutes at Choiseul Sound. The Grupo 4 aircraft escaped without causing damage, and the Mirages refused to be drawn into battle.

The next four days were taken up with supporting 3 Commando Brigade and 5 Brigade in reaching their position for the final assault on Port Stanley. On the 12th, 3 Para fought a vicious battle for Mount Longdon, losing 23 dead and 47 wounded, while 2 Para moved to Wireless Ridge. The Welsh Guards and 42 Commando held Mount Harriet, with 45 Commando on Two Sisters and 22 SAS on Murrel Heights. The Harriers were now able to fly more sorties, although there had been a minor setback on 8 June when one aircraft made a heavy landing at the FOB, putting it out of action for several hours. On the 10th, the first attempt at using laser-guided bombs (LGB) against strongpoints failed through target-marking problems. Early on the 12th, HMS *Glamorgan*, providing NGS, was hit and seriously damaged by a ground-launched MM.38 Exocet, losing her Wessex HAS.3. Shortly afterwards, Port Stanley shook as Vulcan XM607 made the final 'Black Buck 7' raid on the airfield, using conventional airburst bombs.

Later in the day, a Wessex HU.5 of 845 NAS made a risky attack on the Town Hall at Port Stanley, where, it was thought, a major conference was taking place. One AS.12 ASM hit the neighbouring police station, while a second missed any target. On the 13th, the FAA reciprocated with an attack on the British 3 Cdo. Brigade HQ on Mount Kent by A-4B Skyhawks of 5 Grupo. No targets of significance were hit, and most of the aircraft were damaged by groundfire although all returned to base. In the last Argentinian raid of the war, at 2255hrs, Canberra B.62 B-108 of Grupo 2 was shot down over Mount Kent by a Sea Dart fired by *Exeter*. The two days 12 and 13 June saw some of the bitterest fighting on the ground as 2 Para, supported by Scouts firing SS.11 missiles, fought for Wireless Ridge.

To the south, men of the Scots and Welsh

Without the Sea Harrier, it is doubtful whether British forces could have regained the Falklands. This aircraft, finished in Extra Dark Sea Grey, appears to be XZ496/27 of 800 NAS. It is seen here making a vertical landing on HMS *Hermes* after a CAP, with its armament of two AIM-9Ls still in place; also evident are the 100gal drop tanks and twin 30mm Aden gun packs. (BAe via J. Ethell)

TABLE OF UNITS: THE FALKLAND ISLANDS, 1982 (continued)

Unit	Aircraft	Base	Role	Dates
CANA				
2 EH	S-61D-4 Sea King	Bahia Blanca. *Almirante Irizar*. *25 de Mayo*. Rio Grande	Transport. ASW	00/03/82 to 14/06/82
EAS	S-2A	*25 de Mayo*. Bahia Blanca. Port Stanley. Rio Gallegos	ASW. MR	29/03/82 to 14/06/82
EE	SP-2H	Bahia Blanca. Rio Grande	MR	00/04/82 to 15/05/82
1 ESLM	Electra	Rio Grande		
2 ESLM	F-28		Transport	02/04/82 to 30/04/82
1 EA	MB.326GB. MB.339A	Trelew. Bahia Blanca. Rio Grande. Port Stanley	Light ground attack	02/04/82 to 23/04/82. 24/04/82 to 30/05/82
4 EA	T-34C-1	Punta Indio. Rio Grande. Port Stanley. Pebble I.	Light ground attack	15/04/82 to 23/04/82. 24/04/82 to 15/05/82
2 ECA	Super Étendard	Bahia Blanca. Rio Grande	Anti-shipping	19/04/82 to 30/05/82
1 EH	Lynx HAS.23. Alouette III	Various ships	ASW. liaison	25/03/82 to 19/06/82
3 ECA	A-4Q	*25 de Mayo*. Bahia Blanca	Ground attack, anti-shipping	28/03/82 to 14/06/82
PN	Skyvan, Puma	Port Stanley. Pebble I.	Communications. transport	00/04/82 to 15/05/82
CAE				
CAB 601	A-109A, UH-1H, Puma. CH-47C	Various on Falklands	Transport. gunship, liaison	23/03/82 to 17/06/82
FAA				
GAF.1	Learjet	Comodoro Rivadavia. Trelew. Rio Gallegos. Rio Grande	Recce. pathfinder	00/04/82 to 14/06/82
Esc. 1. GTA1	C-130E/H, KC-130H	Comodoro Rivadavia	Transport. recce. air refuelling	01/04/82 to 14/06/82
GTA9	F-27, F-28, Twin Otter. BAC-111, Boeing 737	Comodoro Rivadavia	Transport (air bridge)	02/04/82 to 29/05/82
GA3	Pucará	Santa Cruz. Port Stanley. Goose Green. Pebble I.	Light attack	02/04/82 to 13/06/82
GC17	CH-47C. Bell 212	Various mainland. Port Stanley	SAR, recce, transport	07/04/82 to 14/06/82
GC4	A-4C	San Julian	Anti-shipping, ground attack	11/04/82 to 08/06/82
GC5	A-4B	Rio Gallegos	Anti-shipping, ground attack	14/04/82 to 14/06/82
Esc. 2. GTA1	Boeing 707	Comodoro Rivadavia, El Palomar, Ezeiza	Transport. recce	20/04/82 to 07/06/82
Esc. 2. GC6	Dagger	San Julian	Air defence, escort	25/04/82 to 13/06/82
Esc. 3. GC6		Rio Grande		
Esc. Fenix	Miscellaneous impressed	Various mainland	Communications. SAR, comms. relay, pathfinder	27/04/82 to 14/06/82
GC8	Mirage IIIEA	Comodoro Rivadavia. Rio Gallegos	Air defence, escort	01/05/82 to 14/06/82
GB2	Canberra B.62	Trelew. Rio Gallegos	Day/night bombing	

Guards and Gurkhas were helilifted to Mount Harriet, from where they were to attack Tumbledown Mountain. At midday, Harriers made the first successful LGB attack on a company HQ on Tumbledown, marked by a forward air controller (FAC); later, in a second attack, a 105mm gun was taken out at Moody Brook. Fighting around Tumbledown lasted into the 14th. With Port Stanley surrounded, two Harriers left *Hermes* at midday for an LGB strike on Sapper Hill. At the last minute they were advised to return: white flags were appearing in Port Stanley. By the afternoon the war was over, the surrender being signed at 2359hrs GMT.

The outcome of the war was critically dependent upon the use of sea power, properly supported by air power, to place highly trained ground forces in the right place at the right time. The British supply lines were at all times stretched, and the sinking of a single merchantman created considerable difficulties. With the loss of two destroyers, two frigates, an LSL and a container ship, much was learned about the vulnerability of modern warships. The carriers played a crucial role: without them the invasion could not have proceeded. The Sea Harriers offered the best protection to the Task Force, even without the benefit of AEW. From 1 May to 14 June they flew 1,335 sorties, of which about 1,135 were CAPs; 27 AIM-9Ls were fired, scoring 24 hits and destroying nineteen aircraft, including eleven Daggers and Mirages. Gunfire accounted for six aircraft at the lower end of the speed spectrum. The Harrier family proved remarkably robust, with few losses to enemy action. SAM systems were generally less effective, the ground based variety especially so because of the difficulty of firing horizontally in close proximity to friendly shipping. The Sea Dart accounted for seven aircraft and Seawolf three, plus possibly an incoming Exocet. Stinger, Blowpipe and Rapier brought down one aircraft apiece.

The Falklands conflict also demonstrated the full range of helicopter roles and the importance of this type of aircraft. The loss of three of the four heavy-lift Chinooks on *Atlantic Conveyor*, together with all spares, tools and manuals, placed a considerable burden on the remaining machine, which performed remarkably, and the utility Sea Kings which between them logged over 4,600 hours. The lighter helicopters operated in a range of roles, making over 400 casevac flights alone. The Task Force was protected from submarine threat by two squadrons of Sea King HAS, plus Wessexes, Lynx and Wasps of the Ships' Flights. The Sea Kings undertook 2,253 sorties from 1 May, including record airborne flights.

The long distances involved in supporting a range of activity meant a heavy dependence on airborne refuelling, both between the UK and Ascension and south from Ascension. During the conflict, Vulcan bombers were refitted with probes, and Hercules and Nimrods were adapted in record time. The refuelling load fell on the Victors of 55 and 57 Sqns., who between them flew over 600 sorties in 3,000 hours with only six missions aborted through equipment failure. By way of contrast, the FAA, operating its fighters at extreme ranges over the Falklands, lost a high proportion of sorties through lack of AAR. To supplement the Victors, work was put in hand to convert Hercules and Vulcans as tankers, but these were delivered too late to see active service. The Hercules transports flew 13,000 hours, including, from 16 May, 44 refuelled airdrops to the Task Force. The Nimrods flew 111 sorties, again including many at extreme range, while the Harriers of 1 Sqn. which relied on air refuelling to reach their 'base' on *Hermes* flew 126 sorties in 3½ weeks.

From the time that the decision to send the Task Force south was taken, many developments were designed and tested, and became operational, in amazingly short periods. Apart from refuelling probes, the Nimrods were equipped to use the AIM-9 AAM and AGM-84 ASM supplied by the United States, and Harriers were fitted for the AIM-9 and with electronic support measures (ESM). Not surprisingly, however, in view of the complexity of the task, the most needed facility, AEW, could not be provided in time, although two Sea King HAS.2s were fitted with Searchwater radars and were operational within eleven weeks, sailing south with HMS *Illustrious* in August 1982.

The Argentinian Government must have weighed the decision to invade the Falklands in political rather than military terms. Given a British determination to fight, even at a distance of 8,000 miles, Argentinian equipment was no match for the range of hardware deployed by the British. Argentina's aircraft were old and generally second-hard, and spares were a major difficulty. Without modern electronic aids, they operated at extreme range, generally unable to carry defensive armament; furthermore, their

weapons often failed. Despite an appalling loss rate, the Argentinian pilots pressed home their attacks with great skill and determination, achieving considerable success against well-armed and modern ships. The military and civilian transport crews were flying into Port Stanley to the last minute, usually at night. FAA combat aircraft flew 2,782 hours, transports 7,719 hours and others, including civilian aircraft 1,953 hours. Of 505 combat sorties planned, 445 were launched but only 280 reached their targets. The CANA mounted six Super Étendard and 34 A-4Q sorties.

AIRCRAFT MARKINGS

Argentina
Aircraft of all air arms retained the camouflage schemes in use at the time. After attacks on aircraft by their own defences, yellow identification panels were applied to the fins and wings of some types, as indicated below. Some aircraft, and especially helicopters, wore yellow fuselage bands.

FAA
A-4B Dark olive green/dark brown over, light

The Sea Kings of the Fleet Air Arm were invaluable to the Task Force in their anti-submarine and transport roles. At Port Stanley, immediately after the conflict, is HAS.5 XZ578/21 of 826 NAS, while static in the foreground in HC.4 ZA291/VB of 846 NAS. The first HC.4, ZA290, was flown on a one-way mission to the South American mainland with an SAS detail. It was deliberately destroyed at Agua Fresca, Chile. (MoD).

HMS *Ardent*, a Type 21 frigate, was hit by Argentinian aircraft throughout 21 May. In the end, she was fatally damaged by Skyhawks of 3ECA and sank on the 21st. In all, the Royal Navy lost two destroyers, two frigates and two landing ships with more damaged, some seriously. (via J. Ethell)

blue under, black serial under cockpit and on tailpipe: C-231, C-248 (Grupo 5).

A-4C *Dark brown/light sand over, light grey under, serial not displayed, yellow fin stripe overpainted in light blue: C-321, C-304 (Grupo 4).*

Dagger *Dark green/medium green/tan over, light grey under, contrasting tan or green serial under cockpit and larger on rear fuselage, yellow fin and wing stripes: C-404, C-413 (Grupo 6).*

Mirage IIIEA *Dark green/medium green/tan over, light grey under, black serial under cockpit and rear fuselage: I-014, I-019 (Grupo 8).*

Pucará *All were hastily camouflaged before transfer to Port Stanley, most being light green/tan over, light blue under: A-502, A-514. Later deliveries had yellow wing and fin stripes: A-511, A-531. Last deliveries were dark brown/medium green over, medium grey under: A-515, A-536. All serials black on rear fuselage. All aircraft Grupo 3.*

Canberra B.62 *Dark green/dark grey over, light grey under, white serial on nose and larger on rear fuselage: B-108 (Grupo 2).*

Boeing 707 *White over, medium grey under separated by blue cheat line, black serial on fuselage forward and aft of wing: TC-91 (Grupo 1).*

C-130H *Green/brown over, light blue under, tan serial on nose and rear fuselage: TC-65 (Grupo 1).*

Learjet 35A *White over, grey under separated by blue cheat line, black serial on engine nacelle. T-23, T-24 (Grupo 1).*

CANA

Super Étendard *Glossy dark blue-grey over, white under, white serial on mid fuselage, last two digits on nose: 3-A-203, 3-A-205 (2ECA).*

A-4Q *Light Gull Gray over, white under, black serial on intake: 3-A-305, 3-A-314 (3ECA).*

MB.339A *Dark green/tan over, light grey under, black serial on fin, yellow fuselage band: 4-A-110, 4-A-116 (1EA).*

T-43 *Dark green/tan over, white under, red (training) band around fuselage, black serial on fin: 408, 412 (4EA).*

SP-2H *Dark blue-grey over, light sea grey under, last three digits of serial in black on nose: 3-P-112 (EE).*

S-2E *Dark grey over, light sea grey under, last two digits of serial in black on fin: 2-AS-22 (EA).*

Ejercito

All but one CAB601 helicopters were finished Olive Drab overall with yellow bands around the boom or fuselage. The exception was a Puma used for ambulance duties, which was white overall with a red cross on nose and fuselage.

A-109A *AE-331, AE-337.*

UH-1H *AE-410, AE-418.*

Puma *AE-501, AE-508.*

CH-47C *AE-520, AE-521.*

PN

Skyvan *Medium green over with brown mottle, light grey under, black serial on fin: PA-54.*

Great Britain

No special markings were worn but most types had the white on roundels (if present) overpainted, normally in Roundel Blue. Unit markings were also overpainted, as well as all unnecessary instructions and codes.

RAF

Harrier GR.3 *Dark Green/Dark Sea Grey overall, wing roundel overpainted, red code on outriggers and fin, black serial on rear fuselage: XZ133/10, XZ991/31 (1 Sqn.).*

Vulcan B.2 *Dark Green/Medium Sea Grey over, Dark Sea Grey under, black serial on fin: XM597 (50 Sqn.); XM607 (44 Sqn.).*

Victor K.2 *Dark Green/Medium Sea Grey over, white under, black serial on rear fuselage, squadron markings retained: XH671 (55 Sqn.); XL192 (57 Sqn.).*

Nimrod MR.1 *Hemp over, Light Aircraft Grey under, black code on fin, serial on rear fuselage: XV244/44 (42 Sqn.).*

Nimrod R.1 *XW664/64 (51 Sqn.).*

Nimrod MR2.P *XV232/32 (Kinloss Wing).*

Hercules C.1 *Dark Green/Dark Sea Grey over, Light Aircraft Grey under, black serial on rear fuselage, white code on nose and fin: XV304/304 (Lyneham Wing).*

Hercules C.3 *XV221/221 (Lyneham Wing).*

Hercules C.1P *XV179/179 (Lyneham Wing).*

Chinook HC.1 *Dark Green/Dark Sea Grey over, black under, black serial on rear fuselage, code on rear rotor pylon: ZA718/BN (18 Sqn.).*

VC-10 C.1 *White over, Light Aircraft Grey under separated by blue cheat line, black serial on engine, code on fin, red cross in white square on forward fuselage and under wings: XV107/107 (10 Sqn.).*

Sea King HAR.3 *Golden Yellow overall, black serial on boom: XZ593 (202 Sqn.).*

The RAF Harriers of 1 Sqn. demonstrated the amazing versatility of the V/STOL fighter. The squadron was trained to operate with a high degree of independence and was embarked on HMS *Hermes* from 18 May, although the pilots had never before flown the type from carriers. The aircraft were intended to relieve the Sea Harriers from the ground-attack role, but they were also fitted for Sidewinders, on the outer pylons, for self-defence. Four of the ten aircraft deployed were lost. (MoD)

Phantom FGR.2 *Medium Sea Grey/Mixed Grey over, Light Aircraft Grey under, white serial on rear fuselage, red code on nosewheel door, unit markings removed: XV468/W (29 Sqn.).*

FAA
Sea Harrier FRS.1 *The aircraft of 800 NAS on board* Hermes *had the original top surface Extra Dark Sea Grey extended overall by hand, and most of the markings were obliterated. Codes were on the engine intake in black. Ex 899 NAS aircraft wore black codes beneath the cockpit; 801 NAS aircraft had the top surface finish extended by spraygun and dark blue codes were carried higher up the engine intake; and 809 NAS aircraft were finished, in the UK, Medium Sea Grey over with wing and tailplane undersurfaces Mixed Grey. Roundels were in pink and pale blue on the nose only. Aircraft of 809 NAS on* Hermes *carried two-digit codes in black on the engine intake, while machines on* Invincible *wore pale blue codes higher up the engine intake. Serials were normally in black on the ventral fin, but on some 809 NAS aircraft they were carried on the rear fuselage: XZ492/23, XZ496/27 (800 NAS,* Hermes*); XZ457/14 (ex 899 NAS,* Hermes*); ZA177/77, XZ499/99 (809 NAS,* Hermes*); XZ493/001, ZA175/004 (801 NAS,* Invincible*); ZA174/000 (809 NAS,* Invincible*).*
Sea King HAS.2A *RAF blue-grey overall, black codes and serials: XV672/145 (824 NAS); XV677/595 (825 NAS).*

Sea King HAS.5 *RAF blue-grey overall, black codes and serials: XZ291/17 (820 NAS); ZA133/35 (826 NAS).*
Sea King HC.4 *Olive Drab overall, black serial and codes: ZA295/VM, ZA310/VS (846 NAS).*
Wessex HAS.3 *RAF blue-grey overall, black serial: XM837 (737 NAS, Glamorgan); XP142 (737 NAS, Antrim).*
Wessex HU.5 *Olive Drab overall, black serial and codes: XT484/H (845 NAS); XT480/XQ (847 NAS); XS486/WW (848 NAS).*
Lynx HAS.2 *Oxford Blue overall, black serial, code generally not displayed: XZ251 (815 NAS, Ardent); XZ723 (815 NAS, Antelope).*
Wasp HAS.1 *Black/Light Admiralty Grey/Olive Drab/white overall, black serial: XS527 (829 NAS, Endurance); RAF blue-grey overall: XT429 (829 NAS, Plymouth).*

Army/Royal Marines
All helicopters were finished black/Dark Green overall with black serials and lettering.
Gazelle AH.1 *XX411/X, ZA728/A (3CBAS).*
Scout AH.1 *XW615/DS (3CBAS); XW282 (656 Sqn.).*

The Victors of 55 and 57 Sqns. were another aircraft type vital to the recovery of the Falklands. Based on Ascension, they enabled the Harriers of 1 Sqn. to reach the Task Force and the Vulcans to undertake their record-breaking bombing sorties. XM715 of 55 Sqn. refuelled sister-aircraft XL192 on the first maritime radar reconnaissance sortie of the war, and after supporting various detachments between the UK and Ascension it acted as a tanker for Nimrod and Vulcan missions. (Author's collection)

12.5. Miscellaneous conflicts and incidents

1. On 9 March 1947 there was a revolt by Army elements in Paraguay, specifically at Chaco and Concepción. FAP aircraft in rebel hands, presumably C-45s or C-47s, are reported to have bombed Asunción on the 23rd though causing little damage. The Air Force also attacked rebel Navy gunboats in July, hitting one with a 75kg bomb. A Uruguayan-registered Vought-Sikorsky SV-44A flying boat bringing arms to the rebels crashed in August. The revolution collapsed on 20 August.

2. In Colombia, the decade from 1948 to 1958 saw continuous civil war, known as La Violencia. The FAC was actively involved in coin work, primarily using armed AT-6s and F-47Ds, with C-47s transporting ground forces. Details of the use of aircraft in this protracted war are scarce.

3. In July 1954 General Alfredo Stroessner came to power in Paraguay, forming a right-wing military dictatorship. There was a consequent loss of civil liberties and numerous coup attempts. In 1959 exiles based in Bolivia infiltrated the north-west of the country and fighting broke out. The fighting grew worse, and by April 1960 the

Fuerza Aérea del Paraguay (FAP) was involved. Sorties were flown from Bahia Negra, Fuerte Olimpo and Mariscal Estigarribia using T-6Gs and C-47s fitted with bomb racks. Troops were moved up to Mariscal from Asunción by C-47s and C-54s of Transporte Aéreo Militar (TAM), and Piper L-4A liaison aircraft flew reconnaissance sorties over the lightly inhabited area. By May the rebels had gone to ground.

4. An unidentified submarine was located by Argentinian naval vessels on 30 January 1960 in the Golfo Nuevo. The Naval Aviation Service flew numerous PBM-5 sorties, backed up by FAA Lincoln flights, but the inconclusive search was called off after 26 days. Also involved in the search was the US Navy, one of whose R6Ds collided with a DC-3.

5. In the 1963 revolution in Argentina, naval aircraft fought on behalf of the rebels attempting to overthrow the Government, while the Air Force remained loyal. The Navy took control of Bases Aerea Punta Indio and Commandante Espora on the morning of 2 April; they also took over a radio station in Buenos Aires, which was ineffectively bombed by two MS.760s, while Air Force Meteors conducted armed reconnaissance sorties. During the morning Navy F4U-5s flew reconnaissance sorties and several PBY-5s dropped leaflets. In the afternoon there were several attacks by SNJs on an Army tank unit, during which a dozen Shermans were destroyed. One SNJ and one F9F-2 were shot down by the Army during the strikes. A tank column now made for Punta Indio, and early on the 3rd it was again bombed by SNJs and F4U-5s, but by now it was clear to the rebels that they could not win and many Navy aircraft flew out to Uruguay. At 0800hrs the Air Force launched a bombing raid on Punta Indio by four F-86Fs, four Meteors, four MS.760s and two Lincolns. About ten Navy aircraft were destroyed, and by 2145hrs the revolt was over.

6. There was a border dispute between Chile and Argentina from late in 1965. One Navy F4U-5 was lost in November, and from late 1966 F9F-2s of Esc. de Ataque 1 were deployed to Rio Gallegos. There was no air combat.

7. The revolutionary Ernesto Ché Guevara entered Bolivia in 1965 in an endeavour to apply guerrilla warfare to the overthrow of the right-wing dictatorship of Gen. Barrientos. Although there were underground left-wing activists in the towns and cities, he preferred to work with peasants in the countryside. From March 1967 FAB T-6s, T-28s and F-51Ds of the Esc. de Caza napalmed and rocketed suspected guerrilla targets, but with limited success. The aircraft were involved in Operation 'Cynthia' in July, and Bolivian Government forces tracked Guevara down in October 1967 with the help of the CIA, using radio detection devices and moving troops with the aid of two US-supplied HH-19B helicopters.

8. After Barrientos, the President of Bolivia, was killed in a helicopter crash in April 1969, there was a succession of military coups. During one such, in August 1971, aircraft of the Fuerza Aérea Boliviano (FAB) strafed students occupying areas of La Paz. The aircraft involved were F-51Ds and Cavaliers of Grupo Aéreo 2, based at Colcapirua and acting in support of the new régime of Col. Hugo Banzer Suarez. The FAB was involved in demonstrations in support of his replacement in a further coup on 21 July 1978.

9. In 1970 Dr. Salvador Allende of Chile became Latin America's first democratically elected Marxist head of state. His Government began to institute reforms and, in the process, nationalized US-owned copper mines. On 11 September 1973 there was a military coup headed by General Augusto Pinochet Ugarte and supported by the CIA, who reportedly worked through the International Telephone and Telegraph Corporation (ITT). The Chilean Navy secured key points in Valparaiso port, while the Army surrounded the Moneda Presidential Palace with tanks. At 1130hrs Hunter FGA.71 fighters of Grupo No. 7 bombed the palace, and at 1400hrs Allende ordered resistance to cease. He was later found dead, allegedly having committed suicide. In December 1974 Pinochet was declared President. American confidence in the outcome could be inferred from the fact that, exceptionally, an order for F-5E fighters from the Allende Government was accepted, although delivery was not in the event made until after the coup.

10. There was an internal revolt within the Argentinian Air Force in December 1975 in which Mirages flew demonstration sorties. On the 23rd, Navy A-4Qs of 1 Esc. de Ataque flew a strike against rebels in Buenos Aires.

11. For many years Colombia has maintained a flourishing drug industry, which by 1979 supported no fewer than 150 airstrips. Countering drug smuggling occupies much FAC time, and aircraft are regularly intercepted and forced down.

12. Colombia has attempted to contain insurgency for many years. On 3 February 1986 rebels captured the town of Morales, but they were driven out after A-37 strikes. Rebels regularly fire at helicopters, mostly owned by oil companies, and have shot at least one down. Fighting grew more serious in 1988, at which time the Army was being reorganized.

13. There was a minor border conflict between Ecuador and Peru in January 1981. FAP Su-22s of Grupo 12 and Mirage 5Ps of Grupo 13 flew sorties across the border, as did FAE Mirage F.1Es and Jaguars of Esc. 2111, operating on armed reconnaissance tasks; both air forces are also reported to have flown armed T-37 sorties. The short conflict was inconclusive, and no air losses were reported.

14. Since 1980 there have been several attempts to overthrow the Government of Surinam. In early 1987 rebels captured a Cessna 204 with a view to using it for a bombing raid. A Surinam Airways Twin Otter was also captured; it was intended that it should be sold to purchase arms.

15. From August 1987 there was growing tension between Colombia and Venezuela over territorial claims in the Gulf of Venezuela. Colombian Air Force (FAC) Mirage 5 fighters of Grupo de Combat 1 violated Venezuelan airspace, and the Venezuelans responded by transferring Army units to the border and moving Fighter Group 16 F-16s and Training Group 14 Tucanos from Palo Negro to Maracaibo.

16. At the time of writing, the Peruvian Government is combating guerrillas in Huacano province. Army Mi-8s and Mi-17s are in widespread use to move troops in the region.

Appendices

I. Codes and Serial Numbers

Most military aircraft carry serial numbers or codes, or both. In construction, aircraft are normally given a constructor's code, which is the maker's unique identification for the aircraft regardless of the eventual user. In military service, each aircraft is given a unique serial number which remains with the aircraft, at least for as long as it serves with the particular air arm. Codes usually identify an aircraft within a unit, and they remain with it only for the period of time the aircraft is with the particular unit.

Serials are of many types. In the British air arms a single system is used, comprising two letters followed by three digits, the system having reached the ZF series at the time of writing. Still in service with the RAF are Canberra aircraft conversions from earlier marks, retaining serials in the WH range; for example, WH718, now a TT.18, was originally a B.2. Although serials are assigned in sequence, there are gaps for security reasons.

In the US Air Force a digits-only system is used, the first two numerals of the serial indicating the fiscal year of order. Thus 6714728 was a C-130E ordered in 1967. In recent years only the last few digits have been displayed, normally on the fin. US Navy and Marines Corps serials are known as Bureau of Aeronautics numbers (BuNos). Comprising six digits, they are assigned sequentially; 159316, for example, is a P-3C Orion. The BuNos are carried in 4in high characters on the lower rear fuselage. US-manufactured aircraft are often given US serials which may be retained in overseas service. The C-130K Hercules built for the RAF and given British serials in the XV range were given USAF serials beginning with 65 and 66 (although these were never physically applied to the aircraft).

Coding systems change relatively frequently. In the RAF, the wartime practice of using a two-letter code to indicate the unit, followed by an individual letter to indicate the aircraft, obtained for some years after the war. Fighter aircraft have for many years carried a single identifying letter, but it is increasingly common for two letters to be carried, the first indicating the unit, the second the aircraft within the unit. The unit code is only peculiar to a unit on a particular station. Thus, in 1986, Lightning F.6 XS895 was coded BC (aircraft C of 11 Sqn.), while XS898 was coded AB (aircraft B of 5 Sqn.); both units were based at Binbrook. The code AB was also used by Gutersloh-based Harrier GR.3 XZ967 – aircraft B of 3 Sqn.

The Royal Navy has long used a system of three-digit codes identifying aircraft within a squadron. Until the mid-1950s the codes might be duplicated on units based apart, but from then on the codes have been unique to each squadron. In addition, one-letter (carrier) or two-letter (shore base or ships carrying helicopters) codes have been carried on the fin. Thus Scimitar F.1 XD268/194R indicates that the machine was with 807 Naval Air Squadron on board HMS *Ark Royal*; Lynx HAS.2 XZ241/326AW was from 702 NAS on the frigate HMS *Arrow*; and Sea Hawk F.1 WF199/699FD was from 764 NAS at Ford (HMS *Peregrine*).

The present USAF coding system originated during the Vietnam War, when two letters were applied to the fin of aircraft, identifying the unit. The two-letter system has remained in use, but the letters now identify the normal base, regardless of unit. Thus HO is Holloman AFB, UH is RAF Upper Heyford and HL is Hill AFB. Codes were originally worn by most tactical types, but they are now normally only carried by fighter types.

As with the Royal Navy, the US Navy's code system is based on three-digit, two-letter combinations. Each unit within a Carrier Air Wing is assigned a three-digit series starting with 01. The air defence squadrons are normally assigned 101 on and 201 on, with the attack squadrons given 301 on and 401 on, with other units following. The first aircraft in the series is reserved for the unit commander, and if the Air Wing Commander is qualified on a type his aircraft is given an 00 code. In the days of bright aircraft markings, each unit was required to wear its squadron insignia on the fin in an appropriate colour as follows:

Unit	Code	Colour
1st sqn.	101 on	Insignia red
2nd sqn.	201 on	Yellow
3rd sqn.	301 on	Light blue
4th sqn.	401 on	Orange
5th sqn.	501 on	Light green
6th sqn.	601 on	Black
7th sqn.	701 on	Maroon

The Air Wing Commander's aircraft carried fin markings incorporating all colours.

On carrier-based aircraft, including those of the US Marine Corps, the first letter reflects the broad theatre of operations. Carrier Air Wings operating from the Atlantic coast are coded A, those from the Pacific coast N. The second letter is specific to the Carrier Air Wing, and thus the same two-letter combination is carried by all embarked units on any given carrier. Similarly, on shore-based aircraft, the first letter indicates the home base coast, and for each type of unit the initial letter is the same. A-4F 155022/401NP was thus the unit commander's aircraft of VA-164 from USS *Hancock*.

The French Air Force uses an alphanumeric system. The number(s) indicate the Escadre (Wing). Separated by a hyphen, the letters indicate the escadron (squadron; first letter) and the individual aircraft (second letter). The first-letter (squadron) codes are changed occasionally. Serials carried by aircraft in French military service are sequential, peculiar only to type and generally of up to three digits. They are normally worn in small characters on the fin or rudder. As examples, Mirage F.1C serial 19 was coded 12-ZB (as aircraft B of the 3rd escadron of Escadre de Chasse 12), while aircraft serial 20 was coded 12-YD (aircraft D of the 1st escadron of the same Wing).

II. British Military Aircraft Designations

Most aircraft in British military use are given service names usually in keeping with their roles. Fighters have aggressive names, like Hunter, Swift, Sabre, Meteor and Venom. Bombers, to the late 1940s, had city or town names (Lancaster, Lincoln, Canberra) then aggressive names like Buccaneer, Valiant, Tornado. Transports are given town or city names (Hastings, Valetta,

Andover), except where a type already in commercial use has been taken into service (Comet, VC-10, BAe 146). Trainers have appropriate names like Balliol, Provost and Varsity. Overseas purchases normally retain their original names (Beaver, Sioux, Hercules). Other types are given a role-appropriate name (Neptune, Shackleton) or, in some cases, a name reflecting flying characteristics (Sycamore, Dragonfly). There are many exceptions to these generalized rules, such as Hawk, Dominie and Auster (the last being the manufacturer's name). Some names are re-used after a suitable period (Whirlwind, Bulldog, Tornado).

Designations reflect function and are normally abbreviated to an initial letter or letters (F for Fighter, T for Trainer). Each major variant is given a sequential mark number, occasionally with a letter suffix to indicate a minor variation (Hawk T. Mk. 1A, Buccaneer S. Mk. 2B). In addition, letter suffixes are used to denote modification – K for tanker (e.g., Hercules C. Mk. 1K), P (Probe) for in-flight refuelling (Nimrod MR. Mk. 2P) or T for dual control (Canberra B. Mk. 2T).

The mark numbers were in roman numerals until 1944, after which arabic numerals began to come into use. However, the original designations were frequently kept until the aircraft went out of service. Thus the Tempest F. Mk. VI was often referred to as such until 1953; conversely, in many official records the Mosquito FB. Mk. VI is referred to as the Mosquito FB. Mk. 6. Throughout this book, every attempt has been made to use contemporary forms abbreviated. The strictly correct form of designation of, say, a Hunter fighter, would be, for example, Hawker Hunter Fighter Mark 6. In practice this would be abbreviated to Hunter F. Mk. 6. For reasons of space only, the further abbreviated form Hunter F.6 is used throughout. A full list of designations in use since 1945 is set out below.

AEW	Airborne Early Warning
AH	Army Helicopter
AL	Army Liaison
AOP	Air Observation Post
AS	Anti-Submarine
ASR	Air Sea Rescue
B	Bomber
B(I)	Bomber (Intruder); Bomber (Interdictor)
BK	Bomber Tanker
BPR	Bomber Photo Reconnaissance
B(PR)K	Bomber (Photo Reconnaissance) Tanker
B(SR)	Bomber (Strategic Reconnaissance)
C	Transport
CC	Communications
C(PR)	Transport (Photo Reconnaissance)
D	Drone
E	Electronic
ECM	Electronic Counter Measures
F	Fighter
FAW	Fighter All-Weather
FB	Fighter Bomber
FB(T)	Fighter Bomber (Trainer)
FG	Fighter Ground Attack
FGA	Fighter Ground Attack
FGR	Fighter Ground Attack Reconnaissance
FR	Fighter Reconnaissance
FRS	Fighter Reconnaissance Strike
GA	Ground Attack
GR	General Reconnaissance (pre-1954)
GR	Ground Attack Reconnaissance
HAR	Helicopter Air Rescue
HAS	Helicopter Anti-Submarine
HC	Helicopter Transport
HCC	Helicopter Communications
HR	Helicopter Search and Rescue
HT	Helicopter Trainer
HU	Helicopter Utility
K	Tanker
Met	Meteorological
MR	Maritime Reconnaissance
MRR	Maritime Radar Reconnaissance
NF	Night Fighter
PR	Photographic Reconnaissance
R	Reconnaissance
S	Strike
SR	Strategic Reconnaissance
T	Trainer
TT	Target Tug
TX	Training Glider
U	Unpiloted (target drone)
W	Weather

III. United States Military Aircraft Designations

Since 1962, all United States services have used a common system of designations based on the USAF system. The central component is the type letter, for example C (Transport). The next element is a numerical type sequence number: thus the 130th transport design (since 1925) is the C-130. Each major development incorporated as a new model is given a sequential letter suffix, the second model of the C-130 becoming the C-130B.

Variations in the role within a particular model are given a letter prefix. Hence a version of the C-130B converted for search and rescue became the HC-130B. A second series of prefix letters may be used to designate status; the prototype C-130 was designated YC-130A. Finally there are block numbers and manufacturers' codes, the former indicating minor variations and the latter the factory of manufacture. Block numbers are sequential, but they normally progress by fives or tens. Thus one version of the C-130 was the C-130B-70-LM indicating the seventh block of the C-130B with minor variations and built by Lockheed Marietta. In practice, these last two elements are rarely used.

The type sequence numbers started from 1 again in 1962. In addition, some type letters changed. Many type letters also changed in 1948, when, for example, the P-51D became the F-51D. Occasionally, type letters are misleading in respect of role (U-2 indicating Utility when the aircraft was a reconnaissance type) or outside the approved range. The SR-71 is a case in point. The type was originally designated A-11, which was the manufacturer's type number. In service it was properly designated F-12, but the reconnaissance version was given the improper designation SR-71.

A full list of the pre-1948, 1948–1962 and post-1962 type letters is set out below.

Role	Pre-1948	1948–62	Post-1962
Airship	–	–	Z
Amphibian	OA	A	–
Anti-submarine	–	–	S
Attack	A	–	A
Advanced Trainer	AT	T	T
Aerial Target	OQ	Q	–
Aerial Target Manned	PQ	Q	–
Bomber	B	B	B
Basic Trainer	BT	T	T
Electronic Surveillance	–	R	E
Fighter	P	F	F
Fuel Carrying Glider	FG	G	–
Glide Bomb	GB	–	–
Glide Torpedo	GT	–	–
Glider	CG, FG	G	–
Helicopter	R	H	H
Jet-propelled Bomb	JB	–	–
Liaison	L	L	U
Observation	O	L, R, U	O
Observation Amphibian	OA	A	–
Patrol	OA	A, R	P
Photographic	F	R	R
Powered Glider	PG	G	–
Primary Trainer	PT	T	T

Pursuit (Fighter)	P	F	F
Reconnaissance	F	R	R
Research	S	X	X
Rotary Wing	R	H	H
Supersonic Research	S	X	X
Tactical Support	A	F, B	A
Target, Flying Model	OQ	Q	–
Trainer	AT, BT, PT	T	T
Trainer Glider	TG	G	–
Transport	C	C	C
Transport Glider	CG	G	–
Utility	C, L	U	U
V/STOL	–	V	V

Prefix letters have changed less over time and a schedule is set out below.

Role variant	Pre-1962	Post-1962
Anti-submarine	–	S
Calibration	A	–
Cold Weather Operations	–	L
Drone Director	D	D
Electronics	E	E
Experimental	X	X
Grounded Permanently	–	G
Liaison	L	–
Medical Evacuation	M	–
Missile Carrier	–	M
Obsolete	Z	–
Observation	–	O
Parasite Carrier	G	–
Passenger Transport	P	V
Photographic	F, R	R
Project	–	Z
Prototype, Service Test	Y	Y
Radio-Controlled Drone	Q	Q
Reconnaissance	R	R
Search and Rescue	–	H
Special Tests, Permanent	N	N
Special Tests, Temporary	J	J
Staff Transport	P	V
Tactical Support	–	A
Tanker	K	K
Trainer	T	T
Transport	C	C
Utility	U	U
Weather Reconnaissance	W	W

UNITED STATES NAVY AND MARINE CORPS (PRE-1962)

Navy and Marine Corps designations focused on the manufacturer, for whom a letter code was used. Thus Lockheed designs used the letter V. Designs from a manufacturer were then allotted a sequential number prefix which was in turn prefixed by a role-related letter. The Neptune maritime patrol aircraft was designated P (patrol) 2 (second design from) V (Lockheed), or P2V. Each major variant was then assigned a hyphenated suffix number, for example P2V-6 being the sixth Neptune model. Finally, role-related suffix letters were used to denote variants within the model: the missile carrier version of the P2V-6 was the P2V-6M (when the uniform system was introduced, this designation changed to MP-2F). The manufacturers' codes are set out below.

Bell	L	Interstate	R
Boeing-Vertol	B	Kaman	K
Cessna	E	Lockheed	O, V
Consolidated (Convair)	Y	Martin	M
De Havilland Canada	C	McDonnell	H
Douglas	D	North American	J
Fairchild	Q	Piasecki	P
Globe	G	Piper	O
Goodyear	G	Radioplane	D, R
Grumman	F	Sikorsky	S
Gyrodyne	N	Temco	T
Hiller	E	Vought (LTV)	V

Role prefix letters included the following list, the more usual of which have also been used as suffix letters:

A	Attack	KD	Target Drone
DS	Anti-Submarine Drone	M	Missile
F	Fighter	O	Observation
G	Tanker	P	Patrol
HC	Helicopter, Crane	R	Transport
HJ, HU	Helicopter, Utility	RO	Rotocycle
HN, HT	Helicopter, Training	S	Anti-Submarine
HO	Helicopter, Observation	T	Trainer
HR	Helicopter, Transport	U	Unmanned Drone; Utility (from 1955)
HS	Helicopter, Anti-Submarine	W	Electronic Search
J	Utility (to 1955)	ZP	Airship, Patrol
JR	Utility Transport	ZS	Airship, Anti-Submarine
K	Radio controlled		

IV. United States Aircraft Designations, Manufacturers and Names

Designation	Manufacturer	Name
A-1	Douglas	Skyraider
A-3	Douglas	Skywarrior
A-4	Douglas	Skyhawk
A-6	Grumman	Intruder, Prowler
A-7	Vought	Corsair II
A-10	Fairchild Republic	Thunderbolt II
A-11	Lockheed	See F-12, SR-71
A-16	Grumman	Albatross
A-37	Cessna	Dragonfly
B-17	Boeing	Flying Fortress
B-24	Consolidated	Liberator
B-25	North American	Mitchell
B-26	Douglas	Invader
B-29	Boeing	Superfortress
B-36	Convair	Peacemaker
B-45	North American	Tornado
B-47	Boeing	Stratojet
B-50	Boeing	Superfortress
B-57	Martin	Night Intruder (Canberra)
B-66	Douglas	Destroyer
B-69	Lockheed	Neptune
C-5	Lockheed	Galaxy
C-9	Douglas	Nightingale, Skytrain II
C-10	McDonnell Douglas	Extender
C-45	Beechcraft	Expeditor
C-46	Curtiss	Commando
C-47	Douglas	Skytrain, Dakota
C-54	Douglas	Skymaster
C-78	Cessna	Bobcat
C-82	Fairchild	Packet
C-97	Boeing	Stratofreighter
C-119	Fairchild	Flying Boxcar
C-123	Fairchild	Provider
C-124	Douglas	Globemaster II
C-130	Lockheed	Hercules
C-135	Boeing	Stratotanker, Stratolifter
C-141	Lockheed	Starlifter
E-1	Grumman	Tracer
E-2	Grumman	Hawkeye
E-3	Boeing	Sentry
F-4	McDonnell Douglas	Phantom II
F-5	Northrop	Freedom Fighter
F-5	Lockheed	Lightning
F-6	Douglas	Skyray
F-6	North American	Mustang (RF-51)
F-8	Vought	Crusader
F-10	Douglas	Skyknight
F-12	Lockheed	See A-11, SR-71
F-14	Grumman	Tomcat

F-15	McDonnell Douglas	Eagle	A3D	Douglas	Skywarrior
F-16	General Dynamics	Fighting Falcon	A3J	North American	Vigilante
F-47	Republic	Thunderbolt	A4D	Douglas	Skyhawk
F-51	North American	Mustang	AD	Douglas	Skyraider
F-80	Lockheed	Shooting Star	AF	Grumman	Guardian
F-82	North American	Twin Mustang	AJ	North American	Savage
F-84	Republic	Thunderjet, Thunderstreak, Thunderflash	AM	Martin	Mauler
			AU	Vought	Corsair
F-86	North American	Sabre	F2H	McDonnell	Banshee
F-94	Lockheed	Starfire	F3D	Douglas	Skyknight
F-100	North American	Super Sabre	F3H	McDonnell	Demon
F-101	McDonnell	Voodoo	F4D	Douglas	Skyray
F-102	Convair	Delta Dagger	F4U	Vought	Corsair
F-104	Lockheed	Starfighter	F6F	Grumman	Hellcat
F-105	Republic	Thunderchief	F7F	Grumman	Tigercat
F-111	General Dynamics	'Aardvark'	F7U	Vought	Cutlass
F/A-18	McDonnell Douglas	Hornet	F8F	Grumman	Bearcat
H-1	Bell	Iroquois, HueyCobra, SeaCobra	F8U	Vought	Crusader
			F9F	Grumman	Panther, Cougar
H-3	Sikorsky	Sea King, 'Jolly Green Giant', Pelican	F11F	Grumman	Tiger
			FG	Goodyear	Corsair
H-5	Sikorsky	Dragonfly	FJ	North American	Fury
H-6	Hughes	Cayuse	HO3S	Sikorsky	Dragonfly
H-13	Bell	Sioux	HO4S	Sikorsky	(Model S.55)
H-19	Sikorsky	Chickasaw	HO5S	Sikorsky	(Model S.52)
H-21	Piasecki	Workhorse, Shawnee	HOK	Kaman	Huskie
H-23	Hiller	Raven	HOS	Sikorsky	Hoverfly
H-25	Piasecki	Retriever	HR2S	Sikorsky	(S-56)
H-34	Sikorsky	Choctaw	HRB	Boeing-Vertol	Sea Knight
H-46	Vertol	Sea Knight	HRP	Piasecki	Rescuer
H-47	Boeing-Vertol	Chinook	HRS	Sikorsky	(Model S.55)
H-53	Sikorsky	Sea Stallion, 'Super Jolly'	HSS	Sikorsky	Seabat
			HTE	Hiller	(Model 12)
H-58	Bell	Kiowa	HTL	Bell	(Model 47)
H-60	Sikorsky	Black Hawk, Sea Hawk	HUP	Piasecki	Retriever
			HUS	Sikorsky	Seahorse
L-4	Piper	Cub	J2F	Grumman	Duck
L-5	Stinson	Sentinel	JRB	Beechcraft	Expeditor
L-17	Ryan	Navion	JRC	Cessna	Bobcat
L-18	Piper	Super Cub	JRF	Grumman	Goose
L-19	Cessna	Bird Dog	OE	Cessna	Bird Dog
L-20	De Havilland Canada	Beaver	OY	Stinson	Sentinel
O-2	Cessna	Super Skymaster	P2V	Lockheed	Neptune
P-2	Lockheed	Neptune	P4M	Martin	Mercator
P-3	Lockheed	Orion	P5M	Martin	Marlin
P-38	Lockheed	Lightning	PB4Y	Consolidated	Liberator, Privateer
P-47	Republic	Thunderbolt	PBM	Martin	Mariner
P-51	North American	Mustang	PBY	Consolidated	Catalina
P-63	Bell	Kingcobra	PV	Lockheed	Ventura, Harpoon, Lodestar
P-80	Lockheed	Shooting Star			
S-2	Grumman	Tracker	R4D	Douglas	Skytrain
S-3	Lockheed	Viking	R4Q	Fairchild	Flying Boxcar
SA-16	Grumman	Albatross	R4Y	Convair	Samaritan
SR-71	Lockheed	'Blackbird'	R5C	Curtiss	Commando
T-6	North American	Texan, Harvard	R5D	Douglas	Skymaster
T-11	Beechcraft	Kansan	R6D	Douglas	Liftmaster
T-17	Stearman	Kaydet	S2F	Grumman	Tracker
T-19	Fairchild	Cornell	SB2C	Curtiss	Helldiver
T-28	North American	Trojan, Fennec	SBD	Douglas	Dauntless
T-33	Lockheed	'Tweety Bird', 'T-Bird'	SNB	Beechcraft	Expeditor
T-34	Beechcraft	Mentor	SNJ	North American	Texan
T-41	Cessna	Mescalero	TBF	Grumman	Avenger
TR-1	Lockheed	–	TBM	Eastern (GM)	Avenger
U-2	Lockheed	'Dragon Lady'	UF	Grumman	Albatross
U-21	Beechcraft	King Air	W2F	Grumman	Hawkeye
V-1	Grumman	Mohawk	WF	Grumman	Tracer
V-10	North American	Bronco	WV	Lockheed	Warning Star

V. United States Navy and Marine Corps Unit Names

HC-1	Pacific Fleet Angels	**RVAH-1**	Tigers	**VP-1**	Fleet's Finest	**VX-1**	ASW Pioneers
		VC-1	Unique Antiques	**VQ-1**	Batmen	**HS-2**	Golden Falcons
HS-1	Seahorses	**VF-1**	Wolfpack	**VQ-1**	World Watchers	**VC-2**	Blue Falcons
HU-1	Fleet Angels	**VMO-1**	Yazoo	**VSF-1**	War Eagles	**VF-2**	Bounty Hunters

Designation	Nickname	Designation	Nickname	Designation	Nickname	Designation	Nickname
VMAQ-2	Playboys	VS-21	Red Tails	VA-44	Hornets	VAW-114	Screaming Hawks
VMO-2	Hostage	VA-22	Redcocks	VP-44	Golden Pelicans	VF-114	Aardvarks
HAL-3	Seawolves	VP-22	Blue Goose	VA-45	Blackbirds	VF-114	Executioners
HC-3	Packrats	VS-22	Checkmates	VP-45	Pelicans	VA-115	Arabs
HS-3	Tridents	VA-23	Black Knights	VP-45	Red Darts	VA-115	Chargers
RVAH-3	Sea Dragons	VP-23	Sea Hawks	VA-46	Clansmen	VA-115	Eagles
VC-3	Iron Men	VS-23	Black Cats	VP-46	Gray Knights	VAW-115	Sentinels
VC-3	Targeteers	VF-24	Corsairs	VP-47	Golden Swordsmen	VMFA-115	Silver Eagles
VF(AW)-3	Blue Nemesis	VF-24	Red Checkertails	VP-48	Boomerangers	VAW-116	Sun Kings
HS-4	Black Knights	VP-24	Batmen	VP-49	Woodpeckers	VAW-117	Gamecocks
VAL-4	Black Ponies	VR-24	World's Biggest Little Airline	VP-50	Ancient Mariners	VAW-117	Wall Bangers
VP-4	Skinny Dragons	VS-24	Duty Cats	VP-50	Blue Dragons	RVAW-120	Hummers
VX-4	Vanguards	VA-25	Fist of the Fleet	VRC-50	Cod-Fish Airlines	VAW-121	Bluetails
HS-5	Night Dippers	VP-26	Tridents	VF-51	Screaming Eagles	VF-121	Pacemakers
RVAH-5	Fast Photos	VA-27	Royal Maces	VA-52	Knight Riders	VMA-121	Green Knights
RVAH-5	Savage Sons	VS-28	Hukkers	VA-55	Warhorses	VA-122	Flying Eagles
VC-5	Checkertails	VS-29	Screaming Dragonfires	VA-56	Champions	VAW-122	Steeljaws
VC-5	Workhorse of the Fleet	VS-29	Vikings	VP-56	Dragons	VMFA-122	Crusaders
VP-5	Mad Foxes	HSL-30	Neptune's Horsemen	VF-62	Boomerangs	VAW-123	Cyclops
VX-5	Vampires	VP-30	Crow's Nest	VF-62	Gladiators	VAW-123	Screw Tops
HC-6	Chargers	VP-30	Sea Hawks	VFP-63	Eyes of the Fleet	VF-123	Blue Racers
HC-6	Mercuries	VRC-30	Truckin' Traders	VA-65	First of the Fleet	VAW-124	Bear Aces
HS-6	Indians	VS-30	Diamond Cutters	VA-65	Tigers	VAW-124	Bullseye Hummers
RVAH-6	Fleurs	VS-30	Sea Tigers	VA-66	Mod Squad	VF-124	Gunfighters
VC-6	Skeeters	H&MS-31	31st Aggressors	VA-66	Waldomen	VF-124	Moonshiners
VMO-6	Tomcats	HSL-31	Archangels	VF-71	Hell's Angels	VF-124	Gunfighters
VP-6	Blue Sharks	VF-31	Felix	VA-72	Blue Hawks	VMA-124	Whistling Death
VXE-6	Puckered Penguins	VF-31	Tomcatters	VF-73	Jesters	VA-125	Rough Raiders
HS-7	Big Dippers	VP-31	Genies	VF-74	Be-Devilers	VAW-125	Tiger Tails
HS-7	Shamrocks	VRF-31	Storkline	VA-75	Sunday Punchers	VAW-125	Torchbearers
RVAH-7	Peacemakers	VS-31	Top Cats	VA-76	Spirits	VA-126	Trailblazers
VAH-7	Go-Devils	HSL-32	Tridents	VA-81	Sunliners	VAW-126	Seahawks
HS-8	Eight Ballers	VF-32	Swordsmen	VF-81	Crusaders	VF-126	Sea Hawks
VAH-8	Fireballers	VS-32	Norsemen	VA-82	Marauders	VA-127	Batmen
VC-8	Redtails	VS-32	Yellow Tails	VF-82	Iron Men	VA-127	Royal Blues
VP-8	Tigers	HSL-33	Sea Snakes	VA-83	Rampagers	VA-128	Golden Intruders
VXN-8	World Travelers	VAQ-33	Fire Birds	VF-84	Fighting 84	VAQ-129	Vikings
HS-9	Sea Griffins	VAW-33	Night Hawkers	VF-84	Jolly Rogers	VAQ-130	Zappers
RVAH-9	Hoot Owls	VC-33	Night Hawks	VA-85	Black Falcons	VAQ-131	Blue Bandits
VP-9	Golden Eagles	VF-33	Argonauts	VA-86	Diamond Backs	VAQ-131	Lancers
HS-10	Task Masters	VF-33	Starfighters	VA-86	Sidewinders	VAQ-132	Scorpions
VC-10	Crusaders	VF-33	Tarsiers	VA-87	Golden Warriors	VAQ-133	Wizards
VP-10	Red Lancers	VS-33	Screwbirds	VF-91	Red Lightnings	VAQ-134	Garuda
HC-11	Gunbearers	HSL-34	Green Checkers	VF-92	Silver Kings	VA-135	Thunderbirds
HS-11	Dragon Slayers	VA-34	Blue Blasters	VA-93	Blue Blazers	VAQ-135	Ravens
HS-11	Sub Seekers	HSL-35	Magicians	VA-93	Ravens	VAQ-136	Gauntlets
RVAH-11	Checkertails	VA-35	Black Panthers	VA-94	Shrikes	VAQ-137	Rooks
VF-11	Red Rippers	HSL-36	Lamp Lighters	VA-95	Green Lizards	VAQ-138	Yellowjackets
VP-11	Proud Pegasus	VA-36	Road Runners	VF-96	Falcons	VF-141	Iron Angels
HM-12	Seadragons	HSL-37	Easy Riders	VF-97	Warhawks	VF-142	Ghostriders
HS-12	Wyverns	VA-37	Bulls	VF-101	Grim Reapers	VMA-142	Flying 'Gators
RVAH-12	Speartips	VS-37	Patient Professionals	VF-102	Diamond Backs	VF-143	Pukin' Dogs
VA-12	Flying Ubangis	VS-37	Rooster Tails	VF-102	Prowlers	VA-144	Roadrunners
VA-12	Kiss of Death	VS-37	Sawbucks	VF-103	Sluggers	VF-144	Bitter Birds
RVAH-13	Bats	VS-38	Claw Clan	VA-104	Hell's Archers	VF-144	Roadrunners
VF-13	Aggressors	VS-38	Red Griffins	VA-105	Gunslingers	VA-145	Swordsmen
HM-14	Vanguard	VP-40	Marlins	VA-106	Gladiators	VA-146	Blue Diamonds
HS-14	Chargers	VP-40	Swordfishes	RVAW-110	Firebirds	VA-147	Argonauts
VF-14	Top Hatters	VF-41	Black Aces	VAW-111	Hunters	VA-147	Jasons
HS-15	Red Lions	VS-41	Shamrocks	VF-111	Sundowners	VF-151	Vigilantes
VA-15	Valions	VA-42	Green Pawns	VA-112	Bombing Broncos	VA-152	Wild Aces
HM-16	Seahawks	VA-43	Challengers	VAW-112	Golden Hawks	VF-152	Blue Tail Files
VP-16	Eagles	VF-43	Challengers	VA-113	Stingers	VA-154	Black Knights
VP-17	White Lightning	VA-44	Blackbirds	VAW-113	Black Hawks/ Eagles	VA-155	Silver Foxes
VP-19	Big Red			VAW-114	Hormel Hawgs	HMH-161	Phrog Phlyers
VAH-21	Road Runners					VF-161	Chargers
VF-21	Freelancers					VF-162	Hunters

HMM-163	Ridge Runners	VF-211	Checkmates	VMFA-235	Death's Angels	VMA-332	Polka Dots
HMM-164	Flying Clamors	VF-211	Red Checkertails	VMA-242	Batmen	VMFA-333	Shamrocks
VA-164	Ghost Riders	VMA-211	Wake Island	VMA-251	Thunderbolts	VMFA-333	Triple Trey
VA-165	Boomers		Avengers	HMM-262	Flying Tigers	HMH-363	Red Lions
VF-171	Aces	VA-212	Rampant Raiders	HML-267	Black Aces	VMFA-451	Warlords
VF-172	Blue Bolts	VMFA-212	Lancers	VA-304	Fire Birds	HMH-463	Heavy Haulers
VA-174	Hell's Razors	VF-213	Black Lions	VMA-311	Tomcats	VMA-513	Flying
VA-176	Thunderbolts	VMF-214	Black Sheep	VMA-312	Checkerboard		Nightmares
VF-191	Satan's Kittens	VA-215	Barn Owls		Squadron	VMFA-531	Gray Ghosts
VA-192	Golden Dragons	VA-216	Black Diamonds	VFMA-314	Black Knights	VMA-533	Hawks
VF-193	Ghost Riders	VMA-223	Bulldogs	VMFA-321	Black Barons	VA-702	Rustlers
VF-194	Red Lightnings	VMA-224	Bengals	VMFA-321	Hell's Angels	VS-935	Liberty Bells
VA-195	Dam Busters	VMA-231	Ace of Spades	VMA-322	Gamecocks		
VA-196	Flying Devils	VMFA-232	Red Devils	VMF-323	Death Rattlers		
VA-196	Main Battery	VMGR-234	Thundering Herd	VMA-331	Bumblebees		

VI. Projects, Operations and Call-Signs, Vietnam, 1961–1975

AHB — Assault Helicopter Battalion. US Army, 1965.

AHC — Assault Helicopter Company. US Army, 1965.

ALCC — Airlift Control Center. 1965.

APD — Airborne Personnel Detector (equipment for identifying ammonia smells). 1967.

ASHB — Assault Support Helicopter Battalion. US Army, 1965.

AWADS — Adverse Weather Aerial Delivery System.

Able Mabel — Tactical reconnaissance by 45 and 15 TRS over Laos and South Vietnam. 7 Nov. 1961.

Alleycat — Call-sign of C-130E of 7 ACCS (night), generally over northern Laos. 1965.

Alpha — Large (approx. 30-aircraft) set piece strike by USN against North Vietnamese target. March 1966.

Alpha Lima — Takhli air control call-sign.

Arc Light — B-52 raids. June 1965.

Attleboro — Combined US and ARVN operation 50 miles north of Saigon. 14 Sept. 1966.

BUFF — Common name for B-52 (Big Ugly Fat F***er).

Banish Beach — Forest denial project; C-130 used to drop 'fused' fuel drums to destroy jungle through burning. Believed to have been unsuccessful. 1965.

Barn Door — Co-ordination of USAF and VNAF strike and reconnaissance sorties in South Vietnam. 1 Jan. 1962.

Barrel Roll — Armed reconnaissance strikes on Ho Chi Minh Trail in Laos. 14 Dec. 1964.

Batcat — Common name for EC-121.

Beast — Common name for B-52.

Belfry Express — Unsuccessful USN attempt at drone operations from USS *Ranger*. Nov. 1969.

Bell Tone — Deployment of F-100 and F-102 to Thailand. Dec. 1960.

Big Eagle — A-26A programme, generally over Laos. Det. 9, 1 ACW, from Nakhon Phanom (eight aircraft), lasting for four months. 8 June 1966.

Big Eye — 552 AEWCW EC-121D warning and control operations until March 1967. April 1965.

Big Mother — Common name for USN SH-3 rescue helicopter. 1965.

Big Team — 55 SRW KC-135R and RC-135C elint operations ex Kadena. Sept. 1964.

Black Crow — ASD-5 electronic emission detector ('Pave Pronto' programme). 1967.

Black Spot — NC-123K bombship project using FLIR and LLLTV. 1969.

Blackeye — VNAF A-1G project to fit belly observation windows. 1966.

Blind Bat — Common name for AC-130. 1967.

Blue Bandit — Common name for MiG-21.

Blue Blazer — USMC F-4 night missions.

Blue Chip — Call-sign of 7th AF command centre.

Blue Springs — 4025 RS DC130A drone operational deployment to Bien Hoa. Aug. 1964.

Blue Team — Number of UH-1D or H troop carrying helicopters. 1965.

Blue Tree — Medium level PR over North Vietnam pre- and post-strike. 3 March 1965.

Bolo — Operation by 8 TFW to draw MiGs into combat. 2 Jan. 1967.

Brave Bull — Signal monitoring by EC-97 from Tan Son Nhut. 28 Feb. 1963.

Brigham — Udorn air control call-sign.

Brown Cradles — Deployment of 41 TRS RB-66 to Takhli with ECM for jamming fire control radars. April 1965.

Buffalo Hunter — 4025 RS AQM-34L/U PR drone operation.

Bugle Note — Procedure for dividing target areas into 1 × 2km boxes for three-cell B-52 attack using 'Combat Skyspot' techniques. 15 Feb. 1968.

Bullet Shot — B-52 build-up against increased North Vietnamese infiltration. Feb. 1972.

Bullshit bomber — Common name for C-47 used on psychological warfare missions. 1965.

Bumble Bug — 4025 RS drone operation.

Butterfly — Call-sign of FACs in Laos until replaced by Raven. 1964

CAB — Combat Aviation Battalion (US Army). 1965.

CAG — Combat Aviation Group (US Army). 1966.

CDS — Container Delivery System (C-130).

CIDG — Civilian Irregular Defence Group (South Vietnamese élite Special Forces). 1964.

CRIMP — Consolidated Republic of Vietnam Armed Forces Improvement and Modernization Program. 1968.

CSAB — Combat Support Aviation Battalion (US Army). 1965.

Candle — Call-sign of C-123K flareships of 606 SOS. 1966.

Candy Machine — Air defence of South Vietnam by F-102s of 509 FIS. 31 May 1963.

Carolina Moon — C-130 mine attack on Thanh Hoa bridge. May 1966.

Cedar Falls — Major operation by 1st and 25th Infantry Divisions with airmobile support in 'Iron Triangle'. 8 Jan 1967.

Charging Sparrow — Operational reliability tests in South-East Asia of AIM-7. Dec. 1966.

Chieu Hoi — Open Arms psychological warfare programme over South Vietnam. 1965.

Clementine — Call-sign of UH-2 SAR helicopters. 1965.

Cobra — Common name for UH-1 gunship. 1966.

Cobra Hood — AEW and electronic reconnaissance operations by EC-47s. 1965.

College Eye — Revised name for 'Big Eye'. March 1967.

Combat Angel	AQM-34 project.
Combat Apple	82 SRS RC-135M elint and MiG warning project. Sept. 1967.
Combat Dawn	AQM-34R drone project (147TE/TF model).
Combat Dragon	Evaluation of A-37A with 604 ACS. 26 July 1967.
Combat Hornet	AC-119 Gunship project. 1968.
Combat Lancer	Evaluation of F-111A by 428 TFS. 15 March 1968.
Combat Lightning	Communications relay operation by KC-135As and later EC-135Ls for strike and SAR. 1966.
Combat Martin	44 TFS VHF jammer operations to 1971. 1968.
Combat Proof	Blind bombing by triangulation using MSQ-77 ground radars. 1966.
Combat Sent	RC-135U elint project. 1967.
Combat Skyspot	Later name for Combat Proof. 1966.
Combat Talon	C-130E-I (MC-130E) project (support aircraft for US Special Forces). 1966.
Combat Trap	Landing zone clearance using 10,000lb M121 bomb dropped by CH-54A. 1966.
Commando Hunt	Air strikes against Ho Chi Minh Trail (replaced 'Tiger Hound'). 15 Nov. 1968.
Commando Nail	F-105F fitted with R-14A radar for all-weather and night flying. 1967.
Commando Saber	High speed 'Fast Mover' FAC flown by F-100F and TF-102A. June 1967.
Commando Scarf	C-130 munitions drops in southern Laos.
Commando Scrimmage	'Training' sorties flown by USAF out of Thailand. Aug. 1973.
Commando Vault	C-130 missions involving the dropping of M121 or BLU-82 heavy bombs to blast out clearings normally for helicopter landing sites.
Compass Arrow	AQM-91A drone project (also known as Fire Fly). 1971.
Compass Bin	AQM-34 chaff dispenser project.
Compass Cookie	4025 RS drone operation.
Compass Eagle	'Patricia Lynn' IR equipment project. 1968.
Compass Haste	'Patricia Lynn' IR equipment project. 1967.
Compass Sight	'Patricia Lynn' IR equipment project. 1967.
Constant Guard	Movement of USAF units to South-East Asia in response to North Vietnamese invasion. 31 March 1972.
Credible Chase	Light Gunship project AU-23A and AU-24A, sold to RTAF and Khmer AF respectively. 1971.
Cricket	Call-sign of 7 ACCS C-130E daytime, generally over northern Laos. 1967.
Crown	Original call-sign for HC-130P. 1967.
Deuce	Common USMC name for CH-37 (ex HR2S-1).
Disco	Call-sign of EC-121D.
Dixie Station	Carrier postion 9°30' N, 108°00'E off South Vietnam. 1964.
Dodge City	Common name for Hanoi.
Dragon Lady	U-2 flights by 4080 SRW from Bien Hoa. 31 Dec. 1963.
Dragon's Jaw	Ham Rung bridge at Thanh Hoa.
Dragonseed	Small anti-personnel mines sown over Ho Chi Minh Trail by C-130.
Dragonship	Common name for AC-47 gunship. 1965.
Dressy Lady	Korat air control call-sign.
Drut	Common name for EF-10.
Duck Hook	Infiltration of LRRPs and CIDG into North Vietnam by C-123 out of Nha Trang.
Duel Blade	Revised name for Dye Marker sensor laying on Ho Chi Minh Trail. 1967.
Dump Truck	Revised name for anti-personnel element of 'Muscle Shoals'. 1967.
Dust-Off	Call-sign of UH-1D medevac helicopters. 1965.
Dutch Mill	Infiltration Surveillance Center at Nakhom Phanom to co-ordinate data from sensors laid on Ho Chi Minh Trail as part of 'Igloo White' project. 1968.

Dye Marker	Revised name for Illinois City sensor-laying on Ho Chi Minh Trail; followed by 'Duel Blade'. July 1967.
Eagle Pull	Final evacuation of US personnel from Phnom Penh. 11 April 1975.
Endsweep	Mine clearance of North Vietnamese ports by USN and USMC. Feb. 1973.
Enhance	US programme to re-equip South Vietnamese Armed Forces. 1972.
Enhance Plus	Extension of 'Enhance'. 1972.
Fact Sheet	C-130E leaflet drops over North Vietnam, normally in association with a strike, to 1970 (handled by 6315 Ops. Gp., later 374 TAW out of Ubon). 14 April 1965.
Farm Gate	First USAF support by 4400 CCTS ('Jungle Jim') to VNAF and ARVN. 26 Dec. 1961.
Fat Albert	Large North Vietnamese SAM, possibly SA-4. 22 July 1972.
Feet Wet	Term meaning over sea as opposed to land.
Ferret	Original code-name for 'Wild Weasel' project. Sept. 1965.
Field Goal	RT-33 reconnaissance missions over Laos. April 1961.
Fire Fly	4025 RS drone operation in connection with SA-2 intelligence (AQM-91A drones also under 'Compass Arrow'). 1971.
Firefly	UH-1 fitted with cluster of C-123 landing lights for night illumination. 1965.
Flaming Dart	First US retaliatory strikes on Dong Hoi barracks. 7 Feb. 1965.
Flaming Dart II	Second US retaliatory strikes on Chanh Hoa barracks. 11 Feb. 1965.
Flycatcher	US supply of aircraft to Khmer Air Force. 1971.
Fogbound	USMC VMCJ-1 EF-10B ECM operations. 12 April 1965.
Foreign Legion	KC-135A deployment to Clark AB. 1965.
Frag	Assign (fragment) targets to specific aircraft or units.
Freedom Deal	Secret bombing of Cambodia by, mainly, B-52s under FAC, (succeeded Operation 'Menu'). 26 May 1970.
Freedom Porch	B-52 attacks on Hanoi and Haiphong. 21 April 1972.
Freedom Train	Resumption of the air war. 6 April 1972.
Frequent Wind	Final evacuation of Saigon. 29 April 1975.
GPES	Ground Proximity Extraction System.
Gabby	Call-sign of psywar C-47. 1965.
Game Warden	USN riverine operations in the Mekong Delta. 1 April 1966.
Giant Cobra	Deployment of KC-135A to U-Tapao. Aug. 1966.
Giant Dragon	Revised name for 'Senior Book' U-2 operations. 1966.
Giant Scale	SR-71A Vietnam-related operations. 1967.
Go-Go Bird	Armed ACH-47A. 1967.
Gooney Bird	Common name for C-47.
Gunship II	AC-130 gunship project. 1966.
Gunship III	AC-119 gunship project. 1967.
Hawk Eye	EC-47N radio direction-finding operations against Viet Cong radio communications.
Hell Jelly	USMC common name for napalm.
High Drink	Refuelling of hovering USAF rescue helicopters by USN ships in Gulf of Tonkin. 1966.
Hillsborough	Call-sign of C-130Es of 7 ACCS, generally over South Vietnam or southern Laos. 1965.
Hilo Hattie	Signal monitoring by EC-54 from Tan Son Nhut. 20 April 1962.
Hog	Common name for heavily armed gunship, UH-1B/C or AH-1G. 1965.
Homecoming	Operation to return POWs from North Vietnam (591 returned by 29 March). 12 Feb. 1973.
Hot Soup	Home made napalm (50gal. drums of petrol and detergent with thermite grenade, typically used in Laos and dropped by Caribou).

Huey	Common name for UH-1 (derived from designation). 1964.
Hun	Common name for F-100.
Huss	Common USMC name for UH-34 Sea Horse.
Igloo White	Comprehensive project for sensor laying and tracking on Ho Chi Minh Trail. May 1968.
Illinois City	Revised name for 'Practice Nine' sensor laying on Ho Chi Minh Trail (followed by 'Dye Maker'). May 1967.
Invert	Nakhon Phanom air control call-sign.
Iron Hand	USN SAM-suppression operations. 1965.
JTF-116	SEATO operation deploying aircraft to Thailand to counter North Vietnamese moves into Laos. May 1962.
Jenny	Radio and television entertainment relay by C-121J. Feb. 1966.
Jolly Green Giant	Common name for HH-3 rescue helicopter. Dec. 1965.
Jumping Jack	B-52 post-attack emergency refuelling force. 1965.
Junction City	Major US and ARVN operation around Tay Ninh. 22 Feb. 1967.
Keystone	Evacuation of USMC from South Vietnam. 1969.
Kilo Charlie	Thai air control call-sign (north of Korat).
King	Later call-sign for HC-130P after 'Crown'. 1968.
King Cobra	Deployment of KC-135A to Takhli. Sept. 1965.
Kit Kat	Infiltration of Special Forces into North Vietnam by 20 SOS helicopters.
LAPES	Low-Altitude Parachute Extraction System.
LOH	Light Observation Helicopter.
LRRP	Long-Range Reconnaissance Patrol ('Lurp' in common usage). 1964.
Lamplighter	Call-sign for AC-130 flareships. 1967.
Lead Sled	Common name for F-105.
Left Foot	RU-21E sigint project. 1965.
Lightning Bug	4025 RS component of 'Big Team' SAM-fusing intelligence-gathering. 1964.
Lightning Bug	UH-1 fitted with cluster of C-123 landing lights for night illumination. 1965.
Lima Site	Airstrips constructed by CIA in Laos (over 200 in total). 1964.
Linebacker I	Major air attacks on North Vietnam to prevent supplies from China (involved mainly B-52s; ended 23 Oct. 1972). 8 May 1972.
Linebacker II	Resumption of air strikes against strategic targets for eleven days (otherwise known as the 'Eleven Day War'). 18 Dec. 1972.
Lion	Ubon air control call-sign.
Litter Bug	350 SRS drone leaflet-dropping operation. 1972.
Little Brother	Mini-gunship O-2A project (not proceeded with). 1965.
Little Hummer	Common name for A-7.
Loach	Common name for OH-6A LOH. 1968.
Lucky Dragon	4080 SRW U-2 detachment. Dec. 1963.
Luctar	USN slang for target of opportunity ('lucrative target').
MAD	Mortar Air Delivery system fitted to UH-1. 1966.
Magpie	Call-sign of 2 Sqn. RAAF Canberras. May 1967.
Market Time	Maritime patrol operations in Tonkin Gulf to track supply vessels. Feb. 1965.
Mary Station	SAR and fighter direction ship station 35 miles south-east of Haiphong. 1965.
Masher/White Wing	Search and destroy operation involving 1 Air Cavalry around Bong Son. 24 Jan. 1966.
Menu	Secret bombing of Cambodia by B-52s in support of ground operations in 'Fish Hook' area. 18 March 1969.
MiGCAP	Fighter cover of strike forces to defend against MiG attack.
Misty Bronco	USAF evaluation of OV-10A in light strike role. April 1969.

Moonbeam	Call-sign of C-130Es of 7 ACCS (night), especially over solution Laos. 1965.
Moonglow	Call-sign of 'Patricia Lynn' RB57. 1964.
Moonshine	Call-sign of C-123 flareships. 1965.
Mortar Magnet	USMC common name for C-130. 1967.
Motel	Central Laotian air control call-sign.
Mud River	Revised name for anti-vehicle element of 'Muscle Shoals' Ho Chi Minh Trail marking. 1967.
Mule Train	Tactical transport support to ARVN by 346 TCS (later 315 TCG). 2 Jan. 1962.
Muscle Shoals	Ho Chi Minh Trail marking in Laos (followed by 'Dump Truck'). 1967.
NETT	New Equipment Training Team (AH-1G). Sept. 1967.
NOGS	Night Observation Gunship. YOV-10D light gunship programme (two aircraft operated by VMO-2). 1970.
Neutralize	Air support for besieged combat post at Con Thieu. Sept. 1967.
Niagara	Operation to bomb VC on perimeter of Khe Sanh (first stage intelligence gathering; second stage, from 21 January, bombing itself). 5 Jan. 1968.
Nighthawk	UH-1C night fighter. 1967.
Nimrod	Call-sign of A-26A. Jan. 1966.
Oplan 34-A	US plans for covert operations in North Vietnam. 1964.
Olympic Torch	Revised name for 'Trojan Horse'. 1965.
One Buck	Early USAF TAC and PACAF TDY deployments. 1965.
Paddy	Binh Thuy air control call-sign.
Panama	Da Nang air control call-sign.
Paris	Saigon air control call-sign
Patricia Lynn	RB-57E reconnaissance infra-red flights along Ho Chi Minh Trail, especially by 33 TG (later 6250 CSG). 7 May 1963.
Pave Aegis	AC-130E project with 105mm howitzer (two M61 20mm cannon and a Bofors 40mm cannon). 1968.
Pave Coin	Project to fit AU-24 with 7.62mm Gatling gun as light gunship.
Pave Eagle I/II	QU-22 development to replace EC-121 as sensor relays and flown by 554 RS. Dec. 1970.
Pave Fire	Laser scanner fitted to F-4 to aid optical lock-on of targets.
Pave Gat	B-57G gunship project (not proceeded with). 1967.
Pave Knife	AVQ-10 laser designator and LLLTV camera fitted to F-4. 1966.
Pave Nail	Night observation system fitted to USAF OV-10A. 1966.
Pave Pat	BLU-72 1,100lb propane fuel/air bomb. 1968.
Pave Pronto	AC-130A with 'Black Crow' low-level electronic emission detector. 1967.
Pave Spectre	AC-130E and H gunship programmes. 1971.
Pave Spot	Laser designator fitted to USAF OV-10A. 1967.
Pave Sword	Laser seeker carried by F-4. 1967.
Peacock	Pleiku air control call-sign.
Pedro	Common name for HH-43 rescue helicopter. 1964.
Pegasus	Relief of Khe Sanh by 1 Cavalry Division, 1 and 3 Marine Regiments and 3 ARVN Airborne. 1 April 1968.
Peter Rabbit	Call sign of VQ-1, USN (elint aircraft). Aug. 1964.
Pierce Arrow	Attack on North Vietnamese PTB shore bases. 5 Aug. 1964.
Pink Rose	Attempt by B-52s to fire jungle with incendiaries. 1970.
Pink Team	Offensive support by a pair of helicopters, one LOH plus one gunship.
Pipe Stem	Tactical reconnaissance by 15 TRS in South Vietnam. 18 Oct. 1961.
Plain Jane	Common usage name for AC-130. 1967.

Pocket Money	Mining of North Vietnamese ports. 8 May 1982.
Pony Express	20 SOS CH-3 helicopter operations.
Pop Eye	Project to seed rain clouds to hamper North Vietnamese supply effort (carried out to 1972 by 1 Weather Group WC-130B from Tan Son Nhut). 1967.
Practice Nine	Sensor-laying on Ho Chi Minh Trail (later 'Illinois City'). Late 1966.
Prairie Fire	USAF helicopter missions in Laos.
Prime Choke	B-52 attacks on railway bridges in buffer zone between North Vietnam and China. Sept. 1972.
Prize Crew	US Army Security Agency QT-2PC quiet observation platform evaluation. 1968.
Project 404	Covert USAF programme of operations in Laos and Cambodia. 1964.
Proud Deep	Five days of concerted USN strikes over northern North Vietnam (423 sorties). 26 Dec. 1971.
Puff the Magic Dragon	Popular name for AC-47 gunship. 1965.
Pyramid	Ban Me Thuot air control call-sign.
ROE	Rules of engagement ('Romeo' in common usage).
Ranch Hand	Defoliation by UC-123B of SASF, later under 315 TCG. 10 Jan. 1962.
Raven	Call-sign of FACs in Laos. 1967.
Red Crown	Fighter-direction ship off North Vietnam.
Red Team	Offensive support of two gunships. 1965.
ResCAP	Rescue Combat Air Patrol.
Rivet Brass	6 SW RC-135D elint project. 1964.
Rivet Racer	EB-66 electronic warfare project. 1968.
Rivet Top	522 AEWCW EC-121D project. April 1965.
Rolling Thunder	Air strikes over North Vietnam south of 20th parallel (initial targets of strategic importance numbered 94). 20 Feb. 1965.
Route Package	System of dividing North Vietnam into areas for assignment to USAF and USN for strikes (I, V and VIA to USAF; II, II, IV and VIB to USN). Nov. 1965.
Ruff Puff	Common name for South Vietnamese Regional and Popular Force.
SCOOT	Support Cambodia out of Thailand (campaign to encourage support for Cambodian Government against Khmer Rouge). April 1973.
SLUF	Common name for A-7 (Short Little Ugly F***er).
Sandy	Call-sign of A-1 rescue support aircraft. 1965.
Saw Buck	C-123 operations in 1963.
Scooter	Common name for A-4.
Sea Gap	Collection of SAM guidance and fusing details by USN vessels offshore. Oct. 1967.
Senior Blow	Possible use of Mach 4 GTD-21 drone from B-52s of 4200 TW. 1973.
Senior Book	Revised name for 'Olympic Torch' U-2 operations. 1965.
Shadow	Call-sign of AC-119G. 1968.
Shufly	USMC helicopter detachments, with support, to Da Nang. 15 April 1962.
Sixteen Buck	Operational deployment of FC-47 to 4 ACS. Nov. 1965.
Skoshi Tiger	Evaluation of F-5A by 4503 TFS. 23 Oct. 1965.
Sled	Common name for F-100.
Sleepytime	Call-sign of O-2A FAC. 1966.
Slick	Common name for lightly armed, troop-carrying UH-1D or H. 1965.

Smoke	Call-sign of A-1 smoke-laying rescue support aircraft. 1965.
Snake	Common name for AH-1G gunship. 1967.
Spad	Common name for A-1. 1964.
Spooky	Call-sign of FC-47 (later AC-47) gunship. Nov. 1965.
Squash Bomber	Common name for F-105.
Starlight	USMC air attacks on VC attacking Chu Lai. 18 Aug. 1965.
Steel Tiger	Strikes in southern Laos in support of war in Vietnam. 3 April 1965.
Steve Canyon	Programme for recruiting FAC pilots from USAF via CIA for covert work in Laos. 1966.
Stinger	Call-sign of AC-119K. 1969.
Super Jolly	Common name for CH-53 rescue helicopter. 1967.
Surprise Package	AC-130A project with two 40mm Bofors cannon. 1967.
Tally Ho	USMC strikes into North Vietnam. July 1966.
Teaball	Loatian air control call-sign (south of Luang Prabang).
Thayer	101 Airborne Division operation in Binh Dinh. 1 Sept. 1966.
Thayer II	1 Air Cavalry follow-up to Thayer. 25 Oct. 1967.
Thud	Common name for F-105.
Tiger Claw	Deployment of KC-135A to Korat. June 1972.
Tiger Cub	KC-135A deployment to Don Muang (ex Clark AB). March 1965.
Tiger Hound	Air operations over southern Laos south of 17 parallel (replaced by 'Commando Hunt' programme in 1968). 3 April 1965.
Toan Thang 43	Combined ARVN and 1 Cavalry Division operation into the 'Fish Hook' area of Cambodia. 1 May 1970.
Top Gun	USN fighter pilot school in US following experience in Vietnam. March 1969.
Trojan Horse	U-2 operations. 1965.
Tropic Moon III	Night interdiction system of LLLTV and FLIR fitted to B-57Gs of 13 TBS. Sept. 1970.
Ultra Hog	Common name for F-105.
United Effort	Combined 55 SRW RB-47H and 4025 RS DC-130A operation to determine SA-2 radar settings. 1965.
Viking	Thai-Laos border air control call-sign.
Water Glass	Air defence of South Vietnam by F-102s of 509 FIS and AD-5Ds of VAW-35 on six-weekly turnarounds.
Water Pump	T-28 training for Royal Laos Air Force by Det. 6, 1 ACW, out of Udorn. March 1964.
Waterboy	Quang Tri (Dong Ha) air control call-sign.
Whale	Common name for A-3.
White Star	US Army Special Forces training teams in Laos. 1962.
White Team	Reconnaissance flight of two LOHs. 1965.
Wild Weasel	Aircraft fitted with radar homing and warning (RHAW) and, later, anti-radiation missiles for SAM-suppression sorties. 26 Nov. 1965.
Willie Fudd	Common name for WF-2 (E-1).
Willie Peter	White phosphorous marker rockets.
Willie the Whale	Common name for EF-10.
Yankee Station	Carrier position off North Vietnam. 1964.
Yankee Team	Joint USAF and USN reconnaissance then strike over Laos. 31 March 1964.
Young Tiger	Deployment of KC-135As to Kadena. Jan. 1965.

VII. Soviet Aircraft Designations

As Soviet aircraft are designed, they are given a manufacturer's designation; on entry into service, aircraft are given a military designation of a similar appearance but with a different numbering sequence. As an example, the Tu-104 civil airliner carries the Tupolev design bureau number, but the military bomber counterpart is designated Tu-16. As a general rule, bomber types are given even-numbered service designations, while fighters have odd-numbered designations. The major design bureaux since 1945, with their normal abbreviations, are set out below.

Antonov	An	Mil	Mi
Beriev	B	Myasishchev	M
Ilyushin	Il	Petlyakov	Pe
Kamov	Ka	Polikarpov	Po
Lavochkin	La	Sukhoi	Su
Lisunov	Li	Tupolev	Tu
Mikoyan-Gurevich	MiG	Yakovlev	Yak

Designs, whether civil or military, are given NATO reporting names. These begin with one of five initial letters, depending on function: F for fighters, B for bombers, C for transports, M for miscellaneous types and H for helicopters. In general, single-syllable names are applied to propeller-driven aircraft and two-syllable names to turbojet-powered aircraft. A full list of names applied since 1945 follows.

La-7	Fin	Su-24	Fencer
La-9	Fritz	Su-25	Frogfoot
La-11	Fang	Su-27	Flanker
La-15	Fantail	Tu-28P	Fiddler
MiG-9	Fargo	Tu-128	Fiddler
MiG-15	Fagot	Yak-9	Frank
MiG-17	Fresco	Yak-17	Feather
MiG-19	Farmer	Yak-23	Flora
MiG-21	Fishbed	Yak-25	Flashlight
MiG-21	Faceplate (wrongly	Yak-27	Flashlight-C
	designated)	Yak-28P	Firebar
MiG-23	Flogger	Yak-38	Forger
MiG-23	Flipper (wrongly		
	designated)	A-20	Box (Havoc)
MiG-25	Foxbat	B-25	Bank (Mitchell)
MiG-27	Flogger-D/J	Il-2	Bark
MiG-29	Fulcrum	Il-4	Bob
MiG-31	Foxhound	Il-10	Beast
P-63	Fred (Kingcobra)	Il-28	Beagle
Su-7	Fitter-A	Il-40	Brawny
Su-9	Fishpot-B	Il-54	Blowlamp
Su-11	Fishpot-C	M-4	Bison
Su-15	Flagon-A−D	M-?	Bounder
Su-17	Fitter-C−K	Pe-2	Buck
Su-19	Fencer	Tu-2	Bat
Su-20	Fitter-C	Tu-4	Bull (B-29)
Su-21	Flagon-E/F	Tu-14	Bosun
Su-22	Fitter-F/G/J	Tu-16	Badger

Tu-22	Blinder
Tu-26	Backfire
Tu-91	Boot
Tu-95	Bear
Tu-142	Bear-F/H
Tu-?	Blackjack
Yak-25	Brassard
Yak-28	Brewer
Yak-?	Backfin
An-2	Colt
An-8	Camp
An-10	Cat
An-12	Cub
An-14	Clod
An-22	Cock
An-24	Coke
An-26	Curl
An-28	Cash
An-30	Clank
An-32	Cline
An-72/74	Coaler
An-124	Condor
Il-12	Coach
Il-14	Crate
Il-18	Coot
Il-20	Coot-A
Il-62	Classic
Il-76	Candid
Il-86	Camber
Il-?	Clam
Li-2	Cab (C-47)
Tu-70	Cart
Tu-104	Camel
Tu-110	Cooker
Tu-114	Cleat
Tu-134	Crusty
Tu-154	Careless
Yak-10	Crow
Yak-12	Creek
Yak-16	Cork
Yak-40	Codling
Yak-42	Clobber
Ka-15	Hen
Ka-18	Hog
Ka-25	Hormone
Ka-26	Hoodlum

Ka-27	Helix
Ka-?	Hokum
Mi-1	Hare
Mi-2	Hoplite
Mi-3	Hare
Mi-4	Hound
Mi-6	Hook
Mi-8	Hip
Mi-10	Hake
Mi-10	Harke
Mi-12	Homer
Mi-14	Haze
Mi-17	Hip-H
Mi-24	Hind
Mi-25	Hind
Mi-26	Halo
Mi-28	Havoc
Yak-24	Horse
Be-2	Mote
Be-4	Mug
Be-6	Madge
Be-8	Mole
Be-12	Mail
Il-28U	Mascot
Il-38	May
Il-76 AEW	Mainstay
Il-76 FR	Midas
L-29	Maya
M-12	Mail
MiG-15U	Midget
MiG-21U	Mongol
PBY	Mop (Catalina)
Po-2	Mule
Su-7U	Moujik
Su-9U	Maiden
Su-11U	Maiden
Tu-126	Moss
Yak-7U	Mark
Yak-11	Moose
Yak-14	Mare
Yak-17U	Magnet
Yak-18	Max
Yak-26	Mandrake
Yak-27U	Mangrove
Yak-28U	Maestro
Yak UT-2	Mink

Bibliography

GENERAL

Andrade, J. M. *US Military Aircraft Designations and Serials Since 1909*. Midland Counties Publications, Leicester, 1979.

Armitage, M. J. and Mason, R. A. *Air Power in the Nuclear Age, 1945–82; Theory and Practice*. Macmillan, London, 1983.

Blaxland, G. *The Regiments Depart*. William Kimber, London, 1971.

Bloomfield, L. P. and Leiss, A. C. *Controlling Small Wars: A Strategy for the 1970s*. Allen Lane, London, 1970.

Bowyer, M. J. F. *Bombing Colours 1937–1973: RAF Bombers, Their Markings and Operations*. Patrick Stevens, Cambridge, 1973.

Bowyer, M. J. F. *Fighting Colours: RAF Fighter Camouflage and Markings*. Patrick Stevens, Cambridge, 1969.

Carver, M. *War Since 1945*. Weidenfeld & Nicolson, London, 1980.

Dewar, M. *Brush Fire Wars: Campaigns of the British Army Since 1945*. Robert Hale, London, 1984.

Doll, T. E., Jackson, B. R. and Riley, W. A. *Navy Air Colors 1945–1985*. Squadron/Signal Publications, Carrollton, 1985.

Green, W. and Fricker, J. *The Air Forces of the World*. Macdonald, London, 1958.

Gunston, W. and Spick, M. *Modern Air Combat*. Salamander, London, 1983.

Hartman, T. and Mitchell, J. *A World Atlas of Military History 1945–1984*. Guild Publishing, London, 1984.

Kasulka, D. *USN Aircraft Carrier Units 1946–1956 and 1957–1963*. Squadron/Signal Publications, Carrollton, 1985.

Marriott, L. *Royal Navy Aircraft Carriers 1945–1990*. Ian Allan, Shepperton, 1985.

Mets, D. R. *Land-Based Air Power in Third World Crises*. Air University Press, Maxwell AFB, 1986.

Moyes, P. *Bomber Squadrons of the RAF*. Macdonald, London, 1964.

Nordeen, L. O. *Air Warfare in the Missile Age*. Arms & Armour Press, London, 1985.

Oliver, D. *British Combat Aircraft in Action Since 1945*. Ian Allan, Shepperton, 1987.

Pimlott, J. (ed.). *British Military Operations 1945–1984*. Guild Publishing, London, 1984.

Polmar, N. *The Ships and Aircraft of the US Fleet*. Arms & Armour Press, London, 1981.

Rawlings, J. D. R. *Fighter Squadrons of the RAF*. Macdonald, London, 1969.

Rawlings, J. D. R. *Coastal, Support and Special Squadrons of the RAF*. Jane's, London, 1982.

Robertson, B. *Aircraft Camouflage and Markings 1907–1954*. Harleyford, Marlow, 1956.

Robertson, B. *British Military Serials 1878–1987*. Midland Counties Publications, Leicester, 1987.

Robinson, A. (ed.). *Air Power: The World's Air Forces*. Orbis, London, 1980.

Sturtivant, R. *The Squadrons of the Fleet Air Arm*. Air-Britain, Tonbridge, 1984.

Taylor, J. W. R. et al. *Air Forces of the World*. Salamander, London, 1979.

Thetford, O. *British Naval Aircraft Since 1912*. Putnam, London, 1987.

Thetford, O. *Aircraft of the Royal Air Force Since 1918*. Putnam, London, 1988.

Thompson, R. (ed.). *War in Peace*. Orbis, London, 1981.

Winton, J. *Air Power at Sea 1945 to Today*. Sidgwick & Jackson, London, 1987.

In addition, the following series of books, part-works or magazines are invaluable for reference:

Books
Air-Britain Aircraft Monographs
Aircam Aircraft Monographs
Ian Allan 'At War', 'Postwar Military Aircraft' and 'Modern Combat Aircraft' series
International Institute for Strategic Studies 'Military Balance' and 'Strategic Survey', published annually
Jane's 'All The World's Aircraft', published annually
Osprey Aircraft Monographs
Patrick Stevens Aircraft Monographs and 'Action Stations' series
Putnam Aircraft Manufacturers series
Squadron/Signal Publications, including the 'At War' series
Frederick Warne 'Observer's Book of Aircraft', published annually.

Part-works (UK)
Illustrated Encyclopedia of Aviation, Orbis, 1982–85
War in Peace, Orbis 1983–85
Warplane, Orbis 1985–87

Magazines (UK)
Aeroplane Monthly
Aircraft Illustrated
Air Enthusiast
Air Forces Monthly
Air International
Air Pictorial
Aviation News
Flight
Flypast
Jane's Defence Weekly
Scale Aircraft Modelling

1: EUROPE

The Greek Civil War 1944–1949
Cawthrone, G. (ed.). *Prisoners of ELAS Greeks*. Private, London, 1947.

Kousoulas, D. G. *Revolution and Defeat*. London, 1965.

Matthews, K. *Memories of a Mountain War*. London, 1972.

Albania, 1949–1954
Bethell, N. *The Great Betrayal*. Hodder & Stoughton, London, 1984.

Cyprus, 1955–1959
Byford-Jones, W. *Grivas and the Story of EOKA*. Hale, London, 1959.

Foley, C. and Scobie, W. I. *The Struggle for Cyprus*. Hoover Institute Press, Stanford, 1975.

Stephens, R. *Cyprus*. Pall Mall, London, 1966.

Cyprus, 1963 to date
James, A. *The Politics of Peacekeeping*. Oxford University Press, Oxford, 1973.

Verrier, A. *International Peacekeeping*. Penguin, London, 1981.

Hungary, 1956

Barber, N. *Seven Days of Freedom*. London, 1974.
Lomax, W. *Hungary 1956*. London, 1976.
Pryce-Jones, D. *The Hungarian Revolution*. London, 1969.

Czechoslovakia, 1968

Valenta, J. *Soviet Intervention in Czechoslovakia*. Johns Hopkins Press, Baltimore, 1979.

The Berlin Airlift, 1948–1949

Berlin Airlift. HMSO, London, 1949.
Charles, M. *Berlin Blockade*. Allan Wingate, London, 1959.
Cole, C. and Grant, R. *But not in Anger*. Ian Allan, Shepperton, 1979.
Collier, R. *Bridge Across the Sky*. Macmillan, London, 1978.
Donovan, F. *Bridge in the Sky*. David McKay, New York, 1986.
Jackson, R. *The Berlin Airlift*. Patrick Stevens, Wellingborough, 1988.
Morris, E. *Blockade: Berlin and the Cold War*. Hamish Hamilton, London, 1973.
Phillips Davison, W. *The Human Side of the Berlin Airlift*. Rand Corporation, Washington, 1957.
Phillips Davison, W. *The Berlin Blockade*. Princeton University Press, Princeton 1958.
Rodrigo, R. *Berlin Airlift*. Cassell, London, 1960.

The Berlin Wall Crisis, 1961–1962

Cate, C. *The Ides of August: The Berlin Wall Crisis of 1961*. Weidenfeld & Nicolson, London, 1978.
Galante, P. *The Berlin Wall*. A. Barker, London, 1965.
Heller, D. and D. *The Berlin Wall*. Walker, New York, 1962.
Mander, J. *Berlin: Hostage for the West*. Penguin, London, 1971.
Schick, J. M. *The Berlin Crisis: 1958–1962*. University of Pennsylvania Press, Philadelphia, 1971.
Slusser, R. M. *The Berlin Crisis of 1961*. Johns Hopkins Press, Baltimore, 1973.
Smith, J. E. *The Defense of Berlin*. Johns Hopkins Press, Baltimore, 1963.

Northern Ireland, 1969 to date

Coogan, T. P. *The IRA*. Fontana, London, 1980.
Darby, J. *Conflict in Northern Ireland*. London, 1976.
Kelley, K. *The Longest War: Northern Ireland and the IRA*. Zed Books, London, 1982.
O'Ballance, E. *Terror in Ireland*. Presidio, London, 1981.
O'Brien, C. C. *State of Ireland*. Dublin, 1972.
Utley, T. E. *Lessons of Ulster*. J.M. Dent & Sons, London, 1976.

Strategic Intelligence, 1945 to date

Anderton, D. A. *B-57 and RB-57F* (Profile No. 247). Profile Publications, Windsor, 1973.
Brookes, A. J. *Photo Reconnaissance*. Ian Allan, Shepperton, 1975.
Gunston, W. *Spy Planes*. Salamander, London, 1983.
Hubbard, K. and Simmons, M. *Operation 'Grapple'*. Ian Allan, Shepperton, 1985.
Johnson, R. W. *Shootdown: The Verdict on KAL007*. Chatto & Windus, London, 1986.
Kennedy, W. V. (ed.). *The Intelligence War*. Salamander, London, 1983.
Mikesh, R. C. *B-57 Canberra at War 1964–1972*. Ian Allan, Shepperton, 1980.
Miller, J. *Lockheed U-2*. Aerofax, Austin, 1983.
O'Leary, M. *US Sky Spies since World War I*. Blandford, Poole, 1986.
Peacock, L. T. *Boeing B-47 Stratojet*. Osprey, London, 1987.
Peacock, L. T. *Strategic Air Command*. Arms & Armour Press, London, 1988.
Peebles, C. *Guardians: Strategic Reconnaissance Satellites*. Ian Allan, Shepperton, 1988.
Powers, G. F. *Operation Overflight*. Hodder & Stoughton, London, 1970.

Richardson, D. *Electronic Warfare*. Salamander, London, 1985.
Spick, M. *American Spyplanes*. Osprey, London, 1986.
Streetly, M. *World Electronic Warfare Aircraft*. Jane's, London, 1983.
Taylor, J. W. R. and Mondey, D. *Spies in the Sky*. Ian Allan, Shepperton, 1972.
van der Aart, D. *Aerial Espionage*. Airlife, Shrewsbury, 1985.
Wise, D. and Ross, T. B. *The U-2 Affair*. Cresset Press, London, 1963.

2: THE EASTERN MEDITERRANEAN

Israel – General

Borovik, Y. *Israeli Air Force* (Warbirds No. 23). Arms & Armour Press, London, 1984.
Dupuy, T. N. *Elusive Victory: The Arab-Israeli Wars, 1947–1974*. Macdonald & Jane's, London, 1978.
Gunston, W. *Israeli Air Force*. Salamander, London, 1982.
Herzog, C. *The Arab-Israeli Wars*. Arms & Armour Press, London, 1982.
Hiro, D. *Inside the Middle East*. Routledge & Kegan Paul, London, 1982.
Mansfield, P. *The Arabs*. Penguin, London, 1980.
Morse, S. (ed.). *Modern Military Powers – Israel*. Temple Press, London, 1984.
Rivlin, G. (ed.). *Israel Defence Army 1948–58*. IDF, Tel Aviv, 1958.
Rodinson, M. *Israel and the Arabs*. Penguin, London, 1968.
Rubinstein, M. and Goldman, R. *The Israeli Air Force Story*. Arms & Armour Press, London, 1979.
von Pivka, O. *Armies of the Middle East*. Patrick Stephens, London, 1979.

Israel, 1948–1949

Azcárate, P. de. *Mission in Palestine, 1948–1952*. Middle East Institute, Washington, 1966.
Kurzman, D. *Genesis 1948: The First Arab-Israeli War*. Vallentine Mitchell, London, 1972.
Lorch, N. *The Edge of the Sword: Israel's War of Independence 1947–1949*. Putnam, London, 1961.
O'Ballance, E. *The Arab-Israeli War 1948*. Faber & Faber, London, 1956.

Sinai, 1956

Browne, H. *Suez and Sinai*. Longman, Harlow, 1971.
Dayan, M. *Diary of the Sinai Campaign*. Weidenfeld & Nicolson, London, 1966.
Henriques, R. A. *A Hundred Hours to Suez*. Collins, London, 1957.
Marshall, S. *Sinai Victory: Israel's Hundred Hour Conquest of Egypt*. Morrow, New York, 1958.
O'Ballance, E. *The Sinai Campaign 1956*. Faber & Faber, London, 1959.

Suez, 1956

Barker, A. J. *Suez, the Seven Day War*. Weidenfeld & Nicolson, London, 1967.
Beaufre, A. *The Suez Expedition 1956*. Faber & Faber, London, 1969.
Bromberger, M. and S. *Secrets of Suez*. Pan Books, London, 1957.
Browne, H. *Suez and Sinai*. Longman, Harlow, 1971.
Cavenagh, S. *Airborne to Suez*. William Kimber, London, 1965.
Childers, E. *The Road to Suez*. Macgibbon & Kee, London, 1962.
Eden, Sir A. *Full Circle: The Memoirs of Anthony Eden*. Cassell, London, 1960.
Eisenhower, D. D. *Waging Peace, 1956–1961*. Heinemann, London, 1966.
Finer, H. *Dulles over Suez*. Heinemann, London, 1964.
Fullick, R. and Powell, G. *Suez, the Double War*. Hamish Hamilton, London, 1979.
Gaujac, P. *Suez 1956*. Charles-Lavauzelle, Paris, 1986.

Jackson, R. *Suez 1956: Operation Musketeer.* Ian Allan, London, 1980.

Lloyd, S. *Suez, 1956.* Jonathan Cape, London, 1978.

Mansfield, P. *Nasser.* Methuen, London, 1969.

Nutting, A. *No End of a Lesson: The Story of Suez,* Constable, London, 1967.

Parliamentary Debates (Hansard), Vol. 558. HMSO, London, 1956.

Proceedings 3, Royal Air Force Historical Society. RAFHS, London, 1988.

Robertson, T. *Crisis: The Inside Story of the Suez Conspiracy.* Hutchinson, London, 1965.

Thomas, H. *The Suez Affair.* Weidenfeld & Nicolson, London, 1966.

Watt, D. *Documents on the Suez Crisis, 26 July to 6 November 1956.* Royal Institute for International Affairs, London, 1957.

The Six-Day War 1967

Abu-Lughod, I. (ed.). *The Arab-Israeli Confrontation of June 1967: An Arab Perspective.* Arab Information Center, New York, 1968.

Associated Press. *Lightning out of Israel: The Six Day War in the Middle East.* The Press, New York, 1967.

Byford-Jones, W. *The Lightning War.* Hale, London, 1967.

Caufriez, G. *Du Sinai au Golan, 1967/1979.* Fleurus, Paris, 1981.

Churchill, R. and W. *The Six Day War.* Heinemann, London, 1967.

Eshel, T. *The Six Day War.* Eshel-Dramit, Tel Aviv, 1979.

IDF. *The Six Days' War.* Israeli Defence Force, Tel Aviv, 1967.

Kimche, D. and Bawley, D. *The Sandstorm. The Arab-Israeli War of June 1967: Prelude and Aftermath.* Secker & Warburg, London, 1968.

Laquer, W. *The Road to War, 1967: The Origins of the Arab-Israeli Conflict.* Weidenfeld & Nicolson, London, 1968.

MacLeish, R. *The Sun Stood Still: Perspectives on the Arab-Israeli Conflict.* Macdonald, London, 1968.

Stevenson, W. *Israeli Victory.* Corgi, London, 1967.

Young, P. *The Israeli Campaign 1967.* William Kimber, London, 1967.

The War of Attrition

Strategic Survey 1969. Institute for Strategic Studies, London, 1970.

Strategic Survey 1970. Institute for Strategic Studies, London, 1971.

Israel, 1973

Adan, A. *On the Banks of the Suez.* Arms & Armour Press, London, 1980.

Herzog, C. *War of Atonement.* Weidenfeld & Nicolson, London, 1975.

Laquer, W. *Confrontation 1973: The Middle East War and the Great Powers.* Wildwood House, London, 1974.

Monroe, E. and Farrar-Hockley, A. H. *The Arab-Israel War, October 1973: Background and Events* (Adelphi Paper 111). International Institute for Strategic Studies, London, 1974.

Sherman, A. *When God Judged and Men Died.* Bantam, New York, 1973.

Sunday Times, The. Insight on the Middle East. André Deutsch, London, 1974.

Sunday Times, The. The Yom Kippur War. André Deutsch, London, 1975.

Lebanon, 1958

Mongold, P. *Superpower Intervention in the Middle East.* Croom Helm, London, 1978.

Lebanon, 1978 to date

'Bekaa Valley Combat'. *Flight International.* London, 16 October 1982.

Bullock, J. *Final Conflict: The War in Lebanon.* Century Press, London, 1983.

Gilmour, D. *Lebanon: The Fractured Country.* Sphere, London, 1983.

Nordeen, L. O. *Air Warfare in the Missile Age.* Arms & Armour Press, London, 1985.

Randall, J. *The Tragedy of Lebanon.* Chatto & Windus, London, 1983.

3: NORTH AND WEST AFRICA

Algeria, 1954–1962

Gordon, D. C. *The Passing of French Algeria.* London, 1966.

Horne, A. *A Savage War of Peace.* Penguin, London, 1977.

O'Ballance, E. *The Algerian Insurrection.* Faber & Faber, London, 1967.

Roy, J. *The War in Algeria.* New York, 1961.

Portuguese Guinea, 1963–1974

Abshire, B. M. and Samuels, M. A. *Portuguese Africa: A Handbook.* London, 1969.

Bruce, N. *Portugal: The Last Empire.* David & Charles, London, 1975.

Bruce, N. *Portugal's African Wars* (Conflict Studies No. 34). London, 1973.

Davidson, B. *The Liberation of Guiné.* Penguin, London, 1969.

Minter, W. *Portuguese Africa and the West.* Penguin, London, 1972.

Nigeria, 1967–1970

Forsyth, F. *The Biafra Story.* Hutchinson, London, 1969.

Hilton, B. *Highly Irregular: A Biafran Relief Story.* Collier Macmillan, Toronto, 1969.

Kirk-Greene, A. H. M. *Crisis and Conflict in Nigeria: A Documentary Source Book.* Oxford University Press, Oxford, 1971.

Mockler, A. *The New Mercenaries.* Sidgwick & Jackson, London, 1985.

Rosen, C. von. *Le Ghetto Biafrais, tel que Je l'ai Connu.* Arthaud, Paris, 1969.

St. Jorre, D. S. J. de. *The Nigerian Civil War.* Macmillan, London, 1972.

Zumbach, J. *On Wings of War.* André Deutsch, London, 1975.

4: CENTRAL AND SOUTHERN AFRICA

General

Andrade, J. M. *Spanish and Portuguese Military Aviation.* Midland Counties Publications, Leicester, 1977.

Burchett, W. and Roebuck, D. *The Whores of War.* Penguin, London, 1977.

Mockler, A. *The New Mercenaries.* Sidgwick & Jackson, Lodon, 1985.

The Congo, 1960–1964

Hempstone, S. *Katanga Report.* Faber & Faber, London, 1962.

Kanza, T. *Conflict in the Congo.* Penguin, London, 1972.

Lumumba, P. *Congo, My Country.* London, 1969.

O'Brien, C. C. *To Katanga and Back.* Hutchinson, London, 1962.

Zumbach, J. *On Wings of War.* André Deutsch, London, 1975.

The Congo, 1964–1967

Hoare, T. M. B. *Congo Mercenary.* Robert Hale, London, 1967.

Angola, 1961–1975

Abshire, B. and Samuels, M. A. *Portuguese Africa: A Handbook.* London, 1969.

Bruce, N. *Portugal: The Last Empire.* David & Charles, London, 1975.

Davidson, B. *In the Eye of the Storm.* Penguin, London, 1975.

Duffy, J. *Portugal in Africa.* Penguin, London, 1962

Humbaraci, A. and Muchnik, N. *Portugal's African Wars.* Macmillan, London, 1974.

Wheeler, D. and Pelissier, R. *Angola.* Pall Mall, London, 1971.

Angola, 1975 to date
Dempster, C. and Tomkins, D. *Firepower*. Corgi, London, 1978.
Legum, C. and Hodges, A. *After Angola*. Rex Collings, London, 1976.
Moss, R. *Castro's Secret War*. The Sunday Telegraph, London, 1977.
Stockwell, J. *In Search of Enemies*. André Deutsch, London, 1978.

Rhodesia, 1965 to date
Brent, W. A. *Rhodesian Air Force: A Brief History 1947–1980*. Freeworld Publications, Kwambonambi, 1987.
Henriksen, T. and Gann, L. *The Struggle for Zimbabwe*. Praeger, New York, 1981.
Hudson, M. *Triumph or Tragedy: Rhodesia to Zimbabwe*. Hamilton, London, 1981.
Johnson, P. and Martin, D. *The Struggle for Zimbabwe*. Faber & Faber, London, 1981.
McLaughlin, P. and Moorcraft, P. *Chimurenga! The War in Rhodesia 1965–1980*. Sygma, Marshaltown, 1982.
Stoneman, C. *Zimbabwe's Inheritance*. St. Martin's Press, New York, 1982.
Thomas, A. 'Rhodesian Air Force'. *Scale Aircraft Modelling*, Vol. 4/11. Berkhamsted, 1982.

South Africa, 1966 to date
Davenport, T. R. H. *South Africa: A Modern History*. Macmillan, London, 1977.
Duigan, P. and Gann, L. *South Africa: War, Revolution or Peace?* Hoover Institute Press, Stanford, 1978.
Green, R., Kiljunen, M. and Kiljunen R. *Namibia, The Last Colony*. Longman, Harlow, 1981.
Heitman, H.-R. *South African War Machine*. Galago Publishing, Bromley, 1985.
Potgieter, H. and Steenkamp, W. *Aircraft of the South African Air Force*. Jane's, London, 1981.

5: EAST AFRICA

Kenya, 1952–1956
Clayton, A. *Counter-Insurgency in Kenya*. Transafrica Press, Nairobi, 1976.
Garbett, M. and Goulding, B. *Lincoln at War*. Ian Allan, Shepperton, 1979.
Kitson, F. *Gangs and Counter Gangs*. Barrie & Rockliff, London, 1960.
Kitson, F. *Low Intensity Operations*. Faber & Faber, London, 1971.
Lathbury, G. 'The Kenya Emergency 1955–56'. MoD, London, 1958.
Lee, D. *Flight from the Middle East*. HMSO, London, 1980.
Majdalaney, F. *State of Emergency*. Faber & Faber, London, 1962.

Uganda, 1972
Avirgan, A. and Honey, M. *War in Uganda: The Legacy of Idi Amin*. Tanzania Publishing House, Dar-es-Salaam, 1982.

Entebbe, 1976
Stevenson, W. *90 Minutes at Entebbe*. Bantam Books, New York, 1976.

The Seychelles, 1981
Hoare, B. M. T. *The Seychelles Affair*. Bantam Press, London, 1986.
Mockler, A. *The New Mercenaries*. Sidgwick & Jackson, London, 1985.

6: THE ARABIAN PENINSULA, IRAQ AND IRAN
General
Blaxland, G. *The Regiments Depart*. William Kimber, London, 1971.
Lee, D. L. *Flight From the Middle East*. HMSO, London, 1980.

South Arabia, 1945–1967
Paget, J. *Last Post: Aden 1963–67*. Faber & Faber, London, 1969.
Shagland, P. 'The Dhala Road'. *Royal Engineers Journal*. London, 1969.
Stevens, T. 'Operations in the Radfan 1964'. *RUSI Journal*. London, 1965.
Trevaskis, H. *Shades of Amber*. Hutchinson, London, 1968.

The Yemen, 1962 to date
Seagrave, S. *Yellow Rain*. Sphere Books, London, 1981.
Smiley, D. *Arabian Assignment*. Leo Cooper, London, 1975.

Oman, 1952–1959
Allfree, P. S. *War Lords of Oman*. Robert Hale, London, 1967.
Geraghty, A. *Who Dares Wins*. Arms & Armour Press, London, 1980.
Townsend, J. *Oman: The Making of the Modern State*. Croom Helm, London, 1977.

Dhofar, 1965–1975
Akehurst, J. *We Won a War: The Campaign in Dhofar 1965–1975*. Michael Russell, Salisbury, 1982.
Clements, F. *Oman, the Reborn Land*. Longman, London, 1980.
Geraghty, T. *Who Dares Wins*. Arms & Armour Press, London, 1980.
Jeapes, T. *SAS: Operation Oman*. William Kimber, London, 1982.

The Gulf War, 1980–1988
Cordesman, A. H. *The Iran-Iraq War and Western Security 1984–87*. Jane's, London, 1987.
El Azhary, M. S. *The Iran-Iraq War*. Croom Helm, London, 1984.
Hiro, F. *Iran Under the Ayatollahs*. Routledge & Kegan Paul, London, 1985.
Strategic Survey. International Institute for Strategic Studies, London, 1980–86.

Kurdestan, 1945 to date
Ghareeb, E. *The Kurdish Question in Iraq*. Syracuse University Press, Syracuse, 1981.

Iraqi Reactor Raid, 1981
Perlmutter, A. et al. *Two Minutes Over Baghdad*. Corgi, London, 1981.

The Yemen, 1972–1979
Strategic Survey 1972. International Institute of Strategic Studies, London, 1973.

7: THE INDIAN SUB-CONTINENT
General
Amin, M. et al. *Defenders of Pakistan*. Midland Counties Publications, Leicester, 1988.
Chaturvedi, M. S. *History of the Indian Air Force*. Vikas, New Delhi, 1978.
Green, W. (ed.). *The Indian Air Force and its Aircraft*. Ducimus, London, 1982.
Singh, P. *Aircraft of the Indian Air Force*. The English Book Store, New Delhi, 1975.

India – Pakistan, 1965
Brines, R. *The Indo-Pakistan Conflict*. Pall Mall, London, 1968.
Fricker, J. *Battle for Pakistan: The Air War of 1965*. Ian Allan, Shepperton, 1979.

India – Pakistan, 1971
Ayoob, M. and Subrahmanyam, K. *The Liberation War*. Indian Book Co., New Delhi, 1972.
Kaul, B. M. *Confrontation with Pakistan*. Vikas, Delhi, 1971.
Mankekar, D. R. *Pakistan Cut to Size*. Indian Book Co., New Delhi, 1971.
Palit, D. K. *The Lightning Campaign: The Indo-Pakistan War 1971*. Compton Press, Salisbury, 1972.

Afghanistan, 1980–1988

Fullerton, J. *The Soviet Occupation of Afghanistan.* Methuen, London, 1984.

Girardet, E. *Afghanistan: The Soviet War.* Croom Helm, London, 1985.

Hammond, T. *Red Flag over Afghanistan.* Westview Press, 1984.

Hyman, A. *Afghanistan under Soviet Domination.* Macmillan, London, 1984.

Isby, D. *Russia's War in Afghanistan.* Osprey, London, 1986.

Newell, N. P. and R. S. *The Struggle for Afghanistan.* Cornell University Press, Ithaca, 1981.

Ryan, N. *A Hitch or Two in Afghanistan.* Weidenfeld & Nicolson, London, 1984.

Urban, M. *War in Afghanistan.* Macmillan, London, 1988.

8: CHINA, KOREA AND JAPAN

The Chinese Civil War, 1945–1949

Alexander, G. *Silent Invasion.* Macdonald, London, 1973.

Bonds, R. (ed.). *The Chinese War Machine.* Salamander, London, 1979.

Corr, G. H. *The Chinese Red Army.* Osprey, Reading, 1974.

Korea, 1950–1953

Davis, L. *Air War over Korea.* Squadron/Signal Publications, Carrollton, 1982.

Davis, L. *MiG Alley.* Squadron/Signal Publications, Carrollton, 1978.

Farrar-Hockley, A. *The Edge of the Sword.* Frederick Muller, London, 1954.

Field, J. A. *A History of US Naval Operations, Korea.* Naval History Division, Washington, 1962.

Futrell, G. F. *The United States Air Force in the Korean War.* Office of Air Force History, Washington, 1983.

Hallion, R. P. *The Naval Air War in Korea.* Nautical & Aviation Publishing Co., Baltimore, 1986.

Hastings, M. *The Korean War.* Michael Joseph, London, 1987.

Linklater, E. *Our Men in Korea.* HMSO, London, 1954.

Lowe, P. *The Origins of the Korean War.* Longman, London, 1986.

Montross, L. and Canzona, N. A. *US Marine Operations in Korea, 1950–53.* Historical Branch US Marine Corps, Washington, 1957.

Rees, D. *Korea: The Limited War.* Hamish Hamilton, London, 1964.

Ridgway, M. B. *The Korean War.* Doubleday, New York, 1967.

Scutts, J. *Air War over Korea* (Warbirds No. 11). Arms & Armour Press, London, 1982.

Miscellaneous conflicts and incidents

Strategic Survey 1969. Institute for Strategic Studies, London, 1970.

9: INDO-CHINA

Indo-China, 1945–1954

Asprey, R. B. *War in the Shadows.* Macdonald & Jane's, London, 1976.

Bail, R. *Les Pingouins d'Indochine: L'Aéronavale de 1945 à 1954.* Editions Maritimes et d'Outre-Mer, Paris, 1979.

Buttinger, J. *Vietnam: A Dragon Embattled.* Praeger, New York, 1967.

Chassin, L. M. *Aviation Indochine.* Amiot Dumont, Paris, 1954.

Fall, B. B. *The Two Vietnams.* Pall Mall, London, 1963.

Fall, B. B. *Street Without Joy – Insurgency in Indo-China 1946–63.* Pall Mall, London, 1964.

Fall, B. B. *Hell in a Very Small Place: The Siege of Dien Bien Phu.* Pall Mall, London, 1967.

Giap, V. N. *Big Victory, Great Task.* Pall Mall, London, 1968.

Hammer, E. J. *The Struggle for Indo-China 1940–55.* Stanford University Press, Stanford, 1966.

O'Ballance, E. *The Indo-China War.* Faber, London, 1964.

Paret, P. *French Revolutionary Warfare from Indochina to Algeria.* Pall Mall, London, 1964.

Roy, J. *Dien Bien Phu.* Faber, London, 1965.

Teulières, A. *La Guerre du Vietnam 1945–1975.* Editions Lavauzelle, Paris, 1978.

van Haute, A. *French Air Force. Vol. 2: 1941–1974.* Ian Allan, London, 1975.

Vietnam 1954–1975
General

Baker, M. *Nam.* Sphere, London, 1982.

Beckett, B. *The Illustrated History of the Vietnam War.* Blandford Press, Poole, 1985.

Bonds, R. *The Vietnam War: The Illustrated History of the Conflict in Southeast Asia.* Salamander, London, 1979.

Bowman, J. *The World Almanac of the Vietnam War.* Bison Books, New York, 1985.

Caputo, P. *A Rumour of War.* Macmillan, London, 1977.

Herring, G. *America's Longest War: The United States and Vietnam 1950–1970.* Wiley, New York, 1979.

Karnow, S. *Vietnam: A History.* Viking, New York, 1983.

Kolko, G. *Vietnam: Anatomy of War 1940–1975.* Pantheon, New York, 1986.

Lewy, G. *America in Vietnam.* Oxford University Press, Oxford, 1978.

Maclaear, M. *The 10,000 Day War.* St. Martin's Press, New York, 1981.

Palmer, B. *The 25 Year War. America's Military Role in Vietnam.* University of Kentucky Press, Lexington, 1984.

Sharp, S. *Strategy for Defeat: Vietnam in Retrospect.* Presidio Press, Novato, 1978.

Thompson, R. *Peace is not at Hand.* Chatto & Windus, London, 1974.

Turley, W. *The Second Indo-China War.* Westview Press, New York, 1985.

The Air War

Ballard, J. *The United States Air Force in Southeast Asia: Fixed Wing Gunships.* Office of Air Force History, Washington, 1982.

Bell, D. *Air War over Vietnam. Vols. I–IV.* Arms & Armour Press, London, 1982–84.

Berger, C. *The United States Air Force in Southeast Asia.* Office of Air Force History, Washington, 1977.

Broughton, J. *Thud Ridge.* Lippencott, New York, 1969.

Buckingham, W. A. *Operation Ranch Hand: The Air Force and Herbicides in Southeast Asia 1961–1971.* Office of Air Force History, Washington, 1982.

Chinnery, P. *Air War Vietnam.* Bison Books, London, 1987.

Davis, L. *Wild Weasel: The SAM Suppression Story.* Squadron/Signal Publications, Carrollton, 1986.

Davis, L. *Gunships: A Pictorial History of Spooky.* Squadron/Signal Publications, Carrollton, 1982.

Doll, T. E., Jackson, B. R. and Riley, W. A. *Navy Air Colors: Vol. 2, 1945–1985.* Squadron/Signal Publications, Carrollton, 1985.

Dorr, R. F. *Air War Hanoi.* Blandford Press, London, 1988.

Drendel, L. *Air War over Southeast Asia: A Pictorial Record. Vols. 1–3.* Squadron/Signal Publications, Carrollton, 1982–84.

Drendel, L. *. . . and Kill MiGs.* Squadron/Signal Publications, Warren, 1974.

Drendel, L. *USAF Phantoms in Combat.* Squadron/Signal Publications, Carrollton, 1987.

Dunstan, S. *Vietnam Choppers: Helicopters in Battle 1950–1975.* Osprey, London, 1988.

Fails, W. R. *Marines and Helicopters 1962–1973.* US Marine Corps, Washington, 1978.

Francillon, R. *Tonkin Gulf Yacht Club.* Conway Maritime Press, London, 1988.

Francillon, R. *Vietnam Air Wars.* Hamlyn, London, 1987.

Futrell, R. F. *The United States Air Force in Southeast Asia: The Advisory Years to 1965*. Office of Air Force History, Washington, 1981.

Gropman, A. L. *Airpower and the Airlift Evacuation of Kham Duc*. Office of Air Force History, Washington, 1979.

Harvey, F. *Air War – Vietnam*. Bantam Books, New York, 1967.

Hopkins, C. K. *SAC Tanker Operations in the Southeast Asia War*. Office of the Historian, SAC, Offutt AFB, 1979.

Jones, O. L. *Organization, Mission and Growth of the Vietnamese Air Force, 1949–1968*. HQ Pacific Air Forces, Hickam AFB, 1968.

Ky, N. C. *Twenty Years and Twenty Days*. Stein & Day, New York, 1976.

Lavalle, A. J. C. *The Tale of Two Bridges and The Battle for the Skies over North Vietnam*. Office of Air Force History, Washington, 1976. Reprinted in *Air War Vietnam*, Arms & Armour Press, London, 1978.

Lavalle, A. J. C. *Airpower and the Spring 1972 Invasion*. Office of Air Force History, Washington, 1976. Reprinted in *Air War Vietnam*, Arms & Armour Press, London, 1978.

Lavalle, A. J. C. *The Vietnamese Air Force 1951–1975 and Fourteen Hours at Koh Tang*. Office of Air Force History, Washington, 1977.

Lavalle, A. J. C. *Last Flight from Saigon*. Office of Air Force History, Washington, 1978.

Leary, W. M. *Perilous Mission: Civil Air Transport and CIA Covert Operations in Asia*. University of Alabama Press, Tuscaloosa, 1984.

Littauer, R. and Uphoff, N. *The Air War in Indochina*. Beacon Press, Boston, 1971.

McCarthy, J. R. and Allison, G. B. *Linebacker II: A View from the Rock*. Office of Air Force History, Washington, 1979.

Mason, R. *Chickenhawk*. Corgi, London, 1983.

Mersky, P. B. and Polmar, N. *The Naval Air War in Vietnam*. Nautical & Aviation Publishing Company of America, Annapolis, 1981.

Mesko, J. *Airmobile: The Helicopter War in Vietnam*. Squadron/Signal Publications, Carrollton, 1984.

Mikesh, R. C. *Flying Dragons: The South Vietnamese Air Force*. Osprey, London, 1988.

Nalty, B. C. *Air Power and the Fight for Khe Sanh*. Office of Air Force History, Washington, 1973.

Nalty, B. C., Watson, G. M. and Neufeld, J. *An Illustrated Guide to the Air War over Vietnam: Aircraft of the Southeast Asia Conflict*. Salamander, London, 1981.

Nichols, J. B. and Tillman, B. *On Yankee Station: The Naval Air War over Vietnam*. Airlife, Shrewsbury, 1987.

Pierson, J. E. *A Special Study of Electronic Warfare in SEA 1964–1968*. United States Air Force Security Service, San Antonio, 1973.

Scutts, J. *Wolfpack: Hunting MiGs over Vietnam*. Airlife, Shrewsbury, 1988.

Shulimson, J. *US Marines in Vietnam: An Expanding War, 1966*. HQ US Marine Corps, Washington, 1982.

Thompson, J. C. *Rolling Thunder: Understanding Policy and Program Failure*. University of North Carolina Press, Chapel Hill, 1980.

Tilford, E. H. *Search and Rescue in Southeast Asia, 1961–1975*. Office of Air Force History, Washington, 1980.

Trotti, J. *Phantom Over Vietnam*. Presidio Press, New York, 1985.

Laos, 1954 to date

Branfman, F. *Voices from the Plain of Jars*. Harper & Row, New York, 1972.

Dommen, A. J. *Conflict in Laos: the Politics of Neutralization*. Praeger, New York, 1971.

Drury, S. *My Secret War*. Aero Publishers, Fallbrook, 1979.

Fall, B. *Anatomy of a Crisis: The Laotian Crisis of 1960–61*. Doubleday, New York, 1969.

Langer, P. F. and Zasloff, J. J. *North Vietnam and the Pathet Lao: Partners in the Struggle for Laos*. Harvard University Press, Cambridge, 1970.

Robbins, C. *The Invisible Air Force*. Pan, London, 1981.

Robbins, C. *The Ravens*. Bantam Press, New York, 1988.

Sananikone, O. *The Royal Lao Army and US Army Advice and Support*. US Army Center of Military History, Washington, 1981.

Schanche, D. A. *Mister Pop: The Inside Story of the American Involvement in Laos*. McKay, New York, 1970.

Seagrave, S. *Yellow Rain: Chemical Warfare – The Deadliest Arms Race*. Evans, New York, 1981.

Souvana Phouma, M. *L'Agonie du Laos*. Plon, Paris, 1976.

Stevenson, C. A. *The End of Nowhere: American Policy toward Laos since 1965*. Beacon, Boston, 1972.

Cambodia, 1954 to date

Burrs, R. and Leitenburg, M. *The Wars in Vietnam, Cambodia and Laos, 1945–1982: A Bibliographic Guide*. ABC-Cleo Information Services, Santa Barbara, 1984.

Isaacs, A. *Without Honor: Defeat in Vietnam and Cambodia*. Johns Hopkins Press, Baltimore, 1983.

Kiernan, B. *How Pol Pot Came to Power*. Schocken Books, New York, 1985.

Ponchard, F. *Cambodia: Year Zero*. Holt Rinehart & Winston, New York, 1978.

Shawcross, W. *Kissinger, Nixon and the Destruction of Cambodia*. Simon & Schuster, New York, 1979.

Sutsakhan, S. *The Khmer Republic at War and the Final Collapse*. US Army Center of Military History, Washington, 1980.

Tro, T. D. *The Cambodian Incursion*. US Army Center of Military History, Washington, 1979.

10: INDONESIA, MALAYSIA AND THE PHILIPPINES

General

Carter, G. J. (ed.). *Sixty Squadron*. Private, 1967.

Lee, D. *Eastward: A History of the Royal Air Force in the Far East 1945–1972*. HMSO, London, 1984.

Legge, J. D. *Sukarno: A Political Biography*. Penguin, Middlesex, 1972.

The Netherlands East Indies, Indonesia

Bloomfield, L. P. and Leiss, A. C. *Controlling Small Wars: A Strategy for the 1970s*. Alfred A. Knopf, New York, 1969.

Fischer, L. *The Story of Indonesia*. Harper, New York, 1959.

Kahin, G. *Nationalism and Revolution in Indonesia*. Cornell University Press, Ithaca, 1952.

Pauker, G. *The Role of the Military in Indonesia*. Rand Memorandum RM-2637-PC, Santa Monica, 1960.

Wehl, D. *The Birth of Indonesia*. Allen & Unwin, London, 1948.

Wolf, C. *The Indonesian Story*. John Day, New York, 1948.

Malaya, 1948–1969

Barber, N. *The War of the Running Dogs: The Malayan Emergency 1948–1960*. Collins, London, 1971.

Clutterbuck, R. *The Long, Long War*. Cassell, London, 1967.

Conduct of Anti-Terrorist Operations in Malaya, The. HQ Malaya, Kuala Lumpur, 1952.

Henniker, M. C. A. *Red Shadow over Malaya*. Blackwood, London, 1955.

Majdalaney, F. *State of Emergency*. Longman Green, London, 1962.

Miers, R. *Shoot to Kill*. Faber & Faber, London, 1959.

Miller, H. *The Story of Malaya*. Faber & Faber, London, 1965.

O'Ballance, E. *Malaya: The Communist Insurgent War*. Faber & Faber, London, 1966.

Paget, J. *Counter-insurgency Campaigning*. Faber & Faber, London, 1967.

Royal Air Force: The Malayan Emergency 1948–1960.
Unpublished report, MoD, London, 1970.
Scurr, J. *The Malayan Campaign 1948–60.* Osprey, London, 1982.
Taber, P. *The War of the Flea.* Paladin, London, 1966.

Borneo, 1962–1966
Blaxland, G. *The Regiments Depart.* William Kimber, London, 1971.
Dickens, P. *SAS, The Jungle Frontier: 22 Special Air Service Regiment in the Borneo Campaign, 1963–1966.* Arms & Armour Press, London, 1983.
James, H. D. and Sheil-Small, D. *The Undeclared War: The Story of the Indonesian Confrontation 1962–1966.* Leo Cooper, London, 1971.
Mackie, J. A. C. *Konfrontasi.* Oxford University Press, Oxford, 1974.

Nuclear tests
Hansen, C. *US Nuclear Weapons: The Secret History.* Orion Books, New York, 1988.
Hubbard, K. and Simmons, M. *Operation Grapple: Testing Britain's First H-Bomb.* Ian Allan, Shepperton, 1985.

11: THE CARIBBEAN AND CENTRAL AMERICA
General
Andrade, J. M. *Latin-American Military Aviation.* Midland Counties Publications, Leicester, 1982.
Dienst, J. and Hagedorn, D. *North American F-51 Mustang in Latin American Air Force Service.* Aerofax, Arlington, 1985.

The Bay of Pigs, 1961
Cuban Government. *Playa Girón: Derrota del Imperialismo.* Imprenta Burgay y Cia., Havana, 1961.
del Pino, R. *Amanecer en Girón.* Instituto Cubano del Libro, Havana, 1969.
Ferrer, E. *Operación Puma.* International Aviation Consultants, Miami, 1975.
Johnson, H. *The Bay of Pigs.* Norton, New York, 1964.
Meyer, C. and Szulc, T. *The Cuban Invasion.* Praeger, New York, 1962.
Prendes, A. *En el Punto Rojo de mi Kolimador.* Editorial de Arts y Literatura, Havana, 1976.
Wise, D. and Ross, T. B. *The Invisible Government.* Random House, New York, 1964.
Wyden, P. *Bay of Pigs: The Untold Story.* Simon & Schuster, New York, 1980.

The Cuban Missile Crisis, 1962
Abel, E. *The Missiles of October.* Macgibbon & Kee, London, 1969.
Detzer, D. *The Brink: The Cuban Missile Crisis of 1962.* Dent, London, 1980.
Kennedy, R. F. *13 Days.* Macmillan, London, 1969.

Grenada, 1983
O'Shaughnessy, H. *Grenada: Revolution, Invasion and Aftermath.* Sphere, London, 1984.
Russell, L. E. and Mendez, M. A. *Grenada 1983.* Osprey, London, 1985.

Honduras and El Salvador, 1969
Strategic Survey 1969. Institute for Strategic Studies, London, 1970

12: SOUTH AMERICA
General
Andrade, J. M. *Latin-American Military Aviation.* Midland Counties Publications, Leicester, 1982.

The Falklands, 1982
Braybrook, R. *Battle for the Falklands (3): Air Forces.* Osprey, London, 1982.
Critchley, M. *Falklands: Task Force Portfolio* (Pts. 1 and 2). Maritime Books, Cornwall, 1982.
English, A. and Watts, A. *Battle for the Falklands (2): Naval Forces.* Osprey, London, 1982.
Ethell, J. and Price, A. *Air War South Atlantic.* Sidgwick & Jackson, London, 1983.
Falkland Islands: The Facts, The. HMSO, London, 1982.
Falklands – The Air War. BARG, Middlesex, 1986.
Fowler, W. *Battle for the Falklands (1): Land Forces.* Osprey, London, 1982.
Fox, R. *Eyewitness Falklands.* Methuen, London, 1982.
Franks, Lord. *Falkland Islands Review* (Cmnd., 8787). HMSO, London, 1983.
Frost, J. *2 Para Falklands.* Buchan & Enright, London, 1983.
Godden, J. *Harrier: Ski-jump to Victory.* Brassey's, Oxford, 1983.
Hastings, M. and Jenkins, S. *The Battle for the Falklands.* Pan, London, 1983.
Hooper, A. *The Military and the Media.* Gower, Aldershot, 1982.
Sunday Times Insight Team, The. *The Falklands War.* Sphere, London, 1982.
Tinker, D. *A Message from the Falklands.* Junction Books, London, 1982.
Witherow, J. *The Winter War.* Quartet, London, 1982.

Glossary

AA	**1.** Air America. **2.** Anti-aircraft. **3.** Armada Argentina (Argentine Navy). **4.** Armée de l'Air (French Air Force). **5.** Armeiskaya Aviatsiya (Army Aviation). Detached helicopters, V-VS.
AAA	Anti-aircraft artillery.
AAC	Army Air Corps. British.
AAM	Air-to-air missile.
AB	**1.** Aero Brigata (Air Brigade). Equivalent to Wing. AMI. **2.** Aerodromos-Base (aerodrome). FAP. **3.** Air Base. **4.** Aliyah Bet. Palestinian organization for smuggling immigrants. **5.** Aviation Battalion. US Army.
AC	Aviation Company. US Army.
ACCS	Airborne Command and Control Squadron. USAF.
ACF	Aden Communications Flight.
ACP	Air Control Post.
ACS	Air Commando Squadron. USAF.
ACT	Air Contact Team.
ACW	Air Commando Wing. USAF.
AD	**1.** Airborne Division. **2.** Air Division. USAF.
AdA	Aviation d'Artillerie (Artillery Aviation). French Army.
ADIZ	Air Defence Intercept Zone.
ADSID	Air-Delivered Seismic Detection.
AEC	Atomic Energy Commission. US.
AEW	Airborne Early Warning.
AEWCW	Airborne Early Warning and Control Wing. USAF.
AFB	Air Force Base.
AFME	Air Forces Middle East. RAF.
AFP	Armed Forces of the Philippines.
AFPLA	Air Force of the People's Liberation Army. China; Laos, from 1975.
AFZ	Air Force of Zimbabwe.
AG	Aviation Group. US Army.
AHC	Assault Helicopter Company. US Army.
ALA	Arab Liberation Army. Anti-Israel, 1948.
ALAT	Aviation Légère de l'Armée de Terre (French Army Aviation).
ALCC	Airlift Control Center. USAF.
Al-Fatah	Palestine National Liberation Organization.
ALN	Armée de Liberation Nationale (National Liberation Army). Algeria, Chad.
AMAW	Aero Medical Airlift Wing. USAF.
AMI	Aeronautica Militare Italiano (Italian Air Force).
AN	Aéronautique Navale, Aéronavale (Naval Air). French.
ANC	Armée Nationale Congolaise (Congolese National Army).
ANG	Air National Guard. US.
ANS	National Sihanoukist Army. Kampuchea.
Anya-nya	Southern Sudanese rebels.
APC	**1.** Armament Practice Camp. **2.** Armoured personnel carrier.
APL	Aden Protectorate Levies.
APODETI	Associacao Popular Democratica dos Timorenses (People's Democratic Association of the Timors).

APRF	Arabian Peninsula Reconnaissance Flight. RAF.
AR	Air Regiment. DRAAF.
ARAMCO	Arabian-American Oil Company.
ARC	Aviation Royale Cherifienne (Royal Maroc Air Force).
ARDE	Alianza Revolucionaria Democratica (Democratic Revolutionary Alliance). Nicaragua.
ARG	**1.** Air Refueling Group. USAF. **2.** Air Resupply Group. USAF.
ARM	Anti-radiation missile.
ARRS	Aerospace Rescue and Recovery Squadron. USAF.
ARS	**1.** Air Reconnaissance Squadron. HHP. **2.** Air Refueling Squadron. USAF. **3.** Air Rescue Squadron. USAF.
ARVN	Army of the Republic of Vietnam.
ARW	Air Refueling Wing. USAF.
AS	Attack Squadron. USAF, VNAF.
ASA	Army Security Agency. US.
ATF	Aero Transport Flugbetriebsgesellschaft.
ATG	Air Task Group. USN.
ATS	Air Transport Squadron. USAF.
ATU	Air Transport Unit. RCAF.
ATW	Air Transport Wing. USAF.
AURI	Angkatan Udara Republik Indonesia (Air Force of the Republic of Indonesia).
AVG	American Volunteer Group.
Aviron	Aeroplane (Israel).
AV-MF	Aviatsiya Voenno-Morskogo Flota (Naval Aviation). USSR.
AWACS	Airborne Warning and Control System.
AWADS	All-Weather Aerial Delivery System.
AWCS	Airborne Warning and Control Squadron. USAF.
AWCW	Airborne Warning and Control Wing. USAF.
BA	**1.** Base Aerea (Main Air Base). FAP. **2.** Brigada Aerea (Air Brigade). Spanish.
BAFO	British Air Forces of Occupation.
BAM	Base Aérea Militar (Military Air Base). Argentina.
BARCAP	Barrier combat air patrol. USAF.
BAT	Base (Ile) Aero-Terrestre (Air-Ground Base) French Indo-China.
BATT	British Army Training Team.
BDF (AW)	Bangladesh Defence Force (Air Wing).
BFSUAI	British Forces Support Unit Ascension Island.
BG	Bomb Group. USAF.
BG(L)	Bomb Group (Light). USAF.
BG(M)	Bomb Group (Medium). USAF.
BRITFORBEL	British Force in Belize.
BRITFORLEB	British Force in Lebanon.
BS	Bomb Squadron. USAF.
BS(L,NI)	Bomb Squadron (Light, Night Intruder). USAF.
BST	British Summer Time.
BUA	British United Airways.
BW	Bomb Wing. USAF.
BW(L)	Bomb Wing (Light). USAF.

BW(P)	Bomb Wing (Provisional). USAF.
C³	Command, Control and Communications.
CAB	1. Combat Aviation Battalion (Batallon de Aviacion de Combate). Argentina. 2. Combat Aviation Battalion. US Army.
CAE	Comando de Aviacion del Ejercito (Army Aviation Command). Argentina.
CAG	Carrier Air Group.
CAH	Corps d'Aviation d'Haiti (Haitian Air Force).
CALTF	Combined Air Lift Task Force. Berlin.
CANA	Comando Aviacion Naval Argentina (Argentine Naval Aviation Command).
CAP	Combat air patrol.
CARAMAR	Caribbean Marine Aero Corporation.
CAS	Continental Air Services.
CASF	Composite Air Strike Force. USAF.
CAT	Civil Air Transport.
CATC	Central Air Transport Company. China.
CB	Chemical and biological (weapons).
CBU	Cluster Bomb Unit.
CCC	Combat Cargo Command. USAF.
CCTS	Combat Crew Training Squadron. USAF.
CDS	Container Delivery System.
CEAM	Centre d'Experience Aériennes Militaires (Military Aviation Experimental Centre). French.
CEOPECON	Centro de Operaciones Conjuntas (Joint Operations Centre). Argentina.
CG	Phosgene gas.
CGS	Central Gunnery School.
CHES	Compagnie d'Hélicoptère d'Evacuation Sanitaire (Medical Evacuation Helicopter Company). French.
Chish	(C)hish. Mobile Field Force. Haganah.
CIA	Central Intelligence Agency. US.
CIC	Centro de Informacion y Control (Control and Information Centre). Argentina.
CMF	Ceasefire Monitoring Force. Rhodesia.
CNAC	China National Aviation Corporation.
CNAF	Chinese Nationalist Air Force (Chung-kuo Kung Chuan).
CNRRAAT	China National Relief and Rehabilitation Administration Air Transport.
Coin	Counter-insurgency.
Comint	Communications intelligence.
Contra	Contrarevolucionarios (Counter-revolutionaries). Nicaragua.
CONUS	Continental United States.
CPAFAF	Chinese People's Armed Forces Air Force.
CPVA	Chinese People's Volunteer Army.
CSS	Combat Support Squadron. USAF.
CT	Communist Terrorist. Malaya.
CVA	Attack Carrier. USN.
CVE	Escort Carrier. USN.
CVG	Carrier Air Group. USN.
CVL	Light Carrier. USN.
CVN	Carrier, Nuclear. USN.
CVS	Carrier, Anti-Submarine. USN.
CVW	Carrier Air Wing. USN.
DA	1. Dal'naya Aviatsiya (Long-Range Aviation). V-VS. 2. Direct-action (bombs)
Det.	Detachment.
DG	Dragoon Guards. British.
DIC	Division d'Infantrie Coloniale (Colonial Infantry Division). French.
DLF	Dhofar Liberation Front.
DMZ	Demilitarized Zone.
DPAW	Dubai Police Air Wing.
DPH	Detachement Permanent d'Hélicoptères (Permanent Helicopter Detachment). ALAT.
DPK	Democratic Party of Kurdistan.
DRA	Democratic Republic of Afghanistan.
DRAAF	Democratic Republic of Afghanistan Air Force (De Afghan Hanoi Quirah).
DSE	Dimokratikos Stratos Ellados (Greek Democratic Army).
DTA	Direccao dos Transportes Aereos (Air Transport Directorate). Angola.
EA	1. Elliniki Aeroporia (Greek Air Force). 2. Escuadrilla de Ataque (Attack Squadron). Argentina.
EAA	1. East African Airways. 2. Escadron d'Appui Aerien (Attack Squadron). AA.
EAF	Egyptian Air Force (Al Quwwat Aljawwiya Ilmisriya).
EAH	Ethiopian Air Force (Ye Ethiopia Ayer Hail).
EALA	Escadrille d'Aviation Légère d'Appui (Light Air Attack Flight). AA.
EAM	Ethnika Apeleftherotikon Metopon (National Liberation Front). Greece.
EAN	Estacion Aeronaval (Naval Air Station). Argentina.
EAS	Escuadrilla Antisubmarina (Anti-Submarine Squadron). Argentina.
EATS	European Air Transport Service. USAF.
EB	Escuadron/Escuadrilla de Bombardeo (Bomber Squadron/Flight). Spanish.
EC	1. Escadre de Chasse (Fighter Wing). AA. 2. Escuadron/Escuadrilla de Caza (Fighter Squadron/Flight). Spanish.
ECA	Escuadrilla de Caza y Ataque (Fighter-Bomber Squadron). Argentina.
ECB	Escuadron/Escuadrilla de Caza-Bombardeo (Fighter-Bomber Squadron/Flight). Spanish.
ECCM	Electronic counter-countermeasures.
ECM	Electronic countermeasures.
ECN	Escadron de Chasse Nuit (Night Fighter Squadron). AA.
ECS	Electronic Combat Squadron. USAF.
EE	Escuadrilla Exploracion (Reconnaissance Flight/Squadron). Spanish.
EH	1. Escadre d'Hélicoptères (Helicopter Wing). AA. 2. Escuadrille de Helicopteros (Helicopter Squadron). Argentina. 3. Escuadrille de Helicopteros (Helicopter Flight/Squadron). Spanish.
EHL	Escadrille d'Hélicoptères Légères (Light Helicopter Squadron). AA.
EHM	Escadrille d'Hélicoptères Moyens (Medium Helicopter Squadron). AA.
ELA	Escadrille de Liaison Aérienne (Air Liaison Flight). AA.
ELAS	Ellinikos Laikos Apeleftherotikon (National Popular Liberation Army). Greece.
ELF	Eritrean Liberation Front.
Elint	Electronic intelligence.
EMEO	Escadrille de Marche d'Extrême-Orient (Far East Transport Squadron). AA.
Enosis	Union with Greece. Cyprus.
ENT	Escadrille Nationale Tchadienne (Chad Air Flight).
EOGB	Electro-optical guided bomb.
EOKA	Ethniki Organosis Kyprion Agoniston (National Organization of Cypriot Fighters).

EOKA-B	Ethniki Organosis Kyprion Agoniston-B (National Organization of Cypriot Fighters). Post-1960.
EOM	Escadrille d'Outre Mer (Overseas Flight). AA.
EPFF	Eritrean Police Field Force.
EPG	Escuadrilla de Propositas Generales (General communication Flight/Squadron). Spanish.
EPLF	Eritrean People's Liberation Force.
ER	Escadron de Reconnaissance (Reconnaissance Squadron). AA.
ERALA	Escadrille Reserve d'Aviation Légère d'Appui (Reserve Light Air Attack Flight). AA.
ERV	Escadre de Ravitailement en Vol (Flight Refuelling Wing). AA.
Esc. El.	Escadron Electronique (Electronic Squadron). AA.
ESL	Escuadrilla de Sosten Logistico (Logistic Supply Flight/Squadron). Spanish.
ESLM	Escuadrilla de Sosten Logistico Movil (Transport Squadron). Argentina.
ESM	Electronic support measures.
Esq.	Esquadra (Squadron). Portuguese.
EST	Eastern Standard Time.
ET	1. Escadre de Transport (Transport Wing). AA. 2. Escuadron/Escuadrilla de Transporte (Transport Squadron/Flight). Spanish.
ETOM	Escadrille de Transport d'Outre Mer (Overseas Transport Flight). AA.
EVA	Elliniki Vassiliki Aeroporia (Royal Hellenic Air Force).
EW	Electronic warfare.
F	Flotille (Squadron). Aéronavale.
F(AW)S	Fighter (All Weather) Squadron. USAF.
FA	Frontovaya Aviatsiya (Frontal Aviation). V-VS.
FAA	1. Fleet Air Arm. 2. Fuerza Aérea Argentina (Argentine Air Force).
FAB	1. Force Aérienne Belge (Belgian Air Force). 2. Fuerza Aérea Boliviano (Bolivian Air Force).
FAC	1. Force Aérienne Congolaise (Congolese Air Force). 2. Forward air control(ler). 3. Fuerza Aérea Colombiana (Colombian Air Force). 4. Fuerza Aérea de Chile (Chilean Air Force).
FAD	Fuerza Aérea Dominicana (Dominican Air Force).
FAE	Fuerza Aérea Ecuatoriana (Ecuadoran Air Force).
FAEC	Fuerza Aérea del Ejercito de Cuba (Cuban Army Air Force).
FAF	1. French Air Force (Armée de l'Air). 2. Front de l'Algérie Française (Front for French Algeria).
FAG	1. Force Aérienne de Guinea (Guinea Republic Air Force). 2. Fuerza Aérea Guatemalteca (Guatemalan Air Force).
FAH	Fuerza Aérea Hondurena (Honduran Air Force).
FAK	Force Aérienne Katangaise (Katanga Air Force).
FAL	Force Aérienne Libanaise (Lebanese Air Force).
FAN	1. Forces Armées du Nord (Army North). Chad. 2. Fuerza Aérea de Nicaragua (Nicaraguan Air Force).
FANT	Forces Armées Nationales Tchadiennes (Chad National Armed Forces).
FAP	1. Fôrça Aérea Portuguesa (Portuguese Air Force). 2. Fuerza Aérea del Peru (Peruvian Air Force).
FAPA	Fôrça Aérea Popular de Angola (Angolan People's Air Force).
FAPLA	Fôrça Arma Popular de Liberacione Angola (Angolan People's Liberation Armed Forces).

FAPM	Fôrça Aérea Popular de Moçambique (Mozambique People's Air Force).
FAR	1. Fighter Aviation Regiment. V-VS. 2. Force d'Assistance Rapide (Rapid Response Force). French. 3. Fuerza Aérea Revolucionaria (Cuban Air Force).
FARM	Force Aérienne Royale Marocaine (Royal Moroccan Air Force).
FAS	1. Fuerza Aérea Salvadorena (Salvadoran Air Force). 2. Fuerza Aérea Sandinista (Sandinista Air Force). Nicaragua.
FASRON	Fleet Air Support Squadron. USN.
FAV	1. Formacoes Aéreas Voluntarias (Voluntary Air Formation). Portuguese. 2. Fuerza Aérea Venezolana (Venezuelan Air Force).
FAW	Fleet Air Wing. USN.
FAZ	Force Aérienne Zaïroise (Zaïrean Air Force).
FB	Fragmentation bomb.
FBG	Fighter Bomber Group. USAF.
FBI	Federal Bureau of Investigation. US.
FBR	Fighter-Bomber Regiment. V-VS.
FBS	Fighter-Bomber Squadron. USAF.
FBW	Fighter-Bomber Wing. USAF.
FCS	Fighter Commando Squadron. USAF.
FDN	Fuerza Democratica Nicaraguense (Nicaraguan Democratic Force).
FEAF	Far East Air Force. RAF.
FECAEF	Far East Casualty Air Evacuation Flight. RAF.
FECS	Far East Communications Squadron. RAF.
Fedayeen	Patriotic suicide squad/commandos. Arab.
FEG	Fighter Escort Group. USAF.
FES	Fighter Escort Squadron. USAF.
FFMLN	Frente Farabundo Marti de Liberacion Nacional (National Liberation Front – Farabundo Marti). El Salvador.
FG	1. Fighter Group. USAF. 2. Frontier Guard. Aden.
FIG	Fighter Interceptor Group. USAF.
Firquat	Group (paramilitary). Arab.
FIS	Fighter Interceptor Squadron. USAF.
FIW	Fighter Interceptor Wing. USAF.
FLEC	Frente de Libertacao de Enclave Cabinda (Cabinda Enclave Liberation Front).
FLIR	Forward-looking infra-red.
FLN	Front de la Liberation National (National Liberation Front). Algeria.
FLNC	Front de Liberation Nationale Congolaise (Congolese National Liberation Front).
FLOSY	Front for the Liberation of Occupied South Yemen.
FNLA	Frente Nacional de Libertacao de Angola (National Front for the Liberation of Angola).
FOB	Forward Operating Base.
FPLM	Fôrça Popular de Libertacao Moçambique, (People's Army of Liberated Mozambique).
FRA	Federal Regular Army. Aden.
Frantan	Frangible tank (napalm). Rhodesia.
FRELIMO	Frente de Libertacao de Moçambique (Mozambique Liberation Front).
FRETILIN	Frente Revolucianaria Timorense de Libertacao e Independencia (Revolutionary Front for Timorese Liberty and Independence)
Frog	Free Range Over Ground (Rocket).
FROLINAT	Front de Liberation Nationale de Tchad (Chadian National Liberation Front).
FS	Fighter Squadron. USAF, VNAF.
FSLN	Frente Sandinista de Liberacion Nacional (Sandinista National Liberation Front). Nicaragua.

GA	**1.** Grupo de Aerofotografico (Photo-Reconnaissance Squadron). Argentina. **2.** Grupo de Ataque (Attack Squadron). Argentina.
GAAD	Guards Airborne Assault Division. USSR.
GALA	Groupe d'Aviation Légère d'Appui (Light Air Attack Group). AA.
GANI	Groupement Aéronavale Indochine (Naval Air Group, Indochina).
GAOA	Groupe Aérienne d'Observation d'Artillerie (Artillery Observation Squadron). ALAT.
GATAC	Groupe Aérienne Tactique (Tactical Air Group). AA.
GB	**1.** Groupe de Bombardement (Bomber Group). AA. **2.** Grupo de Bombardeo (Bomber Squadron). Argentina.
GC	**1.** Groupe de Chasse (Fighter Wing). AA. **2.** Grupo de Caza (Fighter Squadron). Argentina.
GCC	Gulf Co-operation Council.
GCI	Ground control intercept (radar).
GFH	Groupement des Formations d'Hélicoptères (Helicopter Group). AA.
GH	Groupe d'Hélicoptères (Helicopter Group). AA.
GLS	Groupe de Liaison et Sauvetage (Liaison and Rescue Group). AA.
GM	**1.** Groupe de Marche (Fighting Wing). AA. **2.** Groupes Mobiles (Mobile Groups). French.
GMT	**1.** Greenwich Mean Time (often Z). **2.** Group de Marche du Tchad (Chad Transport Group). AA.
GMTEO	Groupe de Marche de Transporte d'Extrême-Orient (Far East Transport Group). AA.
GMU	Guided Missile Unit. USN.
GNA	Greek National Army.
GOM	Groupe d'Outre Mer (Overseas Group). AA.
GP	General-purpose (bomb)
GPES	Ground Proximity Extraction System.
GPRA	Gouvernement Provisoire de la Republique Algérienne (Provisional Government of the Algerian Republic).
GSRA	Groupe Saharien de Reconnaissance et d'Appui (Sahara Reconnaissance and Attack Group). AA.
GT	Groupe de Transport (Transport Group). AA.
GTA	Grupo de Transporte Aéreo (Air Transport Squadron). Argentina.
HA	Heyl (Chel) Ha'Avir (Air Force). Israel.
Haganah	Irgun Haganah (Defence Organization). Palestine.
HAL	Light Attack Helicopter Squadron. USN.
HAS	**1.** Hardened aircraft shelter. **2.** Heavy Airlift Squadron. HHP.
Hawk	Homing All-the-Way Killer.
HBL	Hadrami Bedouin League. Aden.
HC	Helicopter Combat Support Squadron. USN.
HDU	Hose drum unit.
HE	High explosive.
HEDRON	Headquarters Squadron. USMC.
HFB	Honvedelmi Forradalmi Bizottmany (Military Revolutionary Committee). Hungary.
HHP	Hukbong Himpapawid Pilipinas (Philippines Air Force).
HIAC	High-altitude camera.
Histadrut	Labour Organization. Palestine.
HM	Helicopter Mines Countermeasures Squadron. USN.
HMA	Attack Helicopter Squadron. USMC.
HMB	Hukbong Mapagpalaya ng Bayan (People's Liberation Army). Philippines.

HMH	Heavy Helicopter Squadron. USMC.
HML	Light Helicopter Squadron. USMC.
HMM	Medium Helicopter Squadron. USMC.
HMR	Helicopter Squadron. USMC.
HMS	Headquarters and Maintenance Squadron. USMC.
HN3	Mustard gas
HS	Helicopter Squadron. USN, VNAF.
HU	**1.** Helicopter Unit. IAF. **2.** Utility Helicopter Squadron. USN.
Huk	Hukbong Bayan Laban Sa Hapon; Hukbalhap (People's Anti-Japanese Army). Philippines.
Humint	Human Intelligence.
HVAR	High-Velocity Aircraft Rocket.
IAF	**1.** Indian Air Force (Bharatiya Vayu Sena). **2.** Iraqi Air Force (Al Quwwat Aljawwiya Aliraqiya).
ICAR	Independent Composite Aviation Regiment. V-VS.
ICBM	Intercontinental ballistic missile.
IDF	Israeli Defence Force (Tsvah Haganah le Israel).
IDF/AF	Israeli Defence Force/Air Force (Tsvah Haganah le Israel/Chel Ha'Avir).
IEAF	Imperial Ethiopian Air Force (Ye Ethiopia Ayer Hail).
IG	Irish Guards.
IGAAS	Independent Guards Attack Aviation Squadron. V-VS.
IHR	Independent Helicopter Regiment. V-VS.
IHS	Independent Helicopter Squadron. V-VS.
IIAF	Imperial Iranian Air Force (Nirou Hayai Shahanshahiye Iran).
IIBG	Imperial Iranian Battle Group.
IN	Indian Navy.
INAS	Indian Naval Air Squadron.
INLA	Irish National Liberation Army (extreme IRA split).
IPKF	Indian Peace-Keeping Force. Sri Lanka.
IR	Infra-red.
IRA	Irish Republican Army. Catholic, 1919.
IRBM	Intermediate-range ballistic missile.
IRF	Independent Reconnaissance Flight. British Army.
IRGC	Islamic Revolutionary Guards Corps (Pasdaran).
IRHS	Independent Reconnaissance Helicopter Squadron. V-VS.
IRIAF	Islamic Republic of Iran Air Force.
ISF	Internal Security Flight. RAF.
ITRS	Independent Tactical Reconnaissance Squadron. V-VS.
IZL	Irgun Zval Leumi (National Military Organization). Palestine.
JEHU	Joint Experimental Helicopter Unit. RAF/Army.
JHU	Joint Helicopter Unit. RAF/Army.
JOC	Joint Operations Centre.
JSP	Jewish Settlement Police.
JTF	Joint Task Force.
KAF	**1.** Kenyan Air Force. **2.** Khmer Air Force.
KAL	Korean Airlines.
KAR	King's African Rifles.
KAU	Kenya African Union.
KHAD	Khedemati-e-Dolati (Security Police). Afghanistan.
KKE	Komounisitikon Komma Ellados (Greek Communist Party).

KLu	Koninklijke Luchtmacht (Royal Netherlands Air Force).
KMT	Kuomintang. China.
KNIL	Koninklijk Nederlands Indische Leger (Royal Dutch Indies Army).
KOB	King's Own Border Regiment.
KPAFAC	Korean People's Armed Forces Air Corps.
KPAFAF	Korean People's Armed Forces Air Force.
KPNLF	Khmer People's National Liberation Front.
KPRAW	Kenyan Police Reserve Air Wing.
KPU	Kurdish Patriotic Union.
LAAS	Laotian Army Air Service.
LACSA	Lineas Aeres Costarricenses SA (Costa Rican Air Lines).
LANICA	Lineas Aereas de Nicaragua (Nicaraguan Airlines).
LAPES	Low-Altitude Parachute Extraction System.
LARAF	Libya Arab Republic Air Force (Al Quwwat Aljawwiya Al Libiyya).
LCI	Landing Craft, Infantry.
LCSFA	Limited Contingent of Soviet Forces in Afghanistan.
LGB	Laser-guided bomb.
LHI	Lohamei Herut Israel (Fighters for the Freedom of Israel).
LLF	Light Liaison Flight. British Army.
LLLTV	Low Light-Level Television.
LPH	Landing Platform, Helicopter. USN.
LS	1. Landing strip ('Lima Site'). US. 2. Liaison Squadron. USAF.
LSD	Landing Ship, Dock.
LSK	Luchtstrijdkrachten (Air Force). Netherlands.
LSL	Landing Ship, Logistic.
LTTE	Liberation Tigers of Tamil Eelam. Sri Lanka.
LWR	Launch warning receiver.
LZ	Landing zone.
MAAF	Malayan Auxiliary Air Force.
MAAG	Military Assistance Advisory Group. US.
MAC	Military Airlift Command. USAF.
MACV	Military Assistance Command Vietnam. US.
MAG	Marine Air Group. USMC.
MAMS	Aircraft Maintenance Squadron. USMC.
MASH	Mobile Army Surgical Hospital. US Army.
MATS	Military Air Transport Service. USAF.
Mau Mau	Kenyan terrorists. Derivation unknown.
MAW	1. Marine Air Wing. USMC. 2. Military Airlift Wing. USAF.
MCAS	Marine Corps Air Station. USMC.
MCP	Malayan Communist Party.
MD	Medical Detachment. US Army.
MDRM	Mouvement Democratique de la Rénovation Malagache (Democratic Movement for the Renewal of Madagascar).
MECS	Middle East Communications Squadron. RAF.
MEZ	Maritime exclusion zone.
MFG	Marinefleigergeschwader (Naval Air Wing). W. Germany.
MIAF	Mauretanian Islamic Air Force (Force Aérienne Islamique de Mauritanie).
MIB	Military Intelligence Battalion. US.
MiGCAP	MiG combat air patrol. USAF.
Min Yuen	People's Movement. Malaya.
MISURA	Miskito, Sumo, Rama (Nicaraguan Contra Indians).
ML	1. Magyar Legiero (Hungarian Air Force). 2. Militaire Luchtvaart (Army Aviation). Netherlands.

MLD	Marine Luchtvaartdienst (Naval Air Service). Netherlands.
MNF	Multi-National Force. Lebanon, 1983.
MNLF	Moro National Liberation Front. Philippines.
MoD	Ministry of Defence. UK.
MOFF	Muscat and Oman Field Force.
MPABA	Malayan Peoples' Anti-British Army.
MPAJA	Malayan Peoples' Anti-Japanese Army.
MPLA	Movimento Popular de Libertacao de Angola (Popular Movement for the Liberation of Angola).
MR	Maritime reconnaissance.
MRBM	Medium-range ballistic missile.
MRD	Motor Rifle Division. USSR.
MRLA	Malayan Races Liberation Army.
MRR	Maritime radar reconnaissance.
MTLD	Movement pour le Triomphe des Libertés Democratiques (Movement for the Triumph of Democratic Freedom). Algeria.
NADK	National Army of Democratic Kampuchea.
NAF	Nigerian Air Force.
Napalm	Naphtha and palm oil (inflammable jelly).
NAS	1. Naval Air Squadron. FAA. 2. Naval Air Station.
NEAF	Near East Air Force. RAF.
NGS	Naval gunfire support.
NICRA	Northern Ireland Civil Rights Association. 1967.
NKAF	North Korean Air Force.
NKPA	North Korean People's Army.
NLF	National Liberation Front. Aden.
NOGS	Night observation gunship.
NPA	New People's Army. Philippines.
NRA	National Resistance Army. Uganda, 1982.
NSA	National Security Agency. US.
NVA	North Vietnamese Army.
NVAF	North Vietnamese Air Force.
OAS	1. Organisation Armée Secrète (Secret Army Organization). Algeria. 2. Organization of American States.
OAU	Organization for African Unity.
OCU	Operational Conversion Unit. RAF.
OL	Operating location.
OLA	Omani Liberation Army.
OLF	Oromo Liberation Front.
OLOS	Organization for the Liberation of the Occupied South. Yemen.
ONUC	Force de l'Organisation des Nations Unies au Congo (United Nations Forces in the Congo).
OS	1. Observation Squadron. VNAF. 2. Operation Squadron. USAF.
PACAF	Pacific Air Force. USAF.
PAF	1. Pakistan Air Force (Pakistan Fiza'ya). 2. Philippines Air Force (Hukbong Himpapawid Pilipinas).
PAIGC	Partido Africano de Independencia da Guine e Capo Verde (African Party for Independence of Guinea and Cape Verde).
Palmach	Plugot Mahatz. Shock troops of Haganah.
PASC	Palestine Armed Struggle Command.
PAVN	People's Army of Vietnam. Post-1975.
PC	Philippines Constabulary.
PDPA	People's Democratic Party of Afghanistan.
PDRY	People's Democratic Republic of the Yemen.
Peshmerga	Forward to Death. Kurdish independence fighters.
PFLO	Popular Front for the Liberation of Oman.

PFLOAG	Popular Front for the Liberation of the Occupied Arabian Gulf.
PFLP	Popular Front for the Liberation of Palestine.
PG	Provisional Group. USAF.
PIA	Pakistan International Airlines.
PJ	Para-jumper.
PKI	Partai Kommunis Indonesia (Indonesian Communist Party).
PKP	Partido Kommunista ng Pilipinas (Philippines Communist Party).
PLA	People's Liberation Army. China.
PLO	Palestinian Liberation Organization.
PMF	Photo-Mapping Flight. USAF.
PMO	People's Mujahideen Organization. Iran.
PMW	Photo-Mapping Wing. USAF.
PNA	Prefectura Naval Argentina (Argentine Coastguard).
POL	Petroleum, oil and lubricants.
POLISARIO	Popular Front for the Liberation of Saguiet el Hamra and Rio.
POW	Prisoner-of-war.
PPP	People's Progressive Party. British Guiana.
PR	Photographic reconnaissance.
PRC	People's Republic of China.
PRKAF	People's Republic of Kampuchea Air Force.
PRU	Photographic Reconnaissance Unit. RAF.
PSP	People's Socialist Party. Aden.
PUP	People's United Party. Belize.
QDG	Queen's Dragoon Guards.
QRA	Quick-Reaction Alert.
R&R	Rest and recuperation/relaxation/recovery.
RA	Royal Artillery.
RAAF	1. Royal Afghan Air Force. 2. Royal Australian Air Force.
RAC	Royal Armoured Corps.
RADALT	Radio altimeter.
RAE	Royal Aircraft Establishment. UK.
RAF	Royal Air Force.
RAFIO	Royal Air Force Intelligence Officer.
RAMC	Royal Army Medical Corps.
RATG	Rhodesian Air Training Group.
RAZON	Range and azimuth only (guided 1,000lb bomb).
RC	Route Coloniale (Colonial Route/Road). French.
RCAF	Royal Canadian Air Force.
RCP	1. Régiment de Chasseurs Parachutistes (Infantry Parachute Regiment). French. 2. Regimento de Cacadores Paraquedistas (Parachute Rifle Regiment). Portuguese.
RCT	Regimental Combat Team. US.
RCyAF	Royal Ceylon Air Force.
RE	Royal Engineers.
REAF	Royal Egyptian Air Force.
Rekhesh	Haganah arms acquisition organization.
RENAMO	Resistancia Nacional Moçambicana (Mozambique National Resistance)
REP	Régiment Etranger Parachutiste (Foreign [Legion] Parachute Regiment). France.
RFA	Royal Fleet Auxiliary.
RHA	Royal Horse Artillery.
RHAF	Royal Hellenic Air Force (Elliniki Vassiliki Aeroporia).
RhAF	Rhodesian Air Force.
RHAW	Radar homing and warning.
RHC	Régiment d'Hélicoptères de Combat (Helicopter Combat Regiment). ALAT.

RIAF	1. Royal Indian Air Force. 2. Royal Iraqi Air Force.
RJAF	Royal Jordanian Air Force (Al Quwwat Aljawwiya Almalakiya Alurduniya).
RKA	Royal Khmer Aviation (Aviation Khmer Royale).
RLAF	Royal Lao Air Force.
RLI	Rhodesian Light Infantry.
RMAF	1. Royal Malay(si)an Air Force (Tentera Udara Diraju Malay(si)a). 2. Royal Maroc Air Force (Al Quwwat Aljawwiya Almalakiya Marakishiya).
RMC	Royal Marine Commando.
RNethAF	Royal Netherlands Air Force (Koninklijke Luchtmacht).
RNF	Royal Northumberland Fusiliers.
RNZAF	Royal New Zealand Air Force.
ROE	Rules of engagement.
ROK	Republic of Korea.
ROKAF	Republic of Korea Air Force (Hankook Kong Goon).
RP	Route Package. US.
RPAF	Royal Pakistan Air Force.
RRAF	Royal Rhodesian Air Force.
RRC	Radio Research Company. US Army.
RRF	Radar Reconnaissance Flight. RAF.
RS	Reconnaissance Squadron. USAF, VNAF.
RSAF	1. Royal Saudi Air Force (Al Quwwat Aljawwiya Assa'udiya). 2. Royal Swedish Air Force (Flygvapnet).
RTAF	Royal Thai Air Force.
RTP	Reinforced Theatre Plan. Kuwait.
RTR	Royal Tank Regiment.
RUC	Royal Ulster Constabulary.
RVAH	Heavy Attack and Reconnaissance Squa-dron. USN.
RW	Reconnaissance Wing. USAF.
RWRW	Rescue and Weather Reconnaissance Wing. USAF.
SA	1. Sherut Avir (Military Air Service). Haganah. 2. Shin Aleph (Military Air Service). Haganah.
SAA	South Arabian Army.
SAAF	1. South African Air Force (Suid-Afrikaanse Lugmag). 2. Syrian Arab Air Force (Al Quwwat al-Jawwiya al Arabia as-Suriya).
SAC	1. Somali Aeronautical Corps (Dayuuradaha Xoogga Dalka Somaliyeed). 2. Strategic Air Command. USAF.
SAF	1. Sudan Air Force (Silakh al-Jawwiya as-Sudaniya). 2. Sultan's Armed Forces. Oman. 3. Swedish Air Force (Svenska Flygvapnet). 4. Syrian Air Force (Al Quwwat al-Jawwiya as-Suriya).
SAL	South Arabian League.
SAM	Surface-to-air missile.
SAMS	Special Air Missions Squadron. HHP.
SAP	South Arabian Police.
SAR	Search and rescue.
SARF	Search and Rescue Flight. RAF.
SARS	Search and Rescue Squadron. HHP.
SAS	Special Air Service (Regiment). British.
SAT	Southern Air Transport.
SBS	Special Boat Squadron.
SDECE	Service de Documentation Extérieure et Contre-Espionage. (External Intelligence and Counter-Espionage Service). French.
SDR	Somali Democratic Republic.
SEATO	South-East Asia Treaty Organization.

Shifta	Bandit. Tribes around the Horn of Africa.
SHORAN	Short-range navigational radar.
Sigint	Signals intelligence.
SLA	Secteur Liaison Air (Area Air Liaison) AA.
SLAF	Sri Lankan Air Force.
SLAR	Side-looking airborne radar.
SLS	Section de Liaison at de Servitude (Liaison and Communications Flight). Aéronavale.
SMS	Special Missions Squadron. VNAF.
SNS	Special Night Squads. Haganah.
SOAF	Sultan of Oman's Air Force (Al Quwwat Aljawwiya Alsultanat Oman).
SOE	Special Operations Executive.
Sonar	Sound navigation and ranging.
SOS	Special Operations Squadron. USAF.
SOW	Special Operations Wing. USAF.
SPLA	Sudan People's Liberation Army.
SRFW	Strategic Reconnaissance Fighter Wing. USAF.
SRS	Strategic Reconnaissance Squadron. USAF.
SRW	Strategic Reconnaissance Wing. USAF.
SS	Support Squadron. USAF.
St.	Staffel (Squadron). W. Germany.
STANO	Surveillance, Target Acquisition and Night Observation.
Stern Gang	LHI
STOL	Short take-off and landing.
SW	Strategic Wing. USAF.
SW(P)	Strategic Wing (Provisional). USAF.
SWAD	Special Warfare Aviation Detachment. US Army.
SWAPO	South-West Africa People's Organization.
SYL	Somali Youth League.
TAAG	Transportes Aéreos de Angola (Angola Air Transport).
TAC	Tactical Air Command. USAF.
TAFTS	Tactical Air Force Transport Squadron. USAF.
TAM	Transportes Aéreos Militares (Military Air Transport). Portugal.
TAP	Transportes Aéreos Portugueses (Portuguese Air Transport).
TARZON	Targeted range and azimuth only (12,000lb guided bomb).
TAS	Tactical Airlift Squadron. USAF.
TASS	Tactical Air Support Squadron. USAF.
TAW	Tactical Airlift Wing. USAF.
TBS	Tactical Bomb Squadron. USAF.
TC	Transportation Company. US Army.
TCG	Troop Carrier Group. USAF.
TCS	1. Tactical Control Squadron. USAF. 2. Troop Carrier Squadron. USAF.
TCW	Troop Carrier Wing. USAF.
TDY	Temporary Duty.
Telint	Telemetry intelligence.
TEWS	Tactical Electronic Warfare Squadron. USAF.
TEZ	Total exclusion zone.
TF	Task Force.
TFS	Tactical Fighter Squadron. USAF.
TFW	Tactical Fighter Wing. USAF.
TG	1. Tactical Group. USAF. 2. Task Group.
TH	Tenuat Humeri (United Resistance). LHI, IZL, Haganah.
THI	Tsvah Haganah le Israel (Israeli Defence Force).
THK	Turk Hava Kuvvetleri (Turkish Air Force).
TNI-AU	Tentara Nasional Indonesia – Angkatan Udara (Indonesian Armed Forces – Air Force).
TNKU	Tentara Nasional Kalimantan Utara (North Kalimantan National Army).

TOAS	Teatro de Operaciones del Atlantico Sur (South Atlantic Theatre of Operations). Argentine.
TOL	Trucial Oman Levies.
TOS	Trucial Oman Scouts.
TPDFAW	Tanzania People's Defence Force Air Wing (Jeshi la Wanachi la Tanzania).
TPLF	Tigre People's Liberation Front.
TRIM	Trail and road interdiction, multisensor. USN.
TRS	Tactical Reconnaissance Squadron. USAF.
TRS(NP)	Tactical Reconnaissance Squadron (Night Photo). USAF.
TRW	Tactical Reconnaissance Wing. USAF.
TS	1. Test Squadron. USAF. 2. Transport Squadron. VNAF, HHP.
TSG	Tactical Support Group. USAF.
TUDM	Tentera Udara Diraju Malaysia (Royal Malaysian Air Force).
TUF	Tamil United Front. Sri Lanka.
TULF	Tamil United Liberation Front. Sri Lanka.
TW	Training Wing. USAF.
UAAF	Uganda Army Air Force.
UAR	United Arab Republic.
UBAF	Union of Burma Air Force (Tandaw Lay).
UDA	Ulster Defence Association. Protestant, 1971.
UDEL	Union Democratica Liberacion (Democratic Liberation Union). Nicaragua.
UDI	Unilateral Declaration of Independence.
UDR	Ulster Defence Regiment. Part-time army, 1971.
UDT	Uniao Democratica de Timor (Timor Democratic Union).
UHF	Ultra-high frequency.
UN	United Nations.
UNCIVPOL	United Nations Civilian Police. Cyprus.
UNFICYP	United Nations Force in Cyprus.
UNIFIL	United Nations Interim Force in Lebanon.
UNITA	Uniao Nacional para a Independencia Total de Angola (National Union for the Total Independence of Angola).
UNLF	Ugandan National Liberation Front.
UNRRA	United Nations Relief and Rehabilitation Agency. China.
UNTSO	United Nations Truce Supervision Organization. Sinai 1969.
UPA	Uniao dos Populacoes de Angola (Angolan People's Union).
UPDA	Ugandan People's Democratic Army.
UPF	Ugandan Popular Front.
USAAF	United States Army Air Force.
USAF	United States Air Force.
USAFE	United States Air Forces Europe.
USASA	United States Army Security Agency.
USMC	United States Marine Corps.
USN	United States Navy.
UTA	Union de Transports Aériens (Air Transport Union).
UTTC	Utility Tactical Transportation Company. US Army.
UVF	Ulster Volunteer Force. Protestant 1912, banned 1966.
VA	Attack Squadron. USN.
VAH	Heavy Attack Squadron. USN.
VAL	Light Attack Squadron. USN.
VAP	Reconnaissance Attack Squadron. USN.
VAQ	Attack and Electronics Squadron. USN.
VAQW	Attack and Electronic Warfare Squadron. USN.
VAW	Airborne Warning Squadron. USN.

VC	1. Fleet Composite Squadron. USN. 2. Viet Cong.	**VSF**	Anti-Submarine Fighter Squadron. USN.
VDV	Vozduyushno Desantniki Voisk (Air Assault Forces). USSR.	**VT**	Variable-timed (bomb).
Vertrep	Vertical replenishment.	**V-TA**	Voenno-Transportnaya Aviatsiya (Military Transport Aviation). V-VS.
VF	Fighter Squadron. USN.	**VU**	Fleet Utility Squadron, USN.
VFA	Fighter/Attack Squadron. USN.	**V-VS**	Voenno-Vozdushnye Sily (Soviet Air Force).
VFP	Fighter Reconnaissance Squadron. USN.	**VW**	Warning Squadron. USN.
VHF	Very high frequency.	**VX**	Air Test and Evaluation Squadron. USN.
VMA	Marine Attack Squadron. USMC.		
VMAQ	Marine Attack and Electronics Squadron. USMC.	**WG**	Weather Group. USAF.
		WGN	West Germany Navy (Marineflieger).
VMCJ	Marine Composite Squadron. USMC.	**WRS**	Weather Reconnaissance Squadron. USAF.
VMF	Marine Fighter Squadron. USMC.	**WRSP**	Weather Reconnaissance Squadron Provisional. USAF.
VMF(N)	Marine Night Fighter Squadron. USMC.		
VMFA	Marine Fighter/Attack Squadron. USMC.	**WRW**	Weather Reconnaissance Wing. USAF.
VMGR	Marine Air Refueling Transport Squadron. USMC.	**WSLF**	Western Somali Liberation Front.
		WW	Wild Weasel. USAF.
VMJ	Marine Photo Reconnaissance Squadron. USMC.		
		YAR	Yemen Arab Republic.
VMO	Marine Observation Squadron. USMC.	**Yishuv**	Jewish settlement movement.
VMR	Marine Transport Squadron. USMC.	**YSP**	Yemeni Socialist Party.
VNAF	Vietnamese Air Force. South Vietnam, to 1975.		
VP	Patrol Squadron. USN.	**Zahal**	Army. Israel, post-1948.
VPAF	Vietnam People's Air Force.	**ZANLA**	Zimbabwe African National Liberation Army.
VQ	Fleet Air Reconnaissance Squadron. USN.	**ZANU**	Zimbabwe African National Union.
VR	Fleet Logistics Support Squadron. USN.	**ZAPU**	Zimbabwe African People's Union.
VS	Anti-Submarine Squadron. USN.	**ZIPRA**	Zimbabwe People's Revolutionary Army.
		ZNA	Zimbabwe National Army.

Index

For reasons of space this index has been simplified; for example, air forces are listed by name of country (the full titles appear in the Glossary), and only those aircraft types appearing in the text (i.e. not necessarily all those listed in the tables) are included, by name or by designation. To avoid confusion US types used by British services are indexed under their British names and cross-referenced; those in the service of any other air arm appear under their US designations. The names of US types relative to designation are listed in Appendix IV. Where basically similar types are in civil and military use they are grouped under the military designation but, again, are cross-referenced. Thus the R4D and DC-3 appear within the C-47 entry while the Dakota (RAF) has a separate entry. Manufacturers are shown only where to have omitted them might have caused confusion. Aircraft of Soviet origin are shown by their manufacturer's designations; a full list of NATO reporting names appears as Appendix VII. Key place names only are shown; to have included airfields would have occupied too much space. Reference to the Contents pages should identify the sections within which given airfields are likely to be found. Similarly units, both army and air arm, are excluded; for air arms, reference to the appropriate air force entry should limit searching. Words indexed in *italics* refer to ships.